CW00433699

LONDON
RECOLLECTED

THE VILLAGE LONDON SERIES

Other titles already published in hard back are:

VILLAGE LONDON Volume I
VILLAGE LONDON Volume II
LONDON RECOLLECTED Volume I
LONDON RECOLLECTED Volume II
LONDON RECOLLECTED Volume III

Other titles already published in paperback

VILLAGE LONDON Pt. 1 West and North
VILLAGE LONDON Pt. 2 North and East
VILLAGE LONDON Pt. 3 South-East
VILLAGE LONDON Pt. 4 South-West

OLD FLEET STREET
CHEAPSIDE AND ST. PAUL'S
THE TOWER AND EAST END

THE MARYLEBONE SCHOOL-HOUSE IN 1780.

4

LONDON RECOLLECTED

ITS HISTORY, LORE AND LEGEND

by

EDWARD WALFORD.

VOLUME IV

THE ALDERMAN PRESS
London

First published in 1872-8 by Cassell, Petter, Galpin & Co.
under the title *Old and New London*.

British Library Cataloguing in Publication Data.

    [Old and new London].
    London recollected: its history, lore and legend.
    Vol. 4
    1. London (England)_____History
    I. Walford, Edward
    942.1   DA677

ISBN 0-946619-04-2

Published by The Alderman Press, 1986
1/7 Church Street, London N9 9DR

Printed in Great Britain by
Dotesios Printers Ltd. Bradford-on-Avon, Wiltshire
and bound by Dorstel Press Limited.

CONTENTS.

—◆—

CHAPTER I.

WESTMINSTER.—A SURVEY OF THE CITY: MILLBANK, AND ITS NEIGHBOURHOOD.

CHAPTER II.

WESTMINSTER.—TOTHILL FIELDS AND NEIGHBOURHOOD.

CHAPTER III.

WESTMINSTER.—KING STREET, GREAT GEORGE STREET, AND THE BROAD SANCTUARY.

CHAPTER IV.

MODERN WESTMINSTER.

CHAPTER V.

ST. JAMES'S PARK.

CONTENTS.

CHAPTER XII.
PALL MALL.—CLUB-LAND.

CHAPTER XIII.
ST. JAMES'S STREET.—CLUB-LAND (*continued*).

CHAPTER XIV.
ST. JAMES'S STREET AND ITS NEIGHBOURHOOD.

CHAPTER XV.
ST. JAMES'S SQUARE AND ITS DISTINGUISHED RESIDENTS.

CHAPTER XVI.
THE NEIGHBOURHOOD OF ST. JAMES'S SQUARE.

CHAPTER XVII.
WATERLOO PLACE AND HER MAJESTY'S THEATRE.

CONTENTS.

CONTENTS.

CONTENTS.

CONTENTS.

CONTENTS.

CHAPTER XLIII.

QUEEN SQUARE, GREAT ORMOND STREET, &c.

CHAPTER XLIV.

RUSSELL AND BEDFORD SQUARES, &c.

CHAPTER XLV.

GORDON AND TAVISTOCK SQUARES, &c.

LIST OF ILLUSTRATIONS.

LIST OF ILLUSTRATIONS.

LONDON.

CHAPTER I.

WESTMINSTER.—A SURVEY OF THE CITY: MILLBANK, AND ITS NEIGHBOURHOOD.

> " London, thou comprehensive word
> What joy thy streets and squares afford!
> And think not thy admirer rallies
> If he should add, thy "lanes and alleys."
> *P. Egan, " Tom and Jerry."*

Millbank—Inigo Jones and Ben Jonson—Great College Street— Little College Street—Barton and Cowley Streets—Abingdon Street — Thomas Telford, the Engineer — Wood Street — John Carter, F.S.A.—North Street—Elliston, the Actor—Peterborough House—" High Livings "—Annual Procession of Stage Coaches —The Manor of Neyte—The Church of St. John the Evangelist—Lord Grosvenor's Residence — Fanciful Style of Street-naming —Vine Street—Vineyards in the Olden Times—Horse-ferry Road—Escape of Queen Mary of Modena—Flight of King James—The Great Seal of England thrown into the Thames— A Lucky Ferryman — Vauxhall Regatta — Works of the Gas Light and Coke Company—The " White Horse and Bower "— Page Street—Millbank Prison—Vauxhall Bridge—Holy Trinity Church—Vauxhall Bridge Road—Residence of Cardinal Manning —A New Cathedral—Vincent Square—Church of St. Mary the Virgin — Rochester Row — Emery Hill's Almshouses—St. Stephen's Church—Tothill Fields Prison—The Old Bridewell— Grey-Coat School—Strutton Ground—Dacre Street.

" THE old City of Westminster proper, with its venerable Abbey, and its gloomy and narrow streets, once the residence of peers, courtiers, and poets, constitutes perhaps the most interesting district of the great metropolis.

So writes Mr. J. H. Jesse, in his pleasant and interesting work on "London." Let us then endeavour to show our readers a few of the chief points of interest which lie around the Abbey. As lately as the reign of Elizabeth, the Middlesex shore opposite to Lambeth was a mere low and marshy tract of land, almost wholly free from buildings, except the Abbey and Palace, and some few public edifices which adjoined them and had grown up under their shadow. The region now known as Millbank was so called from a mill on the bank of the river which occupied the site on which stood Peterborough House, delineated in Hollar's "View of London." This house was pulled down and rebuilt about the year 1735, by the then head of the Grosvenor family, shortly after his marriage with Miss Davis, the heiress of Ebury Manor, by which he acquired the property now known as Belgravia; the Grosvenors continued to occupy it as their town mansion till early in the present century, when they removed to their present house in Upper Grosvenor Street. In St. John's Church, Westminster, between the Abbey and their former home, is one proof of their connection with the parish, in the shape of a panel recording the fact of King George and Queen Charlotte, in 1800, standing there as sponsors at the baptism of "Thomas, second son of Viscount Belgrave," who succeeded whilst still young to the Earldom of Wilton.

But the neighbourhood of which we write has still more ancient associations. Late in life, when he had quarrelled with Inigo Jones, with the Court, and the City, who had been his friends and patrons, we find Ben Jonson living almost under the shadow of Westminster Abbey, "in the house under which you pass," says Aubrey, "to go out of the churchyard into the old Palace." At this time he, whose "mountain belly," "prodigious waist," and stooping back, are familiar to all readers of his works, was suffering from the double misfortune of the palsy and of poverty, from the latter of which he was rescued to some extent by the Earl of Newcastle. Here, probably, he died (his death occurred in August, 1637); and he was buried in the Abbey hard by, where it is a tradition that "Jack Young," happening to pass by, gave a stonemason eighteen pence to carve on the pavement where he lay, the well-known words, "O rare Ben Jonson!"

Immediately to the south of the Abbey precincts is Great College Street, which runs westward from Abingdon Street to Tufton Street. It was formerly known simply as the "Dead Wall," from the wall built by Abbot Litlington round the Infirmary Garden, which once extended, in a semi-circular form, from the place where it now ends in College Street, to the Gate House. Gibbon's aunt, Mrs. Porter, "the affectionate guardian of his tender years," lived in College Street, where for some time she kept a boarding-house for the town boys of Westminster School.

Beyond is Little College Street, which, in the reign of Queen Anne, rejoiced in the name of Piper's Ground, and consisted of "a few houses built, the rest lying waste." Wealthy and well-born families, and even bishops, lived about its neighbourhood. From his house in College Court, in May, 1703, Edward Jones, Bishop of St. Asaph, was borne to his grave in the chancel of St. Margaret's Church.

Barton Street and Cowley Street, both of which branch out of College Street, are stated to have been built by Barton Booth, the actor, whom we have mentioned as a Westminster schoolboy under Dr. Busby. To the former street Booth gave his own Christian name, and to the latter that of his favourite poet, who also, as we have already seen, was an "old Westminster." There is a large old house at the end of Cowley Street, having a fine double staircase; indeed, there are fine staircases, and other marks of aristocratic occupation, in many of the houses round about this spot.

Abingdon Street, which forms the connecting link between Old Palace Yard and Millbank, was, at the commencement of the last century, known as Lindsay Lane, down the narrow length of which the lumbersome state carriage and eight heavily-caparisoned horses were driven into the court-yard of Lindsay House (at the south-west end of the thoroughfare), afterwards the residence of the Earl of Abingdon, and subsequently that of the Earl of Carnarvon, in order to be turned round to take up the King when he went to open Parliament.

At No. 24 in this street, in September, 1834, died, at an advanced age, Thomas Telford, the engineer. He was buried in the Abbey.

Wood Street, the thoroughfare extending from the south end of Abingdon Street to Tufton Street, was described, in 1720, as "very narrow, being old boarded hovels, ready to fall." Here resided John Carter, Esq., F.S.A., the distinguished author of "Specimens of Ancient Sculpture and Painting." He first became known to the public by his etchings engraved in the "Sepulchral Monuments," and other valuable antiquarian works. He died in September, 1817. In North Street, which leads from Wood Street to Smith Square, resided Mr. R. W. Elliston, the celebrated actor of his day, and some time manager of Drury Lane and the Olympic Theatres.

Millbank is described by Strype as "a very long place, which beginneth by Lindsay House, or, rather, by the Old Palace Yard, and runneth up into Peterborough (afterwards Grosvenor) House, which is the farthest house. The part from against College Street unto the Horseferry hath a good row of buildings on the east side, next to the Thames, which is most taken up with large wood-mongers' yards and brewhouses. The north side is but ordinary, except one or two houses by the end of College Street; and that part beyond the Horseferry hath a very good row of houses, much inhabited by gentry, by reason of the pleasant situation and prospect of the Thames. The Earl of Peterborough's house hath a large court-yard before it, and a fine garden behind it, but its situation is but bleak in the winter, and not over-healthful, as being so near the low meadows on the south and west parts."

Pennant speaks of Millbank not as a "very long place," or a district, but as a single mansion. He says it is "the last dwelling in Westminster," and describes it as "a large house, which took its name from a mill which once occupied its site." He says that it was purchased from the Mordaunts, Earls of Peterborough, by the ancestor of Sir Robert Grosvenor, whose hospitality he had often experienced as a boy. In the plan of London by Hollar, the site is marked as Peterborough House, and was owned by that family till, at least, the middle of the eighteenth century, though occasionally let to wealthy merchants. The wall round the garden, with an outer footpath along the river-side, was not removed till about 1810. The Earl of Wilton, brother of the late marquis, and uncle of the Duke of Westminster, was born here, and baptised, as we have said, in the adjoining church of St. John the Evangelist.

It was whilst living here, in 1735, that Charles, third Earl of Peterborough, married, as his second wife, Mrs. Anastasia Robinson, the celebrated singer. His lordship died the same year, after which the house was rebuilt by the Grosvenor family.

The mansion—or its occupant—at this time became the subject of a joke in Joe Miller's "Jest Book," under the head of "High Living," which will bear re-telling:—"Peterborough House, which is the very last in London, one way, being rebuilt, a gentleman asked another who lived in it. His friend told him Sir Robert Grosvenor. 'I don't know,' said the first, 'what estate Sir Robert has, but he ought to have a very good one; for nobody lives beyond him in the whole town.'"

As Congreve was being rowed in a wherry up the Thames, at Millbank, the boatman remarked that, owing to its bad foundation, Peterborough House had sunk a story. "No, friend," said he, "I rather believe it is a story raised."

Holywell Street, erected on the grounds of Peterborough House, was so called after an estate belonging to Lord Grosvenor, in Flintshire.

The Government contractor, Mr. Vidler, lived in a house which had been built in the middle of Millbank by a Sir John Crosse, and to it, as Mr. Mackenzie Walcott informs us, the mail-coaches, before the unromantic days of railroads, used to be driven in annual procession, upon the King's birth-day, from Lombard Street. At noon the cavalcade set out—the horses belonging to the different mails being decked out with new harness, the guards and coachmen decorated with beautiful nosegays, and the postboys in scarlet jackets on horseback in advance. The king's birthday, in 1790, was the occasion of the first of these processions, when sixteen set out with plated harness and hammer-cloths of scarlet and gold.

In the Clause Rolls, 28 Henry VIII., is a grant wherein is mentioned "the manor of Neyte, with the precinct of water called the Mote of the said manor." Some buildings which afterwards occu-pied the site were known as the "Neat Houses." Stowe mentions them as "a parcel of houses most seated on the banks of the Thames, and inhabited by gardeners." John, fifth son of Richard, Duke of York, was born at the Manor House of Neyte, in 1448; and Edward VI., in his first year, granted the "House of Neyte" to Sir Anthony Brown. Pepys mentions going to take his amusement in these "Neat gardens;" and, if we may believe the *Domestic Intelligencer* of August 5th, 1679, "the mother of Nell Gwyn fell into the water near this spot, by accident, and was drowned."

In Smith Square, which lies between Wood Street and Romney Street, is a singular building, which a stranger would never be likely to take for a church, and yet it *is* a church—that of St. John the Evan-gelist; and it is one of the fifty churches built in and about the metropolis in the reign of Queen Anne. The Act of Parliament under which this church was built is commemorated by Tickell in his "Epistles" thus :—

"The pious Town sees fifty churches rise."

Its architect was not Vanbrugh, as is often stated, but a Mr. Archer, who certainly seems to have defied all the rules of architecture, loading the heavy structure with still heavier ornamenta-tion, by building at each of the four angles a stone tower and a pinnacle of ugliness that passes description. In front is a portico supported by

Doric columns, and the same order is continued, after a fashion, in pilasters round the building. It has, also, on the north and south sides other porticos, supported by massive stone pillars. Over the communion-table is a painted window, representing the "Descent from the Cross." The author of "A New Review of the Public Buildings," &c., published in 1736, speaks of "the new church with the four towers at Westminster" as an ornament to the city, and deeply regrets that a vista was not opened from Old Palace Yard, so as to bring its "beauty" fairly into view! Some idea of the writer's taste may be formed when our readers learn that he proposed, as a further improvement, to dwarf the said four towers, "cutting them off in the middle, like those of Babel!"

Lord Grosvenor lived at Millbank till the beginning of the present century; his house stood near the river, and had a pretty garden attached to it. Pennant, the antiquary, used to visit his lordship there, as he tells us in his work on London. At that time the locality was a fashionable resort on Sundays, and the bank of the river was edged with pollard oaks, presenting a view almost as rural as that which we now see at Fulham or Putney.

Marsham Street, Earl Street, and Romney Street, in this immediate neighbourhood, were all named after the owner of the property, Charles Marsham, Earl of Romney. Of the same fanciful style of naming streets we have already given an instance in our account of "George," "Villiers," "Duke," and "Buckingham" Streets, close by Charing Cross. Nearly the whole of one side of Earl Street is occupied by the Westminster Brewery, and the other side by Messrs. Hadfield's marble works and gallery of sculpture, which were established here in 1804.

Vine Street—the old name of Romney Street—which we pass on our right, recalls the time when, as was the case also at Smithfield, in Hatton Garden, and in St. Giles's, there was here a flourishing vineyard. "There was a garden," says Stow, "they called the Vine Garden, because perhaps vines anciently were there nourished, and wine made." Under date of 1565, in the Overseers' Book, a rate is made for "the Vyne Garden," and "Myll," next to Bowling Alley. In the first year of Edward VI., as we learn from Brayley's "History," payment was made to "Rich. Wolward, keeper of the King's house at Westminster, j mark to repair the King's vineyard there." In that reign the place appears to have been inclosed with houses and other buildings. "With a parcel of ground called the Mill-bank, valued at 58s., it was given by Edward VI., in the third year of his reign, to Joanna Smith, in consideration of service."

Churchill, the satirist, was born in this street in the year 1731. He writes :—

"Famed Vine Street,
Where Heaven, the kindest wish of man to grant,
Gave me an old house and a kinder aunt!"

The aunt, however, so far as we know, left him no memorial of her kindness, in recompense for the immortality which he has bestowed upon her.

It is enough to make the mouth of one bred in the country to water when one reads of a Vine Street near Piccadilly Circus, and another in the heart of Westminster, and remembers that these names were not given and written up in irony and mockery, but point to the fact that vineyards, most probably the property of the Abbot of Westminster, did once exist on the slopes which existed near the Abbey. As Mr. Matthew Browne remarks in "Chaucer's England:"—"It is not difficult for a man who wanders as far as he can into the heart of the purlieus of Westminster Abbey, to imagine in that old garden there, with the well in the midst, that the Abbot's orchery and vinery are close at hand somewhere, with a pond fringed by fallen leaves blown off the beeches, and peopled with delicious fish—so strong is the sense that comes over you of shade and monastic stillness." It need, however, be no matter of surprise to find that even in Westminster there were vineyards, where wine was squeezed from the juice of grapes grown on the spot. At Beaulieu Abbey, near Southampton, there are fields still known as the Vineyards; and the late Lord Montagu, who died in 1845, had in his cellar brandy made from the vines grown on that estate. In Barnaby Googe's "Four Books of Husbandry," published in 1578, we find several remarks on the former growth of vineyards in England. The author quaintly adds, "There hath, moreover, good experience of late years been made by two noble and honourable barons of this realm—the Lord Cobham and the Lord Willyams — who had both growing about their houses as good wines as are in many parts of France." Stow also mentions an old MS. roll, in his time extant in the Gate House of Windsor Castle, in which was to be seen the yearly account of the charges of the planting of vines that, in the time of Richard II., "grew in great plenty in the Little Park, and also of the wine itself, whereof some part was spent in the King's house." If this was certainly the case at Windsor, there is no reason to doubt that the vine may have grown and flourished in vineyards on the southern slopes that looked down what was St. James's Park; indeed, a plot of ground in that park in the last century was called "the King's Vineyard."

Horseferry Road, which we may be supposed to have reached, leads to that part of the river between Westminster and Lambeth, where was the only horse-ferry allowed on the Thames in London. The ferry was granted by patent to the Archbishop of Canterbury; and the ferry-boat station on the Lambeth side was near the palace-gate. On the opening of Westminster Bridge the ferry practically ceased, and compensation, amounting to upwards of £2,200, was granted to the see of Canterbury; but, as we learn from a work styled "Select Views of London and its Environs," published in 1805, the ferry was still in use in the early part of the present century, though its traffic was sadly diminished. Indeed, it may be said to have continued more or less as a ferry, down to the building of Lambeth Bridge, in 1862. This bridge, which is constructed of iron, on the suspension principle, has three spans of 280 feet. As our readers may perhaps feel interested in learning what were the rates charged at the horse-ferry, we here give them :—For a man and horse, 2s.; horse and chaise, 1s.; coach and two horses, 1s. 6d.; coach and four horses, 2s.; coach and six horses, 2s. 6d.; a laden cart, 2s. 6d.; cart or wagon, 2s. Mr. Mackenzie Walcott tells us that close to the ferry a wooden house was built for a small guard, which was posted here at the time of the Commonwealth.

Here, on the shore of the dark wintry waters, on the 9th of December, 1688, Mary of Modena, the ill-starred consort of James II., having quitted Whitehall for the last time, stepped into the boat that was to convey her across the river to Lambeth. Passing through the Privy Gardens into the street, the Queen with her infant son, his two nurses, and two male attendants, got into a coach, and threading her way through the narrow lanes which surrounded the east and south of the old Abbey precincts, drove to the horse-ferry, where a boat awaited her. "The night was wet and stormy, and so dark," writes St. Victor, in his "Narrative of the Escape of the Queen of England," "that when we got into the boat we could not see each other, though we were closely seated, for the boat was very small." Thus, literally "with only one frail plank between her and eternity," did the Queen cross the swollen waters, her tender infant of six months old in her arms, with no better attendants than his nurses, and having no other escort than the Count de Lauzun and the writer (St. Victor), who confessed that he felt an extreme terror at the peril to which he saw personages of their importance exposed, and that his only reliance was in the mercy of God, "by whose especial providence,"

he says, "we were preserved, and arrived at our destination. Our passage," he adds, "was rendered very difficult and dangerous by the violence of the wind and the heavy and incessant rain. When we reached the opposite side of the Thames, . . . the coach was still at the inn." Thither St. Victor ran to hasten it, leaving Lauzun to protect the Queen. Her Majesty meantime withdrew herself and her little company under the walls of Lambeth Old Church, without any other shelter from the wind and bitter cold. The child fortunately slept through it all; the coach was soon found, and the party arrived safely at Gravesend, where a yacht was ready to convey them to the coast of France. History tells us that they reached Calais without further disaster, and that they never set eyes on the shores of England again.

A curious print of the time represents the boat in which the Queen effected her escape as in no little danger, and the two gentlemen as assisting the rowers, who are labouring against wind and tide. The Queen herself is seated by the steersman, enveloped in a large cloak, with a hood drawn over her head : her attitude is expressive of melancholy; and she appears most anxious to conceal the little prince, who is asleep on her bosom, partially shrouded among the ample folds of her drapery. The other two females betray alarm. The engraving is rudely executed, and printed on coarse paper; but the design is not without merit, being bold and original in its conception and full of expression. It was probably intended as an appeal to the sympathies of the humbler classes on behalf of the royal fugitives.

Two evenings after the departure of his Queen and Consort, King James quitted Whitehall, and took at the horse-ferry a little boat with a single pair of oars, with which he crossed over to Vauxhall, where horses awaited him. He took with him the Great Seal of England, doubtless with the idea that he might have to use it when safe in France; but, induced by some motive or other, he threw it into the river while crossing. He effected his escape as far as Feversham, where he was recognised, and whence he was brought back to Whitehall. A few days later, however, the Prince of Orange ordered his Dutch guards from St. James's Palace to enter Whitehall, and the King was compelled to depart. He dropped down the river in his barge as far as Gravesend, whence, as history tells us, he effected his escape to the shores of France. On the last night that he slept at Whitehall, when he was about to retire to bed, "Lord Craven came to tell him that the Dutch guards, horse and foot, were marching through the park in order of battle, in order to take possession of White-hall. The stout old earl, though in his eightieth year, professed his determination rather to be cut to pieces at his post than to resign his post at Whitehall to the Dutch. But this bloodshed the King forbade, knowing that it would be useless. The English guards reluctantly gave place to the foreigners, by whom they were superseded, and the next day the King left Whitehall for the last time."

Probably the last person of consequence who crossed the river here was the Princess Augusta of Saxe-Gotha, on Tuesday, April 27, 1736, on her way to be married to the Prince of Wales, the father of George III.

It sounds strange to hear that there was a Horse-ferry and Vauxhall Regatta as recently as 1840, but it is nevertheless true. In Colburn's "Calendar of Amusements" we read that "the arrangements.

MILLBANK ABOUT 1800. (*See page* 3.)

His subsequent sojourn and his death at St. Ger-main-en-Laye, near Paris, are matters known to every reader of English history.

The Great Seal, we may add, was afterwards re-covered, in a net cast at random by some poor fishermen, who delivered it into the hands of the Lords of the Council.

Mr. Mackenzie Walcott, in his amusing manner, tells us how that "very early one morning, while the watermen were dreaming of fares when they should have been at the river-side, the Duke of Marlborough with his hounds desired to cross. By good fortune one Wharton chanced to be at hand, and the duke rewarded him by obtaining a grant of the 'Ferry house' for him: the present owner is a descendant of Wharton."

made by the parochial authorities and others of the parish of St. John's, in getting up this regatta, are deserving of every encomium. The prizes, which bring into competition the watermen of Vauxhall and Westminster Horseferry, are really worth con-tending for — viz., two excellent wherries, and various sums of money. A steamer is engaged for the accommodation of the subscribers."

The works belonging to the Gas Light and Coke Company, which occupy a considerable space of ground between Peter Street and Horseferry Road, stand partly on the site of what was, at the begin-ning of the present century, the residence of a market-gardener, known as the "Bower" ale-house and tea-gardens—a name still perpetuated in that of the adjacent public-house—"The White Horse

THE OLD HORSEFERRY ABOUT 1800.

and Bower," in the Horseferry Road. These gas-works (one of the three earliest stations established by the first gas company in the metropolis, which received its charter of incorporation in 1812) owe their origin to the enterprise of a Mr. Winsor, the same who, on the evening of the King's birthday, in 1807, made a brilliant display of gas along the wall between the Mall and St. James's Park. It may be worth while to note here that the general lighting of the metropolis with gas began on Christmas Day, 1814. Branch establishments in connection with these gas-works have since been erected further westward, and more recently a larger establishment has been opened at Beckton, North Woolwich. There are also branches at Silvertown, Bromley, Bow Common Lane, Great Cambridge Street (Hackney Road), Haggerston, Nine Elms, Kensal Green, King's Cross, Fulham, &c.

The only other buildings in Horseferry Road which we need mention are the small Roman Catholic Chapel of St. Mary, served by the Jesuit Fathers (see *post*, p. 41) ; a Wesleyan Chapel ; the Westminster Training College for Schoolmasters and Practising Schools ; and the Westminster Mortuary and Coroner's Court, a substantial and well-designed structure which stands on ground presented by the Duke of Westminster, and dates from 1893.

Page Street, a clean and broad thoroughfare running parallel with Horseferry Road, presents a striking contrast to most of the streets and lanes which surround it. The graveyard belonging to St. John's Church occupies the greater part of one side ; it is railed in from the street, and with its surrounding trees, and level surface of turf, appears like an oasis in the wilderness. Its conversion into a public recreation ground has proved to be an immense boon to the children of this crowded neighbourhood.

A short distance from Page Street, with its frowning gateway overlooking the river, was Millbank Prison, formerly called the Penitentiary. In 1799 a plan was formed of penitentiary confinement calculated to reform offenders, and an Act of Parliament was drawn up under the direction of Sir William Blackstone, according to the suggestions of Mr. Howard, the prison philanthropist. Fifteen years after another Act was passed for carrying out the design, and a contract was entered into with Mr. Jeremy Bentham, the economist and philanthropist. It was intended as a realisation of a plan which Bentham had put forward on paper, and which he called " The Panopticon, or Inspection House," in recommendation of which scheme he published a work under that title, addressed

to Mr. Pitt. The latter, though a strong Tory, entered keenly into the views of the great social reformer, but the obstinacy of George III. prevented any experiment being made in the direction of the " separate system " in London for more than twenty years. Charles Knight tells us that the cost of the site was £12,000, and that of the building exceeded half a million, or about £500 for each cell. So it seems that felons are rather expensive luxuries for the country.

In the " Picture of London," published in the reign of George III., we read that this prison was established " for the punishment of offenders of secondary turpitude, usually punished by transportation for a term of years, since the disputes began which terminated in the separation from this country of the American States. The plan for colonising New South Wales led to a general system of expatriation to the antipodes ; which, as applied to definite periods, was cruel and unjust, because the wretched objects were generally precluded from the power of returning, however short might be the intended period of their punishment ! A strong and affecting memorial of the sheriffs of London led, however, to several Parliamentary notices and remonstrances against this indiscriminate mode of transportation, which was, in nearly all cases, *in effect*, for life ; and in consequence, this place of punishment and reform was projected at Millbank, and no culprits are, we understand, in future to be sent to New South Wales, except in those enormous cases that justify irrevocable transportation."

The building stood on ground purchased of the Marquis of Salisbury ; and although the Parliamentary grant for its erection was made as far back as 1799, it was not completed till 1821. It was a mass of brickwork, which, in its ground-plan, resembled a wheel, the governor's house occupying a circle in the centre, from which radiated six piles of buildings, terminating externally in circular towers with conical roofs, which gave to the prison the aspect of a fortress. The ground on which it stood is raised but little above the river, and was at one time considered unhealthy. It was the largest prison in London, and contained accommodation for about 1,100 prisoners. Every convict sentenced to penal servitude in Great Britain was sent to Millbank for a term previous to the sentence being carried into effect. The external walls formed an irregular octagon, and enclosed an area of eighteen acres of ground, and within that space the various ranges of buildings were so constructed that the governor, from a room in the centre, was able to view every one of the rows of cells. The circular towers are connected by what may be termed curtains, which has the effect of giving the appearance of a multiplicity of sides to the building. It was first named "The Penitentiary," or "Penitentiary House for London and Middlesex," but in 1843 the name was altered, by Act of Parliament, to "Millbank Prison." Here Arthur Orton, the "claimant" of the Tichborne title and estates—the "unfortunate young nobleman doomed to languish in a prison," in the eyes of certain "fools and fanatics"—spent the first six months of his fourteen years of penal servitude.

A broad esplanade or embankment extends the whole length of the river front of Millbank Prison, and, with a broad and open thoroughfare called Ponsonby Street, leads to the foot of Vauxhall Bridge.

Vauxhall Bridge was at first called "Regent" Bridge, probably from the circumstance that the first stone on the Middlesex side was laid by Lord Dundas, as proxy for the Prince Regent (George IV.). The works were commenced in May, 1811. The first stone of the abutment on the Surrey side was laid in September, 1813, by Prince Charles of Brunswick, eldest son of the Duke of Brunswick, the same who fell soon afterwards on the field of Waterloo. The bridge was finished in August, 1816. It was built from the designs of Mr. James Walker, and cost about £300,000. The iron superstructure, consisting of nine equal arches, each seventy-eight feet in span, is supported on eight rusticated stone piers, built on a foundation of wooden framing cased with stone. The length of the bridge is about 800 feet. The proximity of the bridge to the once famous gardens of Vauxhall, and the facility it was likely to afford to visitors, led to the original name being soon changed to Vauxhall. As we have now lost the gardens for ever, it is pleasant —to quote the words of Mr. Charles Knight—" to have some memorial of the spot made so familiar to us by the writings of our great men."

In Bessborough Gardens, at the foot of Vauxhall Bridge, is the beautiful church of the Holy Trinity, which was built at the expense of the Rev. W. H. E. Bentinck, Archdeacon and Prebendary of Westminster; the first stone of it was laid by Mrs. Bentinck, in November, 1849. The ground on which the church is built was given by Mr. Thomas Cubitt, M.P.; and the building—which is in the "Early Decorated" style of architecture of the time of Edward I. and II.—was erected from the designs ot Mr. John L. Pearson, at a cost of about £10,000. The church can accommodate about 850 worshippers. It consists of a lofty nave, transepts, chancel, and a vestibule at the north-east

corner of the chancel. The tower has a double-lighted belfry, windows and pinnacles at the corner, crocketed at the angle; and on the top of the tower is a spire rising to the height of about 200 feet.

Vauxhall Bridge Road, which extends from the Bridge and Bessborough Gardens to the western end of Victoria Street, may be regarded as forming the termination of Westminster in this direction. A large house on the eastern side of it, formerly built as a club and library for the Guards, was bought about the year 1870, by the Roman Catholic body, in order to form a residence for the "Archbishop of Westminster" for the time being, and shortly afterwards Cardinal Manning took up his abode in it. The rooms are large and lofty, but, in spite of some fine pictures of Roman Catholic prelates which grace its walls, the house has anything but a palatial appearance. Not far off, and between Rochester Row and Victoria Street, it is ultimately intended to erect the Westminster Cathedral of the future; but many centuries must elapse before it equals in historic interest the venerable Abbey hard by. Its plan is that of a lofty Gothic structure of the Decorated or Edwardian style, with nave, chancel, transepts, side chapels, tower, and lofty spire.

It may, perhaps, appear strange to think of finding a Regent Street in the purlieus of Westminster; nevertheless there is one, and in passing through it, one may, of course, look in vain for such fashionable establishments as those which meet the eye in the street which most persons know by that name. Crossing Regent Street at right angles is Vincent Street, and by this latter turning we enter Vincent Square, a large space of ground covering about ten acres, which once formed part of Tothill Fields, of which we shall have more to say in our next chapter. In 1810, this plot of land was marked out as a playground for the Westminster scholars, the sum of £3 being paid for a plough and a team of horses to drive deep furrows round the site, and £2 4s. more for the digging of a trench at the north-east end, to prevent carts from passing over it, as it was then open and unfenced. Further sums were paid for levelling the surface for cricket, and for railing the ten acres in, and fixing gates. It was named after the learned Dean Vincent, who then presided over the Abbey Church.

The church of St. Mary the Virgin, in this square, was built from the designs of Mr. Edward Blore, and was consecrated in October, 1837. The Dean and Chapter gave the ground, and also granted a site for schools which have since been erected, for the accommodation of 600 children.

Rochester Row, running parallel with Vincent Square on its north side, is so called after the bishopric of that name, which was held conjointly with the deanery of Westminster by Dolben, Sprat, Atterbury, Bradford, Wilcocks, Pearce, Thomas, and Horsley. George III., it is said, condoled with Dr. Vincent on the separation of the see and the deanery. Many others of the neighbouring streets are named from clergymen connected with Westminster, as Carey and Page Streets, from the head-masters of St. Peter's College; Fynes Street, from Dr. Fynes-Clinton, of St. Margaret's; and Douglas Street, from the Rev. Prebendary Douglas.

On the north side of Rochester Row are Emery Hill's almshouses, founded in 1708, to provide homes for twelve poor persons, and also the Rev. James Palmer's almshouses, to be homes for a like number of poor persons. The latter were founded in 1656, and re-erected in 1881-2.

Opposite these almshouses is St. Stephen's Church, which was erected and endowed about the year 1847, by Miss (now Baroness) Burdett-Coutts. It is from the designs of Mr. Benjamin Ferrey. It is built in the Decorated Gothic style of the fourteenth century, with a tower and spire on the northern side, nearly 200 feet high. The church, which is most richly decorated and picturesque, will hold about 1,000 worshippers. On the south side of the west front is a group of schools attached to the church, which afford accommodation for about 400 children; together with a parsonage, or presbytery, a portion of which forms a tower surmounted by a quaint, foreign-looking louvre.

In Francis Street, an out-of-the-way thoroughfare on the north side of Rochester Row, and only a few yards from the new and noble thoroughfare of Victoria Street, is a building of more interest, perhaps, to the criminal classes than to Londoners in general, called Tothill Fields Prison, or Bridewell, as it used to be termed. It stands out of sight, being screened from view on almost every side by new mansions taller than itself, justifying the saying of Jeremy Bentham, to the effect that "if a place could exist of which it could be said that it was in no neighbourhood, that place would be Tothill Fields."

The old Bridewell occupied the plot of ground adjoining the north side of the Green-Coat School site, on the west side of Artillery Place, and leading into Victoria Street; so that, as this same school, or "St. Margaret's Hospital," as it was formerly called, was dedicated as far back as the year 1633, to the relief of the poor fatherless children of St. Margaret's parish, it is probable that the hospital, or "abiding house," for the poor, and its next-door

neighbour, the Bridewell, or "house of correction," for the compulsory employment of able-bodied but indolent paupers, were originally joint parish institutions—the one for granting relief to the industrious poor, and the other for punishing the idle. Hence these twin establishments—the one erected under James I., and the other under Charles I.— were probably among the first institutions raised for carrying out the provisions of the first Poor Law, enacted in 1601.

The Bridewell itself, which Sir Richard Steele mentions as existing in Tothill Fields at the beginning of the eighteenth century, was erected nearly a hundred years earlier, namely, in 1618, as may be seen from an inscription let into the wall of the House of Correction. "This ancient prison," says the London chronicles, "was altered and enlarged in the year 1655;" and "in corroboration of the statement," writes the author of "The Great World of London," "we find in the garden surrounding the present building the stone frame, or skeleton, as it were, of the old prison gateway, in shape like the Greek letter Π, standing by itself as a memorial at the back of Bridewell." This cromlech-like relic is covered with ivy, and looks at first more like some piece of imitation ruin-work than the remains of a prison portal, for the doorway is so primitive in character (being not more than five feet ten inches high and three feet wide) that it seems hardly bigger than the entrance to a cottage; nevertheless, an inscription painted on the lintel assures us that it was "The Gateway, or Principal Entrance, to Tothill Fields Prison; erected 1665; taken down and removed to this site A.D. 1836." Colonel Despard was imprisoned in the former Bridewell in 1803.

Although originally designed as a Bridewell for *vagrants*, Tothill Fields was converted, we are told, in the reign of Queen Anne, into a gaol for the confinement of criminals also; and Howard, writing towards the end of the last century (1777), describes it as being "remarkably well managed" at that period, holding up its enlightened and careful keeper, one George Smith, as "a model to other governors." In 1826, however, the erection of a new prison was decided upon, and an Act for that purpose obtained. Then a different site was chosen, and eight acres of land on the western side of the Green-Coat School, and near the Vauxhall Bridge Road, were purchased for £16,000. The designs were furnished by Mr. Robert Abraham, and the building, which cost £186,000, was completed and opened for the reception of prisoners in the year 1834; soon after which the old prison was pulled down, and the relics already described transferred to the new one, as we have said, in 1836.

The new prison, which will accommodate about 900 prisoners in all, is situate on the southern side of Victoria Street. It is a solid and even handsome structure, and one of great extent as well as strength. "Seen from Victoria Street," says one London topographer—though, by the bye, it is in no way visible in that direction—"it resembles a substantial fortress." The main entrance is on the Vauxhall side of the building in Francis Street, and the doorway here is formed of massive granite blocks, and immense iron gates, ornamented above with portcullis work. "Viewed from this point," the author of "London Prisons" describes the exterior (though there is nothing but a huge dead wall and the prison gateway to be seen) as being "the very ideal of a national prison—vast, airy, light, and yet inexorably safe."

The building is said to be one of the finest specimens of brickwork in the metropolis, and consists of three distinct prisons, each constructed alike, on Bentham's "panopticon" plan, in the form of a half-wheel, i.e., with a series of detached wings, radiating, spoke-fashion, from a central lodge, or "argus," as such places were formerly styled. One of such lodges is situate, midway, in each of the three sides of the spacious turfed and planted court-yard; so that the outline of the ground-plan of these three distinct, half-wheel-like prisons resembles the ace of clubs, with the court-yard forming an open square in the centre.

The building is good in its sanitary conditions, and the death-rate is said to be lower than that of most prisons in the kingdom.

On the face of the building is a memorial stone, with the inscription recording the original purpose of its erection:—"Here are several sorts of Work for the Poor of this Parish of St. Margaret, Westminster, as also the County, according to Law, and for such as will beg and live Idle in this City and Liberty of Westminster, Anno 1655." From this it will be seen that it was originally intended as a Bridewell or House of Correction, and a place of "penitentiary amendment" of such vagrants and "sturdy beggars," and "valiant rogues" as objected to work for their living. In fact, it was meant to be a sort of penal establishment in connection with the Poor House, and, like it, maintained at the expense of the City.

Mr. Hepworth Dixon finds fault with this building as ill planned, and a "costly blunder;" and possibly such may be the case. Down to 1850 it had been appropriated to the reception of all classes of convicted prisoners, but from and after

that date it has been set apart for convicted female prisoners, and for males below seventeen years old.

Speaking of Tothill Fields Prison, the witty author of the "Town Spy," published in 1725, quaintly remarks: "In the fields of this parish stands a famous factory for hemp, which is wrought with greater industry than ordinary, because the manufacturers enjoy the fruits of their own labour, a number of English gentlemen having here a restraint put upon their liberties."

The names of the various courts and alleys to the south of this prison still serve to keep in remembrance the once rural character of the locality: here is Willow Walk; close by are Pool Place, and Pond Place, and so on. Here, also, are two lofty brick buildings, which will at once attract attention: one is the hospital for the Grenadier Guards, which was erected about the year 1860, on a vacant plot of ground between Rochester Row and Francis Street; the other rejoices in the name of the Guards' Industrial Home. Close by the latter is the large and spacious building already mentioned as the residence of Cardinal Manning.

At the east end of Rochester Row, facing Grey-Coat Place, is the Grey-Coat School, or Hospital, so named from the colour of the clothing worn by its inmates. It was founded in the year 1698, for the education of seventy poor boys and forty poor girls. The hospital presents a considerable frontage towards Grey-Coat Place, from which it is separated by a large court-yard. It is composed of a central building, ornamented with a clock, turret, and bell, above the royal arms of Queen Anne, with the motto "Semper eadem," flanked by a figure on either side, dressed in the former costume of the children. The south side, which looks out upon an open garden and spacious detached play-grounds (the whole surrounded by an extensive wall), contains the school-rooms. Above is a wainscoted dining-hall, used also for the private prayers of the inmates of the hospital. The dormitories occupy the whole attic storey. In the board-room—a noble panelled apartment—are portraits of the royal foundress, Queen Anne; Dr. Compton, Bishop of London; Dr. Smalridge, Bishop of Bristol; and those of other former governors. In July, 1875, the first distribution of prizes to the children was made by the Duke of Buccleuch, who congratulated the children and visitors upon the successful working of the school under the new scheme. The number of children had increased from twenty-eight to upwards of one hundred.

In Strutton Ground, not far from Grey-Coat

Place, was formerly a house named "the Million Gardens," where, in 1718, tickets were to be purchased for a lottery of plate, as we learn from the *Weekly Journal*. "The name, in reality," observes Mr. Larwood in his "History of Sign Boards," "refers to the Melon Gardens, a fruit which was often pronounced as 'Million' in the seventeenth and eighteenth centuries."

Strutton (or, as it ought more properly to be called, Stourton) Ground perpetuates the name of

the other side, at the entry into Tothill Field, Stourton House, which Giles, the last Lord Dacre, purchased and built anew; whose lady and wife, Anne, left money to build a hospital for twenty poor men and so many children, which hospital," the old historian adds, "her executors have now begun in the field adjoining." This institution is now known as Dacre's Almshouses, or Emmanuel Hospital, and stands in Hopkins' Row, at the

THE GREYCOAT SCHOOL. *From an Original Sketch.* (*See page* 11.)

called, Stourton) Ground perpetuates the name of the Lords Stourton, whose town-house, surrounded by fair garden-grounds, once stood here. The mansion became afterwards the residence of the Lords Dacre. Opposite to Stourton House, in the days of the Stuarts, stood the residence of Lord Grey de Wilton. Both these houses are shown in Norden's Map of London in 1603.

A little to the north of the district which we have been describing is, or rather was, Tothill Street, for it is now all but swept away. According to honest John Stow, it "runneth" from the west gate of the old Palace at Westminster, which gate, as we know, formerly stood at the entrance to Dean's Yard. "Herein," as Stow informs us, "is a house of the Lord Grey of Wilton; and on

back of York Street. The house of the Lords Dacre is, or was in the year 1856, still standing in Dacre Street, leading out of the Broadway, and its gardens occupied the site of what is now termed Strutton Ground—not a very elegant variation of the name Stourton.

In an old map of Westminster, bearing date 1776, the City of Westminster seems limited within its south-western boundary to that ancient causeway, the Horseferry Road. Beyond this, toward Pimlico and Chelsea, spread the open fields, with but here and there scattered buildings. Ponds and marshy ground appear at the western end of Rochester Row, and patches of garden-ground distinguish the cultivated from the generally waste character of the soil. On the site of the present gas-works was Eldrick's Nursery, which supplied the district with fruit and flowering shrubs, as the Abbey vineyard had supplied the monks in the olden time with many a vintage, and the site of which, as we have shown above, might be traced in the thoroughfare till a recent date known as Vine Street.

It will be seen from these remarks that it has been often said that Westminster proper—the trian-

recently, more almshouses, more charity schools, and more prisons, more ancient mansions, and more costermongers' hovels, more thieves' dens and low public houses, than in any other part of the metropolis of equal extent.

It has been sarcastically, but perhaps not undeservedly, remarked, that the City of Westminster is, and has long been, the centre of dissipation of the whole empire; and such perhaps it may be,

THE "FIVE HOUSES." *From an Engraving published in* 1796. (*See page* 14.)

gular slip of the metropolis which lies between the Thames, St. James's Park, and the Vauxhall Bridge Road—can boast at once of some of the noblest and the meanest structures to be found throughout London; the grand old Abbey contrasting with the filthy and squalid Duck Lane almost as strongly as do the new Houses of Parliament and the Palace of which they form a part with the slums about the Broadway, which well nigh equal the dingy tenements which till lately stood about the Almonry, now almost absorbed into the Westminster Palace Hotel. But such is really the case. In Westminster we have the contrast between rich and poor as marked as in St. Giles's and St. James's; for almost within a stone's throw of the seat of the great Legislature of England there are, or were till

for the region to the north of Pall Mall has been, ever since the institution of "clubs," the headquarters of luxury; while a visit to the purlieus of Westminster proper—to the south of the Abbey and Victoria Street—would serve to convince the most incredulous that dissipation does not belong to the upper classes exclusively. Here, however, as in other parts of the great metropolis, recent years have witnessed vast improvements. The building of Victoria Street, and the demolition of old buildings for the construction of the Metropolitan District Railway, necessitated the removal of some of the worst neighbourhoods of Westminster. Still, in the district bordering on the river, the general aspect of the dwellings is to a great extent unchanged.

CHAPTER II.

WESTMINSTER.—TOTHILL FIELDS AND NEIGHBOURHOOD.

"No mead so fit
For courtly joust or tourney brave."—*Cavalier Song.*

Origin of the Word "Tothill"—Punishment of Necromancers—Grant of a Market and Fair to be held in "Tuthill"—Burials in Tothill Fields—The "Five Houses" or "Seven Chimneys"—The Pest-house—The "Maze" and Public Recreation Ground—The "Butts"—Trial by Wager of Battle—The Last "Affair of Honour"—"Masked Highwaymen in Tothill Fields"—Tothill Fields in the time of Charles I.—Westminster Fair—St. Edward's Fair—Tothill Street—Strutton Ground—Southern, the Dramatic Poet—Drinking-houses in the Olden Time—The Old Swan-yard—The "Cock" Tavern—Royal Aquarium and Summer and Winter Garden—Old and New Pye Streets—The Broadway—Westminster Town Hall—York Street—Van Dun's Almshouses—Westminster Panorama—Milton's Residence—Emmanuel Hospital—Westminster Chapel—The Infirmary—James Street—Richard Glover—William Gifford.

THE origin of the word "Tot-hill" is probably the "toot," or beacon hill, from the Welch word "twt," a spring or rising; and the name was probably given to this district from a beacon placed here, as the highest spot in and around the flat region of Westminster. The antiquary, Mr. Wykeham Archer, however, derives the name from Teut, the chief divinity of the Druids, and the equivalent of Thoth, the Egyptian Mercury, adding that the "Tot," "Teut," "Tut," or "Thoth" Hill, often, by the way, styled "Tuttle" and "Tut-hill," was the spot on which solemn proclamations were made to the people. Another derivation may also be suggested. The Normans, as we happen to know, often spoke of these parts as "Thorny Island, *et tout la champ.*" What more easy than the corruption of these two words into "Tuttle?" It should, however, be stated that in Rocque's Map (1746), "Toote Hill" is marked at a bend in the Horseferry Road. "Toot," also, in one of its varied forms, is not an uncommon prefix to the names of other places in different parts of England, as, *Tot*nes, *Tot*ham, *Tut*bury, *Toot*ing, *Tott*enham, &c.; and it may be added that all these are places of considerable elevation compared with the surrounding parts.

"Tothill Fields," says Mr. Archer, in his "Vestiges of Old London," "were, within three centuries, part of a marshy tract of land lying between Millbank and Westminster Abbey, and on which stood a few scattered buildings, some of them the residences of noble personages." They must have witnessed some extraordinary scenes in the Middle Ages. Here necromancers were punished by the destruction of their instruments; for we read that, in the reign of Edward III., a man was taken "practising with a dead man's head, and brought to the bar at the King's Bench, where, after abjuration of his art, his trinkets were taken from him, carried to Tothill, and burned before his face." And, again, in the time of Richard I., Raulf Wigtoft, chaplain to Geoffrey, Archbishop of York, "had provided a girdle and ring, cunningly intoxicated. wherewith he meant to have destroyed Simon (the Dean of York) and others; but his messenger was intercepted, and his girdle and ring burned at this place before the people."

These fields, according to Stow, in the reign of Henry III., formed part of a manor in Westminster, belonging to "John Mansell, the King's counsellor and priest, who did invite to a stately dinner (at his house at Totehill) the kings and queens of England and Scotland, with divers courtiers and citizens, and whereof there was such a multitude that seven hundred messes of meat did not serve for the first dinner." By an Act passed in the same reign, 34 Henry III., the Abbot of Westminster obtained "leave to keepe a markett in the Tuthill every Munday, and a faire every yeare, for three days." Here, in 1236, "royal solemnities and goodly jousts were held" after the coronation of Queen Eleanor, consort of Henry III. Two centuries afterwards, the fields in the neighbourhood were used for appeals by combat; and Stow describes "a combate that was appointed to have been fought" the 18th of June, "in Trinity Terme, 1571," for a "certain manour or demaine lands," in the Isle of Harty, "adjoining to the Isle of Sheppey, in Kent," and for which "it was thought good," says the historian, that "the Court should sit in Tuthill Fields, where was prepared one plot of ground, one and twenty yardes square, double railed, for the combate, without the West Square." In the time of Nicholas Culpepper, the author of the well-known "Herbal," these fields were famous for their parsley. In 1651 (August 25th) "the trained bands of London, Westminster," &c., to the number of 14,000, we are told, "drew out into Tuttle Fields." Here, too, were built the "Five Houses," or "Seven Chimneys," as pest-houses for victims to the plague, and in 1665 many of those who had fallen victims to that direful scourge were buried here. Under date of July 18, 1665, Samuel Pepys writes in his "Diary:"—"I was much troubled this day to hear at Westminster how the officers do bury the dead in the open Tuttle Fields, pretending want of room elsewhere; whereas the New Chapel churchyard was walled in at the publick charge in the last plague-time, merely for want of room, and now none but such as are able to pay dear for it can be buried there." Here, a short while previously, some "1,200 Scotch prisoners, taken at the battle of Worcester," were interred; for in the accounts of the churchwardens of St. Margaret's, Westminster, there is the payment of "thirty shillings for sixty-seven loads of soil laid on the graves of Tothill Fields, wherein," it is added, "the Scotch prisoners are buried." Some of the Scotch were "driven like a herd of swine," says Heath's "Chronicle," "through Westminster to Tuthill Fields," and there sold to several merchants, and sent to the island of Barbadoes.

The "Five Houses," if we may trust the *Builder*, retained much of their primitive appearance in 1832. "With the moss and lichens growing on the roofs and walls, and their generally old-fashioned quaint-ness, a very small stretch of the imagination re-moved the buildings which had surrounded them even then, and brought them once more into the open ground. They marked the site of a battery and breastwork when the fortifications around the cities of London and Westminster were hurriedly thrown up in 1642, by an order of Parliament. This battery is marked as about midway between the Chelsea Road and the bank of the river oppo-site Vauxhall."

The Pest Houses were built by Lord Craven as a lazaretto for the reception of the victims of the Great Plague which preceded the Fire of London. We have already mentioned this nobleman in our account of Craven House, Drury Lane; and it deserves to be recorded to his credit that at that awful season he was not satisfied with building this hospital, but that he sheltered many of the sufferers by that disease who had no residences except in the doomed city, remaining himself on the spot, "with the same coolness with which he had fought the battles of his mistress, the Queen of Bohemia," in order to maintain order and to mitigate the horrors of the scene.

These "pest-houses" consisted of a row of red-brick buildings, and were erected at a cost of £250. At the beginning of the last century they were made into almshouses for twenty-four aged married people. Some remains of them are—or were re-cently—to be seen near Vauxhall Bridge Road.

"Many a torch or lanthorn-lighted group of mysterious-looking figures have borne the litter of the stricken to this then solitary spot, not so much with hope of recovery, as from fear of spreading the dire infection by retaining them within the frighted and unhealthy town." In connection with the surrounding fields, there are several incidents recorded illustrative of the days of old. Prior to the Statutes of Restraint, they were considered to be within the limits of the sanctuary of the Abbey.

In the seventeenth century the people used to resort to a "Maze" in these same Tothill Fields, which, according to an old writer, was "much frequented in the summer-time, in fair afternoons," the fields being described as "of great use, plea-sure, and recreation," to the King's Scholars and neighbours. And Sir Richard Steele, writing in "The Tatler," in 1709, says, "Here was a military garden, a bridewell, and, as I have heard tell, a racecourse." A bear-garden, kept by one William Wells, stood upon the site of the present Vincent Square during the reign of Queen Anne. Mr. Mackenzie Walcott says that, as lately as 1793, there was a famous bear-garden in these fields; and near Willow Walk resided one Haverfield, a noted highwayman, who kept two bears in his rooms as myrmidons. Willow Walk was formerly noted for its "monster" tea-gardens. Bull-baiting occasion-ally took place here as recently as 1820; and the three days' fair, held in honour of St. Edward, was not finally discontinued till some time afterwards.

Upon the spot now occupied by Artillery Place, the men of Westminster used to practise at the "butts," which were provided by the parish in the year 1579, in obedience to an ordinance of Queen Elizabeth. In the beginning of the last century it is described as a large inclosure, "made use of by those who delight in military exercises." The butts were a large mound of turf, and at them the volunteers used to shoot. They were close to the "Five Chimneys." The ground was inclosed within a ditch, and a "shooting-house" was pro-vided for shelter and retirement. The actual butts were removed before the battle of Waterloo, and the name of "The Butts" has almost perished from the memory of the present generation, here as elsewhere.

"The open Tothill Fields, as they were called," observes a writer in the *Builder*, "existed in this state till 1810, with a group of lonely cottages standing in their midst, when the note of prepara-tion for an altered site might have been heard in the construction of the iron bridge at Vauxhall. Dr. Vincent had already inclosed a portion of the fields for the square which bears his name, and the Westminster Gas and Coke Company removed their offices, and commenced their new buildings in the Horseferry Road, on the site of the before-mentioned nursery. In 1830, the Vauxhall Road was not entirely built upon, and bits of the hedgerow were still to be seen.   Patches of greensward might as yet be observed beneath the litter of old iron, which Andrew Mann so liberally spread over any plot of waste ground; and the site of the present South Belgravia remained open market-garden ground, intersected by bridle-paths, for some ten years subsequently.   The present War-wick Street, uniting Westminster with Chelsea, occupies the precise site of the 'Willow Walk.'"

Tothill Fields, in the days of trial by wager of battle, was the place where the judges sat in all the majesty of their official robes, wigs, and gold chains, as arbiters of these encounters—one of the last remnants of the barbarous laws of another age. It is related that in 1441 such a one occurred in a combat between "two theves."   The " pælour " (appellant) is described to have " hadde the felde and victory within three strokes."   This absurdity was not formally set aside until 1819, when an Act of Parliament was passed forbidding all such trials both in civil and criminal matters.

Tothill Fields was also, in the seventeenth cen-tury, a celebrated duelling-ground ; the last "affair of honour" fought there, of which we have any account, took place, it is said, in 1711, when a Kentish gentleman, Sir Cholmley Dering, was killed by a Mr. Richard Thornhill—the fools fighting with pistols so near that the muzzles touched each other.

There is extant a curious etching, by Hollar, of Tothill Fields as they were in the time of Charles I. They appear to be a dead level, broken only by a clump of trees in the centre, forming a sort of maze.   The foreground is broken by a row of slight terraces, not unlike the " butts ; " and some ladies are promenading leisurely, dressed in the fashionable costume of the day.

In an able article on this interesting locality, a writer in the *Builder*, of January, 1875, observes : —"The solitary character of this tract of land, spreading out to the Chelsea Road, beyond which lay the 'Five Fields' extending to Knightsbridge, is illustrated by an incident not uncommon to the neighbourhood at a period when the highwayman would lie in ambush for the belated pedestrian, or for the chaise, which in this instance is conveying not the most loyal subjects of George II. from one of those political meetings when the 'mug-house riots' were at their height.   Such was the disturbed condition of society at this period, that two wit-nesses were sufficient for the immediate arrest of any party suspected of harbouring either Romish priest, or other of proven Jacobite politics, and great abuses were consequent upon this hasty legis-lation.   The panic created by the rumoured march

of the Highlanders, with the numerous party of the disaffected in London, kept the alarmed citizens wakeful in their beds ; for the Highlanders were feared as a terrible race, and possibly no antici-pated result had been surrounded with greater doubt and uncertainty, but that the energy of the King, backed as it was by the commercial interests of the Londoners, threw the balance in favour of the new dynasty.   In the summer of 1745, two adherents of the House of Stuart—one a young officer in the Pretender's army—had hired a chaise to convey them from Westminster to the then remote village of Chelsea.   To avoid the rioting in the town, they had taken a route across the less-disturbed fields.   They had not proceeded very far, however, before two well-mounted men made their appearance, and so suddenly that had they risen out of the earth it could not have surprised them more.   Both men wore masks; and whilst one of them stopped the postboy, the other rode up to the window of the chaise, and scrutinised the occu-pants within.   The post-boy spoke in too low a tone to be heard by the travellers, but whatever might have been the nature of the conversation, it was sufficiently talismanic to relieve the party of their apprehensions.   Making a sign to his com-panion, both men turned their horses' heads in the direction of the town, and the post-boy proceeded on his journey.   Upon reaching their destination, they asked the 'boy' who his rather suspicious-looking friends were, to which he gave no answer, but upon being pressed again on the subject, said, 'It's not much matter who they are, but they belong to those who don't care to meddle with Prince Charley's boys!'   The mystery seemed now greater than before, and further inquiry might only have involved further difficulty.   It was evident the post-boy knew too much, but in what manner he had become acquainted with their political bias it was impossible for them to conceive.   Treating the matter, however, as a joke, and paying the boy handsomely, the matter ended, but their anxiety only terminated by their quitting London for the North.   The widow of one of these gentlemen died in 1824, at the advanced age of ninety-five years.   After the amnesty, her husband, who fought at the battle of Culloden, had, in common with others, some curious restraints laid upon him, one of which was that he could not ride a horse of a higher value than £10 without forfeiture of it to any one who chose to avail himself of the pro-hibition."   But this restraint was also imposed on all Roman Catholics in the seventeenth and the early part of the eighteenth century.

On that part of Tothill Fields which is now

covered by the Westminster House of Correction and some neighbouring streets, was held, in ancient times, Westminster Fair, locally named "St. Magdalen's," or "Magdalen's," from the day on which it was celebrated. Mr. Frost, in his "Old Showmen of London," tells us that it was established in 1257, under a charter granted by Henry III. to the Abbot and Canons of St. Peter's Church. From the same authority we learn that the three days to which it was originally limited were extended by favour of Edward III. to thirty-one; but the fair never proved a dangerous rival to that of St. Bartholomew's, in Smithfield, and gradually fell into discredit and disuse.

In the reign of Henry III., St. Edward's Fair, originally held in St. Margaret's Churchyard, was removed hither, and in 1302, the Abbot of Westminster was allowed to levy tolls upon all traders who sold their wares at the time, even within the precincts of the Palace. In 1628 was preserved in the muniment-room of St. Margaret's Church, King Henry III.'s patent to the Abbot of Westminster, giving him leave to keep a market in Tothill every Monday, and a fair every year for three days. The fair was held in Rochester Row, in the space between Emery Hill's Almshouses and the ground now occupied by the Church of St. Stephen the Martyr. The fair was in existence in 1819, but died away gradually, previously to the general suppression of fairs in 1840.

Tothill Street, which extends to the Broadway from the Broad Sanctuary, near the west front of the Abbey, is the most ancient street in Westminster. It was at one time inhabited by noblemen "and the flower of the gentry." Here the Bishop of Chester was residing in 1488, and in 1522 Lord Dudley rented a house here from the fraternity of St. Mary. Sir Andrew Dudley also lived and died here. At the north-west end of the street, in what is now called Strutton Ground, were the residences of Lord Dacre of the South and Lord Grey de Wilton, as stated in the previous chapter. In 1612 Sir George Carew died at Carew House in this street; and in a house near the Gate House, at one time towards the end of the last century, lived the famous Edmund Burke. Lincoln House was the office of the Revels, when Sir Henry Herbert was master in 1644-5. Southern, the dramatic poet, and author of "Oroonoko," for the last ten years of his life, resided in Tothill Street, where he died in the year 1746. The poet Gray, in a letter to Horace Walpole, dated Burnham, Bucks, 1737, says, "We have old Mr. Southern at a gentleman's house a little way off, who often comes to see us. He is now seventy years old, and has almost wholly lost his memory; but is as agreeable an old man as can be—at least I persuade myself so, when I look at him, and think of 'Isabella' and 'Oroonoko.'" He is said to have been wealthy, but very mean; he used to print tickets on his benefit nights, and press them for sale upon his aristocratic friends. Thomas Betterton, the actor, and friend of Pope, was born in this street.

In the reign of Elizabeth, there were houses on both sides of Tothill Street; those on the north side had large gardens reaching to St. James's Park, and those upon the south had likewise extensive grounds, extending as far as Orchard Street. Very few houses were then built in Petty France (now York Street); a few detached residences appear on the south side only of Orchard Street; and some villas in St. Anne's Lane, Pye Street, and Duck Lane, with gardens along a stream.

Most of the signs of the old inns of Westminster were either religious charges, or else the cognisances of sovereigns or of noblemen residing in the neighbourhood. Such were the "Salutation" (of the Blessed Virgin), in Barton Street; the "Maidenhead," or, more properly, the "Maiden's Head"—in other words, that of "Our Lady;" the "St. George and the Dragon," the "Swan," the "Antelope" (the badge of Henry V.), the "Sun" (that of Richard II.), and the "Blue Boar," the cognisance of the Veres, Earls of Oxford. The "Chequers," in Abingdon Street, was the bearing of the Earls of Arundel, who at one time were empowered by the king to grant licenses to public-houses. Hence the frequency of the "Chequers" as a sign, especially in Westminster, where it was constantly to be seen painted on the walls and door-posts of hostelries; and so the "needy knife-grinder" of Canning was neither the only nor the latest toper who has spent last night in this fair city "a drinking at the Chequers."

Swan Yard was so called after the old hostelry, noted as a resort for highwaymen, "The Swan with Two Necks." The latter word is, as most persons know, a corruption from "nicks"—the marks set upon the birds by the Lord Mayor, in his annual "swan-upping," or, as it is called, vulgarly, "swan-hopping," when he makes his yearly progress up the Thames to count the young cygnets and old swans within the civic jurisdiction.

One of the oldest taverns in the metropolis, bearing the sign of "The Cock," surrounding a quaint old inn-yard, stood till 1871, on the north side of Tothill Street. An ancient coat of arms, those of England and France carved in stone, discovered in this house, was walled up in the front of the building. "Tradition," writes Mr. Larwood in his "History of Sign-boards," "says that the work-men employed at the building of the east end of Westminster Abbey, in the reign of Henry VII., used to receive their wages here." Later, it enjoyed a reputation on quite another account, as having been the inn from which the first stage-coach to

an inn of considerable importance, as its rafters and timbers were principally of cedar intermixed with oak. It was formerly entered by steps. The building exhibited traces of great antiquity, and appears at one time to have been a house of some pretensions. There was a curious hiding-

MILTON'S HOUSE. *From a Drawing by J. W. Archer.* (*See page 22.*)

Oxford started, some two centuries ago. Those who knew the inn down to a very recent date say that in the back parlour there was a picture of a jolly and bluff-looking man in a red coat, who is said to have been its driver. The house was built so as to inclose a quaint and spacious inn-yard, much frequented by carriers, not unlike some of those still standing in Bishopsgate Street and the Borough. The house in all probability was in former times

place on the staircase, which may have secreted either a "mass-priest" or else a highwayman in the days when both were in open hostility to the law of the land. In the house was also formerly a massive carving of Abraham about to offer his son Isaac; and another, in wood, representing the adoration of the Magi, said to have been kept in pledge, at some remote period, for an unpaid score. The cock may have been adopted as a

THE OLD "COCK TAVERN." *From an Original Drawing in the possession of J. G. Crace, Esq.* (*See page 17.*)

sign here on account of the vicinity of the Abbey, of which St. Peter was the patron, for in the Middle Ages a cock crowing on the top of a pillar was often one of the accessories in a picture of the Apostle. This certainly was a very unkind allusion for the saint, particularly when accompanied with such a sneering rhyme as that under the sign of the Red Cock in Amsterdam in 1682. On the one side was written :—

> " When the cock began to crow
> St. Peter began to cry."

On the reverse :—

> " The cock does not crow for nothing ;
> Ask St. Peter, he can tell you ! "

The " Cock and Tabard " in Tothill Street is described by Stow as having existed as far back as the reign of Edward III. He also says that at this tavern the workmen were paid during the building of the Abbey, when the wages of most of the artificers did not exceed one penny per day. On the demolition of the ancient inn, a new one bearing the sign of the " Cock " was built on the opposite side of the street. Shortly after its erection, while some draymen were in the act of placing a supply of porter in the cellars, it was discovered that an additional wedge was required, and accordingly one of the men looking round perceived a piece of oak, which had formed part of one of the girders of the ancient building. This, it was conceived, would answer the purpose, if it could be riven asunder, and this process was accordingly pursued. " Much to the amazement, however, of all present," we read in a newspaper account of the discovery, " in the course of the operation there suddenly emerged, from one of the mortise-holes or some other aperture, a considerable quantity of gold coins, consisting of forty-one rose nobles, and thirteen marks. The former coins were of the date of Edward III., the first reign in which gold coin was struck in this country. The marks were of the reign of Henry VII. and VIII." The whole of the coin is stated to have been in an admirable state of preservation.

The north side of Tothill Street is almost entirely taken up by the Royal Aquarium, and the Imperial Theatre, which forms its western extremity. The buildings occupy an irregular parallelogram of nearly three acres, extending from Princes Street to the corner of Dartmouth Street, and receding to the north nearly as far as the backs of the houses in Queen Street. The Aquarium, which was erected in 1875-6 from the designs of Mr. Bedborough, is in the Classical style, constructed of red brick and Portland stone, with an arched roof of glass, similar in general plan to that of the Crystal Palace, though widely different in its details. It is two storeys in height, and contains in the basement a great central tank of salt and fresh water, holding no less than 600,000 gallons. On the ground floor, at the eastern end, is a large vestibule, or ante-chamber, leading to the central hall, or promenade, and containing a series of table-tanks for the reception of the smaller fish, the zoophytes, sea-anemones, and the like. The Aquarium is utilised for concerts and exhibitions.

New Tothill Street was in the last century called White Hart Street. In the New Way, not far from where the present Workhouse stands, resided the well-known Sir Robert Pye, from whom Old and New Pye Streets derive their names, and the husband of Anne Hampden, the "patriot's" daughter. The New Way Chapel stood, according to Hopwood's map of 1801, at the west end of the Great Almonry, opposite the entrance to Jeffery's Buildings from New Tothill Street : here the celebrated Calvinist, Romaine, used to preach, previous to his election as Lecturer of St. Dunstan's-in-the-West. "At this time," says Mr. Mackenzie Walcott, " Dr. Wilson, then Rector of St. Margaret's, was a suitor at Court for a bishopric ; and being asked by King George III., ' What news from his parish ? ' he replied that there was ' that fellow Romaine, who had got a chapel in the New Way, and drew all his parishioners from the church.' The king quickly replied, ' Well, we will make a bishop of him ; that will silence him ! ' " During the last century, the Government rented the New Way Chapel from the Dean and Chapter, and the Guards attended divine service there for many years.

One side of the Broadway is now nearly occupied by the St. James's Park station on the Metropolitan District Railway. Here James I. granted a hay-market to be held for a certain number of years ; a further term was obtained by licence of Charles II., but it had expired long before 1730. In a survey made in 1722 mention is made of " the White Horse and Black Horse Inns, for the entertainment of man and horse ; there being none in the parish of St. Margaret, at Westminster, for stage-coaches, wagons, or carriers."

Dick Turpin, the notorious highwayman, it is said, lodged in an obscure court hard by, and used to set out from this place on his marauding expeditions, upon his famous mare, Black Bess, from which one of these taverns took its name.

Christ Church, in the Broadway, rebuilt in the Early Pointed style, from the designs of Mr. A. Poynter, in 1843, stands upon the site of a former edifice which was known as the New Chapel.

It consists of chancel, nave and aisles, and a lofty tower. Several of the windows are filled with stained glass, illustrative of the life of our Saviour. The New Chapel was erected upon a piece of waste ground belonging to the Dean and Chapter; its founder being Mr. George Darrell, Prebendary of St. Peter's, who, in the year 1631, bequeathed £400 to build it, provided it was used for "publick prayers on Sundays, Wednesdays, and Fridays, and for prayers and plain catechisings on Sunday afternoons." The bequest was insufficient to complete the building, and was therefore increased by voluntary subscriptions.

Archbishop Laud was a liberal contributor to this chapel, and in its churchyard was interred Sir William Waller, one of the heroes of the Parliamentary army, who died in 1668. In this burial-ground is a memorial of a parishioner, Margaret Pattens, who was buried here in 1739. Her portrait is preserved in St. Margaret's Workhouse, in which she died (as asserted) at the advanced age of 136 years.

In March, 1882, the foundation-stone of a new Town Hall, for the parishes of St. Margaret and St. John, was laid by Lady Burdett-Coutts, on a piece of ground in the rear of Christ Church. The building will be constructed of red brick and stone in the Renaissance style of architecture.

York Street, the thoroughfare running westward in continuation of the Broadway, was formerly known by the name of "Petty France." There were two districts in this locality with foreign names, says Widmore—"Petty Calais," where the wool-staplers principally resided; and "Petty France," where lived the French merchants, who came over to trade at the Staple. An Act of an interchange between the King and the Abbot of Westminster, in the reign of Henry VIII., mentions "a certain great messuage or tenement commonly called 'Pety Caleys,' and all messuages, houses, barns, stables, dove-houses, orchards, gardens, pools, fisheries, waters, ditches, lands, meadows, and pastures." The street received its present name, by a vote of the inhabitants, from Frederick, Duke of York, son of George II., who for some time had a residence among them.

Between Chapel Street and the narrow turning known as Ermin's or Hermit's Hill, stood until very recently a charitable institution—one of a similar character to many others in this neighbourhood—known as the Red Lion Almshouses, but more commonly as Van Dun's Almshouses. These houses contained, originally, twenty rooms, to be inhabited rent free by as many poor women. They were founded in the reign of Elizabeth, under

whom and whose predecessors Van Dun officiated as Yeoman of the Guard. His monument in St. Margaret's, Westminster, has a good bust and the following inscription :—" Cornelius Van Dun lieth here, borne at Breda, in Brabant; soldier with King Henry at Turney, Yeoman of the Guard, and Vsher to King Henry, King Edward, Queen Mary, and Queen Elizabeth : of honest and vertuous life, a careful man for poore folke, who in the end of this towne did build for poore widowes twenty houses at his own cost." Round the figure is inscribed :—" Obijt anno Dom. 1577, buried the 4 of September, ætatis suæ 94."

The tenements founded by Van Dun were of the smallest and plainest description. Not being endowed, they were appropriated to the parish pensioners of St. Margaret's, Westminster. The site of these humble edifices was formerly called St. Hermit's Hill, probably from a cell or hermitage there situate. A chapel dedicated to St. Mary Magdalen is mentioned by Stow as standing near this spot, " wholly ruinated."

These almshouses retained much of their primitive character down to the year 1862; but the alterations in the neighbourhood since the building of the St. James's Park Station of the Metropolitan District Railway have at length swept them away. Stow, in his survey of London and Westminster, mentions them as standing upon "St. Hermit's" Hill; and in Rocque's map this hill is clearly marked as bordering on the fields. Even at the beginning of the last century this neighbourhood retained enough of its rural or suburban character for the churchyard of the New Chapel (now Christ Church) to be considered the "pleasantest about London and Westminster."

The author of the article in the *Builder* to which we have referred in the commencement of this chapter, observes that—"Some interest is awakened by the circumstance that the site on which these almshouses once stood was a spot sacred alike to the Briton, the Roman, and the Saxon. The 'Thoth' of the Egyptian," he argues, "is identical with the Hermes or Mercury of the Greek and Roman, as also with the Tuisco or Teut of the Saxon. The hill of 'Hermes' and the 'teut-hill' of the Saxon are the same; and the name which Stow gives it, and by which it seems to have been known, is a curious coincidence, since the transition from 'Hermes' to St. Hermit is not very difficult of solution. The mound once sacred to this tutelary divinity of merchants and wayfarers is now a heap of rubbish; the caduceus and petasus have taken refuge in the locomotive and telegraph hard by; but through the long vista of time perhaps this transition is not greater than the annual setting up of the May-pole on the neighbouring village green, or the wayside inn and cottages with their gardens yet in the remembrance of the octogenarian."

The Westminster Panorama, in York Street, was opened in 1881. The picture on view, representing the Battle of Waterloo, covers upwards of 22,000 feet of canvas, and was painted by M. Castellani.

The house No. 19 lately standing in York Street occupied the site of the residence of John Milton, the author of "Paradise Lost." Part of the grounds had long been walled up, and appropriated to the house formerly inhabited by Jeremy Bentham. The cotton willow-tree planted by the great poet has now entirely disappeared, and in the place of the garden workshops and other buildings have sprung up. It is evident that the original front of the house was that facing the Park. On that side Jeremy Bentham placed a small tablet, with the following inscription :—" Sacred to Milton, Prince of Poets." In the old wall which bounded the garden on the Park side, opposite the house, were the indications of a door, long built up, which was probably used by Milton in passing between his house and Whitehall during his intercourse with Cromwell in the capacity of Latin secretary. In the house itself, which was pulled down in 1881–2, the arrangement of the windows was entirely changed. It is probable that they formerly extended along the whole front, with sliding frames or lattices, divided by panelled spaces. The original panelling remained in the large room on the first floor. The upper rooms were small, and the staircase, which had not been altered, was steep and narrow. The ground floor seemed to have been comprised in one large room, as the original fireplace was evidently situated about the centre of the wall on the west side. This was probably the family room, or compromise between kitchen and parlour, so common to the economy of houses of respectable pretensions in the olden time. This distinguished house was, in later years, the residence of William Hazlitt, the critic and essayist.

An American paper of 1874 stated that the Historical Society of Pennsylvania has recently received from the Hon. Benjamin Rush an original baluster or newel-post from the stairway of the house formerly inhabited by John Milton, the poet, accompanied by a water-colour sketch of the building, with the following certificate from the hand of the celebrated English jurist, Jeremy Bentham :—" A.D. 1821, August 15. Sketch of a house for some time inhabited by John Milton. It is situated in Westminster, in the street then called Petty France, but on the occasion of the French Revolutionary War, newly named York Street, in horror of France and honour of the Duke of York. This sketch was this day taken from the garden attached to the residence of Jeremy Bentham, into which garden the house has a door, being, under the Dean and Chapter of Westminster, his property. From this house, August 14th, 1821, under the direction of the said Jeremy Bentham, was cut the balustrade pillar, composed of four twisted columns, presented by him, in company with this sketch, to his truly dear and highly-respected friend Richard Rush, Envoy Extraordinary to the United Kingdom of Great Britain and Ireland. Witness my hand, JEREMY BENTHAM."

In Little James Street is Emmanuel Hospital, known also by the name of Lady Dacre's Almshouses. It was founded and built in the year 1600, under the will of Ann, widow of Gregory Fiennes, Lord Dacre, for the support of ten men and ten women, as pensioners ; and also for ten boys and ten girls, with a master for the former and a mistress for the latter. The children, when educated and grown up, were formerly apprenticed to different trades. The buildings and gardens of the hospital occupy about three and a half acres. The original buildings becoming decayed, the present almshouses were erected in the reign of Queen Anne, the chapel in that of George II., and the schoolrooms in the present century. In 1873 the Endowed Schools Commission successfully carried a "scheme" for the "reform" of the schools attached to the hospital. This institution, therefore, was the first of the kind which the "reforming" tendencies of the age may be said to have touched. These schools afford a good middleclass education to sixty-three children, selected from Westminster, Chelsea, and the village of Hayes, near Uxbridge, and also from the City of London and Brandesburton, near Beverley, Yorkshire. All the children are fed, clothed, sheltered, and educated, free of all expense to their relatives. In the education of the girls domestic work has always occupied a prominent position.

The will of Lady Dacre, under which this hospital was established, has often been printed. The testatrix provides, after declaring that her husband in his lifetime, and herself, designed to erect a hospital for the poor in Westminster or its neighbourhood, that her executors, if she should not perform it before her decease, should cause to be erected "a neat and convenient house, with room of habitation for twenty poor folk and twenty poor children," and that it should be entitled "Emmanuel Hospital." She expresses her design to be "the relief of aged people, and the bringing up of children in virtue and good and laudable arts, whereby they may the better live in time to come by their own honest labour," and enjoins her executors to be humble suitors to the Queen for a charter of incorporation. Accordingly a charter was obtained in 1601, ordaining "the house in Tuttle Fields an hospital for the poor, under the name of Emmanuel Hospital," and appointing, after the decease of the last-surviving executor, the Lord Mayor and Aldermen of London governors in perpetuity. The terms of this charter, however, are somewhat peculiar and contradictory; whilst allowing the governors very direct authority in the management of the charity, it nevertheless entrusts the alms-people themselves with very considerable powers of self-government, and incorporates them as "a body corporate of themselves for ever." This corporation is authorised "to purchase land, to grant leases, to have a common seal, to sue and be sued," &c., to choose its own warden, and "to have the custody of all deeds, writings, and surplus moneys in the common chest provided in the chapel." Practically, by custom, long disuse, and by an Act of Parliament passed in 1794, this corporation is defunct, and the jurisdiction entirely in the hands of the aldermen as the governing body. The statutes of 1601 are interesting, as showing the kind of persons which, in the opinion of Lady Dacre's executors, ought to have preference as pensioners :—" 1. Decayed and distressed servants of Lady Dacre. 2. Former servants of this family who have grown poor, lame, or diseased 'in the service of their prince,' or 'without their own fault.' 3. Any poor, honest, godly people past labour. 4. Those born blind, or lamed, or disabled in the service of their prince. 5. Those brought down from riches to poverty without their own fault." The present inmates are entirely of the third class. It would appear from the founder's will that she did not contemplate a school, but rather a cluster of industrial houses, in which each of the aged pensioners, in return for shelter and support, should "bring up and instruct in virtue, and good and laudable acts," one child. But, "as the present poor people are not capable of instructing children, the governors were of opinion that some honest and industrious clergyman who has a wife should be nominated and appointed to read prayers twice a day in the chapel, and instruct the children." Accordingly the school was founded, and the first clerical master appointed in 1735. In 1793 the pensioners' allowance (originally £5 only, and subsequently £15) was increased to £18, and is now fixed at £20 per annum.

In 1794, the lease of the Brandesburton estate having fallen in, the governors obtained an Act of Parliament to "increase and extend the objects of the charity." Ten out-pensioners were added to the almshouse branch, and the benefits of the in-pensioners were increased by the addition of twenty chaldrons of coals to their annual pension. In 1821 the number of children was increased from twenty to forty, which number was finally raised to sixty, in 1845, when the new schools were erected. In 1846 the chapel was enlarged, by the addition of an apex on the west side, to serve the purpose of a chancel. Before this time there had been no means of celebrating the holy communion. The altar-piece was purchased at the taking down of the church of St. Benet Fink, near the Royal Exchange. The pulpit is of elaborately-carved oak, and apparently of the time of James I. Under an arch at the north end of the chapel is a small model of the tomb of the founder, Lady Dacre, in Chelsea Church.

Of the masters of the hospital the only man of eminence was the Rev. William Beloe, the translator of Herodotus, who retained the office from 1783 to 1808, when he was appointed Rector of Allhallows, London Wall, and Assistant Librarian in the British Museum.

The most valuable endowments of this ancient charity consist of the manorial estate of Brandesburton, the greater part of which parish belongs to the "poor of Emmanuel Hospital." The aldermen of London, as "trustees of the poor of Emmanuel Hospital," have been liberal and popular landlords. In 1843 they rebuilt the Brandesburton Schools, which had already been founded and endowed by a Yorkshire lady in the reign of George I.

In 1869 was passed the "Endowed Schools' Act," bringing this and other hospital schools under the stern and reforming hands of the "Endowed Schools' Commission." In 1873 this commission carried in Parliament a "scheme" for the reconstruction of this hospital, and the separation of the schools from the almshouse branch of the charity. Under the provisions of this scheme the endowments of four hospital schools in Westminster were to be united under the management of one body of governors, viz., Emmanuel, St. Margaret's, Palmer's, and Emery Hill's hospitals. Out of these endowments it was proposed to establish three large middle-class schools, namely, a boarding-school, to be erected within twenty miles of London, and two day-schools in Westminster, each providing accommodation for 300 boys, of whom 200 in each should pay a small sum for their education, whilst the other 100 free places were to be reserved as scholarships and exhibitions for deserving candidates, principally for those belonging to the public elementary day-schools of Westminster and Chelsea. The governing body, or trustees, as at present constituted, consist of the Lord Mayor of London, the Aldermen, the Recorder, and nine elected inhabitants of Westminster. It may be added that the school will be as soon as possible removed into the country. The almshouse branch of the

best acoustical arrangements, were the main considerations. The chapel is constructed of brick, and, with its semicircular-headed windows and doorways, has an elegant appearance. The campanile, at the north-east corner, rises to a height of about 160 feet. The interior is commodious and admirably adapted for the purpose for which it was built. There are two galleries, the fronts of which are of open iron-work, supported on a wooden

VAN DUN'S ALMSHOUSES, 1820. (*See page* 21.)

hospital is not touched by the above scheme, and one-third of the revenues of the charity is henceforth set aside for its support.

The hospital forms three sides of a quadrangle, the fourth side, opening to the street, being enclosed with iron railings and gates. The chapel has an enriched pediment, and is in the centre of the west side of the building.

On the north side of Emmanuel Hospital, and at the corner of James Street and Castle Lane, is a Nonconformist edifice called Westminster Chapel, which was rebuilt in 1864, from the designs of Mr. W. F. Poulton. In an architectural sense it is an adaptation of the Lombardic style to the requirements of a building in which convenient accommodation for a large number of persons, and the

basement of such a height as to secure the advantages of an enclosed gallery front; the two ends of the chapel are semi-circular. The ceiling is flat in the centre and coved at the sides; the whole being divided into panels by moulded ribs, springing at the base of the cove from semi-detached stone columns, which divide the wall in bays of equal width round the whole chapel. The coved part of the ceiling is groined between each bay in order to admit of the windows being continued above the caps of the columns.

The Infirmary, out of which Westminster Hospital originated, stood formerly on the east side of Castle Lane.

James Street, which extends from York Street to Buckingham Gate, is so called from its vicinity to the Park. On the west side of this street was formerly Tart Hall, built in 1638, by Nicholas Stone, for Alethea, Countess of Arundel, and belonging to the family of the Howards. It was the residence of William, Viscount Stafford, who was beheaded, on the evidence of Titus Oates, in the

At No. 11 in this street lived the poet, Richard Glover, whose song of "Hosier's Ghost" roused the nation to a war with Spain. Another distinguished writer who resided in James Street was William Gifford, editor of the *Quarterly Review* for the first fifteen years of its existence : he died

WENCESLAUS HOLLAR. (*See page* 29.)

reign of Charles II. Having been used for some time as a place of entertainment, it was demolished early in the last century. The old gateway of Tart Hall, which stood till 1737, was not opened after the condemned nobleman passed under it for the last time. According to Strype, the old hall was partly in the parish of St. Martin's-in-the-Fields, and partly in that of St. James's : we shall have more to say of it in a subsequent chapter. At the garden wall, on the site of which now stands Stafford Row, a boy was whipped annually, in order to keep the parish bounds in remembrance.

here in 1826. His early history is prefixed to his translation of " Juvenal."

A native of Devonshire, and eminently a self-made man, Gifford was a political writer and critic of no small influence in his lifetime. His early life was spent as a cabin-boy on board a little coasting-vessel; but at the age of fifteen he was apprenticed to a shoemaker at Ashburton. In spite of a neglected education, his talents showed themselves in a strong thirst for knowledge. Mathematics at first were his favourite study ; and he relates that, in want of paper, he used to hammer scraps of leather smooth, and work his problems on them with a blunt awl. Through the kindness of Mr. Cookesley and the Earl Grosvenor, the poor and friendless orphan was enabled ultimately to manifest his talents, and to gain admission into the most brilliant literary and political circles, members of which were Pitt, Canning, Lord Liverpool, and the Marquis Wellesley.

In James Street, at the house of Thomas Harley, occurred the secret interview between Harley and the Duke of Marlborough—who, we are informed, entered by the garden door at the back of the house looking into the Park—when Harley discovered the existence of the secret negotiations between the French King and the General, a discovery which placed Marlborough's life in the Minister's hands.

CHAPTER III.

WESTMINSTER.—KING STREET, GREAT GEORGE STREET, AND THE BROAD SANCTUARY.

"Urbs antiqua fuit."—*Virg.*, "*Æn.*," i.

Ancient Gates in King Street—Distinguished Residents in King Street—Oliver Cromwell's Mother—A Strange Incident in the Life of Cromwell—King Charles on his Way to his Trial—The Plague—Ancient Hostelries and Coffee-houses—Death of Hollar, the Engraver—Deldhay Street—Duke Street and its Distinguished Residents—Judge Jeffreys—Fludyer Street—Great George Street—Lying in State of Lord Byron's Body—Institution of Civil Engineers—National Portrait Gallery—Burial of Sheridan—The Buxton Memorial Drinking Fountain—Statue of George Canning—The Sessions House—Westminster Hospital—Training School and Home for Nurses—The National Society. Anecdote about Sir John Hawkins's "History of Music"—Her Majesty's Stationery Office—Parker Street—John Wilkes—The Westminster Crimean Memorial.

KING Street, which we have already mentioned incidentally in our notice of Whitehall, was the ancient thoroughfare between the regions of the Court and the Abbey. It runs parallel to its modern sister, Parliament Street, between it and the Park. King Street was formerly extremely, and, it would appear, even dangerously narrow. Pepys thus commemorates it in his "Diary," November 27, 1660:—"To Westminster Hall; and in King Street there being a great stop of coaches, there was a falling out between a drayman and my Lord of Chesterfield's coachman, and one of his footmen killed."

At the north end of this street was the Cock-pit Gate; at the south end, the High Gate, which is shown in one of Hollar's etchings. The latter Gate House, which was taken down in 1723, was occupied at one time by the Earl of Rochester. Part of the land in King Street, extending as far southward as the Bars, was conveyed by the Abbot of Westminster to King Henry VIII., when he was bent on enlarging Whitehall. After the burning of Whitehall Palace, it was resolved to make a broader street to the Abbey, and in course of time Parliament Street was formed, as we have already stated in a previous chapter. Although part of King Street still remains, it is as narrow as ever, though somewhat better paved, and latterly its length has been considerably curtailed at the northern end by the erection of the new India and Foreign Offices.

Narrow as it was, King Street was the residence of many distinguished personages, doubtless owing to its proximity to the Court and the Parliament

House. In it lived Lord Howard of Effingham, the High Admiral who, Roman Catholic as he was, went forth to fight the cause of his country against the Spanish Armada. Here, too, Edmund Spenser, the author of "The Faery Queen," after his escape from the troubles in Ireland, spent the last few weeks of his life, and died in actual penury and even in want of bread. Such was the end of the man who had sung the praises of the great Elizabeth in higher than mere courtly strains. But his sad end is only another example of the fate that too often waits on poetic genius. "The breath had scarcely departed from his body when the great, the titled, and the powerful came forward to do honour to his memory and to shower laurels on his grave. His remains were carried in state from King Street to Westminster Abbey, the expenses of the funeral being defrayed by the great favourite of the Court, the Earl of Essex." "His hearse," writes Camden, "was attended by poets, and mournful elegies, and poems, with the pens that wrote them, were thrown into his tomb." And it may be added that Anne, the Countess of Dorset, erected the monument over his grave. "The armorial shield of the Spencers," justly observes Gibbon, "may be emblazoned with the triumphs of a Marlborough, but I exhort them to look upon the 'Faery Queen' as the brightest jewel in their coronet."

In King Street, too, resided that most graceful of the courtier poets of the time of Charles I., Thomas Carew, who wrote the masque of "Cœlum Britannicum" for that prince, and who was the friend and boon-companion of Ben Jonson and Sir

John Suckling, and the author of that charming song which begins :—

> " He that loves a rosy cheek,
> Or a coral lip admires."

Here, too, lived Charles, Lord Buckhurst, afterwards Earl of Dorset, the witty and accomplished courtier and poet, and the author of the famous song addressed to the gay ladies of Charles II.'s court, the first stanza of which runs thus :—

> " To all you ladies now on land
> We men at sea indite ;
> But first would have you understand
> How hard it is to write ;
> The Muses now, and Neptune, too,
> We must implore to write to you."

Here the Lord Protector assigned to his mother a suite of apartments, which she occupied until the day of her death, in 1654 : she was buried in Westminster Abbey. She was devotedly fond of her son, and lived in constant fear of hearing of his assassination ; indeed it is said, in Ludlow's " Memoirs," that she was quite unhappy if she did not see him twice a day, and never heard the report of a gun without calling out, " My son is shot." Mr. Noble, in his " Memoirs of the Cromwell Family," tells us that " she requested, when dying, to have a private funeral, and that her body might not be deposited in the Abbey ; but that, instead of fulfilling her request, the Protector conveyed her remains, with great solemnity, and attended with many hundred torches, though it was daylight, and interred them in the dormitory of our English monarchs, in a manner suitable to those of the mother of a person of his then rank." He adds that, " the needless ceremonies and great expense to which the Protector put the public in thus burying her gave great offence to the Republicans."

It would have been well for her if her wish had been granted, for, at the Restoration, Mrs. Cromwell's body was taken up and indecently thrown, with others, into a hole made before the back door of the lodgings of the canons or prebendaries, in St. Margaret's Churchyard. Mrs. Cromwell appears to have been an excellent and amiable person ; and it is worthy of note that she is styled " a decent woman " by so strong a royalist as Lord Chancellor Clarendon.

The house occupied by Mrs. Cromwell, according to Mr. John Timbs, stood a little to the north of Blue Boar's Head Yard, on the west side of the street. If we may accept the testimony of Mr. G. H. Malone, its identity was ascertained by a search into the parish rate-books, and fixed to the north of the above-mentioned yard, and south of the wall of Ram's Mews. Among the Cole MSS. in the British Museum is a copy of a letter written by Cromwell at Dunbar, and addressed to his wife in this street.

One day a strange incident occurred to the Lord Protector as he was passing in his coach through this street, accompanied by Lord Broghill, afterwards better known by his superior title as Earl of Ossory, from whom the story has come down to us through his chaplain and biographer, Morrice :—" It happened that the crowd of people was so great that the coach could not go forward, and the place was so narrow that all the halberdiers were either before the coach or behind it, none of them having room to stand by the side. When they were in this posture, Lord Broghill observed the door of a cobbler's stall to open and shut a little, and at every opening of it his lordship saw something bright, like a drawn sword or a pistol. Upon which my lord drew out his sword with the scabbard on it, and struck upon the stall, asking who was there. This was no sooner done but a tall man burst out with a sword by his side, and Cromwell was so much frightened that he called his guard to seize him, but the man got away in the crowd. My lord thought him to be an officer in the army in Ireland, whom he remembered Cromwell had disgusted, and his lordship apprehended he lay there in wait to kill him. Upon this," adds Morrice, " Cromwell forbore to come any more that way, but a little after sickened and died."

And yet there was, at all events, one other occasion on which the Lord Protector passed along this narrow thoroughfare, and that was to his funeral in the Abbey. He died at Whitehall, in September, 1658 ; and as he died in the midst of his power and state, his obsequies were celebrated with the pomp and magnificence of a king. It would tax the pen of Macaulay to describe the scene : the road prepared for the passage of the hearse by gravel thrown into the ruts; and the sides of the street lined with soldiery, all in mourning, as in solemn state the body was conducted to the great western entrance of the Abbey, where it was received by the clergy with the usual ceremonials.

Among the other residents in King Street were Sir Thomas Knevett, or Knyvett, who seized Guy Fawkes ; and Dr. Sydenham, on the site of Ram's Mews. Here, too, lived Erasmus Dryden, brother of " glorious " John Dryden, supporting himself by trade before his accession to the baronetcy as head of the family.

Dudley, the second Lord North, had a house in this street, about 1646, which was remarkable as being the first brick house in it. His son, Sir Dudley, as we learn in the "Lives of the Norths," was stolen by beggars, and retaken in an alley leading towards Cannon Row, while he was being stripped of his clothes. Bishop Goodman, during the Great Rebellion, lived here in great obscurity, and chiefly in the house of Mrs. Sybilla Aglionby, employing the greater part of his time in frequenting the Cottonian Library.

But there are other and more gloomy reminiscences which attach to King Street. Through it Charles I. was carried on his way to Westminster Hall on the first and last days of his trial. "On both these occasions," writes Mr. Jesse, "his conveyance was a sedan chair, by the side of which walked, bare-headed, his faithful follower, Herbert —the only person who was allowed to attend him. As he returned through King Street, after his condemnation, the inhabitants, we are told, not only shed tears, but, unawed by the soldiers who lined the streets, offered up audible prayers for his eternal welfare." Strange to say, among the residents in this street at the time was Oliver Cromwell himself; and it was from his abode here that, some months after the murder of his sovereign, he set forth in state, amid the blare of trumpets, to take upon himself the Lord Lieutenancy of Ireland. The house which was traditionally said to have been occupied by the Protector, was at the northern end, near Downing Street, and it was not demolished, says Mr. Jesse, until the present century.

Owing to its narrowness and want of light and air, and the crowded courts by which it was hemmed in on either side, King Street was among the first parts of Westminster to suffer from the plague in the year 1665. On its appearance so close to the gates of the royal palace, Charles II. and his train of courtiers, male and female, left Whitehall for Oxford. Accordingly, we find gossiping Samuel Pepys writing, under date June 20th:—"This day I informed myself that there died four or five at Westminster of the plague, in several houses, upon Sunday last, in Bell Alley, over against the Palace Gate." Again, on the 21st: "I find all the town going out of town, the coaches and carriages being all full of people going into the country." And, shortly after, on the 28th and 29th:—"In my way to Westminster Hall, I observed several plague-houses" (that is, houses smitten with the plague) "in King Street and the Palace. . . . To Whitehall, where the court was full of waggons and people ready to go out of town. This end of the town every day grows very bad of the plague." It appears from contemporary history that the example set by the King and Court was largely followed by the nobility and the "quality;" and that so great was the exodus that the neighbouring towns and villages rose up to oppose their retreat, as likely to sow the seeds of the disease still more widely, and to carry the infection further a-field. It is usually said by historians that the Great Plague in 1665 broke out at the top of Drury Lane, but Dr. Hodges, in his "Letter to a Person of Quality," states it as a fact that the pestilence first broke out in Westminster, and that it was carried eastwards by contagion.

King Street would seem to have been at one time noted for its coffee-houses, for in the fifth edition of Izaak Walton's additions to the "Complete Angler," (1676), "Piscator" says:—"When I dress an eel thus, I will he was as long and big as that which was caught in Peterboro' river in the year 1667, which was 3¾ feet long; if you will not believe me, then go and see it at one of the coffee-houses in King Street, Westminster."

Among these coffee-houses and hostelries was the "King's Head" Inn, where there was held an "ordinary," as far back as two centuries ago. Here a Mr. Moore told Pepys, in July, 1663, "the great news that my Lady Castlemaine is fallen from Court, and this morning retired;" and the next day, at the same place, the same bit of scandal, he tells us, is confirmed by a "pretty gentleman," who, however, is in ignorance of the cause.

At another house in this street—the Bell Tavern —the "October Club" met early in the last century. The club, which consisted of about 150 members, derived its name from being composed of High Church Tory country gentlemen, who when at home drank October ale. The large room in which the club assembled was adorned with a portrait of Queen Anne, by Dâhl. After Her Majesty's death and the break-up of the club, the picture was purchased by the corporation of the loyal city of Salisbury, in whose council-chamber it may still be seen suspended.

In this street, also, the beautiful and talented actress, Mrs. Oldfield, earned her livelihood when a girl as a sempstress; and through it she was carried, at the age of forty-seven, to her grave in the Abbey, her pall supported by noblemen and gentlemen, and her body being allowed to lie in state in the Jerusalem Chamber, as stated in a previous chapter. Such is the tide of destiny; and well might it have been written on her hearse, "Voluit fortuna jocari."

Mr. John Timbs tells us, in his "Curiosities of London," that near the southern end of King Street, on the west side, was Thieven (Thieves) Lane, so called as being the regular passage along which thieves were led to the Gate House prison, so that they might not escape into the Sanctuary and set the law at defiance.

In Gardener's Lane, which leads from King Street to Duke Street, died in March, 1677, Hollar, the master of early etchers; he was buried on the 28th of that month in St. Margaret's Churchyard. He seems to have been as child-like and improvident as the rest of his fraternity. At all events, at the time of his last illness the bailiffs were in his rooms ; and the dying artist, who had been the favourite of Lord Arundel, and the honoured inmate of his house, had to beg as a favour that the bed on which he lay might not be taken away till after his death. Hollar's widow survived him many years, and some time after his death sold to Sir Hans Sloane a large collection of the artist's works. This collection was subsequently acquired by the British Museum, and formed the nucleus of the magnificent collection of Hollar's works there existing. Hollar was of Bohemian extraction and of gentle blood ; he was born at Prague in 1607. He came to England in the suite of Lord Arundel, whom we have already mentioned* as a lover and patron of art; and it was the death of his patron that plunged him into difficulties. It is probable that it was through Lord Arundel's influence that he became a member of the Roman Catholic faith, to which his father had formerly belonged.

Delahay Street, between King Street and St. James's Park, was so called from a family of that name formerly resident in the parish of St. Margaret's. At the southern end, at the corner of Great George Street, lived Lady Augusta Murray, the first wife of the Duke of Sussex.

At No. 19 in this street are the branch offices of the Society for the Propagation of the Gospel in Foreign Parts, Dr. Bray's Institution for Founding Libraries, the Colonial Bishoprics' Fund, the Ladies' Association for Promoting Female Education in India, and the Universities' Mission to Central Africa.

Duke Street, which ran in a line with Delahay Street and is now absorbed into it, was a poor and narrow thoroughfare at its best. Pope, in one of his Letters, tells an amusing anecdote relating to this street, but which serves to illustrate the cruel snares laid by the penal laws in force in his time against persons professing the Roman Catholic religion, who were not allowed to keep either carriages or horses of their own ! He writes :—" By our latest account from Duke Street, Westminster, the con-

version of T. G. ——, Esq., is reported in a manner somewhat more particular. That, upon the seizure of his Flanders mares, he seemed more than ordinarily disturbed for some hours, sent for his ghostly father, and resolved to bear his loss like a Christian ; till, about the hour of seven or eight, the coaches and horses of several of the nobility passing by his window towards Hyde Park, he could no longer endure the disappointment, but instantly went out, took the oath of abjuration, and recovered his dear horses, which carried him in triumph to the Ring. The poor distressed Roman Catholics, now unhorsed and uncharioted, cry out with the Psalmist, ' Some trust in chariots, and some in horses, but we will invocate the name of the Lord.'"

In this street died in 1826, aged eighty, Sir Archibald Macdonald, Bart., formerly M.P. for Hindon, &c., and Solicitor-General, and afterwards Chief Baron of the Exchequer. He was educated at Westminster School, to which he was so attached that he never omitted to be present at every college election and at every performance of the Westminster Play.

Here, too, lived Matthew Prior, in a house facing Charles Street. Bishop Stillingfleet, author of the " Origines Britannicæ," died here in 1699; Archbishop Hutton in 1758; and Dr. Arnold, the musical composer, in 1802.

The house once inhabited by the " infamous Judge " Jefferys, when Lord Chancellor, has been demolished during subsequent improvements in this locality. Down to the time of its removal, it was easily distinguished from its neighbours by a flight of stone steps, which James II. permitted the cruel favourite to make into the Park for his special accommodation ; they terminated above in a small court, on three sides of which stood the once costly house. One portion of the mansion was used as the Admiralty House, until that office was removed by William III. to Wallingford House. The north wing of the house, in which Judge Jefferys heard cases, when he found it inconvenient to go to Lincoln's Inn or Westminster Hall, was afterwards converted into a chapel : Dr. John Pettingale, the antiquary, was for some time its incumbent.

The State Paper Office stood at the north end of Duke Street for many years. It was erected in 1833, to contain the documents of the Privy Council and Secretaries of State, formerly kept in Holbein's Gatehouse, and first arranged during the time when Lord Grenville was Premier.

In lodgings in Fludyer Street lived the eminent surgeon, Sir Charles Bell, in the early part of his career, before he joined the Middlesex Hospital.

---

* See Vol. III., p. 74.

This street was so named after Sir Samuel Fludyer, the ground-landlord, who, when Lord Mayor in 1761, entertained George III. and Queen Charlotte at Guildhall. It is said to occupy the site of the ancient Axe Yard, a haunt of Sir William of the "George and the Dragon." The houses in Great George Street were built shortly after the erection of Westminster Bridge, and the street covers ground which formed at that time an arm of the Thames. The tide flowed up from Bridge

THE BUXTON DRINKING FOUNTAIN. (*See page* 33.)

Davenant. The site is mentioned in a document of the time of Henry VIII., as "on the west side of Kynge Street, a great messuage or brew-house, commonly called the Axe." Pepys at one time had a house here.

Great George Street, the broad thoroughfare leading in a direct line from Bridge Street to Bird-cage Walk and St. James's Park, derives its name from standing on the site of an old stable-yard which belonged to an inn close by, bearing the sign

Street, until it found its way into the canal of St. James's Park. From the frequency of inundations, Flood Street, which stood between the entrances of Dean's Yard and Tothill Street, derived its significant name.

In Great George Street lived, in 1763, John Wilkes, whilst carrying on his *North Briton* and fighting duels. It was in the front drawing-room of a house, No. 25 in this street, that in July, 1824, lay in state the body of Lord Byron, which had been brought over in the ship *Florida* from Missolonghi, in Greece, where he died fighting in the cause of Grecian independence. It was hoped that a grave would have been found for the author of "Childe Harold" in Poets' Corner in the Abbey hard by, but the Dean and Chapter refused to

Street, Westminster. At the house of Sir Edward it lay in state for two days, and was visited by hundreds of persons, who paid their last tributes to the genius of the mighty slumberer by gazing on his coffin-lid. After the lying in state had terminated, it was found necessary to remove the

HOUSE IN WESTMINSTER, SAID TO HAVE BEEN OCCUPIED BY OLIVER CROMWELL. (*See page* 27.)

allow his body to rest there; so, a day or two afterwards, the poet's remains were taken down into Nottinghamshire, and consigned to their last resting-place in Hucknall Church, near his home at Newstead Abbey. The scene itself is thus described by an American gentleman who was present:—"On being landed from the *Florida*, the body was removed to the house of Sir Edward Knatchbull, who then resided in Great George

body, for the purpose of placing it in a better constructed leaden coffin than that which had been prepared in Greece. A friend of mine kindly offered to procure me admission to the chamber where the removal of the body was to be effected—an offer which, I need not say, I gladly accepted. Accordingly, on the afternoon of the 11th of July, I proceeded to Sir Edward Knatchbull's, and found three or four gentlemen, attracted thither, like myself, to witness the solemn face of the poet for the last time, ere it should be shut up in the darkness of death. Mr. Samuel Rogers, the author of the 'Pleasures of Memory,' Mr. (now Sir) John Cam Hobhouse, and John Hanson, Esq. (the two last Lord Byron's executors), Dr. (afterwards Sir John) Bowring, Fletcher, his faithful valet, and one or two others, whose names I did not learn, were present.

"The body lay in the large drawing-room, on the first storey, which was hung with black cloth and lighted with wax candles. Soon after my arrival, the work of opening the coffin commenced. This was soon effected, and when the last covering was removed, we beheld the face of the illustrious dead, 'all cold and all serene.'

"Were I to live a thousand years, I should never, never forget that moment. For years I had been intimate with the mind of Byron. His wondrous works had thrown a charm around my daily paths, and with all the enthusiasm of youth I had almost adored his genius. With his features, through the medium of paintings, I had been familiar from my boyhood; and now far more beautiful, even in death, than my vivid fancy had ever pictured, there they lay in marble repose.

"The body was not attired in that most awful of habiliments—a shroud. It was wrapped in a blue cloth cloak, and the throat and head were uncovered. The former was beautifully moulded. The head of the poet was covered with short, crisp, curling locks, slightly streaked with grey hairs, especially over the temples, which were ample and free from hair, as we see in the portraits. The face had nothing of the appearance of death about it— it was neither sunken nor discoloured in the least, but of a dead, marble whiteness—the expression was that of stern repose. How classically beautiful was the curved upper lip and the chin! I fancied the nose appeared as if it was not in harmony with the other features; but it might possibly have been a little disfigured by the process of embalming. The forehead was high and broad—indeed, the whole head was extremely large—it must have been so to contain a brain of such capacity.

"But what struck me most was the exceeding beauty of the *profile*, as I observed it when the head was lifted in the operation of removing the corpse. It was perfect in its way, and seemed like a production of Phidias. Indeed, it far more resembled an exquisite piece of sculpture than the face of the dead—so still, so sharply defined, and so marble-like in its repose. I caught the view of it but for a moment; yet it was long enough to have stamped upon my memory as 'a thing of beauty,' which poor Keats tells us is 'a joy for ever.' It is, indeed, a melancholy joy to me to have gazed upon the silent poet. As Washington Irving says of the old sexton who crept into the vault where Shakespeare was entombed, and beheld there the dust of ages, 'it was something even to have seen the dust of Byron.'"

This same house, which has a handsome architectural front, is now the home of the Institution of Civil Engineers. The institution was established in 1818, and was formally incorporated in June, 1828. It originated in a few gentlemen then beginning life, who, being impressed, "by what they themselves felt, with the difficulties young men had to contend with in gaining the knowledge requisite for the diversified practice of engineering, resolved to form themselves into a society for promoting a regular intercourse between persons engaged in its various branches, and thereby mutually benefiting by the interchange of individual observation and experience." The profession of the civil engineer is defined in the charter of incorporation as "the art of directing the great sources of power in nature for the use and convenience of man, as the means of production and of traffic in states, both for external and internal trade, as applied in the construction of roads, bridges, aqueducts, canals, river navigation, and docks, for internal intercourse and exchange; and in the construction of ports, harbours, moles, breakwaters, and lighthouses; and in the art of navigation by artificial power for the purposes of commerce; and in the construction and adaptation of machinery; and in the drainage of cities and towns."

The institution itself consists of four classes, viz., members, associates, graduates, and honorary members. Members are civil engineers by profession, or mechanical engineers of very high standing; associates are not necessarily civil engineers by profession, but their pursuits must in some way be connected with civil engineering; graduates are elected from the pupils of civil and mechanical engineers; honorary members are individuals who are eminent for scientific acquirements, and are enabled to assist in the prosecution of public works.

Here is a portrait of Thomas Telford, the engineer of the Menai Bridge, and for fifteen years president of the institution. Telford was the first president. His successors have been Mr. James Walker, Sir John Rennie, Sir M. I. Brunel, Sir William Cubitt, Mr. Thomas Hawksley, and Mr. J. F. Bateman.

At No. 29 in this street was established, at its first formation, in 1857, the National Portrait Gallery. This institution arose out of a suggestion of the late Earl of Derby; its object is the collection of a series of portraits of English men and women of note and celebrity, and forming them into a representative gallery belonging to the nation. The collection is largely recruited by gifts, as might naturally be expected, and a sum of £2,000 is voted annually in Parliament for its maintenance and support. In 1870, the portraits were removed to South Kensington, a portion of the building erected for the International Exhibition having been fitted up for their reception. In Great George Street were, till lately, the town mansions of several of the highest nobility. At No. 15, Edward Lord Thurlow resided, and from it in September, 1806, his remains were removed for interment in the Temple. Bishop Tomline, Pitt's tutor, lived for some time at No. 28. At his house here, on the 12th of December, 1849, died Sir Marc Isambart Brunel, the architect of the Thames Tunnel. At No. 31 died, in 1881, William Page Wood, Lord Hatherley, some time Lord Chancellor.

In July, 1816, the body of Richard Brinsley Sheridan was removed from Savile Row to the house of Peter Moore, Esq., in this street, whence it was carried to the grave in the Abbey, attended by several noblemen and gentlemen.

At the corner of Great George Street and St. Margaret's Churchyard is a conspicuous structure, with a spire and cross of imposing height, known as the Buxton Memorial Drinking Fountain. The base is octagonal, about twelve feet in diameter, having open arches on the eight sides, supported on clustered shafts of polished Devonshire marble around a large central shaft, with four massive granite basins. Surmounting the pinnacles at the angles of the octagon are eight figures of bronze, representing the different rulers of England; the Britons represented by Caractacus, the Romans by Constantine, the Danes by Canute, the Saxons by Alfred, the Normans by William the Conqueror, and so on, ending with Queen Victoria. The fountain bears an inscription to the effect that it is "intended as a memorial of those members of Parliament who, with Mr. Wilberforce, advocated the abolition of the British slave-trade, achieved in 1807; and of those members of Parliament who, with Sir T. Fowell Buxton, advocated the emancipation of the slaves throughout the British dominions, achieved in 1834. It was designed and built by Mr. Charles Buxton, M.P., in 1865, the year of the final extinction of the slave-trade and of the abolition of slavery in the United States." Mr. S. S. Teulon was the architect, and the fountain was erected at a cost of about £1,200.

Close by this fountain, and facing the Houses of Parliament, is a fine bronze statue of George Canning, standing upon a granite pedestal. It was executed by Sir Richard Westmacott, and erected in 1832. It formerly stood nearer to Westminster Hall, but was removed hither a few years ago, when sundry alterations were made in the laying out of the open space between King Street and the north door of the Abbey.

Soon after Canning's statue was put up in all its verdant freshness, the carbonate of copper not yet blackened by the smoke of London, Mr. Justice Gaselee was walking away from Westminster Hall with a friend, when the judge, looking at the statue (which is colossal), said, "I don't think this is very like Canning; he was not so large a man." "No, my lord," replied his companion, "nor so green."

On the western side of the Broad Sanctuary, and on the very foundations of the old belfry-tower of the Sanctuary, stands the Sessions House, which, as its name imports, is the place of meeting for the magistrates for the City and Liberties of Westminster. It is an octagonal building of no great architectural pretensions, with a heavy portico, supported by massive columns of the Doric order. It was erected in 1805 from the designs of Mr. S. P. Cockerell. The old Guildhall, apparently of great antiquity, stood on the west side of King Street; and an ancient painting, representing the foundation of this building, said to be a gift of the Duke of Northumberland, was transferred to the walls of the present Sessions House.

Fronting the Broad Sanctuary and the northern side of the nave of the Abbey, between the Sessions House and Victoria Street, stands the Westminster Hospital. It was established in 1719 for the relief of the sick and needy from all parts, and was the first subscription hospital erected in London. It was incorporated in 1836. Patients are admitted by order from a governor, except in cases of accident, which are received, without recommendation, at all hours of the day or night. The institution took its origin from the exertions of a few gentlemen, who set an infirmary on foot, inviting all kindly-disposed persons to aid them. Mr. Henry Hoare was the chief promoter of this charity; and at first the society was known as that "for relieving the sick and needy at the Public Infirmary in Westminster." In 1720, a house was taken for the purpose of an infirmary in Petty France; from which, in 1724, the institution was removed to Chapel Street, and some time after to James Street. The present spacious edifice was completed and opened in 1834. The building is an embattled structure of quasi-Gothic character, and was erected in 1834 by Messrs. Inwood. It has a frontage of about 200 feet, but has no pretensions to taste or beauty. The centre projects slightly, and is raised one storey higher than the wings. The entrance is by a flight of steps to a porch in three divisions, and is surmounted by an oriel. The hospital accommodates about 200 in-patients, and the total number of patients relieved annually is about 20,000.

The following document, which may be styled the first annual report of this institution, dated 1720, hangs framed and glazed on the wall of the secretary's room :—" Whereas a charitable proposal was published in December last (1719), for relieving the sick and needy, by providing them with lodging, with proper food and physick, and nurses to attend them during their sickness, and by procuring them the advice and assistance of physicians or surgeons, as their necessities should require ; and by the blessing of God upon this undertaking, such sums of money have been advanced and subscribed by several of the nobility and gentry of both sexes and by some of the clergy, as have enabled the managers of this charity (who are as many of the subscribers as please to be present at their weekly meetings), to carry on in some measure what was then proposed :—for the satisfaction of the subscribers and benefactors, and for animating others to promote and encourage this pious and Christian work, this is to acquaint them, that in pursuance of the foresaid charitable proposal, there is an infirmary set up in Petty France, Westminster, where the poor sick who are admitted into it, are attended by physicians, surgeons, apothecaries, and nurses, supplied with food and physick, and daily visited by some one or other of the clergy ; at which place the society meets every Wednesday evening for managing and carrying on this charity, admitting and discharging patients, &c."

Close to and in connection with the hospital, an institution has been opened, styled the Westminster Training School and Home for Nurses, having for its object the training of a superior class of nurses for the sick, for hospitals, and private families. An agreement has been entered into by its managers with the Westminster Hospital to undertake the whole of the nursing there. A limited number of probationers are received at the home, and to those who may be accepted is given the efficient training and practical instruction required.

The central schools of the National Society for Promoting the Education of the Poor in the Principles of the Church of England are situated contiguous to Westminster Hospital. These schools were instituted in 1811, and incorporated in 1817.

The institution, which has for its object the " Christianising of the children of millions in the densely-crowded streets of the metropolis, amid the ignorance of an agricultural population, and the restlessness of the manufacturing and mining districts," is supported by voluntary contributions. The number of schools in union with it amounts to upwards of 12,000. Here is the National Society's central depository for the sale, at a cheap rate, of books and apparatus for schools.

In May, 1789, Sir John Hawkins, the author of the " History of Music," and of a " Life of Dr. Johnson," whose executor he was, died at his house near the Broad Sanctuary—the same which had formerly been the residence of the famous Admiral Vernon—in a street leading towards Queen Square. The following anecdote about Sir John Hawkins's "History of Music" is taken from the *Harmonicon* :—" The fate of this work was decided, like that of many more important things, by a trifle, a word, a pun. A ballad, chanted by a fille-de-chambre, undermined the colossal power of Alberoni ; a single line of Frederick the Second, reflecting not on politics but the poetry of a French minister, plunged France into the Seven Years' War ; and a pun condemned Sir John Hawkins's sixteen years' labour to long obscurity and oblivion. Some wag wrote the following catch, which Dr. Callcott set to music :—

'Have you read Sir John Hawkins's History ?
Some folks think it quite a mystery ;
Both I have, and I aver
That Burney's History I prefer.'

Burn his History was straightway in every one's mouth ; and the bookseller, if he did not follow the advice *à pied de la lettre*, actually wasted, as the term is, or sold for waste paper, some hundred copies, and buried the rest of the impression in the profoundest depth of a damp cellar, as an article never likely to be called for, so that now hardly a copy can be procured undamaged by damp and mildew. It has been for some time, however, rising—is rising, and the more it is read and known the more it ought to rise—in public estimation and demand."

In Prince's Street, immediately behind the Westminster Hospital, and on the site of the Westminster Mews, stands a large building of no great architectural pretensions, which is entered by an archway, and surrounds a court. It is divided into two parts, the one of which, to the south, having formerly been a police-barrack, has been devoted, since 1854, to the purposes of Her Majesty's Stationery Office. This public office was first established as a separate department about the year 1790, the stationery used in the public service having been previously supplied by individuals who had lucrative patents. A yearly estimate is published of the amount required " to defray the expense of providing stationery, printing, binding, and printed books, for the several departments of Government in England, Scotland, and Ireland, and some dependencies ; and of providing stationery, binding, printing, and paper for the two Houses of Parliament ; and to pay the salaries and expenses of the establishment of the Stationery Office. The late Mr. J. R. M'Culloch, the eminent statistician, was for many years the Comptroller of this department.

Princes Street was formerly called "Long Ditch." At one time it contained an ancient conduit, the site of which has since been marked by a pump. At the bottom of the well, it is said, is a black marble image of St. Peter, and some marble steps. The southern extremity of this street was called " Broken Cross."

Parker Street, on the west side of Princes Street, was formerly called Bennet Street, so named after Bennet (now Corpus Christi) College, Cambridge, to which the land belongs. Its name was changed some years ago, when a number of disorderly occupants were ejected, and new tenants admitted. The new name refers to Archbishop Parker, who, having bequeathed his valuable library to Corpus Christi College, is regarded as one of its chief benefactors.

At the west end of Prince's Court—a narrow turning out of Prince's Street—resided, in 1788, the great civic notoriety, John Wilkes. It has been noticed that his name, and the offices which he successively filled, coupled with it, were composed of forty-five letters :—

John Wilkes, Esquire, Sheriff for London and Middlesex.
John Wilkes, Esquire, Knight of the Shire for Middlesex.
John Wilkes, Esquire, Alderman for Farringdon Without.
John Wilkes, Esquire, Chamberlain of the City of London.
The Right Honourable John Wilkes, Lord Mayor of London.

Opposite the Broad Sanctuary is a Gothic column, or cross, nearly seventy feet high, erected, in 1861, as a memorial to Lord Raglan, and other "old Westminster scholars," who fell in the Crimea, in 1854–5. It is of Aberdeen granite, and very picturesque, although somewhat incongruous, which is perhaps owing to its having been executed by various artists. Around the polished shaft, which rises from a decorated pedestal, are shields bearing the arms of those whom it commemorates. At the top of the sculptured capital are four sitting figures, under Gothic canopies, representing the successive founders and benefactors of the School and Abbey—Edward the Confessor, Henry III., Queen Elizabeth, and Queen Victoria. The whole is surmounted by a figure of St. George and the Dragon. The architect of this beautiful column was Sir G. Gilbert Scott ; the figures of St. George and the Dragon, however, are by Mr. J. R. Clayton. In 1870, the memorial having become somewhat dilapidated, a sum of £30 towards its repair was voted by the Elizabethan Club, of which we have already spoken in our account of Westminster School.

CHAPTER IV.

MODERN WESTMINSTER.

"But times are altered."—*Goldsmith.*

Great Smith Street—St. Margaret's and St. John's Free Public Library—Public Baths and Washhouses—Mechanics' Institution—Bowling Alley —Little Dean Street—Tufton Street—Royal Architectural Museum—A Cock-pit—Great Peter Street—St. Matthew's Church—The Residence of Colonel Blood—St. Anne's Lane—Old and New Pye Streets—Westminster Working Men's Club and Lodging House—Orchard Street The " Rookery"—A Good Clearance—Palmer's Village—Victoria Street—The Palace Hotel—Westminster Chambers—Metropolitan Drinking-fountain and Cattle-trough Association—Duck Lane—Horseferry Road—Roman Catholic Chapel—Queen Anne's Gate— The Mission Hall—Jeremy Bentham—Mr. Towneley's *Réunions*—The " Three Johns "—The Cock-pit in Birdcage Walk—Distinguished Residents in Westminster in the Olden Times.

HAVING in the preceding chapters dealt with the streets and thoroughfares forming the centre of the City of Westminster, we will now endeavour to point out some of the chief features of interest, and penetrate into some of the courts and alleys that lie scattered through its outlying regions.

Starting from the Broadway, skirting the south-western corner of Dean's Yard, and running parallel to Abingdon Street, is Great Smith Street : this, with Little Smith Street, which joins it at right angles, and also Smith Square, derive their names, says Mr. Mackenzie Walcott, from a person who was clerk of the works at the time of the erection ; but according to Hutton, from Sir James Smith, the ground-landlord, who resided here. At the commencement of the last century there was a turnpike in Smith Street. In Great Smith Street is St. Margaret's and St. John's Free Public Library, and also the Public Baths and Washhouses, two very useful institutions, the benefits of which are highly appreciated by a large number of that particular class of the inhabitants for whose service

days amused themselves at the game of bowls. The memory of the spot is still preserved in the name of Bowling Alley.

In Little Dean Street stood one of the chapels of the French Huguenot Refugees, removed hither about the year 1700, from Berwick Street, Soho.

JUDGE JEFFREYS' HOUSE IN DUKE STREET.   *From an Original Drawing by Shepherd.*   (*See page* 29.)

they were specially erected. In 1840, Dr. H. H. Milman, afterwards Dean of St. Paul's, laid in this street the first stone of the City of Westminster Literary, Scientific, and Mechanics' Institution. The building comprised a spacious lecture-room, reading-rooms, class-rooms for drawing and music, a museum, and a library.

To the south of College Street was the bowling-green, where the members of the convent in other

Tufton Street was built by Sir Richard Tufton, after whom it was named. He died in 1631, and was buried in the Abbey.

At No. 18 in this street is the Royal Architectural Museum. The building in itself has little or nothing architectural about it to merit special mention. It is simply a lofty plain brick edifice on the west side of the street, and is entered through an arched doorway and vestibule. The interior is lighted from the roof only, the walls being entirely covered with the various objects exhibited, such as castings of capitals and bases of columns, bosses, and other kinds of ornament. Two galleries run round the building, each of them likewise filled with specimens. The Museum was founded in 1851, in practical object is to improve and perfect the art-workmanship of the present time, and to afford art-workmen the opportunity of studying casts or copies of those works, the originals of which neither their time nor their means will allow them to visit. Accordingly, a large collection of casts and actual

COLONEL BLOOD'S HOUSE. *From a Drawing in Mr. Crace's Collection.* (*See page* 38.)

Cannon Row, as the nucleus of a National Museum of Architectural Art, and subsequently for several years formed part of the collection exhibited at the South Kensington Museum. The intention of its founders was to supply to architects, artists, and art-workmen, the means of referring to and studying the architecture of past ages, and in combination with those arts which have their origin in or are dependent on architecture itself. Its direct specimens has been formed from the finest mediæval examples, English and foreign, of complete architectural works, arranged, as far as possible in the order of their dates; and of details, comprehending figures, animals, foliage, mouldings, encaustic tiles, mural paintings, roof ornaments, rubbings of sepulchral brasses, stained glass, impressions from seals, and other objects. Schools of Classical Art are also represented, though not so fully or systemati-

148

cally. A special collection of marble reliefs from the ruins of one of the ancient capitals of India, situated in the great desert of Rajpootana, of the date of about 1100 A.D., is due to the generosity of Sir Bartle Frere. The museum is open to the public free; but a small fee is charged for the drawing and modelling classes.

In Tufton Street there was formerly a building devoted to the brutal and unmanly amusement of cock-fighting. It comprised a large circular area, with a slightly elevated platform in the centre, surrounded by benches, rising in gradation to nearly the top of the building. The cock-pit existed in this street long after that near St. James's Park was deserted.

Great Peter Street bears the name of the patron-saint of the Abbey. Upon the front of a house in it might be seen the following inscription, rudely cut: "This is Sant Peter Street, 1624. R. [a heart] W." In this street is the principal entrance to the gas-works, noticed in a preceding chapter. Here, too, stands the Church of St. Matthew, which was erected in 1849, to meet the wants of the over-crowded parish of St. John the Evangelist. The church is situated in a very close and poor neigh-bourhood, its site having been purchased piecemeal as the different miserable houses by which it was partly covered could be procured. It is of a very irregular and unfavourable form, something resem-bling the letter L, and presenting one narrow frontage to Peter Street, and one still narrower to St. Anne's Lane; the remainder is almost buried by houses. The architect has succeeded, however, in placing the church east and west, and in so arranging it as to present all the usual ecclesiastical features and proportions; and though the building externally is but little seen, the part exposed to view is bold and effective; while the interior, though simple, suffers but little from the cramped nature of the position, excepting that the north aisle is deprived of its side windows by the row of houses by which it is flanked. The chancel is lighted by a bold east window of five lights, and by three windows on the south, and one on the north side, the remainder of that side being occu-pied by a chancel-aisle and vestry. The nave, with its aisles, consists of five bays or arches in length, and is chiefly lighted from the clerestory and from a large west window which obtains light from above the surrounding houses. The nave and chancel occupying the whole available area of that part of the ground which lies east and west, but not affording the required accommodation, a third aisle is projected into the southern arm of the ground, so that the nave has one aisle on the

north and two on the south. The principal en-trance is through the tower, which projects again southward from the last-mentioned aisle and faces Peter Street. There are also a western entrance and one from St. Anne's Lane. The style is the later fashion of the geometrical variety of Middle-pointed, or, what is more frequently called, "Early Decorated." It is, however, very simple though bold in its details. The church is built to accom-modate 1,200 worshippers, and the cost of its con-struction was about £6,000.

At a house at the corner of Great Peter Street and Tufton Street, overlooking Bowling Alley, if tradition is correct, resided, during the latter part of his life, the notorious Colonel Blood, who, as told by us in a previous volume,* endeavoured to steal the Crown and Regalia from the Tower. While Edwards, the keeper, who so bravely saved the crown, was literally left to starve, Blood is stated to have retired hither—with a pension, too— after his daring exploit at the Tower, King Charles not only having pardoned, but actually conferred upon him an estate in Ireland, worth £500 a year. Truly, therefore, may we add, in the words of the poet of old—

"Ille crucem sceleris pretium tulit, hic diadema."

Colonel Blood was cast in a suit for libel against his former patron, the Duke of Buckingham, and sentenced to pay £10,000, by way of damages. This sentence he could not survive. He died here in August, 1680, and was buried in New Chapel Yard, near the Broadway. He had, how-ever, been such an eccentric scamp during his life, that the populace thought that his death was only a *ruse* and a sham; so his body was taken up and an inquest held upon it. It was identified beyond dispute by a malformation of the thumb, and ac-cordingly was put back into its grave, only to be again disturbed by the formation of Victoria Street.

In the Luttrell Collection of Broadsides in the British Museum is to be seen "An Elegy on Colonel Blood, notorious for stealing the crown," in which occur the two following lines:—

"Thanks, ye kind fates, for your last favour shown, For stealing Blood, who lately stole the crown."

The house is mentioned in 1820 as "no longer standing." It was distinguished by a shield and coat of arms, raised in relief on the brickwork on the front of the house.

St. Anne's Lane, a narrow turning out of Great Peter Street, was so named from the Chapel dedi-cated to the mother of the Virgin Mary. Henry Purcell, the musician, who was born in Westminster,

---

* See Vol. II., page 81.

lived for some time in this lane. One of the most important features of St. Anne's Lane at the present time is a range of spacious and convenient baths and wash-houses, which have been erected at a cost of about £10,000.

An amusing story with reference to St. Anne's Lane is related in the *Spectator*, No. 125 :—"Sir Roger de Coverley was a schoolboy, at the time when the feuds ran high between the Roundheads and Cavaliers. This worthy knight, being then a stripling, had occasion to inquire which was the way to St. Anne's Lane, upon which the person to whom he spoke, instead of answering his question, called him 'a young Popish cur,' and asked him 'who had made Anne a saint?' The boy, in some confusion, inquired of the next he met which was the way to Anne's Lane ; but was called 'a prick-eared cur,' and, instead of being shown the way, was told she had been 'a saint before he was born, and would be one after he was hanged." 'Upon this,' says Roger, 'I did not think fit to repeat the former question, but going into every lane in the neighbourhood, asked what they called the name of the lane.'"

There were two St. Anne's Lanes which might have cost Sir Roger some trouble to find : one "on the north side of St. Martin's-le-Grand, just within Aldersgate Street," according to Stow; and the other—which it requires sharp eyes to find in Strype's map—turning, as we have said, out of Great Peter Street. Mr. Peter Cunningham, in his "Handbook for London," prefers supposing that Sir Roger inquired his way in the latter neighbourhood.

There is an old saying among Londoners, quoted in Moryson's "Itinerarie," to the effect that "woe be to him who buys a horse in Smithfield, or who takes a servant from St. Paul's, or a wife out of Westminster." Judging from the appearance of the female part of the community inhabiting many of the narrow courts and alleys abounding in this neighbourhood, one would be almost inclined to feel that the latter part of the saying above quoted holds good even in the present day, notwithstanding the sweeping change that has been effected in this neighbourhood within the last few years under the auspices of the Westminster Improvements Commission.

Old and New Pye Streets, part of which has disappeared since the year 1845 in the formation of Victoria Street, derive their names from the well-known Sir Robert Pye, who resided in the New Way close by. He was by marriage a cousin of Oliver Cromwell.

In Old Pye Street is a large brick building devoted to the comfort and intellectual improvement of the poorest classes of the population of Westminster. It is known as the Westminster Working Men's Club and Lodging-house. About the year 1860 a very useful little institution was established in a small room in Duck Lane, near Strutton Ground, on the south side of Victoria Street. It was the first attempt made in London at a working men's club as distinguished from a mechanic's institute—a place of repose and recreation, opened every evening from six till half-past ten, on payment of a weekly subscription of one halfpenny. Several daily and weekly papers, with some monthly periodicals, were provided, besides draughts and chess ; coffee and ginger-beer were supplied at cost price, no alcoholic beverages being admitted. Educational classes were held three times a week, and lectures, free to members and their families, were given every fortnight. A religious service (quite unsectarian) was also held for one hour on Sunday evenings. A penny bank was opened three nights a week, and in six months from the commencement, a labour loan society, enrolled by Mr. Tidd Pratt, was started. The institution soon proved so successful that it was necessary to enlarge the accommodation. Another room was built over the first one, and opened in December, 1861 ; the lower room was thus left free for general conversation, coffee, or smoking ; the classes, lectures, and quiet reading being carried on upstairs. A temperance association was now formed by some of the members, with a sick benefit society attached, formed by paying a penny a week, the use of a room for the temperance meetings being accorded free of expense. A barrow club was also commenced in 1862, for furnishing the members who were costermongers with barrows. The cost of a barrow is 55s. ; a weekly sum is paid, and when the price is liquidated the barrow becomes the property of the owner, instead of the latter always continuing to pay for the hire of one. In 1863, the accommodation having again become insufficient for its numerous members, an adjoining house was taken in, and the club entirely remodelled and improved, at a cost of more than £500, and re-opened in November of that year.

The demolition of Duck Lane, to make way for the progress of "the Westminster improvements," led to the erection, in Old Pye Street, of the pile of buildings above mentioned, which consists partly of a working men's club and partly of a dwelling-house, to accommodate between fifty and sixty of those families who are ineligible, from the lowness of their weekly wages or from their occupations, for any other lodging-houses, Mr. Peabody's included, where none but men earning 18s. or 20s. a week are admitted. The new Working Men's Club was opened in May, 1866. In the club building, which is quite distinct from the dwelling-house, there is, on the ground-floor, a spacious club-room, with a lavatory and other accommodation attached, as also a kitchen and library. A portion of the club at the corner of Old Pye Street and St. Ann's Lane has been fitted up as a double-fronted shop, where a co-operative store has been established by the members. Over the club-room are a lecture-room, a committee-room, and an office; the lecture-room can be at any time divided into two by a movable partition, so as to form a reading-room and a class-room.

In Pye Street lived for some time De Groot, the great-nephew of the learned Hugo Grotius, who was afterwards admitted as a poor brother into the Charter House, on the friendly intercession of Dr. Johnson.

Orchard Street was so called from being erected on the old orchard-garden of the monastery. Here, in 1757, the eccentric Thomas Amory, author of "Memoirs of John Buncle," lived the life of a recluse, venturing out only in the evening. He died in 1789, at a great age.

To the south-west of the Abbey is a district, between Great Smith Street and Victoria Street, which was and is known as "The Rookery." These "rookeries" or vagabond colonies, which meet us in various parts of "Modern Babylon," were originally the sites of sanctuaries and refuges for debtors and felons, or else of some "'spital" or "loke" for the reception of the poor, the maimed, and the lepers; the districts in which these asylums were located proving each the nucleus or nest of a dense pauper and criminal population. For just as the felon of our own days is too often found among the inmates of our "casual wards," so it is probable that of old the "sanctuary men" mixed with the diseased crowds and hordes of beggars that swarmed around a "'spital," associating of course with women of the lowest class, and so perpetuating the breed of outcasts and thieves, and turning the once "religious houses" into nests of poverty, misery, disease, and vice.

The region above alluded to formerly covered a much larger area than it does now, comprising as it did New Pye Street, Duck Lane, New Tothill Street, and portions of Orchard Street and Old Pye Street, together with a vast number of courts which diverged from them, all of which have been swept away since the year 1845, when the work of clearance was taken in hand by the Westminster

Improvement Commission. It was in Orchard Street that Oliver Cromwell had one of his palaces; in those days Palmer's Village was close beside it, and was the seat of gentlemen's country residences. Lady Dacre, the foundress of Emmanuel Hospital, left to the City an estate of between two and three acres of ground—the garden ground—called "Palmer's Village" from the Rev. James Palmer, who here founded, in 1654, almshouses for twelve poor persons, and a school for twenty boys, known as the "Black-Coat School." This institution is now located in Rochester Row, where the almshouses were rebuilt in 1881. Palmer's Village at the early part of the present century, boasted of its village green, upon which the Maypole was annually set up; and there was an old wayside inn, bearing the sign of "The Prince of Orange." All this rurality, together with the nest and labyrinth of vile and dirty lanes and courts which surrounded it, has now disappeared, and in its place has been formed the broad and open thoroughfare, Victoria Street, which was commenced in 1845, and publicly opened in 1851.

"Nobody," writes the author of "A New Critical Review of the Public Buildings" in 1736, "will wonder, I presume, that I am for levelling the Gate House, demolishing a large part of Dean's Yard, and laying open a street at the west end of the Abbey, at least to an equal breadth with the building." Had the writer of these remarks lived to our own days he would have seen his wishes gratified.

Apropos of the improvements that have been of late years effected here, we may add that in 1766 was published Gwyn's "London and Westminster Improved," an important work, dedicated by permission to the King; the dedication and the preface, as we learn from Boswell, being from Dr. Johnson's pen. Mr. Croker thus remarks on it in his notes on Boswell:—"In this work Mr. Gwyn proposed the *principle*, and in many instances the *details*, of the most important improvements which have been made in the metropolis in our day. A bridge near Somerset House; a great street from the Haymarket to the New Road; the improvement of the interior of St. James's Park; quays along the Thames; new approaches to London Bridge; the removal of Smithfield Market; and several other suggestions on which we pride ourselves as original designs of our own times, are all to be found in Mr. Gwyn's able and curious work. It is singular that he denounced a row of houses *then* building in Pimlico, as intolerable nuisances to Buckingham Palace, and of these very houses the public voice now calls for the destruction.

Gwyn had what Lord Chatham calls 'the prophetic eye of taste.'"

Victoria Street is upwards of a thousand yards in length, extending from the Broad Sanctuary to Shaftesbury Place, Pimlico; it is eighty feet wide, and the houses on either side upwards of eighty feet high, mostly cut up into "flats." At the corner of this street, about three hundred yards west of the Abbey, stands the Westminster Palace Hotel, erected in 1861. Here the office of the Secretary of State for India was accommodated for a few years, until the new quarters for that department could be made ready for its reception. The hotel was built from the designs of Mr. A. Moseley. The hotel is traditionally said to stand on the site of the press set up in the Almonry, as already stated, by William Caxton, to whose memory the directors have subscribed a sum for the purpose of placing a statue of the first English printer in the entrance-hall.

A block of buildings of great magnitude, called Westminster Chambers, having a frontage of about 450 feet, stands immediately opposite the Hotel, and with it forms a striking entrance to this great street. The building contains about 530 rooms, disposed on the basement, ground, first, second, third, and fourth floors. It consists of two parallel ranges of building, each about 430 feet in length, separated by court-yards, access to the whole being obtained by seven stone staircases of easy gradients, and from seven arched entrances from Victoria Street. Each suite of rooms is approached from a separate entrance-door on the landings of these staircases, and consists of four or five rooms, as the case may be, with a few sets of two rooms each. There are 120 of these suites in the entire building. Party walls separate the building into fourteen compartments; making, as it were, fourteen separate self-contained houses; and thus, in case of fire, limiting the damage to the division or compartment in which it may occur.

In this street are the offices of the Metropolitan Drinking-fountain and Cattle-trough Association, of which the Duke of Westminster is the president. This is the only society which provides free supplies of water for animals in the streets of London, and the relief which it affords to horses, dogs, sheep, and oxen is well-nigh incalculable. The number of metropolitan fountains and troughs at the end of the year 1874 was as follows:—276 fountains, 72 large cattle-troughs, and 199 small troughs for sheep and dogs. In some cases the committee of the Association have to pay nearly £50 a year for the water consumed at a single trough. It is calculated that more than 1,200

horses, besides a large number of oxen, sheep, and dogs, frequently drink at a single trough in the course of one day. This invaluable association, we may add, as a hint to the charitable friends of dumb animals, is entirely "supported by voluntary contributions."

Duck Lane, which has quite disappeared in the formation of Victoria Street, probably took its name from the number of those birds which frequented the straight canals and runnels by which early maps represent the immediate vicinity to have been divided. There was a noted piece of water, called the Duck Pond, afterwards built over by the houses of this lane. In Duck Lane was first kept, in 1688, the Blue-Coat School, for boys only, and supported by voluntary contributions; and in 1709, a Mr. William Green built a school and masters' house in Little Chapel Street. A great part of the extensive grounds, including parts of Allington Street, Brewers' Green, St. Peter's Street, the Horseferry Road, and Orchard Street, was purchased by Mr. Green, who founded the Stag, or Elliot's Brewery.

In Horseferry Road, between the river and Victoria Street, about half a mile from the west end of the venerable Abbey, is a small and unpretending building, which for many years was the only chapel for the accommodation of the Roman Catholic poor who crowd the close courts abutting on the old Almonry. Down to 1792 they had no chapel at all, but were forced to practise their religion as best they could, in garrets and cellars, for fear of prosecutions under the penal laws. In that year a small chapel was opened in York Street, near Queen Square (now called Queen Anne's Gate), but it was closed for want of funds six years afterwards. In 1803 another attempt was made to maintain a chapel in Great Smith Street, under the auspices of the Chaplains of the Neapolitan Embassy, but this, too, came to an end after a three years' struggle. A temporary chapel in Dartmouth Street was next secured, and this lasted until 1813, when the present chapel was opened, mainly through the energy of the Rev. W. Hurst, the learned Professor of Theology at Valladolid, and translator of the writings of the Venerable Bede. It was enlarged and beautified in 1852, and is now served by Fathers of the Jesuit Order. The sculpture over the altar, representing the Annunciation of our Lady, by Phyffers, is much admired.

Between Victoria Street and St. James's Park is Queen Square, called by Strype "Queen Anne Square," and now altered by the authority of the Metropolitan Board of Works to "Queen Anne's

Gate." It tells its own tale so far as the date of its erection. It is a small oblong parallelogram, extending about fifty yards from east to west, but very narrow from north to south. Hatton, writing in 1708, speaks of it in terms of glowing, and, we fear must be added, undiscriminating praise, as "a beautiful square of very fine buildings." When Park Street was erected, the inhabitants of Queen Square, apprehending that carriages on their way

also as a school and lecture-room, but formerly a chapel of ease to St. Peter's parish. It was originally a royal gift for the special use of the judges of Westminster, and was frequented by the members of the Royal Household. In it is a very handsomely carved pulpit, apparently of the seventeenth century, with an inscription, "Look upon me." In 1840 the chapel was much injured by fire; the altar-piece, then nearly destroyed, is

PALMER'S ALMSHOUSES, 1850. (See page 40.)

to Ranelagh would pass through the New Street, and make their hitherto quiet square a noisy thoroughfare, in order to avoid King Street, the Sanctuary, and Tothill Street, erected, by subscription, the wall and railing which separates Queen Square and Park Street. At the eastern entrance of the square, set up against one of the houses on the south side, is a statue of Queen Anne; it is, however, a poor specimen of art, and is so placed that it scarcely strikes the eye of the passer-by. The queen is dressed in her state robes, and has the sceptre and orb in her hands. At the beginning of this century, Mr. Henry J. Pye, poet laureate, resided in this square.

In the south-west corner of the square is a dull, heavy building, now used as a Mission Hall, and

a fine specimen of wood-carving. The communion-table is said to be the same at which Queen Elizabeth made her first communion.

In Queen Square Place, where he had resided nearly half a century, died, in the year 1832, Jeremy Bentham, the eminent jurist, and writer on the philosophy of legislation. It was here that his brother, Sir Samuel Bentham, on his return from Russia, began to make machinery for all kinds of woodwork before unknown, and planned and constructed ships for the Admiralty, in which for the first time powder magazines were made safe. A singular anecdote is told concerning Jeremy Bentham, which we give for what it is worth :— "One day, returning to his home through Tothill Street, dressed in a suit of grey, of ancient cut, and

STOREY'S GATE, ST. JAMES'S PARK, IN 1820. (*See page 47.*)

with long grey hair falling over his shoulders, he sat down, tired, on a door-step. A lady passing, struck with his appearance, and taking him for a poor man, gave him a penny. He took it, enjoying the jest, and ever after kept it in his writing-desk." It is related of Jeremy Bentham, that he bequeathed his body to Dr. Southwood Smith, for the purposes of anatomical science.

In 1874 Queen Square and Park Street were re-numbered throughout, and together re-named Queen Anne's Gate, as stated above.

At No. 7, Park Street, on Sunday evenings, Mr. Towneley, the collector of the Towneley Marbles, &c., in the British Museum, one of the earliest revivers of the arts, was accustomed to entertain distinguished *literati* and artists, members of the Dilettanti Club; and Nollekens, Sir Joshua Reynolds, and Zoffany were generally found at his hospitable table. Here, in 1772, Mr. Towneley first assembled his collection of marbles, bronzes, and other works of art, which he had commenced in 1768 at Rome. We shall have more to say about this collection when we come to the British Museum.

In Little Park Street there was a curious alehouse called the "Three Johns," and the same sign, it is said, was also to be seen till lately near Queen Anne's Gate. It is thus described by Mr. Larwood:—"It represented an oblong table, with John Wilkes in the middle, John Horne Tooke at one end, and Sir John Glynn, serjeant-at-law, at the other. There is a mezzotint print of this picture, or the sign may have been taken from the print, and engraved by R. Houston in 1769. John Wilkes, on whom the popular gratitude for writing the Earl of Bute out of power has conferred many a sign-board, still survives in a few other spots also."

We have already seen that the Palace of Whitehall had its cock-pit,* and therefore our readers may be surprised to hear that there was a second cock-pit—called also the Royal—within three or four hundred yards off, in Birdcage Walk, facing the Park. It stood at the junction of Queen Square with Park Street, just at the top of Dartmouth Street, and was ornamented with a cupola. It was taken down in 1816; but in Ackermann's "Microcosm of London," published in 1808, there is a picture of its interior, as it was a few years previously, in a style worthy of Hogarth, who, by the way, has also immortalised it. It is drawn by Rowlandson and Pugin, and coloured, showing the style of dress worn by all grades, from the lord to

the Westminster "rough." Some of the figures introduced are evidently portraits of "peers and pick-pockets, grooms and gentlemen," mixed up in a strange medley. The rival cocks are being backed up by two boys, called feeders, dressed in red jackets and yellow trowsers—a sort of "royal" livery; the chief figure in the front row is an elderly gentleman, who seems to anticipate the loss of the battle, as also does his fat neighbour on the left, while a stupid look of despair in the countenance of a grim individual on the right proclaims that all is lost. The smiling gentleman on the left appears to be the winner, actual or expectant. The clenched fists and earnest looks of those in the two front rows show that a goodly sum of money is risked on the issue. Nearly in the centre of the back row of all are two figures apparently hurling defiance at the whole company; they are certainly offering odds which no one is disposed to take. At the back sits an officer in a cocked hat, and above him are the royal arms, the lion and the unicorn, to all appearance, looking down with composure on the fray, whilst some of the "roughs" are laying whips and thick sticks on the heads and shoulders of their neighbours. The whole picture is a study, and gives a far more perfect idea of such a scene than any words can convey. It seems strange that such scenes were tolerated and approved by royalty in the "good old days when George III. was king." In some families in the seventeenth century the patronage of cock-fighting would appear to have been as hereditary as is the keeping of hounds with certain nobles of a later date; for instance, the Herberts, concerning whom there is an old doggerel verse, often quoted:—

"The Herberts every cock-pit day,
　Do carry away, away, away!
　The gold and glory of the day."

It was at the Cock-pit in St. James's Park that Robert Harley, afterwards Earl of Oxford, was stabbed, though not fatally, with a penknife, by a French noble refugee, the Marquis de Guiscard, who was brought before him and the rest of the Cabinet Council by the Queen's Messenger, charged with treacherous correspondence with the rival Court at St. Germain, whilst drawing a pension from the English Court.

In the records of the Audit Office is an entry of a payment of "xxx*l.* per annum to the keeper of our Playhouse called the Cockpitt, in St. James's Parke."

Cock-fighting, and the still more barbarous sport of throwing at cocks, it may interest some of our readers to learn, was, in the days of our forefathers,

---

* See Vol. III., p. 370.

the chief amusement on Shrove Tuesday. Hence Sir Charles Sedley, in his epigram on a cock at Rochester, prays:—

" May'st thou be punished for St. Peter's crime,
   And on Shrove Tuesday perish in thy prime ! "

Such sports, it is fortunate to add, are now very nearly extinct among the educated classes, for public opinion has declared against them in an unmistakable manner. " Cock-fighting and bear-baiting," as Dr. Johnson said, " may raise the spirit of a company, just as drinking does, but they will never improve the conversation of those who take part in them."

Near the Cock-pit resided Sir John Germaine, who was tried for running off with the Duchess of Norfolk, whom her husband divorced in consequence. She was by birth a Mordaunt, a daughter of the Earl of Peterborough. It was sworn on the trial that Sir John and the duchess used to frequent Vauxhall almost daily in each other's company, a fact on which the divorce was based to a large extent, and which does not speak very much in praise of the morals of that place of amusement.

Much of the incongruous character of the Westminster of the era of Victoria may be traced back to the peculiarities of the ancient city. Du Chatelet, the celebrated French statistician, shows that the " Quartier de la Cité "—now the head-quarters of the thieves of Paris—was formerly the site of a well-known "sanctuary ;" and just so it was also with the City of Westminster itself. " The church at Westminster," writes Stow, " hath had great privilege of sanctuary within the precinct thereof, from whence it hath not been lawful for any prince or any other to take any person that fled thither for any cause. The charter granted to it by Edward the Confessor conferred this privilege in the following terms :— ' I order and establish for ever that whatever person, of what condition or estate soever he be, from whence soever he come, or for what offence or cause it be, cometh for his refuge into the said Holy Church of the Blessed Apostle St. Peter, at Westminster, he be assured of his life, liberty, and limbs ; . . . . and whosoever presumeth or doeth contrary to this my grant, I will that he lose his name, worship, dignity, and power, and that, with the great traitor, Judas, that betrayed our Saviour, he be in the everlasting fire of hell.' "

The neighbourhood of the Abbey two centuries, or even a century ago, it is to be feared, was low and disreputable. Pope tells us, for instance, how Curll's hack authors hung about this part : his historian at " the tallow-chandler's under the blind arch in Petty France ; his two translators sharing a bed together ; and his poet in the cockloft in Budge Row, where the ladder to get at it is in the hands of the landlady."

The author of " A New Critical Review of the Public Buildings, &c.," in the reign of George II., with the shallow and false taste of his time, dismisses the fair city in a very few words, as " though famous for its antiquity, yet producing very little worthy of attention and less of admiration." He would have written far otherwise, had he lived till the days of Queen Victoria.

Till within about a century most of the shops in the Strand and Westminster, as in the City, were open, as those of butchers are to the present day ; and in this way not only articles of dress, but watches and jewellery were exposed for sale. In fact, they did not begin to be enclosed and glazed, as now, until about the year 1710. Thus, in the *Tatler* (No. 162), we find mentioned as novelties, " Private shops that stand upon Corinthian pillars, and whole rows of tin pots showing themselves through a sash window," the appearance of "pillars" and " sash-windows " being equally unwarrantable innovations. The appearance, too, of the master, under the first two Georges, if not to a later date, was equally unlike the dress of a modern trades-man. Then the old shopkeeper might be seen walking the quarter-deck of his own shop, with his hair full-powdered, his silver knee and shoe buckles, and his hands surrounded with the nicely-plaited ruffle hanging down to his knuckles, and his apprentices wearing the same livery, only with distinctions to mark their grade.

" By an Act of Parliament of the fourteenth and fifteenth of Henry VIII., c. 2, the jurisdiction of the City corporations was to extend two miles beyond the City ; namely, the town of Westminster, the parishes of St. Martin-in-the-Fields and Our Lady in the Strand, St. Clement's Danes without Temple Bar, St. Giles's-in-the-Fields, St. Andrew's in Holborn, the town and borough of Southwark, the parishes of Shoreditch, Whitechapel, St. John's Street, Clerkenwell, and Clerkenwell, St. Botolph without Aldgate, St. Katharine's near the Tower, and Bermondsey.

" Such were the suburbs of our great metropolis in 1524. They were greatly detached, and the intervals were principally public fields. The Strand was then occupied by mansions and dwellings of the nobility, which were surrounded by large and splendid gardens ; and a considerable portion of the parishes of St. Martin and St. Giles were literally, as they are still called, in the fields, as were also a great portion of the City of Westminster, and the villages of Clerkenwell, Shoreditch, and Whitechapel, and the borough of Southwark."

D'Israeli, in his "Curiosities of Literature," after noting the gradual union of Westminster and London, in spite of all edicts and Acts of Parliament, remarks that "since their happy marriage their fertile progenies have so blended together, that little Londons are no longer distinguishable from their ancient parents. We have succeeded in spreading the capital into a county, and have verified the prediction of James I., that 'England will shortly be London, and London England.'"

In Rymer's "Fœdera" (vol. xvi.) is given a proclamation of Elizabeth, issued for the purpose of restraining the increase of buildings about the metropolis. In it the high-handed Queen commands all persons, on the pain of her royal displeasure, and of sundry punishments besides, to desist from all new buildings of houses or tenements within three miles of any of the gates of London; and in the same document it is ordered that unfinished buildings or new foundations are to be summarily pulled down. A strange contrast this to the policy of Queen Victoria, under whom the buildings and population of London and its suburbs have been more than doubled, without any let or hindrance on the part of the sovereign. The spirit of Elizabeth's proclamation was in due course repeated by James I. on his accession to his southern throne.

The fair city has numbered among its residents many distinguished and many eccentric personages, and has witnessed many freaks of fortune in the sudden rise or fall of individuals of less or more merit. Thus, we read in Erskine's "Dramatic Biography" the following bit of luck which befell a servant maid:—"Mrs. Jane Wiseman, who wrote a tragedy, entitled 'Antiochus the Great, or the Fatal Relapse' (1702, 4to), was a servant in the family of Mr. Wright, Recorder of Oxford, where, having leisure time, she employed it in reading plays and novels. She began there that tragedy which she finished in London, and, soon after, marrying one Holt, a vintner, they were enabled, by the profits of her play, to set up a tavern in Westminster." It is devoutly to be hoped that this worthy pair made a fortune and "lived happily ever after."

Among the distinguished residents of Westminster in former times, as we learn from the "New View of London" (published in 1708), were Lord Scarsdale, who was living at a mansion in Duke Street; Lord Stafford, at Tart Hall; Lord

Rochester, "near Westminster Gate;" Lord Essex, near Whitehall; the Lord Portland, near the Banqueting House in Whitehall; the Bishop of Norwich and the Archbishop of York in Petty France. Peterborough House, near the Horseferry, belonged to the Earl of Peterborough, but was let to a merchant, Mr. Bull. In Queen Square were living Lords North, and Grey, and Guernsey. Robert Harley, Principal Secretary of State under Queen Anne, lived in "York Buildings, near the waterside."

In the Market Place at Westminster was formerly an inn bearing the sign of "The Old Man." This probably refers to "Old Parr," of whom we have already spoken in our account of the Strand,* and who was celebrated in the ballads of the day as "The olde, olde, very olde manne." "The token of the inn," says Mr. Larwood, "represents a bearded bust in profile, with a bare head."

James I., with all his learning and pedantry, was, apparently, a patron of sports and pastimes; at all events, we read that he granted to his groom-porter, one Clement Cottrell, the privilege of licensing, within the limits of London and Westminster, and within two miles therefrom, no less than forty taverns "for the honest and reasonable recreation of good and civil people, who for their quality and ability, may lawfully use the games of bowling, tennis, dice, cards, tables, nine-holes, or any other game hereafter to be invented."

We cannot turn our backs on Westminster without remarking that the two cities of London and Westminster for a number of years were totally distinct and separate—the one inhabited chiefly by the Scots, and the other by the English. It is believed that the union of the two crowns conduced not a little to unite these several cities; "for," says an old writer, Howel, "the Scots greatly multiplying here, nestled themselves about the court, so that the Strand, from the mud walls and thatched cottages, acquired that perfection of building it now possesses;" and thus went on the process which made London, according to the quaint fancy of the writer just named, like a Jesuit's hat, the brims of which were larger than the block; and that induced the Spanish ambassador, Gondomar, to say to his royal mistress, after his return from London, and whilst describing the place to her, "Madam, I believe there will be no city left shortly, for all will run out of the gates to the suburbs."

* See Vol. III., p. 74.

CHAPTER V.

ST. JAMES'S PARK.

" A spark
That less admires the Palace than the Park."—Pope.

Storey's Gate—Origin of "Birdcage Walk"—The Wellington Barracks—Origin of the Guards—Mr. Harrington's House—Office of the Duchy of Lancaster—St. James's Park in the Reign of Henry VIII.—Rosamond's Pond—Charles II. and his Feathered Pets—Duck Island—Le Notre employed in Laying out and Improving the Park—The Decoy—The King and his Spaniels—William III.'s Summer-house—St. James's as a Deer-park—Le Serre's Description of the Park—Pepys' Account of the Works carried out here by Charles II.—The "Physicke Garden"—Waller's Poetic Description of the Park—The Canal—The Ornithological Society—The Waterfowl—Woodcocks and Snipes—Historical Associations of St. James's Park—Cromwell and Whitelock—Oliver Goldsmith—Peace Rejoicings after the Battle of Waterloo—Albert Smith's Description of St. James's Park and its Frequenters—The Mohawks—The Chinese Bridge—Skating on the "Ornamental Water"—Improvements in the Park by George IV.—The Horse Guards' Parade—Funeral of the Duke of Wellington—Robert Walpole and the Countryman—Dover House.

AT the western end of Great George Street, which we have already described, we find ourselves at Storey's Gate, the entrance of St. James's Park. This gate was so called from one Master Edward Storey, the "keeper of the king's birds," whose house stood on the spot. This fact has been doubted; but that Storey's Gate was so named after a real personage is proved by the entry in the registers of Knightsbridge Chapel, in the reign of Charles II., of the marriage of one Thomas Fenwick, "of St. Margaret's, servant to Storey, at ye Park Gate, and Mary Gregory, of ye same."

The birds, which were among the most innocent toys and amusements of the "merry monarch," were kept in aviaries ranged in order along the road which bounds the south side of the Park, and extends to Buckingham Palace, and which is still known by the significative name of "Birdcage Walk." To corroborate this derivation, we may mention here that the carriage-road between Storey's Gate and Buckingham Gate was, until 1828, open only to the Royal Family and to the Hereditary Grand Falconer, the Duke of St. Albans.

About one-half of the south side of Birdcage Walk, extending from Queen Anne's Gate to Buckingham Gate, is occupied by the Wellington Barracks, which consist of lofty and commodious ranges of buildings, for the use of the household troops. The barracks were first occupied by troops in the year before the battle of Waterloo. In the Military Chapel, which was opened in 1838, are preserved the tattered standards which were taken by Marlborough at Blenheim, and the colours of the Grenadier Guards which were used at Waterloo.

As there were no barracks during the reign of Charles II., and as by the Petition of Right it was declared unlawful to billet soldiers on private families, the alehouses and smaller inns of Westminster were always filled with privates of the regiments of Guards, which, from the first establishment of a standing army, have been generally stationed on duty near Whitehall and St. James's. Macaulay thus gives us the history of the origin of the Guards :—" The little army formed by Charles II. was the germ of that great and renowned army which has in the present century marched triumphant into Madrid and Paris, into Canton and Candahar. The Life Guards, who now form two regiments, were then distributed into three troops, each of which consisted of two hundred carabineers, exclusive of officers. This corps, to which the safety of the king and royal family was confided, had a very peculiar character. Even the privates were designated as 'Gentlemen of the Guard.' Many of them were of good families, and had held commissions in the Civil War. Their pay was far higher than that of the most favoured regiment of our time, and would in that age have been thought a respectable provision for the younger son of a country squire. Their fine horses, their rich houses, their cuirasses, and their buff coats, adorned with ribbons, velvet, and gold lace, made a splendid appearance in St. James's Park. A small body of grenadier dragoons, who came from a lower class, and received lower pay, was attached to each troop. Another body of household cavalry distinguished by blue coats and cloaks, and still called the Blues, was generally quartered in the neighbourhood of the capital. Near the capital lay also the corps which is now designated as the First Regiment of Dragoons, but which was then the only regiment of dragoons on the English establishment."

At the commencement of the present century a handsome building of one storey high, in the Chinese style, was, by order of Government, erected on the left angle of the recruiting-house, in Birdcage Walk, for the purpose of serving as the armoury for the whole brigade of Guards. It consisted of four archways on the basement for the field-pieces, the room over it being for the small arms, and a range of rooms in the back, for cleaning. The two front angles had each a small house, one for a serjeant-major, and the other for a guard-room. This, we may infer, was the beginning of the barracks on this spot.

Near this part, as Aubrey tells us, a Mr. James Harrington had a "versatile timber house." He describes it as "built in Mr. Hart's garden, opposite to St. James's Park." "This eccentric individual," says Aubrey, "fancied that his perspiration turned to flies and bees, *ad cætera sobrius*. To try the

longing to the Hospital for Lepers, which in due course of time was converted, by the royal will and pleasure of "Bluff King Hal," into "our Palace of St. James's."

It was by the order of Henry that the meadow was drained and enclosed, formed into a "nursery for deer," and made also "an appendage to the Tilt-yard at Whitehall." At first this was but a small enclosure inside four brick walls; but in

WESTMINSTER ABBEY FROM ST. JAMES'S PARK, ABOUT 1740.

experiment, he would turn this house to the sun and sit towards it; then he had fox-tayles there, to chase away and massacre all the flies and bees." Mr. Harrington is said to have spent the last twenty years of his life in a house in the Little Almonry, near Dean's Yard, of which Aubrey gives us a curious description. "In the upper storey he had a pretty gallery, which looked into the yard, over a court, where he commonly dined and meditated, and smoked his tobacco."

At the western end of Birdcage Walk is the Duchy of Lancaster office, where all business relative to the revenues of the Prince of Wales, in right of that duchy, is transacted.

St. James's Park itself, which we now enter, was originally a low and swampy meadow, be-

course of time Henry VIII. added a "chase," which he threw out, like a wide open noose, from his palace at Westminster, forming, where the line of it fell, a large circle, which ran from St. Giles-in-the-Fields, up to Islington, round Highgate and Hornsey and Hampstead Heath, and so back again by Marylebone to St. Giles's and West-minster; and he forbade all his subjects of every degree either to hawk or hunt within those boundaries. Though little more than three centuries and a half have passed away since this royal proclamation was issued, yet almost every mark of it has long since been blotted out. Edward VI. and Mary possessed no share of their "bluff" father's destructiveness, and the whole chase was gradually "disafforested."

Still, however, St. James's Park retains its verdant and rural character, and in it there are spots where the visitor may sit or walk with every trace of the great city around him shut out from his gaze, except the grey old Abbey, against the tall roof of which the trees seem to rest, half burying it in their foliage, just as they must have done three centuries ago.

In the south-west corner, near Birdcage Walk,

"This the blest lover shall for Venus take,
And send up vows from Rosamonda's lake."

The same is the drift of a dialogue in Southerne's comedy, *The Maid's Last Prayer.*

"Rosamond's Pond," writes the author of "A New Critical Review of the Public Buildings," &c., "is another scene where fancy and judgment might be employed to the greatest advantage; there is something wild and romantic round the sides of

"ROSAMOND'S POND" IN 1758.

and opposite to James Street and Buckingham Gate, was formerly a small sheet of water, known as "Rosamond's Pond," to which reference is constantly made in the comedies of the time as a place of assignation for married ladies with fashionable *roués.* The pond was made to receive the water of a small stream which trickled down from Hyde Park, and it is shown in one or two very scarce prints by Hogarth. It was filled up in 1770, soon after the purchase of Buckingham House by the Crown.

It is to its character as recorded above, and as being, in the words of Bishop Warburton to Hurd, "long consecrated to disastrous love and elegiac poetry," that Pope thus mentions it in the *Rape of the Lock* :—

it, of which a genius could make a fine use, if he had the liberty to improve it as he pleased." He adds, "The banks of it ought to be kept in better repair; and if a Venus in the act of rising from the sea with the Graces round her were raised in the midst of it, it would be neither an improper nor an useless decoration." From the same essay we gather that at this date the vineyard close by was in a most scandalously neglected state, and required much labour and art to make it a tasteful addition to the park. As to the Birdcage Walk, the writer calls it "exceeding pleasant, the swell of the ground in the middle having an admirable effect on the vista," and commanding a "simple and agreeable view down to the canal." He urges, however, that variety should be studied in its arrangement, and that the circle of trees should be made the " centre of a beautiful scene ; " in which case it would become " one of the most delightful arbours in the world." " Its romantic aspect, the irregularity of the ground, the trees which over-shadowed it, and the view of the venerable Abbey, not only rendered it," writes Mr. Jesse, "a favourite resort of the contemplative, but its secluded situation is said to have tempted a greater number of persons, and especially of 'unfortunate' females, to commit suicide than any other place in London."

St. James's Park must have been a rural and pleasant enclosure in the reign of Charles II., when the avenues of trees were first planted along the northern side of the park, where now is the gravel walk known as "The Mall," under the direction of Le Notre, the French landscape gardener, who was also commissioned to lay out and improve the whole ; and when the south side was really, as its name still implies, a walk hung with the cages of the king's feathered pets. Its rural character, at that time, may be inferred from the title of Wycherley's successful comedy, *Love in a Wood, or St. James's Park*, which was first acted in 1672. Close by, at the east end of the water, which was in those days straight, and generally known as the " Canal," was a small decoy and an island, called "Duck Island," over which the celebrated St. Evremond was set as "governor" with a small salary. To this we find Horace Walpole alludes in a tone of pleasant banter when, recording in 1751 the appointment of Lord Pomfret as ranger of St. James's Park, he adds, " By consequence, my Lady [Pomfret] is queen of the Duck Island."

As to the island in the canal, the writer of the " New Critical Review " (1736) speaks of it—with some exaggeration, no doubt—as being on the one side a wilderness and a desert, and on the other " like a paradise in miniature ; " he complains that " the water is allowed to grow stagnant and putrid, and that the trees, shrubs, and banks all wanted attention "—remarks which show that whoever at that time was the "ranger" of the park must have had little eye for either beauty or taste. The canal itself appears to have been 100 feet in breadth and 2,800 feet long.

Duck Island was abolished and made into *terra firma* towards the close of the last century. In fact, "the island," says Pennant in 1790, " is lost in the new improvements."

Pope, who did not approve of Le Notre's stiff and formal style, censures him for the want of good sense—in company, it may be observed, with no less a master than Inigo Jones :—

" Something there is more needful than expense,
And something previous e'en to taste—'tis sense ;
Good sense, which only is the gift of Heaven,
And, though no science, fairly worth the seven ;
A light which in yourself you must perceive,
Jones and Le Notre have it not to give."

It is difficult to say to what omission Pope here makes special allusion. Le Notre was largely employed by Le Grand Monarque, Louis XIV., who also ennobled him. He died at Paris in the year 1700.

The "decoy" above mentioned consisted of five or six straight pieces of water all running parallel to each other and to the canal itself, with which they communicated by narrow openings.

King Charles appears to have been particularly fond of St. James's Park. We are told he would sit for hours on the benches in the walk, amusing himself with some tame ducks and his dogs, amidst a crowd of people, with whom he would talk and joke. It is fancied by some persons that no dogs are now left of the breed popularly called King Charles's breed, except a few very beautiful black-and-tan spaniels belonging to the late Duke of Norfolk, and which used to run riot over Arundel Castle much in the same way that their canine forefathers were formerly allowed to range about the palace at Whitehall. Charles was foolishly fond of these dogs ; he had always many of them in his bedroom and his other apartments ; as also so great a number of these pets lounging about the place, that Evelyn declares in his " Diary" that the whole court was made offensive and disagreeable by them.

Hard by, in a grove which rose round and between the miniature canals, a little later was a " tea-house " or rather summer-house, erected by order of William III. ; a place where that saturnine king would sometimes spend a summer evening with those of his friends whom he admitted into his confidence.

Although the park comprises less than ninety acres, Charles II. made a strict enclosure of the centre portion, which he surrounded with a ring fence for deer. " This day," writes Samuel Pepys, in his " Diary," under date August 11, 1664, " for a wager before the King, my Lord of Castlehaven, and Lord Arran, a son of my Lord Ormond's, they two alone did run down a stout buck in St. James's Park." During the reigns of Elizabeth and the first two Stuarts, the park was little more than a nursery for deer, and an appendage to the Tilt-yard of Whitehall. In the reign of Charles I. a sort of royal menagerie took the place of the deer with which the " inward park " was stocked in the days of Henry and Elizabeth. It was often called the

Inner or Inward Park, and apparently was not freely accessible to the public at large. At all events, Pepys tells us on one occasion in 1660 that when he went to walk there, he "could not get in," and saw "one man basted by the keeper for carrying some people over on his back through the water."

Le Serre, a French writer, in his account of the visit of the Queen-Mother, Mary de Medicis, to her daughter, Henrietta Maria, and Charles I., in the year 1633, mentions several particulars of St. James's Palace, as well as of the park, and the then state of the neighbourhood. The palace he calls the "Castle" of St. James's; and describes it as embattled, or surmounted by crenelles on the outside, and containing several courts within, surrounded by buildings, the apartments of which (at least, those which he saw) were hung with superb tapestry, and royally furnished. "Near its avenue," says he, "is a large meadow, continually green, in which the ladies always walk in the summer. Its great gate has a long street in front, reaching almost out of sight, seemingly joining to the fields, although on one side it is bounded by houses, and on the other by the Royal Tennis Court;" then, after noticing the gardens, and the numerous fine statues in them, he adds, "These are bounded by a great park, with many walks, all covered by the shade of an infinite number of oaks, whose antiquity is extremely agreeable, as they are thereby rendered the more impervious to the rays of the sun. This park is filled with wild animals; but, as it is the ordinary walk of the ladies of the court, their [viz., the ladies'] gentleness has so tamed them, that they all yield to the force of their attractions rather than the pursuit of the hounds."

Pepys, in his gossiping manner, records from time to time the progress of the works carried out here by Charles II. Thus, in his "Diary," September 16, 1660, he writes:—"To the park, where I saw how far they had proceeded in the Pell Mell, and in making a river through the park, which I had never seen before since it was began." Again, a month later, October 11: "To walk in St. James's Park, where we observed the several engines to draw up water, with which sight I was very much pleased. Above all the rest, I liked that which Mr. Greatorex brought, which do carry up the water with a great deal of ease." Further, under date July 27, 1662, we find this entry:—"I to walk in the park, which is now every day more and more pleasant, by the new water upon it."

Evelyn, in his "Diary," in April, 1664, tells us how that he went "to the Physicke Garden in St. James's Parke," and there "first saw orange-trees and other fine trees." The exact position of these gardens is not known now; and as allusions to them are of rare occurrence, in all probability they were allowed to pass away and be forgotten, when a botanic garden on a larger scale was commenced under the highest auspices at Chelsea.

In 1661 we find the courtly Waller thus commemorating the improvements which had then been recently made in the park :—

> "For future shade, young trees upon the banks
> Of the new stream appear, in even ranks ;
> The voice of Orpheus, or Amphion's hand,
> In better order could not make them stand.
> *　　*　　*　　*　　*　　*
> All that can, living, feed the greedy eye,
> Or dead the palate, here you may descry;
> The choicest things that furnish'd Noah's ark,
> Or Peter's sheet, inhabiting this park,
> All with a border of rich fruit-trees crown'd,
> Whose lofty branches hide the lofty mound.
> Such spacious ways the various valleys lead,
> My doubtful Muse knows not what path to tread.
> Yonder the harvest of cold months laid up,
> Gives a fresh coolness to the royal cup ;
> There ice, like crystal, firm and never lost,
> Tempers hot July with December's frost;
> *　　*　　*　　*　　*　　*
> Here a well-polished Mall gives us the joy,
> To see our Prince his matchless force employ."

The most beautiful parts of St. James's Park are the walks beside the Ornamental Water, which is still called "the canal," in memory of its former unsightly shape. The water is alive with water-fowl, for whose comfort and protection a quiet and secluded island, with the Swiss cottage of the Ornithological Society, is reserved, at the south-eastern extremity, nearly on the site of the old "decoy." The waterfowl here are natives of almost every climate in the world, and the Zoological Society itself has scarcely a finer or more varied collection. Those which are not foreign are mostly descendants of the ducks which Charles II. took such pleasure in feeding with his own royal hands. Around the "canal" stand many fine trees, which throw their green shadows into the water, "broken at times by a hundred tiny ripples which have been raised by the paddles of some strange-looking duck, or thrown up by the silver-breasted swans," as Mr. Thomas Miller quaintly remarks in his "Picturesque Sketches of London." It is almost needless to add that the banks of the "canal," and the bridge which spans it, are the haunt of children and their nurses, and the pieces of bread and biscuit which are given daily to the ducks, geese, and swans would well-nigh feed the inmates of a workhouse. At the western end of the lake there is a small island richly clothed with verdure, and also a fountain. The "Swiss cottage" above mentioned was erected in 1841, by means of a grant of £300 from the Lords of the Treasury. It contains a council-room, keeper's apartments, and steam-hatching apparatus; contiguous are feeding-places and decoys, and the aquatic fowl breed on the island, making their own nests among the shrubs and grasses. The water-fowl of the park can, at all events, boast that they have held undisturbed possession of the lake for more than two centuries. Pepys writes, under date of August, 1661 :—"To walk in St. James's Park, and saw a great variety of fowls which I never saw before."

In *Land and Water* of November 6th, 1869, Lord Lansdowne mentions having picked up a snipe, on the 26th of the previous month, under the wall of the Treasury Gardens, on the Horse Guards' Parade. It lay at the foot of a lamp, among some leaves, which had prevented the attention of passers-by being attracted. The spot was out of the line which any one carrying dead game could have taken, and the position in which the bird lay was that in which it might have fallen rather than been dropped. The lamp spoken of is opposite the end of the piece of water in St. James's Park. On examination at the office of *Land and Water* it was found to be a common jack-snipe. Its bill was fractured across, just at the point where it unites with the skull. It was probably flying at a great pace, and, attracted by the light of the lamp, flew against the iron post, when the force of the concussion killed it on the spot.

In the same publication, in March, 1873, a correspondent writes :—" As I was walking through St. James's Park, about ten a.m. on the 21st inst., a woodcock crossed me, flying rapidly and low, from the direction of the barracks towards Marlborough House. It was well within gun-shot when I first saw it, and as my view of it as it crossed the water was quite unimpeded, I cannot for a moment question the accuracy of my observation, though in the case of such a *rara avis* I regret that I cannot produce a witness. In sending you this notice I am induced to add a list of the birds which I have noticed in St. James's Park during the past twelvemonth, as likely to interest those who think there are no birds but sparrows in London. They are :—1, sparrow-hawk, seen once flying from the east, in early morning; 2, great tit; 3, cole-tit; 4, blue tit, all occasionally seen; 5, fly-catcher, constant in summer; 6, rook; 7, jackdaw; 8, starling in small flocks when not breeding; 9, missel-thrush, once; 10, fieldfare, a small flock once in late autumn, one foggy morning; 11, song-thrush, constant; 12, blackbird, constant, the males seeming much more numerous than the females; 13, swallow; 14, martin; 15, swift, only once or twice; 16, pied wagtail, not unfrequent, but not apparently constant; 17, skylark, rare, generally flying high, and apparently moving on: 18, chaffinch, not common; 19, sparrow (*passer, passim*); 20, greenfinch, not common; 21, hedge-sparrow, constant; 22, robin-redbreast, constant; 23, whitethroat, constant in summer on the eastern island, where its song is unmistakable; 24, wren, probably constant; 25, golden-crested wren, once only; 26, wood-pigeon, flying over in flocks in early morning, also once or twice birds probably strayed from Kensington Gardens, where they are common; 27, peewit, once, a flock flying north one foggy morning; 28, woodcock, once. Besides these I may mention the linnet, blackcap, willow-warbler, and wryneck, of which I cannot be quite positive, and last, not least, the Guards' raven, constant while his battalion is in town, on the trees near Buckingham Gate. Perhaps some other Cockney ornithologist will be able to verify and add to the above list."

A good story is told by Mr. W. C. Hazlitt respecting the waterfowl in this park and a young gentleman, a clerk in the Treasury, not over-gifted with brains, who used to feed the ducks with bread as he went daily from his home in Pimlico to the office. One day, having called the birds, as usual, he found that he had no bread in his pockets, and so threw a sixpence into the water, telling them to buy some. On reaching the office, he told the story with perfect simplicity to his fellow-clerks, with one of whom he was engaged to dine the next day. His friend accordingly ordered ducks for dinner, telling the cook to put a sixpence in the stuffing of one of them. The next day came, and with it the dinner, in the course of which the sixpence was found inside one of the birds, and the young man vowed that he would have the poulterer prosecuted for robbing the king, " for," said he, " I assure you, on my honour, that only yesterday I gave this very sixpence to one of the ducks in the park !"

St. James's Park is replete with historical associations, not the least interesting of which is the fact of Charles I. having passed through it on foot on the morning of his execution, from his bedchamber in St. James's Palace to the scaffold at Whitehall. The king, as he passed along on that fatal morning, is said to have pointed to a tree which had been planted by his brother, Prince Henry, near Spring Gardens.

Strype, the historian, gives us a picture of the Princess Elizabeth's life during the reign of her brother, Edward VI., under date March 17th, 1551:—"The Lady Elizabeth, the King's sister, rode through London into St. James's, the King's Palace, with a great company of lords, knights, and gentlemen ; and after her a great company of ladies and gentlemen on horseback, about two hundred. On the 19th she came from St. James's through the Park unto the Court (at Whitehall), the way from the Park gate unto the Court being spread with fine sand. She was attended with a very honourable confluence of noble and worshipful persons of both sexes, and received with much ceremony at the Court gate." What would one not have given to have seen the young princess, thus gaily caparisoned, and in all her pride and beauty, before time had ploughed wrinkles on her brow, and ere the strong passions of middle life had stamped her countenance with their tell-tale marks !

Here Cromwell, as he walked with Whitelock, asked the latter, "What if a man should take upon him to be a king?" To which the memorialist replied, "I think that the remedy would be worse than the disease."

It is said that late in life Milton met James II., then Duke of York, whilst taking the air in the park. The duke, addressing him, asked whether the poet's blindness was not to be regarded as a judgment from Heaven upon him for daring to take up his pen against Charles I., his (the duke's) father, and his "own sovereign?" "Be it so, sir," replied Milton ; "but what then must we think of the execution of your Royal Highness's father upon a scaffold?" The story may be true or false : at all events it has been often told, and told as having happened here : we may say of it certainly, "*Si non e vero, e ben trovato.*"

It may be added that the Princess Anne escaped twice from Whitehall through St. James's Park, once when she joined her husband and the Prince of Orange, and again when the palace was in flames.

This park was a favourite resort of Oliver Goldsmith. In his "Essays" we read that, "If a man be splenetic, he may every day meet companions on the seats in St. James's Park, with whose groans he may mix his own, and pathetically talk of the weather." The strolling player takes a walk in St. James's Park, "about the hour at which company leave it to go to dinner. There were but few in the walks, and those who stayed seemed by their looks rather more willing to forget that they had an appetite than to gain one."

Between the years 1770 and 1775 some ex-tensive repairs and improvements were made in the park ; but notwithstanding this fact, the "rough, and intolerable" manner in which the walks were still kept caused much discontent and grumbling among its more fashionable *habitués*. Thus, for instance, in October, 1775, a letter appeared in the *Middlesex Journal*, addressed to Lord Orford, the ranger of the park, complaining bitterly of the disgraceful state of the walks. After some sarcastic remarks upon the delays of the workmen's wages, the writer plainly says that the public intend to petition his Majesty "on the subject of this unbearable grievance," and to "sign their real names ; which," he adds, "my lord, if all the complainants should do, I presume their number would far exceed that of any address ever presented." The writer finally proceeds to give vent to his feelings, and to entreat his Majesty for some instalment of reform, in the following lines, which he heads with the words—

AN ADDRESS TO THE KING.

" 'Tis yours, great George, to bless our safe retreats,
And call the Muses to their native seats,
To deck anew the flow'ry sylvan places,
And crown the forest with immortal graces.
Though barb'rous monarchs act a servile strain,
Be thine the blessings of a peaceful reign ;
Make James's Park in lofty numbers rise,
And lift her palace nearer to the skies."

The park, in 1780, was occupied as a camp by several regiments of militia, during the alarm and panic caused by the Gordon riots. A print is extant which shows the long line of tents extending from east to west, from the "decoy" to "Rosamond's Pond," and to the south of the canal, and the king paying to the camp his daily visit."

On the occasion of the visit of the Allied Sovereigns, in 1814, Mr. Redding writes in his "Fifty Years' Recollections," "I stood without the iron palisades of Buckingham Old House. It was a childish affair there. But the illumination of the streets was really fine. Every window was lit up, and the blaze of light, from so great a mass of buildings, was thrown grandly upon the heavens. The park of St. James was prettily arranged with lamps in the trees, like another Vauxhall. A wooden bridge with a sort of tower, over the canal in St. James's Park, was illuminated too brightly. The edifice took fire, and the tower was consumed. One or two persons were killed."

The grand *fête*, which had long been in preparation, took place on the 1st of August, and an official programme was issued, in which the public were informed that a beautiful Chinese bridge had been thrown over the canal, upon the centre of which had been constructed an elegant and lofty pagoda, consisting of seven pyramidal storeys. "The pagoda to be illuminated with gas lights; and brilliant fireworks, both fixed and missile, to be displayed from every division of the lofty Chinese structure. Copious and splendid girandoles of rockets to be occasionally displayed from the summit, and from other parts of this towering edifice, so covered with squibs, Roman candles, and *pots de brin*, as to become in appearance one

remembered in connection with humorous frolics. In passing daily along the Mall he noticed a care-worn-looking man, with threadbare clothes, whom he discovered to be an officer on half-pay, with a wife and a large family, whom, for the sake of economy, he had been obliged to send down into Yorkshire. One day the duke sent a message asking him to dine with him next Sunday, and when his guest arrived he told him that he had

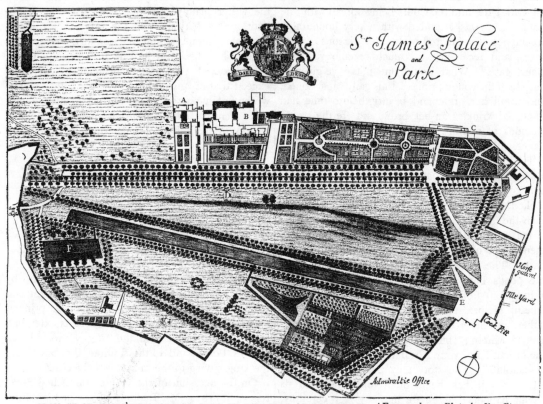

PLAN OF ST. JAMES'S PALACE AND PARK IN THE TIME OF CHARLES II. (*From a large Plate by Knyff.*)

A. Cleveland House. B. St. James's Palace. C. The Spring Garden. D. The Mall. E. The Canal. F. Rosamond's Pond. G. Birdcage Walk. H. Duck Island and the Decoy.

column of brilliant fire. Various smaller temples and columns on the bridge to be vividly illuminated; and fixed fireworks of different devices on the balustrade of the bridge to contribute to heighten the general effect." The fireworks set light to the pagoda and burnt its three upper storeys. The canal was well provided with handsomely decorated boats at the disposal of those who wished to avail themselves of this amusement. The whole margin of the lawn was surrounded with booths for refreshment, open marquees with seats, &c. The Mall and the Birdcage Walk were illuminated with Chinese lanterns.

Among the residents in St. James's Park was the eccentric Duke of Montagu, whose name is still

asked a lady to meet him who had a most tender regard for him. On entering his grace's dining-room he found his wife and children, whom the duke had brought up to London from York-shire; and before he left the house the duke's solicitor brought out, and the duke signed, a deed settling on him an annuity of £200 a year. It is a pity that such practical jokes are not more often played by wealthy dukes and noble lords.

Here, at one time, used to take his daily walk the jovial and genial wit and poet, Matthew Prior, whom Gay calls, "Dear Prior, beloved by every muse." Swift and Prior were very intimate, and the latter is frequently mentioned in the "Journal to Stella." "Mr. Prior," writes Swift, "walks to

TWO OLD VIEWS IN ST. JAMES'S PARK, ABOUT 1680. (From Engravings by S. Rawle published in 1804 by J. T. Smith.)

make himself fat, and I to keep myself down: we often walk round the park together."

Englishmen, as a rule, are not fond of out-door lounging, and, except in the extreme heat of the summer, they prefer taking the air on horseback or on a river steamer, or even on a railway, to sitting still on chairs and gazing leisurely on a green lawn and green trees, as they do in Paris by thousands. But in spite of this national tendency to in-door comforts, the Park of St. James's asserts its attractions so strongly, that at whatever time of the day we visit it, the seats have no lack of occupants; and in the hot days of July and August, when the West-End is emptied of all rank and ·fashion, thousands of "roughs" and idlers may be seen lying sound asleep on the grass under the shade.

Albert Smith has left us a graphic description of the scenes witnessed daily in the park, both in our own day and in days long gone by, which we here take the liberty of quoting :—"Although we do not find such crowds of idlers in the park at the present day, possibly the types encountered are more distinct. We say at the present day, because formerly the gayest of the gay thronged the walks, including royalty itself, with its attendant suite. Dear old Pepys has left us a mass of little mems thereanent. See where he says, on the 16th of March, 1662, that, while idling there in the park, 'which is now very pleasant,' he 'saw the King and Duke come to see their fowle play.' In 1661, in April, he says, 'To St. James's Park, where I saw the Duke of York playing at pall-mall, the first time that ever I saw the sport.' And later, which is quaintly interesting, he writes : 'Dec. 15. To the duke, and followed him into the park, where, though the ice was broken, he would go slide upon his skaits, which I did not like, but he slides very well.' We can imagine that Pepys was not strong upon skates. The first tumble—and nobody learns to skate without being sorely contused—would have been quite sufficient to have disgusted him with this then novel amusement. We find, however, that the love of feeding the ducks and skating in the park has not diminished. Afterwards, he tells us how he saw the King and Queen, with Lady Castlemaine and Mrs. Stuart *cum multis aliis*, walking about. He adds : ' All the ladies walked, talking and fiddling with their hats and feathers, and changing and trying one another's heads, and laughing. But it was the finest sight to see, considering their great beauties and dress, that ever I did see in all my life.' " Evelyn is a little more scandalous. He says, on March 1, 1671 :—' I once walked with the King through St. James's Park to the garden, where I

both saw and heard a very familiar discourse between Mrs. Nellie, as they called an impudent comedian; she looking out of her garden on a terrace at the top of the wall, and ——— standing on the green walk under it. I was heartily sorry at this scene. Thence the King walked to the Duchess of Cleveland' (the Lady Castlemaine of Pepys), 'another lady of pleasure, and curse of our nation.' Horace Walpole, eighty years afterwards, speaks of receiving a card from Lady Caroline Petersham to go with her to Vauxhall. 'And the party that sailed up the park, "with all our colours flying,"' he says, 'consisted of the Duke of Kingston, Lady Caroline, Lord March, Mr. Whitehead, 'a pretty Miss Beauclerc, and a very foolish Miss Sparre.' He adds, that 'Lady Caroline and little Ashe—or the Pollard Ashe, as they called her—had just finished their last layer of red, and looked as handsome as crimson could make them, and that they marched to their barge with a boat of French horns attending, and little Ashe singing.'

" Now-a-days the idlers in the park remind us but little of the personages in the above extracts. Poverty is far more frequently encountered there than wealth ; and more, we fear, walk there to dine with ' Duke Humfrey ' than to get an appetite for a meal elsewhere. At early morning, when the air is clearest, you encounter few persons ; nor, somewhat later, do you find the crowds assembled to read the papers and discuss the politics after breakfast, as in Paris. You may, perhaps, encounter a student reading hard at some uninviting-looking book, and stumbling over the withies bent into the shuffled-out grass, as he moves along ; or, perchance, an actor, as he threatens the lower boughs of the larger trees with his stick (most actors carry sticks), while he is rehearsing his part in some forthcoming play. And yet, lonely as the park is at this time, and half deserted, it is seldom chosen for the purpose of tender declarations, avowals, promises, oaths, quarrels, and all the other usual accompaniments of courtship. No : in this respect, perhaps, those chiefly concerned show their wit. The world—with its broad daylight, its tumultuous noise, and its distracted eyes—is far more adapted for secrecy than the shade and the retreat ; and more than this, society will always lend itself as an accomplice of things which are not sought to be concealed.

" Towards noon, a movement of laughing mirth and noise commences by the arrival of the children and their nursery-maids ; and in the children lies, in our opinion, the greatest attraction here offered —even beyond the ducks—the real zoological ducks. Not that we think slightingly of feeding them. We have heard, by the way, that it was one of the great O'Connell's favourite *délassemens*, and that he enjoyed it as much as the smallest fellow capable of tossing a bit of biscuit. It is great fun to see the rush made after a morsel: how the birds flash through the water to obtain it, and how, as in every community, the strongest always gets it. But if you want to enjoy the sport to perfection, throw in one of the small round rolls you get at evening-party supper-tables, and a fearful tumult is created. The prize is much too large for them to get hold of, as it is too valuable to be relinquished; and so it is pushed and floated about, and vainly pecked at, surrounded by the whole tribe, squabbling, splashing, and fluttering—swayed, like large crowds, here and there—until it gets sufficiently soft to be accessible to their bills, when its consumption is speedily achieved.

"But to return to the children. We mean especially those who have not yet numbered eight years, and whose limbs have still all the smooth roundness of infancy. There is something very pleasing in their graceful movements, their fresh cheeks, and their beautiful hair, and a perfect charm in their gaiety; in the innocent joy sparkling in their eyes, and the pure and living blood colouring their cheeks, which our brightest belles would give so much to imitate. This attraction, perhaps, belongs only to those who run about; albeit it takes a great deal to beat the saucy beauty of an English baby. It is almost enough to make one a convert in favour of matrimony, even in these 'fast' times. The only pity is that these little people should ever be destined to become men."

The parks, though nominally they belong to royalty, are yet always regarded as somehow or other the property of the people. It was but an assertion of this principle that was uttered by Walpole, when, in reference to a design that was at one time entertained by one of the early Georges, of shutting up St. James's Park and converting it into a royal garden, and in answer to the question as its probable cost, he answered, "May it please your Majesty, only three crowns."

Since the time of Charles II., succeeding kings have given the people the privilege of walking in the park, and William III. granted to the public an entrance through the Spring Garden. The walks in the enclosure and the seats scattered about in such profusion beneath the shade of its trees have been a celebrated spot for love-making ever since the days of Charles II., and the park itself is often mentioned in this association in the works of the comic dramatists of the Stuart times. Horace

Walpole tells us that "pretty ladies" who walked in the park were sometimes "mobbed" by the crowd—a proof, if proof be needed, that other ages were not less marked by vulgarity than our own.

Like other parts of town, the park appears to have been frequented by those lawless rascals, the Mohocks, or Mohawks, of whom we have already made mention. Swift, for instance, writes under date of March, 1712, that he "walked in the park, and came home early to avoid the Mohocks;" and apparently not without good reason, for, a day or two afterwards, a party of these armed ruffians assaulted a female servant of Lady Winchilsea's, at her mistress's garden-gate, "cutting her face and beating her without provocation."

It had been for many previous years the favourite amusement of dissolute young men to form themselves into clubs and associations for the cowardly pleasure of fighting and sometimes maiming harmless foot-passengers, and even defenceless women. They took various slang designations. At the Restoration they were Muns and Tityre-Tus; then Hectors and Scourers; later still, Nickers (whose delight it was to smash windows with showers of halfpence), Hawkabites, and lastly Mohocks. These last, as we learn from No. 324 of the *Spectator*, took their title from "a sort of cannibals in India, who subsist by plundering and devouring all the nations about them." Nor was the designation inapt; for if there was one sort of brutality on which they prided themselves more than another, it was in tattooing, or slashing people's faces with, as Gay wrote, "new invented wounds." They began the evening at their clubs, by drinking to excess in order to inflame what little courage they possessed; they then sallied forth, sword in hand. Some enacted the part of "dancing masters," by thrusting their rapiers between the legs of sober citizens in such a fashion as to make them cut the most grotesque capers. The hunt spoken of by Sir Roger de Coverley was commenced by a "view hallo!" and as soon as the savage pack had run down their victim, they surrounded him, and formed a circle with the points of their swords. One gave him a puncture in the rear, which very naturally made him wheel about; then came a prick from another; and so they kept him spinning like a top till in their mercy they chose to let him go free. An adventure of this kind, in which the savages figure under the name of "Sweaters," is narrated in No. 332 of the *Spectator*.

Mr. John Timbs, in his "Curiosities of London," tells us that the park, as well as the palace, sheltered persons from arrest; for, in 1632, one John Perkins, a constable, was imprisoned for serving the

Lord Chief Justice's warrant upon John Beard in St. James's Park. To draw a sword in the park was also a very serious offence. Congreve, in his *Old Bachelor*, makes Bluffe say, "My blood rises at that fellow. I can't stay where he is; and *I must not draw in the park*." Traitorous expressions, when uttered in St. James's Park, were punished very severely. Thus, Francis Heat was whipped, in 1771, from Charing Cross to the upper end of the Haymarket, fined ten groats, and ordered a month's imprisonment, for here saying aloud, "God save King James III., and send him a long and prosperous reign!" and in the following year a soldier was whipped in the park for drinking a health to the Duke of Ormond and Dr. Sacheverel, and for saying he "hoped soon to wear his right master's cloth." The Duke of Wharton, too, was seized by the guard in St. James's Park for singing the Jacobite air, "The king shall have his own again."

Faithorne's plan of St. James's, taken shortly after the Restoration, shows the north half of the parade occupied by a square enclosure, surrounded by trees, with one tree in the centre; and in the lower part of the parade broad running water, with a bridge of two arches in the middle. Later views show the park with long rows of young elm and lime trees, fenced with palings, and occasionally relieved by some fine old trees. A view of this park is worked in as a background to one of Hollar's charming and well-known etchings of the "Four Seasons."

Over the canal in this park during the Regency, when a taste for Eastern monstrosities of the kind was so prevalent, was built a little Chinese bridge, mainly of wood; but already, in 1823, it was beginning to fall to decay. Canova, when asked what struck him most forcibly during his visit to England in the year 1815, is said to have replied, "that the trumpery Chinese bridge in St. James's Park should be the production of the Government, whilst that of Waterloo was the work of a private company."

During the winter months, when the "ornamental water" is frozen over, this spot is much resorted to for the purposes of skating and sliding; but the scene presented is doubtless very different now from what it was two centuries ago, when, as Pepys tells us in his "Diary" (December 1, 1662), he went "to my Lord Sandwich's, . . . and then over the parke, where I first in my life, it being a great frost, did see people sliding with their skates, which is a pretty art." Evelyn, too, has the following entry under the same date :—"Having seene the strange and wonderful dexterity of the sliders

in the new canal in St. James's Park, performed before their Majesties by divers gentlemen and others, with scheets, after the manner of the Hollanders, with what swiftness as they pass, how suddenly they stop in full career on the ice, I went home."

The park appears soon to have become a resort for all classes, for under date December 4, 1683 (when there was a very hard frost), the Duke of York records—"This morning the boys began to slide upon the canal in the park."

St. James's Park, much as we now see it, was laid out by George IV. between the years 1827 and 1829. In form, the enclosure takes somewhat the shape of a boy's kite, the head or broad part of which, towards Whitehall, is bordered by some of the principal Government offices—the Admiralty, the Horse Guards, the Treasury, and the India and Foreign Offices; at the opposite end is Buckingham Palace. In 1857, a suspension bridge for foot-passengers was thrown across the water, so as to form a direct communication between Queen Anne's Gate and St. James's; the bed of the lake was at the same time cleared out and raised, so that its greatest depth of water does not exceed four feet.

"Amongst the many improvements which have contributed to the convenience and ornament of the metropolis," writes Walker, in his "Original," in 1835, "none are more striking than those in the parks. The state in which they are kept does great credit to those who have the management of them. The right-lined formalities of St. James's Park seemed almost to defy the efforts of taste; and I could not have conceived that without any advantages of ground the straight 'canal' and unpromising cow-pasture could have been metamorphosed into so graceful a piece of water, and so beautiful a shrubbery. In walking round the water, almost at every step there is a new and striking point of view of buildings and foliage. Buckingham Palace, Carlton Terrace, the Duke of York's Column, St. Martin's Church, the Horse Guards, Westminster Abbey, and other inferior objects, seen between and over the trees, form a combination and a variety I have never before seen equalled. . . . What a pity it is that the original design of making a gradual descent from Waterloo Place into St. James's Park was not allowed to be carried into execution! Besides the beauty of the plan, a horse-entrance there would have been an immense convenience to a numerous class. As that, however, is now out of the question, the nearest practical approach to it seems to be by the macadamisation of Pall Mall, with an entrance into the Park, if that could be permitted, between Marlborough House and the Palace. I know not how that would affect the Palace, but if it would be no inconvenience to royalty, it certainly would be a great boon to the equestrian public."

It is a pleasant task to record here the fact that in little more than a quarter of a century after the above-quoted words were written the entrance to St. James's Park between Marlborough House and St. James's Palace was thrown open, by permission of Her Majesty and the Ranger, not only to the "equestrian public," but to the commonalty who employ cabs and hired carriages, and that for such vehicles a right of way has been granted by the Queen to Pimlico and South Belgravia, across the once sacred precinct of the Royal Mall in St. James's Park, and under the very windows of Buckingham Palace.

It had always been the tradition of the Court to grant as little as possible to the public a right of way through St. James's Park. The following story, told of George I., shows that the privilege was not always allowed even to the children of a Stuart sovereign :—"Soon after his accession to the throne, the Duchess of Buckingham, a natural daughter of James II., asked for a passage for her carriage through the park, but was met with a polite refusal. She at once wrote off a letter to the king, abusing him in the grossest terms compatible with her character as a lady, affirming that he was an usurper, and that she had a better right to go through the park than a Hanoverian upstart. The king, instead of being offended, laughed, saying, ' The poor woman is mad, let her pass;' and thereupon gave an order that both her Grace and any other mad daughter of a Stuart king, who cared to obtain the privilege, might use it freely."

The park is still regularly patrolled at night by two of the horse guards whenever Her Majesty is in town—a standing proof of the old feeling of the insecurity of retired parts of London when entrusted to the old watchmen, or "Charlies." It was not till 1822 that St. James's Park was lighted with gas, although Pall Mall, adjoining, had been so lit fifteen years before.

The large open space laid down with gravel in front of the Horse Guards is popularly called the Parade, from the fact that the household troops are paraded here almost every day. Here, too, reviews of the troops occasionally take place ; as, also, such ceremonies as the presentation of medals to those of our " brave defenders" who may have taken part in foreign campaigns.

Here are two military trophies, curious pieces of foreign ordnance : the one is a large Turkish gun, captured by the English troops in Egypt, under Sir Ralph Abercromby ; the other is an immense mortar, cast at Seville by command of the great Napoleon ; it was used by the French under Marshal Soult at the siege of Cadiz, in 1812, but abandoned by them subsequently at Salamanca. Mr. Larwood, in his amusing book on the "London Parks," states that the carriage of the mortar was made at Woolwich under the direction of the Earl of Mulgrave : its ornamentation is said to bear reference to King Geryon, a monster with three bodies and three heads, whom Hercules slew at Cadiz, after "lifting" his anthropophagous cattle. Jekyll, the famous punster, however, explained it differently, and said that the dogs' heads were merely placed on it in order to justify the Latin inscription, which is certainly of a somewhat canine species.

As to the "Parade," a writer calls it (in the reign of George II.) a "grand and spacious area," and capable of being made one of the chief beauties "about the town," if surrounded by "noble and august buildings," and adorned with an equestrian statue to the memory of some departed hero. He suggests that it would be a fit place for the erection of one in particular to "the great and immortal Nassau "—meaning King William III.—and adds, " It is true that he has once been denied this piece of justice, but they were not soldiers who were guilty of so great an indignity." It is not, however, clear to what abortive attempt at doing justice to the "pious and immortal memory" of King William the writer means to allude.

Upon the Parade was marshalled the state funeral procession of the great Duke of Wellington, on the 18th of November, 1852. The body was removed from Chelsea Hospital on the previous midnight, and deposited in the audience-chamber at the Horse Guards. Beneath a tent erected on the parade-ground was stationed the funeral car, whereon the coffin being placed, and the command given, the *cortége*, in a slow and solemn manner, moved down the Mall, past Buckingham Palace, whence the procession was seen by Her Majesty and the Royal Family, before it made its way to St. Paul's.

We have already mentioned the fact that Sir Robert Walpole, when Prime Minister, lived constantly at the Treasury, at the corner of Downing Street. In the last century there was a carriage entrance to his house on the side of the park. A good story is told of a scene which occurred here. A countryman from Norfolk, having failed to obtain a post under Government, though recommended by one of Sir Robert Walpole's supporters in Parliament, resolved to trudge up to London, and to push his own request in person. Accordingly, he took up his quarters at the "Axe and Crown," an hostelry close by the Premier's house, and knocked at Sir Robert's door, but without success. The servants, however, told him that if he could speak to Sir Robert in person as he stepped into his

Between the Treasury and the Horse Guards is seen the back of Dover House (already mentioned in a former chapter), where the late Lord Dover made a very choice gallery of paintings. His early death, which took place in July, 1833, was much regretted by society at large. He was the author of a "Life of Frederick the Great;" "The True History of the State Prisoner, the Man in the Iron Mask;" and "Historical Enquiries respecting the

THE INDIA OFFICE, FROM ST. JAMES'S PARK. (*See page* 58.)

chariot, he would be sure to get what he wanted. Accordingly, for two or three days he watched the Premier go out, and at last waylaid him in the act of entering his chariot, and came out plump with his demand, adding that the post had been asked for him by his friend the M.P. for ——. "Well, my good man," said Sir Robert, "call on me another morning." "Yes, an please your honour, I'll be here and call on you every morning until I get the place." The man was as good as his word, and every day for at least a fortnight was at the same spot at the same hour, and made his bow to the Premier, who was either so amused or wearied with his blunt importunity, that he sent him back to Norfolk the richer and, it may be hoped, the happier, by the gift of a tide-waitership.

Character of Edward Hyde, Earl of Ciarendon." He also edited "Horace Walpole's Correspondence" and "The Ellis Correspondence."

In the reign of the two first Georges, and perhaps even more recently, the situation of Dover House was quite rural; so much so indeed that the author of "A New Critical Review of the Public Buildings," in 1736, thus expresses himself about it :—"We will now step into the park, where we shall see a house in the finest situation, with the whole canal and park in prospect, yet so obscured with trees that, except in the garrets, it cannot have the advantage of either. Surely there can be no excuse for so egregious a mistake but that the house itself is in so wrong a taste that it was the owner's interest to hide it."

ARLINGTON HOUSE, 1700. (*See page* 62.)

CHAPTER VI.

BUCKINGHAM PALACE.

"The pillar'd dome magnific heaves
Its ample roof, and luxury within
Pours out its glittering stores."—*Thomson.*

The Palaces of England and France compared—The Mulberry Garden—John Dryden's Fondness for Mulberry Tarts—Arlington House—The House originally called Goring House—The First Pound of Tea imported into England—Demolition of Arlington House—Description of the First Buckingham House—John Sheffield, Duke of Buckingham—Singular Conduct of his Widow—The House purchased by George III., and called the "Queen's House"—Northouck's Description of Buckingham House in the Time of George III.—Dr. Johnson's Interview with George III.—Josiah Wedgwood and Mr. Bentley's Visits to the Palace—The Gordon Riots—Princess Charlotte—The Use of the Birch in the Royal Nursery—Queen Charlotte and her Christmas Trees—Building of the Present Palace—The Edifice described—The Gardens and Out-buildings—Queen Victoria takes up her Residence here—Royal Guests from Foreign Parts—"The Boy Jones"—Marriage of the Princess Augusta of Cambridge—The Queen and Charles Dickens—The Board of Green Cloth—Officers of the Queen's Household—Her Majesty's "Court" and "Drawing-rooms."

IT has often been said by foreigners that if they were to judge of the dignity and greatness of a country by the palace which its sovereign inhabits, they would not be able to ascribe to Her Majesty Queen Victoria that proud position among the "crowned heads" of Europe which undoubtedly belongs to her. But though Buckingham Palace is far from being so magnificent as Versailles is, or the Tuilleries once were, yet it has about it an air of solidity and modest grandeur, which renders it no unworthy residence for a sovereign who cares more for a comfortable home than for display. Indeed, it has often been said that, with the ex-

ception of St. James's, Buckingham Palace is the ugliest royal residence in Europe ; and although vast sums of money have been spent at various times upon its improvement and embellishment, it is very far from being worthy of the purpose to which it is dedicated—lodging the sovereign of the most powerful monarchy in the world. It fronts the western end of St. James's Park, which here converges to a narrow point ; the Mall, upon the north, and Birdcage Walk, upon the south, almost meeting before its gates.

The present palace occupies the site of what, in the reigns of Charles I. and Charles II., was known as the Mulberry Garden, then a place of fashionable resort. It was so called from the fact that the ground had been planted with mulberry-trees by order of James I., one of whose whims was the encouragement of the growth of silk in England as a source of revenue. With this object in view, he imported many ship-loads of young mulberry-trees, most of which were planted round the metropolis. Indeed, he gave by patent to Walter, Lord Aston, the superintendence of " the Mulberry Garden, near St. James's;" but all Lord Aston's efforts were unable to secure success; the speculation entered into by King James proved a failure, and the Mulberry Garden was afterwards devoted to a public recreation-ground.

Every reader of John Evelyn and Samuel Pepys will remember how they describe these gardens in their day—the former as "the best place about the towne for persons of the best quality to be exceedingly cheated at ;" and the latter as "a silly place, with a wilderness somewhat pretty."

The Mulberry Garden is said by Mr. J. H. Jesse to have been a favourite resort of John Dryden, where he used to eat mulberry tarts. To this the author of " Pursuits of Literature " refers when he speaks of "the mulberry tarts which Dryden loved." It was in the years prior to his marriage, in 1665, as we learn from a note in his Life by Sir Walter Scott, that Dryden would repair hither, along with his favourite actress, Mrs. Reeve. " I remember," writes a correspondent of the *Gentleman's Magazine* for 1745, " plain John Dryden, before he paid his court with success to the great, in one uniform clothing of Norwich drugget. I have ate tarts with him and Madame Reeve at the Mulberry Garden, when our author advanced to a sword and a Chadreux wig." It would appear from the Epilogue of Otway's " Don Carlos," in 1676, that in all probability the connection of this fair lady with Dryden was brought to an end by her retreat into a cloister.

The public recreation-ground does not appear, however, to have lasted long, for in the course of a few years we find standing upon the southern portion of it a mansion known as Arlington House, the residence of Henry Bennet, Earl of Arlington, one of the "Cabal" Ministry, under Charles II. Dr. King thus alludes to these changes in his "Art of Cookery :"—

" The fate of things lies always in the dark :
  What cavalier would know St. James's Park?
  For ' Locket's ' stands where gardens once did spring,
  And wild ducks quack where grasshoppers did sing :
  A princely palace on that space does rise,
  Where Sedley's noble muse found mulberries."

The house was originally called Goring House ;

but its name was subsequently changed to that of Arlington House on its being occupied by the Earl of Arlington, whose name is, or ought to be, indissolubly linked with it, on one account at all events ; for in the year of the great plague his lordship brought hither from Holland the first pound of tea which was imported into England, and which cost him sixty shillings ; so that, as John Timbs remarks, "in all probability the first cup of tea made in England was drank where Buckingham House now stands."

On the demolition of Arlington House, in 1703, its site was purchased by John Sheffield, Duke of Buckingham, who built on it a mansion of red brick.

In the " New View of London," published in 1708, the original building is described as " a graceful palace, very commodiously situated at the westerly end of St. James's Park, having at one view a prospect of the Mall and other walks, and of the delightful and spacious canal ; a seat not to be contemned by the greatest monarch. It was formerly," adds the writer, " called Arlington House, and being purchased by his Grace the present Duke of Bucks and Normanby, he rebuilt it, in the year 1703, upon the ground near the place where the old foundation stood. It consists of the mansion house, and at some distance from each end of that, conjoined by two arching galleries, are the lodging-rooms for servants on the south side of the court ; and opposite, on the north side, are the kitchen and laundry, the fronts of which are elevated on pillars of the Tuscan, Dorick, and Ionick orders, thereby constituting piazzas. The walls are brick ; those of the mansion very fine rubb'd and gagg'd (*sic*), adorned with two ranges of pilasters of the Corinthian and Tuscan orders. On the latter (which are uppermost) is an acroteria of figures, standing erect and fronting the court ; they appear as big as life and look noble." They are thus described :—" 1. Mercury with his winged chapeau. 2. Secret, reposing its right arm on a pillar, and in the left hand a key. 3. Equity, holding a balance and a plummet. 4. Liberty, having in his right hand a sceptre, and a cap in the left. 5. Truth, holding the sun in his right hand, and treading on a globe. 6. Apollo, holding a lyre. Also, backward, are four figures beholding the west—Spring, Summer, Autumn, and Winter. Moreover, on the front of this mansion are these words, depensiled in capital gold characters : —' Sic siti lætantur Lares ; ' ' Spectator fastidiosus sibi molestus ; ' ' Rus in urbe ; ' and ' Lente suscipe, cito perfice.' The hall, partly paved with marble, is adorned with pilasters, the intercolumns are noble painture in great variety, and on a pedestal near the foot of the great staircase (whose steps are entire slabs) are the marble figures of Cain killing his brother Abel. In short, the whole structure is spacious, commodious, rich, and beautiful, but especially in the finishing and furniture. This house is now in the occupation of his Grace the Duke of Buckingham." Defoe in his " Journey " (1714) describes Buckingham House as "one of the great treasures of London, both by reason of its situation and its building," an opinion which will hardly be echoed now.

Sheffield's history furnishes another example of the instability of human greatness, and especially of titles. His only son, who held the title but a few short years, died, unmarried, in 1735, when the family honours became extinct. His father's great wealth was carried by his mother into her family by a previous marriage—the Phippses, now Marquises of Normanby. The duchess was grandmother of Mr. Phipps, afterwards Lord Mulgrave, who married the eldest daughter of Lepel, Lady Hervey, the friend of Pope and Horace Walpole. Lady Hervey was often a visitor at Buckingham House, the mansion being at the time an abode of mirth and cheerfulness, if we may judge from her letters.

In a letter to the Duke of Shrewsbury, printed in "London and its Environs," the Duke of Buckingham describes the house, and his style of living there, in the most minute detail. It is said that, at an annual dinner which he gave to his spendthrift friends, he used to propose as a toast, "May as many of us as remain unhanged till next spring meet here again !" He died in this house, and here his remains lay in state previous to their removal to Westminster Abbey, where they were consigned to their tomb in the stately chapel of Henry VII.

The duke's proud widow, Catherine Darnley, the natural daughter of James II. by Catherine Sedley, Countess of Dorchester, lived here after his death. "Here," writes Mr. J. H. Jesse, "on each successive anniversary of the execution of her grandfather, Charles I., she was accustomed to receive her company in the grand drawing-room, herself seated in a chair of state, clad in the deepest mourning, and surrounded by her women, all as black and as dismal looking as herself. Here, too, that eccentric lady breathed her last." "Princess Buckingham," writes Horace Walpole, "is either dead or dying. She sent for Mr. Anstes, and settled the ceremonial of her burial. On Saturday she was so ill that she feared dying before the pomp was come home. She said, 'Why don't they send the canopy for me to see ? Let them send it, even though all the tassels are not finished.' But yesterday was the greatest stroke of all. She made her ladies vow to her that, if she should lie senseless, they would not sit down in the room before she was dead." By her own express directions, she was buried with great pomp beside her lord in the Abbey, where there was formerly a waxen figure of her, after the usual royal fashion, adorned with jewels, prepared in her life by her own hands. She was succeeded in her ownership of the house by the duke's natural son, Charles Herbert Sheffield, on whom his Grace had entailed it after the death of his son, the young duke.

George III., in his second year, bought the house for the sum of £21,000, and shortly afterwards removed hither from St. James's Palace. Here all his numerous family was born, with the exception of the Prince of Wales (afterwards George IV.), whose birth took place at St. James's. The King and Queen grew so fond of their new purchase that they took up their abode entirely here ; and during their reign, St. James's Palace was kept up for use only on Court days and other occasions of ceremony.

In 1775 the property was legally settled, by Act of Parliament, on Queen Charlotte (in exchange for Somerset House, as we have stated in the previous volume) ; and henceforth Buckingham House was known in West-end society as the "Queen's House."

Northouck describes Buckingham House, in 1773, in terms which do not imply that the King and Queen had shown much taste in its approaches. " In the front it is enclosed with a semi-circular sweep of iron rails, which are altered very unhappily from the rails which enclosed it before it became a royal residence. Formerly an elegant pair of gates opened in the middle ; but now, though a foot-opening leads up to where an opening naturally is expected in front, all entrance is forbidden, by the rails being oddly continued across without affording an avenue through. Whoever seeks to enter must walk round either to the right or left, and in the corners perhaps he may gain admittance. The edifice," he adds, " is a mixture of brick and stone, with a broad flight of steps leading up to the door, which is between four tall Corinthian pilasters, which are fluted and reach up to the top of the second storey." The illustration of the front which he gives shows a great resemblance to Kensington Palace. "Behind the house," he adds, "is a garden and terrace, from which there is a fine prospect of the adjacent country." The house is described, at the beginning of the present century, as having a mean appearance, being low and built of brick, though "it contains within," adds the writer, "apartments as spacious and commodious as any palace in Europe for state parade." On the marriage of the Prince of Wales (George IV.), "a suite of the principal rooms was fitted up in the most splendid manner ; the walls of two of the levee rooms being hung with beautiful tapestry, then recently discovered with its colours unfaded in an old chest at St. James's. In the grand levee room," adds the writer, "is a bed of crimson velvet, manufactured in Spitalfields. The canopy of the throne likewise is of crimson velvet, trimmed with broad gold lace, and embroidered with crowns set with fine pearls of great value. This was first used on Queen Charlotte's birthday, after the union of the kingdoms of Great Britain and Ireland, and the shamrock, the badge of the Irish nation, is interwoven with the other decorations of the crown with peculiar taste and propriety."

At the south-east angle of the old house was an octagonal apartment, which contained for many years the cartoons of Raphael (now in the South Kensington Museum). They were transferred to Windsor Castle, and subsequently exhibited for a time at Hampton Court. The saloon was superbly fitted up as the throne-room, and here Queen Charlotte held her public drawing-rooms. Thus the mansion remained till the reign of George IV., externally "dull, dowdy, and decent ; nothing more than a large, substantial, and respectable-looking red brick house," as it was styled by a writer of the time.

At the Queen's House, in February, 1767, when his Majesty had been seated little more than six years upon the throne, Dr. Johnson was honoured by George III. with a personal interview, as related by his biographers. Boswell tells us that the doctor had frequently visited those splendid rooms and noble collection of books, which he used to say was more numerous and curious than he supposed any person could have made in the time which the king had employed. "Mr. Barnard, the librarian, took care that he should have every accommodation that could contribute to his ease and convenience while indulging his literary taste in that place ; so that he had here a very agreeable resource at leisure hours.

"His Majesty having been informed of his occasional visits, was pleased to signify a desire that he should be told when Dr. Johnson came next to the library. Accordingly, the next time that Johnson did come, as soon as he was fairly engaged with a book, on which, while he sat by the fire, he seemed quite intent, Mr. Barnard stole round to the apartment where the king was, and, in obedience to his Majesty's commands, mentioned that Dr. Johnson was then in the library. His Majesty said he was at leisure, and would go to him ; upon which Mr. Barnard took one of the candles that stood on the king's table, and lighted his Majesty through a suite of rooms, till they came to a private door into the library, of which his Majesty had the key. Being entered, Mr. Barnard stepped forward hastily to Dr. Johnson, who was still in a profound study, and whispered him, 'Sir, here is the king.' Johnson started up, and stood still. His Majesty approached him, and at once was courteously easy."

The king conversed with his learned subject freely and agreeably on the studies of Oxford, the two University libraries, the literary journals in England and abroad, the "Philosophical Transactions," Lord Lyttelton's "History," and other literary topics. Boswell continues : "During the whole of this interview Johnson talked to his Majesty with profound respect, but still in his firm, manly manner, with a sonorous voice, and never in that subdued tone which is commonly used at the levee and in the drawing-room. After the King withdrew, Johnson showed himself highly pleased with his Majesty's conversation and gracious behaviour."

Dr. Johnson, on this occasion, was pleased to pass a high compliment on the elegant manners of the sovereign. In speaking of this interview, the biographer writes : "He said to Mr. Barnard, the king's librarian, 'Sir, they may talk of the king as they will, but he is the finest gentleman I have ever seen.' And he afterwards observed to his friend Langton, 'Sir, his manners are those of as fine a gentleman as we may suppose Louis XIV. or Charles II.'" It was not often that Dr. Johnson condescended to express himself so approvingly of anybody, least of all of one whose position was one of direct antagonism to his beloved Stuart line ; but we may well imagine that even the learned doctor's head was a little turned by the unexpected and flattering marks of condescension which he, so lately a poor and struggling man, had received from the King of England.

It is remarkable that Dr. Johnson should have seen four, if not five, of our sovereigns, and been in the actual presence of three, if not four, of them. Queen Anne "touched" him ; George I. he probably never saw ; but George II. he must frequently have seen, though only in public ; George III. he conversed with on the occasion above mentioned ; and he once told Sir John Hawkins that, in a visit to Mrs. Percy, who had the care of one of the young princes, at the Queen's House, the Prince of Wales (afterwards George IV.), being a child, came into the room, and began to play about; when Johnson, with his usual curiosity, took an opportunity of asking him what books he was reading, and, in particular, inquired as to his knowledge of the Scriptures. The Prince, in his answers, gave him great satisfaction. It is possible, also, that at that visit he might have seen Prince William Henry (William IV.), who, as well as the Duke of Kent, was afterwards under Mrs. Percy's care.

Among the occasional visitors to Queen Charlotte here were Josiah Wedgwood and his partner Bentley, who often had the opportunity of showing to their Majesties the "newest things" in the way of artistic pottery. "Last Monday," writes Bentley, in 1770, to a friend at Liverpool, "Mr. Wedgwood and I had a long audience of their Majesties, at the Queen's palace, to present some *bas-reliefs* which the Queen had ordered, and to show some new improvements, with which they were well pleased. They expressed in the most obliging and condescending manner their attention to our manufacture, and entered very freely into conversation on the further improvements of it, and on many other subjects. The King is well acquainted with business, and with the characters of the principal manufactures, merchants, and artists, and seems to have the success of all our manufactures much at heart, and to understand the importance of them. The Queen has more sensibility, true politeness, engaging affability, and sweetness of temper, than any great lady I ever had the honour of speaking to."

During the first two nights of the Gordon Riots, the King sat up with some of the general officers in the Queen's Riding House, whence messengers were constantly dispatched to observe the motions of the mob. "Between three and four thousand troops were in the Queen's Gardens, and surrounded Buckingham House. During the first night the alarm was so sudden, that no straw could be got for the troops to rest themselves on; which being told his Majesty, he, accompanied with one or two officers, went throughout the ranks, telling them, 'My lads, my crown cannot purchase you straw to-night; but depend on it, I have given orders that a sufficiency shall be here to-morrow forenoon; as a substitute for the straw, my servants will instantly serve you with a good allowance of wine and spirits, to make your situation as comfortable as possible; and I shall keep you company myself till morning.' The King did so, walking mostly in the garden, sometimes visiting the Queen and the children in the palace, and receiving all

messages in the Riding House, it being in a manner head-quarters. When he was told that part of the mob was attempting to get into St. James's Palace, he forbade the soldiers to fire, but ordered them to keep off the rioters with their bayonets. The mob, in consequence of that, were so daring as to take hold of the bayonets and shake them, defying the soldiers to fire or hurt them; however, nothing further was attempted on the part of the rioters in that quarter."

In 1809 the King gave a reception to the Persian Ambassador, when an honour was conferred upon him that was hitherto confined to the Royal Family, namely, "the great iron gates fronting the park were thrown open for his entrance."

One of the ladies of the Court of the Princess of Wales thus mentions Buckingham House, in 1811: —"I was one of the happy few at H——'s ball, given in B——m House—a house I had been long anxious to see, as it is rendered classical by the pen of Pope and the pencil of Hogarth. It is in a woful condition, and, as I hear, is to be pulled down."

From its doors, in 1816, Princess Charlotte went forth to Carlton House, attired for her wedding with Leopold of Saxe-Coburg. The nation even now does not forget how, within a few short months, that brightest gem in the English crown was carried to the tomb.

George III. and Queen Charlotte, while living here, it appears, were strong believers in the literal application of the precept of Solomon, "Spare the rod and spoil the child." "The King," writes the Honourable Amelia Murray, in her "Recollections," "was most anxious 'to train up his children in the way they should go;' but severity was the fashion of the day; and although naturally a tender and affectionate father, he placed his sons under tutors who imagined that the 'rod' of Scripture could mean only bodily punishment. Princess Sophia," she adds, "once told me that she had seen her two eldest brothers, when they were boys of thirteen and fourteen, held by their arms at Buckingham Palace, to be flogged like dogs with a long whip!" Was it wonderful that the results proved anything but satisfactory?

Christmas-trees are now quite a common sight in almost every English household. But this was not the case half a century ago. Queen Charlotte, however, true to her German associations, as we learn in the work quoted above, regularly had one dressed up, either here or at Kew Palace, in the room of her German attendant. "It was hung," writes the authoress, "with presents for the children, who were invited to see it; and I well remember the pleasure that it was to hunt for one's own name, which was sure to be attached to one or more of the pretty gifts."

In 1825 the present edifice was commenced, from the design of John Nash, by command of George IV.; but as William IV. did not like the provements were effected, and new buildings added on the south side. The principal of these is the private chapel, which occupies the place of the old conservatory. It was consecrated in 1843. The pillars of this building formed a portion of the screen of Carlton House. Four years later other

THE KING'S LIBRARY, BUCKINGHAM HOUSE, 1775. (See page 64.)

situation or the building, Buckingham House was not occupied until the accession of Queen Victoria. It was at first intended only to repair and enlarge the old house; and therefore the old site, height, and dimensions were retained. This led to the erection of a clumsy building, as it was considered that Parliament would never have granted the funds for an entirely new palace. On the accession of her present Majesty, several alterations and im- and more extensive alterations were effected by the erection, at a cost of about £150,000, of the east front, under the superintendence of Mr. Blore. The palace, as constructed by Nash, consisted of three sides of a square, Roman-Corinthian, raised upon a Doric basement, with pediments at the ends; the fourth side being enclosed by iron palisades. In front of the central entrance stood, formerly, the Marble Arch, now at the north-east

BUCKINGHAM HOUSE IN 1775. (*See page* 63.)

corner of Hyde Park. It was removed to its present situation in 1851. On it was displayed the royal banner of England, denoting the presence of the sovereign. This flag is now displayed on the roof in the centre of the eastern front. The new east front of the palace is the same length as the garden front; the height to top of the balustrade is nearly eighty feet, and it has a central and two arched side entrances, leading direct into the quadrangle. The wings are surmounted by statues representing "Morning," "Noon," and "Night;" the "Hours and the Seasons;" and upon turrets, flanking the central shield (bearing "V. R. 1847"), are colossal figures of "Britannia" and "St. George;" besides groups of trophies, festoons of flowers, &c. Around the entire building is a scroll frieze of the rose, shamrock, and thistle.

It has been asserted that the mismanagement on the part of the Government nearly ruined the artist of the magnificent gates of the arch. Their cost was 3,000 guineas, and they are the largest and most superb in Europe, not excepting the stupendous gates of the Ducal Palace at Venice, and those made by order of Buonaparte for the Louvre at Paris. Yet the Government agents are reported to have conveyed these costly gates from the manufacturer's in a "common stage wagon," when the semi-circular head, the most beautiful portion of the design, was irretrievably mutilated; and, consequently, it has not been fixed in the archway to the present day.

The most important portions of the palace are the Marble Hall and Sculpture Gallery, the Library, the Grand Staircase, the Vestibule, the state apartments, consisting of the New Drawing-room, and the Throne-room, the Picture Gallery (where her present Majesty has placed a valuable collection of paintings), the Grand Saloon, and the State Ballroom.

The Entrance-hall is surrounded by a range of double columns, with gilded bases and capitals, standing on a continuous basement; each column consists of a single piece of Carrara marble. The Grand Staircase is of white marble, the decorations of which were executed by L. Gruner. The State Ball-room, on the south side, was finished in 1856, from Pennethorne's design, and decorated within by Gruner; and it has been more than once stated in print that it cost £300,000. It has ranges of scagliola porphyry Corinthian columns, carrying an entablature and coved ceiling, elaborately gilt. In this room are Winterhalter's portraits of the Queen and the late Prince Consort, also Vandyke's Charles I. and Henrietta Maria. This splendid room was the scene of two superb costume balls in 1842 and 1845: the first in the style of the reign of Edward III.; and the *fête* in 1845 was in the taste of George II.'s reign. The Library, which is also used as a waiting-room for deputations, is very large, and decorated in a manner combining comfort with elegance; it opens upon a terrace, with a conservatory at one end and the chapel at the other, whilst over the balustrade are seen the undulating surface of the palace gardens. From this noble apartment, as soon as the Queen is ready to receive them, deputations pass across the Sculpture Gallery into the Hall, and thence ascend, by the Grand Staircase through an ante-room and the Green Drawing-room, to the Throne-room. The Sculpture Gallery contains busts of eminent statesmen and members of the Royal Family, and extends through the whole length of the central portion of the front of the edifice. The Green Drawing-room, which opens upon the upper storey of the portico of the old building, is a long and lofty apartment. Visitors on the occasions of state balls and other ceremonies are conducted through the Green Drawing-room to the Picture Gallery and the Grand Saloon. On these occasions refreshments are served in the Garter-room and Green Drawing-room, and supper laid in the principal Dining-room. The concerts, invitations to which seldom exceed 300, are given in the Grand Saloon. The Throne-room, which is in the eastern front, is upwards of sixty feet in length, and has the walls hung with crimson satin, the alcove with crimson velvet, and both are relieved by a profusion of golden hues; the ceiling is richly carved and gilt, emblazoned with armorial bearings, and the fringe adorned with bas-reliefs, illustrative of the Wars of the Roses.

The palace includes a Picture Gallery, containing a choice and extensive collection of specimens of ancient and modern masters; it can be viewed by orders from the Lord Chamberlain, which are granted only to persons who can give good references and guarantees of respectability. The Queen's Gallery contains a variety of the works of Dutch and Flemish artists, together with a few pictures of the Italian and English schools, collected by King George IV., who purchased the nucleus of the whole from Sir Thomas Baring, and was aided in his selection of others by Sir Charles Long, afterwards Lord Farnborough, whose taste in all that concerned fine arts was unquestioned. The gallery itself is an extensive corridor, upwards of 150 feet long, and lighted from the roof by skylights of ground glass, on which are exhibited all the stars of the various European orders. The "private apartments" of the Queen, which are very rarely shown, contain some fine portraits and miniatures of the late and present Royal Families, by Vandyck, Lely, Kneller, Gainsborough, Copley, Lawrence, &c.

The Yellow Drawing-room is generally considered the most magnificent apartment in the palace ; the whole of the furniture being elaborately carved, overlaid with burnished gold, and covered with broad-striped yellow satin. Several highly-polished syenite marble pillars are ranged against the walls. In each panel is painted a full-length portrait of some member of the Royal Family. This room, which is on the north side of the palace, communicates with the Queen's private apartments. The saloon, in the centre of the garden front, is superbly decorated ; the shafts of the Corinthian columns are composed of purple scagliola, in imitation of lapis lazuli ; the entablature, cornice, and ceiling are profusely enriched ; and the remaining decorations and furniture are of corresponding magnificence. The South Drawing-room contains three compositions in relief, by the late William Pitts—namely, the apotheosis of Spenser, of Shakespeare, and of Milton.

The last of the state rooms is the Dining-room, which is a very spacious and handsome apartment, lighted by windows on one side only, opening into the garden ; the spaces between these windows are filled with immense mirrors. At the southern end is a deep recess, the extremity of which is nearly filled by a large looking-glass, in front of which, during state balls or dinners, the buffet of gold plate is arranged, producing a most magnificent effect. The ceiling is highly enriched with foliage and floral ornamentation. On the eastern side are portraits of former members of the royal family, and Sir Thomas Lawrence's whole-length portrait of George IV. in his coronation robes, which was originally in the Presence Chamber at St. James's Palace.

The garden, or west front, of the palace, architecturally the principal one, has five Corinthian towers, and also a balustraded terrace, on the upper portion of which are statues, trophies, and bas-reliefs, by Flaxman and other distinguished sculptors.

The pleasure grounds cover a space of about forty acres, five of which are occupied by a lake. Upon the summit of a lofty artificial mound, rising from the margin of the lake, is a picturesque pavilion, or garden-house, with a minaret roof. In the centre is an octagonal room, with figures of "Midnight" and "Dawn," and eight lunettes, painted in fresco, from Milton's "Comus," by Eastlake, Maclise, Landseer, Dyce, Stanfield, Uwins, Leslie, and Ross. Another room is decorated in the Pompeian style, and a third is embellished with romantic designs, suggested by the novels and poems of Sir Walter Scott.

The Royal Stables—or mews, as they are generally called—are situated on the west side of the garden, and are concealed from the palace by a lofty mound. They contain a spacious riding-school, a room expressly for keeping the state harness, stabling for the state horses, and houses for forty carriages. The magnificent state coach, which is kept here, was designed by Sir William Chambers, in 1762, and painted by Cipriani with a series of emblematical subjects ; its entire cost is said to have been little short of £8,000.

In 1837 it was a common joke of the day that Buckingham Palace could boast at all events of being the cheapest of all royal residences, having been "built for one sovereign and furnished for another." It was in July of the above year that Queen Victoria took up her residence here, since which period this palace has been the constant abode of Her Majesty, when in town. Here, in 1840 and 1841, were born the Princess Royal and the Prince of Wales ; and it has been the birthplace of most of the other children of Her Majesty. It is, too, occasionally set apart as the temporary residence of royal guests from foreign parts, when on visits to this country.

In March, 1841, a young lad, named Jones, caused some alarm to the inmates of the palace by making his way into the Queen's private apartments. Unlike the poor demented youth who in more recent times levelled an empty worn-out pistol to Her Majesty as she was leaving her carriage to enter the palace, the only object of "the boy Jones," as he was called, appears to have been notoriety, and this gratification certainly he obtained. Mr. Raikes, in commenting on this incident in his "Journal," says—"A little scamp of an apothecary's errand-boy, named Jones, has the unaccountable mania of sneaking privately into Buckingham Palace, where he is found secreted at night under a sofa, or some other hiding-place close to the Queen's bed-chamber. No one can divine his object, but twice he has been detected and conveyed to the police-office, and put into confinement for a time. The other day he was detected in a third attempt, with apparently as little object. Lady Sandwich wittily wrote that he must undoubtedly be a descendant of *In-I-go* Jones, the architect."

Here, in 1843, the Princess Augusta of Cambridge was married with great state to Frederick William, Grand Duke of Mecklenburg-Strelitz.

The King of Hanover came over for the occasion. Shortly afterwards, Mr. Raikes happening to be breakfasting with the Duke of Wellington, the latter told the following story :—"When we proceeded to the signatures of the bride and bridegroom, the King of Hanover was very anxious to sign before Prince Albert, and when the Queen approached the table, he placed himself by her side, watching his opportunity. She knew very well what he was about, and just as the Archbishop was giving her the pen, she suddenly dodged round the table, placed herself next to the Prince, then quickly took the pen from the Archbishop, signed, and gave it to Prince Albert, who also signed next, before it could be prevented. The Queen," added the duke, "was also very anxious to give the precedence at Court to King Leopold before the King of Hanover, and she consulted me about it, and how it should be arranged. I told Her Majesty that I supposed it should be settled as we did at the Congress of Vienna. 'How was that,' said she ; 'by first arrival?' 'No, Ma'am,' said I, 'but alphabetically ; and B. comes before H.' This pleased her very much ; and it was done."

It was by Buckingham Palace that the Duke of Wellington's funeral cortége passed, in November, 1852, on its way from St. James's Park to St. Paul's Cathedral ; and it was also in front of the Palace that the Scots Fusilier Guards paraded in the early dawn of a bleak March day in 1854, *en route* from the Wellington Barracks to Portsmouth, to embark for the Black Sea. The Queen, accompanied by the Prince Consort, the Prince of Wales, and three others of her elder children, looked down from the balcony to bid her soldiers farewell.

It was here, too, that Her Majesty favoured Mr. Charles Dickens with an interview, in the last few weeks of his life : the true account of this interview is given by Mr. John Forster, in his "Life" of the great novelist, in terms of which the following is the substance :—

"It had been hoped to obtain Her Majesty's name and patronage for some amateur theatrical performances on behalf of the family of Douglas Jerrold, in 1857 ; but, being a public effort on behalf of a private individual, it was feared that offence might be given if a like request should be refused in another case. The Queen, however, sent a request through Sir Charles Phipps, that Charles Dickens would select a room in the palace, and let her see the performance there. There were difficulties, however, in the way, and in return, Dickens proposed that Her Majesty should come on a private night to the Gallery of Illustration, having the room entirely at her own disposal and inviting her own company. This proposal the Queen accepted ; and she was so pleased with the performance, that she sent word round to the greenroom, requesting Mr. Dickens to come to the royal box, and accept her thanks. This, however, he could not do, being undressed and begrimed with dirt. Next year the Queen expressed a wish to hear Dickens read 'The Carol ;' but this, too, came to nothing. At last," writes Mr. Forster, "there came, in the year of his death, the interview with the author whose popularity dated from her accession, whose books had entertained a larger number of her subjects than those of any contemporary writer, and whose genius will be accounted one of the stories of her reign. Accident led to it. Dickens had brought with him from America some large and striking photographs of the battle-fields of the Civil War, and the Queen, having heard of this through Mr. Arthur Helps, expressed a wish to look at them. Dickens sent them alone, and went afterwards to Buckingham Palace with Mr. Helps, at Her Majesty's request, that she might see them and thank him in person. This was in the middle of March . . . . . The Queen's kindness left a strong impression on Dickens. Upon Her Majesty's expressing regret that she had not heard his readings, Dickens intimated that they had now been a thing of the past, while he acknowledged gratefully the compliment of Her Majesty in regard to them. She spoke to him of the impression made upon her by his acting in 'The Frozen Deep ;' and on his stating, in reply to her inquiry, that the little play had not been very successful on the public stage, said that this did not surprise her, since it no longer had the advantage of his performance in it. . . . . . She asked him to give her his writings, and could she have them that afternoon ? but he begged to be allowed to send a bound copy. Her Majesty then took from the table her own book upon the 'Highlands,' with an autograph inscription 'to Charles Dickens,' and saying that 'the humblest of writers' would be ashamed to offer it to 'one of the greatest,' but that Mr. Helps, being asked to give it, had remarked to her that it would be valued most from herself ; so she closed the interview by placing the book in his hands." Just two months from the day of the above interview with the Queen, Dickens was buried in Westminster Abbey.

The "Board of Green Cloth," the head-quarters of which are at Buckingham Palace, comprises five of the chief officers of Her Majesty's Household —namely, the Lord Steward, the Treasurer, the Comptroller, the Master of the Household, and the Secretary. They have the oversight and government of the Queen's Court bearing the above title, and also the supervision of the Household accounts, the purveyance of the provisions and their payment, and the good government of the servants of the Household. In Murray's "Official Handbook of Church and State," we learn that "the palace anciently formed an exempt jurisdiction, which was subject to the Court of the Lord Steward of the Household, held in his absence by the Treasurer, the Comptroller, or the Steward of the Marshalsea. This Court formerly possessed the power to try all treasons, murders, felonies, and other offences committed in the palace and within the verge; but this extensive jurisdiction, which was in part repealed by George IV., had long previously fallen into disuse, and the civil jurisdiction, which the Court continued to exercise till 1849, was abolished in that year by Act of Parliament. The Lord Steward of the Household fills an ancient office of great trust and dignity. He is the chief officer of the Queen's Household, all the officers and servants of which are under his control, except those belonging to the Chapel, the Chamber, and the Stable. His authority extends over the offices of Treasurer, Comptroller, and Master of the Household. The Lord Steward is at the head of the Court of the Queen's Household—the Board of Green Cloth. He is always sworn a member of the Privy Council. He has precedence before all peers of his own degree. He has no formal grant of his office, but receives his charge immediately from the Queen by the delivery of his white staff of office. He holds his appointment during pleasure, and his tenure depends upon the political party of which he is a member. His salary is £2,000 per annum. The Lord Steward has the selection and appointment of all the subordinate officers and servants of the Household, and also of the Queen's tradesmen, except those connected with the royal stables. The Treasurer of the Household acts for the Lord Steward in his absence. He is always a member of the Privy Council, and a political adherent of the Government in power. His salary is £904 per annum. The Comptroller is subordinate to the two preceding officers, for whom he acts in their absence. He is usually a member of the Privy Council. His particular duty consists in the examination and check of the Household expenses. His office is also dependent upon the Government of the day. His salary is £904 per annum. The Master of the Household stands next in rank to this department. He is an officer under the Treasurer, and examines a portion of the accounts; but his duties consist more especially in superintending the selection,

qualification, and conduct of the Household servants. His salary is £1,158 per annum. His appointment is during pleasure, and is not dependent upon party."

In this department an office was held by Mr. William Bray, F.S.A., some years Treasurer of the Society of Antiquaries, and the author (conjointly with Mr. Manning) of the "History of Surrey." He died in November, 1832, aged ninety-six.

It is at Buckingham Palace that Her Majesty usually holds her "Courts" and "Drawing-rooms." A court is held for the reception of the diplomatic and other official bodies, the general circle on the court list, and other persons having special invitations, the presentations being few in number. A writer in the *Graphic* gives us the following observations on these State receptions:—"A Court," he says, "is not so 'interesting' in some respects as a Drawing-room. The few presentations are principally of an official character, and the youthful *débutantes* who give such grace to Drawing-room days are but little represented. There is beauty you may be sure, as there must be in any assembly where English ladies compose a large proportion; and, apart from the splendour of the dresses, it forms the chief charm of the scene. And if the *débutante* element be wanting, there is no lack of youth as well as of beauty; charming faces indeed are everywhere, and fix the attention even more than the dazzling dresses of their owners. At Drawing-rooms, where people attend voluntarily, precautions are always taken to prevent an undue proportion of men being present, as most of us would prefer such an occasion to pay our respects to that of a Levee; so gentlemen have a polite invitation to stay away unless forming the escort of ladies. But here, where notifications are expressly sent by everybody, there is no necessity for the restriction; and the ladies are certainly in no danger of being overshadowed by members of the harder sex. As regards the latter, we notice one peculiarity: there are fewer military uniforms than on Levee and Drawing-room days, when the scarlet of Her Majesty's Forces is just a little in excess. But the dresses present not the less magnificent an appearance on that account. Apart from the foreign costumes, our own official uniforms are splendid enough; and the new general court dress is decidedly more pleasant to the eye than the old style, which, though still represented, is fast giving way to the new fashion sanctioned by authority. One obvious advantage which it possesses is in being something like the garments which gentlemen are accustomed to wear, instead of being a great deal like the garments which gentlemen are accustomed to put upon their foot-men. Indeed, the footmen have the best of it as far as splendour is concerned; for the old court dress has none of the bravery of Queen Anne's time, and that of the earlier Georges. It belongs to the period of the middle of the reign of George III., and is rather sombre than otherwise, except in respect to the variegated waistcoat, which is 'fine' in a certain sense of the term, but decidedly ugly

a dress of the kind when he wandered through the gallery at Whitehall, and scandalised himself— in the cause of his "Diary"—at the lax manners of Charles II.'s court. It would have been scarcely gay enough for Pepys. In our own day it ought to suit even the simple taste of Mr. Bright, who respectfully but firmly declined to costume himself in the old court style.

"Among the fair owners of the headdresses, of

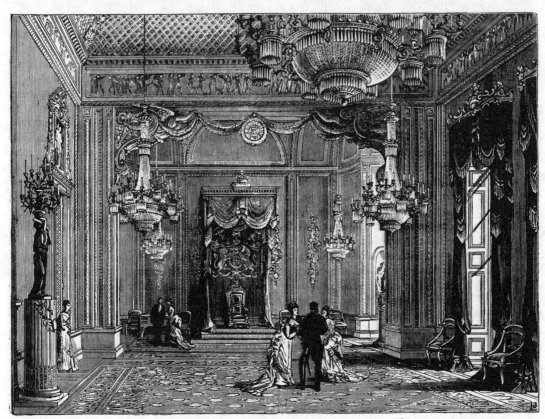

THE THRONE-ROOM, BUCKINGHAM PALACE. (*See page* 68.)

to the eye of taste. The new dress is a little formal in cut; but this is a necessity where regula-tion is imperative; it would never do to have very marked peculiarities of style when the same cos-tume is to be worn by persons of all sizes and variations of figure. There is room, too, for some exercise of the fancy. Private persons—that is to say, persons having no military or official uniform —may wear the coloured cloth suit, embroidered with gold, or they may disport themselves in black velvet from head to foot, with white lace at the collars and wrists. The cloth with its ornaments is more gay; but the velvet has the decided advantage in point of dignity, and the scholarlike appearance which it gives to the wearer. One can fancy Evelyn himself being appropriately clad in

feathers, blonde-lappets, and diamonds, the trains, and other elaborations, are, of course, a large num-ber of men in military uniform, which is, after all, the most effective of any dress, if only for the reason that it seems to belong to the wearers. Not the least gorgeous of these are the Gentlemen-at-Arms, each of whom looks like a field-marshal in his own right, though he bears only the rank of a captain. They are on duty to-day, as may be supposed, and so are the Yeomen of the Guard, in their quaint uniform of the time of Henry VIII.; and a Guard of Honour of the Coldstream Guards is mounted in the court of the palace.

"All these important matters pass under our notice while the company is assembling preparatory to entering the royal presence. At the appointed

BUCKINGHAM PALACE: GARDEN FRONT. (*See page* 69.)

151

hour Her Majesty, who has arrived from Windsor, takes her place, having been joined by the Prince and Princess of Wales, and other members of the Royal Family, to say nothing of the Maharajah Duleep Singh, and the Nawab Nazim of Bengal— who goes everywhere just now—with their respective attendants. The scene on the staircase— the company being on their way to the Throne-room—is very splendid, and in the Throne-room itself it is gorgeous in the extreme.

" See the lady clad in black, with the coronet of diamonds and sapphires, and the white veil covered with large diamonds also; with the necklace, cross, and brooch of yet more diamonds ; on her breast the blue riband and the Star of the Order of the Garter, the Orders of Victoria and Albert and Louise of Prussia, and the Coburg and Gotha Family Order. The dignity of her bearing, apart from all these insignia, would proclaim her to be the principal personage present. As she stands, surrounded by the members of her family, and the ladies and gentlemen of her household, she is evidently *reigning* actively, as a Queen is always supposed to do ; and yet she is the same gentle lady who in her private life has made herself so pleasantly familiar to her subjects.

" Of the assembly who approach her a few are presented in form and kiss the Royal hand ; the rest pass by Her Majesty in rotation, and file off by a sidelong retiring movement from the presence. The ceremony occupies a considerable time, as must be, owing to the large number present ; and the scene during the continuance could scarcely be surpassed for splendour and costly state. The apartment in which it is enacted, too, is well worthy of the occasion, with its glass, and its gilding, and its crimson draperies.

"When the last lady and gentleman have passed the throne, Her Majesty retires with her suite ; then there is a movement downstairs, a general call for carriages, and the first ' Court' of the season has fairly come to an end."

CHAPTER VII.

THE MALL AND SPRING GARDENS.

"The ladies gaily dress'd the Mall adorn
With various dyes and paint the sunny morn."— *Gay's* " *Trivia.*"

The Game of Mall—Discovery of Mailes and Balls used in playing the Game—Formation of the Mall, and Mr. Pepys' Visits thither—The Mall a Powerful Rival to the Ring in Hyde Park—Charles II. and Dryden—Courtly Insignia worn in Public—Congreve, the Poet— A Capuchin Monastery—French Huguenot Refugees—The Duke of York's Column—" Milk Fair "—Spring Gardens—A Bowling-green established there—Duels of frequent occurrence there—The Spring Garden closed, and a Rival Establishment opened—A Part of the Royal Menagerie kept in Spring Gardens—Courtier Life in the Reign of Charles I.—Mistaken Notions as to the Origin of the Name of Spring Gardens—King Charles on his Way to Execution—Thomson, the Poet—The " Wilderness "—Berkeley House—The Metropolitan Board of Works—The Celebrated Mrs. Centlivre—" Locket's Ordinary "—Drummond's Bank—The Old Duchess of Brunswick—Sir Astley Cooper and other Noted Residents—Spring Gardens Chapel—Its Destruction by Fire—St. Matthew's Chapel-of-Ease—The Medical Club—The Tilt-yard Coffee House—Warwick Street and Warwick House—Escape of Princess Charlotte in a Hackney Coach—Her Return to Warwick House—Exhibitions and Entertainments in the Neighbourhood—The " Rummer " Tavern—Prior, the Poet—Dr. Isaac Barrow and the Earl of Rochester—Pepys in the Hands of the Modeller—Miscellaneous Exhibitions in Cockspur Street—Origin of the Name of Cockspur Street— The " British Coffee House."

ON leaving Buckingham Palace, we walk through the Mall, on the north side of St. James's Park. This once fashionable lounge and promenade is described by Northouck as " a vista half a mile in length, at that time (Charles II.) formed with a hollow smooth walk skirted round with a wooden border, and with an iron hoop at the further end, for the purpose of playing a game with a ball called mall." The iron hoop was suspended from a bar of wood at the top of a pole, and the play consisted in striking a ball through this ring from a considerable distance.

In Timbs' " Curiosities of London " we read that in 1854 were found in the roof of the house of the late Mr. B. L. Vulliamy, No. 68, Pall Mall, a box containing four pairs of the mailes, or mallets, and one ball, such as were formerly used for playing the game of pall-mall upon the site of the above house, or in the Mall of St. James's Park. " Each maile was four feet in length, and made of lance-wood ; the head was slightly curved, measuring outwardly $5\frac{1}{2}$ inches, the inner curve being $4\frac{1}{2}$ inches ; the diameter of the maile-ends was $2\frac{1}{2}$ inches, each shod with a thin iron hoop ; the handle, which was very elastic, was bound with white leather to the breadth of two hands, and terminated by a collar of jagged leather. The ball was of box-wood, $2\frac{1}{2}$ inches in diameter." These relics of a bygone, almost forgotten game were presented to the British Museum by Mr. George Vulliamy.

The " Mall " is the name now conventionally

given to the wide gravel walk running under the windows of Carlton Terrace, from the Green Park as far as Spring Gardens. This was not the original "Mall" of the days of Charles II., which seems to have lain to the north, and to have been as nearly as possible identical with "the present street of Pall Mall." No doubt, when a new and broad thoroughfare like the old one, and so close to it, was opened in its place to the public, the name was transformed the more easily and obviously, as the former, like the present, was the northern boundary of the park, and indeed formed part of it.

Under date of April 2, 1661, there is an entry in Pepys' "Diary" which implies that the "Pell Mell" was then newly finished :—" To St. James's Park, where I saw the Duke of York playing at Pellmell,

opportunity for displaying a carriage, horses, and smart livery. Equipages at that time became more and more the fashion, and to be seen afoot in the Mall was by many considered the height of vulgarity. There appeared in 1709 a satire, entitled "The Circus, or the British Olympus," in the preface of which occurs the following remark :—" If gentlemen are never such dear companions now, they must have no conversation together but upon equal terms, lest some should say to the man of figure, 'Bless me, sir! what strange, filthy fellow was that you bow'd to parading in the Mall, as you were driving to the Ring?'"

The following story of the Mall, though told in "Spence's Anecdotes," will amuse many of our readers to whom it may be news :—" It was Charles II. who gave to Dryden the hint for writing his

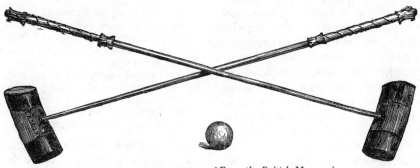

PALL MALL IMPLEMENTS.   (*From the British Museum.*)

the first time that ever I saw the sport." And on the 15th of May, 1663, he tells us how that he "walked in the parke, discoursing with the keeper of the Pell Mell, who was sweeping it." It appears to have been covered with fine gravel, mixed with cockle-shells finely powdered and spread to keep it fast; which, "however," complains Mr. Samuel Pepys, "in dry weather turns to dust and deads the ball." In the following January the diarist is here again, and in his record of this visit, says it pleased him "mightily" to "hear a gallant, lately come from France, swear at one of his companions for suffering his man (a spruce blade) to be so saucy as to strike a ball while his master was playing on the Mall."

Since the reign of Charles II. the Mall had become a powerful rival to the Ring in Hyde Park. In Etheredge's "Man of Mode" (1676), a young lady observes that the Ring has a better reputation than the Mall; "but," says she, "I abominate the dull diversions there, the formal bows, the affected smiles, the silly bywords and amorous tweers in passing; here [in the Mall] one meets with a little conversation now and then." On the other hand, the Ring had this advantage, that it gave the

poem called 'The Medal.' One day, as the king was walking in the Mall and talking with Dryden, he said, 'If I were a poet . . . . . I would write a poem on such a subject in the following manner, and then gave him the plan for it. Dryden took the hint, carried the poem as soon as it was written to the king, and had a present of a hundred broad pieces for it."

The Mall was a fashionable lounge, and is constantly alluded to in the anecdote literature and gossip of the Stuart and Hanoverian times. Thus Swift tells "Stella" that "when he passes the Mall in the evening, it is prodigious to see the number of ladies walking there;" and, speaking of St. John says, "His father is a man of pleasure that walks the Mall, and frequents St. James's Coffee House, and the Chocolate House."

In the time of the first and second Georges it was usual for noblemen of the highest rank to wear the insignia of their orders in public places. The writer of the "Town Spy" for instance, tells us, in 1725, how he was walking in the Mall with a gentleman whom he had met "at a coffee-house within the verge," when there passed before them "a nobleman vested with a blue Garter." His servants, he adds, "were worried about by the people to know what duke it was. It turned out, however, to be only an earl after all."

Congreve, the poet, was one of the gallants who were fond of displaying their fine dress in the haunts of fashion. Hence Thackeray's remark, that "Louis Quatorze in all his glory is hardly more splendid than our Phœbus Apollo of the Mall and the Spring Garden."

Close to St. James's Palace, nearly on the site where now stands the German chapel, was built, in the reign of Charles II., a monastery for the use of the Capuchin monks who attended Catherine of Braganza. It is thus described by Pepys in his "Diary," under date January 23, 1666-7 :—"My Lord Brounkir and I walking into the park, I did observe the new buildings ; and my lord seeing I had a desire to see them, they being the place for the priests and friers, he took me back to my Lord Almoner ; and he took us quite through the whole house and chapel, and the new monastery, shewing me most excellent pieces in wax-worke ; a crucifix given by a Pope to Mary Queene of Scotts, wherein is a piece of the Cross ; two bits set in the manner of a cross in the foot of the crucifix ; several fine pictures, but especially very good prints of holy pictures. I saw the dortoire and the cells of the priests, and we went into one ; a very pretty little room, very clean, hung with pictures, set with books. The priest was in his cell, with his hair-clothes to his skin, bare-legged with a sandall only on, and his little bed without sheets, and no feather bed ; but yet, I thought, soft enough. His cord about his middle ; but in so good company, living with ease, I thought it a very good life. A pretty library they have, and I was in the refectoire, where every man has his napkin, knife, cup of earth, and basin of the same ; and a place for one to sit and read while the rest are at meals. And into the kitchen I went, where a good neck of mutton at the fire, and other victuals boiling. I do not think they fared very hard. Their windows all looking into a fine garden and the park ; and mighty pretty rooms all. I wished myself one of the Capuchins."

In the reign of William III. we find a congregation of the French Huguenot refugees established in the "French Chapel Royal," St. James's.

On the site of what is now the basement or substructure of Carlton House Terrace, which nearly the whole distance eastward bounds the north side of the Mall, was once a row of fine old trees, which overhung the road by the park-wall. Half way along the Terrace is an opening from Waterloo Place, formed by command of William IV., as had

been the Spring Garden Gate, more than a century earlier, by William III.

The column which crowns the steps leading up from the park into Waterloo Place was erected by public subscription in 1830-33, to the memory of the late Duke of York, many years Commander-in-Chief. The cost of it was £26,000. It consists of a plain circular shaft of Aberdeen granite about 120 feet high, from the designs of Mr. B. Wyatt. The statue of the duke which surmounts it is the work of the late Sir Richard Westmacott, R.A.

The column and statue, as might be expected, was the subject of many witticisms. Take, for instance, the following lines in the *New Monthly Magazine :—*

> " Thou pillar, longitudinally great,
> And also perpendicularly straight.
>
>   *   *   *   *   *
>
> Thou art, I fear, but flattery's handiwork,
> Being a tribute unto royal York.
> *Thy* royal highness (ah ! too like to *His*)
> Prompts us somewhat to stare, somewhat to quiz,
> Railing surrounds above thy lofty brow,
> And passers-by do likewise rail below.
> That mortal Prince whom thou to Cherubim
> Wouldst raise, what record canst thou give of him ?
> Of his great deeds few words the Muse can dish up ;
> But, for his virtues, was he not a bishop ?"

The allusion in the last line is to the fact that the duke enjoyed by courtesy the lay title of Prince-Bishop of Osnaburg.

At the end of the Mall, in the shade of the tall trees, near the Spring Gardens entrance, is an "institution "—if we may so call it—of considerable date, and a proof of the former rural character of the spot, which has flourished here perhaps almost since the formation of the Mall. It is known as "Milk Fair," and is held by a privilege granted from royalty to the gatekeepers. In Tom Brown's time (1700) the noisy milk-fools in the park cried, "A can of milk, ladies ! A can of red cow's milk, sir ! " If we may judge from a fashionable conceit in Gay's "Trivia," we may conclude that not only cows' but asses' milk was at one time sold here as a restorative for bodily ailments—

> "Before proud gates attending asses bray,
> Or arrogate with solemn pace the way ;
> These grave physicians with their milky cheer,
> The love-sick maid and dwindling beau repair."

It may be added, that the vendors of milk of the present day in Spring Gardens are almost, without exception, descendants from those who have had their stalls here for the last century or more.

Spring Gardens—more properly "The Spring Garden"—as late as the reign of Elizabeth, and possibly down to a still more recent date, was a rural garden. This spot bears its name from a fountain or "spring" of water, which in the days of Queen Bess was set in motion by the spectator treading on some secret machinery, which proved a novel puzzle for the good people of Westminster.

Hentzner, in his "Travels" (1598), thus describes the scene :—"In a garden belonging to this palace there is a *jet d'eau*, with a sun-dial, at which, while strangers are looking, a quantity of water forced by a wheel which the gardener turns at a distance, through a number of little pipes, plentifully sprinkles those that are standing around." Mr. P. Cunningham assures us that such water-springs as this were common in gardens in the days of Queen Bess, and that one of the same kind was to be seen at Chatsworth as late as 1847. Be this, however, as it may, Nares, in his "Glossary," tells us that the Spring Garden described by Plot was in existence at Enstone, in Oxfordshire, in 1822.

This place appears to have been a sort of adjunct to the Royal Palace of Whitehall, though "across the road," and to have been covered occasionally with scaffolds, in order to enable "the quality" to see the tilting in the Tilt-yard. It contained a pleasant yard, a pond for bathing, and some butts to practise shooting.

Charles I., by royal patent in 1630, made it a "bowling-green," but the patent was revoked, and the "bowling-green" brought to an untimely end four years later. The reason of the withdrawal of its licence may be gathered from the following extract from a letter addressed by a Mr. Gerrard to Lord Strafford :—"There was kept in it an ordinary of six shillings a meal, when the king's proclamation allows but two elsewhere ; continual bibbing and drinking wine all day under the trees ; two or three quarrels every week. It was grown scandalous and insufferable ; besides, my Lord Digby being reprehended for striking in the king's garden, he said he took it for a common bowling place, where all paid money for their coming in." It is clear from this that Lord Digby thought that if he only paid for admission, he had a right to "strike" where and whom he pleased ; and if this was the general idea entertained by "persons of quality," it is not difficult to see how "two or three quarrels "— or, in other words, duels—would arise there every week.

One result of the shutting up of the "Spring Garden" was the opening of a rival, the "New Spring Garden," by one of the Lord Chamberlain's household, too. It appears, however, that the old place was re-opened ere long ; for in June, 1649, John Evelyn paid it a visit, "treating divers ladies of his relations," as he tells us in his "Diary."

Under date May 10, 1654, however, he writes :—"My Lady Gerrard treated us at Mulberry Garden, now the only place of refreshment about the towne for persons of the best quality to be exceedingly cheated at ; Cromwell and his partisans having shut up and seized on the Spring Garden, which till now had been the usual rendezvous for the ladies and gallants at this season." In spite of the sour-visaged Puritans, however, its gates were again thrown open ; for the writer of "A Character of England," published five years later, thus speaks of it, and in the present tense :—"The inclosure is not disagreeable, for the solemnness of the grove, and the warbling of the birds, and as it opens into the spacious walks at St. James's." He adds :—"It is not unusual to find some of the young company here till midnight ; and the thickets of the garden seem to be contrived to all advantages of gallantry, after they have refreshed with collation, which is here seldom omitted, at a certain cabaret in the middle of this paradise, where the forbidden fruits are certain trifling tarts, neats' tongues, salacious meats, and bad Rhenish."

Soon after the Restoration, a part at least of the ground occupied by these rival places of amusement seems to have been built over, and distinguished as the "inner" and the "outer" Spring Garden respectively ; a trace of which doubtless still remains in the present name of Spring Garden*s*. Prince Rupert occupied a house in Spring Gardens from 1674 until his death.

We have already in a previous chapter spoken of the "menagerie" which James I. established in St. James's Park ; some of the animals, however, appear to have been located in Spring Gardens. "At all events," says Larwood, in his "Story of the London Parks," "they were there in the second year of the reign of Charles II. This appears from a document preserved among the State papers, being an order dated January 31, 1626, for £75 5s. 10d. a year to be paid for life to Philip, Earl of Montgomery, 'for keeping the Spring Garden, and the *beasts and fowls* there.' "

The Parliament passed a decree in March, 1647, in the true spirit of Puritan intolerance, ordering "That the keeper of the Spring Garden be hereby required and enjoined to admit no person to come into or walk in the Spring Garden on the Lord's Day or any of the public fast days, and that no wine, beer, ale, cakes, or other things be sold there either upon the Lord's Day or public fast days."

Isaac D'Israeli, in his "Curiosities of Literature," tells us an amusing story illustrative of courtier life in Spring Gardens in the early days of Charles I.

"The king and the Duke of Buckingham," he writes, "were in the Spring Garden looking at the bowlers; the duke put on his hat. One Wilson, a Scotchman, first seizing the duke's hand, snatched it off, saying, 'Off with your hat before the king!' Buckingham, not able to restrain his quick feelings, kicked the Scotchman; but the king interfering, said, 'Let him alone, George; he is either mad or a fool.' 'No, sir,' replied Wilson; 'I am a sober

apparently another writer, R. Brome, who asks his friend, "Shall we make a fling to London, and see how the spring appears there in the Spring Gardens?"

Mr. J. H. Jesse tells us that down to the present day every house in Spring Garden Terrace has its separate well. He also gives currency to a tradition to the effect that as he walked through the park from St. James's Palace to the scaffold at

PLAYING AT PALL MALL. (*From a Contemporary Print.* (*See page* 75.)

man; and if your Majesty would give me leave, I would tell you that of this man, which many know, and none dare speak.'"

Evelyn tells us in May, 1658, how he went to see the coach race in Hyde Park, and afterwards "collationed" in Spring Gardens; and it would seem from other sources that the latter formed an agreeable house of call on the way to and from the park.

Margaret, the learned Duchess of Newcastle, tells us that when young she and her sisters used to ride in their coaches about the streets to see the concourse and recourse of people, and in the spring time to visit the Spring Gardens, Hyde Park, and the like places. From this it is probable that her Grace mistook the origin of the name, as does

Whitehall, King Charles stopped, weary and faint, to drink a glass of water at one of the springs, at the same time, as we have before remarked, pointing out to Bishop Juxon and Herbert a tree close by as having been planted by the hands of his elder brother, Prince Henry.

Among the inhabitants of this place enumerated by Mr. Peter Cunningham are Sir Philip Warwick (after whom Warwick Street is named), Philip Earl of Chesterfield (1670), Prince Rupert, the "mad" Lord Crofts, Sir Edward Hungerford, Colley Cibber, and, last but not least, George Canning. An advertisement in the *Daily Courant* of January, 1703, gives us Cibber's *locale* as "near the 'Bull Head' Tavern, in Old Spring Garden." John Milton, too, during the Commonwealth, occupied lodgings at the house of a tradesman named Thomson, "next door to the 'Bull Head Tavern.'"

In a room over the shop of one Egerton, a bookseller, near this spot, where he resided on first coming to London, a raw Scottish lad, James Thomson wrote part of his "Seasons." We are told that at this time he was "gaping about the town listlessly, getting his pockets picked, and forced to wait on great persons with his poem of

denominated the 'Wilderness' so lately as 1772, in which year Frederick Augustus, Earl of Berkeley, obtained leave to build messuages and gardens in a place called 'the Wilderness,' on the north-west side of the passage from Spring Gardens to St. James's Park. This grant, no doubt, occasioned the disappearance of the last vestige of the once famous place of amusement."

At the northern end of Spring Gardens, at the

THE MALL IN 1450.

'Winter,' in order to find a patron." Most luckily, fond as he was of freedom, he did not carry his love of freedom so far as to close against himself the doors of powerful patrons. "He obtained," writes Leigh Hunt, "an easy place, which required no compromise of his principles, and passed the latter part of his life in his own house at Richmond," where he died and is buried.

As late as the reign of George I., the Spring Gardens are laid down in maps as forming an enclosure limited by rows of houses in Warwick Lane and Charing Cross, and containing a house with a large flower-garden in front, situated in the midst of an orchard or a grove of trees. "It is this plantation, perhaps," says Mr. Jacob Larwood, in his "Story of the London Parks," "which was

corner of the footway leading into the Mall of St. James's Park, stood the above-named dull and unattractive mansion, known as Berkeley House, from having been the town residence of the Earls of Berkeley for the best part of a century. Here George Prince of Wales, and many of his boon companions, were frequent visitors. It was purchased by the Government in 1862, and pulled down. On its site are built the offices of the Metropolitan Board of Works. This edifice is spacious and lofty, and well adapted to the purposes for which it was erected. It is in the Italian style of architecture, and has at once a bold and striking appearance. The Metropolitan Board of Works was established in 1855. Under the Metropolitan Building Act, passed in the same year, it exercises a supervision over all buildings erected within the limits of its jurisdiction. The powers of the Board were extended in 1858, to enable it to effect the purification of the Thames by constructing a new system of Main Drainage on both sides of the river. The construction of the Thames Embankments was also carried on under its supervision. It is empowered by the Act under which it is constituted to raise loans for carrying out public works of this nature, the repayment and interest of which are guaranteed by Government, and secured by a tax of 3d. in the pound on property in the metropolis. The principal general duties of the Board comprise the control over the formation of streets, and the maintenance of the Fire Brigade, the Main Drainage system, and of the parks and commons.

In Buckingham Court, at the southern end of Spring Gardens, died, December 1, 1723, the celebrated Mrs. Centlivre, the witty and pretty dramatist, author of *The Busybody*, and *The Bold Stroke for a Wife*, and the wife of three husbands in succession. She is said to have been a great beauty, an accomplished linguist, and a good-natured, friendly woman. Pope immortalised her in his " Dunciad," it is said, for having written a ballad against his translation of Homer, when she was a child. " But," as Leigh Hunt suggests, "the probability is that she was too intimate with Steele, and other friends of Addison, while the irritable poet was at variance with them. It is not impossible, also, that some raillery of hers might have been applied to him—not very pleasant from a beautiful woman against a man of his personal infirmities, and who was actually jealous of not standing well with the fair sex." Mrs. Centlivre is said to have accompanied her first lover, Anthony Howard (the father of the author of " Love Elegies"), to Cambridge, in boy's clothes. This, however, did not hinder her from marrying a nephew of Sir Stephen Fox, who died a year afterwards, nor from having two other husbands in succession. Her second husband was an officer of the name of Carroll, who was killed in a duel. Her third husband, Mr. Centlivre, who had the formidable title of " Yeoman of the Mouth," being chief cook to Queen Anne, fell desperately in love with her when she was playing the part of Alexander the Great, at Windsor; for she seems to have acted on the stage in the provinces, though she did not appear on London boards. Leigh Hunt says of her plays that " they are not after the taste of Mrs. Hannah More, but the public seem very fond of them. They are still," he adds, in 1835, " acted as often as if they had just come out. The reason is that, careless as they are in dialogue,

and not very scrupulous in manners and morals, they are full of action and good humour."

Her house must have stood near the spot where now is Messrs. Drummond's bank; close by was a house known as " Locket's," or " Locket's Ordinary," a house of entertainment much frequented by the gentry and " persons of quality" in the reign of Queen Anne, and partaking very much of the old character of the gardens on which it rose. Dr. King thus commemorates it, in his " Art of Cookery," with a quaint and not very first-rate pun :—

" For Locket's stands where Gardens once did spring."

The exact site of " Locket's Ordinary " is not known, though Leigh Hunt is inclined to identify it with the " Northumberland " Coffee House of a later date. " It is often mentioned," observes the writer of a MS. in Birch's "Collection," quoted in the Notes to the *Tatler*, "in the plays of Colley Cibber, Vanbrugh, &c., where the scene is sometimes laid. It was much frequented by Sir George Etheredge, as appears from the following anecdotes, picked up in the British Museum :—Sir George and his company, provoked by something amiss in the entertainment or the attendance, got into a violent passion, and abused the waiters. This brought in Mrs. Locket. ' We are so provoked,' said Sir George, ' that I could find it in my heart to pull that nosegay out of your bosom, and throw all the flowers into your face.' This turned all the anger of the guests into a loud fit of laughter. Sir George Etheredge, it appears, discontinued Mrs. Locket's ordinary, having run up a score which he could not conveniently discharge. Mrs. Locket sent a man to dun him, and to threaten him with a prosecution. He bade the messenger tell her that he would kiss her if she stirred a step further in the matter. When this answer was brought back to her, she called for her hood and scarf, and told her husband, who interposed, that ' she'd see if there was any fellow alive who had the impudence to do so.' ' Pry'thee, my dear,' replied her husband, ' don't be so rash; you don't know what folly a man may do in his passion.' "

The banking-house of Messrs. Drummond stands at the corner of Spring Gardens and Charing Cross. It was founded early in the eighteenth century, and is consequently one of the oldest West-end banks. At a day when it was customary for the younger sons of Scottish noblemen to seek their fortunes by commerce, Andrew Drummond, fifth son of Sir John Drummond, the third Laird of Machany, younger brother of the fourth Viscount Strathallan, came to London as an agent for some of the chief Jacobite houses, about the year 1713, and founded this business on the opposite side of Charing Cross as a banker and a goldsmith. The business was removed to its present site a year or two afterwards. Mr. A. Drummond is represented by Malcolm, in his "Genealogical Memoirs of the House of Drummond," as a man of great integrity and ability. He married a Miss Strahan, daughter of a London banker, and bequeathed the business to his three sons. Messrs. Drummond have had, and still have, a large Scottish connection.

Mr. Peter Cunningham tells us that the founder of Drummond's bank obtained his great position by advancing money to the Pretender, and by the king's consequent withdrawal of his account. This step on the part of the king led to a rush of the Scottish nobility and gentry with their accounts to Charing Cross, and to the ultimate advancement of the bank to its present position.

There is a tradition in the house that Sir Robert Walpole, in his zeal for the House of Hanover, wished to inspect the books of Messrs. Drummond's bank, in order to keep his eye on the adherents of the Pretender. It is needless to add that his wish was not gratified, and Mr. Drummond, on meeting Sir Robert soon afterwards at Court, turned his back on the Minister, in order to mark his sense of the affront; and the King, so far from being offended with him, showed Mr. Drummond a special mark of his royal favour, either then or at a later date.

On one occasion, it is said, Messrs. Drummond refused to advance the sum of £500 to the Princess of Wales, when she was in pecuniary difficulties. Hence that lady writes to a friend :—"Messrs. Drummond certainly shall not be the banker to George IV.'s Queen; for any historian, who would write the biography of the ex-Princess of Wales, would not a little astonish the world, in relating that she could not procure the sum of £500, at the rate of paying £500 a *year* per annum for it!!" It is only fair to add that this statement, coming from an angry lady's pen, may very possibly be mere gossip and scandal after all.

There is a portrait of the founder of the bank, painted by Zoffany; an engraved copy of it hangs in the inner room of the bank. Pope had an account at this bank, though few poets of modern times are so fortunate as to enjoy the luxury of a banker. The bank was rebuilt in 1881.

In 1810, the old Duke and Duchess of Brunswick, the parents of Princess (afterwards Queen) Caroline, were living in a dingy and old-fashioned house in New Street. Neither the road nor the royal carriages would appear to have been of the best, for we find one of the ladies of the princess's suite at Kensington writing thus to a friend. "We rumbled in her (the princess's) old tub all the way to New Street, Spring Gardens, much to the discomfiture of my bones . . . We were ushered into the dirtiest room I ever beheld, nearly empty and devoid of comfort. A few filthy lamps stood on a sideboard, common chairs were placed around very dingy walls, and in the middle of this empty space sat the old duchess, a melancholy spectacle of decayed royalty."

In New Street lived Sir Astley Cooper, in the height of his fame as a surgeon. Excellent as was his surgical skill, he liked to display it, and was often accused of a sort of anatomical sleight of hand. "No one," writes the author of the "Family Joe Miller," "will deny that the first requisite for an operating surgeon is nerve, and that to a degree which appears to spectators to amount to want of feeling. Sir Astley Cooper possessed this quality thoroughly. He always retained perfect self-possession in the operating theatre; and his unrivalled manual dexterity was not more obvious than his love of display during his most critical and dangerous *performances* on the patient, whose courage he tried to keep up by lively and facetious remarks. When Sir Astley was in the zenith of his fame, a satirical Sawbones sang thus :—

' Nor Drury Lane, nor Common Garden,
  Are, to my fancy, worth a farden ;
    I hold them both small beer.
  Give me the wonderful exploits,
  And jolly jokes between the sleights,
    Of *Astley's Amphitheatre.*' "

In 1815 Sir Astley Cooper settled in Spring Gardens, and a few years afterwards he was employed professionally by George IV. He long enjoyed a very large share of public patronage, and his reputation both at home and abroad was such as rarely falls to the lot of a professional man.

Lord Campbell—then "plain John Campbell"—was living in New Street, Spring Gardens, in his early Parliamentary days, 1830–35. In the same street, at the same time, lived Sir James Scarlett (afterwards Lord Abinger), whose daughter Campbell married, and whom he helped to raise to the peerage. Joseph Jekyll, the witty contemporary of Selwyn and friend of the Prince Regent, was also an inhabitant of New Street.

In the reign of William III. we find some of the French Huguenot refugees established in Spring Gardens Chapel. The chapel itself was set on fire in the year 1726, when King George I. was in Hanover; and his son, the Prince of Wales (afterwards George II.), happening to take an active part in the work of extinguishing it, the following epigram was written off-hand by Nicholas Rowe, with a covert comparison or rather contrast of the Prince of Wales with Nero, who "fiddled while Rome burnt :"—

> "Thy guardian, blest Britannia, scorns to sleep,
> When the sad subjects of his father weep.
> Weak princes by their fears increase distress :
> He faces danger, and so makes it less.
> Tyrants on blazing towns may smile with joy,
> George knows to save is greater than destroy."

Great alarm was caused in the neighbourhood, as the chapel adjoined some depôts of gunpowder ; but these were saved. The chapel, however, and an inn called the "Thatched House Tavern" adjoining, were destroyed.

In 1731, a new chapel was built by the Hon. Edward Southwell. A chapel subsequently erected by one of the De Clifford family still stands at the corner of New Street ; it is dedicated to St. Matthew, and is a monument of the low architectural taste of the time ; it was styled a chapel-of-ease to St. Martin's parish, but it is to be feared that it proved in the event a frequent bone of clerical contention between Lord De Clifford and the Vicar of St. Martin's.

Nearly the whole of Spring Gardens is about to be removed, to make room for new public offices, and to form a thoroughfare from Whitehall to St. James's Park.

We have already spoken of the Tilt-yard, which formerly occupied part of the space now known as Spring Gardens. Close by it, in Stow's time, "were divers handsome houses lately built before the park." One of these "handsome houses" afterwards became Jenny Man's "Tilt-yard Coffee House," upon the site afterwards occupied by the Paymaster-General's office. It was the resort of military officers, until supplanted by "Slaughter's" in St. Martin's Lane, which more recently was, in its turn, ruined by the military clubs. The *Spectator* states that the mock military also frequented the Tilt-yard Coffee House—"fellows who figured in laced hats, black cockades, and scarlet suits ; and who manfully pulled the noses of such quiet citizens as wore not swords." As Theodore Hook wrote in "Sayings and Doings," no doubt with a retrospect of his own youthful days : "When he fell really in love, Bond Street lounges and loungers became a bore to him; he sickened at the notion of a jollification under the piazza ; and even the charms of the pretty pastry-cooks at Spring Gardens had lost their piquancy."

Warwick Street, built in 1681, was named after Sir Philip Warwick. Strype says that in his day it led to the back gate of the king's garden, "for

the conveniency of her late Majesty's principal gardener."

At the western end of this street, which formed a *cul de sac*, stood Warwick House, adjoining Carlton House Gardens, for some time the residence of the Princess Charlotte, in her girlish years, when heiress to the throne. Here she was brought up by Lady De Clifford, as her governess; and hence in 1814 she "bolted off" in a hackney coach to her mother's house at Connaught Place, from which it required the united pressure of the Lord Chancellor Eldon and the Archbishop of Canterbury (Dr. Manners Sutton) to induce her to return ; and even this was not accomplished without much difficulty and remonstrance from her friends, until an early hour next morning, when she was brought back in one of the royal carriages.

"On the 7th of July, 1814," to use Lady Brownlow's words in her "Reminiscences of a Septuagenarian," "all the London world was startled by hearing that the Princess Charlotte on the previous evening had left Warwick House unobserved, and gone off in a hackney coach to the Princess of Wales in Connaught Place. The cause of this sudden and unaccountable proceeding has never transpired to the world at large. That it was perfectly unexpected and unwished-for by the Princess of Wales there seems no doubt. The Duke of York, the Duke of Sussex, Lord Eldon, and Mr. Brougham all repaired to Connaught Place, and after several hours of discussion the Princess Charlotte returned to Warwick House."

We learn accidentally that the Lord Chancellor (Clarendon) was living at Warwick House in 1660, for in that year Pepys records the fact of having carried a letter thither to him from Whitehall.

In this street, close to where stood old "Warwick House," is to be seen a small public-house, with the sign of "The Two Chairmen"—referring, of course, to the time when "sedan chairs," or as they were commonly called "chairs," were in vogue.

At a time when Regent Street was not built, and when Bond Street was too near to Marylebone to be central, Spring Gardens were the head-quarters of those exhibitions which abound in town in "the season," and disappear at its close. Here, towards the end of the last century, the Incorporated Society of Arts held its exhibitions ; and "here in 1806," as Mr. Timbs reminds us, "at Wigley's Rooms, were shown Serre's Panorama of Boulogne, and other foreign cities, and sea pieces ; also Maillardet's automatic figures, including a harpsichord-player, a rope-dancer, and a singing bird. Here also was exhibited Marshall's 'Peristrophic' Panorama of the Battle of Waterloo"—so called because the spectators themselves were turned round by machinery whilst they viewed it. A similar contrivance more recently was adopted at the Coliseum, when the Panorama of London was exhibited here.

In the reign of Queen Anne there was to be seen "over against the Mews' Gate, at Charing Cross, close to the 'Spring Gardens,' by Royal permission, a collection of strange and wonderful creatures from most parts of the world, all alive." It certainly was most miscellaneous, including a black man, a dwarf, a pony only two feet odd inches high, several panthers, leopards, and jackalls, and last not least, "a strange monstrous creature brought from the coast of Brazil, having a head like a child, legs and arms very wonderful, and a long tail like a serpent, wherewith he feeds himself as an elephant does with his trunk." Mr. Frost, in his "Old Show-men," conjectures that this last-named "monstrous creature" may have been, after all, only a spider-monkey, one variety of which is said by Humboldt to use its prehensile tail for the purpose of picking insects out of crevices.

Among the other objects of curiosity exhibited here from time to time, not the least attractive was the "Mechanical and Picturesque Theatre," which was, as the advertisements of the day tell us, "illustrative of the effect of art in imitation of nature, in views of the island of St. Helena, the city of Paris, the passage of Mount St. Bernard, Chinese artificial fireworks, and a storm at sea."

"Punch," if not a native of this locality, at all events first here made his appearance in England. Mr. Frost, in his "Old Showmen of London," says: "The earliest notices of the representation in London of 'Punch's moral drama,' as an old comic song calls it, occur in the overseers' books of St. Martin's-in-the-Fields, for 1666 and 1667, in which there are four entries of sums ranging from twenty-two shillings and sixpence to fifty-two shillings and sixpence, as 'Received of Punchinello, yᵉ Italian popet player, for his booth at Charing Cross.'"

Somewhere on this side of Charing Cross, though its actual site is unknown, stood the tavern called the "Rummer," where Prior was found reading "Horace" when a boy. In 1685 it appears to have been kept by one Samuel Prior; and this would tally with what Dr. Johnson tells us in his "Lives of the Poets." Prior is supposed to have fallen, by his father's death, into the hands of his uncle, a vintner near Charing Cross, who sent him for some time to Dr. Busby, at Westminster School; but not intending to give him any education beyond that of the school, took him, when he was well educated in literature, to his own house, where the Earl of Dorset, celebrated for his patronage of genius,

found him by chance (as Burnet relates) reading Horace, and was so well pleased with his proficiency that he undertook the care and cost of his academical education. It is well known that all through his life the poet showed a strong propensity for tavern life and pleasures; and Johnson probably is not far from the truth when he adds: "A survey of the life and writings of Prior may exemplify a sentence which he doubtless well understood when he read Horace at his uncle's house. 'The vessel long retains the scent which it first receives;' for in his private relaxation he revived the tavern."

In mean lodgings over a shop close by the entrance to Spring Gardens, which down to our own times was a saddler's, died the celebrated divine and preacher, Dr. Isaac Barrow, one of the most illustrious scholars and writers; and his wit has been spoken of by no less an authority than Dr. Johnson, as the "finest thing in the language." We quote an instance of the doctor's ready wit. In meeting the Earl of Rochester one day, the worthy peer exclaimed, "Doctor, I am yours to the shoe-tie;" to which the clergyman replied, "My lord, I am yours to the ground." The peer rejoined, "Doctor, I am yours to the centre." "My lord," retorted the doctor, "I am yours to the antipodes." Determined not to be outdone, his lordship blasphemously added, "Doctor, I am yours to the lowest pit of hell;" on which Barrow turned on his heel and said, "And *there*, my lord, I leave you."

There is a tradition mentioned by Pyne, that with the intention of painting the proclamation of George III., Hogarth stood at a window near Charing Cross, making sketches of the yeomen of the guard, the heralds, and the sergeant and trumpeter's band, who had their rendezvous hard by. So, at least, says Mr. Timbs, who accepts the statement as probably true.

This would appear to have been the neighbourhood in which ingenious devices of new arts and trades abounded even in the Stuart era. Pepys writes, under date February 10, 1668-9:—"To the plaisterer's at Charing Cross, that casts heads and bodies in plaister: and there I had my whole face done; but I was vexed first to be forced to daub all my face over with pomatum. Thus was the mould made; but when it came off there was little pleasure in it as it looks in the mould, nor any resemblance, whatever there will be in the figure when I come to see it cast off."

In 1748 a female dwarf, the "Corsican Fairy," was shown in Cockspur Street, at half-a-crown a head, drawing almost as large levees as "General Tom Thumb" in our own days. In the same year was exhibited, "in a commodious room facing

Cragg's Court," a strange monstrosity, a "double cow." From the work of Mr. Frost, on "Old Showmen," we learn of yet another and still stranger sight exhibited in the same year at the "Heath Cock, at Charing Cross," namely, "a surprising young mermaid, taken on the coast of Aquapulca, which" (says the prospectus), "though the generality of mankind think there is no such thing, has been seen by the curious, who express their

with the "Mews" which adjoined it. It probably derived its name from some association with the Cock-pit at Whitehall, which we have already mentioned. As it now stands it is quite a modern street, having been built towards the close of the last or beginning of the present century.

As the tide of fashion gradually set westwards from Covent Garden, this street became more and more frequented by the wits and critics of *bon ton ;*

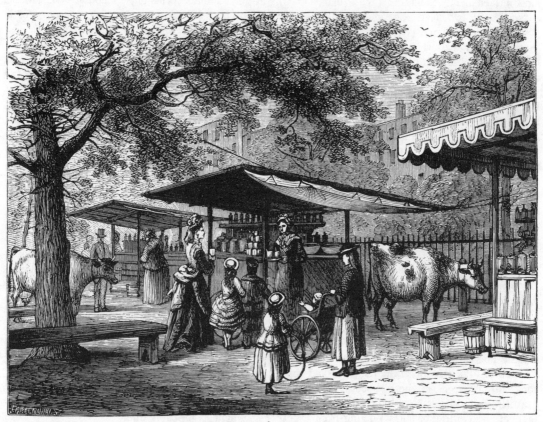

MILK FAIR, ST. JAMES'S PARK. (*See page* 76.)

utmost satisfaction at so uncommon a creature, being half like a woman and half like a fish, and is allowed to be the greatest curiosity ever exposed to the public view." Here, too, was exhibited O'Brien, the Irish giant, whom we have already mentioned (vol. iii., p. 46) ; and here he died.

In 1772, and again in 1775 and in 1779, in a large room in Cockspur Street, appeared the conjuror Breslau, whose tricks of legerdemain were interspersed with a vocal and instrumental concert, and imitations by an Italian, named Gaietano, of the notes of the "blackbird, thrush, canary, linnet, bullfinch, skylark, and nightingale."

The origin of the name of Cockspur Street is uncertain ; and Mr. Peter Cunningham can suggest no better derivation of it than a fancied connection

and among its most pleasant memories is the name of the "British Coffee House," which was largely frequented by gentlemen from "the north of the Tweed." Its northern connection, kept together by hosts and hostesses from Scotland, is incidentally to be gathered from a letter of Horace Walpole to his friend Sir H. Mann, in which, speaking of some Scottish question pending in the House of Lords, he writes :—"The Duke of Bedford . . . had writ to the sixteen [Scotch representative] peers to solicit their votes ; but with so little difference, that he enclosed all their letters under one cover, directed to the 'British Coffee House.'"

Concerning a dinner at this coffee-house, Mr. Cyrus Redding tells a sad story in his "Fifty Years' Reminiscences :"—"While on this short visit to town, the proprietors of the 'Pilot' gave a dinner to some of the officers of the Horse Guards at the 'British Coffee House.' After a sumptuous repast, in the fashion of the time, we sat down to wine. There was present a bustling little man, a Scotch colonel, named Macleod, with his son, a fine young

Mall East stands an equestrian statue of King George III. It is of bronze, between ten and eleven feet high, and stands upon a granite pedestal about twelve feet high. It was executed by Mr. Matthew C. Wyatt, and the cost of its erection amounted to £4,000, the sum being

WARWICK HOUSE, ABOUT 1810. (*See page* 82.)

man, about twenty years old, who sat by me. He was an only son, with a number of sisters. The bottle was pushed hard. The youth partook too freely for one of his years. He was seized with fever and died. The estate entailed went by his death to distant relatives; and his mother and sisters, who would have had to depend on him, were left penniless on the father's demise."

At the junction of Cockspur Street with Pall

defrayed by public subscription. It was set up about the year 1836. Although the likeness of the king is good, the statue is not generally admired, on account of its costume; and the pig-tail at the back of the royal head has often been made the subject of waggish and uncomplimentary remarks. Altogether, it can hardly be said that this statue is calculated to raise the credit of English sculpture in the eyes of foreign visitors.

CHAPTER VIII.

CARLTON HOUSE.

"At domus interior regali splend?da luxu
Instruitur."   *Virgil: Æneid.*

Carlton House in the Reign of George II.—A Facetious Remark—The Screen, or Colonnade—The Building described—The Gardens—The Riding House—"Big Sam," the Royal Porter—Carlton House from a Foreigner's Point of View—A Secret Conclave—The Miniature Court of Frederick Prince of Wales—Carlton House occupied by the Princess of Wales—Lord Bute—Carlton House a Focus of Political Faction—How the Marriage of the Prince of Wales and the Princess Caroline was brought about—The Regency of George IV.—Mrs. Fitzherbert—The Reckless Way in which the Princess of Wales would speak of her Unhappy Life—The *Début* of Princess Charlotte—The Prince of Orange and Prince Leopold of Belgium—Death of Princess Charlotte—Life at Carlton House under the Regency—"Romeo" Coates—George Colman, the Younger—"Beau Brummell"—General Arabin—Mike Kelly, the Actor—Death of George III. and Proclamation of the New King—Demolition of Carlton House—Carlton Terrace and its Principal Residents.

As stated in the previous chapter, the north side of the Mall, in St. James's Park, is nearly all occupied by the lofty mansions of Carlton House Terrace. They cover the site of Carlton House, the palace of Frederick, Prince of Wales, father of George III., and subsequently for many years the residence of George IV., when Prince of Wales. The building is mentioned by the author of the "New Critical Review of the Public Buildings" in the reign of George II., as "now belonging to his Royal Highness," meaning Prince Frederick. He describes it as "most delightfully situated for a palace of elegant and costly pleasure," adding, however, that "the building itself is tame and poor," and that "hardly any place is capable of greater improvements, and hardly any place stands in more need of them."

The house was distinguished by a row of pillars in front; whilst York (now Dover) House, Whitehall, the residence of the Prince's brother, the Duke of York, was marked by a circular court, serving as a sort of entry hall, which still remains. These two buildings being described to Lord North, who was blind during the latter period of his life, he facetiously remarked, "Then the Duke of York has been sent, as it would seem, to the *Round-House*, and the Prince of Wales to the *Pillory*." John Timbs attributes this *bon mot* to Sheridan.

The house itself stood opposite what is now Waterloo Place, looking northward, and the forecourt was divided from Pall Mall by a long range of columns, handsome in themselves, but supporting nothing. Hence the once famous lines—

"Care Colonne, qui state qua?
Non sapiamo in verità:"

thus Anglicised by Prince Hoare—

"Dear little columns, all in a row,
What *do* you do there?
Indeed we don't know."

Lord North's allusion to these columns, quoted above, was scarcely much more complimentary.

This screen, or colonnade, of single pillars, with the long line of cornice or entablature which rested upon them, formed a disagreeable impediment to the view of the front of the palace. "When I first saw England," writes Thackeray in "The Four Georges," "she was in mourning for the young Princess Charlotte, the hope of the empire. With my childish attendant I remember peeping through the colonnade at Carlton House, and seeing the abode of the Prince Regent. I can yet see the guards pacing before the gates of the palace. What palace? The palace exists no more than the palace of Nebuchadnezzar. It is but a name now."

The façade of the palace consisted of a centre and two wings, rusticated, without pilasters, and an entablature and balustrade which concealed the roof. The portico, by Holland, was of the Corinthian order, consisting of six columns, with details taken from the Temple of Jupiter Stator, in the Forum at Rome. Above this was an enriched frieze, and a tympanum, adorned with the Prince's arms. All the windows were plain and without pediments, except two in the wings.

There were in the building several magnificent apartments, which were fitted up and furnished in the most luxurious manner; and there was also an armoury, said to be the finest in the world. The collection was so extensive as to occupy five rooms, and consisted of specimens of whatever was curious and rare in the arms of every nation, with many choice specimens of ancient armour.

The building was modernised at a vast expense in the year 1788, and in 1815 further alterations were made in the interior. The edifice at this period is thus described in the "Beauties of England and Wales:"—"From the hall, which is exceedingly magnificent, you pass through an octagonal room, richly and tastefully ornamented, conducting to the grand suite of apartments on the one side, and to the great staircase on the other. The latter cannot be seen till you advance close to it, when the most brilliant effect is produced by the magical management of the light. Opposite the entrance is a flight of twelve steps, thirteen feet long, and on either side of the landing-place at the top of these is another flight of steps of the same length, which takes a circular sweep up to the chamber floor. Underneath is another staircase descending to the lower apartments. On a level with the first floor are eight divisions, arched over; two of these are occupied by Time pointing to the hours on a dial; and Æolus supporting a map of a circular form, with the points of the compass marked round it. The central division forms the entrance to an ante-room; and the others are adorned with female figures of bronze, in the form of termini, supporting lamps. The railing is particularly rich, glittering with ornaments of gold, intermixed with bronze heads. The skylight is embellished with rich painted glass, in panes of circles, lozenges, Prince's plumes, roses, &c."

One of the most splendid apartments in the palace was the crimson drawing-room, in which the Princess Charlotte was married, in 1816, to Prince Leopold of Saxe-Coburg. This apartment was embellished with the most valuable pictures of the ancient and modern schools, bronzes, ormolu furniture, &c. The other state apartments on the upper floor were the circular cupola room, of the Ionic order; the throne-room, of the Corinthian order; the splendid ante-chamber; the rose-satin drawing-room, &c., all of which were furnished and embellished with the richest satins, carvings, cut-glass, carpetings, &c. On the lower level, towards the gardens and St. James's Park, were other equally splendid suites of apartments, used by the Court for domestic purposes, and for more familiar parties. These rooms, which were designed by Mr. Nash, consisted of a grand vestibule, of the Corinthian order; the Golden Drawing-room, the Gothic Dining-room, a splendid Gothic Conservatory, and the Library.

The mansion was first erected for Lord Carlton, in 1709, and was bequeathed to his nephew, the Earl of Burlington, from whom it was purchased by Frederick, Prince of Wales, in 1732. The house in its original state was of red brick, and differed but little from any of the houses of noblemen and gentlemen which surrounded it. The necessary alterations for the reception of the Prince were at once begun, and the palace was new-fronted with stone. Flitcroft is said to have drawn for the Prince, in 1734, a plan intended as an improvement on the existing house; and Kent designed a cascade in the same year for the garden, where a saloon was afterwards erected, and paved

with Italian marble brought to England by Lord Bingley and Mr. George Dodington. The walls were adorned with statuary and paintings, and the chair of state was of crimson velvet embroidered with gold, said to have cost five hundred pounds. Rysbrack sculptured statues of Alfred and Edward the Black Prince, which were placed on marble pedestals in the garden. The grounds, which extended westward as far as Marlborough House, were in summer a perfect mass of umbrageous foliage; and in them men of the last generation remember to have heard nightingales singing. Indeed, the grove of trees was so tall and so thick, that it contained a rookery so lately as the year 1827. This fact is commemorated by some amusing verses entitled "The Emigration of the Rooks from Carlton Gardens," published in "Hone's Table Book," in that year.

Adjoining the palace was a Riding House, which, when the palace was demolished, was allowed to stand for some years, and was converted into a storehouse for some of the public records. It was long known as Carlton Ride. Its antiquarian contents were subsequently transferred to the great central building in Fetter Lane.

In one of the lodges dwelt "Big Sam," the royal porter to George III. and IV.; he is said to have stood nearly eight feet high.

The whole of Carlton House was pulled down in 1828, in order to make room for the central opening of Waterloo Place. Some of the Corinthian columns, which formed the colonnade in front of the house, were used in the portico of the National Gallery, and others were made use of in the chapel at Buckingham Palace.

The author of an amusing "Tour of a Foreigner in England," published in 1825, thus expresses himself (or herself) with respect to Carlton House:— "Though the royal or government palaces are among the most remarkable in London, they serve to show how little the dignity of the sovereign is respected in England in comparison with other countries of Europe. To say nothing of St. James's Palace (which the present sovereign has not thought fit for his residence) there are in Paris many hotels preferable to Carlton House. This pretended palace is adorned with a Corinthian portico, the elegance of which, at first glance, pleases the eye, but its columns support nothing except the entablature which unites them. On one of these pillars an Italian artist chalked the following lines in the name of Pasquin and Marfori:—

'Belle colonne che fate la?
Io no lo so en verita.' "

The shadowy and extravagant court kept up

here by Frederick, as described by one who knew several of its members, Sir N. W. Wraxall, was not such as to convey a very favourable impression of the good sense of the father of George III. "His court," writes that author, "seems to have been the centre of Cabal, torn by contending candidates for the guidance of his future imaginary reign. The Earl of Egmont and Dodington were avowedly at the head of two great hostile parties. In November, 1749, we find his royal highness, in a secret conclave held at Carlton House, making all the financial dispositions proper to be adopted on the demise of the king his father, and even framing a new Civil List. At the close of these deliberations he binds his three assistants to abide by and support his plans, giving them his hand, and making them take each other's hands as well. The transaction, as related by Dodington, who was himself one of the party, reminds the reader of a similar convocation commemorated by Sallust, and is not unlike one of the scenes in 'Venice Preserved.' It was performed after dinner, however, which may perhaps form its best apology. The diversions of the prince's court appear equally puerile. Three times within thirteen months preceding his decease, Dodington accompanied him and the Princess of Wales to fortune-tellers; the last of which frolics took place scarcely nine weeks before his death. After one of these magical consultations, apparently dictated by anxiety to penetrate his future destiny, the party supped with Mrs. Connor, the Princess's midwife. From Carlton House, too, Frederick used to go disguised to Hockley-in-the-Hole to witness bull-baiting; and either Lord Middlesex or Lord John Sackville was commonly his companion on such expeditions. As far as we are authorised from these premises to form a conclusion, his premature death before he ascended the throne ought not to excite any great national regret."

It was partly at Carlton House that Frederick, Prince of Wales, in the lifetime of his father George II., held his miniature court, and amused himself with sketching out future administrations, in which his friends the Duke of Queensberry, the Earl of Middlesex, "Jack" Spencer, Lord John Sackville, and Francis, Earl of Guildford, were to have their parts. Sir N. W. Wraxall tells us in his "Memoirs" that Lady Archibald Hamilton, the Prince's *chere amie*, resided close to Carlton House, the Prince having allowed her to construct some apartments, the windows of which commanded a view over the gardens of that house, and which, indeed, communicated with the house itself.

Among the guests here in the time of Frederick, Prince of Wales, was Pope, who paid his royal highness very many compliments. "I wonder," said the Prince, "that you, who are so severe on kings, should be so complimentary to me." "Oh, sir," replied the crafty poet, "that is because I like the lion before his claws are full grown."

After the accession of George III. Carlton House was occupied by the Princess of Wales; and hither the young king was accustomed to repair of an evening, and pass the hours with his mother and her special favourite, Lord Bute, the world supposing that the trio formed a sort of interior cabinet, which controlled and directed the ostensible administration. Here, too, the lucky Scotchman whom good fortune, almost in a jest, raised to the premiership, used to pay his mysterious visits to the Princess of Wales—the mother of George III.—in Miss Vansittart's sedan chair, to the great scandal of the entire court.

The extraordinary degree of favour accorded to Lord Bute, and the predilection with which he was known to be regarded by the Princess of Wales, afforded fuel to popular discontent; and the public mind was inflamed by a series of satirical prints, in which her royal highness was held up to odium and reproach, the most odious comparisons being drawn between the Premier and herself and Mortimer and the Queen-Dowager Isabella, of the time of Edward III. The *North Briton* employed the pen of most powerful satire in the same direction.

One of the maids of honour in the establishment of the Princess of Wales at this house was Miss Elizabeth Chudleigh, better known a few years later as the Duchess of Kingston. When reproached for some irregularities by her royal mistress, whose *penchant* for the society of Lord Bute was notorious, she replied, with her usual wit and insolence, "Ah! madame, votre altesse royale sait bien que chacune ici a son *But*."

It is well known that throughout his boyhood and youth, and even in his early manhood, George III. lived a very quiet and secluded life: how quiet and how secluded, may be gathered from Sir N. W. Wraxall's "Memoirs of his Own Time." He writes: "During near ten years which elapsed between the death of his father, early in 1751, and the decease of his grandfather, a period when the human mind is susceptible of such deep impressions, he remained in a state of almost absolute seclusion from his future people, and from the world. Constantly resident at Leicester House or at Carlton House when he was in London; immured at Kew whenever he went to the country; perpetually under the eye of his mother and of Lord Bute, who acted in the choicest unity of design; he saw comparatively few other persons, and those only chosen individuals of both sexes. They naturally obtained, and long preserved, a very firm ascendancy over him. When he ascended the throne, though already arrived at manhood, his very person was hardly known, and his character was still less understood, beyond a narrow circle. Precautions, it is well ascertained, were even adopted by the Princess-dowager to preclude as much as possible access to him, precautions which, to the extent of her ability, were redoubled after he became king. It will scarcely be believed, but it is nevertheless true, that in order to prevent him from conversing with any persons, or receiving written intimations, anonymous or otherwise, between the drawing-room and the door of Carlton House, when he was returning from thence to St. James's or Buckingham House after his evening visits to his mother, she never failed to accompany him till he got into his sedan-chair."

Carlton House, from time to time, proved a focus of political faction. Sir N. W. Wraxall describes with great minuteness the entertainment given here by the Prince of Wales in May, 1784, in honour of the return of Fox for Westminster, after a prolonged and exciting contest in which both parties put forth all their strength. In order to give piquancy to the event, the Prince chose the day after the election, when all the rank, beauty, and talent of the opposition (Whig) party were assembled by invitation on the lawn of his palace for the *fête*, precisely at the time when the King, his father, was proceeding in state down St. James's Park to open the new Parliament. The wall of Carlton Gardens, and that barrier only, formed the separation between them. Then, while the younger part of the company were more actively engaged, there might be contemplated under the shade of the trees an exhibition such as fancy places in the Elysian Fields. . . Lord North, dressed, like every other individual invited, in his new livery of buff and blue, beheld himself surrounded by those very persons who, scarcely fifteen months earlier, affected to regard him as an object of national execration, deserving of capital punishment. Lord Derby and Lord Beauchamp, two noblemen long opposed to each other, Colonel North and George Byng, lately the most inveterate enemies, Fitzpatrick and Adam, depositing their animosities at the Prince's feet, or either at the altar of ambition or interest—were here seen to join in perfect harmony."

A few days afterwards, a second banquet even more magnificent was given by the Prince in the same interest—antagonistic, of course, to his father and his father's ministers—"a banquet," if we may believe the same writer, "prolonged, in defiance of usage and almost of human nature, from the noon of one day to the following morning. Every production," adds the gossiping writer, "that taste and luxury could assemble, was exhausted, the foreign ministers resident in London assisting at the celebration. A splendid banquet was served up to the ladies, on whom, in the spirit of chivalry, his royal highness and the gentlemen present waited while they were seated at table. It must be owned that on these occasions, for which he seemed peculiarly formed, the Prince appeared to great advantage. Louis XIV. himself could scarcely have eclipsed the son of George III. in a ball-room, or when doing the honours of his palace, surrounded by the pomp and attributes of luxury and royal state."

Here, also, in 1789, the Prince used to give dinners on Saturdays and Sundays to the hangers-on of the Whig party, in the hope of confirming them in their allegiance to Fox. The guests were often thirty or forty in number. Sir N. W. Wraxall says, "Wine, promises, and personal attentions were not spared. Governments, regiments, offices, preferments, titles, here held out in prospect, retained the wavering and allured the credulous and discontented; private negotiations were likewise set on foot to gain over supporters to the Government." Here the Prince of Wales, in 1789, received the deputation from the House of Commons, with Pitt at its head, which first offered the Regency to his acceptance.

It is well known that George II. and his eldest son, Frederick, Prince of Wales, during several years previous to the early death of the latter, lived "at daggers drawn" with each other, and without even the veil of decency being drawn before their expressions of mutual dislike. To a certain extent, though not to the same degree, the court of Carlton House under George IV., as Prince of Wales, was maintained in constant hostility to that of the King his father at St. James's and at Kew.

In Mr. T. Raikes's "Journal," we get some insight of the manner in which the unfortunate marriage of the Prince of Wales was brought about. The author, as he tells us, was often in the company of the Duke of Wellington, who talked much about the Royal Family in his time, and on one occasion more especially with reference to the above marriage. "'The marriage,' he said, 'was brought about by Lady ——, who exercised great influence over him: the Prince, who was easily led, imparted his wishes to the King, which were immediately and readily complied with; and as soon as his marriage was accomplished with the Princess Caroline of Brunswick, Lady —— promoted their separation.' I said that this was amply corroborated by what I had lately read in Lord Malmesbury's Papers, who was selected by King George III. to go over to Brunswick, to make the formal proposals and bring the bride over to England. They had a wretched journey home, accompanied by the old Duchess, attempting to go through Holland, and embark at Rotterdam, where the squadron was waiting for

Queen Caroline on reaching England could not speak a word of English. So Samuel Rogers tells us in his "Diary."

It is impossible at this interval of time to conceive the bitterness with which Queen Caroline was assailed by the Tory press, at the head of which,

GRAND STAIRCASE IN CARLTON HOUSE, 1820. (*See page* 87.)

them, but they were stopped by the French armies, and confined for a long time at a miserable Dutch inn, where they met with so many hardships, that the old Duchess was taken ill, and obliged to return home. Lord M——— and his charge were also forced to beat a retreat, countermand the orders given to the men-of-war, and, after six or seven weeks' miserable adventures, they at last embarked at Embden and arrived in England."

for wit and influence, stood the *John Bull*, with Theodore Hook as its editor. It is with a dash of dry humour that Hook's biographer, in an article in the *Quarterly*, makes these observations:— "There is little to be said in defence of the early virulences of *John Bull* except that they were, we believe without exception, directed against the Queen and her prominent partisans; and that the Whig leaders, both in Parliament and in society,

FRONT OF CARLTON HOUSE, 1820. (*See page 86.*)

had, from the commencement of the Regency, countenanced attacks equally malignant on the private life and circle of George IV.—nay, encouraged, in times then freshly remembered, the long series of libels by which the virtues and the afflictions of King George III. were turned into matter of contemptuous sport. The truth is, the Liberals—as they about this period began to style themselves—had shown a fervid desire to domineer in a haughty monopoly of wicked wit : their favourites among the literati almost resented any interference with it as an intolerable invasion of 'vested rights.' The ultimate result of the struggle was, we think, highly beneficial to both parties. In the words of Thomas Moore—

> ' As work like this was unbefitting,
> And flesh and blood no longer bore it,
> The Court of Common Sense then sitting
> Summoned the culprits both before it.'

On either side, when there came coolness enough for measuring the mutual offences and annoyances, all persons of influence seem to have concurred in the determination that such things should no longer be tolerated."

On the meeting of both Houses of Parliament on the 30th of November, 1810, a report of the physicians on the state of the King's health was brought in and laid before the members. The final issue of all the debates which followed was, that the Prince of Wales should be Regent, under certain restrictions ; and that the Queen should have the care of the King's person, her Majesty being assisted by a council. The ceremony of conferring the regency on the Prince was performed at Carlton House with great pomp, on the 5th of February, 1811 ; and in the following June, the Prince Regent gave here a grand supper to 2,000 guests, a stream with gold and silver fish flowing through a marble canal down the central table.

One of the first acts of the Regent, after his being sworn in in due form before the Privy Council, was to receive here the address of the Lord Mayor and Common Council of the City of London on the occasion ; and as he on the same day held a council, all the Ministers of State were present, when it was read in a very solemn manner. The address of the City was partly condoling and partly congratulatory. Among the grievances was specified " the present representation in the Commons House of Parliament, a reform in which was necessary for the safety of the Crown, the happiness of the people, and the independence of the country." To this the Prince Regent returned a kind and dignified answer, assuring the City that he should esteem it as the happiest moment of his life, when he could

resign the powers delegated to him into the hands of his sovereign, and that he should always listen to the complaints of those who thought themselves aggrieved.

The household of the Prince Regent here was full of bickerings and quarrels. As a proof of the absurd stress laid by his Royal Highness upon the merest trifles, it may be mentioned that on one occasion the sub-governess of the Princess Charlotte was obliged to resign her situation at Court because her youthful ward, in a freak, had made a childish will in rhyme, leaving her poll parrot to ———, and all her *non*-valuables to Miss Campbell, as residuary legatee. Indeed, it is said by Miss Amelia Murray, in her " Recollections," that the sub-governess was even accused before the Privy Council of treason, for allowing the heiress presumptive to the throne to make a will, even in jest ! It is to be hoped that the authoress is guilty here of a little feminine exaggeration.

The Princess of Wales herself, as is too well known, had anything but happiness in her married life. On one occasion, as we learn from the " Diary of the Times of George IV.," when all her Royal Highness' ladies had been invited by the Prince Regent to a *fête*, from which she herself was excluded, she presented each of them with a very handsome dress ; and to one her Royal Highness wrote : " Dear ———, pray do me de favour to accept and wear de accompanying gown ; and when you are in de ball at Carlton House, tink of me, and wish me well. For ever your affectionate, C. R."

If the Prince ever really cared for any woman, it was for Mrs. Fitzherbert. After his accession to the throne, and the trial of Queen Caroline, he shut himself up almost wholly from the public gaze, and lived chiefly within the walls of Carlton House, his table being presided over by the beautiful Marchioness of Conyngham, whose brilliant wit, according to his Majesty's estimate, surpassed that of all his friends, male or female.

The Princess of Wales always spoke highly of Mrs. Fitzherbert ; she would say :—" That is the Prince's true wife ; she is an excellent woman ; it is a great pity for him he ever broke vid her. Do you know, I know de man who was present at his marriage, the late Lord Bradford. He declared to a friend of mine, that when he went to inform Mrs. Fitzherbert that the Prince had married me, she would not believe it, for she knew she was herself married to him."

The author of " Memories of the Times of George IV." mentions several instances of the unguarded and reckless way in which the Princess would speak of the situation in which she was then placed, and also of her previous life. She would dwell, in conversation with her friends, on the drunken habits of her husband, which were then notorious to the world. How he spent the first night of his marriage in a state of intoxication is known by all the readers of the "Memories" above mentioned, the author of which says that after the birth of the Princess Charlotte, the unhappy lady received through Lord Cholmondeley a message to the effect that in future the Prince and she would occupy separate establishments. "Poor Princess!" continues the writer, "she was an ill-treated woman, but a very wrong-headed one. Had she remained quietly at Carlton House, and conducted herself with silent dignity, how different might have been her lot. It is true, as her Privy Purse, Miss Hamilton, once told a person of my acquaintance, she was so insulted whilst there, that every bit of furniture was taken out of the room she dined in, except two shabby chairs; and the pearl bracelets, which had been given her by the Prince, were taken from her to decorate the arms of Lady Jersey. Still, had the Princess had the courage which arises from principle, and not that which is merely the offspring of a daring spirit, she would have sat out the storm, and weathered it."

For the following description of the *début* of the Princess Charlotte at Carlton House in the year 1813, we are indebted to Captain Gronow, who was present as a guest. He writes: "At the period to which I refer, Carlton House was the centre of all the great politicians and wits who were friends of the Prince Regent. The principal entrance of the palace in Pall Mall, with its screen of columns, will be remembered by many. In the rear of the mansion was an extensive garden that reached from Warwick Street to Marlborough House; green sward, stately trees (probably two hundred years old), and beds of the choicest flowers, gave to the grounds a picturesque attraction perhaps unequalled. It was here that the heir to the throne of England gave, in 1813, an open-air *fête*, in honour of the battle of Vittoria. About three o'clock p.m. the *élite* of London society, who had been honoured with invitations, began to arrive— all in full dress; the ladies particularly displaying their diamonds and pearls, as if they were going to a drawing-room. The men were, of course, in full dress, wearing knee-buckles. The regal circle was composed of the Queen, the Regent, the Princesses Sophia and Mary, the Princess Charlotte, the Dukes of York, Clarence, Cumberland, and Cambridge.

"This was the first day that her Royal Highness the Princess Charlotte appeared in public. She was a young lady of more than ordinary personal attractions; her features were regular, and her complexion fair, with the rich bloom of youthful beauty; her eyes were blue and very expressive, and her hair was abundant, and of that peculiar light brown which merges into the golden; in fact, such hair as the middle-age Italian painters associate with their conceptions of the Madonna. In figure her royal highness was somewhat over the ordinary height of women, but finely proportioned and well developed. Her manners were remarkable for a simplicity and good-nature which would have won admiration and invited affection in the most humble walks of life. She created universal admiration, and I may say a feeling of national pride, amongst all who attended the ball. The Prince Regent entered the gardens giving his arm to the Queen, the rest of the royal family following. Tents had been erected in various parts of the grounds, where the bands of the Guards were stationed. The weather was magnificent, a circumstance which contributed to show off the admirable arrangements of Sir Benjamin Bloomfield, to whom had been deputed the organisation of the *fête*, which commenced by dancing on the lawn.

"The Princess Charlotte honoured with her presence two dances. In the first she accepted the hand of the late Duke of Devonshire, and in the second that of the Earl of Aboyne, who had danced with Marie Antoinette, and who, as Lord Huntly, lived long enough to dance with Queen Victoria. The Princess entered so much into the spirit of the *fête* as to ask for the new fashionable Scotch dances. The Prince was dressed in the Windsor uniform, and wore the garter and star. He made himself very amiable, and conversed much with the Ladies Hertford, Cholmondeley, and Montfort. Altogether, the *fête* was a very memorable event."

Lady Clementina Davies writes in her "Recollections of Society:"—"The Princess Charlotte was treated by all parties as the brightest hope of England. When she made her *début* at Carlton House a brilliant circle attended. The Queen, the Regent, the Princesses, and the four Royal Dukes, were there, but all eyes were engrossed by the royal girl."

The Princess could not well help resenting the affronts offered to her mother. Indeed, as a child, and throughout her girlhood, she had a most difficult part to play, for, as she often used to say, "if she showed affection or respect for one of her parents, she tacitly blamed the other, and, of course, was blamed in return."

It has often been asked what induced the Princess Charlotte so suddenly to give his *congé* to the Prince of Orange, and suddenly to accept Prince Leopold of Saxe-Coburg in his stead. The Hon. Amelia Murray in her "Recollections," writing of the visit of the Allied Sovereigns in 1814, thus solves the mystery :—"The Prince of Orange was not particularly attractive ; Prince Leopold, on the contrary, was a handsome young man, though not then specially noticed ; but very soon it was discovered that the Princess Charlotte preferred him to her former lover. Small blame to the young Princess ! but I have strong reason to believe that it was through a Russian intrigue that she had been thrown in the way of the handsomest prince in Germany, and that the Grand Duchess of Russia came here for the purpose of disgusting the Princess of England with her intended husband. It did not suit Russian views that England and Holland should be so closely connected. The Grand Duchess of Oldenburg came to this country, I verily believe, for the purpose of ' putting a spoke into that wheel.' She took an hotel in Piccadilly ; she earnestly sought the acquaintance of Miss Elphinstone, who was known to be on intimate terms with the Princess. She gave grand dinners, and took care to invite the Prince of Orange on the night when he was to waltz in public with the Princess as her *fiancé*. The Grand Duchess plied him well with champagne, and a young man could hardly refuse the invitations of his hostess. In fact, he was made tipsy, and the Princess was disgusted. Then, in Miss Elphinstone's apartments, the charming Prince Leopold was presented. Was it to be wondered at that a girl of seventeen should prefer him to the former lover ? The Prince of Orange accordingly was speedily dismissed, and in due time he married the Duchess of Oldenburg's sister. This intrigue accounts for all that happened subsequently."

The story of the engagement of the Princess Charlotte to Prince Leopold of Saxe-Coburg is told, however, somewhat differently in the gossiping pages of Captain Gronow's "Anecdotes and Reminiscences." He writes : "The Duke of York said one day to his royal niece, ' Tell me, my dear, have you seen any one among the foreign princes whom you would like to have for a husband ?' The Princess replied, with much *naïveté*, that she was most agreeably struck with Prince Leopold of Coburg. She had heard of his bravery in the field, and especially of his famous charge in the battle of Leipsic, for which he was rewarded by the Order of Maria Theresa. In a few months afterwards she became the wife of the man whom she so

much admired, and from whom she was so soon afterwards torn away by the hand of death." It will be remembered that she died in childbirth having given birth to a dead infant. Her death was felt as a blow by the whole nation. Miss Amelia Murray, who held a post at Court, and may be supposed to have been well informed on such subjects, does not hesitate to express her opinion that "the Princess Charlotte was starved to death," her medical attendant, Sir Richard Croft, having forbidden her to eat meat so as to keep up her strength. Sir Richard was so much affected by the calamity that he committed suicide shortly afterwards.

It was wittily said of those who were admitted in former days to the circle of Carlton House, that they learnt there the value of being good listeners, or else afterwards came to lament the want of that qualification. Hear what you like, but say as little as possible, was the rule with that gay and heartless coterie who gathered round the Prince Regent in those gilded *salons*.

Cyrus Redding wrote in the *Times* a witty "Dialogue between Carlton House and Brandenburg House," which caused a sensation in town.

The following is an extract from a letter dated February 23rd, 1812 :—" The Prince Regent went yesterday in grand state to the Chapel Royal—the first time of his appearance as virtual sovereign. As he proceeded from Carlton House to St. James's surrounded by all his pomp, &c., not a single huzza from the crowd assembled to behold him ! Not a hat off ! Of this I was assured by a gentleman present, on whom I can depend."

Of the Prince Regent himself, who so long held his court here, Captain Gronow, who was much behind the scenes, has but little that is favourable to say. According to the Captain's anecdotes, the Prince, so far from being "the first gentleman in Europe," was "singularly imbued with a petty and vulgar pride. He would rather be amiable and familiar with his tailor than agreeable and friendly with the most illustrious of the aristocracy of the kingdom ; and would rather joke with ' Beau ' Brummell than admit to his confidence a Howard or a Somerset. And yet he took good care always to show good manners in public. His misfortune was his marriage with a most unattractive and almost repulsive woman, Caroline of Brunswick ; and his debts were at the bottom of his ill-starred union. He sold himself, in fact, for a million sterling."

Sir N. W. Wraxall tells a good anecdote about Lord Carhampton, who, as Colonel Luttrell, had contested the representation of Middlesex against

John Wilkes:—"In 1812, soon after the restrictions imposed by Parliament on the Prince Regent were withdrawn, Lord Carhampton was lying in an apparently hopeless state at his house near Berkeley Square, whence premature intelligence of his death was carried by some officious person to Carlton House. The Prince, who was at dinner at the time, immediately gave away his regiment, the Carabineers, to a general officer present, who actually 'kissed hands' on his appointment. No sooner did the report reach Lord Carhampton next day, than he dispatched a friend to Pall Mall with a message for the Prince, informing his Royal Highness that he was still happily in the land of the living, and humbly entreating him to dispose of any other regiment in the service except the Carabineers. Lord Carhampton, with much humour, added, that the Prince might rest assured that, in case of his own death, he would give special directions to his servants to lose not a moment, when he was really no more, in notifying the fact at Carlton House. The Prince very much enjoyed the joke, and Lord Carhampton got well enough to laugh at it in his company."

Another story is told of one of Theodore Hook's hoaxes, the scene of which was Carlton House under the Regency. On the 17th of June, the Prince gave here a *fête* of "surpassing magnificence." "Romeo" Coates was at this time in all his glory—murdering Shakespeare at the Haymarket, and driving his bright-pink cockle-shell, with the life-like chanticleers in gilt traps, about the parks and the streets of the West-end. Hook, who could imitate almost any and every hand-writing, contrived to get into his possession one of the Chamberlain's tickets for this *fête*, and produced a fac-simile commanding the presence of Signor Romeo at Carlton House. He next equipped himself in a gorgeous uniform of scarlet, and delivered in person the flattering missive at Mr. Coates's door. The delight of Romeo must be imagined. "Hook," says one of his biographers, "was in attendance when the time for his sallying forth arrived, and had the satisfaction of seeing him swing into his chariot, bedizened in all his finery, with a diamond-hilted sword and the air of Louis le Grand. Theodore was also at the front entrance of Carlton House when the amateur's vehicle reached its point. He saw him mount up the broad steps and enter the vestibule. The stranger passed in without remark or question; but when he had to show his ticket to the Private Secretary, that eye caught the imposture. Mr. Coates was politely informed that a mistake had occurred, and had to retrace his course to the portico. The blazoned chariot had driven off; in wrath and confusion he must pick his steps as he might to the first stand of hackney-coaches. Hook was at his elbow well muffled up. No such discomfiture since the Knight of the Woeful Countenance was unhorsed by the Bachelor Sampson Carrasco. We must not omit that the Prince, when aware of what had occurred, signified his extreme regret that any one of his household should have detected the trick, or acted on its detection. Mr. Coates was, as he said, an inoffensive gentleman, and his presence might have amused many of the guests, and could have done harm to no one. His Royal Highness sent his secretary next morning to apologise in person, and to signify that as the arrangements and ornaments were still entire, he hoped Mr. Coates would come and look at them. And Romeo went. In this performance Hook had no confidant. To do him justice, we believe he never told the story without some signs of compunction."

One day, at a party at Carlton House, the Prince Regent gaily observed that there were present two "Georges the Younger," alluding to himself and George Colman, Junior, but that he should like to know which was "George the Youngest." "Oh!" replied Colman, with a happy sally of wit, "I could never, sir, have had the rudeness to come into the world before your Royal Highness." The Prince was highly amused, and never forgot the joke or its author.

In April, 1814, as we learn from Allen's "History of London," "when Marshal Blucher arrived at Carlton House, all attempts to keep the populace out of the court-yard were in vain : the two sentinels at the gate, with their muskets, were laid on the ground ; and the porter was overpowered. To indulge the public, the doors of the great hall were thrown open on the occasion ; and here the first interview of the General with the Prince Regent took place."

One of the most constant frequenters of Carlton House in the days of George Prince of Wales was George Brummell, or "Beau Brummell," as he was known to his friends, and is still known to history. He was born in 1777, and sent to Eton, where he enjoyed the credit of being the best scholar, the best oarsman, and the best cricketer of his day. His father was under-secretary to Lord North, and is said to have left to each of his children some £30,000. Whilst at Eton, he made plenty of aristocratical friends ; and being regarded as a sort of "Admirable Crichton," obtained the *entrée* to the circle of Devonshire House, where the Duchess of Devonshire introduced him to the Prince Regent, who gave him a commission in the 10th Hussars.

When he left the army he lived in Chesterfield Street, where he often had the Prince to sup with him in private. Notwithstanding the great disparity of rank, the intimacy continued for several years. He spent his days mainly at Brighton and at Carlton House, keeping a well-appointed resi-

bidden to approach the royal presence. Even this, however, blew over, and having been lucky enough to win a large sum at cards, he was once more invited to Carlton House. Here, in joy at meeting once more with his old friend, the Prince, he took too much wine. The Prince said quietly

OLD CARLTON HOUSE, 1709. (*See page* 87.)

dence in town, and belonging to "White's" and other clubs, where high play prevailed. His canes, his snuff-boxes, his dogs, his horses and carriage, each and all were of the first class, and distinguished for taste ; and the cut of his dress set the fashion to West-end tailors, who vied with each other in their efforts to secure his patronage. After a few years, however, a coolness sprang up between him and the Prince, as he espoused the cause of Mrs. Fitzherbert, and finally, the mirror of fashion was for-

to his brother, the Duke of York, "I think we had better order Mr. Brummell's carriage before he gets quite drunk," so he left the palace never to return. It is said by Captain Gronow, that in treating his guest thus, the Regent merely retaliated on him for an insult which he had received from him a year or two before at Lady Cholmondeley's ball, when the "Beau," turning to her ladyship, and pointing to the Prince, inquired, "And pray who is your fat friend?" Another version of the rupture between the Prince and "Beau" Brummell is, that one day he risked some freedom of speech to his royal patron, to whom he is reported to have said, "George, ring the bell !" This he always denied ; but it is certain that whatever his words were, they never were forgotten or forgiven by the Prince. Every one knows Brummell's subsequent career and fate. For a few

Late in life he "cut" the Prince, like George Brummell, and revenged himself by writing a volume of scurrilous memoirs of Carlton House and its inmates. The book is mentioned by Cyrus Redding as in MS., and we do not think it has ever yet seen the light.

Then there was a man named Lade, who, from having had the management of the royal stables,

BEAU BRUMMELL. *From a Miniature by John Cooke in Jesse's "Life of Brummell."* (*See page* 95.)

years he was a hanger-on at Oatlands, the seat of the Duke and Duchess of York ; then, having lost large sums at play, was obliged to fly the country, and, having lived in obscurity for some years at Calais, obtained the post of British Consul at Caen, where he died, in anything but affluent circumstances, in 1840—another proof, if any proof be needed, of the precarious existence of those who live by basking in the sunshine of royalty.

Another of the friends and companions of the Prince Regent was General Arabin, the writer of witty prologues and epilogues for lords and ladies.

and having married a very pretty wife, formerly a cook in the royal establishment, received the honour of knighthood from the Prince Regent. Sir John Lade's ambition, however, even after he became a "Knight Batchelor," was to imitate the groom in dress and in language. "I once heard him," writes Mr. Raikes in his "Journal," "asking a friend on Egham racecourse to come home and dine. 'I can give you a trout spotted all over like a coach-dog, a fillet of veal as white as *alablaster* (*sic*), a pantaloon cutlet, and plenty of pancakes.' It was then the fashion to drive a phaeton and four-in-hand. The Prince of Wales used to drive a phaeton and six as more magnificent. . . . As a boy, I have often seen the Prince driving round and round the park in this equipage, followed by a dozen others of the same description, including Lord Sefton, Lord Barrymore, and other notorious 'whips.'"

Tommy Moore was a constant guest here, under George IV., who, as Regent and as King, "played the cheap and easy part of Polycrates to the Irish Anacreon." Some of our readers will not have forgotten Moore's whimsical description of the Prince Regent's breakfast-room at Carlton House during the London season :—

> " Methought the Prince in whisker'd state
> Before me at his breakfast sate ;
> On one side lay unread petitions,
> On t'other hints from five physicians ;
> Here tradesmen's bills, official papers,
> Notes from ' my lady,' drams for vapours ;
> There plans for saddles, tea and toast,
> Death-warrants, and—the *Morning Post.*"

Mike Kelly, the Irish comedian, was another frequent visitor here, and of him Cyrus Redding, in his " Recollections," tells us many anecdotes :— " Kelly was a good after-dinner man. He told many stories of the characters of his time, and of the ' Prince, God bless him !' to use his own words in relation to George IV. All the boon companions of the Prince were friends of Kelly's. After the ' true prince,' Sheridan was Kelly's hero. The veteran composer spoke of one tainted in appearance from such a connection during his life's prime. He looked flaccid from past indulgences. The best of those, high or low, who had come within the influence of the same circle, exhibited similar resemblances to half-worn rakes."

When Dr. Parr dined at Carlton House by royal command, the Prince Regent most good-naturedly allowed him to sit after dinner and quietly smoke his pipe.

The likeness so often drawn between the Regent in his youth to the Hal of Shakespeare, and the similar change of conduct with that Prince when he came to the throne, and which is made an excuse for every caprice of humour and every change of system, has told the tale long ago of an heir-apparent and a crowned monarch. There was, however, nothing new in the conduct of the Prince Regent: all princes who scorn their father's ministers and measures during their minority, generally adopt both when they come to reign.

It was whilst residing here, in 1780—soon after attaining the dignity of a separate royal household —that the Prince of Wales became passionately attached to Mrs. Mary Robinson, the popular actress, better known by her name of " Perdita." In vain did George III. remonstrate with his son upon his infatuation. The Prince appeared in public with the lovely " Perdita" by his side ; and the assumed name of " Florizel," under which royalty sought her plebeian hand, became known to, and was commented on, by the fashionable world without any reserve. It was only a more honourable love for Mrs. Fitzherbert, which dated from the following year, that induced the then heir-apparent to the British throne to give up the most foolish of semi-romantic unions by which a royal personage was ever entangled. " Florizel," in due course, became king ; but " poor Perdita" died in debt and broken-hearted less than twenty years afterwards, and lies at rest in the parish churchyard of Old Windsor, where she had spent the last few years of her life.

At Carlton House the Prince was privately married, on the 21st of December, 1785, by a clergyman of the Established Church, to Mrs. Fitzherbert, a Roman Catholic lady of high family and connections —just a week after writing a letter to Charles James Fox, denying the truth of a rumour to the effect that he had contracted a morganatic marriage.

On the 29th of January, 1820, the venerable King, George III., died at Windsor Castle ; and on the following morning, in pursuance of established usage, the cabinet ministers assembled at Carlton House, and here George IV. held his first court. This was numerously and brilliantly attended by all ranks and parties, who eagerly offered their homage to the new king ; the re-appointment of the Lord Chancellor, and several ministers, was the first exercise of sovereign power, the oaths of allegiance being administered to those present. A council was, in compliance with the royal ordinance, immediately holden ; and all the late king's privy councillors then in attendance were sworn as members of the new council, and took their seats at the board accordingly.

The proclamation of the new king took place publicly in the metropolis, on Monday, January 31st. The first proclamation was made on the steps of Carlton House, in the presence of his Majesty, his royal brothers, and the principal officers of state. The procession then formed in the following order, and proceeded to Charing Cross :—Farriers of the Life Guards with their axes erect ; French horns of the troop ; troop of Life Guards ; the beadles of the different parishes in their long cloaks ; constables ; two knights marshals' officers ; knight marshal and his men ; household drums ; kettle drums ; trumpets ; the pursuivants ; Blue Mantle ;

Rouge Croix; Rouge Dragon and Portcullis; the Kings of Arms in their tabards and collars; Garter, Sir I. Heard, knt., supported by two sergeants at arms, with their maces; Clarencieux and Norroy; heralds in their full dress; the procession being concluded by a troop of Life Guards.

On arriving at Charing Cross, the proclamation was again read, and the procession proceeded to Temple Bar, where the usual formalities of closing the gates, and admitting one of the heralds to shew his authority, having been gone through, the cavalcade entered the City, and were joined by the Lord Mayor, sheriffs, and several of the aldermen; the proclamation was read at the end of Chancery Lane, at the end of Wood Street, Cheapside, and at the Royal Exchange, when the heralds and the military returned.

In the year 1828, as above stated, Carlton House was demolished; much of the ornamental interior details—such as marble mantelpieces, friezes, and columns—being transferred to Buckingham Palace. Upon the site of the gardens have been erected the York Column and Carlton House Terrace; the balustrades of the latter originally extended between the two ranges of houses, but were removed to form the present entrance to St. James's Park, by command of William IV., soon after his accession to the throne. Upon the site of the court-yard and part of Carlton House are the United Service and the Athenæum Club-houses, and on the east side of the intervening area facing Waterloo Place, have been set up, on granite pedestals, bronze statues of Field-Marshal Lord Clyde, the hero of the Punjab and Lucknow, who died in 1863, and of Lord Lawrence, some time Viceroy of India. The latter statue was erected in 1882. On the west side of the area is a statue, also of bronze, of Sir John Franklin, the Arctic navigator; the pedestal is ornamented with bas-reliefs of scenes in the Arctic regions.

The house in Carlton House Terrace next but one eastward from the Duke of York's Column was the residence of Mr. Gladstone for some years before and during his premiership, in 1868-74. Curiously enough, it was occupied for a time, some thirty years earlier, by another Prime Minister, the late Earl of Derby, then Lord Stanley. A curious and interesting anecdote is told concerning this house by Mr. Forster in his "Life of Charles Dickens." He writes:—"The story is, that Lord Derby, when Mr. Stanley, had on some important occasion made a speech which all the reporters found it necessary greatly to abridge; that its essential points had, nevertheless, been so well given in the *Chronicle* that Mr. Stanley, having need of it for himself in greater detail, had sent a request to the reporter to meet him in Carlton House Terrace and take down the entire speech; that Dickens attended and did the work accordingly, much to Mr. Stanley's satisfaction; and that, on his dining with Mr. Gladstone in recent years, and finding the aspect of the dining-room strangely familiar, he discovered afterwards, on inquiry, that it was there he had taken the speech. The story, as it actually occurred, is connected with the brief life of the 'Mirror of Parliament.' It was not at any special desire of Mr. Stanley's, but for that new record of debates, which had been started by one of the uncles of Dickens, and professed to excel 'Hansard' in giving verbatim reports, that the famous speech against O'Connell was taken as described. The young reporter went to the room in Carlton Terrace because the work of his uncle Barrow's publication required to be done there; and if, in later years," adds Mr. Forster, "the great author was in the same room as the guest of the Prime Minister, it must have been but a month or two before he died, when, for the first time, he visited and breakfasted with Mr. Gladstone."

The house No. 9 has been for some years the official residence of the German Ambassador, and here, in 1873, died Count Bernstorff. At No. 14, Lord Lonsdale's, is a very fine collection of old furniture of various styles and dates, with a profusion of Sèvres china, among which is the splendid service given by Louis XV. to the Empress Catharine. At No. 1, Mr. George Tomline has a fine gallery of paintings, including some Murillos. No. 18, the last on the southern side, was the Duke of Hamilton's; but its contents were sold off under the auctioneer's hammer in 1870, and the house afterwards occupied by Earl Granville.

In 1840 the Prince Louis Napoleon (afterwards Emperor of the French) was living here, in the house of Lord Ripon, No. 1, in Carlton Gardens. This mansion accordingly became the centre of preparations for his famous descent upon Boulogne in the August of that year—an abortive attempt to revive the "Napoleonic Idea" in France, which led to the Prince's imprisonment in the fortress of Ham. It is said, indeed, by Mr. B. Jerrold, in his "Life of the Emperor," that in this house the Prince and his friends amused themselves with coining military buttons for a "regiment of the future."

CHAPTER IX.

ST. JAMES'S PALACE.

"The home and haunt of kings."—Spenser.

A Hospital for Leprous Women—The Structure demolished by Henry VIII., and the Palace built—The Gate-house, and Vicissitudes of the Clock—The Colour Court, and Proclamation of Queen Victoria—The Chapel Royal—Perseverance of George III. in his attendance at Chapel—Doing the "Civil Thing"—Royal Marriages—The Gentlemen and Children of the Chapel Royal—"Spur-money"—The "Establishment" of the Chapel Royal—The Chair Court and the State Apartments—The Yeomen of the Guard—The Chapel of Queen Catharine of Braganza, and Pepys' Visit there—The Lutheran Chapel—The Ambassadors' Court—The Royal Library—Office of the Lord Chamberlain's Department—Clarence House—Charles Dartineuf and his Partiality for Ham-pie—Historical Reminiscences of St. James's Palace—Marie de Medicis and her Miniature Court—Charles I. and his last parting from his Children—King Charles II. and Dr. South— La Belle Stewart, afterwards Duchess of Richmond—Dissolute Hangers-on about the Court—Court Balls of the Time of Charles II.— Marriage of William Prince of Orange—Mary Beatrice of Modena and her Court—Morality of the Court under the Georges—Death-bed Scene of Queen Caroline—Strange Conduct of an Irish Nobleman—The Palace partially destroyed by Fire—The Duke of Cumberland and his Italian Valet.

SOME quarter of a mile to the westward of Charing Cross, there stood, in very early times, a hospital for leprous women: it was a religious foundation, and was dedicated to St. James the Less, Bishop of Jerusalem.

St. James's Palace now occupies the site of the above-mentioned hospital, showing what changes a place may undergo by the operation of the whirligig of time. The endowment of the hospital was for women only, "maidens that were leprous" being the sole objects of the charity. Eight "brethren," however, were attached to the house, in order to solemnise the religious services, and to discharge the "cure of souls."

According to Stow, the house had appended to it "two hides of land," with the usual "appurtenances," in the parish of St. Margaret, Westminster; "it was founded," he goes on to say, "by the citizens of London, before the time of man's memory, for fourteen sisters, maidens, that were lepers, living chastely and honestly in divine service. Afterwards," Stow continues, "divers citizens of London gave six-and-fifty pounds rents thereto. . . . . After this, sundry devout men of London gave to the hospital four hides of land in the fields of Westminster, and in Hendon, Chalcote, and Hampstead, eight acres of land and wood."

King Edward I. confirmed these gifts to the hospital, granting to its inmates also the privilege and profits of a fair "to be kept on the eve of St. James, the day and the morrow, and four days following;" "and this," says Mr. Newton, "was the origin of the once famous 'May Fair,' held in the fields near Piccadilly."

Henry VIII., however, set his covetous eyes on the place; and seeing that it was fair to view, while the sisters were defenceless, he resolved to possess himself of it, much as Ahab resolved to become master of Naboth's vineyard. He pulled down the old structure, "and there," as Holinshed tells us, "made a faire parke for his greater comoditie and

pleasure;" and also erected a stately mansion, or, as Stow denominates it, "a goodly manor." This was in the year of his marriage with Anne Boleyn, when he had every motive for wishing to break off with the ancient faith.

St. James's was at that time more of a country seat than would now be supposed; indeed, more than had been any of the other residences of our sovereigns near London, except Kennington. The latter was now abandoned; the sovereign came to dwell on the Middlesex instead of on the Surrey side of the Thames; and St. James's, no doubt, was intended by the fickle-minded monarch to take its place. It stood in the middle of fields, well shaded with trees; and these fields, now the park, were enclosed as the private demesne of the palace. Incredible as it may now seem, they were then well stocked with game. The king lost no time in surrounding himself here with all the appliances for amusement, and there were both a cock-pit and a tilt-yard in front of Whitehall, nearly on the site of the present Horse Guards, as we have stated in a previous chapter.

From the gates of St. James's Palace, Miss Benger tells us, in her "Life of Anne Boleyn," Henry VIII. delighted, on May morning, to ride forth at daybreak, having risen with the lark, and with a train of courtiers all gaily attired in white and silver, to make his way into the woods about Kensington and Hampstead, whence he brought back the fragrant May boughs in triumph.

"The gateway, a part of which now forms the Royal Chapel, and the chimney-piece of the old presence chamber," says Mr. A. Wood, "are all that remain of the palace erected by Henry. The last bears on its walls the initials of Henry and Anne," twined, as he might have added, in that love-knot of which he was then so fond, but which he severed by the axe in four short years afterwards.

Henry, even whilst residing here, held his court still at the old palace, first at Westminster, and then at Whitehall, after he had taken the latter from Wolsey, thus curiously anticipating the present day, when St. James's Palace is "our Court of St. James's," and contains the Throne Room and other state apartments, though it is no longer the residence of the sovereign.

Henry's gatehouse and turrets, built of red brick, face St. James's Street, and with the Chapel Royal, which adjoins them on the west side, cover the site of the ancient hospital, which, to judge from the many remains of stone mullions, labels, and other masonry found in 1838, on taking down some parts of the Chapel Royal, was of the Norman period. The lofty brick gatehouse bears upon its roof the bell of the great clock, dated A.D. 1731, and inscribed with the name of Clay, clockmaker to George II. The clock originally had but one hand. When the gatehouse was repaired, in 1831, the clock was removed, and was not put up again on account of the roof being reported unsafe to carry the weight. The inhabitants of the neighbourhood then memorialised the king (William IV. for the replacement of the time-keeper, when his Majesty, having ascertained its weight, "shrewdly inquired how, if the palace roof was not strong enough to carry the clock, it was safe for the number of persons occasionally seen upon it to witness processions, &c." The clock was forthwith replaced, and a minute-hand was added, with new dials; the original dial was of wainscot, "in a great number of very small pieces, curiously dovetailed together."

The archway of the gatehouse leads into the quadrangle, or "Colour Court," as it is usually called, from the colours of the military guard of honour being placed there. Here, according to ancient practice, a regiment of the sovereign's "foot-guards" parade daily at eleven a.m., accompanied by their band, for the purpose of exchanging the regimental standard, and handing over the keys of the palace to the incoming commandant. Here each new sovereign is formally proclaimed on his (or her) accession to the throne. It was on the 21st of June, 1837, that Her Majesty Queen Victoria was proclaimed "Queen of the United Kingdoms of Great Britain and Ireland, Defender of the Faith." Soon after nine in the morning a troop of the 1st Life Guards drew up in line across the quadrangle, and at ten the youthful sovereign made her appearance at the opened window of the Tapestry Room, where she was so overcome by the affecting scene—the exclamations of joy and clapping of hands, the waving of hats and handkerchiefs—in conjunction with the eventful occurrences of the preceding day, that she instantly

burst into tears; and, says an eye-witness, "notwithstanding her earnest endeavours to restrain them, they continued to flow in torrents down her now pallid cheeks until she retired from the window; Her Majesty, nevertheless, curtsied many times in acknowledgment of her grateful sense of the devotion of her people." Meanwhile the heralds and pursuivants, dismounted and uncovered, had taken up their accustomed position immediately beneath the window at which the Queen was standing; and silence being obtained, Clarencieux King of Arms, Sir William Woods, in the absence of Garter King at Arms, read the Proclamation, which had been issued at Kensington Palace on the preceding day. At its conclusion, Sir William gave the signal by waving his sceptre, and loud and enthusiastic cheering followed, which Her Majesty graciously and frequently acknowledged. A flourish of trumpets was then blown, and the Park and Tower guns fired a salute in token that the ceremony of proclamation had been accomplished.

On the west side of the great gateway is the Chapel Royal. It is oblong in plan, and plain, and has nothing about it to call for particular mention, excepting, perhaps, the ceiling, which is divided into small painted squares, the design of which was executed by Hans Holbein. The Royal Gallery is at the west end, opposite the communion-table. In this chapel there is a choral service on Sundays, at twelve o'clock, which is largely attended by the aristocracy when in town for the London season. The Duke of Wellington, during the last twenty or thirty years of his life, was a constant attendant. Entrance is to be obtained, we fear it must be added, most effectively by aid of a silver key.

George III., when in town, used to attend the services in this chapel, a nobleman carrying the sword of state before him, and heralds, pursuivants-at-arms, and other officers walking in the procession. So persevering was his Majesty's attendance at prayers, that Madame d'Arblay, one of the robing-women, tells us "the Queen and family, dropping off one by one, used to leave the King, the parson, and his Majesty's equerry to freeze it out together."

It is to be feared that not all the frequenters of the Chapel Royal come to attend its services with very devout hearts, if the following story, amusingly told by Mr. Raikes, may be taken as a specimen of the body at large:—"One Sunday morning the Dowager Duchess of Richmond went with her daughter to the Chapel Royal at St. James's, but being late they could find no places.

After looking about some time, and seeing the case was hopeless, she said to her daughter, 'Come away, Louisa; at any rate, we have done the *civil* thing.'" This was completely realising the idea of the *card-leaving* dowager of her day.

Here were married Prince George of Denmark

the 10th of February, 1840, when was celebrated the marriage of Her Majesty Queen Victoria and Prince Albert. The ceremony was performed by the Archbishop of Canterbury, assisted by the Archbishop of York and the Bishop of London, the latter officiating as Dean of the Chapel Royal.

CHAPEL ROYAL, ST. JAMES'S. (*See page* 101.)

and the Princess Anne; Frederick Prince of Wales and the daughter of the Duke of Saxe-Coburg; George IV. and Queen Caroline; Queen Victoria and Prince Albert; and the Princess Royal and the Crown Prince of Germany. Before the building of the chapel at Buckingham Palace, Her Majesty and the Court used to attend the service here.

Upon no occasion, perhaps, did the chapel present a gayer appearance than on the morning of

The Duke of Sussex "gave away" his royal niece, and at that part of the service where the archbishop read the words, "I pronounce that they be man and wife together," the Park and Tower guns were fired. When the wedding ring was put by Prince Albert on the Queen's finger, we are told, Lord Uxbridge, as Lord Chamberlain, gave a signal, and the bells of Westminster rung a merry peal. The fittings of the chapel and palace on this occasion are stated to have cost upwards of £9,000.

VIEW OF ST. JAMES'S PALACE, TIME OF QUEEN ANNE. *(From an Old Engraving.)*

The "Gentlemen and Children of the Chapel Royal," as the members of the choir are styled, were the principal performers in the religious drama, or "mysteries," when such performances were in fashion; and a "Master of the Children" and "singing children" occur in the chapel establishment of Cardinal Wolsey. In 1583 the "Children of the Chapel Royal," afterwards called the "Children of the Revels," were formed into a company of players, and thus were among the earliest performers of the regular drama. In 1731 they performed Handel's *Esther*, the first oratorio heard in England; "and they continued to assist at oratorios in Lent," says Mr. John Timbs, "as long as those performances maintained their ecclesiastical character entire."

In *Notes and Queries*, No. 30, we read that the "spur-money"—a fine upon all who entered the chapel with spurs on—"was formerly levied by the choristers, at the door, upon condition that the youngest of them could repeat his gamut; if he failed, the spur-bearer was exempt." In a tract dated 1598, the choristers are reproved for "hunting after spur-money;" and the ancient chequebook of the Chapel Royal, dated 1622, contains an order of the Dean, "decreeing" the observance of the custom. "Within my recollection," writes Dr. Rimbault, in 1850, "the Duke of Wellington (who, by the way, is an excellent musician) entered the Royal Chapel 'booted and spurred,' and was, of course, called upon for the fine. But his Grace calling upon the youngest chorister to repeat his gamut, and the 'little urchin' failing, the impost was not demanded." As stated above, the Duke used to attend the service here regularly; and Mr. A. C. Coxe, an American clergyman, devotes half a chapter of his "Impressions of England" to a description of an early service here, at which he knelt side by side with the hero of Waterloo.

The establishment of the Chapel Royal consists of a Dean (usually the Bishop of London), a Sub-Dean, Lord High Almoner, Sub-Almoner, Clerk of the Queen's Closet, deputy-clerks, chaplains, priests, organists, and composer; besides "violist" and "lutanist" (now sinecures), and other officers; and, until 1833, there was also a "Confessor to the Royal Household." The forty-eight "Chaplains in Ordinary" to Her Majesty are appointed by the Lord Chamberlain. They receive no payment for their services, and their duties are confined to the work of preaching one sermon each in turn yearly; but the appointment is generally regarded as a stepping-stone to something better. The Dean of the Chapel Royal is nominated by the sovereign; he has a salary of £200 a year.

In spite of modern alterations this is substantially the same chapel as that in which Evelyn so often anxiously marked the conduct of King Charles, and of his brother the Duke of York, at the celebration of the sacrament. The gold plate and offertory basin are the same as those used in the days of our last Stuart sovereign.

Eastward of the Colour Court are the gates leading to the quadrangle formerly known as "the Chair Court." The State Apartments, in the south front of the Palace, face the garden and St. James's Park. The sovereign enters by the gate on this side; it was here, on the 2nd of August, 1786, that Margaret Nicholson made an attempt to assassinate George III. as he was alighting from his carriage.

The State Apartments are said by the guide-books to be commodious and handsome, but they certainly are not very imposing, and indeed may, with truth, be pronounced mean, with reference to the dignity of English royalty. They are entered by a passage and staircase of great elegance. At the top of the latter is a gallery or guard-room converted into an armoury. The walls are tastefully decorated with daggers, muskets, and swords, arranged in various devices, such as stars, circles, diamonds, and Vandyke borders. This apartment is occupied by the Yeomen of the Guard on the occasion of a Royal levee. The Yeomen of the Guard are 140 in number; it is part of their duty to carry up the dishes to the royal table. They also take care of the baggage when the sovereign removes from one place to another. Their principal duty, however, consists in keeping the passages about the palace clear on state days. In former days the yeomen dined together, and kept a good table too. "Cannot one fancy," writes Thackeray, "Joseph Addison's calm smile and cold grey eyes following Dick Steele, as he struts down the Mall to dine with the Guard at St. James's, before he himself turns back, with his sober pace and threadbare suit, to walk back to his lodgings up the two pair of stairs in the Haymarket?"

The old Presence Chamber—or, as it is now called, the Tapestry Chamber—is the next room entered. The walls are covered with tapestry, which was made for Charles II., but was never actually hung until the marriage, in 1795, of the Prince of Wales, it having lain, by accident, in a chest undiscovered until within a short time of the event. In this room, over the fire-place, are some relics of the period of Henry VIII.; among which may be mentioned the initials "H. A." (Henry and Anne Boleyn) united, as stated above, by a true-lover's knot; the fleur-de-lis of France, formerly emblazoned with the arms of England; the portcullis of Westminster; and the rose of Lancaster.

When a drawing-room is held, a person attends here to receive the cards containing the names of the parties to be presented, a duplicate being handed to the lord in waiting, to prevent the presentation of persons not entitled to that privilege. From this room is obtained entrance to the state apartments, the first of which is very splendidly furnished; the sofas, ottomans, &c., being covered with crimson velvet, and trimmed with gold lace. The walls are covered with crimson damask, and the window curtains are of the same material; here is a portrait of George II., in his robes; paintings of Lisle and Tournay; and an immense mirror, reaching from the ceiling to the floor. The apartment is lighted by a chandelier, hanging from the centre of the ceiling, and by candelabra at each end.

The Great Council Chamber was the place where the accession and birthday odes of the Poet Laureate were performed and sung in the last century. During the present century, as far back, at least, as the memory of man runneth, these productions have been "taken as read."

The second room is called Queen Anne's Room; it is fitted up in the same splendid style, and contains a full-length portrait of George III., in his robes of the Order of the Garter; on each side of him hang paintings of the great naval victories of the First of June and Trafalgar. Here the remains of Frederick Duke of York lay in state, in January, 1827. From the centre of the ceiling hangs a richly-chased Grecian lustre, and on the walls are three magnificent pier-glasses, reaching the full height of the apartment.

The third room is called the Presence Chamber; in it Her Majesty or her representative holds levees; although similar in style of decoration, it is far more gorgeous than the two described above. The throne, which is on a raised daïs, is of crimson velvet, covered with gold lace, surmounted by a canopy of the same material. The state chair is of exquisite workmanship. The window-curtains are of crimson satin trimmed with gold lace. Here are placed paintings of the battles of Vittoria and Waterloo, by Colonel Jones. The "Royal Closet" is the name conventionally given to the room in which the Queen gives audiences to ambassadors, and also receives an address annually on her birthday from the clergy of the Established Church.

On the east side of the Palace, close to where now stands Marlborough House, as already stated

in our chapter on the Mall (see page 76 of the present volume), was in former times a friary, occupied by some Capuchin priests, who came into England with Catharine of Braganza, on her marriage with Charles II. The buildings included a refectory, dormitory, chapel, and library, with cells for the religious. Pepys, in his "Diary," gives us an account of a visit which he paid to the place, where he was shown a crucifix that had belonged to Mary Queen of Scots—which we may suppose he believed—and contained a portion of the true cross, which he probably did *not* believe.

The chapel, as prepared for the use of Queen Catharine of Braganza, is thus described by Pepys, in his "Diary," September 21st, 1662:—"To the parke; the Lord's Day. The Queen coming by in her coach going to her chapel at St. James's (the first time that it hath been ready for her), I crowded after her, and I got up to the room where her closet is, and there stood and saw the fine altar, ornaments, and the fryers in their habits, and the priests come in with their fine crosses, and many other fine things. I heard their musique, too, which may be good, but it did not appear so to me, neither as to their manner of singing, nor was it good concord to my ears, whatever the matter was. The Queen very devout; but what pleased me best was to see my dear Lady Castlemaine, who, tho' a Protestant, did wait upon the Queen to chapel. By and by, after masse was done, a fryer with his cowl did rise up and preach a sermon in Portuguese, which I not understanding, did go away, and to the King's Chapel, but that was done; and so up to the Queen's presence-chamber, where she and the King were expected to dine; but she staying at St. James's, they were forced to remove the things to the King's presence, and there he dined alone."

Pepys alludes to the Roman Catholic services in the Royal Chapel at Whitehall in terms which would seem to imply that he had a strong dislike for them. Thus he writes, 10th May, 1663: "Put on a black cloth suit, with white lynings under all, as the fashion is to wear, to appear under the breeches. I walked to St. James's, and was there at masse, and was forced in the crowd to kneel down"—no bad thing, by the way, for such a worldly and sceptical Christian.

When Charles I. married Henrietta Maria it had been stipulated that the Queen should be allowed the free practice of her religion in London, in spite of the severe laws in force against Roman Catholics in England; but the King found it convenient in this, as in other matters, to forget his promise, and ordered "the French," as he contemptuously called them, to be driven out of St. James's Palace. From thence they went in a body to Somerset House, where for some time they performed mass and heard confessions, until "Steenie," Duke of Buckingham, was ordered to dislodge them thence also, and to pack them off without ceremony to their own country.* On leaving St. James's, we are told, "the women howled and lamented as if they had been going to execution, but all in vain, for the Yeomen of the Guard, by Lord Conway's appointment, thrust them and all their country folk out of the Queen's lodging, and locked the doors after them." A contemporary account adds: "The Queen, when she understood the design, grew very impatient, and brake the glass windows with her fist; but since, I hear, her rage is appeased, and the King and she, since they went together to Nonsuch, have been very jocund together."

A community of the Benedictine order was established at St. James's in the reign of James II., but it was suppressed after the Revolution.

On the site of the chapel above mentioned now stands the Lutheran or German Chapel, which seems almost to intrude upon the grounds of Marlborough House. It was here that the late Queen Dowager Adelaide used to attend on Sundays, preferring the simplicity of its service to the Chapel Royal. In 1851, its use was granted, by permission of the Bishop of London, to the foreign Protestants who had flocked to see the Great Exhibition in Hyde Park.

Westward of the Colour Court is the Ambassadors' Court, where are the apartments of the ex-King of Hanover, and of certain other branches of the Royal Family, and beyond it the Stable Yard, so named from covering the site of the ancient stable-yard of the Palace. Here are now Stafford House, the mansion of the Duke of Sutherland, and Clarence House, the residence of the Duke of Edinburgh; besides a few other mansions inhabited by the nobility.

Mr. Cunningham says that, in 1814, during the visit of the Allied Sovereigns, Marshal Blucher was lodged in the dingy brick house on the west side of the Ambassadors' Court, or West Quadrangle, where he would frequently sit at the drawing-room windows and smoke, and bow to the people, pleased with the notice that was taken of him. At this time the state apartments were fitted up for the Emperor of Russia and the King of Prussia.

In the reign of George II. the Royal Library stood nearly on the site of the present Stafford House, detached from the rest of the buildings of the Palace; there is no print of it in existence,

and it is said to have possessed few architectural pretensions. In fact, literature was not one of the "hobbies" of the first two monarchs of our Hanoverian line.

Here, in the Ambassadors' Court, is the office of the Lord Chamberlain's Department. It is poor and mean enough, and gives but little idea of the importance of the work transacted within its walls. Persons to be "presented at Court," either at levees or drawing-rooms,† are required to send their cards to the Lord Chamberlain; and it is his duty to see that such persons are entitled, by station and character, to be presented to the sovereign. Levees only, however, now take place at St. James's Palace. "The Lord Chamberlain," as we learn from Murray's "Official Handbook," "is an officer of the Household of great antiquity, honour, and trust. He has the supreme control over all the officers and servants of the royal chambers (except those of the bedchamber); also over the establishment of the Chapel Royal, and the physicians, surgeons, and apothecaries of the Household. He has the oversight of the Queen's band, and over all comedians, trumpeters, and messengers. All artificers retained in Her Majesty's service are under his directions. The ancient office of Keeper of the Great Wardrobe was abolished in 1782, and the duties, which consisted in providing the state robes of the royal family, the household, and the officers of state, were transferred to the Lord Chamberlain. The public performance of stage plays in the metropolis and at Windsor, and wherever there is a royal palace, is not legal unless in a house or place licensed by the Lord Chamberlain, who may suspend or revoke his licence. Nor is the performance of any new play, or part of a play, anywhere in Great Britain, legal until his licence has been obtained."

Clarence House was for many years the residence of the Duchess of Kent. In 1874 it was assigned as a residence for the Duke and Duchess of Edinburgh, and greatly enlarged, a storey being added to it in height, and its entrance being made to face the Park on the south instead of being in the narrow passage on the west. The entrance portico was formerly on the west side, facing Stafford House; but this has now been pulled down, and in its place, and also in the balcony above, have been substituted three large windows. Fronting St. James's Park, a new portico entrance, with a conservatory, supported on four columns, has been erected, and two gateways for ingress and egress, flanked by lodges and a stone sentry-box,

---

* See Vol. III., p. 91.

† A levee is confined to gentlemen only; a drawing-room is attended by gentlemen and ladies, the latter forming the larger proportion.

have been constructed on the south-west side. The old court-yard, and a number of ancient buildings extending to St. James's Palace, have been demolished, and the area thus obtained has been thrown into the basement, which is set apart for the general domestic offices and servants' apartments; and on the old court-yard site a one-storey building has been erected as a dormitory for the servants. On the west side of the building is the *bijou* "Greek Church," fitted up for the private devotions of the Duchess of Edinburgh; the altar, flooring, walls, &c., are inlaid with rich mosaic work. A portion of St. James's Palace has been thrown into the new premises, thus affording increased accommodation, while the gardens of the two establishments have been thrown into one, and laid out in uniform terraces and slopes.

In 1806, just before his death, Charles James Fox was residing at Godolphin House (the site of which is now covered by Stafford House), in the Stable Yard.

Among the now forgotten dwellers in the out-quarters of the Palace was Charles Dartineuf, or Dartinave, said by some to have been a son of Charles II., by others a member of a refugee family. He was Paymaster of the Board of Works, and Surveyor of the Royal Gardens and Roads in 1736. He was, as Swift describes him, a "true epicure," and a man "that knows everything and everybody; where a knot of rabble are going on a holiday, and where they were last." His partiality for ham-pie has been confirmed by Warburton and Dodsley. Pope, he said, had done justice to his taste; if he had given him *sweet pie*, he never could have pardoned him. Lord Lyttelton, in his "Dialogues of the Dead," has introduced Dartineuf discoursing with Apicius on the subject of good eating, ancient and modern. His favourite dish, ham-pie, is there commemorated; but Dartineuf is made to lament his ill fortune in having lived before turtle-feasts were known in England.

In the "New View of London," published in 1708, St. James's Palace is said to be "pleasantly situated by the Park;" the writer adds, "Though little can be said of its regular design in appearance, yet it contains many noble, magnificent, and beautiful rooms and apartments."

This edifice was the London residence of our sovereigns from 1697, when Whitehall Palace was consumed by fire, until about the middle of the last century, when George III. made Buckingham Palace his home in London. Since 1809, when part of the south-eastern wing was destroyed by fire, a part only of the palace has been rebuilt, but it was put into ornamental repair on the accession of George IV., during the years 1821–23. In this palace died Queen Mary I.; Henry, Prince of Wales, eldest son of James I.; and Caroline, Queen of George II. Here also were born Charles II., James, "the Old Pretender," son of James II., and George IV.

In 1638 this palace was given up by Charles I. as a residence for Marie de Medici, the mother of his consort, Henrietta Maria; but in this, as in nearly all his other acts of imprudent generosity, the King came in for a large share of unpopularity. She was welcomed to London with a public reception and a procession through the streets, and a copy of most courtly verses by the court poet, Edmund Waller; as witness these lines :—

"Great Queen of Europe! where thy offspring wears
   All the chief crowns; where princes are thy heirs;
   As welcome thou to sea-girt Briton's shore,
   As erst Latone, who fair Cynthia bore
   To Delos, was."

The miniature court, however, which she maintained here for three years, was never acceptable to the nation, who regarded her as the symbol of arbitrary power. In the end, the Parliament voted to her a sum of £10,000 if she would only leave the country; and she quitted England for the free city of Cologne in August, 1641. Lilly thus notices her departure :—"I saw the old Queen-mother of France departing from London. A sad spectacle it was, and produced tears in my eyes and those of many other beholders, to see an aged, lean, decrepit, poor queen, ready for her grave, necessitated to depart hence, having no other place of residence left her but where the courtesy of her hard fate assigned. She had been the only stately and magnificent woman of Europe, wife to the greatest king that ever lived in France, mother unto one king and two queens." She died at Cologne in 1642, in a garret, and with scarcely more than the bare necessaries of life!

It was at St. James's that Charles I., so soon about to earn the title of "the Martyr," took his farewell of his young children, who were brought from Sion House for that purpose—an affecting scene, which has been a favourite subject for pictorial representation; and here the King's last night on earth was spent. "He slept," as the historians tell us, "more than four hours; his attendant, Herbert, resting on a pallet by the royal bed. The room was dimly lighted by a great cake of wax, set in a silver basin. Before daybreak the king had aroused his attendant, saying, 'He had a great work to do that day.' Prayer, communion, and the announcement of the executioners waiting for their victim—the glass of claret and the morsel of bread, lest faintness on the scaffold might be felt, and be misinterpreted—the long procession to Whitehall—the silent and dejected faces of the soldiers—the mutual prayers, and the last inquiry, 'Does my hair trouble you?'—the outstretched hands for the signal—all these, and many more

It must have been trying to the proud spirit of Queen Henrietta Maria in her widowhood, when she had seen the bodies of Cromwell, Ireton, and Bradshaw dragged on hurdles to Tyburn, and their heads set, as we have said, on the front of West-minster Hall, to have been compelled, in deference

COUNCIL CHAMBER, ST. JAMES'S PALACE, 1840. (*See page* 105.)

such gloomy sights, go to make up a mournful picture. As the cloak of the king falls from his shoulders, the faithful Juxon receives from the hand of his beloved master, with the single and mysterious word, 'Remember!' the 'George' which he had removed from his neck. So ended the domestic history of poor King Charles; and with him, in one sense, for a long time, the domestic happiness of his country."

to the will of her son, the King, to salute here publicly at court as Duchess of York, and consort of the presumptive heir to the throne, the offspring of Lord Chancellor Hyde and his low-born wife.

We learn from Whitelock that St. James's was temporarily occupied by Monk, Duke of Albemarle, before he had made up his mind that it was time to effect the Restoration.

In former times a dinner was laid regularly every

day in the out-quarters of the Palace for the royal chaplains. A good story is told about this dinner and the witty Dr. South, who obtained a reprieve for it when there was a talk of its being discontinued. King Charles II. one day came in to dine with the reverend gentlemen; and it was Dr. South's turn to say grace. Instead of using the regular form, "God *save* the King, and *bless* our dinner," he transposed the verbs, saying, "God *bless* the

queen to marry her, and was half distracted when, by her clandestine marriage with the Duke of Richmond, she eluded his grasp. The personal charms of La Belle Stewart have been commemorated by Grammont, Pepys, and others. The secretary, indeed, was enraptured with her appearance—her "cocked hat and a red plume," her "sweet eye," and "little Roman nose." Miss Stewart had been so annoyed by the attentions of

COURT-YARD OF ST. JAMES'S PALACE, 1875. (*See page* 101.)

King, and *save* our dinner." "How say you, Dr. South?" said the King; "and it *shall* be saved, I promise, on the word of a king." It is to be hoped that on this occasion his Majesty did not break his word.

One of the chief ornaments of the Court of St. James's in the reign of Charles II. was La Belle Stewart, afterwards Duchess of Richmond, to whom Pope has alluded as the "Duchess of R.," in the well-known line—

"Die and endow a college or a cat."

She was Frances Stewart, grand-daughter of Lord Blantyre, and as such she inspired Charles II. with the purest and strongest passion he seemed capable of entertaining. He would have divorced his

Charles and the manners of his profligate court, that she had already resolved to marry any gentleman of £1,500 a year, when, fortunately, the Duke of Richmond solicited her hand. Her consent was, according to Pepys, "as great an act of honour as ever was done by woman!" In a few years the duchess became a widow, and continued so for thirty years, dying October 15, 1702. The endowment satirised by Pope has been favourably explained by Warton. She left annuities to certain female friends, with the burden of maintaining some of her cats: a delicate way of providing for poor, and probably proud, gentlewomen, without making them feel that they owed their livelihood to her mere liberality. It would have been easy, however, to have effected the same object in a way less liable to ridicule. The "effigy" of the duchess still exists, along with some others, in Westminster Abbey. She left money by her will, desiring that her image, as well done in wax as could be, and dressed in coronation robes and coronet, should be placed in a case, with clear crown glass before it, and should be set up in Westminster Abbey. A more lasting and popular "effigy" is the figure of Britannia on our copper coins, which was originally modelled from a medal struck by Charles II. in honour of the fair Stewart.

In addition to the "sweet little Barbara," Countess of Castlemaine *in esse*, and Duchess of Cleveland *in posse*, there hung about the Court, here and at Whitehall, the Duke of Buckingham and the Earl of Rochester, the handsome Sidney, the pompous Earl of St. Albans, and his vain and giddy nephew, Harry Jermyn; the Earls of Arran and Ossory, and the dissolute Killigrew, who together governed the privacy of their master as readily and easily as Clarendon and Ormond controlled his public measures. King Charles II. being here, on one occasion, in company with Lord Rochester and others of the nobility, Killigrew, the jester, came in. "Now," said the king, "we shall hear of our faults." "No, faith," said Killigrew, "I don't care to trouble my head with that which all the town talks of."

Here, in the bedroom of the Princess, took place, on the 4th of November, 1677, the marriage of Mary, daughter of James Duke of York and of his first wife, Anne Hyde, with William Prince of Orange—a marriage so fatal afterwards to her father and her step-mother, Mary of Modena, who at the time was hourly expecting her confinement. Three days afterwards the boy was born, but he did not live to the end of the year, being carried off by the smallpox. Waller, the Court poet, in a graceful little poem on the death of this infant, alludes to the extreme youth of the royal mother, to which he ascribes the early deaths of her other offspring, and from the same circumstance insinuates consoling hopes for the future :—

> "The failing blossoms which a young plant bears
> Engage our hopes for the succeeding years.
> *   *   *   *   *
> Heaven, as a first-fruit, claimed that lovely boy ;
> The next shall live to be the nation's joy."

When, in 1688, the Prince of Orange, with the forces at his command, was advancing towards London, King James sent him an invitation to take up his quarters here. The Prince accepted it, but at the same time hinted to the King, his father-in-law, that he must leave Whitehall. With

respect to this event, Dalrymple, in his "Memoirs," tells the following story :—"It was customary to mount guard at both palaces. The old hero, Lord Craven, was on duty at the time when the Dutch guards came marching through the Park to relieve, by order of their master. From a point of honour he had determined not to quit his station, and was preparing to maintain his post ; but, receiving the command of his sovereign, he reluctantly withdrew his party, and marched away in sullen dignity."

Here Mary Beatrice of Modena spent the first years of her wedded life with James Duke of York ; and even after she became Queen Consort she always preferred its homely apartments to the gilded and gorgeous rooms of the great Palace at Whitehall. Here, too, when she found that she was once more about to become a mother, in the summer of 1688, she resolved that the child should be born, who, if a son, was destined thereafter to become the heir to the English throne. "Mary Beatrice," writes Miss Strickland, "never liked Whitehall, but always said of it that it was one of the largest and most uncomfortable houses in the world. But her heart always clung to her first English home, which had been endeared to her by those tender recollections that regal pomp had never been able to efface."

Here, too, the son of James II. and Mary Beatrice, afterwards so well known to history as "the Elder Pretender," was born on Sunday, the 10th of June, 1688, being Trinity Sunday, between nine and ten in the morning. This chamber is memorable as the scene of the alleged fraud by which the king and queen were said to have tried to foist upon the nation as its future sovereign a child brought into the palace in a warming-pan. Mr. Peter Cunningham tells us that there is extant "a contemporary plan of the palace, dotted with lines to show the way by which the child was said to have been conveyed to her Majesty's bed in the great bedchamber." Those who would wish to read in detail the narratives of this event cannot do better than study them in the "Life" of that queen by Miss Strickland, who states that nearly every member of the court was present on the occasion, to the number of sixty-seven persons, and all saw that a son was born to the queen.

"The Court of Mary Beatrice at St. James's Palace," writes Miss Strickland, "was always magnificent, and far more orderly than that at Whitehall." Like Whitehall, St. James's Palace, under the Stuart sovereigns, was constantly the scene of the ceremony of "touching for the King's evil." Many instances of its performance are on record. Thus we are told that on the 30th of

March, 1712, some 200 persons were brought before Queen Anne at St. James's Palace to be healed by the "royal touch." Among this number was one whose name was destined to become great—Samuel Johnson, then a child about two years and a half old. His mother had brought him from Lichfield to London to be touched by the Queen on the advice of Sir John Floyer, a physician of fame in Lichfield ; a proof of the high estimation in which the royal "healing" was generally held early in the last century. When asked, late in life, if he could remember Queen Anne, the doctor used to state that he had "a confused but somehow a sort of solemn recollection of a lady in diamonds and a long black hood."

The morals of the Court of Charles II. are matters of history ; and even the court balls at St. James's, in his reign, in spite of the influence of his excellent queen, were not marked with any great propriety, if contemporary diaries may be trusted. But, if the Palace was the scene of much that was discreditable and immoral under the Stuarts, it did not gain much in morality under the first two Georges, who kept here their dull English and German mistresses, just as Charles and James had maintained their more attractive French ladies. In the court chronicles and scandalous memoirs of the time we may read plenty of anecdotes of such court ladies as the Duchess of Kendal and Miss Brett, the rival favourites of George I. ; and of Mrs. Howard, afterwards Countess of Suffolk, who, in the reign of George II., had "apartments" within its walls, under the very nose and eyes of Queen Caroline, who apparently cared little about her existence. Those who are interested in such scandals may read in Mr. Peter Cunningham's "Handbook of London" an interesting account of a passage at arms between the above-mentioned Miss Brett and her "protector's" granddaughter, the Princess Anne, who ordered to be bricked up again a door which that lady had made to connect her apartments with the Palace garden. The strife was at its height when the sudden death of the King put an end to the reign of Miss Brett, and the Princess triumphed. And Horace Walpole tells us how the accident of Lord Chesterfield having won a heavy sum of money, and having deposited it late at night with Mrs. Howard, led the Queen to suspect him of too great intimacy in that quarter, and so almost forced him into opposition to the Ministry.

Cunningham adds further, as a separate bit of scandal, that Mrs. Howard's husband presented himself one night in the quadrangle of the Palace to claim his wife ; but, after many noisy protesta-tions, was induced to desist, "selling to the King," as Walpole had heard, "his noisy honour and the possession of his wife for a pension of twelve hundred a year !" While such scenes were transacted in the eighteenth century, it certainly cannot be allowed that either of the first two Georges had a right to throw the first stone at Charles II. or James II.

Lord Orford, in his "Reminiscences," tells an amusing story of one of the German ladies who came over with King George I. On being abused by the mob, she put her head out of the coach, and cried in bad English, "Good people, why you abuse us ? We come for all your goods." "Yes," answered a fellow in the crowd, "and for our *chattels* too."

The death-bed scene of Queen Caroline has been told by Lord Hervey and other writers of the time. It was on the 9th of November, 1737, that the Queen was taken ill, and continued getting worse. On the 11th, the Prince of Wales—who, as our readers will have already seen, was then living at enmity with his parents—sent to request that he might see her ; but the King said it was like one of the *scoundrel's* tricks, and he forbade the Prince to send messages, or even to approach St. James's. The Queen herself was no less decided. She was then dying from the effects of a rupture, which she had courageously concealed for fourteen years, and she would have died without declaring it, had not the King communicated the fact to her attendants. This delicacy was not, as Lord Hervey says, merely an ill-timed coquetry at fifty-four, that would hardly have been excusable at twenty-five. She feared to lose her power over the King, which she had held firmly in spite of all his mistresses, and was in constant apprehension of making herself distasteful to her husband. The Prince of Wales continued to send messages to the dying Queen, and the messengers got into the Palace ; but the Queen wished to have the *ravens* (who, she said, were only there to watch her death, and would gladly tear her to pieces whilst she was alive) turned out of the house, and the old King was inexorable. About the seventh day of the Queen's illness, the Archbishop of Canterbury (Dr. Potter) was sent for. He continued to attend every morning and evening, but her Majesty did not receive the sacrament.

Some of Lord Hervey's revelations are curious enough. Her Majesty, it appears, advised the King, in case she died, to marry again. George sobbed and shed tears. "Whilst in the midst of this passion, wiping his eyes and sobbing between every word, with much ado he got out this answer :

'Non, j'aurai des maîtresses;' to which the Queen made no other reply than 'Ah! mon Dièu! cela n'empêche pas.'

"When she had finished all she had to say on these subjects, she said she fancied she could sleep. The King said many kind things to her, and kissed her face and her hands a hundred times; but even at this time, on her asking for her watch, which hung by the chimney, in order to give it to him to take care of her seal, the natural *brusquerie* of his temper, even in these moments, broke out, which showed how addicted he was to snapping without being angry, and that he was often capable of using those worst whom he loved best; for, on this proposal of giving him the watch to take care of the seal with the Queen's arms, in the midst of sobs and tears, he raised and quickened his voice, and said, 'Ah, my God! let it alone : the Queen has always such strange fancies. Who should meddle with your seal? Is it not as safe there as in my pocket?'"

During their night watches, the King and Lord Hervey had many conversations, all which the Court Boswell reports fully. George wished to impress upon the Privy Seal that the Queen's affectionate behaviour was the natural effect of an amorous attachment to his person, and an adoration of his great genius! He narrated instances of his own intrepidity, during a severe illness and in a great storm; and one night while he was discoursing in this strain, the Princess Emily, who lay upon a couch in the room, pretended to fall asleep. Soon after, his Majesty went into the Queen's room. When his back was turned, Princess Emily started up, and said, 'Is he gone? How tiresome he is!' Lord Hervey replied only, "I thought your Royal Highness had been asleep. 'No,' said the Princess Emily, 'I only shut my eyes that I might not join in the *ennuyant* conversation, and wish I could have shut my ears too. In the first place, I am sick to death of hearing of his great courage every day of my life; in the next place, one thinks now of mamma, and not of him. Who cares for his old storm? I believe too, it is a great lie, and that he was as much afraid as I should have been, for all what he says now.'"

Other glimpses of the interior of this strange Court at this time are furnished by Lord Hervey. At length the last scene came. There had been about eleven days of suffering :—"On Sunday, the 20th of November, in the evening, she asked Dr. Tesier—with no seeming impatience under any article of her present circumstances but their duration—how long he thought it was possible for all this to last? to which he answered, 'Je crois que

votre Majesté sera bientôt soulagée.' And she calmly replied, 'Tant mieux.' About ten o'clock on Sunday night, the King being in bed and asleep, on the floor, at the foot of the Queen's bed, and the Princess Emily in a couch bed in a corner of the room, the Queen began to rattle in the throat; and Mrs. Purcel giving the alarm that she was expiring, all in the room started up. Princess Caroline was sent for, and Lord Hervey, but before the last arrived the Queen was just dead. All she said before she died was, 'I have now got an asthma; open the window.' Then she said, 'Pray:' upon this the Princess Emily began to read some prayers, of which she scarce repeated ten words before the Queen expired. The Princess Caroline held a looking-glass to her lips, and finding there was not the least damp upon it, cried, ''Tis over.'"

George did not marry again, but contented himself with "des maîtresses." He survived nearly twenty-three years, dying suddenly on the 25th of October, 1760. He directed that his remains and those of the Queen should be *mingled together;* and accordingly, one side of each of the wooden coffins was withdrawn, and the two bodies placed together in a stone sarcophagus.

George III., at his accession, was not much more popular than his grandfather had been before him; and on several occasions the populace showed that he held the throne by a very precarious tenure. Sir N. W. Wraxall tells us, in his gossiping "Memoirs of his Own Time," that in one popular outbreak, in 1769, a hearse, followed by an excited mob, decorated with insignia of most unmistakable meaning, was driven into the court-yard of St. James's Palace, an Irish nobleman, Lord Mountnorris, personating an executioner, holding an axe in his hands, whilst his face was covered over by a veil of crape. "The king's firmness, however," adds Wraxall, "did not forsake him in the midst of this trying ebullition of democratic rage. He remained calm and unmoved in the drawing-room, whilst the streets surrounding his palace echoed with the shouts of an enraged multitude, who seemed disposed to proceed to those extremities to which, eleven years later, they actually went, in the 'Gordon' riots."

On the 22nd of January, 1809, as stated above, about half-past two in the morning, a fire was discovered in St. James's Palace, near the King's back stairs. The whole of the private apartments of the Queen, those of the Duke of Cambridge, the King's court, and the apartments of several persons belonging to the royal household, were destroyed; the most valuable part of the property was preserved. The Hon. Miss Amelia Murray tells us this fire was believed at the time to be the work of an incendiary.

About the year 1810 the Palace was the scene of a horrid tragedy, which, for a time at least, drew down great popular indignation on one member of the royal family. The Duke of Cumberland had an Italian servant named Sellis, who made his way into his master's bedroom and tried to assassinate him in the night. The duke awoke, and was able not only to defend himself, but to drive away the would-be assassin, who, when he found himself foiled in his dastardly attempt, crept back to his own room and cut his throat. A coroner's inquest being held on the body, a verdict of "felo-de-se" was returned. The affair, nevertheless, caused great excitement at the time, and many suspicions were entertained, and many cruel insinuations made against the duke, who was, from youth, the most unpopular member of the royal house; and even to the present day there is a sort of floating tradition to the effect that the duke—who, in 1837, left England on becoming King of Hanover, and scarcely ever afterwards came to this country—was the murderer of his valet.

A good story is told by Miss Murray, in her "Recollections," concerning the wife of the Duke of Cumberland, who in early life was more than suspected of levity of conduct. Old Queen Charlotte was resolved to keep her court pure, in the persons of its female part, at least; and when her eldest son, the Prince Regent, endeavoured to smooth over the Duchess's faults, and procure for her a public reception at Court, her Majesty replied, that "she would receive the Duchess of Cumberland as a daughter-in-law when she received the Princess of Wales also. But this arrangement did not suit the Prince Regent's book."

With regard to the kitchen of St. James's Palace in the time of George III., it need only be said that it was very similar in its appearance to the kitchens of other large establishments. Our illustration (page 120) shows the principal features of the place at the above period. It may be added here that the grass-plot which lies beneath the southern windows of the Palace, now enclosed with high walls, is substantially the same as it was in the reign of Charles II., who, on a summer evening, was often to be seen here, playing at bowls with the fair ladies of his court.

CHAPTER X.

ST. JAMES'S PALACE (continued).

"They say there is a Royal Court,
Maintained in noble state,
Where every able man and good
Is certain to be great."—Tom Hood.

A Drawing-room in the Reign of Queen Anne, and one of the Present Day—Court Wits—Sedan Chairs at St. James's—Influence of Monarchical Institutions on Social Etiquette—Sociality of Great Kings—Courtly Leaders of Fashion—Court Dresses—Costume in the Reign of George III.—Queen Elizabeth's Partiality for Black Silk Stockings—Killigrew and King Charles's Tailor—Hair-powder and Full-bottomed Wigs—Farthingales and Crinoline—The Poet-Laureate and his Butt of Sherry—Royal Patronage of Poetry and Literature—Stafford (formerly Cleveland) House—Appearance of St. James's at the Beginning of the Seventeenth Century.

FOR upwards of two hundred years—indeed, even before the burning of Whitehall—the name of St. James's has been identified in English literature with the English Court, and all that is refined and courtly. Mr. Harrison Ainsworth, therefore, has only given expression to a popular idea of long standing, when he names one of his works "St. James's and St. Giles's," as the very antipodes of each other; and it is almost superfluous to add, that in his historical romance of St. James's he has given us an insight into the inner life of the Court of Queen Anne, scarcely inferior in minuteness to the picturesque peeps of the same court which we find in the "Diaries" of Samuel Pepys and John Evelyn. Here, for instance, is a picture of St. James's Street en fête in February, 1707,

on the occasion of a "drawing-room" held in celebration of the birthday of Queen Anne. It is worth giving entire, as a sketch taken from life:—"The weather was in unison with the general festivity, being unusually fine for the season. The sky was bright and sunny, and the air had all the delicious balminess and freshness of spring. Martial music resounded within the courts of the Palace, and the trampling of the guard was heard, accompanied by the clank of their accoutrements, as they took their station in St. James's Street, where a vast crowd was already collected.

"About an hour before noon the patience of those who had taken up their positions betimes promised to be rewarded, and the company began to appear, at first somewhat scantily, but speedily in great numbers. The science of the whip was not so well understood in those days as in our own times, or perhaps the gorgeous and convenient though somewhat cumbersome vehicles then in vogue were not so manageable; but from whichever cause, it is certain that many quarrels took place among the drivers, and frequent and loud oaths and ejaculations were poured forth. The footpath was invaded by the chairmen, who forcibly pushed the crowd aside, and seemed utterly regard-

respective habiliments, military and naval commanders in their full accoutrements, foreign ambassadors, and every variety of character that a court can exhibit. The equipages were most of them new, and exceedingly sumptuous, as were the liveries of the servants clustering behind them.

"The dresses of the occupants of the coaches were varied in colour, as well as rich in material, and added to the gaiety and glitter of the scene. Silks and velvets of as many hues as the rainbow

AMBASSADORS' COURT, ST. JAMES'S PALACE, 1875. (*See page* 106.)
(*Showing the Room in which the Duke of Cumberland's Valet died.*)

less of the ribs and toes of those who did not make way for them. Some confusion necessarily ensued; but though the crowd were put to considerable inconvenience, jostled here, squeezed there, the utmost mirth and good-humour prevailed.

"Before long the tide of visitors had greatly increased, and coaches, chariots, and sedans were descending in four unbroken lines towards the Palace. The curtains of the chairs being for the most part drawn down, the attention of the spectators was chiefly directed to the coaches, in which sat resplendent beauties bedecked with jewels and lace, beaux in their costliest and most splendid attire, grave judges and reverend divines in their

might be discovered, while there was every kind of peruke, from the courtly and modish Ramillies just introduced, to the somewhat antiquated but graceful and flowing French Campane. Neither was there any lack of feathered hats, point-lace cravats and ruffles, diamond snuff-boxes and buckles, clouded canes, and all the *et cetera* of beauish decoration."

Another writer in describing the scene witnessed at St. James's on the occasion of a Drawing-room in more recent times, remarks that, "after all, magnificence is a tawdry thing, when viewed under the searching blaze of sunshine. Jewels lack lustre—gold appears mere tinsel—the circumstantialities of dress are too much seen to admit of any general

OLD VIEW OF ST. JAMES'S PALACE, BEFORE THE GREAT FIRE OF LONDON.

effect ; and even beauty's self becomes less beautiful. The complexion becomes moistened by the stifling atmosphere of the crowded rooms. As to ladies of a certain age," continues the writer, "let them, above all things, avoid the drawing-room : such a revelation of wrinkles, moles, beards, rouge, pearl-powder, pencilled eyebrows, false hair and false teeth, as were brought to light, I could scarcely have imagined. Many faces, which I had thought lovely at 'Almack's,' grew hideous when exposed to the tell-tale brightness of the meridian sun ; the consciousness of which degeneration rendered them anxious, fretful, and doubly frightful. Two or three dowagers, with mouths full of gold wire, chinstays of blond to conceal their withered deficiencies, and *tulle illusion* tippets, were really horrific ; painted sepulchres—ghastly satires upon the hollowness of human splendour.

"I have often heard it asserted that an English girl, with the early bloom of girlishness on her cheek, is the prettiest creature in the world ; and have thence concluded that a drawing-room, where so many of these rosebuds are brought forward to exhibit their first expansion, must present a most interesting spectacle. This morning I particularly noticed the *demoiselles* to be presented ; and the ghastliness of the ladies of a certain age was scarcely less repulsive than a *niaiserie* of several of these budding beauties. Nothing but a young calf is so awkward as a girl fresh from the schoolroom, with the exhortations of the governess against forwardness and conceit still echoing in her ears ; knowing no one—understanding nothing—afraid to sit, to stand, to speak, to look—always in a nervous ague of self-misgiving. The blushing, terrified, clumsy girls I noticed yesterday will soon refine into elegant women ; but what will then become of the delicacy of their complexion and the simplicity of their demeanour?"

A "Drawing-room," therefore, is an institution organised to fulfil the object of every fair young *débutante's* ambition, by enabling her to be "presented at court," the event which marks her entry into "fashionable life," and gives her an *entrée* and passport in every European capital.

A Levee or a Drawing-room has always formed the head-quarters of witty retort and polite badinage. Of all Court wits perhaps George Selwyn was the readiest and the happiest. Among other witticisms uttered by him within the precincts of the Court, was one related by Mr. W. C. Hazlitt in his "New London Jest Book." "Lord Galloway was an avowed enemy to the Bute administration. At the change of the Ministry consequent on Lord Bute's fall, he came to St. James's for the first time in George III.'s reign. He was dressed in plain black, and in a very uncourtly style. When he appeared at the Levee, the eyes of the company were turned on him, and inquiries were murmured as to who he could be. George Selwyn being asked, replied that he was not sure, but thought he was 'a Scotch undertaker, come up to London to bury the late administration.'"

There are extant many sketches of the front of the Palace Gate on the day of a Levee or a Drawing-room under the later Stuarts and the Hanoverian sovereigns. The illustration on page 103 shows the king arriving in his coach with the company in carriages and sedan-chairs. As they look at it, some of our readers may possibly remember the lines ascribed to Pope :—

" Roxana, from the Court returning late,
  Sighed her soft sorrow at St. James's Gate ;
  Such heavy thoughts lay brooding in her breast,
  Not her own chairmen with more weight oppressed."

In 1626 sedan chairs were novelties confined to the upper classes and persons " of quality." They were introduced at the West-end by Sir Sanders Duncombe, who represented to the King that "in many parts beyond the seas people are much carried in chairs that are covered, whereby few coaches are used among them," and prayed for the privilege of bringing them into London. Duncombe was patronised by the royal favourite, Buckingham, through whose influence he obtained a concession of the privilege for fourteen years, and made, no doubt, a good round sum of money by the monopoly.

Sedan chairs, which once were as common at the West-end as hansom cabs, and as much used by men as well as ladies of "the quality," figure frequently in Hogarth's pictures of London life. In his day the sedan chair was the courtly vehicle, and in one of the plates of the "Modern Rake's Progress" we see the man of fashion using it in attending court. The chair continued to be in use all through the Georgian era, and even to a later date ; and in some large houses, in the early part of Her Majesty's reign, a specimen of it was to be seen in the hall or lobby of large houses in the West-end, laid up like a ship in ordinary. It was used even to a later date occasionally at Bath, Cheltenham, and Edinburgh, where the chairmen were a very quaint and humorous body, mostly natives of the Highlands.

It is far from uninteresting to mark the introduction of such modes of conveyance, as they become curious in the retrospect, and give us a very fair insight into the habits and manners of past years.

The Sedan chair, though so called from the place where it was originally made, did not come to England from France, but from Spain, being introduced from Madrid by Charles I., when, as Prince of Wales, he went to that city to look for a wife. On his departure from Spain, as we learn from Mendoza's "Relation of what passed in the Royal Court of the Catholic King, our Lord, on the departure of the Prince of Wales," the Prime Minister of Spain, and favourite of Philip IV., Olivarez, gave the Prince "a few Italian pictures, some valuable pieces of furniture, and three sedan chairs of curious workmanship." Another contemporary writer tells us that on his return to England, Charles gave two of these chairs to his favourite, the Duke of Buckingham, who raised a great clamour against himself by using them in the streets of London. Bassompierre, the French Ambassador, in his "Memoirs of the English Court," states that "the popular outcry arose to the effect that the Duke was reducing freeborn Englishmen and Christians to the condition of beasts of burden." When, however, the populace found out that money was to be made out of them, and that to start a "sedan" was a good speculation, they swallowed their scruples, and, like shrewd and sensible persons, invested their savings in building and buying them, so that in a short time they came into common use, not only in London, but in the chief provincial towns. In the country they were never popular.

Amongst those who came to St. James's in "a chair" was John Duke of Marlborough, after his crowning victory of Ramillies, then at the summit of his popularity, and almost worshipped by the people, who measure everything by success. He tried to smuggle himself into the levee in a chair, but in spite of his attempt at privacy he was discovered, and in a few minutes was surrounded by thousands who rent the air with their acclamations.

A courtly and polished condition of society among the wealthier circles is a natural consequence of our monarchical institutions. Mr. N. P. Willis, the American writer, confesses as much when he writes, "The absence of a queen, a court, and orders of nobility, gives us in the States a freedom from trammel in such matters which would warrant quite a different school of polite usages and observances of ceremony. Yet up to the present time," he adds, "we have followed the English punctilios of etiquette with almost as close a fidelity as if we were a suburb of London." So deeply engrained in human nature is the observance of an orderly and regulated ceremonial, even in the minutiæ of daily life.

Johnson remarked that it had been suggested that kings must be unhappy, because they are deprived of the greatest of all satisfactions, easy and unreserved society. "That is an ill-founded notion. Being a king does not exclude a man from such society. Great kings have always been social. The King of Prussia, the only great king at present, is very social. Charles II., the last king of England who was a man of parts, was social; and our Henrys and Edwards were all social."

It is one of the least observed but perhaps not among the least equivocal proofs of a great advancement in the ideas of freedom entertained by the British people, that their king and queen for the time being may be said to be the only sovereigns in Europe who have ceased to have the power of dictating the fashions to their people.

In days of old—nay, so late as the reign of George II.—it was with the English, as it is still with the other nations: the first personages in the kingdom (from being supposed to be the best informed) led the fashions. As the king and queen, so their whole court, and all the higher ranks of the public, were habited, from the celebrated ruff of the good Queen Bess to the elegant head-dress of the amiable Queen Caroline. But the reign of George III. introduced a new era. "Queen Charlotte, on her arrival in this country, evinced a desire to fall in with its national modes, and a chasteness in her own ideas of improvement in dress, which well entitled her to take the lead of her adopted countrywomen in this respect; but English ladies, it seemed, were not now to be led, even by their queen. Her Majesty's first endeavour was to reduce their toupee to a size more suited to the length and breadth of the face, than it had been usual to wear them; and next to introduce a cap neither so diminutive as to be nearly invisible, nor of such a magnitude as to bury the features of the wearer. But in vain were her efforts. Broad and towering head-dresses continued still the rage; and so continued till a love of novelty induced the ladies, of their own accord, to change to something less absurd. As for the gentlemen of those days, they seemed more inclined to follow the manners and dresses of the King's Guards than of the King himself. His Majesty's wig and large hat found as few imitators among his subjects as his domestic virtues. Nor at any time during the many years which George III. and his virtuous consort presided over society in this country, could their influence over the fashions be said to have much increased. The annual fashions among the ladies continued as usual to take date from the day on which her Majesty's birthday was celebrated; but the fashions themselves had little or no regard to what her Majesty wore on such occasions, but rather to what was the most admired among the very splendid varieties presented for general imitation."

This may not be literally true, for the dress of her present Majesty and her mode of arranging her hair on first ascending the throne, were most servilely followed by nearly all the young ladies of England.

The court dress of ladies has varied to a very great extent with the fashions of the age, and the sovereign from time to time has laid down very precise regulations as to what is, and what is not, allowable in the female costume on court occasions. The court dress of gentlemen, however, has undergone but very slight modification during the past century: though wigs and hair-powder are no longer worn, yet the plum-coloured suit of livery with light silk facings, worn till our own time at levees by men, would remind us of so many lacqueys, were it not for the sword which accompanies them. Some slight modifications in this dress were made a few years ago by the authority of the Lord Chamberlain, the most important being the admission of velvet as an optional substitute for the plum-coloured cloth above-mentioned, and the recognition of trousers instead of knee-breeches; but the court costume of the male sex is still somewhat of an anachronism.

At the commencement, and indeed to almost the middle of the reign of George III., a nobleman or a gentleman of "quality" was known by his dress, which he wore not only on "court" days and special occasions, but in the streets, and at evening parties or other gatherings, at home, or at the coffee-houses and clubs. "That costume," writes Sir N. W. Wraxall in 1814, "which is now confined to the levee or drawing-room, was forty years ago worn by persons of condition, with few exceptions, everywhere and every day. Mr. Fox and his friends, who might be said to dictate [social laws] to the town, affecting a style of neglect about their own persons, and manifesting a contempt of all the usages hitherto established, first threw a discredit on the court dress. From the House of Commons and the Clubs in St. James's Street, it spread through the private assemblies of London. But though gradually undermined, and insensibly perishing of an atrophy, dress never totally fell till the era of Jacobinism and equality, in 1793 and the following year. It was then that pantaloons, cropped hair, and shoe-strings, as well as the total abolition of buckles and ruffles, together with the disuse of hair-powder, characterised the dress of Englishmen." To the same influence he traces the decline of a distinctive dress among the ladies also; and expresses a hope, and indeed a prophecy, that "it will be necessary at no very distant period to revive the empire of dress."

The huge hoops worn by the ladies of a century or more ago have occasionally been of service. Sir Robert Strange, for instance, the eminent engraver, being "out in '45," as the phrase then went, being hard driven for shelter from the searchers of the victorious army, hid himself under the ample folds of the petticoats of a Miss Lumsden, whom he requited for the service by marrying her soon afterwards.

The first pair of silk stockings brought into England from Spain was presented to Henry VIII., who greatly prized them. In the third year of Elizabeth's reign, her "tiring" woman, Mrs. Montagu, presented her Majesty with a pair of black silk stockings as a new-year's present; whereupon her Majesty asked if she could have any more, in which case she would wear no more cloth stockings. Silk stockings were equally rare things in the Royal Court of Scotland, for it appears that before James VI. received the ambassadors sent to congratulate him on his accession to the English throne, he requested one of the lords of his court to lend him his pair of silk hose, that he "might not appear as a scrub before strangers."

Apropos of court dresses, we may be pardoned for extracting the following from "Joe Miller's Jest-book:"—"King Charles II. having ordered a new suit of clothes to be made, just at a time when addresses were coming up to him from all parts of the kingdom, Tom Killigrew went to the tailor, and ordered him to make a very large pocket on one side of the coat, and one so small on the other, that the king could hardly get his hand into it; which seeming very odd, when they were brought home, he asked the meaning of it. The tailor said, "Mr. Killigrew ordered it so." Killigrew being sent for and interrogated, said, "One pocket was for the addresses of his Majesty's subjects, and the other for the money they would give him."

Hair-powder was introduced into Europe in the year 1614. It is said that at the accession of George I., only two ladies wore powder. At the coronation of George II. there were but two hairdressers in London: in 1795, there were 50,000 in England.

The full-bottomed wigs which envelope and cloud some of the most distinguished portraits of the Stuart era were still in fashion during the reign of William and Mary. Lord Bolingbroke was one of the first to reduce them by tying them up. At this Queen Anne was much offended, and said to a bystander, that "he would soon come to court in a night-cap." Soon after this, tie-wigs, instead of being regarded as undress, became part and parcel of the high court dress at St. James's and Kensington.

Archbishop Tillotson, who was the first English prelate represented in a wig, says :—"I can well remember since the wearing the hair below the ears was looked upon as a sin of the first magnitude ; and when ministers generally, whatever their text was, did either find or make occasion to reprove the great sin of long hair ; and if they saw any one in the congregation guilty in that kind, they would point him out particularly, and let fly at him with great zeal." It is stated that as far as the women were concerned, there was nothing to blame in this innocent fashion of long locks let free from unnatural constraint ; and the glossy ringlets of the young gentlewomen of 1640, confined only by a simple rose, jewel, or bandeau of pearls, was one of the most elegant head-dresses ever invented to please the eye of man : this, as is well known, is the style that has been transmitted to us in the bewitching portraits of the beauties of the court of Charles II. The decorations of the men's heads were not anything half so simple, for, after the frizzing up the hair from the forehead, and then suffering it to fall in the wild luxuriance that called forth the censures of the clergy, they next proceeded to ornament themselves with borrowed hair ; and the odious invention of the peruke, or periwig, made in imitation of the long, waving curls of the "Grand Monarque," came next into fashion. Charles II., it is well known, adopted this fantastic fashion ; and very soon not a gentleman's head or shoulders were considered to be complete without a French wig.

The farthingale of the sixteenth and beginning of the seventeenth centuries was—as our readers, no doubt, well know—the originator of the hooped petticoat of the eighteenth and of the crinoline of the nineteenth century ; but in many respects the men offered a still broader mark for the satirist, the cavalier being adorned in silk, satin, or velvet of the richest colours, with loose, full sleeves, slashed in front ; the collar, too, of this superb doublet was of the costliest point lace ; his sword-belt, of the most magnificent kind, was crossed over one shoulder, whilst a rich scarf, encircling the waist, was tied in a large bow at the side.

Charles II. curtailed the doublet of its fair proportions, made it excessively short, and opened it in front to display a rich shirt, bulging out without any waistcoat, wearing at the same time Holland sleeves of extravagant size and fantastic contrivance. The ladies' dresses, however, and their drapery were not much affected by the example of royalty.

That the dress of the court fops in the Georgian era was a somewhat expensive commodity, we may infer from " Beau" Brummell's answer to a question once put to him. Being asked by a lady how much she ought to allow her son for dress, he replied, that it might be done for £800 a year, *with strict economy!*

Among the curious customs and ceremonies of the Court, which have been handed down to us from the Stuart times, is that of presenting the poet-laureate—who, by the way, is an "officer of the household of the sovereign"—with a butt of sherry from the royal cellars. Although .the earliest mention of a poet-laureate in England occurs in the reign of Edward IV., it was not till 1630 that the first patent of the office seems to have been granted. Since 1670 the following poets have held the office of laureate :—Dryden, Tate, Rowe, Colley Cibber, William Whitehead, Warton, Pye, Southey, Wordsworth, and Alfred Tennyson.

Mention of the office of poet-laureate leads us naturally to speak of the success attending the poetical and literary efforts of such as have owed their rise in life to royal and courtly patronage. Most of the persons mentioned in the following extract from a modern periodical must have frequently crossed the threshold of St. James's Palace to worship the rising or risen sun of royalty :—
" In the reigns of William III., of Anne, and of George I., even such men as Congreve and Addison would scarcely have been able to live like gentlemen by the mere sale of their writings. But the deficiency of the natural demand for literature was at the close of the seventeenth, and at the beginning of the eighteenth century, more than made up by artificial encouragement—by a vast system of bounties and premiums. There was, perhaps, never a time at which the rewards of literary merit were so splendid—at which men who could write well, found such easy admittance into the most distinguished society, and to the highest honours of the state. The chiefs of both the great parties into which the kingdom was divided, patronised literature with emulous munificence. Congreve, when he had scarcely attained his majority, was rewarded for his first comedy with places which made him independent for life. Smith, though his ' Hippolytus and Phædra' failed, would have been consoled with £300 a year but for his own folly. Rowe was not only poet-laureate, but land surveyor of the Customs in the port of London,

Clerk of the Council to the Prince of Wales, and Secretary of the Presentations to the Lord Chancellor. Hughes was Secretary to the Commissions of the Peace. Ambrose Philips was Judge of the Prerogative Court in Ireland. Locke was Com-

unconquerable prejudice of the Queen, would have been a bishop. Oxford, with his white staff in his hand, passed through the crowd of suitors to welcome Parnell, when that ingenious writer deserted the Whigs. Steele was a Commissioner of Stamps

KITCHEN OF ST. JAMES'S PALACE IN THE TIME OF GEORGE III.

missioner of Appeals, and of the Board of Trade. Newton was Master of the Mint. Stepney and Prior were employed in embassies of high dignity and importance. Gay, who commenced life as apprentice to a silk-mercer, became a Secretary of Legation at five-and-twenty. It was to a poem on the death of Charles II., and to the 'City and Country Mouse,' that Montague owed his introduction into public life, his Earldom, his Garter, and his Auditorship of the Exchequer. Swift, but for the

and a Member of Parliament. Arthur Mainwaring was a Commissioner of the Customs, and Auditor of the Imprest. Tickell was Secretary to the Lords Justices of Ireland. Addison was Secretary of State."

On the western side, and within what we may style the precincts of St. James's Palace, commanding a view both of St. James's Park and the Green Park, stands Stafford House, or as it was called till recently, Cleveland House. The old house derived its name from Barbara, Duchess of Cleveland, one of the mistresses of Charles II. By birth she was a Villiers, the daughter and heiress of the Irish Viscount Grandison; and she was created Baroness of Nonsuch, Countess of Northampton, and Duchess of Cleveland, by her royal admirer, to whom she had borne two sons—Charles Fitz Roy, Earl of Southampton, and George Fitz Roy, Duke of Northumberland.   This lady died

his state of health, and catch at every hope of his amendment.   As he grew worse he ceased to go out in his carriage, and was drawn in a garden chair, at times, round the walks. . . . His manner was as easy and his mind as penetrating and vigorous as ever; and he transacted business in this way, though heavily oppressed by his disorder, with perfect facility."   After his death at the Duke of Devonshire's villa at Chiswick, his body rested

CLEVELAND HOUSE.   (*From a Print published in* 1799.)

at Chiswick in 1709.   Seven years before that, apparently she had resigned her interest in this house, as in 1702 we find it granted by the Crown to Henry, Duke of Grafton: it was then called Berkshire House, from its former owner.   The present house covers also very nearly the site of a smaller mansion, Godolphin House, which at the beginning of the present century was occupied by the Duke of Bedford.   It is deserving of a passing note as having been the residence of Charles James Fox during his last illness.   We learn from his biographer, Trotter, that during this anxious period " the garden of the house in the Stable Yard was daily filled with anxious inquirers; the foreign ambassadors and ministers, and private friends of Mr. Fox, walked there, eager to know

here for a night or two previous to his public funeral in Westminster Abbey.   In the last century Godolphin House became the residence of the Duke of Bridgewater, who new-fronted the mansion with stone.

Stafford House was built about the year 1825 by the Duke of York.   It is said by Mr. Chambers, in his " Handy Guide to London," that it was built with money lent to him by the Marquis of Stafford, whose grandson is the present owner. Be this as it may, the Stafford family became possessed of it, and have spent at least a quarter of a million upon it and its decorations.   The mansion was built by the Duke of York on the site of a former residence, where he and the duchess gave pleasant dinners and receptions, devoting the evenings to whist, at which the duke was a first-rate player. Among his most constant guests were Lords Alvanley, Lauderdale, De Ros, and Hertford, " Beau " Brummell, and the Duke of Dorset. It is said that he planned and built the house from his own designs. The duke was very fond of collecting here curiosities of every description—jewels, bronzes, coins, and articles of *vertu;* he also spent large sums in purchasing old chased plate, with which his sideboards groaned ; and on his walls he had a fine collection of portraits of officers in curious old uniforms. When he left the Stable Yard the duke took up his abode at Cambridge House, in South Audley Street. He died at Rutland House, at the north-western corner of Arlington Street, but his body was afterwards brought to St. James's Palace, where it lay in state, in January, 1827.

It may be mentioned here that Stafford House marks the extreme south-western limit of the parish of St. James's, Piccadilly.

The money received for the sale of Stafford House by the Crown was devoted in 1842 to the purchase of Victoria Park in the East-end of London as a recreation-ground for the people. The form of the mansion is quadrangular, and it has four perfect fronts, all of which are cased with stone. The north or principal front, which is the entrance, exhibits a portico of eight Corinthian columns. The south and west fronts are alike ; they project slightly at each end, and in the centre are six Corinthian columns supporting a pediment. The east front differs a little from the preceding, as it has no projecting columns. The vestibule, which is of noble dimensions, leads to the grand staircase. The library is situated on the ground floor ; and on the first, or principal floor, are the state apartments, consisting of dining-rooms, drawing-rooms, and a noble picture gallery, 130 feet in length, in which is placed the Stafford Gallery, one of the finest private collections of paintings in London ; it is particularly rich in the works of Titian, Murillo, Rubens, and Vandyck. The private rooms contain many valuable art treasures.

The noble suite of drawing-rooms have been often lent by the late and the present Duchesses of Sutherland for the purposes of meetings of gentlemen and ladies who are interested in social reforms, so that the interior of the house is known to very many persons. One of the most novel exhibitions, perhaps, which have taken place here, or anywhere, was in the summer of 1875, when there was held in the garden a show of wicker coffins of all sorts, sizes, and patterns—*apropos,* of course, of the much-vexed question of " earth to earth," which at the time had been so frequently agitated in the newspapers.

Even so lately as 1660, St. James's Palace stood in somewhat open country, as shown by a drawing of that date in the Towneley Collection, which corresponds very closely to the description of the place given by Le Serre in his " Entrée Royale," &c., fol. 1639. " Near the avenues of the palace," says the latter, " is a large meadow, always green, in which the ladies walk in summer ; its great gate has a long street in front, reaching nearly to the fields." A long low wall runs eastwards, along what is now the south side of Pall Mall, and a thick grove of trees covers what is now the site of Marlborough House. As nearly as possible, where now stands the Junior Carlton Club, on the north side of Pall Mall, is a small barn or shed and a haystack ; and in the front of the print, not far from the centre of what is now St. James's Square, stands a handsome conduit, with ornamental brickwork and a lofty crenellated roof ; and the meadow in which it stands, apparently, was not at that time surrounded even by a hedge.

We fear it must be owned to be as true in 1875 as it was half a century before, that the sovereign of England is still without a London residence becoming the head of so great an empire. Though Windsor Castle is unequalled as a mediæval stronghold, we have in London nothing that answers to what the Tuileries was ; and Hampton Court is at best but a poor substitute for the Château of Versailles.

With reference to the mean appearance of St. James's Palace, the author of the " Beauties of England and Wales " writes, in 1815 :—" Few ideas of superior grandeur or magnificence are excited by a partial view of the exterior of this royal palace. And when it is considered that, in fact, this is the only habitation which the monarch of a mighty empire like ours possesses in his capital, strangers are at a loss whether to attribute the circumstance to a penuriousness or meanness of our national character. It arises, in fact, from neither. It has been justly remarked that the disparity between the appearance of this palace, and the object to which it is—or rather has been—appropriated, has afforded a theme of wonder and pleasantry, especially to foreigners, who, forming their notions of royal splendour from piles erected by despotic sovereigns, with treasures wrung from a whole oppressed nation, cannot at once reduce their ideas to the more simple and economical standard which the head of a limited monarchy is compelled to adopt in its expenditure."

CHAPTER XI.

PALL MALL.

" Oh, bear me to the paths of fair Pall Mall !
Safe are thy pavements, grateful is thy smell ;
At distance rolls along the gilded coach,
Nor sturdy carmen on thy walks encroach ;
No lets would bar thy ways were chairs denied—
The soft supports of laziness and pride :
Shops breathe perfumes, through sashes ribbons glow,
The mutual arms of ladies and the beaux."—*Gay's* "*Trivia*," Book ii.

Appearance of Pall Mall in the Time of Charles II.—Charles Lamb prefers Pall Mall to the Lakes of Westmoreland—Bubb Dodington—Cumberland House—Schomberg House—Bowyer's Historic Gallery—The "Celestial Bed"—The *Beggar's Opera* concocted—The Society for the Propagation of the Gospel in Foreign Parts—Nell Gwynne's House—A Relic of Nell Gwynne—The First Duke of St. Albans—Messrs. Christie and Manson's Sale-rooms in Pall Mall—Buckingham House—Lord Temple and Lord Bristol—The Duchess of Gordon as the Tory "Queen of Society"—The War Department—Statue of Lord Herbert of Lea—Marlborough House—The Great Duke of Marlborough—Sarah, Duchess of Marlborough—The Mansion bought by the Crown—Its Settlement upon the Prince of Wales—The Vernon Gallery—Literary Associations of Pall Mall—The "Tully's Head"—The "Feathers"—The Shakespeare Gallery—Notable Sights and Amusements—The British Institution—*Habitués* of Pall Mall during the Regency—The "Star and Garter" Hotel—Duel between Lord Byron and Mr. Chaworth—Introduction of Gas.

PALL MALL is described by Strype, in his edition of Stow, as "a fine long street," adorned with gardens on the south side, many with raised mounds and fine views of the royal gardens and St. James's Park beyond ; nevertheless, three centuries ago, the whole of the space between St. James's Palace and Charing Cross was only a tract of fields. In the time of Charles II. it was sometimes styled Catharine Street, out of compliment to the king's unhappy and neglected consort, Catharine of Braganza. We know that at a far later period it was the favourite haunt of the beaux and dandies of the Regency in a summer afternoon ; and few will have forgotten the popularity of the song of the jovial and genial Captain Morris—

"Oh ! give me the sweet shady side of Pall Mall !"

In the days of Pepys, Pall Mall had really a "sweet shady side," as there grew along it a row of elm-trees, a hundred and fifty in number, "in a very decent and regular manner on both sides of the walk ;" and the few houses which stood on the south side of it were "fair mansions enclosed with gardens." The north side was entirely open, and one or two hay-stacks might be seen on the spot now occupied, as has already been mentioned, by the Junior Carlton Club. At that time the Mall was the fashionable walk of the "upper ten thousand," who afterwards transferred their affections, when the trees were cut down, to the Long Walk in Kensington Gardens.

Some celebrated characters have been remarkable for their fondness for London, and especially for the West-end. The reader may possibly remember that when Charles Lamb was invited by Wordsworth to come down and stay with him by the side of the Westmoreland Lakes, he sighed for the silversmiths' shops about Charing Cross, and the "sweet shady side of Pall Mall."

On the south side, in a house which overlooked the Park and its gardens, resided George Bubb Dodington, afterwards Lord Melcombe, whom Pope immortalised as "Bubo." Lord Hervey tells us in his "Memoirs," that his house "stood close to the garden which the Prince (Frederick, Prince of Wales) had bought of Lord Chesterfield," and that "during Dodington's favour, the Prince had suffered him to make a door out of his house into his garden, which, upon the first decay of his interest, the Prince shut up—building and planting before Dodington's house, and changing every lock to his own house, to which he had formerly given Dodington keys." Dodington was a witty, generous, ostentatious, and, in a political sense, unprincipled man ; but he was the kind patron of James Thomson (who dedicated to him his "Summer"), and also the early friend of Richard Cumberland. To him Dr. Young inscribed his third Satire, and Lord Lyttelton his second Eclogue. The unwarrantable publication of his "Diary" by a person to whom he had left his papers on condition of his printing such only as would do credit to his memory, reveals him to the light as politically the type of profligacy, though probably he was not worse than many of his cotemporaries, who were wise enough not to commit their thoughts to paper. Dodington is thus portrayed by Walpole :—"A man of more wit and more unsteadiness than Pulteney ; as ambitious, but less acrimonious ; no formidable enemy, no sure political, but an agreeable private friend. Lord Melcombe's speeches were as daring and pointed as Lord Bath's were copious and wandering from the subject. Ostentatious in his person, houses, and furniture, he wanted in his expense the taste which he never wanted in his conversation. Pope and Churchill treated him more severely than he deserved—a fate that may attend a man of the greatest wit, when his parts are more suited to society than to composition. The verse remains; the *bon mots* and sallies are forgotten."

"Soon after the arrival of Frederick, Prince of Wales, in England," says his biographer, "Dodington became a favourite, and submitted to the Prince's childish horse-play, being once rolled up in a blanket, and tumbled down stairs; nor was he negligent in paying more solid court, by lending his Royal Highness money. 'This is a strange country, this England,' said his Royal Highness once; 'I am told Dodington is reckoned a clever man; yet I got £5,000 out of him this morning, and he has no chance of ever seeing it again." In 1761 he was advanced to the peerage, under the title of Lord Melcombe Regis; and in the following year he died, at the age of seventy-one." "Poor Lord Melcombe," writes Lady Hervey, "an old friend, and a most entertaining and agreeable companion, has lately been subtracted from the friends I had left. He is really a great loss to me; I saw him often; and he kept his liveliness and his wit to the last."

A good anecdote is told of Lord Melcombe; when his name was Bubb, he was appointed ambassador to Spain. Lord Chesterfield told him it would not do, as the Spaniards could not suppose a man to possess any dignity whose name was a monosyllable. "You must make an addition to it." "But how?" answered Lord Melcombe. "Oh," replied Lord Chesterfield, "I can help you to one: suppose you make it *Silly* Bubb."

As nearly as possible on the site of what is now Carlton Gardens, stood as lately as 1786, if not much later, Cumberland House. It was a large brick mansion, retiring from the street. According to Thornton's "Survey of London," it was built for Edward, Duke of York, but afterwards became the residence of his brother, whose name it bore. Thornton describes it as "a lofty and regular building, with a back-front commanding a beautiful prospect of the Park." The house fell into a neglected state after the duke's death, in 1790. When the union of England and Ireland was in agitation, it was resolved to establish a club in honour of the event; a number of gentlemen then purchased the house and fitted it up for an hotel. It bore the name of the "Albion."

The houses Nos. 81 and 82 formed originally one mansion, known as Schomberg House, which was built during the Commonwealth. Like the adjoining house of Nell Gwynne, it had in its rear a garden with a handsome raised terrace commanding a view of the royal gardens and of the Park beyond. At the Restoration it was tenanted by Edward Griffin, one of the high officers of the court of Charles II. Here afterwards lived the Duke of Schomberg, one of the Dutch generals brought over in his train by William, Prince of Orange, and who fell at the battle of the Boyne: the house was named after him. It was beautified for Frederick, the third and last duke, for whom Peter Berchett painted the grand staircase with landscapes in lunettes. The rest of the history of the mansion shall be told in the words of the author of "Curiosities of London:"—"In 1699 the house was near being demolished by a body of disbanded soldiers; and in the Gordon Riots of 1780 attempts were made to sack and burn it. William, Duke of Cumberland, the hero of Culloden, became tenant of the house in 1760. John Astley, the painter and the 'beau,' who lived here many years, divided the mansion into three, and placed the bas-relief of 'Painting' above the middle doorway. Astley built also on the roof a large painting-room—his country-house, as he called it—overlooking the Park, to which and to some other apartments he had a private staircase. After Astley's death, Cosway the portrait-painter became the tenant of the central portion. Gainsborough occupied the west wing from 1777 to 1788, when he died in a second-floor room. He sent for Sir Joshua Reynolds and was reconciled to him; and then exclaiming, 'We are all going to heaven, and Van Dyke is of our number,' he immediately expired. Part of the house was subsequently occupied by Robert Bowyer for his 'Historic Gallery,' and by Dr. Graham, the empiric, for his 'Celestial Bed,' and other impostures, advertised by two gigantic porters stationed at the entrance, with gold-lace cocked hats and liveries. The house was a good specimen of the red-brick mansion of the seventeenth century. It was partly occupied by Messrs. Payne and Foss, with their valuable stock of old books, until 1850, soon after which the eastern wing was taken down and rebuilt in the Italian style, though incongruously, for the War Department." The house is still remarkable for its foreign design, with wings, pediment, and caryatide porticos.

Many years after the duke's death it was bought from the Earl of Holdernesse, who then owned it, by a portrait painter named John Astley, who, as stated above, divided it into three houses. Gainsborough and his works of art have made one of these houses known far and wide. Astley himself occupied the central house, and raised it by a storey. During the latter part of the eighteenth century it was hired by various speculators in succession as a gallery for the exhibition of pictures, &c., and it is said that more shillings were taken at its doors than at any other house in the time of George III. Early in the present century it was converted to more strictly literary uses, becoming the bookshop of Mr. Thomas Payne, whose father, "honest Tom Payne of immortal memory," had been for forty years a bookseller at the Mews Gate. It was here that was first concocted the dramatic scheme of the *Beggars' Opera*. It was originally proposed to Swift to be named the *Newgate Opera*, as the first thought of writing such a gross and immoral drama originated with him. Swift also, who was an ardent admirer of the poetic talents of Gay, delighted to quote his Devonshire pastorals, they being very characteristic of low, rustic life, and congenial to his taste ; for the pen of the Dean revelled in vulgarity. Under the influence of such notions, he proposed to Gay to bestow his thoughts upon the subject, which he felt assured he would turn to good account, namely, that of writing a work to be entitled " A Newgate Pastoral ; " adding, " and I will, *sub rosâ*, afford you my best assistance." This scheme was talked over at Queensberry House, and Gay commenced it, but soon dropped it, with something of disgust. It was ultimately determined that he should commence upon the *Beggar's Opera*. This proposal was approved, and the opera written forthwith, under the auspices of the Duchess of Queensberry, and performed at the theatre in Lincoln's Inn Fields, under the immediate influence of her Grace, who, to induce the manager, Rich, to bring it upon his stage, agreed to indemnify him all the expenses he might incur, providing that the *daring* speculation should fail.

No. 79, adjoining Schomberg House, was for very many years the head-quarters of the venerable Society for the Propagation of the Gospel in Foreign Parts, prior to its removal, about the year 1870, to Park Place, St. James's Street. The house has been identified as that occupied by Nell Gwynne during the heyday of her career as the favourite of King Charles II. To the south side of it was attached a garden, adjoining that of the King ; and we have already told our readers how Evelyn was a witness on this spot to " a familiar discourse between the King and Mrs. Nelly, as they call an impudent comedian ; she looking out of her garden on a terrace on the top of the wall, the King standing on a green walk under it." According to Mr. John Timbs, part of this " terrace," or raised mound of earth, is still to be seen " under the Park wall of Marlborough House," and the same authority tells us that a bill for erecting this very mound was found among Nell Gwynne's papers. It is interesting to learn that whilst basking in the sunshine of the royal favour Nelly did not forget her poor mother, and that the same doctor's bill which mentions the medicine sent for her own use and that of her little son, includes also " a cordial for old Mrs. Gwynne." Maintained in decent comfort after the King's death, whose last words were " Do not let poor Nelly starve," she died in Pall Mall in November, 1687, and was buried in the church of St. Martin's-in-the-Fields, the vicar, Dr. Tenison, preaching her funeral sermon.

With respect to this residence of Nell Gwynne, Mr. Peter Cunningham writes :—" Nelly at first had only a lease of her house, which as soon as she discovered, she returned the conveyance to the King, with a remark characteristic alike of her wit and of the monarch to whom it was addressed. The King enjoyed the joke, and perhaps admitted its truth ; so the house in Pall Mall was conveyed *free* to Nell and her representatives for ever. The truth of the story," he adds, " is confirmed by the fact that the house which occupies the site of the one inhabited by her, No. 79, is the only freehold on the southern or Park side of Pall Mall. No entry, however, of the grant is to be found in the Land Revenue Record Office." The house rebuilt upon the site of that given by Charles II. to Nell Gwynne was some years since occupied by Dr. Heberden.

Previously to living on this side of Pall Mall, Nell Gwynne had occupied a house on the north side, whither she had removed in 1670, soon after the birth of her eldest son by Charles II. That house is described by Pennant as the first good one on the left hand of St. James's Square, as we enter from Pall Mall. Its site is now covered by the Army and Navy Club. When Pennant wrote, it belonged to Mr. Thomas Brand, afterwards Lord Dacre ; it subsequently was the town residence of Lord De Mauley. Pennant says, " The back room on the ground floor was, within memory, entirely of looking-glass, as also was said to have been the ceiling. Over the chimney was her picture, and that of her sister was in a third room." Mr. John Timbs adds the fact that in Lord De Mauley's house was a relic of Nell Gwynne—namely, her looking-glass ; " this," he tells us, " was bought with the house, and is now in the Visitors' Room of the Club."

Bishop Burnet calls Nell Gwynne the indiscreetest and wildest creature that was ever in a king's court, and says she was maintained at a great expense. The Duke of Buckingham, he says, told him that at first she asked only £500 a year ;

but at the end of the fourth year she had received from the King £60,000. Throughout her whole life she continued negligent in her dress, but that might have arisen from the acknowledged fact that whatever she wore became her. Her eldest son, the name of Beauclerk, and created him Earl of Burford; and shortly before his death made him Duke of St. Albans. In the next house west to Schomberg House lived Mrs. Fitzherbert, of whom we have already spoken.

MESSRS. CHRISTIE AND MANSON'S ORIGINAL AUCTION ROOMS.
From an original Drawing in the possession of Mr. Crace. (See p. 128.)

by Charles II., was born in May, 1670, and the tradition of his first elevation to the peerage is as follows:—Charles one day going to see Nell Gwynne, and the little boy being in the room, the King wanted to speak to him. "Come hither, you little bastard, and speak to your father." "Nay, Nelly," said the King, "do not give the child such a name." "Your Majesty," replied Nelly, "has given me no other name by which I may call him!" Upon this the King conferred upon him

Pall Mall is styled by Malcolm, in 1807, a "handsome street, but subject to the endless rattle of coaches, and the lounging place of strings—or rather links, or chains—of men of fashion, and their humble imitators, during the months in which London is tolerable, that is, from December to June." It could not at this time have been well kept or watered, for he complains that "it becomes a desert when the pavements are dry and the carriage way is fit for crossing." He enumerates

MRS FITZHERBERT'S HOUSE, 1820.

NELL GWYNNE'S HOUSE, 1820.

SCHOMBERG HOUSE, 1820.

(From original Drawings in the possession of Mr. Crace.)

as its chief attractions, Carlton House, Kelly's Opera Saloon, or rather music shop—"made fashionable by an odd set of lattices, distributed over the west front,"—and lastly by Christie's Auction Room, which then stood on the south side, next to Schomberg House.

"The late Mr. Christie," observes Malcolm, "was perhaps the most eminent auctioneer in the world"—George Robins, it may be observed by us in passing, was not then known to fame—"and the value of property which waited the tap of his hammer would almost baffle the powers of calculation. The manors, estates, jewels, plate, and collections of pictures which he sold, were situated in or collected from all parts of the kingdom ; and he had the singular fortune to dispose of the rich articles and paintings of but too many noble fugitives from France, Italy, and Holland during the French Revolution. This house was and is," he adds, "the exhibition of everything curious in the arts, under his son and successor, who to his father's abilities adds a rich stock of classical attainments." It may be added that the first auction in London is said to have been held in 1700.

Among the other various relics which here passed under the hammer of Messrs. Christie, was the famous Shakspeare Cup, which is thus described by Mr. J. T. Smith :—"The much-famed cup, carved from Shakespeare's mulberry-tree, lined with and standing on a base of silver, with a cover surmounted by a branch of mulberry leaves and fruit, also of silver-gilt, which was presented to Mr. Garrick on the occasion of the Jubilee at Stratford-upon-Avon." It was sold early in the present century by Mr. Christie, who addressed the assembly, adjuring them "by the united names of Shakespeare and Garrick" to offer biddings worthy of the occasion. The first bid was 100 guineas ; and it was knocked down ultimately for 121 guineas, the purchaser being Mr. J. Johnson, of Southampton Street, Covent Garden.

How thoroughly these rooms held their position not merely as a mart and market, but also as a criterion of the arts, may be inferred from the first stanza of a poem by Mr. Richard Fenton, published just a century ago :—

" As Painting and Sculpture now bending with years
    Proclaimed an assembly at Christie's great room,
For adopting an heir, and reflected with tears
    On the days when they boasted their vigour and bloom;
The doors were scarce opened, when thronging the space
    With different pretensions the candidates pressed."

And so on. What happened does not much matter; but the lines certainly imply that there was at that time no other "repository" in London where the special works of two at least of the Muses would be likely to find competent critics. Messrs. Christie's sale room was removed in the year 1823 to King Street, St. James's Square.

It is mentioned incidentally by Miss Meteyard, in her "Life of Wedgwood," that in 1768 the great master of pottery was in treaty for some premises in Pall Mall, which had been formerly used as auction rooms, but were then occupied as an "Artists' Exhibition Gallery;" and she gives a print of the house as it then stood. The negotiation, however, passed off.

On the south side also, nearly opposite to the entrance leading to the west side of St. James's Square, is a mansion of the last century, built by Sir John Soane, formerly belonging to Lord Temple, and afterwards to his son, the Marquis of Buckingham, and sometimes therefore called Buckingham House. One night, if we may believe Sir N. W. Wraxall, Mr. (afterwards Lord) Nugent was at a party at Lord Temple's, when, in a foolish frolic, he laid a bet with his host that he would spit in Lord Bristol's hat. He coolly did so, then pretended to apologise for the indecorum, and asked to be allowed to wipe off the affront with his pocket-handkerchief. With a coolness and high breeding which marks the perfect gentleman, Lord Bristol took out his own handkerchief, and performed that office for himself, and then sat down to a rubber of whist. Next morning, however, Lord Bristol addressed him a note demanding an apology or instant satisfaction. Mr. Nugent, judging the matter serious, and not wishing to be made the laughing-stock of the town by fighting a duel for so silly a freak, found himself obliged to tender an apology, to which Lord Temple also was forced to subscribe, both asking his pardon at White's Club. Lord Bristol declared himself satisfied, and there the matter happily ended without blood being shed. This Lord Bristol was George, the eldest son of the famous Lord Hervey, whom Pope has most unjustly handed down to posterity as "Sporus" and "Lord Fanny," and like his father, he had an effeminate manner, which led Mr. Nugent to take the liberty of insulting him—with what result we have seen.

Mr. Nugent is the same individual of whom the same writer tells us another capital story. When he was a member of the House of Commons, in the early part of the reign of George III., a bill was introduced for the better watching of the streets of London and Westminster. One of the clauses proposed that watchmen should be made to go to sleep in the day-time, so as to make them the more active at night. Mr. Nugent, with admirable humour, got up, and in his usual Irish accent, begged the Ministers to include him personally in the provisions of the bill, as he was frequently so tormented with the gout that he could sleep neither by day nor by night. Glover, in speaking of this Mr. Nugent, describes him in very just terms, as " a jovial and voluptuous Irishman, who had left Popery for the Protestant religion, widows, and money." Singularly enough, a great part of his wealth in the end came to the son of this same Lord Temple, afterwards Marquis of Buckingham, by his marriage with Lord Nugent's daughter and heiress.

Buckingham House was the head-quarters of the Tory party in the eventful days of the struggles between Pitt and Fox. Accordingly it suffered some indignities from the mob who marched from Covent Garden to Devonshire House, carrying Mr. Fox in triumph on their shoulders as member for Westminster, in 1784. Five years later, the mansion of Lord Buckingham was tenanted by the Duchess of Gordon, whom Pitt and Dundas put forward as the Tory " Queen of Society," in opposition to the Duchess of Devonshire. With her five unmarried daughters she brought together here the leaders of the " constitutional" party, both Lords and Commons, summoning doubtful members to her receptions, questioning and remonstrating with them, and using all other feminine arts for confirming their allegiance to Pitt.

Buckingham House now forms part of the Government Offices, having been purchased by the War Department. The department of the Secretary for War, the duties of which were formerly performed at the Horse Guards, was established in the year 1856. Up to that time, as we learn from " Murray's Official Handbook," the business had formed part of the duty of the Secretary of State; but the consolidation of the finance of the army in his department had become so inconvenient, that this separate office was then created. Since the remodelling of the administration of our military department after the Crimean war, the Secretary of State for War has been really the supreme controller of the army, assuming and exercising a power which essentially minimises that of the Commander-in-Chief. " Not a soldier can be moved," writes the author of the " Personal History of the Horse Guards," " not an alteration effected, or a comfort administered which involves the expenditure of a shilling, unless it pleases the Secretary for War; he is the prime originator, the Commander-in-Chief the instrument; the one pulls the strings, the other is the puppet."

Before the War Office is a statue of Lord Herbert of Lea, its pedestal inscribed with the name by which he is better known, " Sidney Herbert." " It stands," observes the writer above quoted, " in front of the office which he had dignified by his labours and accomplishments."

At the western end of Pall Mall, and on the south side, almost completely shut out from view by the walls and out-buildings which partially enclose it, and also by the buildings forming the southern side of the street, stands Marlborough House, the town residence of the Prince of Wales. Built in 1709-10, by Sir Christopher Wren for John, Duke of Marlborough, on ground leased on easy terms to his Duchess by Queen Anne; it occupies the site of the old pheasantry of St. James's Palace, and of the garden of Mr. Secretary Boyle, the latter of which was taken out of St. James's Park. The supplement to the *Gazette* of April 18th, 1709, says:—" Her Majesty having been pleased to grant to his Grace the Duke of Marlborough the Friary next St. James's Palace, in which lately dwelt the Countess du Roy, the same is pulling down in order to rebuild the house for his Grace; and about a third of the garden lately in the occupation of the Right Hon. Henry Boyle, her Majesty's Principal Secretary of State, is marked out in order to be annexed to the house of his Grace the Duke of Marlborough." The lease of the site was for fifty years, at a low rental; and this was nearly the only boon which the haughty and grasping Duchess of Marlborough obtained from her royal mistress, as she boasts in a letter of Vindication which was published in her name. How true this statement is will be seen presently.

Marlborough House is thus described by Defoe in his " Journey through England" in 1722:— " The palace of the Duke of Marlborough is in every way answerable to the grandeur of its master. Its situation is more confined than that of the Duke of Buckinghamshire, but the body of the house is much nobler, more compact, and the apartments better composed. It is situated at the west end of the King's Garden on the Park side, and fronts the Park, but with no other prospect but that view. Its court is very spacious and finely paved; the offices are large, and on each side as you enter; the stairs, mounting to the gate, are very noble."

The building is a stately red-brick edifice, ornamented with stone. The front is very extensive; and the wings on each side are decorated at the corners with stone rustic-work. A small colonnade extends on the side of the area next the wings; the opposite side of the area is occupied by sundry offices. The top of the house was originally finished with a balustrade, but that was subsequently altered, and the first storey crowned by an attic raised above the cornice. The front towards the Park resembles the other; only instead of there being two wings, there are niches for statues; and instead of the area as in front, there is a descent by a flight of steps into the gardens. The vestibule was painted with a representation of the battle of Hochstet, in which the most remarkable incident was the taking of Marshal Tallart, the French general, and several other officers of distinction, prisoners; the long series of battles in which the illustrious duke was engaged, including of course those of Malplaquet and Blenheim, were painted by La Guerre as ornaments for the house.

If Marlborough House, even now, is quiet and retired, what must it have been when it was first built, when it was shut in upon two sides by a grove of chestnut-trees, its west front open to the gardens of the Palace, its south to the Park, then private? "Here, and at Blenheim," observes Malcolm, "it might have been supposed that the conqueror of so many battles would have enjoyed the honours lavished on him; but party, ambition, and peculation stepped in, and prevented him from enjoying repose. Had he fallen in battle on the day of his last victory, his memory would have been more gratefully remembered by his countrymen."

It is well known to readers of history that the Duke of Marlborough outlived not only his fame but his reason, and during his latter years was reduced to a state of imbecility, of which he was so conscious that he never liked to be seen by strangers, becoming, as it has been said, a "driveller and a show;" though Archdeacon Coxe, in his "Life" of the duke—the substance of which was inspired by the family—appears to represent him as having retained his powers to the last. One day the witty Dr. Monsey being at Marlborough House, and wishing to get slily a view of the duke, hid himself behind a door in the hall, but did not manage to escape detection. Taylor tells us in his "Recollections" that "the duke, all the while that he was getting into his (sedan) chair, and when he was seated, kept his eye fixed on the doctor, and at the moment when the chairmen were carrying him away, the doctor saw the duke's features gather into a whimper like those of a child, and the tears start into his eyes."

Lord Sackville used to say that one of his earliest memories was that of being carried, when a child of five years old, to the gate of St. James's Palace, in order to see the great Duke of Marlborough, as he came away from court. "He was then (1721) in a state of caducity, but he still retained the vestiges of a most graceful figure, though he was obliged to be supported by a servant on either side, whilst the tears ran down his cheeks, just as he is drawn by Dr. Johnson. The populace cheered him as he passed through the crowd to enter his carriage. I have, however, heard my father say," adds Lord Sackville, "that the duke by no means fell into settled or irrecoverable dotage, as is commonly supposed, but manifested at times a sound understanding till within a very short period of his decease, occasionally attending the Privy Council, and sometimes speaking in his official capacity on matters of business with his former ability."

For the Duke of Marlborough's first step on the ladder of advancement, as Macaulay hints in his "History of England," he was perhaps indebted to the fact of his sister Arabella Churchill being the mistress of James II., as this led to his introduction to the gay scenes of court life. Of the duke in his early days, Macaulay tells a story to the effect that he was one day nearly surprised by the King in the chamber of the Duchess of Cleveland, but effected his escape by leaping out of the window in time to shield his paramour. The duchess rewarded her youthful lover with a present of £5,000, which the prudent young officer laid out in the purchase of a well-secured annuity. Pope adds, it is to be hoped untruly, though we know that the duke grew very avaricious in his old age:—

"The gallant, too, to whom she paid it down,
    Lived to refuse his mistress half-a-crown."

So intense was the avarice of the old duke, who at his death in 1722 left a million and a half behind him, that he would walk home from the Palace or from his neighbour's house, however cold the night, in order to save sixpence in the hire of a sedan chair.

Pope often satirised the Duke of Marlborough. In the early editions of the "Moral Essays" the following lines were inserted, though subsequently suppressed:—

"Triumphant leaders at an army's head,
    Hemm'd round with glories, pilfer cloth, or bread;
    As meanly plunder as they bravely fought,
    Now save a people, and now save a groat."

The satire here is general as respects the army —and nothing could be more lax or extravagant than the system of military accounts and supplies—

but the poet evidently points to Marlborough, whose avarice he frequently condemns. The general did not *pilfer*, but he had taken presents from army contractors. One of the most striking illustrations of his penurious habits, and the best comment on Pope's verses, is an anecdote related by Warton, on the authority of Colonel Selwyn. The night before the battle of Blenheim, after a council of war had been held in Marlborough's tent, at which Prince Louis of Baden and Prince Eugene assisted, the latter, after the council had broken up, stepped back to the tent to communicate something he had forgotten, when he found the duke giving orders to his aide-de-camp at the table, on which there was now only a single light burning, all the others having been extinguished the moment the council was over. "What a man is this," said Prince Eugene, "who at such a time can think of saving the ends of candles!"

After her husband's death his widow, Sarah, continued to live here, and, as we know from the diaries of the time, delighted to speak of "neighbour George," as she styled the Hanoverian King who lived in St. James's.

The readers of English history, and of Mr. Harrison Ainsworth's historical romance of "St. James's," will not need to be reminded of the character of this imperious and ambitious woman, who kept Queen Anne, as well as her court, in awe of her power. It may be well, however, to say that, from the day of that Queen's accession, she lost no opportunity of aggrandising her husband's family and her own at the cost of the patient and long-enduring public. She quickly obtained from the personage whom she styled "her royal mistress," besides large pensions, the posts of Groom of the Stole, Keeper of the Great and Home Parks, and of the Privy Purse, and Mistress of the Robes, whilst she extended her female influence by uniting her eldest daughter, Lady Henrietta Churchill, to the eldest son of the Earl of Godolphin, the Lord High Treasurer; her second daughter, Lady Anne, to the Earl of Sunderland; her third, Lady Elizabeth, to the Earl of Bridgewater; and her youngest, Lady Mary, to the Marquis of Monthermer, afterwards by her interest created Duke of Montagu. Hence the Marlborough and Godolphin party, having almost a monopoly of court influence and favour, were called by their opponents "The Family."

The duchess was accustomed to give here an annual feast, to which she invited all her relations, many of whom were expectant legatees in case of her demise. At one of these family gatherings, she exclaimed, "What a glorious sight it is to see such a number of branches flourishing from the same root!" "Alas!" sighed Jack Spencer to a first cousin next him, "the branches would flourish far better if the root were under ground."

Here, too, in October, 1744, having survived all her children but one, and her husband by more than twenty years, the duke's haughty and imperious widow died at the age of eighty-four. The youngest of the three daughters of a plain country gentleman, Mr. Richard Jennings, of Holywell, on the outskirts of the town of St. Albans, she was sent to London at twelve years old, to become the playmate of the Princess Anne at the court of James II., in each of whose wives she found a patroness in succession. At nineteen she married Colonel John Churchill, "the handsome Englishman," whose merits Turenne had even then acknowledged. Though fond of her husband almost to a fault, she became so intimate a friend of the Princess that they agreed to call each other "Mrs. Freeman" and "Mrs. Morley" respectively. She had apartments in the "Cock-pit" at Whitehall before the abdication of James, and so played her cards as to become a necessary adjunct to the courts of Mary and of Anne, in both of which successively she reigned as "Queen Sarah," at once a beauty and a wit. For the first ten years of Anne's reign she governed the Queen herself without a rival, her husband's successes in war serving to consolidate her power. The accession of Harley and the Tory and High Church party to place and power to some extent shook her influence at Court, which was still further imperilled by her opposition to Queen Anne's wish to exclude the Hanoverian succession. She now became head of the opposition, and exerted in this capacity a really formidable power. She was attacked by Swift, and waged war to the knife with Sir John Vanbrugh, all the years during which he was building Blenheim, and also with Sir Robert Walpole, in spite of his Whig principles. To attempt to give an outline of her career, however, would be to write the history of three reigns, which would be foreign to our purpose here.

Many anecdotes of the Duchess of Marlborough are to be gleaned from books of cotemporary memoirs; none, however, show her character more forcibly than the following:—After the death of her husband, the great Duke of Marlborough, her hand was solicited—partly, no doubt, on account of her wealth—by Charles Seymour, the "Proud" Duke of Somerset, whose first wife had been the heiress of the Percies, and who thought that he honoured her by making the offer of his hand. "The widow of Marlborough shall never become the wife of any other man," was her haughty reply. Whilst she filled the *salons* of Marlborough House with the leaders of the Whig party, the "queen" of the Jacobite Tory circles was the Duchess of Buckingham, a natural daughter of James II. For

retorted her Grace of Buckingham; "since I made the request, I have seen the undertaker, who tells me that he can make as good a one for twenty pounds."

Many other stories, as may easily be imagined,

MARLBOROUGH HOUSE, 1710. *From a contemporary Engraving.* (*See p.* 129.)

her rival she felt both contempt and aversion. Her Grace of Buckingham, on being left a widow, made for him a funeral just as splendid as that with which "Queen" Sarah had honoured her lord; and when her son died, she even sent to Marlborough House to borrow the funeral car on which the hero of Blenheim had been conveyed to his tomb. "It carried my Lord of Marlborough," cried the duchess fiercely, "and it never shall carry any other." "It is of no consequence,"

are current respecting the Duchess of Marlborough. It is said she once pressed the duke to take a medicine, adding, with her usual warmth, "I'll be hanged if it do not prove serviceable." Dr. Garth, who was present, exclaimed, "Do take it, then, my lord duke, for it must be of service one way or the other." Among the duchess's constant guests was Bishop Burnet, whose absence of mind was notorious. Dining with her Grace after her husband's fall, he compared that great general to

Belisarius. "But," said the duchess, eagerly, "how came it that such a man was so miserable, and universally deserted?" "Oh, madam," exclaimed the *distrait* prelate, "he had such a brimstone of a wife!"

Horace Walpole tells an amusing anecdote about

never been removed. The reason is given by Thornton in his "Survey of London and Westminster:"—"When this noble structure was first finished, the late Duchess of Marlborough intended to have opened a way to it from Pall Mall, directly in the front, as appears from the manner in which

SARAH, DUCHESS OF MARLBOROUGH. (*From the Portrait by Lely.*)

the haughty duchess in her last days. He writes:— "Old Marlborough is dying; but who can tell? Last year she had lain a great while ill, without speaking. Her physician said, 'that she must be blistered, or she will die.' She called out, 'I won't be blistered, and I won't die!' And she kept her word; at all events, she recovered for a time."

Many Londoners, no doubt, have often wondered why the houses between Marlborough House and Pall Mall, which so obstruct the view, have

the court-yard is formed. But she reckoned without her host: Sir Robert Walpole having purchased the house before it, and not being on good terms with the duchess, she was prevented from executing her design."

The mansion was bought by the Crown, in the year 1817, for the Princess Charlotte and Prince Leopold, but the Princess died before the purchase was actually completed. Her widower, however (afterwards King of the Belgians), lived in it for several years.

In 1828 there was a talk, but only a talk, as we learn from the Correspondence of the Duke of Wellington, about pulling down Marlborough House and building a street upon its site. The question appears to have been discussed among the Lords of the Treasury on financial grounds, and then to have died away; probably their decision, if any was arrived at, was based on the experience gained at Carlton House.

In 1837 the mansion was thoroughly repaired, decorated, and furnished, and settled by Act of Parliament on Queen Adelaide as a Dowager house. She occupied it till her death in 1849.

Considering that Marlborough House has been the residence of the Prince and Princess of Wales ever since their marriage in 1863, having been settled in 1850 on the Prince on his coming of age, it seems strange to find the following paragraph in the *Weekly Post* of 1714:—"The Duke of Marlborough has presented his house to the Prince and Princess of Wales; and it is said a terrace walk will be erected, to join the same to St. James's House (*sic*)." The mansion then lent to the one Prince of Wales is now the property of the other.

Shortly after the settlement of Marlborough House upon the Prince of Wales, the lower part of the building was appropriated to the accommodation of the Vernon collection of pictures, and others of the English school, until they could be fitly hung in the National Gallery. The upper rooms were set apart for the use of the Department of Practical Art, for a library, museum of manufactures, the ornamental casts of the School of Design, a lecture-room, &c. Here, in 1852, was designed the Duke of Wellington's funeral car, which was subsequently exhibited to the public in a temporary building in the court-yard.

A few of the literary associations of Pall Mall in the last century are thus briefly recorded by Mr. John Timbs in his "Curiosities of London:"— "In gay bachelor's chambers in this street lived 'Beau Fielding'—Steele's 'Orlando the Fair;' here he was married to a supposed lady of fortune, brought to him in a mourning coach and dressed in widow's weeds, which led to his trial for bigamy. Fielding's namesake places Nightingale and Tom Jones in Pall Mall, when they leave the lodgings of Mrs. Miller in Bond Street. Letitia Pilkington for a short time kept here a pamphlet and print shop. At the sign of 'Tully's Head,' Robert Dodsley, formerly a footman, opened a shop in 1735, with the profits of a volume of his poems and of a comedy, published through the kindness of Pope; and this soon afterwards was followed by the 'Economy of Human Life,' and Sterne's

'Tristram Shandy.' Robert Dodsley retired in 1759, but his brother James, his partner, continued the business until his death in 1797; he is buried at St. James's, Piccadilly." The "Tully's Head" was the resort of Pope, Chesterfield, Lyttelton, Shenstone, Johnson, and Glover, as also of Horace Walpole, the Wartons, and Edmund Burke.

The sign of Dodsley's house—which, by the way, was in an age before shops were designated by numbers—was set up out of his regard for Cicero. It is thus mentioned in a newspaper of the time:—

> "Where Tully's bust and honour'd name
> Point out the venal page,
> There Dodsley consecrates to fame
> The classics of the age.
> Persist to grace this humble post
> Be Tully's head the sign,
> Till future booksellers shall boast,
> To sell their tomes as thine."

At Dodsley's, in the winter of 1748-49, was held a meeting at which Warton, Moore, Garrick, Goldsmith, Dr. Johnson, and other literary men were present: on this occasion the title of the then newly intended periodical, the *Rambler*, was discussed. "Garrick," says Boswell, "proposed that it should be called the 'Salad,' on account of the variety of its ingredients"—a name which, by a curious coincidence, was afterwards applied to himself by Goldsmith:—

> "Our Garrick's a salad, for in him we see
> Oil, vinegar, sugar, and saltness agree!"

Dodsley proposed that it should be called the *World*, and at last the company parted without any suggestion of which they all approved being offered. Johnson, it is well known, the same night sat down by his bedside, and resolved that he would not go to sleep till he had fixed a title. "The *Rambler* seemed to me the best," he says, "and so I took it."

At Dodsley's shop was published in 1759 the first volume of the *Annual Register*, planned and prepared by Edmund Burke, whose name had recently become known to the world by his "Essay on the Sublime and Beautiful." To it Burke contributed for many years the department entitled "The Historical Chronicle," as well as some philosophical and other essays. The result was to establish the reputation of the *Annual Register* as a standard work of reference and general information, and for a century and more a fit companion for our library shelves to the *Gentleman's Magazine*.

Dodsley's shop, as already remarked, was the

recognised rendezvous and centre of all who were learned or who cultivated a literary taste. Hence when Burke anonymously published his "Vindication of Natural Society" as a satire on and imitation of Lord Bolingbroke, we read that the poet David Mallet rushed into Mr. Dodsley's when it was most crowded, and made an open disclaimer of its authorship on behalf of both Bolingbroke and himself.

In 1780, Mr. H. Payne, whose shop, as we learn from his title-pages, stood "opposite Marlborough House in Pall Mall," published for an unknown and unbefriended writer named George Crabbe, "The Candidate; a Poetical Epistle to the Authors of the *Monthly Review*." Crabbe was poor; within a few weeks his publisher failed; and the young poet was plunged into great perplexity, which led him to seek aid—but in vain—in high circles, where afterwards, when he no longer needed it, he found ready assistance and support. So selfish and blind is human nature.

Apropos of the literary character or reputation of this locality in former times, it may be stated that Pall Mall has given a name to more than one newspaper, all of which perhaps have almost passed clean out of memory. In 1865 was commenced the evening paper bearing the title of the *Pall Mall Gazette;* this, however, has little or nothing to do with Pall Mall, except that it is supposed to retail much of Club talk and gossip. There was published in the reign of George II. a collection of loose tales and biographical sketches, mainly taken from West-end life, and named the "Pall Mall Miscellany." It went through several editions.

As a proof of the rural character of this part of the town, it may be mentioned that in the reign of Charles II. there was in Pall Mall—as at a later time in Piccadilly—an inn rejoicing in the name of the "Hercules' Pillars," denoting, of course, the very westernmost extremity of what then was the metropolis.

"The Feathers" is, of course, the symbol of the Prince of Wales; and there can be no doubt that, considering the fact of the Prince and Princess of Wales being resident at Marlborough House, the sign of "The Feathers" would be by far the most popular now-a-days, if it were still the fashion to denote the houses in Pall Mall and elsewhere by signs instead of numbers.

There was a sign of "The Feathers" in Pall Mall during the time of the Great Plague, as is clear from the following advertisement in one of the newspapers published at that time :—"The late Countess of Kent's powder has been lately experimented upon divers infected persons with admirable success. The virtues of it against the plague and all malignant distempers are sufficiently known to all the physicians of Christendom, and the powder itself, prepared by the only person living that has the true receipt, is to be had at the third part of the ordinary price at Mr. Calvert's, at 'The Feathers,' in the old Pall Mall, near St. James's," &c.

On the north side of Pall Mall, a little to the east of St. James's Street, stood formerly the Shakespeare Gallery, the creation of that real and true patron of art, and especially of historical painting and engraving, Alderman Boydell, whose name is far less well known than it deserves to be among artists and men of taste. Beginning life as an engraver, he spent a larger sum than any nobleman had done up to that time in encouraging a British school of engraving; for, as he tells us in one of his appeals, "when he commenced business nearly all the fine engravings sold in England were imported from abroad, and more especially from France." The outbreak of the French Revolution seriously embarrassed his venture in this artistic business, and in 1789 he was obliged to make arrangements for disposing of his Gallery. He brought out, happily, a costly edition of the works of Shakespeare, the profits of which, together with a Shakesperian lottery, saved him from bankruptcy. After his death, however, the Gallery was for some years vacant, and Malcolm in 1807 speaks of it as "a melancholy memento of the irretrievable ruin of the arts in England."

When Alderman Boydell first proposed, in the interest of the fine arts, to issue his superb edition of Shakespeare, an envious cotemporary imputed his patriotism to sheer vanity, and the following lines appeared in one at least of the journals :—

"Old Father Time, as Ovid sings,
Is a great eater up of things,
 And without salt or mustard
Will gulp down e'en a castle wall
As easily as at Guildhall
 An alderman eats custard.

But Boydell, careful of his fame,
By grafting it on Shakespeare's name,
 Shall beat his neighbours hollow :
For to the Bard of Avon's stream
Old Time has said, with Polypheme,
 'You'll be the last I'll swallow.'

In the last century, the pillory was occasionally set up here, as well as at Charing Cross; one of the last sufferers from this punishment in Pall Mall was a notorious lady of the stamp of Mrs. Cornelys, who was pelted with rotten eggs by the gentry as well as by the rabble, and, if tradition may be believed, by the soldiery as well. She had probably been plying her trade in the neighbourhood of St. James's.

John Timbs reminds us that Pall Mall had at an early date its notable sights and amusements. "In 1701 were shown here models of William III.'s palaces at Loo and Hunstaerdike, 'brought over by outlandish men,' with curiosities disposed of 'on public raffling days.' In 1733 'a holland smock, a cap, checked stockings, and laced shoes,' were run for by four women in the afternoon, in Pall Mall; and one of its residents, the High Constable of Westminster, gave a prize laced hat to be run for by five men, which created so much riot and mischief that the magistrates issued precepts to prevent future runs to the very man most active in promoting them!" In the old "Star and Garter" house, westward of Carlton House, was exhibited, in 1815, the Waterloo Museum of portraits and battle scenes, cuirasses, helmets, sabres, firearms, and trophies of Waterloo; besides a large picture of the battle painted by a Flemish artist. At No. 121 Campanani exhibited his Etruscan and Greek Antiquities, in rooms fitted up as the "Chambers of Tombs."

At No. 52, on the north side, now the Marlborough Club, the British Institution was founded as far back as 1805 for the encouragement of native art, by affording to English artists facilities for the exhibition and sale of their productions. The Institution had two exhibitions every year; the former from February to May for the works of living artists, and the latter from June to the end of the summer for the works of old masters, lent by their owners for the occasion. Here was exhibited West's large picture of "Christ healing the Sick in the Temple," bought by the British Institution for 3,000 guineas, and presented to the National Gallery. Pall Mall has always been a place for exhibitions, especially of pictures. In the present year (1882) here are three or four galleries devoted to the fine arts :—No. 53 is the Institute of Painters in Water Colours; the British Gallery of Art is at No. 57; and No. 120, further eastward, is the Exhibition of Paintings by Continental Artists.

On the site of the British Institution, in the early part of the reign of George III. (1764-5), was "Almack's Club." It was celebrated as the home of Macaronis and high play. It was afterwards known as "Goose-tree's" Club, and William Pitt was one of its frequenters. It was here that he made the acquaintance of Wilberforce. Of the association so long known as "Almack's" we shall have more to say when we come to King Street. Mr. Timbs mentions here a club called the "*Je ne sais quoi*" Club, of which he says that the Prince of Wales, the Dukes of York, Clarence, Orleans, Norfolk, and Bedford, were members; but no details of its history are known to exist.

Among the *habitués* of Pall Mall, in the days of the Regency, was George Hanger, the eccentric "Lord Coleraine." Mr. C. Redding says in his "Recollections :"—"He might be seen in Pall Mall riding his grey pony without a servant; then dismounting at a bookseller's shop, he would get a boy to hold his horse, and sit upon the counter for an hour, talking to Burdett, Bosville, or Major James, who used to haunt that shop, Budd and Calkin's then or afterwards. He was a very rough subject, but honest to the backbone, and plain speaking. He carried a short, thick shillelagh, and now and then took his quid. A favourite of the Prince of Wales, he administered a well-merited reproof to the Prince and the Duke of York one day at Carlton House for the grossness of their language. His name in consequence became no longer on the list of guests there. Upon this, as often related by others, he advertised himself as a coal merchant. Meeting the Prince one day on horseback afterwards, the former addressed him, 'Well, George, how go coals now?' 'Black as ever, please your Royal Highness,' was the quick reply."

In this street was living Lord George Germain, when Secretary of State for the American department in 1781; and here Sir N. W. Wraxall, Lord Walsingham, and a large party were dining in the November of that year, when a messenger arrived announcing the defeat and surrender of the forces in America under Lord Cornwallis. The tidings sent on to the King at Kew, Wraxall tells us, never disturbed the King's dignity nor affected his self-command, deeply as it grieved his heart.

At her residence in Pall Mall, in 1815, at the age of eighty-three, died the celebrated Mrs. Abington, the first actress who played the part of *Lady Teazle* in the "School for Scandal." "Of all the theatrical ungovernable ladies under Mr. Garrick's management," says Mr. Raikes, in his "Book for a Rainy Day," "Mrs. Abington, with her capriciousness, inconsistency, injustice, and unkindness, perplexed him the most. She was not unlike the miller's mare, for ever looking for a white stone to shy at. And though no one has charged her with malignant mischief, she was never more delighted than when in a state of hostility, often arising from most trivial circumstances, discovered in mazes of her own ingenious construction. Mrs. Abington, in order to keep up her card-parties, of which she was very fond, and which were attended by many ladies of the highest rank, absented herself from her abode to live *incog*. For this purpose she generally took a small lodging in one of the passages leading from Stafford Row, Pimlico, where plants are so placed at the windows as nearly to shut out the light, at all events, to render the apartments impervious to the inquisitive eye of such characters as Liston represented in 'Paul Pry.' Now and then, she would take a small house at the end of Mount Street, and there live with her servant in the kitchen, till it was time to reappear; and then some of her friends would compliment her on the effects of her summer's excursion."

In the year 1756 a gentleman named William Backwell, one of the partners in the banking-house of Messrs. Child, of Temple Bar, started on his own account a bank in Pall Mall, and named it "The Grasshopper." It dragged on its existence, in anything but prosperity, down to 1810, when it closed its accounts, and its business was absorbed into other establishments. The Army and Navy Club occupies the site of the bank.

As one of the leading thoroughfares in the neighbourhood of the Court and the aristocracy, Pall Mall is very naturally associated in our minds with the coaches and sedan chairs of our grandfathers' days. Nor will the English reader probably have forgotten how Gay alludes to the latter in his "Trivia:"—

> " For who the footman's arrogance can quell,
> Whose flambeau gilds the sashes of Pall Mall,
> When in long ranks a train of torches flame,
> To light the midnight visits of the dame?"

But of these we have already spoken in our chapter on St. James's Palace.

In this street was an old and fashionable hotel, now long forgotten, named the "Star and Garter." Here, as we learn from the title-page of a small publication on the rules of that English game, were "The Laws of Cricket revised on February 25, 1774, by a committee of noblemen and gentlemen." The "Rules" are prefaced by a woodcut of the bat then in use, which appears to have been curved, and with a face perfectly flat, whereas the modern bat is quite straight, and has a face slightly convex. Perhaps the best information about the early history of the game is to be found in "The Young Cricketer's Tutor, by John Nyren," who was for many years a celebrated member of the Hambledon Club.

In one of the public rooms of the "Star and Garter," in 1762, was fought the fatal duel between William, fifth Lord Byron, and his neighbour in Nottinghamshire, old Mr. Chaworth. The ground of the quarrel was a trivial one, arising out of a heated argument over a dinner-table; but in little more than an hour from its commencement, Mr. Chaworth received a mortal wound from his opponent. Lord Byron — who was the great-uncle and immediate predecessor of the poet—was tried for the capital offence; but the House of Lords found him guilty of manslaughter only, and, as he pleaded his privilege of peerage, he was let off, and discharged from custody on payment of the fees! The "Star and Garter" was famous for its choice dinners and its exorbitant prices, as we learn from the *Connoisseur* of 1754.

It may sound strange when we tell our readers that, as late as the year 1786, a highway robbery was committed on one of his Majesty's mails in Pall Mall. At all events, Horace Walpole writes in January of that year: "On the 7th, half an hour after eight, the mail from France was robbed in Pall Mall—yes, in the great thoroughfare of London, and within call of the Guard at the palace. The chaise had stopped, the harness was cut, and the portmanteau was taken out of the chaise itself. What think you of banditti in the heart of such a capital?"

The Hon. Amelia Murray writes, in her "Recollections," under the year 1811: "It was about this time that gas was first introduced into England; a German of the name of Winsor gave lectures about it in Pall Mall. He had made his first public experiments at the Lyceum, in the Strand, in 1803. He afterwards lighted with gas the walls of Carlton Palace Gardens, on the king's birthday, in 1807, and during 1809 and the following year he lighted a portion of Pall Mall. He died in 1830. My eldest brother," she adds, "and my uncle were so convinced of the importance of the discovery, that they exerted themselves to get a bill through Parliament which gave permission for an experiment to be made; and my uncle established the first gas-works. Like all the pioneers in great works, he was ruined, and his country place, Farnborough Hill, came to the hammer. Since then the old house has been taken down, and a modern mansion has been built by the present possessor of the property; and it is a curious circumstance that the new house is lit throughout by gas made upon the spot. The greatest chemists and philosophers may be mistaken. In 1809, Sir Humphry Davy gave it as his opinion that it would be as easy to bring down a bit of the moon to light London, as to succeed in doing so with gas!" Walker says, in his "Original:" "The first exhibition of gas was made by Winsor, in a row of lamps in front of the colonnade before Carlton House, then standing on the lower part of Waterloo Place; and I remember hearing Winsor's plan of lighting the metropolis laughed to scorn by a company of very scientific men." To our disgrace, Grosvenor Square was the last public place in the West-end of London where gas was adopted.

Macaulay thus records the state of the metropolis, in respect to lighting, two centuries ago :— " It ought to be noticed that, in the last year of the reign of Charles the Second, began a great of one night in three. But such was not the feeling of his contemporaries. His scheme was enthusiastically applauded, and furiously attacked. The friends of improvement extolled him as the greatest of all the benefactors of his city. What, they asked, were the boasted inventions of Archimedes, when compared with the achievement of the man who had turned the nocturnal shades into noon-day? In spite of these eloquent eulogies

THE SHAKESPEARE GALLERY, PALL MALL.   *From a Drawing in Mr. Crace's Collection.*   (*See p.* 135.)

change in the police of London, a change which has perhaps added as much to the happiness of the body of the people as revolutions of much greater fame. An ingenious projector, named Edward Heming, obtained letters patent conveying to him, for a term of years, the exclusive right of lighting up London. He undertook, for a moderate consideration, to place a light before every tenth door, on moonless nights, from Michaelmas to Lady Day, and from six to twelve of the clock. Those who now see the capital all the year round, from dusk to dawn, blazing with a splendour beside which the illuminations for La Hogue and Blenheim would have looked pale, may perhaps smile to think of Heming's lanterns, which glimmered feebly before one house in ten during a small part the cause of darkness was not left undefended. There were fools in that age who opposed the introduction of what was called the new light, as strenuously as fools in our age have opposed the introduction of vaccination and railroads. Many years after the date of Heming's patent there were extensive districts in London in which no lamp was seen."

Those who may wish for further information on the subject of gas will find it in a work called " Angliæ Metropolis," 1690, sect. 17, entitled, " Of the New Lights," and in two works on gas-lighting by the late Mr. Samuel Clegg, jun. (son of the inventor of the gas-meter), and by Mr. Samuel Hughes, both published some years ago in Weale's " Educational Series."

OLD HOUSES IN PALL MALL, ABOUT 1830. (*From an Original Drawing in Mr. Crace's Collection.*)

CHAPTER XII.

PALL-MALL.—CLUB-LAND.

"Man is a social animal."—Aristotle, "Politics."

Advantages of the Club System—Dr. Johnson on Club-Life—Earliest Mention of Clubbing—Club-Life in Queen Anne's Time—The "Albion" Hotel—The "King's Head" and the "World" Club—Usual Arrangements of a Club House—The "Guards'" Club—"Junior Naval and Military"—The "Army and Navy"—The "United Service"—The "Junior United Service"—The "Travellers'"—The "Oxford and Cambridge"—The "Union"—The "Athenæum"—Sam Rogers and Theodore Hook—An Anecdote of Thomas Campbell, the Poet—The "Carlton"—The "Reform"—M. Soyer as *Chef de Cuisine*—The Kitchen of the "Reform" Club—Thackeray —at the "Reform" Club The "Pall Mall" "Marlborough," and "Century" Clubs—Sociality of Club-Life.

As Pall Mall and the immediate neighbourhood of St. James's have been for a century the head-quarters of those London clubs which have succeeded to the fashionable coffee-houses, and are frequented by the upper ranks of society, a few remarks on Club-land and Club-life will not be out of place here.

As Walker observes in his " Original," the system of clubs is one of the greatest and most important changes in the society of the present age from that of our grandfathers, when coffee-houses were in fashion. " The facilities of life have been wonderfully increased by them, whilst the expense has been greatly diminished. For a few pounds a year, advantages are to be enjoyed which no fortunes, except the most ample, can procure. . . . For six guineas a year, every member has the command of an excellent library, with maps ; of the daily papers, London and foreign, the principal periodicals, and every material for writing, with attendance for whatever is wanted. The building is a sort of palace, and is kept with the same exactness and comfort as a private dwelling. Every member is a master without the troubles of a master. He can come when he pleases, and stay away as long as he pleases, without anything going wrong. He has the command of regular servants, without having to pay or to manage them. He can have whatever meal or refreshment he wants at all hours, and served up with the cleanliness and comfort of his own home. He orders just what he pleases, having no interest to think of but his own. In short, it is impossible to suppose a greater degree of liberty in living. To men who reside in the country and come occasionally to town, a club is particularly advantageous. They have only to take a bed-room, and they have everything else they want, in a more convenient way than by any other plan. Married men whose families are absent find in the arrangements of a club the nearest resemblance to the facilities of home ; and bachelors of moderate incomes and simple habits are gainers by such institutions in a degree beyond calculation. They live much cheaper, with more ease and freedom, in far

better style, and with much greater advantages as to society, than formerly. Before the establishment of clubs, no money could procure many of the enjoyments which are now within the reach of an income of three hundred a year. . . . Neither could the same facilities of living, nor the same opportunities of cultivating society, have been commanded twenty years since " [he wrote this in 1835] " on any terms. . . . In my opinion, a well-constituted club is an institution affording advantages unmixed with alloy."

In these remarks Mr. Walker draws for his experience on the club to which he belonged, the " Senior Athenæum ;" and he enters into some interesting calculations as to the cost of living, if a man makes such a club his head-quarters. From the accounts of his club in 1832, it appeared that the daily average of dinners was forty-seven and a fraction, and that the dinners for the year, a little over 17,000 in number, cost on an average two shillings and ninepence three farthings, and that the average quantity of wine drunk by each diner was a small fraction over half a pint ! It is to be feared that all the clubs in the West-end could not show an equally abstemious set of diners; but still, it may fearlessly be said that the majority of them exhibit a simplicity which contrasts very favourably with the old taverns and coffee-houses of fifty or sixty years ago, and the excesses to which they too often ministered occasion. And although the ladies, as a body, do not like "those clubs," because they are more or less antagonistic to early marriages, yet Mr. Walker defends them on even what may be called the matrimonial ground, asserting that " their ultimate tendency is to encourage marriage, by creating habits in accordance with those of the married state ;" and he adds emphatically : " In opposition to the ladies' objections to clubs, I would suggest . . . . that they are a preparation, and not a substitute, for domestic life. Compared with the previous system of living, clubs induce habits of economy, temperance, refinement, regularity, and good order ; and as men are in general not content with their condition as long as it can be improved, it is a natural step from the comforts of a club to those of matrimony, and . . . there cannot be better security for the good behaviour of a husband than that he should have been trained in one of these institutions. When ladies suppose that the luxuries and comforts of a club are likely to make men discontented with the enjoyments of domestic life, I think they wrong themselves. One of the chief attractions of a club is, that it offers an imitation of the comforts of home, but only an imitation, and one which will never supersede the reality."

The London system of clubs, grouping, as it does, around Pall Mall and St. James's, finds its outward expression in buildings that give dignity and beauty to the thoroughfare in which they stand by their architectural splendour. They afford advantages and facilities of living which no fortunes, except the most ample, could procure, to thousands of persons most eminent in the land, in every path of life, civil and military, ecclesiastical, peers spiritual and temporal, commoners, men of the learned professions, those connected with literature, science, the arts, and commerce, in all its principal branches, as well as to those who do not belong to any particular class. These are represented by the "Carlton," the "Reform," the "University," the "Athenæum," the "Union," the "United Service," the "Army and Navy," the "Travellers'," and a host of others.

The opinion of Dr. Johnson on the subject of clubs and club-life is well known to every reader of Boswell. A gentleman venturing one day to say to the learned doctor that he sometimes wondered at his condescending to attend a club, the latter replied, "Sir, the great chair of a full and pleasant town club is, perhaps, the throne of human felicity." Again, the learned doctor touches on this phase of life in the great metropolis, in the following conversation, also related by Boswell :— "Talking of a London life," he said, "the happiness of London is not to be conceived but by those who have been in it. I will venture to say, there is more learning and science within the circumference of ten miles from where we now sit, than in all the rest of the kingdom." Boswell : "The only disadvantage is the great distance at which people live from one another." Johnson : "Yes, sir; but that is occasioned by the largeness of it, which is the cause of all the other advantages." Boswell : "Sometimes I have been in the humour of wishing to retire to a desert." Johnson : "Sir, you have desert enough in Scotland."

Addison, who knew something about the coffee-house, and what we may call the "club-life" of his day, has given us, in his own graphic style, a sketch of St. James's Coffee-house, which stood near the western end of Pall Mall. We have already spoken of him as a frequenter of "Button's"* in Covent Garden, and as a member of the celebrated Kit-cat Club,† in Shire Lane ; indeed, he modestly surmised that his detractors had some colour for calling him the King of Clubs, and oracularly said that "all celebrated clubs were founded on eating and drinking, which are points where most men agree, and in which the learned and the illiterate, the dull and the airy, the philosopher and the buffoon, can all of them bear a part." But it is not every club that has avowed itself by its name or title as formed on this basis. "The Kit-Kat itself," says Addison, in illustration of the proposition quoted from him above, "is said to have taken its original from a Mutton-Pye. The Beef-Steak and October Clubs are neither of them averse to eating and drinking, if we may form a judgment of them from their respective titles."

The truth is, that two centuries ago clubs were the natural resorts of men who, though socially inclined, did not enjoy the social position, and could not, therefore, command the introductions into high circles which were accorded to Pepys or Evelyn in the seventeenth, and to Horace Walpole in the eighteenth century.

Pall Mall, if we may trust John Timbs, was noted for its tavern clubs more than two centuries since. "The first time that Pepys mentions it," writes Peter Cunningham, "is under date 26th July, 1660, where he says, 'We went to Wood's, our old house for clubbing, and there we spent till ten at night.'" The passage is curious, not only as showing how, even at that time, Pall Mall was famous for houses of entertainment, but also as the earliest instance of the use of the verb "to club" in the sense in which we now commonly use it.

Thackeray describes the club-life at the West-end, in Queen Anne's day, with his usual felicity : "It was too hard, too coarse a life, for the sensitive and sickly Pope. He was the only wit of the day . . . . who was not fat. Swift was fat; Addison was fat; Steele was fat; Gay and Thomson were preposterously fat. All that fuddling and punch-drinking, that club and coffee-house boozing, shortened the lives and enlarged the waistcoats of the men of that age." "The chief of the wits of his time, with the exception of Congreve," he writes again, "were what we should now call 'men's men.' They spent many hours of the four-

* See Vol. III., p. 277.　　　† See Vol. III., p. 20.

and-twenty, nearly a fourth part of each day, in clubs and coffee-houses, where they dined, drank, and smoked. Wit and news went by word of mouth: a journal of 1710 contained the very smallest portion of either the one or the other. The chiefs spoke; the faithful *habitués* sat around; strangers came to wonder and to listen. . . . The male society passed over their punch-bowls and tobacco-pipes almost as much time as ladies of that age spent over spadille and manille."

We see few traces of club-life in the gossiping writings of Horace Walpole, though so many of his personal friends—George Selwyn, for example —were devoted to its pleasures. For himself, it is scarcely uncharitable to add that he was scarcely robust enough to live in such an element.

The clubs in London in the days of the Regency belonged exclusively to the aristocratic world. In the words of Captain Gronow: "My tradesmen," as King Allen used to call the bankers and the merchants, had not then invaded White's, Boodle's, Brookes's, or Wattier's, in Bolton Street, Piccadilly; which, with the Guards', Arthur's, and Graham's, were the only clubs at the West-end of the town. "White's" was decidedly the most difficult of entry; its list of members comprised nearly all the noble names of Great Britain. Its politics were decidedly Tory. Here play was carried on to an extent which made many ravages in large fortunes, the traces of which have not disappeared at the present day. General Scott, the father-in-law of George Canning and the Duke of Portland, was known to have won at "White's" a large fortune; thanks to his notorious sobriety and knowledge of the game of whist. The general possessed a great advantage over his companions by avoiding those indulgences at the table which used to muddle other men's brains. He confined himself to dining off something like a boiled chicken, with toast and water; by such a regimen he came to the whist-table with a clear head, and possessing as he did a remarkable memory, with great coolness and judgment, he was able to boast that he had won honestly no less than £200,000.

It is traditionally said that the first modern mansion in Pall Mall which was used as a club in the present sense of the word was No. 86, now part of the War Office, and originally built for Edward Duke of York, brother of George III. It was opened as a "subscription house," and called the "Albion Hotel." This must have been towards the end of the last century.

Cyrus Redding tells us that in 1806, when he first came up from Cornwall to London, single men, of all classes, including the best, still passed

a good part of their time in coffee-houses; the great objection to which plan, he seems to think, was the bad ventilation of these places, and fatal to young men fresh from their country hills. They used to be crowded, especially in the evening, and the conversation in them was general. "The sullen club-house, united with the *rus in urbe* dwelling, and the out-of-town life, not further off than the suburbs, have diminished sociality, and changed the aspect of town intercourse." He means to add, no doubt, "for the worse;" and possibly the accusation may be true.

Spence tells us in his "Anecdotes" that there was a club held at the "King's Head" in Pall Mall, which arrogantly styled itself "The World." Among its members was Lord Stanhope, afterwards Earl of Chesterfield. "Epigrams were proposed to be written on the glasses by each member after dinner: once, when Dr. Young was invited thither, the Doctor would have declined writing because he had no diamond. Lord Stanhope lent him his own diamond, and the Doctor at once improvised the following :—

" Accept a miracle instead of wit:
     See two dull lines with Stanhope's pencil writ."

Dr. Johnson, as we have already seen, considered that "the full tide of human life could be seen nowhere save in the Strand;" but in fifty years after his death the centre of social London had moved somewhat further west, and Theodore Hook, in the reign of William IV., maintained that "the real London is the space between Pall Mall on the south, and Piccadilly on the north, St. James's Street on the west, and the Opera House to the east." At this period, it is to be observed that he himself lived just outside that world which he defined with such geographical precision, being then tenant of a house in Cleveland Row.

Many of the old clubs have passed away, for though some of them, or similar societies, may still exist, they live behind the scenes, instead of figuring conspicuously upon the stage of London life. Quite a new order of things has come up: from small social meetings held periodically, the clubs have become permanent establishments, luxurious in all their appointments—some of them indeed occupy buildings which are quite palatial. No longer limited to a few acquaintances familiarly known to each other, they count their numbers by hundreds, and, sleeping accommodation excepted, provide for them abundantly all the comforts and luxuries of an aristocratic home and admirably-regulated *ménage*, without any of the trouble inseparable from a private household, unless it be one whose management is, as in a club-house, confided to responsible superintendents. Each member of a club is expected to leave his private address with the secretary; but this, of course, remains unknown to the outside world, and considerable advantage frequently results from the arrangement, inasmuch as it was some years ago determined by a County Court judge, who before his elevation to the bench had been sadly annoyed by such visitants, that the interior of a club was inviolable by the bearers of writs, summonses, orders, executions, and the like. Besides those staple features, news-room and coffee-room, the usual accommodation of a club-house comprises library and writing-room, evening or drawing-room, and card-room, billiard and smoking rooms, and even baths and dressing-rooms; also a "house dining-room," committee-room, and other apartments, all appropriately fitted up according to their respective purposes, and supplied with almost every imaginable convenience. In addition to the provision thus amply made for both intellectual and other recreation, there is another important and tasteful department of the establishment— namely, the *cuisine*.

As to the management of a club household, nothing can be more complete or more economical, because all its details are conducted systematically, and therefore without the slightest confusion or bustle. Every one has his proper post and definite duties, and what contributes to his discharging them as he ought is that he has no time to be idle. The following is the scheme of government adopted:—At the head of affairs is the committee of management, who are generally appointed from among the members, and hold office for a certain time, during which they constitute a board of control, from whom all orders emanate, and to whom all complaints are made and irregularities reported. They superintend all matters of expenditure and the accounts, which latter are duly audited every year by others, who officiate as auditors. The committee further appoint the several officers and servants, also the several tradespeople. The full complement of a club-house establishment consists of secretary and librarian, steward, and housekeeper; to these principal officials succeed hall-porter, groom of the chambers, butler, under butler; then, in the kitchen department, clerk of the kitchen, *chef*, cooks, kitchen-maids, &c.; lastly, attendants, or footmen, and female servants, of both which classes the number is greater or less, according to the scale of the household. It may be added that most of the clubs distribute their broken viands to the poor of the surrounding parishes.

So far as the general arrangement of the club-houses is concerned, one description may serve for the whole, as there is little difference between the majority of them. The kitchen, cellars, store-rooms, servants' hall, &c., are situated in the basement of the building. On the ground floor the principal hall is usually entered immediately from the street; in other instances it is preceded by an outer vestibule of smaller dimensions and far more simple architectural character. At a desk near the entrance is stationed the hall-porter, whose office it is to receive and keep an account of all messages, cards, letters, &c., and to take charge of the box into which the members put letters to be delivered to the postman. The two chief apartments on this floor usually are the morning-room and coffee-room, the first of which is the place of general rendezvous in the early part of the day, and for reading the newspapers. In some club-houses there is also what is called the "strangers' coffee-room," into which members can introduce their friends as occasional visitors. The "house dining-room" is generally on this floor. Here, although the *habitués* of the club take their meals in the coffee-room, some of the members occasionally—perhaps about once a month—make up a set dinner-party, for which they previously put down their names, the day and number of guests being fixed: these, in club parlance, are styled "house dinners." Ascending to the upper or principal floor, we find there the evening or drawing room, and card-room; the library, the writing-room. So far as embellishment or architectural effect is concerned, the first mentioned of these rooms is generally the principal apartment in the building. The writing-room is a very great accommodation to members, for many gentlemen write their letters at, and date them from, their club. Upon this floor is generally the committee-room, and likewise the secretary's office. The next, or uppermost floor—which, however, in most cases does not show itself externally, it being concealed in the roof—is appropriated partly to the billiard and smoking rooms, and partly to servants' dormitories, the divisions being kept distinct from each other. Being quite apart from the other public rooms, those for billiards, &c., make no pretensions to outward appearance.

With these preliminary remarks as to our present club system and the usual arrangements of a club-house, we will proceed to speak more individually of the clubs which abound in Pall Mall.

The Guards' Club, which is restricted to the officers of Her Majesty's Household Troops, is the oldest club now extant, having been established in 1813. It was formerly housed in St. James's Street, next to "Crockford's." The present club-house, however, was erected only as far back as 1848; it was built from the designs of Mr. Henry Harrison, and is said to be "remarkable for its compactness and convenience, although its size and external appearance indicate no more than a private house. As Captain Gronow tells us in his "Anecdotes and Reminiscences," it was established

child betwixt its jaws. On the right side of the entrance hall, which is paved with encaustic tiles, is the smoking-room, and in the rear is a noble dining-room. The entire frontage of the first floor is occupied by the morning-room; in the rear is the billiard-room. The second floor consists of billiard and card rooms, and five bed-rooms for members, others being also on the third and fourth floors. In the rear of the fourth floor a large roof

WAR OFFICE, PALL MALL, 1850. (*See page* 129.)

for the three regiments of Foot Guards, and was conducted on a military system. Billiards and low whist were the only games indulged in. The dinner was, perhaps, better than at most clubs, and considerably cheaper.

Close by the Guards' Club, and adjoining the grounds of Marlborough House, is the Beaconsfield Club. The edifice, which was erected in 1875, originally belonged to the Junior Naval and Military Club. It is six storeys high, and is built of Portland stone; the base and columns of the entrance are of polished Aberdeen granite, and over the doorway at each side are two life-sized recumbent female figures supporting shields bearing medallions of Nelson and Wellington; whilst over the centre of the doorway is a huge lion's head with the head of a

or flat has been carried out, overlooking the grounds of Marlborough House; this is paved with encaustic tiles, and during the summer it can be converted into a covered lounge for smokers.

The Army and Navy Club—or rather a part of it—covers the site of what was once Nell Gwynne's house. Pennant thus describes it: "As to Nell Gwynne, not having the honour to be on the Queen's establishment, she was obliged to keep her distance (from the Court) at her house in Pall Mall. It is the first good one on the left hand of St. James's Square, as we enter from Pall Mall. The back room on the ground floor was within memory (he wrote in 1790), entirely of looking-glass, as was said to have been the ceiling also. Over the chimney was her picture, and that of her sister was in a third room. At the period I mention this house was the property of Thomas Brand, Esq., of the Hoo, in Hertfordshire "—an ancestor, we may add, of the Lords Dacre.

This club—which bears the colloquial nickname as far back as the end of the war in 1815, stands at the corner of Pall Mall and the opening into St. James's Park. This club took its rise, says the author of "London Clubs," when so many of the officers of the army and navy were thrown out

FRONT OF THE ARMY AND NAVY CLUB.

of the "Rag and Famish," arising out of a joke in *Punch*—was originally held at a private mansion in St. James's Square, and the present club-house was finished in 1850, at the cost of nearly £100,000. The house is luxuriously furnished, and the smoking-room has the reputation of being one of the best in London.

The "United Service," which was established of commission. Their habits, from old mess-room associations, being gregarious, and their reduced incomes no longer affording the luxuries of the camp or barrack-room on full pay, the late Lord Lynedoch, on their position being represented to him, was led to propose some such institution as a mess-room, in peace, for the benefit of his old companions in arms. A few other officers of influence in both branches of the service concurred, and the United Service Club was the result. It was first established at the corner of Charles Street, Waterloo Place, where the junior establishment of the same name now stands; but the funds soon becoming large, and the number of candidates for admission rapidly increasing, the present large and classic edifice was erected. The building, which is devoid of much architectural embellishment—the decorations being simple almost to severity—was erected from the designs of Mr. John Nash.

This is considered to be one of the most commodious, economical, and best managed of all the London club-houses. Among the pictures that adorn the walls of the principal rooms are Clarkson Stanfield's "Battle of Trafalgar," and the "Battle of Waterloo," by George Jones, R.A. There are also several portraits of the sovereigns of England, of the Stuart and Brunswick lines. Among them are James I., James II., Charles II., William III., and Queen Mary, original picture, by Sir Godfrey Kneller; Queen Anne, the four Georges, William IV., and Queen Victoria, by Sir Francis Grant; and an original portrait of the late Prince Consort, by J. Lucas. The members of this club consist of princes of the blood royal, and officers of the army, navy, marines, regular, militia, and Her Majesty's Indian Forces, of the rank of commander in the navy, or major in the army, in active service or retired; the lords lieutenants of counties in Great Britain and Ireland, &c., are also eligible.

The "Junior United Service," although perhaps not quite within the limits of "Club-land," standing as it does at the corner of Charles Street and Waterloo Place—may be introduced here. It was established in 1827, to provide for officers not of field rank, and also for those general officers whom the Senior Club was unable to receive. The house was rebuilt and enlarged in 1857, from the designs of Messrs. Nelson and Innes. The club accommodates fully as many members as the old club, as well as four or five hundred additional, or "supernumeraries." Many of the senior members of each club now belong to both, it having been considered a high honour, when the Junior was established, for the more distinguished individuals in the ranks of the Senior Club to be elected as honorary members, although those belonging to the new institution could not, of course, attain a similar distinction, unless of the requisite grade.

The Travellers' Club dates its existence from the year 1819. Sir Charles Barry was the architect of the club-house, which was built in the year 1831. In 1850 it had a narrow escape from destruction by fire; the damage, however, was principally confined to the billiard-room, in which it originated. This club is exceedingly select, numbering among its members the highest branches of the peerage, and the most distinguished of the lower House of Parliament. It consists of only about 700 members, but they are amongst the *élite* of the land; and Talleyrand, with some of the most eminent representatives of foreign powers, have been enrolled in the list of its honorary members. When ambassador to this country from the French Court, the veteran diplomatist was wont to pass his leisure hours at this favourite retreat in Pall Mall, and, we are told, "steered his way as triumphantly through all the mazes of whist and *écarté,* as he had done amid the intricacies of the thirteen different forms of government, each of which he had sworn to observe."

The "Oxford and Cambridge," in Pall Mall, midway on the "sweet shady side," and the "United University," at the corner of Suffolk Street, in Pall Mall East, may both be mentioned together as being restricted to University men, and, indeed, to such only as are members of Oxford or Cambridge. The former is a handsome structure, and was built from the joint designs of Mr. Sidney Smirke and his brother, Sir Robert. In panels over the upper windows, seven in number, are a series of bas-reliefs, executed by Mr. Nicholl, who was also employed on those of the Fitzwilliam Museum at Cambridge. The subject of that at the east end of the building is Homer; then follow Bacon and Shakespeare. The centre panel contains a group of Apollo and the Muses, with Minerva on his right hand, and a female, personifying the fountain Hippocrene, on his left. The three remaining panels represent Milton, Newton, and Virgil. The "Oxford and Cambridge," which is the more recent of the two in its origin—having been established in 1830, whereas the "University" dates from 1822 —consists chiefly of the younger spirits of the universities, and is less "donnish." The other is, for the most part, composed of the old and graver members. The serious members of Parliament who have received university education are almost invariably to be found in the latter. It also contains a considerable number of the judges, and no small portion of the beneficed and dignified clergy.

The "Union," at the corner of Trafalgar Square and Cockspur Street, is one of the oldest of the clubs, and for many years enjoyed the reputation of being one of the most *recherché* of all. It was founded in 1822, and consists of politicians, and the higher order of professional and commercial men, without reference to party opinions. The club-house itself was built in 1824, from the designs of the late Sir Robert Smirke, R.A.

The "Athenæum" was established in 1824, and the club-house, built by Mr. Decimus Burton, was opened about two years later. The building showed considerable progress with regard to ornateness and finish, for it presented the then somewhat extravagant novelty of a sculptured frieze. It is surmounted by an imposing statue of Minerva, by Baily, R.A. In the interior the chief feature is the staircase. The library, as perhaps may be expected, is very extensive, consisting of several thousand volumes. A sum of £500 a year from the funds of the club was, several years ago, voted to be set apart for the purchase of new works of merit in literature and art. Above the mantelpiece is a portrait of George IV., painted by Lawrence, upon which he was engaged but a few hours previous to his decease, the last bit of colour this celebrated artist ever put upon canvas being that of the hilt and sword-knot of the girdle; thus it remains, unfinished.

The expense of building the club-house, we are told, was £35,000, and £5,000 for furnishing; the plate, linen, and glass cost £2,500; library, £4,000; and the stock of wine in the cellar is usually worth £4,000. The yearly revenue is about £9,000. It does not admit strangers to its dining-room under any circumstances. The economical management of the club has not, however, been effected without a few sallies of humour from various quarters. In 1834 we read, "The mixture of Whigs and Radicals, *savants*, foreigners, dandies, authors, soldiers, sailors, lawyers, artists, doctors, and members of both Houses of Parliament, together with an exceedingly good average supply of bishops, render the *mélange* very agreeable, despite some two or three bores, who 'continually do dine,' and who, not satisfied with getting a 6s. dinner for 3s. 6d., 'continually do complain.'"

The "Athenæum" was founded by a number of gentlemen connected with the learned professions and higher order of the fine arts and literature; and, with the exception, perhaps, of the "United Service," it is the most select establishment of the kind in London. Previous to the year 1824, if we except the occasional festive gatherings of the Royal Society, there was no place in London where those gentlemen who were more interested in art and literature than in politics could meet together for social intercourse. To remedy this acknowledged want, a preliminary meeting was held in the February of that year, at the rooms of the Royal Society, at Somerset House, at which it was resolved to institute a literary club. Among those present were Sir Walter Scott, Sir Francis Chantrey, Richard Heber, Thomas Moore, Davis Gilbert, Mr. J. W. Croker, Sir Humphry Davy, Lord Dover, Sir Henry Halford, Sir Thomas Lawrence, Joseph Jekyll, and other well-known celebrities. It was at first called "The Society," but the name was subsequently changed to its present. Its members made their rendezvous at the Clarence Club until 1830.

For many years after its establishment, smoking was not permitted within the walls of this club. At last, however, about 1860, a concession was made, and a smoking-room added—apart, however, from the rest of the house, a part of the garden on the south front being sacrificed.

The number of ordinary members is fixed at twelve hundred. Samuel Rogers and Thomas Campbell, the poets, were among the first to join it, and Theodore Hook, too, was also one of its most popular members. Almost all the judges, bishops, and members of the Cabinet belong to it; and the committee have the privilege of electing annually, without ballot, nine persons, eminent in art, science, or literature. It is said that at the "Athenæum" the dinners fell off in number by upwards of 300 yearly after Theodore Hook disappeared from his favourite corner near the door of its coffee-room. "That is to say," observes one of his biographers, "there must have been some dozens of gentlemen who chose to dine there once or twice every week of the season, merely for the chance of his being there, and allowing them to draw their chairs to his little table in the course of the evening. . . . The corner alluded to will, we suppose, long retain the name which it derived from him, "Temperance Corner.'" It may be added, by way of explanation, that when Hook wanted brandy or whisky, he asked for it under the name of tea or lemonade, in order not to shock the grave and dignified persons who were members of the "Athenæum" in his day.

A falling-off in the number of its members being at one time anticipated, says the writer of an able article in the *New Quarterly Review*, a report was foolishly set abroad that "the finest thing in the world was to belong to the 'Athenæum,' and that an opportunity offered for hobnobbing with archbishops, and hearing Theodore Hook's jokes. Consequently, all the little crawlers and parasites, and gentility-hunters, from all corners of London, set out upon the creep; and they crept in at the windows, and they crept down the area steps, and they crept in, unseen, at the doors, and they crept in under bishops' sleeves, and they crept in in peers' pockets, and they were blown in by the winds of chance. The consequence has been that ninety-nine hundredths of this club are people who rather seek to obtain a sort of standing by belonging to the 'Athenæum,' than to give it lustre by the talents of its members. Nine-tenths of the intellectual writers of the age would be certainly black-balled by the dunces. Notwithstanding all this, and partly on account of this, the 'Athenæum' is a capital club. The library is certainly the best club library in London, and is a great advantage to a man who writes."

As may well be supposed from its literary constituency, no modern club in London, except the Garrick, is richer than the Athenæum in anecdotes and *bons mots*. In the library of this club lounging-chairs, writing-tables, and like conveniences are abundantly provided; and it was in some such apartment as this, probably in this identical room, where creditors pressed him, that, as we are told, " the unhappy, the defiant, the scorning, but eventually scorned and neglected Theodore Hook wrote the greater part of his novels, undisturbed by all the buzz and hum of the more fortunate butterflies around."

Mr. E. Jesse used to tell a story to the effect that Thomas Campbell, the poet, was led home one evening from the Athenæum Club by a friend. There had been a heavy storm of rain, and the kennels were full of water. Campbell fell into one of them at the steps of the club, and pulled his friend after him, who exclaimed, in allusion to a well-known line of the poet's, " It is not *I*ser rolling rapidly, but *We*ser."

The "Athenæum" has reckoned among its members at least half of the illustrious names of the last half century; among others, Mr. D'Israeli, Lord Granville, Lord Coleridge, Thackeray, Sir John Bowring, Sir Roderick Murchison, Sir Benjamin Brodie, Sir Charles Wheatstone, Dr. Hooker, Sir Henry Holland, George Grote; Professors Sedgwick, Darwin, Tyndal, Huxley, Willis, Owen, Phillips, Maurice, and Conington; Lord Lytton, Macaulay, Bishop Thirlwall, Charles Dickens, Dean Stanley, Lord Shaftesbury, Bishop Wilberforce, Lord Romilly, Ruskin, Maclise, Thackeray, Serjeant Kinglake, Dean Milman, Lord Mayo, and Sir Edwin Landseer. The first secretary was no less eminent a person than Professor Faraday, but he retained the post only for a year.

In 1832—during the exciting era which culminated in the passing of the First Reform Bill—the friends of the Constitution, somewhat alarmed perhaps at the "sweeping measures" which were supposed to be about to follow, founded the

" Carlton," bestowing upon it this name from the terrace where the club was originally held. In the April of the above year we find the following entry in Mr. Raikes's " Journal :"—" A new Tory club has just been formed, for which Lord Kensington's house in Carlton Gardens has been taken. . . . The object is to have a counterbalancing meeting to ' Brooks's,' which is purely a Whig *réunion ;* ' White's,' which was formerly devoted to the other side, being now of no colour, and frequented indiscriminately by all (parties)."

The club-house, built from the designs of Mr. Sydney Smirke and his brother, Sir Robert, was finished about 1856. It bears upon its exterior a degree of richness almost unprecedented in the metropolitan architecture. The façade in Pall Mall is upwards of 130 feet in length, with nine windows on a floor ; between each of the windows are columns of highly polished red Peterhead granite. The design is said to be founded on the east front of the Library of St. Mark's at Venice.

The Carlton is the head-quarters of Conservative, as the Reform Club is of Liberal politics. The Conservative Club in St. James's Street was started for the reception of the Tory rank and file, but in Pall Mall congregate the leading men of the party. Here are concerted the great political " moves " which are to upset a Whig or Liberal Administration ; here the grand mysterious tactics of a general election are determined upon, and here are the vast sums subscribed which are to put the whole forces of the party in motion in the country boroughs. This club still retains its original name, though removed from the lordly terrace which gave rise to it, to the " shady side of Pall Mall." Passing to what may be called the " inner life " of the club, we may state that the first head of its *cuisine* was a French " artist " who had lived with the Duc d'Escars, chief *maître d'hôtel* to Louis XVIII., and who is said to have made that famous *pâté* which killed his master.

The " Reform," which is situated between the " Carlton " and the " Athenæum," was built from the designs of the late Sir Charles Barry, R.A., and was for a long time considered one of the " lions " of the metropolis. The style is purely Italian, and partakes largely of the character of many of the celebrated palaces in Italy. The building is chiefly remarkable for simplicity of design, combined with grandeur of effect, as well as for the convenience and elegance of its internal arrangements. It differs from most of the other club-houses, in having two ranges of windows above the ground floor instead of a single range. The latter feature has been regarded as rendering the metropolitan club-houses eminently characteristic of their purpose, and highly favourable to architectural dignity.

On the first establishment of the "Reform" by the Liberal party, Gwydyr House, in Whitehall, was hired, and in that mansion the club was located until the present club-house was erected. This, although of severe simplicity, by the utter absence of exterior ornament, is nevertheless an imposing structure. Some critics, indeed, have compared it to an inverted chest of drawers; but the chief beauty of the Reform Club is *ab intra*. On entering the vestibule one is immediately struck by the splendid proportions of the hall and the elegance of the staircase, reminding one of the magnificent *salles* of Versailles and of the glories of the Louvre. In the upper part of the building are a certain number of "dormitories" set apart for those who pass their whole existence amid club gossip and politics—one of the peculiarities of the establishment.

The author of "The London Clubs" writes—"It is in the lower regions, where Soyer reigns supreme, that the true glories of the Reform Club consist; and here the divine art of cookery—or, as he himself styles it, gastronomy—is to be seen in all its splendour. Heliogabalus himself never gloated over such a kitchen; for steam is here introduced and made to supply the part of man. In state the great dignitary sits, and issues his inspiring orders to a body of lieutenants, each of whom has pretensions to be considered a *chef* in himself. 'Gardez les rôtis, les entremets sont perdus,' was never more impressively uttered by Cambacères, when tormented by Napoleon detaining him from dinner, than are the orders issued by Soyer for preparing the refection of some modern attorney; and all the energies of the vast establishment are at once called into action to obey them—steam eventually conducting the triumphs of the cook's art from the scene of its production to a recess adjoining the dining-room, where all is to disappear.

"Soyer is, indeed, the glory of the edifice—the *genus loci*. Peers and plebeian *gourmands* alike penetrate into the recesses of the kitchen to render him homage; and, conscious of his dignity, —or, at least, of his power—he receives them with all the calm assurance of the *Grand Monarque* himself. Louis XIV., in the plenitude of his glory, was never more impressive; and yet there is an aspect—we shall not say assumption—of modesty about the great *chef*, as he loved to be designated, which is positively wondrous, when we reflect that we stand in the presence of the great 'Gastronomic Regenerator'—the last of his titles, and that by which, we presume, he would wish by posterity to be known. Soyer, indeed, is a man of discrimination, and taste, and genius. He was led to conceive the idea of his immortal work, he tells us, by observing in the elegant library of an accomplished nobleman the works of Shakespeare, Milton, and Johnson, in gorgeous bindings, but wholly dust-clad and overlooked, while a book on cookery bore every indication of being daily consulted and revered. 'This is fame,' exclaimed Soyer, seizing the happy inference; and forthwith betaking himself to his chambers and to meditation, his divine work on Gastronomic Regeneration was the result."

The breakfast given by the Reform Club on the occasion of the Queen's coronation obtained for Soyer high commendation; and in his O'Connell dinner, the "soufflés à la Clontarf" were considered by gastronomes to be a rich bit of satire. The banquet to Ibrahim Pacha, in 1846, was another of Soyer's great successes, when "Merlans à l'Égyptienne," "La Crême d'Égypte," and "à l'Ibrahim Pacha," mingled with "Le Gâteau Britannique à l'Admiral (Napier)." Another famous banquet was that given to Admiral Sir Charles Napier, in March, 1854, as Commander of the Baltic Fleet; and the banquet given in July, 1850, to Viscount Palmerston, who was a popular leader of the Reform, was, gastronomically as well as politically, a brilliant triumph. It was upon this occasion that Mr. Bernal Osborne characterised the Palmerston policy in this quotation:—

"Warmed by the instincts of a knightly heart,
    That roused at once if insult touched the realm,
He spurned each state-craft, each deceiving art,
    And met his foes no visor to his helm.
This proved his worth, hereafter be our boast—
    Who hated Britons, hated him the most."

The following description of the kitchen of the Reform Club is from the pen of Viscountess de Malleville, and appeared originally in the *Courrier de l'Europe*:—"It is spacious as a ball-room, kept in the finest order, and white as a young bird. All-powerful steam, the noise of which salutes your ear as you enter, here performs a variety of offices. It diffuses a uniform heat to large rows of dishes, warms the metal plates upon which are disposed the dishes that have been called for, and that are in waiting to be sent above; it turns the spit, draws the water, carries up the coal, and moves the plate like an intelligent and indefatigable servant. Stay awhile before this octagonal apparatus, which occupies the centre of the place. Around you the water boils and the stew-pans bubble, and a little further on is a movable furnace, before which pieces of meat are converted into savoury *rôtis:* here are sauces and gravies, stews, broths, soups, &c.　In the distance are Dutch ovens, marble mortars, lighted stoves, iced plates of metal for fish, and various compartments for vegetables,

as a whole, and in their relative bearings to one another, all are so intelligently considered, that you require the aid of a guide to direct you in exploring them, and a good deal of time to classify in your mind all your discoveries.　Let all strangers

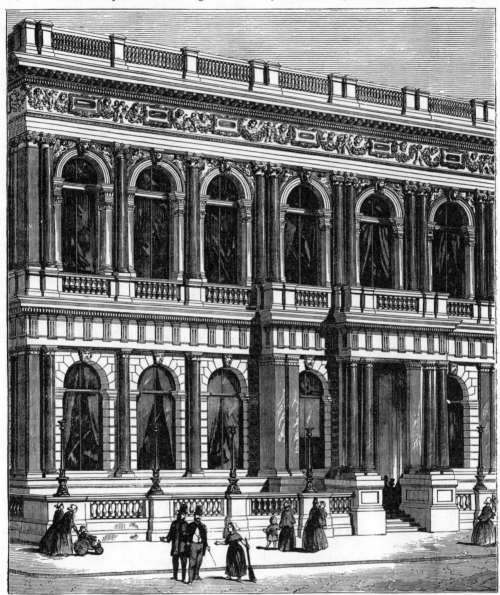

ENTRANCE TO THE CARLTON CLUB.　(*See page* 148.)

fruits, roots, and spices.　After this inadequate, though prodigious, nomenclature, the reader may perhaps picture to himself a state of general confusion—a disordered assemblage, resembling that of a heap of oyster-shells.　If so, he is mistaken; for, in fact, you see very little or scarcely anything of all the objects above described.　The order of their arrangement is so perfect, their distribution

who come to London for business, or pleasure, or curiosity, or for whatever cause, not fail to visit the Reform Club.　In an age of utilitarianism and of the search for the comfortable like ours, there is more to be learned here than in the ruins of the Coliseum, of the Parthenon, or of Memphis."

Thackeray was a member of the Reform, the Athenæum, and Garrick Clubs—perhaps of others,

LIBRARY OF THE REFORM CLUB. (*See page* 148.)

but it was in those here named that his leisure was usually spent. "The afternoons of the last week of his life," writes one of his biographers, "were almost entirely passed at the Reform Club, and never had he been more genial or in such apparently happy moods. Many men sitting in the libraries and dining-rooms of these clubs have thought this week of one of the tenderest passages in his early sketches—'Brown the Younger at a Club'—in which the old uncle is represented as telling his nephew, while showing him the various rooms in the club, of those who had dropped off —whose names had appeared at the end of the club list, under the dismal head of 'members deceased,' in which (added Thackeray) 'you and I shall rank some day.'"

Among the latest additions to the batch of clubs that line Pall Mall are the "Junior Carlton" and the "Marlborough." The former, which was established in 1864, numbers about 1,500 members. It is a political club, in strict connection with the Conservative party, and designed to promote its objects. The "Marlborough"—so named in honour of the Prince of Wales—was started about 1868, and numbers among its members the Prince of Wales and several of the aristocratic patrons of the turf.

The "Century Club" has its abode at 6, Pall Mall Place, and there is a tradition that the premises were once inhabited by Nell Gwynne.

Whatever may have been the "rules and regulations" of the now defunct species of club of the last century—such as the "Essex Street," the "Literary," and others of which we have spoken in the previous volume—a wide difference exists between them and those of the present day in the matter of bacchanalian festivities. It may with truth be said that high play and high feeding are no longer the rules; in fact, clubs are to many persons even dull and unsociable. In most of the clubs of the Johnsonian period, the flow of wine or other liquor was far more abundant than that of mind, and the conversation was generally more easy and hilarious than intellectual and refined. The bottle, or else the punch-bowl, played by far too prominent a part, and sociality too frequently took the form of revelry—or, at least, what would be considered such according to our more temperate habits. Though in general the elder clubs encouraged habits of free indulgence as indispensable to good fellowship and sociality, the modern clubs, on the contrary, have done much to discourage them, as low and ungentlemanly. "Reeling home from a club" used formerly to be a common expression, whereas now inebriety, or the symptom of it, in a club-house, would bring down disgrace upon him who should be guilty of such an indiscretion.

The pleasures and comforts of clubs and club-life to the bachelor whose means and position allow of such luxuries have been often graphically and humorously described in serious and ephemeral publications for the past century and a half, but nowhere in a more amusing manner than in the "New Monthly Magazine," in 1842; and it has been wittily observed by Mrs. Gore in one of her novels that, "after all, clubs are not altogether so bad a thing for family-men; they act as conductors to the storms usually hovering in the air. There is nothing like the subordination exercised in a community of equals for reducing a fiery temper."

CHAPTER XIII.

ST. JAMES'S STREET.—CLUB-LAND (*continued*).

"The Campus Martius of St. James's Street,
Where the beaux' cavalry pace to and fro,
Before they take the field in Rotten Row."—*Sheridan.*

Origin of "Brooks's Club"—Hazard-playing—St. James's Coffee-house—The "Thatched House" Tavern—An Amusing Story about Burke and Dr. Johnson—Origin of Goldsmith's Poem, "Retaliation"—The "Neapolitan Club"—The Dilettanti Society—The "Civil Service," now the "Thatched House" Club—The "Conservative"—"Arthur's"—The "Old and Young Club"—The "Cocoa Tree"—Dr. Garth and Rowe, the Poet—Familiarity of Menials—"Brooks's"—How Sheridan was elected a Member—The "Fox Club"—The "New University" —The "Junior St. James's"—The "Devonshire"—"Crockford's"—"White's"—The Proud Countess of Northumberland—Lord Montford's "important Business" with his Lawyer—Colley Cibber at "White's Club"—Lord Alvanley—A Waiter at "White's" elected M.P.— "Boodle's"—Michael Angelo Taylor and the Earl of Westmorland.

THE spread and increase of our clubs are remarkable signs of the times; their uses and advantages are such as to make one wonder not only why such things were not established very much earlier than they were, but how "men about town" existed without them. "White's," "Brooks's," and "Boodle's" were *the* clubs of London for many years; "White's" being the oldest, and famous as a "chocolate-house" in the time of Hogarth. The origin of "Brooks's" was the "blackballing" of

Messrs. Boothby and James, at "White's;" they established it as a rival, and it was at first held at "Almack's." Sir Willoughby Aston subsequently originated "Boodle's;" but these clubs were clubs of amusement, politics, and play, not the matter-of-fact meeting-places of general society, nor did they offer the extensive and economical advantages of breakfast, dinner, and supper, now afforded by the present race of establishments. And, connected with this subject in some degree, what a wonderful change in the state of affairs has taken place since it was the custom of the king to play "hazard" publicly at St. James's Palace, on Twelfth Night! In the *Gentleman's Magazine* for 1753 is the following account of the result of this annual performance for that year :—

"*Saturday, Jan.* 6.—In the evening his Majesty played at hazard for the benefit of the groom-porter; all the Royal Family who played were winners — particularly the duke, £3,000. The most considerable losers were the Duke of Grafton, the Earl of Huntingdon, the Earls of Holderness, Ashburnham, and Hertford. Their Royal Highnesses the Prince of Wales and Prince Edward, and a select company, danced in the little drawing-room till eleven o'clock, when the Royal Family withdrew."

The custom of hazard-playing was discontinued after the accession of George III.; but it is odd, looking back scarcely a century, to find the sovereign, after attending divine service with the most solemn ceremony in the morning, doing that in the evening which, in these days, subjects men to all sorts of pains and penalties, and for the prohibition and detection of which a bill has been passed through Parliament, arming the police with the power of breaking into the houses of Her Majesty's lieges at all hours of the day and night.

It is obvious that the gradual improvement of the club-houses, together with the changes which passed over West-end society, would almost of its own accord develop the club system out of that which preceded it. There is, therefore, little need for dwelling on the subject, in the way of explanation, and so we will at once pass on up St. James's Street.

At the south-west corner of St. James's Street, next door to the corner house, and commanding the view up Pall Mall, was the "St. James's Coffee-house," the great rendezvous of the Whig party for nearly a hundred years, beginning with the reign of Queen Anne. Its very name has become classical, and indeed immortal, by being so repeatedly mentioned in the pages of the *Spectator*, *Tatler*, &c. Thus we find, in a passage already quoted by us

from the first number of the *Tatler*—"Foreign and domestic news you will have from the St. James's Coffee-house;" and thus Addison, in one of his papers in the *Spectator* (No. 403), remarks—'That I might begin as near the fountain-head [of information] as possible, I first of all called in at the St. James's, where I found the whole outward room in a buzz of politics. The speculations were but very indifferent towards the door, but grew finer as you advanced to the upper end of the room; and were so much improved by a knot of theorists who sat in the inner rooms, within the steams of the coffee-pot, that I heard there the whole Spanish monarchy disposed of, and all the line of the Bourbons provided for, in less than a quarter of an hour." This house was much frequented by Swift, who here used to receive his letters from "Stella," and who tells us in his "Journal to Stella," how in 1710 he christened the infant of its keepers, a Mr. and Mrs. Elliot, and afterwards sat down to a bowl of punch along with the happy parents. Being so close to the palace it was also frequented by the officers of the household troops, who, it is said, would lounge in to listen to the learned Dr. Joseph Warton, as he sat at breakfast in one of the windows. Mr. John Timbs reminds us that, "in the first advertisement of the 'Town Eclogues' of Lady Mary Wortley Montagu, they were stated to have been read over at the St. James's Coffee-house, where they were considered by the general voice to be the productions of a lady of quality."

In 1665 there appeared a poem with the title of "The Character of a Coffee House, wherein is contained a description of the persons usually frequenting it, with their discourse and humours, as also the admirable virtues of coffee; by an Ear and Eye Witness." It begins thus :—

> "A coffee-house the learned hold,
> It is a place where coffee's sold;
> This derivation cannot fail us,
> For where ale's vended, that's an alehouse."

It is evident from what follows that these coffee-houses soon became places of general resort—

> "—— of some and all conditions,
> E'en vintners, surgeons, and physicians,
> The blind, the deaf, the aged cripple,
> Do here resort, and coffee tipple."

At the door of the St. James's Coffee-house, a globular oil-lamp, then described as "a new kind of light," was first exhibited in 1709, by its inventor, Michael Cole. To this house, in early life, the elder D'Israeli, as his son tells us, would repair to read the newspapers of the day, returning to his home at Enfield in the evening, sometimes "laden with journals."

The St. James's Coffee House continued to exist for some few years into the present century, when, its Whig friends having deserted its doors, it passed quietly away, superseded, no doubt, in a great degree, by Brooks's Club.

The "Thatched House Tavern," the name of which implies a very humble and rural origin, was probably an inn which had existed in the days when St. James's was a veritable hospital and not a palace. It stood near the bottom, on the western side of the street. When the Court settled at St. James's, it was frequented by persons of fashion, and grew gradually in importance, as did the suburb of which it formed part. We should like to have seen it in the days when the frolicsome maids of honour of the Tudor and Stuart days ran across thither from the Court to drink syllabub and carry on sly flirtations. In the absence of documents, it is impossible to trace its growth down to the days of Swift, who speaks in his "Journal to Stella," in 1711, of "having entertained our society at dinner at the Thatched House Tavern;" it was, however, a small hotel at that date, for the party were obliged to "send out for wine, the house affording none." It was possibly on account of this and other proofs of its earlier stage of existence, that even when the "Thatched House" had grown into a recognized rendezvous of wits, politicians, and men of fashion, Lord Thurlow alluded to it during one of the debates on the Regency Bill as the "ale-house." By the time of Lord Shelburne, or at all events in the days of Pitt and Fox, it had become one of the chief taverns at the West-end, and had added to its premises a large room for public meetings.

Here the Earl of Sunderland, the great Duke of Marlborough's son-in-law, having shaken off the cares of state, would dine off a chop or steak, in a quiet way, along with Lord Townshend, or his constant companion, Dr. Monsey. The tavern was for many years the head-quarters of the annual dinners or other convivial meetings of the leading clubs and literary and scientific associations. Mr. Timbs gives the following as the list of such gatherings in 1860, on the authority of the late Admiral W. H. Smyth—The Institute of Actuaries, the Catch Club, the Johnson Club, the Dilettanti Society, the Farmers', the Geographical and the Geological, the Linnæan and Literary Societies, the Navy Club, the Philosophical Club, the Club of the Royal College of Physicians, the Political Economy Club, the Royal Academy Club, the Royal Astronomical Society, the Royal Institution Club, the Royal London Yacht Club, the Royal Naval Club, the Royal Society Club, the St. Alban's Medical Club, the St. Bartholomew's Cotemporaries, the Star Club, the Statistical Club, the Sussex Club, and the Union Society of St. James's.

The Literary Society (or Club) was limited to forty members, and its meetings in 1820 were held here. At that time Canning was a member of it; so were Sir William Scott (Lord Stowell), Sir William Grant, and Mr. J. H. Frere.

Mr. Cradock tells us in his "Memoir," that one evening he dined with the club, being introduced by Dr. Percy, and met, *inter alios*, Edmund Burke and Oliver Goldsmith. "The table that day was crowded, and I sat next Mr. Burke; but as the great orator said very little, and as Mr. Richard Burke talked much, I was not aware at first who my neighbour was." He adds an amusing story which brings in both Burke and Johnson, and may therefore well bear telling here:—"One of the party near me remarked that there was an offensive smell in the room, and thought it must proceed from some dog that was under the table; but Burke, with a smile, turned to me and said, 'I rather fear it is from the beef-steak pie that is opposite us, the crust of which is made of some very bad butter which comes from my country. Just at that moment Dr. Johnson sent his plate for some of it; Burke helped him to very little, which he soon dispatched, and returned his plate for more; Burke, without thought, exclaimed, 'I am glad that you are able so well to relish this beef-steak pie.' Johnson, not at all pleased that what he ate should ever be noticed, immediately retorted, 'There is a time of life, sir, when a man requires the repairs of a table.'

"Before dinner was finished, Mr. Garrick came in, full-dressed, made many apologies for being so much later than he intended, but he had been unexpectedly detained at the House of Lords; and Lord Camden had absolutely insisted upon setting him down at the door of the hotel in his own carriage. Johnson said nothing, but looked a volume.

"During the afternoon some literary dispute arose; but Johnson sat silent, till the Dean of Derry very respectfully said, 'We all wish, sir, for your opinion on the subject.' Johnson inclined his head, and never shone more in his life than at that period. He replied, without any pomp; he was perfectly clear and explicit, full of the subject, and left nothing undetermined. There was a pause; and he was then hailed with astonishment by all the company. The evening in general passed off very pleasantly. Some talked perhaps for amusement, and others for victory. We sat very late; and the conversation that at last ensued was the direct cause of my friend Goldsmith's poem, called ' Retaliation.' "

Here, in the beginning of the present century, the " Neapolitan Club" used to dine, the Prince of Wales or the Duke of Sussex taking the chair. Beckford was frequently a guest, and so were " Beau" Brummell, Sir Sidney Smith, Richard Brinsley Sheridan, and Tommy Moore, then quite a young man. Here, too, the members of the Old Royal Naval Club—not a club in the modern West-end sense, but a charitable institution for the dispensing of charity among old " salts" and their families—used to dine on the anniversary of the battle of the Nile.

At the " Thatched House Tavern" were formerly held, on Sunday evenings during the London season, the dinners of the Dilettanti Society, the portraits of whose members—many of them painted by Sir Joshua Reynolds—adorned the walls of a room which was devoted exclusively to their accommodation.

This society, composed of lovers of the fine arts, was founded in 1734 by some gentlemen who had travelled in Italy, and who thought that that fact, coupled with a taste for the beautiful and for the remains of antiquity, was a sufficient bond of union. The members, though they have enjoyed a " name" for a century and a half, have never had a " local habitation." They met originally at Parsloe's, in St. James's Street, but removed to the " Thatched House Tavern" in 1799. By the time that the society was thirty years old, its finances were found to be so prosperous, that its members resolved to send out properly-qualified persons to the East, in order to collect information as to such antiquities as the hands of time and of man had spared, and to bring back their measurements, and correct drawings and elevations. The first persons so sent abroad were Mr. Chandler, a Fellow of Magdalen College, Oxford, an architectural draughtsman named Rivett, and Mr. J. Stuart, whose name will long be remembered as the author of " The Antiquities of Athens." This noble work, published under the auspices of the Dilettanti Society, in instalments, had the effect of rescuing Grecian architecture and art from the contempt into which it had fallen, and to revive a taste for the majestic and beautiful. This book was followed, at distant intervals, by similar works, magnificently illustrated; among these were "Specimens of Sculpture, Egyptian, Etruscan, Greek, and Roman," published in 1809 ; " The Unedited Antiquities of Attica," in 1817 ; a large treatise on " Ancient Sculpture," in 1835 ; and Professor Cockerell's elaborate work on " The Temples of Jupiter in Ægina, and of

Bacchus at Phigaleia," published in 1860. It was, no doubt, the interest excited by the early meetings of the Dilettanti Society which first woke up the Earl of Aberdeen, or, to give him Lord Byron's title—

" The travell'd Thane, Athenian Aberdeen,"

to write and publish his " Enquiry as to the Principles of Beauty in Grecian Architecture ;" Sir William Gell to explain the Troad, Argolis, and Ithaca ; whilst the Earl of Elgin, our ambassador at Constantinople, rescued from destruction and sent over to England that collection of Athenian sculpture which is known to every visitor to the British Museum as the Elgin Marbles. Among the best-known members of the Dilettanti Society, besides those above-mentioned, were Sir William Chambers, Mr. John Towneley, the Marquises of Northampton and Lansdowne, Sir Richard Westmacott, Henry Hallam, the Duke of Bedford, Mr. H. T. Hope, Sir Martin Archer Shee, Mr. Richard Payne Knight, the Earl of Holderness, Sir Bourchier Wrey, Sir Henry Englefield, and Lord Le Despencer (better known by his former name of Sir Francis Dashwood), Lord Northwick, George Selwyn, Charles James Fox, Garrick, Colman, Lord Holland, Lord Fitzwilliam, Sir William Hamilton, and the Duke of Dorset.

Mr. Peter Cunningham says that the original " Thatched House Tavern" stood on the site of the present Conservative Club, to build which it was pulled down in 1843, when it was moved to another house a few doors nearer to the gate of the palace. When he wrote, in 1850, the Dilettanti still numbered fifty members, and continued to hold their Sunday evening meetings. Horace Walpole, in 1743, had described it in one of his letters to Sir H. Mann, as " a club for which the nominal qualification is having been in Italy, and the real one, being drunk ; the two chiefs," he adds, " are Lord Middlesex and Sir Francis Dashwood, who were seldom sober the whole time they were in Italy." Mr. Cunningham, however, assures us, that in the middle of the present century " the character of the club was considerably altered "—it may be hoped and believed for the better. If Horace Walpole's words are true, it could not well be for the worse.

An interesting account of the Dilettanti Society will be found in the *Edinburgh Review*, vol. 107. Since the demolition of their old house, the Dilettanti have held their weekly festive gatherings at Willis's Rooms, where the pictures belonging to the society now grace the walls. Their publications, however, are no longer such as those which were produced under their auspices in the last century.

The original "Thatched House Tavern" was taken down in 1814. "Beneath its front," says Mr. John Timbs, "was a range of low-built shops, including that of Rowland, the fashionable *coiffeur* of 'Macassar fame.' Through the tavern was a

Adjoining the "Thatched House Club," on the south, is one of the most recent additions to club-land, the "United Eton and Harrow Club." It occupies a portion of the house No. 87.

Higher up, at the corner of Little St. James's

THE "THATCHED HOUSE" TAVERN. (*See page* 154.)

passage to the rear, where, in Catharine Wheel Alley, in the last century, lived the widow Delaney, some of whose fashionable friends then resided in Dean Street, Soho.

On the site of the new "Thatched House Tavern" was built, in 1865, the "Civil Service Club," which was modified in 1873, and changed its name to the "Thatched House Club." It is still, however, mainly recruited from the Civil Service of the Crown, including county magistrates, ex-high sheriffs, and deputy-lieutenants.

Street, stands the "Conservative Club." This was established in 1840, in order to supply accommodation for those who could not procure admission into the "Carlton." The building was erected from the designs of Messrs. Basevi and Sydney Smirke. It is at once ornate and stately in its external appearance, and the interior is well arranged, but the club is not rich in anecdote or in incident.

On the same side of the street, only two or three houses intervening, is "Arthur's Club House." This club was so named after its founder, who was also, at one time, the keeper of "White's." Dr. King, in his "Anecdotes of his Own Times," alludes to these two clubs in the following terms, which imply that they were both addicted to high play :—"If I were to write a satire against gaming, and in the middle of my work insert a panegyric on the clubs at 'Arthur's,' who would not question the good intention of the author, and who would not condemn the absurdity of such a motley

Some of Horace Walpole's dilettante friends at Strawberry Hill once beguiled a dull and wet day by devising for this club a satirical coat of arms. The shield was devised by Walpole, Sir C. H. Williams, George Selwyn, and the Hon. R. Edgecumbe, and drawn by the last. The drawing formed a lot in the Strawberry Hall sale ; and a copy of it, with an explanation of its punning or "canting" allusions to card-playing, the great end

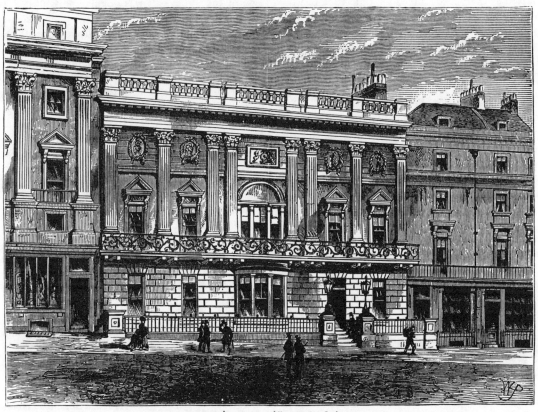

WHITE'S CLUB. (*See page* 161.)

piece ?" Here used to meet an inner club—an *imperium in imperio*—called "the Old and Young Club." Lady Lepel Hervey gives a clue to its name when she laments, in a letter dated 1756, that "luxury increases. All public places are full, and 'Arthur's' is the resort of old and young, courtiers and anti-courtiers—nay, even of ministers." By way of a sneer at the wide-spread habit of presenting civic freedoms to Mr. Pitt and his colleagues in office, this same Lady Hervey writes, under date 1757, "I hear Mr. George Selwyn has proposed to the old and new clubs at 'Arthur's' to depute him to present the freedom of each club in a dice-box to the Right Hon. William Pitt, and the Right Hon. Henry Bilson Legge. I think it ought to be inserted in the newspapers."

and object of the club, will be found in Chambers' "Book of Days."

"Arthur's Club" has always embraced a goodly list of members of the titled classes and the heads of the chief county families, though less aristocratic than "White's" or "Brooks's." A most painful circumstance, however, took place within it in the year 1836. To use the words of Captain Gronow's "Reminiscences," "A nobleman of the highest position and influence in society was detected in cheating at cards, and after a trial, which did not terminate in his favour, died of a broken heart."

At No. 64, on this side of the street, is the "Cocoa Tree Club." In the reign of Queen Anne there was a famous chocolate-house known as the "Cocoa Tree," a favourite sign to mark that new and fashionable beverage. Its frequenters were Tories of the strictest school. De Foe tells us in his "Journey through England," that "a Whig will no more go to the 'Cocoa Tree' . . . . than a Tory will be seen at the Coffee House of St. James's." In course of time, the "Cocoa Tree" developed into a gaming-house and a club. In its former capacity, Horace Walpole, writing in 1780, mentions an amusing anecdote connected with it :—"Within this week there has been a cast at hazard at the 'Cocoa Tree,' the difference of which amounted to an hundred and fourscore thousand pounds. Mr. O'Birne, an Irish gamester, had won £100,000 of a young Mr. Harvey, of Chigwell, just started from a midshipman into an estate by his elder brother's death. O'Birne said, 'You can never pay me.' 'I can,' said the youth ; 'my estate will sell for the debt.' 'No,' said O'Birne, 'I will win ten thousand, and you shall throw for the odd ninety thousand.' They did, and Harvey won." It is to be hoped that he left the gaming-house a wiser man thenceforth.

The anecdotes connected with the "Cocoa Tree" when it was really "the Wits' Coffee House," would fill a volume. One of them may be quoted here. Dr. Garth, who used often to appear there, was sitting one morning in the coffee-room conversing with two persons of " quality," when the poet Rowe, who was seldom very attentive to his dress and appearance, though fond of being noticed by great people, entered the door. Placing himself in a box nearly opposite to that in which the doctor sat, Rowe looked constantly round with a view to catch his eye, but not succeeding, he desired the waiter to ask him for the loan of his snuff-box, which he knew to be a very valuable one, set with diamonds, and the gift of royalty. After taking a pinch he returned it, but again asked for it so repeatedly that Garth, who knew him well, and saw through his purpose, took out a pencil and wrote on the lid two Greek characters, Φ and P, "Fie! Rowe." The poet's vanity was mortified, and he left the house.

As an instance of the familiarity that would sometimes show itself between the menials and the aristocratic visitors at these fashionable rendezvous, this anecdote may be given. A waiter named Samuel Spring having on one occasion to write to George IV., when Prince of Wales, commenced his letter as follows :—" Sam, the waiter at the Cocoa Tree, presents his compliments to the Prince of Wales," &c. His Royal Highness next day saw Sam, and after noticing the receiving of his note, and the freedom of the style, said, " Sam, this may be very well between you and me, but it will not do with the Norfolks and Arundels."

As a club, the "Cocoa Tree" did not cease to keep up its reputation for high play. Although the present establishment bearing the name dates its existence only from the year 1853, the old chocolate-house was probably converted into a club as far back as the middle of the last century. Lord Byron was a member of this club ; and so was Gibbon, the historian.

"Brooks's," pre-eminently the club-house of the Whig aristocracy, occupies No. 60 on the west side of the street. It was originally established at "Almack's," in Pall Mall, in 1764, by the Duke of Portland, Charles James Fox, and others. They afterwards removed it to St. James's Street, and the club-house, designed by Holland, was opened in 1778. The early history of this club, so long the head-quarters of the leaders of the old Whig party, is thus told in the " Percy Anecdotes : "— " When the Whigs, with Mr. Fox for their leader, commenced their long opposition to the Tory party under Pitt, they formed themselves into a club at 'Almack's,' for the joint purpose of private conference on public measures, and of social intercourse. In 1777, a Mr. Brooks built, in St. James's Street, a house for the accommodation of the club, and had the honour of conferring on it the name by which it has ever since been known. The number of members is limited to four hundred and fifty. . . . . A single black ball is sufficient to exclude. The members of the club are permitted by courtesy to belong to the club at Bath, and also to 'Miles's' and other respectable clubs, without being balloted for. The subscription is eleven guineas a year. Although, strictly speaking, an association of noblemen and gentlemen for political objects, gaming is allowed. . . . It was in the bosom of this club that Fox may be said to have spent the happiest hours of his life. Here, when the storm of public contention was over, would the banished spirit of true kind-heartedness return to its own home. Here, with Sheridan, Barré, Fitzpatrick, Wilkes, and other men of the same stamp, did his spirit luxuriate in its natural simplicity ; and hence, after a night of revelry, he would hasten off to the shades of St. Anne's Hill, near Chertsey, and with a pocket Horace—his favourite companion—bring back his mind to contemplative tranquillity."

If we may trust Captain Gronow's " Anecdotes and Reminiscences," at "Brooks's," for nearly half a century, the play was of a more gambling character than at " White's." Faro and macao were indulged in to an extent which enabled a man to win or to lose a considerable fortune in one night. It was here that Charles James Fox, Selwyn, Lord Carlisle,

Lord Robert Spencer, General Fitzpatrick, and other great Whigs won and lost hundreds of thousands, frequently remaining at the table for many hours without rising. On one occasion Lord Robert Spencer contrived to lose the last shilling of his considerable fortune given him by his brother, the Duke of Marlborough. General Fitzpatrick being much in the same condition, they agreed to raise a sum of money, in order that they might keep a faro bank. The members of the club made no objection, and ere long they carried out their design. As is generally the case, the bank was a winner, and Lord Robert bagged, as his share of the proceeds, one hundred thousand pounds. He retired, strange to say, from the fetid atmosphere of play, with the money in his pocket, and never again gambled. George Harley Drummond, of the famous banking-house at Charing Cross, played once only in his whole life at "White's" at whist, on which occasion he lost twenty thousand pounds to Brummell. This event caused him to retire from the banking-house of which he was a partner. Lord Carlisle was one of the most remarkable victims amongst the players at "Brooks's," and Charles Fox was not more fortunate, being subsequently always in pecuniary difficulties.

The membership of "Brooks's Club," in the days of Pitt and Fox, was a sort of crucial test by which the members of the Whig party of the time were distinguished. It was a passport to Holland and Devonshire House, and also to Carlton House, while the Prince of Wales was at war with his father and his ministers. Hence, on Sheridan's entrance into the House of Commons, in 1789, one of the first objects of Fox and his friends was to procure his admission inside the doors of "Brooks's." But he was, personally, most unpopular with two of the leaders of the Whig *coterie*, George Selwyn and Lord Bessborough, who were resolved to keep him out. As one black ball at that time excluded a candidate, the Foxites resolved to get him in by a *ruse*. Aided by Georgiana, Duchess of Devonshire, the presiding genius of the Whig party, when the time for the ballot came on, they sent false messages, conveying alarming news of the illness of near relatives, to both of the dissentients. The bait took in both cases, each no doubt supposing that the other would be in his place to give the black ball; and the result was the election of Richard Brinsley Sheridan, wit, dramatist, orator, and statesman in one.

Even after he had published the first volume of his "History," Gibbon observes that his forced residence in London was sad and solitary. "The many forgot my existence when they saw me no longer at 'Brookes's,' and the few who sometimes had a thought on their friend were detained by business or pleasure; and I was proud if I could prevail on my bookseller, Elmsley, to enliven the dulness of the evening."

Unlike his proud and haughty rival Pitt, it was in the nature of Fox to unbend in social intercourse. The latter, when away from London or from his club, found his home at St. Anne's Hill, at Chertsey, where he derived amusement from his library, from his garden, from conversation, and from a variety of domestic and literary avocations.

Here, William, the fifth Duke of Devonshire, would spend his evenings, at whist or faro, whilst his Duchess, the beautiful Georgiana, was laying down the law to her political allies in the saloons of Devonshire House. At one time O'Connell was a member; but he was not at all a man after the hearts of the old English Whigs, who on one occasion, if we may believe Mr. Raikes' "Journal," had serious thoughts of expelling him.

Mr. Raikes, under date of 1832, recording the defeat of the Reform Bill in the House of Lords, and the refusal of the king to create fresh peers, writes: "'Brooks's' is full of weeping and of gnashing of teeth, so little was the Whig party prepared for this sudden catastrophe." "In the evening," he adds, "there was a most violent meeting of Whigs at 'Brooks's,' where the virulence of the speeches, and especially that of Mr. Stanley, the Irish secretary, who got on the table, showed the exasperated feelings of the party." This Mr. Stanley, it may be added, is the same individual who became afterwards the Tory premier, as the Earl of Derby.

Like "Arthur's Club," of which we have spoken above, "Brooks's" contains a sort of *imperium in imperio* in the "Fox Club," an association of the admirers of the statesman whose name it perpetuates. The members of the Fox Club dine together constantly during the London season. Though nearly eighty years have passed away since the death of Charles James Fox, in the upper room at Chiswick House, yet his name and memory are fresh among the sons and grandsons of his old personal and political friends. It may be asked why there is not still equally green and fresh amongst us a "Pitt Club," as once there was? Englishmen as a rule are "conservative" as well as "progressive" in their tastes and likings; but, as a matter of fact, the "Pitt Club" is particularly extinct, while that named after the great Premier's rival, Fox, still exists. Can the reason be after all that while Pitt was stern and haughty, Fox was pleasant and genial, and made friends instead of repelling them? If so, it is good to know that amiable traits of character are not soon forgotten.

"Brooks's Club," according to Mr. Rush, the American Minister, at the time of the Regency, consisted of 400 members.

A little below Bennett Street is the "New University Club," founded in 1864. The house, which is semi-Gothic in its style of architecture, reaches back into Arlington Street. It consists mainly of the younger members of the Universities of Oxford and Cambridge.

At the corner of Bennett Street, the house No. 54 has been, since 1871, successively the "Junior St. James's" and the "Verulam;" and next door, occupying part of the building formerly known as "Crockford's," is the "Devonshire Club." Like its neighbour, this club is of recent origin (1874), but it nevertheless numbers among its members most of the *élite* of the Liberal party. It was at one time proposed that its name should be altered to the "Liberal," so as to place it in direct antagonism to the "Conservative," but this proposal was ultimately negatived. Whenever the club begins to build, it will probably take the site hitherto occupied by the late Duke of Buckingham's house on the south side of Pall Mall adjoining to the War Office, and at present used for some of the clerks of that department.

Lord Hartington was chosen as the first chairman of the "Devonshire Club," so called after his father. Among its trustees and members of its committee appeared the names of the Duke of Westminster, Lords Huntly, Cork, Wolverton, Kensington, and Lansdowne; Mr. Gladstone and Mr. John Bright; the Right Hons. W. F. Cogan, H. C. E. Childers, and W. P. Adam; Sir Henry James, Q.C., Mr. A. D. Hayter, Sir William Drake, and several leading members of Parliament.

"Crockford's Club-house," at which we have now arrived, was built for its founder, the late Mr. John Crockford, in 1827, by Wyatt. It was erected at a vast cost, and in the grand proportions and palatial decorations of the principal floors, "had not been surpassed in any similar building in the metropolis." On the ground floor are the entrance-hall and inner-hall opening into a grand suite of rooms of noble proportions; on the principal floor are a suite of very lofty and splendid reception-rooms, gorgeously decorated *à la Grand Monarque*, approached from a superb staircase, itself an architectural triumph, and a great feature of the building.

This club was founded by Mr. John Crockford, of whom we have already made mention in speaking of the shop just outside Temple Bar,

where his money was made; and during the last twenty years of his life-time it was frequented by wealthy and aristocratic gentlemen. It lost its character at his death in 1844, and soon afterwards was closed. It was re-opened, after a few years' interval, as the "Naval, Military, and Civil Service Club;" it then was converted into a dining-room, called the "Wellington;" and, lastly, it was taken by a Joint-Stock Company as an auction-room.

The death of Mr. Crockford, in May, 1844, is thus mentioned in the "Journal" of Mr. T. Raikes:—"That arch-gambler Crockford is dead, and has left an immense fortune. He was originally a low fishmonger in Fish Street Hill, near the Monument, then a 'leg' at Newmarket, and keeper of 'hells' in London. He finally set up the club in St. James's Street, opposite to 'White's,' with a hazard bank, by which he won all the disposable money of the men of fashion in London, which was supposed to be near two millions."

At the time of his decease Mr. Crockford was worth £700,000, if we may trust the above-mentioned authority, though he had lost as much more in mining and other speculations. His death was accelerated by anxiety about his bets on the Derby; a proof of the inconsistency of human nature, which seeks the acquisition of wealth at the risk even of life and health, without which all is valueless.

In a work entitled "Doings in London," with illustrations by Cruikshank, it is not obscurely hinted that Mr. Crockford made his fortune by keeping a "hell" in King Street, St. James's, and that the fashionable club called after his name was in reality little or no better. No doubt very high play was carried on there, and the exact limits of a house so called have never, that we know of, been strictly defined.

Many stories are told about "Crockford's," and most of them certainly not to the credit of its owner. For instance, Mr. B. Jerrold tells us that in 1847 the proprietor of "Crockford's" "was compelled to return to Prince Louis Napoleon £2,000, which a cheat had endeavoured to extort from him inside his walls." It is almost a satisfaction to read the fact which has been stated, that this same proprietor of "Crockford's" became afterwards so reduced in circumstances that in 1865 he begged money of the emperor, at whose "fleecing" he had at all events connived.

Mr. Raikes writes in his "Journal" from Paris, in 1835—"Had a letter from G——, with a detail of what is going on in London society, where the gaming at 'Crockford's,' is unparalleled. Alea quando hos animos?"

"White's Club," near the top of the street, on the east side, occupies the site of the town-house of Elizabeth, Countess of Northumberland, daughter of Theophilus, Earl of Suffolk. Here she lived in her widowhood, if we may trust Horace Walpole, whose information came from the lady's niece by marriage. She was "the last lady who kept up the ceremonious state of the old peerage. When she went out to pay visits, a footman, bareheaded, walked on each side of her coach, and a second coach with her women attended her. I think," adds Horace Walpole, "Lady Suffolk told me that her daughter-in-law, the Duchess of Somerset, never sat down before her without her leave to do so. I suppose old Duke Charles, the 'proud' Duke of Somerset, had imbibed a good quantity of his stately pride in such a school."

"White's" originally stood at the bottom of St. James's Street, on the eastern side, nearly opposite to where are now the Conservative and Thatched House Clubs. Gay, in his "Trivia," thus brings to the mind's eye the scene which in former times might here be witnessed—in the winter, of course :—

"At 'White's' the harness'd chairman idly stands,
And swings around his waist his tingling hands."

The history of the establishment of this club is related as follows in the "Percy Anecdotes :"— "When 'Brooks's' became the head-quarters of the Foxite party, their opponents formed on the other side of the street a club which, from the name of its first steward, took the name of 'White's.' Here those measures which were to agitate Europe were submitted to the country gentlemen, whilst the spirit of resistance to the minister's power and ambition was cherished and fed at the other club. In the morning they met to organise and train their opposing forces ; at night, when debate was over, each party retired, the one to 'White's,' and the other to 'Brooks's,' to talk over triumphs achieved, or to sustain disappointed hopes by new resolves and new projects."

"White's" was the great Tory club, and in the days of the Regency, when Whig and Liberal peers could almost be counted on the fingers, it embraced two-thirds, if not three-fourths, of the "upper ten thousand" among its members. Being so fashionable, it is not a matter of wonder that it should have been extremely difficult to gain entrance to it. Its doors were shut against anybody, however rich, who had made his money by mercantile industry. Its large bow window, looking down into St. James's Street, during the season, was very frequently filled by the leading dandies and beaux, who preferred lounging to politics : such as the Marquis of Worcester, the Duke of Argyll, Lord Alvanley, Lord Foley, Mr. G. Dawson Damer, Hervey Aston, "Rufus" Lloyd, &c.

Mr. Rush, the American ambassador, speaks of "White's" as the Tory Club established in the reign of Charles II., and consisting of five hundred members. He adds that it was generally so full that there was great difficulty in gaining admission ; and that the place of head-waiter was said to be worth five hundred pounds a year. The club was a great place of resort among the "upper ten thousand." "Whenever I lose a friend," said George Selwyn, "I go to 'White's,' and pick up another."

This club was originally one of the head-quarters of the Tories of the old school, who here, in 1832, discussed the advisability of throwing out the first Reform Bill. But from and after that day it adopted a neutral tint, being frequented by members of both sides of the house.

The records of "White's" are said to be perfect from 1736. It may be questioned whether any entry on the books of "this famous academy" (as Swift once described it) has more interest than that which records an event in the year 1854—viz., when the leading members of the club gave a complimentary dinner to their fellow-member, the Duke of Cambridge, on his departure to take a command in the military expedition about to proceed to the East.

To this club belonged Sir Everard Fawkner, an official high in the Post Office department, who was celebrated for playing cards for high stakes, and very badly too. In allusion to his office, George Selwyn used to say, that some one who played with him was "robbing the mail."

At this club, on the last night of the year 1754, the first Lord Montfort supped and played at cards, as usual, and on leaving told the waiter to send his lawyer to wait on him the next day at eleven, as he had important business to transact. The important business was simply the work of blowing out his brains with a horse-pistol. Lady Hervey says that the sole cause of this rash act was a *tædium vitæ*, quite unaccountable in a man who had enjoyed all the success of public life.

Colley Cibber, "player, poet, and manager," not only an excellent actor, but the author of a treatise on the stage, which Horace Walpole terms "inimitable," was a member of "White's Club." Davies, in his "Life of Garrick," tells us the following story about him :—"Colley, we are told, had the honour to be a member of the great club at 'White's ;' and so, I suppose, might any other man who wore good clothes, and paid his money when he lost it. But on what terms did Cibber live with this society?

Why, he feasted most sumptuously, as I have heard his friend Victor say, with an air of triumphant exultation, with Mr. Arthur and his wife, and gave a trifle for his dinner. After he had dined, when the club-room door was opened and the laureate was introduced, he was saluted with a loud and joyous acclamation of ' O, King Coll!' 'Come in, King Coll!' and 'Welcome, welcome, King Colley!' And this kind of gratulation Mr. Victor thought was very gracious and very honourable."

garded as the author of the chief witticisms in the clubs after the abdication of the throne of dandyism by Brummell, who, before that time, was always quoted as the sayer of good things, as Sheridan had been some time before. Lord Alvanley had the talk of the day completely under his control, and was the arbiter of the "school for scandal" in St. James's. A *bon mot* attributed to him gave rise to the belief that Solomon caused the downfall and disappearance of Brummell; for on some friends of

CROCKFORD'S CLUB ABOUT 1840. (*See page* 160.)

"White's Club" is more than once alluded to by Pope, as a place where high play and loose morality prevailed in his day. In one of Walpole's letters occurs the following rich bit of satire on the folly of betting, which we may imagine was here indulged in to a very large extent:—"Sept. 1st, 1750. —They have put in the papers a good story made at 'White's.' A man dropped down dead at the door, and was carried in; the club immediately made bets whether he was dead or not; and when they were going to bleed him, the wagerers for his death interposed, and said it would affect the fairness of the bet."

By common consent, as it would appear from Captain Gronow, the late Lord Alvanley was re-

the prince of dandies observing that if he had remained in London something might have been done for him by his old associates, Alvanley replied, " He has done quite right to be off: it was Solomon's judgment."

Of "White's Club," Lord Russell tells in his "Recollections" an amusing story. "A noble lord, who owned several 'pocket boroughs' in the good old days of Eldon and Perceval, was asked by the returning officer whom he meant to nominate. Having no 'eligible' candidate at hand, he named a waiter at 'White's,' one Robert Mackreth; but as he did not happen to be sure of the Christian name of his nominee, the election was declared void. Nothing daunted, his lordship persisted in

1. ARTHUR'S CLUB.   (*See p.* 156.)   2. BROOK'S CLUB.   (*See p.* 158.)

his nomination. A fresh election was therefore held, when the name of the gentleman having been ascertained, he was returned as a matter of course, and took his seat in St. Stephen's." In order to do this, he must at that time have been qualified by his patron with freehold land to the value of £300 a year ! Such was the representation of England in the good old days before the first Reform Bill !

About the year 1870 this club was offered for auction, and changed hands, becoming the property of Mr. T. Percivall, of Wansford, in Northamptonshire. Since this period there has been, it is stated, a great falling off in the number of members proposed for election ; and after being so many years the great resort of the dandies, it is rapidly becoming the stronghold of what may be called "fogeydom." This is supposed to be the result of the establishment of the Marlborough Club, which has special attractions for the rising young men of the day. The club nevertheless still counts a goodly number of the wealthy portion of the aristocracy among its members, including the Prince of Wales and the Duke of Edinburgh.

"Boodle's" is the last of the three surviving clubs which have been identified with the names of individuals ; it was so called after its first founder, of whom, however, little or nothing is known. It is still the property of his representatives, though governed by a committee. Like "White's," it has a very modest and unpretending aspect when compared with some of the lordly edifices in its neighbourhood ; but it is said to be marked by most agreeable and comfortable arrangements within. It is frequented mainly by elderly country gentlemen, chosen indifferently from both of the two great political parties. Hence this club has never been identified with politics. It has been sarcastically said to be sacred to Bœotian tastes, but it has had distinguished persons on its list of members— Edward Gibbon, for instance, whose waddling gait and ugly visage convulsed with laughter not merely such fast friends as Lord and Lady Sheffield, but many of his literary friends and compeers.

Among the eccentric members of this club were the late Mr. Michael Angelo Taylor, M.P., and John, tenth Earl of Westmorland. The former was a notorious gossip and retailer of news and small talk ; in fact, quite a "Paul Pry" in his way : the latter was as thin as a lath. Coming in one day, Taylor found Lord Westmorland, who had just dined off a roast fowl and a leg of mutton. "Well, my lord," said Taylor, "I can't make out where you have stowed away your dinner, for I can see no trace of your ever having dined in your lean body." "Upon my word," replied Lord Westmorland, "I have finished both, and could now go in for another helping." His lordship, slim as was his figure, was remarkable for a prodigious appetite : in fact, it is said that he thought nothing of eating up a respectable joint or a couple of fowls at a single meal.

The original name of this club was the "Savoir vivre," and along with "Brooks's" and "White's," it formed a trio of nearly coeval date. In its early years it was noted for its costly gaieties, and its epicurism is thus commemorated in the "Heroic Epistle to Sir William Chambers : "—

> "For what is Nature ? Ring her changes round,
> Her three flat notes are water, plants, and ground ;
> Prolong the peal, yet, spite of all your chatter,
> The tedious chime is still ground, plants, and water.
> So, when some John his dull invention racks,
> To rival Boodle's dinners, or Almack's,
> Three uncouth legs of mutton shock our eyes,
> Three roasted geese, three buttered apple-pies."

A variety of clubs, past and present, have not been mentioned in this or the previous chapter : these, however, will be dealt with as we come to them in our future account of St. James's Square, Piccadilly, and other parts of the West-end of "Modern Babylon."

It may be remarked, by way of a conclusion to the present chapter, that there were from the first too many aristocratic clubs and private mansions in St. James's Street to leave much room for plebeian inns and hostelries on either side of so highly respectable a thoroughfare. Still, Mr. Jacob Larwood is at the pains of reminding us, in his very amusing and entertaining "History of Signboards," that, in the seventeenth century, there was in this street an inn known as "The Poet's Head." He adds, however, "Who the poet was, it is impossible to say now ; perhaps it was Dryden, since the trade's tokens represent a head crowned with bays." The "poet," as such, has not been a favourite as the sign of an inn, though we fail to see why such should be the case if there be truth in the old saying of Horace, that "no poems will last or live that proceed from the pens of water-drinkers."

CHAPTER XIV.

ST. JAMES'S STREET AND ITS NEIGHBOURHOOD.

" Come, and once more together let us greet
The long-lost pleasures of St. James's Street."—*Tickell.*

Original Name of St. James's Street—The Royal Mercatorium—Anecdote of George Selwyn—" Jack Lee " and George, Prince of Wales—Beau Brummell's Quarrel with the Prince—" Hook and Eye "—Manners of the Court Region a Century and a-half ago—Colonel Blood's Attack on the Duke of Ormonde—Dangers of the Streets in the Reign of Charles II.—The Wig Riots—Noted Residents in St. James's Street —Gillray, the Caricaturist—Pero's Bagnio—" Political Betty "—Sams' Library—Louis Napoleon's Residence at Fenton's Hotel—Arlington Street—Park Place—Society for the Propagation of the Gospel in Foreign Parts—" Mother Needham "—Lepel, Lady Hervey—Lord Guildford—Sir Francis Burdett—Robert Smith, Lord Carington—A Jovial Supper Party—Sir Richard Philipps—Samuel Rogers, the Poet —The Public Schools Club—Spencer House—Cleveland Row—Bridgewater House—The Green Park—Peace Illuminations of 1749 and 1814—Constitution Hill.

HAVING in the preceding chapter given an account of the various clubs in St. James's Street, we shall now proceed to notice what may be called the historical memories of the place, then pass rapidly through the various thoroughfares on its western side, and extend our perambulation into the Green Park.

Two centuries ago St. James's Street was called " the long street." Old Strype describes it as " beginning at the palace of St. James's, and running up to the road against Albemarle Buildings ; the best houses, at the upper end, having a terrace-walk before them ; " a little more than half a century later, the parish of St. James's was described as including " all the houses and grounds comprehended in a place heretofore called St. James's Fields, and the confines thereof." St. James's Street dates from the middle of the seventeenth century ; and we read in "Hunter's History of London " that " the road from Petty France to St. James's Palace, that which afterwards became St James's Street," was first paved in the year after the Restoration. The old buildings have nearly all been swept away to make room for the more stately club-houses and hotels of modern times ; and of these the western side of the street in the present day is chiefly composed. The east side, with the exception of " Boodle's " and " White's " Clubs, consists mainly of elegant shops, one of which, at the beginning of the present century, was fitted up as a bazaar, and rejoiced in the name of the " Royal Mercatorium." The busy tenants of this establishment were summoned before the magistrate at the Queen Square Police Office, for " hawking " their goods without a licence ; but the summons was dismissed, it being decided that the occupants of the bazaars did not come under the Hawkers' Act.

For upwards of a century this noble thoroughfare —for such it really is—has maintained its character as an aristocratic lounge, and a place where only the privileged classes have a right to be seen. To what extent this privilege was carried in former times may be judged from the following anecdote :—

George Selwyn happening to be at Bath when it was nearly empty, was induced, from the necessity of having somebody to associate with, to make the acquaintance of an elderly twaddling gentleman whom he invariably met in the rooms. In the height of the following season Selwyn encountered his old associate here, in St. James's Street, and endeavoured to pass him unnoticed, but in vain. " What, sir," asked the *cuttee,* holding out his hand, " don't you recollect me ? We became acquainted at Bath." " I know we did," returned Selwyn, declining the proffered hand, " and when I next go to Bath I shall be happy to know you again—but not till then."

It was in walking up this street one day, and meeting " Jack Lee " arm-in-arm with George, Prince of Wales, that Beau Brummell sarcastically asked him, " Jack, who's your fat friend ? " pretending not to recognise his Royal Highness, with whom he had quarrelled at Carlton House a few days previously. Tommy Moore, in his " Twopenny Post Bag," immortalises the quarrel in a parody on a letter from the Prince to the Duke of York, in which his Royal Highness is made to say—

" I indulge in no hatred, and wish there may come ill
To no mortal, except, now I think on't, Beau Brummell,
Who declared t'other day, in a superfine passion,
He'd cut me and bring the old king into fashion."

Such attacks as these must have turned the warm friend, though a prince of the blood, into a bitter enemy ; and it must be said in "Beau" Brummell's behalf, that it was at Carlton House that he was led to indulge in those gambling tastes and in that dangerous familiarity with royalty which in the end proved his ruin.

Theodore Hook figured once, and once only, in the celebrated " H. B. Sketches " of the elder Doyle. He is represented walking down St. James's Street, arm-in-arm with the then Speaker, Mr. Manners Sutton (afterwards Viscount Canterbury), who— otherwise a fine-looking man—had a notable squint ; hence the title of the engraving—" Hook and Eye ! "

"St. James's, in Westminster," observes the witty author of the "Town Spy," "has a very large share of the nobility and gentry; yet a person of indifferent rank may find a vacant seat in the church on Sunday. The 'quality,' who fly about in their sumptuous equipages, imagine themselves to be the admiration of the vulgar sort, but, on the contrary, they are only the objects of their ridicule, they being too well acquainted with their most private affairs." No man, as we all know, is a hero in the eyes of his valet; and no doubt the morals of the age in which the "Town Spy" was written (1755), and especially in the neighbourhood of St. James's, were such as often would serve to illustrate the assertion.

Thackeray, in one of his "Lectures on English Humorists," describes in minute detail the manners of the Court region a century and a half ago, when a lady of fashion would joke at table with her footmen, and noble lords call out to the waiters, before ladies, "Hang expense, bring us a ha'porth of cheese." "Such," he adds, "were the ladies of St. James's; such were the frequenters of White's Chocolate-house, when Swift used to visit it, and Steele described it as the centre of pleasure, gallantry, and entertainment."

It is often said that London is more like a country made up of several states than an individual city; and it is in keeping with this idea that Addison, in the *Spectator* (No. 340), speaks of the metropolis as composed of different races, instead of being made up, like a town, of one cognate family. "When I consider this great city," he writes, "in its several quarters, or divisions, I look upon it as an aggregate of various nations, distinguished from each other by their respective customs, manners, and interests. The courts of two countries do not differ so much from one another as the Court and the City of London in their peculiar ways of life and conversation. In short, the inhabitants of St. James's, notwithstanding they live under the same laws, and speak the same language, are a distinct people from those of Cheapside, by several climates and degrees, in their ways of thinking and conversing together." If such was the essayist's opinion in the reign of Queen Anne or George I., what, we may fairly ask, would he have said stronger on the subject, had he lived on into the reign of Victoria?

It was in this street that, on a cold December morning in 1670, Colonel Blood—whose name is notorious for his attempt to rob the Tower of the regalia of England—set upon the great Duke of Ormonde, aided by four ruffians, and attempted to assassinate him on his way to Clarendon House, which stood facing the top of the street, upon the site of what is now Albemarle Street. The duke was dragged out of his carriage by Blood and his associates, tied to one of them on horseback, and carried along Piccadilly towards Tyburn, where it was their intention to have hung him, in revenge, it is said, for a punishment inflicted upon some companions of theirs in Ireland during the duke's administration of that country. The alarm being given at Clarendon House, the servants followed, and recovered his grace from a struggle in the mud with the man to whom he was tied, and who, on regaining his horse, fired a pistol at the duke, and escaped. In the "Historian's Guide" (1688), it is stated that there were "six ruffians mounted and armed," and that the duke's six footmen, who usually walked beside his carriage, were absent when the attack was made—probably having dropped in at a sideway hostelry, in quest of "something to keep out the cold."

As to the dangers of the streets at the West-end at the period in which the above incident occurred, we are not left in the dark by Macaulay. He writes:—"When the evening closed in, the difficulty and danger of walking about London became serious indeed. The garret windows were opened and pails were emptied, with little regard to those who were passing below. Falls, bruises, and broken bones were of constant occurrence; for, till the last year of the reign of Charles II., most of the streets were left in profound darkness. Thieves and robbers plied their trade with impunity; yet they were hardly so terrible to peaceful citizens as another class of ruffians. It was a favourite amusement of dissolute young gentlemen to swagger by night about the town, breaking windows, upsetting sedans, beating quiet men, and offering rude caresses to pretty women. Several dynasties of these tyrants had, since the Restoration, domineered over the streets. The 'Muns' and 'Tityre Tus' had given place to the 'Hectors,' and the 'Hectors' had been recently succeeded by the 'Scourers.' At a later period arose the 'Nicker,' the 'Hawcubite,' and the yet more dreaded name of 'Mohawk,' as we learn from Oldham's 'Imitation of the Third Satire of Juvenal' (1682), and Shadwell's 'Scourers' (1690). Many other authorities will readily occur to all who are acquainted with the popular literature of that and the succeeding generation. It may be suspected that some of the 'Tityre Tus,' like good Cavaliers, broke Milton's windows shortly after the Restoration. I am confident that he was thinking of those pests of London when he dictated the noble lines—

' And in luxurious cities, where the noise
  Of riot ascends above their loftiest towers,
  And injury and outrage, and when night
  Darkens the streets, then wander forth the sons
  Of Belial, flown with insolence and wine.' "

"There were," writes Macaulay, "at the end of Charles II.'s reign, houses near St. James's Park, where fops congregated, their heads and shoulders covered with black or flaxen wigs, not less ample than those which are now worn by the Lord Chancellor and the Speaker of the House of Commons." He adds, " that the wigs and most of the dress of these fops came from Paris, and that they spoke a peculiar and affected dialect, called a 'Lord' a 'Lard.' "

In the year 1764, owing to changes in the fashion, people gave over the use of that very artificial appendage, the wig, and wore their own hair, when they had any. In consequence of this, the wig-makers, who were very numerous in London, were suddenly thrown out of work, and reduced to great distress. For some time, we are told, both town and country rang with their calamities, and their complaints that men should wear their own hair instead of perukes; and at last it struck them that some legislative enactment ought to be at once procured in order to oblige gentlefolks to wear wigs, for the benefit of the suffering wig-trade. Accordingly they drew up a petition for relief, which, on the 11th of February, 1765, they carried to St. James's to represent to his Majesty George the Third. As they went processionally through the town, it was observed that most of these wig-makers, who wanted to force other people to wear them, wore no wigs themselves; and this striking the London mob as something monstrously unfair and inconsistent, they seized the petitioners, and cut off all their hair *par force*. Horace Walpole, who alludes to this ludicious petition, in his Letters to the Earl of Hertford, asks, with his usual wit, " Should one wonder if carpenters were to remonstrate, that since the peace their trade decays, and that there is no demand for wooden legs ? "

St. James's Street in its time has had many distinguished residents. Waller, the poet, as Mr. John Timbs tells us, lived on the west side from 1660 until 1687, when he died at Beaconsfield, in Buckinghamshire. Pope lodged "next door to ye Golden Ball, on ye second terras." Gibbon, the historian, died in January, 1794, at No. 76, then Elmsley's, the bookseller's. Horace Walpole says: " I was told a droll story of Gibbon the other day. One of those booksellers in Paternoster Row, who publish things in numbers, went to Gibbon's lodgings in St. James's Street, sent up his name,

and was admitted. ' Sir,' said he, ' I am now publishing a History of England done by several good hands. I understand you have a knack of these things, and should be glad to give you every reasonable encouragement.' As soon as Gibbon had recovered the use of his legs and tongue, which were petrified with surprise, he ran to the bell, and desired his servant to show this encourager of learning down stairs."

At his residence in this street, in February, 1723, died Sir Christopher Wren, the architect of St. Paul's; in 1811, Lord Byron was living in lodgings at No. 8, just after attaining his majority.

At No. 29, next door to Boodle's Club, lived the caricaturist Gilray, who here committed suicide, in 1815, by throwing himself from the window on to the pavement below. The shop was well known as that of Miss Humphrey, the caricature print-seller, sister of the conchologist, and the vendor of his works. Gilray was first the pupil of Mr. Ashby, the celebrated writing engraver; but afterwards studied under Bartolozzi. The author of the " Book for a Rainy Day " says that Gilray engraved several portraits and other subjects in a steady mechanical way, but soon followed the genuine bent of his genius, though, it must be acknowledged, it was too often at the expense of honour and even common honesty. " He would, by his publications, either divulge family secrets which ought to have been ever at rest, or expect favours for the plates which he destroyed. This talent, by which he made many worthy persons so uneasy, was inimitable; and his works, though time may destroy every point of their sting, will remain specimens of a rare power, both for character and composition." Among numerous instances, he suffered himself to bear evidence against Samuel Ireland, the publisher of the pretended Shakespeare papers. Ireland had given away an etching, a portrait of himself. This print Gilray copied, and offered a few impressions publicly for sale in Miss Humphrey's shop-window, in December, 1797. Gilray, it may be remarked, lies buried in the churchyard of St. James's, Piccadilly.

At the commencement of the last century, Peyrault's, or Pero's, " Bagnio," in this street, was high in fashion. It occupied the site of what is now Fenton's Hotel, on the west side of the street; this was a bagnio of old standing, as appears by the title of a catalogue of the " valuable collection of pictures, the property of the late Mr. Bartrum Aumailkey, *alias* Pero, who kept the bagnio previous to 1714." Next door to the above establishment was a tavern bearing the sign of the " Bunch of Grapes," where, as we learn from the newspapers

ST. JAMES'S STREET IN 1750. (*From an Original Drawing in Mr. Crace's Collection.*)

of 1711, "was sold extraordinary good cask Florence wine, at 6s. per gallon."

The next house of notoriety is now No. 62, some time occupied by Lauriere, the jeweller. It was formerly held by an old lady well known under the appellation of "Political Betty," and was famous in Horace Walpole's time.

At the corner opposite the Palace, the shop which is now occupied by a firm of booksellers was, until recently, well known in the fashionable and

year 1827, was for some time published at Sams' Library, and called "Sams' Peerage."

In 1838-9, Louis Napoleon, then in exile, between the "affair" of Boulogne, and the "affair" of Strasburg, took up his quarters for a time at Fenton's Hotel, leading the life of a young man of fashion. From Fenton's he removed with a suite of seventeen friends and servants into Waterloo Place, and thence to Carlton Terrace and Carlton Gardens, where we have already mentioned him.

ST. JAMES'S PLACE. (*See page* 170.)

aristocratic circles as "Sams' Library." Mr. W. H. Sams, who died in 1872, had here for some time carried on his father's business as librarian and publisher. In former times its windows were often crowded with gazers at the caricatures of well-known political and other celebrities, before the days when Sig. Pellegrini made *Vanity Fair* famous.

"There, where you stop to scan the last 'H. B.',
   Swift paused and muttered, 'Shall I have that see?'"

wrote Lord Lytton in the "New Timon;" and, in truth, upon the site of Sams' shop the great satirist, coming out of St. James's Palace, might often have stood and quieted his fervid indignation at the baseness of the Court of Queen Anne. "Lodge's Peerage," the first edition of which appeared in the

It was in 1843-44, whilst residing in chambers at 88, St. James's Street, close to where now stands the Conservative Club, that Thackeray began and finished "The Luck of Barry Lyndon," which many consider the most original of his earlier writings.

Branching off from the west side of St. James's Street are Bennett Street, Park Place, St. James's Place, and Little St. James's Street. The highest and northernmost of these turnings leads into Arlington Street, a thoroughfare running at right angles with Piccadilly. This street has always been inhabited by statesmen and public men. The first house on the west side was for many years the house of the Duke of Beaufort, and then of the Duke of Hamilton, before it passed into the hands of

Lord Wimborne. It has on the ground floor a magnificently-carved ceiling, painted with the heraldic insignia of the house of Somerset.

In this street was for many years the town residence of the Dukes of Rutland. It was lent by the then Duke, in 1826, to the Duke of York, who died there quite suddenly in his arm-chair, on one of the first days of the following year. His body was removed to St. James's Palace, where it lay in state, and was buried in St. George's Chapel, at Windsor, on the 20th of January, 1827.

In 1708 the Duke of Richmond, Lord Cholmondeley, Lord Kingston, and Guildford Brooke were living in this street. In 1745 the first Earl of Orford, the great Sir Robert Walpole, died here. Here the old Marchioness of Salisbury, one of the leaders of "society" in the reign of George IV., used to hold her Sunday evening receptions, of which we find many notices in "Raikes's Journal," and other books of cotemporary anecdote. They were frequently attended by royalty, ambassadors, &c. The Marchioness was burnt to death at Hatfield House, in December, 1834.

Lord Carteret was living in this street both before and after he was promoted to an earl's coronet, as Lord Granville.

The writer of "A New Review of the Public Buildings, &c.," in the reign of George II., is enthusiastic in his praises of the side of Arlington Street which faces the Green Park, as "one of the most beautiful situations in Europe for health, convenience, and beauty, and combining together the advantages of town and country." The only fault that he can find with the mansions is the "want of uniformity."

In Park Place, in 1835, Vernon House, now the residence of Lord Redesdale, was occupied by Lord William Bentinck, some time Governor-General of India. Close by it are the offices and head-quarters of the Society for the Propagation of the Gospel in Foreign Parts, which was founded in 1701. This institution was formerly in Pall Mall, as we have mentioned. Its aim is to establish and support bishops and clergy of the Church of England abroad, and chiefly in our own colonies. There also is the office of the Colonial Bishoprics Fund, which was established in 1861 for founding and endowing additional Colonial bishoprics.

As a set-off to the good work carried on by the society above mentioned, we may state that in the early part of the last century the noted "Mother Needham" was "convicted of keeping a lewd and disorderly house in Park Place; she was fined one shilling, to stand twice in the pillory, and find sureties for her good behaviour for three years."

The memory of this woman is perpetuated by a couple of lines in the "Dunciad;" and a note on the passage says she was "a matron of great fame, and very religious in her way; whose constant prayer it was, that she might get enough by her profession to leave it off in time, and make her peace with God. This, however, was not granted to her, as she died from the effects of her exposure in the pillory."

No. 4 is the home of the Road Club, which was established here in 1874, by a number of gentlemen who take an interest in figuring as amateur "Jehus."

St. James's Place dates from about the year 1694. At the present time it forms the headquarters of bachelor members of Parliament, almost every other house being let out in apartments; it has been in past time also the abode of several individuals whose names have become as familiar as "household words." Here, in 1712, Addison had lodgings; and a few years later we find John Wilkes living here in "very elegant lodgings." Here, too, resided Parnell, the poet, Mr. Secretary Craggs, Bishop Kennett, the antiquary, and Mrs. Robinson (Perdita), the actress, already mentioned by us in speaking of Carlton House.

At the western end of St. James's Place, overlooking the Green Park, the learned Lepel, Lady Hervey, in 1748, built a house, which was subsequently occupied by Lord Hastings, and ultimately divided into two. Lady Hervey speaks of its windows as commanding a view towards Chelsea and the country, as also of the Duke of Devonshire's house, when the dust in Piccadilly permitted it. Within its walls Lord Chesterfield and other wits and learned persons used to meet constantly.

Lord John Hervey, who in 1720 married the "fair Lepel," one of the maids of honour to the Princess of Wales, was the eldest son of the first Earl of Bristol, and was early attached to the court of the Prince and Princess at Richmond. His marriage was signalised by Pulteney and Lord Chesterfield by a ballad in honour of both bride and bridegroom, in which the noble poets declared that never had been seen—

> "So perfect a beau and a belle,
> As when Hervey the handsome was wedded
> To the beautiful Molly Lepel."

His connection both with the world of politics and with that of poets is known to every reader of his memoirs, and of the life of Pope, who cruelly satirised him under the name of "Sporus."

At No. 25 lived Lord Guildford, who, as John Timbs tells us in his "Curiosities of London," "had his library lined with snake-wood from Ceylon, of which island he was at one time governor." The next tenant was Sir Francis Burdett, so many years the popular member for Westminster, who resided here from about 1820 to his death in 1844.

The life of Sir Francis Burdett affords a remarkable illustration of the political vicissitudes a popular man may encounter. Every reader of the political events of the present century will know how he was idolised by the people during the reign of George III.; and the story of his standing a siege of horse and foot for two days in his house in London, before the warrant could be executed, rather than surrender to the warrant officer who came to convey him to the Tower of London on a charge of libelling the House of Commons, stands out in strong contrast to the staunch Conservatism which marked the later years of his life.

Mr. Raikes, in his "Journal," tells the following anecdote of Sir Francis Burdett :—"Early in life he passed three years in France, at the outbreak of the Revolution, when he attended the meetings of the National Assembly and the Political Clubs, which, during that period of public agitation, were so numerous. When he returned home in 1793, dazzled by the political doctrines he had imbibed, he became a notorious reformer in Parliament, and married the second daughter of Thomas Coutts, the wealthy banker. He was a votary of Horne Tooke; and through the Radical interest of Westminster was elected member for that borough, without a shilling of expense to himself, in 1807, as the man of the people. He was imprisoned in the Tower in 1810, by order of the House of Commons, for addressing a printed letter to his constituents on the commitment of Mr. Gale Jones. Having seen the favourite object of Parliamentary Reform carried by the Whigs, and probably the inefficiency of his former wild theories to confer real happiness on his country, he gradually moderated his views on national politics, and settled down into a good Conservative, which brought upon him the abuse and obloquy of his own party, who then gave him the name of ' Old Glory.' It was a singular coincidence, that he died ten days after his wife, Lady Burdett, to whom he was most tenderly attached. Sir Francis was a great fox-hunter, and a type of the ' fine old English gentleman,' of which he preserved to the last the characteristic dress—leather-breeches and top-boots. When young, he was for a long time the notorious lover of Lady Oxford—*cum multis aliis*. He had a very large fortune, which goes to his eldest son Robert. His daughter, who inherited the Coutts's fortune, is the richest heiress in all England. He had once a dispute

with Mr. Paul about the Westminster election after the death of Mr. Fox, which terminated in a duel, in which both parties were severely wounded ; and there being no medical persons present, and but one carriage on the spot, it became necessary to remove both the combatants to town in the same vehicle."

The death of Sir Francis was as pathetic as his parliamentary life had been famous. His wife was a daughter of Mr. Coutts, the celebrated banker, and for the long period of fifty years they lived happily together ; and when death took away Lady Burdett, in January, 1844, her husband, then in his seventy-fourth year, became inconsolable, and felt that he had nothing left to live for. Wrapping himself up in his sorrow, he refused all consolation and all nourishment. In spite of the most earnest entreaties he would taste no food, and at last nature gave way, and he died on the 23rd of the same month ; and the husband and wife were buried at the same hour, on the same day, in the same vault, in Ramsbury Church, Wiltshire. The above-mentioned daughter of Sir Francis Burdett, Angela Georgina, assumed in 1837 the additional surname and arms of Coutts, under the will of her grandfather's widow, Harriet (afterwards Duchess of St. Albans). Miss Burdett Coutts was raised to the peerage in 1871, by having conferred upon her the title of a Baroness, in recognition of her large-hearted charity and general philanthropy.

In 1790 one of the fine houses on the west side of St. James's Place was occupied by Mr. Robert Smith, a London banker, and M.P. for Nottingham, who, most reluctantly on the part of George III., was created a peer as Lord Carington. This was the first instance in which a peerage was ever bestowed on the moneyed interest as distinct from the ownership of broad acres ; and it was believed, not only by Pitt's enemies but by his friends, that the bestowal of the coronet in this case was the discharge of some pecuniary obligations of the Premier, who forced the King to sign the patent.

Readers of Mr. Harrison Ainsworth's historical romance of " St. James's " will scarcely need to be reminded of two chapters in the early part of that work, in which he gives us a picture of a jovial supper party at St. John's residence in this street, at which Wycherley, Congreve, Tickell, Mrs. Bracegirdle, Mrs. Oldfield, Addison, Vanbrugh, Steele, Rowe, Tom D'Urfey, Dr. Garth, Kneller, Harley, Mr. Markam, Mrs. Manley, and the other wits, poets, and painters of that truly Augustan era, were present, when Mrs. Oldfield and Mrs. Bracegirdle settled a quarrel as to which should sing first, by pistols—not, however, after the way of a duel, but by trying to snuff a candle by a shot at twelve paces. We should like to have been present at the break-up of the party at early dawn, and to have seen the ladies' chairs arrive, and take their departure ; Mrs. Bracegirdle escorted home by Congreve, Mrs. Old-field by Maynwaring, and Mrs. Centlivre by Prior, who persisted in calling her " Chloe " all the way ; whilst Steele and Wycherley, walking along by Mrs. Manley's chair, and being rather excited by St. John's port wine, assaulted the watch, and for their pains were arrested by the "Charlies," and lodged in the St. James's Round House.

Sir N. W. Wraxall, in his gossiping "Memoirs of his own Time," tells the following amusing story about one of the residents of St. James's Place towards the close of the last century :—

" Sir Richard Phillipps, a Welsh baronet of ancient descent, when member for Pembrokeshire, in the year 1776, having preferred a request to his Majesty, through the first Minister, Lord North, for permission to make a carriage-road up to the front of his house, which looked into St. James's Park, met with a refusal. The king, apprehensive that if he acceded to Sir Richard's desire, it would form a precedent for many similar applications, put a negative on it ; but Lord North, in delivering the answer, softened it by adding, that if he wished to be created an Irish peer, no difficulty would be ex-perienced. This honour being thus tendered him, he accepted it, and was forthwith made a baron of that kingdom by the title of Lord Milford. His intimate friend and mine, the late Sir John Stepney, related this fact to me not long after it took place."

At No. 22, a house built by James Wyatt, R.A., lived from 1808 until his death in December, 1855, Samuel Rogers, the poet. Here Sheridan, Lord Byron, Sir James Mackintosh, Thomas Moore, Macaulay, Sharp, and almost all the other literary celebrities of the first half of the present century, were often guests. The house, which is com-paratively small, and is distinguished by its bow windows, fronting the Green Park, contained a choice collection of pictures, Etruscan vases, sculp-ture, antique bronzes, and literary curiosities, and a variety of lesser objects of art—all distinguished for rare excellence; some of the pictures were be-queathed to the nation, and the remainder of the collection was ultimately disposed of. Among the most valued treasures in the house there was to be seen framed and hung on one of the walls of his library, the original agreement by which Milton assigned to the publisher, Symons, his poem of " Paradise Lost," for the sum of five pounds. This historical document bears the undoubted autograph signature of the poet.

Samuel Rogers was a banker as well as a poet ; he knew how to spend his wealth, and his name will live as at once a poet and as a patron of litera-ture. Born in the year 1763, he lived to the great age of ninety-two. His first publication was his "Ode to Superstition, and other Poems," which appeared in 1787 ; five years later he published his " Pleasures of Memory," the work by which his fame as a poet was established, and by which his name came to be most widely and permanently known. In 1798 he gave to the world his " Epistle to a Friend, and other Poems ;" in 1814, appeared his " Vision of Columbus and Jacqueline ;" in 1819, " Human Life ;" and in the following year the first part of his " Italy," on the printing and illustrating of which he is said to have spent not less than £10,000.

The Rev. A. C. Coxe, of the United States, in his " Impressions of England," writes :—" Among the authors of England, I had desired to see especially Mr. Samuel Rogers, who is now the last survivor of a brilliant literary epoch, and whose long familiarity with the historical personages of a past generation would of itself be enough to make him a man of note, and a patriarch in the republic of letters. Though now above ninety years of age, he still renders his elegant habitation an attractive resort, and I was indebted to him for attentions which were the more valuable, as he was at that time suffering from an accident, and hence pecu-liarly entitled to deny himself entirely to strangers. His house, in St. James's Street, has been often described, and its beautiful opening on the Green Park is familiar from engravings. Here every Englishman of literary note, during the last half century, has been at some time a guest; and if its walls could but *Boswellise* the wit which they have heard around the table of its hospitable master, no collection of *Memorabilia* with which the world is acquainted could at all be compared with it. Here I met the aged poet at breakfast ; Sir Charles and Lady Lyell completing the party. He talked of the past as one to whom the present was less a reality, and it seemed strange to hear him speak of Mrs. Piozzi, as if he had been one of the old circle at Thrale's. When a boy, he rang Dr. Johnson's bell, in Bolt Court, in a fit of ambition to see the literary colossus of the time, but his heart failed him at the sticking point, and he ran away before the door was opened. Possibly the old sage himself responded to the call, and as he retired in a fit of indignation, moralising on the growing impertinence of the age, how little did he imagine that the inter-ruption was a signal tribute to his genius, from one who, in the middle of the nineteenth century, should be himself an object of veneration as the Nestor of Literature ! "

But it must be owned, with every wish to speak well of those who are gone, that Samuel Rogers was not a man gifted with such qualities as to make real friends. Acquaintances and hangers-on he numbered by scores; but of friends he had very few. He was full of spleen and sarcasm, though the sun of fortune had smiled on him through life, and accordingly, if he had been a poor man, he would have had many enemies. The following passage from Mr. William Jerdan's " Men I have Known " will serve to illustrate our meaning, though an admission to Mr. Rogers's breakfasts was one of the greatest privileges accorded to men of literary tastes and abilities, who wished to get on in London :—

" Rogers was reputed a wit, and did say some good things ; but many of the best were said by others, and fathered upon him (as the use is), especially when there was any bitterness in the joke, which was his characteristic. His going to Holland House by the Hammersmith stage-coach (in the days when cabs and omnibuses were unknown), and asking the loitering driver what he called it, is not one of his worst : being answered ' The Regulator,' he observed that it was a very proper name, as all the rest *go by it*. Luttrell and Rogers were intimate friends and rival wits, and disliked each other accordingly. I have used the word ' friend,' but it did not appear that the nonogenarian (whatever he might have enjoyed half a century before) had any friends. I never saw about him any but acquaintances or toadies. Had he outlived them ? No ; he was not of a nature to have friends. He was born with the silver spoon in his mouth, and had never needed a friend in his long, easy journey through life. The posthumous laudation lavished upon him by his political cronies was purely of the *de mortuis nil nisi bonum* kind. He never received that coin when alive ; for, if the truth be told, his liberality and generosity were small specks which could not bear blazon, and he was radically ill-tempered. Now, nobody can love a cantankerous person, even though placed in such fortunate circumstances as not to be always offensive. His whole career was too sunny. There were neither clouds nor showers to nourish the sensitive plants which adorn humanity—nothing but showy sunflowers. No lovely dew-dipped blossoms ; no sweet buddings of refreshing scent ; no soft green tufts sending up grateful incense, as when varying seasons produce their beneficial influence, and the breezes and the rains (ay, the storms) from heaven serve but to root and expand the spirit's growth.

" Few men who have had nothing but an even tenor of their way, are duly touched with feeling for the distresses of their fellow-creatures, which they have never experienced. In the absence of any higher motive to benevolence, there was not even a trace of *bonhomie* about Rogers. Sarcasm and satire were his social weapons. Kindness and geniality do not crop out in any account of him that I have seen ; and this negative describes the individual, of whom I did not care to know much. The constant little bickering competitions between him and Luttrell were very entertaining to some minds. They met once, and did not squabble. It was in the Crystal Palace in Hyde Park, into which they were both wheeled in chairs, when no longer able to walk ! "

On one occasion the venerable poet was visited by Wordsworth and Haydon the painter. They had been to Paddington together, and had afterwards walked across the Park to Rogers's house. He had a party to lunch, so Haydon went into the pictures, and studied Rembrandt, Reynolds, Veronese, Raffaelle, and Tintoretto. Wordsworth remarked, " Haydon is down-stairs." " Ah," said Rogers, " he is better employed than chattering nonsense up-stairs." As Wordsworth and Haydon crossed the Park, the latter remarked, " Scott, Wilkie, Keats, Hazlitt, Beaumont, Jackson, Charles Lamb are all gone—we only are left." He said, " How old are you ? " " Fifty-six," replied the painter; " how old are you ? " " Seventy-three," said Wordsworth, " in my seventy-third year ; I was born in 1770." " And I in 1786." " You have many years before you." " I trust I have ; and you, too, I hope. Let us cut out Titian, who was ninety-nine." " Was he ninety-nine ? " said Wordsworth. " Yes," said his friend, " and his death was a moral ; for as he lay dying of the plague, he was plundered, and could not help himself."

" Eminent as he was, both by position and genius," says his biographer, " Rogers's opinion was frequently sought by authors and by artists. He was shy of praise—shy of censure. In an age when almost every poet of any name was a reviewer, Rogers was *not* a reviewer. When in the presence of the painter of any picture, he had constant recourse to the safe and general criticism of Sir Joshua : ' Pretty, very pretty,' were the words that conveyed satisfaction to the eager ears of many a clever artist." The critic who annoyed Mr. Rogers in the *Quarterly Review* was never more in the wrong than when he asserted that his author was a hasty writer. A man of letters and of fortune from his birth, whose literary life extended over sixty years, cannot be called a hasty writer when the produce of his life can be placed with ease in an ordinary pocket volume, for such is the shape his works assume in the latest edition. The fact is, that his were hard-bound brains, and not a line he ever wrote was produced at a single

Mr. Rogers with which he had nothing whatever to do. In the early days of the *John Bull* newspaper, "Sam Rogers" had fathered on him many a smart saying, and many a clever and many a stupid jest. Once, when a certain M.P. wrote a review of his poems, and said he wrote very

SAMUEL ROGERS. (*From a Portrait taken shortly before his death.*)

sitting. This was well exemplified in a favourite saying of Sydney Smith : " When Rogers produces a couplet he goes to bed, the knocker is tied, and straw is laid down, and the caudle is made, and the answer to inquiries is, that Mr. Rogers is as well as can be expected." How many smart sayings have been assigned to Sheridan and Selwyn, to Jekyll and Rose, to Walpole and others of Walpole's contemporaries, which in truth they never uttered ! Many were, and still are, assigned to

well for a banker, Rogers wrote, in return, the following :—

" They say he has no heart, and I deny it :
    He has a heart, and—gets his speeches by it."

The principal front of the house once tenanted by Samuel Rogers overlooks the Green Park, where it forms a conspicuous object by the side of Spencer House. "Within that house," writes Mr. Miller in 1852, "every distinguished literary man of the last century has been a guest. Here Scott,

Byron, Shelley, Coleridge and Campbell have many a time discoursed with the venerable poet. What a rich volume would that be, were it possible to write it, that contained all the good sayings that have been uttered beneath that roof! Here I first sat as a guest, roaring with laughter at the wit of

received, would require the hand of another Horace Walpole to illustrate it. The name of Samuel Rogers," he adds, "alone would save the Green Park from oblivion, and give it a popularity which, but for him, it would never have possessed."

About the year 1863 was established, at No. 17

SAMUEL ROGERS' HOUSE, GREEN PARK FRONT. (See page 174)

Sydney Smith; here also I have listened 'with bated breath' to the music murmured by the lips of Tommy Moore. Within those walls I first saw that true poetess and much-injured lady, Caroline Norton, and from the host himself in my early career as an author received that kindness and encouragement without which I might have 'fallen on the way.' A description of this celebrated house, of all it contains, and of all the guests it has

in St. James's Place—previously the residence of Lord Lyttelton—the Public Schools Club; which, however, had but a transient existence. Its name was subsequently changed to the Phœnix, but the club does not appear to have been more flourishing under its new name, and in a short time it ceased altogether, and the premises were converted into a private hotel.

The mansion of Earl Spencer, which stands at

the south-west angle, with one front facing the Green Park, is by some considered one of the finest designs of Inigo Jones; by others it is said to have been built by Vardy, a scholar of Kent, and architect of the Horse Guards. It consists of an admixture of the Grecian style of architecture, and is highly, though not profusely, ornamented. The principal ornament of the interior is the library, an elegant room, containing one of the finest collections of books in the kingdom. This noble and even palatial edifice was built for John, first Lord Spencer, who died in 1783. The front towards the Park, which is of Portland stone, with attached columns, is surmounted by a pediment adorned with statues and vases, very tastefully disposed.

Retracing our steps into St. James's Street, we now descend towards the Palace gates and Cleveland Row. How different now is the scene to be witnessed here from what it was before the introduction of coaches or even of sedan-chairs. On the happiness of those days, Gay thus descants in his " Trivia : "—

" Thus was of old Britannia's city bless'd
    Ere pride and luxury her sons possess'd ;
Coaches and chariots yet unfashion'd lay,
Nor late-invented chairs perplex'd the way :
Then the proud lady tripp'd along the town,
And tucked up petticoats, secur'd her gown ;
Her rosy cheek with distant visits glow'd,
And exercise unartful charms bestowed ;
But since in braided gold her foot is bound,
And a long trailing manteau sweeps the ground,
Her shoe disdains the street ; the lazy fair
With narrow step affects a limping air."

At the time of which Gay speaks, of course it was but a rare thing for a country dame to be seen in London. Lord Clarendon tells us that his mother, though she was the daughter of a peer, and though her husband had been a member of Parliament, was never in London in her life, " the wisdom and frugality of that time being such that few gentlemen made journeys to London, or any other expensive journeys, but upon important business, and their wives never."

A very different state of things is this from that which meets our eyes in the reign of Victoria, when every nobleman and country gentleman who has a wife and family brings them up yearly to London, for the whole, or at least for a part, of the " season." Young ladies a century ago, as Mr. Cradock observes in his amusing " Library Memoirs," were "not so deeply read as at present;" and " if, when married, they went once a year up to London to see the fashions and attend the theatres, it was thought sufficient. They neither

wished to be presented at court, nor to retain a box at the opera-house."

Mr. F. Locker in the following lines gives us an imaginary picture of St. James's Street and Place in those " good old times : "—

" At dusk, when I am strolling there,
    Dim forms will rise around me ;
Lepel flits by me in her chair,
    And Congreve's airs astound me.

" And once Nell Gwynne, a frail young sprite,
    Looked kindly when I met her ;
I shook my head, perhaps—but quite
    Forgot to quite forget her."

It has been said that Campbell's " Last Man " owed its composition to a chance conversation in St. James's Street. With reference to this " moot point," Cyrus Redding writes in his " Recollections :"—" I had a singular dispute with Campbell, who, if he once adopted an idea, was very difficult to convince of being in error. He had written a letter to the editor of the *Edinburgh Review*, in consequence of the reviewer having stated that his poem of the 'Last Man' had been suggested by Byron's 'Darkness.' He stated that in a conversation with Byron, in St. James's Street, he had mentioned the subject of the extinction of the creation and of the human species to Byron, as a fit subject for a poem. I happened to know that Byron and Shelley were once standing together looking at the splendid view of the Alps across the Leman, and Shelley remarked—'What a thing it would be if all were involved in darkness at this moment—the sun and stars to go out. How terrible the idea !' Such a thought was likely to arise in the minds of more persons than one. Barry Cornwall had told Campbell that some friend of his thought of writing a poem on that subject. The date of the conversation of Shelley and Byron I cannot state exactly, but I know it was years before the 'Last Man' of Campbell appeared. I told the poet this, and contended that the idea was not new."

Extending towards the Green Park, from the south-west corner of St. James's Street, is Cleveland Row. Here Lord Stowell resided when known as Sir William Scott, the honoured M.P. for the University of Oxford. Theodore Hook lived here from 1827 till he removed to Fulham, in 1831. His residence was handsome, and extravagantly too large for his purpose. He was admitted a member of divers clubs ; shone the first attraction of their house-dinners ; and in such as allowed of play he might commonly be seen in the course of his protracted evening. Presently he began to receive invitations to great houses in the country, and, for week after week, often travelled from one to another such scene, to all outward appearance in the style of an idler of high condition. In a word, he had soon entangled himself with habits and connections which implied much curtailment of the time for labour at the desk, and a course of expenditure more than sufficient to swallow all the profits of what remained from his editorial salary and literary gains. We shall have more to say of him when we come to Fulham.

But the spot we are upon has earlier associations. In the spring of the year 1668 Lady Castlemaine, who had just before made up a quarrel with the King, became possessed, by royal gift, of Berkshire House, to the north-west of the Palace Gate, which had been the town residence of the first two Earls of Berkshire, and subsequently occupied by Lord Clarendon. Adjoining the house was a large walled-in Dutch garden, with a summer-house in the north-western corner, in the rear. At the time of which we write it was really a country house, standing quite isolated in its own grounds. The site of the property is now bounded on the south by Cleveland Row and Cleveland Square; on the east by St. James's Street: on the north and west its limits were defined by Park Place and the edge of the Green Park. The house is shown in Faithorne's map of London and Westminster in 1658. The furnishing of the mansion in a style suited to the caprice of the haughty mistress must have been a severe trial for the purse-strings of even a king, for we are told that Berkshire House was most lavishly and sumptuously adorned and decorated.

The dining-room of one of the houses in Cleveland Row, occupied in the reigns of George I. and George II. by Lord Townshend, witnessed the memorable and not very dignified quarrel between its owner, then Secretary of State, and the Premier, Sir Robert Walpole. The two combatants are said by Sir N. Wraxall to have seized each other by the throat—a scene which Gay portrayed in the *Beggar's Opera*, under the characters of "Peachum" and "Lockitt."

At the western end of Cleveland Row stands Bridgewater House, the town residence of the Earl of Ellesmere. Erected in 1847-50, from the designs of the late Sir Charles Barry, the mansion occupies the site of what was formerly Berkeley House, which Charles II. presented to the Duchess of Cleveland. Jarvis, the portrait-painter, died in the old house in 1739. Afterwards, when Berkeley House was named Cleveland Court, it was occupied by Mrs. Selwyn, mother of George Selwyn. It is said of George Selwyn, who died here in 1791,

aged seventy-two, that "he lived for society, and continued in it until he looked like the waxwork figure of a corpse."

The plan of Bridgewater House approaches a square, the south front being about 140 feet in length, and the west 120 feet; and there are two small courts within the mass to aid in lighting the various apartments. The ground-plan itself comprises a perfect residence—drawing-room, dining-room, ladies' rooms, chamber, dressing-rooms, &c. The first floor is, with a small exception, appropriated to state-rooms, dining-room, drawing-room, the splendid picture-gallery, &c. The gallery occupies the whole of the north side of the house, and is carried out a few feet beyond the east wall. The building, in both interior and exterior decoration, is worthy of the splendid collection of works of art which are here brought together. The main portion of this collection, so well known as the "Bridgewater Gallery," was made by the Duke of Bridgewater, who, dying in 1803, left his pictures, valued at £150,000, to his nephew, the first Duke of Sutherland (then Marquis of Stafford), with remainder to the marquis's second son, Francis, afterwards Earl of Ellesmere. This gallery of paintings is in many respects the most valuable in this country; in no gallery is the school of Carracci so well represented. One of the gems of Lord Ellesmere's gallery is the "Chandos" portrait of Shakespeare, which is believed to have belonged once to Sir William Davenport, and then to Betterton, the actor, and while in the possession of the latter was copied by Sir Godfrey Kneller for Dryden, who considered it an original likeness, and who has thus celebrated the copy:—

> "Shakespeare, thy gift I place before my sight:
> With awe I ask his blessing ere I write,
> With reverence look on his majestic face,
> Proud to be less—but of his godlike race."

The portrait was bought by the first Lord Ellesmere, at the Stowe sale, for 355 guineas.

The Green Park, which we now enter, is separated from St. James's along part of its southern side by the Mall, and covers a large triangular piece of ground, extending westwards as far as Hyde Park Corner, the line of communication from the end of the Mall being by Constitution Hill. It was formerly called Little or Upper St. James's Park, and was reduced in extent in 1767, by George III., in order to add to the gardens of Buckingham House. Old maps of London show us that the spot of ground situated between the wall of St. James's Palace, and "the way to Reading," as Piccadilly was formerly called, was before the Restoration merely a piece of waste ground—in fact, a meadow. It is represented in those maps as planted with a few willow-trees, and intersected with ditches, among which must have been "the drie ditch-bankes about Pikadilla," in which old Gerarde, the author of "The Herbalist" (1596), used to find the small buglosse or ox-tongue. In October, 1660, as stated in Rugge's "Diurnal," ice-houses were built in Upper St. James's Park, "as the mode is in some parts of France and Italy, and other hot countries, for to cool wines and other drinks for the summer season." Old plans show that these ice-houses were situated in the middle of what is now called the Green Park, and here they remained till the beginning of the present century. At the western extremity, close to the road leading into Hyde Park, Charles II. formed a deer-harbour.

We read that when, in 1642, it was resolved by the Parliament to fortify the suburbs of the metropolis, "a small redoubt and battery on Constitution Hill" were among the defences ordered to be erected.

Dr. King, in his "Anecdotes of his Own Time," tells an amusing story about the "witty monarch" and his saturnine brother James, which we may as well tell in this place :—"King Charles II., after taking two or three turns one morning in the Park (as was his usual custom), attended only by the Duke of Leeds and my Lord Cromarty, walked up Constitution Hill, and from thence into Hyde Park. But just as he was crossing the road, the Duke of York's coach was nearly arrived there. The duke had been hunting that morning on Hounslow Heath, and was returning in his coach, escorted by a party of the guards, who, as soon as they saw the king, suddenly halted, and conse-quently stopped the coach. The duke, being ac-quainted with the occasion of the halt, immediately got out of his coach, and, after saluting the king, said he was greatly surprised to find his Majesty in that place with such a small attendance, and that he thought his Majesty exposed himself to some danger. 'No danger whatever, James,' said Charles, 'for I am sure that no man in England would take my life to make you king.'"

Like most other lonely places a little distance out of London, it soon became a favourite spot for the gentlemanly diversion of duelling. On Saturday night, January 11, 1696, Sir Henry Colt having been challenged by "Beau" Fielding, these two gentlemen here fought a duel. The spot chosen for this little passage of arms was at the back of Cleveland Court, which, as above stated, stood on the site of what is now Bridgewater House. This place was chosen, it is said, because the "Beau," like the knights of old, wished to fight under the beautiful eyes of his mistress and future wife, the notorious Duchess of Cleveland. It was stated at the time that Fielding, whose courage was none of the brightest, ran Sir Henry through the body before he had time to draw his sword; but the baronet disarmed him, notwithstanding this wound, and so the fight ended.

From the "Foreigner's Guide to London," pub-lished in 1729, we learn that early in the last century Constitution Hill had become as much frequented for the purpose of fighting duels as the favourite little spot at the back of Montague House. The year after this was written, there occurred another duel in this park, which occa-sioned a great noise. The combatants were William Pulteney (afterwards Earl of Bath) and John, Lord Hervey—the "Sporus" of Pope—

    "———— that thing of silk,
Sporus, that mere white curd of asses' milk."

The latter, it appears, had written several defences of Sir Robert Walpole, in answer to attacks on him in the *Craftsman*. To one of these Pulteney pub-lished an answer, entitling it "A Proper Reply to a late Scurrilous Libel." The "Reply," it must be owned, was grossly personal; Hervey therefore challenged his rival, and they fought with swords in St. James's Park. The duel took place on Monday, January 25, 1730, between three and four o'clock in the afternoon, behind Arlington Street, Mr. Fox and Sir John Rushout acting as seconds. The "affair of honour," however, turned out to be a bloodless one; no serious bodily harm ensued to either combatant, and Lord Hervey was left to the vengeance of Pope's satire. The germ of Pope's "Sporus" will be found in these party pasquinades out of which the duel arose.

One evening in May, 1771, a duel was fought here between Edward, Viscount Ligonier, nephew of the celebrated general, and Count Alfieri, the Italian poet, in which the latter was slightly wounded.

"Queen Caroline, who made so many useful improvements in Hyde Park," says Mr. Larwood, in his "History of the London Parks," "also extended her patronage to the Green Park. In February, 1730, the Board of Works received orders to pre-pare a private walk in Upper St. James's Park, for the Queen and the royal family to divert them-selves in the spring. This walk extended along the row of mansions at the eastern extremity of the Park; but that plan never came to anything farther than the erection of a sort of pavilion, called the 'Queen's Library.' Indeed, her Majesty's death was caused by her partiality for this spot. On the

9th of November, 1737, she walked to the 'Library' and breakfasted there. On that occasion she caught such a severe cold that she had to retire to her bed immediately on her return to the palace : ten days after she was a corpse." All traces of this "Library," and of a curious fountain which was once here, have long since passed away.

In 1749, on the publication of the Peace of Aix-la-Chapelle, the centre of the Green Park was selected for an exhibition of fireworks, which in grandeur could not have been surpassed in the last century. A huge and substantial building was constructed, running from north to south, with a solid centre and wings ; if we may judge from a rare print of the time, it must have been upwards of 400 feet in length : it contained pavilions for the Engineers, ten "arcades for planting the cannon," a grand musical gallery in the centre, surmounted by the arms of the Duke of Montague, at whose cost, in all probability, it was put up. Over the music-gallery was an allegorical figure of Peace attended by Neptune and Mars, and above, a grand basso-relievo, representing the King in the act of giving peace to Britannia. This was illuminated in the evening, and on a pole at the top of all was an illumination representing the sun, which burnt nearly all the night long. The print shows Buckingham House surrounded with a long square wall, extending westwards to Chelsea College. The ground is all open up to Hyde Park Corner, where St. George's Hospital and "Lord Chesterfield's new house" figure as almost the only buildings ; a carriage and pair, with outriders, is making its way up an open road marked as "Constitution Hill" towards the spot where now stands Apsley House.

Thursday, the 27th of April, was the grand day appointed for the fireworks. All the entrances into the Green Park were opened, and a breach of fifty feet was made into the Park wall on the Piccadilly side in order to give admittance to the vast concourse of spectators. A gallery was erected for the Privy Council, the Peers, the House of Commons ; and the rest of the places were given to the Lord Mayor. The King, who had in the fore-part of the day reviewed the three regiments of Foot-guards from the garden wall of St. James's, witnessed the fireworks from a pavilion in the Park which had been erected for his reception. The Prince and Princess of Wales, who were on bad terms with the King, kept aloof, and saw the display from the house of the Earl of Middlesex, in Arlington Street. The performance began with a grand military overture, composed by Handel, in which "one hundred cannon, fired singly with the music," formed

a distinctive feature. Shortly after the commencement of the fireworks, the temple accidentally took fire, and part of it was consumed.

During the peace *fêtes* of 1814, the Green Park was again chosen for the scene of a grand pyrotechnical display. Near Constitution Hill a building was erected from the design of Sir William Congreve (of rocket celebrity), which, with all its palings, and the cordon of sentries round it, covered one-third of the Green Park. This building received the name of the Temple of Concord. The materials of this structure, and of the other erections set up on that occasion, were sold afterwards by auction, and fetched only about £200.

Coming down to more recent times, we may state here that on Constitution Hill, near Buckingham Palace, three diabolical attempts have been made to shoot Her Majesty, Queen Victoria. In June, 1840, a lunatic, named Edward Oxford, deliberately fired twice at Her Majesty as she was riding past in her carriage, in company with Prince Albert. Oxford was tried at the Central Criminal Court, when a verdict was returned of "Guilty, but insane," and the prisoner was accordingly removed to be "confined during Her Majesty's pleasure." The second attempt on the life of the Queen was made by Francis, another lunatic, in May, 1842 ; and the third by an idiot, named Hamilton, in 1849.

On the 29th of June, 1850, at the upper end of Constitution Hill, Sir Robert Peel was thrown from his horse, and very severely injured. He died at his house, in Whitehall Gardens, about three days afterwards.

The rest of the history of the Green Park is soon told. In 1829 the Chelsea Waterworks Company constructed an immense reservoir in the north-east corner of the park, opposite Stratton Street ; it was capable of containing 1,500,000 gallons. This reservoir was removed about 1855, and the entrance close by was at the same time considerably widened. "Amidst all the improvements of late years," writes Walker in "The Original," in 1835, "it is much to be lamented that the Green Park has been so much neglected, seeing that it is most conspicuously situated, and, notwithstanding its inferior size, is by much the most advantageously disposed as to ground. There was some years ago a talk of its being terraced in part, and wholly laid out in a highly ornamental style ; which, by way of variety, and with reference to its situation, seems a judicious plan. I would that his Majesty would give orders to that effect ; and then, as its present name would become inappropriate, it might be called after its royal patron. It is to be hoped that, whenever the opportunity occurs, the Ranger's house will not be allowed to stand in the way of the very great improvement which its removal would cause both to the park and to Piccadilly. I do not believe that anything would add so much to the ornament of London as

As Thomas Miller remarks in his "Picturesque Sketches of London," the Green Park "possesses but little to interest, beyond a walk beside the gardens which run up in a line with St. James's Street." But those who know the locality will not

BRIDGEWATER HOUSE. (*See page* 177.)

the embellishment of the Green Park to the extent of which it is capable."

The Ranger's lodge spoken of above stood near the north-west corner, and was removed about the year 1847. The two stags from the pillars at the entrance now adorn the Albert Gate, Hyde Park. The entire park had a few years previously been drained, and the surface re-laid and planted. The Rangership of the Green Park is at present, together with the rangership of St. James's and Richmond Parks, held by the Duke of Cambridge.

pass without gazing at one residence (a little above Spencer House), conspicuous by its large bow-windows, the upper one of which is encircled by a gilt railing. This was the house of the banker-poet, Samuel Rogers, of whom we have already spoken. The gardens of the several houses on this side of the park are leased of the Crown. Owing to its happy site on a sloping ground, the view from the upper walk is very extensive; and whenever the atmosphere is unobscured by fog or smoke, a lovely panorama presents itself.

An Horizontal View of the Public Fireworks ordered to be exhibited on occasion of the General Peace concluded at Aix le Chapelle on November 7ᵗʰ 1748.

THE EXPLANATION.

From A to A is the full length of the Scheme including, 1 Pavilions or store Houses for the Engineers use. 2 Arcades for planting the Cannon. 3 Flight of Steps ascending to the Music-Gallery. 4 The grand Area or Music Gallery. N.B. over the Entrance is the D. of Montagu's Arms: above the Music is PEACE attended by Neptune and Mars: higher is a grand Bas-relievo to be illuminated in which the King is represented giving PEACE to BRITANNIA, over all is the Kings Arms: from remence rise a Pole 50 feet high with a Sun at Sig. 32 feet diameter, which will burn some hours. 5 The Passage from the Mall in S.t James's Park into the Green Park. 6 Constitution Hill: 7 Hide Park Corner: 8 The E. of Chesterfields new House. 9 S.t Georges Hospital: 10 The Footway. 11 Chelsea College. 12 Chelsea Church. 13 Surry Side. 14 Buckingham House. 15 A piece of Water in the Green Park.
N.B. This Prospect is taken from the Library at S.t James's Palace

THE PEACE REJOICINGS IN THE GREEN PARK. *From a Contemporary Print.* (See page 179)

CHAPTER XV.

ST. JAMES'S SQUARE AND ITS DISTINGUISHED RESIDENTS.

" The lordly region of St. James's Square."

Character of the Square in the Seventeenth and Eighteenth Centuries—Patriotism of Dr. Johnson and Savage—Ormonde House—The Duke and the Irish Peer—Romney House—The Fireworks at the Peace of Ryswick—Distinguished Residents—Norfolk House—"Jockey of Norfolk"—"All the Blood of all the Howards"—A Duke over his Cups—The Residence of the Bishop of London—The Bishop of London's Fund—Allen, Lord Bathurst—The Roxburgh Club—The Windham Club—The London Library—The "Lichfield House Compact"—The Residence of Mrs. Boehm—Receipt of News of the Victory of Waterloo—The East India United Service Club—Lady Francis and Queen Caroline—"Jack Robinson" and Lord Castlereagh—The Copyhold, Inclosure, and Tithe Commission.

STANDING as it does so near to "our palace of St. James," St. James's Square was for many years the most fashionable square in London, and though fashion is now fast migrating—perhaps has already migrated—to Belgravia, still it retains much of its long-established character. In the last century its claim was undisputed, as may be gathered from some lines which were favourites of Dr. Johnson—

> " When the Duke of Leeds shall married be
>   To a fine young lady of quality,
>   How happy that gentlewoman will be
>   In his Grace of Leeds' good company !
>   She shall have all that's fine and fair,
>   And ride in a coach to take the air,
>   And have a house in St. James's Square."

This square is mentioned in the comedies of the time of George I. as the *ne plus ultra* of fashion. Thus Shadwell, in his *Busy Fair*, writes, "We call it London, and it outdoes St. James's Square and all the squares in dressing and breeding."

This square is built on the site of the old "St. James's Fields," and the surrounding streets were named, with the usual loyalty of the time, after King Charles II. and his royal brother, the Duke of York (afterwards James II.), namely, King Street, Charles Street, Duke Street, and York Street. On account of their central situation, most of the houses in these side streets are occupied as hotels, or let out in furnished apartments for gentlemen who live mainly at their clubs.

There was a time, however, when the square was not as yet known to the leaders of fashion. "St. James's Square," says Macaulay, "in 1685 was a receptacle for all the offal and cinders, and for all the dead cats and dogs of Westminster. At one time a cudgel-player kept the ring there. At another time an impudent squatter settled himself there, and built a shed for rubbish under the windows of the gilded *salons* in which the first magnates of the realm, Norfolk, Ormond, Kent, and Pembroke, gave banquets and balls. It was not till these nuisances had lasted through a whole generation, and till much had been written about them, that the inhabitants applied to Parliament for permission to put up rails and plant trees."

It would appear, by the few notices of the time that can be found, that the central area of the square was but little cared for even in the last century; indeed, it may be justly remarked that it must have presented in 1773 much the same appearance which all London noticed in Leicester Square as lately as 1873. The Chevalier David in 1721 endeavoured, but in vain, to collect a sum of £2,000 towards erecting in its centre an equestrian statue of George I., which, most disinterestedly of course, he hoped to be commissioned to execute; but an adequate sum was not collected, and the project fell through. Four years later, according to a statement laid before Parliament, the surface of the interior of the square was still a " common laystall for dust, and for the refuse of kitchens and dead animals;" and, worse than all, because less easily dispossessed, we are told that a coachmaker had the audacity to put up a shed some thirty feet in length, and to pile a stack of wood in the area. Under these circumstances, at last it became necessary " to do something;" and accordingly the courtly and, for the most part, titled personages who lived on the north, east, and west sides of the square asked, and obtained, permission to tax themselves for the common benefit, in order to cleanse and improve the square.

From Sutton Nichols' print of the square, published in 1720, it appears that there was in the centre of the area a small lake or reservoir, and a fountain which played to about the height of fifteen feet; as also that there was a pleasure-boat on the water, and that numerous posts were placed at a small distance from the houses all round the square. Another print dated 1773 shows the enclosure of iron rails to have been octagonal, and the interior of it to have been still occupied by a circular pond, edged round with stone. It is described by Northouck, who wrote at the same date, as "the most pleasing square in all London;" and he instances as an example of "true taste" the contrast between the square formed by the houses and the circular nature of the enclosed area. He says, however, that the houses in it are grand individually rather than collectively, each being built on a scale and plan of its own. He writes: "The largest house is Norfolk House, at the south-east corner, a building which gives great offence to a late critic, who observes that in such mansions we expect something beyond roominess and convenience, the mere requisites of a packer or a sugar-baker. Would any foreigner, beholding an insipid length of wall broken with a regular row of windows, ever figure from thence the residence of the first duke of England?"

In a like spirit the author of "A New Critical Review of the Public Buildings, &c.," observes, too, that this square is superior in grandeur of appearance to any other, though it has not in it a single "elegant" house; he bitterly complains of the irregularity of the southern side, and the want of a statue or obelisk in the middle of the large oval basin of water which, as we have said, then occupied the centre. This sheet of water, which was six or seven feet in depth, had subsequently placed in its centre a fine equestrian statue of William III. According to Lambert's "History of London," the basin was 150 feet in length. Into the water in this lake the mob in the "Gordon Riots" of 1780 threw the keys of Newgate, which they had broken open and burnt. They were not found for several years afterwards. Mr. John Timbs tells us that "a pedestal for the statue was erected in the centre of the square in 1732; but the statue, cast in brass by the younger Bacon, was not set up until 1808; the bequest in 1724 for the cost having been forgotten, until the money was found in the list of unclaimed dividends."

Such must have been the appearance of the square at the time that Dr. Johnson and his friend Savage, in early life, when friendless and penniless, spent a summer night walking round the enclosure, now and then resting on a stray cart or friendly bench, and bellowing out all sorts of wild denunciations of the then Government. To use Boswell's own words, "They were not at all depressed by their situation; but in high spirits, and brimful of patriotism, they traversed the square for several hours, inveighed against the Minister, and resolved that they would stand by their country." By prudence and perseverance, and the help of friends, Johnson lived to rise above this obscurity; whilst Savage, although perhaps endowed with even more genius, only sank lower and lower. When he was employed upon his tragedy of *Sir Thomas Overbury*, "he was," says Johnson, "often without lodgings and often without meat, nor had he any other conveniences for study than the fields or the streets allowed him. There he used to walk, and form his speeches, and afterwards step into a shop, beg

for a few moments the use of pen and ink, and write down what he had composed upon paper which he had picked up by accident."

But it is time to pass from these general remarks on the square to a more detailed account of its houses and its residents.

In 1684, the Duchess of Ormonde died at her residence, Ormonde House, on the north side of the square. The Duke of Ormonde, who was living here in the reign of Queen Anne and George I., was said to have been the best bred man of his day. He entertained largely and liberally, but he allowed the bad practice of his servants taking money from his guests. Dr. King tells the following story in his "Anecdotes of his Own Times:"— "I remember a Lord Poer, a Roman Catholic peer of Ireland, who lived upon a small pension which Queen Anne had granted him: he was a man of honour, and well esteemed; and had formerly been an officer of some distinction in the service of France. The Duke of Ormonde had often invited him to dinner, and he as often excused himself. At last the duke kindly expostulated with him, and would know the reason why he so constantly refused to be one of his guests. My Lord Poer then honestly confessed that he could not afford it; 'but,' says he, 'if your Grace will put a guinea into my hands as often as you are pleased to invite me to dine, I will not decline the honour of waiting on you.' This was done; and my lord was afterwards a frequent guest in St. James's Square."

From the *Post Boy*, No. 411, published in 1698, it appears that the house was taken for the Count de Tallard, the French ambassador. The rent paid by the Count is stated to have been no less than £600 per annum, a large rental in those days, even for a house in the very centre of the fashionable world. Ormonde House stood on the east side of James Street, in the north-east corner of the square. In the rear of the houses which at present cover its site is Ormonde Yard, now a mews. Romney House was also on the north side of the square; and here in 1695 and again in 1697, as we learn from the *Flying Post*, the *Post Boy*, and the *Post Man*—the fashionable papers of the day—King William III. visited the Earl of Romney to witness the fireworks in the square; and in 1697, on the conclusion of the treaty of peace of Ryswick, the Dutch Ambassador made before his house a bonfire of 140 pitch-barrels, and wine was "kept continually running among the common people." We learn accidentally, from an anecdote in Joe Miller's "Jest Book," that the author of these fireworks being in company with some ladies, was highly commending the epitaph just then set up in the

Abbey on Mr. Purcell's monument—" He has gone to that place where only his own harmony can be exceeded." " Well, Colonel," said one of the ladies, " the same epitaph might serve for you by altering one word only: 'He has gone to that place where only his own fireworks can be exceeded.' "

In 1708 the following noblemen resided in this square—namely, the Dukes of Norfolk, Northumberland, and Ormonde; and Lords Ossulston, Kent, Woodstock, and Torrington. The Earl of Sunderland (one of the Chief Secretaries of State), the Duke of Kent, and Lord Bathurst were living there in 1724. No. 2 is still Lord Falmouth's town residence. "The street-posts," Mr. John Timbs tells us in his " Curiosities of London," are made of cannon captured by Lord Falmouth's ancestor, Admiral Boscawen, off Cape Finisterre."

In one of the houses in this square, in the reign of Queen Anne, was living Lord Pembroke, whom Pope celebrates as a connoisseur in such matters as " statues, dirty gods, and coins." The house No. 6, on the north side, the town-house of the Marquis of Bristol, has been the residence of his ancestors, the Herveys, since the first laying out of the square in the reign of Charles II. It is not often, however, that the family of any nobleman, except of a Duke like their Graces of Norfolk and Northumberland, has owned one and the same town-house for two centuries without a break. It was of this " noble family "—who are stated to have produced so many eccentric characters—that the Dowager Lady Townshend remarked, a century or more ago, that " God had created three races of bipeds —men, women, and Herveys ! "

The Earl of Radnor—the handsome Sydney of De Grammont's Memoirs—who died in 1723, had his mansion enriched with paintings by Vanson over the doors and chimney-pieces; the staircase was painted by Laguerre, and the various apartments hung with pictures by many of the celebrated masters. An advertisement in the *Postman*, of August, 1703, offers a reward of two guineas for the detection of a thief who had mischievously cut down and carried off one of the trees in front of Lord Radnor's house. Here afterwards lived Josiah Wedgwood, and here his stock of classic pottery was dispersed by auction. The building was afterwards converted into a club, called the Erectheum, and celebrated for its good dinners. About 1854 the club was joined to the Parthenon in Regent Street, and the house was taken as the office of the Charity Commissioners. It is now the Junior Oxford and Cambridge Club.

Among the other notable personages who have lived here at various times may be mentioned Lewis, Earl of Faversham; Lawrence Hyde, Earl of Rochester; Arabella Churchill, the mistress of James, Duke of York, and mother by him of the Duke of Berwick; Sir Allen Apsley, at whose house the Duke of York put up on his sudden return from Brussels; Barillon, Ambassador from the Court of France, the same (says Mr. P. Cunningham) " whose despatches to Louis XIV. revealed the bribes received by Charles II. and his ministers, and even by a patriot so professedly pure as Algernon Sydney ;" Aubrey de Vere, the twentieth and last Earl of Oxford of the old line of that illustrious name; Lord Chancellor Thurlow; the Countess of Warwick, 1676; and Lord Halifax, 1676.

The west side of the square, when first built, does not appear to have been very respectably tenanted. At all events, in 1676, we find the houses occupied by three titled personages, Lord Purbeck, Lord Halifax, and Sir Allen Apsley, and by two notorious ladies, " Moll Davis," one of the King's mistresses, and Madame Churchill, mistress of James, Duke of York, and mother of the Duke of Berwick. In later times, however, and more especially within the last century, some of the houses on this side have got a little better reputation, having been held by different members of the aristocracy; one being the residence of the Duke of Cleveland, Sir Watkin Williams-Wynn, Bart., and another the town residence of the Bishop of Winchester. The latter was sold in 1875, for the purpose of raising a sum for founding the new Bishopric of St. Albans.

In the house of the Duke of Cleveland is the well-known original portrait of the beautiful Duchess of Cleveland, by Sir Peter Lely ; and the mansion of the late Earl De Grey, afterwards that of the Dowager Countess of Cowper (No. 4), is mentioned by Dr. Waagen as containing a fine gallery of portraits by Vandyke, Salvator Rosa, Titian, Vandevelde, and other foreign masters.

The large house in the south-eastern corner of the square has been since 1684 the residence of the Dukes of Norfolk, who migrated hither from the Strand. The old house which they occupied, which was tenanted by Frederick, Prince of Wales, and in which George III. was born in 1738, is still standing in the rear of the present mansion, which was built by Mr. R. Brittingham, and dates from 1742. The portico was added in 1824. The old mansion—which occupies part of the site of the residence of Henry Jermyn, Earl of St. Albans —formerly had in front of it a court-yard. It is a plain, dull, heavy building, of no architectural pretensions, and is now used as a lumber-house and a laundry. The room in which the future king was born is on the first floor. It is a spacious apartment with a roof slightly arched, and divided into compartments or panels, on which some remnants of the ornamental colouring are still visible.

The house of Norfolk has stood for nearly four centuries at the head of the peers of England, since its ancestor, "Jockey of Norfolk," who fell at Bosworth Field, was raised to the dukedom by Richard III., and during that time its members have held or still hold no less than twenty-five patents of creation to separate peerages, such as the Earldoms of Surrey, Suffolk, Northampton, Stafford, Effingham, and Carlisle. Though its founder was only a lawyer, it has produced statesmen, generals, admirals, and also poets, including that flower of chivalric grace, the Earl of Surrey. With one or two temporary breaks, its head and most of its members have adhered steadily to the Roman Catholic religion; and Henry, Earl of Surrey, the only son of the third duke, had the honour of laying his head on the block and seeing an attainder passed upon his coronet by the tyrant, Henry VIII.

Charles, the eleventh duke, finding himself excluded on account of his hereditary faith from his seat in the Legislature, professed himself a member of the Established Church, and sat in Parliament first as Earl of Surrey in the Commons, and afterwards in the Upper House as Duke. Sir N. W. Wraxall, who comments in terms of surprise at the spectacle, new to the House of Peers—namely, a Protestant Duke of Norfolk taking an active part in the legislative proceedings of that body—describes him as "cast in Nature's coarsest mould, and with a person so clumsy that he might have been mistaken for a grazier or a butcher." He tells about him many anecdotes, which show that he could play to perfection the part of a Tribune of the People. He lived mainly in clubs and coffee-houses, and was never so happy as when dining at the "Beefsteaks" or the "Thatched House," or breakfasting or supping at the "Cocoa Tree," in St. James's Street. When under the influence of wine, he would say that, "in spite of his having swallowed the Protestant oath, there were, at all events, three good Catholics in Parliament, Lord Nugent, Gascoyne, and himself;" so little store did he set on religion. This duke, who really deserved the title of a "Jockey" far more than his ancestor, was remarkable for the amount of wine which he could swallow. He would spend the whole night in excesses of every kind. Sir N. W. Wraxall, who knew him well, and constantly met him at his midnight revels, tells us that "when drunk he would

lie down to sleep in the streets or on a block of wood." For personal uncleanliness he was nearly as remarkable as for his drunken habits, "carrying his neglect of his person so far that his servants were accustomed to avail themselves of his fits of intoxication for the purpose of washing him, and to strip him as they would a corpse in order to perform the necessary ablutions. Nor did he change his linen more frequently than he washed himself. One day he complained to Dudley North that he was a martyr to the rheumatism, and had ineffectually tried every remedy for its relief. 'Pray, my lord,' was North's reply, 'did you ever try a clean shirt?'" It is to be hoped that such a specimen of humanity must not be regarded as a fair sample of our hereditary legislators a hundred years ago; and it is only right to add that the duke had many good and amiable qualities to compensate for his follies and vices.

Very naturally, his Grace was proud of his undisputed headship of "all the blood of all the Howards." When sitting at breakfast with him at the "Cocoa Tree Coffee-house" one day, his Grace told Sir N. W. Wraxall that he purposed in the year 1783 to commemorate the "ter-centenary" anniversary of the creation of his dukedom by giving a dinner at his house in St. James's Square to every person whom he could ascertain to be descended in the male line from the loins of the first duke. "But having discovered already," he added, "nearly six thousand persons sprung from him, a great number of whom are in very obscure or indigent circumstances, and believing, as I do, that as many more may be in existence, I have abandoned the design." It is to be feared that even the hall and long suite of rooms in Norfolk House would scarcely have contained such a "family party."

The above-mentioned duke, whose name figures so prominently in the political history of the reign of George III., and who was so frequent a speaker at public meetings at the "Crown and Anchor Tavern," and was deprived of his command of a militia regiment for proposing as a toast, "The People, the Source of Power," was the first member of the House of Lords who laid aside the "pig-tail" and hair powder, which remained so long in use as a relic of the old court dress. His Grace's object, no doubt, was to identify himself with the principles of the French encyclopædists. It was probably this duke who is the hero of a ludicrous story told as follows in the pages of Joe Miller's "Jest Book:"— "Mr. Huddlestone, whose name was admitted to be a corruption of Athelstone, from whom he claimed descent, often met the Duke of Norfolk over a bottle, to discuss the respective pretensions of their pedigrees; and on one of these occasions, when Mr. Huddlestone was dining with the duke, the discussion was prolonged till the descendant of the Saxon kings fairly rolled from his chair upon the floor. One of the younger members of the family hastened by the duke's desire to re-establish him; but he sturdily repelled the proffered hand of the cadet. 'Never,' he hiccuped out, 'shall it be said that the head of Huddlestone was lifted from the ground by

with the Church of England societies for the relief of the spiritual destitution of the metropolis, and to distribute the fund through such agencies and in such manner as may be deemed desirable, as well as by sending earnest and active men to labour among the masses, by opening new churches and schools, and, where necessary, by originating efforts of a strictly missionary character.

The mansion adjoining London House on the

THE FOUNTAIN IN THE GREEN PARK, 1808. (See page 179.)

a younger branch of the house of Howard.' 'Well, then, my good old friend,' said the good-natured duke, 'I must try what I can do for you myself. The head of the house of Howard is too drunk to pick up the head of the house of Huddlestone, but he will lie down beside him with all the pleasure in the world;' so saying, the duke also took his place on the floor."

Next to Norfolk House is the official town residence of the Bishops of London. It was rebuilt about the year 1820. Here was started by Bishop Blomfield the "Bishop of London's Fund," for providing for the spiritual wants of the metropolis. The raising of this fund is entrusted to a board, with the Bishop of London as its president, with authority to direct its investment, and co-operation

north side, at the corner of Charles Street, is the town residence of the Earl of Derby.

In St. James's Square was residing the French ambassador, Barillon, during the autumn of 1688, when the popular frenzy broke out against the Catholics, and in which the representatives of the great Catholic powers of Europe were insulted and assaulted by a mob that showed but slight respect for the law of nations. Macaulay tells us in his "History" that though an excited multitude collected before his doors, yet Barillon fared better than some of his brother ambassadors, "for, though the Government which he represented was held in abhorrence, his liberal housekeeping and exact payments had made him personally popular. Moreover, he had taken the wise precaution of asking for

ST. JAMES'S SQUARE IN 1773. (*See page* 182.)

a guard of soldiers, and, as several men of rank who lived near him had done the same thing, a considerable force was collected in the square. The rioters, therefore, when they were assured that no arms or priests were concealed under his roof, left him unmolested."

In this square resided Pope's friend, Allen, Lord Bathurst, who was created a peer by Queen Anne in 1711, and who, living for sixty years longer, was the last of that great knot of men of wit and genius who rendered illustrious in one way the short but inglorious ministry of Oxford and Bolingbroke. Pope addressed to him the Third Epistle of his "Moral Essays;" and it is to him, in conjunction with the famous architect, Lord Burlington, that the poet alludes when he asks—

"Who then shall grace, or who improve the soil?
Who plants like Bathurst, or who builds like Boyle?"

Lord Bathurst lived to a patriarchal age, in possession of all his faculties, passing the evening of his life among those woods and in those shades which he had reared with his own hand, at Oakley, near Cirencester, and which Pope has immortalised, and enjoying the rare felicity of seeing his son Lord Chancellor.

The house, No. 10, on the north-west side of the square, was in 1880 opened as the Salisbury Club.

No. 11, now the Windham Club, was formerly the residence of John, third Duke of Roxburgh, the bibliophilist (not to say biblio-maniac) of his time. After his death the sale of his books in May, 1812, occupied no less than forty-two days. Many rare specimens of printing, an early Shakespeare, a few Caxtons and Wynkyn de Wordes, wonderful and unique editions of works on theology, poetry, philosophy, and the drama, were fought for with spirit and even recklessness, as one by one they fell beneath the hammer of the auctioneer, Mr. Evans. At last, what Dr. Dibdin calls "the Waterloo of book battles" commenced when Boccaccio's "Decameron," printed at Venice in 1471, was put up. The volume had been bought by the duke for a hundred guineas, and, after a fierce and spirited competition with Lord Spencer, it was knocked down to the Marquis of Blandford for £2,260. Seven years later, the noble purchaser was glad to part with his treasure for £918, and it now forms one of the treasures of the library of his old antagonist, Lord Spencer, at Althorp. It may be added, that on the evening after the sale of the duke's library, some sixteen of the leading bibliophilists or "biblio-maniacs" of the day dined together at the "St. Alban's Tavern" to celebrate the battle. Lord Spencer, the defeated bidder,

occupied the chair, and Dr. Dibdin acted as croupier. At this dinner was originated the Roxburgh Club. This Club may justly be said to have suggested the publishing societies of the present day; as the "Camden," "Shakespeare," "Percy," &c. Among the club were several noblemen, who, we are told, in other respects, were esteemed men of sense. Their rage was to estimate books not according to their intrinsic worth, but for their rarity. Hence any volume of trash, which was scarce merely because it never had any sale, fetched fifty or a hundred pounds; but if it were only one out of two or three known copies, no limits could be set to the price. Books altered in the title-page, or in a leaf, or in any trivial circumstance which varied a few copies, were bought by these *soi-disant* maniacs at one, two, or three hundred pounds, though the copies were not really worth more than threepence per pound. Specimens of first editions of all authors, and editions by the first clumsy printers, were never sold for less than £50, £100, or £200. To gratify the members of this club, *fac-simile* copies of clumsy editions of trumpery books were reprinted; and, in some cases, it became worth the while of more ingenious people to play off forgeries upon them. This mania after a while abated, and in future ages it will be ranked with the tulip mania, during which estates were given for single flowers.

The Roxburgh Club, however, became less celebrated for its publications than for its dinners, which were held at Grillon's, at the St. Alban's, and at the Clarendon Hotels. Some particulars of these feasts, with their bills of fare, were published in the *Athenæum*, from an account of one of its members. On one occasion the bill was above £5 10s. per head, and the list of toasts included the "immortal memory" not only of John, Duke of Roxburgh, but of William Caxton, Dame Juliana Berners, Wynkyn de Worde, Richard Pynson, the Aldine family, and "the cause of Bibliomania all over the world." In one year, when Lord Spencer presided over the feast, the account above mentioned thus records the fact: "Twenty-one members met joyfully, dined comfortably, challenged eagerly, tippled prettily, divided regretfully, and paid the bill most cheerfully."

The mansion of the Duke of Roxburgh had previously been the residence of William Windham; after the death of the duke it was occupied for some time by Lord Chief-Justice Ellenborough, and at a later date by the Earl of Blessington, who possessed a fine collection of pictures. The Windham Club, which was afterwards established here, was founded by the late Lord Nugent for gentlemen "connected with each other by a common bond of literary or personal acquaintance."

Adjoining the Windham Club is the mansion once tenanted by Lord Amherst, when Commander-in-Chief, and formerly known as Beauchamp House. It is now the London Library. This library, which dates its origin from 1840, is conducted upon the subscription and lending plan, and its books may be borrowed by subscribers and taken to their homes. It embraces every department of literature and philosophy. The library was opened on the 3rd of May, 1841, with a collection of about 3,000 volumes, which, by the following March, when the first catalogue was published, had increased to 13,000. "The additions of subsequent years," as we learn from the report published in 1870, "have raised the number of volumes in the library to more than 80,000. Purchased on the most advantageous terms, there has been brought together in the course of thirty years, by the expenditure of little more than £20,000, a noble collection of books, offering to members of the library a choice of standard works in all the various departments of literature." It may be added that its contents have since continued to increase. A striking proof of the success with which the library has fulfilled and continues to fulfil the purpose for which it was created, will be found in the names of the many illustrious writers which appear in the various published lists of its members, and in the use they have made of its treasures. In addition to this silent testimony to the usefulness of the institution, may be quoted the opinion of M. Guizot, given in evidence before a Committee of the House of Commons on Public Libraries in 1849, an opinion which is supported by that of many other participants in the benefits of the library. "If the London Library," says M. Guizot, "had not existed, I should have felt great inconvenience. It is a very useful library : there are a great many excellent books about English history which I have found there. It is a great inconvenience to me to be obliged to go to the British Museum, and not to be able to work in my own room with my own books ; that is a great part of the pleasure of working."

Here also the Statistical Society of London and the Institute of Actuaries hold their meetings periodically.

The house No. 13, formerly the residence of the Earl of Lichfield, when Postmaster-General in Lord Melbourne's Ministry, was the scene of the "Lichfield House Compact," as the friendly understanding between the Whigs of that day and Daniel O'Connell was often jestingly styled.

The house two doors beyond the London Library, in the direction of King Street, was at the beginning of the present century in the occupation of Mrs. Boehm. Here the Prince Regent, Lord Castlereagh, and many of the leading politicians of the day, were dining, on the 21st of June, 1815, when the news was brought of the victory of Waterloo, thus putting an end to and confirming the rumours by which London had been kept in suspense for more than twenty-four hours. The scene is thus described by Lady Brownlow in her "Reminiscences of a Septuagenarian :"—

"Never shall I forget that evening. . . . I was sitting quietly alone at Lord Castlereagh's, when suddenly there came the sound of shouting and the rush of a crowd ; and on running to the window to discover the cause of all this noise, I saw a post-chaise and four, with three of the French eagles projecting out of its windows, dash across the square to Lord Castlereagh's door. In a moment the horses' heads were turned, and away went the chaise to Mrs. Boehm's."

It was, of course, the work of a few minutes for Lady Brownlow to dress and join Lady Castlereagh at Mrs. Boehm's house. She continues thus : —"The ladies had left the dining-room, and I learnt that Major Henry Percy had arrived, the bearer of despatches from the Duke of Wellington, with the intelligence of a glorious and decisive victory of the Allies over the French army, commanded by Buonaparte in person. The despatches were being then read in the next room to the Prince, and we ladies remained silent, too anxious to talk, and longing to hear more. Lord Alvanley was the first gentleman who appeared, and he horrified us with the list of names of the killed and wounded. . . . What I heard stupefied me ; I could scarcely think or speak. The Prince presently came in, looking very sad, and he said, with much feeling, words to this effect : 'It is a glorious victory, and we must rejoice at it ; but the loss of life has been fearful, and *I* have lost many friends ;' and, while he spoke, the tears ran down his cheeks. His Royal Highness remained but a short time, and soon after the party broke up."

With reference to Mrs. Boehm, Captain Gronow, in his "Anecdotes and Reminiscences," says :— "This lady used to give fashionable balls and masquerades, to which I look back with much pleasure. The Prince Regent frequently honoured her *fêtes* with his presence. Mrs. Boehm, on one occasion, sent invitations to one of her particular friends, begging him to fill them up, and tickets were given by him to Dick Butler (afterwards Lord Glengall) and to Mr. Raikes. Whilst they were deliberating in what character they should go, 'Dick Butler'—for by that name he was only then known—proposed that Raikes should take the part of Apollo, which the latter agreed to, provided Dick should be his 'lyre.' The noble lord's reputation for 'stretching the long bow' rendered this repartee so applicable that it was universally repeated at the clubs."

This house is now the home of the East India United Service Club, which was established here about the year 1860.

The next house (No. 15) was once the property of Lady Francis, the widow of Sir Philip Francis, to whom the "Letters of Junius" are usually attributed. Lady Francis lent this house to the unfortunate Queen Caroline, in the month of August, 1820; and it was from its doors that her Majesty proceeded every day in state to the House of Peers during the progress of the attempted Bill of "Pains and Penalties."

In this square lived Mr. Robinson—"Jack Robinson"—the Secretary of the Treasury under Lord North. He is described by Sir N. W. Wraxall as knowing the secrets of ministerial and political affairs better than any man of his day.

Lord Castlereagh was residing at No. 16 in December, 1813, when dispatched abroad to enter into negotiations with Napoleon. In March, 1816, during the riots at the West-end, on account of the rejection of the Corn-Law Alteration Bill, his lordship's house was attacked by the mob, together with that of Mr. Robinson, from the parlour window of which shots were fired, which proved fatal to two innocent persons. The cavalry appearing, the rioters desisted and retired, to vent their fury by damaging the mansions of Lord Bathurst, Lord King, &c. The riots continued more or less to the latter end of the week.

Lady Brownlow records an instance of the coolness and self-possession of Lord Castlereagh. One night, when an excited mob attacked his house in this square, and paving-stones were being thrown at his windows, he quietly mixed with the crowd outside, till some one whispered to him, "You are known; you had better go in." He did so, and then went to the drawing-room, and, with the utmost composure, closed the shutters while a shower of stones fell all around him. "When I called next day," adds her ladyship, "I found him on the point of walking out, and as I knew that he would have the mob to encounter, I with difficulty persuaded him to let me take him in my carriage.".

Lord Castlereagh was always unpopular with the mob. In 1819, Mr. Rush, in his "Diary of a Residence at the Court of London," speaks of several official interviews which he had here with Lord Castlereagh, then Secretary of State for Foreign Affairs, and describes the mansion as having lately suffered much, especially in its windows, from the effects of the violence of the mob in a late Westminster election.

Lord Castlereagh played a foremost part in effecting the union of Ireland with England, and in 1801 entered the first Imperial Parliament as member for County Down. He held the post of President of the Board of Control during Mr. Addington's administration, and Secretary of State for War and the Colonies in the ministries of Mr. Pitt and the Duke of Portland. In 1809, the year of the Walcheren expedition, occurred his duel with Canning, then Foreign Secretary. In this affair Canning was wounded, and both the duellists resigned their offices. Before the end of the year, however, Lord Castlereagh succeeded his antagonist as Secretary for Foreign Affairs, an office which he retained till his death, in 1822. His remains were buried in Westminster Abbey, between Pitt and Fox. Mr. Rush, in the work above mentioned, avers of him that "no statesman ever made more advances, or did more in fact towards placing the relations of England and America on an amicable footing;" and in his description of the funeral he adds, "Nor did I ever see manly sorrow more depicted on any countenance than that of the Duke of Wellington, as he took a last look of the coffin when lowered down into the vault."

Near the north-east corner of the square are the offices of the Copyhold, Inclosure, and Tithe Commission. The Tithe Commissioners for England and Wales were appointed in 1836 to provide the means for an adequate commutation and compensation for the tithes payable to the clergy of the Established Church. The Copyhold Commissioners were appointed in 1841, and the Inclosure Commissioners some four years later. The duties of the commissioners are "to facilitate the enclosure and improvement of all lands subject to any rights of common whatsoever, and the exchange of lands inconveniently intermixed or divided; and to provide remedies for the incomplete execution of powers of enclosure made under local and general Enclosure Acts."

Nearly the whole of the south side of the square is occupied by an uneven row of houses, the fronts of which face Pall Mall; and a considerable part is taken up by the back of the Junior Carlton Club, which we have already described in our chapter on Pall Mall.

CHAPTER XVI.

THE NEIGHBOURHOOD OF ST. JAMES'S SQUARE.

" John his dull invention racks,
To rival Boodle's dinners, or Almack's."

Heroic Epistle to Sir W. Chambers.

King Street—Nerot's Hotel—St. James's Theatre—*Début* of John Braham—An Amusing Story of him—Mr. Hooper opens the St. James's Theatre—Mr. Bunn and German Opera—The Name of the Theatre changed to "The Prince's"—The Theatre opened with English Opera—Willis's Rooms—"Almack's"—The Dilettanti Society and their Portraits—Curious Comments on Quadrilles—A Ball in Honour of the Coronation of George IV.—Christie and Manson's Sale-rooms—Famous Residents in King Street—Louis Napoleon—Crockford's Bazaar—Duke Street and Bury Street—A Famous Lawyer and his Will—Steele—Swift and Crabbe—Yarrell, the Naturalist—York Street and its Foot Pavement—Charity Commission Offices—Jermyn Street—A Strange Story of a Truant Husband—The Brunswick Hotel—The Museum of Practical Geology—The Society for the Prevention of Cruelty to Animals—The Turkish Bath—An Artists' Quarter—"Harlequin's" Account of the Neighbourhood.

EXTENDING from the west side of the square to St. James's Street, parallel with Pall Mall and Jermyn Street, runs a thoroughfare to which the loyalty of the Stuart times gave the name of King Street. On the south side of this street, on the site now occupied by the St. James's Theatre, formerly stood a large building, long known as Nerot's Hotel. The premises were old, probably dating from the time of Charles II.; it had a large heavy staircase, carved after the fashion of the time, its panels being adorned with a series of mythical pictures of Apollo and Daphne and other heathen deities. The front of the house was pierced with no less than twenty-four windows.

The St. James's Theatre, like the New Royalty, owes its existence to one of those unaccountable infatuations which stake the earnings of a lifetime upon a hazardous speculation. It was built in 1835, from a design by Mr. Beazley, and at a cost of £26,000, by the celebrated John Braham, then sixty years of age. The great tenor, who was of Jewish origin, having from childhood developed remarkable vocal powers, made his *début* at the old Royalty Theatre in 1787, at the age of thirteen, as a pupil of Leoni; in the bills he is called "Master Abrahams." Here he is said to have attracted the notice of the wealthy Abraham Goldschmidt, who placed him under the tuition of Rauzzini, the director of the Bath concerts, in which city Braham first established his reputation as a vocalist. He returned to London in 1796, and made his appearance in Storace's opera of *Mahmoud.* Subsequently he proceeded to Italy, where he completed his musical studies, and returned to England in 1801, from which time he pursued his professional career with uninterrupted success. His delivery of the recitative "Deeper and deeper still," from Handel's *Jephthah,* is said to have been one of the finest specimens of tragic vocalisation ever heard. Charles Lamb says of him:—"There is a fine scorn in Braham's face. . . . . . The Hebrew spirit is strong

in him, in spite of his proselytism. He cannot conquer the shibboleth: how it breaks out when he sings 'The children of Israel passed through the Red Sea!' The auditors for the moment are as Egyptians to him, and he rides over our necks in triumph. The foundation of his vocal excellence is sense." Henry Russell relates the following amusing story of him:—"His father's name was Abraham, and as he was short and stout, his neighbours nicknamed him 'Aby Punch.' Braham on one occasion was performing in an absurd *pasticcio* with Mrs. Crouch, Mrs. Bland, Kelly, and Jack Bannister. The scene represented the interior of an old country inn. [*Enter Braham with a bundle slung to a stick on his shoulder.*] 'I have been traversing this desolate country for days with no friend to cheer me. [*Sits.*] I am weary—yet no rest, no food, scarcely life. O Heaven, pity me! Shall I ever realise my hopes? [*Knocks on the table.*] What ho there, house! [*Knocks again.*] Will no one come!' [*Enter Landlord.*] 'I beg pardon, sir, but—[*starts*]. I know that face [*aside*]. What can I do for you, sir?' *Braham:* 'Gracious Heaven! 'tis he — the voice, the look — the — [*with calmness*]—Yes; I want food.' *Landlord:* 'Tell me, what brings one so young as thou appearest to be through this dangerous forest?' *Braham:* 'I *will.* For days, for months, oh! for years, I have been in search of my father.' *Landlord:* 'Your father!' *Braham:* 'Yes; my father. 'Tis strange—but that voice—that look—that figure —tell me that *you* are my father.' *Landlord:* 'No, I tell thee, no; I am *not* thy father.' *Braham:* 'Heaven protect me! Who, tell me, WHO IS MY FATHER?' Scarcely had Braham put this question when a little Jew stood up in an excited manner in the midst of a densely-crowded pit, and exclaimed, 'I knowed yer father well. His name was Abey Punch!' The performance was suspended for some minutes by the roars of laughter which followed this revelation."

Braham's theatre opened under the most favourable auspices on the 14th of December, 1835, with an original operatic burletta by Gilbert A'Beckett, entitled *Agnes Sorel*, in which the principal parts were sustained by Messrs. Braham and Morris Barnett, and the Misses Glossop and P. Horton.

nist, were engaged at the St. James's Theatre during Lent, 1836, Mrs. Honey appearing in the parts of "Captain Macheath," in the *Beggar's Opera*, and "Kate O'Brien," in *Perfection*. It seems rather ominous of the future that the first season of the

ST. JAMES'S THEATRE. (*See page* 191.)

An original interlude, *A Clear Case*, followed the opera, and an original farce, *A French Company*, concluded the performances. Braham appears to have been a liberal patron of dramatic writers, as we find an unusual number of "new and original" pieces produced at this theatre during his too brief reign, although far more numerous audiences assembled on the nights when he performed in his famous parts of "Fra Diavolo" and "Tom Tug," in *The Waterman*. Mrs. Honey and Love, the polypho-

new theatre lasted little more than three months, when Braham was glad to let it to Madame Jenny Vertpré for French plays, which commenced April 8th, 1836, and in which Mdlle. Plessis appeared. Braham re-opened his theatre on September 29th, 1836, with the somewhat pompous announcement that "The theatre having been, during the recess, perfected in all parts, was now admitted to be the most splendid in Europe!" The performances commenced on this occasion with *The Strange*

Gentleman, by "Boz," followed by *The Sham Prince,* by John Barnett, concluding with *The Tradesmen's Ball,* all three being burlettas, and all "new and original." Dr. Arne's operetta of *Artaxerxes* was produced the following month, with Miss Rainforth as "Mandane," and Braham as

run of more than fifty nights, while the former disappeared from the bills after fifteen representations. By this time Wright and Mrs. Stirling had joined the already powerful company ; yet, in spite of the combination of talent which he had assembled in his elegant little theatre, the unfortunate proprietor

WILLIS'S ROOMS. (*See page* 196.)

"Artabanes." "Boz" again appears in December, 1836, as the author of the libretto of *The Village Coquettes,* the music being by John Hullah, in which the chief performers were Miss Rainforth and Messrs. Braham, Morris Barnett, Harley, and John Parry—a strong caste, indeed, and one which might have been supposed to ensure the success of any piece of average merit. *The Village Coquettes* seem, however, to have met with less favour than *The Strange Gentleman,* the latter having had a

found himself at the close of the season of 1838 a ruined man, forced, at the age of sixty-four, to seek a maintenance in America by the exercise of his profession. Here he achieved as great a popularity as he had enjoyed in England, and on his subsequent return a few years later to his native land, his old age was made happy by the dutiful affection of his daughter, the Countess Waldegrave. He died in 1856, in his eighty-third year, leaving a name which will always be remembered as one of the greatest of English singers. His fame did not rest solely upon his remarkable skill as a scientific vocalist in operas and oratorios, but upon his exquisite and most pathetic rendering of the homely ballads and patriotic songs so dear to the heart of the people of every country, and to an especial degree of the people of England.

But to return to the history of the St. James's Theatre, which was opened by Mr. Hooper in 1839, with a company comprising Messrs. Dowton, Wrench, Alfred Wigan, Mdmes. Glover, Honey, Nisbett, and several other excellent performers from the Haymarket Theatre. As he was a sufficiently wise man in his generation to profit by the unfortunate experience of his predecessor, Hooper resolved not to depend upon talent alone for success. Van Amburgh, the lion-tamer, with his formidable *troupe* of wild beasts, had at this time gained such a triumph over Macready and the legitimate drama at Drury Lane, that, as Mr. Bunn, the lessee, tells us, whereas the latter had been playing (at £16 a night) to comparatively empty benches, the former now nightly exhibited his intrepidity before crowded audiences, including on several occasions the young Queen, who highly eulogised this fascinating exhibition ! Mr. Hooper therefore announced that the St. James's Theatre would re-open on the 4th of February, 1839, with three new pieces, and a dozen lions and tigers of extraordinary size. The three new pieces consisted of a burletta, *Friends and Neighbours*, by Haynes Bayley ; *The Young Sculptor*, by Henry Mayhew; and *The Troublesome Lodger*, by Bayley and Mayhew. Dowton, although at that time the oldest actor on the stage, having passed his seventieth year, was a universal favourite, as also were both Wrench and Mrs. Glover ; but the manager soon found that the taste of the day gave four-legged performers so decided a preference over bipeds, that he started off to Paris and obtained the services of a *troupe* of highly-trained monkeys, dogs, and goats. The event proved his sagacity ; the attraction was irresistible, and all the rank and fashion of the metropolis crowded to witness the antics of " Madame Pompadour, Mademoiselle Batavia, Lord Gogo, and his valet Jacob !" So, at least, says Theodore Hook, in an essay written during this year upon " The Decline of the Drama :"—

"Perhaps as great an alteration as any which has occurred during the present generation is to be found in the theatrical taste of the people—not to go back to the theatrical reign of Garrick, which terminated in 1811, during which the acceptance or rejection of a comedy formed the subject of general conversation. Then there were but two theatres, the seasons of which were limited from the 15th of September to the 15th of May. Then each theatre had its destined company of actors, a change in which, even in an individual instance, created a sensation in society. Theatrical representations had a strong hold upon the public, up to a much later period—in fact, until that which modern liberality denounced as a gross monopoly was abolished, and theatres sprung up in almost every street of the metropolis. The argument in favour of this extension was that the population of London and the suburbs had so much increased, that the demand for playhouses was greater than the supply, and that 'more theatres' were wanted. We have the theatres, but where are the authors and the actors to make them attractive? Monkeys, dogs, goats, horses, giants, lions, tigers, and gentlemen who walk upon the ceiling with their heads downwards, are all very attractive in their way, and they will sometimes, not always, fill the playhouses. But as to the genuine drama, the public taste has been weaned from it, first by the multitude of trashy diversions scattered all over the town, and, secondly, by the consequent scattering of the theatrical talent which really does exist. At each of these minor theatres you find some three or four excellent actors, worked off their legs, night after night, who if collected into two good companies, as of old, would give us the legitimate drama well and satisfactorily."

On the marriage of Her Majesty with Prince Albert, in February, 1840, a scheme was set on foot for the establishment of a German opera in London. An arrangement was effected with Herr Schuman, director of the opera at Mayence, and the St. James's Theatre, of which Mr. Bunn had become the lessee, was selected as a suitable *locale* for the purpose, and its name changed to "The Prince's Theatre," in honour of the illustrious bridegroom. Public expectation was wrought up to the highest pitch : a new entrance was made for Her Majesty and the Queen Dowager through Mr. Braham's private house ; the Duke of Brunswick engaged the box next to that of the Queen for the season, and long before the opening night every box and stall had been disposed of. The German company, headed by their director, Herr Schuman, duly arrived in London, and the procession of carriages and baggage wagons, containing the stage wardrobes, decorations, and other articles, resembled, said the *Era*, " a troop of soldiers rather than a *troupe* of actors; it was, indeed, more like a military than a Thespian corps."

With all this flourish of trumpets, and under this distinguished patronage, "The Prince's" opened on the 27th of April, 1840. " Never was it our lot," says one of the weekly papers of that date, " to witness such a fashionable and crowded audience in the walls of any theatre. Many families of the highest rank were obliged to be contented with seats in the public and upper boxes, while the private ones were filled by their noble subscribers, including the Cambridge family, and a portion of that of the Queen Dowager. The two queens were prevented from attending by the death of the Countess of Burlington." The well-known and ever-popular *Der Freischütz*, by Weber, was judiciously chosen for the opening performance. Among the operas subsequently produced at this theatre were Spohr's *Jessonda ;* his *Faust*, of which it was remarked that "the opera of *Faust* might be set to the text of the oratorio of *The Day of Judgment*, and would be as much in character with the one as with the other ;" Weber's *Euryanthe*, said, on account of its dulness, to have been nicknamed in Germany *Ennuianthe ;* Glück's *Iphigenia in Tauris ;* and Beethoven's *Fidelio*.

The German singers were not generally admired. The *Era* remarks, *apropos* of the performance of Weber's *Euryanthe : "* Herr Poeck sang with great spirit and power, Schmerzer was good in some parts of the opera ; but the ladies, whom out of gallantry we ought to praise, can only claim it on that head. If they had but moderate execution, and could but sing tolerably in tune, we would willingly excuse their badness of school, for we should at least hear the composer without being offended ; but really (and the ladies must pardon us for saying so) such singers as Madame Fischer Schwartzböck and Madame Michalesi are sufficient to destroy the effect of any opera, however fine it may be." In spite of these trifling drawbacks, the Prince's Theatre continued to be both fashionably and fully attended up to the close of the season, and Herr Schuman, previous to his departure, is said to have expressed himself "confident that he had laid the foundation of a permanent German opera in England, and that he should return the following year, this, his experimental season, having proved that it would be worth his while to bring over the *élite* of the German singers."

These " great expectations " were never destined to be fulfilled. The late German opera-house re-opened in November, 1840, under the management of Mr. Morris Barnett, with *Fridolin*, a new opera by Frank Romer, which, not proving a success, terminated the winter season before Christmas, and with it ended the career of this theatre as " The Prince's." In 1841 we find it was taken by Mr. Mitchell, and opened for French plays, in its old name of the St. James's, which it has ever since retained. Under the lesseeship of Mr. Mitchell, which lasted twelve years, the English public had an opportunity of witnessing the best works of the French dramatists, represented by the best native artists, such as the veteran Perlet, Achard, Ravel, Levasseur, Lemaitre, Mdlle. Plessy, the famous Dejazet, and the gifted Rachel, who, to use the fashionable cant, "created" the parts of "Adrienne Lecouvreur," of Racine's *Phèdre*, and of Corneille's "Camille " in *Les Horaces*. At the close of each of his last two seasons of French plays Mr. Mitchell essayed the experiment of a brief series of German dramas, but with no encouraging result. In 1855, the St. James's Theatre, then under the management of Mrs. Seymour, produced the lyrical drama of *Alcestis*, adapted from the Greek of Euripides, set to music by Glück, the choruses, &c., being under the direction of Sir Henry Bishop. This scarcely classical entertainment was lightened by two after-pieces, *Abon Hassan*, an extravaganza, and *The Miller and his Men*. *Alcestis* was not appreciated by the public, and was withdrawn after a few nights.

In June, 1859, an English opera by Edward Loder, entitled *Raymond and Agnes*, was brought out at this theatre, under the management of Augustus Braham, a son of the great tenor. The principal parts were sustained by Hamilton Braham, George Perren, Mdmes. Rudersdorf and Susan Pyne. But the St. James's Theatre would seem to have been the evil genius of the Braham family ; for, although the opera was highly commended by musical authorities, and the caste unobjectionable, *Raymond and Agnes* proved an utter failure, and after being performed five nights to nearly empty benches disappeared on the sixth, to be seen and heard no more. From 1859 to 1863 the St. James's was successively leased to Messrs. F. B. Chatterton, Alfred Wigan, Frank Matthews, and B. Webster, the short tenure of each lease proving that the speculation was in no case satisfactory. The company during the greater part of the time comprised the two clever couples, Mr. and Mrs. Alfred Wigan and Mr. and Mrs. Frank Matthews, Miss Rainforth, and Miss Herbert. The last-named lady became lessee of the theatre in 1864, but, although an elegant and highly popular actress, she, like her predecessors, failed to make a fortune out of the proverbially unfortunate place. In 1868 the management was assumed by Mrs. John Wood, a lively lady, whose piquant performance of " La Belle Sauvage " was the great hit of the season of 1869. In 1874, the St. James's acquired an un-enviable notoriety from the nature of the entertainment offered, which fell under the ban of the Lord Chamberlain ; but its character has improved of late years, under the joint management of Messrs. Kendal and Hare.

We learn casually from Forster's " Life of Charles Dickens," that when in 1846 the idea of giving readings from his published works first came into his head, he at first proposed to take the St. James's Theatre for that purpose.

Apropos of Mr. Braham's management of the St. James's, a story is told, which may be worth repeating here. Mr. Bunn was passing through Jermyn Street late one evening, and seeing Kenney at the corner of St. James's Church, swinging about in a nervous sort of manner, he inquired the cause of his being there at such an hour. He replied, " I have been to the St. James's Theatre, and, do you know, I really thought Braham was a much prouder man than I find him to be." On asking why, he answered, " I was in the green-room, and hearing Braham say, as he entered, ' I am really proud of my pit to-night,' I went and counted it, and there were but seventeen people in it ! "

Close by the St. James's Theatre are " Willis's Rooms," a noble suite of assembly-rooms, formerly known as " Almack's." The building was erected by Mylne, for one Almack, a tavern-keeper, and was opened in 1765, with a ball, at which the Duke of Cumberland, the hero of Culloden, was present. Almack, who was a Scotchman by birth, seems to have been a large adventurer in clubs, for he at first "farmed " the club afterwards known as " Brooks's." The large ball-room is about one hundred feet in length by forty feet in width, and is chastely decorated with columns and pilasters, classic medallions, and mirrors. The rooms are let for public meetings, dramatic readings, concerts, balls, and occasionally for dinners. Right and left, at the top of the grand staircase, and on either side of the vestibule of the ball-room, are two spacious apartments, used occasionally for large suppers or dinners.

In these rooms are held the re-unions of the Dilettanti Society. This society, as we have stated in a previous chapter, was established in the year 1734, and originally met at the " Thatched House " Tavern, St. James's Street, its object being " the promotion of the fine arts, combined with friendly and social intercourse." The members of this association dine nere every fortnight during the " London season." The walls of the apartment are still hung with the portraits of the members, most of which were removed hither on the demolition of the old " Thatched House." Many of the

portraits are in the costume familiar to us through Hogarth, others are in Turkish or Roman dresses, and several of them are so represented as to show the convivial nature of the gatherings for which they were famous : for instance, Sir Francis Dashwood, afterwards Lord Le Despenser, who figures as a monk at his devotions—the object on which his gaze is intently fixed, however, is *not* a crucifix, nor an image of " Our Lady ; " Charles Sackville, Duke of Dorset, appears as a Roman soldier. The three principal pictures in the room are those by Sir Joshua Reynolds, who was himself a member of the Dilettanti Society : one of these represents a group containing portraits of the Duke of Leeds, Lord Dundas, Lord Mulgrave, Lord Seaforth, the Hon. Charles Greville, Charles Crowle, Esq., and Sir Joseph Banks ; another is a group treated in the same manner, containing portraits of Sir William Hamilton, Sir Watkin W. Wynn, Mr. Richard Thomson, Sir John Taylor, Mr. Payne Gallwey, and Mr. Spencer Stanhope ; the third is a portrait of Sir Joshua himself, attired in a loose robe, and without the addition of his customary wig. There are also portraits of the late Lord Broughton (better known as Sir John Cam Hobhouse), and Lord Ligonier, and, in fact, nearly every man of note in the early part of the present century. The latest addition to the collection is the portrait of Sir Edward Ryan, who died in August, 1875.

" Almack's " was already established as a place of public amusement as far back as 1768, for in the *Advertiser* of November 12th, in that year, we find the following notice :—" Mr. Almack humbly begs leave to acquaint the nobility and gentry, subscribers to the Assembly in King Street, St. James's, that the first meeting will be Thursday, 24th inst. N.B. Tickets are ready to be delivered at the Assembly Room."

In a satire on the ladies of the age, published in 1773, we read—

" Now lolling at the Coterie and ' White's,'
We drink and game away our days and nights.

* 　　 * 　　 * 　　 * 　　 *

No censure reaches them at Almack's ball ;
Virtue, religion—they're above them all."

The assembly which bore the title of "Almack's" was in its palmy days under the regulation of six lady patronesses, of the first distinction, whose fiat was decisive as to admission or rejection of every applicant for tickets, and became a most autocratic institution—quite an *imperium in imperio*. In fact, the *entrée* to " Almack's " was in itself a passport to the highest society in London, being almost as high a certificate as the fact of having been presented at Court.

Lady Clementina Davies writes in her " Recollections of Society : "—" At 'Almack's,' in 1814, the rules were very strict. Scotch reels and country dances were in fashion. The lady patronesses were all powerful. No visitor was to be admitted after twelve o'clock, and once, when the Duke of Wellington arrived a few minutes after that hour, he was refused admission."

A writer in the *New Monthly Magazine* (1824) observes : " The nights of meeting fall upon every Wednesday during the season. This is selection with a vengeance, the very quintessence of aristocracy. Three-fourths even of the nobility knock in vain for admission. Into this *sanctum sanctorum*, of course, the sons of commerce never think of intruding on the sacred Wednesday evenings ; and yet into this very 'blue chamber,' in the absence of the six necromancers, have the votaries of trade contrived to intrude themselves."

Mr. T. Raikes tells us in his " Journal" that the celebrated *diplomatiste*, the Princess Lieven, was the only foreign lady who was ever admitted into the exclusive circle of the lady patronesses of this select society, into the *tracasseries* of which establishment she entered very cordially, though her manner, tinctured at times with a certain degree of *hauteur*, made her many enemies.

"At the present time," writes Captain Gronow, in 1862, "one can hardly conceive the importance which was attached to getting admission to 'Almack's,' the seventh heaven of the fashionable world. Of the three hundred officers of the Foot Guards, not more than half a dozen were honoured with vouchers of admission to this exclusive temple of the *beau monde*, the gates of which were guarded by lady patronesses, whose smiles or frowns consigned men and women to happiness or despair as the case might be. These 'lady patronesses,' in 1813, were the Ladies Castlereagh, Jersey, Cowper, and Sefton, Mrs. Drummond Burrell, afterwards Lady Willoughby d'Eresby, the Princess Esterhazy, and the Princess Lieven.

"The most popular amongst these *grandes dames*," he adds, "was unquestionably Lady Cowper, now Lady Palmerston. Lady Jersey's bearing, on the contrary, was that of a theatrical tragedy queen ; and whilst attempting the sublime, she frequently made herself simply ridiculous, being inconceivably rude, and in her manner often ill-bred. Lady Sefton was kind and amiable, Madame de Lieven haughty and exclusive, Princess Esterhazy was a *bon enfant*, Lady Castlereagh and Mrs. Burrell *de très grandes dames*.

" Many diplomatic arts, much finesse, and a host of intrigues, were set in motion to get an invitation to 'Almack's.' Very often persons whose rank and fortunes entitled them to the *entrée* anywhere, were excluded by the cliqueism of the lady patronesses ; for the female government of 'Almack's' was a pure despotism, and subject to all the caprices of despotic rule : it is needless to add that, like every other despotism, it was not innocent of abuses. The fair ladies who ruled supreme over this little dancing and gossiping world, issued a solemn proclamation that no gentleman should appear at the assemblies without being dressed in knee-breeches, white cravat, and *chapeau bras*. On one occasion, the Duke of Wellington was about to ascend the staircase of the ball-room, dressed in black trousers, when the vigilant Mr. Willis, the guardian of the establishment, stepped forward and said, ' Your Grace cannot be admitted in trousers ; ' whereupon the Duke, who had a great respect for orders and regulations, quietly walked away.

" In 1814, the dances at 'Almack's' were Scotch reels and the old English country dance ; and the orchestra, being from Edinburgh, was conducted by the then celebrated Neil Gow. It was not until 1815 that Lady Jersey introduced from Paris the favourite quadrille, which has so long remained popular. I recollect the persons who formed the first quadrille that was ever danced at 'Almack's :' they were Lady Jersey, Lady Harriet Butler, Lady Susan Ryder, and Miss Montgomery ; the men being the Count St. Aldegonde, Mr. Montgomery, Mr. Montague, and Charles Standish. The 'mazy waltz' was also brought to us about this time ; but there were comparatively few who at first ventured to whirl round the *salons* of 'Almack's ;' in course of time Lord Palmerston might, however, have been seen describing an infinite number of circles with Madame de Lieven. Baron de Neumann was frequently seen perpetually turning with the Princess Esterhazy ; and, in course of time, the waltzing mania, having turned the heads of society generally, descended to their feet, and the waltz was practised in the morning in certain noble mansions in London with unparalleled assiduity."

Mr. T. Raikes thus commemorates the arrival of the German waltz in England :—" No event ever produced so great a sensation in English society as the introduction of the German waltz in 1813. Up to that time the English country dance, Scotch steps, and an occasional Highland reel, formed the school of the dancing-master, and the evening recreation of the British youth, even in the first circles. But peace was drawing near, foreigners were arriving, and the taste for Continental customs and manners became the order of the day. The young Duke of Devonshire, as the 'magnus Apollo' of the drawing-rooms in London, was at the head of these innovations; and when the *kitchen* and country dance became exploded at Devonshire House, it could not long be expected to maintain its footing even in the less celebrated assemblies. In London, fashion is or was then everything. Old and young returned to school, and the mornings which had been dedicated to lounging in the Park, were now absorbed at home in practising the figures of a French quadrille, or whirling a chair round the room, to learn the step and measure of

persevered in spite of all the prejudices which were marshalled against them, every night the waltz was called, and new votaries, though slowly, were added to their train. Still the opposition party did not relax in their efforts, sarcastic remarks flew about, and pasquinades were written to deter young ladies from such a recreation.

"The waltz, however, struggled successfully through all its difficulties; Flahault, who was *la fleur des pois* in Paris, came over to captivate Miss Mercer, and with a host of others drove the prudes

LORD WORCESTER.   LADY JERSEY.   CLANRONALD MACDONALD.   LADY WORCESTER.

THE FIRST QUADRILLE DANCED AT "ALMACK'S." (*From Gronow's "Reminiscences."*)

the German waltz. Lame and impotent were the first efforts, but the inspiring effect of the music, and the not less inspiring airs of the foreigners, soon rendered the English ladies enthusiastic performers. What scenes have we witnessed in those days at 'Almack's,' &c.! What fear and trembling in the *débutantes* at the commencement of a waltz, what giddiness and confusion at the end!

"It was perhaps owing to this latter circumstance that so violent an opposition soon arose to this new recreation on the score of morality.

"The anti-waltzing party took the alarm, cried it down, mothers forbade it, and every ball-room became a scene of feud and contention; the waltzers continued their operations, but their ranks were not filled with so many recruits as they expected. The foreigners, however, were not idle in forming their *élèves;* Baron Tripp, Neumann, St. Aldegonde, &c.,

into their entrenchments; and when the Emperor Alexander was seen waltzing round the room at 'Almack's,' with his tight uniform and numerous decorations, they surrendered at discretion."

The author of "Memoirs of the Times of George IV." favours us with the following curious comments on quadrilles, then (1811) newly exhibited in England:—"We had much waltzing and quadrilling, the last of which is certainly very abominable. I am not prude enough to be offended with waltzing, in which I can see no other harm than that it disorders the stomach, and sometimes makes people look very ridiculous; but after all, moralists, with the Duchess of Gordon at their head, who never had a moral in her life, exclaim dreadfully against it. Nay, I am told that these magical wheelings have already roused poor Lord Dartmouth from his grave to suppress them. Alas! after all, people set about it as gravely as a company of dervises, and seem to be paying adoration to Pluto rather than to Cupid. But the quadrilles I can by no means endure; for till ladies and gentlemen have joints at their ankles, which is impossible, it is

In July, 1821, a splendid ball was given here in honour of the coronation of George IV. by the special Ambassador from France, the Duc de Grammont. The King himself was present, attended by some of his royal brothers, the Duke

THE BALL-ROOM, WILLIS'S ROOMS.

worse than impudent to make such exhibitions, more particularly in a place where there are public ballets every Tuesday and Saturday. When people dance to be looked at, they surely should dance to perfection. Even the Duchess of Bedford, who is the Angiolini of the group, would make an indifferent *figurante* at the opera; and the principal male dancer, Mr. North, reminds one of a gibbeted malefactor, moved to and fro by the winds, but from no personal exertion."

of Wellington, and a numerous circle of courtiers. "Whatever French taste, directed by a Grammont, could do," writes Mr. Rush in his "Court of London," "to render the night agreeable, was witnessed. His suite of young gentlemen from Paris stood ready to receive the British fair on their approach to the rooms, and from baskets of flowers presented them with rich bouquets. Each lady thus entered the ball-room with one in her hand; and a thousand posies of sweet flowers displayed their hues, and exhaled their fragrance as the dancing commenced."

Here, from 1808 to 1810, Mrs. Billington, Mr. Braham, and Signor Naldi gave concerts, in rivalry with Madame Catalini at Hanover Square Rooms. In 1839 Master Bassle, a youth only thirteen years of age, appeared here in an extraordinary mnemonic performance; and in 1844 the rooms were taken by Mr. Charles Kemble, for the purpose of giving his readings from Shakespeare. In 1851, while the Great Exhibition was attracting its thousands, Thackeray here first appeared in public as a lecturer, taking as his subject "The English Humorists." Mr. Tom Taylor tells us an anecdote which belongs to his very first evening :—"Among the most conspicuous of the literary ladies at this gathering was Miss Brontë, the authoress of 'Jane Eyre.' She had never before seen the author of 'Vanity Fair,' though the second edition of her own celebrated novel was dedicated to him by her, with the assurance that she regarded him ' as the social regenerator of his day—as the very master of that working corps who would restore to rectitude the warped state of things.' Mrs. Gaskell tells us that, when the lecture was over, the lecturer descended from the platform, and making his way towards her, frankly asked her for her opinion. 'This,' adds Miss Brontë's biographer, ' she mentioned to me not many days afterwards, adding remarks almost identical with those which I subsequently read in "Villette," where a similar action on the part of M. Paul Emanuel is related.' The remarks of this singular woman on Thackeray and his writings, and her accounts of other interviews with him, will be found scattered about Mrs. Gaskell's biography of her."

As far back as 1840 it was pretty evident that "Almack's" was on the decline; as a writer in the *Quarterly Review* of that time puts it, there was " a clear proof that the palmy days of exclusiveness are gone by in England ; and," he adds, "though it is obviously impossible to prevent any given number of persons from congregating and re-establishing an oligarchy, we are quite sure that the attempt would be ineffectual." Such an attempt, made in 1882, proved quite abortive.

Opposite Willis's Rooms are the auction-rooms of Messrs. Christie and Manson, still celebrated as ever for sales of pictures and articles of *vertu.* The sale-rooms of Messrs. Christie, as stated in a previous chapter, were originally in Pall Mall, but were removed hither in 1823. The eldest son of him who raised the firm to its lofty position, and who subsequently was himself its principal, was Mr. James Christie, no less distinguished as the scholar

and the gentleman than as an auctioneer. His first literary production was a disquisition upon Etruscan vases, a subject suggested to him through his intimacy with the collection of the famous Townley Marbles. Works of a similar character followed at different times ; and, without entering into particulars, it will be sufficient to transcribe the opinion of the author of a memoir in the *Gentleman's Magazine,* " that the originality of his discoveries is not less conspicuous than the taste and talent with which he explains them." To this we may add, from the same eloquent tribute to his memory, that it will not seem surprising to find that such a man " raised the business he followed to the dignity of a profession. In pictures, in sculpture, in *vertu,* his taste was undisputed, and his judgment deferred to, as founded on the purest models and the most accredited standard. If to these advantages we add that fine moral feeling and that inherent love of truth which formed the basis of his character, and which would never permit him for any advantage to himself or others to violate their obligations, we may then have some means of judging how in his hands business became an honourable calling, and how that which to many is only secular, by him was dignified into a virtuous application of time and talents." This, the best of auctioneers, if we may credit the portrait here drawn of him, died in 1831.

The prices realised in these rooms for books, pictures, prints, old china, and other curiosities and antiquities, have almost always been high, though they have varied according to the direction taken by each passing mania of the day. It is stated that a pair of Sevrès china vases, for which in 1874 Lord Dudley gave £6,000 at Christie's, were not worth more than as many hundreds. It appears that a rival commission for this was given by one of the Rothschilds. A story is also told of a nobleman who sent an agent to a sale here with directions to buy a certain picture. The work was knocked down for a very large sum. "Well," said his lordship a few days after the sale, " did you bring the picture home ?" "No," said the steward, " it fetched an enormous price, I did not think it worth the money, so I did not buy it." " Sir," said his lordship, " I did not say anything about the price ; I told you to buy the picture." Similarly, these two agents of china-loving millionaires were told to buy the vases, and it is a good thing for one of the purchasers that both of them were not guided by the story of the noble lord, who, by the way, finished his rebuke to the steward with the remark, " Sir, it was your duty to buy that picture if you and your opponent had remained bidding for it until Doomsday."

Among the most important sales that have taken place here of late years were those of the art treasures belonging to Mr. Charles Dickens, and removed hither from his residence at Gad's Hill, near Rochester, where he died ; and the works of art, *virtu*, pictures, &c., belonging to the Duke of Hamilton, and brought from Hamilton Palace, which were sold here in 1882.

It may be interesting to record here the fact that the first book-auction in England, of which there is any record, was held in 1676, when the library of Dr. Searnan was brought to the hammer. Prefixed to the catalogue there is an address to the reader, saying, " Though it has been unusual in England to make sale of books by auction, yet it hath been practised in other countries to advantage." For general purposes this mode of sale was scarcely known till 1700.

In this street was born, in 1749, Mrs. Charlotte Smith, well known as a poet and a novelist. She was the daughter of Nicholas Turner, Esq., of Bignor Park, Sussex. She was the author of " The Old Manor House," " Rural Walks," and other works which enjoyed a wonderful popularity near the close of the last century. She died in October, 1806, at the age of fifty-seven.

At the beginning of 1847 the future Emperor of the French, then known as Prince Louis Napoleon, and an exile, took up his abode at No. 1*c*, on the north side of King Street, which bears on its front a tablet commemorating the fact. There he amused himself by collecting his books, portfolios, and family portraits, and made it his regular home. He was elected an honorary member of the Army and Navy Club, where he spent much of his spare time, rode in Hyde Park constantly, and frequented "Crockford's" in the evening. Here he entertained his friends quietly and unostentatiously, living quite a retired life in his " furnished apartments ; " and it is pleasant news to learn, on the authority of Mr. B. Jerrold, that here the Prince made some clever sketches of decorations for Lady Combermere's and Lady Londonderry's stalls at the great military bazaar for the benefit of the Irish, which was held in the barracks of the Life Guards. Louis Napoleon was still living here in the following spring, when he served as one of 150,000 special constables who had been sworn in to keep order in anticipation of a Chartist rising. And here, too, he was residing when summoned to Paris a few months later by the events of the Revolution, which speedily raised him to the presidential chair, and ultimately to the imperial throne. When he entered London in 1855 along with his bride, the Empress Eugenie, he was seen to point out to her

with interest and pleasure the street in which he had spent those months of weary waiting, as, amid the cheering of the crowds, the *cortége* drove slowly up St. James's Street.

At one corner of King Street, in the year 1832, a large saloon, nearly 200 feet in length, was built for Mr. Crockford, and opened by him as the St. James's Bazaar. It was not, however, successful in attracting visitors. Here were exhibited, in 1841, three dioramic *tableaux* of the second obsequies of the great Napoleon in Paris ; and in 1844 the first exhibition of decorative works for the New Houses of Parliament was held here.

Two main thoroughfares connect King Street on the north with Jermyn Street—namely, Duke Street and Bury Street. In the former, on the 12th of February, 1781, was born Edward Burtenshaw Sugden, Lord Chancellor of Ireland, and subsequently of England also, and one of the most consummate lawyers of the nineteenth century. His father was a fashionable hairdresser and wig-maker ; and it is said—we know not with how much of truth—that the future occupant of the woolsack and " keeper of Her Majesty's conscience," as a boy, often held the bridles of the horses of customers who stopped to make their purchases at the shop of Mr. Richard Sugden. On one occasion, later in life, on the Sussex hustings, when reproached with his being the son of a barber, Mr. Sugden made the brave and noble reply, " The gentleman before me asks me if I remember that I am the son of a tradesman ? Yes ; I remember it, and know it, and am proud of it. But the difference between my assailant and myself is, that I, being a barber's son, have raised myself to the position of a barrister, while he, if he had been born like me, would doubtless have remained a barber's son, and perhaps a barber, all his life." As it was, he netted in middle life an income of twenty thousand a year, and no doubt was a great loser in money by accepting a seat upon the judicial bench. It was late in life that he took a peerage, his patent as Lord St. Leonard's being dated 1st of March, 1852, certain obstacles to its acceptance being then removed. His lordship died in January, 1875, having reached the good old age of ninety-four. His will was afterwards the subject of litigation, the result of which was to establish, under certain conditions, the validity of a formal declaration of a testator's intentions, if satisfactorily proved and corroborated, as equivalent to a written will, where that will was known to exist, but was accidentally lost.

In this street Edmund Burke was living in 1795 when his hopes and parental pride were raised to the highest pitch by the election of his only son,

Richard, in his own room, as M.P. for Malton. These hopes, however, were destined to be speedily and rudely cast down, for no sooner had the father and son returned thither from Yorkshire than the latter was seized with a fatal illness, and died a week later at Brompton. The aged statesman was never himself again, and he survived the heavy blow only just two years.

At No. 10, now called Sussex Chambers, was formerly the Association of the Friends of Poland, over which the late Lord Dudley Coutts Stuart so long presided. This association was founded in 1832, for the purpose of diffusing information about Poland, of relieving poor Polish refugees, and of educating their children. The building, now the head-quarters of the Catholic Union of Great Britain, is, or once was, a very fine mansion, with a noble staircase, ornamental ceilings, and doors of the finest mahogany. It has below it large cellars and vaults, which, tradition says, went under Pall Mall and St. James's Park, and led to the Houses of Parliament. This, however, must be a fiction. There may, perhaps, be more truth in the story that the house was once occupied for a time by Oliver Cromwell.

Bury (or, more properly, Berry) Street, being so named after its original builder, being mainly let out as "apartments for bachelors," has had the honour of accommodating some distinguished residents; among others, Sir Richard Steele and Dean Swift, George Crabbe and Thomas Moore. Swift, as we learn from his writings, occupied a first-floor set of rooms, for which he paid eight shillings a week rent, "plaguy dear," as he remarks; but it is as well that he did not live here in our own day, and in the "season," or we fear that he would have found himself far more heavily rented.

Here, upon his marriage, in September, 1707, "Captain" (afterwards Sir Richard) Steele, the wit and essayist, took for his lady a house, "the third door from Germain [Jermyn] Street, left hand of Berry [Bury] Street." But it is clear, from autograph letters still to be seen at the British Museum, that the rent of this nuptial house, so sacred to "Prue," and to the tenderness and endearments of the honeymoon, was not paid until the landlord had put in an execution upon Steele's furniture. He appears soon after this to have migrated to Blooms-bury Square, where the same fate befell his establishment. Steele and "Prue" were married, in all probability, about the 7th of September in the above-mentioned year. "There are traces," writes Thackeray, "of a 'tiff' between them in the middle of the next month; she being as prudish and fidgety as he was impassioned and reckless."

Swift shared his lodgings here with his "Stella," Hester Johnson. Five doors off lived the rival lady, who flattered him and made love to him so outrageously, and in the end died for hopeless love of him—his "Vanessa." Thackeray tells us that Mrs. Vanhomrigh, "Vanessa's" mother, was the widow of a Dutch merchant who had held some lucrative posts in the time of King William. The family settled in London in Anne's reign, and had a house in Bury Street—"a street," he adds, "made notable by such residents as Steele and Swift, and in our own times by Moore and Crabbe." In one of his letters Swift describes his lodging in detail: he has "the first floor, a dining-room and bed-chamber, at eight shillings a week." He often lounged in upon the Vanhomrighs. In his journal to Stella, he writes: "I am so hot and lazy after my morning's walk that I loitered at Mrs. Vanhomrigh's, where my best gown and my periwig were, and, out of mere listlessness, dine there very often: so I did to-day."

On coming up to London from Trowbridge, late in life, George Crabbe took lodgings in this street, to be near Rogers and some other literary friends. Whilst here, he was a frequent visitor at Holland House, at Mr. Murray's, in Albemarle Street, and at Lansdowne House, from the doors of which he had been repulsed by its former owner, Lord Shelburne. At Holland House he made the acquaintance of Thomas Campbell, and Tommy Moore, and Brougham, and Sylvester Douglas, and the Smiths of the "Rejected Addresses," and Sydney Smith, and Ugo Foscolo. He writes in his "diary" on his return, "This visit to London has been indeed a rich one. I had new things to see, and was, perhaps, something of a novelty myself. Mr. Rogers introduced me to almost every man he is acquainted with; and in this number were comprehended all I was previously very desirous to obtain a knowledge of." It is only fair to add that by all that the quiet country parson-poet saw in the gay world of London he seems to have been quite unaltered, and that he returned to Trowbridge and his parochial duties with his head unturned and his kind heart unchanged.

At the corner of Ryder Street and Duke Street for many years lived William Yarrell, the naturalist, the author of "British Fishes," "British Birds," &c. He followed the trade of a news-agent. In 1849 he was elected a vice-president of the Linnæan Society. He died in 1856. His collections of British fishes, and the specimens illustrative of his papers in the "Transactions" of the Linnæan Society, were secured by the trustees of the British Museum at the sale of Mr. Yarrell's effects.

York Street, a short thoroughfare extending from the north side of St. James's Square to Jermyn Street, was the first street in London paved for foot-passengers. Strype, in his edition of Stow, describes it as " a broad street coming out of St. James's Square ; " but, he adds, " the greatest part is taken up by the garden walls of the late Duke of Ormond's house on the one side, and on the other by the house inhabited by the Lord Cornwallis." On the eastern side of this street stood, till the present year, St. James's Chapel, a dull and poor-looking chapel-of-ease to the parish church. It was formerly occupied by Josiah Wedgwood, as a show-room for his pottery and porcelain from Etruria, in Staffordshire. In previous time this had been the residence of the Spanish ambassador, the chapel being used as a Roman Catholic place of worship under the ambassador's wing. It was subsequently used by Dissenting congregations, and from 1866 down to the time of its demolition the Rev. Stopford Brooke officiated here.

At No. 8 in this street were formerly the offices of the Charity Commission,* now located at Gwydyr House, Whitehall. The endowed charities amounted, in 1786, according to returns then made to Parliament under the Gilbert Act, to £528,710 a year. A Committee of the House of Commons, moved for by Mr. Brougham in 1816, recommended an inquiry into their condition. The first commission for this purpose was appointed by the Crown, under an Act of 1818, and further commissions of inquiry were issued and prosecuted under that and several subsequent Acts, until 1837. During many years after this time, numerous ineffectual proposals were made, in and out of Parliament, for the establishment of some jurisdiction for the permanent superintendence and control of these endowments. In 1853, an Act for the better administration of charitable trusts was, however, obtained, appointing commissioners and inspectors, but with the very minimum of power which could be given without rendering the commission altogether nugatory. Beyond a veto on suits by any one but the Attorney-General, the commissioners had only powers of inquiry, of advice, and of rendering assistance in a few cases in which trustees might seek it. Under the above Act the Lord Chancellor, in 1854, appointed official trustees of charity funds. In 1855, another Act empowered the Board to apportion parish charities under £30 a year; but with regard to new schemes, its operations were still subordinate, not only to Chancery, but to the County Courts. An Act

* See Vol. III., p. 377.

passed in 1860 for the first time gave the commissioners judicial power over charities of £50 a year, and like power, with the consent of the trustees, over larger charities ; but being judicial, they can only be called into operation at the suit of persons interested in each case. Under the jurisdiction thus given, the Charity Commission has aided in establishing improved schemes in several cases ; but a public department, which Parliament did not at its outset place even as high as a County Court, and which has ever since remained in the same position, cannot be expected to exercise influence enough with the public to originate and carry out any enlarged principles of administration on a subject in which so many individual and local prejudices are to be encountered. The Education Commissioners have proposed to vest the control of charities in a committee of the Privy Council, which might be governed less by technical and narrow rules than by an enlightened public opinion.

Abutting on York Street is Ormond Yard, so called after the Duke of Ormond, who suffered so severely in the royal cause during the Civil War. Mr. P. Cunningham reminds us that " the gallant Earl of Ossory " was his son, and the beautiful Countess of Chesterfield, of De Grammont's " Memoirs," his daughter, and that his grandson and heir was attainted in 1715 for his share in the rebellion of that year.

Jermyn Street, which runs parallel with Piccadilly on the north side of St. James's Square, and extends from St. James's Street to the Haymarket, was named from Henry Jermyn, Earl of St. Albans. This nobleman's residence, called St. Albans House, was on the south side of the street, and its site was afterwards occupied by part of Ormond House, of which we have already spoken. Like many other staunch loyalists, the Earl of St. Albans was little remembered by Charles II. He was, however, an attendant at court, and one of his Majesty's companions in his gay hours. On one of these occasions a stranger came with an importunate suit for an office of great value just vacant. The King, by way of joke, desired the Earl to personate him, and commanded the petitioner to be admitted. The gentleman, addressing himself to the supposed monarch, enumerated his services to the royal family, and hoped the grant of the place would not be deemed too great a reward. " By no means," answered the Earl, " and I am only sorry, that as soon as I heard of the vacancy, I conferred it on my faithful friend, the Earl of St. Albans," pointing to the King, " who constantly followed the fortunes both of my father and myself, and has hitherto gone unrewarded." Charles granted, for this joke, what the utmost real service would not have received. The Earl was supposed to have been privately married to the Queen Dowager, Henrietta Maria, who, as Pennant puts it, "ruled her first husband, *a king;* but the second, a *subject,* ruled her." The Earl died here in 1683.

In Jermyn Street, near the church, there was living, in the reign of Queen Anne, a Mrs. Howe, of whom, or rather of whose husband, we find an amusing account in Dr. W. King's "Anecdotes of

Church, Piccadilly (being so placed that she could not see him); and even frequented a coffee-house, from the window of which he could see his own wife at her meals. The strangest thing is, that the coffee-house keeper, supposing him to be an elderly bachelor, recommended to him the deserted lady and supposed widow as a wife. At the end of seventeen years, Mr. Howe sent to his wife an anonymous letter, begging her to be the next night, at a particular hour, in Birdcage Walk. On

BURY STREET. (*See page* 202.)

his Own Time." Her maiden name was Mallett; she was of a good family in the West of England, and married a Mr. Howe, who had a fortune of some £700 or £800 a year. Seven or eight years after his marriage, when he had two children, apparently without any reason he disappeared from his home in Jermyn Street, leading his wife to suppose that he had gone abroad. For seventeen years she heard no tidings of him, and, her two children having died, she removed into a smaller abode in Brewer Street, Golden Square. It appears that during all this long period Mr. Howe had gone no further away than Westminster, where he lived under an assumed name, and disguised in dress; that he constantly saw his wife at St. James's

repairing thither, the truant husband declared himself, and they lived happily together ever afterwards. It appears that the eccentric old gentleman was in the habit of even reading in the newspapers his wife's petition for a private Act of Parliament, entitling her and her children to a maintenance out of his estate; but that, in spite of this, he continued to keep up his incognito. The story is improbable, and would make the subject of a comedy.

At the Brunswick Hotel, in this street, Louis Napoleon took up his residence, under the assumed name of the Comte d'Arenenberg, on his escape from his captivity in the fortress of Ham, in May, 1846.

On the north side, extending through to the

south of Piccadilly, is the Museum of Practical Geology and Government School of Mines. It occupies an area of 70 feet by 153 feet, specially designed and built for its purposes by Mr. James Pennithorne, architect, at a cost of £30,000. The building comprises, on the ground storey, a spacious apartment having two galleries along its sides to give access to the cases with which the walls are lined. At the north and south ends are model-rooms, containing a gallery, and connected with the principal museum. The principal object of the Government School of Mines, which is engrafted on

TURKISH BATH, JERMYN STREET. (*See page* 206.)

hall, formed into three divisions by Doric columns, for the exhibition of building-stones, marbles, the heavier geological specimens, and works of art. Adjoining is a theatre for lectures upon scientific subjects, capable of accommodating upwards of 600 persons. There is also a library, librarian's apartments, and reception-room. On each side the entrance-hall is a staircase, joining in a central flight between Ionic columns, leading to the principal floor, containing the museum, a splendid

the Museum of Practical Geology and Geological Survey, is to discipline the students thoroughly in the principles of those sciences upon which the successful operations of the miner and metallurgist depend. During the session, viz., from October to June, courses of lectures are delivered on chemistry, natural history, physics, mining, mineralogy, geology, applied mechanics, and metallurgy.

At No. 105, on the south side, is the Royal Society for the Prevention of Cruelty to Animals.

This institution, the only one having for its object the protection of dumb and defenceless animals, was founded in 1824, and is under the patronage of Her Majesty. The labours of this institution embrace the circulation of appropriate tracts, books, lectures, and sermons, and the prosecution of persons guilty of acts of cruelty to the brute creation.

At No. 76, on the same side of the street, is the London and Provincial Turkish Bath Company, which was established about the year 1860. Here, as in establishments of a similar kind which have sprung up in various parts of the United Kingdom, the plan of the old Roman bath is strictly followed. There is the Tepidarium, the Sudatorium (heated to a temperature of 120), and the Calidarium, in which the heat is exalted to 160 degrees. Next to this is the Lavatorium, in which the washing and shampooing process is carried on. *Apropos* of such baths, a writer in *Once a Week* has remarked that "the barbarian Turk has been the medium of keeping alive one of the most healthful practices of the ancients. There is scarcely a spot throughout the United Kingdom in which the remains of these very baths have not been disinterred and gazed at by the curious during the last half century. We turn up the flues, still blackened with the soot of fourteen centuries ago; we find, as at Uriconium, the very furnaces, with the coal fuel close at hand; and we know that the hot bath was not only used by the legionaries who held Britain, but by the civilised Britons themselves; yet we must go all the way to the barbarian Turk for instruction upon one of the simplest and most effective methods of maintaining the public health."

In 1768 Dr. Hunter gave up his house in this street to his brother John, and took possession of one which he had built in Windmill Street, whence ultimately he moved, as we have noticed in a previous chapter, into Leicester Square.

Jermyn Street appears to have been at one time inhabited by artists. In 1782, at his rooms in this street, Mrs. Siddons gave sittings to Sherwin, for her portrait, in the character of the "Grecian Daughter," which was afterwards engraved; the print from which, in consequence of a purse having been presented to Mrs. Siddons by gentlemen of the long robe, was dedicated to the Bar.

In this neighbourhood meets a Bohemian club called the "Century," composed of worshippers of the philosophy of Herbert Spencer, and other thinkers of the "advanced" school. The rest of the street is now mainly devoted to private family hotels, and to apartments for members of Parliament and aristocratic bachelors. A few years ago it was one of the head-quarters of gambling-houses.

In some papers in the *London Magazine* for 1773, signed "Harlequin," the whole of the neighbourhood of St. James's and Pall Mall, which we have described in this and the preceding chapters, is fictitiously traversed by a sprite, who peeps in at St. James's, at Carlton House, in Pall Mall, at "Boodle's," and at the "stately mansion of the Northumberlands, at Charing Cross." It is amusing, at the distance of a century or more, to note the scenes witnessed by "Harlequin." In St. James's Palace he saw the interior of the royal nursery, where "Madame Schulenberg was teaching the young Prince of Wales to play leap-frog," while his brother, the "Bishop of Osnaburg," was "riding a wooden horse called Hanover;" and at Carlton House, Prince George and the Earl of Bute were standing in a bow window, while the Queen and the princess were engaged in working a flowered waistcoat for the simple and easy-going king!

CHAPTER XVII.

WATERLOO PLACE AND HER MAJESTY'S THEATRE.

"Hic alta theatris
Fundamenta locant."—*Virgil,* "*Æn.,*" i.

St. James's Fields in the Time of Charles I.—St. James's Market—The "Mitre Tavern" and Mrs. Oldfield, the Actress—Hannah Lightfoot and her Union with the Prince of Wales (afterwards George III.)—The "Hoop and Bunch of Grapes"—The Criterion Theatre and Restaurant—The "White Bear"—The "Piccadilly Saloon"—The Gallery of Illustration—The Parthenon and Raleigh Clubs—St. Philip's Chapel—Charles Street—The Junior United Service Club—Waterloo Place—Catlin's American Indian Collection—The Guards' Memorial—Her Majesty's Theatre—Supposed Origin of Operatic Performances—The First Opera House and its Struggles—Assumes the Name of "The King's Theatre"—Prohibition of Masquerades—The First Oratorio ever performed in England—Walpole's Criticism upon Vaneschi's Opera of *Fetonte*—Destruction of the First Opera House by Fire—Description of the First Theatre—The Theatre rebuilt—John Braham and Madame Catalani—Management of the Theatre in the Time of George IV.—Reconstruction of the Theatre in 1818—The Italian Opera from a Frenchman's Point of View—Triumphs of the King's Theatre—The Name changed to "Her Majesty's"—The "Omnibus" Row—First Appearance of Jenny Lind—Sims Reeves and Catherine Hayes—The "Black Malibran"—Mdlle. Titiens—Piccolomini and Christine Nilsson—Destruction of the Theatre by Fire in 1867—The New Theatre—The Building advertised for Sale—Messrs. Moody and Sankey's Services.

PREVIOUS to the year 1560, the tract of ground which we are about to traverse, and indeed as far north and north-west as the parish of St. Marylebone, was a vast extent of fields. There were no houses, excepting three or four in the immediate neighbourhood of what is now called Pall

Mall East. In the time of Charles I., the whole of the district was unbuilt upon, and was known by the name of "St. James's Fields." In the middle of these fields stood a solitary dwelling, called "Pickadilly," mentioned by Clarendon, in his "History of the Rebellion," as "a fair house for entertainment and gaming," with handsome gravel walks and shade, and where there was an upper and a lower bowling-green, whither many of the nobility and gentry of the best quality resorted for exercise and recreation. In Charles Knight's "Old London" reference is made to a petition from Colonel Thomas Panton, read in 1671, before the Privy Council, setting forth that the petitioner having been at great charge in purchasing "a parcel of ground lying at Pickadilly," part of it being two bowling-greens fronting the Haymarket, the other lying on the north of the Tennis Court, on which several old houses were standing, and praying for leave to build on this ground, notwithstanding the royal proclamation against building on new foundations within a certain distance of London. No doubt the colonel must have had influential friends about him, for we find that, "in consequence of Sir Christopher Wren's favourable report, he obtained leave to erect houses in Windmill Street, on the east corner towards the Haymarket, and also in the two bowling-greens between the Haymarket and Leicester Fields."

In the reign of Charles II., mention is made of the Hay Market and Hedge Lane; but they were at that time literally lanes, bounded by hedges. In Faithorne's plan of London, published in 1658, no traces of houses are to be found in the north, except a single one, called the Gaming House, at the end next to Piccadilly. In the upper part of this district, on the north side of Jermyn Street, and on the site now partly covered by the Criterion Restaurant and Theatre and Lower Regent Street, a market was established in 1664. Malcolm tells that the market for all sorts of provisions was proclaimed "to be kept in St. James's Fields on Mondays, Wednesdays, and Saturdays; and for all kinds of cattle in the Hay Market, in the parish of St. Martin-in-the-Fields." According to Gay's "Trivia," St. James's Market was famous for its supply of veal. From Pepys we learn that the market owed its foundation to Jermyn, Earl of St. Albans, whose name is still preserved in Jermyn Street.

At the "Mitre Tavern," in the market, the mother of the charming and accomplished actress, Mrs. Oldfield, was living when the latter was quite young. One day the girl was overheard reading a play with so much power and expression, that Sir John Vanbrugh obtained for her an introduction to Rich, the patentee of Covent Garden Theatre, by whom she was engaged. Here she soon made herself a name, and became so popular, that she obtained access to the first circles. She became the mistress of General Churchill, a nephew of the great Duke of Marlborough, by whom she had a son, who married a natural daughter of Sir Robert Walpole, and obtained the rank and precedence of an earl's daughter. In the end Mrs. Oldfield had the honour of a funeral in Westminster Abbey.

In the house which stood at the corner of Market Street, in St. James's Market, at the shop of a linen-draper named Wheeler, lived Hannah Lightfoot, the early flame of King George III., and indeed, if report may be credited, privately married to him. The fair Quakeress—for such was Hannah—is said to have contracted her marriage with royalty in 1759, in Kew Church. She afterwards married a Mr. Axford, and died in obscurity. The story of Hannah Lightfoot has been thoroughly sifted and discussed by Mr. W. J. Thoms in the pages of *Notes and Queries*, the conclusion arrived at leaving little or no doubt as to the legality of her union with the young Prince.

"The 'Hoop and Bunch of Grapes,'" says Mr. Larwood, "was the sign of a public-house in St. Albans Street (now part of Waterloo Place), kept, at the beginning of the present century, by the famous Matthew Skeggs, who obtained his renown from playing, in the character of Signor Bombasto, a concerto on a broomstick at the Haymarket Theatre, adjoining. His portrait was painted by King, a friend of Hogarth, engraved by Houston and published by Skeggs himself."

About the year 1815, some low and mean houses that stood between the market and Pall Mall were demolished, and these were soon afterwards followed by the market itself, in order to form the broad and spacious thoroughfares of Lower Regent Street and Waterloo Place. At the upper or northern end of Lower Regent Street a junction is formed right and left with Piccadilly. In that part of Piccadilly lying to the east is the "Criterion" Restaurant and Theatre. This handsome building, which combines under one roof the advantages of a restaurant on an unusually large scale, reading, billiard, hair-dressing rooms, cigar divan, concert-hall, ball-room, and theatre, was built for Messrs. Spiers and Pond, in 1873, from a design by Mr. Thomas Verity. The sum originally named as the probable cost, exclusive of decorations and fittings, was £25,000, but the actual expense to the proprietors, before the vast establishment was opened, is said to have exceeded £80,000.

The " Criterion " has two façades; the principal one, in Piccadilly, is of Portland stone, decorated in the style of the French Renaissance. The doorway is arched and deeply recessed, the arch being supported by four handsome bronze columns. Figures, beautifully sculptured, representing the seasons, are placed in niches above. The frontage in Jermyn Street is of brick, picked out with Portland stone. The great dining-room, capable of accommodating 200 persons, is on the right of the central vestibule; on the left is the refreshment-buffet, at the south end of which is the smoking-divan. The grand staircase leads to the ball-room, which occupies the entire width of the Piccadilly frontage. The whole interior is richly decorated; mosaics, parquetry, painted frescoes, mirrors, gildings, and carvings, meet the eye in every direction. The upper floor is occupied by kitchens and sculleries. The right-hand entrance in Piccadilly leads to the grill-room, also to the balcony and orchestra stalls of the theatre, while the entrance to the amphitheatre stalls and parterre is from Jermyn Street, the whole theatre being below ground. It will accommodate 800 persons, and is fitted up in the most luxurious manner. It was opened on the 21st of March, 1874, with two new pieces—*An American Lady*, by Mr. H. J. Byron; and *Topsyturveydom*, by Mr. W. S. Gilbert. The company being an excellent one, and principally consisting of popular favourites, and the two authors being equally well and favourably known, the opening night was a triumphant success, giving a favourable augury of its future career. The entertainments since given have been principally of the class known as *opera bouffe*.

The " Criterion " stands on the site of an inn, the " White Bear," which for a century and more was one of the busiest coaching-houses in connection with the west and south-west of England. Mr. Larwood, in his " History of Sign-boards," tells us that at this inn Benjamin West, the future President of the Royal Academy, put up and spent the night on his first arrival in London from America. Here, too, he tells us, died Luke Sullivan, the engraver of some of Hogarth's most famous works, and another engraver, Chatelain—the latter in such poverty, that he was buried, at the expense of friends who had known him in better days, in the poorground attached to St. James's workhouse.

A few doors to the eastward of the " Criterion " stood for many years a house notorious from the commencement of the present century as " The Piccadilly Saloon," a house of refreshment and gambling, which was open nearly all night, and formed a scene of dissipation which, even at that time, was unparalleled in London. Its aristocratic patrons, however, did not protect it from the fate which awaits all such dens sooner or later, and it is now a thing of the past.

On the eastern side of Lower Regent Street is a large building, which till recently bore the name of the " Gallery of Illustration." It was erected from the designs of Mr. Nash, who intended it as a residence for himself. It was used occasionally for dramatic readings, and also for a class of amusements popularly known as " drawing-room entertainments." The northern wing of the building, formerly the Parthenon Club-house, is now the home of the Raleigh Club; the other portion of the edifice (formerly the Gallery of Illustration) has been converted into a restaurant, and bears the name of the " Pall Mall." The long gallery was decorated from a *loggia* of the Vatican at Rome.

St. Philip's Chapel, or, as it is often called, Waterloo Chapel, on the opposite side of the street, was built in 1820 from the designs of Mr. Repton. The tower is a reproduction of the Choragic Monument of Lysicrates, at Athens. The front is adorned with a portico, supported by four Doric columns. The interior has the appearance of a public secular assembly-room rather than of a church, being nearly square, with a double gallery, supported below by heavy piers, and above by Corinthian columns of scagliola. The ceiling is formed of a double cove, and is lighted from above.

Crossing Regent Street, and extending from St. James's Square to the Haymarket, is Charles Street. Here Burke was living in the year 1781, when he received from a poor and friendless young man, named George Crabbe, a letter asking for aid. Burke read the note, and at once responded; asked Crabbe to call on him; read, and admired his verses. " From that hour," writes Mr. Serjeant Burke, " Crabbe was a made man. Burke not only relieved his more pressing necessities, but domesticated him in his own house, introduced him to a large circle of noble and literary friends, afforded him the inestimable advantage of his critical advice, and, having established his poetical reputation to the world, finally crowned the most ardent aspirations of his *protégé* by getting him admitted into the Church." Such deeds of kindness deserve to be recorded to the honour of the great orator.

Here, too, in 1806, the sculptor Chantrey, then quite a young man, was living; and whilst residing here he exhibited some of his early busts.

The Junior United Service Club, of which we have already spoken in our chapter on " Clubland," stands at the corner of Charles Street and Regent Street.

Waterloo Place, which we now enter, was, like Regent Street, built from the designs of Mr. Nash. Some time after the death of the architect, the *New Monthly Magazine* gave the following eulogium on his memory :—" Whether the stranger traverses the splendid line of Regent Street, the Quadrant, and Portland Place, until he reaches the Regent's Park—beautifully disposed, and laid out in walks and groves, ornamented with sheets of water, dotted with elegant villas, and encircled by rows of houses of noble elevation, from classic architectural designs —or takes his way from Waterloo Place towards Somerset House, and sees before him streets, and places, and arcades, occupying the sites of the filthiest courts imaginable, and finds himself in front of the splendid parish church of St. Martin-in-the-Fields—able to admire its beauties, because cleared away from the wretched dwellings by which it was surrounded—we think his first inquiry will be—to whose taste, genius, and enterprise, are these improvements owing ? He will be answered by being told that they are all attributable to the genius, energy, and talent of Mr. Nash, to abuse and ridicule whom was the fashion of the time in which he lived. This is the best answer to the senseless cry raised against him by those whose enmity arose from their jealousy of the estimation in which he was held by the munificent monarch in whose regency and reign these wonderful changes in this part of the metropolis were effected. Mr. Nash is in his grave ; and, standing in the midst of the vast alterations for which we are indebted to him, we feel inclined to say, in the words of Wren's epitaph, *Si monumentum requiris, circumspice.*"

On the eastern side was, in 1851, and for some time afterwards, Mr. Catlin's American Indian Collection, one of the most interesting and successful of the many exhibitions that have been opened in London.

In the centre of Waterloo Place, facing the Duke of York's Column, stands the Guards' Memorial, which was erected from the designs of Mr. John Bell. It consists of a massive granite pedestal, the front of which, some eleven feet from the ground, is occupied by three bronze figures, representing a Grenadier, a Fusilier, and one of the Coldstream Guards, " in their full marching costume, as they fought at Inkerman." These figures are about eight feet high, and behind them are placed their respective flags, thus forming a pyramidal group. The front of the pedestal is inscribed with the word " Crimea." Upon this pedestal rises a smaller one, having upon either side the words " Alma," " Inkerman," " Sebastopol;" whilst

the back of this upper block of granite is ornamented with a pyramidal pile of cannon—the *actual* broken Russian guns, burst and mutilated, as they were found in Sebastopol—having beneath it this inscription :—" To the memory of 2,162 officers and men of the Brigade of Guards who fell during the war with Russia, 1854, 1855, 1856." The whole is surmounted with a bronze figure of Honour, with her arms extended wide, and having in her hands and on her arms wreaths of laurel ; and immediately beneath this figure is inscribed—" Honour to the brave."

Eastward of Waterloo Place stands Her Majesty's Theatre, or, as it is generally called, the Opera House. The building occupies a vast space of ground, with its eastern side in the Haymarket, and extends north and south from Charles Street to Pall Mall.

The species of dramatic performance which we now style an opera, in which the various emotions incidental to the action of the piece are interpreted by the aid of music, vocal and instrumental, is supposed to have originated with the Chinese. Their dramas, almost interminable (a single representation of one being an affair of many nights, and sometimes even of weeks), instead of being declaimed in the natural voice, have been, from time immemorial, delivered in a carefully intoned recitative, mingled with songs. The first work of this description produced in Europe was *The Conversion of St. Paul*, composed by an Italian artist, Francisco Barbarini, and performed in Rome in 1470. England was at that period by no means a musical nation; and it was not until about the commencement of the eighteenth century that, as Colley Cibber writes, " the Italian opera began first to steal into England, but in as rude a disguise as possible, in a lame hobbling translation, with metre out of measure to its original notes, sung by our own unskilful voices, with graces misapplied to almost every sentiment and action."

In 1704 a subscription was started by Sir John Vanbrugh to build a theatre for this special purpose, and £3,000 was raised in shares of £100 from each of thirty persons, who, in addition to their interest in the building, were to have an admission ticket for life to all public entertainments given therein. The foundation-stone was inscribed with the words, " Little Whig," in honour of Lady Sunderland, the most celebrated Whig toast and beauty of her day. The theatre was opened April 9th, 1705, with an Italian opera, *The Triumph of Love*, which was so far from being a " triumph," that it was withdrawn after having been performed three times before a mere handful of spectators. Sir John Vanbrugh and his associate Congreve, the dramatist, were not long in retiring from a management so little profitable to themselves, and the theatre was transferred to a Mr. McSwiney. The first Italian singer who made his mark on these boards was Valentini, who, on his first appearance, sang through his part in his own language, the rest of the company singing in English! The effect must have been grotesque in the extreme, and may partially account

It appears that this species of entertainment has never been truly popular in England. The first masquerade given in London upon the foreign plan, uniting, after the Venetian fashion, elegance with rude mirth and revelry, was given by Henrietta, the queen of Charles I.; but, as it was unfortunately fixed for a Sunday, the populace in front of the Banqueting House, Whitehall, loudly complained of the profanation of the Lord's Day. A scuffle

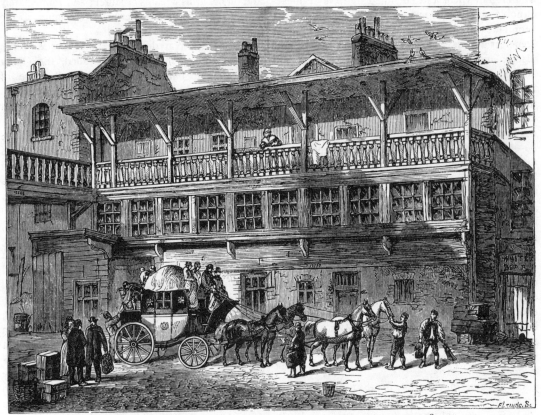

THE YARD OF THE OLD "WHITE BEAR" INN, PICCADILLY, ABOUT 1820.
From an Original Drawing by Shepherd, in the Crace Collection. (*See page* 208.)

for the fact that, during the first twenty-five years of its existence, the Opera House was but very poorly supported, and was frequently made a subject for satire in the *Spectator* and *Tatler*. Under these discouraging circumstances a subscription was raised for its support, and £50,000 was thus obtained, King George I. contributing £1,000 (afterwards continued annually): from this time the theatre assumed the name of "The King's."

In 1729, says Hughson, the Grand Jury of Middlesex "presented" the fashionable and wicked diversion called masquerade, and "particularly the contriver and carrier on of masquerades at the King's Theatre in the Hay Market, in order to be punished according to law."

ensued between the soldiers and the people, in which half a dozen of the latter and two or three of the former were killed.

The most splendid masquerade ever known in England, as we learn from Colburn's "Kalendar of Amusements," took place at the Opera House in 1717, and was provided by Mr. Heidegger. It was allowed to exceed anything that had been known in Italy or any other country. The masquerades formerly given at the Pantheon were very celebrated. In 1783 Delphini, the famous clown, got up a grand masquerade there, in honour of the birthday and coming of age of the Prince of Wales. The tickets were sold at three guineas each, yet Delphini was a loser by the speculation.

In 1724 the Bishop of London preached a sermon against masquerades, which made such an impression, that orders were issued for their discontinuance. After the lapse of some years they were again introduced. Some excellent reasons for the renewal of the prohibited amusement appeared in the *Morning Chronicle*, March 7, 1770. We have already spoken of masquerades in our account of Mrs. Cornelys' house in Soho Square.

The first oratorio ever performed in England

Fetonte. "It is," writes he, "in what they call the French manner, but about as like it as my Lady Pomfret's hash of plural persons and singular verbs was to Italian. They sing to jigs, and dance to church-music. 'Phaeton' is run away with by horses that go a foot's pace, like the 'Electress's' coach, with such long traces, that the postilion was in one street and the coachman in another. Then comes 'Jupiter' with a farthing candle, to light a squib and a half; and that they call fireworks. 'Regi-

PICCADILLY CIRCUS, FROM COVENTRY STREET.

was Handel's *Esther*, which was produced at this theatre in 1732, and followed, later in the same year, by his *Acis and Galatea*. The opera must, by this time, have made vast strides in the estimation of the public, as in the year 1734 we find the famous Farinelli—at whom the newspapers of the day directed many a pointed sarcasm—receiving for the season a salary of £15,000, as well as a free benefit, which realised an additional profit of £2,000. Such, however, is the uncertain tenure of the public favour, that scarcely two years later Farinelli had the mortification of singing to a house containing but £35.

Horace Walpole, in a letter written in 1747, gives a piquant criticism upon Vaneschi's opera of

nello,' the first man, is so old and so tall, that he seems to have been growing ever since the invention of operas. The first woman has had her mouth let out to show a fine set of teeth, but it lets out too much bad voice at the same time. Lord Middlesex, for his great prudence in having provided such very tractable steeds to 'Prince Phaeton's' car, is going to be Master of the Horse to the Prince of Wales ; and, for his excellent economy in never paying the performers, is likely to continue in the Treasury."

In the year 1789 the usual fate of theatres befell the Opera House, which was burnt to the ground on the night of the 17th of June. The fire was supposed to have been the work of an incendiary, and suspicion attached to Pietro Car-nivalli, the leader of the orchestra, who owed a grudge to Signor Ravelli, the manager, for whose benefit the performance was to have taken place the evening after the catastrophe. The company were at rehearsal when the fire broke out, and the wife of Signor Ravelli owed her life to the intrepidity of the firemen. In this conflagration the favourite opera of *La Laconda*, by Paesiello, was destroyed—score, separate parts, and all. It is said that Mazzinghi, who then presided at the harpsichord, undertook to reproduce from memory the whole of the instrumental accompaniments, and this he did successfully. There still exists a print of the original building, taken from a drawing made on the spot by W. Capon, published in Smith's " Historical and Literary Antiquities." It shows the front of the edifice, much as it must have been when built by Sir John Vanbrugh, in the reign of George I. It was a dull plain building, not unlike a Quaker's meeting-house. The front was " of red brick, rusticated with good gauged work." It had three circular-headed doorways, with three windows of a similar shape above; in the second floor, instead of windows, were three oblong recesses of a very heavy character, and the roof was covered with black glazed tiles. The front was thirty-four feet in width. Over the entrance-hall was " Ridant's Fencing Academy," shown by a conspicuous notice in the print. On the piers below are seen some handbills of the time, including the name of Signor Rauzzini, and of Signora Carnivalli, the wife of the man whose hand is supposed to have set fire to the theatre.

The first stone of the succeeding structure, the entrance to which is shown on page 216, was laid in April, 1790, by the Earl of Buckingham-shire, the architect being Michael Novosielski. The new theatre commenced its career under weighty liabilities, for which it was by no means fairly responsible, and of which there will be occasion to speak more in detail in our history of the Pantheon. Chancery or the Insolvent Court generally terminated the career of its first half-dozen managers, as, in addition to its hopeless load of debt, the current expenses were so enormous as to swallow up all the receipts.

The great English tenor, John Braham—as mentioned in our notice of the St. James's Theatre—made his *début* here in 1796, and rose at one step to the height of public favour. The year 1806 was distinguished by two great events in the history of this theatre—the introduction of Mozart's music, never before performed in England, and the *début* of Madame Catalani. This marvellous singer, the

versatility of whose talents rendered her equally admirable in a tragic or comic *rôle*, received the sum of £15,000 for the season of 1809, her benefit and the various concerts which she gave amounting to £11,000 more.

Catalani is pronounced by Captain Gronow, who well recollected her, the greatest vocalist that he ever heard. He writes: " In her youth she was the finest singer in Europe, and she was much sought after by all the great people during her *séjour* in London. She was extremely handsome, and was considered a model as wife and mother. Catalani was very fond of money, and would never sing unless paid beforehand. She was asked, with her husband, to pass some time at Stowe, where a numerous but select party had been invited; and Madame Catalani, being asked to sing soon after dinner, willingly complied. When the day of her departure came, her husband placed in the hands of the Marquis of Buckingham the following little billet—' For seventeen songs, seventeen hundred pounds.' This large sum was paid at once without hesitation, proving that Lord Buckingham was a refined gentleman in every sense of the word."

" I visited Catalani in town," writes Cyrus Redding, " and always found her the same elegant and amiable creature, with the same sweet simple smile and modest manners. She stood unrivalled in her profession. As an actress she was by no means remarkable; yet she looked so attractive on the boards, that the audience forgave any little fault of action. And then her voice was transcendent. She sang in a private room more charmingly than in the theatre. I had known her previously. Of all the females attached to the opera, before or since, that I have seen, she pleased me most. She was a kind generous creature, without a particle of pretension, an excellent mother, and exemplary wife, wedded to a narrow-minded man, who sometimes got her an ill name from his avarice. He managed all her money transactions, and used to call her ' ma poule d'or.' I hear her now singing ' God save the King,' with her heavenly voice and pretty foreign accent, set off by a person, one of the sweetest on the stage I ever saw. For mind she was not remarkable; I never met with a singer of either sex that was so. There was an openness and candour about her quite charming. ' Monsieur Redaing, I speak no language propre. I speak one Babylonish tongue. I speak not my own tongue, nor French, nor your tongue propre.'

" Her husband, before Junot entered Lisbon, used to blaze away in the pit of the opera in a dashing French uniform, speculating upon his future *poule d'or*, which to him she afterwards most fully proved. He was rarely invited with his wife to the houses of people of consideration. A person I knew, half a Roman, said one day to Catalani, 'My dear half-countrywoman, how did you come to marry Valabreque?'—'I will tell you. I was at Lisbon; the Portuguese are fond of music. Great men, princes, and counts talk to me of love, and a number of fine things, but none of them talk of marrying. M. Valabreque talked of marriage—I marry M. Valabreque.'"

Captain Gronow writes thus in his "Anecdotes and Reminiscences:"—"When George IV. was Regent, this theatre was conducted on a very different system from that which now prevails. Some years previous to the period to which I refer, no one could obtain a box, or a ticket for the pit, without a voucher from one of the lady patronesses, who, in 1805, were the Duchesses of Marlborough, Devonshire, and Bedford, Lady Carlisle, and some others. In their day, after the singing and ballet were over, the company used to retire into the concert-room, where a ball took place, accompanied by refreshments and a supper. There all the rank and fashion of England were assembled, on a sort of neutral ground. At a later period the management of the Opera House fell into the hands of Mr. Waters, when it became less difficult to obtain admittance; but the strictest etiquette was still kept up as regarded the dress of the gentlemen, who were only admitted with knee-buckles, ruffles, and *chapeau-bras*. If there happened to be a drawing-room, the ladies would appear in their court dresses as well as the gentlemen; and on all occasions the audience of Her Majesty's Theatre was stamped with aristocratic elegance. In the boxes of the first tier might have been seen the daughters of the Duchess of Argyle, four of England's beauties; in the next box were the equally lovely Marchioness of Stafford and her daughter, Lady Elizabeth Gower, now the Duchess of Norfolk; not less remarkable were Lady Harrowby and her daughters, Lady Susan and Lady Mary Ryder. The peculiar type of female beauty which these ladies so attractively exemplified is such as can be met with only in the British isles: the full round, soul-inspired eye of Italy, and the dark hair of the sunny South, often combined with that exquisitely pearly complexion which seems to be concomitant with humidity and fog. You could scarcely gaze upon the peculiar beauty to which I refer without being as much charmed with its kindly expression as with its physical loveliness."

The theatre was reconstructed, in 1818, by Messrs. Nash and Repton, with great improvements. The interior was the first in England to be modelled in the horse-shoe shape, so favourable both for sight and sound. The dimensions were within a few feet of those of the Grand Opera House at Milan. The length from the front of the curtain to the back of the boxes was 102 feet; the extreme width, 75 feet; the stage measured 60 feet in length and 80 in width. The edifice was of brick and Bath stone, with a bas-relief on the Haymarket front representing Apollo and the Muses. It was in this year that the music of Rossini was first presented to the English public.

A French nobleman remarks, in a letter to an English friend, in 1823—"I must acknowledge that the whole universe does not offer a more splendid *coup d'œil* than that which is presented by the Italian Opera in London on a Saturday night. The beauty of the theatre, the richness of the decorations, the loveliness of the women, the variety and brilliancy of their dresses and jewels, the blaze of light, the number of distinguished characters who are often found in the ranks of the audience, the general appearance of wealth and prosperity, and the total absence of all features of an opposite kind, form altogether such a picture of gaiety and magnificence as is indeed unrivalled."

From 1824 to 1840 the history of the King's Theatre is that of a series of triumphs. Pasta, Veluti (the wonderful male soprano), Sontag, Grisi, Rubini, Tamburini, Lablache, and Mario successively appeared upon the stage; the five last named, who were all in their zenith about the same time, forming a brilliant constellation of talent unequalled before or since.

In 1837 the name of the theatre was changed to "Her Majesty's," in honour of the accession of Queen Victoria. The year 1841 witnessed the "Omnibus" row, almost as famous in history as the O. P. riots. The manager, Laporte, who had long been at issue with several of the talented quintette, who were the glory of his establishment, and who had formed a *clique* against him, had declined the further services of Tamburini. His choice of a victim was determined by the fact that he was enabled to replace the great baritone by Coletti, a singer who had achieved a great success at La Scala. But Laporte had miscalculated his power. Madame Grisi, at whose fair shrine all the *jeunesse dorée* of that day bowed down, induced her aristocratic admirers to organise a disturbance, which burst out on the appearance of Coletti in the place of Tamburini. The omnibus boxes were crowded with lords of high degree, foremost among whom was a prince of the blood; and Coletti was saluted with yells, hisses, and cries of "Off, off!" "Tamburini!" "Laporte!" shouted with all the force of aristocratic lungs; and finally the whole party, headed by the scion of royalty, leaped upon the stage, and the curtain fell on their shouts of "Victory." Negotiations were subsequently entered into with Tamburini, through the good offices of Count D'Orsay, and the discarded baritone was persuaded to overlook the affront and resume his place.

This battle royal is handed down to posterity in the "Ingoldsby Legends," as "A Row in an Omnibus (Box):"—

> " Dol-drum, the manager, sits in his chair,
>   With a gloomy brow and dissatisfied air;
>   And he says, as he slaps his hand on his knee,
>   ' I'll have nothing to do with Fiddle-de-dee.
>   Though Fiddle-de-dee sings loud and clear,
>   And his tones are sweet, yet his terms are dear.
>   The glove won't fit !
>   The deuce a bit—
>   I shall give an engagement to Fal-de-ral-tit !'
>
> " The prompter bow'd, and he went to his stall;
>   And the green baize rose at the prompter's call ;
>   And Fal-de-ral-tit sang fol-de-rol-lol ;
>   But scarce had he done,
>   When a row begun ;
>   Such a noise was never heard under the sun.
>   ' Fiddle-de-dee,
>   Where is he ?
>   He's the *artiste* whom we all want to see.
>   Dol-drum ! Dol-drum !
>   Bid the manager come !
>   It's a scandalous thing to exact such a sum
>   From boxes and gallery, stalls and pit,
>   And then fob us off with Fal-de-ral-tit !' "

The manager, being thus peremptorily summoned by the audience—

> " Smooth'd his brow,
>   As he well knew how ;
> And he walk'd on, and made a most elegant bow ;
> And he paused, and he smiled, and advanced to the
> In his opera hat, and his opera tights.　　　[lights,
> ' Ladies and gentlemen,' then said he,
> ' Pray what may you please to want with me? '
>   ' Fiddle-de-dee !
>   Fiddle-de-dee !'
>
> " Folks of all sorts, and of every degree,
>   Snob, and snip, and haughty grandee,
>   Duchesses, countesses, fresh from their tea,
>   And shopmen who had only come there for a spree,
>   Halloo'd, and hooted, and roared with glee—
>   ' Fiddle-de-dee,
>   None but he !
>   Subscribe to his terms, whatever they be !
>   Agree, agree, or you'll very soon see,
>   In a brace of shakes, we'll get up an O. P. !' "

M. Laporte, who must have had rather a hard time of it among his imperious *troupe*, resigned his uneasy throne in 1842, and was succeeded by Mr. Lumley, who had long been his colleague.

The year 1847 was an eventful one for Her Majesty's Theatre, which had been for more than half a century the only temple of Italian opera in London. Then took place the secession of Grisi, Mario, Persiani, and Tamburini, with the mighty Costa, to the new Opera in Covent Garden ; then began the struggle to solve the problem whether two Italian Opera Houses could be made to pay in London—a vexed question, which seems hardly settled even yet.

The same year (1847) witnessed also the first appearance of Jenny Lind, who had been persuaded to break her engagement with Mr. Bunn, the lessee of Drury Lane, in favour of Mr. Lumley. No words can describe the *furore* excited by this far-famed lady from the night of her *début* until the time when she finally quitted the stage. As much as £30 was frequently paid for a stall on a "Jenny Lind night." As Lumley tells us in his "Reminiscences:"—" The newspapers teemed with descriptions of wild scenes of ' crushing, crowding, and squeezing ; of ladies fainting in the pressure, and even of gentlemen carried out senseless ; of torn dresses, and evening coats reduced to rags.' " These triumphs were, however, partially counterbalanced by the result of an action brought by Mr. Bunn against the *prima donna*, for her breach of contract with him. He laid the damages at £10,000, and gained a verdict for £2,500—a loss which fell entirely on Mr. Lumley, who had undertaken to bear the vacillating fair one scathless. The operatic career, however, of the celebrated songstress was as brief as it was brilliant ; for on the 18th of May, 1849, Jenny Lind made her last appearance upon any stage, as "Alice," in *Roberto il Diavolo*.

In 1850 the chief stars of the Italian opera at Her Majesty's were native artists, Mr. Sims Reeves and Miss Catherine Hayes. An attempt was made in the same year to produce a sensation through the introduction of the *Black Malibran*. The lady bearing this pretentious title was Donna Maria Martinez, a negress, who appeared in a *divertissement* called *Les Delices du Serail*, in which she sang quaint Spanish melodies, accompanying herself on the guitar. " Her songs," writes Lumley, " were full of original charm, her execution excellent, her voice sweet, pure, and true ; but the whole performance was small almost to meagreness, and, although it might well be regarded as a piquant musical curiosity, it failed in any real power of attraction." In 1852 Mdlle. Titiens, the only worthy successor of Grisi in such parts as " Norma," " Lucrezia Borgia," or " Semiramide," appeared as " Valentina " in *Les Huguenots*.

The year 1856 produced another " great sensation" in the young, charming, and high-born Marietta Piccolomini, of whom Lumley writes:— " Once more frantic crowds struggled in the lobbies of the theatre ; once more dresses were torn and hats crushed in the conflict. In what lay the charm of this new fascinator of all hearts ? It would be difficult to tell, although this much is undeniable, that she exercised an almost magical power over the masses. The statistics of a ' treasury' are indisputable facts. Her voice was a high and pure soprano, with all the attraction of youth and freshness, not wide in range, sweet rather than powerful, and not gifted with any perfection of flexibility. Her vocalisation was far from being distinguished by its correctness or excellence of school ; to musicians she appeared a clever amateur, but never a really great artist." This fascinating little lady created an equal *furore* in Paris, yet the French criticisms on her performance seem to agree with those of Lumley—as, for example, the following :—" Mdlle. Piccolomini sings with infinite charm, but is not a *cantatrice*. She acts with talent, but is not an actress. She is a problem—an enigma ! "

Pecuniary difficulties having terminated Mr. Lumley's long managerial career, Mr. E. T. Smith became the lessee of Her Majesty's Theatre in 1860, to be succeeded, two years afterwards, by Mr. Mapleson.

Mdlle. Christine Nilsson appeared in 1867 with great success ; perhaps the only *artiste* who has ever succeeded in realising to the full the poet's exquisite conception of " Marguerite," in *Faust*. This triumph was the last reserved for the old " King's Theatre," which was once more destroyed by fire on the 6th of December, 1867. At the time of the catastrophe the Earl of Dudley, as assignee of Mr. Lumley, was the lessee under the Crown, on a lease terminating in 1891. In 1862 Lord Dudley had sub-let the theatre to Mr. Mapleson for twenty-one years, at a yearly rental of £8,000, payable in advance. The earl was fully insured ; but Mr. Mapleson, who unfortunately was not so, was a loser to the extent of £10,000. The great organ, valued at £800, the chandeliers, scenery, costumes, interior fittings, the whole of the musical library, besides several invaluable manuscripts of Rossini, were all destroyed. The origin of the fire was never ascertained.

Lord Dudley having decided upon rebuilding the theatre without loss of time, the site was cleared early in 1868, and the works were commenced at midsummer. The architect was Mr. Charles Lee, and the contractors Messrs. George Trollope and Sons, who undertook to complete their task in forty weeks, under a penalty of £1,000 for every following week in case of failure. This promise was so strictly fulfilled, that before the end of March, 1869, the new theatre, complete at all points, at a cost of about £50,000, was in a condition to open its doors to the public. The old edifice having been considered deficient in stage accommodation, care had been taken in the present case to increase the size of the stage, which had been effected, as it was stated, without materially lessening the area of the auditorium. There are four tiers of boxes in front of the stage, and five tiers on either side ; the space above the fourth tier in front being occupied by amphitheatre stalls, with a spacious amphitheatre behind them. As in the case of Covent Garden Theatre, the partitions between the boxes are constructed in such a manner as to be easily removed, so as to form the ordinary dress circle of a theatre, if required. Every possible precaution has been adopted to reduce the risk by fire, throughout the whole of the building, to a minimum. It is calculated that the new theatre will accommodate about 1,800 for operatic, and 2,500 for dramatic performances. So much stress had been laid upon the completion of the new edifice by the contractors before the commencement of the opera season of 1869, that both the public and the press were daily speculating upon the probable date of the opening night ; when the *Times* of the 24th of March, 1869, published a notice from the " Directors " of Her Majesty's Theatre, to the effect that no performances would be given there during that season. Great was the surprise and consternation at this announcement, and higher still rose popular amazement when the solution of the enigma leaked out by degrees. The construction of the interior is such that, the greater part of the boxes and stalls being held on lease, the expenses must necessarily be in excess of the receipts, even in the case of a full attendance every night. In 1874 the theatre was advertised for sale by public auction ; but it does not appear that any sale was effected. In 1875 the theatre was hired for the " revival " services of Messrs. Moody and Sankey, and since 1876 it has been under the management of Mr. Mapleson, and has been occasionally used for the performance of English, Italian, and German Opera.

Even the Italian Opera House has had its " ups and downs "—its days of popularity and the reverse. It went out of fashion, through the caprice of the day, in the reign of George II., the nobility supporting their own favourite house in Lincoln's Inn Fields. What the Court then patronised was but in ill odour with the rest of the aristocracy.

"The opera, on its first introduction into England," writes a well-known author, "divided the wits, literati, and musicians of the age. By those esteemed the best judges, the English language was thought too rough and inharmonious for the music of the opera ; and by men of common sense a drama in a foreign and unknown tongue was considered very absurd. However, Addison, who opposed the Italian opera on the London stage, wrote the English of *Rosamond*, which seemed an attempt to reconcile the discordant opinions. But this, though a beautiful poem, is said by Dr. Burney to have shown Addison's total ignorance of the first principles of music."

ENTRANCE TO THE OLD OPERA HOUSE, 1800.

CHAPTER XVIII.

THE HAYMARKET.

"From the Haymarket canting rogues in grain."—"*Rejected Addresses.*"

The Old Market for Hay and Straw—A Seller of 'Sea Coal"—Foreign Ambassadors in Peril—Rogues "in Grain"—Addison in a Garret—Thackeray on Addison—Sir John Suckling's Heroine—Tiddy Dol and his Gingerbread—Lord Eldon's Pint of Wine—Dr. Wolcott and Madame Mara—Michael Kelly's Wine Vaults—Assault on Sir John Coventry—Baretti: his Trial for Murder—Shows in the Haymarket—The Animal Comedians—The Cat's Opera—O'Brien, the Irish Giant—Weeks's Museum—The "Little Theatre in the Haymarket:" its History—Foote : his "Cat Music"—Anecdotes of Foote—"Romeo" Coates—The Theatre in Colman's Hands—A Sad Accident—Reconstruction of the Theatre by Nash—Liston's Appearance in *Paul Pry*—Subsequent Managers and Actors at the Haymarket: Mr. Benjamin Webster, Mr. Buckstone, Mr. Charles Mathews—"Lord Dundreary."

THE broad street denominated the Haymarket, connecting Pall Mall East with the eastern end of Piccadilly, was a place for the sale of farm-produce as far back as the reign of Elizabeth ; and in Aggas's plan it appears under its present name It was then evidently a rural spot, as there were hedgerows on either side, and few indications of habitations nearer than the "village of Charing."

At that time, as may be gathered from an inspection of the plan referred to, the air was so pure and clear, that the washerwomen dried their linen by spreading it upon the grass in the fields, as nearly as possible on the spot where now stands Her Majesty's Theatre. Down to the reign of found to violate a part of the Charter granted by Edward III. to the City of London, and was accordingly annulled. At the beginning of the eighteenth century we find the Crown, however, leasing the tolls of the Haymarket for ninety-nine years to one Derick Stork. The market for hay and straw, three

JOSEPH ADDISON. *From an Authentic Portrait.* (*See page* 218)

William III. it was the public highway, in which carts loaded with hay and straw were allowed to stand for sale toll-free; but in 1692 the street was paved, and a tax levied on the carts according to their loads. But this was not the first market held here; for, as far back as the reign of Charles II., John Harvey and another person received a grant empowering them, and their heirs after them, to hold markets here for the sale of oxen and sheep on Mondays and Wednesdays; but the grant was

times a week, continued to be held here as lately as the reign of George IV., when it was removed to Cumberland Market, near Regent's Park.

In 1708 Hatton speaks of the Haymarket as "a very spacious and public street, in length 340 yards, where is a great market for hay and straw;" and it is described by Malcolm in 1807 as "an excellent street, 1,020 feet in length, of considerable breadth, and remarkably dry, occasioned by the descent from Piccadilly."

Apart from the obstruction arising from the heavy-laden carts, which on certain days occupied the middle of the street, the Haymarket, and especially its eastern side, is described by Malcolm as a " pleasant promenade ; " and he speaks of that side as being occupied by several eminent tradesmen's houses and the " Theatre Royal," of which we shall have to say more presently.

On the opposite, or western side, he adds, is the " King's Theatre for Italian operas," which he describes as " fronted by a stone basement in rustic work, with the *commencement* of a very superb building of the Doric order, consisting of three pillars, two windows, an entablature, pediment, and balustrade." " This," he adds, " if it had been continued, would have contributed considerably to the splendour of London ; but the unlucky fragment is fated to stand as a foil to the vile and absurd edifice of brick pieced to it, which I have not patience to describe." How little could he anticipate the future glories of the Italian opera on this very spot !

One of the earliest tradesmen in the Haymarket appears to have been a coal-merchant, or, as he was then styled, a vendor of sea-coal. A " token " used by him is in the British Museum ; it bears this inscription—" Nathanil Robins, at the Sea-coale seller, 1666." Reverse—" Hay Markett, in Piccadilla, his half-penny." About half-way down, on the east side, at the south-west corner of James Street, and on the site of the building now known as Clarence Chambers, stood till very recently a large house which dated from the time of Charles II. ; tradition says that it was frequented by that monarch and the Duke of York, who used to walk through it to the Tennis Court at the back.

During the riots which ensued on the accession of William and Mary to the throne vacated by James II., the house of the minister of the Duke of Florence, which was in this street, had a narrow escape of being burnt and sacked by the mob, as was also that of the Spanish ambassador. Sir Henry Ellis, in his second series of " Original Letters," quotes one from an eye-witness, dated December 13, 1688, who describes the scene, the " train-bands coming up only just in time to save the house from destruction, and that only after the officer at their head being shot through the back." The attack, however, was renewed a day or two afterwards, when Macaulay tells us that the house above mentioned was destroyed by the infuriated mob, who paraded the streets, almost unchecked, with oranges on the top of their drawn swords and naked pikes. " One precious box," he adds, " the Tuscan minister was able to save from the marauders. It contained some volumes of memoirs written in the hand of King James himself."

The authors of the " Rejected Addresses," in their imitation of Crabbe, as shown in the line quoted as a motto for this chapter, would seem to give a bad name to the Haymarket and its inhabitants, on the score of moral character, if we are to take literally the expression " rogues in grain." But if the meaning of the adjective " canting " as applied to them is to be understood in its ordinary sense, some explanation of it is certainly required ; for we never heard of the Haymarket assuming even the appearance of rigid virtue.

In a garret in this street, literally up " three pair of stairs," was living Joseph Addison, when he was waited on by the Hon. H. Boyle, Chancellor of the Exchequer under Lord Godolphin, and requested to write a poem on the battle of Blenheim. The Whig hack jumped at the offer, and penned " The Campaign," which led to his immediate appointment as a Commissioner of Appeals, and to his subsequent advancement by the Whig party. Unfortunately, it is impossible, by the help of letters or of the parish rate-books, to identify the house in which Addison actually lived here ; for though Pope visited the house for that purpose, and " made a note of it," saying to his companion, " In this garret Addison wrote his 'Campaign,'" yet he has forgotten to record its exact whereabouts. D'Israeli, in his " Curiosities of Literature," in noticing this incident, adds—" Nothing less than a strong feeling impelled the poet to ascend this garret—it was a consecrated spot to his eye ; and certainly a curious instance of the power of genius contrasted with its miserable locality! Addison, whose mind had fought through 'a campaign' in a garret, could he have called about him 'the pleasures of imagination,' had probably planned a house of literary repose, where all parts would have been in harmony with his mind. Such residences of men of genius have been enjoyed by some ; and the vivid descriptions which they have left us convey something of the delightfulness which charmed their studious repose."

Thackeray, in his own peculiar manner, thus deals with this incident in Addison's career :—" At thirty-three years of age that most distinguished wit, scholar, and gentleman was without a profession and an income. His book of ' Travels ' had failed ; his ' Dialogue on Medals ' had no particular success ; his Latin verses, even though reported the best since Virgil, or Statius, at any rate, had not brought him a Government place ; and Addison was living up two shabby pair of stairs in the Haymarket, in a poverty over which old Samuel Johnson rather chuckles, when in these shabby rooms an emissary from Government and fortune came and found him. A poem was wanted about the Duke of Marlborough's victory of Blenheim. Would Mr. Addison write one? Mr. Boyle, afterwards Lord Carleton, took back to Lord Treasurer Godolphin the reply that Mr. Addison would. When the poem had reached a certain stage, it was carried to Godolphin; and the last lines which he read were these :—

> " 'But oh, my muse ! what numbers wilt thou find
> To sing the furious troops in battle join'd?
> Methinks I hear the drum's tumultuous sound
> The victor's shouts and dying groans confound ;
> The dreadful burst of cannon rend the skies,
> And all the thunders of the battle rise.
> 'Twas then great Marlborough's mighty soul was proved,
> That in the shock of charging hosts unmov'd,
> Amidst confusion, horror, and despair,
> Examined all the dreadful scenes of war,
> In peaceful thought the field of death surveyed,
> To fainting squadrons lent the timely aid,
> Inspired repulsed battalions to engage,
> And taught the doubtful battle where to rage.
> So when an angel by Divine command,
> With rising tempests shakes a guilty land,
> Such as of late o'er pale Britannia passed,
> Calm and serene he drives the furious blast ;
> And, pleased th' Almighty's orders to perform,
> Rides on the whirlwind and directs the storm.' "

" Addison," continues Thackeray, " left off at a good moment. That simile was pronounced to be one of the greatest ever produced in poetry. That angel, that good angel, flew off with Mr. Addison, and landed him in the place of Commissioner of Appeals ! . . . . In the following year Mr. Addison went to Hanover with Lord Halifax, and the year after was made Under-Secretary of State. Oh ! angel-visits ! you come 'few and far between' to literary gentlemen's lodgings ! Your wings seldom quiver even at second-floor windows now ! "

The " Hay Market " originally stretched down to Charing Cross ; for Northumberland House was really the scene of the wedding of the young lady so prettily celebrated in the cavalier song of Sir John Suckling, in which occur the oft-quoted lines :—

> " Her feet beneath her petticoat
> Like little mice stole in and out
> As if they fear'd the light ;
> But oh ! she dances such a way !
> No sun upon an Easter day
> Is half so fine a sight."

The place is identified by the second verse, which runs thus :—

> " At Charing Cross, hard by the way,
> Where we (thou know'st) do sell our hay,
> There is a house," &c.

Among the eccentric characters who had their haunts in and about the Haymarket, was " Tiddy

Dol," the celebrated vendor of ginger-bread and the king of itinerant dealers in such wares, who figures in Hogarth's picture of the "Idle Apprentice" at Tyburn. His proper name was Ford ; and Mr. Frost, in his " Old Showmen," records the fact that he was so well-known a character, that once, being missed from his usual stand in the Haymarket on the occasion of a visit which he paid to a country fair, a "catch-penny" * account of his alleged murder was printed, and sold in the streets by thousands.

But in spite of its alleged production of " rogues in grain," we find that, in the reigns of Anne and of George I., the Haymarket was inhabited by a few of " the quality." Thus, Lord Sackville was born in 1716 in the Haymarket, where his father, he is careful to tell us, then resided.

Cyrus Redding tells us that he well remembered Lord Eldon often stealing into the " George Coffee House " at the top of the Haymarket, to get a pint of wine, as Lady Eldon did not permit him to enjoy it in peace at home. Redding did not like Eldon, either as a Tory or as a man. " His words," he writes, " were no index of his real feelings. He had a sterile soul for all things earthly except money, doubts, and the art of drawing briefs."

The Haymarket is said to have been the scene of the meeting between Dr. Wolcott (" Peter Pindar ") and Madame Mara, with reference to the sale of the manuscript of the song, "Hope told a Flattering Tale," which the doctor had written expressly for Madame Mara, and which she had sung for the first time at one of her own benefits. The next day she sold the manuscript. The doctor, it appears, had already done the same, and the two purchasers, after a long dispute, which neither had the power to settle, agreed to wait on Mara, and solicit her interference. She consented ; and, as she was going in search of Dr. Wolcott, he happened here to cross her path. He had already heard of the circumstance, and, like the *prima donna*, was not disposed to refund the money he had received. " What is to be done? " said Mara. " Cannot you say you were intoxicated when you sold it? " " Cannot you say the same of yourself? " replied the satirist ; " one story would be believed as soon as the other."

Dr. Wolcott, whose fondness for liquor of all kinds was notorious, might possibly at the time have been making his way to the house of Michael Kelly, the once popular singer and composer, who was in business in this street as a wine merchant. The singer had written over his door in conspicuous letters—" Michael Kelly, Composer of Music and

Importer of Wine." Sheridan, it is said, suggested the following alteration—"'Michael Kelly, Importer of Music and Composer of Wine;' for," observed the wit, "none of his music is original, and all his wine is, since he makes it himself." Sheridan's favourite haunt at this time, it may be remarked, was the "One Tun Tavern" in Jermyn Street, close by.

Hard by was the scene of the famous assault on Sir John Coventry, which occasioned the passing of the "Coventry Act," Sir John being waylaid here on his way to or from his lodgings, and having his nose slit by some young men of high rank for an ill-timed, and perhaps ill-judged, reflection on the theatrical amours of his sovereign.

This episode of Sir John Coventry is mentioned by Sir Walter Scott, in his "Life of Dryden," as a parallel to the assault on that poet by hired ruffians in Rose Street, which we have already mentioned. He observes, that "in the age of the second Charles, a high and chivalrous sense of honour was esteemed Quixotic, and that the Civil War had left traces of ferocity in the manners and sentiments of the people. Encounters where the assailants took all advantages of number and weapons were as frequent, and were held as honourable, as regular duels." The assault on Sir John Coventry, he adds, "caused the famous statute against maiming and wounding, called the 'Coventry Act;' an act highly necessary, since so far did our ancestors' ideas of manly forbearance differ from ours, that Killigrew introduces the hero of one of his comedies, a cavalier and the fine gentleman of the piece, as lying in wait for and slashing the face of a poor courtesan who had cheated him."

On the 3rd of October, 1769, as we learn from Boswell's "Life of Johnson," another assault of a very similar nature to the above took place here. It appears that Mr. Baretti, the author of the well-known "Italian Dictionary," was going hastily up the street, when he was accosted by a woman, who behaving with great rudeness, he was provoked to give her a blow on the hand; upon which three men immediately interfering and endeavouring to push him from the pavement, with a view to throw him into a puddle, he was alarmed for his safety, and rashly struck one of them with a knife (which he constantly wore for the purpose of cutting fruit and sweetmeats), and gave him a wound, of which he died the next day. Baretti was arraigned at the Old Bailey for murder, and among the numerous witnesses called to give evidence as to character, appeared Dr. Johnson himself. This, his biographer supposes, was the only time in his life that the doctor ever appeared as a witness in a court of justice. "Never," he adds, "did such a constellation of genius enlighten the awful Sessions-house, emphatically called Justice-hall; there were Mr. Burke, Mr. Garrick, Mr. Beauclerk, and Dr. Johnson: and undoubtedly their favourable testimony had due weight with the court and jury. Johnson gave his evidence in a slow, deliberate, and distinct manner, which was uncommonly impressive. It is well known that Mr. Baretti was acquitted."

Situated in the centre of the pleasure-going West-end population, the Haymarket is a great place for hotels, supper-houses, and foreign *cafés;* and it need hardly be added here, that so many of its taverns became the resort of the loosest characters, after the closing of the theatres, who turned night into day, and who were so constantly appearing before the sitting magistrates in consequence of drunken riots and street rows, that the Legislature interfered, and an Act of Parliament was passed, compelling the closing of such houses of refreshment at twelve o'clock.

The street and its neighbourhood have long been noted for places of amusement, and for those kinds of entertainment which are generally known as "popular." About the year 1750 a collection of performing dogs and monkeys from Italy, and exhibited under the name of the "Animal Comedians" at a place in the Haymarket known as "Mrs. Midnight's Oratory," became so famous that they were made the subject of a paper in the *Adventurer.* The writer discourses in a most learned style on the various animal prodigies and strange biped performers that had lately appeared "within the bills of mortality"—such as the "modern Colossus;" the "female Samson;" the "famous negro, who swings about his arms in every direction;" the "noted ox with six legs and two bellies;" the "beautiful panther-mare;" the "noted fire-eater, smoking out of red-hot tobacco pipes, champing lighted brimstone, and swallowing his infernal mess of broth;" the "most amazing new English *chien savant;*" the "little woman that weighs no more than twenty-three pounds;" the "wonderful little Norfolk man;" the "wonderful Stentor;" the "wonderful man who talks in his belly;" the "wire-dancer;" the "five dancing bears;" and the "much-applauded stupendous ostrich."

In 1758, or the following year, Bisset, the famous animal-trainer, hired here a room, in which he announced a public performance of the "Cat's Opera," supplemented by tricks of a horse, a dog, and some monkeys. Mr. Frost, in his "Old Showman," tells us that, "besides the organ-grinding and rope-dancing performances, the monkeys took wine together, and rode on the horse, pirouetting and somersaulting with the skill of a practised acrobat. One of them also," he adds, " danced a minuet with the dog. The 'Cat's Opera' was attended by crowded houses, and Bisset cleared a thousand pounds by the exhibition in a few days. He afterwards taught a hare to walk on its hind legs and beat a drum; a feathered company of canaries, linnets, and sparrows to spell names, tell the time by the clock, &c.; half-a-dozen turkeys to execute a country dance; and a turtle (or more probably a tortoise) to write names on the floor, having its feet blackened for the purpose. After a successful season in London, he sold some of the animals, and made a provincial tour with the rest, rapidly accumulating a considerable fortune." " At the Opera Room in the Haymarket," in the reign of George II., were exhibited by Fawkes, the showman, some wax-work figures, which went through the comical tragedy of " Tom Thumb."

According to a placard immortalised by Mr. John Timbs in his " Romance of London," at No. 61 in this street, O'Brien, the Irish Giant, whose skeleton is to be seen in the Museum of the College of Surgeons, as already stated by us,* was exhibited in 1804. He is thus described :—" He is indisputably the tallest man ever shown; is a lineal descendant of Brian Boru, and resembles that great potentate. All the members of the family are distinguished by their immense size. The gentleman alluded to measures near nine feet high." Owing to his great height he was most unwieldy, and could scarcely walk up an incline, so that he had to rest his hands for support on the shoulders of two men in walking up Holborn Hill. When he wished to light his pipe, Mr. Timbs tells us, he used to take the top off a street-lamp. Once on a journey in his own carriage he was stopped by a robber ; but when he looked out of the window, the thief rode off, frightened at his height. He exhibited himself for more than twenty years, and realised a large sum ; and we are told that he was seldom absent from Bartlemy Fair. He died in 1806.

Another of the principal places of amusement in the Haymarket, in the early part of the present century, was Weeks's Museum. The grand room, which was upwards of one hundred feet in length, was hung entirely with blue satin, and contained a variety of figures, which exhibited the powers of mechanism.

At the top of the street, at the north-east corner, facing Weeks's Museum, stood a place of public amusement — in fact, a gaming-house, familiar

to the readers of the comedies of the time as " Shaver's Hall ; " its name being derived from the barber of Lord Pembroke, who built it out of his earnings. It occupied the whole of the southern side of Coventry Street from the Haymarket to Hedge Lane. It is described by Garrow in a letter to Lord Strafford, in 1635, as " a new Spring Garden, erected in the fields beyond the Mews." For the following minute description of it we are indebted to the industry and research of John Timbs :— From a survey of the premises made in 1650, we gather that Shaver's Hall was strongly built of brick, and covered with lead; its large cellar was divided into six rooms ; above these were four rooms, and the same in the first storey, to which there was a balcony commanding a view of the bowling-alleys that sloped to the south. In the second storey were six rooms, and over the same a walk with leads, and enclosed with rails, " very curiously carved and wrought," as was also the staircase throughout the house. On the west were large kitchens and coal-house, with lofts over it. At the entrance-gate to the upper bowling-green was a " parlour-lodge," close to which a double flight of steps led down to the lower bowling-alley. There was still beyond this another bowling-alley, and an orchard well planted with choice fruit-trees, as also " one pleasant banqueting house, and one other fair and pleasant apartment called the Green Room, and one other Conduit House, and two turrets adjoining the walls." Beyond, to the south, was also "one fair Tennis Court, of brick, tiled, well accommodated with all things fitting for the same." This is the Tennis Court which till recently stood at the corner of James Street, the last building shown on Faithorne's plan in 1658.

On the east side of the upper part of the Haymarket, in the year 1720, if not still later, was living the widow of Colonel Thomas Panton, the successful gamester, who, having realised a sudden fortune as the keeper of a gaming-house in Piccadilly, had the good sense to invest his gains in a house and land, and abandon cards and the dicebox. His name is still kept up in that of Panton Street, and of Panton Square ; but the bulk of his wealth was carried by his daughter on her marriage into the family of Lord Arundell of Wardour, who gave his name to Arundell Street adjoining, and also, as we have said, to Wardour Street, in Soho.

On the same side of the street, opposite Charles Street, stands the Haymarket Theatre. Its early history runs as follows :—

In the year 1720 an enterprising carpenter named John Potter built a small playhouse in the Haymarket, on the site of the " King's Head Inn."

* See Vol. III., p. 46.

The cost of the building was £1,000, and Potter further expended £500 in decorations, scenery, and dresses. He leased the theatre, immediately after its completion, to a company of French actors, who were at that time much favoured by the English aristocracy, and who performed under a temporary licence from the Lord Chamberlain. This company styled themselves " The French Comedians of his Grace the Duke of Montague," that nobleman

dropped from the clouds." His opening piece was entitled *Pasquin*, and, being a social satire of the most caustic nature, it achieved great popularity, and had a run of more than fifty nights. Elated by his success, Fielding produced a second piece, called *The Historical Register*, a political satire, which contained so audacious a caricature of Sir Robert Walpole, under the name of " Quidam," that the Prime Minister's resentment led to the

THE OLD HAYMARKET THEATRE.

being their principal patron, and opened the new house on the 29th of December, 1720, with the comedy of *La Fille à la Morte, ou le Badeaud de Paris*. At this time, and for several years afterwards, Potter's speculation was known to the play-going world as " The New French Theatre." About ten years later, being then occupied by an English company, it began to be spoken of as " The Little Theatre in the Haymarket "—a title which it retained until the original edifice was pulled down in 1820, having just completed a century of existence. Its site is now occupied by the " Café de l'Europe." In 1734 it was in the occupation of Henry Fielding, the great novelist and dramatist, with a congenial band, styled in the play-bills " The Great Mogul's Company, recently

passing of that Act which requires all dramatic pieces to be submitted to the approval of the Lord Chamberlain before they can be performed.

We are told by Mr. Frost, in his " Old Showmen," already quoted, that " Punch's celebrated company of comical tragedians from the Haymarket performed the most comical and whimsical tragedy that ever was tragedised by any tragical company of comedians, called *The Humours of Covent Garden*, by Henry Fielding, Esq."

In 1745 the " Little Theatre," having passed through the hands of several managers, each of whom had only a temporary licence, was opened without the ceremony of a licence of any sort by Theophilus Cibber, who succeeded in evading the usual penalty by the manner in which his advertisements were worded. They ran thus:—"At Cibber's Academy, in the Haymarket, will be a concert; after which will be exhibited *gratis* a rehearsal in the form of a play, called *Romeo and Juliet*." It is probable, however, that in spite of this ingenious artifice, Mr. Cibber received an

Apropos of Foote's entertainment, a good story of the silly Duke of Cumberland is told by Mr. W. C. Hazlitt, in his "New London Jest Book." One night he was in the green-room here. "Well, here I am, Mr. Foote," said he, "ready to swallow all your good things." "Your royal highness,"

SAMUEL FOOTE.

official hint which induced him to announce, in the autumn of the same year, that "Mr. Cibber's company, being busily employed in reviving several pieces, are obliged to defer playing until further notice."

In 1747 the house was daily crowded by fashionable audiences to witness Samuel Foote's humorous entertainments, entitled "Foote giving Tea," &c., which included life-like imitations of the most notable characters of the day.

answered the witty actor, "must have the digestion of an ostrich, for I never knew you to throw up any again!"

When Foote first opened this theatre, amongst other projects, he proposed to entertain the public with an imitation of cat music. For this purpose he engaged a man famous for his skill in mimicking the mewing of cats. This person was called "Cat Harris." As he did not attend the rehearsal of this odd concert, Foote desired Shuter would endeavour to find him out and bring him with him. Shuter was directed to some court in the Minories where this extraordinary musician lived; but not being able to find the house, Shuter began a cat solo; upon this the other looked out of the window, and answered him with a cantata of the same sort. "Come along," said Shuter, "I want no better information that you are the man. Mr. Foote stays for us—we cannot begin the cat opera without you."

All sorts of stories are told of Foote, and some of them on very good authority. A few of them will bear repeating here.

Foote could not bear to see anybody or anything succeed in the Haymarket but himself and his own writings, and forgot that a failure of the new scheme might possibly endanger the regular payment of his annuity. His pique broke out sometimes in downright rudeness. One morning he came hopping upon the stage during the rehearsal of the *Spanish Barber*, then about to be produced; the performers were busy in that scene of the piece where one servant is under the influence of a sleeping draught, and another of a sneezing powder. "Well," said Foote, dryly, to the manager, "how do you go on?" "Pretty well," was the answer; "but I cannot teach one of these fellows to gape as he ought to do." "Can't you?" replied Foote; "then read him your last comedy of *The Man of Business*, and he'll yawn for a month."

On another occasion he was not less coarse, though more laughable, to an actor than he had been to the manager. This happened when Digges, of much celebrity out of London, and who had come to town from Edinburgh, covered with Scottish laurels, made his first appearance in the Haymarket. He had studied the antiquated style of acting; in short, he was a fine bit of old stage-buckram, and "Cato" was therefore selected for the first essay. He "discharged the character" in the same costume as it is to be supposed was adopted by Booth when the play was originally acted; that is, in a shape, as it was technically termed, of the stiffest order, decorated with gilt leather upon a black ground, with black stockings, black gloves, and a powdered periwig. Foote had planted himself in the pit, when Digges stalked on before the public thus formidably accoutred. The malicious wag waited till the customary round of applause had subsided, and then ejaculated, in a pretended under-tone, loud enough to be heard by all around him, "A Roman chimney-sweeper on May-day!" The laughter which this produced in the pit was enough to knock up a *débutant*, and it startled the old stager personating the Stoic of Utica; the sarcasm was irresistibly funny, but Foote deserved

to be kicked out of the house for his cruelty and insolence too.

The theatre barely escaped being destroyed, in 1749, by an enraged mob, the victims of a hoax planned by the eccentric Duke of Montague, who had caused an advertisement to appear, stating that, "on the 16th of January, a conjurer would jump into a quart bottle at the Little Theatre." On the appointed day thousands of persons were assembled in and around the theatre to witness the exploit, and a furious riot was the result of their disappointment.

In 1766 the Duke of York, who was Foote's staunch patron, obtained for him a royal patent for his life, in virtue of which the "little" playhouse became a "Theatre Royal," and Foote, who had leased it as a summer theatre since 1762, now purchased the premises on which it was built, and greatly altered and enlarged the building. It is said that on one occasion, when out on a party of pleasure with the Duke of York and other illustrious personages, Foote met with an accident which in the end was overruled to his advantage. He was thrown from his horse, and his leg being broken, he was forced to submit to amputation. It was in consequence of this accident the duke obtained for him the patent above mentioned. "Strange as it may appear, with the aid of a cork leg he performed his former characters with no less agility and spirit than before, and continued by his laughable performances to draw together crowded houses."

Remarkable for his wit as well as for his marvellous power of mimicry, neither friend nor patron was sacred from Foote's merciless satire, provided the person were sufficiently well known to be worth the trouble. It must, however, be urged in his defence, that his friends were no more troubled with scruples of delicacy than himself, and seem to have considered gross personalities to be the soul of wit. Foote's uncle, Captain Goodere, having been executed for the murder of his brother, Sir John Goodere, Mr. Cooke, the translator of "Hesiod," once presented Foote to a select society, with the agreeable introductory remark, "This is the nephew of Captain Goodere, the gentleman who was lately hung in chains for murdering his brother."

Another little episode in the annals of the Haymarket Theatre is perhaps worth mentioning here. In the early days of the Regency—about the year 1810—there suddenly appeared at the West-end a wealthy gentleman, of middle age, and of West Indian extraction, named Robert Coates. He was of good-figured appearance, dressed well, and even showily, and always wore a quantity of fur. At evening parties, to which he gained an entrance, his buttons and knee-buckles were studded with diamonds. There was a great mystery about his antecedents, and the public curiosity was heightened by the announcement that he proposed to appear at the Haymarket Theatre in the character of "Romeo." By hook or by crook he contrived to arrange for this appearance, and on the night the house was crowded to suffocation, the play-bill having given out that an "amateur of fashion" had consented to perform "for one night only;" and it was generally whispered that the rehearsal gave unmistakable signs that the tragedy would be turned into a comedy. But his appearance outdid all expectations. Mr. Coates's dress was grotesque in the extreme. In a cloak of sky-blue silk, profusely spangled, red pantaloons, a vest of white muslin, and a wig of the style of Charles II., capped by an opera hat, he brought down the whole house with laughter before he opened his lips, and the laughter was increased by the fact that his nether garments, being far too tight, burst in seams which could not be concealed. But when his guttural voice was heard, and he showed his total misapprehension of every part of the play, especially in the vulgarity of his address to "Juliet," and in his equally absurd rendering of the balcony scene, the whole thing was so comic, that gallery and pit were equally convulsed with laughter, and the piece ended in an uproar. It is needless to add that, for the character of the theatre, "Romeo" Coates, as he was afterwards called, was not allowed to appear again upon the stage at the Haymarket, though he possibly amused his friends by amateur performances in private.

To this theatre belongs the somewhat eccentric and amusing story of Lady Caroline Petersham, told by Horace Walpole :—

"Your friend Lady C—— P—— has entertained the town with a new scene. She was t'other night at the play with her court—viz., Miss Ashe, Lord Barnard, M. St. Simon, and her favourite footman, Richard, whom, under pretence of keeping places, she always keeps in her box the whole time to see the play at his ease. Mr. Stanley, Colonel Vernon, and Mr. Vaughan arrived at the very end of the farce, and could find no room but a row and a half in Lady C——'s box. Richard denied their entrance very impertinently. Mr. Stanley took him by the hair of his head, dragged him into the passage, and thrashed him. The heroine was outrageous; the heroes not at all so. She sent Richard to (Sir John) Fielding for a warrant : he could not grant it ; and so it ended." On this incident Lady Lepel Hervey remarks, "Come and hear a little of what is going on in town. . . . . You will

hear of ladies of quality who uphold footmen in insulting gentlemen."

In 1770 the theatre was engaged by one Maddox, a performer on the slack wire ; and it is said that his were the most prosperous entertainments ever carried on in this house. His profits in one season are stated to have amounted to £11,000, being £2,500 more than Garrick's a few years earlier.

In 1776 Foote sold his interest in the theatre to George Colman the elder for an annuity of £1,600, and Colman, on Foote's death, early in the following year, obtained the whole property for £800. And now, for a period of nearly fifty years, the Haymarket Theatre was the property of George Colman, passing, in 1794, on the death of George the elder, into the hands of George the younger, under whose management it was one of the most prosperous theatres in London.

On the 3rd of February, 1794, a dreadful accident happened here, through the pressure of the crowd, who had assembled in great numbers, in consequence of the play on that night having been commanded by their Majesties. On opening the pit door, the rush was so strong, that a number of persons were thrown down, and fifteen persons deprived of life, and upwards of twenty others materially injured by bruises and broken limbs. Most of the sufferers were respectable persons, and among the dead were two of the heralds.

An old lady named Wall, for whom Colman, from early associations, appears to have had a kind consideration, had been an actress in a subordinate situation for many seasons in this theatre. We must all pay the debt of nature ; and, in due time, the old lady died. Somebody from the theatre went to break the intelligence to Colman, who, on hearing it, inquired "whether there had been any bills stuck up !" The messenger replied in the negative, and ventured to ask Mr. Colman why he had put that question. Colman answered, "They generally paste bills on a *dead wall*, don't they?"

In 1820, Colman having sold his entire interest in the theatre, the old edifice was pulled down, and the present building erected, on almost the same site, from a design by John Nash. The front is of stone, and is about sixty feet in length, and nearly fifty in height. The entrance is through a handsome portico, the entablature and pediment being supported by six columns of the Corinthian order; above are circular windows connected by sculpture of an ornamental character. Under the portico are five doors, leading respectively to the boxes, pit, galleries, and box-office. The shape of the interior differs from that of every other theatre in London, being nearly a square, with the side facing the stage very slightly curved. The expense of the new building was about £20,000. It is a remarkably neat and pretty house, having two tiers of boxes, besides other half-tiers parallel with the lower gallery, and will seat about 1,500 persons with comfort.

The first great success of the new theatre was Poole's comedy of *Paul Pry*, which was produced in 1825, with Liston in the principal character, supported by William Farren, Mrs. Waylett, Mrs. Glover, and Madame Vestris. With such a caste it cannot be a matter of surprise that the piece had a run of 114 nights, and that the price of a box was sometimes paid for a seat in the gallery.

In 1837 Mr. Benjamin Webster became the lessee, and collected around him a brilliant company. Messrs. Macready, Charles Kean, Tyrone Power, Sheridan Knowles, Charles Mathews the younger, Mrs. Glover, Mrs. Nisbet, Miss Ellen Tree, Madame Vestris, Miss Cushman, Miss Helen Faucit, and Mrs. Stirling, were the most notable stars which shone in the Haymarket Theatre during Mr. Webster's management. In 1843 the lessee made a spirited effort in behalf of the modern drama, by offering a competition prize of £500 for the best comedy. The piece selected was *Quid pro Quo*, by Mrs. Gore, which was performed in the year 1844, and turned out a dead failure, a result partly compensated by the enormous success of Charles Mathews in *Used Up*, which was produced here shortly afterwards. Mr. Webster relinquished his connection with the Haymarket in 1853, after having effected great improvements at his own expense. He widened

the proscenium eleven feet, introduced gas at an expense of £500 per annum, and presented the central chandelier to the proprietors. The theatre then passed into the hands of Mr. Buckstone, under whose management it has run a career of uninterrupted prosperity. For several years it was the only house in London where the standard English comedies, such as *The School for Scandal*, *The Rivals*, &c., were regularly performed, the *pièce de résistance* being as regularly followed by a farce in which Mr. Buckstone sustained the principal part. For a quarter of a century since Mr. Buckstone became the lessee of the Haymarket he was the life and soul of his company; and just as in those days his "Tony Lumpkin" and "Bob Acres" seemed the chief features of the old comedies, so now the humours of "My Lord Dundreary" and the exquisite grace of Mr. Gilbert's fairy dramas would be accounted insipid, without the pinch of Attic salt with which the veteran actor flavours the dainty dish.

In a work published in 1808 it is made a subject of complaint that there were only two theatres, whereas London, in the reign of Elizabeth and James I., the golden age of the English drama, was not a tenth part of its then size, and yet nevertheless it contained seventeen theatres. "More theatres are therefore wanted," adds the writer; and he complains bitterly of the restrictions imposed on the dramatic muse by the exclusive privileges conferred on Drury Lane and Covent Garden. It is perhaps worthy of note that the first new theatre to break the ice of these restrictions was the Haymarket, as already related in this chapter.

CHAPTER XIX.

PALL MALL EAST, SUFFOLK STREET, &c.

The University Club-house and the Royal College of Physicians—The Society of Painters in Water-Colours—Benjamin West's *Chefs d'Œuvres*— Messrs. Colnaghi's and Messrs. Graves' Print-shops—The Assassination of Thomas Thynne—Grant of Land to Edward Russell in 1692—The Old Horse-pond—Suffolk House—Suffolk Street—Miss Vanhomrigh and Dean Swift—Stanislaus, King of Poland—Mr. Chenevix's Toy-shop—The "Cock-Tavern" and Mr. Pepys—The "Calves' Head Club"—The Gallery of British Artists—Suffolk Place and "Moll Davis"— Dorset Place and Whitcomb Street—Hedge Lane—Supposed Remains of the Old Royal Mews—Oxendon Street Chapel—The Attack on Sir John Coventry—James Street—The Royal Tennis Court—Fawkes, the Conjuror—Orange Street Chapel—Sir Isaac Newton's Residence —Panton Street—Royal Comedy Theatre—Goldsmith's and Burke's Visit to the Puppets—Hamlet, the Jeweller—Messrs. Ambroise and Brunn's Entertainments—The Société Française de Bienfaisance—A Singular Atmospheric Phenomenon—Arundell Street—Coventry Street—Coventry House—Sights and Amusements—Messrs. Wishart's Tobacco and Snuff Manufactory—The Kilted Highlander as a Sign for Snuff-shops.

EXTENDING eastward from the southern end of Her Majesty's Theatre to Trafalgar Square, and skirting the northern end of Cockspur Street, is Pall Mall East. Here, at the corner of Suffolk Street, stands the United University Club-house, of which we have already spoken* in our chapter on "Club-

land," and also the principal front of the Royal College of Physicians, described in the previous volume.†

At No. 5 are the rooms of the old Society of Painters in Water-Colours. Externally the building possesses nothing to call for special mention,

---

* See above, p. 146.

* See Vol. III., p. 142.

excepting, perhaps, a new and elegant doorway, which was erected in 1875; this, alike in design and workmanship, is worthy of the gallery to which it gives access. The society itself originated in 1808, when its first exhibition of water-colour drawings took place. It was at first blended with that of the Royal Academy; but in 1821 the painters in this branch of art determined to exhibit their productions separately from other artists, and erected the house in Pall Mall East expressly for the purpose. The exhibition is open during the greater part of the year, and comprises usually about 500 pictures of various kinds, among which, as might be expected, landscapes generally predominate. This society has always limited the exhibition entirely to its own members; but the body of artists showed a gradual and steady increase.

Here, in the year 1819, were exhibited the *chefs d'œuvres* of Benjamin West, President of the Royal Academy, including his "Christ rejected by the Jews," and "Death on the White Horse." The former contains nearly two hundred figures, in their appropriate costumes, all these displaying some passion of grief, pity, astonishment, revenge, exultation, or total apathy. The principal figures of Christ, the High Priest, Pilate, and many others, taken as single objects, are scarcely to be equalled in the entire compass of art. It is enriched with a splendid frame, carved after the model of the gate of the Temple of Theseus at Athens.

From its central position, Pall Mall East has always been a favourite locality in the world of art; and the two old-established shops for the sale of prints and engravings—that of Messrs. Colnaghi, adjoining the College of Physicians, and of Messrs. Graves, close by the Royal Opera Arcade—have tended to keep up its reputation in this respect. At No. 9, on the north side of the street, are the offices of the Palestine Exploration Fund, to which Biblical scholars are so largely indebted for bringing to light many objects in Jerusalem and elsewhere, which throw light on the narrative of the Holy Scriptures, as well as on the manners and customs of the Jewish people two thousand years ago.

Nearly opposite the south-west corner of what is now the Opera House, on Sunday, February 12th, 1681, Mr. Thomas Thynne was "most barbarously shot with a musketoon in his coach, and died next day." The instigator of this crime, as we have already related in describing Thynne's monument in Westminster Abbey,* was Count Köningsmark, who was in hopes of gaining the hand of the rich

heiress, Lady Elizabeth Ogle, to whom Thynne was either already married or else contracted. The sentiment of Köningsmark on this occasion furnishes a curious insight into the ideas as to violence current in the days of the early Stuarts. We learn from the "State Trials" that he "allowed that the assassination of Mr. Thynne by his bravoes was a stain on his blood, but only such a one as a good action in the wars . . . would easily wash out!" Three of the ruffians whom he hired to do the deed were tried at the Old Bailey, found guilty, and hanged on the spot whereon the murder was committed. The cowardly villain, the Count himself, however, escaped the just punishment of his crime, getting off by securing the favour of a corrupt jury. Strangely enough, the jury who acquitted the real and principal agent, condemned the actual perpetrator of the deed, Colonel Vrats, who was hung, and, being of good family in Holland, was allowed to have his body embalmed and carried thither; so Evelyn, at least, tells us in his "Diary."

Two parcels of waste ground—no doubt, a part of the old site of the Royal Mews, containing about three acres, bounded on the east by the once rural Hedge Lane, by the Haymarket on the west, and by Cockspur Street on the south, including Suffolk and Little Suffolk Streets—were granted by the Crown, in 1692, to Edward Russell, no fine being taken "on account of the eminent services" of the grantee. It may be added, in excuse for the grant, that in the good old days before George III. was king, when Leicester *Square* was Leicester Field—a "dirty place where ragged boys used to assemble to play at chucks"— between the bottom of the Haymarket and "the King's Mews" there was a horse-pond, where stray horses were taken to water, and in which pickpockets were ducked when caught in the act.

Mr. Peter Cunningham considers that in early times there was a town mansion of the Earls of Suffolk on the site of what is now Suffolk Street; and quotes, in support of his views, the commencement of the ballad of Suckling, already given above on page 219. The Suffolks, however, subsequently became possessed of what was afterwards Northumberland, but was for a time called Suffolk, House, at Charing Cross, when they removed to their new quarters.

In this street, which now consists almost entirely of modern houses, and has been transformed partly into Pall Mall East, and partly into Dorset Place, formerly resided the unhappy Miss Vanhomrigh, the poor "Vanessa" of Dean Swift, a lady who died of a broken heart through her unfortunate

---

* See Vol. III., p. 419.

attachment to the Dean. The witty Dean, when in London on the affairs of the Irish Church, made the acquaintance of this young lady and her mother, the widow of a Dutch merchant, and became so constant a visitor at their house, as to leave there "his best gown and cassock for convenience." As he was a man of middle age, while she was not twenty, it was thought quite a matter

for she was always known by the latter, and never by the former name—that surely "Vanessa" must have been an extraordinary woman to have inspired the Dean to write such fine verses upon her. "That's not at all clear," said the lady, offended with and yet proud of her husband, and hurt besides in her own vanity, "for it is very well known that the Dean could write finely upon a broomstick."

THE COLLEGE OF PHYSICIANS. (*See page 226.*)

of course that he should direct her studies; but this direction of her reading soon ripened into quite another affair, and it was only when Miss Vanhomrigh's affections were deeply and irrevocably engaged that she discovered, on following the Dean back to Ireland, that he had a wife living— his "Stella." This discovery was shortly afterwards followed by the young lady's death.

While the melancholy fate of Miss Vanhomrigh was the common topic of conversation in London circles, and while every one was reading the Dean's "Cadenus and Vanessa," somebody is said to have remarked to Mrs. Swift, or rather to Mrs. Johnson—

Malcolm tells us that the last and most unfortunate King of Poland, Stanislaus Augustus lodged in 1754, in Suffolk Street, at the house of a Mr. Cropenhole. We also learn incidentally that "over against Suffolk Street, Charing Cross," in the reign of George II., was the celebrated toy-shop of Mr. Chenevix, where tickets for most of the West-end "shows" and exhibitions were sold.

In Suffolk Street was an old hostelry, the "Cock," much praised by Samuel Pepys, who thus writes, under date March 15, 1669: "Mr. Hewes and I did walk to the Cocke, at the end of Suffolk Street, where I never was (before): a great ordinary mightily cried up, and there bespoke a pullet; which, while dressing, he and I walked into St. James's Park, and thence back, and dined very handsome, with a good soup and a pullet for 4s. 6d. the whole." It would appear that on the whole the diarist was well pleased with the accommoda-

occasion, was held one of the meetings of this club, which, in the year 1735, produced a serious riot. At this meeting it is said by tradition that a bleeding calf's head, wrapped in an old napkin, was thrown out of the window into the street below, while the members of the club inside were drinking

THE OLD TENNIS COURT, NEAR THE HAYMARKET. (*See page* 231.)

tion; for in less than a month afterwards he took his wife and some other friends thither, where they were "mighty merry," the house being "famous for good meat, and particularly for pease-porridge."

A tavern in this street—possibly the "Cock," already mentioned—appears to have been at one time the head-quarters of the famous, or rather infamous, "Calves' Head Club," established by the Puritans and Roundheads in ridicule of the memory of Charles I. At all events, here, on one

the pious toast of confusion to the Stuart race! Lord Middlesex, however, who was one of those present on the occasion, denies the truth of this indictment in a letter to Mr. Spence, which is published in "Spence's Anecdotes." In this letter he says that there happened to be a bonfire of straw made by some boys in the street under the windows, and that some of the company, "wiser or soberer than the rest," proposed drinking some loyal and popular toasts to the mob outside, and that the only toasts drank by the members were the King, the Queen, the Royal Family, the Protestant Succession, Liberty and Property, and the present Administration. Stones were then flung, the windows of the tavern were broken, and a regular row ensued, which was only suppressed by the arrival, an hour later, of "the justice, attended by a strong body of guards, who dispersed the populace."

The author of the "Secret History of the Calves' Head Club, or the Republicans Unmasked" (supposed to be "Ned Ward," of alehouse memory), ascribes the origin of this association to Milton and other partisans of the Commonwealth, who, in opposition to Bishop Juxon, Bishop Sanderson, and other loyalists, used to meet together on the 30th of every January, having compiled for their own use a form of prayer for the day, not very unlike that which was till lately to be found in the Book of Common Prayer. " After the Restoration," observes the writer of this pamphlet, "the eyes of the Government being on the whole party, they were obliged to meet with a great deal of precaution ; but in the reign of King William they met almost in a public manner, apprehending no danger. . . . They kept in no fixed house, but moved about from place to place, as they thought convenient." The place where they met when his informant was present was in a blind alley near Moorfields, where " an axe was hung up in the club-room, and was reverenced as a principal symbol in this diabolical sacrament. Their bill of fare was a large dish of calves' heads, dressed in several ways, by which they represented the king, and his friends who had suffered in his cause ; a large pike with a smaller one in his mouth, as an emblem of tyranny ; a large cod's head, by which they intended to represent the person of the king singly ; a boar's head with an apple in his mouth, to represent the king as bestial, as by their other hieroglyphics they had made him out to be foolish and tyrannical. After the repast was over, one of their elders presented an ' Icon Basilicé,' which was with great solemnity burnt on the table, whilst anthems were being sung. After this, another produced Milton's ' Defensio Populi Anglicani,' upon which all present laid their hands, and made a protestation in form of an oath ever to stand by and maintain the same. After the table-cloth was removed, the anniversary anthem, as they impiously called it, was sung, and a calf's skull, filled with wine or other liquor, and then a brimmer, went about to the pious (?) memory of those worthy patriots who had ' killed the tyrant,' and relieved their country from his arbitrary sway ; and lastly, a collection was made for the mercenary

scribbler [probably meaning John Milton], to which every man contributed according to his zeal for the cause and the ability of his purse. The company consisted only of Anabaptists and Independents ; and the famous Jeremy White—formerly chaplain to Oliver Cromwell, who, no doubt, came to sanctify with his pious exhortations the ribaldry of the day—said grace before and after dinner." " Although no great reliance," says Wilson, in his " Life of Defoe," " is to be placed upon the faithfulness of Ward's narrative, yet in the frighted mind of a high-flying Churchman, continually haunted by such scenes, the caricature would easily pass for a likeness. It is probable, therefore, that the above account must not be accepted without many grains of salt to qualify it. The name and idea of the club is sufficiently disgusting, and a lasting dishonour, not to the murdered king, but to its founders."

On the east side of Suffolk Street stands the Gallery of British Artists. The building, which was completed in 1824, is entered by a Doric portico, designed by Mr. Nash, and consists of a suite of six octagonal galleries, all on one floor, and lighted from above, designed by Mr. James Elmes.

In consequence of the limited size of the rooms at Somerset House, where the Royal Academy held its exhibitions, the Society of British Artists was instituted in 1823 for the annual display of the works of living artists in the various branches of painting, sculpture, architecture, and engraving. The fund raised for the erection of the building, &c., was by donations and subscriptions, which were divided into eight classes, and admissions awarded in accordance with the amount given or subscribed.

In a notice of the building printed in the *Mirror*, in 1824, it is stated that it was "intended as a building for the reception of ancient models, casts, &c., and students ; the ground storey is occupied by a portico of the Grecian Doric, having coupled *antæ*, the proportions, apparently, from the Temple of Theseus, at Athens ; the upper storey is a continuation of the *antæ* throughout the front ; in the centre is a window with a pediment, frieze, architrave, &c., from the Temple of Erectheus, at Athens, ornamented with *paterœ*, as are also the *antæ ;* the ornaments are of terra cotta, the whole surmounted by a bold cornice."

Suffolk Place, leading to Suffolk Street, is mentioned by Strype as consisting of handsome houses. They do not, however, appear to have been aristocratically tenanted. At all events, here lived the notorious " Moll Davis," in a mansion which Charles II. had furnished expensively for her—an arrangement of which even Pepys speaks as "a most infinite shame;" she kept also, as he tells us, "a mighty pretty fine coach."

Running up northwards from Pall Mall East, in the rear of Suffolk Street, are Dorset Place and Whitcomb Street, its continuation, which leads towards Coventry Street. This follows the course of the old "Hedge Lane," which, till about 1830, commemorated the once rural character of the neighbourhood of the Haymarket and Leicester Fields.

It is related of Steele, Budgell, and Phillips, that one evening, when they were coming out of a tavern or coffee-house in Gerrard Street, they were warned that there were some suspicious characters waiting to waylay any stray foot-passengers in Hedge Lane. "Thank ye," said the wits, and each hurried off home by a different way.

Hedge Lane is marked in the map of Ralph Aggas, *temp.* Elizabeth, and was, even in the days of Charles II., what the name implied—a lane running into the fields, and bordered by hedges. The Duke of Monmouth is said to have lived here before taking up his abode in Soho, where we have already seen him located. According to Mr. Peter Cunningham, Maurice Lowe, the painter, was also a resident of this lane. It was still called Hedge Lane in the days of Dr. Johnson, of whom Boswell tells us that, in April, 1778, on his way to dine at the West-end, he got out of the hackney-coach at the bottom of Hedge Lane in order to leave a letter containing charitable aid for a " poor man in distress," probably a hungry author.

The Royal Mews, already mentioned, in the reign of Henry VIII., as standing near the bottom of the lane, was burnt in 1534, and some remains (or what were supposed to be remains) of its charred walls were discovered in 1821.

In Oxendon Street, which runs parallel to the Haymarket, from north to south, about half way between it and Leicester Square, formerly stood, on its western side, a Nonconformist chapel, which had become historical. It was built by no less a man than that " prince of Independents," Richard Baxter, " adjoining the wall of the house of Mr. Secretary Coventry," to whom Baxter's principles were so unpalatable that it is said he caused the soldiers to beat drums under the chapel windows to drown the preacher's voice. The Secretary was so far successful in this outrageous conduct that he forced Baxter to give up the chapel, which afterwards became a chapel-of-ease to the parish in which it stood. The following curious notice respecting it will be found in the *Spectator*, under date November 30, 1711: "This is to give notice to all promoters of the holy worship, and to all

lovers of the Italian tongue, that on Sunday next, being the 2nd of December, at five in the afternoon, in Oxendon Chapel, near the Haymarket, there will be divine service in the Italian tongue, and will continue every Sunday at the aforesaid hour, with an Italian sermon, preached by Mr. Casotti, Italian minister, author of a new method of teaching the Italian tongue to ladies," &c. Malcolm, in his "Londinium Redivivum," after quoting the advertisement, adds a waggish remark, to the effect that the chapel is still (1807) in use, though " not for the above purpose of teaching the Italian language." The chapel, after serving as a chapel-of-ease to St. Martin's, passed to the " Scottish Secession." It was pulled down about 1875, its connection removing to Haverstock Hill.

It was in this street that Sir John Coventry was living at the time of the attack made on him in the Haymarket, as noticed in the preceding chapter. It appears that Sir John had been supping with some friends at the Cock Tavern in Bow Street, and was, at the time, on his way home. A motion had recently been made in the House of Commons to lay a tax on playhouses. The Court opposed the motion. The players, it was said (by Sir John Birkenhead), were the king's servants, and a part of his pleasure. Coventry asked, "Whither did the king's pleasure lie, among the men or the women that acted?" perhaps recollecting more particularly the king's visit to Moll Davis in Suffolk Street, where Charles had furnished a house for her, provided her with " a mighty pretty fine coach," and given her a ring of £700, " which," says the page (like Pepys), " is a most infinite shame." The king determined to *leave a mark* upon Sir John Coventry for his freedom of remark, and he was marked on his way home. " He stood up to the wall," says Burnet, " and snatched the flambeau out of the servant's hands; and with that in one hand, and the sword in the other, he defended himself so well, that he got more credit by it than by all the actions of his life. He wounded some of them, but was soon disarmed, and " they cut his nose to the bone, to teach him to remember what respect he owed to the king." Burnet adds, that " his nose was so well sewed up, that the scar was scarcely to be discerned."

Eastward from the Haymarket, a little north of the theatre, stretches James Street, on the south side of which is a building which was till lately occupied by the Royal Tennis Court. Tennis, if we may trust old writers, derives its name from the French Hand-ball or Palm-play, and was played in London as far back as the sixteenth century, in covered courts erected for that special purpose. Henry VII. and

Henry VIII. were both fond of tennis; the latter added a tennis-court to his palace at Whitehall. James I., we know, recommended tennis to his son as a game well becoming the dignity of a prince. Charles II. was an accomplished master of the game, and had a particular dress which he wore when playing it here. Timbs tells us that there was another tennis-court not far off, in Windmill Street, belonging to and attached to Piccadilly Hall. He also mentions "one called Gibbons's in Clare Market, where Killigrew's comedians sometimes performed," and others in Holborn, Blackfriars, and Southwark, where there were (and possibly still are) small thoroughfares still bearing the name of Tennis Courts. The court in James Street, it may be added, was one of the favourite haunts of Charles II. It was closed about the year 1863, and has lately been converted into a storehouse for military clothing.

In this street, in the reign of George II., the conjuror Fawkes used to locate his "show" in the intervals between the various London and suburban fairs, at which he put in his appearance, anticipating the tricks of Colonel Stodare of our own time.

The eastern end of James Street is continued by Orange Street—so called after the Prince of Orange, William III.—which is crossed by St. Martin's Street, running northwards into the centre of the south side of Leicester Square. The corner of Orange and St. Martin's Street is occupied by a Nonconformist chapel. Next to the chapel stands a house which is still visited by pilgrims from all parts of the world, as having been the last London residence of Sir Isaac Newton. He removed hither in 1710 from Jermyn Street, but did not die here, as is erroneously said by Dr. Burney in an anecdote related to Boswell, and mentioned in his "Life of Johnson." The house is now a school; on its roof was till lately a small observatory built by a subsequent tenant, but often supposed to have been Newton's own. The house had subsequently as its tenants Dr. Burney and his daughter Frances, who here composed her once (and still) popular novel, "Evelina." Frances Burney (Madame D'Arblay) dates from this house many of the letters published in her diaries; and Mr. Henry Thrale—Johnson's friend and host—writing to Miss Burney, playfully styles the inmates of the house his "dear Newtonians."

Panton Street, which forms one of the connecting links between the Haymarket and Leicester Square, was so called after its ground landlord, Colonel Panton, of whom we have spoken in the preceding chapter as having won his money at the card-table, and refusing to touch a card again. It has been said, though erroneously, that the street received its name from a kind of horse-shoe called a panton. At the corner of Panton and Oxendon Streets stands the Royal Comedy Theatre, which was erected in 1881. The class of entertainment given here is implied by the name of the theatre.

In a large room in Panton Street, Messrs. Ambroise and Brunn gave a "variety entertainment," consisting of "Ombres Chinoises," "danses de caractère," and sundry "metamorphoses" by a veritable magician; this being patronised by the Court, the price of admission was raised to five shillings. This same room was occupied, in a subsequent season, by the conjuror Breslau.

Forster tells us in his "Life of Goldsmith" that poor Oliver and Edmund Burke once paid a visit to some very ingenious puppets exhibited here. Burke praised in particular the dexterity of one puppet, who tossed a pike with military precision. "Psha!" remarked Goldsmith, with some warmth, "I could do it better myself." Boswell adds that Goldsmith afterwards went home to supper with Burke, and broke his shin by attempting to show the company how much better he could jump over a stick than the puppets themselves.

It is, perhaps, worth noting that Hamlet, the great jeweller of the time of the Regency, who had nearly all the aristocracy on his books, and of whom we have already spoken in our notice of Cranbourn Alley, Leicester Square, at one time had his business in Panton Street. He made a colossal fortune, but afterwards hastening to be rich in excess, he lost it through unfortunate speculations.

At No. 5 in this street was established, in 1842, a charitable institution, entitled the Société Française de Bienfaisance, for the relief of the distressed French in London. Its chief operations consist in giving temporary help in money and bread to numerous French artisans out of work.

Before quitting Panton Street, we may add, on the authority of Hughson's "London," that in the afternoon of the 9th of June, 1803, a most singular phenomenon happened here. He writes: "The inhabitants were alarmed by a violent and tremendous storm of rain and hail, which extended only to Oxendon Street, Whitcomb Street, Coventry Street, and the Haymarket, a space not exceeding 200 acres. For about seven minutes the torrent from the heavens was so great that it could only be compared to a cataract rushing over the brow of a precipice. In the midst of the hurricane an electric cloud descended in Panton Street, which struck the centre of the coachway, and sunk in to a great depth, forming a complete pit, in which not a vestige of the materials which had before occupied the space could be found. The sulphurous odour from the cloud was so powerful that for several seconds the persons near the spot were almost suffocated. No further damage was done, except filling the neighbouring kitchens and cellars with water, which soon escaped through the gulf formed by the electric fluid."

Arundell Street, which leads from Panton Square to Coventry Street, preserves the memory of its original ground landlord, Lord Arundell of Wardour; and still remains in the possession of the family.

Coventry Street derived its name from Mr. Henry Coventry, Secretary of State in the reign of Charles II., whose private mansion stood on its south side, with a garden wall running down behind what now is the west side of Oxendon Street. In the *London Gazette* for July — August, 1674, is an advertisement offering a reward for the recovery of a white, long-haired landspaniel, lost between London and Barnet, on application to "the porter at Mr. Secretary Coventry's house in Pickadilly." Coventry House, according to Pennant, stood on the site of a building called in the old plans of London "The Gaming House."

The Secretary, it may be added, died here in 1686, and was buried in the church of St. Martin's-in-the-Fields. Coventry Street was continued eastwards beyond Leicester Square into St. Martin's Lane about the year 1842; the compensation paid to the freeholder of the ground, the Marquis of Salisbury, exceeded £70,000.

Like the rest of this neighbourhood, Coventry Street in its time has had its places of amusement. At one of these, in 1835, was exhibited the "Parisian infernal machine." This extraordinary exhibition comprised a likeness of the murderer Gerard (*alias* Fieschi), before and after the perpetration of his crime, attempting to assassinate the French king and his sons; also a model of the room and of the infernal machinery, taken from drawings made on the spot by distinguished artists, sent to Paris expressly for that purpose. The advertisements announcing this place of entertainment state that "Ladies may visit this exhibition, where the most scrupulous attention has been observed not to wound the most fastidious delicacy."

In 1851, one of the most popular entertainments given here was that of a French wizard, named Robin.

The tobacco and snuff manufactory of Messrs. Wishart, now in the Haymarket, was located in this street for many years. The house has lately been demolished to make room for improvements. The "card" of the firm a century and a half ago, and still used, is a curiosity in its way. A fac-simile of it is here given.

Mr. J. Larwood humorously remarks in his "History of Sign-boards," "Since the Highlander's love of snuff and whisky was such, that he wished to have a Ben Lomond of the former and a Loch Lomond of the latter, nobody could make a better public-house sign than the 'Highland Laddie,' nor a better sign for a snuff-shop than the kilted Highlander, who generally stands guard at the door of these establishments."

The following skit appeared shortly after the Rebellion of 1745, when every effort was made to suppress the nationality of the Scotch, down to their ballads and their kilts:—" We hear that the dapper wooden Highlanders who so heroically guard the doors of snuff-shops intend to petition the Legislature in order that they may be excused

WISHART'S SHOP-CARD.

from complying with the Act of Parliament with respect to the change of dress, alleging that they have ever been faithful subjects to his Majesty, having constantly supplied his guards with a pinch out of their mulls when they marched by; and so far from engaging in any rebellion, they have never

In Coventry's known street, near Leicester Fields,
At the 'Two Heads,' full satisfaction yields.
Teeth artificial he fixes so secure,
That as our own they usefully endure;
Not merely outside show and ornament,
But every property of teeth intent;
To eat as well as speak, and form support

SIR ISAAC NEWTON'S HOUSE, 1850. (*See page* 232.)

entertained a rebellious thought: whence they humbly hope that they shall not be put to the expense of buying new clothes."

The "Two Heads" in this street was, in 1760, the sign of an advertising dentist, who thus makes known his profession in the *London Evening Post:*

" Ye beauties, beaux, ye pleaders at the bar,
Wives, husbands, lovers, every one beside
Who'd have their heads deficient rectify'd,
The dentist famed, who by just application
Excels each other operator in the nation,

To falling cheeks and stumps from further hurt.
Nor is he daunted when the whole is gone,
But by an art peculiar to him known,
He'll so supply, you'll think you've got your own.
He scales, he cleans, he draws; in pain gives ease,
Nor in each operation doth fail to please.
Doth the foul scurvy fierce your gums assault?
In this he also rectifies the fault
By a fam'd tincture. And his powder, nam'd
A Dentifrice, is also justly fam'd.
Used as directed, 'tis excellent to serve
Both teeth and gums—cleanse, strengthen, and preserve.

"Foul mouth and stinking breath can ne'er be lov'd ;
But by his aid these evils are remov'd."

In this street, towards the close of the last century, if the tradition runs aright, there was a famous fish-shop which numbered Sir Joshua Reynolds (who lived hard by in Leicester Square) among its daily customers. The great painter would generally stroll so far before breakfast, examine the fish that lay on the leads, turn them over and reverse their position ; then, having chosen what was to his taste, he would go back to breakfast, report the state of the fish-market, and send his sister to effect the purchase. " Miss Reynolds," the old fishmonger used to say, " never chose ; Sir Joshua never paid ; and both were good hands at driving bargains."

THE LION BREWERY. (*See page* 239.)

CHAPTER XX.

GOLDEN SQUARE AND ITS NEIGHBOURHOOD.

" Fallentis semita vitæ."—*Horace,* "*Epistles.*"

The Neighbourhood of Golden Square Two Centuries ago—Great Windmill Street—Piccadilla Hall—Noted Residents—Anatomical School—Argyll Rooms—St. Peter's Church—Golden Square—Lord Bolingbroke—Mrs. Cibber—Angelica Kauffmann—The Residence of Cardinal Wiseman—Chapel for French Refugees—Wardour Street—Dr. Dodd's Residence—Princes Street—The " Star and Crown " and the " Thirteen Cantons " —Berwick Street—St. Luke's Church—Bentinck Street—Sherwin, the Engraver—Broad Street—William Blake—" The Good Woman "—The Lion Brewery- Warwick Street—Roman Catholic Chapel of the Assumption—Carnaby Street—The Pest Houses—Great Marlborough Street—Distinguished Inhabitants—Argyll Street—Northcote the Painter—Madame de Staël—The " Good " Lord Lyttelton—Argyll House —Argyll Street Rooms—Chabert, the " Fire King "—The Harmonic Institution—Oxford Street—The Pantheon—Miss Linwood's Exhibition of Needlework—The " Green Man and Still "—The " Hog in the Pound "—The " North Pole "—The " Balloon " Fruit-shop.

In the second year after the Restoration orders were issued for the paving of the way from St. James's northwards, which was a quagmire, and also of the Haymarket "about Piquadillo." The Piccadilly line of road is said to have formed at its eastern end the line of demarcation between the courtly mansions then in the course of erection in " St. James's Fields," and the mean and small dwellings which, in Sir C. Wren's words, "will prove only a receptacle for the poorer sort, and for offensive trades, to the annoyance of the better inhabitants, the damage of the parishes already too much burdened with poor, the choking of the air of his Majesty's palace and park and the houses of the nobility, and the infecting of the waters." These dwellings were some lately erected in Dog's Fields, Windmill Fields, and the fields adjoining Soho. This is the first mention that we find of the neighbourhood of which Golden Square and Wardour Street now form the western and eastern limits. The property in this vicinity of old belonged to Lord Craven, who erected the famous pest-house here for the reception of those struck by the plague. The lazaretto itself consisted, we are told, of thirty-six small tenements; and near it, at the lower end of Marshall Street, was a common cemetery, in which some thousands of poor persons found a last resting-place during the continuance of that pestilence. "Out of Wardour Street," we are told by Strype, in 1720, "goeth Peter Street, which crosseth Berwick Street, and falleth into waste and unbuilt ground; a street not over-well inhabited. Here is a small court, but the right name is not given. Further northward is Edward Street, which also crosseth Berwick Street, and falleth into waste and unbuilt ground; nor is this street over-well inhabited." Berwick Street, mentioned as running on the west of Wardour Street as far to the north as "Tyburn Road," is described as a "pretty, handsome, straight street, with new well-built houses, much inhabited by the French, where they have a church." About the middle of the street was a place designed for a hay market, and a great part of the low ground raised, with some of the houses built piazza-wise. "Westward of this," adds the annalist, "is a large tract of waste ground, reaching to the wall of the pest-house builded by the Earl of Craven, which runneth from the back side of Golden Square to a piece or close of meadow ground which reacheth to Tyburn Road."

Passing northward from Coventry Street, in a direct line from the Haymarket, is Great Windmill Street, so called from a mill which stood there till the reign of Charles II.; it was designed at one time to be made the main thoroughfare from Charing Cross and the Haymarket to Oxford Street; the removal of Carlton House, however, deflected this to Swallow (now Regent) Street. At the corner of Great Windmill Street formerly stood a noted gaming-house, called Piccadilly Hall, mentioned by Lord Clarendon, in his "History of the Rebellion," under date 1640. Referring

to himself, Clarendon says: "Mr. Hyde going to a house called Piccadilly, which was a fair house for entertainment and gaming, with handsome gravel walks and with shade, and where were an upper and a lower bowling-green, whither very many of nobility and gentry of the best quality resorted for exercise and conversation."

In explanation apparently of this incidental mention, Pennant tells us that "at the upper end of the Haymarket stood Piccadilla Hall, where piccadillas, or turn-overs, were sold, which gave name to that vast street called from that circumstance Piccadilly." This street was completed in 1642 as far westwards as Berkeley Street. The explanation, however, does not solve the mystery which surrounds the word, unless we suppose that the "fair house for entertainment" mentioned by Lord Clarendon derived its name from the articles sold in the neighbouring houses. The tennis-court attached to the hall was not pulled down till our own day. Its last owner was the celebrated and successful gamester, Colonel Panton. The gaming-house itself figures in Faithorne's plan of London, published in 1658, as almost the only house standing in this locality.

In Great Windmill Street lived Colonel Godfrey, whose wife, Arabella Churchill, sister of John, Duke of Marlborough, had been the mistress of James II., when Duke of York.

Here, in the early part of the present century, was the great Anatomical School of the metropolis, in which nearly all the most distinguished surgeons of the last two generations taught as lecturers and professors. This school of surgery owed its establishment to Dr. William Hunter, who erected the building, and in whose "Medical Commentaries" will be found a full account of its origin and progress. Its lecturers were chiefly members of the staff of St. George's Hospital. The list included such names as Sir C. Bell, Sir B. Brodie, Dr. Baillie, and Dr. Wilson. Some interesting details respecting the introduction of Sir Charles Bell to it, and his long connection with it, will be found in a work entitled "Extracts from the Correspondence of Sir Charles with his Brother, Mr. George Joseph Bell." After flourishing with great prestige for half a century or more, it began to decline, mainly owing to the establishment of other schools of the same kind in connection with University and King's College Hospitals. It may be added that the fine museum in which Sir Charles Bell used to lecture, with its miscellaneous collection of curiosa, which the Government refused to buy, was sold to the Royal College of Surgeons at Edinburgh. The house occupied by the Medical School became afterwards a printing-office, and is now a foreign restaurant.

On the site of the tennis-court of Piccadilly Hall stand the Argyll Rooms, which were formerly opened for promenade concerts and dancing; such, however, was the character that the rooms acquired, that a renewal of the licence was refused about 1878. The place is now known as the "Trocadero." It was for some time a restaurant, but has recently obtained a licence to open as a music-hall. The rooms originally bearing the name of "The Argyll" stood, as we shall presently see, at the corner of Little Argyll Street.

Adjoining the above-mentioned rooms is St. Peter's Church, an edifice of Gothic design, erected in 1861, from the designs of Mr. Raphael Brandon. The church owes its origin mainly to the Rev. J. E. Kempe, the Rector of St. James's, Piccadilly; the money for the work, amounting to some £12,000, having been chiefly obtained through his influence among his wealthy congregation.

Golden Square, which is connected with Windmill Street by two narrow thoroughfares, called respectively Denman and Brewer Streets, though so close to Regent Street, still lies out of the beaten path, and few Londoners know it, unless business happens to call them in its direction. It has been said of it that it is "not exactly in anybody's way, to or from anywhere." Even in the summer time it wears a dull and dingy look, and seems as if it had seen better days. And yet it stands immortalised, not only in Charles Dickens's "Nicholas Nickleby," but in the older and more venerable pages of "Humphrey Clinker" by Tobias Smollett, whilst the authors of the "Rejected Addresses," in their imitation of Crabbe, speak of "bankrupts from Golden Square and Riches Court." It is said to have derived its name from the person by whom it was laid out for building, and Hatton describes it in the reign of Queen Anne, within a few years of its erection, as a "very new and pleasant square." Pennant, however, says that the name was derived from a neighbouring inn, the "Gelding," which the good taste of its inhabitants changed gradually into "Golden"—a change, it must be owned, for the better, if true in fact. Pennant dismisses it with the remark that it is "of dirty access;" and certainly none of the thoroughfares which lead into it can be accused of being broad or clean. This square, which was at one time surrounded with wooden rails, was built a little before the Revolution of 1688, as is clear from its being mentioned by that name in an advertisement in the *Gazette* of that year.

One of its earliest inhabitants was the great Lord Bolingbroke, Pope's friend, when holding the office of Secretary-at-War, in the beginning of the last century; and Mrs. Cibber, the singer, whose name is so well known in connection with that of Lord Peterborough, was living here in the reign of George II. The small and very common-place statue of George II., in the centre of the square, was brought from Lord Chandos's seat at Canons, near Edgware.

In the centre house on the south side of this square resided, for many years, Angelica Kauffmann, one of the original members of the Royal Academy, and who lived till 1807. Of this lady a very amusing story is told, illustrative of female folly and vanity. She was a great coquette, and pretended to be in love with several gentlemen at the same time. Once she professed to be enamoured of Nathaniel Dance; to the next visitor she would divulge the great secret that she was dying for Sir Joshua Reynolds. However, she was at last rightly served for her duplicity, by marrying a very handsome fellow who pretended to be "Count Horn," an adventurer of the type of the Duc de Roussillon of more recent times. With this alliance she was so pleased, that she made her happy conquest known to Queen Charlotte, who was much astonished that the Count should have been so long in England without coming to Court! However, the real Count's arrival was some time afterwards announced at Dover; and Angelica Kauffmann's titled husband turned out to be no other than the real Count's *valet de chambre!* He was prevailed upon subsequently to accept a separate maintenance. After this man's death she married an Italian, named Zucchi, and settled in Rome, where she spent her declining years. There is a portrait of Angelica, by Sir Joshua Reynolds, engraved by Bartolozzi.

The large house in the centre of the north side was for many years the residence of the Roman Catholic vicars-apostolic of the London district, as the heads of that communion in England were designated previous to the restoration of the hierarchy in 1850. Here, about 1835, were living Bishops Bramston and Griffiths, who successively held that office; and the house was the residence of Dr. Wiseman, when he obtained, in 1850, the honour of the archiepiscopal mitre, and the red hat of a cardinal, in spite of Lord John Russell's ineffective opposition.

In 1875, Childs, an old servant of Lord Byron, and the last survivor of his personal attendants, was still acting as a beadle in this square.

In Glasshouse Street, close by the south side of the square, was founded, in 1689, a chapel for one of the French refugee congregations ; but it was removed before long to Leicester Fields.

From what we have said, it is evident that the whole of this district was covered with small buildings towards the beginning of the eighteenth century, though here and there on the north there were a few open spaces left. A piece of stone, let into one of the houses in New Street, on the north side of the square, bears the date 1704. Thirty years before, as already stated, Sir C. Wren complained of the small streets which were being run up, and of the poverty of their inhabitants, as if he could foresee the day when St. Giles' and St. James' would be placed in close and painful contrast ; and Fielding, in the reign of George II., describes the mob, whom he calls the "fourth estate of the realm," as "encroaching upon people of fashion," and driving them fast from their seats in Leicester, Soho, and Golden Squares, to Cavendish Square and other spots in that more distant locality, where there was more light and fresher air, as the breezes blew across the green lanes of St. Marylebone.

The streets to the north and east of the square were the scene of a very violent outbreak of cholera in the year 1853, on account of the overflowing of cess-pools into a well whence the inhabitants drew their supply of water.

To the east of the square lies Wardour Street, renowned as the head-quarters of the dealers in old furniture, and other curiosities, and which serves as a line of demarcation between this district and the parish of Soho. Here, we may add, lived Dr. Dodd in 1751, when, a little over age, he had married a penniless girl, and had not even yet taken orders. We shall have more to say of his career when we come to Pimlico.

"A large fort with four half bulwarks across the road (now Oxford Street), at the corner of Wardour Street," is mentioned among the fortifications ordered to be set up around London by the Parliament in 1642.

Wardour Street, with Princes Street, opens up a direct line of communication between Oxford Street and Leicester Square. In Princes Street was, in 1785, the "Star and Crown," the sign of a fashionable haberdasher, who, amongst other articles of female luxury, dealt in "dress and undress hoops." Branching off on the east from Princes Street is King Street, where there is a tavern called "The Thirteen Cantons." This sign was put up in compliment to the thirteen Protestant cantons of Switzerland, or more strictly speaking, to the numerous natives of those districts who were settled in the neighbourhood of Soho.

Parallel with Wardour Street, and opening into Oxford Street, is Berwick Street, which is described by Hatton (in 1708) as "a kind of a row ;" whilst "the fronts of the houses, resting on columns, make a small piazza." The appearance of the houses in the present day, however, is very much changed. This street was a haunt of artists of little note, and of trades subservient to an artist's requirements. Mr. Peter Cunningham records the fact that Sir Joshua Reynolds's portrait of Sheridan was engraved by a resident in this street, John Hall, a man of some little fame in his day. The only building in this street which merits special mention is St. Luke's Church. This edifice serves as the church of a district cut off from St. James's, Westminster. It was built in 1838-9, from the designs of Mr. Blore, and in the Gothic style of architecture ; but it has, nevertheless, a somewhat poor and mean appearance. The cost of the building and the site on which it stands amounted to about £14,000.

In Bentinck Street, which runs out of Berwick Street, was the studio of Sherwin, the engraver. Mr. J. T. Smith tells the following anecdote of this place, which brings up the remembrance of one of the most famous actresses of the last century :—

"The Bishop of Peterborough (Dr. Hinchliffe), one of my father's patrons, prevailed on Sherwin to let me in at half-price ; and under his roof I remained for nearly three years. Here I saw all the beautiful women of the day ; and being considered a lively lad, I was noticed by several of them. Here I received a kiss from the beautiful Mrs. Robinson.

"This impression was made upon me, nearly as I can recollect, in the following way :—It fell to my turn that morning, as a pupil, to attend the visitors, and Mrs. Robinson came into the room singing. She asked to see a drawing which Mr. Sherwin had made of her, which he had placed in an upper room. When I assured her that Mr. Sherwin was not at home, 'Do try to find the drawing of me, and I will reward you, my little fellow,' said she. I, who had seen 'Rosetta,' in *Love in a Village*, the preceding evening, hummed to myself as I went upstairs, 'With a kiss, and a kiss, I'll reward you with a kiss." I had no sooner entered the room with the drawing in my hand, than she imprinted a kiss on my cheek, and said, 'There, you little rogue.' I remember that Mrs. Berby, her mother, accompanied her, and had brought a miniature, painted by Cosway, set in diamonds, presented by 'a high personage,' of whom Mrs. Robinson spoke with the highest respect to her last hour. The colour of her carriage was a light blue, and upon the centre of each panel a basket of flowers was so artfully painted, that as she drove along it was mistaken for a coronet."

In Broad Street, a little to the north-east of this square, where his father kept a hosier's shop, was born, in 1757, William Blake, the gifted poet and painter, the author of "Songs of Innocence," "Songs of Experience," &c. Here, too, after his marriage, in 1784-7, he established himself as a print-seller and engraver. In the latter year he removed into Poland Street, hard by, and after many wanderings he died at Fountain Court, in the Strand, in 1827. In this street there was a most ill-natured sarcasm levelled against the fair sex on a sign-board, representing a headless female figure, and styled "The Good Woman." No doubt this sign was older than the Reformation, and represented St. Osyth, the Saxon martyr, who is said to have been beheaded. The legend runs that where her head fell a spring of clear water bubbled up. The same sign—said to be the only good woman in Essex—curiously enough, still exists at Widford, near Chelmsford, a parish in which the Priory of St. Osyth formerly held lands. In Broad Street is the Lion Brewery, represented on page 235.

But to return to Golden Square. On its west side, running parallel with Regent Street, and forming a communication between Glasshouse Street and Great Marlborough Street, is Warwick Street, on the eastern side of which stands the Roman Catholic Chapel of the Assumption, long known as the Bavarian Chapel, from having been originally erected, in the time of the penal laws, under the shelter and protection of the Bavarian Embassy. It is probable that it was founded under the later Stuarts, though its registers go back only to 1747. To it most of the noble Roman Catholic families, during the last century, when this was a fashionable quarter of the town, resorted for the celebration of divine service, and of marriages and baptisms. It was burnt down in the Gordon riots of 1780, and not rebuilt, or, at all events, re-opened till eight years afterwards, so great and so real was the panic caused by that outbreak of fanaticism. According to the trust deed, the chapel was built as a sanctuary, not for the West-end of London only, but for the whole Roman Catholic body of England. In 1839 the Auxiliary Catholic Institute was established in connection with this chapel. Here, it is said, the first modern "mission service" was held; and within its walls the first English pilgrimage to Paray le Monial was projected, organised, and sent forth in September, 1873, in honour of the Sacred Heart, a devotion first taught in England very near this

spot by F. Colombiere, chaplain to Queen Mary Beatrice, wife of James II.

The chapel, when rebuilt, stood a little back from the line of the street, being made so to retreat in order to avoid attracting notice, as is or was till lately the case with Roman Catholic chapels even in Dublin. It is a poor, shapeless, and unsightly edifice, built after the commonest type of Noncon-formist chapels of the time, with heavy galleries and round-headed windows. The decorations of the interior, especially about the altar, redeem it to some extent from the charge of being hideous; and in 1875 a large subscription was entered into by the Roman Catholic body for the enlargement and adornment of the structure, the old walls being retained as memorials of a state of things which happily has long since passed away.

This chapel, it may be added, serves as a centre of ministration for a very large number of Roman Catholics of the middle classes about the southern parts of Soho. The residence of the priests who officiate in this chapel is in Golden Square, with which it has a communication in the rear. The schools attached to the chapel are among the most efficient in the Roman Catholic arch-diocese of Westminster.

Carnaby Street, which extends from the north side of the square to Great Marlborough Street, is thus described by Strype:—"An ordinary street which goes out of Silver Street, and runs northward almost to the bowling ground. On the east side of this street are the Earl of Craven's pest-houses, seated in a large piece of ground, inclosed with a brick wall, and handsomely set with trees, in which are buildings for the entertainment of persons that shall have the plague, when it shall please God that any contagion shall happen."

Maitland, in his "History of London," mentions the Pest Field in the following terms :—"The site whereon Marshall Street, part of Little Broad Street, and Marlborough Market are now erected, was denominated the Pest Field, from a lazaretto therein, which consisted of thirty-six small houses, for the reception of poor and miserable objects of this neighbourhood that were afflicted with the direful pestilence of 1665. And at the lower end of Marshall Street, contiguous to Silver Street, was a common cemetery, wherein some thousands of corpses were buried that died of that dreadful and virulent contagion." When Carnaby Street and other streets were built, a "field on the Pad-dington estate" was assigned as a pest-field in place of that which we have described.

The parish authorities of St. James's do not appear to have been very popular with the poor in

GOLDEN SQUARE IN 1750.

the reign of the first Georges, if we may take literally the following paragraph which occurs in the *St. James's Evening Post*, of August 4, 1726 :—"Some days since, while the officers of the parish of St. James, Westminster, were making merry at a tavern, the workhouse in the Pest-Fields (nearly finished) was then " esteemed one of the finest in Europe." The writer adds, however, that its only claim to such a character lies in its length and breadth, " the buildings on each side being trifling and inconsiderable, and the vista ending either way in nothing great or extraordinary." To the eyes of

THE PANTHEON THEATRE. (*See page 244.*)

for the reception of the poor was blown down by a sudden gust of wind, to the no small satisfaction of the lazars, who testified their joy by loud acclamations, bonfires, and other illuminations in the evening."

Great Marlborough Street, which we now enter, runs parallel with Oxford Street, extending from Poland Street to Regent Street. If we may believe the author of the "New Critical Review of the Public Buildings of London," in 1736, this street

persons in the nineteenth century, the street will, we fancy, present little ground for admiration, even of this limited kind : it is a broad, heavy, dull street, and that is all.

A century or so ago the appearance of the street must have been very different from what it is in the present day ; for, as we learn, it formed one of the principal promenades for the belles and beaux of the day, when the piazza in Covent Garden had become deserted by them, and the shady walk along the Mall in St. James's Park had lost for a time its attraction. Its chief literary note arises from the fact that a house on the north side was for many years the publishing office of the late Mr. Henry Colburn, to whom we are so much indebted for cheap light literature. After his death his business passed into the hands of Messrs. Hurst and Blackett.

That talented but unfortunate genius, B. R. Haydon, in the earlier part of his career, had lodgings on the southern side of this street, which at that time had not quite lost its fashionable character. Cyrus Redding tells us, in his "Autobiography," how he breakfasted with Haydon and Wilkie at the "Nassau Coffee House" at the corner of Nassau and Gerrard Streets, close to the home of John Dryden, which we have already mentioned, between Leicester Fields and Soho.

This street had also another distinguished inhabitant, in the person of the miser, John Elwes, who, on one occasion, had a narrow escape of his life here. The story is thus told:—It was the custom of Mr. Elwes, whenever he went to London, to occupy either of his houses that might be vacant. On one occasion when he had come to town, and, as usual, had taken up his abode in one of the empty houses, Colonel Timms (his nephew), who wished much to see him, in vain inquired at his banker's and at other places. Some days elapsed, and he at length learned from a person whom he met by chance in the street that Mr. Elwes had been seen going into an uninhabited house in Great Marlborough Street. The colonel proceeded to the house, knocked very loudly at the door, but could obtain no answer. Feeling alarmed, he sent for a person to join him, and they entered the house together. In the lower part all was shut and silent, but on ascending the stairs they heard the moans of a person seemingly in distress. They went to the chamber, and there on an old pallet-bed they found Mr. Elwes, apparently in the agonies of death. For some time he seemed quite insensible, but on some cordials being administered he recovered.

At the western end of the street, near the Argyll Baths and Argyll Street, is the Marlborough Street Police Court.

Argyll Street, which here branches off from Great Marlborough Street, and forms the connecting link between its western end and Oxford Street, runs northwards parallel with Regent Street. Here Sir Joseph Banks was born, as already stated by us, in the reign of George II. Here, too, Northcote the painter lived and died. Of him Cyrus Redding writes in his "Recollections:"—"I used to visit Northcote before I went abroad, and often sat in Argyll Street talking to him about the West country, while he was painting. He was a vain man, of a contracted mind, an excellent small story-teller, not over good-natured. He owed to the assistance of others all the attempts he made in literature, and to no one was he so deeply in debt as to Hazlitt. His offence with that writer was pretended. When he died he left him a hundred pounds as a memento of their intimacy—rather an odd mode of exhibiting his wrath!"

In 1811 Madame de Staël, that brilliant and learned woman, was living in lodgings here; and here she put in force and exercised the prerogative of intellect, by actually making even the Prince Regent pay her a visit, before she would wait on him at Court. But we need not wonder at her boldness or her success, for she was the only human being before whom the great Napoleon quailed, and whom he owned that he could not conquer.

The house which was occupied by Madame de Staël is to be identified by the description of it in Mr. Cyrus Redding's "Fifty Years' Recollections." It was about the middle of the western side of the street, "nearly opposite to Lord Aberdeen's." Madame de Staël has been so often described, that it is difficult to say about her anything that is fresh. Redding records the fact that when he called, between one and two o'clock, he was long before her time of seeing visitors, as she spent her mornings in reading and writing in bed, and never left her room till after two o'clock. She was plain and unattractive in her appearance, and was so conscious of the fact, that she told him, as well as others, that "she would willingly exchange her literary reputation for personal beauty." And yet she was so far from aiming at what is generally thought a woman's empire, that she professed herself especially fond of men's society, on the ground of their being less disposed than women to frivolous conversation. She was seen, he tells us, at her best in a small circle, where her good sayings secured attention, though she was "fond of a large company in her drawing-room, on the ground, perhaps, that an actor likes to see a full house." He adds— "Madame de Staël's drawing-room in Argyll Street was a daily levée. All the world went to see her, and she to see all the world. If she had some little vanity, she had a just claim to be excused that fault. It would be difficult to find any female writer since to approach her in ability. She thus gained a precedence she never used ungracefully. Her critical remarks on Teutonic literature, her extensive acquirements and reading, and the aim she had in her writings of fiction, always elevated, and never downward or mean in tendency, showing the worthiest aspirations, made me, as I still am, one of the admirers of that renowned lady."

It is of Madame de Staël,—

"Necker's fair daughter, Staël the Epicene,"

that the story is told that, when she first came to London, she had hardly reached her lodgings when she inquired of the servant of the house if he could direct her to the tomb of Richardson. The man knew nothing of poems or comedies, and sent her to a tavern-keeper at Covent Garden, of that name, who had lately lost his father; but, of course, that was not the Richardson whom she wanted. At last, after sundry adventures, which took her to Cornhill and to Paternoster Row, she learned that Richardson lay buried in St. Clement Danes Churchyard. Off she packed at once, dark and drizzly as the evening was, in quest of the tomb of her favourite English writer, and, when she had found it, prostrated herself upon the cold and mud-sprinkled stone with such reverence and zeal that on returning to Argyll Street, it took her landlady and servant the whole evening to brush her dress, and make her presentable.

In this street lived George, Lord Lyttelton— the "good" Lord Lyttelton—the friend of Pope, Thomson, and Mallet. To him Pope alludes in these lines:—

"Sometimes a patriot, active in debate,
Mix with the world and battle for the State,
Free as young Lyttelton her cause pursue,
Still true to virtue, and as warm as true."

Lord Lyttelton's "Poems," "Dialogues of the Dead," "History of Henry II.," and "Dissertation on the Conversion of St. Paul," have given him a respectable rank in literature. It appears from his "Correspondence" that he wrote his treatise on St. Paul's conversion chiefly with a view to meet the case of Thomson, who, in that sceptical age, was troubled with doubts. Lyttelton was anxious that the amiable poet should unite the *faith* to the *heart* of a Christian, "for the latter he always had." The circumstance is highly honourable to Lyttelton, and is another instance of that warmth of friendship which Thomson inspired.

About the centre of this street, on the eastern side, there formerly stood a dull, heavy mansion of no architectural pretensions, called Argyll House, after the Dukes of Argyll, to whom it had originally belonged. It had a small paved court-yard before it, with a wall and gates of the approved pattern. Early in the present century it became the property of "the travell'd Thane, Athenian Aberdeen," as Lord Byron calls the late Earl of Aberdeen, who resided here both previously and whilst Premier

at the beginning of the Crimean war. His lordship was the last nobleman who lived on the eastern side of Regent Street, showing how thoroughly fashion's tide, like that of empire, sets to the westward amongst us. The house was pulled down about the year 1865, and the site was used for building. In its place arose an edifice which has been used for various purposes, being at one time the Corinthian Bazaar, and at another as Hengler's Circus.

At the corner of Little Argyll Street formerly stood the Argyll Rooms. The establishment was founded under the auspices of Colonel Greville, a noted sportsman and "man about town" under the Regency, who purchased a large house and turned it into a place of entertainment, as a rival to the Pantheon. The fashionable world worshipped at Colonel Greville's shrine, and its balls, masquerades, and amateur balls soon became part of the recognised amusements of West-end society.

In 1811 Lady Margaret Crawford, a lady of eccentric and individual character, gave a ball here "to all her friends, or rather her enemies." It is made a matter of complaint by a French gentleman of fashion in London, in 1823, addressing an English friend, "The wives and daughters of your most respectable country gentlemen no sooner arrive in London than, forgetting all high feelings of conscious virtue and hereditary pride, they seem anxious to purchase, at any price, the honour of belonging to 'The Argyll Street Rooms,' and of frequenting the Wednesday balls at 'Almack's.' Even mothers of families, who have gone through life with untainted reputation, if unable to gain the envied distinction themselves, will condescend to court the 'patronage' of women of very different characters, and to entrust their fair young daughters to the care of peeresses, whose 'indiscretions' would long since have banished them from all association with the best of their own sex, had not their lords been conveniently blind to their failings. No costs or pains are spared to propitiate these deities of fashion—the 'lady patronesses.'"

In 1818 the rooms were rebuilt in a handsome style, by Mr. John Nash, the architect. Here the *contralto* singer, Velluti, gave a concert in June, 1829. In the same year, M. Chabert, who rejoiced in the title of the "fire king," here exhibited his power of resisting the effects of poisons, and withstanding extreme heat. Among other things, we are told that he "swallowed forty grains of phosphorus, sipped oil at 333° with impunity, and rubbed a red-hot shovel over his tongue, hair, and face unharmed; that he swallowed a piece of a burning torch; and then, dressed in coarse woollen, entered an oven heated to 380°, sung a song, and cooked two dishes of beef-steaks!" "These performances," it is added, "were suspected of being a chemical juggle."

The building was burnt down in 1830. On this occasion, Mr. Braithwaite first publicly applied steam-power to the working of a fire-engine; and we are informed that "it required eighteen minutes to raise the water in the boiler to 212°, when the engine threw up from thirty to forty tons of water per hour to a height of ninety feet."

Adjoining the Argyll Rooms was a long range of buildings, formerly known as the "Harmonic Institution" of Messrs. Welsh and Hawes. It was originally a species of joint-stock company, associated for the publication of musical compositions, and other objects connected with that art. But from about the year 1828 it was conducted entirely by the two eminent musical professors whose name it bore. It had a portico, with capitals formed of female heads.

Oxford Street, the south side of which we now enter, has always been a street of shops, and for the most part of good shops also, as was eminently fitting for one of the two great westerly thoroughfares of the city of this "nation of shopkeepers." Less fashionable than Regent Street, because further from the court and courtly influences, and less devoted to pleasure than the Strand, owing to its greater distance from the theatres, it has always preserved the happy medium of respectability. It seems strange, indeed, now that we are bowled at the rate of nine or ten miles an hour in a hansom cab over the level pavement of Oxford Street, or at a slower rate in an omnibus, to learn that, within the memory of the antiquary Pennant (who died in 1798), it was little better than a quagmire, dangerous on account of its roughness, and on account of the "cut-throats" who frequented it, malgré the "Charlies" and the night-watch. But so it was. In spite of its containing the Oxford Music Hall, the Soho Bazaar, the Princess's Theatre, and the old Pantheon, it has, on the whole, steered clear of fashionable dissipation; and it now is content to be the chief thoroughfare in which the well-to-do, but not over-rich, classes purchase the necessaries and comforts of life, in the way of clothing, dresses, haberdashery, domestic wares, and generally those articles which form the delight and the comfort of the British matron.

Of the Soho Bazaar we have already spoken in the previous volume, and of the Oxford Music Hall we shall have to speak when describing the northern side of this great thoroughfare; but of the Pantheon, which may now (except in name) be reckoned among the places that have been, we may here state that it occupied a large space of ground between Argyll Street and Poland Street, and that it extended from Oxford Street back into Great Marlborough Street. The building, with a portico projecting over the pavement, is still called the "Pantheon," and was formerly known under that name as a bazaar. Its exterior has few pretensions to architectural beauty; but a guide-book of London, published in 1851, assures us that at that time "the interior, in point of extent, design, convenience of arrangement, and beauty of execution united," was "unequalled by anything of the kind in London, or even in Europe." Perhaps this may have been the case; but its interior beauty, and that of its fair bevy of marchandes, did not prevent it from running to the end of its career as a bazaar. About the year 1870 it was closed, and converted into wine stores.

The Pantheon, a century ago, was celebrated for its masquerades. In the London Magazine for 1773, we read: "The play-houses, the operas, the masquerades, the Pantheon, Vauxhall, Ranelagh, Mrs. Cornelys, the London Tavern, &c., are all crowded. . . . . The money squandered at the last masquerade was computed to be £20,000, though tradesmen go unpaid, and the industrious poor are starving." We are sorry to read this remark of a contemporary, who could scarcely be ignorant of facts, or have been allowed to pervert them uncontradicted; but hitherto we always supposed that such extravagances were defensible, mainly on the ground that they were "good for trade."

The Pantheon was originally built in 1770–1, as a place of public amusement, including concerts, balls, promenades, &c., with the view of cutting the wind out of the sails of Mrs. Cornelys, whose successes at Soho Square (as already recorded) roused feelings of jealousy in her rivals, the more strongly, perhaps, because she was a foreigner. The building was erected from the designs of James Wyatt, and was opened early in 1772. It was intended by its founders to be a sort of winter Ranelagh in London, and it cost £60,000. It was destroyed by fire in 1792; rebuilt on the same plan, and pulled down in 1812, the Oxford Street front being preserved from the original building. Having served as a place of amusement of various kinds, in 1834 it was remodelled, and made into a bazaar, similar to its rival in Soho Square.

The original Pantheon is immortalised by Sheridan, in one of his comedies, and is thus described by gossiping Horace Walpole, in May, 1770, in a letter to his friend, Sir Horace Mann:—"The new winter Ranelagh in the Oxford Road is nearly finished. It amazed me myself. Imagine Balbec in all its glory. The pillars are of artificial *giallo antico*. The ceilings even of the passages are of the most beautiful stuccos in the best taste of grotesque. The ceilings of the ball-rooms and the panels are painted like Raphael's *loggias* in the Vatican: a dome like the Pantheon glazed. It is to cost fifty thousand pounds."

In the year 1783, a masquerade took place here in honour of the coming of age of the Prince of Wales; it was got up by a noted clown of the period, named Delpini, and a charge of three guineas was made for each ticket. In the following year, a concert in commemoration of Handel was performed here, which was attended by the king, queen, and royal family.

Here, in September and October, 1784, was exhibited the balloon in which Lunardi had made his first successful ascent (September 15) from the Artillery Ground at Moorfields. He gained a large sum by the exhibition, and became the lion of the season, being presented at Court, to receive the king's and queen's congratulations on account of his achievement; although, if the truth must be told, the very first ascent in Great Britain had been made about three weeks before by a poor man at Edinburgh.

In 1788, after the destruction of the King's Theatre, the Pantheon was fitted up as an opera-house by Mr. O'Reilly, at a rent of £3,000. After that, in 1812, a lease of these premises was taken by Mr. Cundy, the builder, and some other persons, and the interior was reconstructed as a theatre, on a plan analogous to that of the Great Theatre at Milan, for the performance of Italian comic operas, burlettas, &c. The boxes, 171 in number, were disposed into four regular tiers, besides the upper or slip boxes. They were supported by gilt columns, furnished with curtains and chairs, and illuminated by chandeliers. The pit would accommodate about 1,200 and the gallery 500 persons. The stage was 56 feet wide and 90 feet deep. The devices and designs before the curtain were by Signio; the scene-painter was Marinari. A saloon, measuring 49 feet by 21 feet, was appropriated to the boxes, and a refreshment-room was attached to the pit. It was opened on the 25th of February, 1812, at opera prices, with T. Dibdin's opera of *The Cabinet*. In 1814 everything movable was sold, in which state it remained many years, only the bare walls being left. Several applications were made by Mr. Cundy for a renewal of a lease to open it again as a winter theatre, but failed.

In 1796-8 Miss Linwood's collection of needle-work was exhibited at the Pantheon, previous to its establishment at the Hanover Square Rooms. Miss Linwood died in 1845, at the age of ninety, seventy-six years after working the earliest of her pictures. "The designs," says Mr. Timbs, "were executed with five crewels, dyed expressly for her, on a thick tammy, and were entirely drawn and embroidered by her own hand."

The Pantheon has also its political recollections. Here, in 1806, Gale Jones, and other Radicals of the time of Pitt and Fox, used to meet and discuss the necessity of Parliamentary Reform, in spite of informers.

Close to the corner of Argyll Street, near Regent Circus, is a noted booking-office for heavy goods and parcels, called the "Green Man and Still." "This is," says Mr. Larwood, "a liberty taken with the arms of the distillers, the supporters of which are two Indians. The latter were transformed by the sign-painters into wild men, or green men, and the green men, again, into foresters; and then it was said that the sign arose from the partiality of foresters, as such, for the produce of the still!" In all probability, however, the reference is really to a "green man"—that is, a seller of green herbs and other produce of what used to be called a physic-garden, in which case the still would be easily understood as an adjunct.

The "Hog in the Pound" was the name of an inn in this street, commonly known as "The Gentleman in Trouble." It was a great starting-point for coaches to the western parts, and it gained notoriety by a murder committed by its landlady, Catherine Hayes. Having formed an improper acquaintance, she was induced by her paramour to murder her husband, after which she cut off his head, put it in a bag, and threw it into the Thames. It floated ashore; and being set up in the churchyard of St. Margaret's at Westminster, it was recognised, and by a train of events the murder was brought home to its perpetrators. The man was hanged, and Mrs. Hayes was burnt alive at Tyburn, in the year 1726.

The "North Pole" inn, which stands near Wardour Street, commemorates one of those expeditions which have been sent out to explore the Arctic regions, from the days of Frobisher to those of Franklin, M'Clintock, and Nares.

It may here be mentioned that a house in this street, near Soho Square, known as "the Balloon" fruit-shop, was the first in London to commemorate on its sign the conquest over nature which was thought to have been achieved in September, 1783, when the first "air-balloon" ascended at Versailles, in the presence of Louis XVI. and his family.

OLD STABLES IN SWALLOW STREET, 1820. (*See page* 249.)

CHAPTER XXI.

REGENT STREET AND PICCADILLY.

"Westward the tide of empire holds its way."

Westward Extension of the Metropolis—Albert Smith's and Horace Walpole's Remarks thereon—Origin of the Name of Piccadilly—Tradesmen's Tokens—Gradual Extension of Piccadilly—Appearance of the Site of Regent Street in the Last Century—The County Fire Office—The Quadrant—Regent Street—Archbishop Tenison's Chapel—Foubert's Riding Academy—*Fraser's Magazine* and its Early Contributors—A "Literary Duel"—Hanover Chapel—Anecdote of the Poet Campbell—Little Vine Street—The "Man in the Moon"—Swallow Street—Chapel of the Scotch Presbyterians—St. James's Hall—Piccadilly—Fore's Exhibition—M. Daguerre's Experiments—Lady Hamilton—Mr. Quaritch's Book-Store—The Genealogical and Historical Society—St. James's Church—Sir William Petty, the Political Economist—Eminent Publishers—Bullock's Museum—The Egyptian Hall—The Albany—"Dan" Lambert—Arlington Street—The Old "White Horse Cellar," and the Glories of Stage-coaching.

WHAT the poet has said so pithily about the tide of empire may be said also of the tide of fashion in this great metropolis, which for these two centuries and more past has set steadily westward. As Mr. Albert Smith remarks, in his "Sketches of London Life:"—"Proceeding in two parallel directions, divided by Oxford Street, Hanover Square gradually declined before that of Grosvenor, and Portman rose above that of Manchester. Still fashion kept marching on—the former division tending towards May Fair, and the latter to the Edgware Road; until the first, turned aside in its course by Hyde Park, reached the site of Belgravia, and the second, heedless of the associations connected with the gallows, and

the decaying foliage of the Bayswater tea-gardens, colonised Tyburnia for its territory."

That old prince of gossips, Horace Walpole, writes thus to Miss Berry and her sister, in 1791:—"Though London increases every day, and Mr. Herschel* has just discovered a new square or circus somewhere by the New Road, in the 'Via Lactea,' where the cows used to be fed, I believe you will think the town cannot hold all its inhabitants, so prodigiously the population is augmented. I have twice been going to stop my coach in Piccadilly (and the same has happened to Lady Ailesbury), thinking there was a mob, and it was only nymphs and swains sauntering

* The great astronomer.

SWALLOW STREET DURING ITS DEMOLITION.   (*See page* 249)

or trudging. T'other morning, *i.e.*, at two o'clock, I went to see Mrs. Garrick and Miss Hannah More at the Adelphi, and was stopped five times before I reached Northumberland House; for the tides of coaches, chariots, curricles, phaetons, &c., are endless. Indeed, the town is so extended, that the breed of chairs is almost lost; for Hercules and Atlas could not carry anybody from one end of the enormous capital to the other. How magnified would be the error of the young woman at St. Helena, who some years ago said to the captain of an Indiaman, 'I suppose London is very empty when the India ships come out.'"

And again, in the same letter: "There will soon be one street from London to Brentford—aye, and from London to every village within ten miles round. . . . . London is, I am certain, much fuller than ever I saw it. I have twice this spring been going to stop my coach in Piccadilly, to inquire what was the matter, thinking there was a mob: not at all; it was only foot-passengers." He adds a few remarks, by way of consolation, to the effect that, in spite of the enormous increase of London, there was as yet no complaint that the country was coming to be depopulated, as Bath "shoots out into new crescents, circuses, and squares every year; while Birmingham, Manchester, Hull, and Liverpool would serve any king in England for a capital, and even make the Empress of Russia's mouth to water."

The origin of the name of Piccadilly is wrapped in obscurity, and has frequently been discussed in *Notes and Queries*, and in other quarters. Mr. Peter Cunningham and Mr. John Timbs, among modern antiquaries, have started the inquiry as to its derivation rather than solved it; and we must be content to believe, with them, that the street gradually took its name from a place of amusement, spoken of in the preceding chapter as formerly standing at its eastern or town end, styled Piccadilly Hall, which in its turn was so styled after the ruffs, called "pickadils," or "peccadillos," worn by the gallants of the reign of James I., the stiffened points of which, as Mr. Timbs observes, resembled spear-heads, or "picardills," a diminutive of the Spanish and Italian word *pica* (Latin *spica*) a spear. Ben Jonson writes, in his "Underwoods:"—

"And then leap mad on a neat pickardill."

To this line Mr. Robert Bell appends a note to the effect that the latter word is the name of "a stiff collar, or ruff, generally with sharp points, and derived from 'picca,' a spear-head. The ruff came into fashion, as we see by contemporary portraits, early in the reign of James I.; and, according to

some authorities, gave its name to the street of Piccadilly." But then, the further difficulty arises, how to connect Piccadilly Hall with so fanciful a word. Was it, as is sometimes said, because the man who built it—one Higgins, a draper—made his fortune by the sale of "pickadils" when they were the height of fashion? or was the Hall itself originally a way-side inn, so named by chance or caprice? or does some subtle and fanciful analogy underlie the name? and are we to suppose that it was so styled by the Londoners, as being "the utmost or skirt house of the suburbs that way?" This supposition is too far-fetched, and savours too much of poetry, we think, to be ascribed to the ordinary and commonplace Londoners. Then, again, an old writer, Blount, in his "Glossographia," interprets the word as denoting "the round hem about the edge or skirt of a garment, or a stiff collar or band for the neck and shoulders;" whence Butler, in his "Hudibras," styles the collars in the pillory "peccadilloes." If so, may not the name have originated from the pillory having been often set up here in the good old Tudor times? Pennant, again, has another derivation to offer, suggesting that it comes from a sort of cakes or turnovers called "piccadillas,' which were sold in the fields about here. Whatever the connecting link may be, however, it is clear that the name, as applied to these parts, dates from the sixteenth century; for Gerard, in his "Herbal," published in 1596, speaks of the small wild buglosse which grows upon the dry ditch-banks about "Pickadilla." D'Israeli, in his "Curiosities of Literature," tells us that Piccadilly "was named after Piccadilla Hall, a place of sale for piccadillies, or turnovers, a part of the fashionable dress which appeared about the year 1814. It has preserved its name uncorrupted; for Barnabe Rich, in his 'Honesty of the Age,' has this passage on 'the body-makers that do swarm through all parts, both of London and about London.' He says, 'The body is still pampered up in the very dropsy of excess.' He that some forty years sithence should have asked after a Pickadilly, I wonder who should have understood him, or could have told what a Pickadilly had been, either fish or flesh.'" So we must be content to leave the inquiry where we found it, and pass on.

The name Piccadilly is found written in a variety of ways. Mr. Akerman, in his work on "London Tradesmen's Tokens," enumerates eleven different specimens, in the shape of copper coins, which bear date, "Piccadily," between 1660 and 1670. Some of these are issued by grocers, some by "sea-coal" dealers, and others apparently by the keepers of forges. They do not agree in their orthography, for the name is spelt "Peckadille," "Pickedila," "Pickadilla," and other ways.

The first thoroughfare bearing the name of Piccadilly, says Mr. Peter Cunningham, was a very short line of road, running no further west than the foot of Sackville Street; and the name Piccadilly Street occurs, for the first time, in the rate-books of St. Martin's, under the year 1673. Between Sackville and Albemarle Streets, or, as some say, to Stratton Street, or even to Hyde Park, at different times, the thoroughfare was called Portugal Street, after Catherine of Braganza, Queen of Charles II.; all beyond that point being the great Bath Road, or, as it is called in Aggas's map (1560), "the way to Reding." The Queen, however, was never a favourite with the people, and gradually the name of Piccadilly displaced her memory altogether. "The north side," says Pennant in 1790, "consists of houses, most of them mean buildings; but it finishes handsomely with the magnificent new house of Lord Bathurst, at Hyde Park Corner." It is amusing to compare the state of the street at that date with what it is in the reign of Victoria. The Green Park, opposite, was shut in by a brick wall, in which, however, were inserted, here and there, some "benevolent" railings, to enable the passers-by to catch a glimpse of the trees inside.

The first mansion built along Piccadilly was Goring House, which stood on what is now Arlington Street; it was bought by Bennett, Lord Arlington, after whom both Bennett and Arlington Streets were named. Nearly opposite it, about 1688, rose Clarendon House, and Burlington House, built by Sir John Denham, and re-fronted by the celebrated amateur architect, Boyle, Earl of Burlington. This negatives the hackneyed story of Lord Burlington having chosen the site of his mansion so far out of town that no one could build beyond him. Immediately to the east were the house and garden of the Earl of Sunderland, the treacherous minister of James II.; the site is now occupied by the Albany.

"In 1711," according to Hunter's "History of London," "the town extended as far west as Devonshire House. Beyond Clifford Street was built Bond Street, which took its name from the family of a baronet, now extinct, who owned the ground. But New Bond Street was still an open field, called Conduit Mead, from one of the conduits which supplied that part of the town with water, and from which Conduit Street, adjoining, derived its name. All beyond was open ground, a receptacle for dunghills, and every kind of refuse . . . Oxford Street was then built on the south side, as far as Swallow Street (now absorbed in Regent Street), but almost unbuilt on the north side. It was a deep hollow road, full of sloughs, with here and there a ragged house, the lurking-place of cut-throats."

The head-quarters of the fashionable world, as lately as the beginning of the reign of George IV., lay between Piccadilly and Oxford Street. Hence, a witty personage, when giving advice to a rich country friend as to how to make a good show in London, says—

" Hire a house in the purlieus of *ton*, and take care
   That it stands in a street near some smart-sounding square,
   Such as ' Hanover,' ' Grosvenor,' or ' Portman,' at least."

A better incidental proof could not well have been given that Belgrave and Eaton Squares were not as yet erected. In fact, at that date Belgravia was a swamp, and its squares were cabbage-gardens.

Near the eastern extremity of Piccadilly the thoroughfare is intersected by Regent Street, which commences at Waterloo Place, and proceeds northward for nearly a mile. It crosses Piccadilly, by a circus, to the County Fire Office, whence it passes to the north-west by a curved road, called the Quadrant, and then again in a direct line northward, crossing Oxford Street to Langham Place. On the whole, this street—at all events in its lower parts—follows the line of Swallow Street, which it superseded. To judge from its appearance, as preserved to us in the prints of the time, the latter was a long, ugly, and irregular thoroughfare. The tradition is that it bore a reputation by no means good, and contained, among its other houses, a certain livery-stable, which in the last century was a noted house-of-call for highwaymen.

Of the appearance of this district in the last year of the reign of Charles II., Lord Macaulay gives us the following picture:—"He who then rambled to what is now the gayest and most crowded part of Regent Street, found himself in a solitude, and was sometimes so fortunate as to have a shot at a woodcock.* On the north the Oxford road ran between hedges. Three or four hundred yards to the south were the garden-walls of a few great houses, which were considered as quite out of town. On the west was a meadow, renowned for a spring, from which, long afterwards, Conduit Street was named. On the east (near where now stands Golden Square) was a field not to be passed without a shudder by any Londoner of that age. There, as in a place far from the haunts of men, had been dug, twenty years before, when the great plague was raging, a pit into which the dead-carts had nightly shot

---
* General Oglethorpe, who died in 1785, used to boast that he had shot such birds here in Queen Anne's reign.

corpses by scores. It was popularly believed that the earth was deeply tainted with infection, and could not be disturbed without imminent risk to human life. No foundations were laid there till two generations had passed without any return of the pestilence, and till the ghastly spot had long been surrounded by buildings. It may be added, that the 'pest-field' may still be seen marked in maps of London as late as the end of the reign of George I."

The County Fire Office, which stands at the commencement of the Quadrant, was built from the designs of Mr. Abraham. It is a stately pile, of the Composite order, with a rustic basement and arcade, above which rise six three-quarter columns, and pilasters at the angles, supporting the entablature; the latter is surmounted by a balustrade and parapet, on the centre of which is a colossal figure of Britannia, standing with her spear and shield, and at her side the British lion couchant.

The Quadrant had, originally, a Doric colonnade on either side, projecting over the foot-pavements. The columns—some 270 in number—were of cast-iron, sixteen feet high, exclusive of the granite plinth, and supported a balustraded roof. The effect of this novel piece of street architecture was generally considered as very fine and picturesque. The colonnades, however, in consequence of the darkness which they imparted to the shops, were removed in 1848, at which time a balcony was added to the principal floor. In the centre of the Quadrant, on the south-west side, is one of the entrances to the St. James's Hall. Cyrus Redding fixes the Quadrant as the scene of the following incident. He writes in his "Recollections:"— "Campbell and myself set off one morning to walk to Dulwich College, to see the pictures and dine. We were passing along the Quadrant, when we met Sir James Mackintosh, looking serious. 'What a melancholy affair this is,' was his remark, without a 'good morning.' 'What affair?' 'The death of Sir Thomas Lawrence.' Campbell, who had been with Sir Thomas the evening but one before, was thunderstricken. When Sir James had passed on, I could not help remarking I thought he would be the next to depart—he looked so ill. My surmise was confirmed. It was not long before I visited his resting-place, with his daughter, in Hampstead churchyard. Campbell became too disturbed in his mind to proceed to Dulwich, and a walk we had often talked about was never taken."

The long vista of Regent Street, as seen from the Quadrant, is very fine, exhibiting, as it does, a remarkable variety of architectural features. It was erected principally from the designs of Mr. John Nash, who deserves to be remembered as the author of this great metropolitan improvement; and it was named from the architect's patron, the Prince Regent. The expenditure of the Office of Woods and Forests in its construction was a little in excess of a million and a half. Of course, being a thoroughfare of so recent a date, having been commenced in 1813, Regent Street has scarcely a back history for us to record here, like Pall Mall and St. James's Street. It belongs to "new," and not to "old" London.

In his design for Regent Street, Nash adopted the idea of uniting several dwellings into a *façade*, so as to preserve a degree of continuity essential to architectural importance; and it cannot be denied that he has produced a varied succession of architectural scenery, the effect of which is picturesque and imposing, superior to that of any other portion of the then existing metropolis, and far preferable to the naked brick walls at that time universally forming the sides of our streets. The plaster fronts of the houses have given rise to some severe criticism, and the perishable nature of the brick and composition of which the houses in this street are built, gave rise to the following epigram in the *Quarterly Review* for June, 1826 :—

> " Augustus at Rome was for building renown'd,
> And of marble he left what of brick he had found ;
> But is not our Nash, too, a very great master ?
> He finds us all brick, and he leaves us all plaster."

Regent Street is full of handsome shops, and during the afternoon, in the height of the London season, is the very centre of fashion, and with its show of fine carriages, horses, and gay company, forms one of the most striking sights of the metropolis. At the close of the London season "everybody who pretends to be anybody" goes away from town, and the West-end becomes comparatively a desert. As Mr. Albert Smith remarks, in his "Sketches of London Life and Character"— "The thousands who leave London make no difference to the stream of life that daily flows along its business thoroughfares; but Regent Street assimilates to Pompeii in its loneliness. There are no more lines of carriages at the kerb; no concert programmes at the music-shops; nor bouquets and lap-dogs on the pavements. Men run in and out of their clubs in a shy and nervous manner, as though they were burrows; not caring to be seen, and inventing lame reasons for their continuance in London. You may wander all round Eaton Square without finding a single window lighted up, or meeting one carriage rolling along, with its lamps like two bright eyes, to a party. All have departed—the handsome girls to recruit their somewhat jaded strength, and recover from the pallor induced by late hours and the thousand fretting emotions of society; the men to shoot, and ride, and sail; the heads of the families to retain their caste, because it is proper to do so; but all to get away as soon and as fast as they can, when Parliament is prorogued, and the grouse are reported to be ready for slaughter."

On the east side, about half way up, near Chapel Court, stood "Archbishop Tenison's Chapel," so called after its founder, who conveyed this chapel, or "tabernacle," to certain trustees (one of whom was the great Sir Isaac Newton), as a chapel of ease, or "oratory," for the parish of St. James's. The archbishop added to it an endowment for two "preachers," as also for a "reader" or chaplain, to say prayers in it twice daily, and for a school-master to teach sundry poor boys of the parish to read, write, and cast accounts. The chapel was opened in 1702. It was re-fronted when Regent Street was built; but about the year 1860, its endowment not being adequate to its maintenance, the west end of the building was cut off and turned into shops.

Higher up, on the same side of the street, a certain M. Foubert had, in the reign of Charles II., a riding academy, and his name is still retained in Foubert's Passage. Evelyn writes in his "Diary," under date September 17, 1684, that M. Foubert had "lately come from Paris for his religion, and resolved to settle here." In the following December he was again here, and gives a list of the performances, and also the names of the principal of the nobility present. On the site of Foubert's academy had previously stood the mansion of the Countess of Bristol.

In this street was the publishing office of Mr. James Fraser, the starter and proprietor of *Fraser's Magazine*. In the January number of that magazine for 1835, we have, from the pencil of Maclise, a sketch of an editorial banquet at the residence of Mr. Fraser, at which some eminent men were present. Mr. Mahony, the "Father Prout" of the magazine, in his account of this banquet, written some years later, tells us that it was a reality, and not a fiction. In the chair appears Dr. Maginn in the act of making a speech; and around him are some of the contributors, including Bryan Waller Procter (better known then as "Barry Cornwall"), Robert Southey, William Harrison Ainsworth, Samuel Taylor Coleridge, James Hogg, John Galt, Fraser the publisher, having on his right Mr. J. G. Lockhart, Theodore Hook, Sir David Brewster,

Thomas Carlyle, Sir Egerton Brydges, the Rev. G. R. Gleig, Edward Irving, and William Makepeace Thackeray, the last-named being easily recognised by his double eye-glass, for he was short-sighted even as a young man. Alas! of that pleasant and distinguished party, how few survive! Whilst speaking of *Fraser's Magazine*, we may add that in the zenith of its popularity, in the year 1837, its pages, or rather the connection of Dr. Maginn with it as editor, led to a duel, happily a bloodless one. As usual, there was "a lady in the case;" and the Hon. Grantley Berkeley, then M.P. for West Gloucestershire, came forward to espouse the cause of the lady, who conceived that she had been injured by Maginn. Mr. Berkeley was warned by Lady Blessington that Maginn would be sure to look out for some opportunity of revenge. The opportunity came very soon afterwards; for Mr. Grantley Berkeley wrote and published a novel, which Dr. Maginn reviewed in *Fraser's Magazine*, not, however, confining himself to fair criticism, but using malignant insinuations against Lady Euston, a cousin of the author. Accordingly, Mr. Grantley Berkeley, accompanied by his brother Craven, called at Mr. Fraser's shop to demand the name of the writer, and not obtaining it, administered to the publisher a severe chastisement. This was made, very naturally, the subject of a civil action; but, meantime, it leaked out incidentally that Dr. Maginn was the writer. The consequence was a duel, which was fought with pistols. Three shots were fired, but without effect, Major Fancourt being Mr. Berkeley's second, whilst Mr. Fraser acted in that capacity for Dr. Maginn. The ridiculous nature of this "literary duel" and its bloodless termination, literally "in smoke," helped to seal the doom of the once fashionable practice of duelling; and the publicity gained for the transaction, to use the words of the *Times*, "put a wholesome restraint upon the herd of libellers who, in the *Age* and *Satirist* newspapers, and in *Fraser's Magazine*, had for years been recklessly trading upon scandals affecting families of distinction." The *Age* and the *Satirist* are both happily defunct; and *Fraser's Magazine* has long since abandoned bad habits of this kind.

At the junction of Regent Street with Oxford Street is another circus. Of the portion of the street lying beyond this point we shall speak in a future chapter.

On the west side of the way, between Hanover and Princes Streets, stands Hanover Chapel, which was built, in 1823, from the designs of the late Mr. Cockerell, R.A.; it is of the Ionic order, and in its internal arrangement somewhat resembles St.

Stephen's Church, Walbrook.   The altar is enriched with carved work, and the fabric generally
forms a fine architectural display, though utterly
unsuited to a church.

Before resuming our account of Piccadilly, we
may be pardoned for introducing the following
anecdote of the poet Campbell, as narrated by
Southey :—"Taking a walk with Campbell one
day up Regent Street," he says, "we were accosted

us he would turn us both out; that he believed we
came there to kick up a row for some dishonest
purpose.   So here was a pretty dilemma.   We
defied him, but said we would go out instantly, on
his apologising for his gross insult.   All was uproar.
Campbell called out—'Thrash the fellow! thrash
him!'   'You will not go out, then?' said the
mercer.   'No, never, till you apologise.'   'Well,
we shall soon see.   John, go to Vine Street, and

THE QUADRANT, REGENT STREET, BEFORE THE REMOVAL OF THE COLONNADE.   (See page 250.)

by a wretched-looking woman, with a sick infant
in her arms, and another starved little thing at her
mother's side.   The woman begged for a copper.
I had no change, and Campbell had nothing but a
sovereign.   The woman stuck fast to the poet, as
if she read his heart in his face, and I could feel
his arm beginning to tremble.   At length, saying
something about it being his duty to assist poor
creatures, he told the woman to wait; and, hastening into a mercer's shop, asked, rather impatiently,
for change.   You know what an excitable person
he was, and how he fancied all business must give
way till the change was supplied.   The shopman
thought otherwise; the poet insisted; an alterca-
tion ensued; and in a minute or two the master
jumped over the counter and collared him, telling

fetch the police.'   In a few minutes two policemen
appeared; one went close up to Mr. Campbell,
the other to myself.   The poet was now in such
breathless indignation that he could not articulate a sentence.   I told the policeman the object
he had in asking change, and that the shopkeeper had most unwarrantably insulted us.   'This
gentleman,' I added, by way of a climax, 'is Mr.
Thomas Campbell, the distinguished poet, a man
who would not hurt a fly, much less act with the
dishonest intention that person has insinuated.'
The moment I uttered the name the policeman
backed away two or three paces, as if awe-struck,
and said, 'Guidness, mon, is that Maister Cammell,
the Lord Rector o' Glasgow?'   'Yes, my friend,
he is, as this card may convince you,' handing it

to him. 'All this commotion has been caused by a mistake.' By this time the mercer had cooled down to a moderate temperature, and in the end made every reparation in his power, saying he was very busy at the time, and had he but known the

to the day when a vineyard, belonging to the Abbey of Westminster or to some wealthy lord, flourished and yielded the fruit of the grape on a sunny slope. Here, in 1805, was living, in comparative obscurity, a young artist, who after-

SIR ISAAC NEWTON.   (*See page* 232.)

gentleman, he would have changed fifty sovereigns for him. 'My dear fellow,' said the poet, who had recovered his speech, 'I am not at all offended;' and it was really laughable to see them shaking hands long and vigorously, each with perfect sincerity and mutual forgiveness."

But we must proceed. Between Regent's Quadrant and Piccadilly runs Little Vine Street, a thoroughfare remarkable now-a-days mainly for its police station; but carrying back our memories

wards became known as Sir Francis Chantrey, the eminent sculptor.

In this street there is to be seen the sign of the "Man in the Moon"—a sign representing, as antiquaries tell us, either Cain, or Jacob, or the man who was stoned for gathering sticks on the Jewish Sabbath (Numbers xv. 22, &c.), and so old as to be alluded to by Shakespeare and Dante. There were other houses bearing this sign in Cheapside and other parts of London.

We have already stated that a considerable part of Swallow Street was absorbed in the formation of Regent Street; a small portion, however, is still left between the Quadrant and Piccadilly, and into that we now pass. Here there has been a chapel belonging to the Scotch Presbyterians since 1710, when it was bought by a Dr. James Anderson from the French Huguenots, who had used it as one of the principal churches of their worship not long after their arrival in England after the revocation of the Edict of Nantes. Mr. Smiles, in his work on the Huguenots, tells us that "the congregation had originally worshipped in the French Ambassador's chapel in Monmouth House, Soho Square, from which they removed to Swallow Street in 1690." The records of their church, which are still preserved at Somerset House, show that it was the principal place for receiving back into church membership such refugees as had lapsed from their first fervour.

St. James's Hall, which covers a large space of ground between the Quadrant and Piccadilly, and is almost wholly concealed by houses and shop-fronts, was built in 1857, from the designs of Mr. Owen Jones, in the Arabesque or Moorish Alhambra style. The building, which has entrances in both thoroughfares, consists of one large room and two smaller ones. The principal hall is beautifully decorated, and surrounded on three sides with a gallery; the western end is apsidally constructed, and is so arranged that concerts may be given on an extensive scale, a class of entertainment for which the Hall was originally intended. Among the principal concerts given here are those of the New Philharmonic Society, and those widely-celebrated chamber concerts known as the "Monday Popular Concerts." The first public dinner held here was on June 2, 1858, under the presidency of Mr. Robert Stephenson, M.P., when a testimonial of the value of more than £2,500 was presented to Sir F. P. Smith, in recognition of services in the introduction of the screw-propeller into our steam fleet. Here Charles Dickens gave the second series of his "Readings," in the spring of 1861. In one of the smaller apartments entertainments on a humbler scale—such as panoramas, &c.—are given. In 1875, handsome and spacious dining-rooms, &c., were added to the building. Adjoining each room is a small kitchen, communicating, by means of a lift, with the general kitchen upstairs; the general fittings and furniture are handsome throughout, and in good keeping, marble and glazed tiling being largely employed in the panelling of the walls.

At Fore's Exhibition, which, towards the end of the last century, was in a house near the eastern end of Piccadilly, was to be seen the largest collection of caricatures by Gilray, Rowlandson, and the elder Cruickshank, including many political squibs and songs.

At No. 7, close to Regent Circus, in August, 1839, were made the first experiments in this country with the newly-discovered process of M. Daguerre, in the presence of a large body of scientific persons.

At a short distance westward from the circus, probably in the house now occupied by Mr. Quaritch, the eminent second-hand bookseller, but what was at the time No. 23, resided, in 1805, Emma Lyon, afterwards Lady Hamilton. She was born in Cheshire, and came to London, while a girl, in 1777, and lived in several families as a nurse-maid. In 1791 she was married to Sir William Hamilton. She became acquainted with Lord Nelson at Naples, in 1799, and here the great naval hero used to visit her. By him she had a child, named Horatia, who afterwards married a clergyman. It has been remarked by a writer in *Blackwood*, that "of her virtues, unhappily, prudence was not one. After the death of Nelson, and the disgraceful disregard of her claims by the Government, her affairs became greatly embarrassed. Those who owed wealth and honour to Nelson, and who had sunned themselves in her prosperity, shrank away from her. In her distress she wrote a most touching letter to one who had courted her smiles in other days, the Duke of Queensberry, imploring him to buy the little estate at Merton, which had been left to her by Nelson, and thus to relieve her from the most pressing embarrassments. The cold-hearted old profligate turned a deaf ear to the request. In 1813 Emma Hamilton was a prisoner for debt in the King's Bench. Deserted by the great, the noble, and the wealthy, abandoned by the heir of his title and the recipient of his hard-earned rewards, she, whom Nelson had left as a legacy to his country, might have died in a gaol. From this fate she was saved by one whose name is not to be found in the brilliant circle who surrounded her but a few short years before. Alderman Joshua Jonathan Smith (let all honour be paid to his most plebeian name) redeemed his share of his country's debt and obtained her release. She fled to Calais, where she died in destitution, and was buried by the hands of charitable strangers."

Mr. Quaritch's establishment is by far the most extensive of the kind in London, and probably in the world; and his catalogue, a most voluminous production, larger and more varied than even that of Mr. H. G. Bohn, is of itself of such interest in the literary world as to have merited a long and elaborate notice in the *Times*.

On the southern side of Piccadilly, nearly opposite the entrance to St. James's Hall, is the Museum of Practical Geology, of which we have spoken in a previous chapter.

At No. 208, on this side of the street, between the Circus and St. James's Church, are the Rooms of the Genealogical and Historical Society of Great Britain, an association which, though it has been in existence for twenty years, has hitherto published no "Transactions" or records of its proceedings, nor even the names of its president and council, or a list of its members!

St. James's Church, which is separated from the roadway by a paved court and brick wall, with handsome iron gates, owes its erection to the great increase in the parish of St. Martin-in-the-Fields. It was originally a chapel of ease only, and was built at an expense of about £8,500, chiefly by Henry Jermyn, Earl of St. Albans, and the neighbouring inhabitants.

It is well known that Sir Christopher Wren always regarded this as one of the best of his churches. He is said to have taxed his powers to the utmost here to provide "a room so capacious as with pews and galleries to hold 2,000 persons, and all to hear the service and see the preacher." It is divided in the interior into a nave and side aisles. The principal merit is in the formation of the roof, which is described by the late Professor Cockerell as "singularly ingenious and economical; its simplicity, strength, and beauty being a perfect study of construction and architectural economy." The writer of "A New Critical Review of the Public Buildings" draws attention to its beautiful and commanding situation, while he expresses his regret that the architect troubled himself but little about beauty in his design.

The walls of this church are of brick and stone, with rustic quoins, &c.; the roof is arched, and supported by Corinthian pillars. The interior of the roof is beautifully ornamented, and divided into panels of crotchet and fret-work. The galleries have very handsome fronts, and the door-cases are highly enriched; that fronting Jermyn Street (originally the principal one) has above it the arms of the Earl of St. Albans. The font was carved by Grinling Gibbons, and represents the Fall of Man, the Salvation of Noah, &c. In Brayley's "Londoniana" it is asserted that the cover of the font, which was held by a flying angel and a group of cherubim, was stolen about the beginning of the present century, and subsequently hung up as a sign at a spirit-shop in the neighbourhood. The great east window was filled with stained glass in 1846, the subjects represented being Christ's Agony in the Garden, Bearing the Cross, the Passion, the Burial, Resurrection, and the Ascension. Of the altar-piece, which is very spacious, and highly enriched with carved work, Evelyn, in his "Diary," under date December 16, 1684, gives us the following particulars:—"I went to see the new church of St. James's, elegantly built. The altar was especially adorned, the white marble inclosure curiously and richly carved, the flowers and garlands about the walls by Mr. Gibbons, in wood; a pelican, with her young at her breast, just over the altar in the carved compartment, and border environing the purple velvet fringed with (black) I.H.S. richly embroidered, and most noble plate, were given by Sir R. Greere, to the value (as was said) of £200. There was no altar anywhere in England, nor has there been any abroad, more handsomely adorned." The organ, which is considered very good, was built for James II., and intended for his Roman Catholic Oratory at Whitehall, but it was given to this parish by Queen Mary in 1691. At the north-west corner of the church is a tower and spire, rising to the height of about 150 feet. The spire, says Mr. Timbs, was a later addition, planned by a carpenter, whose design was preferred to that of Wren, from motives of economy. In 1850, the spire was coated with lead, when the exterior of the church was repaired throughout.

The church was consecrated in 1684, and many of its rectors have become bishops and high dignitaries in the Church. One of the earliest was Dr. Hoadly, afterwards Bishop of Winchester. Dr. Tenison, vicar of St. Martin's, and subsequently Archbishop of Canterbury, was appointed the first rector. The third rector, Dr. Wake, and the seventh, Dr. Secker, likewise at a later date became Archbishops of Canterbury. One of the rectors of St. James's in the last century was Dr. Samuel Clarke, the well-known latitudinarian divine, whose writings were so severely censured by the Lower House of Convocation as to cause a breach with the Upper House, and eventually to suspend the sittings of both Houses for nearly a century. He was a great favourite of Queen Anne (who placed his bust in her Hermitage) and of Queen Caroline, though disliked by Bolingbroke and Pope. On the death of Sir Isaac Newton he was offered the Mastership of the Mint, but refused it as "inconsistent with his profession," though in all probability he would have been better placed there than in a Trinitarian pulpit. Another of its rectors was Dr. Gerrard Andrewes, some time Dean of Canterbury, who refused the Bishopric of Chester, which was offered to him by Lord Liverpool in 1812. Another rector was Dr. Ward, Dean of Lincoln, who was succeeded by Dr. Jackson, since Bishop of London.

In 1762, a fire broke out most unaccountably in the vaults of this church, and destroyed two hundred coffins and their contents.

In this parish lived and died, at the age of eighty-seven, the Hon. Frederick Byng, a well-known member of the world of fashion, both before and under the Regency. He was always known as "Poodle Byng," on account of his curly hair. Of late years he took an active interest in the parochial affairs of St. James's, having lived for sixty years in the region of the clubs and of St. James's Place, where he resided. He was the subject of sundry caricatures by Dighton, in 1817.

In St. James's Church is buried the learned anatomist, Mr. Joshua Brookes, F.R.S., whose lectures at his theatre in Blenheim Street are said to have been attended by seven thousand pupils. His museum was almost a rival of that belonging to John Hunter, of whom we have already spoken in our account of Leicester Square : its doors were always open to scientific men of this and other countries. It was, however, dispersed on his death, in 1833.

Here, too, is buried Sir John Malcolm, the distinguished Indian general, who died in 1833. James Dodsley, many years an eminent bookseller in Pall Mall, of whom we have already spoken, is likewise interred here. There is a monument to his memory near the communion-table. Here, too, lies Mary Delaney, niece of Granville, Lord Lansdowne. Benjamin Stillingfleet, the naturalist, Charles Cotton, the friend and companion of Izaak Walton, and Dr. Sydenham, are also buried here. The latter is commemorated by a marble tablet, erected by the College of Physicians. Among other notabilities interred in this church may be mentioned Hayman and Michael Dahl, the portrait painters; G. H. Harlow, the painter of "The Trial of Queen Katharine;" Dr. Akenside, the author of the "Pleasures of the Imagination," and also the two Vanderveldes, the marine painters.

Here, as at St. Giles's-in-the-Fields, unfortunately, the earlier volumes of the parish rate-books have disappeared; so that it is impossible to glean the same accurate information as to its inhabitants in the reigns of the earlier Stuarts, which meets us at every turn in those of St. Martin's-in-the-Fields and of St. Paul's, Covent Garden.

With reference to this parish, and to the line of roadway running westward, it may be stated that in an Act of Parliament, in the reign of James II., mention is made of the "mansion-house of the Earl of Burlington, fronting Portugal Street;" and a "toft of ground" in Piccadilly is assigned to the rector of St. James's parish.

In a house at the corner of Sackville Street, "over against St. James's Church," in the year 1687, died Sir William Petty, the eminent writer on political economy, and an ancestor of the Lansdowne family. The son of a clothier in humble circumstances, he was born at Romsey, in Hampshire, in 1623, and was educated at the grammar school of his native town. He afterwards determined to improve himself by study at the University of Caen, in Normandy. Whilst there, he contrived to support himself by carrying on a small pedlar's trade with a "little stock of merchandise." Wishing to return to England, he bound himself apprentice to a sea-captain, who beat him most unmercifully. Leaving the navy in disgust, he took to the study of medicine, and having studied at Leyden and Paris, he took his degree, and was subsequently made professor of anatomy. During this part of his life he was reduced to such poverty that he subsisted for two or three weeks entirely on walnuts. But again he began to trade in a small way, and, "turning an honest penny," returned to England with money in his pocket. Steadily applying himself to his profession, he then became a successful London physician, and was one of the first fellows of the Royal Society, to which he presented the model of a double-bottomed ship, to sail against wind and tide. In 1652 he was appointed physician to the army in Ireland, and secretary to Henry Cromwell, by whom he was employed in surveying the forfeited lands, for which charges were alleged against him in the House of Commons, and he was dismissed from his appointments. At the Restoration he was knighted, and made Surveyor-General of Ireland. Sir William suffered much by the Great Fire of London; but by marriage and various speculations he recovered his losses, and died very rich, in the year 1687. In his will, which is a curious document, singularly illustrative of his character, he writes, with a certain amount of self-pride, "At the full age of fifteen, I had obtained the Latin, Greek, and French tongues," and at twenty years of age "had gotten up threescore pounds, with as much mathematics as any of my age was known to have had." Sir William was buried in the fine old Norman church of Romsey. A plain slab, cut by an illiterate workman, with the inscription, "Here layes Sir William Petty," covers his tomb.

Next door but one to Sir William Petty, Verrio,

the Italian painter, was residing in the reign of William and Mary ; the reader will not have forgotten the often-quoted line which records his decorations of the ceiling of Whitehall—

"Where sprawl the saints of Verrio and Laguerre."

In a shop opposite St. James's Church there was, in 1819, a curious collection of live animals, which had a run of popularity, but was unable to stand as a rival against Exeter 'Change.

Continuing our walk along Piccadilly, we pass on our left the publishing-houses of Messrs. Chapman and Hall, Messrs. Hatchard, and others. From the first-named shop were issued the successive numbers of "Pickwick" and "Nicholas Nickleby," which electrified and amazed the world in 1837-9, and made the name of "Boz" a "household word." Messrs. Chapman and Hall were the publishers of Charles Dickens's serial works down to and inclusive of "Martin Chuzzlewit" and the "Christmas Carol," which appeared in 1843-4 ; from that date, however, Messrs. Bradbury and Evans became his publishers, and those relations lasted until 1858, when he started *All the Year Round* on his own account. The publication of Charles Dickens's works is now again in the hands of the house in connection with which he first "made his mark" with "Pickwick." At the shop of Mr. Hardwicke, No. 192, were issued for some time the publications of the Ray Society. This society, which was formed in 1844, takes its name from John Ray, the celebrated naturalist.

The booksellers' shops here, at the close of the last century, had not ceased to be what those of Tonson, in the Strand, and Dodsley, in Pall Mall, had been—the resort of literary characters. At this time, Mr. D'Israeli tells us that Debrett's was the chief haunt of the Whigs, and Hatchard's that of the Tories. It was at Hatchard's that the elder D'Israeli was first introduced to Mr. Pye, the Poet Laureate, who was then busy on his translation of Aristotle's Poetics, and who, in passing Debrett's door, requested his new friend, who was then unknown, to go in and buy a pamphlet which he dared not be seen going in to purchase for himself.

The house No. 169 is remarkable as having been not only the shop where the *Anti-Jacobin* was published, but also the house in which its editor (William Gifford) and its writers used to meet in council ; a fact worthy of note, when we add that among the contributors to its columns were the younger Pitt, George Canning, and John Hookham Frere. This shop, then kept by a Mr. Wright, was much frequented by the friends of Mr. Pitt's

ministry. It was here that Dr. Wolcott was severely "castigated" by Gifford. No. 117 was the shop of William Pickering, the eminent publisher. The Aldine anchor, revived by the late Mr. Pickering on his title-pages, gave a celebrity to the books, mostly reprints of the poets and prose writers of the past, and works in curious paths of literature, which he issued from his shop.

The Egyptian Hall, the front of which forms one of the most noticeable features on the southern side of Piccadilly, nearly opposite to Bond Street, was erected in the year 1812, from the designs of Mr. G. F. Robinson, at a cost of £16,000, for a museum of natural history, the objects of which were in part collected by William Bullock, F.L.S., during his thirty years' travel in Central America. The edifice was so named from its being in the Egyptian style of architecture and ornament, the inclined pilasters and sides being covered with hieroglyphics ; and the hall is now used principally for popular entertainments, lectures, and exhibitions. Bullock's Museum was at one time one of the most popular exhibitions in the metropolis. It comprised curiosities from the South Sea, Africa, and North and South America ; works of art ; armoury, and the travelling carriage of Bonaparte. The collection, which was made up to a very great extent out of the Lichfield Museum and that of Sir Ashton Lever, was sold off by auction, and dispersed in lots, in 1819.

Here, in 1825, was exhibited a curious phenomenon, known as "the Living Skeleton," or "the Anatomic Vivante," of whom a short account will be found in Hone's "Every-Day Book." His name was Claude Amboise Seurat, and he was born in Champagne, in April, 1798. His height was 5 feet 7½ inches, and as he consisted literally of nothing but skin and bone, he weighed only 77¾ lbs. He (or another living skeleton) was shown subsequently—in 1830, we believe—at "Bartlemy Fair," but died shortly afterwards. There is extant a portrait of M. Seurat, published by John Williams, of 13, Paternoster Row, which quite enables us to identify in him the perfect French native.

Of the various entertainments and exhibitions that have found a home here, it would, perhaps, be needless to attempt to give a complete catalogue ; but we may, at least, mention a few of the most successful. In 1829, the Siamese Twins made their first appearance here, and were described at the time as "two youths of eighteen, natives of Siam, united by a short band at the pit of the stomach—two perfect bodies, bound together by an inseparable link." They died in America in the early part of the year 1874. The American dwarf, Charles S. Stratton, "Tom Thumb," was exhibited here in 1844; and subsequently, Mr. Albert Smith gave the narrative of his ascent of Mont Blanc, his lecture being illustrated by some cleverly-painted dioramic views of the perils and sublimities of the Alpine regions. Latterly, the Egyptian Hall has been almost continually used for the exhibition of feats of legerdemain, the most successful of these—if one may judge from the

owner, exchanged it with the Duke of York and Albany for his mansion in Whitehall, now Dover House. Near or on this site, says Pennant, stood the house of "that monster of treachery, that profligate minister, Charles Spencer, Earl of Sunderland, who, by his destructive advice, premeditatedly brought ruin on his unsuspecting master, James II. . . . . At the very time that he sold him to the Prince of Orange, he encouraged his Majesty

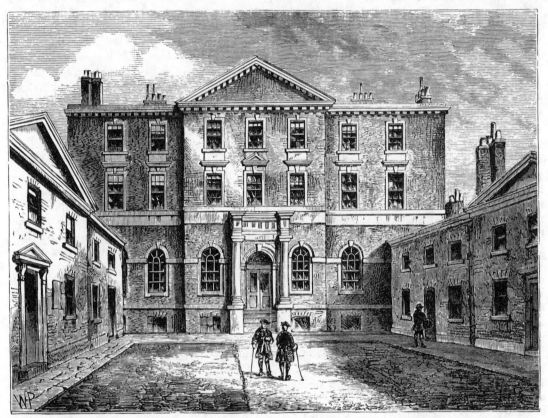

THE ALBANY, IN 1805.

"run" which the entertainment has enjoyed—being the extraordinary performances of Messrs. Maskelyne and Cooke.

In 1819, there was, adjoining Bullock's Museum, the Pantherion, a separate exhibition, "intended to display quadrupeds in such a manner as to convey a correct notion of their haunts and habits. In one orange-tree were disposed sixty species of the genus *Simia*, or monkeys. Besides animal nature, Mr. Bullock exhibited, in connection with it, many exotic trees."

Nearly opposite the Egyptian Hall is "The Albany." This building, which is separated from the main thoroughfare by a small paved courtyard, was known in the last century as Melbourne House. Lord Melbourne, however, the then

in every step which was certain of involving him and his family in utter ruin."

The present central building, designed by Sir William Chambers, was sold by Lord Holland, in 1770, to the first Lord Melbourne. In 1804 the mansion was altered and enlarged, and first let in chambers, and named the Albany, after the second title of the Duke of York. It extends in the rear as far as Burlington Gardens, having a porter's lodge and entrance at either end. It is entirely occupied by bachelors (or widowers), and comprises sixty sets of apartments, each staircase being marked by one of the letters of the alphabet. Most of the occupants of these suites are members of one or other of the Houses of Parliament, or naval or military officers. Among those who have occupied chambers here in their day were Lord Byron, George Canning, Lord Macaulay (who here wrote the greater part of his "History of England"), Lord Lytton, Lord Glenelg, and Sir John C. Hobhouse. Here, too, as we learn from his Autobiography, Lord Brougham was living in bachelor chambers

Clarges' house, which is described, in the year 1675, as being "near Burlington House, above Piccadilly."

In 1806, the house adjoining the Albany was occupied, for the purposes of exhibition, by Daniel Lambert, a Leicestershire man, who bore the repu-

THE NEW "WHITE HORSE CELLAR." (*See page* 261.)

from 1806, when studying for the Bar, down to 1808, when he removed to chambers in the Middle Temple. It is said that no person who carries on a trade or commercial occupation is allowed to reside on the premises; and that, as a rule, "ladies are not admitted," excepting the mothers, sisters, grandmothers, and aunts of the occupants of the chambers; but this rule, we fancy, is not very strictly adhered to.

The Albany adjoins the site of Sir Thomas

tation of being the "heaviest man that ever lived." His weight, at the age of thirty-six, was upwards of eighty-seven stone. It is stated that, although in most instances, when the body exceeds the usual proportions, the strength correspondingly diminishes, this was not the case with Lambert, for it is recorded that, notwithstanding his excessive corpulency, he tested his ability by carrying more than four hundredweight and a half—a feat that many a sinewy athlete would fail to accomplish. During his stay here, "Dan" Lambert was as fashionable a celebrity as Albert Smith or "General" Tom Thumb became in later years, at the Egyptian Hall opposite. Thousands went to see him daily, and from morning till night his reception-room was thronged with men in cocked hats and ladies in furbelows, coming alike from Kensington and Cheapside.

On the opposite side of the road, between St. James's Street and the Green Park, is Arlington Street, of which we have already spoken.* The exact date of building this street is not known, but it must have been between 1680 and 1690. The street stands partly on the site of Goring House. Evelyn, in his "Diary," under date of 29th March, 1665, tells us how that he "went to Goring House, now Mr. Secretary Bennet's; ill built, but the place capable of being made a pretty villa." The same diarist records its destruction by fire, November 21, 1674, when a fine collection of pictures, as well as much handsome plate, hangings, and furniture, perished; and he elsewhere describes the appointments of the house as "princely." From Pepys we learn that a sister of John Milton was married here in July, 1660.

We might add here, as one of the residents of this street in former times, the name of Lady Mary Wortley Montagu, who, before her marriage, was living here in the house of her father, the Marquis of Dorchester, afterwards Duke of Kingston. She was the author of those charming, lively, and witty letters, written at Constantinople, and addressed by Lady Mary to friends at home, descriptive of Turkish life and society, and in which, it has been said, she displays "the epistolary talents of a female Horace Walpole." She was very eccentric in her attire; indeed, Horace Walpole once described her dress as consisting of "a groundwork of dirt, with an embroidery of filthiness."

Horace Walpole himself resided in this street for many years, before removing further west into Berkeley Square (where he died); and from Arlington Street are dated many of his letters to Lady Ossory. At Horace Walpole's house, on one occasion, there was a large party present at dinner, when Bruce, the celebrated African traveller, was talking in his usual style of exaggeration. Some one asked him what musical instruments were used in Abyssinia. Bruce hesitated, not being prepared for the question, and at last said, "I think I saw a lyre there." George Selwyn, who was one of the party, whispered to his next man, "Yes, there is one less since he left the country." Admiral Lord

Nelson, too, was living in this street when his wife separated from him, in 1801.

Close by Arlington Street was a well-known hostelry, the old "White Horse Cellar." In the "good old days," before the power of steam had been developed, or railways planned, even Londoners rejoiced, on summer evenings, to lounge about this noted house, and watch the mails drive down Piccadilly, *en route* for the West of England. On the king's birthday, especially, the scene was picturesque, and of special interest. The exterior of the "Cellar" was studded over with oil lights of many colours, arranged in tasty lines and capital letters. The sleek-coated horses stepped along as if they were proud of their new harness, and the bright brass ornaments on their trappings glittered in the light. The coachmen and guards, too, were dressed in unsullied scarlet coats, which they wore for the first time on that day—woe for them if it was wet—and there were gay rosettes of ribbons and bunches of bright flowers at each of the horses' heads, as well as in the coachman's button-hole. The coaches themselves were, if not newly painted, at all events, freshly "touched-up" with the brush, and the post-horn sounded pleasantly as the ostlers cried, "All right; off they go!" In the reign of George IV., many of the coaches which left London were driven by gentlemen, and in some cases the reins were handled by peers of the realm. Sir St. Vincent Cotton drove the Brighton "Age;" another coach on the same road was horsed and driven by the Marquis of Worcester, afterwards Duke of Beaufort; Sir Thomas Tyrrwhitt Jones drove the "Pearl;" and the Reading coach was driven by Captain Probyn.

Hazlitt has thus described, in his own graphic manner, the scene presented on the starting of the old mail-coaches:—"The finest sight in the metropolis," he writes, "is the setting off of the mail-coaches from Piccadilly. The horses paw the ground and are impatient to be gone, as if conscious of the precious burden they convey. There is a peculiar secrecy and dispatch, significant and full of meaning, in all the proceedings concerning them. Even the outside passengers have an erect and supercilious air, as if proof against the accidents of the journey; in fact, it seems indifferent whether they are to encounter the summer's heat or the winter's cold, since they are borne through the air on a winged chariot. The mail-carts drive up and the transfer of packages is made, and at a given signal off they start, bearing the irrevocable scrolls that give wings to thought, and that bind or sever hearts for ever. How we hate the Putney and Brentford stages that draw up when they are

* See p. 169, *ante*.

gone! Some persons think the sublimest object in nature is a ship launched on the bosom of the ocean; but give me for my private satisfaction the mail-coaches that pour down Piccadilly of an evening, tear up the pavement, and devour the way before them to the Land's End." Poor Hazlitt! in the fall of the mail-coach he sees a type of the rapid changes to which all mortal inventions and fashions are subject. In Cowper's day the mail-coach had scarcely superseded the post-boy and stage; and in Hazlitt's time they had entered on their decline and fall; and we have lived to see the Putney and Brentford stages superseded by omnibuses!

At the old "White Horse Cellar," when it served as the head-quarters of the departure of the passengers by the country coaches, there used to stand a small confraternity of Jews, who sold oranges, pencils, sponges, brushes, and other small wares; but these, of course, disappeared when the system of travelling was changed, and the old house came, in the end, to be converted into a railway booking-office for luggage.

A new house on the opposite side of the way, it is true, rejoices in the sign of the "White Horse Cellar;" and at Hatchett's Hotel, which adjoins it, an attempt has been made, within the last few years, to revive the taste for coaching, and, with this aim in view, stage-coaches have been run daily during the summer to Sevenoaks, Tunbridge Wells, Windsor, Brighton, Dorking, &c. The history of this movement is worth epitomising, in the words of a well-known writer on sporting subjects :—
"The Brighton road was the last to give up the old-fashioned stage-coach, and the first selected by the amateurs who are the stage-coach owners of to-day. Up to about 1862, the 'Age,' the property of and driven by 'Old Clark,' ran during the summer, viâ Kingston and Dorking (where the 'coach' dined), to Brighton. In its latter days the Duke of Beaufort and Mr. Charles Lawrie, of Bexley, Kent, helped the proprietor in a substantial and practical manner, but the 'Age' was like any other business speculation, and soon after it ceased to pay it stopped. In the year 1866, and chiefly through the exertions of Mr. Lawrie, a little yellow coach, called the 'Old Times,' was subscribed for in shares of £10 each, and made its appearance on the 'Brighton' road, the Duke of Beaufort, Mr. Chandos Pole, Lord H. Thynne, and Mr. C. Lawrie being among the shareholders. The success was so considerable, that in the April of the following year the Brighton was 'doubled,' and two new coaches built especially for the work, and horsed by the Duke of Beaufort and his friends, ran during

that summer. Alfred Tedder and Pratt were the coachmen, and the lunching-place (where the coaches met) was the 'Chequers,' at Horley, an inn now kept by Mr. Tedder (the driver of the Brighton coach of to-day). At the close of the season of 1867, Mr. Chandos Pole determined to carry on one coach by himself. This he did through the entire winter; and further, with his brother's (Mr. Pole-Gell's) aid (the latter found twelve of the horses), 'doubled' the coach in the succeeding summer. At the season's close, after the horses had been dispersed by the auctioneer's hammer at Aldridge's, a few lovers of the road gave 'the Squire' (Mr. Chandos Pole) a dinner at 'Hatchett's,' Piccadilly, and presented him with a handsome silver flagon (value £50) to commemorate his plucky behaviour, and in admiration of his wonderful ability as a 'whip.' At a later date there was presented to Tedder, the coachman, a smaller flagon (value £20), as a token of the appreciation of his friends of his ability on the 'bench' (i.e., the driving-seat). In 1869, Mr. A. G. Scott first took the position of honorary secretary to the Brighton coach, which then made the 'Ship' at Charing Cross its starting-place. This was the best year the coach has known, as it never once had a clean bill up or down. The proprietors were Lord Londesborough, Colonel Stracey-Clitheroe, Mr. Pole-Gell, and Mr. G. Meek, who each provided the horses for one stage; while Mr. Chandos Pole again took the largest responsibility by providing the horses for two stages. But the example of the Brighton coach was followed. Towards the end of the season of 1867, Mr. Charles Hoare started a coach between Beckenham and Sevenoaks. This developed the following year into the Sevenoaks coach, starting from Hatchett's, and this carried such good loads, that in 1868 its proprietor carried it on to Tunbridge Wells, to the delight of thousands who have since enjoyed the exquisite scenery it has introduced them to. Since 1868 the Brighton has continued a single coach, but several new candidates for public favour have appeared."

Apropos of the subject of coaching, we may add that Mr. Larwood tells us in his " History of Sign-boards," that there is still (1866) a sign of the " Coach and Six " to be seen in Westminster; but he does not specify the exact spot. It does not appear, however, in the " Post Office Directory" for 1876. The sign, however, speaks of the day when the roads even near London were so bad in the winter time that four horses were not enough to carry a coach safe out of the deep and miry ruts. Mr. Larwood also tells us, that in 1866 there were still no less than fifty-two public-houses, exclusive of beer-houses, coffee-houses, &c., which rejoiced in the sign of the " Coach and Horses," in spite of the progress made by railways.

While on the subject of sign-boards, we may state that Piccadilly was the place in which the " Cat and Fiddle" first appeared as a public-house sign. The story is that a Frenchwoman, a small shopkeeper at the eastern end, soon after it was first built, had a very faithful and favourite cat, and that, in lack of any other sign, she put up over her door the words, " Voici une Chat fidèle." From some cause or other the " Chat Fidèle " soon became a popular

sign in France, and was speedily Anglicised into the " Cat and Fiddle," because the words form part of one of our most popular nursery rhymes. We do not pledge ourselves for the correctness of the derivation, but simply tell the story as told to us.

It has often been observed that while the fashionable world flitting westwards occupied the streets to the north and south of Piccadilly—its tributaries —the great thoroughfare itself was given up to tradesmen and shopkeepers, with the exception of two or three great mansions, which, though *in* it, were scarcely *of* it.

CHAPTER XXII.

PICCADILLY.—BURLINGTON HOUSE.

" Burlington's fair palace still remains :
Beauty within—without, proportion reigns ;
There Handel strikes the strings, the melting strain
Transports the soul, and thrills through every vein ;
There oft I enter, but with cleaner shoes,
For Burlington's beloved by every muse."—*Gay's "Trivia."*

The Earl of Burlington's Taste for Classical Architecture—Walpole's First Visit to Burlington House—A Critical Reviewer's Opinion of the Old Entrance and Colonnade—Pope lampooned by Hogarth—Anecdotes of Pope and Dean Swift—Burlington House under the Regency—Visit of the Allied Sovereigns—The Elgin Marbles—The Mansion purchased by Government—Various Plans drawn up for rebuilding it—Description of the New Buildings—The Royal Society—Charles II. and his Piscatorial Query—Scientific Experiments under the Auspices of the Royal Society—How Sir Isaac Newton became a Member—Remarkable Events connected with the Royal Society—Principal Presidents, Secretaries, and Fellows of the Society—Society of Antiquaries of London—The Linnæan Society—The Geological Society—The Royal Astronomical Society—The Chemical Society—The Royal Academy—Burlington Arcade.

THIS splendid mansion, now the home of the Royal Academy, the Royal Society, and other learned and scientific associations, dates its existence from the time of Charles II., having been erected by Richard Boyle, third Earl of Burlington, on the site of a house built by Sir John Denham, the poet, whose wife was the mistress of James II. when Duke of York, and is said to have been poisoned. Lord Burlington was a man actuated by a fine public spirit. He was at the expense of repairing St. Paul's Church, Covent Garden, the work of Inigo Jones; and by his publication of the "Designs" of that great architect, and of the " Antiquities of Rome " by Palladio, he contributed to form a taste for classical architecture in England. To this Pope alludes in his fourth Epistle, at the same time expressing his fear that the public will be slow to profit by such works :—

" You show us Rome was glorious, not profuse,
   And pompous buildings once were things of use :
   Yet shall, my lord, your just and noble rules
   Fill half the land with imitating fools,
   Who random drawings from your sheets shall take,
   And of one beauty many blunders make."

Lord Burlington also deserves to be held in honour for having helped that pure and simple-

minded philosopher, Dr. Berkeley, by his powerful recommendation, to attain the dignity of an Irish bishopric.

It is to this Lord Burlington that the author of the " New Critical Review of the Public Buildings, &c., in and about London and Westminster, in 1736," most appropriately dedicated his work, as one of those few persons who " have the talent of laying out their own fortunes with propriety, and of making their own private judgment contribute to the public ornament." We have already mentioned one instance of this public spirit in the part which he took towards the rebuilding of the great dormitory at Westminster School.[*]

At the time when Pope dedicated his " Epistle on Taste " to Lord Burlington, his lordship was in his thirty-sixth year. He was then engaged in ornamenting his gardens, and building his villa at Chiswick. The celebrated front and colonnade at Burlington House had been erected some years before, in 1718. There is reason to believe that, in this splendid improvement, his lordship, then very young, had the assistance of a practical architect, Colin Campbell, though Walpole considers that the

* See Vol. III., p. 469.

design is too good for the latter. The same lively and picturesque writer thus describes the effect which the Burlington colonnade had upon him when he first beheld it:—"Soon after my return from Italy, I was invited to a ball at Burlington House. As I passed under the gate by night it could not strike me. At daybreak, looking out of the window to see the sun rise, I was surprised with the vision of the colonnade that fronted me. It seemed one of those edifices in fairy tales that are raised by genii in a night-time."

The author of the "Critical Review," above mentioned, observes that "in this street we are entertained with a sight of the most expensive wall in England, namely, that before Burlington House." This he criticises, and, on the whole, favourably. "The grand entrance," he says, "is august and beautiful, and by covering the house entirely from the eye, gives pleasure and surprise at the opening of the whole front, with the area before it, at once." He complains, however, of the columns of the gate, as "merely ornamental, and supporting nothing." The colonnade remained till the last, but the dead wall in front concealed from the public all view of the fine architecture within.

During the life of Lord Burlington, the town mansion which bore his name was the haunt of all the wits, poets, and learned men of his day. Pope was a frequent visitor; and it was in allusion to his noble host's talents as an architect that he wrote—

"Who plants like Bathurst, or who builds like Boyle?"

In satire of Pope's adulation of Lord Burlington, and his fierce onslaught on the "princely" Duke of Chandos, under the character of "Timon," Hogarth made a humorous design, in which the poet was represented as standing on a builder's stage or platform, engaged in whitewashing the gate of Burlington House, and at the same time bespattering the coach of the duke as it passed by along Piccadilly.

Dr. King, in his "Anecdotes of his Own Times," tells a story about Pope, which shows that, at all events, he was not a teetotaler, and had no idea of sinking down into one of those water-drinkers whose poems, according to Horace, have no chance of immortality. He writes: "Pope and I, with my Lord Orrery, and Sir Harry Bedingfield, dined with the late Earl of Burlington. After the first course Pope grew sick, and went out of the room. When dinner was ended, and the cloth was removed, my Lord Burlington said he would go out, and see what was become of Pope. And soon after they returned together. But Pope, who had been casting up his dinner, looked very pale, and complained much. My lord asked him if he would have some mulled wine, or a glass of old sack, which Pope refused. I told my Lord Burlington that he wanted a dram. Upon which the little man expressed some resentment against me, and said he would not taste any spirits, and that he abhorred drams as much as I did. However, I persisted, and assured my Lord Burlington that he could not oblige our friend more at that instant than by ordering a large glass of cherry-brandy to be set before him. This was done, and in less than half an hour, while my lord was acquainting us with an affair which engaged our attention, Pope had sipped up all the brandy. Pope's frame of body did not promise long life; but he certainly hastened his death by feeding much on highly-seasoned dishes, and drinking spirits."

Sir John Hawkins tells us, in his "History of Music," that Handel lived for three years an honoured guest here.

Swift also was a frequent guest here, and he did not always carry to the table of its hospitable owner the manners of a gentleman. For instance, in Scott's "Life of Swift" an anecdote is related, to the effect, that on the last occasion of the Dean being in London, he went to dine with the Earl of Burlington, then recently married. The earl, it is supposed, being willing to have a little diversion, did not introduce him to his lady, nor mention his name. After dinner, said the Dean, "Lady Burlington, I hear you can sing; sing me a song." The lady looked on this unceremonious manner of asking a favour with distaste, and positively refused. He said "she should sing, or he would make her. Why, madam, I suppose you take me for one of your poor English hedge-parsons; sing when I bid you." As the earl did nothing but laugh at this freedom, the lady was so vexed that she burst into tears, and retired. His first compliment to her when he saw her again was, "Pray, madam, are you as proud and ill-natured now as when I saw you last?" To which she answered, with great good-humour, "No, Mr. Dean, I'll sing for you if you please." From which time he conceived a great esteem for her ladyship.

Lord Burlington died in the year 1753, and with his demise a title honoured and ennobled through three generations by genius, virtue, and public spirit, became extinct. It was afterwards revived in the person of a member of the ducal house of Cavendish, who had inherited part of his fortune. Nightingale says that the mansion was left to the Cavendishes on the express condition that it should not be pulled down, but the statement is questioned.

BURLINGTON HOUSE, ABOUT 1700.

Pennant says, that long after the year 1700, Burlington House was the last house westwards in Piccadilly; but the statement may be questioned. It will be remembered that the nobleman who had built the mansion in the seventeenth century, had placed it there, "because he was certain that no one would build beyond him." This aim, however, if it was ever true in fact, was speedily frustrated, for shortly afterwards we read that to the west of

House, and of building a crescent of houses on its site. "I do not know," she writes, "why the plan fell to the ground; but in 1814, the great *fêtes* in honour of the Allied Sovereigns were given in these gardens, which were enclosed for the purpose; and now," she adds, "in 1868, the site is likely to be applied to still better purposes"—alluding, probably, to the University of London. "The whole garden of Burlington House was

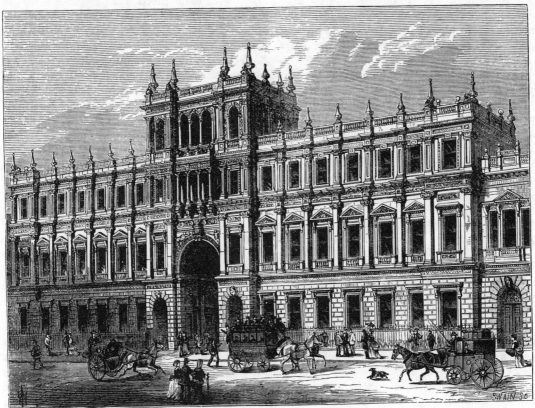

BURLINGTON HOUSE, 1875. (*See page* 266.)

Burlington House rose Clarges House, named after Sir Thomas Clarges, and two others, inhabited, according to Strype, by "Lord Sherbourne and the Countess of Denby" (*sic*).

Burlington House, in 1811, was tenanted by the Earl of Harrington, who gave there a grand ball. Under the Regency and in the reign of George IV., the mansion became occasionally the rallying-point of the Liberal party. In 1817, as Lord Russell tells us in his "Recollections," there was held here a meeting, at which Lord Grey, as the leader of the party, sketched out the policy of Lord Liverpool's ministry, and his own plan of opposition tactics. The Honourable Miss Amelia Murray tells us in her "Recollections," that about the year 1812 there was an intention of pulling down Burlington

enclosed by tents and temporary rooms. I did not think the Emperor of Russia a handsome man; he looked red, and stiff, and square: but Nicholas, the future Emperor, was a magnificent young prince. Among the numerous followers of the Emperor of Russia, there were the 'Hetman' Platoff, and twelve of his Cossacks, who were lodged by Lord James Murray, in Cumberland Place."

At Burlington House were exhibited the Elgin marbles, on their first arrival from the East, till they could find a permanent home at the British Museum. Cyrus Redding, in his "Fifty Years' Recollections," records his first visit to them here, in company with Haydon the painter.

In 1854, the mansion was purchased by the Government, and some five years later Lord John

Manners (then First Commissioner of Works) instructed Messrs. Banks and Barry to prepare a plan for buildings covering the entire site, which were then intended to comprise " a new Royal Academy, the University of London, and a Patent Office much enlarged, and to be connected with an extensive museum of patented invention for public reference, and also accommodation for at least six of the principal learned and scientific societies, who, it was considered, by past usage had acquired claims to be lodged at the public expense." The design consisted of two spacious quadrangles, each communicating with the other, and having arched gateways in the centre of the façades to Piccadilly and Burlington Gardens, thus connecting all together internally, and giving a thoroughfare through the building from the one part to the other. By this arrangement the Royal Academy would have had allotted to it nearly the whole of the Piccadilly façade, and the whole side of the first quadrangle on the west. This appropriation of the site, however, involved the removal of Old Burlington House, and, as the *Builder* remarks, "the sentimental ideas of its architectural importance and beauty were allowed to set aside this arrangement."

It was subsequently proposed by the Government to remove the national collection of pictures from Trafalgar Square, giving up the whole building there to the Royal Academy only, and to construct a National Gallery on the Burlington House lands. Accordingly, in 1863, fresh plans were prepared to meet this arrangement, by which the old mansion was to remain, the screen-wall in Piccadilly was to be replaced by a handsome open railing, the colonnades being retained, and, with the old building, being made to furnish the access to the new galleries. Again their plans met with the approval of the trustees of the National Gallery, after most careful deliberation, and also of the Government; but the vote for carrying this scheme into effect was refused by Parliament, partly on the same grounds as before—namely, the much-feared interference with the architectural glories of Old Burlington House.

" At last," says the *Builder*, " in the year 1866, it was proposed to reverse the above scheme, and that the National Gallery should remain in Trafalgar Square, and the Royal Academy should have a lease for 999 years, at a nominal rent, of the centre portion of Old Burlington House, with about half the garden in the rear, on which latter area they should erect new galleries and schools at their own cost, and under the direction of one of their members, Mr. Sydney Smirke; the access

to the same being through the old building, which was to accommodate the administration."

The grounds in the rear, extending to Burlington Gardens, were to be given as a site for the University of London, and their new edifice has been erected accordingly, under the direction of Sir James (then Mr.) Pennethorne. The wing-buildings, the colonnades, and the wall to Piccadilly were to be removed, and Messrs. Banks and Barry were again called upon to prepare designs for the erection of the new buildings, which were to accommodate six of the learned and scientific societies, namely, the Royal Society, the Linnæan Society, and the Chemical Society, who had hitherto occupied Old Burlington House, and the Society of Antiquaries, the Geological Society, and the Astronomical Society, who at that time were occupying parts of Somerset House. Arrangements having once more been made with the governing bodies of each society, as to the accommodation which they considered would be necessary for them respectively, and the plans having been finally approved by the then Government and by Parliament, and obtaining the Royal assent, the foundations for the present buildings were commenced in November, 1868.

The space now occupied by Burlington House extends from Piccadilly northwards into Burlington Gardens, having a frontage to each of about 200 feet, and a depth between them of nearly 600 feet. The old mansion, which still remains, stands at a distance of about 225 feet back from Piccadilly. The site of the south wall and the colonnades and wings is now covered with lofty and spacious buildings, forming three sides of a quadrangle, which, in the shape of an oblong square, has replaced the old court-yard. In the new façade towards Piccadilly, the most peculiar feature is the grand central archway leading into the court-yard ; it is probably the largest archway of the sort in London, being 20 feet clear in width and about 32 feet in height. The façade of Burlington House (now the Royal Academy of Arts) is fully seen from Piccadilly through this archway. The colonnade mentioned above was removed in 1868-9, and has found a temporary resting-place in Battersea Park.

The style of architecture adopted by Messrs. Banks and Barry is pure Italian ; and, as the authority above quoted observes, " taking as the key-note the general features and proportions of the façade of Old Burlington House, which was to form one side of the quadrangle, the architects have endeavoured to blend it with their new composition, with sufficient similarity of design to effect this, but with more finished details."

On the completion of the new building intended for the learned societies, those which at that time occupied the old mansion vacated their apartments, and that building was wholly made over to the Royal Academy, with the proviso that the Academy should, at their own expense, heighten their building by the addition of an upper storey. The portions of the buildings occupied by the members of the several societies are arranged on two floors, on the upper of which are situated the libraries—with the exception of that of the Geological Society, which is on the ground floor—each fitted with galleries, and lighted from the roof as well as at the sides. The Geological Society has its museum on the first floor, and this is fitted with two tiers of galleries.

The Royal Society has on the first floor a noble suite of reception-rooms, available for the annual *soirées* of the president, and a library which it is computed will give room for nearly 35,000 volumes, enabling it to continue what it now is, one of the most perfect scientific libraries in the world. The libraries of the Linnæan and Antiquarian Societies are very spacious, and all of them two storeys in height, with internal galleries.

The resident officers of the various societies located here have their apartments on the first and second floors of the building, in positions convenient to the scene of their daily labours. Dispersed throughout the rooms occupied by the Royal Society are the portraits of the presidents, distinguished Fellows, and other great luminaries of science, painted by Van Somer, Sir Peter Lely, Sir Godfrey Kneller, Sir Joshua Reynolds, Sir Thomas Lawrence, and other great artists.

It will not be out of place to introduce in this place a brief mention of some of our chief learned societies which have the advantage of free quarters here.

First and foremost, of course, stands the Royal Society. This is the oldest scientific society, with a consecutive history, in Europe, and stands with the French Institute at the head of the science of the world. As stated already (Vol. I., page 104), it dates its existence from the year 1645, and its early meetings were held sometimes at the lodgings of Dr. Goddard (one of its originators) in Wood Street, sometimes in Cheapside, and on other occasions in Gresham College. In 1648 and the following year, some of the supporters of these meetings became connected with the University of Oxford, and instituted a similar society in that city. Ten years later, several of the members of this philosophical society came to London, and held their meetings at Gresham College, where they were joined by Lord Brouncher, John Evelyn, and others; but owing to the political troubles of the times, their meetings were not long continued. In 1660, it was agreed to constitute a society for the study of science, when, in accordance with this resolve, a president, secretary, and registrar were elected; the president was Sir Robert Moray.

During the two centuries of the society's life it has occupied several dwellings. First at Gresham College; then at Arundel House, which was lent by Henry Howard, afterwards Duke of Norfolk; and again at Gresham College, where the society remained until 1710, when it removed to Crane Court. It continued here, in its own house, until 1780, when apartments in Somerset House were provided for it; and in these it remained till its removal to Burlington House, but its annual dinners were held at the "Thatched House Tavern" until the latter was taken down.

In 1859, the dinner party of the Royal Society would appear to have been remarkably cosmopolitan; the Electric Telegraph having been represented by Professor Wheatstone, the Railway System by Mr. Robert Stephenson, the Penny Post by Rowland Hill, and Astronomy by Sir Thomas Maclear, now Astronomer Royal at the Cape of Good Hope.

Charles II. presented the society with a silver-gilt mace, which is still placed on the table whenever the council or society meets, and without which no meeting can be legally held. This mace was for long supposed to be the "bauble" that Cromwell so unceremoniously ordered to be taken away from the table of the House of Commons, but Mr. Weld unluckily proved that it was made expressly for the society by command of the king. Another benefactor was Henry Howard, who presented the Arundel Library, which is still in the possession of the society; but the collection of antiquities and curiosities was presented to the British Museum when the apartments at Somerset House were found to be too contracted for its reception. The society still possesses several relics of Newton; as the sun-dial which he cut in the wall of his father's house when he was a boy; the first reflecting telescope, made, in 1671, with his own hands; and the original mask of his face, taken by Roubiliac.

The meetings of the society take place once a week, from the third Thursday in November to the third Thursday in June. A record of these meetings is published in the octavo "Proceedings," and a selection of the best papers is printed in the quarto "Transactions." These last were first printed in 1665, under the title of "Philosophical Transactions, giving some Account of the present Undertakings, Studies, and Labours of the Ingenious in many considerable Parts of the World;" and the series now extends to upwards of 160 volumes.

The society has at its disposal four medals, in the distribution of which it is able to mark its appreciation of scientific investigations and distinguished discoveries. The first award of the Copley medal was made in 1731, and of the Rumford medal in 1800 to the founder himself (Benjamin, Count Rumford) for his various discoveries respecting light and heat. In the year 1825, George IV. communicated through Sir Robert Peel his intention "to found two gold medals of the value of fifty guineas each, to be awarded as honorary premiums under the direction of the president and council of the Royal Society in such manner as shall by the excitement of competition among men of science seem best calculated to promote the objects for which the Royal Society was instituted." These medals were first awarded, in the year 1826, to John Dalton and James Ivory. William IV. and Queen Victoria have continued the gift of these royal medals, and they are, therefore, annually awarded. Besides these, the society undertakes the distribution of the annual grant of £1,000, which is voted by Parliament to be employed in aiding the promotion of science in the United Kingdom; and it also performs the office of scientific adviser to the Government on the difficult questions that arise in the various public departments. Through a committee of its Fellows, the Royal Society has made itself gratuitously useful to Her Majesty's Government for many years by directing the business of the Meteorological Department, which was formerly part of the duty of the Board of Trade.

In 1874, an attempt was made, though unsuccessfully, to limit the number of fellows to be elected in each year to fifteen. The proposal was carefully considered by a committee, to whom it was referred; but after a long discussion, a resolution was passed by the Council not to make any change in the existing rules.

Many particulars about the society and its convivial meetings, &c., may be learnt from a privately printed history of the club by the late Admiral Smyth, one of its most active and zealous members.

The following story of the merry monarch and of the learned society, though often told before, will bear being told again in the present chapter:— When King Charles II. dined with the members on the occasion of constituting them a Royal Society, towards the close of the evening he expressed his satisfaction at being the first English monarch who had laid a foundation for a society which proposed that their whole studies should be directed to the investigation of the arcana of nature, and added, with that peculiar gravity of countenance he usually wore on such occasions, that among such learned men he now hoped for a solution to a question which had long puzzled him. The case he thus stated:—Suppose two pails of water were fixed in two different scales that were equally poised, and which weighed equally alike, and two live bream, or small fish, were put into either of the pails; he wanted to know the reason why that pail, with such addition, should not weigh more than the other pail which was against it. Every one was ready to set at quiet the royal curiosity; but it appeared that every one was giving a different opinion. One at length offered so ridiculous a solution, that another of the members could not refrain from a loud laugh; when the king, turning to him, insisted that he should give his sentiments as well as the rest. This he did without hesitation; and told his Majesty, in plain terms, that he denied the fact; on which the king, in high mirth, exclaimed: "Odds fish, brother, you are in the right!" The jest was not ill designed, and the story is often useful to cool the enthusiasm of the scientific visionary, who is apt to account for what never existed.

All sorts of scientific experiments have been made from time to time under the auspices of the Royal Society. The following may be taken as a specimen:—In 1667, the Royal Society successfully performed the experiment of transfusing the blood of a sheep into a man in perfect health. The subject of the experiment was Arthur Coga, who, as Pepys says, was a kind of minister, and, being in want of money, hired himself for a guinea. Drs. Lower and King performed the experiment, injecting twelve ounces of sheep's blood, without producing any inconvenience. The patient drank a glass or two of canary, took a pipe of tobacco, and went home with a stronger and fuller pulse than before. The experiment was in a day or two afterwards repeated on Coga, when fourteen ounces of sheep's blood was substituted for eight ounces of his own. Pepys went to see him, and tells us that he heard him give an account in Latin of the operation and its effects.

The following is Sir David Brewster's account, in the *North British Review*, of the circumstances under which the great Sir Isaac Newton became a member of the society:—" Mr. Isaac Newton, Professor of Mathematics at Cambridge, was proposed as a Fellow by Dr. Seth Ward, Bishop of Sarum. Newton, then in his thirtieth year, had made several of his greatest discoveries. He had discovered the different refrangibility of light; he had invented the reflecting telescope; he had deduced the law of gravity from Kepler's theorem; and he had discovered the method of fluxions. When he heard of his being proposed as a Fellow, he expressed to Oldenburg, the secretary, his hope that he would be elected, and added, that he would endeavour to testify his gratitude by communicating what his poor and solitary endeavours could effect towards the promoting their philosophical design. The communications which Newton made to the society excited the deepest interest in every part of Europe. His little reflecting telescope, the germ of the colossal instruments of Herschel and Lord Rosse, was deemed one of the wonders of the age."

The most remarkable events connected with the society during the last century were the bequest of £100 by Sir George Copley in 1709, which resulted in the institution of the Copley medal; the measures taken for observing the transit of Venus, which, according to Halley, was to occur in 1761 and 1769, and the grand discovery of the composition of water in 1784, by some attributed to Cavendish, by others to Watt. In the early part of the present century Sir Humphry Davy commenced his well-known scientific career, and after having had all the honours of the Royal Society showered upon him, in 1820 took his seat as president in the chair previously occupied by Wren, Sir Isaac Newton, Sloane, and Banks.

The first list of Fellows includes such names as Sir Kenelm Digby, Sir William Petty (of whom we have spoken in the preceding chapter *), Matthew Wren, Robert Boyle, John Dryden, and Isaac Barrow. The signatures of all the Fellows, from the time of Charles II., when the society received the royal charter, down to the latest elected, are preserved in a vellum charter-book, which is a treasure of the highest interest. The number of presidents of the society, from Lord Brouncker—the first after its incorporation—down to Dr. Hooker, who was chosen in 1874—is thirty-two, among whom have been Sir Christopher Wren, Sir Hans Sloane, Sir Isaac Newton, Samuel Pepys, Lord Chancellor Somers, Sir John Pringle, Sir Joseph Banks, Sir Humphry Davy, Sir Benjamin Brodie, the Duke of Sussex, and the Earl of Rosse. The list of secretaries is specially rich in great names, such as John Evelyn, Dr. Halley, Sir John Herschel, Bishop Wilkins, Robert Hooke, Sir Humphry Davy, and many others.

The Society of Antiquaries of London, already mentioned in our account of Somerset House,† was founded by Archbishop Parker, in 1572. The members assembled at the house of Sir Robert Cotton, near Westminster Abbey, for twenty years. They applied to Elizabeth for a charter and a public building; but their hopes were frustrated by the queen's death. James I. took umbrage at some of the society's proceedings, and dissolved it. It would appear, however, to have existed privately during the seventeenth century, for in Ashmole's "Diary" we read of the "Antiquaries' feast on July 2, 1659," probably their annual dinner, which has now fallen into desuetude.

In 1707, we hear of their resuming their meetings in a more public form, and under the presidency of Le Neve. With him were associated Dr. William Stukeley, Humphrey Wanley, Roger Gale, Vertue, Browne Willis, and many others well known to fame. The minutes of the society commence in 1717, and in the same year they resolved to issue the first of that great series of prints which grew up into the work known as the "Vetusta Monumenta." We may here mention that the society has recently (1875) issued some *fasciculi* of great interest in completion of the sixth volume of this valuable collection.

In 1751, a royal charter of incorporation was granted to the society. In 1776, the king gave orders, when Somerset House was rebuilt, that the society should be accommodated with apartments in the new building. The whole of the fittings were put up at the expense of the Government, and in 1781 the society was formally inducted into possession of their new apartments.

The Society of Antiquaries was no favourite, strange to say, in spite of his antiquarian tastes, with Horace Walpole, who writes: "I dropped my attendance there four or five years ago, being sick of their ignorance and stupidity, and have not been three times amongst them since."

When the Royal Society removed to Burlington House, some changes were effected as to the rooms occupied by this society. In 1866, a scheme was submitted to the society by Her Majesty's Government for -accommodating the society in Burlington House. To this scheme the society acceded, not without some reluctance, and only on the understanding that adequate accommodation should be provided, and that the expense of the fittings should be borne by the Government.

The services which the society has rendered are patent to the world. Its "Transactions" can only

---

be compared with the "Memoirs" of the Académie des Inscriptions et Belles Lettres for range and depth. Among the more recent and public services rendered by the society may be mentioned the restoration of the Chapter House at Westminster, which was undertaken mainly at the instance and through the zeal of its council. The late Lord Stanhope, better known by his former title of Lord Mahon, held the presidential chair of the Society

the Royal Society, Sir Joseph Banks, to whom it was indebted for pecuniary assistance, and for large additions to its library and collections.

From an early period of its existence, the Linnæan Society took a high station in the world of science, and it stands now, as it always has done, at the head of the natural history societies of the United Kingdom, and on a level with the most distinguished of similar societies abroad.

CLARENDON HOUSE, IN 1666. (*See page* 273.)

of Antiquaries from 1846 down to his death at the close of 1875.

The Linnæan Society, so called after the great naturalist, Linnæus, was founded, as stated in our account of Soho Square,* in 1788, for the study of natural history, more especially that of the British Islands, and was incorporated by royal charter in 1802. It was the earliest offset of the Royal Society, the separation taking place with the ready assent and concurrence of the parent body, it being felt that natural history was a science of sufficient extent and importance to demand the entire attention of a distinct society. The infant society was warmly aided by the then president of

Its "Transactions" now include about thirty copiously-illustrated quarto volumes, and form, unquestionably, the most important series of memoirs on natural history which this country has produced. In addition, it has now for many years published an octavo journal in two sections, Zoology and Botany, where those papers appear which have less need of illustration.

The library and collections of the society are very extensive, including those of Linnæus (invaluable in themselves, and in illustration of the works of the great Swedish naturalist), which, together with the additions made by its founder, Sir J. E. Smith, were purchased by the society, in 1829, for £3,000, and the extensive herbarium of Indian plants, munificently presented by the

* See Vol. III., p. 191.

Court of Directors of the East India Company in 1832.

The funds of the society, with the exception of a very small return, in proportion to the outlay, from the sale of its publications, are wholly derived from the contributions of its Fellows, to whom the "Transactions" and "Journal" are distributed without further payment.

By the cost of printing and illustrating these

1828, the late Sir Robert Peel, then Secretary of the Treasury, assigned to it the apartments in Somerset House which it continued to occupy till its removal to Burlington House in 1874. Previously it had occupied a house in Bedford Street, Strand. The charter says: "Whereas the Reverend William Buckland, B.D., Arthur Aikin, esquire, John Bostock, M.D., George Bellas Greenough, esquire, Henry Warburton, esquire, and several

CLARGES HOUSE, PICCADILLY. (*From Mr. Crace's Collection.*)

publications, and in other necessary expenses, the society was, for a long period, seriously cramped in its operations. When, therefore, in 1856, the Government offered to put the Royal Society in possession of the main building of Burlington House, on the understanding that suitable accommodation therein should be assigned to the Linnæan and Chemical Societies, the Linnæan, although it had recently renewed, for a long term, its lease of the house in Soho Square, availed itself of the proposal, which, in the first place, promised to place its library and collections out of danger from fire, and would relieve the funds of the society from the outlay for rent.

The Geological Society was established in 1807, and incorporated by royal charter in 1826. In

others of our loving subjects, being desirous of forming a society for investigating the mineral structure of the earth, and having for promoting such investigation expended considerable sums of money in the collection and purchase of books, maps, specimens, and other objects, and in the publication of various works, the said William Buckland, Arthur Aikin, John Bostock, George Bellas Greenough, and Henry Warburton have humbly besought us to grant unto them and unto such other persons as shall be appointed and elected Fellows of the Society, as hereinafter is mentioned, our Royal Charter of Incorporation, for the better carrying on the purposes aforesaid." A charter was accordingly granted, Dr. Buckland being appointed first president. The early publications of the society consisted of "Proceedings" in octavo, and "Transactions" in quarto : of the former, four volumes were published ; and of the latter, twelve volumes in two series (of five and seven). The "Transactions" ceased in 1856, but in 1845 a quarterly journal was started, and has been carried on ever since in their place. The society also publishes Mr. Greenough's Geological Map of England. The society possesses an extensive library, and a museum consisting of fossils, minerals, &c. ; the collection of foreign fossils being particularly interesting.

The Royal Astronomical Society was founded in the year 1820 by the exertions of the Rev. Dr. Pearson, Mr. Francis Baily, and other gentlemen at that time eminent in the science of astronomy, its objects being "the encouragement and promotion of astronomy." We need scarcely add that it has been eminently successful in carrying out these objects, having published thirty-eight volumes of "Memoirs," and thirty volumes of "Monthly Notices," which are held in much estimation both by English and foreign astronomers.

The only remaining learned body located here is the Chemical Society. This was founded in 1841, and incorporated under royal charter in 1848. Its objects are defined to be "the promotion of chemistry and of those branches of science immediately connected with it, by the reading, discussion, and subsequent publication of original communications." The society holds fortnightly meetings during eight months of the year, and publishes a journal in monthly numbers. Its management is vested in a president and a council, chosen, for the most part, annually by ballot.

Of the rise and progress of the Royal Academy we have already spoken in our notice of the National Gallery, Trafalgar Square.* It only remains to add that, since the removal hither, the exhibitions of the Royal Academy have gone on steadily increasing in popularity, and that during "the season" not only are the spacious apartments here crowded with the *élite* of society, but the exhibitions have become sufficiently attractive to induce artisans and others belonging more to the working classes to flock thither, and in such numbers as to warrant the council in allowing the works of art annually brought together to be exhibited during the evening by gas-light. *Apropos* of the good work achieved by the Royal Academy, it may be stated that the choice of Angelica Kauffmann and Mrs. Montague among its first members

gave an impetus to female education, and helped to keep alive till a more enlightened period the claims of women to take their place side by side with men in the battle of life, and in following the professions. As a proof that their example was not without effect, we may add that, in the year 1778, the publisher of "The Ladies' Pocket-book" gave, as a frontispiece, a group of nine ladies celebrated in art or in literature, namely, Miss Carter, Mrs. Barbauld, Angelica Kauffmann, Mrs. Sheridan, Mrs. Lennox, Mrs. Montague, Miss Moore, Mrs. Macaulay, and Miss Griffith, each lady in the fanciful character of one of the nine Muses.

On the west side of Burlington House is the Burlington Arcade, which was built as a bazaar by Lord George Cavendish, afterwards Earl of Burlington, in 1819. This arcade, upwards of 200 yards in length, forms a covered pathway between Piccadilly and Burlington Gardens ; it has shops on each side for the sale of millinery, jewellery, and, in fact, almost every article of fashionable demand. It is closed at night by gates at each end under the charge of a beadle in livery. It is stated by Mr. Peter Cunningham that the rents of the shops in this arcade amount to upwards of £8,000 a year, only about half of which finds its way into the pockets of its owners, the Cavendishes.

We have given on page 264 a view of the original Burlington House, with its gardens in the rear, laid out on the square formal French fashion. It shows the little temporary church or chapel in Conduit Street, standing quite isolated from every other building. There is also a view, by Kip, of the first Burlington House, built by Sir John Denham, the author of the poem called "Cooper's Hill," and also Surveyor of Buildings under the Crown.

With reference to the old court-yard and colonnade, of which we have already spoken, we may add that it is represented in the first of the above-mentioned views, and that to it Sir William Chambers thus alludes :—" In London, many of our noblemen's palaces towards the street look like convents. Nothing appears but a high wall, with one or two large gates, in which there is a hole for those who are privileged to go in and out. If a coach arrives, the whole gate is indeed opened ; but this is an operation that requires time, and the porter is very careful to shut it up again immediately, for reasons to him very weighty. Few in this vast city, I suspect, believe that behind an old brick wall in Piccadilly there is one of the finest pieces of architecture in Europe."

* See Vol. III., pp. 146—149.

CHAPTER XXIII.

NOBLE MANSIONS IN PICCADILLY.

" Est via declivis."—*Ovid.*

Clarendon House—Lord Clarendon incurs the Displeasure of the Populace—Extracts from the Diaries of Evelyn and Pepys referring to Clarendon House—The Name of " Dunkirk House " given to the Mansion—Its Demolition—Berkeley House : Descriptions of the Building—Devon. shire House : Description of the Building—The Picture Galleries and Library—The Earl of Devonshire, and the Murder of Mr. Thynne of Longleat—Anecdote of the First Duke of Devonshire—Devonshire House as a " Pouting Place of Princes "—The Mansion as a Rendezvous of the Whig Party—Georgiana, Duchess of Devonshire—Walpole's Compliment to the House and its Owner— Fashionable Entertainments and Dramatic Performances at Devonshire House—Stratton Street—Mrs. Coutts, afterwards Duchess of St. Albans—Sir Francis Burdett : his Seizure, and Committal to the Tower—Pulteney Hotel—Bath House—Anecdotes of Lord Orford and Lord Bath—Watier's Club—The Dilettanti Society—Grafton House, now the Turf Club—Egremont House, now the Naval and Military Club—Hertford House—Coventry House, now the St. James's Club—The Rothschilds—Viscountess Keith—Hope House, now the Junior Athenæum Club— John, Earl of Eldon—Gloucester House—The Duke of Queensberry, " Old Q."—Lord Byron's Residence—Lord Palmerston's House— The " Hercules Pillars"—The " Triumphal Chariot"—Historical Remarks.

ALONG the line of Piccadilly, when the district was more or less open country, besides Burlington House, stood some of the mansions of the nobility of the seventeenth century.

Westward of Burlington House, facing the top of St. James's Street, and on the site of what is now Bond Street, Stafford Street, and Albemarle Street, formerly stood Clarendon House. Pennant places the mansion as far to the north as Grafton Street ; but the existing maps would seem to show that Stafford Street would mark more precisely the spot on which it stood. In a plan of London etched by Hollar, in 1686, it is evident that the centre of Clarendon House must have occupied the whole of the site of Stafford Street. No. 74, in Piccadilly, the publishing house of the late Mr. J. C. Hotten—now Messrs. Chatto and Windus—is said to be built of the old materials of the mansion. It was a heavy, high-roofed house, standing a little back from the street, with projecting wings; it had square-headed windows, including a row of attic windows which pierced the roof. A flight of stone steps led up to the door, which was in the centre.

Lord Clarendon, when Lord Chancellor under Charles II., having built his magnificent house soon after the sale of Dunkirk to Louis XIV., about the year 1664, found that he had incurred in the eyes of the people the full blame of the transaction, and that his mansion was called by the public not Clarendon but Dunkirk House, on the supposition that it had been built with French money. No sane person can doubt the fact of Charles II. having received large sums from the Court of Versailles for purposes hostile to the interests of his people ; but there is no proof what- ever that Lord Clarendon was privy to such trans- actions, much less that he derived any personal profit from them. It was, in his case, the old story repeated—

" Delirant reges, plectuntur Achivi."

A view of Lord Clarendon's house as it appeared during its brief decade of existence, may be found in the first volume of Charles Knight's " London," and there is also an engraving of it in the *Gentle- man's Magazine* for August, 1789.

From the Diaries of Evelyn and Pepys we learn something of the varying fortunes of Clarendon House during its brief existence. Under date 15th October, 1664, Evelyn writes : " After dinner, my Lord Chancellor and his lady carried me in their coach to see their palace now building at the upper end of St. James's Street, and to project the garden." Pepys, in January, 1665-6, makes this entry in his Diary : " To my Lord Chancellor's new house which he is building, only to view it, hearing so much from Mr. Evelyn of it ; and indeed it is the finest pile I ever did see in my life, and will be a glorious house." Evelyn, about the same time, wrote to Lord Cornbury, the Chancellor's eldest son : " I have never seen a nobler pile . . . Here is state, use, solidity, and beauty, most symmetrically combined together. Nothing abroad pleases me better, nothing at home approaches to it." Besides the laying out of the gardens, Evelyn appears to have contributed to the internal adornment of this magnificent mansion, for in March, 1666-7, he sent the Chancellor a list of " pictures that might be added to the assembly of the learned and heroic persons of England which your lordship has already collected ;" and on a subsequent occasion, in recording the fact of his dining here with Lord Cornbury, after the Chancellor's flight, Evelyn remarks that it is " now bravely furnished, especi- ally with the pictures of most of our ancient and modern wits, poets, philosophers, famous and learned Englishmen, which collection I much commended, and gave a catalogue of more to be added." Pennant says it was built with the stones intended for the rebuilding of St. Paul's.

The whole place, according to Charles Knight, " would seem to have resembled in stately dignity the style of the ' History of the Great Rebellion.' " " The plague, the Great Fire, and the disgraceful war with Holland," says the above authority, " had goaded the public mind into a temper of savage mutiny; and the 'wits and misses,' to aid their court intrigues against the Chancellor, had done what in them lay to direct the storm against his head. The marriage of the Chancellor's daughter to the Duke of York and the barrenness of the Queen were represented as the results of a plot; the situation of Clarendon House, looking down on St. James's, and the employment of stones collected with a view to repair St. Paul's, were tortured into crimes." At length the storm of public wrath fairly burst over Clarendon House, as the following entry in Pepys's "Diary" will show. Under date 14th of June, 1667, he writes :—" Mr. Harter tells me, at noon, that some rude people have been, as he hears, at my Lord Chancellor's, where they have cut down the trees before his house, and broke his windows; and a gibbet either set up before or painted upon his gate, and these words writ, 'Three sights to be seen—Dunkirk, Tangier, and a barren Queen.'"

In a volume of rare London ballads and broadsides in the British Museum is one entitled, "A Hue and Cry after the Earl of Clarendon," dated in 1667. Our readers may gather how strong was the popular feeling against him on account of the sale of Dunkirk from the opening lines :—

" From Dunkirk House there lately ran away
A traitor whom you are desired to slay.
You by these marks and signs may th' traitor know,
He's troubled with the gout in feet below.

* * * * * * * * *

This hopeful blade being conscious of his crimes,
And smelling how the current of the times
Ran cross, forsakes his palace and the town
Like some presaging rat ere th' house fall down."

Evelyn mentions, in the following terms, a journey made by him in June, 1683, along Piccadilly, doubtless on the way to his residence in Dover Street :—" I returned to town in a coach with the Earle of Clarendon, when, passing by the glorious palace his father had built but few years before, which they were now demolishing, being sold to certain undertakers [contractors], I turned my head the contrary way till the coach was gone past it, lest I might minister occasion of speaking of it, which must needs have grieved him that in so short a time their pomp was so sadly fallen."

"The sumptuous palace," writes Macaulay, "to which the populace of London gave the name of Dunkirk House, is among the many signs which indicate the shortest road to boundless wealth in the days of Charles II." The enormous gains then made by prime ministers, partly by salaries, and partly by the sale of posts and places, were the real secret of the tenacity with which men clung to office in those days.

Lord Clarendon seems to have been particularly fond of this mansion, though it was so offensive to the public. The day before his lordship's flight, Evelyn "found him in his garden at his new-built palace, sitting in his gowte wheel-chaire, and seeing the gates setting up towards the north and the fields. He looked and spake very disconsolately. Next morning I heard he was gone." His lordship, even in his exile, after writing that " his weakness and vanity" in the outlay he made upon it, "more contributed to that gust of envy that had so violently shaken him than any misdemeanour that he was thought to have been guilty of," confesses that, when it was proposed to sell it, in order to pay his debts and to make some provision for his younger children, "he remained so infatuated with the delight he had enjoyed, that, though he was deprived of it, he hearkened very unwillingly to the advice."

Under date of September, 1683, Evelyn thus writes in his "Diary :"—"I went to survey the sad demolition of Clarendon House, that costly and only sumptuous palace of the late Lord Chancellor Hyde, where I have often been so cheerful with him, and sometimes so sad. . . . The Chancellor gone and dying in exile," he continues, "the earl, his successor, sold the building, which cost £50,000, to the young Duke of Albemarle for £25,000 to pay debts, which how contracted remains yet a mystery, his son being no way a prodigal. . . . However it were, this stately palace is decreed to ruin, to support the prodigious waste the Duke of Albemarle had made of his estate since the old man died. He sold it to the highest bidder, and it fell to certain rich bankers and mechanics, who gave for it and the ground about £35,000; they design a new town, as it were, and a most magnificent piazza. . . . See the vicissitude of earthly things! I was astonished at the demolition, nor less at the little army of labourers and artificers levelling the ground, laying foundations, and contriving great buildings, at an expense of £200,000, if they perfect their design."

In Smith's "Streets of London" it is stated that "the earliest date now to be found upon the site of Clarendon House is cut in stone and let into the south wall of a public-house, the sign of ' The Duke of Albemarle ' in Dover Street, thus : ' This is Stafford Street, 1686.' "

It is said by Isaac D'Israeli, in his "Curiosities of Literature," that the two Corinthian pilasters on either side of the gateway of the "Three

Kings," on the north side of Piccadilly, are the only remains of the house built by the great Earl of Clarendon, whose name, however, has been perpetuated, at all events, down to the year 1870, in the Clarendon Hotel hard by.

Berkeley House, a little further to the west, according to Pepys, was built about the same time as Clarendon House. It was so called because it was built for Lord Berkeley, of Stratton, an able officer in the Royal army under Charles I., and whose name is still commemorated in the neighbourhood, by Berkeley Square and by Berkeley and Stratton Streets. Slightly at the rear, as it would seem, was a farm-house, from which Hay Hill, possibly, derives its name.

"Before the date of Burlington House," writes Pennant, "there was built here a fine mansion belonging to the Berkeleys, Lord Berkeley (of Stratton). It stood between the south end of Berkeley Square and Piccadilly, and gave the name to the square and an adjacent street (Berkeley Street). The misery and disgrace which the profligacy of one of the daughters brought on the house, by an intrigue with her brother-in-law, Lord Grey (afterwards engaged in the Monmouth Rebellion), is too lastingly recorded in our State Trials ever to be buried in oblivion."

Evelyn tells us that the mansion was "very well built," and that it had "many noble rooms; but," he adds, "they are not very convenient, consisting but of one *corps de logis*. They are all rooms of state, without closets. The staircase is of cedar; the furniture is princely; the kitchen and stables are ill placed, and the corridor worse, having no respect to the wings they join to. For the rest, the fore-court is noble, so are the stables, and, above all, the gardens, which are incomparable, by reason of the inequality of the ground, and a pretty *piscina* [a fish-pond]. The holly hedges on the terrace I advised the planting of. The porticos are in imitation of a house described by Palladio, but it happens to be the worst in his book, though my good friend, Mr. Hugh May, his lordship's architect, affected it."

In the "New View of London," published in 1708, Berkeley House is described as "a spacious building on the north side of Portugal Street, near Piccadilly, with a pleasant, large court, now in the occupation of the Duke of Devonshire. The house," it is added, "is built of brick, adorned with stone pilasters, and an entablature and pitched pediment, all of the Corinthian order, under which is a figure of Britannia carved in stone. At some distance on the east side is the kitchen and laundry; and on the west side stables and lodg-

ing-rooms, which adjoin to the mansion by brick walls, and two circular galleries, each elevated on columns of the Corinthian order, where are two ambulatories."

Independently of the beauties of the mansion and gardens, there is but little interest attaching to Berkeley House. Its founder is represented by Pepys as "a passionate and but weak man as to policy; but, as a kinsman, brought in and promoted by my Lord St. Albans." It was destroyed by fire on the 16th of October, 1733, soon after it had passed into the hands of William, first Duke of Devonshire.

"On the site of the house," continues Pennant, "fronting Piccadilly, stands Devonshire House. Long after the year 1700 it was the last house in this street, at that time the portion (*sic*) of Piccadilly." He means, no doubt, that the Piccadilly of that day formed only a portion of the present long street.

The old house, according to Pennant, was frequented by Waller, Denham, and many others of the wits and poets of the reign of Charles II.; and he speaks of it as containing, in his own time, an excellent library and a very fine collection of medals. He also enumerates the pictures, which are very much the same as now, adding, that the collection of specimens by the great Italian masters "is by far the finest private collection now in England."

The author of the "New Critical Review of the Public Buildings" speaks in very high terms of the former Devonshire House, the ruins of which were still standing in 1736, when he wrote. He attributes its destruction to the carelessness of the duke's servants, and their disregard of the family motto, "Cavendo tutus." He describes it as simple in plan, yet very elegant, and quite worthy of the master hand of Inigo Jones, its only fault being the great number of its chimneys, which he calls "a heavy Gothic incumbrance to the whole." He laments the loss of a fine statue of Britannia, which, having escaped the flames, was accidentally destroyed by a second act of carelessness.

The present Devonshire House is briefly dismissed by Mr. J. H. Jesse with the curt remark that, "except during the brief period when the beautiful Georgiana, Duchess of Devonshire, held her court within its walls, and when Fox, Burke, Windham, Fitzpatrick, and Sheridan did homage at her feet, little interest attaches to the present edifice." But we think that this remark is scarcely just; for the court of Georgiana, the beautiful duchess (of whom we have made mention in our account of the Westminster election at Covent

Garden), was not a very "brief" one, nor does it deserve to be put aside out of memory after so summary a fashion.

The mansion, which for more than a century has divided with Holland House the reputation of being the head-quarters of the leaders of the great Whig party, was built about the year 1737, by William, third Duke of Devonshire, on the site of part of the property of Lord Berkeley of Stratton.

on the north side, of marble and alabaster, with rails of solid crystal, was erected by the late duke. The ornamentation of the great staircase, and of most of the rooms in the house, is by Mr. Crace.

The picture-galleries in this house are scattered through the long range of rooms which passes all round it on the first floor. It would be impossible, in this work, to give a complete list of the art treasures that are to be found here, but we may

DEVONSHIRE HOUSE, ABOUT 1800.

The design of the house was by Kent; and it cost upwards of £20,000. The house recedes a little from the rest of the houses in this street. It has little or nothing in its exterior appearance to recommend it to particular notice, but its interior is richly stored with some of the finest works of art in any private collection.

The entrance to the house was originally up a double flight of stone steps, arranged as an external staircase, in the front, and leading straight into the reception-rooms on the first floor; but this arrangement was done away by the late duke, who made the entrance on the ground level into a hall of low elevation, beyond which he threw out on the north or garden side a semi-circular apse, containing a new staircase. The interior staircase

mention a few of the most important. In the large north room hang "The Madonna and Child and St. Elizabeth," by Rubens; "The Prince and Princess of Orange," by Jacob Jordaens; and also "a Portrait," unknown, by Titian. In the green-room adjoining is "Jacob's Dream," by Salvator Rosa, and "Samson and Delilah," by Tintoretto. In the blue drawing-room is "Moses in the Bul-rushes," by Murillo. A small room on the north side is hung almost entirely with specimens of Van Dyke, including a noble portrait of the great Lord Strafford; in the same room is Lord Richard Cavendish, by Sir Joshua Reynolds. In addition to the portraits mentioned above, the list also comprises John Hampden's friend, Arthur Goodwin, by Van Dyke, and his daughter Jane, wife of

Philip, Lord Wharton; a head of the virtuous and accomplished Lord Falkland; Sir Thomas Browne (author of the "Religio Medici"), his wife, and daughters; a Jewish Rabbi, by Rembrandt; a head of Titian, by himself; Philip II., by the same; and the old Countess of Desmond. A list

laid down in turf as lawns, and contain some fine elm-trees.

But to pass from the bricks and mortar of the house to the personal history of its owners. We have already mentioned the murder in Pall Mall of Mr. Thynne, of Longleat. The then Earl of

SIR FRANCIS BURDETT. (*See page* 281.)

of some of the finest pictures to be seen in this mansion is printed in Dr. Waagen's work on "Art and Artists in England."

In the library here is kept John Philip Kemble's celebrated collection of old English plays, probably the finest in existence. It was made at the cost of £2,000, and was purchased by the sixth duke, after the collector's death. The library is very rich also in other departments of early English literature. The gardens in the rear of the house are mostly

Devonshire, as friend of Mr. Thynne, desired to avenge his death, and challenged the dastardly foreigner, who had plotted his assassination, to meet him in a duel. The Count (says Pennant) accepted the challenge, but afterwards his conscience (!) prevented him from meeting the Earl. It is some comfort to know that on returning to his own country the Count met with that fate which he so richly deserved here.

A good story is told in the "Apology for the

Life of Colley Cibber" respecting the Earl of Devonshire, who was raised to the dukedom in reward for the leading part which he took in the Revolution of 1688. Being one day in the Royal Presence Chamber shortly before that event, and being known to be no friend of the Court or the Ministry, he was insulted by a person who trod purposely on his foot. The insult was returned on the spot by a blow, which brought the offender to his senses. But as the act was committed within the king's court, the striker was sentenced to a fine of thirty thousand pounds. Having, however, time allowed for paying it, he retired to Chatsworth, whither King James sent a messenger to him with offers to mitigate the fine if he would pay it promptly. The earl, knowing the "lie of the land," replied, that if his Majesty would allow him a little time longer, he would rather choose to play "double or quits" with him. The Revolution being near at hand, there was no time for any further parley; and the king speedily found himself in a position in which he might inflict, but could not enforce, the fine.

It is stated of the above nobleman, by Dr. W. King, in "Anecdotes of his Own Times," that he received, after the accession of George I., more than £200,000 in places and pensions, without having done any service to his country or his sovereign. Let us hope that this censure was not well deserved, or else that the money has since been recouped to the country by the services of his descendants.

Like Leicester House, already mentioned,* Devonshire House played for two years the part of a "pouting place of princes." From 1692 to the death of her sister Mary, Anne, Princess of Denmark, and her husband lived here, not being on the best of terms with their then Majesties.

For a century and a half this house has been one of the special rendezvous of the Whig party. "Three palaces in the year 1784," writes Sir N. W. Wraxall, "the gates of which were constantly thrown open to every supporter of the 'Coalition' (against Pitt), formed rallying-points of union." One of these was Burlington House, then tenanted by the Duke of Portland; the second was Carlton House, the residence of George, Prince of Wales; the third was Devonshire House, which, "placed on a commanding eminence opposite to the Green Park, seemed to look down upon the Queen's House, constructed by Sheffield, Duke of Buckingham, in a situation much less favoured by nature."

At this time its leading spirit was Georgiana, Duchess of Devonshire, a lady whose character

formed a perfect contrast to the indolence of her husband, and who, in respect of her beauty, her accomplishments, and the part which she played in the world of politics, may be compared with Anne Genevieve de Bourbon, Duchesse de Longueville, in the French annals. She is described by Sir N. W. Wraxall as "one of the most distinguished ladies of high rank whom the last century produced. Her personal charms," he adds, "constituted her smallest pretension to universal admiration; nor did her beauty consist, like that of the Gunnings, in regularity of features and faultless formation of limbs and shape; it lay rather in the graces of her deportment, in her irresistible manners, and the seduction of her society. Her hair was not without a tinge of red, and her face, though pleasing, had it not been illumined by her mind, might have been considered an ordinary countenance. Descended, in the fourth degree, lineally from Sarah Jennings, the wife of John Churchill, Duke of Marlborough, she resembled the portraits of that celebrated woman. In addition to the external advantages which she received from nature and fortune, she possessed an ardent temper, susceptible of deep as well as strong impressions, a cultivated understanding, illumined by a taste for poetry and the fine arts, and much sensibility, not exempt, perhaps, from vanity and coquetry."

In our account of Covent Garden,† and the scenes witnessed there in former times in connection with the elections for Westminster, we had occasion to speak of the part taken by the Duchess of Devonshire in securing the return of Mr. Fox in 1784. The following lines were written in consequence of her Grace's canvass on his behalf:—

"Arrayed in matchless beauty, Devon's fair
    In Fox's favour takes a zealous part;
But oh! where'er the pilferer comes—beware!
    She supplicates a vote, and steals a heart."

The lines quoted above were, no doubt, intended as complimentary to the duchess; she had, however, a more elegant compliment paid to her one day at Chatsworth by a gentleman who, after viewing the garden and the library, applied to her the words of Cowley:—

"The fairest garden in her looks,
    And in her mind the choicest books."

Towards the close of her life, however, the beautiful duchess would often say "that of all the compliments paid her, the drunken Irishman, who asked to light his pipe by the fire of her beautiful eyes, paid her the highest."

It was at Devonshire House, however, and not at

---

* See Vol. III., p. 164.

† See Vol. III., p. 257.

Carlton Palace, that the procession of the multitude was brought to an end on the occasion of Fox's election to which we refer ; and so great was the excitement that, according to Sir N. W. Wraxall, " on the procession entering the great court in front of the house, the Prince of Wales, who had already saluted the successful candidate from the garden wall on the side of Berkeley Street, appeared within the balustrade before the mansion, accompanied by the most eminent members of the Whig Coalition, both male and female, Fox dismissing the assembled mob with a brief harangue."

The Duke of Devonshire, if not a man of very great abilities, was a man of his word and the soul of honour. Dr. Johnson said of him that he was " a man of such ' dogged veracity,' that if he had promised an acorn, and not one had grown in his woods that year, he would have sent to Denmark for one !" A strong testimony to a Whig nobleman's honour from so staunch a Tory as the learned doctor.

William, the third duke, who is satirised by Pope for his meanness, as " dirty D——," was a staunch Whig, like the rest of his family. Horace Walpole said of him, that " his outside was unpolished and his inside unpolishable."

It is said that one day, not long after the erection of the present mansion, the great Sir Robert Walpole looked in to make a morning call on its owner, and not finding him at home, left on his table the following Latin epigram :—

> " Ut dominus domus est ; non extra fulta columnis
> Marmoreis splendet : quod tenet, intus habet."

A higher or more graceful compliment could hardly be paid to either the house or its owner, than to say that they were both " all glorious within."

George IV., as Prince of Wales, was a constant frequenter of the coteries and parties of Devonshire House, which was at that time the resort, not only of the Whig Opposition, but of all the wits and *beaux esprits* of the time. Among the rest were Sheridan, Grey, Whitbread, Lord Robert Spencer, Fox, Hare, Fitz-Patrick, and George Selwyn, all members of the society of *bon ton* in their day.

Mr. T. Raikes thus mentions Devonshire House in his " Journal :"—" In these entertainments, which many years ago engrossed all the wit and fashion of London society for a long period, since quoted as the era of refinement and pleasure, Lady Bessborough was a leading character. Even Lady Grenville now, when she meets an ancient votary of those days, illustrated by her mother, will say, ' He, too, remembers Devonshire House.' "

Here, in 1814, William, the sixth Duke of Devonshire, gave several splendid entertainments to the Emperor of Russia, the King of Prussia, and the other military personages who accompanied the Allied Sovereigns to England. Here the Prince of Orange was present at a grand ball on the evening before he returned to the Continent in the character of the discarded lover of the Princess Charlotte. Shortly before, Lady Brownlow tells us in her " Reminiscences," she had seen the royal affianced pair at a party given by the Prince Regent at Carlton House, when the Emperor of Russia and the King of Prussia were present. " At this party I well remember seeing the Princess Charlotte and the Prince of Orange sitting together and walking about arm-in-arm, looking perfectly happy and lover-like. What were the intrigues and influences that changed the princess's feelings and caused her to break off the marriage is a mystery, known, I believe, to few. There were many rumours—many stories afloat, but none to be relied on ; the only thing positive being the fact that the prince was dismissed."

The entertainments at Devonshire House have not been confined to balls and such-like aristocratic amusements, but have had a much wider range. Here the celebrated dwarf, Count Boruwlaski, was received by the Duke and the Duchess at one of their entertainments and presented by their Graces to the King, the Queen, and the Prince of Wales, and the rest of the nobility, with whom he became a " lion," and by whom he was *fêted* and caressed to an extent which would strike us as absurd and incredible if we did not remember the more recent visit of " Tom Thumb " to this metropolis and the fuss that was made with him.

But Devonshire House has its literary as well as its fashionable and political associations. As very many of our readers will remember, it was more than once, in the time of the late duke, the scene of amateur private theatricals given on a scale of magnificence which reminds us of the days when English actors were " the king's " and the duke's " servants." When, in 1850, Charles Dickens, in concert with Sir E. Bulwer Lytton, was endeavouring to set afloat the " Guild of Literature and Art " by the proceeds of a farce written by the former, and a comedy by the latter, the Duke of Devonshire, as Mr. Forster tells us in his " Life of Dickens," " offered the use of his house in Piccadilly for their first representations, and in his princely way discharged all the expenses attending them. A movable theatre was built and set up in the great drawing-room, and the library was turned into a green-room. *Not so Bad as we Seem* was played for the first time at Devonshire House on the 27th of May, 1851, before the Queen and the Prince

Consort, and as large an audience as could be found room for. *Mr. Nightingale's Diary* was the name of the farce." The representation was a great success. It was repeated several times over at the Hanover Square Rooms, and continued at intervals both in London and in the country during that and the following year. Among the distinguished authors and artists who took part in the performance at Devonshire House, besides Lord Lytton and Dickens, were Douglas Jerrold, John Leech, and Mr. Maclise.

The western side of Devonshire House is bounded by a street without a thoroughfare, called Stratton Street, after Lord Berkeley of Stratton, by whom it was built in the year 1694. At No. 12 the gallant Lord Lynedoch died, at the age of ninety-four, in 1843. This street, and also Berkeley Street, on the east side of Devonshire House, it would seem, were laid out after a design of John Evelyn, who thus writes under date June, 1684 :— "I went to advise and give directions about building two streets in Berkeley Gardens, reserving the house and as much of the garden as the breadth of the house. In the meantime I could not but deplore that sweet place (by far the most noble gardens, courts, and accommodations, stately porticos, &c., anywhere about town) should be so much straitened and turned into tenements. But that magnificent pile and gardens contiguous to it, built by the late Lord Chancellor Clarendon, being all demolished and designed for piazzas and buildings, was some excuse for Lady Berkeley's resolution of letting out her gardens, also for so excessive a price as was offered, advancing near £1,000 per annum, in mere ground rents ; to such a mad intemperance was the age come of building about a city by far too disproportionate already to the nation."

In the corner house of Piccadilly and Stratton Street, noticeable for its fine bow windows, overlooking the Green Park, lived for many years the rich and benevolent Mrs. Coutts, widow of Thomas Coutts, the banker, originally Miss Harriet Mellon, the actress, and afterwards Duchess of St. Albans. As an instance of her benevolence, it is recorded that, in the year 1836, when a fund was set on foot for the relief of the Spitalfields weavers, she not only sent a subscription equal in amount to that of royalty, but also gave the weavers an order for a suite of damask curtains for her drawing-rooms, at the price of a guinea a yard, an example which was followed by other wealthy families.

Captain Gronow tells us, in his "Anecdotes and Reminiscences," an amusing story connected with this house. On the day after the coronation of George IV., Mr. Hamlet, the jeweller, came to the house, expressing a wish to see the wealthy banker. It was during dinner ; but owing, no doubt, to a previous arrangement, he was at once admitted, when he placed before Mr. Coutts a magnificent diamond cross which had been worn the previous day by the Duke of York. It at once attracted the admiration of Mrs. Coutts, who loudly exclaimed, "How happy I should be with such a splendid specimen of jewellery !" "What is it worth ?" immediately exclaimed Mr. Coutts. "I could not allow it to pass out of my possession for less than £15,000," said the wary tradesman. "Bring me a pen and ink," was the only answer made by the doting husband, and he at once drew a cheque for that amount upon the bank in the Strand ; and with much delight the worthy old gentleman placed the jewel upon the fair bosom of the lady.

"Upon her breast a sparkling cross she wore,
Which Jews might kiss, and infidels adore."

The following anecdote of the early life of this lady, as related by herself, may be of interest :— "When I was a poor girl," she used to say, "working very hard for my thirty shillings a week, I went down to Liverpool during the holidays, where I was always kindly received. I was to perform in a new piece, something like those pretty little affecting dramas they get up now at our minor theatres, and in my character I represented a poor, friendless orphan girl, reduced to the most wretched poverty. A heartless tradesman prosecutes the sad heroine for a heavy debt, and insists on putting her in prison unless some one will be bail for her. The girl replies, 'Then I have no hope—I have not a friend in the world.' 'What ! will no one be bail for you, to save you from prison ?' asks the stern creditor. 'I have told you I have not a friend on earth,' was my reply. But just as I was uttering the words I saw a sailor in the upper gallery springing over the railing, letting himself down from one tier to another, until he bounded clear over the orchestra and footlights, and placed himself beside me in a moment. 'Yes, you shall have *one* friend at least, my poor young woman,' said he, with the greatest expression in his honest sunburnt countenance ; 'I will go bail for you to any amount. And as for *you*,' turning to the frightened actor, 'if you don't bear a hand, and shift your moorings, you lubber, it will be worse for you when I come athwart your bows.' Every creature in the house rose ; the uproar was perfectly indescribable ; peals of laughter, screams of terror, cheers from his tawny messmates in the gallery, preparatory scrapings of violins from the orchestra; and amidst the universal din there stood the unconscious cause of it, sheltering me, 'the poor, distressed young woman,' and breathing defiance and destruction against my mimic persecutor. He was only persuaded to relinquish his care of me by the manager pretending to arrive and rescue me with a profusion of theatrical bank-notes."

The Duchess of St. Albans, who died in 1837, left her immense fortune, amounting, it is said, to £1,800,000, to Miss Angela Burdett, who thereupon assumed the additional name of Coutts. It was stated in the newspapers at the time, that the weight of this enormous sum in gold, reckoning sixty sovereigns to the pound, is 13 tons 7 cwt. 3 qrs. 12 lbs., and would require 107 men to carry it, supposing that each of them carried 298 lbs., equivalent to the weight of a sack of flour. This large sum may be partially guessed, by knowing also that, counting at the rate of sixty sovereigns a minute for eight hours a day, and six days, of course, in the week, it would take ten weeks, two days, and four hours to accomplish the task. In sovereigns, by the most exact computation (each measuring in diameter $\frac{17}{20}$ of an inch, and placed to touch each other), it would extend to the length of 24 miles and 260 yards, or about the distance between Merthyr and Cardiff; and in crown pieces, to $113\frac{1}{2}$ miles and 280 yards. It may be noted that £1,800,000 was the exact sum also left by old Jemmy Wood, the banker and millionaire of Gloucester, who died in 1836. After inheriting the property in question, Miss Burdett-Coutts distinguished herself by furthering works of charity and benevolence, and in recognition of her large-heartedness she was, in the year 1871, raised to the peerage as Baroness Burdett-Coutts.

Close by, during his demagogue days, lived Sir Francis Burdett, the father of Lady Burdett-Coutts. The old baronet enjoyed the distinction of being the last political or state prisoner who was confined in the Tower of London. On April 6, 1810, a vote passed the House of Commons for his committal to the Tower, on account of a letter written and published by him in *Cobbett's Register* of a week or two previously, which was considered to be "libellous and scandalous, and a breach of privilege." Sir Francis resisted the Speaker's warrant for his committal "upon principle," wishing, of course, to make political capital out of the affair, and to be regarded by the mob as a patriot. Accordingly that part of Piccadilly which lay opposite his house was blocked up by a mob from Westminster and the southern suburbs, who kept on shouting "Burdett for ever!" till the Guards were

called out and rode up to the spot. They were received on their arrival with a volley of stones. The Guards charged the mob, whence they were nicknamed the "Piccadilly Butchers." The whole of the West-end of London was in uproar and confusion, and the windows of the chiefs of the party who had procured the warrant for his arrest were smashed. At length, on the third day, Sir Francis Burdett, believing further resistance vain, was taken prisoner in the king's name, and carried off in a glass coach; but, in spite of this being done with all possible privacy, the mob tried to stop the carriage on Tower Hill, and a conflict ensued between the soldiers and the people, in which one rioter lost his life, and others were wounded.

The riot arose out of the following circumstances, the account of which we abridge from Hughson :—

"On the 21st of February, a Mr. John Gale Jones, a well-known orator at various debating societies in the metropolis, was committed to Newgate by an order of the House of Commons for a gross breach of the privileges of that House. The breach complained of was contained in a bill issued from a debating society, called the 'British Forum,' of which Jones was president. The question in the bill was, 'Which was a greater outrage on the public feeling, Mr. Yorke's enforcement of the standing order to exclude strangers from the House of Commons, or Mr. Windham's recent attack on the liberty of the press?'

"On the 12th of March, Sir Francis Burdett moved in the House of Commons that John Gale Jones should be discharged on the ground of the illegality of the measure. This motion, however, was lost; and on the 24th of March there appeared in *Cobbett's Political Register* a letter inscribed, 'Sir Francis Burdett to his constituents, denying the power of the House of Commons to imprison the people of England,' accompanied with the arguments by which he had endeavoured to convince the gentlemen of the House of Commons that their acts in the case of Mr. Jones were illegal. On the 26th, the publication was brought before the House of Commons by Mr. Lethbridge, who desired the Speaker to ask Sir Francis Burdett whether he acknowledged himself to be the author of the letter, which Sir Francis did. The next day Mr. Lethbridge resumed the subject, and laid the number of *Cobbett's Register* before the House. Sir Francis Burdett made a short but very able defence; and after some further discussion the House adjourned till next day, March the 28th, and then to the 5th of April, when the resumed debate was continued till half-past seven in the morning;

the House then voted that Sir Francis Burdett should be committed to the Tower, the letter in question being a libellous and scandalous paper, reflecting upon the just rights and privileges of that House. The sergeant-at-arms found great difficulty in serving his warrant; and it was not until the fourth day after he had received it from the Speaker, that Sir Francis was conveyed to the Tower, and only then by means of breaking into his house, attended by a posse of constables and soldiers."

door east from the corner of Bolton Street, as that from which Sir Francis was carried a state prisoner to the Tower, and he quotes the following *jeu d'esprit* on the arrest :—

> " The lady she sat and she played on the lute,
>   And she sang, ' Will you come to my bower ?'
> The sergeant-at-arms had stood hitherto mute,
>   But now he advanced, like an impudent brute,
>   And said, ' Will you come to the Tower ?' "

The house was subsequently occupied by the Duke

CAMBRIDGE HOUSE, IN 1854. (*See page* 285.)

On the prorogation of Parliament, June 21st, the captive was set free, but he did not care to return home with the same demonstrations. The populace had planned a triumphal procession from the Tower to Piccadilly; but Sir Francis contrived to give his friends the slip, crossed the river in a boat, and drove off in a carriage. which was waiting for him on the south side of London Bridge, for his country residence at Wimbledon. The story of his committal to the Tower narrated above stands out in strong contrast to the staunch Conservatism which marked his later years; nevertheless he was

> " Through good and ill report, through calm and storm,
>   For forty years the pilot of reform."

Mr. J. H. Jesse identifies the house No. 80, one

of St. Albans, who, however, migrated two or three doors more to the east when he married the widow of Thomas Coutts, of whom we have spoken above.

Late in life Sir Francis Burdett, who was known among his constituents at Westminster as "Old Glory," changed his colours, abandoned his Radical allies, and died a most loyal and peaceable Conservative. About the year 1820 he had removed to St. James's Place, where he died, and as we have already seen in a previous chapter,* his death was as pathetic as his parliamentary life had been famous.

At the western corner of Bolton Street, facing Piccadilly, stands Bath House, the residence of

---

* See *ante*, p. 171.

OLD HYDE PARK CORNER IN 1820. *From Mr. Crace's Collection.* (*See page 290.*)

Lord Ashburton. It contains a fine collection of pictures, chiefly of the Dutch and Flemish schools, formed by the builder of the mansion, Mr. Alexander Baring, afterwards the first Lord Ashburton of the present creation. Dr. Waagen gives a list of the pictures to be seen here, in his work on "Art and Artists in England." The house occupies the site of the Pulteney Hotel, where many royal personages were lodged during their visits to London; among others the Emperor Alexander of Russia, during the sojourn of the Allied Sovereigns in 1814. It was so called because it had been formerly the residence of Pulteney, Earl of Bath, the great rival and antagonist of Sir Robert Walpole. Pulteney, who up to about 1741 had been, as a commoner, the most violent and popular patriot of his day, dwindled down, in 1742, into the Earl of Bath. Sir Robert Walpole, when forced, about the same time, to retire into the peerage, had laid this trap for his antagonist, who readily fell into it. On their first meeting, after what one of them called their respective "falls up-stairs," Lord Orford said to Lord Bath, with malicious good humour, "My lord, you and I are now the most insignificant fellows in England." A coronet, in fact, as well as a mitre, has often proved an extinguisher, and this fact well illustrates Pope's line with reference to William Pulteney :—

" He foams a patriot to subside a peer."

Walpole relates the following story concerning the earl, which appears almost too amusing to be true :—" Lord Bath once owed a tradesman eight hundred pounds, and would never pay him. The man determined to persecute him till he did; and one morning followed him to Lord Winchilsea's, and sent up word that he wanted to speak with him. Lord Bath came down, and said, ' Fellow, what do you want with me?' ' My money,' said the man, as loud as ever he could bawl, before all the servants. He bade him come next morning, and then would not see him. The next Sunday the man followed him to church, and got into the next pew; he leaned over, and said, ' My money; give me my money.' My lord went to the end of the pew; the man too—' Give me my money.' The sermon was on avarice, and the text, ' Cursed are they that heap up riches.' The man groaned out, ' O Lord!' and pointed to my Lord Bath; in short, he persisted so much, and drew the eyes of all the congregation, that my Lord Bath went out and paid him directly." Lord Bath died not long after the accession of George III.

At the opposite corner of Bolton Street stood, from 1807 to 1819, Watier's Gambling Club. Con-

cerning the origin of this club—or rather, gaming-house, for it was nothing more—the following anecdote is told by Captain Gronow:—"Upon one occasion, some gentlemen of both 'White's' and 'Brooks's' had the honour to dine with the Prince Regent, and during the conversation the Prince inquired what sort of dinners they got at their clubs; upon which Sir Thomas Stepney, one of the guests, observed that their dinners were always the same, the eternal joints or beef-steaks, the boiled fowl with oyster sauce, and an apple tart. 'That is what we have at our clubs, and very monotonous fare it is.' The Prince, without further remark, rang the bell for his cook, Watier, and in the presence of those who dined at the royal table, asked him whether he would take a house and organise a dinner-club. Watier assented, and named the Prince's page, Madison, as manager, and Labourie, from the royal kitchen, as cook. The club flourished only a few years, owing to the night-play that was carried on there. The favourite game played there was 'Macao.'" The Duke of York patronised it, and was a member. Tom Moore also tells us that he belonged to it. The dinners were exquisite; the best Parisian cooks could not beat Labourie.

Mr. John Timbs, in his account of this club, remarks, with sly humour, " In the old days, when gaming was in fashion, at Watier's Club both princes and nobles lost or gained fortunes between themselves;" and by all accounts "Macao" seems to have been a far more effective instrument in the losing of fortunes than either " Whist" or " Loo."

Mr. Raikes, in his " Journal," says that Watier's Club, which had originally been established for harmonic meetings, became, in the time of " Beau" Brummell, the resort of nearly all the fine gentlemen of the day. "The dinners," he adds, "were superlative, and high play at 'Macao' was generally introduced. It was this game, or rather losses which arose out of it, that first led the ' Beau' into difficulties." Mr. Raikes further remarks, with reference to this club, that its pace was "too quick to last," and that its records show that none of its members at his death had reached the average age of man. The club was closed in 1819, when the house was taken by a set of "black-legs" who instituted a common bank for gambling. This caused the ruin of several fortunes, and it was suppressed in its turn, or died a natural death.

At the end of the last or early in the present century it was proposed that the Dilettanti Society, already mentioned by us in our account of the " Thatched House Tavern," should erect a permanent home for itself in Piccadilly, either near the

Pulteney Hotel, or else near the foot of the descent, opposite the Ranger's Lodge; but the proposal was never carried out.

At the south-west corner of Clarges Street is the Turf Club. This club was originally established in Grafton Street. The former building, known as Grafton House, was dull, heavy, and ugly, probably the *ugliest* house in London. It was built, says Charles Knight, by the father of Mr. Michael Angelo Taylor, M.P., but others say by the duke himself, who forgot to insert a door, and who therefore had to buy the adjoining house in Clarges Street to make an entrance. The house was taken by the Turf Club in 1875, and a noble new club-house has since been erected.

Passing along Piccadilly, we soon arrive at No. 94, the Naval and Military Club. The building, the site of which was once occupied by an inn, was originally erected for the Earl of Egremont, and called Egremont and afterwards Cholmondeley House. The house has a noble appearance; it is fronted with stone, and overlooks the Green Park. It has a small court-yard in front of it. For many years it was the residence of Adolphus, late Duke of Cambridge, who died here in 1850, and whose name it bore also when occupied by Lord Palmerston, whose body was brought hither from Brockett Hall, where he died, in 1865, the day before it was deposited in Westminster Abbey. Shortly after his lordship's death the house was purchased by the Naval and Military Club, who have greatly improved and enlarged it.

Between White Horse and Engine Streets (No. 105) is a noble Italian mansion, called Hertford House, after the late Marquis of Hertford, who built it about the year 1850, from the designs of a Polish or Russian architect, named Novosielski. It was left by Lord Hertford to his natural son, Sir Richard Wallace, who sold it to one of the family of the Goldsmids. Though his lordship built the house, he chose, with his usual eccentricity, never to reside in it, because the parishioners of St. James's refused to allow him to pave the street in front of it after a fashion of his own. The house contained a very fine collection of works of art, purchased by Lord Hertford from the galleries of Cardinal Fesch, the late King of Holland, and Lord Ashburnham, and many others from the Saltmarshe collection.

The next house westward, at the opposite side of Engine Street, is Coventry House, now the St. James's Club. It was for a century the residence of the Earls of Coventry, one of whom procured, by his influence, the abolition of the "May Fair" in the rear of his mansion. It occupies the site of the old "Greyhound Inn," and, as Mr. John Timbs informs us, it was bought by the Earl of Coventry of Sir Hugh Hunlocke, in 1764, for 10,000 guineas.

The house adjoining the St. James's Club is the residence of the Baroness Meyer de Rothschild, widow of Baron Meyer Amschel de Rothschild, of Mentmore, Buckinghamshire, who was many years M.P. for Hythe, and who died in 1874. The house of another member of this wealthy family is situated further westward, next to Apsley House. The Rothschilds, who began by sweeping out a small shop in the Jews' quarter of the city of Frankfort, over which hung suspended the sign of the "Red Shield," whence they derive their name, have become the metallic sovereigns of Europe. From their different establishments in Paris, London, Vienna, Frankfort, St. Petersburg, and Naples they have obtained a control over the European exchanges which no party ever before could accomplish, and they now seem to hold the strings of the public purse. No sovereign without their assistance now could raise a loan. When the first Baron Rothschild was at Vienna, having contracted for the Austrian loan, the emperor sent for him to express his satisfaction at the manner in which the bargain had been concluded. The Israelite replied, "Je peut assurer votre Majesté que la maison de Rothschild sera toujours enchantée de faire tout ce qui pourra être agréable à la maison d'Autriche."

Nathan Meyer de Rothschild, the father of the two sons mentioned above, and himself the third son of the founder of the wealth and influence of this great commercial family, was a native of Frankfort; he was naturalised as a British subject by royal letters patent in the reign of George III., and subsequently was advanced to the dignity of a Baron of the Austrian Empire. He died in 1836, leaving a family of four sons, all Austrian barons. Ten years later, in 1846, an English baronetcy was conferred on his second son, Anthony, with remainder, failing his own male issue, to the sons of his elder brother Lionel. Sir Anthony died in January, 1876, when his English title accordingly passed to his nephew, Mr. Nathan Meyer de Rothschild, M.P. for Aylesbury.

A few doors westward, at No. 110, lived for many years Hester Maria, Viscountess Keith. She was the last remaining link between the present generation and that brilliant literary circle which congregated around Johnson at "the Club," and which thronged the hospitable mansion of her mother, Mrs. Thrale, at Streatham. During the first eighteen years of her life she was surrounded by Johnson, Reynolds, Garrick, Boswell, Beau-clerk, and Bennet Langton. Johnson was her tutor, and Baretti her language-master. From her mother she learnt to value and to cultivate intellectual pursuits, while from her excellent father she derived those solid and sterling qualities which belong more especially to the true English character. On the death of Mr. Thrale, and the re-marriage of her mother to Signore Piozzi—a marriage highly disapproved by the Leviathan of literature—Miss Thrale retired to her late father's house at Brighton, where she applied her mind to several courses of severe study, and acquired a knowledge of many subjects rare in a woman at all times, and especially so in the less cultivated days of the last century. Here she remained until the time arrived for her to take possession of the fortune left her by her father, when she settled herself in a handsome mansion in London. In the meantime she had the misfortune to lose her valued friend and preceptor, the illustrious Johnson, whose death-bed she assiduously attended. A few days before his death the venerable philosopher addressed Miss Thrale in these words :—" My dear child, we part for ever in this world ; let us part as Christians should : let us pray together." He then uttered a prayer of fervent piety and deep affection, invoking the blessing of Heaven on his pupil. In 1808, Miss Thrale became the wife of George Keith Elphinstone, Admiral Viscount Keith, one of the most distinguished commanders by whom the naval honour of Great Britain was so greatly exalted during the war against the great Napoleon. Lady Keith was left a widow in 1823. For several years she held a distinguished position in the highest circles of the fashionable world in London, and was one of the original patronesses of " Almack's." Having lived to the advanced age of ninety-five, Lady Keith died in March, 1857.

The house standing at the south-east corner of Down Street is the Junior Athenæum Club. This splendid mansion was built for the late Mr. Henry Thomas Hope, M.P., in 1849–50, from the designs of M. Dusillon and Professor Donaldson. The building has some remarkably handsome external decorations in stone and metal, in the modern French style. The decorations were executed chiefly by French artists, and the iron railing is particularly fine, both with regard to design and workmanship. The mansion was for some years known as Hope House, and during the time of Mr. Hope's occupation it was noted as containing one of the finest picture-galleries in London. The pictures were chiefly of the Dutch and Flemish masters, and of the very highest quality of art in

these schools ; they were obtained by Mr. Hope's ancestors (bankers at Amsterdam) principally from the painters themselves. A list of the principal of them is given in Dr. Waagen's " Art and Artists in England." Mr. Hope had also here a fine collection of ancient Greek sculpture. Mr. Hope, who was the owner of Deepdene, in Surrey, and was many years M.P. for Gloucester, &c., died in 1861, leaving an only daughter, who was married in the same year to Alexander, sixth Duke of Newcastle. Shortly after Mr. Hope's death his house was sold, and converted into a club.

The house at the corner of Hamilton Place, facing Piccadilly, was for many years the town residence of John, Earl of Eldon, the distinguished Chief Justice of the Court of Common Pleas, and Lord Chancellor of England, during the early part of the present century. He died in 1838.

Gloucester House, at the corner of Park Lane, now the residence of the Duke of Cambridge, was formerly that of William Henry, the last Duke of Gloucester, who purchased it on his marriage, and who died in 1834. In spite of being Chancellor of Cambridge, he was called "Silly Billy." Mr. Raikes describes him as " a quiet, inoffensive character, rather tenacious of the respect due to his rank, and strongly attached to the ultra-Tory party." The mansion was previously the residence of the Earl of Elgin, at which time it was known as Elgin House. Here, on their first arrival in this country, were deposited the Elgin Marbles, previous to their removal to Burlington House, whence they were taken to the British Museum in 1816. It is in allusion to this fact that Lord Byron, in his " English Bards and Scotch Reviewers," calls Elgin House a " stone shop," and

" General mart
For all the mutilated blocks of art."

The houses now numbered 138 and 139, between Park Lane and Hamilton Place, were, at the beginning of the present century, one mansion, remarkable for its large bow window, and occupied by the eccentric and licentious Duke of Queensberry, better known to society by his nickname of " Old Q." In his old age, when sated with pleasures of the grossest kind, he would sit in sunny weather in his balcony, with an umbrella or parasol over his head, and amuse himself with watching the female passers-by, ogling every pretty woman, and sending out his minions to fetch them in, as a spider will draw flies into his web. The duke had an exterior flight of steps built to aid him in this sport. These steps were removed long subsequently to his death, in 1810.

Mr. T. Raikes, in his " Journal," under date of

1840, writes :—"The late Duke of Queensberry, whom I remember in my early days, called 'Old Q.,' was of the same school as the Marshal Duc de Richelieu in France, and as great a profligate. He lived at the bow-window house in Piccadilly, where he was latterly always seen looking at the people who passed by; a groom on horseback, known as Jack Radford, always stood under the window to carry about his messages to any one whom he remarked in the street. He kept a physician in the house, and, to ensure attention to his health, his terms were that he should have so much per day while he lived, but not a shilling at his death. When he drove out he was always alone in a dark-green vis-à-vis, with long-tailed black horses ; and during winter, with a muff, two servants behind in undress, and his groom following the carriage, to execute his commissions. He was a little, sharp-looking man, very irritable, and swore like ten thousand troopers : enormously rich and selfish."

The duke was one of the three individuals who were said to be the fathers of Maria Fagniani, afterwards Marchioness of Hertford, to whom he left a very large portion of his property ; the title passing to a distant relative, the Duke of Buccleuch.

Of the two houses above mentioned, that numbered 139 maintained its celebrity by being at one time the residence of Lord Byron. Here he was living when the separation between himself and Lady Byron took place a year after their ill-starred marriage ; and here he wrote "Parisina" and the "Siege of Corinth." It was also from this house that Lady Byron left the poet, carrying with her his infant child, whom he commemorates so touchingly as "Ada, sole daughter of my house and heart." "The moment that my wife left me," he writes, "I was assailed by all the falsehoods that malice could invent or slander publish ; . . . . there was no crime too dark to be attributed to me by the moral (?) English, to account for so common an occurrence as a 'separation in high life.' I was thought a devil, because Lady Byron was allowed to be an angel !" Poor man ! bad as he may have been, he deserved to have met with a creature endowed with some small store of sympathy, and at least some little feminine weakness, in the woman whom he made his wife.

At No. 144, one of the mansions between Hamilton Place and Apsley House, Lord Palmerston was living about the time of the Crimean War, and shortly before his acceptance of the Premiership. His lordship removed thence to Cambridge House, of which we have already spoken as being now the Naval and Military Club.

Where Apsley House now stands, if we may accept the statement of Charles Knight, was the tavern called the "Hercules' Pillars," "the same at which the redoubted Squire Western, with his clerical satellite, is represented as taking up his abode on his arrival in London, and conveying the fair Sophia." The sign of the "Hercules' Pillars" was given to the tavern probably as marking, at that time, the extreme "west-end" of London. Its name is recorded by Wycherley, in his *Plain Dealer*, and is said to have been a haunt of the Marquis of Granby, and of other members of the titled classes. The character of the house in Fielding's time may be gathered from the following quotation from "Tom Jones," touching Squire Western's arrival in London :—"The squire sat down to regale himself over a bottle of wine, with his parson and the landlord of the 'Hercules' Pillars,' who, as the squire said, would make an excellent third-man, and would inform them of the news of the town ; for, to be sure, says he, he knows a good deal, since the horses of many of 'the quality' stand at his door."

Mr. J. H. Jesse tells us that the tavern in question stood *between* Apsley House and Hamilton Place, and that, on account of its situation, it was much frequented by gentlemen from the West of England. Wherever may have been the exact spot on which the house stood, it seems at best to have been a comfortable but low inn on the outskirts of the town, where gentlemen's horses and grooms were put up, and farmers and graziers resorted.

In the reign of George II. all the ground to the west of Devonshire House up to Hyde Park Corner was covered by a row of small shops and yards of the statuaries ; nor were the latter of the best and purest kind, if we may judge by the loud complaints against their design and execution uttered by the author of "A New Critical Review of the Public Buildings, &c.," at that date. In fact, the tasteless atrocities in sculpture there perpetrated could not well be exceeded now-a-days by the artists of the "figure-yards" of the Euston Road. On the site of the last remaining "figure-yard" in this neighbourhood was built, in the early part of the reign of George III., a house for the eccentric and notorious Lord Barrymore, but it was burnt down before it had been many years in his occupation.

Between the "Hercules' Pillars " and what now is Hamilton Place, instead of the magnificent houses of the Marquis of Northampton, and Barons Lionel and Ferdinand de Rothschild and others, long known collectively as Piccadilly Terrace, was a row of low and mean tenements, one of which bore conspicuously in the street before it the grand sign of the "Triumphal Chariot." Mr. J. H. Jesse suggests that "this was, in all probability, the 'pretty tavern' to which the unfortunate Richard Savage was conducted by Sir Richard Steele on the occasion of their being closeted together for a whole day, busy in composing a hurried pamphlet which they had to sell for two guineas before they could pay for their dinner," as Johnson tells us in his "Life of Savage." The tavern is stated to have

review-days, when long wooden seats were fixed in the street before the doors for the accommodation of as many barbers, all busily employed in powdering the hair of these sons of Mars!"

Near the "Hercules' Pillars" and "Triumphal Chariot," there would appear to have been quite a cluster of other small inns, "convenient" to the wayfarer as he entered London from the western counties. Mr. Larwood enumerates among these

HAMILTON PLACE IN 1802. *From a Drawing in the Guildhall Library.* (*See page* 291.)

been a "watering-house" for hackney-coaches, &c. Charles Knight says that "by the kerbstone in front of it there was a bench for the porters, and a board over it for depositing their loads;" and he gives a view of just such another "watering-house" still standing at Knightsbridge in 1841, answering in every minute detail to the above, except in the sign, for it is not the "Triumphal Chariot," nor a "chariot" at all, but "The White Hart."

The sign of the "Triumphal Chariot" was probably an allusion to the soldiery from the barracks, who were its chief supporters. Mr. J. T. Smith, in his "Antiquarian Rambles in the London Streets," tells us that, "in the middle of the last century, this and other public-houses were much resorted to by the red-coats on Sundays and

the "Red and the Golden Lion," the "Swan," the "Horse Shoe," the "Running Horse," the "Barley Mow," the "White Horse," and the "Half Moon," of which the last has left the trace of its being in the name of a street running out of Piccadilly.

Thoughtful observers will note the slight but graceful bend of the roadway of Piccadilly, and will see in it with us a proof that the road itself was of ancient date. Modern streets are almost always driven straight; but the earliest roads follow the tracks of cart-wheels and pack-horses; and probably it was by the pack-horses or market-carts of five centuries ago that this road was first gradually worn. The only proof of its existence in the days of antiquity is to be found in the map of Ralph Aggas, where it forms but a continuation of the line marked out at the top of the Haymarket as "the way to Reading," just as what now is Oxford Street is marked "the way to Uxbridge." We find, however, a corroboration of the map in the narrative of the rebellion raised by Sir Thomas Wyatt and his Kentish followers on the unpopular marriage of Queen Mary with Philip of Spain, when it would seem that, in addition to a lower way running past the front of St. James's Palace

that it was upon a hill beyond St. James's, "almost over against the Park Corner, on the hill in the highway, above the new bridge over against St. James's."

How Wyatt passed on first to Charing Cross and then to Ludgate, how he was there captured, and how he was beheaded and afterwards quartered on Tower Hill, are matters well known to nearly every reader of English history. His head as

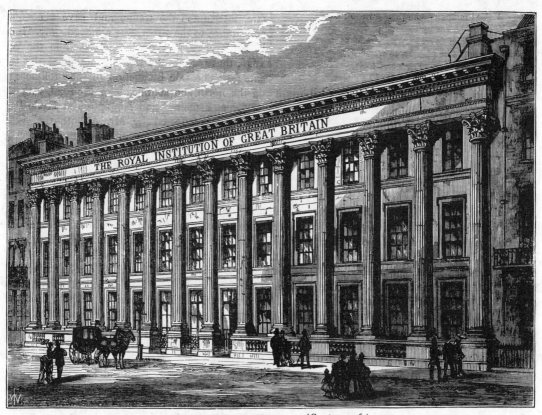

THE ROYAL INSTITUTION. (*See page 296.*)

to Charing Cross, there was also a "highway on the hill," along which some of the rebel forces and ammunition were brought up. This event is, indeed, the earliest matter of historical interest connected with Piccadilly. We read that, unable to effect the passage of London Bridge, Wyatt marched to Kingston, where he crossed the Thames, and so forced his way to Knightsbridge. In our account of Charing Cross* we have already given the narrative of Wyatt's advance on London, as told by honest John Stow, and therefore we need not repeat it here, further than to say that, in all probability, it was in Piccadilly that he "planted his ordenance," for the old chronicler tells us

Stow further informs us, was set up on the gallows at Hay Hill, at that time almost if not quite in sight of the spot where he had left his "ordenance." The "new bridge" spoken of in Stow's narrative probably spanned the brook which ran in this direction down from Tyburn, giving its appellation to the Brook Fields, whence "Brook Street" derives its name, as we shall see in a future chapter.

It was near the western extremity of Piccadilly that the citizens of London fortified themselves against the threatened approach of Charles I. and his army in 1642, when the citizens of the West-end, aided by the female population, and, indeed, even ladies of high birth and blood, lent a helping hand in the trenches, and in throwing up earthworks

* See Vol. III., p. 125.

In this emergency, men, women, and even children, assisted in hundreds and thousands, and speedily a rampart of earth was raised, with batteries and redoubts at intervals. The fort here was armed with four bastions. The active part taken by the women in this undertaking is described with much graphic humour by Butler, in his "Hudibras." He writes that they

"Marched rank and file, with drum and ensign,
T' entrench the city for defence in ;
Raised ramparts with their own soft hands,
To put the enemy to stand ;
From ladies down to oyster-wenches
Laboured like pioneers in trenches,
Fall'n to their pickaxes and tools,
And helped the men to dig like moles."

In spite of its proximity to the Court suburb, it would appear that Piccadilly was not a very secure thoroughfare, even during the reigns of the first Hanoverian kings. For instance, it is on record, that in 1726 the Earl of Harborough was stopped here, whilst being carried in his sedan chair, during broad daylight ; we read that "one of the chairmen pulled a pole out of the chair and knocked down one of the villains, while the earl came out, drew his sword, and put the others to flight, but not before they had raised their wounded companion, whom they took off with them." Indeed, even a quarter of a century later, the neighbourhood of Piccadilly, and, in fact, all the western and northern suburbs of London, were infested with footpads and highwaymen ; and, under cover of the darkness, favoured by the ill-lighted and ill-protected state of the streets, highway robberies continued to be committed with impunity, in the heart of London, up to a much more recent period than is generally supposed. Mr. Jesse tells us that about the year 1810 a near relative of his own, accompanied by a friend, was forcibly stopped in a hackney-coach in Piccadilly, opposite to St. James's Church, by ruffians, who presented their pistols, and forced them to give up their money and watches. He adds, that in this case the driver, in all probability, was in league with the highwaymen.

The modern history of Piccadilly may be soon told. In process of time the thoroughfare has undergone great alteration since buildings were first erected on its northern side. Bath House, of which we have spoken above, was the first mansion of any pretension erected to the west of Devonshire House ; and down to about the year 1770, with the exception of the one just named, there were no houses more than one or two storeys high. Many years ago the pavement on the north side of all the middle portion was raised, and formed a terrace ; and when the name of the terrace ceased to be used in this part of the street, it came to be applied to the larger mansions further westward and lying between Down Street and Apsley House. Now, however, it is restricted to the row of houses situated to the west of Hamilton Place.

About the end of the year 1825 the toll-gate at Hyde Park Corner, which narrowed the thoroughfare, interrupted the traffic, and gave a confined appearance to the street, was removed. Mr. Hone, in his "Every Day Book," published in the year 1826, thus records the sale by auction of this toll-gate :—"The sale by auction of the 'toll-houses' on the north and south side of the road, with the 'weighing-machine' and lamp-posts at Hyde Park Corner, was effected by Mr. Abbott, the estate agent and appraiser, by order of the trustees of the roads. They were sold for building materials ; the north toll-house was in five lots, the south in five other lots ; the gates, rails, posts, and inscription boards, were in five more lots ; and the engine-house was also in five lots." It is not stated what amount was realised by the sale, but Hone gives a graphic illustration representing the auctioneer raising his hammer and calling out, "Going, going, gone !" He adds, "The whole are entirely cleared away, to the great relief of thousands of persons resident in this neighbourhood," and then he moralises as follows : "It is too much to expect everything vexatious to disappear at once ; this is a good beginning, and, if there be truth in the old saying, we may expect a good ending." At the same sale were put up and knocked down the weighing-machine and toll-house at "Jenny's Whim," of which we shall have more to say when we come to Knightsbridge, and also the toll-house near the "Original Bun-house" at Chelsea, with the lamp-posts on the road.

Thanks to the iron roads out of London, which steam has opened of late years, Piccadilly is no longer the great "coaching" thoroughfare which it was in the days "when George III. was King ;" but still, "in the season," it is always lively and well filled, and there is no street in London where the miscellaneous character of London conveyances and "carriage folk," from the outside passengers on a lordly "drag," down to the city clerks on the knifeboards of omnibuses, and even to the donkey-driving costermongers, may be seen in greater variety. All ranks are jostled together in Piccadilly, if anywhere in this great metropolis.

CHAPTER XXIV.

PICCADILLY : NORTHERN TRIBUTARIES.

" Intervalla vides humanè commoda ; verum
Puræ sunt plateæ."—Horace, " Satires."

Hamilton Place and its Noted Residents—White Horse Street—Halfmoon Street—Boswell's Lodgings—Clarges Street—Bolton Street—Berkeley Street—Dover Street—Dr. John Arbuthnot—Residence of the Bishops of Ely—Albemarle Street—Grillon's Hotel and Club—Hotels, Clubs, and Scientific Societies in Albemarle Street—Royal Institution—Professor Faraday—St. George's Chapel—Stafford Street—" Street Clubs "—Grafton Street—Old and New Bond Street—Clifford Street—Burlington Gardens—The London University—Old Burlington Street—Boyle Street—Uxbridge House—Queensberry House—Vigo Street—Sackville Street—Air Street—Cork Street—Savile Row—New Burlington Street.

HAVING already dealt with the various streets abutting on the south side of Piccadilly, and in the preceding chapters described the principal buildings and objects of interest to be met with along the route from the southern Regent Circus to Hyde Park Corner, we now retrace our steps, noting on the way the several streets and outlets on its northern side, or, at least, such as have anything worthy of remark appertaining to them in the way of history and personal associations.

Hamilton Place, the first turning on our way back eastward from Apsley House, brings down to our own times the memory of Colonel James Hamilton, a boon companion of Charles II., who gave him the Rangership of Hyde Park. He was a brother of Anthony Hamilton, the witty chronicler of the Court of Charles II., but perhaps better known to the world in general as the same " Beare " Hamilton who was so amusingly duped by the Countess of Chesterfield at Bretby Park. " Being considerably in the king's favour," writes Mr. J. Larwood, in his "Story of the London Parks," " Hamilton received some grants in connection with the park. One of these was the triangular piece of ground between the lodge (which stood on the site of Apsley House) and the present Park Lane ; during the Commonwealth a fort and various houses had been built upon it. This was now granted to Hamilton, with the covenant that he should make leases to purchasers to be appointed at half the improved rents. Of course, it is from him that this site still bears the name of Hamilton Place. He was shot in an engagement with the Dutch in 1673, on which occasion the king renewed the lease for ninety-nine years to his widow."

The Duke of Wellington was living in Hamilton Place in 1814, during the interval of peace consequent on the abdication of Napoleon and his retirement to Elba ; and here he received a deputation of the House of Commons sent to present him with an address of thanks for his services in the field in Spain. Of No. 1 we have already spoken, as the house of old Lord Eldon. No. 2 was the town residence of the Duchess-Countess of Sutherland, who, by her marriage with the Marquis of Stafford, put the coping-stone to the fortunes of the now ducal house of Leveson-Gower. Hamilton Place, too, was the last residence of Mr. H. A. J. Munro, of Novar, N.B., who was the owner of a fine gallery of paintings, and also of a valuable library.

Park Lane, in the reign of Queen Anne, was a desolate by-road, generally spoken of as " the lane leading from Piccadilly to Tyburn." It is now a noble thoroughfare, built only on the eastern side, the other being open to Hyde Park. We shall have more to say of it in a future chapter when making our way to Oxford Street.

Passing Down Street (which leads to Mayfair, and in which D'Israeli lived in his bachelor days), we arrive at White Horse Street. " The bay-fronted house at the west corner of this street," says Mr. Peter Cunningham, " was the residence of Mr. Charles Dumergue, the friend of Sir Walter Scott ; until a child of his own was established in London, this was Scott's head-quarters when in town."

Halfmoon Street, the next turning eastward, took its name from an inn which stood at the corner, facing Piccadilly. The sign was not an uncommon one ; and it may be well here to remind the reader that the lower half of Bedford Street, Strand, was formerly called Halfmoon Street, and for the same reason. The half-moon or crescent, according to Mr. Larwood, was the emblem of the temporal, as the sun was that of the spiritual power. There was another " Half Moon " tavern at Upper Holloway, famous for its cheese-cakes, which were hawked about London by a man on horseback, and at one time formed one of the established " cries of London." Another " Half Moon " in Aldersgate Street, was connected with the name of Ben Jonson. But our business is with the street bearing the name of the Half-moon. The street may be speedily dismissed, for it has but few literary reminiscences, and has for several generations consisted of respectable houses of the middle class, let out in apartments to members of Parliament and others. The east corner house was formerly the residence of Madame d'Arblay. In this street Boswell, as he tells us in his " Life of Johnson," was lodging in May, 1768, when he was visited by the great lexicographer, who, having expressed a dislike of the publication of a portion of one of his letters, on being asked by his future biographer whether he forbade his letters to be published after his decease, gave the bluff reply, "Nay, sir, when I am dead you may do as you will"—a reply to which posterity is deeply indebted. Here, too, died, in 1797, the celebrated actress, Mrs. Pope ; she was buried in the cloisters of Westminster Abbey.

According to the "New View of London," published in 1708, the Lady Clarges was the owner of a stately new building on the north side of Piccadilly, then in the occupation of the Venetian Ambassador. Its site is now covered by Clarges Street, which was named after Sir Walter Clarges, and was built about the year 1717. At No. 12 in this street Edmund Kean, the tragedian, lived for some few years, and it is said that, in the adjoining house (No. 11) Lady Hamilton was residing at the time of Lord Nelson's death. If this statement be correct, she must have removed to this street only a few days before from Piccadilly. In the year 1826, No. 14 was the residence of William Mitford, the historian of Greece, brother of Lord Redesdale. His opinions disqualified him from appreciating the Athenian constitution, and his work has ceased to be valued. He died in the year 1827.

It was not till many mansions had been built further west that the ground about May Fair came to be utilised. Towards the end of the seventeenth century, indeed, a considerable plot of ground adjoining Clarges Street was leased by Sir Thomas Clarges (whose wife was a Berkeley) to one Thomas Neale, Groom-Porter to his Majesty (of whom Charles Knight tells us that he was the introducer of lotteries on the Venetian plan, and the builder of the Seven Dials, in St. Giles's), on the condition that he should lay out £10,000 in building on it, but the agreement was never carried out, and the lease was forfeited or cancelled. After his son obtained back the lease granted to Neale by Sir Thomas Clarges, the grounds on the slope of the hill in Piccadilly westward, toward Park Lane, were, as we have already stated, soon covered with buildings.

Bolton Street is a dull, narrow, and heavy thoroughfare, with no great interest attaching to its houses. In it, however, lived, in the time of Queen Anne and George I., the celebrated Earl of Peterborough, who, as Mr. John Timbs tells us, "in his biography (fortunately never printed), confesses having committed three capital crimes before he **was** twenty years of age." Pope, however, did

not, on this account, object to stay with him here as a guest. The Hon. Mrs. Norton was living here in 1841, before settling in Chesterfield Street. Hatton, in 1708, speaks of Bolton Street as being "the most westerly street in London, between the road to Knightsbridge south and the fields north." But almost every street in this neighbourhood, at one time or other, might have had the same thing said of it.

Of Stratton Street, which forms a *cul de sac*, we have already spoken ; and of Berkeley Street, which is opposite the north-east corner of the Green Park, we have but little to say, beyond the fact that it dates from the year 1642, at which it was the western extremity of Piccadilly, or, as it was then called, Portugal Street, and that it was named from Berkeley House, which it bounded on the east. In this street was the last town apartment occupied by Pope, who came to live here in order to be near his friend, Lord Burlington. One side of the street is now occupied entirely by the wall of Devonshire House, and the other by a few respectable houses and the stables belonging to the mansions in Dover Street.

Dover Street, which was built in the year 1642, was so called after Henry Jermyn, Lord Dover, the "little Jermyn" of De Grammont's Memoirs ; he resided on the east side of the street, and died in 1782. The street stands on a part of the ground that had been for a few years occupied by Clarendon House, the "Dunkirk House" of the populace, and the princely mansion of Lord Chancellor Clarendon. John Evelyn, who had been "oftentimes so cheerful, and sometimes so sad, with Chancellor Hyde" on that very ground, lived for some time close by Lord Dover's house.

On the west side of this street lived Dr. John Arbuthnot, "Martinus Scriblerus," physician to Queen Anne, and the friend of Pope and other literary celebrities of his time. On the death of the queen, Arbuthnot, like the other attendants at Court, was displaced, and had to leave his apartments at St. James's. He removed into Dover Street, "hoping still," as he said, "to keep a little habitation warm in town, and to afford half a pint of claret to his old friends." It is to this "displacement" that Pope alludes in his well-known apostrophe to Arbuthnot :—

> " O friend ! may each domestic bliss be thine !
> Be no unpleasing melancholy mine :
> Me let the tender office long engage,
> To rock the cradle of reposing age,
> With lenient arts extend a mother's breath,
> Make languor smile, and smooth the bed of death ;
> Explore the thought, explain the asking eye,
> And keep awhile one parent from the sky !

On cares like these if length of days attend,
May Heaven, to bless those days, preserve my friend ;
Preserve him social, cheerful, and serene,
And just as rich as when he served a queen."

Dr. Arbuthnot, the son of a nonjuring clergyman in Scotland, was born at Arbuthnot, in Kincardineshire, about the period of the Restoration. Early in life he settled in London, and for some time gained his livelihood as a teacher of mathematics. He had studied medicine in his native country, but a fortunate accident brought him into practice here as a physician. He happened to be at Epsom on one occasion, when Prince George, who was also there, was suddenly taken ill. Arbuthnot was called in, and having effected a cure, was soon afterwards appointed one of the physicians in ordinary to the queen. He continued to practise, enjoying considerable professional distinction, till his death, in 1735.

No. 37 in this street is the town residence of the Bishops of Ely. It was purchased or built in the year 1772, out of the proceeds of the sale of the ancient Palace of the Bishops of Ely, in Ely Place, Holborn. On the front of the house is a mitre, sculptured in stone. In the adjoining house (No. 38) resided Lord King, the "bishop hater," who wrote a life of his kinsman, John Locke. This work was published in 1829. In 1841, No. 23 was the residence of Lady Byron, widow of the poet.

In this street also was the gun-shop of the celebrated "Joe Manton," who was a favourite with almost all the aristocratic sportsmen of his day. He patented his principal improvements in the manufacture of guns in 1792.

Here, too, for many years, was the publishing house of Mr. Edward Moxon, who continued to surround himself as a publisher with such a host of poetical clients, that his shop may be said to have become a modern temple of the Muses. From this shop were issued the successive volumes of Barry Cornwall, Wordsworth, Tennyson, &c. But this passed away about the year 1870, when the business was transferred elsewhere, and the poetic halo disappeared from Dover Street.

Albemarle Street was so called after Christopher Monk, second Duke of Albemarle, who purchased the mansion of the Earl of Clarendon which stood partly on its site. The street was built towards the close of the seventeenth or beginning of the eighteenth century by Sir Thomas Bond, of Peckham, Comptroller of the Household to Henrietta Maria, the Queen of Charles II., and a loyal friend of James II., whom he accompanied in his exile to St. Germains. Evelyn tells us, in his "Memoirs," that this Sir Thomas Bond bought part of the grounds of Clarendon House, "in order to build a street of tenements to his undoing." Clarendon House was sold by the Duke of Albemarle, when in difficulties, soon after he had purchased it. Hatton, in 1708, describes Albemarle Street as "a street of excellent new buildings, inhabited by persons of quality, between the fields and Portugal Street."

At No. 50A, on the west side of this street, is the shop of John Murray, publisher. It is scarcely necessary here to do more than just remind our readers of the connection of this house with Lord Byron, whose poems were first issued hence to the public, as they came fresh from the anvil of his brain, between 1807 and his death in 1822. Nor will they forget how the poet's fondness for his publisher stands recorded in his lordship's verses and letters. With Byron he was "my Murray." In 1812 appeared the first two cantos of "Childe Harold's Pilgrimage," and so eminently successful were they, that, as Byron himself briefly described in his memoranda, he awoke one morning and found himself famous. The copyright money paid by Mr. Murray, £600, his lordship presented to his friend, Mr. Robert C. Dallas, saying, that he never would receive money for his writings,* "a resolution," as Moore tells us in his "Life of Byron," "he afterwards wisely abandoned." We learn from Alibone, that Mr. Murray paid, at different times, for copyrights of his lordship's poems, certainly over £15,000. As we have already mentioned in another place,† the publishing business was first established in Fleet Street by the grandfather of the present head of the house, Mr. John McMurray, a Scotchman, who came to London after the Jacobite troubles to push his fortunes. It was a bold step of John Murray the elder to venture so far west, and so far not only from Paternoster Row, but from that highway of literature, Fleet Street and the Strand ; but it was amply justified by the result.

The elder Mr. John Murray died in 1793, and was succeeded by his son of the same name, one of whose earliest "hits" was Mrs. Rundell's "Cookerybook," the sale of which, we are told, proved even more remunerative, perhaps, than "Childe Harold." Becoming connected with Thomas Campbell and Sir Walter Scott, in 1809 Mr. Murray projected the *Quarterly Review*, as the recognised organ of the Tory party. The new review soon acquired a hold on the mind of the educated classes, which it had hardly lost at the end of half a century, in spite of the progress made by the cheaper monthly, weekly, and now daily press. The first editor

* See Dallas's "Recollections of Lord Byron."
† See Vol. I., p. 46.

of the *Quarterly* was William Gifford; and among its earliest contributors were George Canning, John Hookham Frere, Sir Walter Scott, Byron, Dean Milman, and Jonathan Croker. "Some of the scholarship notices," says Mr. Cyrus Redding, in his "Fifty Years' Recollections," "are excellent. A selection of these, in three or four volumes, from the mass of high-flown rubbish and falsified prophecies of national ruin would be most useful. In in Albemarle Street. Byron himself has thus de-scribed the scene:—

> "The room's so full of wits and bards,
> Crabbes, Campbells, Crokers, Freres, and Wards."

Mr. Murray's dinner-parties included politicians and statesmen, as well as authors and artists. The second Mr. John Murray died in 1843, and was succeeded by his son, John Murray the third. Under his *régime* the house has published many

LONG'S HOTEL, BOND STREET. (*See page* 302.)

its classical articles, the *Review* as far outshone the *Edinburgh* as the *Edinburgh* outshone the *Quarterly* in the truth of its political predictions and that advocacy of improvement and reform for which its reputation is imperishable." Gifford, like many others who have risen in life, was extremely vain; he would even go so far as to boast that he had the power of distributing literary reputations. "Yes," observed Sheridan, "and you deal them out so largely that you have left none for yourself!"

It was in Mr. Murray's establishment in Albemarle Street that Byron and Scott first met, and here Southey made the acquaintance of Crabbe; indeed, it has been said that almost all the literary magnates of the day were "four o'clock visitors" of the greatest works in history, travel, biography, art, and science of the present age, among which may be mentioned Dr. Livingstone's "Travels," Smiles's "Life of George Stephenson," and Darwin's "Origin of Species by Natural Selection;" and the Handbooks of English Counties and Continental travel of late years brought out by this firm owe much to the personal assistance and superintendence of the head of the house. Mr. Murray has counted among his clients, besides the writers named above, Colonel Leake, Dean Milman, Sir Henry Holland, Henry Hallam, George Grote, Mrs. Somerville, Dean Stanley, and nearly all the most distinguished authors of the present century. We may add that the sign-board of Mr. MacMurray, or Murray, in Fleet Street, was the "Ship in full sail," a sign probably assumed by him in opposition to that of Messrs. Longman, a "Ship at anchor."

No. 7, on the opposite side of the street, now the Royal Thames Yacht Club, was formerly Grillon's Hotel. Here Louis XVIII. of France stayed in 1814, on his journey from Hartwell to France, to take his seat on the throne of the do with politics. To it belonged most of the distinguished public men of the Regency, and of the reigns of George IV. and William IV. Here, every Wednesday during the Parliamentary season, its members dined together, "the feuds of the previous day being forgotten, or made the theme of pleasantry and genial humour at a table where all

PROFESSOR FARADAY. (See page 297.)

Bourbons, to which he had been restored mainly by the intervention of England. He was escorted from London to Dover by the Prince Regent himself. Out of this hotel grew a private club, called "Grillon's Club," which used to hold its meetings here. It was formed in 1813 by some members of both Houses of Parliament, who wished for some neutral ground on which they might meet, politics being strictly excluded. "Grillon's" differed from most of the other clubs of the first half of the present century in having nothing to sets of opinions had their representatives. To this club belonged George Canning, Lord Dudley and Ward, Lord F. Leveson-Gower (afterwards better known as Lord Francis Egerton), Lord Harrowby, Lord Wharncliffe, Lord Clare, Sir Robert Harry Inglis, Mr. G. Agar-Ellis, Sir R. Wilmot-Horton, and Sir James Graham.

Here, and at the Clarendon Hotel, in New Bond Street, were held for many years the Roxburghe Club Dinners. In 1860, there was sold at the rooms of Messrs. Puttick and Simpson a collection of nearly eighty portraits of members of Grillon's Club, almost all of them members of Parliament and of various Governments, mostly engravings from private plates, after drawings by Slater, George Richmond, and other artists.

In this street are several large hotels, such as the Pulteney, the York, the St. George's, and the Albemarle. In the days of the Regency, when the club system was as yet in its infancy, the hotels at the West-end were much more frequented than now-a-days is the case. There was then a very large class of men, including Wellington, Nelson, Collingwood, Sir John Moore, and some few others, who seldom frequented the clubs. The persons to whom we refer, and amongst whom were many members of the sporting world, used to congregate at a few hotels, of which the "Clarendon," "Limmer's," "Ibbetson's," "Fladong's," "Stephens's," and "Grillon's" were the most fashionable. The "Clarendon," mentioned above, was at that time kept by a French cook, Jacquiers, who contrived to amass a large sum of money in the service of Louis XVIII. in England, and subsequently with Lord Darnley. This was the only public hotel where a genuine French dinner could be obtained, but the sum charged seldom amounted to less than three or four pounds ; a bottle of champagne or of claret in the year 1814 usually cost a guinea.

No. 23 has been for many years the home of different clubs, more or less successful. In 1808 the "Alfred" was established here ; it is described by Lord Dudley in his time, as "the dullest place in existence, the asylum of doting Tories and drivelling quidnuncs." Lord Byron was a member of this club, and he tells us that "it was pleasant, a little too sober and literary, and bored with Sotheby and Francis d'Ivernois; but one met Rich, and Ward, and Valentia, and many other pleasant or known people." On the break-up of the "Alfred," another club was started here, called the "Westminster;" but its career does not appear to have been altogether a flourishing one. At the Albemarle Hotel, at the junction of the street with Piccadilly, another club was inaugurated towards the close of 1875, and called "The Albemarle." It was established for the accommodation of both gentlemen and ladies. "This," observes one of the daily papers, "is a noble experiment, and upon its success depends the settlement of the question whether women as a body are *feræ naturâ*, or social and clubable animals."

At No. 22 are the rooms of the Royal Asiatic Society, the London Mathematical Society, and the British Association for the Advancement of Science. The first-mentioned of these societies was founded in 1823, for the investigation and encouragement of arts, science, and literature in connection with Asia. Its museum contains, *inter alia*, a choice collection of Persian, Chinese, and Sanskrit MSS., with Oriental arms and armour, and various other illustrations of the history, arts, and antiquities of the Eastern world. The British Association was established in 1831, for the purpose of affording scientific men, both of this and other countries, an opportunity of assembling together and discussing on scientific subjects, and for which purpose meetings of a week's duration are held annually in different parts of England.

The Royal Institution, near the north-east corner of this street, was established in 1799, mainly through the exertions of Count Rumford, the most able practical philosopher of the day, for the purpose of encouraging improvements in arts and manufactures. Its meetings were commenced in 1800, shortly before which time the proprietors of the original shares obtained a charter of incorporation for the purpose of helping on the introduction of useful and mechanical inventions and improvements, and for teaching, by courses of philosophical lectures and experiments, the application of science to the common purposes of life, whence the motto of the institution—"Illustrans commoda vitæ." The building is spacious and well adapted for the purposes to which it is applied ; it originally consisted of five private houses, which having been purchased by the institution, an imposing architectural front was added, from the designs of Mr. L. Vulliamy, consisting of fourteen fluted halfcolumns, of the Corinthian order, placed upon a stylobate ; and occupying the height of three floors, support an entablature and the attic storey. On the fascia is inscribed, "The Royal Institution of Great Britain." The lectures delivered here are of a very popular class, and are well attended. In the reading-room are deposited choice or rare specimens of art, taste, and *virtu*.

The institution has, since its foundation, undergone a very considerable change in constitution. Some years ago, in consequence of the low state of the funds, the majority of proprietors relinquished their proprietary claim, and became shareholders for life only ; the dissentients from such terms selling their respective shares to the institution for a stipulated sum. By this means and by some personal bequests, the funds were materially improved. About the year 1830 the Royal Institution acquired fresh fame as the scene of Professor Faraday's experimental researches in electricity, the success of which has few parallels in the records of modern science.

A native of Newington, Surrey, and the son of a working smith, Michael Faraday, as a boy, was apprenticed to a bookseller and bookbinder; and during his term of apprenticeship a few scientific works had occasionally fallen into his hands, among them being the treatise on "Electricity" in the "Encyclopædia Britannica," and Mrs. Marcet's "Conversations on Chemistry." The perusal of the first led to the construction of his first electrical machine with a glass phial, and this he speedily followed up by a variety of experiments. Through the kindness of Mr. Dance, a member of the Royal Institution and a customer of his master, young Faraday was enabled to attend the last four lectures delivered by Sir Humphry Davy, in the early part of 1812. In the following year he was appointed Chemical Assistant at the Royal Institution, under Sir Humphry as Honorary Professor, and Mr. Brande as Professor of Chemistry; and shortly afterwards he went abroad, as assistant and amanuensis to his patron, Sir Humphry Davy. On his return, after an absence of three years, Mr. Faraday resumed his duties, and took up his residence at the Royal Institution, where he remained almost till the day of his death. In 1827 he first appeared at the lecture-table in the great theatre, and he continued to deliver lectures on scientific subjects every year from that time. In 1831 he commenced the series of experimental researches in electricity which have been published from time to time in the "Transactions" of the Royal Society. In the year 1833, when Mr. Fuller founded the chair of chemistry called after his name in the Royal Institution, he nominated Mr. Faraday the first professor; and two years later Professor Faraday received from Lord Melbourne's Government a pension, as a recognition of the importance of his scientific discoveries. In 1836 he was appointed scientific adviser on lights at sea to the Trinity House, and in the same year became a member of the Senate of the University of London; and he was subsequently scientific adviser on the same subject to the Board of Trade. Professor Faraday was a corresponding member of the Academy of Sciences at Paris, a fellow of the Royal Society, and a member of several learned and scientific bodies, not only in this country, but also on the Continent, and in America. The University of Oxford conferred upon him the honorary degree of Doctor of Civil Laws. Late in life he settled down in retirement at Hampton Court Green, where he died in the year 1867. The *Athenæum*, in recording his death, observes that "nothing can be written about his career without entering upon the whole history of electricity in connection with

magnetism during the last fifty years;" and that his great talents were "overshadowed in private life by his singular modesty and gentleness."

Among the members of the scientific world who have lectured within the walls of the institution with which Faraday was so long and so honourably connected, have been Murchison, Lyell, Sedgwick, Whewell, Tyndall, and Huxley. The scientific world has likewise been benefited by a "Journal" published at the expense of the Royal Institution, in a less costly, and consequently more available, form than that of the average of "Transactions" and "Proceedings."

Opposite to the Royal Institution is St. George's Chapel, a private "chapel of ease"; it is a building with little or no architectural pretensions. In fact, the religious edifices in this neighbourhood take the shape of proprietary chapels rather than of parish churches. "In this enlightened age," says Pennant, with dry humour, "it was found that 'godliness was profitable to many.' Accordingly the projector, the architect, the mason, the carpenter, and the plasterer united their powers. A chapel was erected, well pewed, well warmed, dedicated and consecrated. A captivating preacher is next provided, the pews are filled, and the good undertakers amply repaid by the pious tenantry."

Lord Orkney and Lord Paulet were living in Albemarle Street in 1708. Here, too, in 1785, died Richard Glover, the poet, the author of "Leonidas" and "Admiral Hosier's Ghost."

In 1852 the Roman Catholics established, at Crawley's Hotel, in Albemarle Street, a club, which they called the "Stafford-Street Club," from its entrance being in that thoroughfare, which crosses Albemarle Street about midway. This was the first and only instance of a London club named from a street, though such a practice is common in Dublin; but, according to Mr. John Timbs, it was common in the last century, in the early part of which many "street clubs" were formed, composed of members all living in the same thoroughfare, so that a man had but to stir a few houses from his own door to enjoy his club and the society of his neighbours. "There was also," observes Mr. Timbs, "another inducement, for the streets of London were then so unsafe that the nearer to his home a man's club lay, the better for his clothes and his purse. Even riders in coaches were not safe from mounted footpads and from the danger of upsets in the huge ruts and pits which intersected the streets. But the passenger who could not afford a coach had to pick his way after dark along dimly-lighted, ill-paved thoroughfares, seamed by filthy open kennels, besprinkled from projecting spouts, bordered by gaping cellars, guarded by feeble old watchmen, and beset with daring street robbers and lawless 'rake-hells,' of the Mohock tribe, who banded into companies, and spread terror and dismay through the streets." The "street club," therefore, arose out of the instinct of mutual protection. It may be added that Stafford Street occupies as nearly as possible the site of Clarendon House, already mentioned by us under Piccadilly.

At the northern end of Albemarle Street, connecting Dover Street and Old Bond Street, is Grafton Street, which consists of spacious and old-fashioned mansions. At the house of Sir Ralph Payne (afterwards better known as the eccentric Lord Lavington) the leaders of the Opposition in Pitt's days frequently met. Erskine, having one day dined there, found himself so indisposed as to be obliged to retire after dinner to another apartment. Lady Payne, who was incessant in her attentions to him, inquired, when he returned to the company, how he found himself. Erskine took out a piece of paper, and wrote on it—

" 'Tis true I am ill, but I cannot complain,
    For he never knew *Pleasure* who never knew *Payne*."

"Sir Ralph, with whom I was well acquainted," writes Sir Nathaniel William Wraxall, "always appeared to be a good-natured, pleasing, well-bred man ; but he was reported not always to treat his wife with kindness. Sheridan, calling on her one morning, found her in tears, which she placed, however, to the account of her monkey, who had expired only an hour or two before, and for whose loss she expressed deep regret. 'Pray write me an epitaph for him,' added she ; 'his name was *Ned*.' Sheridan instantly penned these lines :—

    'Alas ! poor Ned !
    My monkey's dead !
    I had rather by half
    It had been Sir Ralph !' "

At No. 4 in this street Henry, first Lord Brougham, resided during the last nineteen or twenty years of his life. He was born at Edinburgh in 1778, and coming to London to push his fortunes at the Bar, first made himself known to the political world by his advocacy of Queen Caroline, and afterwards by his zeal in the cause of Reform and Education. He was suddenly raised to the woolsack by the Whig party on their attaining to place and power under Lord Grey in 1830 ; but, for reasons never yet fully explained, he was not re-appointed after the Conservative interregnum five years later. He died somewhat suddenly at his residence at Cannes, in the south

of France, in 1868. He was a mathematician, a man of science, a linguist, and an orator, as well as a lawyer and statesman ; indeed, his general knowledge was so extensive that it was said of him in satire, that " if he had only known a little law he would have known a little of everything." His house was afterwards the Turf Club.

Here, at No. 19, lived for the last half century of his life Sir Alleyne Fitzherbert, a distinguished diplomatist, afterwards known as Lord St. Helen's, who, after having tried in early life nearly all the capitals of Europe, used to maintain that there was no other place but London that was worth living in. He was true to his principles, and he seldom if ever quitted the West-end, either winter or summer. He died in 1838.

Sir William Scott, afterwards Lord Stowell, who, in his sixty-eighth year, married the Dowager Marchioness of Sligo, lived for some time in this street. In our description of Doctors' Commons* will be found a detailed account of Sir William's marriage with this lady, as well as an anecdote referring more particularly to his residence in Grafton Street.

No. 10 was for many years the residence of Mr. William Holmes, M.P. for Berwick, and the " whipper-in " of the Tories in the House of Commons. He was an especial favourite of the Great Duke and of Sir Robert Peel, who used often to " drop in " upon him here.

Grafton Street, on account of its retired situation and the absence of a direct thoroughfare, has for several years been, as it were, an offshoot of " Club-land." At the present time there are the Grafton and the Junior Oxford and Cambridge, the latter occupying what was formerly the home of the Marlborough. The Turf Club, mentioned above, removed in 1875-6 to their new quarters in Piccadilly. In the south-east corner of this street Benjamin Tabart, the publisher, for some time had his shop ; his picture-books for children are well known.

Bond Street, which we now enter, dates from the year 1686, when it was built by Sir Thomas Bond. " In 1700," says Pennant, " Bond Street was built no further than the west end of Clifford Street. New Bond Street was at that time an open field, called the Conduit Mead, from one of the conduits which supplied this part of the town with water. Hatton, writing in 1708, describes it as " a fine new street, mostly inhabited by nobility and gentry.'

The *Weekly Journal* of June 1st, 1717, observes,

---

* See Vol. I., p. 290.

"The new buildings between Bond Street and Mary-le-bone go on with all possible diligence, and the houses even let and sell before they are built. They are already in great forwardness." It is obvious to remark that as Old and New Bond Streets are one street, it is the latter to which allusion is evidently made in the above extract. Even a century and a half ago Bond Street was a region of fashion; or, to use the words of Pennant, in spite of the loose expression, "it abounded with shopkeepers of both sexes of superior taste." The same writer remarks, however, in 1805, that if its builder had been able to foresee the extreme fashion in reserve for the street, he would have made it wider. "But this," he philosophises, "is a fortunate circumstance for the Bond Street loungers, who thus get a nearer glimpse of the fashionable and generally titled ladies that pass and repass from two to five o'clock." Indeed, even down to the days of the Regency and the opening of Regent Street, the chief fashionable lounge in the West-end was along Old and New Bond Street; and as lately as the year 1823, the morning was the correct time for putting in an appearance there during "the London season."

The reader will be amused, we think, with the following extract from "A New Critical Review of the Public Buildings of London," in the year 1736:—"There is nothing in the whole prodigious length of the two Bond Streets or in any of the adjacent places, though almost all erected within our memories, that has anything worth our attention; several little wretched attempts there are at foppery in building, but they are too inconsiderable even for censure." How little could the writer of these lines imagine that in the course of a few years Bond Street, Old and New, would become one of the most fashionable streets of the district, and that its shops would be the chief emporium of articles of beauty and taste, only, at a later period, outdone by those of Regent Street.

"In February, 1768," writes Sir Walter Scott, "Lawrence Sterne expired at his lodgings in Bond Street, London, his frame exhausted by a long debilitating illness. There was something in the manner of his death singularly resembling the particulars detailed by Mrs. Quickly, as attending that of Falstaff, the compeer of 'Yorick,' for infinite jest, however unlike in other particulars." In vain did the female attendant, a lodging-house servant, chafe his cold feet, in order to restore his circulation. He complained that the cold came up higher, and he died without a groan. "His death took place much in the manner in which he himself had wished, and the last kind offices were rendered him not in his own house, or by the hand of kindred affection, but in a hired lodging and by strangers." Dr. Ferrier, however, adds, "I have been told his attendants robbed him even of his gold sleeve-buttons while he was expiring." Mr. P. Cunningham, in his "Handbook of London," identifies the house in which he died as No. 41 on the west side, "the silk-bag shop, now (1849) a cheese-monger's shop." His death, the date of which most writers fix as March 18th, 1786, was somewhat sudden, for he had only just "come back to his lodgings in Bond Street" (writes Thackeray) "with his 'Sentimental Journey' to launch upon the town, eager as ever for praise and pleasure, as vain, as wicked, as witty, and as false as he had ever been, when death seized the feeble wretch."

In "Anecdotes of Distinguished Men," we read that "Sterne was no strict priest, but, as a clergyman, not likely to hear with indifference his whole fraternity treated contemptuously. Being one day in a coffee-house, he observed a spruce powdered young fellow by the fireside, who was speaking of the clergy, in a mass, as a body of disciplined impostors and systematic hypocrites. Sterne got up while the young man was haranguing, and approached towards the fire, patting and coaxing all the way a favourite little dog. Coming at length towards the gentleman, he took up the dog, still continuing to pat him, and addressed the young fellow. 'Sir, this would be the prettiest little animal in the world had he not one disorder!' 'What disorder is that?' replied the young fellow. 'Why, sir,' said Sterne, 'one that always makes him bark when he sees a gentleman in black.' 'That is a singular disorder,' rejoined the young fellow; 'pray how long has he had it?' 'Sir,' replied Sterne, looking at him with affected gentleness, 'ever since he was a puppy!'"

Sterne was among the frequenters of Drury Lane Theatre in the days of Garrick. Mr. Cradock one day meeting him there, asked him why he did not try his hand on a comedy, especially as he was so intimate with the great actor. With tears in his eyes, Sterne replied, that there were two reasons which prevented him: firstly, that he had not the gifts of the comic muse; and secondly, that he was wholly unacquainted with the business of the stage. Possibly he was right; but we cannot help regretting that the author of "Tristram Shandy" never made an effort in that direction.

Poor Sterne was interred in the burial-ground belonging to St. George's, Hanover Square, where, curiously enough, a wrong date was cut upon his tombstone. He died poor, if not actually in debt. A letter addressed by him (probably from his lodgings) to Garrick, asking for a loan of ten pounds, just before leaving town on his "Sentimental Journey," is printed in *fac-simile* in Smith's "Historical and Literary Curiosities."

In this street, in 1769, lodged Pascal Paoli, the patriot of Corsica, and here he was constantly visited by Boswell, who, if the truth must be told, made himself somewhat foolishly conspicuous by dancing attendance upon him—so much so, indeed,

was paid for the painting of an English artist during his life-time.

Among the other eminent inhabitants of this street were Sir Thomas Lawrence, the distinguished President of the Royal Academy, and the Countess of Macclesfield, mother of the poet, Richard Savage. "She died here," says Mr. Peter Cunningham, "Oct. 11th, 1753, surviving both Savage and the publication of his 'Life' by Johnson."

GLOUCESTER HOUSE, PICCADILLY. (*See page* 286.)

as to be nicknamed "Corsica Boswell." Here, too, Boswell introduced Dr. Johnson to the General, thereby realising a proud feeling of hope which he thus expressed in his "Journey to Corsica:"— "What an idea may we not form of an interview between such a scholar and philosopher as Johnson, and such a legislator and general as Paoli?"

Here, too, Boswell had lodgings, where he would often entertain Dr. Johnson, Reynolds, and the rest of the literary circle of his time. It was stated in the *Times* of April 26th, 1875, that a picture of the interior of these lodgings, with portraits of the guests, a fancy scene, painted by Mr. W. P. Frith, was sold at Messrs. Christie and Manson's rooms, a few days before the above date, for upwards of £4,000—a larger sum than ever

At No. 24 Old Bond Street are the offices of the Artists' General Benevolent Institution, Artists' Orphan Fund, and the Arundel Society for Promoting the Knowledge of Art. The first-named of these institutions was founded in 1814, and incorporated in 1842; it affords relief to artists, whether members or not, as well as to their widows and children. The Arundel Society, which has for its object the promotion of the knowledge of art, by copying, reproducing, and publishing the most important works of the ancient masters, was founded in 1848, and is called after Thomas Howard, the celebrated Earl of Arundel in the reigns of James I. and Charles I., who has deservedly been called "the Father of *virtu* in England, and the Mæcenas of all politer arts," and whom we have already introduced to our readers in our account of Arundel House in the Strand.* Its members are divided into three classes—associates, life and annual subscribers, and honorary members—and its funds are applied to the publication of essays on art subjects, chromo-lithographs, engravings, photographs, &c., of the highest order of mediæval art; and it may safely be asserted that no society has done more than the Arundel in reviving a general appreciation of mediæval art. A minute account of the results achieved by the society may be found in two works issued by its secretary, Mr. F. W. Maynard, and entitled respectively

we may add, on the authority of Mr J. Larwood, in his "History of Sign-boards," that the sign of the "Coventry Cross" was borne by a mercer in New Bond Street at the end of the eighteenth century, this particular sign evidently being chosen on account of the silk ribbons manufactured in that town.

Of the librarians at different times inhabiting this street was Ebers, who lived at No. 27, and who, as Mr. John Timbs tells us, "in seven years lost £44,080 by the Italian Opera House, Haymarket." Of Hookham's Library, one of the fashionable lounges towards the close of the last

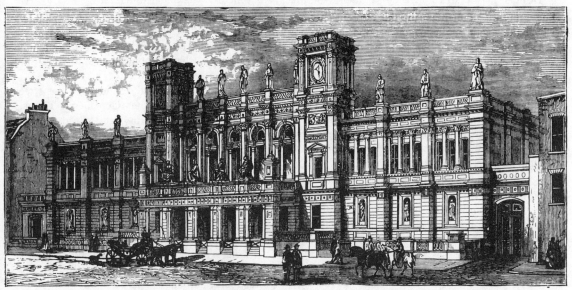

THE LONDON UNIVERSITY, BURLINGTON GARDENS. (*See page* 304.)

"Twenty Years" and "Five Years of the Arundel Society."

In this neighbourhood a club of gentlemen, mostly members of one or other of the Houses of Parliament, calling themselves "The Bohemians," still hold their musical Sunday gatherings, though their exact *locale* is kept a secret from the outer world. Bond Street, in fact, has long ranked high in the musical world for its devotion to the divine art.

The keepers of music-shops, it is well known, have usually adhered to the primitive practice of taking for signs some one or other of the instruments in which they deal, as, for instance, the "Hautboy," "The Violin," "The German Flute;" and Messrs. Novello, the great musical publishers in Cheapside, have so far adhered to the custom as to carry on their trade under the sign of the "Golden Crotchet." While on the subject of signs

century, mention is thus made in George Colman's "Broad Grins:"—

> "For novels should their critick hints succeed,
>   The Muses might fare better when they took 'em;
> But it would fare extremely ill indeed
>   With gentle Mr. Lane and Messieurs Hookham."

In New Bond Street, although, perhaps, not so ostentatious as those in the more general thoroughfares, such as Oxford Street or Regent Street, many of the shops are, nevertheless, extremely elegant, and the articles exhibited for sale are of the most *recherché* description. At the corner of Bruton Street is the shop of Mr. C. Hancocks, the great manufacturing jeweller. At 156 are the show-rooms of Messrs. Hunt and Roskell, formerly Storr and Mortimer, who succeeded to a large part of the connection of Mr. Hamlet. At No. 160 are the extensive show-rooms of Messrs. Copeland and Co. (formerly Messrs. Copeland and Spode), the eminent porcelain manufacturers, of Stoke-upon-Trent, almost the only rivals of Messrs. Wedgwood,

* See Vol. III., p. 71.

whom we have already mentioned in our account of the neighbourhood of Lincoln's Inn Fields.* Mr. Alderman Copeland, formerly Lord Mayor of London, was head of this firm.

At No. 116 in this street, Miss Clark, the great-granddaughter of Theodore, King of Corsica (who was buried at St. Anne's Church, Soho, and of whom we have already given some account in a former chapter †), was established as a miniature-painter early in the present century. Her card of address, with her modest prices and hours of attendance, is given *in extenso* in John Timbs' "Romance of London."

Dealers in pictures and other branches of the fine arts are numerous in this street; besides which the picture-galleries offer opportunities for a pleasing promenade for such as care to avail themselves of them. Foremost among these is the Doré Gallery, situated at No. 35. This exhibition, which includes some of the choicest productions of the distinguished French artist, M. Gustave Doré, is open daily all the year round. Among the pictures exhibited here are the "Massacre of the Innocents," the "Dream of Pilate's Wife," the "Night of the Crucifixion," and "Christ leaving the Prætorium." Of the last-named work the *Examiner* thus observes:—"We must go back to the Italian painters of the sixteenth century to find a picture worthy of being classed with this most stupendous achievement of the young French master. In gravity and magnitude of purpose, no less than in the scope and power of his imagination, he towers like a Colossus among his contemporaries."

At No. 47 is the Hanover Gallery, frequently used for the exhibition of pictures. No. 136 is the Grosvenor Gallery, which has become one of the popular exhibitions of the "London season," the pictures shown here being principally those of the "æsthetic" school. Scores of exhibitions of pictures and other curiosities, too numerous to particularise, have at various times existed in New Bond Street and its neighbourhood. The following curious notice of one such exhibition, quoted from the *Morning Chronicle*, of March 18, 1799, may be of interest to our readers in connection with this street :—"The real embalmed head of the powerful and renowned usurper, Oliver Cromwell, with the original dies for the medals struck in honour of his victory at Dunbar, are now exhibited at No. 5, in Mead Court, Old Bond Street (where the rattlesnake was shown last year); a genuine narrative relating to the acquisition, con-

cealment, and preservation of these articles to be had at the place of exhibition."

Cromwell's head, it appears, was exhibited here by an individual named Cox, who kept a museum of curiosities, and who had purchased it from one of the Russell family, in whose hands it had been for a century. When Cox parted with his museum, he sold the head to three individuals who all in their turn met with sudden deaths, and the head became the property of the daughters or nieces of the last survivor. These ladies, as we have mentioned in a previous chapter, being nervous at the idea of keeping in their house a relic so fatal, sold it to a medical man named Wilkinson.

At No. 21, in New Bond Street, was exhibited, in 1831, Haydon's picture of "Napoleon at St. Helena," painted for Sir Robert Peel, and upon which Wordsworth wrote one of his most beautiful sonnets.

Among the distinguished residents of this street Mr. Cunningham enumerates General Sir Thomas Picton, who fell at Waterloo, and Lord Nelson, who, as Southey tells us in his charming biography, was lodging here in 1797, after the battle of St. Vincent, and at the time when the news reached London of Lord Duncan's victory off Camperdown. By some accident or other the house was not illuminated; but when the mob was told that Admiral Nelson lay there in bed, badly wounded, it went off without breaking the windows.

At Long's Hotel, as we learn from his "Life" by Tommy Moore, Byron dined in company with Sir Walter Scott; and another hotel in this same street, "Stevens's," is mentioned by the same authority as one of Byron's "old haunts."

At No. 148, over a grocer's shop, the eccentric Lord Camelford had lodgings, preferring them to his magnificent mansion of Camelford House. It is recorded of him that in 1801, when all London was lit up with a general illumination on account of "the peace," no persuasion of friends, or of his landlord, could induce him to suffer a candle to be put in his windows. The mob, of course, attacked the house, and saluted his windows with a shower of stones. Lord Camelford rushed out with a pistol in his hand, and it seemed as if the day of public rejoicing was about to be stained with bloodshed. At last a friend and companion induced him to exchange his pistol for a good stout cudgel, which he laid about him right and left, till at length, overpowered by numbers, he was rolled over and over in the gutter, and glad to beat a retreat indoors, for once in his life crest-fallen. A year or two later we find his lordship still living here, when he fought with Captain Best that memorable duel in which he fell mortally wounded "in the fields behind Holland House." The interior of Lord Camelford's lodgings is thus described in a note to the "Rejected Addresses:"—"Over the fire-place in the drawing-room . . . . were ornaments strongly expressive of the pugnacity of the peer. A long, thick bludgeon lay horizontally supported by two brass hooks. Above this was placed parallel one of lesser dimensions, until a pyramid of weapons gradually arose tapering to a horsewhip." No doubt its walls were decorated with portraits of the first "bruisers" of the day, and of the heroes of the "cock-pits," which then were still in vogue.

In this street, too, were the lodgings of "Squire Alworthy," a personage familiar to every reader of Fielding's "Tom Jones;" and many of the most touching scenes in that novel are laid in this thoroughfare.

Between Old Bond Street and Albemarle Street, on the site of a part of the gardens of Clarendon House (already described by us in our walk along Piccadilly), stood, till 1870, the Clarendon Hotel, one of the largest establishments of the kind in London. It had a frontage to either street, and contained large suites of apartments where royal and noble personages used to put up during their stay in London. Official banquets, too, were often held here in the first decade of Her Majesty's reign. Here were held the meetings of the Association of Baronets, instituted by the late amiable visionary, Sir Richard Broun, for the purpose of asserting the right of members of that order to the use of heraldic supporters, a coronet, the prefix of "honourable," and other more tangible and substantial advantages; but the association quietly died a natural death.

Among the records of the house was the *menu* of a dinner given by the late Lord Chesterfield in the year 1835, on resigning his office as Master of the Buckhounds. It is a curiosity in its way—the way of costly luxury; it is printed *in extenso* in the second volume of the "Club Life of London."

The mansion, before its conversion into an hotel, was occupied for two or three seasons by the Earl of Chatham as his town residence.

Stevens's Hotel, in Bond Street, was fashionable in the days of the Regency as the head-quarters for officers in the army, and "men about town." Captain Gronow tells us in his "Reminiscences" that if a stranger wanted to dine there, he would be "stared at by the servants and very solemnly assured that there was no table vacant." He adds that it was no uncommon thing to see thirty or even forty saddle-horses or tilburies waiting outside the doors of this hotel; and that two of his old Welsh friends who resided here in 1815 qualified themselves for residence within its walls—in the eyes of "mine host," at all events—by "disposing of five bottles of wine daily." It is to be hoped that the gallant captain meant to add "between them;" but his phrase is a little ambiguous.

In this street, on its eastern side, about the year 1820, was a bazaar, called the Western Exchange, consisting of only one large room, well furnished with a variety of stalls. It had an entrance in the rear into the Burlington Arcade. The bazaar, however, proved a failure, and soon closed. Another bazaar was built in this street in 1879.

Clifford Street, which connects the north end of Savile Row with Bond Street, cutting Old Burlington Street at right angles, was built about the year 1740, and perpetuates the name of the Cliffords, Earls of Cumberland, the daughter and heiress of the last holder of that title having been the mother of the first Lord Burlington.

The house No. 7 was inhabited by Dr. Anthony Addington, a physician in good practice, and the father of Henry Addington, the first Lord Sidmouth, who was born in 1757, and who succeeded Pitt as Premier in 1801. It will be remembered that the latter, in some of the squibs of the day, was dubbed "The Doctor," partly, perhaps, owing to his parentage, partly to the story that it was by his advice that a pillow of hops was provided to cure the sleeplessness of George III. At No. 5 in this street Robert Liston, the celebrated surgeon, was living in the year 1841.

In this street, towards the end of the last century, was a debating society which lasted some few years. It was styled the Clifford Street Club, and met at the "Clifford Street Coffee House." Among its members were Lord Charles Townshend, and George Canning in his early prime. Political questions were here discussed, generally from a Liberal point of view, while foaming jugs of porter crowned the tables; and it was here that Canning first practised his tongue in political debate, on such subjects as the French Revolution. During the "sittings" of this club, porter was the only beverage indulged in by its members; and on one occasion, as John Timbs tells us, Canning compared a pot of this liquor to the eloquence of Mirabeau "as empty and vapid as his patriotism—'foam and froth at the top, heavy and muddy within.'"

On the north side is the shop of Messrs. Stulz, the fashionable tailors of the days of the Regency, who are said to have had half the members of the clubs of St. James's on their books.

At right angles with Bond Street, and forming,

together with Vigo Street, a direct communication into Regent Street, is the thoroughfare known as Burlington Gardens. Built about the year 1729, it consisted at first of small houses, scattered irregularly up and down. At the south-west corner, where the Gardens join Bond Street, and extending back to the Arcade, is the large warehouse of Messrs. Atkinson, the perfumers, established here in 1799. The opposite corner is occupied by the fashionable haircutters, Messrs. Truefitt, who have held it since 1810.

On the south side of Burlington Gardens, between the Arcade and the Albany, are the new buildings of the London University. The building, which is from the designs of Mr. Pennethorne, and was opened by Her Majesty in person early in the year 1870, occupies a site of about 250 feet long by 150 feet in depth, on which formerly grew two lines of tall poplars, which threw a graceful and grateful shadow over Burlington Gardens. The elevation is in the ornate Italian style, such as would have gladdened the heart of so great an admirer of classical architecture as the old Earl of Burlington, if he could wake up to life again.

As regards its ground-plan, it consists of two oblong blocks, the smaller of which stands behind and to the south of the principal one. The front presents a central portion of 120 feet long, flanked by two square towers, and extended further east and west by wings two storeys in height. These towers carry a clock and a sun-dial, and between them is a projecting portico, with five entrances. The portico, the centre, and the wings are all surmounted by ornate balustrades, on the pedestals of which are placed statues of eminent men, selected as fitting representatives of the various forms of academic culture. The statues over the portico are seated, those on the roof are standing, and there are also other standing figures in niches on the ground floor of each wing. The principal figures are those on the balustrade of the portico. These are by Mr. Joseph Durham—viz., Newton, Bentham, Milton, and Harvey, as representatives of the four Faculties of Science, Law, Arts, and Medicine. The figures on the central roof represent ancient culture in the persons of Galen, Cicero, Aristotle, Plato, Archimedes, and Justinian, the first three by Westmacott, and the last three by Woodington. The eastern wing is devoted to illustrious foreigners. On the roof-line are Galileo, Goëthe, and Laplace, by Wyon; in the niches are Leibnitz, Cuvier, and Linnæus, by MacDowell. The balustrade of the west wing is adorned with English worthies—Hunter, Hume, and Davy, by Noble; the niches being occupied by Adam Smith,

John Locke, and Bacon, by Theed. The individuals chosen to be represented, and also the sculptors, were selected by the joint action of the Senate of the University and the Metropolitan Board of Works. It was at first proposed to put Shakespeare in the place occupied by Milton, but the idea was overruled on the ground that the genius of the great dramatist was quite independent of academic instruction or rules. A statue of Shakespeare, however, has since been placed in the interior of the building.

Opposite to the centre of the portico is the principal entrance, with rooms to the right and left; beyond these is a fine and spacious corridor, running east and west. At the extreme west is the great library, used also as an examination hall, occupying the whole of that wing. To the east is the great theatre, or lecture hall, used for the purpose of conferring degrees, and capable of seating eight hundred persons, the benches rising behind one another after the fashion of an amphitheatre. It is well planned as to its acoustic properties. It is used occasionally, however, for other besides strictly academic purposes, such as for the meetings of the Royal Geographical Society. At each end of the corridor above mentioned are passages leading to the smaller examination halls and private rooms for the use of the examiners. The great staircase occupies a lofty hall, and leads to the first floor, where there is a library and common room for the use of the graduates. The staircase has marble balusters and hand-rails, and the floor of the main landing also is of polished marble. On this floor are also the senate-room and the offices of the registrar of the University.

The building is, perhaps, the finest modern example in England of the most refined and enriched style of Italian or "Palladian" architecture. The decorations are elaborate, abundant, and massive, and remarkable for a general character of flatness which is without a parallel in our time, and helps to subordinate mere ornamentation to the main outlines of form.

It is important to note here that the University of London is an examining, not strictly a teaching body. Its essential function is the bestowal of academical degrees on qualified candidates from all classes and denominations of Her Majesty's subjects, without distinction of caste or creed; and it was long without a home. For many years, in fact, since its commencement in 1838, when it grew out of the University, now University College, in Gower Street, it lived, so to speak, in furnished apartments, and, as a matter of course, had to shift its quarters from time to time. In consequence, it did not hold the position which it deserved in the republic of art, science, and the *belles lettres*. It is now, however, fairly at the head of all the higher education of the kingdom which is not given at Oxford and Cambridge; not, however, conferring it, but testing it from time to time. The number of candidates seeking to pass its examinations has now risen from twenty-three in the first year of Her Majesty's reign to about fifteen hundred annually; and it is honourably distinguished by the firmness with which it has insisted on a high standard being maintained by all who seek to become graduates of it. The Council comprises, or has comprised, many of the most eminent scholars and statesmen of the age, such as Grote, Thirlwall, Brougham, and Macaulay. Its board of examiners consists of men of high standing in the several branches of learning, who hold their appointments from year to year, when they are usually re-elected.

It is not a little singular to record the fact that in the first instance, when the Liberal party were in power, Mr. Pennethorne prepared a classical design for the university, being commissioned by Mr. Cowper-Temple, then Chief Commissioner of Public Buildings, but that when the Conservatives came into office in 1866, Lord John Manners insisted on an ecclesiastical structure being substituted, and that this was carried up some six or eight feet above the ground, when another change of Ministry revived the former commission, and the Palladian style conquered and prevailed.

Opposite, and extending northward to Clifford Street, is Old Burlington Street. If there is to be found in the West-end a dull, heavy, and unattractive street, it is this; and yet, in 1736, the author of "A New Critical Review of the Public Buildings" speaks of it as containing houses "in the finest taste of any common buildings that we can see anywhere; without the least affectation of ornament or seeming design at any remarkable elegance." He adds, "They need no ornament to make them remarkable." It is evident that the standard of architectural merit and beauty has considerably altered since the reign of George II. Mr. Planché tells us, in his agreeable "Recollections," that he remembers seeing blood running in kennels in Burlington Street, into which men, and women too, were dipping sticks and handkerchiefs, in front of the residence of Mr. F. Robinson ("Prosperity Robinson," afterwards Lord Goderich and Earl of Ripon), during the corn-law riots in 1815.

At the north end of this street, facing Boyle Street, a small and unimportant thoroughfare which connects the north end of Savile Row with that of Old Burlington Street, stood a large, heavy, and gloomy building, apparently almost without windows or doors. It was a school founded by Lady Burlington "for the maintenance, clothing, and education of eighty female children." It covered part of what was originally called the "Ten-Acres-Field." A new scheme for the remodelling of this institution was propounded in 1875–6; its endowment has since been made available for the education of boys as well as girls, and the school rebuilt. The name of Boyle Street serves to perpetuate yet another title of the house of Burlington.

Adjoining this building on the east is the office of Messrs. Rushworth and Jarvis, the house agents and auctioneers. It is said to occupy the site of a summer-house which stood at the north-east corner of the gardens of Lord Burlington's mansion. At No. 8 lived Mr. Samuel Pepys Cockerell, F.S.A., father of the late Professor Cockerell, R.A.

At the corner of this street is the Burlington Hotel. Here Miss Florence Nightingale used to stay when in London, before and after the Crimean war, when her name first became known on account of her exertions in the cause of the sanitary condition of the British army.

On the north side of Burlington Gardens, occupying the space between Savile Row and Old Burlington Street, stands a handsome building used as the western branch of the Bank of England, and known as Uxbridge House. It was built by Vardy, assisted by Joseph Bonomi, for the first Earl of Uxbridge, the father of Field-Marshal, the first Marquis of Anglesey, who lost his leg at Waterloo. It was sold by his son and successor about the year 1855. It stands upon the site of a still earlier mansion, known as Queensberry House, which was built by Leoni for the celebrated Duke of Queensberry, the father of the "Piccadilly Duke" already mentioned. The poet Gay lived for many years as an inmate of its hospitable halls, enjoying the patronage and friendship of the duke, and of his eccentric wife, so well known to our readers as the friend of Pope, and celebrated in song as

"Kitty ever bright and young."

If we may believe Pope, who knew him well, Gay was quite a child of nature, wholly without art or design; one who spoke just what he thought and as he thought it. He dangled for twenty years about the Court, and at last obtained the offer of being made usher to the young princess. Secretary Craggs made Gay a present of stock in the South Sea year; and he was once worth £20,000, but lost it all again. He got about £500 by the first *Beggar's Opera*, and £1,100 or £1,200 by the second. Like most literary men, he was negligent of ways and means, and a bad manager. Latterly, however, the Duke of Queensberry took his money into his own hands, letting him have only what was necessary out of it, and as he lived at the duke's table, he could not have occasion for any large outlay; consequently he died worth upwards of £3,000.

Thackeray accuses the Duke and Duchess of Queensberry of having over-fed the poetical Gay, Court. Lord Hervey, in his "Memoirs of the Reign of George II.," has thus characteristically described this *fracas:*—"Among the remarkable occurrences of this winter [1729], I cannot help relating that of the Duchess of Queensberry being forbid the Court, and the occasion of it. One Gay, a poet, had written a ballad opera, which was thought to reflect a little upon the Court, and a good deal upon the minister. It was called *The*

UXBRILGE HOUSE. (*See page* 305.)

who, he says, "was lapped in cotton, and had his plate of chicken, and his saucer of cream, and frisked, and barked, and wheezed, and grew fat, and so ended." Congreve testifies that Gay was a great eater. "As the French philosopher used to prove his existence by *cogito, ergo sum,* the greatest proof of Gay's existence is *edit, ergo est.*" It is not often now-a-days that literature finds itself so liberally rewarded in the persons of its followers.

The high-spirited Duchess of Queensberry, to whose kind intervention with Lord Bute even Thurlow was indebted for his silk gown, was Catherine Hyde, grand-daughter of the great Lord Clarendon. In order to promote the services of Gay, induced by her extraordinary friendship for him, the duchess sacrificed even the favour of the *Beggar's Opera,* and had a prodigious run, and was so extremely pretty in its kind, that even those who were most glanced at in the satire had prudence enough to disguise their resentment by chiming in with the universal applause with which it was performed. Gay, who had attached himself to Mrs. Howard (then one of the ladies of the bed-chamber to Queen Caroline), and been disappointed of preferment at Court, finding this couched satire upon those to whom he imputed his disappointment succeed so well, wrote a second part to this opera, less pretty, but more abusive, and so little disguised that Sir Robert Walpole resolved, rather than suffer himself to be produced for thirty nights together upon the stage in the person of a highwayman, to make use of his friend, the Duke of Grafton's authority, as Lord Chamberlain, to put a stop to the representation of it. Accordingly this theatrical craftsman was prohibited at every playhouse. Gay, irritated at this bar thrown in the way both of his interest and revenge, zested this work with some supplemental invectives, and resolved to print it by subscription. The Duchess of Queensberry set herself at the head

King, when he came into the drawing-room, seeing her Grace very busy in a corner with three or four men, asked her what she had been doing. She answered, 'What must be agreeable, she was sure, to anybody so humane as his Majesty, for it was an act of charity, and a charity to which she did not despair of bringing his Majesty to contribute.' Enough was said for each to understand the other,

RICHARD BRINSLEY SHERIDAN. (*See page* 311.)

of this undertaking, and solicited every mortal that came in her way, or in whose way she could put herself, to subscribe. To a woman of her quality, proverbially beautiful, and at the top of the polite and fashionable world, people were ashamed to refuse a guinea, though they were afraid to give it. Her solicitations were so universal and so pressing that she came even into the Queen's apartment, went round the drawing-room, and made even the King's servants contribute to the printing of a thing which the King had forbid being acted. The

and though the King did not then (as the Duchess of Queensberry reported) appear at all angry, yet the proceeding of her Grace's, when talked over in private between his Majesty and the Queen, was so resented, that Mr. Stanhope, then Vice-Chamberlain to the King, was sent in form to the Duchess of Queensberry, to desire her to forbear coming to Court. His message was verbal. Her answer, for fear of mistakes, she desired to send in writing; she wrote it on the spot, and this is the literal copy :—

"'Feb. 27th, 1728–9.

"'The Duchess of Queensberry is surprised and well pleased that the King hath given her so agreeable a command as to stay from Court, where she never came for diversion, but to bestow a great civility on the King and Queen : she hopes by such an unprecedented order as this is, that the King will see as few as he wishes at his Court, particularly such as dare to think or speak the truth. I dare not do otherwise, and ought not, nor could have imagined that it would not have been the very highest compliment that I could possibly pay the King, to endeavour to support truth and innocence in his house, particularly when the King and Queen both told me that they had not read Mr. Gay's play. I have certainly done right, then, to stand by my own words rather than his Grace of Grafton's, who hath neither made use of truth, judgment, nor honour, through this whole affair, either for himself or his friends.

C. QUEENSBERRY.'

"When her Grace had finished this paper, drawn with more spirit than accuracy, she gave it to Mr. Stanhope, who desired her to think again, asked pardon for being so impertinent as to offer her any advice, but begged she would give him leave to carry an answer less rough than that she had put into his hands. Upon this she wrote another, but so much more disrespectful, that he desired the first again, and delivered it. Most people blamed the Court upon this occasion. What the Duchess of Queensberry did was certainly impertinent ; but the manner of resenting it was thought impolitic. The Duke of Queensberry laid down his employment of Admiral of Scotland upon it, though very much and very kindly pressed by the King to remain in his service."

It was exactly eighteen years after penning the above protocol, that the Duchess of Queensberry found her way back to Court.

The author of the "New Critical Review of the Public Buildings of London," in the year 1736, speaks of Queensberry House as having no other faults but its bad situation, "over against a dead wall in a lane that is unworthy of so grand a building," and the fact that no wings can ever be added to it. The criticism, however, no longer holds good. "This fabric," adds the writer, "is evidently in the style of Inigo Jones, and not at all unworthy the school of that great master."

The large house fronting Burlington Gardens, extending from Old Burlington Street to Cork Street, long occupied by a younger branch of the Cavendish family, has lately been converted into an hotel.

Vigo Street (formerly called Vigo Lane), which, as we have said, connects Burlington Gardens with Regent Street, was named after a town in the north-west of Spain attacked and captured by the English forces under Drake, by Ormond, Rooke, and Stanhope, and also by Lord Cobham at various dates in the seventeenth and eighteenth centuries. It was probably built about the year 1720.

At right angles with this street, and opening out into Piccadilly nearly opposite St. James's Church, is Sackville Street, which was built about 1679-80, and was probably named after Sackville, the witty Earl of Dorset, by those who were anxious to perpetuate his memory. At all events, no proof can be found of any direct connection of its builders or of the former owners of the land on which it stands with the family which gave birth to a Buckhurst and a Dorset. Mr. Peter Cunningham tells us that it is "the longest street in London of any note without a turning on either side." It is now extensively occupied by wholesale warehouses of cloths and woollen fabrics.

The "Prince," an inn in this street, was one of the temporary dining-houses of the Literary Club of Dr. Johnson and his friends after they left the "Turk's Head," in Soho, and before repairing to the "Thatched House Tavern ;" and here the Dilettanti Society met for some time in 1783.

In this street the Board of Agriculture, established in 1793 by the efforts of Sir John Sinclair and of Mr. Arthur Young, used to hold its meetings in the beginning of the reign of George IV. This board was subsidised by a grant of £3,000 annually from Parliament, to be dispensed in improving the practical agriculture of the kingdom.

No. 32 in this street is a perfect "rabbit-warren" of charitable and other institutions, the bare enumeration of which, as they stand mentioned in the "Post Office Directory," will be sufficient here :— The British Hairdressers' Benevolent Society, the British Archæological Association, General Domestic Servants' Benevolent Institution, Governesses' Benevolent Institution, The Irish Society, London Aged Christian Society, the Metropolitan Convalescent Institution, Milliners' and Dressmakers' Provident and Benevolent Institution, Naval and Military Bible Society, Royal Naval Female School Society, Society for the Relief of Distressed Widows, and the Pall Mall, Albany, and Albert Building Societies. Several of these institutions rely to a great extent for their support upon the voluntary contributions of the public ; whilst others are self-supporting. It may not be out of place to remark here, that when M. Guizot was in this country he observed that nothing struck him more forcibly than the number of charitable institutions on the front of which were inscribed the words, "Supported by Voluntary Contributions;" and that they impressed him with a most favourable estimate of the English character. Besides the institutions named above, this house is also the head-quarters of the Albert Freehold Land and Building Society, the Irish Society, and the British Archæological Society. This last-named association is an offshoot of the Archæological Institute, and holds its own rival meetings and publishes its own "Transactions."

Of the distinguished residents in this street, in times past, have been Sir Everard Home (at No. 30), and Sir Gilbert Blane (at No. 8), both members of the medical profession.

Between Piccadilly and Regent Street, at a little distance eastward of Sackville Street, and near St. James's Hall, is Air (or Ayr) Street. It is stated on the authority of the rate-books of St. Martin's-in-the-Fields, that this street was built, at all events, as early as 1659, at which time it must have been quite at the western end of the town. But nothing is known as to the origin of its name, and it is quite innocent of literary or historic associations.

Parallel with Old Burlington Street on its west side, extending from Burlington Gardens to Clifford Street, is Cork Street, which perpetuates the name of one of four distinguished brothers of the House of Boyle, who all held peerages at the same time— a fact paralleled only by the Duke of Wellington and his three brothers. They were (besides Lord Burlington) Lord Cork, Lord Orrery, and Lord Broghill. A fifth brother was no less distinguished —the Honourable Robert Boyle, the philosopher. This street has only four houses on the eastern side. One of these belonged to the celebrated Field-Marshal Wade, for whom Lord Burlington built it in a fit of gratitude. It is described by the author of the "New Critical Review," as small, but chaste and simple in design, though rather overladen with ornament. Yet, he adds, "it is the only fabric in miniature I ever saw where decorations are perfectly proportioned to the space they are to fill, and do not by their multiplicity, or some other mistake, incumber the whole." The house was sold by auction in 1748. Horace Walpole tells us that it was regarded by Lord Chesterfield as such a toy that "he intended to take the house over against it to look at it;" and it was also commonly said of it that "it was too small to live in, and yet too big for a watch." Among the other eminent persons who lived in Cork Street were the haughty and imperious Mrs. (afterwards Lady) Masham, the celebrated bed-chamberwoman of Queen Anne's Court,

and Dr. Arbuthnot, the physician, wit, and man of letters of the reign of Queen Anne. They both died here, the latter in February, 1735.

In this street is a public-house known as the "Blue Posts," for several generations a favourite dining-house for bachelors. Instead of a sign-board, and in the absence of a poetical and inventive taste, some innkeepers chose to denote their hostelry by the colour of some external feature of the fabric. Thus we read that there were "Black Posts" as well as "Blue Posts." Indeed, there was an inn rejoicing in that sign close by in Bond Street, immortalised by Etheredge in his comedy, *She would if she could.*

Savile Row, which extends northward from Burlington Gardens to Boyle Street and New Burlington Street, appears to have been for generations the favoured *locale* for the leading members of the medical profession.

No. 1 is the home of the Royal Geographical Society, which was founded in 1830 for the purposes of cultivating and extending geographical knowledge. It had its head-quarters in 1851 at No. 3, Waterloo Place; it was subsequently for a time settled in Whitehall Place, whence it removed to Savile Row in 1870.

It was this society which took a leading part in sending out Dr. Livingstone on those travels which have opened up a large portion of Central Africa to commerce and civilisation; and it was here that the embalmed body of David Livingstone (who had died in Africa several months previously), on being brought to London, was deposited prior to its being consigned to its last resting-place in Westminster Abbey, in April, 1874. The society has a large and well-selected library of works treating on those subjects which fall within its scope; and it gives an annual gold medal in recognition of services rendered to geographical science.

The adjoining house, No. 2, has been, since the year 1860, the head-quarters of the Roman Catholic body in London, in the shape of a club. It was founded in 1852, as the Stafford Club, so called from its original locality, occupying, as it did, the side of Crawley's Hotel, which faces Stafford Street. This club, however, was dissolved towards the close of the year 1875, after having been in existence for a little more than twenty years. In its place a new club has been established here, called the "St. George's;" the Duke of Norfolk was the chief mover of the establishment of the new club, and its success is largely due to the duke's exertions. It started with its full compliment of 350 members.

In 1826 Lord Maryborough (brother of the "great" Duke of Wellington) was living at No. 3; Sir Charles Mansfield Clarke at No. 10; and the Right Hon. George Tierney, M.P., at No. 11. No. 4 is the home of the Science (originally the Scientific) Club, established in 1874.

At No. 12 resided for many years Mr. George Grote, the distinguished historian of Greece. The eldest son of the late Mr. George Grote, of Badg-moor, Oxon., and a banker in London, he was born at Beckenham, Kent, in 1794. As a youth he entered his father's establishment as a clerk, and his leisure time was for many years afterwards spent in unremitting study. In 1832 he was re-turned to Parliament as one of the representa-tives of the City of London, and he held his seat for nine years as the champion of the ballot. His first publication was a pamphlet in reply to Sir James Mackintosh's "Essay on Parliamentary Reform" in the *Edinburgh Review;* it was printed anonymously in 1821. He afterwards wrote a small work on the "Essentials of Parliamentary Reform," "Plato and other Companions of So-crates," besides numerous essays, &c. His chief work, "The History of Greece," was published between 1846 and 1856. Mr. Grote was a trustee of the British Museum, a member of the Institute of France, Vice-Chancellor of the London Univer-sity, and a Fellow of the Royal Society. He died here in 1871, and his remains were interred in Westminster Abbey. His widow, a lady of an old Kentish family, known as the authoress of "The Life of Ary Scheffer," died in 1878.

At No. 14 lived for many years Sir Benjamin Brodie, the eminent surgeon, and president at one time of the Royal Society. Sir Benjamin, who was of Scottish extraction, though the son of a Wiltshire clergyman, was one of the staff of the Medical School in Great Windmill Street, and a pupil of Sir Everard Home, at St. George's Hospital. He was Surgeon in Ordinary to George IV., and Serjeant-surgeon to William IV., and also to Her Majesty Queen Victoria. He was created a baronet in 1834, and he was the author of several works of the highest repute in the medical profession, espe-cially on the generation of animal heat, the action of poisons, the nervous affections, &c. He was chosen to fill the presidential chair of the Royal Society in 1858. He died in 1862.

The adjoining house (No. 15) has been for some time the home of the Savile Club. At No. 17, formerly the residence of George Basevi, the architect, is the Burlington Fine Arts Club, which till about 1870 had its head-quarters at No. 177, Piccadilly. This club was established in 1866,

"for the purpose of bringing together amateurs, collectors, and others interested in art; to afford ready means for consultation between persons of special knowledge and experience in matters re-lating to the fine arts; and to provide accommoda-tion for showing and comparing rare works in the possession of the members and their friends." In the reading-room all periodicals, books, and cata-logues, foreign as well as English, having reference to the world of art, are provided, so that the opportunity is afforded of obtaining knowledge of all sales of works of art, and of acquiring informa-tion on points relating to the history and condition of the fine arts both at home and abroad. In the gallery and rooms of the club arrangements are made for the exhibition of pictures, rare books, enamels, ceramic wares, coins, &c., and occasion-ally special exhibitions are held, having for their object the elucidation of some school, master, or specific art. When works of more than usual interest are on view, *conversazioni* are held. Two interesting gatherings of this kind took place in 1875. At one of them were exhibited the water-colour paintings of Turner's youthful friend, the artist Girtin (who was cut off at less than thirty years of age), and also the sketch models of the late eminent sculptor, Mr. J. H. Foley, com-prising the designs for many of his most important works in London and elsewhere. On another occasion an almost perfect collection of Hollar's etchings were exhibited. In addition to its galleries of artistic objects, the house affords to members the ordinary accommodation and advantages of a London club.

At No. 20 lived and died Mr. Robert Vernon-Smith, many years one of the most laborious underlings in Lord Melbourne's and Lord John Russell's ministries, and afterwards Lord Lyveden. The house formerly belonged to his father, Mr. Robert Smith, brother of the witty Canon of St. Paul's, Sydney Smith, and known to society, from old Eton days, as "Bobus Smith." He was him-self a wit, and deserves mention here as the founder of "The King of Clubs," which used to meet at the "Crown and Anchor," in the Strand, and which numbered among its members J. P. Curran, James Scarlett (afterwards Lord Abinger), Sam Rogers, the banker-poet, Lord Erskine, and Charles Butler, the Roman Catholic controversialist. Its talk was entirely of books, authors, and literature, politics being rigidly excluded. "Bobus Smith's" wife was one of the charming Miss Vernons, known as Horace Walpole's "Three Graces," the others being Lady Lansdowne and Lady Holland. Their mother was a daughter of the Countess of Ossory.

In this street lived and died Richard Brinsley Sheridan, the dramatist, wit, and politician. The history of the chequered career of this celebrity and bold companion of the Prince Regent has been often told. It has been said that when, by the assistance of his friends, he was installed in his residence in Savile Row, he boasted to one of his relations how carefully and regularly he was living —so much so that everything went on like clock-work. "Oh! that I can easily imagine," was the reply; "it goes on—tick! tick! tick!"

"His last scene," observes Sir N. W. Wraxall, "holds up to us an affecting and painful subject of contemplation. A privy councillor, the ornament of his age and nation, caressed by princes and dreaded by ministers, a man whose orations and dramatic works alike rank him among the most dis-tinguished men of his own or of any period, he expired—though not in a state of destitution, like Spencer, like Otway, or like Chatterton, yet under humiliating circumstances of pecuniary embarrass-ments. His house in Savile Row was besieged by bailiffs, one of whom pressing to obtain entrance, and availing himself of the moment when the front door was opened by a servant, in order to admit the visit of Dr. Baillie, who attended Sheridan during his last illness, that eminent physician, assisted by the footman, repulsed him, and shut the door in his face. Dr. Baillie . . . . refused to accept any fee for his advice; and Earl Grey, who had so long acted in political union with Sheridan as a member of the Opposition, supplied him with every article for his comfort from his own kitchen. Nor, I have heard, did the Prince Regent forsake him in his last moments. If my informa-tion is correct, his Royal Highness sent him two hundred pounds, but Sheridan declined its accept-ance, and returned the money." Sheridan died on the 7th of July, 1816, neglected by all but a few friends, among whom were the poets Rogers and Moore. Three or four days afterwards his body was carried to its last resting-place in Westminster Abbey, the pall being borne by dukes and other high personages, who had stood aloof from him in his difficulties and even in his last illness. Such is the way of the world!

No. 24, at the north-west corner, now a shop below and a private hotel above, is ambitiously styled Byron House, on account of a tradition— which, however, lacks verification—that the poet lived here about the time of his ill-starred marriage with Miss Milbanke.

At No. 34 in this street is an old-established charitable institution, the objects of which are clearly expressed in its title—the "Blind Man's Friend." It was founded by the late Mr. Charles Day, of the well-known firm of Day and Martin, of Holborn, who died towards the end of 1836, leaving £100,000 for the benefit of distressed persons suffering under the deprivation of sight. Between 200 and 300 blind persons are in the receipt of pensions of from £12 to £20 each. The entire income is about £4,000, and the election of the pensioners rests with the trustees.

At the back of Savile Row eastward, and running parallel between it and Regent Street, is Heddon Street, the entrance to which is on the west side of Regent Street. It is narrow and tortuous, and can scarcely be dignified with the name of a thoroughfare. The origin of its name is unknown, and its annals are a blank.

New Burlington Street, which we now enter, is a short thoroughfare, extending from the north end of Savile Row to the west side of Regent Street.

No. 6, on the north side, now the shop of Messrs. R. Cocks and Co., the eminent music publishers, was formerly the town residence of the Earl of Cork. Here, in the days of the Regency and later, the old eccentric Lady Cork held her "recep-tions," which were largely attended by the "upper ten thousand" and the rest of the world of fashion, in spite of her ladyship's well-known vice of "kleptomania"—a weakness in which she indulged so extensively and habitually, that her friends used to place pewter spoons and forks in their halls for her to carry off; in fact, all kinds of "dodges" were resorted to for the purpose of humouring her. "It was supposed," says Captain Gronow, "that she had a peculiar ignorance of the laws of *meum* and *tuum;* for her monomania was such that she would try to get possession of whatever she could place her hands upon; so that it was dangerous to leave in the ante-room anything of value. On applica-tion being made, however, the articles were usually returned the following day, the fear of the law act-ing strongly upon her ladyship's bewildered brain." And yet she reigned for many years a "queen of society" at the West-end, and, in fact, was the notorious "lion-hunter" of her age. At one time she would bring together such people as Sir Walter Scott; Betty, the "infant Roscius;" Belzoni, the Egyptian explorer; old Joseph Lankester, the schoolmaster; and other persons of note. Here, in 1840, the old countess died at the age of upwards of ninety. She was the last of the "Blue Stocking Club," of which we shall have more to say when we reach Portman Square, and was known in her youth as the lively and fascinating Miss Monckton. She "used to have the finest bit of blue at the house of her mother, Lady Galway," which was one of the haunts where that *coterie* assembled.

At Messrs. Colburn's, in this street, was published from its commencement, the *New Monthly Magazine.* It was started as a high Tory rival against the *Monthly Magazine* of Sir Richard Phillips. In 1820 Thomas Campbell became its nominal editor,

Physician." Redding accepted them, and ordered them to be set up in type, and to appear in the magazine. "It will scarcely be credited, but it is a fact," writes Mr. Redding, "that the packet was opened, Mr. Warren's paper canvassed among Colburn's *employés*, represented to him as not worth a sixpence, and returned by him to Mr.

SIR BENJAMIN BRODIE.   (*See page* 310.)

the lion's share of the work, however, falling to Mr. C. Redding, on account of the poet's careless and indolent habits. About the same time it began to number among its writers Serjeant Talfourd. In connection with Mr. Colburn and the *New Monthly Magazine*, Cyrus Redding tells a good story with reference to a writer who subsequently became famous. Mr. Samuel Warren, then unknown to fame, sent for publication in the *New Monthly*, to Tom Campbell, or to his colleague, Cyrus Redding, the first few sheets of his "Diary of a Late

Warren without my knowledge. . . . The intercepted paper came out afterwards in *Blackwood*, and was followed by others equally good. Colburn then apologised, but not till the mischief was done. His regret was the greater because it appeared in his rival's pages." But what is the good of a responsible editor if his judgments are thus liable to revision by every ignorant shopman of a publisher? Other contributors afterwards joined the staff—viz., J. P. Curran, Joanna Baillie, Horace and James Smith, Bryan W. Procter ("Barry Corn-

HANOVER SQUARE, IN 1750.

171

wall "), Sir John Bowring, Henry Roscoe, W. M. Praed, Blanco White, "Morocco" Jackson, Miss Mary R. Mitford, Mrs. Hemans, and R. L. Shiel.

No. 8 is the publishing house of Messrs. Richard Bentley and Son. From this shop were issued the famous "Ingoldsby Legends," by the Rev. R. H. Barham (better known by his literary name of Thomas Ingoldsby); they were first sent as contributions to *Bentley's Miscellany*, and afterwards published separately. Mr. R. H. Barham, the witty author of these "Legends," was a minor Canon of St. Paul's and the vicar of a parish in Kent. He died in 1845. Charles Dickens and other authors frequently met at Mr. Bentley's table, and it was he who was the first editor of the *Miscellany*. At Messrs. Churchill's, the medical publishers (No. 11), are the offices of the British Medical Benevolent Fund, founded in 1836, for the relief of medical men, their widows and orphans, in temporary difficulty or distress, granting annuities to those who are incapable of providing for themselves. About 200 cases, it is stated, are relieved during the year.

In this street lived Mr. Joseph Planta, who for many years held the office of Under-Secretary of State for Foreign Affairs; and here he used to entertain George Canning, Baron Bulow, Lord Strangford, and other celebrities of that time, as his constant guests.

Here, too, lived Admiral Sir Joseph Sydney Yorke, K.C.B., some time M.P. for Sandwich, who was accidentally drowned in 1831. He was the third son of the Hon. Charles Yorke, who was appointed Lord High Chancellor in 1770, and who died suddenly, whilst his patent of creation as Lord Morden was in process of completion.

At No. 16 was, till 1882, the Royal Archæological Institute of Great Britain and Ireland. This body, for many years settled in the Haymarket, was established in 1843 under the title of the British Archæological Association. Its objects are "to investigate, preserve, and illustrate all ancient monuments of history, customs, art, &c., relating to the United Kingdom." The society possesses a good library, and a small but valuable collection of antiquities and drawings. The meetings of the members are held monthly during the London season, and the annual general Archæological Congress takes place in one of the cathedral cities or great towns of the kingdom.

CHAPTER XXV.

HANOVER SQUARE AND ITS NEIGHBOURHOOD.

"O could I as Harlequin frisk,
And thou be my Columbine fair,
My wand should, with one magic whisk,
Transport us to Hanover Square:
St. George's should lend us its aid."—"*Rejected Addresses.*"

Statue of William Pitt—Description of the Square in the Last Century—Harewood House—"Beau" Lascelles—Lord Rodney, and his Daughter's Clandestine Marriage—Lord Palmerston's Residence—Sir William Fairfax and Mrs. Somerville, and other Distinguished Residents—Zoological Society—Royal Agricultural Society—Royal College of Chemistry—The Oriental Club—The Arts Club—Hanover Square Rooms, now the Hanover Club—The building of New Streets in the Neighbourhood—Tenterden Street—Royal Academy of Music—Brook Street—George Street—St. George's Church—Fashionable Weddings—Dr. Dodd's Desire to become Rector—The Parish Burial-grounds—Distinguished Residents in George Street—Junior Travellers' Club—Maddox Street—Architectural Museum—The "Golden Star" Inn—Mill Street—Conduit Street—The Locality Three Hundred Years ago—Limmer's Hotel—The "Coach and Horses"—The "Prince of Wales" Coffee-house—A Batch of Architectural Societies—Trinity Chapel.

THIS square—perhaps in one way among the most popular in London, so closely connected as it is with the fashionable marriages solemnised in St. George's Church—was entirely unbuilt in 1716; but its name, which is mentioned in the plans of London of the year 1720, bears testimony to the loyalty of the Londoners who worshipped the "rising sun" in the person of George I. Both in the square itself, and in George Street adjoining, there are several specimens of the German style of building. The square covers about four acres of ground, and the centre is enclosed with a neat iron railing, within which, on the north side, is a colossal bronze statue of William Pitt, by Sir Francis Chantrey. This statue was not set up until 1831, when the statesman had been dead for more than a quarter of a century; it cost £7,000; and Mr. Peter Cunningham, who was present on the occasion, records the fact, that on the very day of its erection some advanced reformers endeavoured, though in vain, to pull it down with ropes. The figure is upright, in the act of speaking, and is one of the finest statues in London.

The *Weekly Medley*, in 1717, contains the following observations, which are interesting at the present time :—" Round about the new square, which is building near Oxford Road [now Oxford Street], there are so many other edifices that a whole magnificent city seems to be risen out of the ground, and one would wonder how it should find a new set of inhabitants. It is said it will be called by the name of Hanover Square. The chief persons that we hear of who are to inhabit that place when it is finished, having bought houses, are these following:—The Lord Cadogan, a general; also General Carpenter, General Wills, General Evans, General Pepper, the two General Stuarts, and several others whose names we have not been able to learn." It would appear, therefore, that its first tenants were mostly of the military order.

Strype tells us that the houses which in his time were in the process of creation were rapidly taken up; one of them he specifies by name, the mansion of "My Lord Cowper, late Lord High Chancellor of England;" and he adds that it was in contemplation to change the common place of execution from Tyburn to somewhere near Kingsland, in order to spare that square and the houses thereabouts—it must be supposed that he really means their inmates—the inconvenience and annoyance which might be caused by the execution of malefactors, which at that time went on rather by wholesale. But the square, though so aristocratic in its earlier inhabitants, does not appear to have been well looked after. At all events, we find plenty of complaints as to its condition half a century later. "As to Hanover Square," writes the author of "Critical Observations on the Buildings and Improvements of London," published in 1771, "I do not know what to make of it. It is neither open nor enclosed. Every convenience is railed out, and every nuisance railed in. Carriages have a narrow, ill-paved street to turn round in, and the middle has the air of a cow-yard, where blackguards assemble in the winter to play at hustle-cap, up to the ankles in dirt. This is the more to be regretted, as the square in question is susceptible of improvement at a small expense."

We gather from Dr. Hogg's work on "London as it is," published in 1837, that several at all events of the streets near Hanover Square, on the Grosvenor property, were not originally public thoroughfares. But the only gate now existing which bars the passage of carriages in this neighbourhood is that in Harewood Place, between the north side of this square and Oxford Street.

On the north side of the square, with its stables facing Oxford Street, is Harewood House, the residence of the Earl of Harewood. Of the interior of this mansion, Mr. T. Raikes gives us the following peep in his amusing "Journal:"—"The finest collection of old china in England will be found in the house of Lord Harewood, in Hanover Square, a nobleman whose agricultural pursuits and simple habits would give little reason to suppose that he was possessed of such an expensive article of luxury and taste. Fagg, the Chinaman, since the renewed rage in England for *old valuables*, has in vain offered Lord Harewood immense sums for this collection; but it was originally made by his elder brother, well known then as Beau Lascelles, who died unmarried, in 1814, and is always preserved in the family as a *souvenir* of him. The brothers were much attached to each other; but never was a greater contrast seen than in the refinement of the one and the simplicity of the other. Beau Lascelles was the essence of fashion of that day. He was a handsome man, rather inclined to be fat, which gave him a considerable resemblance to George Prince of Wales, whom he evidently imitated in his dress and manner. He was very high bred and amicable in society, and his taste in all that surrounded him was undeniable; his house, his carriages, horses, and servants, without any attempt at gaudy trappings, were the admiration of all the town, from the uniform neatness and beauty of their *tenue*. The *ensemble* of his equipage when he went to Court on a birthday might really be compared to a highly-finished toy. His house, though not large, was a museum of curiosities, selected with great taste and judgment, at a time when he had few competitors; and, had they all been preserved, they would now be of incalculable value. His life was luxurious but short, as he died at the age of fifty."

The gallant admiral, Lord Rodney, was living in this square in 1792. It is well known that his favourite daughter eloped to Gretna Green with Captain Chambers, a son of the eminent architect, Sir William Chambers. At first he was inclined to be angry, but he soon relented, and merely said, "Well, well! what is done can't be undone; but it's odd that my own family is the only crew that I never could manage, and I only hope that Jessy will never mutiny under her new commander!"

The large house in the south-western corner, towards the close of the last century, was the town residence of Lord and Lady Palmerston, the father and mother of the late Premier. The house, which was one of the great centres of political and social reunions, is noted by Lambert, in his "History of London," as "the best piece of brick-work in the metropolis."

In 1816 Mrs. Somerville was residing in this square along with her parents, Sir William and

Lady Fairfax, and gratifying her new-born taste for astronomical and other science by attending the lectures at the Royal Institution. Here the Fairfaxes used to have little evening parties, and it was here that the late Sir Charles Lyell (as recorded in Mrs. Somerville's " Life ") first met his future wife, the beautiful Miss Horner.

Among the other distinguished residents in the square have been Field-Marshal Lord Cobham, the owner of Stowe, and the friend of Pope; Sir James Clark, Physician to Her Majesty the Queen in 1841; and Ambrose Philips, the poet satirised by Pope, and author of the " Distressed Mother," who died in 1749. The mansion at the corner of Brook Street, now rebuilt and turned into the London and County Bank, was formerly called Downshire House. In 1826 it was inhabited by the Marquis of Salisbury. In 1835 it was held by another tenant, Prince Talleyrand, the ex-Minister of State in France, who used to gather round him the wits, *literati*, and diplomatists of the time. We shall meet him again at Kensington.

Of the houses which form the north-east side, one is occupied by the Zoological Society, whose offices have been located here since about 1846. The society was instituted in the year 1826, under the auspices of Sir Humphry Davy, Sir Stamford Raffles, and other eminent individuals, " for the advancement of zoology, and the introduction and exhibition of subjects of the animal kingdom, alive or in a state of preservation." In 1829 the society had a museum in Bruton Street, and subsequently in Leicester Square. This society took the place of the Zoological Club of the Linnæan Society, which had been broken up by internal differences. We shall have more to say about this society presently on reaching its gardens in the Regent's Park.

The Royal Agricultural Society of England has its offices at No. 12 (next door to the above). This society was established in 1838, for improving the general system of agriculture in this country, and engaging talented men in the investigation of such subjects as are of deep practical importance to the British farmer. Agricultural meetings are held annually in London and the country; the latter including a cattle-show, an exhibition of agricultural implements and inventions, and the awarding of prizes in either department. Its presidents, chosen annually, are almost always noblemen of high standing as practical farmers and breeders of stock.

At No. 15, on the north side of the square, and extending back into Oxford Street, is the Royal College of Chemistry. It was founded in 1845 " for the purpose of affording adequate opportunities for instruction in practical chemistry at a moderate expense, and for promoting the advancement of chemical science by means of a well-appointed laboratory and other appliances." The first stone of the laboratory, which has a handsome elevation on the south side of Oxford Street, was laid by the late Prince Consort in January, 1846. The fees for the students are in proportion to the number of days in each week that they attend.

At the north-west angle of the square, facing Tenterden Street, is the Oriental Club, founded about the year 1825, mainly through the influence and exertions of that accomplished writer and traveller, the late Sir John Malcolm. It was at first intended for gentlemen who have belonged to the civil or military services in India, or have been connected with the government of any of our Eastern dependencies. The building is constructed after the manner of club-houses in general, having only one tier of windows above the ground-floor. The interior received some fresh embellishment about the year 1850, some of the rooms and ceilings having been decorated in a superior style by Collman, and it contains some fine portraits of Indian and other celebrities, such as Lord Clive, Nott, Pottinger, Sir Eyre Coote, &c. This club is jocosely called by one of the critics of " Michael Angelo Titmarsh," the " horizontal jungle " off Hanover Square.

At No. 17 was established, about the year 1865, the Arts Club. It was instituted " for the purpose of facilitating the social intercourse of those who are connected, either professionally or as amateurs, with art, literature, or science." Charles Dickens belonged to this club, which numbers among its members very many of the Royal Academicians and others of the most rising artists of the day, with a goodly sprinkling of literary celebrities.

On the east side of the square, at the south-eastern corner of Hanover Street, the large building now known as the Hanover Square Club, or Cercle des Étrangers, had for many years, down to the beginning of 1875, borne the name of the Queen's Concert Rooms, more popularly known as the Hanover Square Rooms. The site of the building was anciently called the Mill Field (from a mill which adjoined it, and which Mill Street, hard by, still commemorates), or Kirkham Close. It was originally in the parish of St. Martin's-in-the-Fields, though in 1778 it was joined on to that of St. George's, Hanover Square. It appears to have formed part of the premises in the occupation of Matthew, Lord Dillon, the ground landlord being the Earl of Plymouth, who sold it to Lord Dunmore, who re-sold it to Sir John Gallini, by whom the house and the original concert-room were erected, in the first half of the reign of George III. Gallini, an Italian by extraction, but a Swiss by birth, who, coming to England, was engaged to teach dancing to the then youthful royal family, realised a fortune at the West-end, received the honour of knighthood, and married Lady Betty Bertie, daughter of Lord Abingdon. In 1774 Gallini, joining with John Christian Bach and Charles F. Abel, converted the premises into an "Assembly Room," no doubt, in order to act as a counter attraction to the fashionable gatherings in Soho Square, under the auspices of Mrs. Cornelys, and other places where music went hand-in-glove with masked balls and other frivolous dissipations. Two years later we find Gallini buying up the shares of his partners and carrying on the rooms upon his own account. Supported by the musical talent of Bach, Abel, and Lord Abingdon, and also, in emergencies, by the purse of the last, Gallini carried on here, from 1785 to 1793, a series of concerts, for which he contrived to gain the patronage of the Court. George III. himself was accustomed frequently to attend these concerts, together with Queen Charlotte; and it is said that his Majesty showed such an active interest in the performances that he had a room added to the side, called the Queen's Tea Room: in this apartment, over the mantelpiece, was fixed a large gilt looking-glass, which he presented to the rooms for ever. In 1776 a committee of noblemen and gentlemen, consisting of Lord Sandwich, Lord Dudley and Ward, the Bishop of Durham, Sir Watkin Williams Wynn, Sir R. Jebb, and the Hon. Mr. Pelham, established the well-known "Concerts of Ancient Music," to the directorship of which soon afterwards were added Lord Fitzwilliam and Lord Paget, subsequently the Earl of Uxbridge. These memorable performances, which commenced their first season at the Tottenham Street Rooms, near Tottenham Court Road (subsequently converted into a theatre), and which from 1794 to 1804 had their head-quarters at the King's Theatre in the Haymarket, were removed hither in the latter year, and continued to flourish under the patronage of royalty and the leaders of the aristocracy—including the late Prince Consort, the Duke of Wellington, Lord Westmoreland, and others—down to June, 1848, when they were discontinued. King George III. took the warmest interest in these concerts, and not only occupied the royal box with his Queen and family night after night, but would constantly write out the programmes of the performances with his own hand. It is said the directors of these concerts paid Sir

John Gallini a rental of £1,000 a year for the use of the rooms. Mr. Greatorex was the conductor of these concerts from the commencement of the century down to his death in 1831, when he was succeeded by Mr. W. Knyvett. "The Concert of Ancient Music, at present more generally known by the appellation of the King's Concert," writes Sir Richard Phillips, in 1804, "is a branch that seceded from the Academy of Ancient Music. . . . It generally commences in February, and continues weekly on Wednesdays till the end of May. Six directors, chosen from among the nobility, select in turn the pieces for the night, and regulate all its principal concerns. The leading feature of its rules is the utter exclusion of all modern music. So rigid are its laws on this head, that no composition less than twenty-five years old can be performed here, without the forfeiture of a considerable sum from the director of the night." He adds, that two difficulties arise out of this stringent rule, a want of variety in the performances, and the "discouragement of living genius."

These rooms were also long used for the Philharmonic Concerts, established by Messrs. Cramer and Co., in 1813, under the auspices of the then Prince Regent. They were first held in the Argyll Rooms, at the corner of Argyll Place, and on those premises being burnt down in 1831, they were given at the concert-room of the Opera House; but they were transferred to Hanover Square in 1833. It may not, perhaps, be out of place to mention here that the annual performance of the *Messiah* for the benefit of the Royal Society of Musicians was given here from 1785 to 1848.

In Jesse's "Life of Beau Brummell," the incident which is said to have given rise to the estrangement between the Prince Regent and the "Beau" is stated to have occurred at these rooms, although other writers have fixed upon St. James's Street as the scene, as we have mentioned in our account of that street; nevertheless, the story told by Jesse will bear repeating:—"Lord Alvanley, Brummell, Henry Pierrepoint, and Sir Harry Mildmay, gave at the Hanover Square Rooms a *fête*, which was called the Dandies' Ball. Alvanley was a friend of the Duke of York; Harry Mildmay, young, and had never been introduced to the Prince Regent; Pierrepoint knew him slightly; and Brummell was at daggers-drawn with his Royal Highness. No invitation, however, was sent to the Prince; but the ball excited much interest and expectation, and to the surprise of the amphitryons, a communication was received from his Royal Highness, intimating his wish to be present. Nothing, therefore, was left but to send him an invitation, which was done in due form, and in the name of the four spirited givers of the ball. The next question was, how were they to receive their guest? which, after some discussion, was arranged thus:— When the approach of the Prince was announced, each of the four gentlemen took, in due form, a candle in his hand. Pierrepoint, as knowing the Prince, stood nearest the door with his wax-light,

were in front, and saw the Prince's face, say that he was cut to the quick by the aptness of the satire."

The entertainments provided in these rooms were not strictly confined to balls and concerts, for lectures, "readings," and public meetings innumerable have been held here; and in 1798 Miss Linwood here exhibited her "needlework pictures," prior to their final removal to Leicester

HAREWOOD HOUSE. (See page 315.)

and Mildmay, as being young and void of offence, opposite. Alvanley, with Brummell opposite, stood immediately behind the other two. The Prince at length arrived, and, as was expected, spoke civilly and with recognition to Pierrepoint, and then turned and spoke a few words to Mildmay; advancing, he addressed several sentences to Lord Alvanley, and then turning towards Brummell, looked at him, but as if he did not know who he was or why he was there, and without bestowing on him the slightest symptom of recognition. It was then, at the very instant he passed on, that Brummell, seizing with infinite fun and readiness the notion that they were unknown to each other, said aloud, for the purpose of being heard, 'Alvanley, who's your fat friend?' Those who

Square. In 1838-9, Dr. Chalmers, the celebrated Scotch divine, here delivered a series of lectures on the Church of England.

In 1845, at the death of the Misses Gallini, Sir John's nieces (the founders of the Roman Catholic Church in Grove Road, St. John's Wood), their freehold interest in Hanover Square Rooms was bought by Mr. Robert Cocks, the eminent musical publisher, who subsequently let them on a lease of twenty-one years to the committee of the club above mentioned. It is not, however, only with the two ancient institutions named above that the history of these rooms was interwoven, but with that of Mr. Henry Leslie's choir, and with the concerts of the Royal Academy of Music in Tenterden Street close by, which renewed its performances here in 1862. The large room, in its original state, was dull and heavy, owing to the architectural style of the date at which it was built; at one end was the ponderous royal box, and almost the only tasteful decoration consisted also gilt. The panels over the looking-glasses were filled with medallions, painted in *bas relief*, of the most celebrated composers—Handel, Beethoven, Bach, Rossini, Purcell, Weber, Haydn—accompanied by their names and dates; and the plinth

GEORGE STREET, HANOVER SQUARE, IN 1800.

of some paintings by the hand of Cipriani. In the winter of 1861-62, however, the rooms underwent a complete restoration and re-decoration, and they became the most comfortable concert-rooms in London, to say nothing of their great superiority to most large buildings in respect of acoustic properties. The large room had a slightly arched roof, richly gilt and ornamented with pictures; the walls on either side of the room were adorned with Corinthian columns with ornamental capitals, round the room was decorated in imitation of marbles of various patterns and colours.

On Saturday evening, December 19, 1874, took place the very last entertainment ever given in these time-honoured rooms. Mr. Cocks having placed them at the disposal of the Royal Academy of Music, a full orchestral and choral concert was given under the direction of Mr. Walter Macfarren. The work of altering the building to suit the requirements of a club was commenced immediately afterwards. The large room has been preserved unaltered, as far as possible; but in other respects the building has undergone a thorough transformation, and has been raised a couple of storeys in height; the additional floors being devoted to chambers for such members as may wish to make the club their home, either permanently or temporarily. On the ground-floor is the newspaper-room, which occupies the position of the old supper-room, to the left of the entrance in Hanover Street; the secretary's office, and also a writing-room. The principal lavatories, &c., are in the basement. The grand staircase, entirely of stone, is ornamented with statues holding jets of gas, and at the top is a large skylight, with an inner light of coloured glass. The first floor contains a smoking-room, card-room, wine-bar, and also the dining-hall. The last-named apartment has been formed out of the old concert-room, which has been somewhat curtailed in length; the east end, where the royal box formerly stood, is new; the pictures in the ceiling, mentioned above, where practicable, have been restored, and new ones inserted where necessary. On the second floor is a billiard-room, and also the drawing-room, which overlooks Hanover Square. The Hanover Square Club, as now established—whose object is much the same as that of the Travellers', embracing the introduction of foreigners—is not the first of that name which has existed; and it is probable that some house in the neighbourhood, in the time of the first two Georges, formed the head-quarters of a political association of persons zealous for the Hanoverian succession, which bore the same name; but the exact house which it occupied is not known.

In 1736 the *General Evening Post* of September 23rd contains the following paragraph, which shows pretty clearly the condition of the immediate neighbourhood of Hanover Square at that time, so far as the building of streets is concerned:—" Two rows of fine houses are building from the end of Great Marlborough Street through the waste ground and his Grace the Duke of Argyll's gardens into Oxford Road, from the middle of which new building a fine street is to be made through his Grace's house, King Street, and Swallow Street [now covered by Regent Street], to the end of Hanover Square, Brook Street, and the north part of Grosvenor Square, the middle of his Grace's house being pulled down for that purpose; and the two wings lately added to his house are to be the corners of the street which is now building." The street here spoken of is now called Princes Street, which opens into the north-east corner of the square.

This and Hanover Street, which connects the square with Regent Street at its south-east corner, were built about the same time, and bear testimony to the strong hold which the succession of the House of Brunswick had already taken on the feelings of the nation. Both streets are deficient in literary or personal associations; but it may be noted, that in the former Miss Emily Faithfull first started her "Victoria Press," through which she inaugurated her efforts to obtain remunerative employment for women.

In Tenterden Street, which connects the square at its north-west angle by a circuitous route with Oxford Street and the northern end of New Bond Street, is the Royal Academy of Music. It has been devoted to its present use almost since the formation of the Academy. The Academy itself was established in the year 1822, and a few years afterwards a charter was obtained from George IV. Here the Academy used to give its concerts until 1862, when the latter were transferred, as already stated, to the Hanover Square Rooms. The object of the Academy is the instruction of youth of either sex in every branch of musical education; and they are taught in classes by the first professors at a trifling charge. Since its foundation, it has supplied a large number of instrumental performers of no mean eminence to the various orchestras of London; and many of its pupils have become leaders and conductors of concerts, and also eminent musicians, whilst several have distinguished themselves as composers. Among the students here was Mr. Charles Dickens's sister Fanny, to fetch whom the future "Boz" would call at its doors every Sunday morning, and bring her back at night after spending the day in their wretched home in Upper Gower Street. The house, No. 4, on the north side, opposite the Oriental Club, was at one time the town residence of the Herberts, Earls of Carnarvon, who here used to entertain King George III. and his family with syllabub and tea in the terraced garden behind, which commanded a view of the Uxbridge or Tyburn Road. On the gardens of Lord Carnarvon's House, at the back, stands the carriage-factory of Messrs. Laurie and Marner, of which we shall have more to say when dealing with Oxford Street.

Brook Street, which connects the south-west angle of the square with New Bond Street and Grosvenor Square, will be more properly treated in a future chapter. Only a few of its houses stand to the east of Bond Street, and to these no literary interest attaches, unless it is worth while to mention the fact that one of them was the last abode of

Messrs. Saunders and Otley, librarians and publishers to the Queen, before the break-up of that firm, about the year 1865.

George Street, which dates its erection from the building of the square itself, and which, as we have observed above, is similar to it in the character of its architecture, passes from the centre of the south side of the square into Conduit Street. Of this street the author of "A New Critical Review of the Public Buildings of London" remarks that there is an inconsistency and a departure from the true rule of taste in making it wider at the upper than at the lower end, as quite reversing the perspective; and yet he says that the view down George Street from the top of the square, with St. George's Church in the front, is fine, and indeed "the most entertaining in the whole city," though it ought properly to end in something more attractive to the eye than the shops which now stand on the site of Trinity Chapel, in Conduit Street.

In a somewhat similar strain, but more rhapsodical style, Ralph remarks: "The sides of the square, the area in the middle, the breaks of building that form the entrance to the vista [of George Street], but above all the beautiful projection of the portico of St. George's Church, are all circumstances that unite in beauty and make the scene perfect." For ourselves, we prefer decidedly the view looking *up* the street towards the square, which throws the portico into bold relief against the sky. An *as*cending view of a church, too, is almost always preferable to what may be called a descending view.

The parish of St. George's was "carved" out of that of St. Martin's-in-the-Fields, and Mr. John Timbs says that the site of the church was given by a General Stewart. The fabric has been much admired by those who think that style of architecture appropriate for religious edifices. It was built in 1722-4; the designer and architect was named James. This was, to use Pennant's quaint expression, "one of the fifty [new churches] voted by Parliament, to give this part of the town the air of the capital of a Christian country." The writer of "A New Critical Review of the Public Buildings of the Metropolis," in 1736, mentions it as "one of the most elegant in London; the portico is stately and august, the steeple handsome and well-proportioned, and the north and east prospects very well worth a sincere approbation;" he complains, however, that its position is such as not to allow its beauties to be seen, for, "though situated in the very centre of the vista that leads to Grosvenor Square," it is so blocked up by houses as "only to be seen in profile." No doubt the beautiful pro-

portions of its lofty Corinthian portico would form a fine object if there had been a broad street leading from Grosvenor Square to its western front; nevertheless, as it is, it is seen to great advantage from the junction of George Street and Conduit Street. The interior has been decorated in an ecclesiastical style, so far as possible, of late years. Over the altar is a fine painting of the Last Supper, ascribed to Sir James Thornhill; it is surmounted by a painted window, said to be of the sixteenth century; but the two ornaments do not harmonise. The window itself is said to have formerly belonged to a convent at Malines. The subject is "The Genealogy of Our Lord, according to His human nature, as derived from Jesse through the twelve kings of Judah, previous to the Babylonian captivity. In the centre of the lower part is the figure of Jesse seated; the roots of a vine are on his head; on his right are Aaron and Esaias; on his left, Moses and Elias."

Till within the last few years—or between the close of the last century and the year 1850, when Grosvenor Square was the centre of rank and fashion—St. George's enjoyed a monopoly of "fashionable" weddings, which has passed into a proverb. Here Sir William Hamilton was married on the 6th of September, 1791, to Emma Harte, afterwards so well known as "Emma Lady Hamilton," the friend of Nelson. Horace Walpole, in announcing the marriage to the Miss Berrys, tells them that "Sir William has just married his gallery of statues," alluding to the fact that his wife used to sit as a model to artists. Here, too, was married in the year 1839, the Marquis of Douro (now Duke of Wellington). The attesting witnesses, whose signatures may be seen in the marriage register, are his noble father, the great duke, and his three brothers—all peers of the realm—the Marquis Wellesley, Lord Maryborough, and Lord Cowley.

Mr. F. Locker, in one of his charming volumes of "Vers de Société," "takes off" to perfection a fashionable wedding at St. George's, and epigrammatically expresses all the good wishes which usually attend the brides who are "led to the altar" there:—

"She pass'd up the aisle on the arm of her sire,
     A delicate lady in bridal attire,
          Fair emblem of virgin simplicity.
     Half London was there, and, my word! there were few
     Who stood by the altar or hid in a pew,
          But envied Lord Nigel's felicity.

"O beautiful bride! still so meek in thy splendour,
     So frank in thy love and its trusting surrender,
          Going hence you will leave us the town dim!
     May happiness wing to thy bosom unbought,
     And Nigel, esteeming his bliss as he ought,
          Prove worthy thy worship, confound him!"

But "fashionable" as the marriages mostly were that were performed in this church, they had their rude accompaniments : for instance, there were fees to be paid to "his Majesty's Royal Peal of Marrow-bones and Cleavers : instituted 1719." "The book of their receipts," says a writer in 1829, "it seems, they carefully preserve. By the proceedings against the St. George's 'Marrow-bone and Cleaver Club' at Marlborough Street Office, by the Dowager Lady Harland, in their attempting to extort from her newly-married daughter, to whom they presented their silver plate, ornamented with blue ribbon and a chaplet of flowers, it appears the constable pre-sented before the magistrate the book belonging to them, containing the names of a great many persons of the first consequence, who had been married at St. George's, Hanover Square ; all of whom had put down their names for a sovereign. In the course of a year, the sum gathered by these greasy fellows, as marriage-offerings, was £416 !"

The rectors of St. George's, in spite of the fashion-able situation of the church, have not been on the whole distinguished, nor have many of them at-tained high dignities in the Church. To obtain this rectory the notorious Dr. Dodd offered to Lady Apsley, wife of the then Lord Chancellor, a *douceur* of three thousand pounds.

There are two burying-grounds belonging to this parish—one in the rear of Mount Street, Grosvenor Square, and the other on the north side of the Bayswater Road, Uxbridge Road. In the latter burial-ground for nearly fifty years reposed the remains of the gallant general, Sir Thomas Picton, who fell at Waterloo ; but in 1859 they were re-moved and deposited, with all due military honours, in St. Paul's Cathedral. There, too, lies poor Law-rence Sterne : we shall speak of him again when we reach Bayswater.

No. 25, about half way down on the eastern side, was the residence, for nearly a century, first of John Copley, the Royal Academician, and afterwards of his son, John Singleton Copley, Lord Lyndhurst, both of whom died here ; the former in 1815, and the latter in 1863. The future Chancellor was born in America in 1772, and at an early age was brought over to England by his parents, who were staunch royalists. The father was presented at Court, obtained the favour of George III. and Queen Charlotte, and enjoyed a prosperous career. The son obtained the highest honours at Cam-bridge, was called to the bar in due course, entered Parliament in middle life, and soon rose to be Solicitor and Attorney-General, and Master of the Rolls, and in 1827 succeeded Eldon as Lord Chancellor. He enjoyed the confidence of the

Duke of Wellington and Sir Robert Peel, and at one time was sent for by the King to form an administration. The Whig party for many years feared nothing so much as the withering sarcasm of his annual reviews of the Parliamentary session, delivered by him in his place in the House of Lords. He again held the Great Seal under Sir Robert Peel in 1834-5 and in 1841-6. The walls of his house in George Street were hung with his father's historical paintings, including the "Death of Wolfe," the "Death of Lord Chatham," &c. It is remarkable that the united ages of the painter, the ex-Chancellor, and a sister amounted to nearly 270 years. After Lord Lyndhurst's death his house and the adjoining one were pulled down, and on their site was built the magnificent mansion of Mr. Gore-Langton.

The house, No. 15, formerly the town residence of the late Sir George Wombwell, one of the leaders of fashion in his day, and a friend of Count D'Orsay and the Fitzclarences, is now the Junior Travellers' Club.

Maddox Street, which runs from Regent Street to the east end of St. George's Church, dates from about 1720, and is probably named after the en-terprising person who built it. In this street is the Museum of Building Appliances, which is in direct communication with, and indeed forms a part of, the Architectural Societies' House in Conduit Street. This museum, which was established in 1866, and enlarged in 1873, is "devoted to the reception of drawings, prospectuses, models, and specimen manufactures of every kind pertaining to the building trades." It was founded chiefly as a means of affording to patentees and inventors an "opportunity for the introduction of their improve-ments to those most interested in their adoption." The museum is open free daily throughout the year.

In this street is an inn now called the "Golden Star," but formerly the "Coach and Horses." It is remarkable that the "Golden Star" does not figure in Mr. Larwood's "History of Sign-boards." Less than half a century ago there were more than fifty inns in London rejoicing in the sign of the "Coach and Horses ;" but their number is much reduced now, having been superseded by railways and steam.

Close by Maddox Street, and also at the back of St. George's Church, is Mill Street, which per-petuates the fact of the mill standing hard by the site of Hanover Square, as mentioned above.

Conduit Street, which extends from Regent Street to Bond Street, across the south end of George Street, still preserves the memory of the conduit which stood in the centre of Conduit Mead—a large field—as lately as the year 1700, on which New Bond Street and its neighbouring streets have since been erected, but whereon Carew Mildmay told Pennant, in 1780, that he remembered shooting woodcocks when a boy. The same thing is said also of his contemporary, General Oglethorpe, who died in 1785, having lived to be upwards of ninety, and who, as Macaulay tells us, had "shot birds in this neighbourhood in Queen Anne's reign."

The Conduit Field in old days was a great "meet" for the Nimrods of the City. "On the 18th of September, 1562," writes Stow, "the Lord Mayor Harper, the aldermen, and divers other worshipful persons, rid to the Conduit-head before dinner. They hunted the hare, and killed her, and thence to dine at the Conduit-head. The Chamberlain gave them good cheer; and after dinner they hunted the fox. There was a great cry for a mile, then the hounds killed him at St. Giles's; great hallooing at his death and blowing of horns; and thence the Lord Mayor and all his company rode through London to his place in Lombard Street." It is amusing, after an interval of more than three hundred years, to read of a Lord Mayor going out from Cheapside and finding the hare and the fox in Marylebone, or possibly even nearer to the City, and thence making his return journey to his home in Lombard Street to the yelping of dogs and the lusty cheer of the huntsman's horn.

At the corner of Conduit Street and George Street is Limmer's Hotel, once an evening resort for the sporting world; in fact, it was a midnight "Tattersall's," where nothing was heard but the language of the turf, and where men with not very clean hands used to make up their books. "Limmer's," says a popular writer, "was the most dirty hotel in London; but in the gloomy, comfortless coffee-room might be seen many members of the rich squirearchy, who visited London during the sporting season. This hotel was frequently so crowded that a bed could not be had for any amount of money; but you could always get a good plain English dinner, an excellent bottle of port, and some famous gin-punch."

At the corner of this and Mill Street is the sign of the "Coach and Horses," serving as a sort of tap to "Limmer's," still bearing testimony to the sporting associations of the neighbourhood. Whilst the gentlemen Jehus put up at "Limmer's," their coachmen and grooms met here, and discussed all sorts of questions connected with horseflesh at a sociable "free and easy."

In this street was the "Prince of Wales" coffee-house, in which the mad Lord Camelford picked up, most gratuitously, his last quarrel with his friend Mr. Best, about a lady named Simmons—a quarrel which led to the duel fought by them in the grounds of Holland House, and his lordship's tragic death.

At No. 9, on the north side, between George Street and Regent Street, is a house formerly the town residence of the Earl of Macclesfield, but now entirely devoted to the architectural and building interests, for it contains within its walls the offices and rooms of the Architectural Association, the Architectural Publication Society, the Architectural Union Company, the District Surveyors' Association, the Photographic Society, the Provident Institution of Builders' Foremen and Clerks of Works, the Royal Institute of British Architects, the Society of Biblical Archæology, the Society for the Encouragement of the Fine Arts, and also an entrance to the Museum of Building Appliances, mentioned above. The rooms and gallery of the Architectural Association are used constantly during the "season" for exhibitions of architectural designs and paintings. The Royal Institute of British Architects was established in 1835 for the purpose of "facilitating the acquirement of architectural knowledge, for the promotion of the different sciences connected with it, and for establishing a uniformity and respectability of practice in the profession." The society has here founded a library of works, manuscripts, and drawings, illustrative, practically and theoretically, of the art; the publication of curious and interesting communications; the collection of a museum of antiquities, models, casts, &c.; with provision for performing experiments on the nature and properties of building materials. Its president is Mr. Horace Jones.

On the south side of the street, nearly facing George Street, is Trinity Chapel, a curious and interesting relic of London in the days of the Stuarts. Although they did not form part of the original edifice, yet the walls of the chapel which now present themselves to our view stand on the site of a movable tabernacle, or chapel on wheels, which was built by order of James II., to accompany him in his royal progresses and on his visits to the camp at Hounslow, in order that mass might be celebrated in his presence by his chaplain. The camp was at Hounslow when in the autumn of 1688 the king withdrew and abdicated; and as soon as his abdication was known to be a fact, the chapel was brought up by road to London, and placed upon the site now occupied by its successor. Dr. Tenison—afterwards Archbishop of Canterbury,

BERKELEY SQUARE. (*See page 327.*)

but at that time rector of St. Martin's-in-the-Fields—begged the new king and queen, William and Mary, to make over to him the structure, in order to turn it into a temporary church, or rather chapel of ease, for the use of the outlying portion of the inhabitants of his then wide and scattered parish. It was actually opened for service according to the rites of the Established Church in July, 1691, and among those who were present to hear the first Protestant

of ease," without a district assigned to it; for the commissioners for church building in those days refused to allow a proposal which he made to that effect, on the ground that the site was not freehold. The latter, it appears, had been bestowed on the vicar and churchwardens of St. Martin's for the benefit of the poor of the parish, by whom it was turned into money, being purchased at the close of the last or very early in the present century for

LANSDOWNE HOUSE, IN 1800. (*See page* 327.)

sermon preached within its walls was John Evelyn, who thus writes in his diary :—" This church, being formerly built of timber on Hounslow Heath by King James for the mass priests, being begged by Dr. Tenison, was set up by that public-minded, charitable, and pious man." Pennant tells us that, " after having made as many journeys as the holy house of Loretto," it was altered into " a good building of brick, and has ever since rested on the same site." The houses on either side of the chapel were erected at the same time, forming part of the same insipid design, but such was the prevailing taste that they were then " considered by the public in general as highly ornamental to the street." It appears not to have been Dr. Tenison's fault that Trinity Chapel remained a mere " chapel

a " proprietary " chapel. The speculation would seem to have been successful, for a writer in the *Gentleman's Magazine* mentions it as one of the most fashionable places of worship at the West-end, " no pulpit being more frequently honoured by voluntary discourses from the most eminent dignitaries." Towards the commencement of the present century, the Rev. Dr. Beamish made it by his fervid and eloquent discourses, if not so fashionable, at all events so crowded, that it was impossible to accommodate the congregations which he drew together, without the erection of galleries. The chapel was plain and ugly enough before, but by this addition it was made fairly the most ugly of the then existing proprietary chapels. In the early part of the year 1875, it was decreed by the ground landlord that the site was required for secular building, and that the services in this chapel should be discontinued, and the fabric itself demolished.

George Canning lived for several years at No. 37, next door to the chapel, afterwards the residence of the excellent and benevolent Dr. Elliotson, to whom we are mainly indebted for the science of mesmerism, a study to which he devoted many years of his life, "and whose name," as Mr. John Forster observes, "was for nearly thirty years a synonym with all for unwearied, self-sacrificing, and beneficent service to every one in need." On the same side of the street was formerly, for very many years, before they removed into Brook Street, the shop of Messrs. Saunders and Otley, booksellers to the Queen, and for some time the publishers of "Lodge's Peerage." In this street died

quite suddenly, in 1832, Mr. E. Delmé Radcliffe, Gentleman of the Horse to George IV., whose racing studs he superintended. In his youth he was the best gentleman jockey in England, and lived much in the sporting circles of Carlton House. Mr. Raikes says, in his "Diary," that "from the time that he left Eton he never changed the style of his dress, wearing a single-breasted coat, long breeches, and short white-topped boots." Michael William Balfe, the composer, also resided in this street.

The eminent surgeon, Sir Astley Cooper, whom we have already mentioned in our account of Spring Gardens, lived in this street towards the end of his most successful professional career, after the futile attempt he made to retire from practice, making the large income of £15,000 a year; and here he died "in harness" in 1841.

CHAPTER XXVI.

BERKELEY SQUARE, AND ITS NEIGHBOURHOOD.

"Fountains and trees our wearied pride do please,
E'en in the midst of gilded palaces;
And in our town the prospect gives delight,
Which opens round the country to our sight."—*Sprat.*

Bruton Street—The "Great" Duke of Argyll—Anecdote of Sheridan—Museum of the Zoological Society—Berkeley Square—Lansdowne House and its Occupants—Horace Walpole—Lord Clive—Lady Jersey—Beau Brummell and his "Harbinger of Good Luck"—The Eccentric Sir John Barnard—Highwaymen and Footpads—Hay Hill—Bolton Row—"The Three Chairmen"—"The Running Footman"—Charles Street and its Noted Residents—Hill Street—The Blue-Stocking Club—Davies Street—Lord Byron and Joe Manton—Farm Street and the Roman Catholic Chapel—Mount Street—Martin Van Butchell, the Quack Doctor—The Coburg Hotel.

UNDOUBTEDLY there is a natural pleasure in a *rus in urbe*, which has no counterpart in any *urbs in rure*. It is this feeling to which must be ascribed the fact that in the most crowded parts of this great metropolis we leave open spaces, and plant them with trees, and rejoice to live in "squares" if our means will allow us. Still it was long before Nature asserted her sway. The majority of our squares, except those of Tyburnia and Belgravia, are the growth of the last century; and few of them existed before the accession of George III., their sites up to that time being mostly sheep-walks, paddocks, and kitchen-gardens.

Mr. Timbs tells us, what few of us remember or know, that it was at first attempted to call the squares by the strange and uncouth name of *quad-rantes;* and Maitland, in his "History of London," retains the term, with only a slight alteration, when he mentions "the stately *quadrant* denominated King Square, vulgarly Soho Square." This name is probably known to few except very learned antiquaries, so wholly has it passed out of use.

We wish that we could endorse the words of Mr. John Timbs when he calls the garden spaces

or planted squares the most "recreative" feature of our metropolis. At all events, to the multitude the recreation is that of the eyes alone; for, except Leicester Square, not one of them is accessible to the weary working man, the public being allowed only to stare at them through the iron railings selfishly set round them.

But to proceed. Again bending our steps towards the west, we pass in a parallel line with Piccadilly, but in a somewhat "higher latitude." Leaving Conduit Street, which was our point of divergence at the conclusion of our last chapter, we step across Bond Street into Bruton Street, which leads direct into Berkeley Square. Bruton Street derived its name from Lord Berkeley of Stratton, whom we have already mentioned in connection with Picca-dilly, and whose ancestors were known as the Berkeleys of Bruton. This street has had some distinguished residents in its time; among others, John, the second and "great" Duke of Argyll, who in the reign of William III. was Ambassador in Spain, and, after the Peace of Utrecht, Com-mander of the Forces in Scotland. He took part in the suppression of the rebellion of 1715. This duke is the same who is immortalised by Pope in the following lines :—

> "Argyll, the state's whole thunder born to wield,
> And shake alike the senate and the field."

It may be remembered also that Sir Charles Hanbury Williams in his poems identifies the duke with this street :—

> "Yes! on the great Argyll I often wait
> At charming Sudbrooke or in Bruton Street."

Sheridan also was living in this street in 1786. At this period his house was so beset with duns that, in spite of his seat in Parliament, even the provisions for his family had to be let down the area between the railings, as he was afraid to open the front door. Sir N. W. Wraxall tells a capital story *apropos* of this house and its occupant in that year :—"Sheridan," he writes, "entertained at dinner here a number of the (Whig) opposition leaders, though he laboured all the time under heavy pecuniary embarrassments. All his plate, as well as his books, were lodged in pawn. Having, nevertheless, procured from the pawnbroker an assurance of the liberation of his plate for the day, he applied to Beckett, the celebrated bookseller in Pall Mall, to fill his empty book-cases. Beckett not only agreed to the proposition, but promised to ornament the vacant shelves with some of the most expensive and splendid productions of the British press, provided that two men, expressly sent for the purpose by himself, should be present to superintend their immediate restoration. It was settled finally that these librarians of Beckett's appointment should put on liveries for the occasion, and wait at table. The company having arrived, were shewn into an apartment where, the book-cases being opened for the purpose, they had leisure, before dinner was served, to admire the elegance of Sheridan's literary taste, and the magnificence of his collection. But, as all machinery is liable to accidents, so in this instance a failure had nearly taken place, which must have proved fatal to the entertainment. When everything was ready for serving dinner, it happened that, either from the pawnbroker's distrust, or from some unforeseen delay on his part, the spoons and forks had not arrived. Repeated messages were dispatched to hasten them, and they at last made their appearance ; but so critically, and so late, that there not being time left to clean them, they were thrown into hot water, wiped, and instantly laid on the table. The evening then passed in the most joyous and festive manner. Beckett himself related these circumstances to Sir John Macpherson."

In this street, for a time, resided Lord Brougham, when Lord Chancellor. No. 16 was the town house of the late and present Lord Granville, and at one time that of Lord Chancellor Cottenham. It passed afterwards into the hands of another well-known statesman, Lord Carnarvon. In 1841 No. 26 was the residence of Sir Matthew Tierney the favourite physician of George IV.

In Bruton Street was formerly the Museum of the Zoological Society, before or about the time of the establishment of its gardens in Regent's Park. The studio of Mr. Matthew Noble, the sculptor, was formerly in this street.

Berkeley Square, which we now enter on its eastern side, was built in 1698, and named after John, Lord Berkeley, of Stratton, whose mansion and grounds we have already described as situated on the north side of Piccadilly. From the rear of Devonshire House they extended back to Hay Hill, in the south-east corner of the square. In the centre of the square, which contains about five acres of ground, are some fine, tall, and shady plane-trees, which impart an air of cheerfulness and picturesqueness to the spot. Within the enclosure there was formerly an equestrian statue of George III., erected by the Princess Amelia. The statue, which was executed by Wilton, stood on a clumsy pedestal, and represented the king in the character of Marcus Aurelius. At one time this square was the most fashionable locality in London. The houses are rather heavy and monotonous in appearance ; and a few link-extinguishers may still be seen flanking the doorways, reminding us of the days of sedan-chairs and cumbrous family coaches.

The magnificent mansion standing within its garden and gates, which occupies the southern side of the square, and has been for four generations the town-house of the Marquises of Lansdowne, was originally built by Robert Adam, the architect of the Adelphi, for John, Earl of Bute, the favourite Premier of George III. in his early days. It was scarcely finished when, in 1762, after an administration of about two years, during which he had brought the war with France and Spain to a close by the Treaty of Fontainebleau, Lord Bute suddenly threw up the reins of government, and retired into private life. The act was most unpopular. This magnificent residence, just completed and newly occupied, exposed his lordship to the most malignant comments ; and his enemies asserted that he could not possibly have erected such a mansion by honest and fair means. They concluded, therefore, that he had either received large presents from the Court of France for signing the treaty, or had made large purchases in the public funds, previous to signing its preliminaries. The accusation was made publicly by others as well as by

"Junius," who in the plainest terms accused the earl of selling his country. It is not a little singular that, when some twenty years later the house passed by purchase into the hands of Lord Shelburne, afterwards Marquis of Lansdowne, the same accusation was revived, the public again raising an outcry to the effect that it could not have been bought except by moneys paid to his lordship for concluding the peace of 1783. Lord Shelburne, however, took no notice of the cry, for, according to Jeremy Bentham, he "was the only minister who did not fear the people."

Lord Bute was known to be, or at all events to have been, a poor man until called to the post of Premier; and his enemies were not slow to draw attention to the fact, that he could never have afforded to build such a house either from his patrimony or from his marriage with the daughter of Lady Mary Wortley Montagu. The "scandal" is recorded in the gossiping pages of Sir N. W. Wraxall, who adds, "As little could he be supposed to have amassed during his very short administration enough to suffice for such a building. The only solution of the difficulty, therefore, lay in imagining, however unjustly, that he had either received presents from France, or had made large purchases in the public funds previous to the signature of the preliminaries of peace" with that country. Whatever may have been the real solution of the mystery, there can be no doubt that the mansion brought nearly as much of public odium on Lord Bute as the building of Clarendon House, as we have already seen, had entailed a century before upon Lord Chancellor Hyde.

The story of Lord Bute's first introduction to royal circles is told at considerable length by Sir N. W. Wraxall. The substance of it is that in 1747, whilst living, from motives of economy, at a villa on the banks of the Thames, he was at Egham races, and that a shower coming on, and the Prince of Wales, accidentally finding him without a conveyance, offered to give him a seat in his own carriage, and took him to Cliefden, near Maidenhead, where he stayed the night. He rendered himself extremely acceptable to their royal highnesses, and thus laid the foundation, under the succeeding reign, of his elevation to the premiership—a promotion which may be said to have been a consequence of this turn in the chapter of accidents. When young he had a very handsome person; and long after he became a constant visitor and almost an inmate of Leicester House and of Cliefden, he would frequently play the part of "Lothario" in the private theatricals exhibited by the Duchess of Queensberry for the amusement

of those royal personages—a fact to which Wilkes alludes more than once with a sly *inuendo* in one of his publications. If this be really the true history of the rise of Lord Bute to place and power, it is but a modern instance of the Latin satirist's remark, "*Voluit Fortuna jocari.*"

In 1762 Dr. Johnson waited here on Lord Bute to thank him for the literary pension which, at his recommendation, the King had settled on him. Lord Bute on this occasion said to him expressly that this mark of royal favour was "given him not for anything he was to do, but for what he had already done." As Boswell remarks, Lord Bute on this occasion behaved in a very handsome manner. "A minister of a more narrow and selfish disposition would have availed himself of such an opportunity to fix an implied obligation on a man of Johnson's powerful talents to give him his support."

Lord Bute does not appear to have long resided here, for very soon after the mansion was completed it was sold to the Earl of Shelburne, afterwards first Marquis of Lansdowne. John Timbs tells us that "the price was £22,000, being some £3,000 less than it cost." He also mentions the *canard* which was current in the last century with respect to the house, namely, that "it was built by one Peace, that made by Lord Bute, in 1762, and paid for by another."

In the spring of 1780, on the failure of his publisher, Mr. H. Payne, of Pall Mall, George Crabbe, poor and unknown, came to this house, in order to ask for temporary aid; but he was refused by Lord Shelburne once and again. Crabbe's son tells us in his "Life" that "often in latter times he would express the feelings with which he contrasted his reception at this nobleman's door in 1780, with the courteous welcome which he received at a subsequent period in that same mansion, now Lansdowne House." "Dined at Lansdowne House," writes the poet, in his "Diary," in 1817. "My visit to Lord Lansdowne's father in this house, now thirty-seven years since!" The only wonder that one feels in reading such an episode, even in a poet's life, is that he could condescend, when his name was known as the author of "The Village," to enter the doors of that Mæcenas from which he was so rudely repulsed when he needed temporary assistance.

With respect to the history of this house and its noble owners, we may be pardoned for drawing largely here upon one of the literary articles of the *Times*:—"In 1805 died the first Marquis of Lansdowne, having by that time passed very much out of popular notice; and the principal cause of public regret for his demise was, that only a fortnight before his death he had declared his knowledge of the Junius secret, and yet among his papers was to be found no indication that could lead to its discovery. He was succeeded by his eldest son, the Earl of Wycombe, whose first act on coming into possession was to sell almost all the literary and artistic treasures which his father had accumulated with so much love and labour. The greater part of these were dispersed under the hammer of the auctioneer, many of the pictures going to enrich the National, the Grosvenor, and other galleries; only the Lansdowne MSS. were kept together, being purchased by the British Museum; while the Gallery of Antique Marbles was the sole portion of the collection for which the marquis showed any appreciation—his opinion being expressed in the fact that he purchased it from his father's executors for £6,000. If, however, this nobleman did not show much respect to his father's cultivated taste, he was not without a certain ancestral pride, for he tried to build a vessel on the principle of Sir William Petty's double-bottomed ship, that was to sail against wind and tide, a model of which was then, and is perhaps still, exhibited in the council-room of the Royal Society. Of nautical habits, he also erected, near the Southampton Water, a marine villa, in which, from dining-hall and private bower to kitchen and scullery, all was pure Gothic, while the gardens belonging to the castle were laid out at Romsey, some ten or twelve miles distant, on a site which formed the original estate of the Petty family. Here, if not in yachting voyages to Ireland or the Continent, he spent most of his time. In London he was a marked man—remarkable for his disregard of dress, and for the pride he took in appearing on the coldest days in winter without a great-coat and without gloves. He died in November, 1809, and was succeeded by his half-brother, the third Marquis, whose first care was to purchase the antique marbles from his sister-in-law; and there, at Lansdowne House, they may now be seen—some of them, as the youthful 'Hercules' and the 'Mercury,' justly considered the finest statues of the kind that have found their way to this country. As for the pictures, when the marquis succeeded to the title, in 1809, there was not one in this splendid mansion, with the exception of a few family portraits; but Lord Lansdowne set himself to the formation of a gallery, which now comprises nearly two hundred pictures of rare interest and value, but miscellaneous in their character, no school or master predominating, unless it be Sir Joshua Reynolds. Some of the portraits in this collection are of great interest. There is the celebrated portrait of Pope, by Jervas; Reynolds's wonderful portrait of Sterne; one of Franklin, by Gainsborough; a beautiful one of Peg Woffington, by Hogarth; Lady Hamilton appears twice—as a bacchante and a gipsy, from the pencil of Romney; Horner, the old college friend of Lord Lansdowne, is not forgotten; and, most interesting of all, there is the lovely portrait of Mrs. Sheridan, as St. Cecilia, painted by Reynolds."

It may recall with some vividness the fashion of those times if we record a little incident connected with this portrait. During the short-lived Ministry of "All the Talents" the Whig leaders celebrated their return to power by a continual round of festivities, in which Sheridan outvied all his colleagues. One Sunday (25th of May, 1806) he gave a grand dinner; on the Monday following a supper and ball, at which the dancing was prolonged to past eight o'clock next morning; on the Tuesday a christening, a masque, and another ball, the Prince being present on each occasion, and the Lord Chancellor Erskine, and the young Chancellor of the Exchequer, Henry Petty, being conspicuous among the dancers. On the occasion of this dinner, the portrait of Mrs. Sheridan was redeemed for one night only from the pawnbroker's, and exhibited in its place in the dining-room. When poor Sheridan died, it was still in possession of the pawnbroker; it then fell into the hands of Sheridan's solicitor, and from him it was purchased for £600 by Lord Lansdowne. In this little incident we get some glimpses of that conviviality for which the Whigs were distinguished. "Le Whig est la femme de votre Gouvernement," says Balzac; and the truth of the remark is especially illustrated in that social influence which the Whigs have always cultivated.

The name of Petty was assumed by the Hon. John Fitzmaurice, second son of Thomas, twenty-first Lord Kerry, and of Anne, only daughter of Sir William Petty, on inheriting the Petty estates on the death of his maternal uncle, Henry Petty, Esq., of Shelburne. He was created a peer of Ireland as Viscount Fitzmaurice, and soon after promoted to the Earldom of Shelburne. His son and successor, William the second earl, and the purchaser of Lansdowne House, was advanced to the Marquisate of Lansdowne in 1784. The above Sir William Petty, of whose talents and public services we have spoken in a previous chapter (page 256), is styled by Aubrey "a person of a great stupendous invention, and of as great prudence and humanity." Sir William was one of the members of the "Rota" or Coffee Club, to which John Milton and Pepys also belonged. The character of the club may be inferred from the lines in "Hudibras:"—

"———as full of tricks
As 'Rota-men' of politics."

Continuing our account of the mansion, we may simply state that it is large and of somewhat heavy proportions, and that the front is of white stone, ornamented with Ionic pillars and a pediment; but it is almost shut out from view by the rich foliage by which the mansion is surrounded; upon the gate-piers is a beehive, one of the crests of the house of Lansdowne. The pictures mentioned above are, for the most part, hung in a gallery of fine proportions (being 100 feet long by 30 wide); and besides these there is in the ante-room a copy of Canova's "Venus." The house also contains some fine specimens of antique busts and statues collected by Gavin Hamilton. The "classic" dining-room served for many years, with Holland House and Devonshire House, to bring together the principal leaders of thought and action belonging to the old Whig *coterie*. Here the Russells and Greys, and Sir James Mackintosh, would often meet around the hospitable table of Henry, the third marquis, so long the venerated "Nestor" of the Liberal party, who divided his time between this house and his seat of Bowood, in Wiltshire, till his death in 1863. Mr. Rush, the American Minister, was a frequent guest here in the days of the Regency, and he speaks of the hospitality of its "classic" dining-room in most glowing terms. We learn from Brougham's "Life" that cabinet councils were occasionally held here.

Among the most constant and most welcome guests here was "Tommy" Moore—"Anacreon Moore," as he was often called, in allusion to his light and sparkling verses.

Horace Walpole lived for the last fifteen years of his life at No. 11 on the east side of this square,

THE SIGN OF "THE RUNNING FOOTMAN." (*See page* 334.)

and here he died on the 2nd of March, 1797, a few years after succeeding to the Earldom of Orford, a title he scarcely ever cared to assume, preferring to be called plain "Horace Walpole" to the end. He thus writes to the Countess of Ossory, under date October, 1779, which fixes the date of his removal hither from Arlington Street, where we have already been introduced to him:—" I came to town this morning to take possession of [my house in] Berkeley Square, and am as well pleased with my new habitation as I can be with anything at present. Lady Shelburne's being queen of the palace over against me" (he is referring, of course, to Lansdowne House) "has improved the view since I bought the house, and I trust will make your ladyship not so shy as you were in Arlington Street."

Walpole was attacked at Strawberry Hill by the cold, about the close of November, 1796, and at the end of that month he removed to his house in Berkeley Square, which he never left again. On this cold supervened an attack of gout. He still amused himself with writing and dictating brief notes, instead of letters, and with the conversation of his friends; and, exhausted by weakness, sunk gradually and died painlessly, on the 2nd of the following March. On the death of Horace Walpole, the house passed to his niece, Lady Waldegrave, who was living here at the beginning of the present century.

It has been said of Horace Walpole, with some justice, by Mr. Charles Knight: "The chief value of his letters consists in his lively descriptions of those public events whose nicer details, without such a chronicler, would be altogether hid under the varnish of what we call history."

The house No. 13, two doors farther to the north, was at one time occupied by the late

Marquis of Hertford, who kept here the nucleus of the fine gallery of paintings now at Hertford House, Manchester Square.

No. 45, on the west side of the square, was the house of the great Lord Clive, the founder of our Indian Empire—"that second Kouli Khan," as

things being not sufficient to move his great mind." The house now belongs to his nearest representative, the Earl of Powis, who, though a Herbert by birth, bears the name of Clive.

An amusing story, showing how Lord Clive obtained his wife, is thus told by Sir Bernard

EXTINGUISHERS IN BERKELEY SQUARE. (See page 327.)

Horace Walpole styles him. Sated with success and honours, his restless spirit seems to have en-feebled his nervous system, and there is too much reason to fear that he fell by his own hand, in November, 1774. Lord Clive in Dr. Johnson's opinion, was a man who, though loaded with wealth and what the world called honours, had yet "acquired his fortune by such crimes that his consciousness of this impelled him to cut his own throat, because he was weary of still life, little

Burke in his "Rise of Great Families:"—"Mr. Maskelyne (brother of Dr. Nevil Maskelyne, the Astronomer-Royal) went as a cadet to India, where he became acquainted with Mr. Clive (afterwards Lord Clive). The acquaintance ripened into inti-mate friendship, and led to constant association. There hung up in Mr. Maskelyne's room several portraits; among others a miniature, which at-tracted Clive's frequent attention. One day, after the English mail had arrived, Clive asked Maskelyne if he had received any English letters, adding, 'We have been very much misunderstood at home, and much censured in London circles.' Maskelyne replied that he had, and read to his friend a letter he then held in his hand. A day or two after, Clive came back to ask to have the letter read to him again. 'Who is the writer?' inquired Clive. 'My sister,' was the reply; 'my sister whose miniature hangs there.' 'Is it a faithful representation?' further asked Clive. 'It is,' rejoined Maskelyne, 'of her face and form; but it is unequal to represent the excellence of her mind and character.' 'Well, Maskelyne,' said Clive, taking him by the hand, 'you know me well, and can speak of me as I really am. Do you think that girl would be induced to come to India and marry me? In the present state of affairs, I dare not hope to be able to go to England.' Maskelyne wrote home, and so recommended Clive's suit, that the lady acquiesced, went to India, and, in 1753, was married at Madras to Clive, then rising to the highest distinction. Lord Clive returned to England in 1767, having done more to extend the English territory and consolidate the English power in India than any other commander. His name stands high on the roll of conquerors; but it is found in a better list—among those who have done and suffered much for mankind. He died at the age of forty-eight, in a fit of insanity, produced by the ingratitude and persecution of his country."

In another house in this square died, in 1762, Martha Blount, the friend and correspondent of Pope. At No. 48 resided Earl Grey for several years both before and after his premiership. In 1842 this square numbered among its residents Sydney Smirke, the architect, and Sir John Cam Hobhouse, afterwards Lord Broughton.

Another celebrated house in this square is No. 38, for half a century or more the residence of the Earl of Jersey. Here the celebrated Lady Jersey, the widow of the fifth earl—one of the female favourites of George IV., in the old days of Carlton House, and in after time one of the most omnipotent and imperious queens of "Almack's"— held her receptions. Half the fashionable world had the *entrée* to these, and the other half sought the privilege in vain, with watering lips. Lady Jersey was the daughter and heiress of Mr. Robert Child, the banker; and her large interest in the bank of Messrs. Child, at Temple Bar, and the income which she drew from it, threw a halo around her which blinded the upper ten thousand to the facts of her early married life.

A curious story which connects this square with a turn—though only a temporary turn—in the fortunes of "Beau" Brummell, of whom we have spoken in our chapter on Carlton House,* is told by Mr. Raikes in his "Journal:"—"At five o'clock on a fine summer's morning, in 1813, he was walking with me through Berkeley Square, and was bitterly lamenting his misfortunes at cards, when he suddenly stopped, seeing something glittering in the kennel. He stooped down and picked up a crooked sixpence, saying, 'Here is an harbinger of good luck.' He took it home, and before going to bed drilled a hole in it, and fastened it to his watchchain. The spell was good: during more than two years he was a constant winner at play and on the turf, and, I believe, realised nearly £30,000."

The blind god, or goddess, of gain, however, appears speedily to have deserted him, for in 1816 he was obliged to fly the country on account of debt, and to retire to Calais, between which place and Caen, where he ultimately became English Consul, he spent his latter days.

Brummell outlived most of the Carlton House set: he died in 1840. Mr. Raikes describes him as tall, well-made, and of a good figure, and a general favourite in ladies' society. "Latterly," he writes, "he became bald, and continued to wear powder to the last of his stay in England, rather piquing himself on preserving this remnant of the *vieille cour* amidst the inroads of the Crops and Roundheads who dated from the French Revolution. He was always studiously, and even remarkably, well-dressed; never at all *outré;* and though considerable time and attention were devoted by him to his toilette, when once accomplished, it never seemed to occupy his attention. His manners were easy, polished, and gentleman-like, stamped with what St. Simon would call *l'usage du monde, et du plus grand, et du meilleur*, and regulated by that same good taste which he displayed in most things. No one was a more keen observer of vulgarism in others, or more piquant in his criticisms, or more despotic as an *arbiter elegantiarum;* indeed, he could decide the fate of a young man just launched into the world by a single word. His dress was the general model; and when he had struck out a new idea, he would smile at observing its gradual progress downwards from the highest to the lowest classes. . . . He was not only good-natured, but thoroughly good-tempered. I never remember to have seen him out of humour. His conversation, without having the wit and humour of Lord Alvanley, was highly amusing and agreeable, replete with anecdotes not only of the present day, but of

---

* See p. 96, *ante*.

society several years back, which his early introduction to Carlton House and to many of the Prince's older associates had given him the opportunities of knowing correctly." " Beau" Brummell, indeed, has never been equalled or paralleled since, not even by Count D'Orsay, whom he in some respects resembled.

In this square died, towards the close of the last century, the eccentric son of Sir John Barnard, sometime alderman of and M.P. for London, and one of those few members whose " price" even Sir Robert Walpole could not find out. This was the more remarkable in his case, as he was extremely penurious. Lord Chatham called him "the Great Commoner," probably in jest; but it is recorded that more than one high Minister of State constantly consulted him on all measures of finance, and that once, at least, he was offered the Chancellorship of the Exchequer. His son inherited his penurious tastes. The circumstances of his death were singular. One Monday morning he woke, having dreamed that he should die in the course of the week. He used to have a cup of chocolate for breakfast daily, and every Monday morning he gave his housekeeper the money for the weekly supply. He was so impressed with his dream, however, that he told her on this occasion to get only half the quantity. Before the fourth morning came he was found dead.

In the days of the Regency Berkeley Square probably vied with Grosvenor Square in being the most fashionable spot in the West-end, and the neighbourhood of both was constantly spoken of in the last century as the very type of London wealth, taste, hospitality, and luxury. Hence the sarcastic remark of Cawthorne—

> " Alas ! no dinners did he eat
> In Berkeley Square or Grosvenor Street."

Nevertheless, in spite of its wealth and luxury, the locality seems to have had its drawbacks, for it enjoyed the unenviable distinction of being infested with highwaymen and footpads. According to Dr. Doran, the district around the square, Hay Hill, Hill Street, &c., continued to be a dangerous one down to the middle of the reign of George III. Lord Cathcart, in an unpublished letter to his son William, dated December, 1774, affords an instance of the peril which people ran on their way to the houses of Mrs. Montagu, Lady Clermont, Lady Brown, and other residents of that neighbourhood. Lord Cathcart tells his son that as his sisters and Mr. Graham (afterwards Lord Lynedoch) were going to Lady Brown's in a coach, they were attacked by footpads on Hay Hill. One opened the door and demanded the company's money.

The future Lord Lynedoch showed the stuff of which that gallant soldier was made. He upset the robber who addressed them, then jumped out and secured him. The confederate took to his heels. We may add, on the authority of Walker's "Original," that George IV. and the Duke of York, when very young men, were stopped one night by highwaymen on Hay Hill, whilst riding in a hackney coach, and robbed of what valuables they had about them.

Then, again, this neighbourhood has more than once been the scene of civil strife and bloodshed ; and Mr. Planché tells us, in his agreeable " Recollections and Reflections," that he remembers seeing artillerymen standing with lighted matches by the side of their loaded field-pieces in Berkeley Square in the days of Lord Liverpool's ministry.

Hay Hill, which connects the south-east angle of the square with Grafton and Dover Streets, is a steep slope, and covers part of the site of the gardens belonging to Berkeley House. It is generally thought to derive its name, like Farm Street, on the other side of the square, from the rural manor of which it once formed a part. But Peter Cunningham considers it is a corruption of the " Eye" or " Aye," a brook which ran at its foot from Tyburn, which he supposes to be a corruption of " Eye-burn" or " Ay-burn."

Near this, in the reign of Queen Mary, as already mentioned, a skirmish took place between a party of insurgents, under Sir Thomas Wyatt, and a detachment of the royal army, in which the former were repulsed. After the subsequent defeat and capture of Sir Thomas Wyatt at Ludgate, he was executed, and, as Stow tells us, his head set up on a gallows at this very place.

According to the " Annual Register " for 1799, " Hay Hill was granted by Queen Anne to the then Speaker of the House of Commons ; but much clamour being made about it as a bribe, . . . the Speaker sold it for £200, and gave the money to the poor. The Pomfret family afterwards purchased it, and it has lately been sold for £20,300."

At the foot of Hay Hill, in a lane leading towards Bruton Mews South, is a small public-house called the " Three Chairmen," pointing back to the days when sedan chairs were in fashion.

A narrow passage between the gardens of Lansdowne and Devonshire Houses leads to Bolton Row and Curzon Street. It is sunk below the level of the ground, and at one end is a flight of steps, with an upright iron bar in the centre. It is said that this bar was put up because a highwayman who had done some deed of violence in May Fair rode his horse through the defile, much to the danger of the foot-passengers. In Bolton Row, in the early part of the present century, resided Mr. Henry Angelo, the noted teacher of the noble art of fencing, who lived all his life in the world of fashion, and whose "Reminiscences" occupy two large volumes.

Charles Street and Hill Street, both on the western side of the square, are handsome thoroughfares; and the houses in both have always been tenanted by the highest and noblest families. In Hayes Mews, running northwards between these two streets, there is a public-house bearing the sign of the "Running Footman," much frequented by the servants of the neighbouring gentry. Upon the sign-board is represented a tall, agile man in gay attire, and with a stick having a metal ball at top; he is engaged in running, and underneath are the words, "I am the only running footman." We have given a copy of this curious sign on page 330. It is obvious that the very word "footman," still in constant use for a man-servant, implies the original purpose for which such a servant was kept—namely, to run alongside his master's carriage.

Chambers tells us in his "Book of Days," that the custom of keeping running footmen survived to such recent times that Sir Walter Scott remembered seeing the state-coach of John, Earl of Hopetoun, attended by one of the fraternity, "clothed in white, and bearing a staff." It is believed that the Duke of Queensberry—the "Old Q." already mentioned—who died in 1810, kept up the practice longer than any other of the London grandees; and Mr. Thoms tells an amusing anecdote of a man who came to be hired for the duty by that ancient but far from venerable peer. The duke was in the habit of trying the pace of candidates for his service by seeing how they could run up and down Piccadilly, watching and timing them from his balcony. They put on a livery before the trial. On one occasion, a candidate presented himself, dressed, and ran. At the conclusion of his performance he stood before the balcony. "You will do very well for me," said the duke. "And your livery will do very well for me," replied the man, and gave the duke a last proof of his ability as a runner by then running away with it.

In Charles Street, at No. 22, lived the Duke and Duchess of Clarence, prior to the accession of the former to the throne as King William IV. In this street, too, have resided at one time or another, the Earl of Ellenborough, some time Governor-General of India; Mr. James R. Hope-Scott, of Abbotsford, who came into possession of that property through his marriage with the grand-daughter and heiress of Sir Walter Scott; Mr. Thomas Baring, M.P., the distinguished master of finance, whose house was noted for its fine gallery of paintings; Admiral Sir Edward Codrington, the victor of Navarino, and subsequently M.P. for Devonport; Lady Grenville, sister of Lord Camelford, and widow of the Premier of 1806–7, the head of the "ministry of all the talents:" she lived till 1864, and died at the age of upwards of ninety.

Of John Street, which connects the western end of Charles Street with Hill Street, there is little or nothing to say, beyond the fact that it bears the Christian name of Lord Berkeley of Stratton, whom we have already mentioned. At the junction of these two streets stands Berkeley Chapel, one of the many proprietary chapels in the parish of St. George's, Hanover Square, to which a conventional district out of that parish has been attached. It dates from about 1750. Sydney Smith, at one time, was its officiating minister. Externally, it has as little to recommend it as most West-end proprietary chapels; but in 1874–5 its interior was decorated in good ecclesiastical taste.

Hill Street, so called from some trifling ascent on the farm of Lord Berkeley already mentioned, was erected in the early part of the last century. It comprises none but fine and handsome houses, and has always been inhabited chiefly by titled families, or, at all events, those of high aristocratic connections. Amongst its former residents Mr. P. Cunningham enumerates the "good" Lord Lyttelton; Mrs. Montagu, before she became a widow and removed to her more celebrated house in Portman Square; the first Lord Malmesbury; and Lord Chief-Justice Camden, who died here in 1794. In this street the late Lord De Tabley, better known by his former name of Sir John Leicester, made his fine collection of paintings of the English school. In 1826, it counted among its residents Mr. Henry Brougham, M.P. for Winchelsea; he lived at No. 5, the same house where, in 1835, resided Lord Albert Conyngham, afterwards Lord Londesborough. At No. 19 lived Mr. N. Ridley Colborne, afterwards Lord Colborne; both the latter were known for their galleries of pictures. At No. 9, in 1841, resided Admiral Sir Philip Durham, the last survivor, it is supposed, of those who escaped from the *Royal George*, when she went down at Spithead, with Admiral Kempenfelt and "twice four hundred men."

Sir N. W. Wraxall, in his "Historical Memoirs in his own Time," gives us a most interesting picture of the gatherings of literary celebrities and fashionable ladies under the roof of Mrs. Montagu, which were nicknamed the Blue Stocking Club, and into which, he tells us, he was introduced by Sir William Pepys. He describes minutely her dinners, and her evening parties, and the good looks and *esprit* of the hostess as she was seen in the season of 1776, when verging on sixty. Here frequently came the ponderous and sententious Dr. Johnson, as a satellite attendant on Mr. and Mrs. Thrale; Edmund Burke, grave and reserved, his society being more coveted than enjoyed; Lord Erskine, then just beginning to be known to fame as an orator; Dr. Shipley, the Bishop of St. Asaph, and his daughter, afterwards married to Sir William Jones, the Orientalist; Mrs. Chapone, who concealed the most varied and superior attainments under the plainest of outward forms; Sir Joshua Reynolds, with his ear-trumpet, prevented by deafness from joining in the general conversation; Horace Walpole, full of anecdote, gathered partly by contact with the world and partly by tradition from his father, the great Sir Robert; the learned and grave Mrs. Carter, the "Madame Dacier of England;" Dr. Burney, and his daughter, afterwards Madame D'Arblay, the author of "Evelina" and "Cecilia;" David Garrick, whose presence shed a gaiety over the whole room; the Duchess Dowager of Portland, grand-daughter of the Lord Treasurer Harley, Earl of Oxford; and Georgina, Duchess of Devonshire, then in the first bloom of youth.

Davies Street, which runs from the north-west corner of Berkeley Square, across Grosvenor and Brook Streets into Oxford Street, is named after Miss Mary Davies, the rich heiress of Ebury Manor, who carried the estate at Pimlico by marriage into the house of Grosvenor; or else, as Mr. Peter Cunningham suggests, after Sir Thomas Davies, some time Lord Mayor of London, who inherited a large part of the fortune of "the great Mr. Audley," whose name is connected with North and South Audley Streets. In this street lived "Joe Manton," the gun-maker, before his removal to Dover Street. When in London Byron used to go to Manton's shooting-gallery, to try his hand, as he said, at a wafer. Captain Gronow, in his agreeable anecdotes and reminiscences, tells us that Wedderburn Webster was present one day when the poet, intensely delighted with his own skill, boasted to Joe Manton that he considered himself the best shot in London. "No, my lord," replied Manton, "not the best, but your shooting to-day was very respectable;" upon which Byron waxed wroth, and left the shop in a violent passion.

The top of Davies Street runs into Oxford Street, not at right angles, as most of the other thoroughfares but diagonally, and appears to follow the course of an old and narrow thoroughfare called Shug Lane, which, in the "New View of London," published in 1708, is mentioned as in a line with Marylebone Lane. The very name of Shug Lane, however, has long since passed away.

Farm Street, for such is the name by which the mews at the rear of the north side of Hill Street is dignified, contains the Jesuit Church of the Immaculate Conception, a handsome and lofty Gothic structure of the Decorated style, designed by Mr. J. J. Scoles, and built in 1848-9.

The fabric is the first possessed by the Jesuits in London since the expulsion of the order from Somerset House and St. James's under the Stuart sovereigns.* The front, which looks south instead of west, is a miniature reproduction of that of the Cathedral of Beauvais. The high altar, designed by the late Mr. A. W. Pugin, was the gift of Miss Tempest, and cost £1,000. The church has two other altars, and dwarf side-aisles. Having houses built up against it on either side, it is lit from a clerestory above.

Mount Street, which was built gradually at various dates, between the commencement and the middle of the last century, commemorates in its name a fort or bastion in the line of fortification so hastily drawn round the western suburbs in 1643, by order of the Parliament, when an attack from the royal forces was expected. There was a mount at the west end of this street, on the eastern border of Hyde Park. The eastern entrance to this street is in the corner of Berkeley Square, at the south end of Davies Street. Most of the street consists of shops, irregular in plan and size, and by no means of the first calibre.

Peter Cunningham tells us that in later times there was in this street a celebrated coffee-house, called "The Mount." It was probably one which was frequented by the charming Lawrence Sterne, towards the end of his life, whilst occupying the lodgings in Bond Street, where he died. From this coffee-house, at all events, many of his love letters to Mrs. Draper and other ladies are dated.

In Mount Street was living, at the commencement of the present century, a singular character, one Martin Van Butchell, a quack doctor and dentist of celebrity, who claimed to be able to cure the king's evil, teeth, ruptures, fistula, and every kind of evil to which flesh is heir, and who, consequently, obtained from his patients fees suited rather to the extent of their credulity than to that of his own merits. He applied, through the Lord Chamberlain of the Household, for the post of

---

* See Vol. III., p. 91.

GROSVENOR SQUARE. (*See page* 339.)

dentist to George III.; but when the consent of his Majesty was obtained, he said that he did not care for the custom of royalty. His wife having died, he had her body embalmed and kept in his parlour; and he outdid even this act of eccentricity by allowing his beard to grow, which at that time was reckoned sheer madness. He is said to have sold the hairs out of his beard at a guinea each to ladies who wanted to become the mothers to make his wife and children dine by themselves, and to come when called by a whistle; he dressed his first wife in black, and his second in white, never allowing either a change of colour. He was also one of the earliest of teetotalers. He died in 1810.

No. 111, now occupied by a detachment of priests of the Order of Jesus, was at one time the manor house of an estate extending southwards to the

THE LOFT USED BY THE CATO STREET CONSPIRATORS, 1820. (*See page* 340.)

of fine children. He described himself in one of his printed circulars as "a British Christian man, with a comely beard full eight inches long." He used to ride about the West-end on a shaggy pony, always unclipped, of course, and painted with spots by the hand of its master. Its bridle was one of Van Butchell's contrivances, being really a blind, which could be let down over both the pony's eyes in case of the animal taking fright. He lived in the same house for nearly half a century, and never would go to visit a patient. "I go to none," he said and wrote, and he was true to his word, though as much as £500 was offered him to induce him to alter his resolution. And yet, when at home, he would sit and sell oranges, cakes, and gingerbread to the children at his doorstep. He used borders of the property of the Berkeleys. In the garden behind it are some fine trees, which once stood, doubtless, in the open fields; and Farm Street in the rear still serves to keep up the tradition of its former rurality. A few doors west, on the southern side of the street, stands the Workhouse of St. George's, Hanover Square, a dingy and gloomy building externally. Nearly opposite to its gates, from the middle of Mount Street to Grosvenor Square, runs a short thoroughfare called Charles Street, of which there is little or nothing to say, beyond the fact that in it is the Coburg Hotel, kept by Francis Grillon, an offshoot of Grillon's Hotel, of Albemarle Street. In 1832, the Duchesse d'Angoulême, in her way from Edinburgh to France, held receptions at this hotel.

In this street, during the years 1767–68, when, as we have seen, he removed into the artistic neighbourhood of St. Martin's Lane, Josiah Wedgwood had his West-end show-rooms of pottery and porcelain, the royal arms over his door denoting— what at that time and in his case was no fiction —the patronage and custom of royalty which his firm enjoyed. Hither Queen Charlotte would drive from Buckingham House to see those art-treasures by the production of which Wedgwood was destined in a few short years to make the name of England famous in Continental courts. The fact is that the rooms here were small, and

as the patronage of the wealthy classes poured in upon him in a stream, he soon found himself quite at a loss for room when large and handsome vases, as well as dishes and dinner-services, had to be displayed.

Charles Street was probably so called after one of the Stuart kings, from whose reign it dates. It may be interesting to record here that in the "Post Office Directory" for 1883 there are as many as forty Charles Streets mentioned as being within the limits of the metropolis, to say nothing of a Charles Square, three Charles Places, and a Charles Mews.

CHAPTER XXVII.

GROSVENOR SQUARE, AND ITS NEIGHBOURHOOD.

A Critical Reviewer's Opinion of the Square in the Last Century—Sir Richard Grosvenor—The Statue of George I.—Linkmen and Oil-Lamps— A House raffled for—Mr. Thomas Raikes—Anecdote of Charles Mathews—Beckford of Fonthill, and Lord Nelson—The Earl of Derby and Miss Farren, the Actress—The Earl of Harrowby and the Cato Street Conspiracy—Lord Stratford de Redcliffe—The Earl of Shaftesbury —Dr. Johnson—Lower Grosvenor Street—A Curious Exhibition—Brook Street and its Distinguished Residents—North and South Audley Streets.

THIS square was the last addition in point of date, and also the farthest addition westward, to the metropolis at the time when "The New Critical Review of the Public Buildings of London" was published, namely, in 1736. It was intended to be the finest of all the then existing squares; but the writer of that work condemns it as hopelessly falling short of any such a design. In fact, he laughs at it as a miscarriage in its execution, utterly wanting in harmony of plan, and irregular in its details. He speaks of the east side as the best of the four; but even this he censures severely, and he cannot find terms bad enough to describe the "triple house on the north side," which, he suggests, "could have been built only with the view of taking in some young heir to buy it at a great rate." He praises, however, the expensive taste with which the centre of the square was laid out, though he condemns the brick enclosure round it as clumsy, and a "blemish to the view which it was intended to preserve and adorn." The brick enclosure happily is no more, having long since given place to iron railings. As for the south and west sides, they are, in the author's opinion, "little better than a collection of whims and frolics in building, without anything like order or beauty, and therefore deserving no further consideration." The purer taste of our own day, however, will see merits, if not beauty, in the variety of styles introduced into the houses which form the square;

and the owner of the freehold, the head of the Grosvenor family, will be able to laugh at the attempt to "write down" his ancestors' fine and important contribution to the grandeur of the West-end. The real fact is that many of the houses are built of red brick, but they have noble stone facings, and being each of a different pattern, though uniform in general appearance, they give to the square a pleasing variety in details, without detracting from its dignity.

That the square was built a long time before the year above mentioned is clear from the fact, that as early as 1716 Pope speaks of it in a letter to his friend and correspondent, Miss Martha Blount.

Previous to the completion of the houses between New Bond Street and Hyde Park, the erections here were called "Grosvenor Buildings;" but in the year 1725, says the author of the "Beauties of England," Sir Richard Grosvenor, Bart. (who was in right of the manor of Wimondham, Herts. Grand Cup-bearer at the coronation of George II., and who died in 1732), assembled his tenants and the persons employed in the buildings to a splendid entertainment, when he named the various streets. At the same period he erected the gate in Hyde Park, now called by his name." Sir Richard, to whom this square owes its origin, was, says Malcolm, "as great a builder as the Duke of Bedford." The landscape garden, which occupies the centre of the square, was laid out by Kent, and the enclosure can boast a few trees, though not so handsome as the plane-trees of Berke.ey Square.

There was formerly in the centre of the square a gilt statue of George I. on horseback, but the pedestal is now vacant. This statue was made by Van Nort, and was erected by Sir Richard Grosvenor in 1726, "near the redoubt called Oliver's Mount." Soon after it was put up, says Malcolm, "some villains dismembered it in the most shameful manner, and affixed a traitorous paper to the pedestal."

Before several of the houses in this square, and indeed in other streets at the West-end, may still be seen specimens of the iron link-extinguishers on the top of the railings. Numerous allusions to the link-boys and their calling are to be found in the plays and lighter poems of the last century, and links were commonly carried before carriages at the West-end until about the year 1807, when the introduction of gas gradually superseded their use. The link-men and link-boys would appear to have been a disorderly class, and the profession to have been followed as a cloak for thieving. Thus Gay writes in his "Trivia:"—

> "Though thou art tempted by the linkman's call,
> Yet trust him not along the lonely wall :
> In the midway he'll quench the flaming brand,
> And share the booty with the pilfering band."

It is worthy, perhaps, of a note, as showing the reluctance of our aristocracy to adopt new-fangled fashions, that Grosvenor Square was the last street or square which was lit with oil; the last oil-lamp there was not superseded by gas until 1842. The inhabitants for many years opposed the intrusion of so vulgar a commodity as gas, and preferred to go on as their fathers had gone on before them. What we have here said about the opposition to the introduction of gas in this locality may serve to remind the reader of Macaulay's words respecting the obstruction offered, less than two centuries ago, to Edward Fleming's first attempt to light the streets of London with oil. "The cause of darkness was not undefended. There were fools in that age who opposed the introduction of what was called 'the new light' as strenuously as fools in our own age have opposed the introduction of vaccination and railroads, and as strenuously as the fools of an age anterior to the dawn of history doubtless opposed the introduction of the plough and of alphabetical writing."

In 1739, says a writer in the *Gentleman's Magazine*, "the centre house on the east side of the square was raffled for, and won by two persons named Hunt and Braithwaite. The possessor valued it at £10,000, but the winners sold it two months afterwards for £7,000 to the Duke of Norfolk." The house was built on ground held by Sir Richard Grosvenor for eighty-four years from 1737, at a ground-rent of £42 per annum.

Malcolm, writing at the commencement of this century, humorously observes that his readers "must know that this square is the very *focus* of feudal grandeur, elegance, fashion, taste, and hospitality," and that "the novel-reader must be intimately acquainted with the description of residents within it, when the words 'Grosvenor Square' are to be found in almost every work of that species written in the compass of fifty years past."

Grosvenor Square, as may naturally be supposed, though only a century and a half old, has had plenty of distinguished inhabitants. In it, in 1832, was living Mr. Thomas Raikes, the accomplished author of the "Journal" from which we have so often quoted. Here Mr. Raikes used to entertain not only many of the leading politicians and statesmen of the day, but also Pope the actor, the elder Mathews, Tom Sheridan, Charles Calvert, and other genial acquaintances. One evening, when the above-named guests were present, a comical incident occurred, which Mr. Raikes records in his "Journal:"—"In the course of conversation, Pope alluded to an old gentleman in the country who was so madly attached to the society of Mathews, that whenever he came to town he went straight to his house, and if he did not find him there, would trace him and follow him wherever he might happen to be. This did not excite much attention, but about nine o'clock we all heard a tremendous rap at the door, and my servant came in saying that there was in the hall a gentleman who insisted on seeing Mr. Mathews. The latter appeared very disconcerted, made many apologies for the intrusion, and said that he would get rid of him instantly, as he doubtless must be the person who so frequently pestered him. As soon as he had retired, we heard a very noisy dialogue in the hall between Mathews and his friend, who insisted on coming in and joining the party, while the other as urgently insisted on his retreat. At length the door opened, and in walked a most extraordinary figure, who sat down in Mathews's place, filled himself a tumbler of claret, which he pronounced to be execrable, and began in the most impudent manner to claim acquaintance with all the party, and say the most ridiculous things to every one. We were all for the moment thrown off our guard ; but we soon detected our versatile companion, who really had not taken three minutes to tie up his nose with a string, put on a wig, and otherwise so to metamorphose himself that it was almost impossible to recognise him."

It had been foretold to Mr. Raikes at Paris some years previously that he would one day be arrested for debt; and the prophecy was thus fulfilled. Mr. Raikes shall tell his own story:—"The repairs of my house were being performed by contract; but the builder failed before his work was concluded, and the assignee claimed of me the whole amount of the sum agreed. This I would not pay further than it had been fairly earned. The difference was only £150; but the assignees sent a bailiff to my house and arrested me, while my carriage was waiting to convey me to dinner at the Duke of York's, where the story caused considerable merriment."

The town residence of Mr. Beckford, the famous owner of Fonthill Abbey, in Wiltshire, was in this square; and on one occasion Lord Nelson was on a visit here, at a time of general scarcity, when persons in every rank of life denied themselves the use of that necessary article of food, bread, at dinner, and were content, for the sake of example, with such vegetables as the season afforded. Lord Nelson, however, contrary to the established etiquette of the dinner-table, called for bread, and was respectfully told by one of the servants in waiting that, in consequence of the scarcity of wheat, bread was wholly dispensed with at the dinner-table of Mr. Beckford. Nelson looked angry; and desiring his own attendant to be called, he drew forth a shilling from his pocket, and commanded him to go out and purchase him a loaf; observing, that after having fought for his bread, he thought it hard that his countrymen should deny it to him.

Here, at No. 23, lived Edward, the twelfth Earl of Derby, after his marriage with Miss Farren, the celebrated actress, whose mother lived with his lordship and her daughter, and died here in 1803. Miss Farren's first patronesses and acquaintances in London were Lord and Lady Ailesbury and Mrs. Damer, to whom she had been introduced by the Duchess of Leinster, who knew something of her family in Ireland. The house was the town residence of the Earls of Derby until about the year 1852, when the then head of the house of Stanley removed to St. James's Square.

It was at No. 39 in this square, then, as now, the house of the Earl of Harrowby, that the Cabinet Ministers of George IV. had arranged to dine on the 23rd of February, 1820, when they were prevented by a preconcerted plan for their assassination, which is known to history as the Cato Street conspiracy, from the place between Marylebone and the Edgware Road where it was concocted, and which is now called Horace Street. The head of this conspiracy was a discharged soldier, named Arthur Thistlewood, who had been imprisoned for twelve months for annoying Lord Sidmouth. Along with a band of a dozen or more desperadoes, it had been arranged that some of them should watch the door of Lord Harrowby's house, where, whilst one of the gang delivered a pretended dispatch-box, the rest were to rush in and kill all the King's ministers, Lords Sidmouth and Castlereagh being especially marked out for vengeance. From Grosvenor Square they were to rush off to the barracks in Hyde Park, and thence to attack the Bank of England and the Tower of London, as they expected that they would have the people with them. Meantime, however, the Government had obtained scent of the intended massacre, through the agency of a spy, and whilst the assassins were assembled in a stable-loft in Cato Street, and arming themselves by the light of a candle for the execution of their plan, they were surprised by a body of Bow Street officers, who made their way up the ladder into the loft. The leader of the officers, on calling upon Thistlewood to surrender, was shot dead; the lights being put out, a fearful *mêlée* followed; in the midst of it Thistlewood managed to escape, but he was captured early next morning. Along with nine of his comrades, he was safely lodged in the Tower next day; and it may be remarked that they were the last prisoners confined in that fortress. In the following April the conspirators were brought to trial, when Thistlewood and three of his chief accomplices were sentenced to death, and the rest were transported for life. It is stated in Mr. John Timbs' "Romance of London," on the authority of the late Sir R. Thierry, a judge in the Australian colonies, that two at least of the persons transported for this crime rose in the course of time to independent positions at Bathurst and Sydney, and became respectable members of society.

The corner house of the square, between Upper Grosvenor and South Audley Streets, was for many years the residence of Lord Stratford de Redcliffe, better known by his former name of Sir Stratford Canning, "the greatest of diplomatists of his age, the highest authority on all subjects connected with Turkey and the East, and the only man in Western Europe of whom the Ottoman Porte was really afraid." Here he produced a drama, a volume of poems, and sundry essays on religious subjects at an age when most men are rather inclined to throw the pen aside than to take it in hand. He died in 1880.

Besides the members of the aristocracy named above, this square has numbered among its inhabitants, at one time or another, Bishop Warburton, author of the "Divine Legation;" Lord Chancellor Hardwicke; Lord North, when Premier; Henry Thrale, of Streatham; Sir Thomas Stamford Raffles; and John Withers and Sir George Beaumont, the great patron of art and artists. He had part of his gallery at the house already mentioned as belonging to Lord Stratford de Redcliffe. In 1841 Lord Canning and Lord Granville (then Lord Leveson) were living together at No. 10. Among its more recent inhabitants may be mentioned the late Mr. Joseph Neeld, M.P., whose fine gallery of paintings was at No. 6; and the Earl of Shaftesbury, who has lived at No. 24 for more than thirty years. The philanthropy of the last-named nobleman, although so well known, is fairly entitled to a word or two of recognition here, particularly in his efforts to ameliorate the condition of the lowest orders of society. The Ragged School movement, of which Mr. John Forster epitomises the history in his "Life of Dickens" by saying that it was begun by a shoemaker of Southampton and a chimney-sweep of Windsor, was carried out to its present length and its present success mainly under the auspices of Lord Shaftesbury; and the same writer tells us that in thirty years the schools had passed some thirty thousand children through them, and that it is computed that for a third of that number honest means of employment have been found by the same agency.

We have already had occasion, more than once, to speak of the conflicts that took place in this neighbourhood during the civil wars. It is said that the line of fortifications thrown up at that time, by order of Cromwell, ran diagonally across the space occupied by this square from the mound, or mount, at the western extremity of what is now, from that circumstance, called Mount Street, as we have already mentioned. Apart from this, there are few, if any, historical events connected with the square; indeed, it may be said that it is almost of too recent growth to have much of a history.

That Johnson was a frequenter of so fashionable a region as Grosvenor Square may be set down by Mr. Timbs, or by others, among "Things not Generally Known." But Mr. Smith, in his "Book for a Rainy Day," tells us that he once saw the burly doctor "follow a sturdy thief who had stolen his handkerchief in Grosvenor Square, seize him by the collar with both hands, and shake him violently; then, letting him loose, give him such a powerful smack on the face as sent him reeling off the pavement." Independent as he was in all his ideas, the learned doctor once fairly owned that if he was not plain Dr. Johnson, of Lichfield, Oxford, and Bolt Court, he would desire to be "Grosvenor of that ilk."

The Count de Melfort, in his "Impressions of England," remarks that Grosvenor and St. James's Squares clearly have the first rank to themselves. This may have been a just remark at the time when he wrote, in the reign of William IV., but it would scarcely be true now that Belgrave Square has come to be the centre of attraction and fashion. However, they all owe their precedence to the fact that they are mainly occupied by the highest of the aristocracy, and that there is not a plebeian "professional" man—not even a titled M.D.—living in them.

At the south-eastern corner of the square, and extending eastward towards Bond Street, is Lower Grosvenor Street. Writing at the commencement of the present century, the author of the "Beauties of England" states that it "consists of a great number of excellent houses, the majority of which are inhabited by titled persons and affluent families. Indeed, a bare list of the persons of distinction residing in this neighbourhood would comprehend a great portion of the present British peers."

Here, in 1784, was living Mr. John Crewe, M.P. for Cheshire, and subsequently Lord Crewe, already mentioned as the last survivor of Fox's friends at "Brooks's" Club. His wife, who was a most zealous Whig, gave at her house a splendid entertainment in commemoration of the return of Mr. Fox for Westminster, in May of the above year. "The intimate friend of Fox, and one of the most accomplished and charming women of her time," writes Sir N. W. Wraxall, "she had exerted herself in securing his election, if not as efficaciously, yet as enthusiastically as the Duchess of Devonshire herself. On this occasion the ladies, no less than the men, were all habited in blue and buff. The Prince of Wales, too, was present in that dress. After supper, a toast having been given by his Royal Highness, consisting of the words 'True blue and Mrs. Crewe,' which was received with rapture, the lady rose and proposed another health, expressive of her gratitude, and not less laconic, namely, 'True blue, and all of you.'"

Mr. Peter Cunningham enumerates among the other residents the Countess of Hertford (celebrated in Thomson's "Seasons," Spring), Miss Vane, the mistress of Frederick, Prince of Wales; Mrs. Oldfield, the actress; Admiral Jervis, afterwards Earl St. Vincent; Dr. Matthew Baillie (brother of Agnes and Joanna Baillie); and last, not least, Sir

Humphry Davy, when he became President of the Royal Society. Mr. Fox Maule, afterwards Lord Dalhousie, and the accomplished Mr. H. Gally Knight, M.P., author of "An Architectural Tour in Normandy," also lived here.

And yet this highly aristocratic street has been occasionally invaded by plebeian exhibitions. At No. 68, for instance, was, in 1818-20, Duburg's Exhibition. This consisted of models in cork of

On the north of the open fields, says Macaulay, the Oxford Road, in the reign of Charles II., ran between hedges. "Three or four hundred yards to the south were the garden walls of a few great houses, which were then considered as quite out of town. Here was a spring from which, long afterwards, Conduit Street was named." From this stream or brook—which came down from Tyburn, and found its way across Piccadilly, as we have

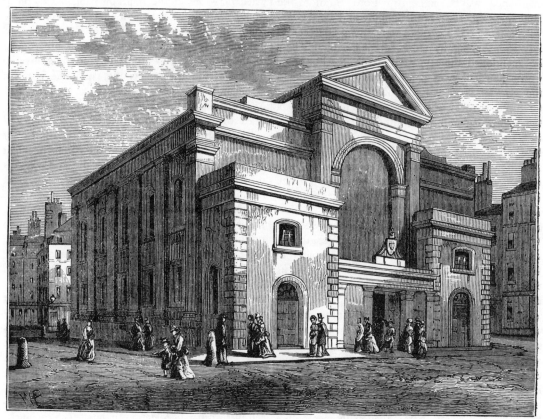

CURZON CHAPEL, MAY FAIR. (*See page* 352.)

ancient temples, theatres, &c., in Rome and other Italian cities, and in the south of France, all formed to a scale, and executed so as to convey a faithful representation of the ruins as they then stood. Mr. Rush, the ambassador from the United States of America, writes in his "Court of London," under date May, 1819: "Went to see the cork models in Lower Grosvenor Street. There was a representation of the amphitheatre at Verona, and of that at Rome; of Vergel's tomb; of the Cascade near Tivoli; of the Grotto of Egeria; of Vesuvius in a state of eruption; and of various other things of antiquity. I rank it among the most curious exhibitions that I have seen in London." No. 16 was for some time the home of the Royal Institute of British Architects.

already seen—the neighbourhood was called the Brook Field. The earliest instance of the name occurring is, perhaps, in the *London Gazette* of September, 1688 :—" His Majesty has been graciously pleased to grant a market for live cattle to be held in Brookfield, near Hyde Park Corner, on Tuesday and Thursday in every week. The first market day will be held on the first Thursday in October next, and afterwards to continue weekly on Tuesdays and Thursdays—the Tuesday market in the morning for cattle, and the afternoon for horses." The land, however, being wanted for building purposes, and the market not proving very attractive, the latter was dropped, and the services of designers and architects were called in. Many of the original houses still remain; they mostly date from the middle of the last century. The principal street that sprung up in these fields—running from Hanover Square across Bond Street, Davies Street, and Grosvenor Square, towards Hyde Park —naturally took the name of Brook Street.

This street has for a century been the residence of successful surgeons and physicians. Hither Sir Charles Bell, in the height of his fame, removed about the year 1831, and here he lived till his final settlement in Edinburgh, in 1835. Sir Henry Holland, the fashionable Court physician, resided for upwards of fifty years at No. 25, formerly the residence of Edmund Burke. His house was a centre of literary and scientific society, and around his table often were gathered the Macaulays, the Wilberforces, and Sydney Smith (whose daughter he married), as well as Lord John Russell, Lord Melbourne, and other political leaders. He attended the deathbeds of no less than five Premiers, and of several members of our own and some other royal houses. He was the physician to the Princess Charlotte, and at a later date to Her Majesty and the late Prince Consort. He was created a baronet

TIDDY DOL.
From a Contemporary Print. (*See page* 346.)

in 1853. He was the author of very many important medical works and books of travel, and he made it a rule of his life, and one which he observed until the very last year of his life, to travel abroad every summer. He died in October, 1873, at the age of eighty-five. Lady Holland's name is well known in the world of letters as the author of the "Life" of her accomplished and witty father, "the Canon of St. Paul's."

Sir William Gull, physician extraordinary to Her Majesty, is another distinguished resident in this street. He was created a baronet in 1872, on the recovery of the Prince of Wales, after a dangerous attack of fever, through which Sir William attended his Royal Highness as his chief medical adviser.

At No. 50 lived Sir Jeffrey Wyatville, the restorer of the architecture of Windsor Castle.

Handel likewise resided in this street. Mr. J. T. Smith, in his "Antiquarian Rambles," fixes the house exactly; it was "No. 57 on the south side, four doors from Bond Street, and two from the gateway." On the same side of the street, between Bond and Davies Streets, is Claridge's—formerly Mivart's—hotel, noted as the place where royal and distinguished personages from foreign countries usually "put up."

At No. 20 was held the first entertainment given by the Society of Painters in Water Colours.

In Woodstock Street, which lies between Oxford Street and Brook Street, Johnson was once living in lodgings, accompanied by his wife, on his second journey to London, in the autumn of 1737, before he took up his residence in Castle Street, and made the acquaintance of Edmund Cave. He does not, however, appear to have remained here long, finding it possibly too far from the scene of his literary labours at Clerkenwell in the days when there were no omnibuses or "underground" railways.

Grosvenor Square is connected with Oxford Street, at its north-east corner, by a thoroughfare of inferior appearance, built about 1770, and called Duke Street, probably after the Duke of Cumberland. It requires no further notice here.

At the north-west corner of the square, which also it connects with Oxford Street, is North Audley Street—so called, not from the Lords Audley, as is often supposed, but after Mr. Hugh Audley, a barrister of the Inner Temple, who, seeing the tendency of London to increase in a westerly direction, bought up the ground hereabouts for building purposes, and having started with a very small capital, died in 1662, leaving property to the tune of nearly half a million. The land taken up by him is described in an old survey, to be seen among the maps of George III., in the British Museum, as "lying between Great Brook Field, and the Shoulder of Mutton Field." The history of this individual may be found in a curious pamphlet, entitled, "The Way to be Rich, according to the practice of the great Audley, who began life, with £200, in the year 1605, and died worth £400,000 this instant November, 1662."

Here lived and here died, in 1770, at the age of upwards of ninety, General Lord Ligonier, one of the last survivors of the Duke of Marlborough's campaigns, and the correspondent of nearly all the eminent statesmen of the reigns of George II. and George III.

In this street was the "Vernon's Head," the sign of Admiral Vernon, the hero of Portobello, set up in commemoration of the capture of that town in 1739. The house was converted into a private residence in 1882-3. Opposite is St. Mark's Church, originally a chapel of ease to St. George's, Hanover Square, though now it has a district assigned to it, and has become, to some extent, independent of the mother church. It is in the Ionic style of Grecian art. It was erected by Mr. John Deering, R.A., in 1828.

South Audley Street, which runs southward from the south-western corner of Grosvenor Square, was not built till many years after North Audley Street, namely, about 1728; it comprises far finer houses, and has been tenanted by the highest families; and many foreigners of distinction, diplomatists, and others, have lived in it temporarily. Charles X. of France, for instance, in his exile, occupied No. 72; Louis XVIII. also lived here at one time, but the house is not identified, even by Mr. P. Cunningham. General Paoli, of Corsican fame; Sir William Jones, the great Eastern scholar; and Sir Richard Westmacott, the sculptor, are also named as residents here. Mr. Cunningham also tells us that Sir Richard Westmacott executed all his principal works at the house No. 14, now the residence of the Hon. Edward Leveson-Gower, brother of Lord Granville.

In this street, too, lived Mr. Robert Berry, the father of the charming Misses Berry, the friends and correspondents of Horace Walpole, of whom we shall have more to say in our next chapter.

Horace Walpole complains, in a letter to one of these ladies, that he has "no Audley Street" to receive him of an evening—alluding, no doubt, to his cousins, the Conways, to whose house he also refers in another letter, complaining that "all Audley Street is off to Yorkshire," and that town is dull and lonely.

No. 74 in this street, lately the residence of the

Earl of Cawdor, was for the best part of a century the house of the Portuguese Ambassador. In this street, at No. 77, was living, in 1820, Alderman (afterwards Sir Matthew) Wood; and here, on the 6th of June in that year, Queen Caroline, the injured consort of George IV., arriving from the Continent, took up her residence. Here she received the formal addresses from the common councilmen and livery of London, and here she would appear on the balcony, and bow to the mob assembled in the street below. Here her Majesty continued to reside till the commencement of her trial in Westminster Hall, which lasted from the 19th of August down to the 10th of November. During these long and weary weeks, the Queen was accommodated with apartments more conveniently situated in St. James's Square, at the house of Sir Philip Francis, as we have already seen. The sad story of the Queen's last few days is thus told by Hughson:—"On the death of George III., the Princess of Wales, who had been several years residing on the Continent, became Queen-consort of England, and resolved on immediately proceeding thither. On the 6th of June, 1820, her Majesty arrived in London, and took up her temporary residence at the house of Alderman Wood, in South Audley Street. The alderman met her Majesty at Montbarde, in France, and accompanied her through the rest of her journey. On the 16th, the common council, and on the 3rd of the following month, the livery of London, presented addresses to her Majesty on her return. On the 19th of August, the proceedings on the Bill of Pains and Penalties commenced in the House of Lords, which lasted till the 10th of November, when her Majesty was acquitted. It is impossible, in the limits of this work, to describe the state of the metropolis during these unpopular proceedings; on their close, the town was illuminated for three nights, and, on the 29th, the Queen went to St. Paul's Cathedral to return thanks." It is difficult to imagine what the special mercies were for which her Majesty gave "thanks" on this occasion. Her death happened in the following August.

Queen Caroline, however, was not the only royal personage who has lived in this street; for, in 1826, at Cambridge House (now Curzon House) resided the Duke of York, after he gave up his newly-built mansion in the stable-yard at St. James's. The house has been, at a later date, the residence of Earl Howe.

In the above year, too, Lord John Russell lived in this street; his house, however, has been converted to business purposes, and now serves as a hairdresser's shop. In 1841 the name of Lord Sydenham occurs among the list of residents here.

Among the inhabitants of this street, in 1763, was Lord Bute, as we learn from a notice in a contemporary journal, which tells us that, " in the July of that year, two women were sent by Lord Bute's order to Bridewell, for singing political ballads before his lordship's door in South Audley Street."

On the eastern side of this street is one of those proprietary chapels of ease, with which we have seen this fashionable district abounds. It is a dull, heavy structure, dating from the last century. In its vaults repose some distinguished characters : Lady Mary Wortley Montagu ; Ambrose Philips, the poet ; Philip, Earl of Chesterfield, who was carried hither from Chesterfield House, in 1773 ; and John Wilkes, who was buried here from Grosvenor Square, in 1797. A mural tablet in the chapel bears an inscription, said to be from his own pen :—" The remains of John Wilkes, a friend to Liberty."

In this street are the pottery-galleries of Messrs. Goode, where are displayed the celebrated productions of the Messrs. Minton. The chief stores of the Lambeth Art *Faience* have for many years past been kept at this establishment, which is said to be the most extensive of its kind in Europe.

At the corner of South Street stands a house of a very marked character, and by many attributed to Inigo Jones. The building is heavy and dull to a degree ; massive cornices, small window-panes set in massive frames, and a bay-window over a portico, projecting partly over the pavement in South Street, are its chief architectural features. The house was formerly the residence of General Gascoyne, the colleague of Canning in the representation of Liverpool.

Audley Square—as it is the fashion to style a few dull, heavy, substantial houses which recede a little from the road on the eastern side of South Audley Street, just above Chesterfield House—scarcely deserves a separate notice, but may be regarded as a part of South Audley Street ; and the only fact recorded in its annals is, that Mr. Spencer Perceval, the premier, whose assassination we have recorded,† was born in it in the year 1762.

Chesterfield House, at the bottom of this street, we shall describe in our next chapter.

CHAPTER XXVIII.

MAY FAIR.

" The morals of May Fair."

Derivation of the Name of May Fair—The Earliest Notice on Record of St. James's Fair—Description of the Fair in the Last Century—Puppet Shows—The Eccentric " Tiddy Dol "—Suppression of the Fair—The Rev. Dr. Keith's Chapel, and the Clandestine Marriages there—The Marriage of " Handsome Tracy "—Miss Elizabeth Gunning and the Duke of Hamilton—Extracts from the Marriage Registers of St. George's, Hanover Square—Curzon Street—The Misses Berry—Epigram by Horace Walpole—Distinguished Residents of Curzon Street— Hertford Street—Dr. Jenner—The " Dog and Duck "—Shepherd's Market—" Kitty Fisher "—Seamore Place—Chesterfield Street—The Hon. Mrs. Norton—Queen Street—Chesterfield House, and its Reminiscences.

THIS spot, which embraces in its somewhat vague and undefined area the present Curzon Street, Hertford Street, and Chesterfield House and gardens, took its name, in the days of Edward I., from an annual fair, which that king privileged the hospital of St. James's to keep " on the eve of St. James', the day, and the morrow, and four days following," as has already been stated in our account of St. James's Palace.* Pepys speaks of it as St. James's Fair, a name which expresses it geographically with sufficient accuracy, at a time when all to the north and west of St. James's Hospital was an open field.

The following amusing notice of " the Fair in St. James's " is quoted from Mackyn's Diary by Mr. Frost, in his " Old Showmen of London," as the earliest on record :—" The xxv. day of June [1560]. Saint James's fayer by Westminster was so great that a man could not have a pygg for money ; and the bear wiffes had nether meate nor drink before iiij. of cloke in the same day. And the chese went very well away for 1d. q. the pounde. Besides the great and mighti armie of beggares and bandes that were there."

Beyond the fact that it was postponed for a few weeks or months in 1603, on account of the plague, nothing more is recorded concerning this fair till 1664, in which year, Mr. Frost tells us, " it was suppressed, as considered to tend rather to the advantage of looseness and irregularity, than to the substantial promotion of any good, common and beneficial to the people."

It is to be hoped that the bad character of the fair, as given by the *Observator* somewhat later, in

* See p. 100, *ante.*

† See Vol. III., p. 530.

the reign of Queen Anne, is a little exaggerated. The editor writes:—"Oh! the piety of some people about the Queen, who can suffer things of this nature to go undiscovered to her Majesty, and consequently unpunished! Can any rational men imagine that her Majesty would permit so much lewdness as is committed at May Fair, for so many days together, so near to her royal palace, if she knew anything of the matter? I don't believe the patent for that fair allows the patentees the liberty of setting up the devil's shops and exposing his merchandise for sale." As to the precise nature, however, of this diabolic ware and "merchandise" he does not enlighten us in detail.

According to Mr. Frost, in his work quoted above, "May Fair" did not assume any importance till about the year 1701, when the multiplication of shows of all kinds caused it to enlarge its sphere of attractions. "It was held," he writes, "on the north side of Piccadilly, in Shepherd's Market, Shepherd's Court, White Horse Street, Sun Court, Market Court, and on the open space westwards, Chapel Street and Hertford Street, as far as Tyburn (now Park) Lane. The ground-floor of the Market House, usually occupied by butchers' stalls, was appropriated during the fair to the sale of toys and gingerbread, and the upper portion was converted into a theatre. The open space westwards was covered with the booths of jugglers, fencers, and boxers, the stands of mountebanks, swings, roundabouts, &c.; while the sides of the streets were occupied by sausage-stalls and gambling-tables. The first-floor windows were also, in some instances, made to serve as the proscenia of puppet-shows."

"I have been able to trace," he adds, "only two shows to this fair in 1702, namely, Barnes and Finley's, and Miller's, which stood opposite to the former, and presented 'an excellent droll called *Crispin and Crispianus*, or a shoe-maker a prince, with the best machines, singing, and dancing ever yet in the fair.'" The fair, on this occasion, drew together a large concourse of persons, and an attempt to exclude some young women of light character resulted in a riot. The young women, arrested for the purpose of being turned out, were rescued by some soldiers; a conflict ensued, other constables came up, and the "rough" element, of course, took part with the accused women. In the end one constable was killed and three others seriously injured. The man who actually dealt the fatal blow to the unfortunate constable managed to escape; but a butcher who had been active in the affray, was tried for his part in the affair, convicted, and hung at Tyburn. This tragical occurrence helped, no doubt, to bring the fair itself into dis-

credit, especially among the respectable inhabitants of the neighbourhood of Piccadilly."

Pennant, who remembered the last "May Fair," describes the locality as "covered with booths, temporary theatres, and every enticement to low pleasure." A more minute description of the scene, evidently drawn from the life, is given by an antiquary named Carter, in the *Gentleman's Magazine* for 1774.

"A mountebank's stage," this person tells us, "was erected opposite the 'Three Jolly Butchers' public-house, on the eastern side of the market area, now the 'King's Arms.' Here Woodward, the inimitable comedian and harlequin, made his first appearance as 'Merry Andrew;' from these humble boards he soon after made his way to those of Covent Garden Theatre. Then there was a 'beheading of puppets,' in a coal-shed attached to a grocer's shop (then Mr. Frith's, now Mr. Frampton's). One of these mock executions was exposed to the attending crowd. A shutter was fixed horizontally, on the edge of which, after many previous ceremonies, a puppet was made to lay its head, and another puppet instantly chopped it off with an axe. In a circular staircase-window, at the north end of Sun Court, a similar performance by another set of puppets took place. In these representations the late punishment of the Scottish chieftain, Lord Lovat, was again brought forward, in order to gratify the feelings of southern loyalty at the expense of that farther north."

"After the Scottish rebellion of 1745," writes Chambers, in his "Book of Days," "the beheading of puppets formed one of the most regular and attractive parts of the exhibitions at the 'May Fair,' and was continued for several years. The last great proprietor of such puppet-shows was a man named Flockton, whose puppets were in the height of their glory about 1790, and who retired soon after on a handsome competence." A puppet-show, we may add, under the name of the Marionettes, was revived at St. James's Hall about the year 1872.

At these annual gatherings in May Fair, too, was to be seen "Tiddy Dol," the eccentric vendor of gingerbread, whom we have mentioned in our account of the Haymarket, and who figures in Hogarth's well-known picture of the "Idle Apprentice" at Tyburn, where he, in his ornamental dress, is seen in the crowd holding up a gingerbread cake in his hand and addressing the mob. Here, too, was to be seen a Frenchman, whose name has passed away, who submitted to the curious his wife's powers of physical endurance. Fragile and delicate as she appeared, she would (so it was stated) raise from the floor a blacksmith's anvil by the hair of her head, which she twisted round it; and then, lying down, she would have the anvil placed on her bosom, while a horse-shoe was forged upon it with the same heavy blows which may be heard and seen in a blacksmith's shop.

In "Malcolm's Anecdotes" (vol. ii.) is preserved an advertisement of this fair from one of the London papers of the time:—"In Brookfield market-place, at the east corner of Hyde Park, is a fair to be kept for the space of sixteen days, beginning with the 1st of May; the first three days for live cattle and leather, with the same entertainments as at Bartholomew Fair, where there are shops to be let, ready built, for all manner of tradesmen that usually keep fairs, and so to continue yearly at the same place."

May Fair, which had long been falling into disrepute, ceased to be held in the reign of George I. It was "presented by the grand jury of Middlesex for four years successively as a public scandal; and the county magistrates then presented an address to the Crown, praying for its suppression by royal proclamation." Its abolition was brought about mainly through the influence of the Earl of Coventry, to whose house in Piccadilly it was an annual nuisance.

In 1721, as we learn from the *London Journal* of May 27th in that year, "the ground upon which the May Fair formerly was held is marked out for a large square, and several fine streets and houses are to be built upon it." The idea of a "square," however, was never realised.

In recording the downfall of May Fair and of its doings, the *Tatler* announces that "Mrs. Saraband, so famous for her ingenious puppet-show, has set up a shop in the Exchange, where she sells her little troop under the name of jointed babies."

The fashionable locality now known as May Fair, in the days of George I. and George II., however, enjoyed, on other grounds than that of the annual fair, a celebrity almost unique, and rivalled only by the Fleet Prison, of which we have already spoken.* Here was a chapel for the celebration of private and secret marriages, which stood within a few yards of the present chapel in Curzon Street. It was presided over by a clergyman, Dr. George Keith, who advertised his business in the daily newspapers, and, in the words of Horace Walpole, made "a very bishopric of revenue." This worthy parson having contrived for a long time to defy the Bishop of London and the authorities of Church and State, was at length

excommunicated for "contempt" of the Church of which he was a minister; but he was impudent enough to turn the tables upon his superior, and to hurl a sentence of excommunication at the head of his bishop, Dr. Gibson, and the judge of the Ecclesiastical Court. Keith was sent to prison, where he remained for several years. His "shop," however, as he called it, continued to flourish under his curates, who acted as "shopmen;" and the public was kept daily apprised of its situation and its tariff, as witness the following advertisement in the *Daily Post* of July 20th, 1744: "To prevent mistakes, the little new chapel in May Fair, near Hyde Park corner, is in the corner house, opposite to the city side of the great chapel, and within ten yards of it, and the minister and clerk live in the same corner house where the little chapel is; and the licence on a crown stamp, minister and clerk's fees, together with the certificate, amount to one guinea, as heretofore, at any hour till four in the afternoon. And that it may be the better known, there is a porch at the door like a country church porch."

But the rank and fashion of May Fair did not care whether the fees demanded were high or low, provided they could get the marriage ceremony performed secretly and expeditiously, yet legally. "Sometimes," writes Charles Knight, in "Once upon a Time," "a petticoat without a hoop was led by a bag-wig and sword to the May Fair altar, after other solicitations had been tried in vain." As an instance of the way in which this marriage, not *à la mode*, worked in West-end society, let us take the following sketch from Horace Walpole in his best style:—"Did you know a young fellow that was named 'Handsome Tracy?' He was walking in the Park with some of his acquaintance, and overtook three girls; one was very pretty. They followed them; but the girls ran away; and the company grew tired of pursuing them, all but Tracy. He followed them to Whitehall Gate, where he gave a porter a crown to dog them. The porter hunted them, and he the porter. The girls ran all round Westminster, and back to the Haymarket, where the porter came up with them. He told the pretty one that she must go with him, and kept her talking till Tracy arrived, quite out of breath, and exceedingly in love. He insisted on knowing where she lived, which she refused to tell him; and after much disputing, went to the house of one of her companions, and Tracy with them. He there made her discover her family, a butter-woman in Craven Street, and engaged her to meet him next morning in the Park; but before night he wrote her four love-letters, and in the last offered to give two hundred pounds a year and a hundred a year to Signora la Madre. Griselda made a confidence to a staymaker's wife, who told her that the swain was certainly in love enough to marry her, if she could determine to be virtuous, and to refuse his offers. 'Ay,' says she; 'but suppose I should, and should lose him by it?' However, the measures of the cabinet council were decided for virtue; and when she met Tracy next morning in the Park, she was

concocted and cemented, turned out a happy one afterwards.

But the butterman's daughter was far from being the only person who found her way through this little chapel into the matrimonial "ship of fools." Everybody has heard of the three Miss Gunnings, whose beauty and attractions set the West-end in a perfect flame in the reign of George II., the eldest of whom was married to the sixth Earl of Coventry.

CLARIDGE'S HOTEL. (*See page* 343.)

convoyed by her sister and brother-in-law, and stuck close to the letter of her reputation. She would do nothing; she would go nowhere. At last, as an instance of prodigious compliance, she told him that if he would accept such a dinner as a butterman's daughter could give him, he should be welcome. So away they walked to Craven Street; the mother borrowed some silver to buy a leg of mutton, and kept the eager lover drinking till twelve o'clock at night, when a chosen committee accompanied the faithful pair to the minister of May Fair. The doctor was in bed, and swore he would not get up to marry the king, but added that he had a brother over the way who perhaps would, and who did marry them." It is to be hoped that the union, thus hastily and thoughtlessly

One of these young ladies here went through the marriage ceremony, which gave her the coronet of a duchess. Horace Walpole thus records the fact in his gossiping letters, under date February 27th, 1752:—" The event that has made the most noise since my last is the extempore marriage of the youngest of the Miss Gunnings, who have made so vehement a noise of late. About a fortnight since, at an immense assembly at my Lord Chesterfield's, made to show the house, which is really most magnificent, the Duke of Hamilton made violent love at one end of the room while he was playing faro at the other; that is, he saw neither the bank, nor his own cards, which were of three hundred pounds each; he soon lost a thousand. . . . Two nights afterwards he found himself so impatient, he sent for a parson. The doctor refused to perform the ceremony without license or ring, so the duke swore he would send for the archbishop. At last they were married with a ring off the bed-curtain at half an hour after twelve at night, at the May Fair Chapel."

At last even the people of rank and "quality," the inhabitants of May Fair, grew frightened at their own practices; and, as a consequence, an

in the little chapel here. The entries in these volumes extend over nearly twenty years; and there is a duplicate set in the Bishop of London's registry covering, probably, a somewhat larger period.

Dr. Keith himself was a clergyman from the north of the Tweed, but he had been driven from Scotland on account of his attachment to Episcopacy. He had set up a marriage office in the Fleet Prison,

CHESTERFIELD HOUSE, 1760. (*See page* 353.)

Act was passed forbidding clandestine marriages. On the day previous to its coming into operation no less than sixty-one marriages were registered here. The Act itself was passed in the previous year, though its operation was delayed till Lady-day, 1754. During this period of suspense, Walpole writes to Montague:—"The Duchess of Argyll harangues against the marriage bill not taking place (*i.e.*, effect) immediately, and is persuaded that all the girls will go off before next Lady-day."

Among the registers of St. George's, Hanover Square, are three dingy volumes, marked "A," "B," and "C," respectively, containing such records as exist of about 7,000 marriages which were performed by the Rev. Mr. Keith and other clergymen

but had been forced to abandon it. He found, however, a better opening here, and a richer class of customers. It is said that, in one morning during the Whitsun holidays, he tied up in the silken bonds of matrimony a greater number of loving couples than had been married at any ten churches within the "bills of mortality." But this surely must have been an exaggeration.

While in prison, Keith seems to have had a keen eye to business. During his incarceration his wife died, and he kept her corpse embalmed and unburied for many months, and by that means ingeniously contrived to turn the circumstance into an advertisement of his trade. At all events, here is a record of his proceedings taken from the *Daily Advertiser* of January 30, 1750:—"We are informed that Mrs. Keith's corpse was removed from her husband's house in May Fair the middle of October last, to an apothecary's in South Audley Street, where she lies in a room hung with mourning, and is to continue there till Mr. Keith can attend the funeral. The way to Mr. Keith's chapel is through Piccadilly, by the end of St. James's Street, and down Clarges Street, and turn on the left hand." Then follows the announcement that the marriages are still carried on as usual by "another regular clergyman," as quoted above.

In the *Connoisseur* for October, 1754, are the following witty and satirical remarks *apropos* of the then recent Act for preventing clandestine marriages, and its effects on Keith's chapel :—" I received a scheme from my good friend Mr. Keith, whose chapel the late Marriage Act has rendered useless on its original principles. The reverend gentleman, seeing that all husbands and wives are henceforth to be put up on sale, proposes shortly to open his chapel on a new and more fashionable plan. As the ingenious Messrs. Henson and Bever have lately opened, in different quarters of the town, repositories for all horses to be sold by auction, Mr. Keith intends setting up a repository for all young males and females to be disposed of in marriage. From these studs (as the Doctor himself expresses it) a lady of beauty may be coupled to a man of fortune, and an old gentleman who has a colt's tooth remaining may match himself with a tight young filly. The doctor makes no doubt but his chapel will turn out even more to his advantage on this new plan than on its first institution, provided he can secure his scheme to himself, and reap the benefits of it without interlopers from the *fleet* (*sic*). To prevent his design being pirated, he intends petitioning the Parliament that, as he has been so great a sufferer by the new Marriage Act, the sole right of opening a repository of this sort may be vested in him, and this, his place of residence in May Fair, may still continue the grant for marriages." Here follows a "Catalogue of Males and Females to be disposed of in Marriage to the best bidder, at Mr. Keith's Repository, in May Fair :"—

"A young lady of £100,000 fortune—to be bid for by none under the degree of peers, or a commoner of at least treble the income.

"A homely thing, who can read, write, cast accounts, and make an excellent pudding—this lot to be bid for by none but country parsons.

"A very pretty young woman, but a good deal in debt, would be glad to marry a member of Parliament, or a Jew.

"A blood of the first-rate, very wild, and has run loose all his life, but is now broke, and will prove very tractable.

"Five Templars—all Irish. No one to bid for these lots of less than £10,000 fortune."

The concluding announcement in the article is as follows :—

"Wanted, a dozen of young fellows, and one dozen of young women, willing to marry to advantage ; to go to Nova Scotia."

The following extracts, taken at random from the register-books at St. George's, above mentioned, will serve to show that the private marriages celebrated in Dr. Keith's little chapel were not confined to the lower or rougher element, but were often taken advantage of by the "upper ten thousand :"—

"1748, March 23.—Hon. George Carpenter and Frances Clifton."

"1749, September 14.—William, Earl of Kensington, and Rachel Hill, Hempstead."

"1751, May 25.—Henry Trelawney, Esq., and Mary Dormer, St. Margaret's."

"1751, July 21.—Edward Wortley Montagu and Elizabeth Ashe, St. Martin's Fields."

"1752, June 30.—Bysshe Shelley and Mary Catherine Michell, Horsham."

"1751, May 25.—Hon. Sewallis Shirley and Margaret, Countess of Oxford."

"1753, March 15.—James Stewart Stewart, Esq., and Catherine Holoway, of St. Matthew's, Friday Street."

"1752, February 14.—James, Duke of Hamilton, and Elizabeth Gunning."

Of the lady whose name is contained in the last-mentioned entry we have already spoken. We may add, however, that she was the second of three fair sisters, of Irish extraction, without fortune, but closely related to the first baronet of the same name. Miss Elizabeth Gunning was not content with a single dukedom, for, after the death of the Duke of Hamilton, she married John, Duke of Argyll, and was eventually created a peeress of Great Britain in her own right, as Baroness Sundridge and Hamilton. The last time she appeared at any public assembly was at a pic-nic ball at Marseilles, during a three months' sojourn of the family in France in 1785. With reference to that event, a writer of that period observes : "I had the honour of dining with them that day, and the duchess, as soon as possible, retired from the company to dress. She came down to coffee in all her splendour; every one was struck with astonishment ; and I could not refrain from saying that I thought her Grace really looked as well as when I first saw her in the court-room in England as Duchess of Hamilton. The duke, with a smile, replied, 'Less aided then, perhaps, than now, sir.' Her Grace could not but be apprised of the wonder that was excited, and the Lieutenant of Police, rather too loudly, exclaimed, 'I have never seen any one so completely beautiful before.'" Her elder sister, Maria, was the wife of George William, sixth Earl of Coventry, and lived close by, in Piccadilly.

The marriages at May Fair Chapel, if not quite so loosely conducted as they were at the Fleet, were at least attended with the same evils, and afforded the same facilities for the accomplishment of forced and fraudulent unions. For instance, marriages could be antedated without limit, on payment of a fee, or not entered at all. Parties could be married without declaring their names. It was a common practice for women to hire temporary husbands at the Fleet, in order that they might be able to plead coverture to an action for debt, or to produce a certificate in case of their being *enceinte*. These hired husbands were provided by the parson for five shillings each; sometimes they were women. It appears that, for half-a-guinea, a marriage might be registered and certified that never took place. The marriage of the Hon. H. Fox, son of the first Lord Holland, to the daughter of the Duke of Richmond, at the Fleet, in 1744, and the increase of these irregular practices, led to the introduction of the Marriage Act. The interval between the passing of the bill and its coming into operation, as we have stated, afforded a rich harvest to the parsons of the Fleet and May Fair. In one register-book there are entered 217 marriages which took place at the Fleet on the 25th of March, 1754, the day previous to the Act coming into force. Clandestine marriages continued at the Savoy till 1756, when a minister and his curate being transported, an effectual stop was put to them.

To return once more to Dr. Keith, we may add that, in spite of being a person of loose morals, and frequently performing the marriage service in a state of intoxication, he published at least one religious treatise—"The Guide; or, the Christian Pathway to Everlasting Life." He lived to be nearly ninety, and died in 1758.

Curzon Street was so named from the ground landlord, George Augustus Curzon, third Viscount Howe, ancestor of the present Earl Howe. In this street, in November, 1852, died at No. 8, at the age of ninety, Miss Mary Berry, one of the two Misses Berry who enjoyed for so many years the friendship of Horace Walpole; and, indeed, the lady to whom, when late in life he succeeded to the earldom of Orford, he made an offer of his hand and his coronet. She and her younger

sister, Agnes, were the daughters of a Yorkshire gentleman, Mr. Robert Berry, who lived in South Audley Street, as already stated in our last chapter. Walpole first met them when on a visit at Wentworth Castle, in Yorkshire, and the friendship there made proved a lasting one. "The young ladies," says Mr. Robert Chambers, in his "Book of Days," "afterwards took up their abode at Twickenham, in the immediate neighbourhood of Strawberry Hill, with whose master a constant interchange of visits and other friendly offices was maintained. Horace Walpole used playfully to call them his 'two wives,' corresponded with them frequently, told them many stories of his early life, and what he had seen and heard, and was induced by these friends, who used to take notes of his communications, to give to the world his 'Reminiscences of the Courts of George I. and II.' On Walpole's death, the Misses Berry were left his literary executors, with the charge of collecting and publishing his writings. This task was accomplished by Mr. Berry, under whose superintendence an edition of Walpole's works was published, in five quarto volumes. He died, a very old man, in 1817; and his daughters, for nearly forty years afterwards, continued to assemble around them all the literary and fashionable celebrities of London. Agnes, the younger sister, pre-deceased Miss Berry by about a year and a half. Miss Berry was an authoress, and published a collection of 'Miscellanies' in 1844. She also edited about sixty letters, addressed to herself and her sister by Horace Walpole, and came chivalrously forward to vindicate his character against the sarcasm and aspersions of Lord Macaulay in the *Edinburgh Review*."

The following epigram on the Misses Berry was written by Horace Walpole, on their paying a visit to his printing-press at Strawberry Hill, soon after their return from a visit to Italy and a stay at Rome:—

" To Mary's lips has ancient Rome
    Her purest language taught;
And from the modern city home
    Agnes its pencil brought.

"Rome's ancient Horace sweetly shouts,
    Such maids with lyric fire;
Albion's old Horace sings nor paints—
    He only can admire.

"Still would his griefs their fame record,
    So amiable the pair is;
But ah! how vain to think his word
    Can add a straw to Berry's."

Sir Henry Halford, the Court physician, during his long reign of successful practice, lived for many years in this street, as also did the Princess Sophia

Matilda of Gloucester. The name of Madame Vestris also appears as the occupier of No. 1, in the year 1826. Here, too, Tobias Smollett was living, in third-rate lodgings, when he heard the news of the victory of Culloden.

Mr. Peter Cunningham enumerates, as residents of this street, Pope's Lord Marchmont, and Richard Stonehewer, the friend and correspondent of the poet Gray, at No. 41. In 1808, Francis Chantrey was living in this street, before his marriage, while first beginning to make his name famous as a sculptor. Whilst here, he received his first great order, from Mr. Alexander, the architect. It was for four colossal busts of Howe, St. Vincent, Duncan, and Nelson, for the Trinity House, with duplicates for the Royal Naval Asylum at Greenwich. He had already occupied rooms in Chapel Street, close by, where we find him in 1804, when he sent his first work for exhibition to the Royal Academy, of which he afterwards became so leading a member.

In the large house on the north side of the street, enclosed in its own grounds, and embowered in a grove of plane-trees, nearly opposite Curzon Chapel, lived Lord Wharncliffe, the great-grandson of Lady Mary Wortley-Montagu, and editor of her works. The house is still the property of his descendants. Curzon Chapel—a chapel of ease—is a large, dull, brick building, on the south side; and it stands within a few yards of the spot whereon Dr. Keith's unlicensed chapel formerly flourished.

Hertford Street—a somewhat dull and heavy thoroughfare, running parallel with Curzon Street on its south side, and crossing the top of Down Street, which it connects with Park Lane—has long been one of the most fashionable thoroughfares in this aristocratic neighbourhood, and is often mentioned as typical of the height of fashion in the days of William IV. and the early part of the reign of Queen Victoria.

In No. 14 lived Dr. Jenner, for a few years, from 1804, a man sadly in advance of his age, as may be inferred from the fact that, in spite of his wonderful discovery of vaccination, which arrested the ravages of the small-pox, he was unable to make a good professional connection at the West-end, and returned to Gloucestershire in disgust. His merits have been somewhat tardily acknowledged by the erection of a statue. The first Earl of Liverpool, father of the prime minister, died here in 1808. At No. 10 lived, in the last century, Lord Sandwich, famous for his musical parties: the house was afterwards inhabited by General John Burgoyne, the unsuccessful hero of the American War;

and subsequently, for a short time, by Richard Brinsley Sheridan. At No. 30 was living, in 1841, Mr. H. B. Trelawny, Lord Byron's companion in his last expedition to Greece, and in whose arms the poet breathed his last. In this street resided the late Sir Charles Locock, Bart., the eminent physician-accoucheur to Her Majesty, who died in 1875; and that consummate lawyer and accomplished scholar, Sir Alexander Cockburn, Lord Chief Justice of England, who died in 1880.

But Hertford Street is rich also in its past memories of quite another kind. As nearly as possible on its site there stood, a couple of centuries ago, a public-house, with gardens attached, called "The Dog and Duck," from the diversion of duck-hunting by spaniels which was carried on there. The fun was to watch the duck dive in order to escape from the dog's jaws; and it was quite a fashionable sport in the suburbs of London till the early part of the present century, when it was superseded by pigeon-shooting. Mr. Larwood, in his "History of Sign-boards," describes it as an old-fashioned wooden house, extensively patronised by the butchers, and other rough characters, during the "May Fair" time. The pond in which the sport took place was situated behind the house, and, for the benefit of the spectators, was boarded round to the height of the knee, in order to preserve the over-excited spectators from involuntary immersions. The pond, he adds, "was surrounded by a gravel walk, shaded by willow-trees."

In the immediate neighbourhood of Curzon and Hertford Streets are a number of small and dingy streets and lanes, the names of which help to perpetuate the market formerly held here, such as Market Street, Shepherd's Market, and Shepherd's Street. But this market, rural as the name may sound, is not so called from any pastoral associations, but from a certain Mr. Shepherd, or Sheppard, to whom once belonged the ground on which the "May Fair" was held. We fear, therefore, that all poetical thoughts of shepherds and shepherdesses going there a-Maying must be dismissed as baseless fictions. In Carrington Street, an insignificant thoroughfare between Down Street and Park Lane, there was a riding-school; and in this street lived the noted "Kitty Fisher."

Seamore Place is the name of a row of handsome but somewhat old-fashioned mansions, which occupy a sort of *cul de sac* at the western end of Curzon Street. They are only nine in number, and their chief fronts look westward over Hyde Park. In one of them, Lady Blessington, with her daughter and her son-in-law, Count D'Orsay, resided during a part of her widowhood, from about

1836 to 1840, surrounded by all the fashionable butterflies of the world of *bon ton*, whose admiration she so much courted. Whilst living here, too, she followed her bent by penning and sending some of her best known contributions to the literature of the day. We shall have to speak of her career hereafter, when we come to Gore House, between Knightsbridge and Kensington. Here, too, at one time, resided Lord Normanton.

Chesterfield Street, which runs out of Curzon Street northwards to Charles Street, was so called out of compliment to the great, or rather the polite, Lord Chesterfield, whose grounds it bounded on the east. In this street lived "Beau" Brummell for some years, after his retirement from the army, and while he still basked in the sunshine of royal favour among the circle of the Prince of Wales at Carlton House. Here, consequently, the Prince would frequently come of a morning in order to see the "Beau" make his toilette, and to learn the art of tying his neckerchief *à la mode*. And here the Prince would continue to sit so late into the evening that he would send his horses home from the door, and insist on taking a quiet chop or steak with his host, but with no intention of returning home till he was half-seas over, and the streaks of early morning were appearing in the sky.

Here, too, was living, in 1847, the gallant admiral, the Earl of Dundonald, formerly known as Lord Cochrane, when his name was formally restored to his rank in the navy and to the roll of the Knights of the Order of the Bath, by an order of the Queen in Council; and from this street he dated his letter of thanks to Mr. Douglas Jerrold for having advertised that tardy act of justice in the public press.

At No. 1 in this street lived that amiable, talented, and eccentric personage, Mr. J. W. Ward, afterwards Mr. Canning's Secretary for Foreign Affairs, and eventually known as Lord Dudley; and No. 11 was for many years the residence of Sir Robert Adair, the distinguished diplomatist. He died here in 1855. In this street, too, at No. 3, has lived, for upwards of thirty years, the Hon. Mrs. Norton, the poetess. By birth a Miss Caroline Sheridan, one of three beautiful grand-daughters of Richard Brinsley Sheridan, in early life she married the Hon. George C. Norton, a brother of the late Lord Grantley. She contributed to the annuals from a date prior to her marriage, and is known to the world as the authoress of several poems, which have taken a high stand in English literature, among which should be mentioned "The Undying One," based on the legend of the Wan-

dering Jew, "The Child of the Islands," "The Dream," and the "Lady of La Garaye."

The next turning on the east of Charles Street is Queen Street, where the ever youthful widow of the last Viscount Saye and Sele died in 1789, at the age of ninety-four, a lady about as celebrated as Queen Elizabeth for her fondness for dancing, in which she indulged almost to the last week of her long life. She was supposed to be the original of the Viscountess delineated in Hogarth's print of the "Five Orders of Periwigs, Coronets, &c." * It may be added that here, too, Lord John Russell was living in 1835, whilst M.P. for South Devon and for Stroud.

Chesterfield House, to which we now turn, stands at the junction of South Audley and Curzon Streets, and was built on ground belonging to Curzon, Earl Howe, by Isaac Ware, the same who edited "Palladio" for Philip, fourth Earl of Chesterfield. From one of Lord Chesterfield's "Letters to his Son," dated "March 31, O.S., 1749, Hotel Chesterfield," and from a quotation in No. 152 of the *Quarterly Review*, we get a fair account of the house when newly built. In the former his lordship writes: "I have yet finished nothing but my *boudoir* and my library; the former is the gayest and most cheerful room in England; the latter the best. My garden is now turfed, planted, and sown, and will, in two months more, make a scene of verdure and flowers not common in London." The writer in the *Quarterly Review* says: "In the magnificent mansion which the earl erected in Audley Street you may still see his favourite apartments, furnished and decorated as he left them—among the rest, what he boasted of as 'the finest room in London,' and, perhaps, even now it remains unsurpassed, his spacious and beautiful library looking on the finest private garden in London. The walls are covered half-way up with rich and classical stores of literature; above the cases are in close series the portraits of eminent authors, French and English, with most of whom he had conversed; over these, and immediately under the massive cornice, extend all round, in foot-long capitals, the Horatian lines—

' NUNC . VETERUM . LIBRIS . NUNC . SOMNO . ET .
   INERTIBUS . HORIS :
 DUCERE . SOLICITÆ . JVCUNDA . OBLIVIA . VITÆ.'

On the mantelpieces and cabinets stand busts of old orators, interspersed with voluptuous vases and bronzes, antique or Italian, and airy statuettes, in marble or alabaster, of nude or semi-nude opera nymphs." The columns of the screen facing the court-yard, and also the spacious marble staircase,

---

* See *Gentleman's Magazine*, vol. lxi., p. 394.

were brought from Canons, near Edgware, the mansion of the "princely" Duke of Chandos, which was pulled down in the year 1744, and the costly materials dispersed by auction. Among the historic relics which found a place here was a lantern of copper gilt, for eighteen candles, which

In 1869 this splendid mansion was—or, rather, so it was reported—doomed to be abolished; but it was purchased by a City merchant, Mr. Charles Magniac. Although it is no longer inhabited by the family of the noble earl whose name it bears, its walls still remain, and doubtless its interior is

THE GRAND STAIRCASE, CHESTERFIELD HOUSE.

was bought at the sale at Houghton, Sir Robert Walpole's seat. An amusing story is told with reference to the portraits of Lord Chesterfield's ancestors, which hung upon the walls of the library. As a piece of satire on the boast of ancestry so common at that time in great families, his lordship, it is said, placed among these portraits two old heads, which he inscribed "Adam de Stanhope" and "Eve de Stanhope." Surely no one could beat that.

but little altered in its general appearance from what it was in the above year, when the following description was written:—"The house itself has many fine points, and in others, it must be owned, it is slightly disappointing. Passing from the porter's lodge across a noble court paved with stones, and entering the hall, the visitor cannot fail to be struck by the grand marble staircase, up and down which the great Chandos must have walked when it stood beneath his own palatial roof at Canons.

And, apart from historical traditions, it is really a staircase for *ideas* to mount, especially when one is met on its first landing, not only by busts of Pitt and Fox, but by a lofty clock, apparently of antique French construction, and which looks as though it had, at some time or other, chimed out the hours at the two fiddles in bas-relief, gilt and crossed one over the other, are scarcely to be compared in appearance with harps, lyres, &c., the usual metaphorical tributes to the Muse of Melody, the Muse of Apollo, to Orpheus, and to Sappho ; and that one is more reminded of the violinists who played

THE EARL OF CHESTERFIELD. (*See page* 356.)

Versailles, long ere gay courtiers there perceived the shadow of the scaffold cast by the coming event of the 'Great' Revolution.

"Entering the music-room by means of this same staircase, we confess to some sense of disappointment. Not, of course, that we had expected to be greeted by any harmony of sweet sounds, any music from the spheres, but that the symbolism of decoration on the walls, on the ceiling, and the mantelpiece, might, on the whole, have been more graceful and more appropriate than it is, considering that prominent parts at the Court of France in the reign of Louis XIV., and at the beginning of that of Louis XV., than of the divine origin of music itself, which such a room ought to suggest. More pleasingly reminded, however, of that same Court is the visitor on descending to the reception-rooms on the lower floor, and entering the drawing-room, which is especially called the French room. There not only do the panelling of the walls, and the construction of the various pieces of furniture transport one back to the glories of the *ancien régime* of the time when Chesterfield enjoyed its society, but the looking-glasses, one over the fire-place and another facing it, appear as though they had mirrored that society, and not only mirrored but *multiplied* it; for these looking-glasses, being severally formed of various panels, fit, mosaic-like, one into another, and the divisions of these panels being ornamented by wreaths of painted flowers, &c., the beholder is reproduced again and again, and, in many a fantastic multiform, may judge of himself under various, not to say versatile, aspects.

"In one of the apartments—another drawing-room, to which this French *salon* leads—hangs a large chandelier, formed of pendent crystal, which once belonged to Napoleon I. Historically, this chandelier is so luminous in interest that it re-quires a narrative to itself; but the effect of it is somewhat heavy, owing to the large size of the crystal drops.

"The mantel-shelf in this room is classically beautiful; and amongst the pictures on the walls is a fine copy of Titian's 'Venus,' the original of which—if we remember aright—hangs in the Uffizii Gallery at Florence. But, perhaps, the most interesting apartment in the whole house is the library. There, where Lord Chesterfield used to sit and write, still stand the books which it is only fair to suppose that he read—books of wide-world and enduring interest, and which stand in goodly array, one row above another, by hundreds. . . In another room, not far from the library, one seems to gain an idea of the noble letter-writer's daily life, for we can still see its ante-chamber, in which the aspirants for his lordship's favour were sometimes kept waiting*—aspirants to favour who afterwards, in various ways, achieved fame for transcending that of ' their then patron.' On the garden-front outside is a stone or marble terrace, overlooking the large lawn, stretching out in lawn and flower-beds behind the house. Upon this terrace Chesterfield, doubtless, often walked, snuff-box in hand, and in company with some choice friends—let us say from France —friends with whom he might gossip on matters connected with the courts, and camps, and cabinets of his day." The old earl, it would seem, was fond of the repose which his garden and court-yard afforded; for the late Earl of Essex, who died in 1839, the husband of Kitty Stephens, used to say that he remembered, as a boy, seeing the courtly old earl sitting on a rustic seat in front of his mansion, and basking in the sun.

Chesterfield House is one of the few private houses in London which M. Grossley, in his " Tour to London," allows to be equal to the hotels of the nobility in Paris. After it was sold to Mr. Magniac, as above stated, that gentleman consider-ably curtailed the grounds in the rear, and erected a row of handsome buildings overlooking Chester-field Street, to which has been given the name of Chesterfield Gardens.

Philip Dormer Stanhope, fourth Earl of Chester-field, was the son of Philip, third Earl, and of Lady Elizabeth Savile, daughter of the Marchioness of Halifax. His grandmother superintended his education till his eighteenth year, when he went to Cambridge. After his university career he spent a few years in foreign travel, mixing freely with the best society of the chief Continental towns, and at the Hague, adding to his many accomplishments the pernicious vice of gaming. While at Paris he received his final polish under the tuition of the beauties of that place, and, no doubt, gained much of the experience which forms the ground-work of the advice, which he afterwards transcribed in his "Letters" for the very questionable benefit of his son.

Before the death of his father, he sat in the House of Commons as representative of two Cornish boroughs, St. Germains and Lostwithiel, and became a distinguished speaker; and after his accession to the title, in 1726, and his con-sequent removal to the Upper House, he soon obtained some slight celebrity as an orator. His Court favour varied greatly. During the life of George I., he was appointed Gentleman of the Bedchamber to the Prince of Wales; but on that prince's accession as George II., he was greatly disappointed by the absence of that royal favour which he conceived he had a right to expect. He was, however, in the following year appointed Am-bassador to Holland, where he greatly distinguished himself by his diplomatic talent; and it was at the expiration of his two years of service there that, on his return to England, he was appointed Lord Steward of the Household; but having joined a strong opposition against Walpole, and incurring the decided enmity of the king, he was dismissed from this situation with marks of strong resentment. There are various stories as to the radical cause of the king's dislike to the brilliant statesman, but probably any one of them would have been suffi-cient to create, at the least, a decided coldness. Archdeacon Coxe's version of it is confirmed by Walpole, who was concerned in it, in his memoir of George II.; but there is a discrepancy as to dates, and a tone of improbability about some of the details, which throw more than a shadow of

---

* The room is immortalised in Mr. E. M. Ward's picture, "Dr. Johnson in the Ante-room of Lord Chesterfield." In this picture the Canons staircase is well shown in the back-ground.

doubt over the whole. Briefly, it runs to the following effect : that Chesterfield had ardently desired the post of Secretary of State, and an arrangement had been made in his favour ; upon which he had an audience of the Queen, to which he was introduced by Walpole, and immediately after paid a longer visit to Lady Suffolk, then reigning favourite, than was approved of by the Queen, who thereupon procured that his appointment should not take place. Here it may be remarked that Chesterfield had been intimately acquainted with Mrs. Howard long before she had attracted the notice of Queen Caroline or George II.; and further, that, having been created Countess of Suffolk in 1731, and thus set at her ease as to money matters, she was well disposed to leave the Court, but did not do so till 1735, three years after the dismissal of Chesterfield, to which Archdeacon Coxe represents her retirement as the ominous preliminary! Walpole relates a similar parallel indiscretion of Chesterfield's ; and it appears that it was not till two years before the earl's death that he was informed, by Horace Walpole himself, that the cause of his disgrace was his having offended the Queen by paying court to Lady Suffolk. Be this as it may, there was another and more probable cause for the royal dislike, which lay in his marriage with the daughter of George I. and the Duchess of Kendal, Melosina de Schulenburg, created, in her own right, Countess of Walsingham, and considered, as long as her father lived, one of the wealthiest heiresses in the kingdom. George I. opposed the inclinations of his tall, dark-haired, and graceful daughter, in consequence of Chesterfield's notorious addiction to gambling ; but, a very few months after Chesterfield's dismissal from court, Lady Walsingham became Lady Chesterfield. Her husband's house in Grosvenor Square was next door to the Duchess of Kendal's, whose society he much frequented ; and it was she who suggested legal measures respecting a will of the late king, which George II. was said to have suppressed and destroyed, and by which, as the duchess alleged, a splendid provision had been made for Lady Walsingham ; and at last, rather than submit to a judicial examination of the affair, George II. compromised the suit by a payment of £20,000 to the Earl and Countess of Chesterfield. These things were not likely to smooth the way for the ex-Lord Steward's return to St. James's ; nor was it facilitated by his inveterate habit of ridiculing and disparaging the Electorate and all its concerns, which he continued to his dying day.

His marriage took place in 1733 ; fourteen years after, in 1747, he commenced building the "rather fine house," as he described it, in May Fair. When the famous boudoir of blue damask and gold, of which much has been said, and more hinted, was finished, and to which Madame de Monconseil contributed the two magnificent *bras de porcelaine* to be placed on each side of the costly mantelpiece, the lordly owner took possession of the house, a year before the other rooms were finished, their slow progress greatly vexing him. In 1745 his lordship was admitted a member of the Cabinet, and in the next year appointed Lord-Lieutenant of Ireland. Three years later we find the earl retiring from the office of principal Secretary of State, to which the king had been constrained, by his undoubted talent, to appoint him ; and thus at the early age of fifty-four, he resigned finally the cares of official life. He was, nevertheless, still an active member of the Upper House, and among the measures with which his name is identified are some of historical importance. In spite of much opposition, within and without of the House, he carried the Bill for the Reform of the Calendar, and gave us the "new style," which set our calculation of the year in harmony with that of the rest of Western Europe.

Dr. King, in " Anecdotes of his Own Times" (1819), says that the earl resigned his employment of Secretary of State because "he would not submit to be a cipher in his office, and work under a man who had not a hundredth part of his knowledge and understanding, and resolved to meddle no more in public affairs. However," he adds, "he was lately so much disgusted with our bad measures, that he could not help animadverting on them, though in his usual calm and polite manner. His petition to the king is an excellent satire, and hath discovered to the whole nation how, at a time when we are oppressed with taxes, and the common people everywhere grown mutinous for want of bread, the public money is squandered away in pensions, generally bestowed upon the most worthless men."

It was during Lord Chesterfield's last brief tenure of the seals of office that Dr. Johnson's eagerly-sought introduction to him took place. The then unknown author, whose dictionary, now a great fact, was then merely an idea floating in the brain of an apparently ordinary mortal, waited in the ante-room of the Secretary of State, and when, having seen Colley Cibber preferred before him, he was admitted, he received, besides approval of his plan, a donation of ten guineas ! Not many months before he had received fifteen guineas for " The Vanity of Human Wishes." And many years after, he remarked to Boswell: "Sir, ten pounds were to me at that time a great sum."

"The world has been for many years," writes Boswell, in his "Life of Johnson," "amused with a story, confidently told, and as confidently repeated, with additional circumstances, that a sudden disgust was taken by Johnson upon occasion of his having been one day kept long in waiting in Lord Chesterfield's ante-chamber, for which the reason assigned was, that he had company with him; and that, at last, when the door opened, out walked Colley Cibber; and that Johnson was so violently provoked when he found for whom he had been so long excluded, that he went away in a passion, and never would return. I remember having mentioned this story to George, Lord Lyttleton, who told me he was very intimate with Lord Chesterfield; and holding it as a well-known truth, defended Lord Chesterfield by saying, that 'Cibber, who had been introduced familiarly by the back-stairs, had probably not been there above ten minutes.' It may seem strange even to entertain a doubt concerning a story so long and so widely current, and thus implicitly adopted, if not sanctioned, by the authority which I have mentioned; but Johnson himself assured me that there was not the least foundation for it. He told me that there never was any particular incident which produced a quarrel between Lord Chesterfield and him; but that his lordship's continued neglect was the reason why he resolved to have no connection with him.

"When the dictionary was upon the eve of publication, Lord Chesterfield, who, it is said, had flattered himself with expectations that Johnson would dedicate the work to him, attempted, in a courtly manner, to soothe and insinuate himself with the sage, conscious, as it should seem, of the cold indifference with which he had treated its learned author; and further attempted to conciliate him, by writing two papers in *The World*, in recommendation of the work; and it must be confessed that they contain some studied compliments, so finely turned, that if there had been no previous offence, it is probable that Johnson would have been highly delighted. Praise, in general, was pleasing to him; but by praise from a man of rank and elegant accomplishments he was peculiarly gratified.

"This courtly device," continues Boswell, "failed of its effect. Johnson, who thought that 'all was false and hollow,' despised the honeyed words, and was even indignant that Lord Chesterfield should, for a moment, imagine that he could be the dupe of such an artifice." His expression to Boswell

concerning Lord Chesterfield, upon this occasion, was: "Sir, after making great professions, he had for many years taken no notice of me; but when my dictionary was coming out, he fell a-scribbling in *The World* about it. Upon which I wrote him a letter, expressed in civil terms, but such as might show him that I did not mind what he said or wrote, and that I had done with him."

Dr. Johnson appeared to have had a remarkable delicacy with respect to the circulation of this letter; for Dr. Douglas, Bishop of Salisbury, informed Boswell that, having many years ago pressed him to be allowed to read it to the second Lord Hardwicke, who was very desirous to hear it (promising at the same time that no copy of it should be taken), Johnson seemed much pleased that it attracted the attention of a nobleman of such a respectable character; but, after pausing some time, declined to comply with the request, saying, with a smile, "No, sir, I have hurt the dog too much already," or words to this purpose.

Dr. Adams expostulated with Johnson, and suggested that his not being admitted when he called on him, to which Johnson had alluded in his letter, was probably not to be imputed to Lord Chesterfield; for his lordship had declared to Dodsley that "he would have turned off the best servant he ever had if he had known that he denied him to a man who would have been always more than welcome." And in confirmation of this, he insisted on Lord Chesterfield's general affability and easiness of access, especially to literary men. *Johnson:* "Sir, that is not Lord Chesterfield; he is the proudest man this day existing." *Adams:* "No, there is one person, at least, as proud; I think, by your own account, you are the prouder man of the two." *Johnson:* "But mine was *defensive* pride." This, as Dr. Adams well observed, was one of those happy turns for which Johnson was so remarkably ready.

Johnson having now explicitly avowed his opinion of Lord Chesterfield, did not refrain from expressing himself concerning that nobleman with pointed freedom. "This man," said he, "I thought had been a lord among wits, but I find he is only a wit among lords!"

Johnson's remark on Lord Chesterfield's "Letters to his Son"—a natural son, of course, for the title passed at his death to a cousin—is well known to most readers of modern literature: "Take out the immorality, and the book should be put into the hands of every young gentleman."

Of Lord Chesterfield we are told by the Hon. G. Agar-Ellis, afterwards Lord Dover, in the *Keepsake*, that "the love of literature, and, still more, any talent for it, was so rare an attribute in a 'man of quality,' that his lordship, in his day, stood almost alone as a noble author, and as the Mæcenas of all others." But the first of these assertions is surely an exaggeration; and as to the latter character, Lord Chesterfield's treatment of Dr. Johnson, in his own courtly mansion, was not very much like that of the courteous and kindly Mæcenas to the poet Horace.

A good story is told by Mr. Frost, in his "Old Showmen," respecting Lord Chesterfield. His lordship once made a wager with Heidigger, a Swiss by birth, and by office Master of the Revels, and who had the reputation of being "as ugly as sin," that he could find an uglier person in the course of a week. The seven days elapsed, and Lord Chesterfield lost his wager.

One of his lordship's most familiar acquaintances was the elder brother of the first Lord Rokeby, called "*Long* Sir Thomas Robinson" on account of his height, and to distinguish him from Sir Thomas Robinson, first Lord Grantham. Hawkins relates how that Lord Chesterfield "employed him as a mediator with Johnson, who, on his first visit, treated him very indignantly." It was on his request for an epigram that Lord Chesterfield made the distich :—

"*Un*like my subject will I make my song:
It shall be witty, and it shan't be *long ;*"

and it was he to whom he said in his last illness,

"Ah, Sir Thomas, it will be sooner over with me than it would be with you, for I am *dying by inches.*" Lord Chesterfield was very short. Sir Thomas did not long survive his witty friend, and died in 1777.

Lord Chesterfield had but one child—the illegitimate son, Philip Stanhope, to whom his famous "Letters" were addressed; and he, after disappointing Chesterfield's expectations, was carried off in the prime of life. The aged peer survived him some five years, and died in 1773, almost an octogenarian.

Lord Chesterfield's wit did not die with him, for even his will contained a grim satire on the Dean and Chapter of Westminster, some of whose lands, adjoining Chesterfield House, were taken by the earl, after a hard bargain, for the purpose of forming Stanhope Street. The substance of the clause in the will referred to is to the effect that, if his "godson," as he calls him, Philip Stanhope, should at any time indulge in horse-racing, or the keeping of race-horses or hounds ; or if he should reside for one night at Newmarket during the time of the races there, or should lose in any one day the sum of £500 by gambling, then he should forfeit and pay out of his estate the sum of £5,000, "to and for the use of the Dean and Chapter of Westminster." As his death took place before that of the earl, the Dean and Chapter could have no claim upon the estate of the "godson," as the contingent interest never accrued in their favour.

CHAPTER XXIX.

APSLEY HOUSE AND PARK LANE.

——— "Tecto quum vidit in illo
Magnum habitatorem."—*Juvenal.*

Situation of Apsley House—George II. and the Apple-stall Keeper—Henry, Lord Apsley, purchases the Site, and builds a Mansion—The First Earl Bathurst—Apsley House purchased by the Nation for the Duke of Wellington—Description of the Building—The Picture-Gallery—The Duke's Temporary Unpopularity, and Attack of the Mob on Apsley House—The Waterloo Banquets—The Waterloo Shield—Biographical Notice of the Duke of Wellington—Memorials of the Illustrious Duke—The "Curds and Whey House"—Hyde Park Corner—A Singular Panic—Park Lane—A Strange Abode—Park Lane Fountain—Holdernesse House—Great Stanhope Street—Tilney Street—Dean Street—Dorchester House—South Street—Chapel Street—Grosvenor House—The Grosvenor Family—Dudley House—Upper Brook Street—Park Street—Green Street—Norfolk Street—The Murder of Lord William Russell—Camelford House.

QUITTING May Fair, we now turn to the southwest, down Hamilton Place, in order to look in upon Apsley House, with which we were obliged to deal very briefly in our walk along the mansions of Piccadilly. This house, so many years the residence of the late, and still the residence of the present Duke of Wellington, forms a conspicuous object on entering London from the west, occupying as it does the corner of Hyde Park and Piccadilly. Its situation is one of the finest in the metropolis, standing upon the rising ground

overlooking the parks, and commanding views of the Kent and Surrey hills in the far distance. Its site is said to have been a present from George II. to a discharged soldier, named Allen, who had fought under that king at Dettingen. His wife here kept an apple-stall, which by the thrifty couple was turned by degrees into a small cottage. The story of this present has been often told, but it will bear telling yet once again :—When London did not exist so far as Knightsbridge, George II., as he was riding out one morning, met Allen, who

doubtless showed by his garments that he had once belonged to the army; the king accosted him, and found that he made his living by selling apples in a small hut. "What can I do for you?" said the king. "Please your majesty to give me a grant of the bit of ground my hut stands on, and I shall be happy." "Be happy," said the king, and ordered him his request. Years rolled on; the apple-man died, and left a son, who from dint of industry became a respectable attorney. The then Chancellor gave a lease

house which he built upon it the name by which it is still known. The mansion was originally of red brick, and though solid and substantial, it had no great architectural pretensions.

The father of Lord Chancellor Apsley, the first Earl Bathurst, was one of the most genial and agreeable of the friends of Pope, who has referred to him in the often quoted lines in terms of respect and affection :—

THE DUKE OF WELLINGTON IN 1842. (*After a Sketch by* "*H. B.*")

of the ground to a nobleman, as the apple-stall had fallen to the ground. It being conceived the ground had fallen to the Crown, a stately mansion was soon raised, when the young attorney put in claims; a small sum was offered as a compromise, and refused; finally, the sum of £450 per annum, ground rent, was settled upon.

In 1784, Allen's son or other kin sold the ground to Henry, Lord Apsley, Lord Chancellor, afterwards second Lord Bathurst, who gave to the

"Oh! teach us, Bathurst, yet unspoiled by wealth,
   That secret rare, between th' extremes to move
   Of mad good-nature and of mean self-love."

His lordship appears to have been of a particularly lively and cheerful disposition, and to have preserved his natural vivacity to the very last. To within a month of his death, which happened on the 16th of September, 1775, at the age of ninety-one, he constantly rode out on horseback for two hours before dinner, and regularly drank his bottle of claret or madeira after dinner. Some amusing anecdotes have been told of this old Lord Bathurst, which will bear telling over again. He used to repeat often, with a smile, that Dr. Cheyne had assured him, fifty years before, that he would not live seven years longer, unless he abridged himself of his wine. About two years before his death, he invited several of his friends to spend a few cheerful days with him at his seat, near Cirencester; and being, one evening, very loth to part with them, his son (then Lord Chancellor) objected to their sitting up any longer, adding, that health and long life were best secured by regularity. The earl suffered his son to retire, but as soon as he left the room, exclaimed, "Come, my good friends, since the old gentleman is gone to bed, I think we may venture to crack another bottle!"

In 1820 the mansion was purchased by the nation, and settled as an heirloom on the illustrious dukedom of Wellington. It was then leasehold only. Mr. Peter Cunningham tells us that "the Crown's interest in Apsley House was sold to the duke by indenture, dated the 15th of June, 1830, for the sum of £9,530, the Crown reserving, however, a right to forbid the erection of any other house or houses on the same site." The principal front, next Piccadilly, consists of a centre with two wings, having a portico of the Corinthian order, raised upon a rusticated arcade of three apertures, leading to the entrance hall. The west front consists of two wings; the centre slightly recedes, and has four windows with a balcony. The front is enclosed by a rich bronzed palisade, corresponding with the gates to the grand entrance to the Park. In the saloon is a colossal statue of Napoleon, by Canova.

In 1828 the mansion was enlarged, and the original exterior of red brick was faced with a casing of Bath stone, designed by Mr. B. Wyatt. At this time the front portico and the west wing were added; but, says Mr. Peter Cunningham, "the old house still remains intact, so much so, indeed, that the hall door and knocker belonged to the original Apsley House." In the upper part of the west wing is the Waterloo Gallery, nearly a hundred feet in length. This noble apartment is splendidly decorated, and richly gilt. The ball-room extending the whole depth of the mansion, and the small picture gallery, which together form a suite, are both superb rooms. On the ground-floor, at the north-west angle, looking into the little garden which divides the house from Hyde Park, is the modest chamber used by the great Duke as a bedroom to the last year of his life. It is plainly furnished, with a small iron bedstead and a plain

writing table; a few books, which were the duke's favourite companions, still remain where their great master left them. This room was shown to the public, along with the rest of the house, for a few days in 1852, the year of the duke's death, and a striking proof it gave of his simplicity and studied avoidance of all that savoured of luxury. The house contains several fine pictures, amongst others a full-length portrait of George IV., in the Highland costume, by Sir David Wilkie. This picture was damaged by a stone during the Reform Bill riots, but the injury has been skilfully repaired. There are also portraits of the Emperor Alexander and the Kings of Prussia, France, and the Netherlands, and of several of the duke's companions-in-arms, and pictures of the battles which he fought. Among the latter is Sir William Allan's celebrated painting of the "Battle of Waterloo, with Napoleon in the Foreground," of which the duke is said to have remarked that it was "good, very good; not too much smoke." Then there are several portraits of his great rival, Napoleon; also Wilkie's "Chelsea Pensioners reading the Gazette of the Battle of Waterloo," which was painted for the duke. The gallery contains besides a collection of other subjects, sacred and profane, by the old masters and painters. Dr. Waagen, in his work on "Art and Artists in England," speaks with great enthusiasm of the specimens of Sir David Wilkie in this collection; as also of a "Christ on the Mount of Olives," by Corregio (captured in Spain from Joseph Bonaparte); besides others by Velasquez, Claude Lorraine, Jan Steen, and Teniers.

In the tumults which broke out in London in 1831 on account of the opposition of the duke and the Tory party to the first Reform Bill, the windows of Apsley House were broken by the mob. In consequence of this, the duke had all his windows cased with iron shutters, like those of shop-fronts in our leading thoroughfares, and made bullet-proof; and though often entreated to have them removed when his popularity returned, he steadily refused to allow the change to be made, as he had no confidence in the smiles of popular favour, and would often say that they were a standing proof of the vanity of the world's applause. With reference to the manner in which the fury of the multitude in the above-mentioned year vented itself on the duke, we glean a little intelligence in the following extract from Mr. Raikes' "Journal:"—
"I can remember well," he writes, "the time when the duke returned to England, after his brilliant campaigns, crowned with the battle of Waterloo; at that time he was cheered by the people wherever he went, and lauded to the skies. Afterwards, at

the period of the Reform Bill, the fickle people forgot all his services, and constantly hooted him in the streets. One morning, as he was coming from the Tower on horseback, the rascally mob attacked him with so much virulence and malice, that he was exposed to considerable personal danger in the street. I was in that year at a ball given by him at Apsley House to King William IV. and his Queen, when the mob were very unruly and indecent in their conduct at the gates ; and on the following days they proceeded to such excesses, that they broke the windows of Apsley House, and did much injury to his property. It was then that he caused to be put up those iron blinds to his windows, which remain to this day as a record of the people's ingratitude. Some time afterwards, when he had regained all his popularity, and began to enjoy that great and high reputation which he now, it is to be hoped, will carry to the grave, he was riding up Constitution Hill, in the Park, followed by an immense mob, who were cheering him in every direction ; he heard it all with the most stoical indifference, never putting his horse out of a walk, or seeming to regard them, till he leisurely arrived at Apsley House, when he stopped at the gate, turned round to the rabble, and then pointing with his finger to the iron blinds which still closed the windows, he made them a sarcastic bow, and entered the court without saying a word."

The shutters remained outside the windows of the house down to the death of the duke in 1852, after which they were removed by his son and successor.

On every 18th of June to the last, the duke celebrated his Waterloo dinner in the large gallery. Mr. Rush, in his " Court of London," mentions dining here in the summer of 1821, when the king (George IV.) was a guest, with most of the royal dukes, the foreign ambassadors, and the duke's old companions in arms. He thus describes the after-dinner scene :—" The king sat on the right hand of the duke. Just before the dessert courses, the duke rose and gave as a toast, ' His Majesty.' The guests all rose and drank it in silence, the king also rising and bowing to the company. A few minutes afterwards the king gave ' The Duke of Wellington,' introducing his toast with a few remarks. The purport of these was, that had it not been for the exertions of ' his friend upon his left ' (it was so that he spoke of the duke), he, the king, might not have had the happiness of meeting those whom he now saw around him at that table ; it was, therefore, with peculiar pleasure that he proposed his health. The king spoke with great emphasis and great apparent pleasure. The duke made no

reply, but took in respectful silence what was said. The king himself continued sitting whilst he spoke, as did the company in profound stillness under his words."

These banquets were continued from year to year down to the duke's death. As years rolled on, the familiar faces gradually fell off, and the number of chairs for his guests—his old comrades in arms— grew smaller and smaller.

AUTOGRAPH OF THE DUKE OF WELLINGTON.

On state occasions, the chief ornament of the duke's sideboard was the celebrated shield presented to him by the City of London. It is of pure gold, and was manufactured by Messrs. Rundle and Bridge, from the designs of Thomas Stothard, R.A. On it are represented, in basrelief and in alto, the most important of the duke's victories ; and it is said that its cost was nearly £15,000. In fact, a dinner at Apsley House has been almost described in anticipation by Virgil, in a passage of his " Æneid," thus translated by Dryden :—

" On Tyrian carpets, richly wrought, they dine ;
With loads of massive plate the sideboards shine ;
And antique vases, all of gold embossed
(The gold itself inferior to the cost
Of curious work), where, on the sides, were seen
The fights and figures of illustrious men,
From their first founder to the present Queen."

Down to within a few weeks of his death, the duke used to ride out every afternoon, on his way to the Horse Guards or the Park. His appearance, as he passed from the gate of Apsley House into Piccadilly, at his accustomed hour, was one of the sights of London which " country cousins " were regularly taken to see ; and, attired in a plain blue frock-coat, with white waistcoat and trousers, with a groom riding behind him, he was " the observed of all observers." " A stranger could recognise him amidst the peers by the marked respect they showed to him. The duke was the best-known and most popular man in London. There were people constantly waiting at the entry to the House of Lords, and not unusually in the vicinity of the Horse Guards, to get a peep at him ; and he had been so long accustomed to acknowledge the homage paid to him by all classes, on his appearing in public, that the habit had become mechanical with him. Every well-bred person raised his hat to the duke ; and the duke, sitting on horseback in his calm, impassive manner, and looking straight before him, lifted two fingers towards his hat to everybody. It was quite a scene when he chanced to walk along Regent Street, or some of the more frequented thoroughfares in the neighbourhood of the Horse Guards or the Houses of Parliament. A knot of followers instantly fell into his wake, augmenting as he proceeded. Shopkeepers rushed to their doors, or peered out of their windows, to catch a glance of him. 'The Duke!' passed from lip to lip. You could see in the countenance of all sorts of people as they approached and passed—and all sorts of people is a wide word in the streets of London—a pleased expression as they recognised the duke. It was less striking to observe the respectful greetings of the better-conditioned classes, than the cordial interest which the common people evinced in the great captain. The omnibus-driver would point him out to his outside passengers; the cad on the steps behind, to his 'insides.' The butcher's boy, as he dashed along on his pony, drew bridle to look at the duke. Cabmen, cadgers, costermongers, and *gamins*, gentle and simple, young and old, paused for a moment to gaze at the man whom they delighted to honour."

To write a complete biography of "the duke" would be altogether beyond our province, for to do that would be almost equivalent to writing a history of Europe during the time in which he lived. Suffice it then for us to say that he was the third son of Garrett, first Earl of Mornington, and brother of the Marquis Wellesley, and that he was born in 1769. Entering the army in 1787, he commenced his actual service in the field in 1794. Shortly afterwards, he was returned to the Irish Parliament for the borough of Trim, County Meath; and in 1806, he was chosen to represent Newport in the House of Commons. In the following year he was appointed Chief Secretary for Ireland. His Grace was for upwards of a quarter of a century Lord Warden of the Cinque Ports, and besides the honours and emoluments bestowed upon him for his brilliant services by the British Government, he received almost every foreign order of distinction, to the number of seventeen. As a parliamentary orator he spoke plain and to the point, and his correspondence was remarkable for its laconic brevity. To sum up, in the words of one of his biographers, it may be said that "throughout his long career, he appears the same honourable and upright man, devoted to the service of his sovereign and his country, and just and considerate to all who served under him. As a general, he was cautious, prudent, and careful of the lives of his

men; but when safety lay in daring, as at the battle of Assaye, he could be daring in the extreme. He enjoyed an iron constitution, and was not more remarkable for his personal intrepidity than for his moral courage. The union of these qualities obtained for him the appellation of the 'Iron Duke,' by which he was affectionately known in his later years. . . . His tastes were aristocratic, and his aides-de-camp and favourite generals were almost all men of family and high connections. Altogether, he was the very type and model of an Englishman; and in the general order issued by the Queen to the Army, he was characterised as 'the greatest commander whom England ever saw.'"

On the 14th of September, 1852, the "great Duke" died at Walmer Castle, his official residence as Lord Warden of the Cinque Ports. On that morning his valet called him as usual at six o'clock. Half an hour afterwards he entered the room and found his master ill. At four o'clock in the afternoon, after an epileptic fit, the great soldier breathed his last. Of all his crowd of illustrious friends, only two were near him—Lord and Lady Charles Wellesley, who were staying on a visit. So little did he anticipate death that he had appointed that day to meet the Countess of Westmoreland at Dover to see her off by packet to Ostend. The chamber in which he died had much the appearance of that at Apsley House described above; it was a little room with a single window, which served as his library and study, and an iron bedstead three feet wide.

Apsley House stood between two other memorials of the illustrious duke—a colossal figure mounted on horseback surmounting the arch at the top of Constitution Hill, and the statue of Achilles in Hyde Park. The first of these statues was modelled by Mr. Matthew C. Wyatt and his son, James Wyatt; it occupied three years, and is said to have taken more than one hundred tons of plaster. It represents the duke upon his horse "Copenhagen," at the field of Waterloo. The entire group weighs forty tons, and is nearly thirty feet high. The erection of this statue, in 1846, which cost about £30,000, originated from the close contest for the execution of the Wellington statue in the City. The archway on which this statue stood was erected by Mr. Decimus Burton, in 1828. It is Corinthian, and on each face are six fluted pilasters, with two fluted columns, flanking the single archway, raised upon a lofty stylobate or plinth, and supporting a richly-decorated entablature, in which are sculptured alternately "G. R. IV.," and the imperial crown within wreaths of laurel. The massive iron gates, bronzed, are enriched with the royal arms in a circular centre. In 1882-3, in order to relieve the block caused by the traffic at Hyde Park Corner, it was decided to set the archway 200 feet back, and to form a new roadway across the corner of the Green Park, connecting Hamilton Place with Halkin Street. At the present time (Jan., 1883), it is undecided where the statue of the duke will be re-erected.

The statue in its original position had always been an object of interest to visitors to the metropolis. "On fine afternoons," writes Mr. John Timbs, "the sun casts the shadow of the duke's equestrian statue full upon Apsley House, and the sombre image may be seen gliding, spirit-like, over the front." But this will now be seen no more.

Of the statue of Achilles, erected in the duke's honour by the ladies of England, we shall have more to say when we come to our chapter on Hyde Park. It has not, however, been by the aid of statuary alone that the memory of the duke has been kept alive; for it is said that within twenty-five years after he fought his last crowning battle, there were already in Europe seven bridges, nine museums, seventeen public squares, and twenty streets, which bore the name of Waterloo. How many more have been added since we can scarcely estimate.

We have already mentioned the toll-gate at Hyde Park Corner, and the old lodge adjoining it, which stood by the entrance into the Park. Appended to it was a small cottage, known to the public as the "Curds-and-Whey House." The lodge was joined on to Knightsbridge by a brick wall, which, as well as the old lodge and the "Curds-and-Whey House," was taken down about the year 1825, when a new lodge of stone was built, and the wall superseded by a light iron railing. About the same time, a small strip of ground was taken off the south-east corner of the Park, in order to form a garden for Apsley House; but the Duke of Wellington was not very popular at the time, and the encroachment on the public rights stirred up not a little bad feeling against him, an invidious parallel being drawn between his Grace and John, Duke of Marlborough, whose house was built on a site subtracted from St. James's Park.

"Hyde Park Corner is a worthy terminal mark to a great metropolis," observes Charles Knight. "To one who has been 'long in city pent,' the view from the Achilles along the elm row, towards the Serpentine, has a park-like appearance, that makes him feel out of town the moment he reaches it. To the traveller from the country, on the contrary, the view across the Green Park, towards West-minster Abbey, is truly courtly and metropolitan. The triumphal archways on either side corroborate the impression of stately polish; the magnificent scale of St. George's Hospital is worthy the capital of a great nation; . . . and Apsley House seems placed there in order that the 'hero of a hundred fights' may keep watch and ward on the outskirts of the central seat of power of the land whose troops he has so often led to victory."

In our view of this spot, on page 283, is shown the old toll-gate which formerly stood here. It had a milestone nestling under it, which gave it quite a rural appearance. It would have been amusing to have stood by the side of the old toll-gate, and to have seen the "quality," as people of rank and fashion were then styled, collecting just before the expected arrival of the great earthquake, which, it was prophesied vehemently, was coming to demolish the City and its suburbs. Charles Knight tells us, in his "London," that "for some three days before the date fixed, the crowds of carriages passing Hyde Park Corner westwards, with whole parties removing into the country, was something like a procession to Ranelagh or Vauxhall." This occurred in the month of April, 1750, and is thus recorded in a newspaper of that date:—

"Incredible numbers of people, being under strong apprehensions that London and Westminster would be visited by another and more fatal earthquake on this night, according to the predictions of a crazy life-guardsman, and because it would be just four weeks from the last shock—as that was from the first—left their houses, and walked in the parks and the fields, or lay in boats all night; many people of fashion in the neighbouring villages sat in their coaches till day-break; others went off to a greater distance, so that the roads were never more thronged, and lodgings were hardly to be procured even at Windsor; so far, and even to their wits' end, had their superstitious fears, or their guilty consciences, driven them."

This going off to Kensington, or Hounslow, or Windsor, to avoid the earthquake, reminds one of the old Duchess of Bolton, who, on Whiston's prophecy of the approaching destruction of the world, prudently resolved to be off to China, in order to escape so inconvenient an accident. Lady Hervey writes to her friend, Mr. Morris, with reference to this silly panic: "The Ides of March are come, and will, I am persuaded, be past in all safety before you receive this letter, in spite of prophets and prophecies. The newspapers are filled with accounts of a hundred little subaltern earthquakes which have been felt in many different places, but which I take to be only the ghosts of the more

considerable one which haunt the timorous. . . . .
Fear is an epidemic distemper; there is scarcely
anything that is more contagious. I dare say at
this minute nine parts in ten of the inhabitants of
Westminster are shaking as much from this fear as
they would from the earthquake if it was really to
happen." That this curious instance of a "popular
delusion" was not altogether a groundless panic,
may be gathered from the following account,

read in the *London Magazine* for 1773 :—" Paris,
May 14.—A report which had prevailed here that
this city was to be destroyed by a comet in the
night between the 12th and 13th of this month,
so terrified many weak and credulous people, that
whole families actually quitted Paris on that account,
and are gone into foreign countries."

But it is time for us to resume our perambulation. Leaving Apsley House, we now travel north-

APSLEY HOUSE IN 1800. (*From Mr. Crace's Collection.*)

quoted from another publication, printed in the
above year :—" On the 8th of March, at half-past
five in the morning, the sky being very clear and
serene, and the air very warm, the inhabitants of
London, and to a great extent round the City, were
alarmed by the shock of an earthquake, that came
with great violence, especially about Grosvenor
Square. This was preceded, about five o'clock, by
a continual though a confused lightning, till within
a minute or two of its being felt, when a noise was
heard resembling the roaring of a great piece of
ordnance, fired at a considerable distance, and then
instantly the houses reeled, first sinking, as it were,
to the south, and then to the north, and with a
quick return into the centre."

A parallel to this "popular delusion" may be

wards, and following in the main the course of
Park Lane, we shall, before long, find ourselves at
Tyburn, which, for the present, must be the limit
of our journeyings in the west of the metropolis,
as we are bound to find our way back to the
central regions of Bloomsbury, by a route embracing
Oxford Street and the large district which lies to
the north of it.

Park Lane, in the reign of Queen Anne, was a
desolate bye-road, generally spoken of as "the lane
leading from Piccadilly to Tyburn." The thoroughfare is, for the most part, open on its west side to
Hyde Park, the other side being chiefly occupied
by lofty and splendid mansions and terraces.
Towards its southern extremity, the "lane" was
formerly very narrow and inconveniently crowded;

but in 1871 it was widened by the Board of Works, by the removal of one of the mansions in Piccadilly, and the throwing open of Hamilton Place. Before the extension of London so far westward, when this was nothing more than a country lane, or bye-road, shaded here and there by trees, and winding its way along by the park palings, from the toll-gate at Hyde Park Corner to Tyburn, it must have presented a very rural appearance. So lately

the property of a lady who died intestate, and whose wealth came into possession of the Government. It having been understood that she had often in her lifetime advocated the erection of a fountain here, this was thought the most desirable way to spend the money. The fountain stands on a very advantageous site, between the new and the old roads leading into Piccadilly, some twenty yards in advance of the point of bifurcation. The space

ENTRANCE TO GROSVENOR STREET FROM HYDE PARK, ABOUT 1780. (See page 370.)

as the beginning of the last century, the lane was almost, if not quite, destitute of habitation, for in it lived, moping away their existence in an unfinished house, commenced by their eccentric father, the sons of George Bushnell, who sculptured the statues which adorn Temple Bar. "This strange abode," says Mr. Walter Thornbury, in "Haunted London," "had neither staircase nor doors. . . . . Vertue, in a MS. dated 1728, describes a visit which he paid to the house, which was 'choked up with unfinished statues and pictures,' the sad relics of their father's wayward and eccentric genius."

At the point where Park Lane and Hamilton Place meet, there was erected, in 1875, at the cost of £5,000, an ornamental fountain by Thornycroft. The money expended on it was a part of

is necessarily somewhat triangular, and the sculptor has adapted his design to the place by making it tri-frontal. The great feature in the work is, in accordance with this form of composition, a group of three heroic-size marble statues of the greatest of English poets—Shakespeare, Milton, and Chaucer; and the summit of the monument, twenty-six feet from the ground, is a gilded bronze-winged figure of Fame, poised with one foot on a globe, blowing her trumpet, and bearing the wreath. Below the columnar pedestal on which these portrait statues stand, are three bronze figures of Muses, seated, and holding their attributes as Tragedy, Comedy, and History. These are so arranged that the Shakespeare is supported by the figures of Tragedy and Comedy, while the Milton stands between

Tragedy and History, and the Chaucer with Comedy and History on each side. The principal front is naturally given to the Shakespeare, facing across the Park, while Fame, lifting her trumpet high in the air, looks upward in the same direction. The statue of Milton faces the spectator coming down Park Lane; while Chaucer, his tablets and stile in hand, greets him with a pleasant half-humorous, half-reflective look, as he passes up the old narrow way from Piccadilly. Thus the sculptor has, with the happiest sense of the harmonies arising from mere position, availed himself of every coigne of vantage, and added interest and meaning to his work beyond its ostensible purpose of a fountain. The poet of all time faces the wide expanse of space, while Milton and Chaucer look over the western paths of busy practical life and work.

The first large mansion as we go up Park Lane is Holdernesse House, at the corner of Hertford Street. It is the residence of the Marquis of Londonderry, and stands on a site formerly occupied by the town mansion of the D'Arcys, Earls of Holdernesse, a title long since extinct. It is said that the father of the first Lord Londonderry travelled in the north of Ireland as a commission agent for a Scottish house of business, and that when his son rose to the surface in the political world, he was glad to petition the Earl of Galloway for leave to hook himself on to an obscure branch of the family tree of the Scottish house of Stewart.

The mansion—one of the most spacious and splendid in London—though little known to the world outside, was built, about the year 1850, from the designs of Messrs. S. and B. Wyatt, and commands a charmingly rural view over the expanse of Hyde Park. Here is a magnificent picture-gallery, containing, among other pictures, some full-length portraits of British and foreign monarchs of the present century by Sir Thomas Lawrence, as also a collection of articles of *virtu*—some of which were presented to the second Marquis of Londonderry by the Allied Sovereigns — vases, and tables of malachite. The sculpture-gallery contains several works by Canova and other great masters.

Great Stanhope Street, a broad thoroughfare, leading up, like an avenue, to the front of Chesterfield House, immortalises the family name of the old Earl of Chesterfield, its builder. Lord Palmerston lived, for many years prior to 1840, at No. 9. Next door, was living Mr. Alexander Raphael, the first Roman Catholic sheriff of London and Middlesex, whose money largely helped to ensure the return of O'Connell to Parliament as member for Carlow. No. 5 was, for many years, the residence of the Duke of Wellington's friend, Lord Fitzroy

Somerset, afterwards Lord Raglan; and from this house he started, in the spring of 1854, to take the command of our army in the Crimea, where he died in 1855. No. 15 was for some time the town residence of the gallant Field-Marshal, the first Viscount Hardinge, formerly Governor-General of India, and successor of the Duke of Wellington as Commander-in-Chief of the British Army. Facing the entrance to this street, and opening into the park, is Stanhope Gate.

Tilney Street, the next turning northward, connects Park Lane with South Audley Street. At his house in this street, in 1787, died, at an advanced age, Soame Jenyns, the well-known man of letters, essayist, poet, and convert from infidelity, and many years M.P. for Cambridge. His kindly and genial character made him very popular in society; but his various writings have come, for the most part, to be forgotten. It is said that no words of ill-nature or personality ever passed his lips, except his memorable epigram and epitaph—for it is both —on Dr. Johnson :—

> " Here lies Sam Johnson. Reader, have a care;
> Tread lightly, lest you wake a sleeping bear.
> Religious, moral, generous, and humane
> He was; but self-sufficient, proud, and vain;
> Fond of, and overbearing in, dispute ;
> A Christian and a scholar—but a brute !"

The house No. 6 in this street was the last town residence of Mrs. Fitzherbert, who was, no doubt, the lawful wife of George IV. She died in 1837, leaving her house to the Damer family. At No. 5, lived the Lord Yarmouth of the Regency, before his father's death raised him to the House of Peers as Marquis of Hertford.

Dean Street is the name by which a narrow and winding thoroughfare, leading behind Dorchester House into South Audley Street, is dignified. It is clearly only an enlargement of a rural bye-road, probably worn by the wheels of carts and wagons proceeding from the market-gardens of Pimlico to the market in the Brook Field, already mentioned. It consists of some half-a-dozen small houses, on one side only of the street, and has few reminiscences, social, literary, or political.

Dorchester House, the residence of Mr. R. S. Holford, the gardens of which face Park Lane on the one side, and Dean Street on the other, is one of the handsomest of the many modern mansions of London. It is in the ornate Italian style, and stands on the site of an older mansion of the same name, which was one of the residences of the late Marquis of Hertford, who died there in 1842. This nobleman, who, as Earl of Yarmouth, was a well-known figure under the Regency, married Mademoiselle

Fagniani, the daughter, according to some, of the Duke of Queensberry ("Old Q."), according to others, of George Selwyn, or George Selwyn's butler. Selwyn, it is recorded, left her a fortune of £30,000, two-thirds of which were to pass to Lord Carlisle's family if she should have no children. Lord Yarmouth was a *roué* and a profligate, but he had one redeeming quality, and that was wit. When Lord Granville resigned his post as ambassador at Paris, Lady Granville gave an evening party, jocosely adding that it was her "funeral." "I believe in a resurrection," said his lordship.

The present mansion was built in 1851-2, from the architectural designs of Mr. Lewis Vulliamy. It is faced with Portland stone, and in plan forms a parallelogram, about 105 feet wide by 135 feet in depth, very nearly the size of Bridgewater House. The grand staircase is of marble, and the interior generally is fitted up with great completeness. The arrangement of the west front, facing Park Lane, is original and effective, the mouldings and dressings generally having been carefully studied. The principal cornice displays a large amount of carving, and its size may be judged from the fact that the stones composing the chief projection of it are each upwards of eight feet square. There is a bold stone screen wall round the house, with a lodge at the south-west corner. "This mansion," says the *Builder*, "is a very good specimen of masonry, and is built for long endurance. The external walls are 3 feet 10 inches thick, with a cavity of about 5 inches, and the proportion of stone is great, and the bonders numerous; the stones are all dowelled together with slate dowells; and throughout, the greatest care appears to have been taken by the architect to ensure more than usually sound construction. If the New Zealander, who is to gaze on the deserted site of fallen London in some distant time to come, sees nothing else standing in this neighbourhood, he will certainly find the weather-tinted walls of Dorchester House erect and faithful, and will, perhaps, strive to discover the meaning of the monogram which appears on the shield beneath the balconies, 'R.S.H.,' that he may communicate his speculations to some 'Tasmanian Society of Antiquaries,' perhaps not more pugnacious, if less erudite, than our own."

Scattered through the principal apartments of Mr. Holford's mansion is a splendid collection of pictures, mostly by the ancient masters, many of them being of first-rate celebrity. The gallery contains, *inter alia*, fine specimens of Titian, Velasquez, Tintoretto, Vandyke, Murillo, Teniers, Wouvermans, and other artists. Among the pictures are two of the Caracci series, painted for the Giustiniani Palace, by Agostino and Ludovico Caracci. These famous pictures came to England in the Duke of Lucca's collection, and not being purchased for the National Gallery, after some negotiation with the trustees, they were subsequently exhibited in most of the cities of the United Kingdom, before they were separated to pass into the hands of private gentlemen. Then there are several of Rubens' exquisite sketches, among them the slight one for his "Entry of Henry IV.," in the Luxembourg collection, and the "Assumption of the Virgin," for the picture over the high altar in Antwerp Cathedral. Claude and the two Poussins are represented by brilliant landscapes. Altogether, the gallery ranks among the most important private collections in England. Mr. Holford has also a magnificent library, well stored with rare and curious books, among which are the *editio princeps* of Walton's "Compleat Angler," and Bunyan's "Pilgrim's Progress," and an extensive collection of English and foreign classics.

On the north side of Dorchester House is South Street, which runs into Hill Street, Berkeley Square. In this street stood the Roman Catholic chapel belonging to the Portuguese Embassy, and called after it the Portuguese Chapel. The building was removed about the year 1845, when it was superseded by the Jesuit Church in Farm Street, as already mentioned. In this street (at No. 39) lived Lord Melbourne, while occupying the post of Premier. In 1835, Mdlle. D'Este, daughter of the Duke of Sussex, lived at No. 36; and at No. 33, Lord Holland. In this street, also, lived Vice-Chancellor Sir John Leach.

Chapel Street is so called on account of its proximity to Grosvenor Chapel. In it, in 1841, lived General Sir Robert Thomas Wilson, who, having gained laurels in Egypt under Sir Ralph Abercromby, and subsequently in the Peninsula under Wellington, became involved in the unfortunate matter of Queen Caroline, and for his censure of the course pursued by the members of the Crown, was degraded and dismissed from the army; he was, however, subsequently reinstated, and attained the rank of general. He was for many years M.P. for Southwark; and for some time, just before his death in 1849, he held the post of Governor of Gibraltar.

Of Mount Street, which runs parallel with Chapel Street, across the middle of South Audley Street, we have spoken in a previous chapter.

A fine and spacious mansion, No. 21, between Mount and Upper Grosvenor Streets, was for many years the residence of the Marquis of Breadalbane,.

and afterwards of Lady Palmerston, who lived here in her widowhood.

In Upper Grosvenor Street lived William, Duke of Cumberland, more frequently known as "the butcher," on account of his wholesale massacre of the conquered Jacobites after the battle of Culloden, in 1746. Here he died, somewhat suddenly, at the end of October, 1765.

brother of George III., for whom it was originally built. It is separated from the street by a handsome open stone colonnade or screen, of classic pillars, connecting a double arching entrance, above which are pediments sculptured with the family arms, and panels with the four seasons above the foot entrances; the metal gates, and other portions of the screen, are enriched with foliage, fruit,

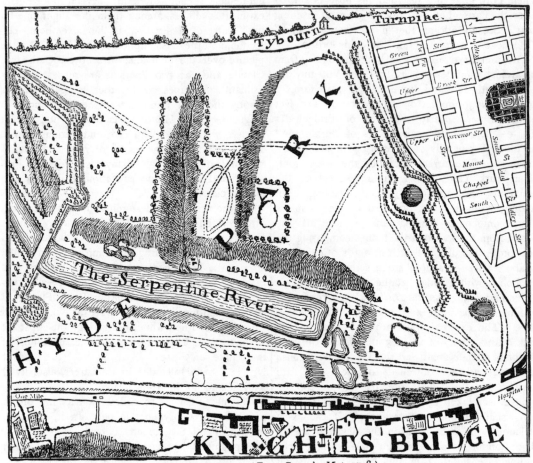

HYDE PARK. (*From Rocque's Map,* 1748.)

The corner house of Park Lane and Upper Grosvenor Street, formerly numbered 1, Grosvenor Gate, was the residence of Lord Beaconsfield, for more than thirty years, including the period of his first Premiership. It had belonged to Mr. Wyndham Lewis, for a short time his colleague in the representation of Maidstone, whose widow (afterwards Lady Beaconsfield) he married in 1839, soon after her first husband's death. He occupied it down to the year before his second Premiership.

On the south side of this street is Grosvenor House, the town residence of the Duke of Westminster. It was formerly called Gloucester House; and in it lived the Duke of Gloucester, younger

flowers, and armorial bearings. This screen was completed in 1842, from the designs of Mr. T. Cundy, who also erected, in 1826, after a beautiful example of the Corinthian order, the western wing of the mansion, containing the picture-gallery, one of the finest private galleries in Europe. Few sights are more attractive to strangers than galleries of paintings and statues; and although we are sadly deficient in public collections of such works of art, yet it may safely be asserted, that no country in Europe can boast of such magnificent private galleries as England, and no capital as London. Unlike Paris in this respect, most of the picture-galleries in London are the property of private individuals ; but they are generally accessible by special application or a personal introduction.

The celebrated "Grosvenor Gallery" was commenced by Richard, first Earl Grosvenor, by the purchase of Mr. Agar's pictures, as a nucleus, for 30,000 guineas. The collection has since been considerably increased by various purchases. The gallery contains specimens of Claude, the Poussins, Raphael, Murillo, Snyders, Rembrandt, Rubens, Velasquez, Titian, Guido, Paul Veronese, Vandyke, Cuyp, Gainsborough, Reynolds, Hogarth, Vandervelde, and, indeed, of nearly all the great masters, ancient and modern. Hogarth's "Sigismonda," which is among them, as we know from one of the painter's private letters, was executed in 1764, the last year of his life, at the earnest request of Sir Richard Grosvenor.

In the words of Dr. Waagen, in his "Art and Artists in England," Grosvenor House gallery "makes a truly princely appearance, by its extent, the value of the pictures, and the manner in which they are hung. . . . . It is rich in the works of the great painters of the Dutch and Flemish schools of the seventeenth century, and in works of Rembrandt it is perhaps the first in England, after the private collection of royalty." Dr. Waagen also singles out for special commendation pictures by Paul Potter, Gerard Dow, Salvator Rosa, Claude Lorraine, Murillo, and Velasquez. The gallery is a magnificent and lofty apartment, lit only by a lantern from above ; a faint and subdued light consequently reaches the lower part, to the great disadvantage of the pictures which are hung low. It contains five fine specimens of Rubens, including "The Wise Men's Offering," "Ixion," and "Sarah sending away Hagar ;" the "Visitation of St. Elizabeth," and four others, by Rembrandt.

The following extract from Mr. H. C. Robinson's Diary, under date May 31, 1833, will give a good idea of the merits of this gallery :—"I accompanied ——— to the Marquis of Westminster's, to see his pictures. The pleasure of seeing them was rather enhanced than diminished by my better acquaintance with the great master-pieces in Italy. There are here some delightful specimens of Claude, which are equal to any on the Continent ; there are also capital Rembrandts and Rubenses. It is true that there are but few of the great Italian masters, yet Guido's 'Fortune' (a duplicate) is one of the most beautiful pictures that I know. Westall was here with ——, and I could hear him giving the preference in colouring to Sir Joshua's 'Mrs. Siddons' over every picture in the room. The 'Blue Boy' of Gainsborough is a delicious painting."

It only remains to add that the duke very freely allows the gallery to be seen by the working classes ; and that, with this end specially in view, has allowed access to it, under certain conditions, on Sundays, an example of liberality and consideration which might be followed in other quarters.

The Duke of Westminster is the head of the family of Grosvenor—a house which, although its connection with the English peerage is scarcely a century old, can lay claim to as noble a descent as any of our Norman houses. In fact, the Grosvenors have been of knightly dignity since the Conquest. Its head was the individual who, towards the close of the fourteenth century, carried on, for five long years, the memorable controversy of Scrope *versus* Grosvenor, before the High Court of Chivalry, the judges being the Lord High Constable, Thomas of Woodstock, Duke of Gloucester, youngest son of Edward III., and the Earl Marshal, Thomas de Mowbray, Earl of Nottingham. " Kings, warriors, mitred abbots, bishops, statesmen, and poets, appear on the scene. Four hundred witnesses, not one of lesser degree than 'a gentleman having knowledge of arms,' were called on to give evidence—among them John of Gaunt, Owen Glendower, Hotspur, and Geoffrey Chaucer. The question before the Court was such as may well raise a smile now-a-days, when everybody is, forsooth, a 'gentleman,' and when everybody who likes to pay the tax can assume what armorial bearings he pleases, without fear of punishment ; it was simply the right to bear a particular plain coat of arms, heraldically described as ' *Azure, a bend or.*' The plaintiff was Sir Richard de Scrope, of Bolton, the friend and comrade of the Black Prince ; the defendant was Sir Robert Grosvenor, a Cheshire knight. We will not attempt to give an outline of the pleadings : suffice it to say, that the decision of the Court was in favour of Scrope, the same arms, ' *within a plain bordure argent,*' being allowed to Grosvenor—the present arms of the family."

The Grosvenors were raised to a baronetcy in 1621, but did not attain the peerage till the early years of the reign of George III., when Sir Richard Grosvenor was created Baron Grosvenor of Eaton, in the County Palatine of Chester. His lordship was advanced to the dignities of Viscount Belgrave and Earl Grosvenor twenty years later. The second earl was raised to the Marquisate of Westminster at the coronation of William IV. The ducal title was conferred by Her Majesty in 1874. The title chosen by Earl Grosvenor for his marquisate is, at all events, appropriate ; for it is from within the boundaries of the fair City of Westminster that the largest portion of the princely rent-roll of the family is derived. It is often said, and generally believed, that the Duke of Westminster's income exceeds that of any other nobleman of the age.

Continuing our walk up Park Lane, we pass, at No. 35, the residence of Sir Moses Montefiore, Bart., the venerable and indefatigable champion of the religious and social interests of the Jewish race in every part of the world.

administration, was somewhat of a *bon vivant*, as may be guessed from some of the anecdotes handed down about him. During the general depression in 1825–7, Lord Dudley remarked to a friend that his coal-mining income had fallen off during one year, £30,000; "but," he added, "I am a moderate man, and don't feel it. Lord Durham, they tell me, has not bread!"

On one occasion, when the *carte* of a forth-

THE FRONT OF GROSVENOR HOUSE. (*See page* 370.)

Dudley House, at the north-western corner of Upper Brook Street, is the residence of the Earl of Dudley, and is also noted for containing a gallery of pictures of the Flemish and Italian schools. The collection formed here by the late earl is described by Dr. Waagen in 1835 as a very mixed one. He enumerates a few by Bellini, Francia, Cuyp, Rysdale, &c., adding, "I looked in vain for the 'Three Graces,' by Raphael, which Passavant saw there." It is understood, however, that the present earl has added considerably to his gallery. There are also several fine specimens of sculpture, including a "Venus" by Canova.

Here lived the eccentric Earl of Dudley, who died in 1833. His lordship, who was Secretary of State for Foreign Affairs under Mr. Canning's

coming dinner at the "Clarendon" was discussed in his presence, his lordship observed: "My wants and wishes are moderate in such matters. I consider a good soup, a small turbot, a neck of venison with asparagus, and an apricot tart, is a dinner for an emperor—when he can't get a better."

Of his lordship's extraordinary absence of mind, and his unfortunate habit of "thinking aloud," many amusing anecdotes have been in circulation. It is told, as a fact, that when he was in the Foreign Office, he directed a letter, intended for the French, to the Russian Ambassador, shortly before the affair of Navarino; and, strange as it may appear, it obtained him the highest honour. Prince Lieven, who possibly never made any mistakes of the kind, set it down as the cleverest *ruse* ever attempted to be played off, and gave himself immense credit for not falling into the trap laid for him by the sinister ingenuity of the English Secretary. He returned the letter with a most polite note, in which he vowed, of course, that he had not read a line of it after he had ascertained that it was intended for Prince Polignac; but could not help telling Lord Dudley at an evening party, that he was "*trop fin*, but that diplomatists of his (Prince L.'s) standing were not so easily caught."

In 1826, No. 40 was occupied by the wealthy and eccentric Mr. Ball Hughes. In 1841, No. 27 was the residence of the celebrated engineer, Sir John Burgoyne; and at No. 49 lived Lord Ashley (since Earl of Shaftesbury). In this street, too, at one time, resided the Hon. Mrs. Damer, the sculptor. She was a daughter of General Conway, and the widow of Mr. John Damer, who, as we have seen,* whilst quite a young man, shot himself at a tavern in Covent Garden. She was a great friend

CAMELFORD HOUSE, 1820. (*See page* 375.)

With high birth, wealth, and everything in his favour, Lord Dudley ended in a ridiculous failure. He is tersely described by one of the ladies of the Court of George IV., as "a man who promised much, did little, and died mad." Madame de Staël, however, said of him, that "he was the only man of *sentiment* whom she had met in England."

Upper Brook Street, which connects Park Lane with the north-west corner of Grosvenor Square, has had at different times some distinguished residents; among others, William Gerard Hamilton, M.P., known as "single-speech Hamilton." In 1763, Lady Molesworth, her brother, and seven other persons, were accidentally burnt in their house in this street.

of Horace Walpole, who left her a life interest in Strawberry Hill.

Portugal Street, which runs north and south from Mount to Chapel Streets, parallel to Park Lane, still commemorates the name of the queen of Charles II. Our readers will not have forgotten that, at one time, this name was given to Piccadilly; and, in all probability, when thus quietly dropped out of use for the great thoroughfare, it was preserved in connection with this modest and retiring street by some lover of the Stuart line of kings. The street is narrow, and consists of little more than a dozen houses, all old-fashioned, and rather

* See Vol. III., p. 258.

gloomy; and there is little more to be said about it.

Park Street, which extends northwards from South Street to Oxford Street, crossing Mount Street, Upper Grosvenor, and Upper Brook Streets, has numbered among its residents at various times a few names which have become famous, such as Sir Humphry Davy, the greatest chemist of his age, who lived at No. 26; Mr. William Beckford, of Fonthill celebrity, who, in 1841, occupied No. 27; Mr. Serjeant Goulburn, who lived at No. 21; and Miss Lydia White, who, in 1827, died at her residence, No. 113. This lady, Mr. Peter Cunningham tells us, was "celebrated for her lively wit and for her blue-stocking parties, unrivalled, it is said, in the soft realm of *blue* May Fair"—except, it may be supposed, by Mrs. Montague. Sir Walter Scott writes, in his diary, under date of 13th May, 1826, that he "went to poor Lydia White's, and found her extended on a couch, frightfully swelled, unable to stir, roughed, jesting, and dying. She has a good heart and head, and is really a clever creature; but, unhappily, or rather, happily, she has set up the whole staff of her rest in keeping literary society about her. The world has not neglected her. She can always make up a circle, and generally has some people of real talent and distinction." At No. 56, now pulled down, lived, for many years, Baron Parke, both whilst a judge, and subsequently to his creation, in 1855, as a "peer for life," by the name, style, and title of Lord Wensleydale.

In Green Street, which runs eastward from Park Lane into North Audley Street, lived and died the Rev. Sydney Smith, the witty canon of St. Paul's. A native of Woodford, in Essex, he was born in the year 1771, and having entered the Church, became curate of Amesbury, in Wiltshire. "The squire of the parish," says Sydney Smith, "took a fancy to me, and requested me to go with his son to reside at the University of Weimar; before we got there, Germany became the seat of war; and, in stress of politics, we put into Edinburgh, where I remained five years." Here, in 1802, in conjunction with a few literary associates, he projected the *Edinburgh Review*. In the following year he removed to London, where he soon became "the delight and wonder of society." After holding various preferments, he was appointed, in 1831, one of the canons residentiary of St. Paul's. He published several pamphlets and sermons, and also his contributions to the *Edinburgh Review* in a collected form; but the work by which he is best remembered is "Peter Plymley's Letters," written to promote the cause of Catholic emancipation, and abounding in wit and irony. Sydney Smith died in February, 1845.

In this street lived Lord Cochrane, whose name became notorious in connection with a certain stock-jobbing fraud of a most extraordinary kind, which was played off in the metropolis, and of which we have already given the particulars,* but which may be briefly summarised here. It appears that between eleven and twelve in the forenoon of Monday, the 21st of February, 1814, a person, wearing a white cockade, passed rapidly by the Royal Exchange, in a post-chaise, drawn by four horses, and decorated with sprigs of laurel. Much about the same time a chaise similarly decorated, and a person of the same description within, was seen in the vicinity of Downing Street—not proceeding directly thither, but wandering about, apparently in want of a guide. Much excitement was caused by the appearance of these individuals, coupled with the rumours which had been spread abroad, to the effect that the mission of the man with the cockade was not to the British Government, but to the French princes here; and that he had certainly arrived at the residences of the Prince of Condé and the Duke of Bourbon. One of the actors engaged in this conspiracy, named De Berenger, was traced to the house of Lord Cochrane, in this street. After some lapse of time in consequence of investigations of the committee appointed by the Stock Exchange, these two persons, together with some four or five others, were brought to trial before Lord Ellenborough, "for conspiring to defraud that body, by circulating false news of Bonaparte's defeat, his being killed by the Cossacks, &c., to raise the funds to a higher price than they would otherwise have borne, to the injury of the public and to the benefit of the conspirators." All the persons indicted were found guilty; Lord Cochrane was sentenced to pay a fine of £1,000 to the king, to be set upon the pillory in front of the Royal Exchange, and to be imprisoned for twelve calendar months; one of the other prisoners received the same judgment, and the remainder were sentenced to a year's imprisonment in the Marshalsea. Lord Cochrane was one of the last persons sentenced to the pillory. This punishment he had not to bear, for Sir Francis Burdett vowed that, if necessary, he would stand by his side; and his presence was, in itself, protection from the mob.

Crossing Green Street, at right angles at its western end, is Norfolk Street. No. 22 in this street was once the residence of Lord Overstone, the eminent and wealthy banker, who here had a fine gallery of pictures. In this street lived the Duchess of Gordon. Though strictly pious in her

---

* See Vol. I., p 478.

later years, as a middle-aged matron she was a leader of fashion, and the admiration of West-end circles. If it be true that she was ambitious and vain, her ambition and vanity must have been gratified by seeing three daughters married to the Dukes of Bedford, Richmond, and Manchester, and a fourth to the Marquis Cornwallis.

In this street resided Lord William Russell, brother of the fifth and sixth Dukes of Bedford, who, on the 6th of May, 1840, was murdered in his bed by his valet, Courvoisier. From the confession which Courvoisier made, after finding his case was hopeless, it appears that, in the middle of the night, when the family had retired to rest, Lord William, feeling indisposed, dressed himself, and went down stairs, where he found the valet busy in packing up the valuables, apparently with intent to carry them away. He taxed him with his crime, and, telling him he should be discharged the next morning, returned to his bed. Courvoisier, in despair, after waiting some time, seized a carving-knife, went up to his master's room, and, finding him fast asleep, savagely cut his throat. The murderer was tried at the Old Bailey, and, being found guilty, was executed in the following July.

Passing once more into Park Lane, we have to direct our attention to two or three more houses before closing this chapter. The first of these, No. 16, was, in 1826, the residence of the late Lord Ellenborough, some time Governor-General of India; at No. 8 were living the Misses Berry, Horace Walpole's friends; and the large house at the northern end, next to Oxford Street, and backing on to Camelford House, was for many years the residence of the late Duke of Somerset, whose wife, one of the fair trio of Sheridan sisters, sat as the "Queen of Beauty" at the Eglinton Tournament. Camelford House, so called after Pitt, Lord Camelford, has nothing to command special attention, unless it be its mean and dingy appearance. The front of the house is towards Oxford Street, and the entrance at the side, whilst the court-yard at the back is open to Norfolk Street. The second Lord Camelford's body, after his death, in a duel fought near Holland House, was brought back hither, in 1804, and was taken hence to be deposited in St. Anne's Church, Soho, as we have already stated. The house then passed to his only sister, Lady Grenville, who lived here, with her husband, the Premier. She died, aged ninety, in 1863. At one time the house was let to Prince (afterwards King) Leopold and the Princess Charlotte. It has been for many years the residence of Sir Charles Mills, Bart., of Hillingdon Court, Middlesex.

Having now reached the northern extremity of Park Lane, we have on our left the Marble Arch; but of this, and also of Cumberland Gate and Tyburn, we shall speak in subsequent chapters.

CHAPTER XXX.

HYDE PARK.

"The show shop of the metropolis, Hyde Park."—*Pierce Egan.*

The Site of the Park in Remote Ages—Its Boundaries—Division of the Manor of Eia—The Manor of Hyde appropriated by Henry VIII., and converted into a Royal Park—Lord Hunsdon appointed Ranger—Fees to the Keepers or Rangers—Entertainments for distinguished Foreign Visitors—Herons and other Water-fowl preserved here—Sir Edward Carey as Ranger—James I. as a hunter—Robert Cecil, Earl of Salisbury, Sir Walter Cope, and Henry Rich, Earl of Holland, as Rangers—The Water-supply for Western London—The City "Trained Bands" exercised in the Park—Sale of the Park by the Government—It again becomes Royal Property—The Duke of Gloucester appointed Keeper—James Hamilton as Keeper—Apples for Cider grown in the Park—Forts and Bastions erected in the Park—Extracts from the Diaries of Evelyn and Pepys referring to Hyde Park—Narrow Escape of Oliver Cromwell—The Park as a Fashionable Resort—Proposal to build a Palace in Hyde Park—The Ring—Reviews and Encampments held in Hyde Park—Duels fought in the Park—Peace Rejoicings in 1814 and 1815.

HAVING travelled to the northern end of Park Lane, and exhausted our store of information respecting the fashionable district which lies on our right hand, we must now retrace our steps as far as Apsley House and Hyde Park Corner, and ask our readers to accompany us into that most famous of recreation-grounds, and chief of the "lungs of London," which all the world, to this day, persists in calling "the Park," as if we had no other park in our metropolis—no doubt because, in the Stuart times, and even later, it was the only park really open to the people at large. We shall find that, in spite of the absence of houses and mansions, and, therefore, of actual inhabitants, it is almost as rich in historical recollections as any other part of London.

In the days of the Roman occupation of England, as Mr. Larwood remarks, in his "History of the London Parks," "the site of the future Hyde Park lay in the far west, in the midst of virgin forests, which for more than ten centuries after continued to surround London to the north and the west. Wild boars and bulls, wolves, deer, and smaller game, a few native hunters, swine-herds, and charcoal-burners, were, in all probability, the only inhabitants of those vast wildernesses." If May Fair had any other inhabitants at that time, it is probable that they were painted savages.

In remote ages the tract of land now enclosed as the Park was bounded on the north by the Via Trinobantina—one of the great military roads—now identified with Oxford Street and the Uxbridge Road. On the east ran another Roman way, the old Watling Street, which crossed the other at Tyburn, and sloped off to the south-east, in the direction of Park Lane. On the west and south its limits were not equally well defined. Under the Saxon kings, it would appear that the Manor of Eia, of which it formed a part, belonged to the Master of the Horse ; and Mr. Larwood most appropriately observes, " Could the shade of that old Saxon revisit the land which he held when in the flesh, no doubt he would be satisfied, for nowhere in the world could he now find finer horses and better riders than those we daily see in Rotten Row."

About the time of Domesday Book, the manor of Eia was divided into three smaller manors, called, respectively, Neyte, Eabury, and Hyde. The latter still lives and flourishes as a royal park, under its ancient name, no doubt of Saxon origin. The manor of Neyte became the property of the Abbey of Westminster, as did also that of Hyde, which remained in the hands of the monks until seized upon by King Henry, at the time of the Reformation. Of the manor of Hyde we know that its woods afforded to the monks both fire-wood and shelter for their game and water-fowl ; and there is extant a document, in which William Boston, the abbot, and the rest of the Convent of Westminster, with their entire assent, consent, and agreement, handed over to his Majesty " the seyte, soyle, circuyte, and precincte of the manor of Hyde, with all the demayne lands, tenements, rentes, meadowes, and pastures of the said manor, with all other pro-fytes and commodities to the same appertayning and belonging, which be now in the tenure and occupation of one John Arnold."

" Henry's main object in appropriating this estate," observes Mr. Larwood, " seems to have been to extend his hunting-grounds to the north and west of London. As we have already seen, the king had previously purchased that plot of ground which afterwards became St. James's Park. Marylebone Park (now the Regent's Park and sur-rounding districts) formed already part of the royal domain ; and thus the manor of Hyde, connected

with these, gave him an uninterrupted hunting-ground, which extended from his palace of West-minster to Hampstead Heath. That some such idea existed in the royal mind appears from a proclamation, for the preservation of his game, issued in July, 1536, in which it is stated that, 'As the King's most royal Majesty is desirous to have the games of hare, partridge, pheasant, and heron preserved, in and about the honour of his palace of Westminster, for his own disport and pastime, no person, on the pain of imprisonment of their bodies, and further punishment at his Majesty's will and pleasure, is to presume to hunt or hawk, from the palace of Westminster to St. Giles'-in-the-Fields, and from thence to Islington, to Our Lady of the Oak, to Highgate, to Hornsey Park, and to Hampstead Heath.' It was, probably, also about this period that the manor of Hyde was made into a park, that is, enclosed with a fence or paling, and thus became still better adapted for the rearing and preserving of game. And here it may be fit to observe, that its extent at that time, and for long after, was much greater than it is at present, reach-ing as far as Park Lane to the east, and almost up to the site of Kensington Palace to the west."

As soon as the church manor was thus turned into a royal park, it was a matter of course for the king to appoint a ranger. The first who held the post was George Roper—perhaps of the same family with William Roper, the worthy husband of good Sir Thomas More's daughter. On his death, two rangers or keepers were appointed, and a lodge assigned to each ; the one lived not far from what now is Hamilton Place ; and the other near the centre of the park, " in a building "—if Mr. Lar-wood's surmise is correct—" afterwards known as the Banqueting House, or the Old Lodge, and which was pulled down at the formation of the Serpentine." Queen Elizabeth gave one of the rangerships to her friend and favourite, Nicholas, Lord Hunsdon, with the handsome salary of " four-pence a day, together with herbage, pannage, and browsage for the deer." In Peck's " Desiderata Curiosa " is the following account, which may, perhaps, cause a smile, particularly if we notice that two men are paid for the same office, the one for holding it and the other for " exercising " it—in another word, for discharging its duties :—

	£	s.	d.
Hyde Park, annual fee of keeper ...	12	13	4
For exercising the said office ...	12	13	4
Keeper of Hyde Park	6	6	8
For his necessaries and costs ...	17	3	4
Keeper of the ponds (there)... ...	10	5	0
Keeper of St. James' Park	6	1	8

Hyde Park, as in the time of Henry VIII.,

says the author above quoted, "was still used as a hunting-ground in the reigns of Edward VI., Queen Elizabeth, and King James." In 1550 we find the boy-king, Edward VI., hunting in it with the French ambassadors. In January, 1578, John Casimir, Count Palatine of the Rhine, Duke of Bavaria, and a general in the service of the Dutch, paid a visit to Queen Elizabeth, lodged in Somerset House, and was by her Majesty made Knight of the Garter. Amongst the entertainments given to this princely visitor was that of hunting at Hampton Court, and shooting in Hyde Park, on which last occasion the old chroniclers relate that the duke "killed a barren doe with his piece from amongst three hundred other deer." Again, an entry in the accounts of the Board of Works for the year 1582 contains a payment "for making of two new standings in Marybone and Hyde Park for the Queen's Majesty and the noblemen of France [i.e., the Duke of Anjou, Elizabeth's intended husband, and his court] to see the hunting." No doubt, these were the "princely standes" to which Norden alludes, in his mention of Hyde Park in 1596, in his "Survey of Middlesex and Hertfordshire." "Perhaps the queen herself, at times, here followed the pursuit of her patroness Diana, for we know that her Majesty took pleasure in hunting. On such occasions the sport would conclude, according to the established law of the chase, by one of the huntsmen offering a hunting-knife to the queen, as the first lady of the field, and her '*taking say*' of the buck—*i.e.*, plunging the knife in its throat with her own fair and royal hand. Again, the pools in the Park must have been a favourite haunt of the heron (which Henry VIII. includes among the game to be preserved in the neighbourhood of his palace), and other water-fowl, and there the queen may have 'cast her hawk' on summer afternoons. We can imagine her riding here on an 'ambling palfrey' through the forest glades, accompanied by the fiery Essex, the courtly Burleigh, the manly Raleigh, or that arch plotter and scheming villain, Leicester, whose name . . . ought to have been for ever connected with a certain spot north-east of the Park, where Tyburn gallows stood."

Before the end of Elizabeth's reign the second rangership was given to Lord Hunsdon's son, Sir Edward Carey. He was a brother of the Countess of Nottingham, whose name is so well known to history in connection with the romantic episode of Lord Essex and the ring. In his time, some forty acres of land on the southern side, not far from Knightsbridge, were added to the park, and fenced in with rails. "No cattle," writes Mr. Larwood, "were allowed to enter this enclosure, as it was

reserved for the deer to graze in; and the grass growing within it was to be mown for hay, on which to feed the deer in winter. The exact locality of these forty acres," he adds, "is not stated; but it is not improbable that it was this very fence that was pulled down by the Londoners on their Lammas crusade in 1592."

Mr. Larwood writes: "King James I., as everybody knows, was a 'mighty hunter before the Lord.' Frequently, no doubt, the dryads and hamadryads of the Park must have witnessed his sacred Majesty in that famous costume which he wore when on his journey from Scotland to England to ascend the throne—'a doublet, green as the grass he stood on, with a feather in his cap and a horn by his side.' Then the clear echoes, nestling in the quiet nooks and corners of the ancient forest, were awakened by the merry blasts of the horn, the hallooing of the huntsmen cheering the dogs, and the 'yearning' of the pack, as they followed the hart to one of the pools where it 'took soil,' and was bravely dispatched by his Majesty. After that followed the noisy 'quarry,' in which, of course, 'Jowler' and 'Jewel,' the king's favourite hounds, obtained the lion's share. When the hunt was over, his Majesty would probably adjourn to the Banqueting House, which stood in the middle of the Park, and refresh himself with a deep draught of sack or canary; and in the cool of the evening, as, returning home to Whitehall, the king crossed over 'the way to Reading' (now Piccadilly), he might see, in the far blue distance, the little village of St. Giles' nestled among the trees, the square steeple of old St. Paul's, and the smoking chimneys of his good citizens of London, whilst the faint evening breeze wafted towards him the sweet silvery sound of Bow bells ringing the curfew."

The next keeper of whom we read, under James I., was Robert Cecil, Earl of Salisbury, with whom, three years later, we find associated Sir Walter Cope, the same person who built the centre and the turrets of Holland House. During their joint keepership various improvements were made in the Park; grants of money were made for planting trees and repairing lodges, fences, palings, pond-heads, &c.; which show that it was then quite a rural park. In 1612 Sir Walter Cope resigned his rangership in favour of his son-in-law, Henry Rich, subsequently created Earl of Holland. This nobleman, it may be remarked, cut but a poor figure in history. In early life he was employed abroad to negotiate the marriage of Charles I. with Henrietta Maria; but after the outbreak of the Civil War he fought at one time on the side of the Parliament, and then again for the King, and being taken prisoner by the Roundheads, was executed.

In the first year of Charles's reign a strange scene was witnessed in the Park. The young queen, Henrietta Maria, just wedded, went through it barefoot, and clad in sackcloth, to Tyburn gallows, an event of which we shall have to speak more fully in our account of Tyburnia.

In the reigns of our early Stuart kings there was in Hyde Park a large number of pools or ponds, all communicating with each other, and variously given as ten, eleven, and twelve. They were fed by a small stream, the West Bourne, which, rising on the western slope of Hampstead, passed through Kilburn and Bayswater, and then intersected the Park, which it quitted at Knightsbridge on its way to join the Thames at Millbank and Chelsea. These pools used to supply the western parts of London with water, until a complaint was made that they were drained so much that there was no water for the deer. This at least, was stoutly asserted by the keepers, and as stoutly denied by the citizens, who petitioned the king to allow the supply to continue. But Charles I. preferred the word of his keepers to the petition of his loyal and faithful subjects; he chose rather to see his subjects than his favourite deer lacking water, and so he rejected the petition—a step which much increased his unpopularity at the time.

During the early part of the Civil Wars in the time of Charles I., Hyde Park was largely used for exercising the "trained bands," as the regular forces of the City were called. This body of men was first enrolled—or, as the phrase went, "drawn forth in arms"—on the side of the monarch; yet, subsequently, the citizens supported the popular cause, and it was principally by their aid that the House of Commons obtained its decided preponderancy. So early as November, 1642, within three months after Charles had set up his standard at Nottingham, the "trained bands" were marched

A LONDON DANDY OF 1646. (*See page* 383.)

out to join the Earl of Essex, on the heath near Brentford, "where," says Clarendon, "they had indeed a full army of horse and foot, fit to have decided the title of a crown with an equal adversary." In the further progress of the war, several auxiliary regiments, both of foot and horse, were raised by the City; and to a part of these forces, joined to two regiments of the "trained bands," "of whose inexperience of danger," remarks the historian just quoted, "or any kind of service beyond the easy practice of their postures in the Artillery Garden, men had till then too cheap an estimation," the Parliament army was indebted for its preservation in the first battle of Newbury, "for they stood as a bulwark and rampire to defend the rest, and, when their wings of horse were scattered and dispersed, kept their ground so steadily," that Prince Rupert himself, who charged them at the head of the choice royal horse, "could make no impression upon their stand of pikes, but was forced to wheel about." The same historian designates London as "the devoted city" of the Commons, and their "inexhaustible magazine of men."

"In April, 1660," says Mr. Allen, in his "History of London," "about six weeks before the restoration of Charles II., and when the artful management of General Monk had disposed the citizens to countenance the measures he was pursuing in favour of royalty, a muster of the City forces was held in Hyde Park: the number of men then assembled amounted to about 18,600—namely, six regiments of 'trained bands,' six auxiliary regiments, and one regiment of horse; the foot regiments were composed of eighty companies, of two hundred and fifty men each; and the regiments of cavalry of six troops, each of one hundred men. The assembling of this force was judged to have been highly instrumental to the success of the plan for restoring the monarchy. Within a few months afterwards the king granted a commission of lieutenancy for the City of London, which invested the

HYDE PARK ON SUNDAY. *From a Print published in 1804.*　(*See page 399.*)

commissioners with similar powers to those possessed by the lords-lieutenants of counties; and by them the 'trained bands' were new-modelled, and increased to 20,000 men; the cavalry was also increased to 800, and divided into two regiments of five troops, with eighty men in each. The whole of this force was, in the same year, reviewed by the king in Hyde Park."[*]

The Act of Parliament which ordered the sale of the Crown lands, after the execution of Charles I., excepted Hyde Park from its provisions, and it became the subject of a special resolution of the 1st of December, 1652, "That Hyde Park be sold for ready money." The Park at that time contained about 621 acres, and the sale realised £17,068 2s. 8d. The purchasers of the three lots were Richard Wilson, John Lacey, and Anthony Deane.

As soon as the king was brought back to Whitehall, Hyde Park very naturally again became what it had been before the Puritan episode—the rendezvous of fashion and pleasure. The sales of the Park to individuals, which we have mentioned, were treated as null and void; Hyde Park became again royal property, and was open to the public once more. The king appointed his brother, the Duke of Gloucester, to the office of keeper; he, however, held it only two months, and after his death it was granted to James Hamilton, one of the Grooms of the Bedchamber, whose name, as we have already seen, survives in Hamilton Place. This place, and other houses about Hyde Park Corner, had been erected during the Protectorate by the then proprietors, and it is uncertain what compensation or tenant-right they obtained for the outlay. Mr. Hamilton was killed in battle, in 1673; and as Charles II. had thrown open St. James's Park to the public, and it was rightly judged that one Ranger could superintend both parks, it is scarcely a matter of surprise to find that his successor, Mr. Harbord, an ancestor of Lord Suffield, was styled Ranger of St. James's Park, the latter taking precedence, as being not only royal property, but the residence of the merry king and his court. It was by Mr. Hamilton's advice that the Park was first enclosed with a brick wall, and re-stocked with deer, the enclosure of the herd being on Buckdean Hill, on the side farthest from the City, and, therefore, the most quiet and retired. This wall stood till the reign of George II., when it was replaced by a more substantial one, six feet and a half high on the inside, and eight feet high on the outside. A horse belonging to a Mr. Bingham leaped this wall in 1792;

this feat, it appears, was done for a wager. The wall was removed in the time of George IV., and an iron railing was substituted. Colonel Hamilton also made a speculation in the growth of apples for cider on an enclosure at the north-west corner, but with what result we are not informed.

But to return to the time of Charles II. The Park was then open ground, with the exception of such fences as were put up for the purposes of pasturage; but in 1664 the Surveyor-General observes in a report that "the king was very earnest with him for walling Hyde Park, as well for the honour of his palace and great city as for his own disport and recreation." Ten years after, a portion of it was so well fenced in as to be replenished with deer. In 1642, a large fort, with four bastions, had been erected at Hyde Park Corner, and another to the south, called Oliver's Mount, the memory of which remains in Mount Street. This latter work was erected by popular enthusiasm, the ladies of rank not only encouraging the men, but, as we have had occasion to remark in a previous chapter, carrying the materials with their own hands. In a note by Nash to the second canto of the second part of "Hudibras," Lady Middlesex, Lady Foster, Lady Anne Waller, and others, are celebrated for their patriotic exertions as serious volunteers in this emergency. Since that period, the military performances in Hyde Park have been of a mimetic character.

In Evelyn's "Diary," under date the 11th of April, 1653, we read:—"I went to take the aire in Hide Park, when every coach was made to pay a shilling, and horse sixpence, by the sordid fellow who had purchased it of the State, as they were called." And in the "Character of England in a Letter to a Nobleman in France," published in the year 1659, it is described as "a field near the town, which they call Hide Park; the place is not unpleasant, and which they use as our course, but with nothing of that order, equipage, and splendour; being such an assembly of wretched jades and hackney-coaches as, next a regiment of carrmen, there is nothing approaches the resemblance." The writer adds that "the Parke was used by the late king and nobility for the freshness of air, and the goodly prospect, but it is that which now (besides all other exercises) they pay for hire in England, though it be free for all the world besides; every coach and horse which enters buying his mouthful, and permission of the publican who has purchased it, for which the entrance is guarded with porters and long staves." It was, therefore, the Restoration which gave the people the free entrance to the Park, but with the entire reservation of the

---

royal rights, as shown in several ways; not the least curious being the obligation of Mr. Hamilton, the Ranger, to deliver to the Lord Steward, or to the Treasurer of the Household, " one-half of the pippins or red streaks, either in apples or cider, as his Majesty may prefer, the produce of the trees he is authorised to plant in fifty-five acres of the north-west corner of the Park, on the Uxbridge Road."

Pepys' " Diary " is invaluable for the minuteness with which he describes London life during the first nine years of the reign of Charles II., and from him we learn much incidentally about the Park and its frequenters. " Gaiety, jollity, and merry life," it has been well observed, "beam through his pages, which rustle with silk and velvet, and sparkle with gold lace and jewellery." A crowd of gay dissolute people still move through them with the same restless flutter which animated them when in the flesh, two hundred years ago and more. By his help we get peep after peep into that bygone world, and obtain a full view of the manners, fashions, and pleasures of those past generations; and we cannot do better than follow him whenever he shows his merry face in the Park. Early in June, 1660, within a few days after the Restoration, Pepys hears from friends that the two royal Dukes of York and Gloucester " do haunt the Park much;" but he has not as yet seen them there with his own eyes. It is not until the 9th of the month that the little Clerk of the Admiralty has had the happiness of seeing his Majesty there face to face, a sight which, he tells us, was " gallantly great." Again, on the 3rd of July, Pepys records his sight of the king's presence there, to which Evelyn adds, " and abundance of gallantry."

Both Evelyn and Pepys, in their " Diaries," bear frequent witness to the gay appearance which the Park presented after the Restoration, especially on May Day. The former tells us that on the 1st of May, 1661, he went to the Park to take the air, and that " there was his Majesty and an innumerable appearance of gallants and rich coaches, being now a time of universal festivity and joy." Our friend Pepys, however, was not a spectator of these gay doings in the Park, he having been ordered away, on his official duties to Portsmouth; much to his personal regret, as he does not forget to tell us.

When Pepys and Evelyn speak thus of the Park, they must not be understood to mean its whole circumference, but simply an inner circle in the centre of its northern half, generally known as " the Ring," round which it was the fashion to ride

and drive. It was on account of this circular movement that Lady Malapert, in the old comedy of *The Maid's Last Prayer*, calls the " Ring " a " dusty mill-horse drive."

Sometimes this " Ring " was called " the Tour;" and in this sense Pepys uses the word. Thus we have the following entry in his " Diary," under date of the 31st of March, 1668 :—" Took up my wife and Deb, and to the Park, where being in a hackney (coach), and they undressed, was ashamed to go into the Tour, but went round the Park, and so with pleasure home."

In the above reign, it seems, horse and foot-races were of frequent occurrence here. Evelyn, under date May 20, 1658, even tells us that he " went to see a coach-race in Hide Park;" and Pepys, in his " Diary," August 10, 1660, records how that he went " with Mr. Moor and Creed to Hyde Park, by coach, and saw a fine foot-race three times round the Park, between an Irishman and Crow, that was once my Lord Claypole's footman." This was followed by a horse-race, and in the interval which occurred between the two performances a milk-maid went about, crying " Milk of a red cow!" which the humbler spectators partook of—the " quality " meanwhile sipping " sillabub with sack in it." The ladies, we are further told, wagered scarlet stockings and Spanish scented gloves on their favourite steeds.

" Hyde Park," says Pennant, " was celebrated by all our dramatic poets in the late century, and in the early part of the present (18th), for its large space railed off in form of a circle, round which the *beau monde* drove in their carriages, and in their rotation, exchanging, as they passed, smiles and nods, compliments or smart repartees." This large space was also, very suitably, the place in which coaches were displayed when first introduced by persons of fashion and " quality." Taylor, the water-poet, tells us that one William Boonen, a Dutchman, was the first who introduced the use of such vehicles into England. The said Boonen was Queen Elizabeth's coachman, and the date of their first appearance in London may be fixed at about 1564. Taylor quaintly observes, " Indeed, a coach was a strange monster in those days, and the sight of them put horse and man into amazement." The introduction of " glass-coaches " is fixed by the " Ultimum Vale of John Carleton," published in 1663. " I could wish her coach, which she said my Lord Taffe bought for her in England and sent it over to her, made of the new fashion, with glasses, very stately."

The railed-off space above mentioned was called the " Ring," and is often spoken of by the poets of the eighteenth century as the central resort of fashion. It was probably on his way hither that Cromwell once had a most narrow escape from sudden death. He was, as the story has been often told, driving his own coach in the Park; his horses ran away and were uncontrollable; the stern Protector, much to the delight of any Royalist who might have been present on the occasion, was thrown off the coach-box, and fell upon the pole between the wheelers, and his feet becoming entangled in the harness, he was dragged along for a considerable distance. He does not, however, appear to have suffered much beyond the necessary fright and a few bruises. On this accident the following lines were written by the old rhyming cavalier, Cleveland :—

" The whip again ! away ! 'tis too absurd
  That thou shouldst lash with whip-cord now, but sword.
  I'm pleased to fancy how the glad compact
  Of hackney-coachmen sneer at the last act.
  Hark how the scoffing concourse hence derives
  The proverb, 'Needs must go when the devil drives.'
  Yonder a whisper cries, ''Tis a plain case,
  He turned us out to put himself i' the place;
  But, God-a-mercy, horses once for aye
  Stood to 't, and turn'd him out as well as we.'
  Another, not behind with his mocks,
  Cries out, ' Sir, faith you were in the wrong box.'
  He did presume to rule because, forsooth,
  He 's been a horse commander from his youth :
  But he must know there 's a difference in the reins
  Of horses fed with oats and fed with grains.
  I wonder at his frolic, for be sure
  Four hamper'd coach-horses can fling a *brewer ;*
  But ' Pride will have a fall,' such the world's course is,
  He who can rule three realms can't guide four horses ;
  See him that trampled thousands in their gore,
  Dismounted by a party but of four.
  But we have done with 't, and we may call
  This driving Jehu, Phaeton in his fall.
  I would to God, for these three kingdoms' sake,
  His neck, and not the whip, had given the crack."

It would be interesting, as Mr. Thomas Miller remarks, in his " Picturesque Sketches of London," to know whether the Lord Protector remembered the uncomplimentary wish contained in the last couplet when the old royalist afterwards had to petition Cromwell for his release from Yarmouth Gaol. If he remembered it, and yet released the writer, he must have had, at all events, a forgiving disposition. Cromwell's fall from his coach-box is likewise commemorated in one of the poems of Sir John Birkenhead, entitled " The Jolt." Cromwell had received from the German Count of Oldenburg a present of six German horses, which he attempted to drive, with his own hands, in Hyde Park, when "the political Phaeton" met with the accident above mentioned. Sir John Birkenhead

was not slow to perceive the benefit of such an event, and more than hints how unfortunate for the country it was that the fall was not a fatal one. During the dominion of Cromwell, Sir John was forced to " live by his wits," which meant nearly to starve. On the Restoration, he was made one of the Masters of Requests, with a handsome salary.

But to pass on to the Restoration and the times of Charles II. " Hardly," writes Mr. Larwood, " were the members of the royal family safely lodged in the palaces of Whitehall and St. James's, when they commenced their round of amusements, Hyde Park forming part of the programme. Both Charles and his brother James were of active habits, fond of open air and exercise; both also found a still more powerful attraction in the Park, for it was the gathering place of all those matchless beauties which still live on the canvas of Lely and Kneller. All Grammont's equivocal heroines, and all their more virtuous and not less beautiful sisters, were daily there, fluttering in the sunshine, and dazzling alike both king and subjects. There were Lady Castlemaine, *la belle* Hamilton, *la belle* Stewart, and *la belle* Jennings, the Countesses of Chesterfield and Southesk, Lady Denham and Mrs. Lawson, Mrs. Middleton, Mrs. Bagot, Miss Price—in a word, that entire galaxy of ladies whose beauty, as Pope says, was an excuse for the gallantries of Charles, and an apology for his Asiatic court. These, in fact, were

' Those days of ease, when now the weary sword
  Was sheath'd, and luxury with Charles restor'd,
  In every taste of foreign courts improv'd,
  All by the king's example lived and lov'd.'

" There still remained some of the picturesque elegance of the Spanish costume which had been in vogue in the reign of Charles I., though it was gradually spoiled more and more by an invasion of exaggerated French fashions. But there was one great and charming novelty, the new riding garb — the *Amazone*, as it was called—the nondescript attire from which the present *habit* is descended. Till then ladies had worn the usual walking-dress on horseback; it was left for the beautiful flirts of Charles's reign to introduce the ' habit.' It was this novelty which puzzled good Pepys so much, when he, for the first time, saw the ladies ' with coats and doublets with deep skirts, just for all the world like men, and their doublets buttoned up the breasts, with periwigs and with hats, so that, only for a long petticoat dragging under their men's coats, nobody would take them for women in any point whatever.' "

The following description of Hyde Park is from

the Memoirs of Count Grammont in the reign of Charles II. :—"Hyde Park, every one knows, is the promenade of London: nothing was so much in fashion, during the fine weather, as that promenade, which was the rendezvous of magnificence and beauty: every one, therefore, who had either sparkling eyes, or a splendid equipage, constantly repaired thither, and the king [Charles II.] seemed pleased with the place."

Our portrait of the "London dandy" (page 378) of the middle of the seventeenth century, the greater part of whose time probably was spent in the Park, shows the exact dress of the fashionable young men of the time; the long locks of hair, hanging down from the temples on either side the face, with tasty bows of ribbon tied at the ends, were called by the ladies "love-locks;" and Prynne, in his zeal, thought this so prominent a folly that he wrote a quarto volume to prove "The Unloveliness of Love-locks." Prynne, however, himself did not kill the fashion, which died a natural death at the end of the reign of Charles I. The stars and half-moons seen on the young man's face are ornamental patches of dark sticking plaster, a mode of embellishment which is in favour with the ladies occasionally, even in the reign of Victoria, as serving to show off a fair white skin. Among the absurdities of the age to which our illustration refers, it would be difficult to find one more ridiculous than that of gentlemen who are not riders wearing spurs on their boots, as part of their walking dress. The spur forms a conspicuous object in the dress of the dandy of 1646; and we learn that it was considered the very height of fashion to have the spurs made so as to rattle or jingle as the wearer walked along, like Apollo, with his rattling arrows, in the first book of Homer's "Iliad."

The "dandies" of that period, however, did not have it all their own way, or assert an entire monopoly to the Park, as a place intended only for promenading and flirtations, for we read that during the plague of August and September, 1665, a large number of the poorer inhabitants of London, who could not escape into the country, brought thither their household goods, and setting up tents, formed in the Park a sort of camp, which is described to the life in a ballad or broadside of the day, preserved in a volume of London songs in the British Museum. But in spite of all these precautions for safety, the plague pursued them thither, and those who died were buried as quickly as possible upon the spot :—

"We pitch'd our tents on ridges and in furrows,
And there encamped, fearing th' Almighty's arrows.

But oh! alas! what did this all avail?
Our men, ere long, began to droop and quail.
Our lodgings cold, and some not us'd thereto,
Fell sick and dy'd, and made no more adoe.
At length the plague amongst us 'gan to spread,
When every morning some were found stark dead.
Down to another field the sick were ta'en,
But few went down that ere came up again.
But that which most of all did grieve my soul,
To see poor Christians dragg'd into a hole."

It must have been with great satisfaction that the poor creatures thus encamped in Hyde Park learned that, by the end of October, the plague had disappeared, and that they were able to return to their homes in London.

The gay circle of "the Ring" being shorn of its old frequenters, in the year of the great plague, no doubt the grass grew where the horsemen and carriages had stirred the dust as often as spring and summer came round. During part of that fatal and fearful summer, however, a regiment of the Guards was quartered in the Park, under the command of Monk, Duke of Albemarle, who, like Lord Craven, refused wholly to quit the doomed city. Two years later, on St. George's Day, the Merry Monarch and the Knights of the Garter, we are told by Mr. Larwood, had the "ridiculous humour" of keeping on their robes all the day, and in the evening made their appearance in "the Ring," still wearing their insignia—cloaks, coronets, and all. The Duke of Monmouth and another noble lord indulged even in a further freak, for thus apparelled they drove about the Park in a hackney coach.

On the re-appearance of the company in the Park, after the plague and the "great fire," we soon come again across the lively figure of Pepys, who, on the 3rd of June, 1668, writes :—"To the Park, where much fine company and many fine ladies; and in so handsome a hackney I was that I believe Sir W. Coventry and others who looked on me did take me to be in one of my own, which I was a little troubled for; so to the Lodge and drank a cup of new milk, and so home." In the reign of Charles II. the Lodge here spoken of by Pepys stood in the middle of the Park, and was used for the sale of refreshments; it was sometimes called Price's Lodge, from the name of Gervase Price, the chief under-keeper.

"Like everything connected with the Park," writes Mr. Larwood, "it is frequently mentioned by the dramatists of that reign. For instance, in Howard's *English Monsieur* (1674) :—'Nay, 'tis no London female; she's a thing that never saw a cheesecake, a tart, or a syllabub at the Lodge in Hyde Park.' In Queen Anne's time it was more generally called the Cake House, or Mince-pie

House; and, according to the fashion which still continued to prevail, the beaux and belles used to go there to refresh themselves. The dainties which might be obtained there in the reign of George II. are thus enumerated in a little descriptive poem of the period :—

> " ' Some petty collation
> Of cheesecakes, and custards, and pigeon-pie puff,
> With bottle-ale, cider, and such sort of stuff.' "

worthy diarist was a frequent stroller in the Park, and his pages, therefore, contain numerous indications of the doings of the fashionable world in his time; he not only brings before us, in brilliant colours, some of the most famous beauties and court gallants, but also gives us an account of the gentle flirtations of the king himself and his more favoured dames.

Mr. Harrison Ainsworth is but recording the

GROUP OF OLD TREES IN HYDE PARK.

The Lodge was a timber and plaster building, and was taken down in the early part of the present century."

As far back as the reign of Elizabeth we find that cheesecakes were to be had at a house near the Serpentine, while branch establishments existed at Hackney and Holloway for the retail of these dainties, and, from the northern heights, persons were employed to cry them in the streets.

Our friend Pepys, in his "Diary," under date May, 1669, describes a visit, with his wife and some friends, to the Park, where, doubtless, they ate cheesecakes before going "thence to the 'World's End,' " a noted drinking-house, which we shall have occasion to mention hereafter, when we reach the neighbourhood of Knightsbridge. The

actual state of things in the reign of Queen Anne, when he writes, in his historical romance of " St. James's :"—" Well may we be proud of Hyde Park, for no capital but our own can boast aught like it. The sylvan and sequestered character of the scene was wholly undisturbed, and, but for the actual knowledge of the fact, no one would have dreamed that the metropolis was within a mile's distance. Screened by the trees, the mighty city was completely hidden from view, while, on the Kensington road, visible through the glade which looked towards the south-west, not a house was to be seen. To add to the secluded character of the place, a herd of noble red deer were couching beneath an oak, that crowned a gentle acclivity on the right, and a flock of rooks were cawing loudly on the summits of the high trees near Kensington Gardens."

As far back as the year 1731, the author of the "Critical Review," chalking out a plan of London improvements, pointed to Hyde Park as "a place possessed of every beauty and convenience which might be required in the situation of the royal palace of the British king." In 1766, a Mr. John Gwynne proposed to build in the Park a palace cost of the erection. The whole of the building was to extend from Knightsbridge to Bayswater, and to be relieved by occasional breaks. This design was much approved by the notorious Lord Camelford, who was then at Rome, where he saw Soane's drawings, and who became a warm friend and patron of the young architect when subsequently he settled in London."

Mr. Larwood also gives a map of Hyde Park,

THE CAKE-HOUSE, HYDE PARK. *From a Drawing in the Crace Collection.* (*See page* 383.)

with a circuit round it of one mile in circumference. In 1779, a correspondent of the *St. James's Chronicle,* writing under the *nom de plume* of "Possible," enumerates several large buildings which he considered ought to be erected in London; "amongst them," he observes, "a palace in Hyde Park is also much wanted." Towards the end of the last century, the subject was again broached by Sir John Soane, "who," writes Mr. Larwood, "in the gay morning of youthful fancy, full of the wonders he had seen in Italy, and inspired by the wild imagination of an enthusiastic mind, proposed, without regard to expense or limit, to erect a royal habitation in the Park. It was to consist of a palace, with a series of magnificent mansions, the sale of which was calculated to defray the entire about the year 1736 or 1737. It shows the turnpike and gallows at Tyburn, and a double row of walnut-trees, with a wide gravel-walk between, runs from north to south, parallel to the Park Lane. In the centre of this avenue is a circular reservoir, belonging to the Chelsea Waterworks, and from which not only Kensington Palace and the suburb were supplied, but also "the new buildings about Oliver's Mount" (now Mount Street) "and the northern parts of Westminster." Mr. Larwood tells us that the machinery used for forcing the supply was at that time so primitive, that the water had to be conveyed to the houses on the high ground near Grosvenor Square by means of a mill turned by horses. It may interest our readers to learn that this avenue was standing till about the year 1810, when most of the trees, being much decayed, and in danger of being blown down whenever the wind was high, were cut down, their wood being destined to make stocks for the muskets of our infantry. In this map the "Ring" is marked with a large circle, apparently about 150 yards to the north of the east end of the Serpentine. Round the "Ring" stands a square of large trees, a few of which may, perhaps, still be standing. There is a small brook, which runs into the Serpentine, near the present boat-house, from the neighbourhood of the Uxbridge Road; and two small ponds of water are marked towards the south-east corner—one nearly where the statue of Achilles now stands, and the other nearer to the rear of Apsley House. The map shows also the two roads running parallel to the Serpentine on the south, marked respectively as "The King's Old Road, or Lamp Road," and "The King's New Road;" the former corresponding nearly with the Rotten Row of our time, and the latter running, as now, inside the Park, close to the Knightsbridge Road and Kensington Gore. On the north of the Serpentine there is, apparently, no regular road, except for about a hundred yards from the eastern end, where it bends to the north, away from the water, towards the "Ring."

The cutting down of trees needlessly, in the neighbourhood of London, is a sin. Evelyn, in his "Book of Forest Trees," as Dr. Johnson more than once reminds us in his "Letters," tells us of wicked men who cut down trees, and never prospered afterwards. It is to be hoped that a like fate awaited those persons who caused the destruction of the walnut-tree avenue mentioned in the preceding paragraph.

The "Ring," of which we have already spoken, was a place of fashionable resort down to the reign of George II., when it was partly destroyed in the formation of the Serpentine River. It is often alluded to in old plays and novels, and is described by a French traveller, in 1719, as being "two or three hundred paces in diameter, with a sorry kind of balustrade, or rather with poles placed upon stakes, but three feet from the ground, and the coaches drive round this. When they have turned for some time round one way, they face about and turn t'other. So rolls the world." * Another foreigner, who lived in England at the end of the seventeenth century, in speaking of the "Ring," says: "They take their rides in a coach in an open field where there is a circle, not very large, enclosed by rails. There the coaches drive slowly round,

some in one direction, others the opposite way, which, seen from a distance, produces a rather pretty effect, and proves clearly that they only come there in order to see and to be seen. Hence it follows that this promenade, even in the midst of summer, is deserted the moment night begins to fall, that is to say, just at the time when there would be some real pleasure in enjoying the fresh air. Then everybody retires, because the principal attraction of the place is gone." †

Pepys, in his "Diary," under date of 4th April, 1663, writes how that he "saw the king in one coach and Lady Castlemaine in another, in the Ring in Hyde Park, they greeting one another at every turn."

The origin of this "Ring" is unknown; Mr. Larwood suggests that "it may have been a remnant of the garden attached to the Banqueting House, or it may simply have been made by the two speculating citizens who hired the ground from Anthony Dean, Esq., and levied toll on the gates." Remnants of it were still traceable at the beginning of this century, on the high ground directly behind the farm-house. A few very old trees are even now to be found on that spot. Some of these are indeed ancient enough to have formed part of the identical trees round which the wits and beauties drove in their carriages, and, as Pennant says, "in their rotation exchanged, as they passed, smiles and nods, compliments or smart repartees." Plain as it was, it must have been a pleasant spot on a summer's afternoon. Situated on an upland space of ground, one may imagine the pleasurable prospect from hence when all around was open country, and nothing intercepted the view from the Surrey hills to the high grounds of Hampstead and Highgate. One can easily imagine how delightful it must have been for the ladies who "came in their carriages from the hot play-house and the close confined streets of the City, to be fanned by soft winds which blew over broad acres of ripening corn, flowering clover, and newly-mown hay, or rustled through the reeds and willows on the banks of the pools."

Walker, in "The Original," in 1835, speaks of the "Ring" as being still traceable round a clump of trees near the foot-barracks, and inclosing an area of about ninety yards in diameter, and about forty-five yards wide. "Here," he adds, "used to assemble all the fashion of the day, now diffused round the whole park, besides what is taken off by the Regent's Park."

In the merry days of our later Stuart sovereigns

* Misson's "Memoirs and Observations in his Travels through England." 1719.

† "Lettres sur les Anglais et les Français." Cologne, 1727.

no equipage in the "Ring" was thought complete unless drawn by six grey Flanders mares, and the owner's coat-of-arms emblazoned conspicuously on the panels. Thus we read in "The Circus, or the British Olympus," professedly a satire on the "Ring:"—

> "Manlius through all the city doth proclaim
> His arms, his equipage, and ancient name;
> For search the Court of Honour, and you'll see
> Manlius his name, but not his pedigree.
> What then? This is the practice of the town;
> For, should no man bear arms but what's his own,
> Hundreds that make the 'Ring' would carry none;
> And that would spoil the beauty of the place."

Mr. Larwood, who quotes these lines, adds his own opinion that the "Manlius" here intended was none other than "Beau Fielding," who pretended to be a cadet of the noble house of the Earl of Denbigh, which is sprung, as every reader of the "Peerage" knows, from the Hapsburgs, cousins to the ancient Emperors of Germany. He gives the following version of the story to which allusion is made in the above verses:—"On the strength of his name he ventured to have the arms of Lord Denbigh painted on his coach, and to drive round the 'Ring,' as proud as the jackdaw with the purloined peacock's feathers. At the sight of the immaculate coat-of-arms on the plebeian chariot all the blood of all the Hapsburgs flew to the head of Basil, fourth Earl of Denbigh; in a high state of wrath and fury he at once procured a house-painter and ordered him to daub the coat-of-arms completely over, and before all the company in the 'Ring.' The beau seems to have thought with Falstaff that 'the better part of valour is discretion;' and as the insult had not been offered to his own arms, he judged it wise to bear it rather than to resent it." From this same satire we may glean a few other illustrations of the way in which the frequenters of the Park, towards the end of the seventeenth century, conducted themselves. For instance, it appears that the beaux bought fruit in the Park, and there, as in the theatres, amused themselves with breaking coarse jests with the orange and nosegay-women, and other female hawkers. Thus we read in the same poem:

> "With bouncing Bell a luscious chat they hold,
> Squabble with Moll, or Orange Betty scold."

The same practice is also alluded to in another satire, Mrs. Manley's "New Atlantis," where a Mrs. Hammond is represented buying a basket of cherries and receiving a *billet-doux* from the "orange-wench." Again, in Southerne's play of the *Maid's Last Prayer* (1693), Lady Malapert says, "There are a thousand innocent diversions more whole-some and diverting than always the dusty mill-horse driving in Hyde Park." But her airy husband is of a different opinion: "O law!" says he, "don't prophane Hyde Park: is there anything so pleasant as to go there alone and find fault with the company? Why, there can't a horse or a livery 'scape a man that has a mind to be witty; and then, I sell bargains to [*i. e.* 'chaff'] the orange-women." It was with such refined amusements, such a delicate way of displaying their wit, that the beaux of that period, like Sir Harry Wildair, acquired the reputation of being "the joy of the play-house, the life of the Park."

During the reign of Queen Anne, the "Ring" held its place as the resort of all the fashion and nobility, even in winter. "No frost, snow, or east wind," writes the *Spectator*, in 1711, "can hinder a large set of people from going to the Park in February, no dust nor heat in June. And this is come to such an intrepid regularity, that those agreeable creatures that would shriek at a hind-wheel in a deep gutter, are not afraid in their proper sphere of the disorder and danger of seven crowded Rings." In the *Tatlers*, *Spectators*, and in the plays of the period, there are constant allusions to the brilliant crowds who frequented the "Ring," around which a full tide of gaudily dressed ladies were whirled day by day. As Mr. Larwood happily remarks:—"It was an endless stream of stout coachmen driving ponderous gilt chariots lined with scarlet, drawn by six heavy Flanders mares; and running footmen trotting in front, graced with conical caps, long silver-headed canes, and quaintly cut silk jackets loaded with gold lace, tassels, and spangles. In those coaches appeared all the beauty and elegance of the kingdom, outvieing each other in splendour and extravagance; for daughters of Eve were scarce who thought, like Lady Mary Wortley Montagu, that 'All the fine equipages that shine in the Ring never gave me another thought than either pity or contempt for the owners that could place happiness in attracting the eyes of strangers.'"

It was in the "Ring" that a curious incident occurred in the life of Wycherley, which Pope related to Spence. "Wycherley was a very handsome man. His acquaintance with the famous Duchess of Cleveland commenced oddly enough. One day as he passed that duchess's coach in the 'Ring,' she leaned out of the window, and cried out loud enough to be heard distinctly by him, 'Sir, you're a rascal; you're a villain.' Wycherley from that instant entertained hopes. He did not fail waiting on her the next morning; and, with a very melancholy tone, begged to know how it was possible for him to have so much disobliged her grace. They were very good friends from that time."

In the days of George II., the machinery used for watering the fashionable drive in Hyde Park was very primitive indeed. "On account of the numerous coaches which drive round in a small circle," observes a German writer, Z. Conrad von Uffenbach, in his "Remarkable Journey through Europe," "we are greatly troubled by the excessive dust. When the heat and dust are very great, however, a man drives round with a barrel of water in a cart; and the tap is taken out of the barrel, so that as he goes on the water runs out into the road, and moistens it, and so lays the dust."

From the time of Cromwell down to the present day the history of Hyde Park is little more than a record of five events, of which from time to time it has been the scene—reviews of the troops and volunteers, encampments, duels, highway robberies, and executions. For a full catalogue of these matters, equally minute and monotonous, we must be content to refer our readers to the pages of Mr. Jacob Larwood's "Story of the London Parks." It will be enough for our purpose to enumerate here a few of the principal occurrences.

The earliest occasion on which the Park was used for a review, so far as we can learn, was in March, 1569, when the Ranger, Lord Hunsdon, caused Elizabeth's pensioners to muster before the Virgin Queen, his men all "well appointed in armour, on horseback, and arrayed in green cloth and white," the Tudor livery, as may be learnt from sundry pictures in the galleries at Windsor Castle and Hampton Court Palace.

Commencing then with the first year of the reign of Charles II., Stow tells us how, only a few months after his accession, the king here reviewed his "trained bands," 20,000 strong and upwards, in the presence of "divers persons of quality, and innumerable other spectators," and how in the following March (1661) the Park witnessed a muster of archers shooting with the long bow. This exercise had always been a favourite with the English people; and a writer named Wood, in his "Bowman's Glory," especially mentions the fact, that so great was the delight, and so pleasing the exercise, that three regiments of foot soldiery laid down their arms to come and see it.

Again in 1662, Charles reviewed here his troops, including the handsome Life Guards, whom he had formed in Holland. Their array was picturesque, and their gallant appearance pleased the people, who were sick of the dull Puritanical troopers. The *Kingdom's Intelligencer* thus describes the scene:

"It was a glorious sight, . . . and, with reverence be it spoken, worthy those royal spectators who came purposely to behold it; for his sacred Majesty, the Queen, the Queen-mother, the Duke and Duchess of York, with many of the nobility, were all present. The horse and foot were in such excellent order that it is not easy to imagine anything so exact; which is the more creditable if you consider that there were not a few of that great body who had formerly been commanders, and so more fit to be guard of the person of the most excellent king in the world."

Again, in July, 1664, we read in Pepys' "Diary" of another grand review of the Guards in the Park, the troops, horse and foot, being four thousand; but the diarist, in the honesty of his heart, speaks rather doubtfully of their real value as troops. In 1668 there was a similar display, in order to do honour to the Duke of Monmouth, who had been appointed Colonel of the Life Guards. Pepys was present on this occasion too, and gives us a picture of the duke in "mighty rich clothes;" but he saw no reason to change his former opinion of the men, though he owned, that he "indeed thought it mighty noble."

In January, 1682, there was another review of the Guards in the Park, in the presence of Charles, and of the ambassadors of the Sultan of Morocco. "The soldiers," says Mr. Larwood, "were gallantly, and the officers magnificently accoutred. After they had gone through their various exercises, to the great admiration of the ambassadors, the Moorish followers of their Excellencies would show what they could do; and though their performances were very different from the military exercises of Western nations, they proved themselves good and active horsemen. Whilst riding at full speed, with their lances they took off a ring, hung up for the purpose, and performed various other surprising feats."

An encampment, it would appear from one of Pope's letters, was formed in Hyde Park about the year 1714. At all events, he writes from the West-end to a lady friend, probably Martha Blount:— "You may soon have your wish to enjoy the gallant sights of armies, encampments, standards waving over your brother's corn-fields, and the pretty windings of the Thames stained with the blood of men. . . . . The female eyes will be infinitely delighted with the camp which is speedily to be formed in Hyde Park. The tents are carried there this morning, new regiments, with new cloaths and furniture, far exceeding the late cloth and linen designed by his Grace (the Duke of Marlborough) for the soldiery. The sight of so many gallant fellows, with all the pomp and glare of war yet undeformed by battles, those scenes which England has for many years beheld only on stages, may possibly invite your curiosity to this place."

In another letter to the Hon. Robert Digby, he thus describes the effect produced by the encampment on West-end society :—" The objects that attract this part of the world are quite of a different nature. Women of quality are all turned followers of the camp in Hyde Park this year, whither all the town resort to magnificent entertainments given by the officers, &c. The Scythian ladies that dwelt in the waggons of war were not more closely attached to the baggage. The matrons, like those of Sparta, attend their sons to the field, to be the witnesses of their glorious deeds ; and the maidens, with all their charms displayed, provoke the spirit of the soldiers. Tea and coffee supply the place of Lacedæmonian black broth. This camp seems crowned with perpetual victory, for every sun that rises in the thunder of cannon, sets in the music of violins. Nothing is yet wanting but the constant presence of the princess to represent the *mater exercitûs*."

In June, 1799, King George III. here reviewed 12,000 volunteers. Of those reviewed on that day, at all events, two survived to take an active part, to the extent, at least, of shouldering a musket and attending drill, in the volunteer movement on its revival in 1858—the late Mr. C. T. Tower, of Weald Hall, Essex, and Mr. James Anderton, of Dulwich, Surrey.

At these reviews there was always a goodly concourse of spectators present, of whom the larger half were ladies, true then, as now, to Ovid's well-known line—

　"They come to see, but also to be seen."

If we may believe Lord Lansdowne, there was among these lady frequenters of the Park on such occasions one whose name is now forgotten, though she was doubtless the "belle of the season" in her day. He calls her only Mira, and we have, alas ! no clue to the secret of Mira's parentage. Was she the daughter of a duke or a marquis ? or was she one of the maids of honour who attended in the train of royalty? Alas ! we cannot tell. But we can quote Lord Lansdowne's lines entitled " Mira at a Review of the Guards in Hyde Park," as certainly not out of place :—

　" Let meaner beauties conquer singly still,
　　But haughty Mira will by thousands kill :
　　Through armèd ranks triumphantly she drives,
　　And with one glance commands a thousand lives.
　　The trembling heroes nor resist nor fly,
　　But at the head of all their squadrons die."

The following anecdote is vouched for by Lady C. Davies, in her " Recollections of Society :"—Marshal Soult attended a review in Hyde Park in 1838, and his stirrups happening to break, a saddler, named Laurie—the same who became afterwards Alderman Sir Peter Laurie—being asked to supply others, sent the identical stirrups which had been used in the Waterloo campaign by Napoleon I."

On the 23rd of October, 1760, George II. held his last review. The king, we are told, " entered the grand pavilion, or tent, under the Kensington Garden wall," where were also present the Prince and Princess of Wales, the Duke of York, Princess Augusta, and some other of the young princesses, besides a host of noblemen. As soon as the review was over, says *Read's Weekly Journal* of October 25, 1760, " some pieces of a new construction, of a globular form, were set on fire, which occasioned such a smoke as to render all persons within a considerable distance entirely invisible, and thereby the better enabled in time of action to secure a retreat." The brave old king had been in bad health for some days previously, and within forty-eight hours after the review he was dead.

We must say a few words respecting some of the duels—many bloody and fatal ones—that have been fought in Hyde Park. The barbarous practice of duelling, no doubt, came down by tradition from the era of the Normans, if not from that of our Anglo-Saxon forefathers. From whatever race it came, it was a national stain and disgrace for centuries. In the reigns of Charles II. and James II. the mania for duelling was at its height, and, indeed, it could scarcely pass away as long as gentlemen wore their swords in every-day life as part of their costume. John Evelyn remarks, in 1686 : " Many bloody and notorious duels were fought about this time. The Duke of Grafton killed Mr. Stanley, brother to the Earl of Derby, indeed upon an almost insufferable provocation. It is to be hoped," he adds, " that his Majesty will at last severely remedy this unchristian custom."

The story of the duel between Lord Mohun and the Duke of Hamilton, which was fought here on the 15th of November, 1712, is thus told by Sir Bernard Burke, in his " Anecdotes of the Aristocracy :"—

" This sanguinary duel, originating in a political intrigue, was fought early one morning at the Ring, in Hyde Park, then the usual spot for settling these so-called affairs of honour. The duke and his second, Colonel Hamilton, of the Foot Guards, were the first in the field. Soon after, came Lord Mohun and his second, Major Macartney. No sooner had the second party reached the ground, than the duke, unable to conceal his feelings, turned sharply round on Major Macartney, and remarked, 'I am well assured, sir, that all this is by your contrivance, and therefore you shall

for him, at this very moment the attention of the colonel was drawn off to the condition of his friend, and, flinging both the swords to a distance, he hastened to his assistance. The combat, indeed, had been carried on between the principals

THE STATUE OF ACHILLES. (*See page* 395.)

have your share in the dance; my friend here, Colonel Hamilton, will entertain you.' 'I wish for no better partner,' replied Macartney; 'the colonel may command me.' Little more passed between them, and the fight began with infinite fury, each being too intent upon doing mischief to his opponent to look sufficiently to his own defence. Macartney had the misfortune to be speedily disarmed, though not before he had wounded his adversary in the right leg; but, luckily

with uncommon ferocity, the loud and angry clashing of the steel having called to the spot the few stragglers that were abroad in the Park at so early an hour. In a very short time the duke was wounded in both legs, which he returned with interest, piercing his antagonist in the groin, through the arm, and in sundry other parts of his body. The blood flowed freely on both sides, their swords, their faces, and even the grass about them, being reddened with it; but rage lent them that

A MEET OF THE FOUR-IN-HAND CLUB. (*See page* 400.)

almost supernatural strength which is so often seen in madmen. If they had thought little enough before of attending to their self-defence, they now seemed to have abandoned the idea altogether. Each at the same time made a desperate lunge at the other; the duke's weapon passed right through his adversary, up to the very hilt; and the latter, shortening his sword, plunged it into the upper part of the duke's left breast, the wound running downwards into his body, when his grace fell upon him. It was now that the colonel came to his aid, and raised him in his arms. Such a blow, it is probable, would have been fatal of itself; but Macartney had by this time picked up one of the swords, and stabbing the duke to the heart over Hamilton's shoulder, immediately fled, and made his escape to Holland. Such, at least, was the tale of the day, widely disseminated and generally believed by one party, although it was no less strenuously denied by the other. Proclamations were issued, and rewards offered, to an unusual amount, for the apprehension of the murderer, the affair assuming all the interest of a public question. Nay, it was roundly asserted by the Tories, that the Whig faction had gone so far as to place hired assassins about the Park to make sure of their victim, if he had escaped the open ferocity of Lord Mohun, or the yet more perilous treachery of Macartney.

"When the duke fell, the spectators of this bloody tragedy, who do not appear to have interfered in any shape, then came forward to bear him to the Cake-House, that a surgeon might be called in, and his wounds looked to; but the blow had been struck too home; before they could raise him from the grass, he expired. Such is one of the many accounts that have been given of this bloody affair, for the traditions of the day are anything but uniform or consistent. According to some, Lord Mohun shortened his sword, and stabbed the wounded man to the heart while leaning on his shoulder, and unable to stand without support; others said, that a servant of Lord Mohun's played the part that was attributed, by the more credible accounts, to Macartney. This intricate knot is by no means rendered easier of untying by the verdict of the jury, who, some years after, upon the trial of Macartney for this offence, in the King's Bench, found him only guilty of manslaughter.

"Lord Mohun himself died of his wounds upon the spot, and with him his title became extinct; but the estate of Gawsworth, in Cheshire, which he had inherited from the Gerards, vested by will in his widow, and eventually passed to her second

daughter, Anne Griffith, wife of the Right Hon. William Stanhope, by whose representative, the Earl of Harrington, it is now enjoyed."

In "Crowle's Illustrated Pennant," now in the British Museum, there is a small drawing of the above duel; and there is also engraved in fac-simile, in Smith's "Historical and Literary Curiosities," a letter of Dean Swift to Mrs. Dingley, describing it. The Dean thus writes concerning this duel:—

"Before this comes to your Hands, you will "have heard of the most terrible accident that "hath almost ever happened. This morning at 9 "my man brought me word that D. Hamilton had "fought with Ld. Mohun and killed him and "was brought home wounded. I immediately "sent him to the Duke's house in St James' Square, "but the Porter could hardly answer him for tears, "and a great Rabble was about the House. In "short they fought at 7 this morning. The Dog "Mohun was killed on the spot, and well (when) "the Duke was over him, Mohun short'ning his "sword stabb'd him in at the shoulder to the heart. "The Duke was help'd towards the Cake-house "in the Ring in Hide Park (where they fought) "and dyed on the grass before he could reach the "House, and was brought home in his Coach by "8 while the poor Dutchess was asleep. Mac-"kartney, and an Hamilton were seconds and "fought likewise, and are both fled. I am told, "that a footman of Ld. Mohun's stabb'd D. "Hamilton, and some say Mackartney did so too. "I am infinitely concerned for the poor Duke "who was an honest good natured man, I loved "him very well and I think he loved me better."

Lord Mohun was a notorious profligate; he had frequently been engaged in duels and midnight brawls,[*] and had been twice tried for murder. The only remark made by his widow, when his corpse was brought home, was an expression of high displeasure that the men had laid the body on her state-bed, thereby staining with blood the rich and costly furniture! The Duchess of Hamilton, who was a daughter of Digby, Lord Gerard of Bromley, continued a widow until her death, in 1744. We have some scanty notices of this lady in Swift's "Journal and Correspondence." The dean visited her on the morning of the fatal occurrence, and remained with her two hours. "I never saw so melancholy a scene," he says. Two months afterwards, he was again on a visit to the duchess, but the tables were turned. She never grieved, but raged, and stormed, and railed:

---

* See Vol. III., p. 161.

"She is pretty quiet now, but has a diabolical temper."

A noteworthy duel took place in Hyde Park, in 1762, between John Wilkes, the witty agitator, and Samuel Martin, a rather truculent member of Parliament. Martin, in his place in the House of Commons, had alluded to Wilkes as a "stabber in the dark, a cowardly and malignant scoundrel." Wilkes prided himself as much upon his gallantry as upon his wit and disloyalty, and lost no time in calling Martin out. The challenge was given as soon as the House adjourned, and the parties repaired at once to a copse in Hyde Park with a brace of pistols. They fired four times, when Wilkes fell, wounded in the abdomen. His antagonist, relenting, hastened up and insisted on helping him off the ground; but Wilkes, with comparative courtesy, as strenuously urged Martin to hurry away, so as to escape arrest. It afterwards appeared that Martin had been practising in a shooting gallery for six months before making the obnoxious speech in the House; and soon after, instead of being arrested, he received a valuable appointment from the ministry.

Wilkes was the cause of another rather amusing than tragical duel in this park several years later. One Captain Douglas, discussing the great demagogue's merits and demerits in a coffee-house, spoke of him as a scoundrel and a coward; and, turning to the company, he added that these epithets equally applied to Wilkes's adherents. A Rev. Mr. Green took up Wilkes's cause, and pulled Captain Douglas's nose, saying he would back Wilkes against a Scot any day. They at once repaired to the Park, though it was late in the evening. The duel was fought with swords, and finally the parson militant ran the captain through the doublet, whereupon the honour of both gentlemen was asserted to be saved, and they left the field of combat, satisfied.

Richard Brinsley Sheridan, in 1772, repaired to Hyde Park with Captain Matthews to fight a duel; but finding the crowd too great, they went to the Castle Tavern, Covent Garden, instead, and there fought with swords. The quarrel was about the beautiful Miss Linley, the singer, to whom Sheridan was already secretly married. Both were severely cut, but neither was seriously wounded.

In 1780 a duel was fought here between the Earl of Shelburne and Colonel Fullarton; and three years later Lieutenant-Colonel Thomas and Colonel Gordon met here in deadly combat, when the former was killed. In 1797 Colonel King and Colonel Fitzgerald fought, the cause of dispute being a lady, a near relation of the former, who had been wronged by his antagonist; Fitzgerald was killed. It will scarcely be credited, that as recently as 1822 a duel was fought here between the Dukes of Bedford and Buckingham.

Mr. Harrison Ainsworth, in his historical romance of "St. James's," describes one of the duels which were fought in Hyde Park in the reign of Queen Anne. He pictures the parties as striking off in the direction of Kensington Gardens, and keeping on the higher ground till they reach a natural avenue of fine trees, chiefly elms, sweeping down to the edge of a sheet of water which has since been amplified into the Serpentine. He states that "about half way down the avenue were two springs celebrated for their virtues, to which, even in those days, when hydropathy was unknown as a practice, numbers used to resort to drink, and which were protected in wooden frames;" and that "at a later period the waters of the larger spring, known as St. Anne's well, were dispensed by an ancient dame who sat beside it with a small table and glasses. . . . A pump," he adds, "now occupies the spot, but the waters are supposed to have lost none of their efficacy." We shall have occasion to mention these springs again.

It is pleasant to pass from these records of bloodshed to the more enlivening accounts of the festivities and rejoicings that took place here in consequence of the Peace in 1814, and the visit of the Allied Sovereigns. Mr. Cyrus Redding describes, with the pen of an eye-witness, the review of the Scots Greys in Hyde Park in the presence of their Majesties. "It was amusing," he writes, "to see the activity of the other princes and of the Duke of Wellington in their movements, and the incapacity of the Prince Regent to keep up with them. Already grown unwieldly and bloated, he was generally left behind in the royal excursions, being too bulky and too Falstaff-like to move about as they did." He describes the Emperor Alexander of Russia as "affable, easy, and good-humoured;" the King of Prussia as being "as milk-and-water as his courtiers and his enemies could have desired;" and the King of Belgium (then simply aide-de-camp to one of their Majesties), as "lodging *au deuxième* in Marylebone Street."

Again, after the battle of Waterloo, the Park was made the centre of the rejoicings for the peace. Mr. Redding tells us how "a mock naval engagement on the Serpentine river in Hyde Park was presented on the occasion. Boats rigged as vessels of war were engaged in petty combat, and one or two filled with combustibles were set on fire in order to act as fire-ships. First a couple of frigates engaged. Then the battle of the Nile was imtated. Later at night the fireworks commenced. I was as close to them as any one could well be placed. There was a painted castle externally made of cloth. This mock fort gave out a pretended cannonade, amid the smoke of which, the scene shifting, changed the whole into a brilliant temple, with transparent paintings, to represent a temple of Peace, quite in a theatrical way. This elicited shouts of admiration from the people.

"The newspapers made merry with these proceedings, of which the Prince Regent was said to have been the designer. They were worthy of the Prince's taste, extravagant and puerile as it was. One of the papers said, that two watermen, each with a line-of-battle ship on his head proceeding up Constitution Hill to the Serpentine, had been met by their reporter that morning. Another stated that a corps of Laplanders, not to exceed three feet six in height, had been reviewed for the purpose of sending them to man the Prince Regent's fleet in Hyde Park, but that they were declared to be eleven inches five lines too tall."

We may conclude this chapter by remarking that the fresh air of the neighbourhood of Hyde Park a century ago was proverbial; for Boswell writes to thank one of his friends for the offer of the use of his apartments in London, but to decline them on the ground that "it is best to have lodgings in the more airy vicinity of Hyde Park."

CHAPTER XXXI.

HYDE PARK (continued).

"Now in Hyde Park she flaunts by day,
All night she flutters at the play."
Foundling Hospital for Wit, vol. i., 1771.

Rural Aspect of the Park, and Purity of the Air—Extent of the Park, and Names of the Principal Entrances—The Chelsea Waterworks, and the Duke of Gloucester's Riding-house—Mineral Waters—The Statue of Achilles—Rotten Row—The "Drive"—Anecdote of Lord Chesterfield —Horace Walpole attacked by Robbers in the Park—The Park as a Lounge for Effeminate Gallants—"Romeo" Coates and his Singular Equipage—The Park as a Place for the display of the "Newest Fashions"—Miss Burdett-Coutts and the "Irrepressible Stranger"— The "Four-in-hand" and the "Coaching" Clubs—The Serpentine—The Royal Humane Society—The Swimming Club—A Favourite Place for Suicides—Proposal for a World's Fair—The Apple-stall Keeper and the Government—The "Reformer's Tree"—The Marble Arch.

THE entrance into Hyde Park from the west end of Piccadilly, at "the Corner," is, as we have already seen, imposing and magnificent in the extreme. "The park itself," writes Mr. James Grant, "is in a fine, open, and airy situation; and what with the trees in Kensington Gardens, and the handsome houses on the east, north, and south, presents a remarkably interesting and pleasant view. Its attractions, indeed, altogether are so great that no other place in the vicinity of London can bear a moment's comparison with it. I question if there be many such places in the world." At the beginning of the present century, however, it wore a different appearance from that of to-day. For instance, from a print of 1808, it is clear that on the left, inside the entrance at Hyde Park Corner, was the under-keeper's lodge, a wooden structure. At the bottom of an old view of Kensington Palace, among the topographical illustrations belonging to George III., is the following inscription:—"The avenue leading from St. James's through Hyde Park to Kensington Palace is very grand. On each side of it landthorns (*sic*) are placed at equal distances, which being lighted in the dark seasons for the conveniency of the courtiers, appear inconceivably magnificent."

Hyde Park far surpasses that of St. James's in pure rural scenery. Its trees may not be greener or leafier, but there is in its appearance less of art and more of nature, and this is evidenced by the beauty—artificial as it is—of the Serpentine river.

The air here, though not equal in purity to that on Epsom Downs, or even Hampstead Heath, is fresh enough, as compared with that of close-packed rooms in the centre of London. "Taking three of Dr. Smith's London tests," observes a writer in *Once a Week*, we find that while the air of the Court of Chancery shows ·20 of carbonic acid, and that of the pit of the Strand Theatre ·32, the air of Hyde Park shows only ·03." The parks, therefore, may well be called the "lungs of London."

The Park reaches from Piccadilly as far westwards as Kensington Gardens, and it lies between the roads leading to Kensington and Bayswater, the former a continuation of Piccadilly, and the latter of Oxford Street. It originally contained a little over 620 acres; but by enclosing and taking part of it into Kensington Gardens, and by other grants of land for building between Park Lane and Hyde Park Corner, it has been reduced to a little under four hundred. It has eight principal entrances. The first (as already mentioned) is at Hyde Park Corner; it consists of a triple archway, combined with an iron screen, and was erected from the designs of Mr. Decimus Burton, in 1828. In Park Lane is Stanhope Gate, opened about 1750; and also Grosvenor Gate, which was erected by a public subscription among the neighbouring residents, and named after Sir Richard Grosvenor. At the north-east corner of the Park, at the western end of Oxford Street, is Cumberland Gate, now adorned with the "Marble Arch," of which we shall have more to say presently. In the Bayswater Road is the Victoria Gate, opposite Sussex Square. The entrances on the south side are the Albert Gate, Knightsbridge, nearly opposite the road leading into Lowndes Square; the Prince of Wales's Gate, near the site of the old "Half-way House," and close by the spot whereon stood the "Great Exhibition" of 1851; whilst further westward is the Kensington Gate.

At a very early period, the Park was fenced in with deer-palings. In the reign of Charles II. these were superseded by a brick wall, which again, in the reign of George IV., gave place to an open iron railing. As late as the year 1826 the south side was disfigured by two large erections—the one a riding-house, and the other an engine-house belonging to the Chelsea Water-works Company. The former building, known as the Duke of Gloucester's Riding House, was built in 1768, but pulled down in 1820, having served as the head-quarters of the Westminster Volunteer Cavalry during the war against Napoleon. Its site was afterwards occupied for a time by an exhibition of a picture of the Battle of Waterloo, painted by a Dutch artist, which enjoyed a season's popularity as one of the sights for "country cousins" in London, and is now in the Royal Museum of the Pavilion, near Haarlem, in Holland. The licence of the Chelsea Water-works Company terminated towards the end of the reign of William IV., when the engine-house opposite Grosvenor Gate was taken down, and the circular space which it occupied was turned into a basin, with a fountain in the centre. This was filled up about the year 1860, and the place converted into a circular Dutch garden.

The enclosure at the north-west corner was well planted with trees, and stocked with cows and deer, and had a keeper's lodge. Sir Richard Phillips writes thus, in "Modern London," published by him in 1804 :—"Beneath a row of trees,

running parallel with the keeper's garden, are two springs, greatly resorted to : the one is a mineral, and is drunk; the other is used to bathe weak eyes with. At the former, in fine weather, sits a woman, with a table, and chairs, and glasses, for the accommodation of visitors. People of fashion often go in their carriages to the entrance of this enclosure, which is more than a hundred yards from the first spring, and send their servants with jugs for the water, or send their children to drink at the spring. The brim of the further spring is frequently surrounded by persons, chiefly of the lower orders, bathing their eyes. The water is constantly clear, from the vast quantity which the spring casts up, and is continually running off by an outlet from a small square reservoir."

Of the recent improvements in this park, Walker speaks thus, in his "Original," in 1835 :—"The widened, extended, and well-kept rides and drives in Hyde Park, with the bridge, and the improvement of the Serpentine, form a most advantageous comparison with their former state."

We have already described Apsley House, the residence of the great Duke of Wellington. "No stranger," writes Mr. T. Miller, in his "Picturesque Sketches in London," "would ever think of entering Hyde Park without first casting a look at Apsley House, the abode of 'the Duke;' and if he did, the statue of Achilles, which seems stationed as if to point it out, would remind him where he was."

The statue here mentioned stands on a gently sloping mound in the Park, facing the entrance, about a hundred yards north of Apsley House. It was executed by Sir Richard Westmacott in 1822. The figure is said to have been copied from one of the antique statues on the Monte Cavallo at Rome. The statue appears as if in the act of striking. On the pedestal is this inscription :—"To Arthur, Duke of Wellington, and his brave companions in arms, this statue of Achilles, cast from cannon taken in the battles of Salamanca, Vittoria, Toulouse, and Waterloo, is inscribed by their countrywomen." This statue, which was erected by a subscription among the ladies of England as a monument in honour of the military successes of the Duke of Wellington, is open to grave objections, besides the fact that the figure is undraped. From the first it was made the subject of very uncomplimentary remarks in English circles of refinement and discrimination, and a rather sharp controversy was carried on as to its merits and demerits, both before and after it was set up.

The author of a "Tour of a Foreigner in England," published in the year 1825, remarks :

"The important monuments of London seem to be chiefly consigned to Mr. Westmacott. This artist excels in grace and harmony of contour. He ought, perhaps, to devote himself wholly to the representation of nymphs. His 'Achilles,' which has been erected as a monument to the Duke of Wellington, is merely a colossal Adonis. West-macott would have succeeded better in representing the youthful hero grouped with the daughters of King Lycomedes. Who would believe that

set up, and excited at first something like wonder, then an ignorant or canting clamour, because it was undraped; but it has been from the first moment regarded by those who knew anything about art matters as a work of truly magnificent execution, and one of the noblest productions of modern art. With respect to its popular or vulgar name, it has no one distinctive trait of the Homeric Achilles, but that is immaterial; it is enough that we have before us a colossal representation of the human

BRIDGE OVER THE SERPENTINE. (*See page* 404.)

this gladiator Achilles could ever have deceived Deidamia and her companions under the disguise of a female? This colossal statue, which is erected in Hyde Park, as a monument to the Duke of Wellington, represents Achilles raising his shield. The illusion is somewhat forced. The ladies who subscribed for the monument affirm that the artist did not consult them respecting this allegorical statue; and that it was completed before the subscription was set on foot. A great outcry has been raised against the undraped figure of Achilles."

In a work entitled "Cities and Principal Towns," Westmacott's statue of "Achilles" is thus dealt with :—"The bronze colossus in Hyde Park, commonly called 'The Achilles,' was a novelty when

figure in the full play of muscle and energetic grandeur of outline. It is a copy, as everybody knows, from a figure forming part of one of two groups on the Quirinal Hill. There it is grouped with a horse against, it is supposed, the original intention. This may be; but still it is quite clear that its detachment has essentially weakened the effect. There is a want of object, and a vagueness. The English sculptor, Mr. Westmacott, to supply this want— *this mancanza*—has placed upon the left arm a shield, from the evidence and authority of shield-straps on the arm of the original. The small dimensions of Mr. Westmacott's shield, so far short of the "orbicular" shields of Homer, which, turned behind, touched with their borders, in walking, the

Hyde Park.]   **"THE ROW."**   397

nape of the neck and the heels, negative the supposition of an Achilles in his mind; and it may be questioned whether, by introducing it at all, he has not rather disenchanted the spectator of the power to supply much more effectually the vagueness of attitude and action, by still grouping the figure, in his imagination, as it is grouped on the Quirinal. As to the straps on the arm, they are far from proving that a shield had ever before been placed upon them. The ancient sculptors addressed themselves by signs and suggestions of this kind to the imagination; and Mr. Westmacott had better, we think, have imitated them in this, as he has rivalled them in other graces. This grand production of English art is unfavourably placed; and as to its destination and inscription, they set language at defiance."

In a newspaper paragraph of January 29th, 1825, we read that public curiosity was excited by the preparations for erecting here a temple for the exhibition of the long-talked-of painting, "The Battle of Waterloo." The ground marked out was in advance of the statue of Achilles, viewing it from the Piccadilly Gate, and to the west of the figure; it adjoined the foot-path by the side of Rotten Row. Another object of attraction at that time was the turning of the road near Grosvenor Gate. The Gloucester riding-house was then rapidly disappearing; and that long useless pile would, it was asserted, make way for a plantation of young trees extending to the canal or basin. The esplanade on the south side of the Serpentine river was then nearly completed. "The gravel terrace," added the writer, "from its width, will no doubt become a fashionable promenade for the beaux and belles in the summer months."

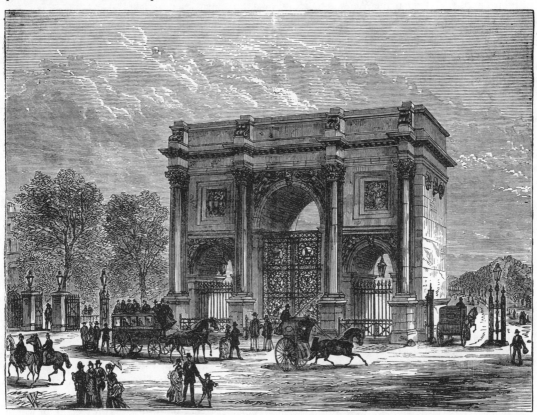

THE MARBLE ARCH. (*See page* 405.)

selves by signs and suggestions of this kind to the imagination; and Mr. Westmacott had better, we think, have imitated them in this, as he has rivalled them in other graces. This grand production of English art is unfavourably placed; and as to its destination and inscription, they set language at defiance."

In a newspaper paragraph of January 29th, 1825, we read that public curiosity was excited by the preparations for erecting here a temple for the exhibition of the long-talked-of painting, "The Battle of Waterloo." The ground marked out was in advance of the statue of Achilles, viewing it from the Piccadilly Gate, and to the west of the figure; it adjoined the foot-path by the side of Rotten Row. Another object of attraction at that time

The part of the Park near the statue of Achilles, between it and "The Row," is, during the London season, what the "Ring" was in the old Stuart times, the very maze and centre of fashion. "Here," writes Mr. Thomas Miller, "the pride and beauty of England may be seen upon their own stage, and on a fine day in 'the season' no other spot in the world can outrival in rich display and chaste grandeur the scene which is here presented." Out of the "season," however, Hyde Park is a dull place enough. Tom Hood the elder thus speaks of it in the dull days of November:—

"No Park, no 'Ring,' no afternoon gentility,
   No company, and no nobility,
   No warmth, no cheerfulness, no healthful ease!"

Lord Byron, in "Don Juan," canto 13, if our

readers remember, says of Rotten Row, when out of season, that it—

"Sleeps from the chivalry of this bright age."

And R. B. Sheridan, in his prologue to *Pizarro*, talks of the horse seen cantering along its sand and gravel in May or June as—

"The hack Bucephalus of Rotten Row."

It has been suggested that the name itself is a corruption of *Route du roi* (the king's road); but Mr. John Timbs says, "the name *Rotten* is traced to *rotteran*, to muster; a military origin which may refer to the Park during the Civil War." Mr. Peter Cunningham, in his "Handbook of London," contents himself with just mentioning this place, as the part of Hyde Park, on the south of the Serpentine, most crowded with equestrians in the height of the London season; but he is wholly silent as to the derivation of its name. The "Row" is about a mile and a half in length, and is laid down with a fine loose gravel, mixed with tan, so that the fair equestrians and their friends can gallop over it without much danger from a fall.

There is extant a most amusing ballad which illustrates the character of the Park and its company shortly after the Restoration, entitled "News from Hyde Park," from which we quote the following stanzas; it is printed at length in the "History of the Parks:"—

"One evening, a little before it was dark,
　Sing tantararara tantivee,
I call'd for my gelding and rid to Hide Parke,
　On tantararara tantivee:
It was in the merry month of May,
When meadows and fields were gaudy and gay,
And flowers apparell'd bright as the day,
　I got upon my tantivee.

"The Park shone brighter than the skyes,
　Sing tantararara tantivee,
With jewels, and gold, and ladies' eyes
　That sparkled and cry'd, Come see me:
Of all parts of England, Hide Park hath the name
For coaches and horses, and persons of fame:
It looked at first sight like a field full of flame,
　Which made me ride up tantivee.

"There hath not been seen such a sight since Adam's,
　For perriwig, ribbon, and feather.
Hide Park may be termed the market of Madams,
　Or Lady-Fair, chuse you whether:
Their gowns were a yard too long for their legs,
They shew'd like the rainbow cut into rags,
A garden of flowers, or a navy of flags,
　When they all did mingle together."

One of the most constant frequenters of the Park, or more especially of the "Drive," about the middle of the last century, was Lord Chesterfield, "the man of the graces," on whom we have already peeped in at Chesterfield House, in May

Fair.* That nobleman late in life had a severe fall from his horse, which took fright whilst drinking at one of the little ponds in the Park.

A few days before his death, one of his friends expressed some astonishment at meeting his lordship again there, considering the precarious state of his health. "Why," replied Chesterfield, "I am rehearsing my funeral;" alluding to his own dark-coloured chariot drawn by four horses, and the string of fashionable carriages which followed behind. Thus Chesterfield remained to the last a seeker after the vanities of this world. His constant endeavour was to be more young and more frivolous than was becoming his age. His days were employed in parading in the Park among youth and fashion, his nights at "White's," gaming and pronouncing witticisms amongst "the boys of quality." The consequence was, as we find from his own letters, that his old age was one of fretfulness and disappointment. He was always attempting to keep up his former reputation, and found it constantly sinking under him.

Here Horace Walpole, as he tells us, was robbed, in the winter of 1749, by the fashionable highwayman, Maclean. He writes: "One night, in the beginning of November, as I was returning from Holland House by moonlight, about ten o'clock, I was attacked by two highwaymen in Hyde Park, and the pistol of one of them going off accidentally, razed the skin under my eye, left some marks of shot on my face, and stunned me. The ball went through the top of the chariot, and if I had sat an inch nearer to the left side, must have gone through my head." Such were the perils of the parks, within half a mile of Piccadilly, in the reign of the second George! Maclean was the son of an Irish dean, and had once kept a grocer's shop in or near Welbeck Street; but losing his only child, of whom he was very fond, he sold off his business and "took to the road," and lived in town lodgings in St. James's Street, "over against White's Club," and in country apartments at Chelsea, whilst carrying on his depredations. He was hung at Tyburn in the year following, when some of the brightest eyes of ladies of high birth were in tears at his loss. Thus Soame Jenyns writes, in his "Modern Fine Lady"—

"She weeps if but a handsome thief is hung."

It is clear that a hundred years ago "The Park" was the lounge of indolent and effeminate gallants; for a writer in the *London Magazine* for 1773 mentions, in terms of ill-disguised contempt, "our emaciated youth, who, shattered by green tea and

* See *ante*, p. 353.

claret, drag their delicate and enervated forms at noon through the Park where their ruddy fore-fathers were wont to exhibit their manly forms."

Among the eccentric characters who figured in "The Park" in the days of the Regency, was a certain Mr. Coates, a wealthy planter from the West Indies, who made a sudden appearance in London, performing "for one night only," at the Haymarket Theatre, in *Romeo and Juliet*. We have already informed our readers * how ludicrously he played "Romeo" on this occasion, so as to be called "Romeo Coates" ever afterwards. His love of notoriety did not end at the Haymarket. He had built for him a singular shell-shaped carriage, in which he drove two fine white horses about the Park almost daily. His harness and every available part of the vehicle was blazoned all over with his self-assumed heraldic device, a cock crowing; and wherever he went his appearance was heralded by half the *gamins* of London running by his side, and crying "Cock-a-doodle-doo!" Eventually, having been the fun and sport of the West-end for a season or two, "Romeo" Coates left London and settled at Boulogne, where he induced a fair lady to become the partner of his existence, in spite of the ridicule of the world.

Hyde Park has always been the chief ground for exhibiting the "newest fashions" among the upper ten thousand; and here, during "the season," a good opportunity is afforded to the stranger of seeing the aristocratic world *en masse*, and of noting the ever varying cut of fashionable attire. Our lady readers will doubtless be amused at the excess to which the belles of even the Georgian era went in the matter of adornment, when we tell them that we read in a newspaper of January, 1796, under the title of "The Height of Fashion," that Lady Caroline Campbell "displayed in Hyde Park the other day a feather four feet higher than her bonnet!"

From a poetic effusion printed in 1808, Sunday would appear to have been the great day for the *beaux* and *belles* of the middle classes, and the City in general, to "do" the Park. Here we read :—

"Horsed in Cheapside, scarce yet the gayer spark
Achieves the Sunday triumphs of the Park;
Scarce yet you see him, dreading to be late,
Scour the New Road, and dash through Grosvenor Gate;
Anxious, yet timorous, too, his steed to show,
The bold Bucephalus of Rotten Row.
Careless he seems, yet, vigilantly shy,
Woos the stray glance of ladies passing by;
While his off-heel, insidiously aside,
Provokes the caper which he seems to chide."

* See *ante*, p. 225.

Captain Gronow says of the Park that, as lately as 1815, it looked a part of the country. Under the trees grazed not only cows, but deer, and the paths across it were few and far between. As you gazed from an eminence, no rows of monotonous houses reminded you of the vicinity of a large city, and its atmosphere was then "much more like what God made it than the hazy, grey, coal-darkened half-twilight of the London of to-day. The company, which then congregated daily about five, was composed of dandies and women in the best society; the men mounted on such horses as England alone could then produce. The dandy's dress consisted of a blue coat with brass buttons, leather breeches, and top-boots; and it was the fashion to wear a deep, stiff white cravat, which prevented you from seeing your boots while standing. All the world watched Brummell to imitate him, and order their clothes of the tradesman who dressed that sublime dandy. One day a youthful beau approached Brummell, and said, 'Permit me to ask you where you get your blacking?' 'Ah!' replied Brummell, gazing complacently at his boots, 'my blacking positively ruins me. I will tell you in confidence; it is made with the finest champagne!'

"Many of the ladies used to drive into the Park in a carriage called a *vis-à-vis*, which held only two persons. The hammer-cloth rich in heraldic designs, the powdered footmen in smart liveries, and a coachman who assumed all the gravity and appearance of a wigged archbishop, were indispensable. The equipages were generally much more gorgeous than at a later period, when democracy invaded the Park and introduced what may be termed a 'brummagem society,' with shabby-genteel carriages and servants. The carriage company consisted of the most celebrated beauties, amongst whom were conspicuous the Duchesses of Rutland, Argyle, Gordon, and Bedford; Ladies Cowper, Foley, Heathcote, Louisa Lambton, Hertford, and Mountjoy. The most conspicuous horsemen were the Prince Regent, always accompanied by Sir Benjamin Bloomfield; the Duke of York, and his old friend, Warwick Lake; the Duke of Dorset on his white horse, the Marquis of Anglesey with his lovely daughters, Lord Harrowby and the Ladies Ryder, the Earl of Sefton and the Ladies Molyneux, and the eccentric Earl of Morton on his long-tailed grey. In those days 'pretty horse-breakers' would not have dared to show themselves in Hyde Park; nor did you see any of the lower or middle classes of London society intruding themselves into regions which, by a sort of tacit understanding, were then given up exclusively to persons of rank and fashion. Such was the

Park and the 'Row' little more than half a century ago."

Some amusing sketches of scenes in Hyde Park during "the season," with an essay on its equipages and throng of loungers that pass idly along the "Row," from the pen of Mr. Cyrus Redding, appeared in the columns of the *Pilot* newspaper in the hey-day of its early prosperity.

In 1823 it was the fashion for the fops of the London season to take a morning stroll in Hyde Park, and then to re-appear there from about five to seven in the afternoon. At that time, however, it was the east side of the Park, parallel to Park Lane, between Cumberland Gate and Hyde Park Corner, Piccadilly, which formed the centre of attraction, the "Drive" and the "Row" at that date not extending westwards. So changeable is custom or fashion, however, that, some twelve or fourteen years later, to have put in an appearance in the Park before the afternoon would have been considered vulgar; now once more it is the custom of the most fashionable persons to take a morning ride in the "Row."

It is hinted by Mr. James Grant in his "Travels in Town," that it was in the "Drive" in Hyde Park that Miss (now Lady) Burdett-Coutts first caught a glimpse of the irrepressible stranger who persecuted her life, and who interpreted an accidental smile as an encouragement to his attentions.

In spite of all rival attractions elsewhere, an afternoon's lounge in the Park during the summer months is still a delightful recreation to a country cousin, for there he will see a splendid assortment, not only of female beauty and lovely dresses, but also of equine symmetry and magnificent "turns out;" and it need hardly be said that the sight of the annual meets of the "Four-in-Hand Club," and "The Coaching Club," near the powder magazine at the north-west end of the Serpentine, is one well worth taking a little trouble to see. To such perfection has the coaching revival of late years been brought, that the present generation has fairly eclipsed not only that of its fathers, but that of its grandfathers. "Not in the most palmy days of the bygone coaching era," observes a writer in the *John Bull*, "when every country gentleman could keep a four-in-hand, and many drove their own coaches, were there to be seen such 'turns out' as now display themselves almost daily." Never were so many first-class animals put to such work, and never were "the ribbons" more artistically handled. Even the "butterfly" coaches which make country trips from London daily during the season are so horsed, so turned out, and so driven, as to be far in advance, in style and appearance, of

the best stages of the olden time. And it must be owned that this revival of coaching skill is by no means an unhealthy symptom of the age.

The vehicles formerly used by the "Four-in-Hand Club" are described as of a hybrid class, "quite as elegant as private carriages, and lighter than even the mails." They were horsed with the finest animals that money could procure; and, in general, the whole four in each carriage were admirably matched—grey and chestnut being the favourite colours. "The master generally drove the team, often a nobleman of high rank, who commonly copied the dress of a mail-coachman. The company usually rode outside; but two footmen in rich liveries were indispensable on the back seat, nor was it at all uncommon to see some splendidly-attired female on the box." Mr. Timbs, in his "Club Life of London," mentions, perhaps, one of the finest specimens of good "coachmanship," as performed by Sir Felix Agar. He had made a bet, which he won, that he would drive his own four-horses-in-hand up Grosvenor Place, down the passage into Tattersall's Yard (which was formerly close by Hyde Park Corner), around the pillar which stood in the centre of it, and back again into Grosvenor Place, *without either of his horses going at a slower pace than a trot*. In our chapter on Piccadilly we have spoken at some length of the good old custom of stage-coaching, and also of its recent revival; so that nothing further need be said here.

Having thus described the general features of the Park, and given these few sketches from its historical annals, it is time that we said something about the lake—or river, as it is called—which forms its chief ornament.

The Park is deeply delved, and abundantly supplied with springs which have been renowned for ages. "Many persons," says a writer in the *Lancet* of October 21st, 1848, "every morning drink of these wells, or have the water brought home for their daily use. A part is conveyed by pipes to Buckingham Palace for drinking purposes, and to Westminster Abbey, the Dean of which still holds a spring, formally granted by one of our Edwards to the Abbots of Westminster. In 1663 Charles II. granted to Thomas Hawes of Westminster all the springs, waters, and conduits in the Park to hold for ninety-nine years, rendering to the Exchequer 6s. 8d. per annum."

It was in 1730 that Queen Caroline, the Consort of George II., being a woman of taste, and of great activity, took into her head the idea of improving and embellishing the Park by forming the several ponds and pools and the brook of Westbourne into one large sheet of water. She consulted the Surveyor-General of Woods and Forests, a gentleman of the name of Withers, who gave to the Serpentine its present shape, the slight bend which it makes in the centre being thought sufficient to justify the name at a time when no ornamental water was allowed in landscape gardening, except perfectly straight and square after the Dutch fashion.* The works were commenced in the October of the year mentioned above; and apparently the Serpentine was intended only as part of a larger plan, including the erection of a new royal palace in Hyde Park, of which we have already spoken. At all events, we read in the *London Journal* of September 26th, 1730: "Next Monday they begin the Serpentine River and Royal Mansion in Hyde Park. Mr. Ripley is to build the house, and Mr. Jepherson to make the river, under the direction of Charles Withers, Esq." The old Lodge in the centre of the Park had to be sacrificed. "Two hundred men," Mr. Larwood tells us, "were employed on the work. A dyke or dam was thrown across the valley of the Westbourne, and with the soil dug out of it was raised a mound at the south-east end of Kensington Gardens, on the summit of which was placed a small temple, revolving on a pivot, so as to afford shelter from the winds." The cost of the works was £6,000, including a sum of £2,500 paid to the Chelsea Waterworks Company to induce them to forego their right of carrying water-pipes through the Park. "The king believed that it was all paid out of the queen's own money, and good-humouredly refused to look at her plans, saying he did not care how much money she flung away of her own revenue. He little suspected the aid which Walpole furnished her from the royal treasury; and it was only at the queen's death that this little trick of Walpole's policy came to light, for then it appeared that £20,000 of the king's money had been expended by her Majesty upon these various improvements."

Considerable alterations and improvements have been effected in the Serpentine at different periods. It originally received the water of a stream which had its rise in the neighbourhood of Hampstead; but as this stream was for many years the Bayswater sewer, the result was that we had about fifty acres of stagnant water and other matters, the depth varying from one to thirty feet. To remedy this state of things the Bayswater sewer was cut from

the Serpentine in 1834, and the loss of water, or rather of sewerage, which the river sustained in consequence was supplied from the Thames by the Chelsea Waterworks Company. The accumulation of putrid matter, nevertheless, still remained for many years in the bed of the river; but in the end it became absolutely necessary, in consequence of the effluvia arising from it during the hot weather, to remove the mud deposits, and to take means for ensuring a constant stream of pure water throughout.

It sounds absurd to our ears, but it is nevertheless true, that in the reign of George IV. Mr. John Martin suggested the following "plan for bringing to London a current of pure water, and, at the same time, materially beautifying the metropolis." He proposed that a stream should be brought from the Colne (the water of which is excellent), to be taken about three-quarters of a mile to the north-east of Denham, near Uxbridge, and to be conveyed, by a somewhat circuitous route, following on the whole the course of the Grand Junction Canal, to the reservoir at Paddington. He calculated that the elevation of the reservoir would ensure the distribution of the water, without the aid of a steam-engine, to all the western end of the metropolis, except the highest parts of Paddington and Marylebone. In order to combine other objects of utility, as well as ornament, with that of affording a supply of wholesome beverage, Mr. Martin proposed that a large bath should be formed, near the great reservoir, capable of containing one thousand persons, with boxes for the bathers; and he had marked out upon a map a route by which he proposed to carry the stream under Grand Junction Street and the Uxbridge Road into Kensington Gardens and the Serpentine, diversifying its course with occasional falls and pieces of ornamental water. From Hyde Park he would carry it underground to the gardens of Buckingham Palace, where "the stream might be made to burst out as from a natural cavern, and spread itself into an ornamental water." Passing under Constitution Hill into the Green Park, and "giving motion and wholesomeness to the water stagnant there," he proposed that the current should be conveyed under the Mall into the ornamental water then formed or forming in St. James's Park, at the two extremities of which he would place fountains. Finally, he suggested that the stream might flow into the Thames at Whitehall Stairs. Although Mr. Martin's plan does not appear to have received the attention it perhaps deserved, thanks to the Board of Works we have now something very nearly approaching what he had proposed.

---

* Lord Bathurst, the friend of Pope, is said to have been the first person who ventured on a departure from this tasteless style, in a rivulet which he widened into a sheet of water at his seat of Ritchings, near Colnbrook.

This sheet of water—something belying its name, it must be owned—is almost straight, instead of being what a stranger might expect to find it—a meandering stream, wandering hither and thither in graceful curves "at its own sweet will."

water is the favourite resort of the lovers of skating, for whose safety the Royal Humane Society has erected on the north side a neat classic edifice as a receiving-house. It is kept well supplied with boats, ladders, ropes, and everything necessary to

OLD OUTFALL OF THE SERPENTINE AT KNIGHTSBRIDGE, IN 1800. (*From the Crace Collection.*)

The Serpentine has been frequently frozen over so strongly as to realise Virgil's description of a real English frost in his days, when it might be said of its water—

" Undaque ferratos a tergo sustinet orbes,
　Puppibus illa prius, patulis nunc hospita plaustris."

In the winter of 1814 a fair was held on the ice ; and in 1825 a Mr. Hunt for a wager drove a coach and four horses across the Serpentine during a severe frost. In severe winters this fine sheet of

the resuscitation and comfort of those who may be suddenly immersed. The building stands on the site of an older one, which had been erected in 1794 upon ground presented by George III. It was erected in 1834, from the designs of Mr. J. Bunning, the first stone being laid by the Duke of Wellington. Over the Ionic entrance is sculptured the obverse of the society's medal—a boy striving to rekindle an almost extinct torch by blowing it, together with the legend, "Lateat scintillula

TYBURN TURNPIKE, 1820. (*See page 407.*)

forsan" (Perchance a spark may be concealed). The Royal Humane Society, whose chief offices are in Trafalgar Square, was founded in 1774, by Drs. Goldsmith, Towers, Heberden, and others; and its receiving-houses in the parks cost about £3,000 a year. This society, which is supported by voluntary contributions, publishes accounts of the most approved and effectual methods for recovering persons apparently drowned or dead; and suggests and provides suitable apparatus for, and also bestows rewards on all who risk their lives in, the preservation or restoration of human life. Its records show that during the past thirty years upwards of 7,000 persons have been granted the society's honorary rewards for exertions in saving life; and that about 16,000,000 persons have bathed and skated in the royal parks and gardens of the metropolis under the care of the society's officers. In that large number accidents in which life was in danger were very numerous, and nearly all were rescued by the society.

Early in the morning in the summer months the Serpentine is much frequented by bathers; and 12,000 have been known to indulge in the luxury of a bath in one summer day. This, as may be seen from the Report of the Royal Humane Society in 1849, was before the purification of its waters had been effected!

We must not omit to mention here the Serpentine Swimming Club, whose members have done much to ensure the safety of bathers in these waters. In connection with this club, a handsome silver challenge cup is contested for over a distance of 100 yards. The trophy has to be won three times in succession by the same swimmer before he can substantiate his claim to retain it as his absolute property, and is contested on the first Tuesday in each month "all the year round."

Close by the receiving-house are the boat-houses where boats are let for hire; and the brightly-painted craft being extensively patronised during the summer, a pleasing and animated scene is presented on the water. The boats were introduced here in 1847, but that was not the first occasion on which a craft had scudded the waters of the Serpentine, for towards the close of the last century the ingenious and inventive Lord Stanhope here launched a model of a steamboat made by his own hands or under his own superintendence. How little did he expect at that time that his son would live to see the day when steam and a pair of paddle-wheels would carry a large ship across the broad Atlantic!

Like "Rosamond's Pond" in St. James's Park, of which we have already spoken in a former chapter,[*] the Serpentine is a favourite place for suicides, and frequently the spot selected by those unfortunate individuals who may have determined upon ending their existence. Here Harriet Westbrook, the unhappy first wife of the poet Shelley, drowned herself in December, 1816.

Somewhat oddly placed, in juxtaposition with the Royal Humane Society's house, is the great Government store of gunpowder. In this magazine it is stated that upwards of one million of ball and blank ammunition are kept ready for immediate use. Spanning the river near its western extremity, and at the point where it joins Kensington Gardens, is a handsome stone bridge of five arches, which was built from the designs of Sir John Rennie. The view of London from this point is much admired.

In 1840 it was proposed by Mr. T. S. Duncombe, then M.P. for Finsbury, that an annual fair should be held in Hyde Park; but the proposition was defeated in the House of Commons. Mr. Raikes, in mentioning the subject in his "Journal," remarks that it would have been "a source of endless riot and disorder among the lower classes, attended with much injury to the localities. It would," he adds, "indeed be preposterous, when all sober men are anxious to abolish Bartholomew Fair in the City, to institute another scene of the same description in the fairest part of the metropolis, and close to the palace." Little did Mr. Raikes or Mr. Duncombe anticipate that, in a few years later—namely, in 1851—the broad piece of ground south of the Serpentine would become the scene of one of the greatest "fairs" the world has ever seen. The Crystal Palace, or "temple of industry and the arts," was indeed frequently spoken of as the "World's Fair." Our notice of this exhibition, together with that of the Prince Consort's Memorial which now marks its site, we must reserve for a future chapter, when dealing with South Kensington and the various Industrial Exhibitions, of which the Great Exhibition of 1851 may be considered the parent.

Some little amusement and excitement, too, was caused in Parliament, in 1850–1, by an old woman named Anne Hicks, who, having been allowed to hold an apple-stall at the east end of the Serpentine, had by sheer importunity contrived to surround herself with a small hovel, and to convert that again into a cottage. When preparations were being made for holding the World's Fair in the Park, it became important to remove this cottage; but Anne Hicks refused to give up possession, and

* See ante, p. 49.

was turned out at last only by force. Her grievance was brought before Parliament, but it was explained that she had no legal rights as against the Crown, and the agitation died away, the poor old woman receiving a small compensation. " Many foreigners were in England at the time," writes Mr. Chambers in his " Book of Days," "and the matter afforded them rather a striking proof of the jealousy with which the nation regards any supposed infraction of the rights of private persons by the Government, even in so small a matter as an apple-stall."

In our time the walk by the "Lady's Mile"—as "Rotten Row" is sometimes called—is frequented by the leaders of fashion; but of late the centre of the Park has come to be looked upon by certain of the working classes as a privileged spot wherein to vent their grievances—real or imaginary—against "the powers that be," and much damage has at times been done by these unruly and disorderly assemblages. On one occasion, in the year 1866, during Mr. Walpole's career as Home Secretary, when the park gates were closed against them, and the right of holding a political meeting in the Park was refused, the mob even went so far as to break down the railings in Park Lane, at the same time doing considerable damage to the shrubs and flowers.

Many of our readers will remember Lord Byron's description of the Park in one of the later cantos of " Don Juan :"—

> " Those vegetable puncheons
> Call'd parks, where there is neither fruit nor flower
> Enough to gratify a bee's slight munchings;
> But, after all, they are the only ' bower,'
> In Moore's phrase, where the fashionable fair
> Can form a slight acquaintance with fresh air."

Thanks to various Chief Commissioners of Public Works and Buildings, it can no longer be said with truth that our parks are wholly destitute of flowers, at least; for all along the south, the east, and the north of the drives in Hyde Park there are beds of the gayest geraniums and roses in the summer, and in the spring there are brilliant displays of tulips and hyacinths to gladden the eyes of the Londoners.

Cumberland Gate, which, as we have said, stands at the north-eastern corner of the Park, at the western end of Oxford Street, was erected about 1744, at the expense of the inhabitants of Cumberland Place and its neighbourhood, and took its name after the "Butcher" Duke of Cumberland, the hero of Culloden. It was at first com-monly called Tyburn Gate, from the gallows which stood close by. The original gateway was a mean brick building, comprising an arch with side entrances, and had wooden gates. Here took place, in August, 1821, a disgraceful conflict between the people and the soldiery at the funeral of Queen Caroline, when two persons were killed by shots from the Horse Guards on duty. In the following year the unsightly brick arch and wooden gates were removed, and in their place some handsome iron gates were set up, at a cost of nearly £2,000; but in 1851 these gates were removed in order to make room for the marble arch (see page 397) which now occupies the site, and the iron gates placed on each side of it.

The marble arch had, up to that time, stood in front of the chief entrance to Buckingham Palace, bearing the royal banner of England, and carrying the imagination back to that age of chivalry, the departure of which was lamented by Edmund Burke. The arch, which was adapted by Mr. Nash from the Arch of Constantine at Rome, was not included in the design for building the new front of Buckingham Palace. It cost £80,000; the metal gates alone cost £3,000. It was originally intended to have been surmounted by an equestrian statue of George IV., by Sir Francis Chantrey. The material is Carrara marble, and it consists of a centre gateway and two side openings. On each face are four Corinthian columns, the other sculpture being a keystone to the centre archway, and a pair of figures in the spandrils, a panel of figures over each side entrance, and wreaths at each end; these were executed by Flaxman, Westmeath, and Rossi. The centre gates are bronzed, and ornamented with a beautiful scroll-work, with six openings, two filled with St. George and the Dragon, two with " G. R.," and above, two lions *passant gardant*. They were designed and cast by Samuel Parker, of Argyll Street, and are said to be the largest and most superb in Europe, not excepting those of the Ducal Palace at Venice, or of the Louvre at Paris. The frieze and semicircle intended to fill up the archway—the most beautiful part of the design—were unfortunately mutilated in the removal, and could not be restored.

Of Tyburn toll-gate, which stood nearly opposite Cumberland Gate, and at the corner of the Edgware Road and Cumberland Place, and also of the old gallows which stood a little beyond, we shall have to speak in future chapters.

CHAPTER XXXII.

OXFORD STREET, AND ITS NORTHERN TRIBUTARIES.

" Inter fœmineas catervas."—Horace.

Oxford Street in the Last Century—Figg's Theatre—Great Cumberland Place—Lady Buggin, afterwards Duchess of Inverness—Walpole's Musings on Popularity—Hyde Park Place—Charles Dickens' Last Residence in London—The Portman Family—Edgware Road—Bryanston Street—Spanish and Portuguese Jews' Synagogue—Upper Seymour Street and its Noted Residents—Old Quebec Street—Quebec Chapel—The Cripples' Nursery—Upper Berkeley Street—The West London Jewish Synagogue—St. Luke's Church, Nutford Place—The "Yorkshire Stingo"—The Christian Union Almshouses, John Street—Crawford Street—Homer Street—The Cato Street Conspiracy—St. Mary's Church, Bryanston Square—Montagu and Bryanston Squares—Gloucester Place—Portman Square and its Distinguished Residents—Montagu House and the "Blue-Stocking" Club—Mrs. Montagu and the Chimney-sweepers—Difference between Montagu Matthew and Matthew Montagu—Anecdote of Beau Brummell—John Elwes, the Miser—Baker Street—Madame Tussaud's Exhibition of Waxwork—The Baker Street Bazaar—Royal Smithfield Club—Portman Chapel—Roman Catholic Chapel of the Annunciation—York Place—Cardinal Wiseman—Orchard Street.

HAVING turned our backs on the fashionable part of London, and reached Tyburn, we may fairly ask for our readers' pardon if, startled and alarmed at the sights which meet us there, we now seek to travel eastwards, retracing our steps towards Bloomsbury by way of Oxford Street, and noting down, as we pass along, all that there is of interest to be told about its northern tributaries. We shall thus be able to look in upon Mrs. Montagu, in Portman Square, to find Lord and Lady Hertford dispensing the hospitalities of their great house in Manchester Square, and to see how the "princely" Duke of Chandos is getting on, not with bricks and mortar, but with marble and cement, in Cavendish Square, before we find ourselves once more in the dull regions which "fashion" has agreed to leave to artists and lawyers. With these few words by way of preface, we proceed along our way.

Oxford Street follows the line of the Via Trinobantina, one of the military roads of the Romans, which bounded the north side of what is now Hyde Park, and continued thence to Old Street (Eald Street), in the north of London. Oxford Street extends from the north-east corner of Hyde Park to the junction of Tottenham Court Road with High Street, St. Giles's, where, as we have already stated, the village pound of St. Giles's formerly stood.* The thoroughfare was formerly called the "Uxbridge Road," "Tyburn Road," and subsequently "Oxford Road," as being the highway to Oxford. Hatton, in 1708, describes it as lying between "St. Giles's pound east, and the lane leading to the gallows west." In a plan published in the above year, the "Lord Mayor's Banqueting House" is shown as standing at the north end of Mill Hill Field, and at the north-east corner of the bridge across Tyburn Brook, which is now covered over by part of Stratford Place. Pennant tells us how that "the Lord Mayor and his brethren of the City used to repair to a building called the City Banqueting House, on the north side of Oxford

Street, on horseback, attended by their ladies in waggons, to inspect the conduits, and then to partake of their banquet." A view of the old house, as it appeared in 1750, is given on page 408.

In Ralph Aggas' map of London, published in 1560, it is almost needless to say, the space to the north of Oxford Street, then "the way to Uxbridge," was open country, with fields and hedges, and dotted irregularly with trees; and in Vertue's plan, about a century later, the only building seen between the village of St. Giles's and Primrose Hill is the little solitary church of Marylebone, and still further away in the fields is the little church of St. Pancras, "all alone, old, and weatherbeaten."

Mr. Peter Cunningham says it "is somewhat uncertain when the thoroughfare was first formed into a continuous line of street, and in what year it was first called Oxford Street." Mr. J. T. Smith, in his "Book for a Rainy Day," tells us that "on the front of the first house, No. 1, in Oxford Street, near the second-floor windows, is the following inscription cut in stone: 'OXFORD STREET, 1725.'" This, however, no longer exists. Lysons, in his "Environs of London," remarks that "the row of houses on the north side of Tybourn Road was completed in 1729, and it was then called Oxford Street. About the same time most of the streets leading to Cavendish Square and Oxford Market were built, and the ground was laid out for several others." There is, it appears, says Mr. Cunningham, "good reason to suppose that it received its present name at a still earlier date; for a stone let into the wall of the corner of Rathbone Place is inscribed: 'RATHBONE PLACE, OXFORD STREET, 1718.'" In a "Tour through Great Britain, by a Gentleman," published in 1825, it is stated that "A new Bear Garden, called Figg's Theatre, being a stage for the gladiators or prize-fighters, is built on the Tyburn Road. N.B.—The gentlemen of the science taking offence at its being called Tyburn Road, though it really is so, will have it called the Oxford Road." Of Figg's theatre we shall have more to say in a subsequent chapter.

---

* See Vol. III., p. 200.

Facing us at the Marble Arch is Great Cumberland Place, formerly Great Cumberland Street, extending northward from Oxford Street to Bryanston Square. This thoroughfare was commenced about the year 1774, and, like the gate opposite leading into the Park, was named after the Duke of Cumberland, the hero of Culloden. On the east side the houses form a semicircle, the original design having been for a complete circus. Here, in 1826, at No. 5, was living Lady Buggin, the widow of Sir George Buggin, and afterwards the morganatic wife of the Duke of Sussex, when she was styled Lady Cecilia Underwood. In 1840 she was created Duchess of Inverness. She died at Kensington Palace, where she had resided for many years, in 1873.

At No. 3 lived for some time at the commencement of this century, Earl Cathcart, K.T., a distinguished general in the army, and colonel of the 2nd Life Guards. His lordship was Commander-in-Chief of the military forces in the expedition to Copenhagen, and died in 1843.

Here is a public-house bearing a portrait-sign of the Duke of Cumberland. Horace Walpole, in 1747, looking upon this sign, and remembering how such signs had everywhere superseded those of Admiral Vernon, the Duke of Ormonde, and other heroes, muses in his agreeable though cynical style on the fleeting nature of popularity, and compares glory itself to a sign-board!

At the western end of Oxford Road stood Tyburn Turnpike (see page 403), whose double gates commanded the Uxbridge and the Edgware Roads, which here branch off, divided by Connaught Terrace. Of the neighbourhood which lies beyond this point, and which is popularly known as "Tyburnia" (just as the district south of Hyde Park is "Belgravia" in common parlance), we shall have more to say hereafter. At present we shall keep ourselves entirely to the eastward of the Edgware Road, and treat it briefly and cursorily.

Hyde Park Place is the name given to a row of mansions overlooking the Park, and built on the right and left of the entrance to Great Cumberland Place. Here, at No. 5, the house of his friend Mr. Milner-Gibson, Charles Dickens, in the spring of 1870, became for a few months a resident, being obliged to stay in London in order to give his farewell readings at St. James's Hall, though his medical advisers in vain dissuaded him from the attempt. Here he wrote more than one number of "Edwin Drood." He left this house at the end of May for the rest and quiet of Gadshill, where he died suddenly on the 9th of the following month.

The moment that we pass to the north of Oxford Street, we find ourselves in far different latitudes from those in which we have lately been travelling. Owing to the comparatively modern period from which the streets and squares hereabouts date, we no longer have the friendly guidance of the honest old chroniclers, Stow and Strype, or even Pennant; and we no longer have before our eyes that *embarras de richesse* under which we laboured in selecting our materials in treating of the Strand and Whitehall, Pall Mall or Piccadilly. All to the north of Oxford Street was quite a *terra incognita* in the Stuart days, and there are no contemporary notices from the pens of Pepys and Evelyn to enliven our pages. We must, therefore, be grateful for even small mercies, and pick up with a thankful heart such scanty crumbs of information as may be found in stray magazines and books of anecdote biography. There is one advantage, however, and that is, that we shall move over the ground at a somewhat quicker pace.

We may remark, *en passant*, that the names of most of the streets and squares in this vicinity are synonymous with the names of the ground landlords, and, in some cases, of their county residences; such, for instance, as Wyndham Street and Place, Orchard Street, Berkeley Street, Portman Square, Bryanston Street and Square, and Blandford Street. These names, of course, were given with reference to the family and estates of the sole landowner of the district of which we are about to speak in this chapter—namely, Edward Berkeley Portman, Viscount Portman, of Bryanston, near Blandford, in Dorsetshire, who was for many years M.P. for Dorset, and for a short time M.P. for Marylebone. The Portmans were a family of distinction in Somerset in the reign of Edward I., but its most distinguished member was Sir William Portman, Lord Chief Justice of England, who died in 1555.

On turning round the corner into the Edgware Road, we notice that there are two houses on our right hand with balconies and verandas, nearly opposite to Connaught Square. These balconies were built in order to accommodate the sheriffs and other officials who were bound to be present at the executions of criminals, who, during the seventeenth and eighteenth centuries, were "turned off" on the gallows which stood about fifty yards on the other side of the road, occupying the site of one of the houses in Connaught Place, or, according to Mr. Peter Cunningham, of a house in Connaught Square. Of this gallows, and of those who suffered the extreme penalty of the law there, we shall have plenty to tell our readers hereafter.

In the early part of the present century the Edgware Road was void of any connected row of houses beyond those already mentioned; but there were one or two public-houses at the corners of rural cross-roads. At one of these, which stood near the corner of Oxford and Cambridge Terrace, it is said that a messenger of Charles I., who was travelling with dispatches *incognito*, had his saddle ripped open, and was robbed of its contents.

At the time of which we speak, Nutford Place and the other streets which connect Edgware Road its architecture. The vestibule leads to stone stairs on either side, leading up to the ladies' gallery; while the floor of the synagogue will accommodate about 150 male worshippers.

Upper Seymour Street, the next turning, leading across Great Cumberland Place into Portman Square, was so named after the family of the Seymours, from whom the Portmans descend. Among the distinguished residents of this street have been

THE LORD MAYOR'S BANQUETING-HOUSE, OXFORD ROAD, IN 1750. *From the Crace Collection.* (*See page* 406.)

with Bryanston Square did not exist; and a gentleman then residing still further north in Chapel Street well remembered that from his back drawing-room windows he could see the troops being reviewed in Hyde Park by George III.

Bryanston Street, the first turning in Edgware Road, and extending eastward to Portman Street, was, like the square bearing the same name, so called, as we have shown above, from Bryanstone, in Dorsetshire, the seat of Lord Portman, the ground landlord. The street, which simply consists of some well-built private houses, has no history attached to it to require special mention.

In Upper Bryanston Street is a synagogue, erected for the use of the Spanish and Portuguese Jews residing at the West-end. It is Saracenic in

"Tom" Campbell, the author of the "Pleasures of Memory," who resided at No. 10 whilst editing the *New Monthly Magazine*, and who here lost his wife. The Corsican General, Paoli, who stood as sponsor to the first Emperor Napoleon, lived for some time at the first house, at the corner of Edgware Road. In Croker's "Boswell" appears a letter from Boswell to Lord Thurlow, dated from "General Paoli's, Upper Seymour Street, Portman Square, 24th June, 1784." According to Mr. Peter Cunningham, it was in the drawing-room of No. 45 in this street, in 1820, then the residence of Lady Floyd, that the late distinguished statesman, Sir Robert Peel, was married to Julia, youngest daughter of General Sir John Floyd, Bart.

Connecting the south side of Seymour Street

with Oxford Street, and running parallel with Cumberland Place, is old Quebec Street, which commemorates the capture of Quebec by General Wolfe, in 1759, and probably dates its erection from about that time. Quebec Chapel, so named from the street in which it is situated, is a chapel of ease to Marylebone. It is a square, ugly edifice, dating from 1787, with no pretensions to ecclesiastical fitness, and has been described as nothing

is the West London Synagogue, for the congregation of Jewish "dissenters." The building, though monumental in character, is erected on leasehold land belonging to the Portman estate, and was built in the year 1870. The main portion of the structure occupies back land, and the exterior is consequently unseen from the surrounding streets; but the stone entrance-front in Upper Berkeley Street forms a fitting entrance.

MRS. MONTAGU'S HOUSE, PORTMAN SQUARE. (*See page* 413.)

but a "large room with sash-windows." Among its ministers have been the amiable and accomplished Dean of Canterbury, Dr. Henry Alford; Dr. Goulburn, afterwards Dean of Norwich; and Dr. Magee, who here first acquired the popularity as a preacher which he carried to so great a height as Bishop of Peterborough.

At No. 14 in this street is a charitable institution bearing the name of the Cripples' Nursery. It was established in 1861, and consists of a home, with religious instruction and medical aid, for infant cripples. This charity has a branch establishment at Margate.

Connecting Edgware Road with the north side of Portman Square is Upper Berkeley Street. In this street, close by the corner of Edgware Road,

The synagogue is constructed of brick, and was erected from the designs of Messrs. Davis and Emanuel, at an expense of about £20,000. The edifice is a domical structure, Byzantine in character, and a square in plan. It has a wide gallery along the two sides and western end, the ceiling consisting of a large central dome, and four small domes in the angles, and four great arches covering the side spaces. This ceiling is supported by four piers of clustered columns of Devonshire marble with carved capitals. At the east end of the building is a domed semi-circular recess, or apse, in which is placed the organ and choir, and in the centre of this apse is placed the ark, which has been constructed of inlaid marble-work. A peculiar feature in this building is the placing of the choir at the east end of the building, facing the congregation, and concealing them from the view of the congregation by a screen of marble containing open-work grilles of gilded metal. The decoration is somewhat peculiar. The highest class of decorative art —namely, subject painting, or figure sculpture—is necessarily absent, the Jews, so far as their religious buildings are concerned, reading literally the Second Commandment.

Many special objects in the building were presented to the synagogue by the wealthier members of the congregation, the ark especially being the gift of the ladies of the Goldsmid family. It may be added that the founders of the congregation of Jewish dissenters, by whom this building was erected, left the orthodox Jewish body some thirty years ago, through just such a communal quarrel as caused old Isaac D'Israeli to leave the religion of his fathers. Starting with a small room in Burton Street, their numbers increased, until about twenty years ago they built for themselves a small synagogue in Margaret Street, and since that time the further increase of their congregation rendered necessary the erection of the building now under notice.

In this street Cyrus Redding occupied lodgings during the greater part of his career as sub-editor of the *New Monthly*. It was then on the very verge of the country, the town ending at Connaught Place, or thereabouts, as we have already stated.

Proceeding on our way along the Edgware Road, we pass Nutford Place and Queen Street, both of which terminate in Seymour Place. In Nutford Place is St. Luke's Church, a large Gothic edifice, with a tower ornamented with pinnacles, erected in gratitude for the exemption of this district from the visitation of the cholera in 1849.

The western end of Marylebone Road, between the bottom of Lisson Grove and the top of Oxford and Cambridge Terrace, forms of necessity what we may call our "north-west passage," in reference to this portion of our work. The chief object of interest in this neighbourhood, on the south side of the Marylebone Road, is the celebrated "Yorkshire Stingo" tavern. At the early part of the present century there were tea-gardens and a bowling-green attached to this rural inn, which was much crowded on Sundays, when an admission-fee of sixpence was demanded at its doors. For that a ticket was given, to be exchanged with the waiters for its value in refreshments—a plan very commonly adopted even then in such places of resort, in order to exclude the "roughs" and lower orders, and such as would be sure to stroll about

without spending anything, because they had no money to spend. It was from this house that the London omnibuses commenced running, in 1829, when first introduced by Mr. Shillibeer.

In John Street, through which we commence our return towards Oxford Street, are the Christian Union Almshouses, for the relief of thirty-eight poor and aged persons, in "full communion with some Protestant church." The almshouses were erected in 1832, and are supported by voluntary contributions.

Extending from John Street to Queen Street is a short thoroughfare called Horace Street. This, it is said, was formerly known as Cato Street, a view of which, as it appeared in 1820, has already been given in this work.* A loft over a stable in this thoroughfare, in the early part of the year 1820, formed the head-quarters of Thistlewood and some other assassins, who designed to murder the leading members of the then Administration. This is known to history as the Cato Street Conspiracy. The building contained but two rooms, which could only be entered by a ladder. The conspirators having mustered to the number of twenty-four, they took the precaution of placing a sentinel below, whilst they prepared for their dreadful encounter. We have already given an account of this affair in treating of Grosvenor Square, the intended scene of the massacre.† Mr. R. Rush, who was residing in London at the time of its occurrence as Minister from the United States, speaks of the conspiracy in the following terms, in his "Court of London :"—

"The assassination plot has continued to be a prevailing topic in all circles since its discovery and suppression. It has caused great excitement, it may almost be said some dismay, so foul was its nature, and so near did it appear to have advanced to success. Thanks were offered up at the Royal Chapel, St. James's, for the escape of those whose lives were threatened. Different uses are made of the events, according to the different opinions and feelings of the people in a country where the press speaks what it thinks, and no tongue is tied. The supporters of Government say that it was the offspring of a profligate state of morals among the lower orders, produced by publications emanating from what they called the 'cheap press,' which the late measures of Parliament aimed at putting down ; and added, that it vindicated the necessity and wisdom of those measures. The opponents of Government, who vehemently resisted the measures, insisted in reply, that it was wrong to suppress, or even attempt to interfere with, such publications, since, if every irritated feeling, however unjust might be deemed its causes, were not allowed vent in that way, it would find modes more dangerous."

We learn from Mr. Rush that the convicted prisoners confessed that it was their design, on getting to Lord Harrowby's house, that one of their number should knock at the door with a note in his hand, under pretence of desiring that it should be sent in to his lordship, doing this in such a manner as to cause no suspicion among the passers-by. The rest of the band, from twenty to thirty in number, were to be close at hand, but divided into small groups, so as to be better out of view. The servant who opened the door was to be knocked down by the bearer of the note, when the whole of the band were to rush forward, enter the house, and make for the dining-room, and there have massacred the whole of the ministers and guests, not sparing even the servants if they offered resistance. It is satisfactory to know that this daring gang stood convicted, out of their own lips, of a cool and deliberate murder in design and intention, and that they were not hung without richly deserving their sentence. The conspirators, as we have already mentioned,* were imprisoned in the Tower, and were the last State prisoners lodged there.

Thistlewood was a Lincolnshire man, by birth a gentleman, but reduced by gambling and bill trans-actions. Cyrus Redding, who met him at Paris, thus speaks of him in his "Recollections:"—"His countenance bespoke indomitable determination. I cannot forget it. He had been subjected to a long imprisonment by Lord Sidmouth, I forget on what account. His unscrupulous character, when driven to extremity, no doubt made him capable of the most revolting crimes." Mr. T. Raikes, in his "Journal," gives the following account of the execution of this villain and his associates :—"It was a fine morning, and the crowd in the Old Bailey was, perhaps, greater than ever was assembled on such an occasion ; all the house-tops were covered with spectators ; and when we first looked out of the window of the sheriffs' room, there was nothing to be seen but the scaffold, surrounded by an immense ocean of human heads, all gazing upon that one single object. At length the procession issued from the debtors' door, and the six culprits came on, one after the other, and were successively tied up to the gibbet. Thistlewood came first, looking as pale as

death, but without moving a muscle of his features or attempting to utter a word, except that when the rope had been adjusted round the neck of him who was next to him, he said, in a low tone to him, 'We shall soon know the grand secret.' Ings, the butcher, appeared in a great state of excitement, almost as if under the influence of liquor ; he gave several huzzas, and shouted out to the crowd, 'Liberty for ever!' twice or thrice ; but it was evidently a feint to try to interest the bystanders. The last in this odd rank was a dirty-looking black man, who alone seemed to be impressed with a sense of his awful situation ; his lips were in con-tinual motion, and he was evidently occupied in silent prayer. At this moment one of the gentle-men of the press, who had posted himself in the small enclosure close to the foot of the scaffold, looked up to Thistlewood with a paper and pencil in his hand, and said, 'Mr. Thistlewood, if you have anything to say, I shall be happy to take it down and communicate it to the public.' The other made him no answer, but gave him a look. As they were about to be launched into eternity, a well-dressed man on the roof of one of the oppo-site houses got up from his seat, and looking at Thistlewood, exclaimed, in a very loud but agitated voice, 'God bless you ! God Almighty bless you !' Thistlewood slowly turned his head to the quarter whence the voice came, without moving his body, and as slowly reverted to his former position, always with the same fixed impassible countenance. The caps were then pulled down, the drop fell, an after some struggles they all ceased to live. The law prescribed that their heads should be severed from their bodies, and held up to public view as the heads of traitors. The executioner had neglected to bring any instrument for the purpose, and we in the sheriffs' room were horrified at seeing one of the assistants enter, and take from a cup-board a large carving-knife, which was to be used instead of a more regular instrument. When we were able to leave the prison, which was not for some time on account of the immense crowd, I drove to Seymour Place, found —— at breakfast, and gave him an account of the scene."

At the east end of John Street, and extending thence to Baker Street, is Crawford Street, out of which on either side branch a number of small courts and streets which we need not particularise, with one or two exceptions. The first turning on the left in this thoroughfare, running northward into Marylebone Road, is a small street called Homer Row. At the angle of this street and Marylebone Road stands a handsome Gothic edifice of red brick, with stone facings, and with a high-pitched

* See Vol. II., p. 76.

roof and bell turret. This is a Roman Catholic church, dedicated to the Holy Rosary; the mission was commenced in 1855, and the church built in 1870. The ground floor of the edifice is used as a schoolroom.

Passing along Crawford Street, we cross Seymour Place, which forms a direct communication between Marylebone Road and Seymour Street, near its junction with the Edgware Road. Wyndham Place, the next turning eastward on the right, leads into Bryanston Square, on its north side; opposite, on the north side of Crawford Street, is St. Mary's Church, chiefly noticeable for its lofty semi-circular portico, supported by Corinthian columns, above which rises a graduating spire, surmounted by a cross. It was built in 1823, from the designs of Sir Robert Smirke. Here, in 1838, Miss Letitia E. Landon, the author of "Zenana," and other poetical works, and better known in literary circles by her initials, "L. E. L." was privately married, by her brother, to Mr. George Maclean, Governor of Cape Coast Castle, the scene of her early death. A former vicar of this church was the Rev. J. H. Gurney, celebrated for his zeal in education.

Upper Montagu Street, together with Old and New Quebec Streets, forms a direct line of communication, through Montagu Square, between the Marylebone Road and the western portion of Oxford Street. Montagu Square and also Bryanston Square, which is immediately contiguous to it on the west side, were, according to Mr. John Timbs, "built on Ward's Field, and the site of 'Apple Village,' by David Porter, who was once chimney-sweeper to the village of Marylebone." It has been the fashion to decry these two squares as scarcely deserving of the name. Thus, a writer in the *Builder* says, " They are mere oblong slips with houses built in dreary uniformity; they are fortunately out of the way, and few people see them." Bryanston Square, however, certainly does not deserve such criticism. In it resided for many years Mr. Joseph Hume, the economical M.P.; and also Sir Francis Freeling, many years Secretary of the General Post Office.

Gloucester Place, the next turning eastward of Montagu Street, extends from Marylebone Road to the north-west corner of Portman Square; it consists of well-built private houses. Making our way down Gloucester Place, we enter Portman Square, one of the most aristocratic of London neighbourhoods. It was formed, or rather commenced, about the year 1764, on land once belonging to the Knights of St. John of Jerusalem. According to Mr. Peter Cunningham, it is described in the last lease granted by the Prior of that Order

as "Great Gibbet Field, Little Gibbet Field, Hawkfield, and Brock Stand; Tassel Croft, Boy's Croft, and twenty acres Furse Croft, and two closes called Shepcott Hawes, parcel of the manor of Lilestone, in the County of Middlesex." The north side of the square was first built, and it was nearly twenty years before the whole was finished. This square takes its name from that of the proprietor of the land upon which it is built—namely, William Henry Portman, of Orchard-Portman, in Somersetshire, who died in 1796, and was the ancestor of the present Lord Portman. According to Lambert, who wrote in the year 1806, it is " one of the largest and handsomest squares in the metropolis;" though he complains of the want of correspondence—*i.e.*, of uniformity—in the houses which surround it.

Portman Square was built on high ground, with an open prospect to the north, which gave it a name as a peculiarly healthy part of London. Mrs. Montagu, whom we have already mentioned at Hill Street, Berkeley Square, but whose name is, more than any other, particularly associated with this square, called it the Montpelier of England, and said she "never enjoyed such health as since she came to live in it." It is one of the largest and handsomest squares in London for its general effect, but the houses have no architectural character; and the central enclosure is laid out as a shrubbery. They were, however, built with due consideration for the requirements of the wealthy, and were inhabited by a large number of the " quality" at their first building. In 1822 the following members of the nobility were living in the square :—Lord Clifford, Lord Teignmouth, Earl of Beverley, Lord Lovaine, Lord Kenyon, Lord Petre, Earl Manvers, Earl of Scarbrough, Duke of Newcastle, Countess of Pomfret, Lady Owen, Earl Nelson, Dowager Duchess of Roxburghe, Earl of Cardigan, Dowager Countess of Clonmell, and the Dowager Countess of Harcourt. In this same year lived, at No. 5, Mr. Thomas Assheton Smith, of Tedworth, who might truly be called the pattern and type of the old English sportsman.

No. 12 was the town-house of the late Duke of Hamilton, who married the daughter of William Beckford, the author of " Vathek," and who took a pride in showing on his walls some of the finest paintings in the collection of that connoisseur, which he inherited in right of his wife. At No. 6 lived General Sir John Byng, afterwards Field-Marshal the Earl of Strafford.

Early in the present century No. 40 was the residence of the Right Hon. Hugh Elliot; and Lord Garvagh, the possessor of the celebrated

"Aldobrandini Madonna" of Raffaelle, now in the National Gallery, lived at No. 26 for many years.

Sir William Pepperell, the eminent loyalist and royalist, of Rhode Island, in North America, and formerly the richest subject of the Crown in that country, died at his house here, in December, 1816. He was created a baronet in recognition of his loyalty and losses, and a handsome pension was settled on his title. But his son dying before him, his title became extinct, and his pension was not continued to his daughters.

M. Otto, the French ambassador at the Court of St. James's, was living in Portman Square at the time of the short-lived Treaty of Amiens. Peace had long been wished for by the people, and the preliminaries were signed at Lord Hawkesbury's office in Downing Street, on the 1st of October, 1801. On the arrival in London of General Lauriston, first aide-de-camp to Napoleon, with the French ratifications, he was greeted with enthusiastic cheers by a vast concourse of people. Some of the men took the horses from his carriage, and drew him to M. Otto's house with tumultuous expressions of joy.

A very curious print is in existence showing the illumination of M. Otto's house in celebration of this event. On the front was a row of large oil-lamps forming the word "Concord," and on either side were the initials "G. R.," for "George III.," and "R. F.," "République Française"—the first time, no doubt, and probably the last, on which those two names stood united. This illumination was somewhat unfortunate, for a London mob, un-wittingly, interpreted "Concord" into "Conquered." All the ambassador's windows were smashed in consequence. When the word "Concord" was removed, its place was supplied by "Amitié;" but the stupid mob read this as "Enmity," and insisted on its removal also. Mr. Planché, who was present, writes: "The storm again raged with redoubled fury. Ultimately, what ought to have been done at first was done: the word 'Peace' was displayed, and so peace was restored to Portman Square for the evening."

The chief interest of Portman Square, however, centres in the large house—lately rebuilt or re-cased with red brick—standing by itself in a garden at the north-west corner; this was originally built for the once celebrated Mrs. Montagu, of "Blue-stocking" notoriety, whose memory has of late years been revived by Dr. Doran, by the publica-tion of some of her letters in a volume entitled, "A Lady of the Last Century." As we have stated in a previous chapter, this distinguished lady re-

moved hither from Hill Street, Berkeley Square, a few years after the death of her husband, Edward Montagu, of whose family Lord Rokeby is the head.

Elizabeth Robinson—for such was Mrs. Mon-tagu's maiden name—was born at York, in 1720, and, as we learn from Dr. Doran's interesting book, she was a lively girl, loving fun and pursuing learning, so that the Duchess of Portland nick-named her *La petite Fidget*. In 1742 she married Edward Montagu, M.P., a mathematician of emi-nence, and a coal-owner of great wealth, after which event she became more sober, and told her friend the duchess that her "fidgetations" were much spoiled. She became a power in the literary world, and was the founder, or, at all events, one of the chief leaders, of the celebrated "Blue-Stocking Club." Her house in Hill Street, as we have already shown, became a favourite resort of states-men, poets, and wits; and the young aspirant for fame felt that he had his foot on the first rung of the ladder when he was invited to her table. Indeed, her name will be known to all our readers as emphatically "the Englishwoman of letters" of the eighteenth century, for in that respect she stood unrivalled. Let us look for a moment at her as portrayed in 1776, by the pen of Sir N. W. Wraxall. He writes: "At the time of which I speak, the 'Gens de Lettres,' or 'Blue Stockings' as they were commonly termed, formed a very numerous, powerful, and compact phalanx in the midst of London. . . . Mrs. Montagu was then the Madame du Deffand of the English capital; and her house constituted the central point of union for all those persons who were already known, or who sought to become known, by their talents and productions. Her supremacy, unlike that of Madame du Deffand, was indeed established on more solid foundations than those of intellect, and rested on more tan-gible materials than any which her 'Essay on Shakespeare' could furnish her. . . . Impressed, probably from the suggestions of her own deep knowledge of the world, with a deep conviction of that great truth laid down by Molière, which no man of letters ever disputed, that '*Le vrai Am-phytrion est celui chez qui l'on dine*,' Mrs. Montagu was accustomed to open her house to a large company of both sexes, whom she frequently en-tertained at dinner. A service of plate, and a table plentifully covered, disposed her guests to admire the splendour of her fortune, not less than the lustre of her talents. She had found the same results flowing from the same causes during the visit which she made to Paris, after the Peace of 1763, where she displayed to the astonished *literati* of that metropolis the extent of her pecuniary as well as of her mental resources. As this topic formed one of the subjects most gratifying to her, she was easily induced to launch out on it with much apparent complacency. The eulogiums lavished on her repasts, and the astonishment expressed at the magnitude of her income, which

countenance bespoke intelligence, and her eyes were accommodated to her cast of features, which had in them something satirical and severe, rather than amiable and inviting. She possessed great natural cheerfulness, and a flow of animal spirits; loved to talk, and talked well on almost every subject; led the conversation, and was qualified to

MADAME TUSSAUD. (*See page* 419.)

appeared prodigiously augmented by being transformed from pounds sterling into French livres, seemed to have afforded her as much gratification as the panegyrics bestowed upon the 'Essay on the Genius and Writings of Shakespeare.'

"Mrs. Montagu, in 1776, verged towards her sixtieth year; but her person, which was thin, spare, and in good preservation, gave her an appearance of less antiquity. From the infirmities often attendant on advanced life she seemed to be almost wholly exempt. All the lines of her

preside in her circle, whatever subject of discourse was started; but her manner was more dictatorial and sententious than conciliating or diffident. There was nothing feminine about her; and though her opinions were usually just, as well as delivered in language suited to give them force, yet the organ which conveyed them was not musical. Destitute of taste in disposing the ornaments of her dress, she nevertheless studied or affected those aids more than would seem to have become a woman professing a philosophic mind intent on higher

MARYLEBONE IN 1740.   (*From an Old Print.*)

pursuits than the toilet. Even when approaching to fourscore, this female weakness still accompanied her; nor could she relinquish her diamond necklace and bows, which, like Sir William Draper's 'blushing riband,' commemorated by 'Junius,' formed of evenings the perpetual ornament of her emaciated person. I used to think that these glittering appendages of opulence sometimes helped to dazzle the disputants whom her arguments might not always convince, or her literary reputation intimidate. That reputation had not as yet received the rude attack made on it by Dr. Johnson at a subsequent period, when he appears to have treated with much irreverence her 'Essay on Shakespeare,' if we may believe Boswell. Notwithstanding the defects and weaknesses that I have enumerated, she possessed a masculine understanding, enlightened, cultivated, and expanded by the acquaintance of men as well as of books. Many of the most illustrious persons in rank no less than in ability, under the reigns of George II. and III., had been her correspondents, friends, companions, and admirers. Pulteney, Earl of Bath, whose portrait hung over the chimney-piece in her drawing-room, and George, the first Lord Lyttelton, so eminent for his genius, were among the number. She was constantly surrounded by all that was distinguished for attainments or talents, male or female, English or foreign; and it would be almost ungrateful in me not to acknowledge the gratification derived from the conversation and intercourse of such a society."

Lord Bath thought there never was a more perfect being than Mrs. Montagu, and Edmund Burke was inclined to agree with him. Hannah More describes her as combining "the sprightly vivacity of fifteen with the judgment and experience of a Nestor;" and Cowper, after he had read her "Essay on the Genius of Shakespeare," no longer wondered that she stood "at the head of all that is called learned."

Boswell tells us that when Reynolds, Garrick, Johnson, Goldsmith, and a knot of literary friends were dining with him in Old Bond Street in 1769, and mention was made of Mrs. Montagu's "Essay on Shakespeare" by Reynolds, who remarked that it "did her honour," Dr. Johnson replied, sharply, "Yes, sir, it does her honour, but it would do honour to nobody else. . . . I will venture to say that there is not one sentence of true criticism in her book." And yet the burly doctor was not above accepting the hospitality of the lady of whom he spoke thus lightly; but then it must be remembered that it was Mrs. Montagu who made the witty and most truthful remark, that "were an

angel called upon to give the *imprimatur* to Dr. Johnson's works, they would not have to be curtailed by a single line."

On another occasion, as his biographer informs us, Johnson had formed one of a party one evening at Mrs. Montagu's, where a splendid company had assembled, consisting of the most eminent literary characters. "I thought," adds Boswell, "he seemed highly pleased with the respect and attention that were shown him; and asked him, on our return home, if he was not 'highly *gratified* by his visit.' 'No, sir,' said he, 'not highly *gratified*; yet I do not recollect to have passed many evenings *with fewer objections.*'"

The Blue-Stocking Club was the name given to a society of ladies who met at Mrs. Montagu's house, which had for its object the substitution of the pleasures of rational conversation for cards and other frivolities. The name, as Mr. Forbes tells us, in his "Life of Beattie," originated in this manner:—

"It is well known that Mrs. Montagu's house was at that time (1771) the chosen resort of many of those of both sexes most distinguished for rank, as well as classical taste and literary talent, in London. This society of eminent friends consisted, originally, of Mrs. Montagu, Mrs. Vesey, Miss Boscawen, and Mrs. Carter; Lord Lyttelton, Mr. Pulteney, Horace Walpole, and Mr. Stillingfleet. To the latter gentleman, a man of great piety and worth, and author of some works in natural history, &c., this constellation of talents owed that whimsical appellation of 'Bas Bleu.' Mr. Stillingfleet being somewhat of a humorist in his habits and manners, and a little negligent in his dress, literally wore grey stockings; from which circumstance Admiral Boscawen used, by way of pleasantry, to call them 'The Blue-Stocking Society,' as if to intimate that when these brilliant friends met, it was not for the purpose of forming a dressed assembly. A foreigner of distinction hearing the expression, translated it literally 'Bas Bleu,' by which these meetings came to be afterwards distinguished." This account is corroborated, we may here remark, by Forbes, in his "Life of Beattie," almost in the very words here used.

If we may rely on the statement of John Timbs, in his amusing sketches of "Clubs and Club Life," the earliest mention of a Blue Stocking, or *Bas Bleu, coterie* is to be found in "a Greek comedy entitled *The Banquet of Plutarch*," but which we rather imagine to be the "Symposium of Plato." He adds, "The term as applied to ladies of high literary tastes, has been traced by Mills, in his 'History of Chivalry,' to 'the Société de la Calza, formed at Venice in A.D. 1400, when consistently with the character of the Italians of marking academies and other intellectual associations by some external sign of folly, the members when they met in literary discussion were distinguished by the colour of their stockings. These colours were sometimes fantastically blended; and at other times a single colour, especially blue, prevailed.' The Société de la Calza lasted till 1590, when the foppery of Italy took some other symbol. The rejected title then crossed the Alps, and found a congenial soil in Parisian society, and particularly branded female pedantry. It then passed from France to England, and for a while marked the vanity of the small advances in literature in female *coteries*." So far Mr. John Timbs.

Boswell, who writes, in his "Life of Johnson," under date 1781, gives a very similar account of the matter to that of Mr. Forbes, already quoted, in the following terms:—"About this time it was much the fashion for several ladies to have evening assemblies, where the fair sex might participate in conversation with literary and ingenious men animated by a desire to please. One of the most eminent members of these societies was a Mr. Stillingfleet (a grandson of the bishop), whose dress was remarkably grave; and in particular it was observed that he wore blue stockings. Such was the excellence of his conversation, and his absence was felt so great a loss, that it used to be said, 'We can do nothing without the blue stockings!' and thus by degrees the title was established." Miss Hannah More has admirably described a Blue-Stocking Club in her "Bas Bleu," a poem in which many of the persons who were most conspicuous there are mentioned; and Horace Walpole speaks of this production as a "charming poetic familiarity, called 'the Blue-Stocking Club!'"

The circle at Mrs. Montagu's used to include nearly all the persons of her time who were celebrated in art, science, or literature, including not only Boswell and Johnson—the latter of whom, in the presence of ladies, forgot his rough and rude manners—but Miss Burney, the author of "Evelina," and also Dr. Monsey, of Chelsea College, the fashionable physician, who used to send to his lady-hostess the compliment of a poem as often as her birthday returned.

After thirty-three years of married life, Edward Montagu left his distinguished wife a widow well provided for, with an income of £7,000 a year. She soon afterwards entertained thoughts of leaving Hill Street for the more northern district of Marylebone, and decided on building for herself a mansion in Portman Square. During its erection, it is related, she watched its progress with much interest. In one of her letters, Mrs. Montagu says, "I will get the better of my passion for my new house, which is almost equal to that of a lover to a mistress whom he thinks very handsome and very good, and such as will make him enjoy the dignity of life with ease;" and in another she writes, "It is an excellent house, finely situated, and just such as I have always wished, but never hoped to have."

In the year 1781, just six years after the death of her husband, the mansion was ready for her occupation, and she at once proceeded to transfer her household goods hither. Some three years previously, as we learn from one of her letters, she had "bought a large glass at the French ambassador's sale, and some other things for my new house, pretty cheap." One of the rooms in the new house was ornamented in a novel manner with "feather hangings," and Mrs. Montagu begged all sorts of birds' feathers from her friends. She tells one correspondent that "the brown tails of partridges are very useful, though not so brilliant as some others;" and another she asks for "the neck and breast feathers of the stubble goose. Things homely and vulgar are sometimes more useful than the elegant, and the feathers of a goose may be better adapted to some occasions than the plumes of the phœnix." On this unique room, where Mrs. Montagu held her court, Cowper wrote, in 1788, some lines commencing as follows:—

"The birds put off their every hue
To dress a room for Montagu;
The peacock sends his heavenly dyes,
His rainbows and his starry eyes;
The pheasant, plumes which round infold
His mantling neck with downy gold;
The cock his arch'd tail's azure show;
And, river-blanched, the swan his snow;
All tribes beside of Indian name,
That glossy shine or vivid flame,
Where rises and where sets the day,
Whate'er they boast of rich and gay,
Contribute to the gorgeous plan,
Proud to advance it all they can.
This plumage neither dashing shower
Nor blasts that shake the dripping bower,
Shall drench again or discompose,
But screen'd from every storm that blows,
It boasts a splendour ever new,
Safe with protecting Montagu."

The excitement that seems to have pervaded the mind of Mrs. Montagu during the erection of her new house, and the satisfaction which she evinced on its completion, does not appear to have worn off after she took up her residence there, notwithstanding that she was then getting well advanced in years, for we find her afterwards writing:—"I am a great deal younger, I think, since I came into my new house; from its cheerfulness, and from its admirable conveniences, less afraid of growing old. My friends and acquaintances are much pleased with it." In this last particular she was quite correct, for Walpole, who was not over-prone to praise the hobbies of others, wrote as follows to Mason:—"On Tuesday, with the Harcourts, at Mrs. Montagu's new palace, and was much surprised. Instead of vagaries, it is a noble, simple edifice. Magnificent, yet no gilding. It is grand, not tawdry, not larded, embroidered, and pomponned with shreds and remnants, and *clinquant* like the harlequinades of Adam, which never let the eye repose an instant."

Mrs. Montagu, however, used to give here, not only splendid entertainments to the Blue-Stocking Club and to a large circle of literary friends and persons of the highest distinction, but also annually, on the 1st of May, a feast on the lawn before her doors to all the chimney-sweepers in London. A writer in *Cassell's Magazine*, for May 24, 1873, remarks : " It is not generally known that this celebration took its rise in a case of kidnapping which occurred—not to one of her children, for she never had any, but to some member of her own or of her husband's family. It is said that the boy whose restoration she thus commemorated was stolen by chimney-sweeps when only three or four years old, and was brought back unintentionally to the house by some members of the sooty confraternity, when sent for to sweep the chimneys of her town mansion. If so, the only wonder is that none of our modern versifiers have seized on the incident as the subject of a poem."

The Blue-Stocking gatherings, however, did not thrive very long in the new house, for many of their chief supporters had passed away. Mrs. Montagu's breakfasts, however, were continued; but they became more sumptuous, and her rooms were often overcrowded. In 1788 Mrs. Montagu adopted giving teas, a fashion introduced from France by the Duke of Dorset. Three years before Cumberland had written an essay in the *Observer* on the assemblies at Montagu House, in which he lightly satirises the hostess as " Vanessa," and her assembly as the " Feast of Reason." Cowper afterwards more politely wrote :—

> " There genius, learning, fancy, wit,
> Their ruffled plumage calm refit."

In the year 1800 Mrs. Montagu died, when the mansion passed to her nephew, Mr. Matthew Montagu, who had taken that surname in lieu of his patronymic Robinson, on being made heir to her estate. In Sir N. W. Wraxall's "Memoirs of his Own Times," there is an amusing anecdote relating to the confusion as to this gentleman's name, after he entered the House of Commons. There appears to have been some difficulty in distinguishing between Matthew Montagu and Montagu Matthew, until "General Matthew himself thus defined the distinction : ' I wish it to be understood,' said he, ' that there is no more likeness between Montagu Matthew and Matthew Montagu than between a chestnut-horse and a horse-chestnut.'"

After Mrs. Montagu's death the house was for some time occupied by the Turkish ambassador, who erected in the garden a "kiosk," or movable temple, where he used to sit and smoke in state, surrounded by his Eastern friends. In the year 1835 Montagu House is given as the address of the Right Hon. Henry Goulburn, M.P., Chancellor of the Exchequer under Sir Robert Peel, who married a daughter of Lord Rokeby, one of the Montagus. The mansion, however, remained in the possession of the Montagu family down to the year 1874, when the lease having expired, it has reverted into the hands of the ground-landlord, Lord Portman, whose family have made it their London residence. The pleasant memory of Mrs. Montagu, however, still survives in the Square, Place, and Street named after her.

In connection with Portman Square, a laughable anecdote is told concerning Beau Brummell, which may bear repeating. It was first related in the *New Monthly Magazine*. It appears that Brummell was once at an evening party in the square. On the removal of the cloth, the snuff-boxes made their appearance, and Brummell's was particularly admired; it was handed round, and a gentleman, finding it somewhat difficult to open, incautiously applied a dessert-knife to the lid. Poor Brummell was on thorns; at last he could not contain himself any longer, and addressing the host, said, with his characteristic quaintness, " Will you be good enough to tell your friend that my snuff-box is not an oyster ?"

" The neighbourhood," writes Malcolm, in 1807, is distinguished beyond all London for its regularity, the breadth of its streets, and the respectability of the inhabitants, the majority of whom are titled persons, and those of the most ancient families."

One of the largest builders of houses in this neighbourhood was John Elwes, the well-known miser and M.P., who is said to have made a very large addition to his fortune by building speculations, especially about Portman Street, which opens into Oxford Street from the south-west corner of the square. In this street Queen Caroline took up her residence, in 1820, in the house of Lady

Anne Hamilton, one of her Ladies of the Bed-chamber.

On the east side of Portman Square, extending north and south, are Baker Street and Orchard Street. The former street, which runs into the Marylebone Road, was named after Sir Edward Baker, of Ranston, a neighbour of the Portmans, in Dorsetshire, and who seems to have lent Mr. Portman a helping hand in developing the capacities of his London estate. It consisted, at the commencement of this century, chiefly of private houses, now, however, mostly turned to business purposes. At No. 64 in this street, in the year 1800, was living Lord Camelford, who, four years later, was killed in a duel with a Mr. Best, in the grounds behind Holland House. In the year 1820 the Right Hon. Henry Grattan, the distinguished Irish orator, died at his residence in this street.

In 1826 No. 3 was in the occupation of Lord William Lennox. Mr. Thomas Spring Rice, M.P., afterwards Lord Monteagle, was at that time living in this street; and No. 69 was the residence of John Braham, the singer, already mentioned by us in our account of St. James's Theatre.*

This street has at various times been the *locale* of exhibitions of a popular character, which have come and gone, and their memory soon perished. One, however, has at all events remained, and shown that it has in it the elements of permanence, and of this we will now proceed to speak. Madame Tussaud's exhibition of wax-work figures of the celebrities of the past and present age has been established in Baker Street for a period of forty years. In our account of Fleet Street we have noticed the wax-works of Mrs. Salmon,† which have passed away, while those of Madame Tussaud seem destined to survive the present era. They were originally commenced in Paris about the year 1780, and brought, in 1802, to London, where they formed for a time the chief attraction of what is now the Lyceum, in the Strand, and after-wards at the Hanover Square Rooms. Madame Tussaud subsequently travelled with her exhibition from town to town, and in the course of twelve years succeeded in forming a goodly collection and a small sum of money. She then resolved to visit Ireland; but in the transit the vessel in which she had embarked her all was wrecked, and with great difficulty the lives of the passengers were saved; so that when she landed at Cork with her boys she found herself penniless. She then began the world anew, and this time with still greater success; and thus she was, as it were, twice the architect

of her own fortune. In 1833 she came again to London, and founded her "unrivalled" collection in Baker Street; and it has since gone on increasing, till it now includes upwards of 300 specimens, ranging from William the Conqueror down to the Duchess of Edinburgh and the impostor Arthur Orton. Of the founder of this collection, Madame Tussaud, who died in 1850, at the age of ninety, we know that she was a native of Berne, in Switzer-land, and that when a child she was taught the art of modelling figures in wax by an uncle. Coming to Paris, she taught drawing and modelling to Madame Elizabeth, the daughter of Louis XVI. and of Marie Antoinette, and mixed in the best society of the French capital, where she became acquainted with Voltaire, Rousseau, La Fayette, Mirabeau, and the other heads of the party opposed to royalty. She found it convenient, however, to accept the hospitality of England, and accordingly settled here as a refugee.

The exhibition is approached through a small hall, and by a wide staircase, which leads to a saloon at its summit, richly adorned by a radiant combination of arabesques, artificial flowers, and mirrored embellishments. From the saloon the great room is at once entered. This is a gorgeous apartment—in fact, almost an "exhibition" in itself. Its walls are panelled with plate-glass, and richly decorated with draperies, and burnished gilt orna-ments in the Louis Quatorze style. The principal statues and groups are placed round the four sides of the room, and the larger scenic combinations of figures in the centre of the room. The objects exhibited here are constantly varied, according to the public interest which they excite. Some, how-ever, are shown *en permanence*, being never out of date. Of these the most noteworthy are the re-cumbent effigies of Wellington and Napoleon; of Henry VIII. and his six wives; Queen Victoria, the Prince Consort, and the different members of the royal family; Voltaire (taken from life a few months before his death), and a coquette of the period; Lord Nelson, the cast taken from his face; and a series of the kings and queens of England, from William the Conqueror to Queen Victoria. The apartment called the "Hall of Kings" has a ceiling painted by Thornhill; and in the richly-gilt chamber adjoining is George IV. in his corona-tion robes, which, with two other velvet robes, cost, it is said, £18,000; the chair is the "homage-chair" used at the coronation. The "Napoleon" room contains an interesting collection of trophies and relics connected with the first emperor, besides a fine series of portraits of the Bonaparte family. The last apartment entered, which bears the not

* See *ante*, p. 193.   † See Vol. I., pp. 45, 46.

very pleasant-sounding name of the "Chamber of Horrors," contains, as may be inferred, an array of portrait-models of some of the greatest criminals of the age, including those of the Mannings, Greenacre, and Wainwright type. Here, too, are casts of the bleeding and dying heads of Robespierre, Marat, Fouquier, and various horrible relics and mementos, even to a model of the guillotine itself. Although to view this chamber an extra charge is

in his "Curiosities of Literature," published in 1791. The author, after mentioning several attempts to produce exhibitions of wax-work in London, though not very successful ones, adds the following:— "There was a work of this kind which Menage has noticed, and which must have appeared a little miracle. In the year 1675 the Duke of Maine received a gilt cabinet, about the size of a moderate table. On the door was inscribed *The Chamber*

THE OLD MANOR-HOUSE, MARY-LE-BONE, IN THE TIME OF QUEEN ELIZABETH. *From an Old Print.* (*See page* 429.)

made, such is the love of the marvellous, that but few persons decline to enter it, the ladies especially liking to "have their flesh made to creep."

Ingenious as these wax-works were, they are but a proof of the old saying, that there is nothing new under the sun; for we have already been introduced[*] to the wax-work effigies of our sovereigns, &c., in Westminster Abbey; and we read in the first volume of the "Entertaining Correspondent," published in 1739, a long account of a group of wax-work figures to be seen in the Maze at Amsterdam, representing the scene of the Nativity of our Lord in the manger at Bethlehem; and the proverb is further confirmed by Mr. Isaac D'Israeli,

of Wit. The inside displayed an alcove and a long gallery. In an arm-chair was seated the figure of the duke himself, composed of wax, the resemblance the most perfect imaginable. On one side stood the Duke de la Rochefoucault, to whom he presented a paper of verses for his examination. M. de Marcillac, and Bossuet, Bishop of Meaux, were standing near the arm-chair. In the alcove Madame de Thianges and Madame de la Fayette sat retired, reading a book. Boileau, the satirist, stood at the door of the gallery, hindering seven or eight bad poets from entering. Near Boileau stood Racine, who seemed to beckon to La Fontaine to come forward. All these figures were formed of wax, and this imitation must have been at once curious and interesting."

---

* See Vol. III., p. 446.

The basement-floor of the building is devoted to other purposes, and is known as the "Baker Street Bazaar." It was originally called the "Portman Bazaar," and had its chief entrance in King Street. It was at first established for the sale of horses; but carriages, harness, furniture, and other household goods are the only commodities now exhibited for sale. Here, in 1829, was given what the advertisements style a "magnificent exhibition of

Show, from 1839 down to 1861, when it was removed to the Agricultural Hall at Islington. The late Prince Consort was an exhibitor on several occasions, and carried off several prizes here in 1844, and again in 1850.

From Mr. Gibbs's "History of the Origin and Progress of the Smithfield Club," we learn that it was founded in 1798 by a party of noblemen and gentlemen, including the Duke of Bedford, Lords

MANCHESTER HOUSE. *(See page* 424.)

musical and mechanical automata, comprising nearly twenty different subjects, including the celebrated musical lady, juvenile artist, magician, ropedancer, and walking figure; also a magnificent classic vase, made by order of Napoleon; together with a serpent, birds, insects, and other subjects of natural history; the whole displaying, by their exact imitations of animated nature, the wonderful powers of mechanism." Here, about the year 1845, was started a field of artificial ice for skating, but it did not take with the public, and was soon given up. It is not a little singular, that the attempt to anticipate the pleasures of the skating-rinks, now so generally popular with the rising generation, should have been a failure. Here, too, the Royal Smithfield Club held its annual Cattle

Somerville and Winchilsea, and Sir Joseph Banks. Its first exhibitions were held in Smithfield, then in Barbican, and in one or two other places in that neighbourhood; and it did not move westwards hither till 1839, when the receipts taken at the doors of the bazaar amounted to only £300. Her Majesty paid a visit to the cattle show here in 1844, and the Prince Consort, who had become a member of the Smithfield Club on his marriage, carried off several prizes at the annual exhibitions held here with his cattle bred at his model farm in Windsor Park. The members of the Smithfield Club made an award of prizes, in the shape of gold and silver medals, silver cups, &c., for the successful competitors with live stock, agricultural implements, &c.

On the east side of Baker Street, at the corner of Adam Street, is Portman Chapel, a chapel of ease to Marylebone Parish Church. Like most of its neighbours, it is a dull, heavy, unecclesiastical-looking structure, and offers little or no subject for remark.

The streets which run crosswise between Gloucester Place and Baker Street, on its western side, such as George, King, Dorset, Crawford, and York Streets, if they have about them little of personal or historic interest, and are even less remarkable in an architectural point of view, at all events bear testimony to the loyalty of the House of Portman, and their attachment to their native county of Dorset. Between King Street and George Street, in a sort of mews and side passage, "gracefully re-treating" from the public view, as became a chapel of Roman Catholics, when they lay under penal laws, but nestling safely under the wing of the French ambassador's house, is the Chapel of the Annunciation. This chapel was built in the reign of George III., and has always been the place whither the sovereigns of France have resorted to hear mass when in this country, and where masses are said for the repose of the souls of French royalty after death; and though a small and poor edifice, and concealed in a back street which is little better than a mews, it has a history of its own which cannot be omitted here. It was founded by some of the *emigrés* who sought an asylum in England on the outbreak of the French Revolution in 1791, and who opened it in 1793, having previously celebrated the divine offices in a house in Paddington Street, not far off. It is said that many of the clergy, and even members of the French court, aided the workmen with their own hands in building the walls. It was solemnly blessed and dedicated on the 15th of March, 1799. Here most, if not all, of the Bourbon kings and princes who have come to England as exiles or as visitors—Louis XVIII., Charles X., Louis Philippe and Queen Amelie, the Duchesse d'Angoulême, &c. —have always heard mass; to say nothing of the Emperor Louis Napoleon, the Empress Eugenie, and their son. Here have been preached the *oraisons funèbres* of the Abbé Edgworth, of the Duc d'Enghien, and of very many royal and distinguished personages of foreign countries, such as the King of Portugal, Queen Mary Josephine of Savoy, Chateaubriand, Count de Montalembert, and others. In this chapel the body of the Duc de Montpensier lay in state, previous to its interment in Westminster Abbey. Here courses of sermons have been annually preached, and "Retreats" have been given, from time to time, by the most eloquent of French preachers, such as Père Ravignan, Père Gratry, and Père Lacordaire. Attached to the chapel are many religious and charitable confraternities, &c., including a branch of the Society of St. Vincent de Paul, for the benefit of the French poor of the metropolis.

York Place is the name given to the last twenty or thirty houses at the upper end of Baker Street, where it joins the Marylebone Road. The houses, which were built about the year 1800, are fine and commodious. At his residence here, in February, 1865, died his Eminence Cardinal Wiseman, at the age of sixty-two. The Cardinal removed his archiepiscopal residence hither from Golden Square, as we have stated in a previous chapter. Born at Seville, in Spain, in the year 1802, Nicholas Wiseman was the son of Irish parents, descended from the younger branch of the ancient Essex family of Sir William Wiseman, Bart. He entered the priesthood at the age of twenty-three; in the following year he was appointed Vice-Rector of the English College at Rome, and in the year 1827 he became Professor of Oriental Literature. In 1840 he was chosen Coadjutor-Bishop to Dr. Walsh, then the Vicar-Apostolic of the Central District in England. He afterwards for some years presided over St. Mary's College, Oscott; and on the transference of Dr. Walsh to the post of Pro-Vicar Apostolic of the London District, Dr. Wiseman was again the coadjutor. On the establishment of the Roman Catholic hierarchy in 1850, Dr. Walsh having died in the meanwhile, Dr. Wiseman was nominated Archbishop of Westminster, and at the same time elevated to the cardinalate. His eminence was acknowledged as one of the first scholars in Europe; he was also a great Biblical scholar, a judicious critic, and a proficient in almost every branch of science. His successor in the see of Westminster, Cardinal Manning, lived in the same house from 1865 down to 1872. The house is now the "Bedford College for Ladies."

In York Place lived for some time Mr. Edward Hodges Baily, R.A., the sculptor. He executed the *bassi relievi* surrounding the throne-room at Buckingham Palace, and also designed several of the figures on the Marble Arch. Among his principal works are "Eve Listening," the group of "The Graces," and "The Fatigued Huntsman;" and among his most recent works are statues of Mansfield and Fox, erected in St. Stephen's Hall, in the Houses of Parliament; and a statue of "Genius," from Milton's Arcades, for the Mansion House of London. His last work was a bust of Mr. Hepworth Dixon. Mr. Baily died in 1867.

Midway between Marylebone Road and Crawford

Street, and extending from York Place westward into Seymour Place, is a broad thoroughfare called York Street; but, like the two or three small streets connecting it with Marylebone Road, its history is a blank. Seymour Place and Street took their designation from the original family name of Lord Portman's ancestor, who was not a Portman, or even a Berkeley by birth, but a Seymour, but took the name of Portman on inheriting the estate of Orchard-Portman.

Making our way back into Oxford Street, we pass through Orchard Street, which runs from the south-east corner of Portman Square, and is called after Orchard-Portman, in Somersetshire, one of the seats of Lord Portman. Here Sheridan, soon after his marriage with the beautiful Miss Linley, took his first town-house, and here he wrote *The Rivals* and *The Duenna*.

There used formerly to be some barracks between Portman Street and Orchard Street; they were removed about the year 1860, and Granville Place built on their site.

In Oxford Street, in the immediate neighbourhood of Orchard Street, was Fladong's Hotel, which in the days of the Regency acquired some celebrity. Captain Gronow, in his "Reminiscences," speaks of it as mostly frequented by "old salts," as at that time there was no club for sailors.

CHAPTER XXXIII.

OXFORD STREET.—NORTHERN TRIBUTARIES (*continued*).

" Oh! who will repair
Unto Manchester Square?"—*T. Moore.*

Duke Street—Somerset and Lower Seymour Streets—The Samaritan Hospital—Manchester Square—The Prince Regent and the Marquis of Hertford—Theodore Hook on the Ladder of Fame—Talleyrand and other Distinguished Residents in Manchester Square—Hinde Street—Thayer Street—A "Fast-Living" Earl—Spanish Place and the Roman Catholic Chapel—Manchester Street—Joanna Southcote—Death of Lady Tichborne—Dorset Street—Charles Babbage and his Calculating Machines—Paddington Street—The Cemeteries—George Canning—Historical Remarks concerning the Parish of Marylebone—Marylebone Lane—Nancy Dawson—The Old Manor House—The Parish Church—Devonshire Terrace, and Charles Dickens' Residence—Nottingham Place—Colonel Martin Leake—The Workhouse—Marylebone Road—A Batch of Charitable Institutions—The Police-court—Marylebone Gardens—Dangerous State of the Neighbourhood—Gallantry of Dick Turpin—Demolition of the Gardens—Wimpole Street—Stratford Place—Archæological Discoveries in Oxford Street—The Deaf and Dumb Association—Laurie and Marner's Coachbuilding Establishment.

As in the previous chapter we have pointed out that most of the streets and squares through which we have passed have been named with direct reference to Lord Portman, his family, and his property, so we shall find in the locality we are about to enter the same with reference to the ducal house of Portland, and to that of Harley, Earl of Oxford.

Duke Street, through which we now pass on our way northward, leads direct into Manchester Square, and was so named in honour of the Duke of Manchester, to whom the square itself owes its origin. Of Somerset Street, the first thoroughfare crossing Duke Street, there is little or nothing to record. In Lower Seymour Street, which runs from Duke Street westward into Portman Square, a valuable freehold property, consisting of two houses, was purchased in 1875, through the influence of Lady Petre, for the purposes of establishing a night home for girls and unmarried women of good character. This charity is to be combined in management with a *crèche*, or infant nursery, in Bulstrode Street, on the east side of Manchester Square. Another charitable institution in this street is the Samaritan Hospital for Women and Children, which was established in 1847, and is supported entirely by voluntary contributions. The hospital provides for "the reception of poor women afflicted with diseases peculiar to their sex, where they have home comforts and hospital treatment without publicity." Attendance is also furnished to poor married women at their own homes in peculiar cases. Close by this hospital is the Quebec Institute, or, as it is sometimes called, Seymour Hall; it is a building where miscellaneous lectures, concerts, &c., are held. In 1835 the Right Hon. Sir John Sinclair, M.P., the eminent writer on agriculture, was a resident in this street. He was President of the Board of Agriculture for Scotland. In this capacity a good story is told of him. He was vain and ambitious enough to tell Pitt that the head of such a board ought to have a peerage. Pitt affected not to understand him, but treated his remark as equivalent to a resignation, and nominated Lord Somerville to the post.

"Manchester Square," observes a writer in the *Builder*, "was erected soon after Portman Square, on a site which had been previously proposed for a square, with a church in the centre, to be called Queen Anne's Square." Her Majesty's death, however, threw a damp upon the suggestion. The ground, after lying waste for a time, was taken by the Duke of Manchester, who, in 1776, commenced the building of Manchester House (now called Hertford House), which occupies nearly all the northern side. Two years later, on the duke's death, it was bought as the residence of the Spanish ambassador. From him it passed into the hands of the second Marquis of Hertford, one of the friends of George, Prince Regent, who used daily to call at the door in his chariot or pony phaeton. To this habit Thomas Moore refers, in his "Diary of a Politician:"—

"Through Manchester Square took a canter just now,
Met the old yellow chariot, and made a low bow."

The marchioness, of course, was the great attraction of the Prince. Moore thus refers to her elsewhere as the reigning beauty of the day :—

"Or who will repair unto Manchester Square,
And see if the lovely Marchesa be there?
And bid her to come, with her hair darkly flowing,
All gentle and juvenile, crispy and gay,
In the manner of Ackerman's dresses for May."

Some idea may be formed of the unpopularity under which royalty laboured in the interval between the commencement of the Regency and the accession of the "first gentleman in Europe" to the throne as George IV., from a facetious mock advertisement which was inserted in the *Scourge* for 1814 :—"Lost between Pall Mall and Manchester Square, his Royal Highness the Prince Regent."

Besides serving as the Spanish embassy, it is said by a writer in the *Builder* that Manchester House was at one time occupied by the French ambassador, and that Talleyrand lived in it; but we have not been able to confirm the statement. The mansion was the property of the late Marquis of Hertford, who left it to Sir Richard Wallace, who remodelled and nearly rebuilt it in 1873-4. The house is built of staring red brick, with white stone dressings, in a very heavy, unattractive style; but it contains a splendid gallery of pictures. The ground on which it stands belongs to the Portman estate.

Manchester House is famous as having been one of those social stepping-stones which helped poor Theodore Hook in his introduction to the fashionable and West-end world. Through the good offices of Sheridan and his son, the gay Tom Sheridan, favourable mention of his talents was made to the Marchioness of Hertford, then one of the lights in the brilliant firmament of the Regency. She was so pleased with his musical and metrical facility that she sang his praises in every direction, and he was called on to minister to the amuse-

ment of the Prince Regent himself at a supper in Manchester Square. He used to describe his presentation to the Prince : his awe at first was something quite terrible, but good-humoured condescension and plenty of champagne by-and-by restored him to himself; and the young man so delighted his Royal Highness, that as he was leaving the room he laid his hand on his shoulder, and said, "Mr. Hook, I must see and hear you again." After a few more similar evenings at Lady Hertford's, and, we believe, a dinner or two elsewhere, the Regent made inquiry about his position, and finding that he was without profession or fixed income of any sort, signified his opinion that "something must be done for Hook."

In spite of his humble extraction, Hook's gaiety and brilliancy soon made him generally acceptable, especially with the ladies, and he speedily became a favourite throughout the regions of May Fair. He saw its boudoirs, too, as well as its salons, and "narrowly escaped various dangers incidental to such a career; among the rest, at all events, a duel with General Thornton, in which transaction, from first to last, he was allowed to show equal tact and temper."

The centre of Manchester Square is formed into a circular enclosure, laid out with grass, shrubs, and a few trees, and surrounded by an iron railing. The houses forming the remaining three sides of the square possess no particular interest, with the exception, perhaps, that between the years 1828 and 1830 No. 12 was the residence of William Beckford, the author of "Vathek," and the owner of the once magnificent mansion of Fonthill, between Salisbury and Shaftesbury.

Hinde Street, which runs out of the square on the eastern side, was called after one Mr. Jacob Hinde, whose name occurs as lessee of part of "Marylebone Park" in the middle of the last century.

In Thayer Street—the thoroughfare connecting Hinde Street with Marylebone High Street—in small lodgings, almost forgotten by the world, died, in July, 1857, the fifth Earl of Mornington, better known by his former name of Mr. W. Long-Pole-Tylney-Wellesley. In the early days of the Regency he was a dandy about town, and distinguished himself by giving sumptuous dinners at Wanstead Park, in Essex, where he owned one of the finest mansions in England, in right of his wife, Miss Tylney-Long, an heiress with £50,000 a year, whom he ruined, and broke her heart. He used to ask his friends down to Wanstead to dine *after* the opera at midnight, the drive from London, through the dreary streets of Whitechapel and Stratford, being deemed by him *appétisant*. Every luxury that money could command he would place upon his table at that unusual hour of the night, and he often protracted the dessert into the next day. Having had the enjoyment of such wealth, although he was the head of the Wellesley family, he died almost a beggar; "in fact," says Captain Gronow, "he would have starved if it had not been for the charity of his cousin, the Duke of Wellington, who allowed him a pension of £300 a year." The authors of the "Rejected Addresses" wrote of him, in 1820—

"And long may Long-Pole-Tylney-Wellesley live."

They had their prayer granted; for his lordship enjoyed for nearly forty years more the lease of life.

The whole of the west side of Spanish Place, which bounds Manchester Square on the east, is formed by the somewhat sombre-looking walls of Manchester House; and the name of Spanish Place, we need hardly say, serves to keep in remembrance the occupancy of the mansion by the Spanish ambassador in the last century. As was the case in other parts of the town, so here the Roman Catholics were glad to be allowed to practise their religion under the shelter of a foreign embassy whilst the penal laws were still in force. The chapel on the eastern side was built from the designs of Bonomi, an Italian architect, in 1796; it is dedicated to St. James, the patron saint of Spain. It was enlarged in 1846, and further beautified and adorned internally under Cardinal Wiseman. The building is disproportionately broad for its length, and is Italian rather than ecclesiastical in its character.

In the north-west corner of the square—crossing George and Blandford Streets, and terminating in Dorset Street—is Manchester Street. Here, in 1814, died the arch-impostor, Joanna Southcote, who deluded hundreds and thousands of credulous persons in London and elsewhere that she was destined to become the mother of the future "Shiloh," and that he was soon to be born of her. Her imposture occupied the public attention for several months, and even well-informed and sensible medical men were victims of her assertions. She was buried at St. John's Wood Chapel, and we shall have more to say about her when we reach that place. Manchester Street is almost wholly occupied by private hotels or houses let out in furnished lodgings. At Howlett's Hotel, No. 36 in this street, died suddenly, in 1868, Lady Tichborne, the mother of Roger Tichborne, who was lost at sea in 1854, and whose title and

estates were claimed by the impostor, Arthur Orton, who pretended to be her long-lost son.

Dorset Street, into which we now pass, was so named, as we have already shown, after the county in which is situated a large portion of the estates of Lord Portman, whose property extends thus far eastwards. At No. 1 in this street, now a branch establishment of the Samaritan Free Hospital for Women and Children, noticed above, formerly lived the celebrated Mr. Charles Babbage, the inventor of the machine for calculating and printing mathematical tables. From the "Percy Anecdotes" we learn that Mr. Babbage constructed several of these machines. One is capable of computing any table by the aid of differences, whether they are positive or negative, or of both kinds. One remarkable property of this machine is, that the greater the number of differences, the more the engine will outstrip the most rapid calculator. By the application of other parts of no great degree of complexity, this may be converted into a machine for extracting the roots of equations, and consequently the roots of numbers. Mr. Babbage likewise constructed another machine, which he says "will calculate tables governed by laws which have not been hitherto shown to be explicitly determinable, and it will solve equations for which analytical methods of solution have not yet been continued. Supposing," continues Mr. Babbage, "these engines executed, there would yet be wanting other means to ensure the accuracy of the printed tables to be produced by them. The errors of the persons employed to copy the figures presented by the engines would first interfere with their correctness. To remedy this evil, I have contrived measures by which the machines themselves shall take from several boxes containing type, the numbers which they calculate, and place them side by side, thus becoming, at the same time, a substitute for the compositor and the computer, by which means all error in copying, as well as printing, is removed." Mr. Babbage died here in 1871.

On the north side of Dorset Street, a thoroughfare called East Street will take us at once into Paddington Street, so called because it led in the direction of the then distant rural village of Paddington, and which forms the connecting link between Crawford Street and High Street, Marylebone. A great part of Paddington Street is taken up on either side with cemeteries for the use of the parish. They are not quite so tastily laid out as that of Père la Chaise, at Paris, nor is the list of their occupants a very interesting or illustrious one. In the cemetery on the south side of the street it is computed that near 100,000 persons have been interred. An inscription here records the deaths of several infants, children of J. F. Smyth Stuart, "great-grandson of Charles II." Among those who lie buried here are Baretti, the friend of Johnson, and the author of the "Italian Dictionary," already mentioned in our account of the father of the Premier; and William Guthrie, the historian. The southern cemetery was consecrated in the reign of George I., the northern early in that of George III.

In "Marylebone, near London," on the 11th of April, 1770, was born George Canning, the future

MARYLEBONE CHURCH IN THE SIXTEENTH CENTURY AND IN 1750. (*See page* 430.)

Haymarket. For many years he lived at the hospitable table of the Thrales at Streatham, but eventually—like Dr. Johnson—he quarrelled with Mrs. Thrale, afterwards Mrs. Piozzi. An account of the quarrel between these irritable and touchy votaries of the Muses may be seen in the *European Magazine*. Baretti was foreign secretary to the Royal Academy, and some members of that learned body attended his funeral here.

Here, too, lie buried Mr. George Canning, the

Premier of England. His father, mentioned above, was a young gentleman of good family, whose father had cast him off for making a poor marriage; and while Canning was an infant, his father died of a broken heart, his mother being glad to support herself and her bairn by keeping a small school. Sent by an uncle to Eton, the boy so distinguished himself that he was entered at Christ Church, Oxford, where he showed himself one of the best scholars of his age, and soon afterwards

MARYLEBONE GARDENS. *From a Print of 1780. (See page 431.)*

J. GREENWAY sc.

entered upon that political career which led him ultimately to the premiership.

In Dorset Mews East, Paddington Street, a house served as the home of the French *emigré* clergy, in 1791-3, and here they said mass and celebrated the divine offices, till they could open their chapel in King Street.

Before proceeding with our perambulation of the streets and thoroughfares lying to the east and south-east of Paddington Street, and crossing the boundary-line which separates the property of Lord Portman from that of the Duke of Portland, we may be pardoned for introducing a few historical remarks concerning the parish of Marylebone. The name is said to be a corruption or an abridgment of "St. Mary-le-Bourne," or "St. Mary on the Brook," so called from a small chapel dedicated to the Blessed Virgin which stood on the banks of a small brook, or bourne, or burn, which still runs down from the slopes of Hampstead, passing under Allsop Buildings, where, of course, it is arched over. This is the derivation of the name as given by most writers, who compare with it the termination of Ty*burn*. Some writers have asserted that the parish was itself originally called Tybourne, or Tyburn, from the brook (bourne) of which we have just spoken, a name which gradually was exchanged for Marylebourne or Marylebone. If, however, we might hazard an opinion, we would suggest that it is possibly a corruption of "St. Mary la Bonne."

But whatever may be its derivation, two centuries ago it was still a rural spot, and Macaulay reminds us that at the end of the reign of Charles II. "cattle fed and sportsmen wandered with dogs and guns over the site of the borough of Marylebone." It was, in fact, nothing more than a small country village, separated from London by green fields. In one of the fields in the neighbourhood, as late as the year 1773, was fought a duel between Lord Townshend and Lord Bellamont, in which the latter was dangerously wounded, being shot through the groin.

Almost at the beginning of the last century, writes Lambert, in his "History of London," published in 1806, "Marylebone was a small village, almost a mile distant from the nearest part of the metropolis; indeed, it was formerly so distinct and separate from London, as not to be included in most histories and topographical works devoted to the metropolis. Its increase began between 1716 and 1720, by the erection of Cavendish Square." Maitland, in his "History of London," in 1739, gives the number of houses in "Marybone" as 577, and the persons who kept coaches—that is,

carriages—as thirty-five. At the beginning of the nineteenth century, the houses had risen to 9,000, and the number of "coaches" is estimated at about 530. But even this is a sorry total in comparison of the Marylebone of to-day, which at the last census had a population of upwards of 477,000 souls, and no less than 32,000 electors, having increased no less than 11,000 since its erection into a Parliamentary borough in 1832. According to Malcolm, in 1807, there were over 7,000 houses, with a population of 27,000 males and 37,000 females.

The parish of Marylebone is now the largest in the metropolis, being more than twice the size of the actual City proper, and having also a larger population; indeed, its population is larger than that of London and Westminster combined, in the reign of Elizabeth. According to the last census returns, the population of this parish numbered 477,532, or nearly double what it was only a quarter of a century ago. Its present population (1876) is estimated at about 600,000.

The manor of Marylebone was granted by King James I. to Edward Forset, in 1611, and afterwards passed into the family of Austen, by the marriage of Arabella Forset to Thomas Austen. In 1710 John Holles, Duke of Newcastle, purchased the manor of John Austen, afterwards Sir John Austen; and his only daughter and heir, Lady Henrietta Cavendish Holles, marrying Edward Harley, second Earl of Oxford and Mortimer, it passed into that family. The only daughter and heir of the Earl and Countess of Oxford, Lady Margaret Cavendish Harley, marrying William, second Duke of Portland, took the property into the Portland family, with whom it still remains, the present duke being lord of the manor. The various names of these noble families are all represented in the streets of the neighbourhood. Lady Henrietta Cavendish Holles gave her names to Henrietta Street, Cavendish Square, and Holles Street; her husband to Harley Street, Oxford Street, and Mortimer Street; and their daughter, Lady Margaret, to Margaret Street. Bentinck, Duke, and Duchess Streets, as well as Portland Place, all take their names from the Duke and Duchess of Portland. One of the titles of the Earl of Oxford was Lord Harley of Wigmore, after which place Wigmore Street was named. Welbeck Abbey, an estate of the Duke of Portland, and Bulstrode, a former seat of the family, are represented by Welbeck and Bulstrode Streets.

In Marylebone was one of the many chapels or churches which the Huguenot refugees established on settling in London after the revocation of the Edict of Nantes, whose number is estimated by

Mr. Smiles at thirty-five, and by Mr. Burn at forty. It was founded about the year 1656.

In a map published in 1742 we see the small village church of Marylebone, or "St. Mary-at-the-Bourne," standing quite alone in the fields. It is approached by two narrow zigzag lanes, one winding up from about the bottom of the east side of Stratford Place—then the western boundary of all continuous houses—following the line of what is still called Marylebone Lane; the other lane crosses the fields diagonally from Tottenham Court Road. This lane, the northern end of which is now called Marylebone High Street, was in olden times a footway through the fields from Brook Field, the site of which is now covered by Brook Street, to Marylebone Manor House. The lane exhibits proofs of its antiquity, by its winding and its narrowness. No doubt it was an old rural lane, along which the farm-horses went to the great city to market from the farmers of the outlying districts. It now terminates on the north side of Oxford Street; but it would seem to have formerly continued in a winding manner by Shug Lane and Marylebone Street to the east end of Piccadilly and the Haymarket, much in the same way that Drury Lane led from St. Giles's-in-the-Fields to St. Clement's Danes, and Tyburn Lane (now Park Lane) from Tyburn to Hyde Park Corner. The Marylebone Street above mentioned was built about the year 1680, and was so called because it led from "Hedge Lane" to Marylebone. It is described in the "New View of London," in 1708, as a "pretty straight street, between Glasshouse Street and Shug Lane, near Pickadilly."

Mr. Smith, in his "Book for a Rainy Day," tells us how that "at this time (1744) houses in High Street, Marylebone, particularly on the western side, continued to be inhabited by families who kept their coaches, and who considered themselves as living in the country, and perhaps their family affairs were as well known as they could have been had they resided at Kilburn. In Marylebone great and wealthy people of former days could hardly stir an inch without being noticed; indeed, so lately as the year 1728, *The Daily Journal* assured the public that 'many persons arrived in London from their country houses in Marylebone.'"

The "Rose of Normandy," a public-house in High Street, is said to be the oldest house in the parish. It is described in the *Gentleman's Magazine*, vol. lxxxiii., p. 524, as having had, in the year before the Restoration, "outside a square brick wall, set with fruit-trees, gravel walks 204 paces long, 7 broad; the circular wall 485 paces long, 6 broad; the centre square a bowling-green, 112

paces one way, 88 another; all, except the first, double set with quickset hedges, full-grown, and kept in excellent order, and indented like town walls." "The street having been raised," writes Mr. Larwood, "the entrance to the house is now (1866) some steps below the roadway. The original form of the exterior has been preserved, but the garden and large bowling-green have dwindled down into a miserable skittle-ground." It is currently reported that the celebrated Nancy Dawson, as a young girl, was employed in setting up the skittles at a bowling-alley in High Street, probably in these identical grounds.

The old Manor House, of which we have given a view on page 420, stood on the south side of what is now called the Marylebone Road, and its site is now occupied by Devonshire Mews. The house, as Mr. Smith tells us, in the work above quoted, consisted of a large body and two wings, a projecting porch in the front, and an enormously deep dormer roof, supported by numerous cantalivers, in the centre of which there was, within a very bold pediment, a shield surmounted by foliage, with labels below it. The back, or garden front, of the house had a flat face with a bay window at each end, glazed in quarries, and the wall of the back front terminated with five gables. The mansion was wholly of brick, and surmounted by a large turret containing a clock and bell. From the style of decorations of the interior, Mr. Smith considers it was probably of the Inigo Jones period: the hand-rails of the grand staircase were supported with richly-carved perforated foliage. The house was turned into a school, kept by a certain clergyman named Fountayne, who had here among his pupils the eccentric and wayward George Hanger, afterwards Lord Coleraine.

In connection with this old manor house, or rather with reference to Mr. Fountayne's academy, Mr. J. T. Smith tells us, that one Sunday morning his mother allowed him, before they entered the "little church in High Street, Marylebone, to stand to see the young gentlemen of Mr. Fountayne's boarding-school cross the road. I remember well," he adds, "a summer's sun shone with full refulgence at the time, and my youthful eyes were dazzled with the various colours of the dresses of the youths, who walked two and two, some in pea-green, others sky-blue, and several in the brightest scarlet; many of them wore gold-laced hats, while the flowing locks of others, at that time allowed to remain uncut at schools, fell over their shoulders. To the best of my recollection, the scholars amounted to about one hundred."

During the time that it was vested in the Crown,

the manor house was occasionally used as a temporary royal residence, particularly by Queen Elizabeth, who appears by many accounts to have used
her various palaces in rapid succession. The park
attached to the manor stretched away northward,
and its site is now the Regent's Park, of which we
shall speak in a future chapter.

There was an old church in Marylebone which
had come down from the times before the Reformation, but having fallen out of repair, it was pulled
down in 1741, to make room for another structure,
which served as the parish church, until the erection
of a third structure in the New Road, some eighty
years later, reduced it to the rank of a mere chapel
of ease. Lambert, in his "History of London,"
places the old village of Tyburn on the site of the
north-west part of Oxford Street, and supposes,
from the number of bones dug up there,* that the
old Marylebone Court House covered the site of
the old church and churchyard of that village.
"This church," he writes, "was dedicated to St.
John the Evangelist, and being left alone by the
highway side, in consequence of the decay of the
village, was robbed of its books, vestments, bells,
images, and other decorations;" therefore the parishioners petitioned the Bishop of London for leave
to build a new church on another site, and this
being dedicated to St. Mary, and standing near the
bourne, came to be called "St. Mary of the Bourne."
This village of Tyborne appears in "Domesday
Book" to have belonged to the abbess and sisters
of Barking in Essex. The first church was the one
selected by Hogarth for the plate in his "Harlot's
Progress," where he has introduced his "Rake at
the Altar with an Old Maid." As the print was
published in 1735, the scene could not have taken
place within the little dingy building now standing
in the High Street: a part of the inscription in
the picture, nevertheless, still remains to be seen
in one of the pews in the gallery. In Smith's
"History of Marylebone," it is stated that "the first
two lines of this inscription are the originals; the
last two were restored in 1816, at the expense of
the Rev. Mr. Chapman, the minister."

Among those baptised in this ugly little structure were the poet Byron, in the year 1788;
and "Horatia," the daughter of Lord Nelson, by
Emma Lady Hamilton, in 1803. The list of those
who are buried here is rather long, including John
Wesley's brother Charles; Gibbs, the architect
of St. Martin's-in-the-Fields; Hoyle, the author
of "Whist" and a work on "Games;" Caroline
Watson, the engraver; Bower, author of a "History

of the Popes;" Allan Ramsay and Vanderbank,
the portrait-painters; John Dominic Serres, the
marine-painter; Rysbrack, the sculptor; Ferguson,
the astronomer; and James Figg, the celebrated
prize-fighter, whose portrait figures in one of the
engravings of Hogarth, in the "Rake's Progress."

The present parish church is situated in the
New (or, as it is now styled, the Marylebone) Road,
opposite York Gate. It was originally intended to
be only a chapel of ease; but it was so much
admired, both externally and internally, that it was
subsequently converted, under an Act of Parliament, to parochial uses. It was erected, under an
Act of Parliament, in 1813–17, at a cost of about
£60,000, its architect being Mr. Thomas Hardwick, a pupil of Sir William Chambers, and one of
a family of architects, his son Philip being the
designer of Lincoln's Inn Hall and Library; and
his grandson, Mr. Philip C. Hardwick, of the new
buildings of the Charter House, on the Surrey
Hills. A double gallery forms a feature of its
interior; and a peculiarity in its construction is
that the portico faces the north, an arrangement
necessitated by the nature of the ground whereon
it is erected. The altar-piece, by Benjamin West,
President of the Royal Academy, was a present
from that celebrated painter to the church: it
represents the Nativity of our Lord.

Here lie buried James Northcote, R.A., the pupil
and biographer of Sir Joshua Reynolds, and also
another Royal Academician, Richard Cosway, who
died in 1821, at his residence in Edgware Road.

In the Marylebone Road, near the east end of
the parish church, and close by the High Street,
is Devonshire Terrace. Here, in 1839, Charles
Dickens took up his abode, when newly married,
and in the first flush of his fame as the author of
"Pickwick," "Nicholas Nickleby," and "Oliver
Twist." His residence is described by Mr. J.
Forster as "a handsome house, with a garden of
considerable size, shut out from the New Road by
a high brick wall, facing the York Gate into the
Regent's Park." Here he used to gather round
his friends, Macready, Stanfield, Landseer, Harrison Ainsworth, Talfourd, and Bulwer; and here
he composed the principal portion of "Master
Humphrey's Clock," the "Old Curiosity Shop,"
and "David Copperfield." How fond Dickens
was of his residence here may be gathered from
his remark, later on in life, "I seem as if I had
plucked myself out of my proper soil when I left
Devonshire Terrace, and could take root no more
until I return to it." A sketch of the house, by
Maclise, will be found in Mr. Forster's "Life of
Dickens."

---

* Several skeletons were dug up here in March, 1876.

Nottingham Place is the name given to the thoroughfare at the west end of the church, running from the Marylebone Road into Paddington Street. Its designation is probably derived from the county in which the chief landed property of the Duke of Portland is situated. Here, at No. 26, lived for many years Colonel William Martin Leake, the accomplished traveller, and author of so many topographical and antiquarian works on Ancient Greece and Asia Minor, &c. Nottingham Place is crossed by a short street bearing the same name.

Marylebone Road, owing to its great breadth, and the houses standing so far back from the road, has always been a favourite place for hospitals, charitable institutions, &c. Within a short distance of the church is the parish workhouse, which stands partly on the Portman estate, and partly on that of the Duke of Portland. It was originally built in 1775, but was greatly altered and enlarged in 1875. The house is conveniently fitted up with workshops, washhouse, laundry, wards, kitchen, bakehouse, chapel, infirmary, and officers' rooms, all of which are well adapted to their different purposes. Close to the workhouse, at the corner of Northumberland Street, is the Home for Crippled Girls, which was established in 1851, and was formerly in Hill Street, Dorset Square. The building, which is known as Northumberland House, was built about the year 1800; no reason can be found for the name. The poor afflicted inmates of this institution occupy their time, so far as their ability serves them, in the manufacture of fancy articles in straw and other material suitable for presents; and there is also a public laundry in connection with the Home.

The New Hospital for Women, at No. 222, was founded in 1866, for the purpose of affording to poor women and children medical and surgical treatment from legally qualified women. This institution was originally established in Seymour Street, but was removed hither in 1875.

In 1830 was established in this road the Western General Dispensary, for the relief of the sick poor in the north-west parts of Marylebone and the parish of Paddington. The number of patients relieved during the year amounts, on an average, to about 15,000. Between York Place and Gloucester Place are the offices of the Marylebone Association for Improving the Dwellings of the Industrious Classes. Judging from the description of some wretched tenements in this parish, as given by the Medical Officer of Health, it would almost seem that there is still work to be done by the above association in this neighbourhood. The dwellings referred to are described as consisting of twenty cottages placed in four parallel rows, which are reached by an avenue twenty-five feet wide, with a narrow, wretchedly-paved footway. "In some of the forecourts of these cottages," says Dr. Whitmore, "there is an attempt to cultivate the soil, while in others rubbish is strewn about, and puddles of filthy stagnant water lie there long after a fall of rain. None of the cottages have rooms above the ground floor; the front rooms have an average of 850 feet of cubic space each, while the backs have only 750 feet. The ceilings are seven feet from the floor, but the flooring is six feet below the level of the forecourt; consequently the eaves of the roof are but little above the level of the ground." An inhabitant of one of these hovels, nevertheless, declared that if she were forced to leave she would soon die.

At the corner of Marylebone Road and Seymour Place are the police-court buildings of the parish. The building, which was erected in 1874-5—the old police-court in the High Street having become unsuited for its purposes—consists of a large and commodious court-room, private rooms for the magistrates, and the requisite offices for other officials. The basement of the edifice is of rusticated Portland stone, and the upper part is built of white Suffolk brick with stone dressings; and the central portion of the front elevation is surmounted by a pediment enclosing a sculptured representation of the royal arms.

A little northward of Manchester and Cavendish Squares, and on the east side of Marylebone Lane, towards the close of the last century, was the place of fashionable amusements so well known to fame as "Marylebone Gardens." These gardens were formed towards the end of the seventeenth century, by throwing together the place of public resort called "The Rose" and an adjoining bowling-green, mentioned above. The chief entrance was in the High Street; and there was also an entrance at the back, from the fields, through a narrow passage, flanked with a small enclosure, known as "The French Gardens," from their having been cultivated by refugees who had settled in London after the passing of the Edict of Nantes. At first, and for many years, the gardens were entered *gratis* by all ranks of the people; but the company resorting to them becoming more respectable, a shilling was charged as entrance-money; for which the party paying was to receive an equivalent in viands. They afterwards met with such success as to induce the proprietor to form them into a regular place of musical and scenic entertainment; and Charles Bannister, Dibdin (who both made their first public appearance here when youths), and other eminent vocalists, contributed to enliven them with their talents. Chatterton wrote a burlesque burletta, after the fashion of Midas, called the *Revenge*, which was performed here in 1770. Splendid *fêtes*, balls, and concerts, during the run of the season, were given here, as at Vauxhall; and their details are to be found advertised in the papers of the day. In one of these *fêtes*, given on the King's birthday, June 4, 1772, after the usual concert and

covered by Beaumont Street and Devonshire Street." It is mentioned by Pepys, two years after the great "fire of London," in his own quaint manner, in these words: "Then we abroad to Marrowbone, and there walked in the garden; the first time I ever was there, and a pretty place it is." Its bowling-alleys were famous in the days of Pope and Gay, and the latter writer alludes to this place more than once in the *Beggar's Opera*, as a

THE "FARTHING PIE HOUSE." *From a Drawing*, 1820. (*See page* 433.)

songs, was shown a representation of Mount Etna, with the Cyclops at work, and a grand firework, consisting of vertical wheels, suns, stars, globes, &c., which was afterwards copied at Ranelagh. On another occasion a great part of the garden was laid out in imitation of the Boulevards at Paris, with numerous shops and other attractions.

In the old time London was surrounded with places of amusement—its Vauxhall, Ranelagh, &c.; but none were more popular than these gardens, the very name of which seems now to have almost passed away. Chambers writes, in his "Book of Days:" "Of these places of amusement in the north-west suburbs, the most important was that known as Marylebone Gardens. It was situated opposite the old parish church, on ground now

rendezvous for the dissipated, putting it on a level with one of bad repute already mentioned. In one of his "Fables" he thus alludes to the dog-fights allowed here:—

> "Both Hockley-hole and Marybone
> The combats of my dog have known."

The gardens and the adjoining bowling-green seem to have been frequented by the rank and fashion of the town. Lady Mary Wortley Montagu alludes to the fondness of Sheffield, Duke of Buckingham, for this place of amusement; she writes—

> "Some dukes at Marybone bowl time away."

Here, at the end of each season, as the actor Quin told the antiquary Pennant, the Duke of Buckingham used to give a dinner to the guests who frequented the place, when he always proposed as a particular standing toast, "May as many of us rogues as remain '*unhanged*' next spring meet here again!" An anecdote book, in recording this toast, amusingly prints the word in italics "*unchanged*."

Smith was a lad, commanded a view of the fields, over hillocks of ground, now occupied by Norfolk Street; and the north and east outer sides of Middlesex Hospital garden wall were entirely exposed. Mr. John Timbs, in his "Romance of London," completes the picture by telling us that

STRATFORD PLACE.   (*See page* 437.)

Although the memory of Marylebone Gardens has perished to a very great extent, we fortunately have, in Mr. J. T. Smith's "Book for a Rainy Day," a quantity of curious information respecting them and the pleasant sights and sounds which there amused the ladies of the western suburbs, whilst the City dames were showing off their finery at such places of amusement as Bagnigge Wells, and the Mulberry Garden in Clerkenwell. The houses of the north end of Newman Street, at the time Mr.

at that time a cottage with a garden and a rope-walk were here; and that "under two magnificent rows of elms Richard Wilson, the landscape painter, and Baretti might often be seen walking." To the right of the rope-walk was a pathway on a bank, which extended northward to the "Farthing Pie House," now the sign of the "Green Man;" it was kept by Price, the famous player on the salt-box, of whom there is an excellent mezzotinto portrait. It commanded fine views of the distant heights of Highgate, Hampstead, Primrose Hill, and Harrow; and Mr. Smith tells us that, as a boy of eight years old, he frequently played at trap-bat beneath the elms. The south and east ends of Queen Anne and Marylebone Streets were then unbuilt: the space consisted of fields to the west corner of Tottenham Court Road, thence to the extreme end of High Street, Marylebone Gardens, Marylebone Basin, and another pond then called "Cockney Ladle," which were the terror of many a mother. Upon the site of the "Ladle" now stands Portland Chapel.

In the *London Gazette*, January 11, 1691, mention is made of "Long's Bowling-green, at the 'Rose,' at Marylebone, half a mile distant from London." The distance here mentioned doubtless refers to the utmost limits of bricks and mortar in the neighbourhood of Oxford Street.

The *Daily Courant*, for Thursday, May 29, 1718, contains the following announcement:—"This is to give notice to all persons of quality, ladies and gentlemen, that there having been illuminations in Marylebone Bowling-green on his Majesty's birth-day every year since his happy accession to the throne, the same is (for this time) put off till Monday next, and will be performed with a *consort* (*sic*) of musick in the middle green, by reason there is a ball in the gardens at Kensington with illuminations, and at Richmond also."

The gardens, as we have observed, were at first opened gratuitously; but in 1738–9 they were enlarged, and an orchestra built. Silver tickets were at first issued, at 12s. each for the season, each ticket admitting two persons. From every one without a ticket 6d. was demanded for the evening; but afterwards, as the season advanced, the admission was 1s. for a lady and gentleman.

About this time, when these gardens were in a flourishing state, selections from Handel's music were often played here, under the direction of Dr. Arne. Concerning one of these performances, Mr. Smith tells an amusing anecdote, which will bear repeating. "One evening," he says, "as my grand-father and Handel were walking together and alone, a new piece was struck up by the band. 'Come, Mr. Fountayne,' said Handel, 'let us sit down and listen to this piece; I want to know your opinion of it.' Down they sat, and after some time Mr. Fountayne, the old parson, turning to his com-panion, said, 'It is not worth listening to; it is very poor stuff.' 'You are right, Mr. Fountayne,' said Handel, 'it is very poor stuff; I thought so myself, when I had finished it.' The old gentle-man, being taken by surprise, was beginning to apologise, but Handel assured him there was no

necessity; that the music was really bad, having been composed hastily, and his time for the pro-duction being limited; and that the opinion was as correct as it was honest."

In 1741 a "grand martial composition of music" was performed here by Mr. Lampe, in honour of Admiral Vernon, for taking Carthagena.

The proprietor of the Mulberry Garden, Clerken-well, apparently stirred up by feelings of envy or jealousy at the success of his brother caterers in the same line of business, indulged in some sar-castic remarks upon five places of similar amuse-ment, in which he described this suburban retreat as "Mary le Bon Gardens down on their marrow-bones."

About the year 1746 robberies accompanied by violence were of so frequent occurrence in this neighbourhood that "the proprietor of the gardens was obliged to have a guard of soldiers to protect the company to and from London."

In 1753 the *Public Advertiser* announced that the gardens had been "made much more extensive by taking in the bowling-green, and considerably improved by several additional walks; that lights had been erected in the coach-way from Oxford Road, and also on the footpath from Cavendish Square to the entrance to the gardens; and that the fireworks were splendid beyond conception." A large sun was exhibited at the top of a picture; a cascade, and shower of fire, and grand air-bal-loons were also most magnificently displayed; and likewise "red fire was introduced." This has been considered as probably the first occasion of air-balloons and "red fire" being exhibited in England.

Towards the end of the reign of George II. the gardens appear to have risen somewhat in popu-larity, and to have had rather more of the aristo-cratic element in its visitors; for we learn that in 1758 "no persons were admitted to the ball-rooms without five-shilling tickets, and only twenty-six tickets were delivered for each night." In the following year we are told that the gardens were opened for breakfasting; nor is it forgotten to be added that "Miss Trusler made the cakes." The father of this young lady was the proprietor of the gardens, and being a cook, gave dinners and break-fasts. In the following year the gardens, having been greatly improved, were opened in May "with the usual musical entertainments." They were opened also every Sunday evening, when "genteel company were admitted to walk gratis, and were accommodated with coffee, tea, cakes, &c." Miss Trusler, it would seem, was an adept in the art of cake-making, for in the *Daily Advertiser* of May

6, 1759, appears the following announcement:— "Mr. Trusler's daughter begs leave to inform the nobility and gentry, that she intends to make fruit-tarts during the fruit season; and hopes to give equal satisfaction as with the rich cakes and almond cheesecakes. The fruit will always be fresh gathered, having great quantities in the garden; and none but loaf sugar used, and the finest Epping butter. Tarts of a twelvepenny size will be made every day from one to three o'clock. New and rich seed and plum cakes," too, we are reminded, "are sent to any part of the town."

In 1761 there was published an engraving, after a drawing made by J. Donowell, representing these gardens, probably in their fullest splendour. "The centre of this view exhibits the longest walk, with regular rows of young trees on either side, the stems of which received the irons for the lamps at about the height of seven feet from the ground. On either side of this walk were latticed alcoves; on the right hand of the walk, according to this view, stood the bow-fronted orchestra, with balustrades supported by columns. The roof was extended considerably over the erection, to keep the musicians and singers free from rain. On the left hand of the walk was a room, possibly for balls and suppers. The figures in this view are well drawn and characteristic of the period."

In 1762 the gardens were visited by the Cherokee Kings; and in the following year the celebrated Tommy Lowe became the proprietor. Among the singers here at that time was Nan Cattley.

Notwithstanding the patronage bestowed upon these gardens by many of the nobility, the place seems in the end to have fallen into bad repute; for in Dodsley's "London and its Environs" we find mention of it as "the noted gaming-house at Marylebone, the place of assemblage of all the infamous sharpers of the time." The security of the outlying districts, too, does not seem to have improved, for we are told that in 1764 Mr. Lowe, the then proprietor, offered "a reward of ten guineas for the apprehension of any highwayman found on the road to the gardens." An attempt, nevertheless, seems to have been made by the Sabbatarian party to render this place of amusement less attractive for visitors on the people's only holy day; for we read that in "this year a stop was put to tea-drinking in the gardens on Sunday evenings."

Well may Sir John Fielding console the public by writing as follows, just a century ago:—"Robberies on the highway in the neighbourhood of London are not very uncommon; these are usually committed early in the morning, or in the dusk of the evening, and as the times are known, the danger may be for the most part avoided. But the highwaymen here are civil, as compared with other countries; do not often use you with ill-manners; have been frequently known to return papers and curiosities with much politeness; and never commit murder, unless they are hotly pursued and find it difficult to escape." That highway robberies here, in Sir John Fielding's time, were no new thing, may be learnt from the *Evening Post* of March 16, 1715–16:—"On Wednesday last four gentlemen were robbed and stripped in the fields between London and Marylebone."

Amongst other distinguished personages whose names are connected by tradition with this place is Dick Turpin, the prince of highwaymen. He was a gay and gallant fellow, and very polite to the ladies. A celebrated beauty of her day, the wife or sister-in-law of a dean of the Established Church, Mrs. Fountayne, was one day "taking the air" in the gardens, when she was saluted by Dick Turpin, who boldly kissed her before the company and all "the quality." The lady started back in surprise and offended. "Be not alarmed, madam," said the highwayman; "you can now boast that you have been kissed by Dick Turpin. Good morning!" and the hero of the road walked off unmolested. Turpin was hanged at York in 1739.

In 1768 Mr. Lowe gave up the gardens, at the same time declaring that his loss in the concern had been considerable. He conveyed his property in the gardens to trustees for the benefit of his creditors; and in the deed of conveyance, Mr. John Timbs tells us, it is recorded that the premises of Rysbrack the sculptor were formerly part of the gardens. The grounds, however, were not finally closed; for in 1770 there was a concert of vocal and instrumental music, in which James Hook, the father of Theodore Hook, is announced as having taken part; and in that same year various alterations were made in the grounds for the better accommodation of the visitors. Two years later, as Mr. Smith informs us, "for the convenience of the visitors, coaches were allowed to stand in the field before the back entrance. Mr. Arnold was indicted at Bow Street for the fireworks. Torre, the fire-worker, divided the receipts at the door with the proprietor."

In 1773, proposals "were issued for a subscription evening to be held every Thursday during the summer, for which tickets were delivered to admit two persons. The gardens were now opened for general admission on three evenings in the week only. On Thursday, May 27th, *Acis and Galatea* was performed, in which Mr. Bannister, Mr. Reinholdt, Mr. Phillips, and Miss Wilde were singers. Signor Torre, the fire-worker, was assisted by Monsieur Caillot, of Ranelagh Gardens. On Friday, September 15th, Dr. Arne here conducted his celebrated catches and glees."

In the following year (1774) the gardens were again opened for promenading, sixpence being charged for admission; and Dr. Kenrick delivered a series of lectures on Shakespeare in the gardens in this year.

The newspaper advertisements of these gardens in 1775 are curious. As a specimen, we quote one which appeared in the *Morning Chronicle and London Advertiser* of May 29th :—

AT MARYBONE GARDENS,

To-morrow, the 30th instant, will be presented
THE MODERN MAGIC LANTERN.

In three Parts, being an attempt at a sketch of the Times in a variety of Caricatures, accompanied with a whimsical and satirical Dissertation on each Character.

By R. BADDELEY, Comedian.

BILL OF FARE.
EXORDIUM.

PART THE FIRST.

A Serjeant at Law.	A Modern Patriot.
Andrew Marvel, Lady Fribble.	A Duelling Apothecary, and
A Modern Widow.	A Foreign Quack.

PART THE SECOND.

A Man of Consequence.	Lady Tit for Tat.
A Hackney Parson.	An Italian Tooth-drawer.
A Macaroni Parson.	High Life in St. Giles's.
A Hair-dresser.	A Jockey, and
A Robin Hood Orator.	A Jew's Catechism.

And Part the Third will consist of a short Magic Sketch called

PUNCH'S ELECTION.

Admittance 2s. 6d. each, Coffee or Tea included. The doors to be opened at seven, and the Exordium to be spoken at eight o'clock.

Vivant Rex et Regina.

At the foot of Mr. Baddeley's subsequent bills the gardens are announced as being still open on a Sunday evening for company to walk in. Some of the papers of this year declare, under Mr. Baddeley's advertisements, that "no person going into the gardens with subscription tickets will be entitled to tea or coffee."

Subsequently, George Saville Carey here gave his Lecture on Mimicry. In 1776 the gardens opened in May, "by authority," when the "Forge of Vulcan" was represented, followed a few days later by some feats of sleight of hand, &c.

After existing for upwards of a century, and undergoing many vicissitudes, the gardens were closed about the year 1778, and the site soon afterwards turned to building purposes. The grounds

were, however, opened again for a short time in 1794, as a sort of last expiring flicker. Some of the trees under which the company promenaded and listened to the sweet strains of music are still standing behind the houses in Upper Wimpole Street.

A Prussian writer, D'Archenholz, at the end of the last century, remarks with great truth of the English people, and especially of the Londoners, that "they take a great delight in public gardens near the metropolis, where they assemble and drink tea together in the open air. The number of these gardens," the writer continues, "in the neighbourhood of the capital is amazing, and the order, regularity, neatness, and even elegance of them is truly admirable. They are, however, rarely frequented by people of fashion; but the middle and lower classes go there often, and seem much delighted with the music of an organ which is usually played in an adjoining building." When he wrote thus it is difficult to persuade oneself that the foreign author had any other place more entirely before his mind's eye than Marylebone Gardens.

These gardens were commemorated by the great London magistrate, Sir John Fielding, in his judgment on Mrs. Cornelys, when he condemned her operas in Soho as "illegal and unnecessary," on the ground that, besides other places such as the three patent theatres, "there was Ranelagh with its music and fireworks, and Marylebone Gardens with music, wine, and plum-cake."

Northouck calls the gardens "small," and contrasts them with those of Vauxhall, with a note of admiration which indicates a sneer. "Marylebone," he says, "may now (1772) be esteemed a part of this vast town (though it is not yet included in the bills of mortality), as the connection by new buildings is forming very fast."

The entire parish of Marylebone, in the last century, appears to have been devoted to the Muses; for Dr. Arne, and Samuel and Charles Wesley, then stars of the first magnitude in the musical firmament, lived in the neighbourhood; and since that time Marylebone has given a home to many painters and sculptors.

The principal thoroughfares now occupying the site of Marylebone Gardens as well as the adjoining bowling-greens, are Devonshire Place, Upper Harley, Weymouth, Upper Wimpole, Marylebone, and Devonshire Streets.

Wimpole Street, down which we now proceed on our return to Oxford Street, was so named after Wimpole, on the borders of Hertfordshire and Cambridgeshire, formerly the country seat of the Harleys, Earls of Oxford, and subsequently that of Lord Chancellor Hardwicke, whose family became possessed of it by purchase in the last century. The street was, at all events, begun before the complete demolition of the gardens, for we find that Edmund Burke took up his residence here in 1757, soon after his marriage with the daughter of an Irish physician at Bath, a Dr. Nugent. He was happy in his wife and his home, and his house became a centre of attraction to his friends. The expenses of housekeeping on a larger scale than that to which he had been accustomed, spurred him on to increased exertions in the field of literature, and the author of the "Essay on the Sublime and Beautiful" here wrote some of those other political and philosophical works which speedily raised him to a high post as an author, including the early volumes of the "Annual Register."

At No. 21 was living, in 1826, Mrs. Cipriani, the widow of the eminent painter, and friend of Wedgwood. At her father's house (No. 50) in this street, lived for some time between 1840 and 1845, Miss Elizabeth Barrett, then known as the author of a volume of poems, and who afterwards was better known to fame as Mrs. E. Browning. Most of her married life was spent, on account of delicate health, at Florence, where she died in 1861. In this street, too, lived the Duchess of Wellington during the Peninsular War.

From the year 1826 to 1841, and probably longer, No. 67 was the residence of Henry Hallam, the historian; here he wrote his "History of the Middle Ages" and his "Constitutional History of England." He died in 1858. In 1841 No. 10 was in the occupation of the fashionable portrait-painter of his time, Mr. Alfred E. Chalon, and of his brother, John James Chalon, both Royal Academicians. These two brothers appear to have been inseparable, for a few years previously they were living together in Great Marlborough Street. At No. 12 in this street lived for some time the gallant Admiral Lord Hood. No 17 was for many years the home of the late Mr. Joseph Parkes, and of his daughter, Miss Bessie R. Parkes.

Of Weymouth Street we have nothing to record beyond the fact that it forms a connecting link between High Street, Marylebone, and Harley Street and Portland Place; that in it Bryan W. Procter ("Barry Cornwall") lived and died; and that it was so called after Lord Weymouth, a son-in-law of the second Duke of Portland.

Great Marylebone Street, as we have said, crosses Wimpole Street about midway, connecting High Street on the west with Harley Street on the east. In this street was lodging Prince Leopold, afterwards King of the Belgians, when he came to England in 1814, at the time of the Peace Re-joicings, as aide-de-camp to one of the Allied Sovereigns, as we have already stated in our chapter on Hyde Park.

In Edward Street—as that part of Wigmore Street lying between Marylebone Lane and Duke Street was formerly called—at No. 21, the remains of General Sir Thomas Picton lay in state, on their arrival here after the battle of Waterloo, prior to their first interment in the burial-ground in the Uxbridge Road, Bayswater.

In Marylebone Lane, near the Oxford Street end, was for many years the Court-house for the parish. It was erected in 1825, adjoining an older court-house and watch-house, on ground on which was formerly situated a pound. The building, however, having become unsuited for its present requirements, a new court-house has been erected at the corner of Marylebone Road and Seymour Place, as we have already stated.

On the west side of Marylebone Lane, and abutting upon Oxford Street, is Stratford Place. This group of buildings comprises two rows of mansions facing each other, with a square court-yard at the northern end, forming a *cul de sac*. On each side of the entrance is a small house for a watchman, on the top of which is the figure of a lion carved in stone. The buildings were erected about the year 1775 by Edward Stratford, second Lord Aldborough, on land which had been leased from the Corporation of London. The place was formerly decorated with a column supporting a statue of George III., commemorative of the naval victories of Great Britain. It was erected by General Strode, and taken down in 1805, in consequence of the foundation giving way. The house in the centre of the northern side, and facing Oxford Street, is that in which Lord Aldborough himself lived for many years. The house has been occupied at various periods by the Duke of St. Albans, Prince Esterhazy, and other persons of distinction. One of these mansions at the commencement of this century was the residence of Richard Cosway, R.A. Shortly before his death, he disposed of a great part of his collection of ancient pictures and other property, and removed to a house in the Edgware Road, where he died in 1821. Two other Royal Academicians have likewise occupied houses here—namely, Sir Robert Smirke, who was living here in 1826, and Mr. H. W. Pickersgill, who died here in 1875, aged upwards of ninety.

The house at the south-east corner, fronting Oxford Street, has been for many years the home of the Portland Club, which is understood to be one of the leading clubs where high play at cards prevails, but is honourably and honestly conducted.

A code of rules for the game of whist is extant, the preparation of which was the work of a committee of gentlemen from many of the West-end clubs, among whom the Portland was largely represented. Of the inner life and history of the Portland Club little is known, and few anecdotes about it are published.

As we have already stated, here in former times stood a building known as the Lord Mayor's

which then spanned the River Fleet and up Ludgate Hill to the conduit at the west end of Cheapside. The head of water in the reservoirs was about thirty feet above the conduit mouth. The King used his influence with the owner of the lands whence the springs issued to grant the water to the Corporation ; and certain merchants of Ghent, Bruges, and Antwerp provided the lead pipe, or gave the money to purchase it, in con-

WIGMORE STREET IN 1850.   (*From a Drawing by Shepherd in the Crace Collection.*)

Banqueting-house, from the fact that the chief magistrate and Corporation of London used to dine here annually for many generations, after officially visiting the springs and reservoirs in this neighbourhood whence the great conduit in Cheapside was supplied with water. The supply came from the gravelly subsoil of Marylebone, where no less than nine springs oozed out of the ground at various places, and trickled down the grassy slopes into the watercourse called the *Tye-bourne*, of which we have spoken above. As far back as the year 1216 the Mayor and Corporation of London collected these springs into some reservoirs, which they constructed near Stratford Place, and laid a six-inch lead pipe from thence to Charing Cross, along the Strand and Fleet Street, over the bridge

sideration of the goods they imported into London being exempt from river dues or tolls for a term of years. For the King's service in the matter the Corporation permitted him to lay a pipe " of the size of a goose-quill " from the main pipe into his stables, which were situated where the north-east part of Trafalgar Square now stands. On the occasion of the Mayor's official visits to these springs, the company used to hunt a hare or a fox in the neighbourhood, and afterwards they dined together with much ceremony near the reservoirs. In course of time the reservoirs were arched over, and a large banqueting-house was erected upon the arches.

In August, 1875, while making some repairs or alterations in the roadway of Oxford Street at the

MARYLEBONE, FROM THE SITE OF THE PRESENT WIGMORE STREET.   (*From a Print of* 1750.)

point, the workmen came upon these reservoirs and arches, which had remained in a fair state of preservation. Shortly afterwards, another interesting archæological discovery was made a short distance westward, at the corner of North Audley Street. Here, close to the curb, two much-worn iron flaps were discovered. The workmen's curiosity being aroused as to where the opening might lead, they applied their pickaxes, and after some difficulty, succeeded in raising the flaps, when they discovered a flight of brick steps, sixteen in number, leading to a subterranean chamber. On descending, they entered a room of considerable size, measuring about 11 feet long by 9 feet wide, and nearly 9 feet high. The roof, which is arched, is of stone, and, with a few exceptions, is in fair repair. The walls to the height of about five feet are built of small red brick, such as was used by the Romans, in which are eight chamfered Gothic arches, with stone panels, as though originally used as windows for obtaining light. The upper part of the wall is of more recent date. In the four corners of the chamber there is a recess with an arched roof, extending with a bend as far as the arm can reach. In the middle of the chamber is a sort of pool or bath, built of stone, measuring about five feet by seven feet. It is about six feet deep, and was about half filled with water, tolerably clear and fresh. A spring of water could be seen bubbling up, and provision was made for an overflow in the sides of the bath. From all appearances the place was originally a baptistery.

In the beginning of the reign of George III. there was only a dreary and monotonous waste between the then new region of Cavendish Square and the village of Marylebone, sometimes called Harley Fields; and even as lately as 1772, the now thickly-peopled district between Duke Street and Marylebone Lane was unbuilt. Within the last century Oxford Road, as it was then called, had houses only on one (the southern) side between the top of New Bond Street and Tyburn Turnpike; the lower parts of many of these, too, were occupied by dustmen, chimney-sweepers, and "purveyors of asses' milk." At the end of South Molton Street there projected into the road a garden, at one corner of which was a wretched mud hovel, rather a contrast to the fine buildings lately erected not far from that very spot by the Duke of Westminster. Even for some years after it was built and inhabited, "Oxford Road" remained a kind of private street, and the few shops which it contained made but little show. It was a solitude indeed compared with its present activity, its silence being principally broken by the tinkling

of the bells of long lines of packhorses proceeding to and returning from the country westwards every day at stated hours. Along this western road, we need hardly remark, the Oxford scholars and the agents of the Bristol merchants travelled, first on packhorses, and then in the long stage-wagons, which in their turn gave place to the stage-coaches of the eighteenth century.

Even down to a very late period of the seventeenth century, or possibly to the beginning of the eighteenth, the high roads in the neighbourhood of London were sadly neglected, and very frequently were in a state almost impassable for vehicles of any and every description. Anthony à Wood, in his "Diary," first mentions a stage-coach under the year 1661; and six years afterwards he informs us that he travelled from London to Oxford by such a conveyance. How much would we give to see him start along the Oxford Road, and nearing Tyburn turnpike in spite of the ruts! The journey occupied, as he tells us, two days. An improved conveyance called the "Flying Coach" was afterwards instituted; it completed the whole distance, about sixty miles, in thirteen hours, and the event was regarded as a wonder; but it was found necessary to abandon the effort during the winter months. It has been well remarked that the days of slow coaches were the Augustan era of highwaymen. Many of the last generation well remember the time when gentlemen desiring to return to town late in the evening would stop for other companions to collect on the road for mutual protection, while the more timid would stay the night at an inn at Acton or Bayswater.

Oxford Street is now the longest thoroughfare in London, being upwards of 2,300 yards in length. Towards the western extremity of the street, on the southern side, the dull monotony of its houses and shops has in some instances been relieved by the erection of spacious edifices of a more ornate character. An instance of this is afforded in the group of buildings erected in connection with the Association in Aid of the Deaf and Dumb, between Queen Street and Duke Street, nearly opposite the thoroughfare leading into Manchester Square. The buildings, which are of red brick with stone dressings, stand on ground leased from the Duke of Westminster, and were erected in 1870 from the designs of Mr. A. Blomfield, son of the late Bishop of London, and the first stone was laid by the Prince of Wales. The chief feature of this block of buildings is the Deaf and Dumb Chapel, dedicated to St. Saviour, which is subordinate to the parent church of St. Mark in North Audley Street. Although the site is somewhat limited, it has been admirably utilised. The lower floor is devoted to a lecture-hall, the upper floor being the church. The ground-plan and the upper floor exhibit nearly the form of a Maltese cross; but in the chapel an apse containing the communion-table is corbelled out over the projecting arm of the cross towards Oxford Street. About twenty feet from the floor-level the angles of the square are cut off with arches and buttressed by the walls of the projecting arms, and the square becomes an octagon. The cruciform projections are arched off, and the simple octagon is left. This has a groined ceiling, pierced with a circular opening in the centre, where there is a sunlight. The four sides of the octagon above the angles of the square are pierced with large three-light windows, and the apse is lighted with five lancets, and groined with stone ribs and brick filling-in. Externally, the main building is covered with a high-pitched octagonal roof, with a circle of small lucarnes or dormer windows near the apex. The other roofs are of a high pitch, and abut on the main building at various levels. The style of the building is Early Pointed, but it is rather French than English in the character of its details. The church affords accommodation for 250 worshippers, and is so planned that, while meeting the requirements of the deaf and dumb, it is equally available for a "hearing" congregation.

A little to the east of this part of Oxford Street, nearly opposite to Cavendish Square, is the carriage manufactory of Messrs. Laurie and Marner, at No. 313, between the top of New Bond Street and the gates of Hanover Square. It stands on a site which formerly was the garden of the town-house of Lord Carnarvon in Tenterden Street (now the Royal Academy of Music), and it still belongs to the Herberts. The garden was bounded on the north by a wall, with a terrace and summer-house inside, where George III. and his family would come and sit under shady trees and look down upon the carriers' wagons and newly-invented "fly coaches" as they made their way along the Tyburn Road. The garden extended nearly as far eastward as Hanover Gates. The premises now used as a carriage manufactory occupy nearly an acre and a half in extent, having a side entrance in Shepherd Street; underneath are vaults which once held Lord Carnarvon's store of port wine. The business of Messrs. Laurie was first established, some 300 or 400 yards further west in Oxford Street, about the year 1820; its founder was the late amiable and eccentric alderman, Sir Peter Laurie, who in 1832-3 occupied the civic chair. The carriage manufactory of Messrs. Laurie and Marner grew gradually into its present large dimensions out of a humble saddle-maker's business.

CHAPTER XXXIV.

OXFORD STREET, AND ITS NORTHERN TRIBUTARIES (*continued*).

"*And business compelled them to go by the way
Which led them through Cavendish Square.*"—*Old Song.*

Progress of Building in Last Century—Number of Houses and Population of Marylebone—Harley Fields—The Harleys, Earls of Oxford—Vere Street—Rysbrack, the Sculptor—St. Peter's Chapel—Henrietta Street—The Old Countess of Mornington—Welbeck, Bentinck, and Wigmore Streets—Cavendish Square—The "Princely" Duke of Chandos, and his proposed Palace—Mr. George Watson-Taylor, M.P.—The Statue of the Duke of Cumberland—Harcourt House—Holles Street—The Birthplace of Lord Byron—Queen Anne Street—Turner's "Den"—Mansfield Street—Duchess Street—The Residence of Mr. Thomas Hope—Harley Street, and its Distinguished Residents—Park Crescent—Portland Place—The Langham Hotel—Langham Place—The Portland Bazaar, or German Gallery—A Skating Rink—The Royal Polytechnic Institution—Cavendish Club—Civil and United Service Club.

AT the beginning of the last century, if we may believe contemporary accounts, Marylebone was a small village, "nearly a mile distant from any part of the metropolis." In the year 1715 the plan for building Cavendish Square and several new streets on the north side of Oxford Street, then, as we have already shown, called indiscriminately by that name and Tyburn Road, was first suggested. About two years afterwards the ground was laid out, and the circular plantation in the centre enclosed, planted, and surrounded by a parapet wall and wooden railings. The buildings, however, seem to have been proceeded with very slowly; for several years

elapsed before either the square or the surrounding streets were actually completed. It was the building of this square that originally gave an impetus to the increase of Marylebone, and Maitland, in his "History of London," published in 1739, gives the number of houses in Marylebone as 577, and the persons who kept coaches (carriages) as thirty-five. "At present," writes Lambert in the year 1806, "the number of houses is near upon 9,000, and the number of coaches must have increased in a proportionate if not even a greater ratio." The present population (1876) is estimated at about 600,000 souls.

The South Sea Bubble, in the year 1720, put a stop for a time to the building of the square, which for many years later remained in an unfinished state. In the view of Hanover Square by Sutton Nicholls, which bears the date of 1754, this square is shown as standing almost alone to the north of Oxford Road, and surrounded by fields, with an uninterrupted view of Hampstead and Highgate. At this particular time Harley Street extended very little way to the north, and Harley Fields were resorted to by thousands who went to hear George Whitefield preach there.

The site of Cavendish Square is said to have been intersected by a shady lane called "Lover's Walk," leading from Margaret Street to where now stands Cavendish Square.

Cavendish Square and the adjoining streets were named after the various relatives of Robert Harley, first Earl of Oxford, K.G., and of his son, Lord Harley, afterwards second Earl. The family titles as they stood in the pages of Lodge and Burke till the extinction of the peerage, were "Earl of Oxford and Mortimer, and Baron Harley of Wigmore Castle." The second earl married the Lady Henrietta Cavendish Holles, only daughter and heiress of John, Duke of Newcastle, who carried all this property by marriage into the family of the Duke of Portland. It is necessary to state these facts in order to account for the names of Cavendish Square, Portland Place, and Henrietta, Harley, Wigmore, Mortimer, and Holles Streets, in the immediate neighbourhood.

The approaches to Cavendish Square from Oxford Street are by Old Cavendish, Holles, and Princes Streets. Another short thoroughfare, called Vere Street, leads into Henrietta Street, which opens into the south-western corner of the square. By Vere Street we now again proceed to make our way northward. The street was so called after the De Veres, who for many centuries previous to the Harleys had held the Earldom of Oxford. In this street resided Rysbrack, the sculptor, and here he died in 1770. Gibbs, the architect, in a letter to Pope, says : " Mr. Rysbrack's house is in the further end of Bond Street, and up across Tyburne Rode (*sic*), in Lord Oxford's grownd, upon the right hand going to his chaple." The chapel here spoken of stands at the corner of Vere Street and Henrietta Street. It is dedicated to St. Peter, and is a nondescript edifice of the reign of George I., built from the designs of Gibbs about the year 1724, and is said in the prints of the day to have been erected at Lord Harley's cost, "to accommodate the inhabitants of his manor." It may cause a smile to add that once it was thought one of the most

beautiful structures of its kind in London. In his " Guide to the London Churches " Mr. C. Mackeson thus remarks : " This is a Government church : the Government collects and reserves the pew-rents, and pays £450 to the incumbent." It has no district assigned to it ; consequently it is not burdened with any poor, and cannot require any free seats. The chief interest of the chapel lies in the fact that the late Rev. F. D. Maurice was its minister for nine years before his death in 1870. This chapel was called, down to a date within the present century, " Oxford Chapel," and is described by Lambert, in 1806, as surmounted by a steeple springing from the centre of the roof, and consisting of three stages. Here, on the 11th of July, 1734, William, second Duke of Portland, was married to the Lady Margaret Harley, the heiress of Lord Oxford, the same lady whom Prior has celebrated as " my noble, lovely, little Peggy."

Henrietta Street, which we now cross, runs from Marylebone Lane into the south-west corner of Cavendish Square. At No. 3 in this street resided for some time the venerable Countess of Mornington, mother of the Duke of Wellington, who, after living to witness the multiplied honours of her children, died in 1831, at the age of ninety. In this street is the studio of Mr. William Theed, the sculptor, to whose chisel we owe the group of " Asia," on the Albert Memorial at Kensington. Mr. Theed numbered among his pupils Count Gleichen, formerly known as Prince Victor of Hohenlohe, and maternally a cousin of Queen Victoria.

Extending from the western end of Henrietta Street to Marylebone Street is Welbeck Street, so named after Welbeck Abbey, near Ollerton, Nottinghamshire, the seat of the Duke of Portland. Here, at No. 59, lived the Right Hon. Henry Ellis, the diplomatist. He died in 1855. At No. 30, in 1826, lived Count Woronzow, of Russia, some time ambassador, and father-in-law of the eleventh Earl of Pembroke. Edmund Hoyle, of whist celebrity, who died here at the age of ninety-seven ; Mrs. Piozzi, and Martha Blount, were also residents in this street at various dates. This street, says Mr. J. P. Malcolm, " will long be famous in the annals of our time as the residence of that mad and honourable (?) imitator of the Wat Tylers and Jack Straws of old times, Lord George Gordon." In this street, too, resided for a short time before his death, the eccentric John Elwes.

Bentinck Street, between Welbeck Street and Manchester Square, was so named after the family surname of the Duke of Portland. In this street Charles Dickens lived for some time with his father, whilst acting as a newspaper reporter at Doctors' Commons, and in the "gallery" of the House of Commons, spending his spare time amongst the books in the library of the British Museum. Here, too, Gibbon, the historian, lived for some time at No. 7, while member for Liskeard, and here he wrote a large portion of his "Decline and Fall of the Roman Empire," and the whole of his "Defence." In a letter to Lord Sheffield, dated 17th January, 1783, Gibbon writes: "For my own part, my late journey has only convinced me in the opinion that No. 7, Bentinck Street is the best house in the world."

Wigmore Street, which extends from Duke Street, Manchester Square, to the north-west corner of Cavendish Square, derives its name from Wigmore, in Herefordshire, whence Robert Harley took his title as Earl of Oxford, Earl Mortimer, and Lord Harley of Wigmore Castle. All these names are perpetuated in the streets in this immediate neighbourhood. In Wigmore Street at one time lived the friend of Alfieri, Ugo Foscolo; and here, at his humble lodgings, he used to entertain at breakfast Samuel Rogers, Tom Campbell, Roscoe the historian, Cyrus Redding, and other celebrities. Whilst residing here he showed in his studies that ardour which marks the man of genius. "I once found him there," writes Cyrus Redding, "at noonday in summer, with his room still shut up, and studying by candlelight, forgetful that it was day. He had prolonged his sitting from the previous night, whilst composing an article for the forthcoming *Quarterly*." We shall have more to say about his eccentric and wayward career when we come to stand by what was once his grave in Chiswick Churchyard.

From Wigmore Street we pass into Cavendish Square, at its north-western corner. In the reign of George II. the building of this square had been commenced, but had not been carried through, and the site lay desolate and incomplete. The writer of the "New Critical Review of the Public Buildings of London," in 1736, is uncertain whether he ought to call it "Oxford" or "Cavendish" Square; but whichever name we choose, he says, "here we shall see the folly of attempting great things before we are sure that we can accomplish little ones. Here it is the modern plague of building was first stayed; and I think the rude, unfinished figure of this project should deter others from a like infatuation. . . . . I am morally assured that more people are displeased at seeing this square lie in its present neglected condition than are entertained with what was meant for elegance or ornament in it. . . . . It is said the imperfect side (the north) of this

square was laid out for a certain nobleman's palace, which was to have extended its whole length, and that the two detached houses which now stand at each end of the line were to have been the wings. I am apt, however, to believe that this is a vulgar mistake; for these structures, though exactly alike, could have been in no way of a piece with any regular or stately building; and it is to be presumed this nobleman would have as little attempted any other, as he would have left any attempt unfinished." The "certain nobleman" to whom allusion is here made, is none other than the "princely" Duke of Chandos, who had succeeded in amassing a splendid fortune as paymaster to the army in Queen Anne's reign. It is said that he proposed building here a palatial residence, and to have purchased all the property between Cavendish Square and his palace of Canons at Edgware, "so that he might ride from town to the country *through his own estate*."

Dodsley writes, in his "Environs of London," 1761: "In the centre of the north side is a space left for a house intended to be erected by the late Duke of Chandos, the wings only being built; there is, however, a handsome wall and gates before this space, which serve to preserve the uniformity of the square." An elevation of the grand house or palace which the duke intended to erect may be seen in the Royal Collection of Maps and Drawings in the British Museum. It bears the inscription, "Designed by John Price, architect, 1720." It is obvious to remark that the connection of the "princely" duke with this square is still commemorated by Chandos Street, which joins its north-eastern corner with the east end of Queen Anne Street.

We shall have more to say about "princely Canons," the duke's seat near Edgware, when we come to treat of the suburban districts. Meanwhile, we may be pardoned for reminding the reader that this duke is the person who figures in Pope's "Epistles" as Timon, the man who builds on a magnificent scale, but with false taste, and the downfall of whose projects the poet prophesied, and had he lived but three years longer, would actually have seen. It is to his palace at Edgware, and not to that in Marylebone, that Pope alludes when he writes—

> " Another age shall see the golden ear
> Imbrow the slope and nod on the parterre;
> Deep harvest bury all his pride has planned,
> And laughing Ceres re-assume the land."

At all events, it is not the fair goddess of corn, but the demon of bricks and mortar, who has "re-assumed" the lordship of the vicinity of Cavendish

Square.   Of the duke's magnificent conceptions in building here, the satirist says that—

> "Greatness with Timon dwells in such a draught
> As brings all Brobdingnag before your thought ;
> To compass this his building is a town,
> His pond an ocean, his parterre a down."

The duke's scheme, we need hardly say, was never carried out, for he died of a broken heart, caused by the death of his infant heir while being

articles of *virtu*, he was quite ruined within ten or twelve years.   It was of him that Sir Robert Peel said, that "no man ever bought ridicule at so high price."

The other wing of the duke's plan is the corresponding mansion at the corner of Chandos Street. It has been for many years the town residence of the Earls of Gainsborough.   The central part is now principally occupied by two splendid mansions,

LANGHAM HOUSE IN 1820. *From a Print in the Crace Collection.* (*See page* 452.)

christened in the midst of the greatest pomp and magnificence.   Of the two wings of the duke's mansion, which we have mentioned above, one is the large house standing at the corner of Harley Street, which has numbered among its distinguished occupants, at different periods, the Princess Amelia, aunt to George III.; the Earl of Hopetoun, and the Hopes of Amsterdam ; and also the late Mr. George Watson-Taylor, M.P., who, as John Timbs informs us, "assembled here a very valuable collection of paintings."   Mr. Watson-Taylor, in 1832, was declared a bankrupt.   At the outset of life he had a private income of £1,500 a year, on which he lived comfortably.   At forty-five he came into an income of £60,000 a year, and by extravagant living, and by squandering sums of money on

the fronts of which are ornamented with Corinthian columns, said to have been designed by James, of Greenwich, who was architect to the duke at Canons.

It was at first intended to place a statue of Queen Anne in the centre of the enclosure, and in the plan above referred to the statue is marked ; the idea, however, was never realised, and the site remained vacant till 1770, when Lieutenant-General William Strode erected an equestrian statue of William, Duke of Cumberland, "the butcher of Culloden," as the inscription sets forth, "in gratitude for private kindness, and in honour of public worth."   The statue, which was of lead, gilt, represented the "hero" in the full military costume of his day ; it has recently been removed.   On the south side, facing Holles Street, is a colossal standing bronze statue of Lord George Bentinck, some time leader of the Conservative party in the House of Commons; this was set up soon after his death, in 1848. The heavy wooden railings which originally surmounted the dwarf brick wall forming belonging to "the quality." These extinguishers sometimes formed a part of the ornamental iron scroll-work with which the front entrances of town mansions were adorned. A good specimen of them is given on page 331 of this volume, in our account of Berkeley Square.

CAVENDISH SQUARE, 1820.

the enclosure were allowed to fall into a sad state of decay, so that in 1761 we are told that they made "but an indifferent appearance;" but the unsightly rails have long since given way to substantial iron railings. In this square, as also in Manchester Square and in Queen Anne Street, there remain, or remained till only a few years since, some good specimens of the flambeaux-extinguisher which a century ago formed an almost necessary adjunct to the front door of a house

The large and heavy mansion called Harcourt House, which occupies the centre of the west side of the square, and which was long the town residence of the Dukes of Portland, was built by Lord Bingley, in 1722-3. It was purchased after his death by the Earl of Harcourt, who had previously built a house on the east side of the square. This mansion is mentioned by the author of the "New Critical Review," already quoted, as "one of the most singular pieces of architecture about the town," and "rather like a convent than the residence of a man of quality; in fact," he adds, "it seems more like a copy of one of Poussin's landscape ornaments than a design to imitate any of the genuine beauties of building." After an interval of a century and a half, the verdict of any man of architectural taste who sees it will be very much the same. It is a dull, heavy, drowsy-looking house, and it has about it an air of seclusion and privacy almost monastic. Its seclusion of late has been increased by three high walls, which have been raised behind the house, the chief object of which appears to be to screen the stables from the vulgar gaze.

This square was the scene of one of the mad freaks of Lord Camelford, who fell in a duel fought near Holland House, at Kensington. On one occasion he and a boon companion, Captain Barry, returning home at a very late, or, more probably, very early hour, found the "Charlies" asleep at their post, and woke them up and thrashed them, an offence for which the assailants were brought up next morning at the Marlborough Street police station, and fined.

Among the celebrated inhabitants of Cavendish Square may be mentioned Lady Mary Wortley Montagu, who was living here, at all events, from 1723 to 1730, during which period she was satirised with great grossness by Pope.

At No. 24 lived for some time George Romney, the painter. He produced such exquisite portraits as to become a dangerous rival to Sir Joshua Reynolds, and by whom Romney was always referred to as "the man of Cavendish Square." Romney forsook his lawful wife, and became entangled with Emma, Lady Hamilton, whom he admitted as a model to his studio, and whom he portrayed in no less than fourteen of his most beautiful paintings; all of them are, however, more or less of the type of the Phrynes and Lesbias of Horace and Catullus. The house had been previously inhabited by Mr. F. Cotes, R.A., another distinguished portrait painter, who built it; it has been a home of arts and artists in its day, for it was subsequently tenanted by Sir Martin Archer Shee, R.A., afterwards President of the Royal Academy, who died in 1850.

The mansion No. 15 was for many years the scene of the fashionable "receptions" of the Dowager Countess of Charleville, the chief rival of Lady Blessington in her day, as a "queen of society." At No. 16 resided Field-Marshal Viscount Beresford, one of the "great Duke's" chief companions-in-arms.

In this square lived, and here died in August, 1769, aged ninety-seven, Edmund Hoyle, registrar of the Prerogative Court, but better known to the world at large as the author of "Hoyle's Games." Here, too, lived Mr. Thomas Hope, F.R.S., F.S.A., the accomplished author of "Anastasius;" and also Matthew Baillie, the fashionable physician. At No. 5, behind the premises of the Polytechnic, was played, in 1851, the great "International Chess Tournament," players from all quarters of the world taking part in the competition. In this square, in 1747, the newly-formed Dilettanti Society purchased ground on which they intended to build a house for their accommodation, but they afterwards abandoned the idea.

As a proof of the once rural character of the neighbourhood of Cavendish Square, we may here mention that Mr. Fox told Samuel Rogers that when Dr. Sydenham was sitting at his window in Pall Mall, with his pipe and a silver tankard on the sill, a fellow made a snatch at the tankard and ran off with it, and that he was not overtaken, for his pursuers could not keep him in sight further than the bushes at the top of Bond Street, where they lost him.

In Old Cavendish Street, close by Oxford Street, was the shop of Mr. Marsh, the publisher, in 1825, of the *Star Chamber*, the paper in which appeared the first literary ventures of Mr. Benjamin Disraeli, subsequently Premier of England, and Earl of Beaconsfield; but it was a periodical of which the public took but little notice. When he published his first novel, "Vivian Grey," Mr. Cyrus Redding tells us that "Disraeli reviewed and extolled his own book in his own columns." The *Star Chamber* was strongly personal. "I have heard," adds Redding, "that the author suppressed it, but not till it had attacked most of the literary men of the day." It appears that Marsh meantime published "A Key to Vivian Grey," professing to be a complete exposition of the royal, noble, and fashionable characters who figure in that most extraordinary work.

Holles Street, which runs from the south side of the square into Oxford Street, was so named after Henrietta Holles, already mentioned as the daughter and heiress of John Holles, Duke of Newcastle. The street, which was originally composed of private houses, at present consists almost entirely of shops and private hotels. At No. 24 in this street Lord Byron was born on the 22nd of January, 1788; and a tablet has been placed on the front of the house by the Society of Arts, in order to record the fact for the benefit of posterity. Lord Byron was baptised in the old parish church of Marylebone.

In May, 1831, Queen Hortense and her son Prince (afterwards Emperor) Louis Napoleon, took up their abode in Holles Street; and "assuming their own proper name and dignity, speedily found themselves the centre of a brilliant circle of sympathising friends."

At No. 10, in Chandos Street, which runs out of the square at its north-east angle, lived, for many years, the Right Hon. Joseph Planta, M.P., Chief Librarian of the British Museum—an office, the duties of which he discharged by deputy, whilst mixing in political and official circles.

Queen Anne Street, which unites the northern end of Chandos Street with Welbeck Street, has numbered among its residents, at different periods, men famous both in literature and the fine arts. Here, in 1770, Richard Cumberland was living when he wrote his play of the *West Indian;* and at the beginning of this century, No. 58 was in the occupation of Malone, the commentator on Shakespeare.

At No. 47 was living, in the year 1836, J. M. W. Turner, the prince of modern English landscape painters; and here he kept for many years the greater part of his stores of pictures, patiently biding his time till they should be worth thousands. He was right in his calculations, as well as in the estimate which he had formed of himself. Indeed, his one hundred and more paintings in the National Gallery, not to mention his drawings on the basement-floor, and at South Kensington, show a versatility and an infinite variety, endless as Nature herself. It has been, perhaps justly, observed, that "after all allowance and deduction, Turner remains the fullest exponent of nature, the man above all others who was able to reflect the glory and the grandeur, the sunshine and the shade, the gladness and the gloom which in the outward landscape respond to the desires and the wants of the human heart."

He was just commencing to climb the hill of fame when he first settled here. As a young man he was slovenly and untidy, and now he gave way to his *penchant* for dirt and disorder. The house was " subsequently known," writes Dr. W. Russell, "as 'Turner's Den.' And truly it was a den. The windows were never cleaned, and had in them breaches patched with paper; the door was black and blistered; the iron palisades were rusty for lack of paint. If a would-be visitor knocked or rang, it was long before the summons was replied to by a wizened, meagre old man, who would unfasten the chain sufficiently to see who knocked or rang, and the almost invariable answer was, 'You can't come in.' After the old man's death,

an elderly woman, with a diseased face, supplied his place."

The same writer records a visit which Turner received at this " Den " from Mr. Gillat, a wealthy Birmingham manufacturer, who called in order to purchase one of Turner's pictures. " He was met at the door by a refusal of admission, and was obliged to make an almost forcible entry. He had hardly gained the hall when Turner, hearing a strange footstep, rushed out of his own particular compartment, and angrily confronted the intruder, 'What do you want here?' 'I have come to purchase some of your pictures.' 'I have none to sell.' 'But you won't mind exchanging them for some of these?' and he took out of his pocket a roll of bank-notes, to the amount of five thousand pounds. The Birmingham gentleman was successful, and carried off his five thousand pounds worth—now, perhaps, worth five times that sum—of the great artist's creations."

A wealthy merchant of Liverpool, at a later date, was less fortunate in his visit to the " Den." He offered a hundred thousand pounds for the art treasures rolled up in dark closets, or hanging from the damp walls, in Queen Anne Street. " Give me the key of the house, Mr. Turner," said the would-be purchaser. " No, I thank you," replied Turner; " I have refused a better offer." And so he had. He could not bear to sell a favourite painting—it was a portion of his being; to part with it was a blotting out of that part of his life which had been spent in its creation. He was always dejected and melancholy after such a transaction; and he would say, with tears in his eyes, " I have lost one of my children."

Mr. C. Redding, in his " Fifty Years' Recollections," claims Turner as a native, not of Maiden Lane, as usually supposed, but of the west country. He writes, " We were sailing on the St. German's River—Turner, Collier, and myself—when I remarked what a number of artists the West of England had produced from Reynolds to Prout. ' You may add my name to the list,' said Turner; ' I am a Devonshire man.' I asked from what part of the county, and he replied, ' From Barnstaple.' I have several times mentioned this statement to persons who insisted that Turner was a native of Maiden Lane, London, where, it is true, he appears to have resided in very early life, whither he must have come from the country. His father was a barber. When Turner had a cottage near Twickenham, the father resided with his son, and used to walk into town to open the gallery in Queen Anne Street, where I well remember seeing him, a little plain, but not ill-made old man—not reserved and austere as his son, in whom the worth lay between a coarse soil."

Some time before his death, Turner abruptly and secretly quitted his "Den" and walked to Chelsea, where he took lodgings next door to a ginger-beer shop close to Cremorne Pier; here, after some days, he was discovered by his faithful housekeeper, Miss Danby; but the hand of death was upon him. He died in December, 1851, and was buried in the crypt of St. Paul's Cathedral, near the grave of Reynolds.

Between 1788 and 1793 the house No. 72 in this street was in the occupation of Fuseli, the painter; he afterwards removed to No. 75. In 1826 No. 48 was the residence of Mr. Charles C. Pepys, while practising at the Bar; he became afterwards Lord Chancellor Cottenham. At that time No. 7 was in the occupation of Prince Nicholas Esterhazy, the Austrian Ambassador, who was still living there in 1836. The prince, it will be remembered by some, at least, of our readers, was noted for the splendour of his attire when taking part in any public state ceremonial; and he is thus commemorated by Ingoldsby in "Mr. Barney Maguire's Account of the Coronation of Queen Victoria :"—

"'Twould have made you crazy to see Esterhazy,
　All jewels from jasey to his di'mond boots."

In this street Edmund Burke took up his residence in 1764-5, on his return from his first public employment at Dublin, in order to resume his literary labours. Whilst living here he used to frequent the "Turk's Head," in Greek Street, and other debating societies of the metropolis; and on spare evenings was to be seen in the Strangers' Gallery in the House of Commons, studying the art of oratory in the best school, from the lips of living orators.

Mr. Serjeant Burke tells us in his life of his kinsman, that the future statesman and orator, when he first came to London to study for the Bar, found in the Strangers' Gallery a powerful attraction, which drew him away even from the tables of his friends. "It was his favourite custom to go alone to the House of Commons, there to ensconce himself in the gallery, and to sit for hours, his attention absorbed and his mind enwrapped in the scene beneath him. 'Some of the men,' he remarked to a friend, 'talk like Demosthenes and Cicero, and I feel, when listening to them, as if I were in Athens or Rome.' Soon these nightly visits became his passion; a strange fascination drew him again to the same place. No doubt the magic of his own master spirit was upon him, and the spell was working. He might be compared to the young eagle accustoming its eyes to the sun before it soars aloft. . . . . . The House of Commons was but his recreation; literature continued to be his chief employment." Burke was still living in Queen Anne Street when he entered Parliament, by Lord Verney's influence, as one of the members for Wendover. It may be added that if Burke really wrote the "Letters of Junius," it is most probable that those letters were composed in this street.

In Queen Anne Street, at the end of Mansfield Street, and looking directly down it, is a spacious mansion, formerly called Chandos House, but now divided into two, built by the "princely" Duke of Chandos as a town residence. The side, or rather back front, of the mansion in Queen Anne Street opens into a garden on the western side adjoining Langham House.

Mansfield Street, a continuation of Chandos Street on the north side of Queen Anne Street, was built by the brothers Adam, of the Adelphi, about the year 1770, on a plot of ground which had previously been a basin or reservoir of water. Some of the houses in this neighbourhood exhibit many good architectural details, especially in the rooms and staircases.

In this street, in 1836, were living the Princess De la Beiza and the Prince of Asturias. This street appears to have been a great rallying-point for the Roman Catholic aristocracy. At various times the families of Lord Clifford, Lord Stourton, Lord Petre, the Howards of Corby, &c., have resided here. Count Woronzow, the Russian diplomatist, died at his residence in this street, in 1832, at the age of eighty-seven.

Duchess Street is a short thoroughfare connecting Mansfield Street with Portland Place. Here was the town mansion of Mr. Thomas Hope, F.R.S., the author of "Anastasius," "The Costumes of the Ancients," &c. Mr. Hope had here formed a valuable collection of works of art altogether unrivalled, and comprising paintings, antique statues, busts, vases, and other relics of antiquity, arranged in apartments, the furniture and decorations of which were in general designed after classic models, by the ingenious possessor himself. Among the specimens of sculpture was the exquisite group representing "Venus rising from the Bath," by Canova. The whole of these valuables were open to the public, under certain restrictions, during "the season."

Mr. John Timbs says that, in the decoration of his mansion in this street, Mr. Hope "exemplified the classic principles illustrated in his large work on 'Household Furniture and Internal Decorations.' Thus, the suite of apartments included the *Egyptian, or Black Room,* with ornaments from scrolls of papyrus and mummy-cases ; the furniture and ornaments were pale yellow and bluishgreen, relieved by masses of black and gold. The *Blue,* or *Indian Room,* in costly Oriental style. The *Star Room :* emblems of Night below ; and above, 'Aurora visiting Cephalus on Mount Ida,' by Flaxman ; furniture, wreathed figures of the Hours. The *Closet,* or *Boudoir,* hung with tent-like drapery ; the mantelpiece, an Egyptian portico ; Egyptian, Hindoo, and Chinese idols and curiosities. *Picture Gallery,* Ionic columns, entablature and pediment from the Temple of Erectheus at Athens, car of Apollo, classic tables, pedestals, &c. The *New Gallery,* for one hundred pictures of the Flemish school, antique bronzes and vases ; furniture of elegant Grecian design." Mr. Hope was one of the earliest patrons of Chantrey, Flaxman, Canova, Thorwaldsen, and George Dawe ; and he died here in 1831.

Harley Street dates from the same period as Mansfield Street, with which it runs parallel on its western side. It was called after the Harleys, Earls of Oxford, to one of whom Pope pays a well-deserved compliment in his " Moral Essays," in which he writes :—

" And, showing Harley, teach the golden mean."

A happy and graceful allusion to the second earl of that line, of whose marriage with the daughter and heiress of the noble house of Holles we have already spoken. Harley died in 1741, regretted by all men of taste and letters, great numbers of whom had experienced the benefits of his munificence. He left behind him one of the most noble libraries in Europe. The collection was formed by himself and his son, and was purchased for the British Museum in 1753. His name is perpetuated in the Harleian MSS. in the Museum, and in the *Harleian Miscellany.*

In this street Lord and Lady Walsingham were accidentally burnt to death in bed in April, 1831. At No. 18 lived Sir William Beechey, the celebrated painter, during the latter years of his life. He was born at Burford, in Oxfordshire, in 1753, and in early life was articled in a solicitor's office, but at nineteen found admission as a student to the Royal Academy, where he became a pupil and close imitator of the great Sir Joshua. Having attracted public notice by his portraits of the Duke and Duchess of Cumberland, he was appointed portrait-painter to Queen Charlotte. In 1793 he was elected an Associate of the Royal Academy, and attained the full honours of R.A. four years

later. He died at Hampstead in January, 1839, in his eighty-sixth year. The house No. 45 was built and occupied by Mr. John Stuart, the author of " Athenian Antiquities," published under the auspices of the Dilettanti Society ; it was afterwards the town-house of Admiral Viscount Keith.

At No. 73 lived for many years Sir Charles Lyell, the eminent geologist. Born at Kinnordy, in Fifeshire, in 1797, he graduated at Exeter College, Oxford, and received the honorary degree of D.C.L. from his University in 1855. He was twice President of the Royal Geological Society, and was the author of a volume of " Travels in North America," " The Antiquity of Man," of treatises on the Elements and Principles of Geology, and of many papers in scientific journals. He was created a baronet late in life, and died here at the beginning of 1875. His house, in 1876, became the residence of Mr. W. E. Gladstone. In this street, too, lived Sir John Herschel, the son of Sir William Herschel, the astronomer. The father, who was of Hanoverian extraction, coming to England in the reign of George II., held for some time the post of organist at Halifax, and also at Bath. Whilst at the latter place he turned his attention to astronomy. He began to contribute to the " Philosophical Transactions " in 1780, and in the following year announced to the world his discovery of a supposed comet, which soon turned out to be the new planet now called Uranus. This announcement drew him immediately into the "full blaze of fame," and he was at once appointed astronomer to King George III. It was the discovery of this planet which gave the impetus to further additions to the solar system by others in more recent times. In the stellar field Herschel also achieved great results. Late in life he was elected President of the Royal Astronomical Society, and he died at Slough, near Windsor, in 1822. Sir John Herschel, who was little inferior to his father, either as an astronomer or as a mathematician, received the honour of a baronetcy at the Queen's coronation, and was for some time Master of the Mint. He died in 1871.

Allan Ramsay, the painter, who lived at No. 67, was appointed " principal painter to George III.," and died in 1784. " Allan Ramsay's house," says Mr. Peter Cunningham, " was in 1800 the residence of Colonel John Ramsay, his son." In 1826 No. 49 was in the occupation of Mr. William Horne, afterwards Sir William Horne, Solicitor-General in 1832-4, and M.P. for Marylebone. In this street, too, lived Viscount Strangford, the diplomatist and poet ; and also Lady Nelson, the relict of the hero of the Nile and Trafalgar.

Dean Swift appears to have been at one time a resident here; at all events, he dates from Harley Street one of his letters to "Stella," in which he alludes with feelings of disgust to the nightly outrages then being perpetrated in London by the "Mohawks," whose street outrages we have already mentioned.* This street is now principally inhabited by physicians and surgeons. On the west side, between Queen Anne Street and Great Mary-

with it, is Portland Place, a thoroughfare remarkable for its width, being upwards of 100 feet wide, in respect of which it contrasts most agreeably with the narrow thoroughfares which prevail in most quarters of London, reminding us of the broad boulevards of Paris and other foreign cities, though falling short of them in beauty because it has no trees. In 1875, however, it was resolved by the parochial and municipal authorities that

FOLEY HOUSE, IN 1800. (*See page 452.*)

lebone Street, are the Queen's College for Ladies and the Governesses' Benevolent Institution. The former was incorporated by Royal Charter in 1853, for the general education of ladies, and for granting certificates of knowledge. Individual instruction is given here in vocal and instrumental music, and there is a Cambridge Scholarship, open to the daughters or granddaughters of a graduate of Cambridge.

The readers of Charles Dickens will hardly need to be reminded that it was in this street that "Mr. Merdle," the gigantic swindler in "Little Dorrit," resided.

Eastward of Harley Street and running parallel

trees should be planted on either side, but as yet the suggestion has not been carried into effect. The two rows of stately houses which form Portland Place were constructed from the designs of Mr. Robert Adam in 1778, and named after the ground landlord. The north end was originally intended to have been terminated by a circus, but only one half was built; and that, now designated Park Crescent, was called, in 1816, by Nash, the architect, "the key to Marylebone Park." Had this design been carried out, it would have been the largest circle of buildings in Europe. The foundations of the western quadrant of it were even laid, and the arches for the coal-cellars turned. For some reasons, however, this plan was abandoned, and the entire chord of the semicircle left

* See Vol. III., p. 243.

J. M. W. TURNER, R.A. (*See page* 447.)

open to the Park, instead of being closed in by the intended half circus. This alteration is a manifest improvement of the entire design, and is productive of great benefit to the houses in the crescent and in Portland Place. Of Park Square, which was erected in its stead, we shall have to speak in a future chapter. In Park Crescent, facing Portland Place, is a bronze statue of the Duke of Kent, the father of Queen Victoria ; it was designed and cast by Gahagan.

Among the residents in Park Crescent have been Mr. Ralph Bernal, who lived at No. 11, before settling in Eaton Square ; Joseph Buonaparte ; the late Sir John Taylor Coleridge and his son Sir

John Duke (afterwards Lord Chief Justice) Coleridge; and also Sir Charles Wheatstone, the inventor of the electric telegraph, and the man who, in conjunction with Sir William Fothergill Cooke, placed that discovery at the service of the nation, and, in fact, of the world. He died at Paris in 1875, but his remains were brought over to England, and buried at Kensal Green.

Although less fashionably inhabited than when first built, Portland Place still numbers among its occupants several members of "the upper ten thousand," including peers, baronets, judges, and ambassadors. In the year 1836 No. 38 was the residence of Lord Denman, Chief Justice of the Court of Queen's Bench; No. 58 was that of Count Batthyani; and at No. 61 lived Sir William Curtis, the eccentric alderman, the advocate of "the three R's"—reading, 'riting, and 'rithmetic. No. 24 at that time was occupied by Mr. J. B. Sawrey Morritt, of Rokeby, the friend and correspondent of Sir Walter Scott. Lord Selborne has lived in Portland Place for over twenty years.

Here, in 1819, was the Spanish Embassy; and here the ambassador gave a splendid entertainment on the 16th of December in that year in honour of the marriage of his master, the King of Spain; the Prince Regent, all the royal dukes, and members of the Cabinet, the Duke of Wellington, &c., were present; the house was brilliantly illuminated, and a squadron of the Royal Horse Guards was on duty in the street in case of any disturbance arising.

In the year 1772, according to a plan and detailed account given in Northouck's "History of London," a new square was intended on the site of Portland Place, to be called Queen Square; it was to be bounded by Foley House and gardens on the south; by houses abutting on Portland Street on the east; by Harley Street on the west; and by an island of mansions on the north; with two grand streets, one on the east, called Highgate Place; and the other, on the west, designated Hampstead Place. Westward, towards the south, is Great Queen Anne Street, and opposite to it, on the east, Little Queen Anne Street. This design, however, was abandoned, and Portland Place built as above described.

It was part of Nash's design, in building Regent Street, that the great thoroughfare should lead through and beyond Portland Place to a magnificent palace to be built for George IV. in the centre of the Regent's Park. This design, also, was abandoned.

Foley House, at the southern end of Portland Place, was the town residence of Lord Foley; it was a large mansion, and with its surrounding grounds occupied a considerable amount of space, stretching away to the north-east corner of Cavendish Square. The house was of the same width as Portland Place, and had a somewhat dwarfed elevation; and the garden in front was separated from Portland Place by a brick wall. The building was pulled down about the year 1820, for the formation of Langham Place, so called after the adjoining mansion, belonging to Sir James Langham. Foley House is still kept in remembrance by the name being given to one of the mansions (No. 6) on the east side of Portland Place, and also by Foley Street, which is immediately contiguous. In Foley Place (now called Langham Street), which also occupied part of the grounds surrounding Foley House, lived John Hayter, the artist. Close by old Foley House, on part of the site now occupied by the Langham Hotel, stood till about 1860 Mansfield House, the town mansion of the Earl of Mansfield. The first Lord Mansfield, it is said, owed his first steps in professional success to the kindness of his friend and neighbour, Lord Foley, who allowed him £200 a year out of his own not very large income, to "keep up appearances" till he could achieve an income for himself.

Lord Mansfield in his early life was a great friend of Pope, who addresses him in his "Moral Essays" as "Dear Murray;" and, in his later days, of Dr. Johnson, who, however, stoutly refused to give Scotland any very great share of the credit arising from his lordship's career, as he was educated in England. "Much may be done with a Scotchman," the prejudiced old doctor would say good-humouredly, "if he is only caught young!"

Close to Foley House stood also the mansion of Sir James Langham, after whom the adjoining Place was named. On its site, about the year 1862, was erected a monster hotel called the "Langham," one of the most spacious and complete establishments of the kind in London. Here families can live, being boarded by contract, escaping all the domestic worries of servants, and petty household expenses.

English inns have not lost their reputation for comfort and the attention paid to guests; but the almost entire alteration in the methods of travelling by the introduction of railways has left them considerably behind the requirements of the age. Except in the smaller towns and villages, they have been superseded by hotels—houses of a more pretentious kind, which contain suites of apartments for families or individuals who choose to be alone, also a larger apartment for travellers generally. About the year 1861 projects were set on foot for the purpose of building several hotels in London worthy of the place, and corresponding to the vastness of modern demands, and the "Langham" was not only one of the first erected, but has ever since remained one of the most important.

The Langham Hotel was originally designed by a company about the year 1858, but the project proved abortive. The design, however, was subsequently taken in hand by another set of shareholders, who employed Messrs. Giles and Murray as the architects, and the foundations were laid in 1863. The hotel, which cost upwards of £300,000, is one of the largest buildings in London, and comprises no less than six hundred apartments. It measures upwards of 200 feet in the façade looking up Portland Place, and is upwards of 120 feet in height, the rooms rising to a sixth storey, and overtops by some forty or fifty feet all the mansions in Portland Place and Cavendish Square. The style of architecture would be called Italian; it is, however, plain, simple, and substantial, and singularly free from meretricious ornament. It includes large drawing-rooms, a dining-room, or coffee-room, 100 feet in length, smoking-rooms, billiard-rooms, post-office, telegraph-office, parcels-office, &c., thus uniting all the comforts of a club with those of a private home, each set of apartments forming a "flat" complete in itself. Below are spacious kitchen, laundry, &c., and water is laid over all the house, being raised by an engine in the basement. Some idea of the extensive nature of this establishment may be formed when we add that its staff of servants numbers about two hundred and fifty persons, from the head steward and matron down to the junior kitchenmaid and smallest "tiger." The "Langham," on an emergency, can make up as many as 400 beds. The floors are connected with each other by means of a "lift" which goes up and down at intervals. It is as nearly fire-proof as art can render it.

The hotel, which may be called, not a monster, but a leviathan of its kind, was opened in June, 1865, with a luncheon at which the Prince of Wales was present; and not long after its opening a dinner was given here, as an experiment towards utilising horse-flesh by the "hippophagists" of this country and of Paris. These monster hotels are no novelties in America; indeed, the Langham is far outstripped in size by the Palace Hotel at St. Francisco; but as this is the first experiment of the kind which has been made in London, it may be as well to add that it has paid a dividend of 20 per cent. upon the outlay.

Langham Place has had, at different times, some noted men among its residents. At No. 15 lived, and here also died, May 30th, 1832, the accom-

plished lawyer, philosopher, and historian, Sir James Mackintosh. His death was occasioned by a small bone of a fowl which accidentally lodged in his throat. He was buried in the churchyard at Hampstead. No. 6 was formerly the house of Sir Anthony Carlisle, the fashionable surgeon; and during the parliamentary season of 1836, No. 10 was the town residence of Daniel O'Connell, the well-known member for Dublin.

In the north-east corner of Langham Place, at the point where the road sweeps boldly round to enter Portland Place, stands All Souls' Church. It was built from the designs of Nash, in 1824, and forms a pleasing termination of the view from the junction of Regent Street and Oxford Street. It has a circular tower surrounded with Ionic columns, and Corinthian peristyle above; the "extinguisher" spire is circular and tapering. The interior arrangement is after the Italian style, being divided into a nave and aisles by colonnades. The altar-piece is a painting of "Christ crowned with Thorns," by Westall. Among the previous incumbents of this church have been Dr. Thomson, Archbishop of York, and Dr. Baring, late Bishop of Durham.

On the east side of Langham Place, about half way between the church and the north end of Upper Regent Street, is St. George's Hall. The building contains a spacious room which is occasionally used for balls, concerts, and other entertainments; and likewise for public meetings and lectures both on week days and Sundays. Here are the offices of the London Academy of Music, which was established in 1861. The academy is open to amateur as well as to professional students, and the instruction in the various branches of musical education is given by some of the first professors of the day.

The Portland Bazaar in Langham Place, better known as the "German Fair," was erected as far back as the year 1835, and was opened as a bazaar in 1839. Fourteen years afterwards it was burnt down and rebuilt with great improvements. The management of this establishment was in one respect unlike that of rival undertakings, as every young person employed had a direct interest in the profits, and was not in any way responsible for stall rents, or the purchase of stock; consequently there was no fear of her losing her little all. From November to the end of January the German Fair was literally crammed with customers, the whole stock being imported direct from Germany, France, and other foreign coun es. When the bazaar was rebuilt after the fire above mentioned, the southern portion of the premises, up to that time used as a furniture warehouse, was converted into the large building known as St. George's Hall, of which we have spoken above. In the winter of 1875–6 the premises were taken for the purpose of forming a large first-class "skating-rink," and the necessary alterations were at once effected in the building. The project was started by a company, and the rink was called the "Langham." It included the conveniences of a club, a restaurant, &c., on the grandest possible scale. The rink comprised a hall fitted up for musical performances, fancy-dress *fêtes*, &c., and was surrounded by galleries which could be used as promenades. The project nevertheless failed, and the building has since been used by "Archdeacon" Dunbar as a ritualist chapel.

The upper part of Regent Street was made by demolishing two narrow and ill-built thoroughfares, called Edward and Bolsover Streets, which formed a continuous line from the east side of Foley House into Oxford Street, nearly opposite to Great Swallow Street, which, as we have shown in a previous chapter, was amplified into Regent Street. On the west side of Upper Regent Street was an institution perhaps as well known to country visitors to London as to Londoners themselves—the Royal Polytechnic. It was founded in 1838, for the exhibition of novelties in "the Arts and Practical Science, especially in connection with Agriculture, Manufactures, and other branches of Industry." The buildings were enlarged in 1848. The premises of this institution were capacious and well-appointed, and extend from the east entrance in Regent Street 320 feet in depth, including the mansion, No. 5, Cavendish Square. The exhibition consisted, for the most part, of mechanical and other models, distributed through various apartments; a hall devoted to manufacturing processes; a theatre, or lecture-room; a very spacious hall; and other apartments.

The "Great Hall," lighted from the roof, contained models and designs. The floor of the hall was for many years principally occupied by two canals, containing a surface of 700 feet of water; attached to which were the appurtenances of a dockyard, locks, water-wheels, steam-boat models, &c. At the west end was a reservoir, or tank, fourteen feet deep; this, with the canals, held nearly 5,000 gallons of water, and could, if requisite, be emptied in less than one minute. Beneath the west-end gallery hung the diving-bell, which had, from the commencement, been the chief and standing attraction of the Poly-

technic, especially with the young folks and country cousins.

Courses of lectures were delivered on the principal topics of the day, and indeed upon almost every subject connected with human interest, accompanied with dioramic illustrations, and various optical illusions; not the least interesting of these was the so-called "Ghost" illusion, which is associated with the name of Professor Pepper, and has obtained great popularity in all the various shapes, dramatic and other, which it has assumed from season to season. The manufacture of spun-glass was carried on in the large room almost from the commencement with great success.

The Royal Polytechnic Institution, we may add, was under the management of a council. Besides the rooms mentioned above, there was an excellent laboratory, where chemical experiments were carried out. Public classes were likewise held, in which instruction was given in the various branches of science, in music, history, geography, in Latin, and also in French, German, and other modern languages. These classes were open to ladies as well as to gentlemen, and they rendered the institution a most valuable assistant to the cause of adult education. These classes were given up after a fire in 1881, and the building was subsequently sold. It is now used as a lecture-hall and class-rooms by the Young Men's Christian Institute.

In the house over the entrance of the Polytechnic Institution was opened, in January, 1855, the Cavendish Club; its founder and proprietor was Mr. Lionel Booth. The club died a natural death at the end of 1872; it was, however, revived at the beginning of 1874, under new management, and with increased resources, especially in the culinary department, but has been again given up.

On the opposite side of the street is another house which has been at different times the home of divers clubs, some of which have had but a transient existence. At one time it was the "Corinthian," and opened professedly with the view of affording the luxury and comforts of a club to the north-west of London; but this proved a failure. In 1873 it was opened as the "Civil and Military," a title which was subsequently altered to the "Civil and United Service." It afterwards became the "Russell," admitted ladies as members, and, under the chairmanship of "Archdeacon" Dunbar, deservedly came to grief, having existed for a year or two as the "Lotus."

CHAPTER XXXV.

OXFORD STREET EAST.—NORTHERN TRIBUTARIES.

"Miratur portas strepitumque, et strata viarum."—Virgil, "Æn." i.

Condition of Oxford Street in the Beginning of the Last Century—The "Adam and Eve" Tavern—Figg, the Prize-Fighter—Selwyn and the Earl of March stopped by a Highwayman—The London Crystal Palace—Mark Lemon's Birthplace—Great Portland Street—"Homes" and Charitable Institutions—St. Paul's Church—The Central Jewish Synagogue—Sir George Smart and Von Weber—David Wilkie and Dr. Waagen—The Woodbury Permanent Photographic Printing Company—The "Girls' Home," Charlotte Street—George Jones, R.A.—Unitarian Chapel, Little Portland Street, and Charles Dickens—Riding House Street—Mortimer Street—Nollekens, the Sculptor—St. Elizabeth's Home for Incurable Women—Margaret Street—David Williams, Founder of the Royal Literary Fund—"Tom" Campbell and Belzoni—Sir Walter Scott—All Saints' Church—All Saints' Sisterhood—Great Titchfield Street—Castle Street—Oxford Market—The Princess's Theatre—Charles Kean's Shakespearian Revivals—Blenheim Street—A Strange Occurrence—Poland Street—The "North Pole" Tavern—Wells Street—St. Andrew's Church—Berners Street—The Hoax played by Theodore Hook—A Batch of Medical Societies—The Middlesex Hospital—Nassau Street—Cleveland Street—Newman Street—A Modern Worker of Miracles—Mr. Heatherley's School of Art —An Eccentric Vow.

THE region upon which we are about to enter dates its existence from the earlier years of the reign of Queen Anne. John Timbs writes thus in his "Curiosities of London:"—"In a map of 1707, on the south side, King Street, near Golden Square, is perfect to Oxford Road, between which and Berwick Street are fields; thence to St. Giles's is covered with buildings, but westward not a house is to be seen; the northern side of Oxford Road contains a few scattered buildings, but no semblance of streets westward of Tottenham Court Road." This would appear to have been literally the case, for a plan of 1708, which he also mentions, shows the "Adam and Eve" as "a detached road-side public-house." It stood, according to this plan, in the "Dung-field," near the present Adam and Eve Court, almost opposite Poland Street; in an adjoining field is represented "the boarded house of Figg, the prize-fighter," standing quite isolated from other buildings. Figg appears to have been a noted character in his time. Hogarth has preserved his face in one of his engravings; and local gossips still quote the lines, by an unknown author—

"Long live the great Figg, by the prize-fighting swains
Sole monarch acknowledged of Marybone plains."

It appears that the amusements at "Figg's" were more varied than select, for we find that even women here could have "sets-to" in a manner marvellous to behold. One advertisement of the time announces that "Mrs. Stokes, the City Championess, is ready to meet the Hibernian Heroine at Figg's." Other advertisements of a more disgusting character we omit to quote, in mercy to our female readers.

That the street in its early days must have been anything but a pleasant or safe thoroughfare for travellers is pretty clear from Pennant's remark that he remembered it "a deep hollow road, and full of sloughs, with here and there a ragged house, the lurking-place of cut-throats; insomuch," he adds, "that I never was taken that way by night

in my hackney-coach to a worthy uncle's, who gave me lodgings in his house in George Street, but I went in dread the whole way." It was this part of Oxford Street that was probably the scene of a highway robbery, recorded in *Lloyd's Evening Post*, about the year 1760:—"Jan. 30.—Saturday last, about ten in the evening, as a post-chaise was coming to town, between the turnpike and Tottenham Court Road, ... with the Earl of March and George Augustus Selwyn, Esq., a highwayman stopped the postilion, and swore he would blow his brains out if he did not stop; on which the Earl of March jumped out of the chaise and fired a pistol, and the highwayman immediately rode off."

But we are now concerned mainly with the northern tributaries of Oxford Street which lie between Regent Street and Tottenham Court Road. We will begin, therefore, with the Circus, and work our way gradually eastwards, very leisurely, for we shall have a good deal to say before we find ourselves at Bloomsbury again.

Near the Regent Circus is the chief entrance to the London Crystal Palace, one of the most elegant bazaars in the metropolis. This building, which has also an entrance in Great Portland Street, was erected in 1858, from the designs of Mr. Owen Jones, the plan of the structure being somewhat similar to that of the Floral Hall, in Covent Garden. It is constructed chiefly of iron and glass, after the manner of its great prototype at Sydenham. The roof, which is of coloured glass, of mosaic appearance, is supported by iron columns. The nave of the building, from the Great Portland Street entrance to the western extremity, is 180 feet in length; from it there is a transept extending southwards to the Oxford Street entrance, which internally has a length of 90 feet, giving, with the entrance-hall on that side, a total length, from north to south, of about 140 feet. On the ground floor is a spacious hall, divided by iron columns on each side into a nave and aisles, the floor being occupied by counters for the exhibition and sale of fancy goods of all descriptions; there is on each side a gallery above, and in and under these galleries there are also convenient and well-lighted stalls. The building was advertised for sale while this sheet was in the printer's hands. In a house on this site was born, in November, 1809, Mark Lemon, the genial editor of *Punch* during the first quarter of a century of its existence.

Great Portland Street is a broad and respectable land Street, is a building called the Langham Hall, which is used for concerts and other entertainments of a similar character. It is also occasionally used for religious services. It was formerly known as the Lyric Hall.

On the same side of the way, about half-way up, stands St. Paul's Church, for many years known as Portland Chapel. It was erected in 1775-6, and stands on a site which formed part of a basin of the Marylebone Waterworks. John Timbs tells us

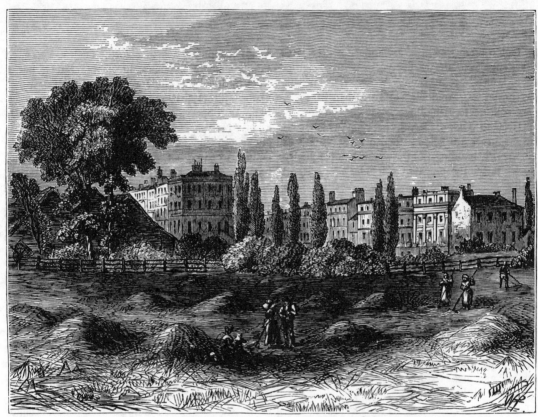

THE ENTRANCE TO PORTLAND PLACE, 1815.

thoroughfare, at present almost entirely consisting of shops, largely occupied by picture-dealers and music-sellers, &c. It extends, in a direct line from Oxford Street to the Marylebone Road, close by the eastern end of Park Crescent. The houses on each side, towards the northern end, stood back from the roadway, with gardens in front; but of late years shops have been thrown out on both sides of the way.

At this end of the street are various charitable institutions, or "homes." Amongst others are the National Dental Hospital, the Western Dispensary for Skin Diseases, and Miss Gladstone's Female Servants' Home.

On the west side of the street, near Little Port-

that there is a view, by Chatelain, of this basin, which was the scene of several fatal accidents and suicides. The chapel was first consecrated in 1831, when it was dedicated to St. Paul.

Near the above church is another religious edifice, which forms a conspicuous architectural feature in the street. It is the central Jewish Synagogue, which was completed and opened in 1870. The building is a fine specimen of Moorish design, its thoroughly Oriental style being especially exemplified in the interior, with its tiers of columns decorated with Saracenic capitals, supporting the gallery, clerestory, and lofty vaulted roof. The ark, in which are placed the sacred scrolls of the law, is situated at the south-east end of the building, looking towards Jerusalem, and is covered by a heavy curtain, embroidered with gold. Immediately over it are the two tables of stone inscribed with the ten Commandments; and above them, through a small circular window, shines the "per-

At No. 204 was originally the West London School of Art, now removed to 155, Great Titchfield Street. This institution has classes in architectural drawing, in drawing from life and the antique, and in design, as applied to mural, textile,

INTERIOR OF THE JEWISH SYNAGOGUE, GREAT PORTLAND STREET.

petual light" which is never extinguished. The ark rests on a platform of white marble, raised several steps above the floor. The *almemar*, a large raised pew, where the readers, choristers, and harmonium are placed, stands conspicuously in the centre of the synagogue, and is richly ornamented with gilt stanchions.

The Rothschild family showed much interest in, and subscribed largely to, the building fund of this new tabernacle.

and other decorations. It is in connection with the Government Department of Science and Art.

Among the eminent residents in this street mentioned by Mr. Peter Cunningham, were William Seward, author of the "Anecdotes" which bear his name; Dr. William Guthrie, author of a well-known grammar; James Boswell, Dr. Johnson's biographer; and Carl Maria von Weber. The two last-mentioned persons died here; the latter very suddenly, on the 5th of June, 1826, at No. 91, for many years the house of the late eminent composer, Sir George Smart. Sir George, we may here remark, is thus celebrated by "Ingoldsby," in "Mr. Barney Maguire's Account of the Coronation of Her Majesty:"—

> " That same Sir George Smart, O !
> Who played the consarto,
> With his four-and-twenty fiddlers all of a row."

Weber was buried at the Roman Catholic Church of St. Mary's, Moorfields, whence his body was afterwards taken to Germany. On his death Mr. J. R. Planché, who knew him well, penned the following exquisite lines, which were set to music, and sung by Braham :—

> " Weep, for the word is spoken !
> Mourn, for the knell hath tolled !
> The master-chord is broken,
> And the master-hand is cold.
> Romance hath lost her minstrel ;
> No more his magic strain
> Shall throw a sweeter spell around
> The legends of Almaine.

> " His fame had flown before him
> To many a foreign land ;
> His lays were sung by every tongue,
> And harped by every hand.
> He came to seek fresh laurels,
> But Fate was in their breath,
> And turned his march of triumph
> Into a dirge of death."

In this street, in a hackney-coach, which was conveying her home from the Seven Dials, his mother, in 1766, gave birth to Mr. J. T. Smith, afterwards the superintendent of the print-room at the British Museum, and the author of " Nollekens and his Times," and of " A Book for a Rainy Day," from which we have quoted very largely in these pages.

In this street lodged Wilkie in the early part of his career in London, as we learn from Cyrus Redding's " Fifty Years' Recollections." In 1835 he was in the very height of his fame and popularity. Dr. Waagen tells us that on one occasion he met Callcott, Eastlake, and Etty the painter at dinner. "Wilkie," he adds, " is now unhappily so overwhelmed with orders for portraits that he has hardly a moment for his good-natured humorous subjects." At No. 157 are the offices of the Woodbury Permanent Photographic Printing Company.

Charlotte Street, between Great Portland Street and Portland Place, and running parallel to both, at one time bore a very bad character for its residents. A clearance, however, was made by the parochial authorities about the year 1860, and now it is largely occupied by public institutions, among which may be mentioned the "Girls' Home," which was instituted in 1867 for the purpose of lodging, clothing, and educating destitute girls, who may not have been convicted of crime—a sister institution to the "Boys' Home" in Regent's Park Road, which we shall describe hereafter. Here also are the offices of the Central Synagogue and of the United Synagogue.

At No. 10, New Cavendish Street, George Jones, R.A., was living in 1806. He was a well-known painter of battle-pieces, and some time Librarian and afterwards Keeper of the Royal Academy. He died in 1869.

In Little Portland Street is the leading West-end Chapel of the Unitarian body. Its minister was for many years Mr. James Martineau, a brother of Harriet Martineau. In this chapel Mr. Charles Dickens for a time held sittings, though in later years he frequented a parish church. Mr. Forster tells us that he was led to frequent the Unitarian worship on account of his " impatience of differences with the clergymen of the Established Church on the subject of creeds and formularies."

The neighbourhood of Great Portland Street, towards the upper end, is largely the home of artists and sculptors' studios; and on the southern side of the Euston Road the marble-yards are not unlike the Piccadilly of a century ago. Clipstone Street and Carburton Street, in this neighbourhood, are both named after villages belonging to the ducal estate; the former in Nottinghamshire, and the latter in Northamptonshire.

Facing the New Road, in the garden of the top house on the east side of what was formerly known as Norton Street, but is now styled Bolsover Street, a few yards east of the top of Great Portland Street, were two fine elm-trees, standing as lately as the year 1853. It was said by the late Mr. Robert Cole, to whom the house then belonged, that Lord Byron had once spent an evening under their shade.

Riding House Street, which connects the top of Regent Street with Great Portland Street, bears witness in its name to an establishment long since forgotten, one of the Riding Academies so popular in the days of our great-grandfathers.

At No. 30, Foley Place (now called Langham Street), Campbell was living in 1822, and here he wrote some of his shorter poems.

Mortimer Street, which crosses Great Portland Street, extending from the north-east corner of Cavendish Square to Charles Street, was so called after the earldom of Mortimer, which was borne by the Harleys, conjointly with that of Oxford. At No. 9 in this street was the studio of the sculptor Nollekens, almost as remarkable for his parsimony as for the artistic power of his chisel. Here Dr. Johnson came to sit to him for his bust, and Mr. J. T. Smith, who was then a boy working at art under Nollekens, was busy drawing in the studio at the time. He thus describes Dr. Johnson to the life:—"The doctor, after looking at my drawing, then at the bust I was copying, put his hand heavily upon my head, pronouncing 'Very well, very well.' Here I frequently saw him, and recollect his figure and dress with tolerable correctness. He was tall, and must have been, when young, a powerful man : he stooped, with his head inclined to the right shoulder : heavy brows, sleepy eyes, nose very narrow between the eye-brows, but broad at the bottom; lips enormously thick; chin wide and double. He wore a stock and wrist-bands; his wig was what is called a *Busby*, but often wanted powder. His hat, a three-cornered one ; coats, one a dark mulberry, the other brown, inclining to the colour of Scotch snuff; large brass or gilt buttons; black waistcoat, and small clothes —sometimes the latter were corduroy ; black stockings; large easy shoes, with buckles; latterly he used a *hooked* walking-stick; his gait was wide and awkwardly sprawling." The late Mr. C. Towneley, the collector of the Towneley Marbles in the British Museum, was also a frequenter of Nollekens' studio, and on one visit he tipped or "pouched" young Smith half-a-guinea to buy a store of paper and chalk. Though an exquisite sculptor, Nollekens was utterly uneducated, and could not even spell his own language. His wife, a daughter of Mr. Justice Welch, was as niggardly as himself. It is said that he attended the Royal Academy Club dinners, at the cost of a guinea a year, because he could carry off in his pockets enough nutmegs to make that difference in his house-keeping. He died in April, 1823, very rich; and eccentric to the last, left a very long drawn will, with no less than fourteen codicils to it.

At No. 67 in this street is a charitable institution in connection with All Saints' Home, in Margaret Street. It is called St. Elizabeth's Home, and its object is to relieve women whom the present London hospitals reject as incurable. The persons received here are chiefly those who have "seen better days," and are unable to support themselves without assistance. In each case it is required that the applicant should be able herself, or through her friends, to guarantee a small annual payment.

Running parallel with Mortimer Street, and extending from the south-east corner of Cavendish Square to Wells Street, is Margaret Street, which keeps in remembrance the name of Lady Margaret Cavendish, the daughter and heiress of the second

and last Duke of Newcastle of that line, and wife of John Holles, Marquis of Clare and Duke of Newcastle. The duke died without male issue, and his daughter married Edward Harley, second Earl of Oxford and Mortimer, whose daughter and heiress became, in her turn, as we have already seen, the wife of the second Duke of Portland. The name of the duke's second title, Marquis of Titchfield, is given to the street running parallel with Great Portland Street, on its eastern side, and reaching from Oxford Street to the Marylebone Road ; whilst Bolsover Street, close by, is named after the duke's estate in Derbyshire.

In Margaret Street was the chapel of the Rev. David Williams, the founder of the Royal Literary Fund. For the facts contained in the following account of him we are indebted to Dr. Robert Chambers' "Book of Days :"—Born in a humble sphere of life, near Cardigan, in 1738, he was originally a minister of the Unitarian body, and settled at Highgate. He next set up a very liberal form of worship in Margaret Street, where he preached mainly on social subjects, such as the bad effects of gaming. We next catch a glimpse of him at Chelsea, where he kept a school, and had Benjamin Franklin for a guest at the time when the American philosopher was subjected to the abuse of Wedderburn before the Privy Council. He wrote works on education, politics, public worship, economy, &c., in all of which he showed a spirit of philanthropy ; but soon after the outbreak of the French Revolution we find him joining the Girondists, whom he helped to frame a constitution. When, however, the rabble at Paris began to thirst for blood, he returned to England, and set to work on the more sensible task of founding a society for the aid of men of letters. In this he succeeded, after many years of persevering labour, in which he collected £6,000. He had the satisfaction of seeing the society regularly constituted and founded in May, 1790. The society distributes between £1,000 and £2,000 a year regularly in aiding poor authors in their struggles. David Williams died in 1816, and was buried in St. Anne's Church, Soho.

In Margaret Street Campbell occupied chambers during the day, whilst editing the *New Monthly Magazine*, though he lived at Sydenham, and went home every night by the stage-coach. Mr. Cyrus Redding writes thus of him in his "Fifty Years' Recollections :"—" When Belzoni returned from Egypt I went to see his exhibition of the Egyptian tombs. He appeared little altered, and as I was going to take coffee with Campbell, I asked him if he would like to be acquainted with the poet,

Campbell being curious about everything relating to the East. He said he should like to go at that moment, and I took him. The king, the queen, and Bergami then occupied the attention of the public. Belzoni and I passing through Bond Street, his remarkable stature and foreign appearance attracted attention. Somebody gave out that it was Bergami. People stopped to stare at us, and a crowd rapidly collected. Belzoni proposed we should get out of the larger thoroughfares, which we did, he moving his Herculean form rapidly onwards. We crossed into Hanover Square, still followed by some of the mob; then crossing Oxford Street, we were soon in Margaret Street, and ensconced in the poet's lodgings. When Belzoni stood by Campbell, I thought of ' Ajax the Less and Ajax the son of Telamon.' I never saw Belzoni but once after this, before he started on the African expedition in which he died. He was an unassuming, quiet man, on whose merit I am convinced there were wrongful attempts made to cast a cloud. His knowledge was strictly practical; indeed, he pretended to nothing more."

On another occasion Cyrus Redding paid a visit to the poet in his apartments here, which he thus records :—"Walter Scott was in town soon after the *New Monthly Magazine* commenced. He was too much engaged, and too 'anti-Whig' to be enrolled at any price in our pages. One day Scott called in Margaret Street; he was going away as I went in. When he was gone, Campbell tried at an impromptu. ' Don't speak for a moment,' said the poet, ' I have it.'

"Quoth the South to the North, ' In your comfortless sky
  Not a nightingale sings.' ' True,' the North made reply;
  ' But your nightingale's warblings, I envy them not,
  When I think of the strains of my Burns and my Scott!'"

Cyrus Redding, like a " Fidus Achates," took the lines down on a letter-cover at the moment, and so saved them from perishing. Let us be grateful for the boon.

In this street, between Great Portland and Regent Streets, was formerly the West London Jewish Synagogue. It was built in 1850, from the designs of Mr. Mocatta, and consisted of a square building, surrounded on three sides with Ionic columns supporting the ladies' gallery, whence rose other columns, receiving semi-circular arches, crowned by a bold cornice and lantern light. The ark, which completed the fourth side, was surmounted by a decorated entablature, above which were placed the tablets of the Ten Commandments. This edifice has been superseded by the new building in Great Portland Street, above described.

In Margaret Street stands All Saints' Church, a handsome modern building of red brick, in the simplest and severest style externally, though its interior is more richly decorated than any other church of the Anglican communion in London. Until about 1850 there stood here a poor, meagre, and gloomy little structure, built in the year 1788, and known as " Margaret Street Chapel." It had been originally a meeting-house belonging to Lady Huntingdon's connection. On the publication of the " Tracts for the Times," this chapel, then under the Rev. W. Dodsworth, became a focus of extreme Tractarian views, and its incumbent and his colleague, the Rev. F. Oakeley, both became Roman Catholics. The new church, of which the architect was Mr. W. Butterfield, was built in 1850–9. The first stone was laid by Dr. Pusey, its first minister being the late Rev. W. Upton Richards. The spire rises to the height of 230 feet. The interior is richly decorated with carving, and with frescoes of the Birth and Crucifixion of our Lord, and the Court of Heaven, showing the saints with our Lord in the centre, by Mr. W. Dyce, R.A. The painted windows are by O'Connor. At the entrance of the church is a baptistery, and adjoining it is a residence for its clergy, who are mostly celibates. The music of this church is of a very ornate and elaborate character; and its ritualistic services attract large congregations, especially of the upper classes, the majority being ladies. There are separate seats provided for the male and female worshippers.

The following *jeu d'esprit*, said to be from the pen of a clerical wit of our day, in all probability contains an allusion to this sacred edifice :—

"In a church that is furnished with mullion and gable,
  With altar and reredos, with gurgoyle and groin,
  The penitents' dresses are seal-skin and sable,
  The odour of sanctity 's Eau de Cologne.

"But if only could Lucifer flying from Hades
  Gaze down on this crowd with its panniers and paints,
  He could say, as he looked at the lords and the ladies,
  Oh ! where is ' All Sinners,' if this is ' All Saints ?'"

At the corner of Margaret and Wells Street, opposite the church, and more or less dependent on it and its clergy, are various religious houses and homes, in which the work of Christian charity is conducted by ladies, who style themselves the " All Saints' Sisterhood ;" they work under the sanction of the Bishop of London. The works in which they are engaged are various. They teach in the night-school of the district, and visit and nurse the poor and sick at their own houses ; and they take charge of orphan girls, and receive aged and infirm women, incurable sick women, and young serving girls into the Home. These latter, as well as the orphans are trained up for service, and are instructed in the various kinds of household work ; and if any show an aptitude for teaching, they are trained to be schoolmistresses.　The Sisters have also an industrial school, in which all kinds of plain needlework are done.　The building once used as the temporary church in Margaret Street has been fitted up as an orphanage.　Attached to the Home is a pharmacy, where medicines are dispensed by the Sisters to the sick and needy, under the supervision of able and experienced physicians, who regularly visit the institution, and give their services gratuitously. The buildings are of red brick, in the severest style of Gothic architecture, and serve the double purpose of a home and national schools.

Great Titchfield Street has had in its time, among its residents, a few men of note in the world of art. Mr. Cunningham mentions the names of Richard Wilson, the landscape painter, who, in 1779, lived at No. 85.　Again, Loutherbourg, the landscape painter, resided for some years at No. 45; and No. 76 was the residence of Mr. Bonomi, R.A.

In this street was formerly a place of worship for the " Independents ;" it was known as " Providence Chapel," and was under the ministry of the eccentric preacher, William Huntington.*　The fabric was burnt down in 1810, and on the minister being spoken to respecting its rebuilding, he is said to have observed that " Providence having allowed the chapel to be destroyed, Providence might rebuild it, for he would not," and in consequence the site was afterwards occupied as a timber-yard.

Cirencester Place, the former name of the north end of Great Titchfield Street, recorded one of the inferior titles of the Duke of Portland, who is also Baron of Cirencester.　Like Norton Street, it was formerly tenanted by an unsatisfactory population ; but these were cleared out a few years ago ; and, the houses being numbered as part of Titchfield Street, the name disappeared.

Castle Street, a thoroughfare extending from Upper Regent Street to Wells Street, and passing across the north of Oxford Market, is probably named after an inn which bore that sign, and it has a history of its own.　At No. 36, James Barry, the Royal Academician, resided in 1773, when in the height of his professional reputation and engagements.　Here Edmund Burke gave him sittings for a portrait painted at the request of their mutual friend, Dr. Brocklesby.　The painter here entertained Burke at a homely dinner, cooking the beefsteak on the fire in his parlour, and availing himself of the great orator's aid in the operation.　Barry

* See Vol. II., p 284.

died in 1806, at the house of his friend and neighbour, Mr. Bonomi.

At No. 6, Dr. Johnson and his wife were living, as we learn from Boswell, in 1738, on his second visit to London ; and it was in this street, at the house of some Miss Cotterells, his opposite neighbours, that the great lexicographer first met and was introduced to Sir Joshua Reynolds.　It was also whilst living here that he made the acquaintance of Edmund Cave, to whom he addressed several letters, and dated from this house.

Oxford Market was so called either from the Oxford Road, to which it was adjacent, or, more probably, after Harley, Earl of Oxford, the original ground landlord.　It was erected in 1721, as shown by the date in the brass vane which surmounted its centre.　The vane bore upon it the initials " H. E. H.," which are probably those of Edward Lord Harley and his wife, Henrietta (the heiress of the house of Holles, Duke of Newcastle), who gave the site.　It is called by the painter Barry "the most classic of London markets;" but it is certainly difficult to see in what its "classic" nature consists. It was originally a plain hexagonal structure, mostly of wood ; this was pulled down, either entirely or to a great extent, about the year 1815, when it was rebuilt, small dwelling-rooms above being added to the shops below.　It was the only daughter of the above-named Lord Harley who carried this and other adjoining property by marriage into the family of the Duke of Portland.　In 1876, the site of the market was disposed of for £27,500 ; the market was removed in 1880–82, and the Oxford Mansions, a block of buildings in the Queen Anne style, erected in its place.

The Princess's Theatre stands on the north side of Oxford Street, about four hundred yards east of the Circus ; it stretches backwards as far as Castle Street.　It occupies the site of a building formerly known as the Queen's Bazaar, which had existed for some years, but never gained popularity.　It was destroyed by fire in 1829, but rebuilt.　In 1833 were exhibited here Mr. Roberts's great picture of the " Departure of the Israelites out of Egypt," and also the " Physiorama," comprising twelve views arranged in a gallery 200 feet long. The edifice, like its successor, had a back entrance in Castle Street.

The building of the original theatre was a costly and unsuccessful speculation, and it nearly ruined Hamlet, the silversmith of Leicester Square.　In 1841 it was entirely remodelled from the designs of Nelson, and decorated by Mr. Crace ; and it was opened in the September of that year with a series of promenade concerts.　It was a chaste, elegant, and commodious house, having three tiers of boxes, besides another row just below the ceiling.

The history of the old theatre is chiefly remarkable for its having been the scene of Mr. Charles Kean's Shakespearian revivals, which were commenced in 1849, and continued for ten years. In putting these plays on the stage Mr. Kean spared no expense, and shirked no amount of study and trouble; and the theatrical world and the public

manager. Shortly afterwards, in recognition of his efforts to raise the dramatic profession and elevate the English stage, Mr. Kean was presented with a handsome service of plate.

The theatre subsequently passed into the hands of Messrs. Webster and Chatterton, of the Adelphi, and Mr. Dion Boucicault for some time figured as the leading actor. In 1864 a drama entitled the *Streets of London* was performed here to overflow-

THE MIDDLESEX HOSPITAL. (*See page* 465.)

at large are largely indebted to his liberality and erudition for the admirably correct costumes and *mise en scène* which were in his time characteristic of the plays at the Princess's. In all this he was ably seconded by Mrs. Kean (formerly known as Miss Ellen Tree), who entered warmly into the spirit of his work of revival. In the first year he adapted and produced Byron's play of *Sardanapalus*, and varied his Shakesperian revivals by putting on the boards at various times Sheridan's *Pizarro, Louis XI.*, and other standard dramas. In the year 1860, on his resigning the management of the theatre, Mr. Kean was invited to a dinner in St. James's Hall, where a large company, with the Duke of Newcastle in the chair, assembled to do honour to the famous tragedian and spirited

ing houses. The play, however, like many others of a similar character which have been since produced, appears to have aimed more at "sensationalism" than to have rested on its literary merits, and, therefore, as stated in Charles Dickens's "Life," may be put down as "but an inferior style of theatrical taste." Mr. Kean died in 1868.

In 1879–80 the theatre was rebuilt on an enlarged and more elaborate scale, and has since been under the management of Mr. Wilson Barrett.

We must here cross for a few minutes to the south side of Oxford Street, in order to speak of one or two matters which escaped us in our wanderings westward. Nearly opposite the Princess's Theatre, in Blenheim Street, was at one

OXFORD MARKET, 1870.

time the residence of Ugo Foscolo, of whom we shall have more to say hereafter.

A strange occurrence is related by tradition as having happened in Blenheim Street about the time that Dr. Johnson lodged in it. A coach drew up late one evening at the door of a surgeon, Mr. Brooks, who was in the habit of buying "subjects" for dissection. A heavy sack was taken out and deposited in the hall, and the servants were about to carry it down the back stairs into the dissecting-room, when a living "subject" thrust his head and neck out of one end, and begged for his life. The servants in alarm ran to fetch pistols, but the "subject" continued to implore for mercy in such tones as to assure them that there was no ground for alarm, for he had been drunk, and did not know how he had got into the sack. Dr. Brooks coming in, ordered the fellow to have the sack tied up again loosely round his chin, and sent him off in a coach to the watch-house, where it is to be hoped that he recovered his senses.

In Poland Street, the next turning eastward on the same side of Oxford Street, was living, in 1765, Mr. Burney, the friend and correspondent of Dr. Johnson, so often mentioned by Boswell. This street has also numbered among its residents Dr. Macaulay, the husband of the authoress, Mrs. Macaulay; Dr. Burney, the author of the "History of Music;" and the old Earl of Cromartie, who was pardoned by George II. for his share in the Scottish rising of 1745.

In Oxford Street, on the same side, not far from Wardour Street, is an inn called the "North Pole," so named, no doubt, to commemorate one of those many arctic expeditions which from time to time have left our shores, and those of adjoining countries, in search of the spot "where there is no north beyond it."

Re-crossing Oxford Street, we now leave the Portland property on our left, and pass into that belonging to Lord Berners' family. Wells Street, which crosses the eastern end of Castle Street, is narrow and crooked, and therefore more ancient than its neighbours. Its name is probably a corruption of Well Street, and so called after Well, in Yorkshire, the seat of the family of Strangeways, from whom Lady Berners descends. Here Dr. Beattie, the author of "The Minstrel," and of the essay on "Truth," &c., was living during his stay in London, in 1771. He was one of the last of Dr. Johnson's contemporaries, surviving till 1803.

In this street is the handsome district church of St. Andrew's, erected in 1846 from the designs of Mr. Dankes. It is in the Early Perpendicular Gothic style, and has a tower and spire upwards of 150 feet high. At the east end is a large painted glass window, by Hardman. The services are intoned, but "plain-song and anthems are used instead of Gregorian compositions;" and the church has been always remarkable for the excellence of its choir.

Berners Street, so called after the family title of its ground-landlord, runs northward a little to the east of Wells Street. It was built about the middle of the last century, and has always been celebrated as the "home and haunt" of artists, painters, and sculptors. Among its former residents are to be reckoned Opie, Fuseli, and Sir William Chambers, the latter of whom we have already mentioned in connection with Somerset House. Opie was buried in St. Paul's Cathedral. His second wife, Amelia, the learned Quakeress, was well known by her writings, "Tales of Real Life," "Poems," "Simple Tales," &c. In this street was the bank in which Fauntleroy, the forger, was a partner.

As we saunter up Berners Street we are irresistibly reminded of one of Theodore Hook's earliest pranks, when his life was already a succession of boisterous buffooneries. This was in the year 1809; and the lady on whom it was practised, says Mr. Peter Cunningham, was a Mrs. Tottingham, living at No. 54. Hook, it appears, had laid a wager that "in one week that nice quiet dwelling should be the most famous in all London." The bet was taken; and in the course of four or five days he had written and dispatched several hundred letters, conveying orders to tradesmen of every sort "within the bills of mortality," all to be executed on one particular day, and as nearly as possible at one fixed hour. From "wagons of coal and potatoes, to books, prints, feathers, ices, jellies, and cranberry tarts," nothing in any way whatever available to any human being but was commanded from scores of rival dealers scattered all over the metropolis. At that time the Oxford Road (as it was then called) was not approachable either from Westminster or from the City otherwise than through a complicated series of lanes. It may be feebly guessed, therefore, what was the crush, and jam, and tumult of that day. We are told that "Hook had provided himself with a lodging nearly opposite the fated house; and there, with a couple of trusty allies, he watched the development of his midday melodrame. But some of the *dramatis personæ* were seldom, if ever, alluded to in later times. He had no objection to bodying forth the arrival of the Lord Mayor and his chaplain, invited to take the death-bed confession of a peculating common-councilman; but he would have buried in oblivion that no less liberty was taken with the Governor of the Bank, the Chairman of the East India Company, a Lord Chief Justice, a Cabinet Minister—above all, with the Archbishop of Canterbury, and his Royal Highness the Commander-in-Chief. They all obeyed the summons—every pious and patriotic feeling had been most movingly appealed to. We are not sure that they all reached Berners Street; but the Duke of York's military punctuality and crimson liveries brought him to the point of attack before the poor widow's astonishment had risen to terror and despair. Perhaps no assassination, no conspiracy, no royal demise or ministerial revolution of recent times was a greater godsend to the newspapers than this audacious piece of mischief. In Hook's own theatrical world he was instantly suspected, but no sign escaped either him or his confidants. The affair was beyond that circle a serious one. Fierce were the growlings of the doctors and surgeons, scores of whom had been cheated of valuable hours. Attorneys, teachers of all kinds, male and female, hair-dressers, tailors, popular preachers, parliamentary philanthropists, had been alike victimised, and were in their various notes alike vociferous. But the tangible material damage done was itself no joking matter. There had been an awful smashing of glass, china, harpsichords, and coach-panels. Many a horse fell, never to rise again. Beer-barrels and wine-barrels had been overturned and exhausted with impunity amidst the press of countless multitudes. It had been a fine field-day for the pickpockets. There arose a fervent hue and cry for the detection of the wholesale deceiver and destroyer."

Hook, after this escapade, found it convenient to have a severe fit of illness, and then to recruit his health by a prolonged country tour. The affair, however, having been a nine days' (or, possibly, a nine weeks') wonder, blew over, and the unknown author of the hoax re-appeared with his usual coolness in the green-room of the theatre.

Berners Street forms the head-quarters of several foreign and charitable institutions, some of which have been established ever since the last century. In 1788 was founded the Society for the Relief of Widows and Orphans of Medical Men. The Medical and Chirurgical Society was established in 1805, and incorporated in 1834, for the cultivation and promotion of medicine and surgery. The society possesses a good library, numbering some 25,000 volumes. Here, too, are the Obstetrical Society of London, instituted in 1858; and the Pathological Society, founded in 1846. The last-named society was instituted for the exhibition and examination of specimens, drawings, microscopic preparations, casts or models of morbid parts, with accompanying written or oral descriptions, illustrative of pathological science. All the above-mentioned medical societies, together with another styled the Clinical Society of London, are accommodated in the same house (No. 53).

No. 54 in this street was originally St. Peter's Hospital for Stone. This charitable institution was established in 1860, and its object is to benefit as large a number as possible of suffering poor by affording them, without a letter of recommendation, the advantages of hospital accommodation; to improve medical and surgical knowledge on the subjects specially treated of here, by bringing together a large number of patients suffering from those diseases, and thus affording opportunities for observation and classification; and, in the cases of patients suffering from stone, to investigate the best means of accomplishing its removal with the least possible danger to the life of the patient, and, whenever practicable, to substitute lithotrity for lithotomy. The hospital is now located in Henrietta Street, Covent Garden.

At No. 22 are the offices of the Ladies' Sanitary Association, and also the Society for Promoting the Employment of Women. At No. 9 was started, about 1875, the Berners Women's Club —one of the first experiments which was made in this direction—but the institution seems to have been soon broken up. The London Association for the Protection of Trade has its office at No. 16. in this street.

In Charles Street, at the top of Berners Street, the view down which it commands, is the Middlesex Hospital. The building, which is of brick, and very extensive, comprises a centre and wings; it is fitted up with baths, laboratory works, ventilating shaft, and, indeed, all the necessary appliances for comfort, &c. The hospital dates from about ten or twenty years after the splendid bequest of Thomas Guy, the penurious bookseller of Lombard Street. It was first established, in 1745, in Windmill Street, Tottenham Court Road, for sick and lame persons, and for lying-in married women. It was removed, in 1755, to its present site, when it stood among green fields and lanes. Since 1807 the midwifery patients, to the number of nearly a thousand yearly, instead of being received as inmates, are attended at their own homes by the medical officers of the hospital. The cancer wards were founded by a gift of £4,000 from Mr. Samuel Whitbread, in 1807, to which other gifts and legacies were added. A remarkable incident in the history of the hospital is that in 1793 it became a refuge for many of the French royalist emigrants driven from France by the Jacobin Reign of Terror. The buildings were enlarged by new wings constructed in 1775, and again in 1834. Lord Robert Seymour, a zealous and munificent friend of this institution, obtained for it the royal patronage of George IV., which is continued by her present Majesty. The medical school, established in 1835, enjoys a high reputation; it is furnished with a museum of valuable collections.

The hospital contains beds for upwards of three hundred patients. Of these twenty-six are devoted to the cancer establishment, instituted in the year 1791, where the patient is allowed to remain "until relieved by art or released by death;" eight are appropriated to women suffering from diseases peculiar to their sex; the remainder of the beds being set apart for general miscellaneous cases. Upwards of nine hundred lying-in married women are attended at their own habitations, and eighteen thousand out-door patients are relieved every year. The hospital is unendowed. The annual subscriptions amount to not more than £2,355, while of late years the expenditure has been increased by some necessary works of improvement.

This hospital has numbered among its surgeons and physicians men of the highest eminence in the medical profession; besides which it has been the cradle of many eminent careers in surgery.

In 1812 Sir Charles Bell was appointed surgeon to this hospital, an important step in his early professional progress. We have spoken of him somewhat later in life, in our account of the Windmill Street School of Surgery (page 236). It was he to whom is ascribed the saying that " London is a place to live in, not to die in;" and his remarks, perhaps, may explain the reason which led him, in the midst of a successful career in the metropolis, to retire to his native city of Edinburgh—a step which few Scotchmen take, if successful on the south of the Tweed.

The southern side of Charles Street, which is continued by Goodge Street into Tottenham Court Road, presents a busy appearance, especially on Friday and Saturday evenings; and as one of the few street markets remaining at the West-end, and probably destined at no long interval to disappear, may claim a short notice. To the long row of stall-keepers on its southern side, who display their stores of fish, fruit, and vegetables in hand-barrows and baskets, and on movable slabs, we may apply the words of Henry Mayhew :—" The scene in these parts has more of the character of a fair than of a market. There are hundreds of stalls, and every stall has its one or two lights; either it is illuminated by the intense white light of the new self-generating gas-lamp, or else it is brightened up by the red

smoking flame of the old-fashioned grease lamps. One man shows off his yellow haddock with a candle stuck in a bundle of firewood; his neighbour makes his candlestick of a huge turnip, and the tallow gutters over its sides; while the boy shouting 'Eight a penny pears!' has rolled his dip in a thick coat of brown paper, that flares away with the candle. Some stalls are crimson with a fire shining through the holes beneath the baked chestnut stove. Others have handsome octohedral lamps; while a few have a candle shining through a sieve. These, with the sparkling ground-glass of the tea-dealers' shops, and the butchers' gas-lights streaming and fluttering in the wind like flags of flame, pour forth such a flood of light, that at a distance the atmosphere immediately above the spot is as lurid as if the street was on fire."

Nassau Street, which runs north and south, a little to the west of the Middlesex Hospital, was so named in compliment to the royal house from which King William III. was sprung.

Cleveland Street, which severs the Portland from the Southampton estate, is a good broad street, extending from Euston Road in a south-easterly direction to the corner of Charles Street, close by Middlesex Hospital, and, together with Newman Street, affords a direct communication into Oxford Street. On the eastern side of Cleveland Street is a dull, heavy building, formerly the Strand Union Workhouse, but which was taken, in 1874, as the Central London Sick Asylum Infirmary, by the joint action of the several parishes of Westminster, St. Pancras, the Strand, and St. Giles's.

Newman Street was built between the years 1750 and 1770, and was, from the first, inhabited by artists of celebrity, and its shops at the present time still having among them several devoted to art studies. Banks and Bacon, the sculptors, both lived in this street; as also did Benjamin West, the president of the Royal Academy. Cyrus Redding, in his " Fifty Years' Recollections," speaks of him as "a man of few words, grave, and I imagine," he adds, "not possessed of much acquired information beyond his art. I remember there were numerous sketches in his gallery, but that of 'Death on the Pale Horse' struck me most as a composition. It was, indeed, of a high character." West's gallery was in the year 1832 converted into a chapel by the Rev. Edward Irving, on his expulsion from the National Scottish Church in Regent Square, Gray's Inn Road.

In 1826, No. 28 was in the occupation of Thomas Stothard, R.A., the designer of the Waterloo shield at Apsley House; and four other royal academicians of lesser note figure in the Royal Blue Book of that year as residents here. In 1836, three of these five R.A.'s have disappeared ; but the name of Copley Fielding, as yet without those mystic letters appended to it, is entered as part occupant of No. 26.

At No. 73 is the Atlas Club. The National Hospital for Diseases of the Heart was for some time located in this street.

In this street is a large public room called St. Andrew's Hall, where lectures on secular and religious subjects are delivered. In 1870 some temporary celebrity was given to it by a man named Newton, who professed to be able to work miraculous cures on all who came to him with a sufficient stock of faith. Numbers of persons responded to his call, most of them being females, of course ; and in some of them faith, or mind, had so great a command over the body and the nervous system, that they went away feeling or regarding themselves as cured. But this strange " popular delusion " soon passed away, and Mr. Newton was forgotten.

At No. 79 is Mr. Heatherley's School of Art, where many, if not most, of the rising artists of the time have made their commencement in artistic practice. It was formerly kept by a Mr. Leigh, who succeeded William Etty, the Royal Academician. Though the artists are " flown to another retreat," yet their aroma still remains in Newman

Street, for half the shops are devoted to the sale of articles subservient to artistic purposes.

Some of the shop-fronts on the north side of Oxford Street about this point are very fanciful and picturesque. At the corner of Berners Street, No. 54, the shop of Messrs. Battam and Co., decorators, has a *Rénaissance* or Elizabethan front, " a picturesque composition of pedestals, consoles, or semi-caryatid figures."

Amid all its bustle and business, Oxford Street has nevertheless had a touch of " the romantic," if a peculiar eccentricity, brought about by disappointment in love affairs, can be called a romance. At all events, we read how a certain Miss Mary Lucrine, a maiden of small fortune, who resided in this street, and who died in 1778, having met with a disappointment in matrimony in early life, vowed that she would " never see the light of the sun ! " Accordingly the windows of her apartments were closely shut up for years, and she kept her resolution to her dying day. It would, of course, be impossible at this distant date to fix with accuracy upon the exact house in which this singular whim of turning day into night was carried out, for, as the lady was merely occupying " apartments," it is probable that her name does not appear on the parish register of ratepayers, and a further search would be profitless.

CHAPTER XXXVI.

OXFORD STREET : NORTHERN TRIBUTARIES.—TOTTENHAM COURT ROAD.

" There is a fiercer crowded misery
In garret-toil and London loneliness
Than in cruel islands in the far-off sea."—*Anon.*

Rathbone Place—Mrs. Mathew and her Literary and Artistic Friends—The " Percy Coffee House" and the " Percy Anecdotes "—Noted Inhabitants of Rathbone Place—Reminiscence of Mr. J. T. Smith—Hanway Street—Jonas Hanway and the Introduction of Umbrellas into England—A Veritable Centenarian—An Ingenious Piece of Glass-painting—The " Oxford" Music Hall—Experiments in Street-paving—Percy Street and Percy Chapel—Charlotte Street—George Morland—The Small-pox Hospital—Tottenham Street—The Prince of Wales's Theatre—St. John's Church—The Hogarth Club—Dressmakers' and Milliners' Association—Fitzroy Square—A Favourite Locality for Artists—Warren Street—Dr. Kitchiner—Whitfield Street—Tottenham Court Road—Tottenham Court Fair—Whitefield's Tabernacle—A Grim Story—An Eccentric Character—" Peg" Fryer, the Actress—The " Blue Posts " Tavern—Dickens' Fondness for Stale Buns.

WE have now fairly turned our backs on the fashionable quarter of London, for a time, at least, and in the last and present chapters find ourselves in quite a different world from that over which we have been travelling ever since we left the neighbourhood of the Strand and the purlieus of Westminster. We no longer move about under the windows of dukes and duchesses, lords and ladies, gay courtiers, or well-dressed wits ; we come back into the midst of a prosaic and work-a-day world— a world which lives in furnished and often in unfurnished lodgings, in garrets and attics, and even in

cellars ; a world which knows more of the interior of the pawnbroker's shop and the gin palace than of a club or a church ; and where poverty is almost hopeless. And yet the view is not all black or dark : intermixed with those low and squalid thoroughfares are some fine streets and handsome squares; there are a few public buildings or private mansions ; but the carriages that roll by, or stand at the doors of some of the residents, are perceptibly fewer ; and, generally speaking, there is about the neighbourhood an air of repose and retirement which contrasts agreeably, in the height of the season, with the bustle which pervades Regent Street, and with what the poet calls—

> " Beatæ
> Fumum et opes strepitumque Romæ."

In this locality have lived and toiled many men who, in after life, have won for themselves names that will remain imperishable in the annals of art and literature ; and some of the streets through which we are about to proceed have been rendered

The above lines, evidently drawn from life, might be applied with equal truth in former times to many a poor struggling artist as to those who wield the pen ; but let us hope that now-a-days, as a rule, genius, whether literary or artistic, is better housed.

Rathbone Place, the first turning to the eastward of Newman Street, perpetuates the name of its builder, a Captain Rathbone, and an inscription on one of the houses, " Rathbone Place, Oxford

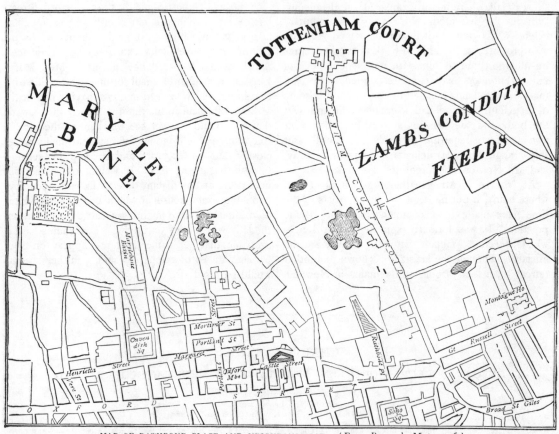

MAP OF RATHBONE PLACE AND NEIGHBOURHOOD. (*From Rocques's Map*, 1746.)

sacred by the early struggles of many an artist who has subsequently reached the highest honours of the Royal Academy.

Few who have read Goldsmith will forget his description of an author's bedchamber in this immediate neighbourhood :—

> " Where the ' Red Lion ' staring o'er the way,
> Invites the passing stranger—that can pay ;
> Where Calvert's butt and Parsons' black champagne
> Regale the drabs and bloods of Drury Lane ;
> There in a lowly room, from bailiffs snug,
> The Muse found Scroggins stretched beneath a rug.
> A window patched with paper lent a ray
> That dimly showed the state in which he lay,
> The sanded floor, that grits beneath the tread,
> And humid walls with paltry pictures spread."

Street, 1718," fixes the date of its erection. As the " Tyburn Road " does not appear to have been generally known as " Oxford Street " till some ten or eleven years later, though occasionally so named in legal documents,* the inscription is the more worthy of being placed on record here. In Ralph Aggas's plan of London, the commencement of this street is designated " The Waye to Uxbridge ; " further on, in the same plan, the highway is called " Oxford Road." In this map cows are represented grazing in a field on the site now occupied by Rathbone Place.

---

* For instance, in the Act of Parliament, in 1678, laying down the boundaries of the new parish of St. Anne's, Soho.

In 1784, according to Mr. J. T. Smith, in his "Book for a Rainy Day," this street consisted entirely of private houses, and its inhabitants were all of high respectability. "I have heard Mrs. Mathew say," he adds, "that the three rebel lords, Lovat, Kilmarnock, and Balmerino, had at different times resided in it."

Mrs. Mathew was the wife of the Rev. Henry Mathew, for whom Percy Chapel, close by, was issued in 1782. We have already spoken of Blake's career in our account of the neighbourhood of Golden Square. In return for the friendly welcome which he always received from Mr. and Mrs. Mathew, Flaxman decorated the walls of their parlour with models of figures in classical and tasteful niches. But these have long since perished.

Rathbone Place has always borne an artistic

EXTERIOR OF THE TOTTENHAM STREET THEATRE, 1830. (*See page* 473.)

built. At their house, towards the close of the last century, used to meet a knot of literary, musical, and artistic celebrities, including Flaxman and William Blake, the long-forgotten artist and poet, who would sometimes recite his verses to the company. Of Blake Mr. Smith predicted, with great judgment, that a day would come when his drawings would be sought after with the most intense avidity, adding that, although little known to the world at large, he was regarded by Flaxman and Stothard with the highest admiration. The prophecy has of late years been fulfilled, and Blake's powers, as an artist and a poet, are now recognised at their true worth. It was through Mr. Mathew's influence, combined with that of Flaxman, that Blake's first volume of poems was reputation, and at present it is the head-quarters of artists' repositories, and of vendors of paints and drawing materials. Mr. Peter Cunningham reminds us in his "Hand-book of London" that "the well-known publication called the 'Percy Anecdotes,' edited by Sholto and Reuben Percy, derives its name from the 'Percy Coffee-house,' in Rathbone Place—now no more—where the idea of the work was first started by two friends, Mr. George Byerley and Mr. Joseph C. Robinson, who assumed the *noms de plume* of the Brothers Percy, of a certain apocryphal monastery." These brothers also wrote a "History of London," in three small volumes; one of them was also editor of the *Mechanics' Magazine* and the other editor of the *Mirror*. Mr. John Timbs, in his "Autobiography," tells us that the idea of the "Percy Anecdotes" was likewise "claimed by Sir Richard Phillips, who stoutly maintained that he suggested to Dr. Tilloch and Mr. Mayne to cut the anecdotes from the many years' files of the *Star* newspaper, of which Dr. Tilloch was then editor, and Mr. Byerley assistant editor; and to the latter over-hearing the suggestion, Sir Richard contended, might the 'Percy Anecdotes' be traced. The *Star* was an evening paper, and well-timed anecdotes were its *spécialité*. Mr. Thomas Boys, the pub-lisher of Ludgate Hill, realised a large sum by the sale of the 'Percy' work; and no inconsiderable portion of its success must be referred to the publisher's taste. The portrait illustrations, mostly engraved by Fry, were admirable. The work had, moreover, this remarkable commendation of Lord Byron, who said, 'No man that has any pretensions to figure in good society can fail to make himself familiar with the 'Percy Anecdotes.'"

Rathbone Place numbered among its residents, in former times, Mr. Nathaniel Hone, R.A., the painter of the picture called the "Conjurer." He died here in 1784. In 1826, Mr. E. H. Baily, R.A., the sculptor, was living here; as also was Mr. Peter De Wint, the water-colour painter. Here lived the learned Baron Maseres, author of the "Scriptores Logarithmici." He died in 1824, at the age of ninety-three. In 1836, all mention of the street is struck out from the "Blue Book." Such is the westward march of fashion.

The locality of Rathbone Place and Windmill Street, which lies immediately to the north of it, is thus mentioned by Mr. J. T. Smith, in "Nolle-kens and his Times:"—

"One day, in a walk with me, Nollekens stopped at the corner of Rathbone Place, and observed that when he was a little boy his mother used often to take him to the top of that street to walk by the side of a long pond near a windmill, which then stood on the site of the chapel in Charlotte Street, and that he recollected that a halfpenny was paid by every person at the hatch belonging to the miller for the privilege of walking in his grounds. He also told me that his mother took him through another 'halfpenny hatch' in the fields between Oxford Street and Grosvenor Square, the northern side of which was then in the course of building. When we got as far as the brew-house, between Rathbone Place and the end of Tottenham Court Road, he told me that he recollected thirteen large and fine walnut-trees standing on the north side of the way, between Hanover Yard and the Castle Inn, a little beyond the Star Brewery."

Passing along Oxford Street for a short distance,

we arrive at Hanway Street, which was originally a zigzag country lane, leading out of the Uxbridge Road into Tottenham Court Road. It was at first, says Mr. J. T. Smith, better known by the vulgar people under the name of "Hanover Yard," and subsequently Hanway Yard, and it was for some time the resort of the highest fashions for mercery, and other articles of dress; and it has continued to this day to be noted for its china-dealers and curiosity shops, as it was in days of yore when high-heeled shoes and stiff brocades were all the rage.

The author of "The Old City," who wrote under the assumed name of "Aleph," and was a native of St. Giles's, remembered this thoroughfare when it was still called Hanway Yard. It was narrow and dirty, and full of old china-shops, including Baldock's, "a sort of museum for Chinese horses and dragons, queer-looking green vases, and doll-sized teacups;" and at the Oxford Street end stood a muffin and crumpet shop, which had about it an air of mystery and romance, as a suspected depository of smuggled goods. Another shop, for the sale of Dutch toys, was kept by an old woman named Patience Flint, a thin, little, shrunken old dame, who dressed in a close-fitting gingham gown, and wore a stiff muslin cap tightly drawn over her forehead. She rarely spoke, but conducted her business by signs, holding up four fingers to denote that the price of a cup or a saucer was fourpence, and scarcely eating, drinking, or sleeping at all. One winter's morning "Aleph" went to the shop, but found it closed, and that the neighbours were about to follow the old woman of Hanway Yard to the burial-ground at St. Pancras. The coffin-plate bore the inscription, "Patience Flint, aged 109 years."

In Hanway Street, in 1808, there was living a certain Mrs. Elizabeth Alexander, aged 106, under a portrait of whom, published in that year, appear the words, "Supposed to be the oldest woman in England."

How Hanway Street came to be so called, we have no definite authority for stating. It may pro-bably have been named after one Jonas Hanway, to whom we are mainly indebted for bringing into general use in England that very necessary article of daily need—in our variable climate, at least—the umbrella. Hanway's name had already become favourably known in London, from his many schemes of benevolence. He originated both the Marine Society and the Magdalen, and, in con-junction with Captain Coram, he was active in pro-moting the foundation of the Foundling Hospital, of which we shall speak in a future chapter. In respect to his courage and perseverance in bringing umbrellas into general use, Hanway was a greater benefactor than at first might be supposed. Gay's poem of "Trivia," it is true, commemorates the earlier use of an umbrella by poor women, "tuck'd-up-sempstresses" and "walking maids;" but even with this class it was a winter privilege, and woe to the woman of a better sort, or to the man, whether rich or poor, who dared at any time so to invade the rights of coachmen and chairmen. But Hanway steadily underwent all the staring, laughing, jeering, hooting, and bullying; and having punished some insolent knaves who struck him with their whips as well as their tongues, he finally succeeded in overcoming the prejudices against it. Jonas made a less successful move when he tried to write down the use of tea.

With reference to the above subject, we quote the following from Chambers's "Book of Days:"—"The eighteenth century was half elapsed before the umbrella had even begun to be used in England by both sexes, as we now see it used. In 1752 Lieutenant-Colonel (afterwards General) Wolfe, writing from Paris, says: 'The people here use umbrellas in hot weather to defend them from the sun, and *something of the same kind to save them from the snow and rain.* I wonder a practice so useful is not introduced in England.' Just about that time a gentleman did exercise the moral courage to use an umbrella in the streets of London. He was the noted Jonas Hanway, newly returned from Persia, and in delicate health, by which, of course, his using such a convenience was justified both to himself and the considerate part of the public. 'A parapluie,' we are told, 'defended Mr. Hanway's face and wig.' For a time no others than the dainty beings called Macaronies ventured to carry an umbrella. Any one doing so was sure to be hailed by the mob as 'a mincing Frenchman.' One John MacDonald, a footman, who has favoured the public with his memoirs, found, as late as 1770, that on appearing with a fine silk umbrella which he had brought from Spain, he was saluted with the cry of 'Frenchman, why don't you get a coach?' It appears, however, as if there had previously been a kind of transition period, during which an umbrella was kept at a coffee-house, liable to be used by gentlemen on special occasions by night, though still regarded as the resource of effeminacy. In the *Female Tatler* of December 12, 1709, there occurs the following announcement: 'The young gentleman belonging to the Custom House, who, in the fear of rain, borrowed the umbrella at Will's Coffee-house, in Cornhill, of the mistress, is hereby advertised that to be dry from head to foot, he shall be welcome to the maid's pattens.' It is a rather early fact in the history of the general use of umbrellas, that in 1758, when Dr. Shebbeare was placed in the pillory, a servant stood beside him with an umbrella to protect him from the weather, physical and moral, which was raging around him. . . . About thirty years ago, there was living in Taunton a lady who recollected when there were but two umbrellas in that town; one belonging to a clergyman, who, on proceeding to his duties on Sunday, hung up the umbrella in the church porch, where it attracted the gaze and admiration of the townspeople coming to church."

We must not, however, be too severe in our censure of the folly of the public in mocking at the use of umbrellas, when we remember in our own day, even so very recently as the beginning of the Crimean War, it was regarded as almost a mark of insanity for a private gentleman to wear a beard.

At No. 15 in Oxford Street, a few doors eastward of Hanway Street, was exhibited, in 1830, a most ingenious piece of glass-painting of the "Tournament of the Field of Cloth of Gold," elaborately worked out from Hall's "Chronicles," and containing upwards of a hundred figures and forty portraits. It cost the designer, a Mr. Wilmhurst, upwards of £3,000, and covered 432 square feet. After it had been exhibited in the metropolis for little more than a year, this painting was accidentally destroyed by fire.

Further eastward, and near the junction of Oxford Street with Tottenham Court Road, is the "Oxford" Music Hall, occupying the site of the old "Boar and Castle Hostelry and Posting House," which dated back to about the year 1620. The "Oxford" was one of the earliest and most popular of the metropolitan music-halls, and the present is the third building of the kind which has occupied the same site, the two previous halls having been destroyed by fire. It consists of a spacious room in the rear of the hotel, facing the street, and to which it is attached; and it has a lofty arched entrance, which, together with the hall itself, is tastefully decorated. The hall is fitted up with a stage, and around the other three sides there is a gallery or balcony. The performances given here consist of selections from popular operas, comic and sentimental singing, glees, duets, &c., with an occasional acrobatic performance.

In 1839 the roadway of Oxford Street was made the subject of some experimental paving. The space between Tottenham Court Road and Charles Street was laid with a dozen different specimens either in wood, stone, bitumen, asphalte, or some other material; the whole, being laid in different patterns, presented a most even and beautiful roadway. The *Mirror* remarks that "the portion to which attention was more particularly directed was that of the wooden blocks, the noiseless tendency of which made the vehicles passing along appear to be rolling over a thick carpet or rug." These experiments being somewhat in advance of the age, and the public taste not being ripe for change, the roadway was suffered to remain unaltered. The subject, in fact, appears at that time to have elicited but little public interest; indeed, one magnate, Sir Peter Laurie, was as strongly resolved to oppose all wood-paving as he was to "put down suicide."

In connection with these experiments, a statement was published by the Marylebone Vestry, which will give the reader some idea of the immense traffic in the streets of London in 1839 :—"On Wednesday, the 16th of January, from six in the morning until twelve at night, by the Pantheon, 347 gentlemen's two-wheel carriages, 935 four-wheel, 890 omnibuses, 621 two-wheel and 752 four-wheel hackney carriages, 91 stage-coaches, 372 wagons and drays, 1,507 light carts and sundries; total, 5,515. By Stafford Place, on Friday, the 18th of January, the total is 4,753, out of which 1,213 were omnibuses; on Tuesday, the 22nd of the same month, by Newman Street, the total was 6,992 ; and on Saturday, by Stafford Place, the total is stated to be 5,943." The number of vehicles passing through Oxford Street at the present time, we need hardly state, is probably double what it was forty years ago, notwithstanding the introduction of underground railways.

Passing from these dry matter-of-fact statements, we may add that this thoroughfare has witnessed some amusing scenes : for instance, the punishment of a Tom and Jerry boy of the older school, as recorded in the *Post Boy* of December 14th, 1747. The culprit, a carpenter, was whipped from the watch-house in Great Marlborough Street to the "Blue Posts" in Poland Street, for stealing the knockers from gentlemen's doors. He had two brass knockers tied round his neck.

A much pleasanter scene, however, was witnessed in Oxford Street, in the early part of 1872, on the occasion of the Prince of Wales returning thanks at St. Paul's Cathedral on his recovery from a dangerous illness. In obedience to the wishes of the inhabitants, the return journey of the Queen and the Royal Family to Buckingham Palace was made by way of Holborn and Oxford Street, and the whole line of route was beautifully decorated with flags and streamers.

At the northern end of Rathbone Place, and

running eastward into Tottenham Court Road, is Percy Street, which is chiefly noticeable on account of the chapel near its western end. The fabric, which is known as Percy Chapel, was erected about 1790 by the Rev. Mr. Mathew, of whom we have spoken above. It was for some years the scene of the pastoral labours of the Rev. Robert Montgomery, the author of "Satan," "Luther," "Oxford," "The Christian Life," "The Omnipresence of the Deity," and other poems, who died in 1855. The article on his poems in "Macaulay's Essays" is probably one of the severest pieces of criticism ever published.

In this street lived the parents of Henry West Betty, "the youthful Roscius," at the time when the child made his first appearance at Covent Garden Theatre, and took the town by storm. We shall have occasion to speak of him further, when we come to Camden Town.

Charlotte Street, the thoroughfare leading from Rathbone Place to Fitzroy Square, was named either after Charlotte, Duchess of Grafton, or after the Queen of George III. Here, in the house formerly occupied by Sir Thomas Apreece, George Morland, the celebrated painter, was living in 1796. Mr. J. T. Smith thus records a visit which he paid him in that year, in company with a generous patron of art and artists, Mr. Wigston:—"He received us in the drawing-room, which was filled with easels, canvases, stretching-frames, gallipots of colour, and oilstones ; a stool, chair, and a three-legged table were the only articles of furniture of which this once splendid apartment could then boast. Mr. Wigston immediately bespoke a picture, for which he gave him a draft for forty pounds, that sum being exactly the money he then wanted ; but this gentleman had, like most of that artist's employers, to ply him close for his picture."

On the east side of Charlotte Street is Windmill Street. Here, in the early part of the reign of George III., the Small Pox Hospital was first established ; it was afterwards removed to King's Cross, and thence to Highgate Rise.

Goodge Street was so called after the speculating builder who erected the houses in it. In 1772, the date of the map in Northouck's "History of London," it appears to have been called Crabtree Street.

Further northward, running parallel with Goodge Street, and crossing Charlotte Street, is Tottenham Street. Here was one of the most fashionable of the London theatres, the Prince of Wales's. The building was originally the concert-room of Signor F. Pasquali, and was purchased and enlarged by the directors of the Concerts of Ancient Music, who built a superb box for George III. and Queen Charlotte. Early in the present century it was fitted up by Colonel Greville for a body of amateur dramatists, called the "Picnics," "whose celebrity," writes Mr. J. Timbs, "rendered them objects of alarm to the professional actors of the day, and exposed them to the attacks of the caricaturist, Gilray." In 1807, or the following year, like the Olympic, it was converted into a sort of circus for equestrian performances, but it never in this respect rivalled Astley's. In 1820 it passed into the hands of Mr. Brunton, whose daughter, Mrs. Yates, was one of its greater stars. The ring had, in due course of time, given place to a pit, which is described, six years later, by Mr. J. R. Planché, as being "about as dark and dingy a den as ever sheltered the children of Thespis." Its out-of-the-way and unfashionable situation, however, did not prevent the "upper ten thousand" from patronising it occasionally.

In some of the earliest bills it is called "The New Theatre," the "King's Ancient Concert Rooms," Tottenham Street; afterwards it took the names of the "Regency," the "Theatre of Varieties," and the "West London," and after the accession of William IV., "The Queen's," out of compliment to Queen Adelaide. An attempt was made, in the year 1831, by Mr. Macfarren, to turn it into a sort of English Opera House, but it was not successful. Two years or so later it acquired a transitory celebrity under the name of "The Fitzroy," as the home of burlesque, and afterwards of French plays. In 1835 it was taken by Mrs. Nesbitt, who re-opened it under its old name of "The Queen's." It was for some time under the management of Madame Vestris; but its career seems to have been anything but flourishing until the year 1865, when it was taken by Miss Marie Wilton (afterwards Mrs. Bancroft), in the joint capacity of lessee and manager, who partly reconstructed the theatre and altered its name to the "Prince of Wales's." On Mrs. Bancroft giving up the management, it was taken in hand by Mr. Edgar Bruce, under whom the theatre continued its popularity till it was finally closed in 1882.

In Charlotte Street, on the east side, between Tottenham and North Streets, is the church of St. John the Evangelist. The edifice, which is in the Norman or Romanesque style, was built from the designs of Hugh Smith, and was consecrated in 1846.

At No. 84 in this street is the "Doric Club." Originally the "Hogarth," it was founded in 1870, and limited to artists, architects, and sculptors. Here *conversazioni* are held during the season, and the pictures and drawings of members are shown

previous to being exhibited publicly at the Royal Academy, the Dudley Gallery, or the Gallery of British Artists.

At No. 98 were the offices of the Association for the Aid and Benefit of Dressmakers and Milliners. This institution, which was founded in 1844, and is now located in Gower Street, provides a home for deserving young persons, and assists them in obtaining employment; it also affords pecuniary and medical aid to those in distress, and almhouses for the aged and decayed.

The erection of Fitzroy Square, which we now enter, was begun about the year 1790. According to Mr. Cunningham, it commemorates the name of Charles Fitzroy, the second Duke of Grafton (whose father, the first duke, was a natural son of King Charles II., by Barbara Villiers, Duchess of Cleveland), to whom the lease of the Manor of Tottenham Court descended in right of his mother, Lady Isabella Bennet, the daughter and heiress of Henry Bennet, Earl of Arlington, one of the five statesmen who composed the "Cabal" Ministry of the above-named king.

In consequence of the stagnation to trade generally, caused by the wars at the close of the last and the beginning of the present centuries, this square remained a long time unfinished, the south and east sides alone being built. In the "Beauties of England and Wales," published in 1815, it is described as "not yet completed. The houses," continues the writer, "are faced with stone, and have a greater portion of architectural embellishment than most others in the metropolis." They were designed by the brothers Adam, already familiar to our readers in connection with the Adelphi and Portland Place.

Between Fitzroy Square and Tottenham Court Road was Fitzroy Market. It consisted of a number of small and dark tenements, and was pulled down in 1875.

The neighbourhood of Fitzroy Square has for a long time been a favourite haunt of painters, no doubt on account of the excellence of the light on the northern side, by reason of the vicinity of the Regent's Park. Indeed, from 1810 to 1830, all the neighbourhood between this square and Oxford Street appears, from an examination of the "Blue Books" and "Court Guides," to have been studded with artists, among whom figure a few R.A.'s, *rari nantes in gurgite vasto.* Among the former, living in Charlotte Street, are the names of Mr. C. L. Eastlake (afterwards President of the Royal Academy), Mr. (afterwards Sir) W. C. Ross, A.R.A., miniature painter to the Queen; in this street, too, lived John Constable, R.A., during the last fifteen years of his life. He died in 1837, and lies buried at Hampstead.

In Russell Place lived Daniel Maclise, the gifted Royal Academician, until a short time before his lamented decease, in 1870, whilst in the zenith of his fame. Maclise was a native of Cork, but settled in London in 1827, and in the following year became a student at the Royal Academy. He became an Associate of the Royal Academy in 1835, and five years later attained the full honours. In 1866, on the death of Sir Charles Eastlake, the presidential chair of the Royal Academy was offered for his acceptance, but was declined. Besides his two large wall-paintings in the new Houses of Parliament—"The Meeting of Wellington and Blucher at Waterloo," and the "Death of Nelson," Maclise will be, perhaps, best remembered by his "Play Scene in *Hamlet*," in the national collection, the "Banquet Scene in *Macbeth*," and the "Vow of the Ladies and the Peacock." One of Mr. Maclise's latest works was "The Earls of Desmond and Ormond," painted in the year of his death. In 1835-6 Mr. Maclise was living in the same neighbourhood, at No. 63, Upper Charlotte Street. At this house a sketching society used often to meet, including Eastlake, Stanfield, David Roberts, Decimus Burton, and the brothers Alfred and John Chalon. They met at each other's rooms, the host of the evening giving out the subject, and an hour was the time allowed for each to work out his conception. When the artists went further a-field into the suburbs, this little coterie broke up. In the "Blue Books" of the period above mentioned there is also a sprinkling of "honourables," and baronets, and knights named as living here; but these have all disappeared when we come to the reign of Victoria.

In London Street, which runs from Cleveland Street into Tottenham Court Road, lived, in 1841, E. W. Wyon, the sculptor, and Miss Chalon, sister

WHITEFIELD'S TABERNACLE, 1820. (*See page* 478.)

THE "ADAM AND EVE" TAVERN, 1750.

THE MANOR HOUSE OF TOTEN HALL. (*From a View published by Wilkinson*, 1813.)

to the brothers Chalon, and herself also an artist of considerable repute. Upper Fitzroy Street, in 1826, had among its residents, Mr. (afterwards Sir) Robert Smirke, R.A., the architect of the General Post Office and other public buildings.

Warren Street, on the north of Fitzroy Square, running parallel to the Euston Road, was so called, probably, after the wife of the first Lord Southampton, Anne, daughter and co-heiress of Admiral Sir Peter Warren. Some of the houses in it have a double frontage. In this street in 1817, and for several years subsequently, resided the celebrated Dr. Kitchiner, author of some works which have made his name widely known—the most celebrated being "The Cook's Oracle," which has passed through several editions. He was the son of a coal merchant residing in Beaufort Buildings, Strand, and was born in 1775. He received his education at Eton, and took his degree at Glasgow ; but as he inherited a good fortune from his father, he did not follow his profession. In Allibone's "Dictionary of English Literature" he is described as "a native of London, celebrated for writing good books and giving good dinners." His hours of rising, eating, and retiring to rest were all regulated by system. His lunches, to which only the favoured few had the privilege of *entrée*, were superb. They consisted of potted meats of various kinds, fried fish, savoury *pâtes*, rich *liqueurs*, &c., in great variety and abundance. His dinners, unless when he had parties, were comparatively plain and simple, served in an orderly manner, cooked according to his own maxims, and placed upon the table invariably within five minutes of the time announced. His public dinners were things of more pomp, ceremony, and etiquette : they were announced by notes of preparation, of which the following will serve as a specimen :—

"Dear Sir,—The honour of your company is requested to dine with the Committee of Taste, on Wednesday next, the 10th inst. The specimens will be placed upon the table at five o'clock precisely, when the business of the day will immediately commence. I have the honour to be your most obedient servant, W. KITCHINER, Secretary.

"At the last general meeting it was unanimously resolved that—1st. An invitation to *Eta, Beta, Pi* must be answered in writing as soon as possible after it is received, within twenty-four hours at latest, reckoning from that on which it is dated, otherwise the secretary will have the profound regret to feel that the invitation has been definitely declined. 2nd. The secretary having represented that the perfection of several of the preparations is so exquisitely evanescent, that the delay of one minute after their arrival at the meridian of concoction will render them no longer worthy of men of taste : therefore, to ensure the punctual attendance of those illustrious gastrophilists who on grand occasions are invited to join this high tribunal of taste for their own pleasure and the benefit of their country, it is irrevocably resolved, ' That the janitor be ordered not to admit any visitor, of whatever eminence of appetite, after the hour which the secretary shall have announced that the specimens are ready.' By order of the Committee, WILLIAM KITCHINER, Secretary."

Dr. Kitchiner possessed an extensive library, for in the introduction to the "Cook's Oracle" he gives a list of the titles of about 217 different books treating of the subject of cookery, all of which, he tells us, he consulted in the preparation of the book above named. Another of his books was entitled, "The Art of Invigorating and Prolonging Life by Food, Clothes, Air, Exercise, Wine, Sleep, &c., and Peptic Precepts," to which is added "The Pleasure of Making a Will." He was likewise a connoisseur in telescopes, and in his "Economy of the Eyes"—a book abounding with many curious facts of great interest to amateur astronomers—he gives a description of fifty-one telescopes, reflecting and achromatic, which he purchased or had made for him during his thirty years' experience as an astronomical amateur, at an expense of more than £2,000. Among other eccentric habits of Dr. Kitchiner which are on record, is one to the effect that it was his practice always to take his own wine with him when he went out to dinner. His will was remarkable for its eccentricity, and it is said that another, making serious alterations in the disposal of his property, was intended for signature on the day following his death, which happened suddenly, on the 26th of February, 1827.

The Euston Road ; Cleveland Street, which runs thence southwards, towards Newman Street ; Grafton Street, which leads from the south-east corner of Fitzroy Square into Tottenham Court Road ; and Southampton Street, which skirts the west side of the square, are all so called after the various family connections of the ducal house of Grafton, and of Lord Southampton.

On the east side of Fitzroy and Charlotte Streets, and running parallel with Tottenham Court Road, is Whitfield Street, so named after the Rev. George Whitfield, or Whitefield, of whom we shall speak on reaching the "Tabernacle" in Tottenham Court Road. Here are two cross streets, bearing the names of Pitt and Lord North respectively, and thereby declaring the date of their erection ; but they are quite barren of incident and history.

Passing through Grafton Street, we enter Tottenham Court Road. This name, like that of Covent Garden, is a popular corruption, sinning, however, rather strangely, by way of elongation instead of abridgment. The country road which, three or four centuries ago, ran northwards from St. Giles's Pound, between green hedges and open fields, was so called from Totten, or Totham, or Totting Hall, the manor-house of which stood at the north-west corner of four cross-ways, on the site of what now is the "Adam and Eve," celebrated in Hogarth's picture in the last century, and of which we shall have to speak in a future chapter. This manor-house, it appears, belonged to one William de Tottenhall, as far back as the reign of Henry III. It is described in "Domesday Book" as belonging to the Dean and Chapter of St. Paul's. After changing hands several times, the manor was leased for ninety-nine years to Queen Elizabeth, when it came popularly to be called Tottenham Court. In the next century it appears to have become the property of the Fitzroys, who erected Fitzroy Square, upon a part of the manor estate, towards the end of the last century; and the property still belongs to the Fitzroys, Lord Southampton. In the map in Northouck's "History of London" (1772), a turnpike-gate is marked at the top of Tottenham Court Road, but this has long since disappeared.

In 1748 Tottenham Court Fair was kept for fourteen days without interruption, but "it does not appear," says Mr. Frost, in his "Old Showmen," "to have been attended by any of the shows which contributed so much to the attractiveness of the fairs of Smithfield and Southwark Green." In fact, although the notices of the fair make mention of a great theatrical booth, it seems to have been devoted rather to wrestling and singlestick than to purely Thespian purposes. These booths were occasionally used for the settlement of "affairs of honour" by means of pugilistic encounters. The challenges were duly announced in the newspapers of the day, in the form of advertisements. Here is one which appeared in 1772:—" Challenge.—I, Elizabeth Wilkinson, of Clerkenwell, having had some words with Hannah Hyfield, and require satisfaction, do invite her to meet me upon the stage, and box me for three guineas; each woman holding half-a-crown in each hand, and the first woman that drops the money to lose the battle." "Answer.—I Hannah Hyfield, of Newgate Market, hearing of the resoluteness of Elizabeth Wilkinson, will not fail, God willing, to give her more blows than words, desiring home blows, and from her no favour; she may expect a good thumping!" The

half-crowns were an ingenious device to prevent scratching. Cock-fighting, bull-baiting, and other "sporting" advertisements, accompany these lady-like diversions.

Mr. J. T. Smith thus writes in his "Book for a Rainy Day:"—"Notwithstanding that Tottenham Court Road was for the most part frequented by persons of the lowest order, who kept in it what they styled a 'Gooseberry Fair,' it was famous at certain seasons, and particularly in the summer, for its booths of regular theatrical performers, who deserted the empty benches of Drury Lane Theatre, under the management of Mr. Fleetwood, and condescended to admit the audience at sixpence a head. Mr. Yates, and other eminent performers, had their names painted on their booths." This must have been about the year 1777.

Tottenham Court Fair appears, from Mr. Frost's "Old Showmen," to have risen into sudden fame and celebrity about the end of George I. or the beginning of George II. Mr. Frost is unable to trace the origin of the fair, but contents himself with telling us that "it began on the 4th of August, and that Lee, Harper, and Petit set up a 'show' in it, behind the 'King's Head,' in the Hampstead Road. The entertainments," he adds, "were *Bateman* and the *Ridolto al fresco*." Of the exact time when this fair was discontinued we have no authority for stating; but the truth is, that when the good people of St. James's ceased to patronise the "Old Showmen," those of Bloomsbury voted them low, and followed in the wake of their wealthier and more aristocratic neighbours.

In a previous chapter we have spoken of the insecurity of these northern districts of the metropolis in the last century, in consequence of the numerous bands of highwaymen infesting the locality; and in the *London Magazine* we read that as lately as 1773 two prisoners were sentenced to death at Newgate for robbing a gentleman and his wife near Tottenham Court turnpike.

The vicinity of Tottenham Court Road, being near to the Middlesex Hospital, appears to have enjoyed an unenviable notoriety as a depository for dead bodies. At all events, Hunter tells us, in his "History of London," that in 1776 the town was startled by the discovery of the remains of more than a hundred corpses in a shed hereabouts, which were "supposed to have been deposited there by traders to the surgeons, many of whom, especially in the Borough, were known to have made an open profession of this traffic."

On the west side of the road, between Tottenham and Howland Streets, is Tottenham Court Chapel, or, as it is generally called, "Tabernacle."

It was designed by the Rev. George Whitefield, the eloquent colleague and fellow-worker of John Wesley. The immediate cause of its erection was the opposition which he met with, as minister of a chapel in Long Acre, from the Vicar of St. Martin's-in-the-Fields, who had no sympathy with the new "Evangelical" doctrines. Hindered thus in his ministry, he obtained from the Fitzroys a lease of a plot of ground in what was then called, in maps and surveys, "The Crab and Walnut-tree Field," close to a pond known as "The Little Sea," on the road which ran from St. Giles's Church to the "Adam and Eve Tavern." In writing to his patroness, the Countess of Huntingdon, Whitefield says, "I have taken a piece of ground not far from the Foundling Hospital whereon to build a new chapel." When he built it, he desired to place it within the pale of the Established Church, and had hoped to have done so all the more easily on account of his position as chaplain to a peeress of the realm; but in this he was disappointed. He sailed, however, as near to the model of the English Church worship as the law allowed him. The foundation-stone was laid in May, 1756, Mr. Whitefield himself preaching on the occasion. It was a large but plain double-brick building, seventy feet square, and capable of holding a large congregation; over the door, we are told, were the arms of Mr. Whitefield. But the preacher was so popular that the edifice had soon to be enlarged; and three or four years later an octagonal front was added, which gave it a singular appearance. Twelve alms-houses and a chapel-house soon grew up by its side, all the result of private subscriptions among the adherents of "Evangelicalism." Indeed, so celebrated was Mr. Whitefield as an orator that he numbered among his occasional hearers the Prince of Wales and several of his brothers and sisters, Lords Chesterfield, Halifax, and Bolingbroke; also David Hume, Horace Walpole, and David Garrick. Ned Shuter, the actor, also, who was acting the *Rambler* at the time, came in one day, when Whitefield, turning to him, implored that in the course of his wanderings he might be led to "ramble" towards his Saviour. Shuter was struck at the unexpected attack on himself, and expostulated with the preacher, but in the end he became a Methodist. Whitefield died in America, in September, 1770, and his funeral sermon was preached here by John Wesley. There is in the chapel a monument to George Whitefield, and another to his wife, who was buried here. There is another to Augustus Toplady, author of the well-known hymn "Rock of ages, cleft for me." John Bacon, R.A., the sculptor, is buried under the north

gallery. The chapel was satirically called by the opponents of the new doctrines, Whitefield's "soul-trap;" on which the latter merely said, "I pray that God may make it indeed a soul-trap to many of his wandering creatures." Whitefield was also burlesqued by Samuel Foote, on the stage of old Drury Lane, in *The Minor* and *The Hypocrite*. This, however, provoked him no further than to observe, with a smile, "I am afraid Satan is angry." There are few anecdotes told in favour of Foote's magnanimity; but one deserves to be recorded. The epilogue to his farce of *The Minor* contained a burlesque of the style and manner of the well-known preacher, under the title of "Dr. Squintem." During the run of the farce it happened that White-field died. The epilogue was withdrawn. On its being loudly called for by the audience, Foote came forward, and said that he was incapable of holding up the dead to ridicule.

Following in the wake of the great preachers of the previous century—South and Barrow—and in a style which was afterwards copied by Rowland Hill at the Surrey Chapel, and by one or two preachers even in the present day, Mr. Whitefield increased his popularity by using eccentric terms and modes of expression in his sermons, and by reference to commonplace and trivial matters. In fact, his discourses often sparkled with wit and fun. Both Whitefield and Wesley contrived, as the Established Church disclaimed their acts, to disown and to defy its authority in turn, and therefore they gradually found themselves forced to take up the position of Nonconformists and Dissenters. A man of superhuman energy and power, John Wesley has been able to exercise the widest influence over the English-speaking race. Macaulay observes of him that "his genius for government and organisation was not inferior to that of Cardinal Richelieu," and others have compared him with St. Ignatius Loyola.

It is recorded in the *Gentleman's Magazine* that during a violent thunder-storm which passed over London, on Sunday, March 15, 1772, a man was killed by the lightning in this chapel. The electric fluid penetrated the roof just over the man's head, and entering a little above his breast, pierced his heart. He had two children by him at the time, neither of whom received the least hurt.

It is said that Whitefield wished to have the ground adjoining consecrated as a burial-ground, but that the Bishop of London refusing to perform the ceremony, he obtained several cart-loads of consecrated earth from a churchyard in the City, conveyed them hither, and spread them over the adjacent surface, which he thenceforth regarded as sacred. How deep the consecration went downwards was a question he did not even attempt to decide.

It would appear that the ministers of the two chapels in Tottenham Court Road and Moorfields often preached alternately in these edifices. At any rate, the eccentric Matthew Wilks, who was minister at Moorfields from 1775 to 1829, is stated to have had the oversight of the two chapels.

On the expiration of Whitefield's lease, in 1828, the chapel was closed for two years, when it was purchased by trustees, and greatly altered in its appearance, the exterior being coated with stucco. About the year 1860 the fabric was enlarged and re-fronted with stone.

There were persons living in 1832, as is clear from a letter published at that date in Hone's "Year Book," who "remembered when the last house in London was the public-house in the corner, by Whitefield's Chapel." The writer remarks that he himself remembered the destruction of a tree which once shadowed the skittle-ground and roadside of the same house. It was cut down and converted into firewood by a man who kept a coal-shed hard by. Persons living at the above date could recollect Rathbone Place ending at Percy Street, and the mill still in position which gave its name to Windmill Street, and the neighbourhood of Charlotte Street being occupied by large open soil-pits. The writer above referred to tells the following grim story about this neighbourhood:—"A poor creature, a sailor, I believe, was found dead near here, and denied burial by the parish on the ground of a want of legal settlement. The body was placed in a shell and carried about the streets by persons who solicited alms for its interment. A considerable sum was collected, but the body was thrown into one of those pits, the money being spent in other ways. After a time the corpse floated, and the atrocity was discovered, but the perpetrators were not to be found. A friend of mine," he adds, "saw the fragments of the coffin floating about on the surface of the pool."

At "King John's Palace," a public-house in this street, lived an eccentric character named Shooter. He had been pot-boy at a tavern in Covent Garden, and became on such friendly terms with the rats in the cellars of the house, by giving them sops from his porter—for at that time everybody, if he liked, might have a bit of toast in his beer—that they would creep about him, and over his hands and face, without fear and without injury. He would carry them about the streets between his shirt and his waistcoat, to the surprise of every one, and even make them answer to their names. Later in life he became a Methodist, through listening to the preaching of Wesley and Whitefield.

Tottenham Court Road in the present day is one of the busiest thoroughfares in London, and can boast of several monster commercial establishments, notably among them being those of Messrs. Moses and Son, outfitters, at the corner of the Euston Road; Messrs. Shoolbred and Co., linen-drapers; and Messrs. Hewetson and Milner, upholsterers. At No. 216 are the offices of the North London Consumption Hospital, of which we shall speak on reaching Hampstead, where the hospital itself is situated.

This thoroughfare being of comparatively recent growth, there is but little to say in the way of anecdote connected with it. Here "Peg" Fryer, a wonderful old actress, who quitted the stage in the reign of Charles II., kept a public-house in her latter days. A farce called the *Half-pay Officer*, by Charles Molloy, was brought out at Drury Lane Theatre in 1720; and to Mrs. Fryer, then eighty-five years of age, was assigned the part of an old grandmother. In the bills it was mentioned:—"The part of 'Lady Richlove' to be performed by Peg Fryer, who has not appeared on the stage these fifty years." The character in the farce was supposed to be a very old woman, and Peg exerted her utmost abilities. The farce being ended, she was brought again upon the stage to dance a jig. She came tottering in, and seemed much fatigued; but on a sudden, the music striking up the Irish trot, she danced and footed it almost as nimbly as any girl of twenty. She resided in Tottenham Court Road until her decease, which took place in 1747, at the reputed age of 117 years.

The "Blue Posts," a tavern still standing at the corner of Hanway Street and Tottenham Court Road, says Mr. J. T. Smith, in his "Book for a Rainy Day," "was once kept by a man of the name of Sturges, deep in the knowledge of chess, upon which game he published a little work, as is acknowledged on his tombstone in St. James's burial-ground, Hampstead Road."

Charles Dickens, as a boy, when living at Camden Town, and acting as a drudge at the blacking shop at Hungerford Stairs, used to frequent the second-class pastry-cooks along this route, and spend his coppers on stale buns at half-price.

At the southern extremity of the road, where it joins Oxford Street, and on the west side, are three or four isolated houses, the little foot-passage behind which is called Bozier's Court. They stand on what was waste land adjoining the old Pound. The removal of these old houses has been often threatened, but never carried into effect.

THE FIELD OF THE FORTY FOOTSTEPS. (*From an Original Sketch, taken in* 1830.)

CHAPTER XXXVII.

BLOOMSBURY.—GENERAL REMARKS.

" By thee transported, I securely stray
Where winding alleys lead the doubtful way ;
The silent court and opening square explore,
And long perplexing lanes untrod before."—*Gay's "Trivia."*

The Locality a Century ago—A Pair of Eccentric Old Maids—The Field of Forty Footsteps—A Singular Superstition—Street Brawls and Roysterers—The Game of Base—Bloomsbury deserted by the Aristocracy—Albert Smith's Remarks on this once Patrician Quarter of London—The "Rookery," or "Holy Land"—Meux's Brewery—The "Horse-shoe" Tavern, New Oxford Street—The Royal Arcade—George Street—Bainbridge and Buckeridge Streets—The "Turk's Head"—Old Dyot Street—"Rat's Castle"—The "Hare and Hounds," originally called "The Beggar's Bush"—A Dangerous Locality—Model Lodging Houses in Streatham Street—Bloomsbury and Duke Streets—Mudie's Library—Museum Street—Great Russell Street.

THE district now known under the general name of Bloomsbury lies on the north side of Holborn, stretching away as far as the Euston Road, and is bounded to the east and west respectively by Gray's Inn Road and Tottenham Court Road. It was originally called Lomsbury, or Lomesbury, and the manor and village are said to have occupied the site of Bloomsbury Square and the surrounding streets. At the time when Lomesbury was a retired village, the royal mews, an establishment for horses and also for hawks, stood here ; but on these stables being burnt down, in 1537, the hawks and steeds were removed to the stabling at Charing Cross, which was altered and enlarged for their reception. "Indeed," remarks Mr. Jesse, in his

work on London, "as late as the middle of the last century it (the mews) would seem to have been still kept up as a branch of the royal stables."

Of this neighbourhood, about the year 1685, Macaulay writes thus in his "History of England :"—"A little way north from Holborn, and on the verge of pastures and corn-fields, rose two celebrated palaces, each with an ample garden. One of them, then called Southampton House, and subsequently Bedford House, was removed early in the present century to make room for a new city which now covers, with its squares, streets, and churches, a vast area renowned in the seventeenth century for peaches and snipes. The other, known as Montagu House, celebrated for its furniture and its frescoes, was, a few months after the death of King Charles II., burned to the ground, and was speedily succeeded by a more magnificent Montagu House, which, having long been the repository of such various and precious treasures of art, science, and learning as were scarce ever before country, the only buildings that met the eye in the interval being Whitefield's Chapel, in Tottenham Court Road, and Baltimore House, which, as we shall see presently, now forms one of the mansions in Russell Square.

Mr. Smith also remarks that when he was a boy

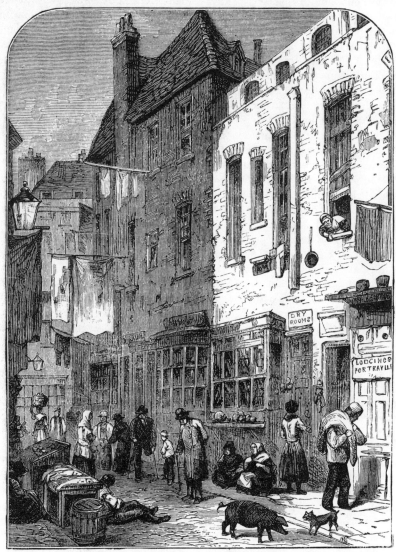

THE "ROOKERY," ST. GILES'S, 1850. (*See page* 484.)

assembled under a single roof, has since given place to an edifice more magnificent still." The building here referred to, we need hardly remark, is the British Museum.

Nor was Bloomsbury only an isolated village, but it was quite rural in its retirement. Mr. Smith tells us, in his "Book for a Rainy Day," that in 1777, when he went on a sketching excursion to St. Pancras Churchyard, the whole of the space between that spot and the British Museum was open

—that is, about 1774—"the ground behind the north-west end of Great Russell Street was occupied as a farm by two old maiden sisters named Capper. They wore riding-habits and men's hats; one rode an old grey mare, and it was her spiteful delight to ride with a pair of shears after the boys who were flying their kites, in order to cut their strings. The other sister's business was to seize the clothes of the lads who trespassed on their premises to bathe. From Capper's farm were several straggling houses ; but the principal part of the ground to the 'King's Head,' at the end of the road, was unbuilt upon. The 'Old King's Head,' opposite to the 'Adam and Eve,' forms a side object in Hogarth's celebrated picture of 'The March to Finchley,' which may be seen, with other fine specimens of art, in the Foundling Hospital."

The whole of the ground north of Capper's farm, so often mentioned as frequented by duellists, was in irregular patches, and many of the fields had turnstiles. The pipes of the New River Company were propped up in several parts to the height of six and eight feet, so that persons walked under them to gather watercresses, which grew in great abundance and perfection, or to visit "The Brothers' Steps," or "Field of the Forty Footsteps."

Dr. E. F. Rimbault, in *Notes and Queries*, gives the following particulars of these remarkable footprints, and of the locality in which they were situated :—" The fields behind Montagu House were, from about the year 1680, until towards the end of the last century, the scenes of robbery, murder, and every species of depravity and wickedness of which the heart can think. They appear to have been originally called the 'Long Fields,' and afterwards (about Strype's time) the 'Southampton Fields.' These fields remained waste and useless, with the exception of some nursery grounds near the New Road to the north, and a piece of ground enclosed for the Toxophilite Society, towards the north-west, near the back of Gower Street. The remainder was the resort of depraved wretches, whose amusements consisted chiefly in fighting pitched battles, and other disorderly sports, especially on Sundays. Such was their state in 1800. Tradition had given to the superstitions at that period a legendary story of the period of the Duke of Monmouth's Rebellion, of two brothers, who fought in this field so ferociously as to destroy each other ; since which their footsteps, formed from the vengeful struggle, were said to remain, with the indentations produced by their advancing and receding ; nor could any grass or vegetable ever be produced where these *forty footsteps* were thus displayed. This extraordinary area was said to be at the extreme termination of the north-east end of Upper Montagu Street. . . . . The latest account of these footsteps, previous to their being built over, with which I am acquainted, is the following, which I have extracted from one of Joseph Moser's Common-place Books :—'June 16, 1800. Went into the fields at the back of Montagu House, and there saw, for the last time, the *forty footsteps ;* the building materials are there ready to cover them from the sight of man. I counted *more than forty*, but they might be the foot-prints of the workmen.' This extract is valuable, as it establishes the period of the final obliteration of the footsteps, and also confirms the legend that *forty* was the original number."

The story is also recorded in Southey's "Common-place Book,"* where, after quoting a letter from a friend, recommending him to "take a view of those wonderful marks of the Lord's hatred to *duelling*, called *The Brothers' Steps*," the author thus records his visit to the spot :—" We sought for nearly half an hour in vain. We could find no steps at all within a quarter of a mile, no, nor half a mile of Montagu House. We were almost out of hope, when an honest man, who was at work, directed us to the next ground, adjoining to a pond. There we found what we sought, about three-quarters of a mile north of Montagu House, and 500 yards east of Tottenham Court Road. The steps are of the size of a large human foot, about three inches deep, and lie nearly from north-east to south-west. We counted only seventy-six ; but we were not exact in counting. The place where one or both the brothers are supposed to have fallen is still bare of grass. The labourer also showed us the bank where (the tradition is) the wretched woman sat to see the combat." Mr. Southey then speaks of his full confidence in the tradition of their indestructibility, even after ploughing up, and of the various conclusions to be drawn from the circumstance.

In the third edition of the "Book for a Rainy Day" appears the following note upon the above mysterious spot :—" Of these steps there are many traditionary stories ; the one generally believed is, that two brothers were in love with a lady, who would not declare a preference for either, but coolly sat upon a bank to witness the termination of a duel which proved fatal to both. The bank, it is said, on which she sat, and the footmarks of the brothers when pacing the ground, never produced grass again. The fact is," adds the writer, "that these steps were so often trodden that it was impossible for the grass to grow. I have frequently passed over them ; they were in a field on the site of Mr. Martin's Chapel, or very nearly so, and not on the spot as communicated to Miss Porter, who has written an entertaining novel on the subject." It may be added here that at Tottenham Street Theatre (afterwards the Prince of Wales's), about the year 1830, was produced an effective melodrama, by the Brothers Mayhew, founded upon the same incident, entitled the *Field of Forty Footsteps*.

* See First Series, Vol. I., p. 217.

Apart from the air of superstition which seems to have settled round the remarkable footprints spoken of above, the Long Fields had, from a much earlier period, been associated with superstitious notions, for Aubrey tells us, that on the eve of St. John Baptist's (Midsummer) Day, in 1694, he saw, at midnight, twenty-three young women in " the parterre behind Montagu House, looking for a coal, under the root of a plantain, to put under their heads that night, and they should dream who would be their future husbands." The superstition, we may here remark, is a very ancient one, and not confined to London or even to England, and is probably connected with the fire and serpent worship, which came at an early date into Europe from the East. But this is a matter foreign to the subject in hand.

The street brawls which disgraced the times of our later Stuart sovereigns frequently ended in a duel on this spot. In the days of Charles II., when there was next to no pavement, and when among the population of London there were so many strange characters that the peaceful way-farer was obliged to pick his steps with circum-spection, and be ready for conflict at the turning of every alley, each passer-by endeavoured to take the wall, and this gave rise to numerous quarrels. Indeed, as Macaulay tells us, " if two roysterers met, they cocked their hats in each other's faces, and pushed each other about till the weaker was shoved into the kennel. If he was a mere bully he sneaked off, muttering that he should find a time. If he was pugnacious, the encounter pro-bably ended in a duel behind Montagu House. The mild and timid gave the wall; the bold and athletic took it."

Occasionally, however, this neighbourhood wit-nessed encounters of a less sanguinary nature. "About the year 1770," writes Strutt, in his " Sports and Pastimes," " I saw a grand match at base (Prisoner's Base) played in the fields behind Montagu House and the British Museum, by twelve gentlemen of Cheshire against twelve of Derbyshire, for a considerable sum of money, which afforded much entertainment to the spec-tators." The game, we may add, is described in detail by Strutt in the chapter from which we make our quotation.

At the above period the grounds at the back of Montagu House were open to the fields extending to Lisson Grove and Paddington ; north, to Prim-rose Hill, Chalk Farm, Hampstead, and Highgate ; and east, to Battle Bridge, Islington, St. Pancras, &c. The north side of Queen Square was left open that it might not impede the prospect. Dr.

Stukeley, many years Rector of St. George's Church, describes (in his MS. diary, 1749) the then sylvan character of Queen Square and its neighbourhood. On the side of Montagu Gardens, next Bedford Square, was a fine grove of lime-trees ; and the gardens of Bedford House, which occupied the north side of the present Bloomsbury Square, reached those of Montagu House. "We can, therefore," adds Dr. Rimbault, " understand how, a century and a half since, coachmen were regaled with the ' perfume of the flower-beds of the gardens belonging to the houses in Great Russell Street,' which then enjoyed 'wholesome and pleasant air.' Russell Square was not built until the year 1804, although Baltimore House was erected in 1763 ; the latter appears to have been the only erection made in this neighbourhood from the publica-tion of Strype's ' Survey' down to this period, with the exception of a chimney-sweeper's cottage, still further north, and part of which is still to be seen in Rhodes's Mews, Little Guildford Street. In 1800 Bedford House was demolished entirely, with its offices and gardens ; this house had been the home where the noble family of the South-amptons and the illustrious Russells had resided during more than 200 years."[*] About the middle of the last century, when the gardens of Gray's Inn became deserted by the beaux and belles of that period, those at the back of Montagu House became for a time fashionable as a lounge and promenade.

Where Euston Square is now, in the year 1820 was a large nursery garden, in which the children of privileged neighbours were glad to be allowed to take their morning walk and to play. There is extant a small print, by Corbould, published in the first decade of this century, showing the distant and quite rustic view of Primrose Hill, and Hampstead with its spire beyond, taken from the top of Woburn Place. In the foreground is a rustic wooden bridge, and a little further off, as nearly as possible where is now the terminus of the London and North-Western Railway, stands a small group of farm-buildings quite isolated.

No doubt the district at present under notice cannot be regarded as fashionable ; it is too near to St. Giles's to have much in common with the courtly region of St. James's. It nevertheless in-cludes within its area as great a number of com-modious dwellings around open spaces as can be met with in any other spot of similar dimensions within the scope of the Registrar-General's func-tions. When we remember that this was, until no

_____

[*] Quoted from John Timbs's "Romance of London."

very distant date, an aristocratic part of London, it is not surprising that the associations which cluster around it, from the memory of great and eminent men, are as abundant and interesting as its claims to be still considered one of the most convenient and sanitary divisions of the modern Babel are well founded. This particular quarter, more especially about Bedford and Russell Squares, appears to have been a highly favoured one with " gentlemen of the long robe ; " indeed, those two squares have had more than a fair share of judicial occupants. Like those parts of the metropolis lying eastward of Temple Bar, this neighbourhood, when once deserted by the wealthier classes, came to be looked upon by them—or some, at least—with a sort of reproachful feeling; indeed, as a witty writer has observed, the very absence of knowledge of its locality " was accounted a mark of high breeding," and this notion was once forcibly illustrated by Mr. Croker's inquiry in the House of Commons, " But where *is* Russell Square ? " *Apropos* of this joke, another may be told, how that a nobleman once commissioned his son to go into the City for him to transact some business, and rung for his carriage to convey the young gentleman. " The City ? the City ? my lord ? " he said, inquiringly ; " I've been told that is a dreadful way off; where shall I change horses ? "

" It is very curious," writes Albert Smith, " to speculate as to what part of England will ultimately be the West-end of London—no less than to watch the gradual progress that the apparent desire of the fashionable world to get still nearer the sunset has made in that direction for many years. Keeping within the recollection of old inhabitants still extant, we find that the anomalous neighbourhood between the Foundling Hospital and Red Lion Square, north and south, and Gray's Inn Lane and Bloomsbury, east and west, was once the patrician quarter of London. The houses, even in their decay of quality, have a respectable look. Their style of architecture is *passé*, it is true ; but they evidently make a great struggle to keep up appearances. If chance leads you into them, you will find that they are all similarly appointed, even to their inhabitants. All the furniture is rubbed up to the last degree of friction polish, and the carpets are brushed cleanly threadbare. The window-curtains, blanched in the sun of thirty or forty summers, until their once crimson hue has paled to a doubtful buff; the large semi-circular fireplace, with its brass-handled poker and latticed fender ; the secretary and large flap-table, on which is the knife-case with its forlorn single leaf, or shell, in *marqueterie* on the cover—all remain as they

were. Even the ancient landladies have given the same conservative care to their flaxen fronts and remarkable caps. They are grave and dignified in their demeanours, for they believe Great Ormond Street still to be the focus of the West-end. It is long since they have been out to learn to the contrary : left stationary, whilst time has flown by them, like an object in the tranquil side-water of a stream, whilst similar ones are hurried past with the torrent, they still regard Russell and Bedford Squares as their *Belgravia*—for at every epoch all fashionable parts of town had an ultra-aristocratic neighbourhood. So, when the superior classes still moved on towards the west, colonising Percy and Newman Streets and the old thoroughfares about Soho, then Fitzroy and Golden Squares were in turn looked up to with respect."

Of that part of Bloomsbury which lies between New Oxford Street and High Street and Broad Street we have already spoken in our account of St. Giles's.* The parish of St. George's is co-extensive with what used to be called the Bloomsbury side of St. Giles's-in-the-Fields ; in other words, with that part of the parish which lay to the north of the old line of Holborn. What is now called " Broad Street, Bloomsbury," still forms part of St. Giles's parish, and of old was called by its proper name of " Broad Street, St. Giles's." Even at the commencement of the present century, the scene which the said " High Street " presented was not very inviting. On both sides of the way were rows of chandlers' shops, low public-houses, cook-shops —or rather cellars—for the accommodation of the poorer Irish, who even then formed a colony here before what was called " the ruins " of St. Giles's were cleared away, and the site devoted to broad and spacious streets. This " colony " was generally known as " The Rookery," but it was also called the " Holy Land " and " Little Dublin," on account of the number of Irish who resided there. It is true, although the place bore anything but a reputable name, some of its residents were honestly employed, even in the humblest walks of industry. Of the inhabitants of the " Holy Land " there was, at least, a floating population of 1,000 persons who had no fixed residence, and who hired their beds for the night in houses fitted up for the purpose. Some of these houses had each fifty beds, if such a term can be applied to the wretched materials on which their occupants reposed ; the usual price was sixpence for a whole bed, or fourpence for half a one ; and behind some of the houses there were cribs littered with straw, where the wretched might

---

* See Vol. III., p. 206, &c.

sleep for threepence. In one of the houses seventeen persons have been found sleeping in the same room, and these consisting of men and their wives, single men, single women, and children. Several houses frequently belonged to one person, and more than one lodging-house-keeper amassed a handsome fortune by the mendicants of St. Giles's and Bloomsbury. The furniture of the houses was of the most wretched description, and no persons but those sunk in vice, or draining the cup of misery to its very dregs, could frequent them. In some of the lodging-houses breakfast was supplied to the lodgers, and such was the avarice of the keeper, that the very loaves were made of a diminutive size in order to increase his profits. Yet amidst so much wretchedness, there was much of wanton extravagance; and those who might have traversed the purlieus of the "Holy Land" on a Saturday night, must have felt convinced that the money squandered away in dissipation would have procured much daily comfort both in bed and board. But the extravagance of beggars is proverbial; and an anecdote is related of old Alderman Calvert going in disguise to one of their suppers, and being much alarmed at hearing some of them ordering an "alderman in chains," until he learnt from the landlord that it was but another name for a turkey and sausages.

At the angle of Tottenham Court Road and New Oxford Street stands the celebrated brewery of Messrs. Meux and Company, one of the largest in London. It was founded early in the reign of George III., by Messrs. Blackburn and Bywell, whose name it bore until Mr. Henry Meux, at that time a partner in the brewery of Messrs. Meux, in Liquorpond Street, joined the firm. He was a cousin of Lord Brougham, and was created a baronet by William IV., in 1831.

The brewery covers nearly four acres, and its interior arrangements are well worth a visit. The stranger is shown over several ranges of buildings, each devoted to some one process or other, by which ale, porter, and stout are manufactured. These we shall not attempt to describe, but will simply state that the brewery contains seven or eight huge vats, one of which holds 1,500 barrels of liquid, and others hold 1,000 or 900. It is said that the firm employ some 150 hands and fifty horses, and that they turn out of their manufactory not very much less than half a million of barrels yearly. The demand for ales, it may be interesting to learn, is steadily on the increase, while that for the dark-coloured liquids shows a slight tendency to diminish.

It may not be out of place here to state the

circumstances under which London "porter" came to be so called. Prior to the year 1722 the malt liquors in general use were ale, beer, and "twopenny," and it was customary for the drinkers of malt liquors to call for a pint or tankard of half and half—*i.e.*, half of ale and half of beer, half of beer and half of twopenny. In course of time it also became the practice to call for a pint or tankard of three-threads, meaning a third of ale, beer, and twopenny, and thus the publican had the trouble to go to three casks and turn three cocks for a pint of liquor. To avoid this trouble and waste, a brewer of the name of Harwood conceived the idea of making a liquor which should partake of the united flavours of ale, beer, and twopenny. He did so, and succeeded, calling it "entire," or entire butt beer, meaning that it was drawn entirely from one cask or butt; and being a hearty, nourishing liquor, it was very suitable for porters and other working people. Hence it obtained its name of "porter."

In 1816 this brewery was attacked by a London mob, who were anxious to wreak upon it—why or wherefore is not clear—their dislike of Lord Liverpool and Lord Sidmouth, and the rest of the Tory ministers.

Adjoining the entrance to Messrs. Meux and Co.'s Brewery is the "Horse-shoe Tavern," so called from the shape of its original dining-room—a shape doubtless assumed for a reason which will presently appear. By absorbing the adjoining premises, and erecting large additions, the modest tavern has lately grown into a monster hotel, where the *table d'hôte* system has been introduced, on a plan similar to that which we have mentioned in our account of the "Langham."

The sign of the "Horse-shoe," though common in combination with other subjects, as Mr. Larwood tells us, in his "History of Sign-boards," is rarely found by itself. Its adoption here is due, doubtless, to the large horse-shoes nailed up at the entrance of Meux's Brewery, and conspicuous both on the trappings of the dray-horses of that establishment, and also as the trade-mark of the firm. There was formerly, and perhaps may be still, a "Horseshoe Tavern" on Tower Hill, and another in Drury Lane, because it is mentioned in connection with Lord Mohun's attempt on Mrs. Bracegirdle,* as the place where he and his comrades drank a bottle of sack while they lay in wait for that lady. It is also mentioned by Aubrey, in his "Anecdotes and Traditions," as the scene of a bloody duel. The horse-shoe, from its pronged shape, was regarded

---

* See Vol. III., p. 82.

MESSRS. MEUX'S BREWERY, 1830. (See page 485.)

in the Middle Ages as a potent charm against witchcraft. Thus Robert Herrick writes :—

" Hang up hooks and speres to scare
Hence the hag that rides the mare ! "

There is, or was till lately, a " Horse and Horse-shoe Tavern " in Great Titchfield Street.

New Oxford Street, which we now enter, extends from the corner of Tottenham Court Road to Bury Place, where it forms a junction with High Holborn.

George Street, crossing New Oxford Street, and leading from Great Russell Street to Broad Street, was formerly known as Dyot Street, being so called after one Richard Dyot, a parishioner of St. Giles's, in the reign of Charles II., and possibly a man of considerable importance at that time. Bainbridge and Buckeridge Streets were built prior to 1672, and were named after their respective owners ; of these streets the latter disap-

ENCAMPMENT IN THE GARDENS OF MONTAGU HOUSE, 1780.   (*See page* 493.)

It runs through what once was the thickest part of St. Giles's " Rookery," and was opened in 1847. Many of the houses, particularly on the north side, have a pleasing appearance, built as they are of red brick and stone dressings, in the domestic Tudor and Louis XIV. style of architecture, whilst some of the house-fronts are of Ionic and Corinthian character. In about the centre is what is called the Royal Arcade, a glass-roofed arcade of shops extending along the rear of four or five of the houses, and having an entrance from the street at each end. The shops here are mostly confined to the sale of drapery and haberdashery. This arcade was opened about 1852, with great expectations, but it never " took " with the public, and is almost unknown and unnoticed.

peared in the general clearance which was effected in the formation of New Oxford Street. In old Dyot Street was a public-house called the " Turk's Head," where Haggarty and Holloway, in November, 1802, planned the murder of Mr. Steele, on Hounslow Heath, and to which they returned after the murder. It may be here mentioned that at the execution of the murderers at the Old Bailey twenty-eight people were crushed to death. " Rat's Castle " was another rendezvous in Dyot Street for some of the vilest denizens and outcasts of the " Rookery." The Rev. T. Beames, in his " Rookeries of London," in speaking of this famous thieves' public-house, says : " In the ground floor was a large room, appropriated to the general entertainment of all comers ; in the first floor, a free-and-easy, where dancing and singing went on during the greater part of the night, suppers were laid, and the luxuries which tempt to intoxication freely displayed. The frequenters of this place were bound together by a common tie, and they spoke openly of incidents which they had long since ceased to blush at, but which hardened habits of crime alone could teach them to avow." In our account of the beggars of St. Giles's we have already mentioned one curious character, "Old Simon," who used to take up his quarters in this den of infamy,* appearing in the street near the church in the daytime.

During the improvements which were effected about the year 1844-5, when the greater part of the "Rookery," or the "Holy Land," was swept away, one at least of the houses which disappeared had a history of its own. This was a public-house called the "Hare and Hounds." It stood nearly in the centre of what is now New Oxford Street, and, says Mr. Jacob Larwood, in his "History of Sign-boards," "it was one of those places associated with 'the good old customs of our ancestors.'" "The 'Hare and Hounds,'" writes Mr. Richardson in his "Recollections of the Last Half Century," "was to be reached by those going from the West-end towards the City, by going up a turning on the left hand, nearly opposite St. Giles's Churchyard. The entrance to this turning or lane was obstructed or defended by posts with cross bars, which being passed, the lane itself was entered. It extended some twenty or thirty yards towards the north, through two rows of the most filthy, dilapidated, and execrable buildings that could be imagined; and at the top or end of it stood the citadel, of which 'Stunning Joe' was the corpulent castellan. I need not say that it required some determination and some address to gain this strange place of rendezvous. Those who had the honour of an introduction to the great man were considered safe, wherever his authority extended, and in this locality it was certainly very extensive. He occasionally condescended to act as a pilot through the navigation of the alley to persons of aristocratic or wealthy pretensions, whom curiosity, or some other motive best known to themselves, led to his abode. Those who were not under his safe-conduct frequently found it very unsafe to wander in the intricacies of this region. In the *salon* of this temple of low debauchery were assembled groups of all 'unutterable things,' all that class distinguished in those days, and, I believe, in these, by the generic term 'cadgers.'

* See *ante*, Vol. III., p. 207.

'Hail cadgers, who, in rags array'd,
　　Disport and play fantastic pranks,
Each Wednesday night in full parade,
　　Within the domicile of Banks'.'

A 'lady' presided over the revels, collected largess in a platter, and at intervals amused the company with specimens of her vocal talent. Dancing was 'kept up till a late hour,' with more vigour than elegance, and many Terpsichorean passages, which partook rather of the animation of the 'Nautch' than the dignity of the minuet, increased the interest of the performance. It may be supposed that those who assembled were not the sort of people who would have patronised Father Mathew, had he visited St. Giles's in those times. There was, indeed, an almost incessant complaint of drought, which seemed to be increased by the very remedies applied for its cure; and had it not been for the despotic authority with which the dispenser of the good things of the establishment exercised his rule, his liberality in the dispensation would certainly have led to very vigorous developments of the reprobation of man and of woman also. In the lower tier, or cellars, or crypt, of the edifice, beds or berths were provided for the company, who, packed in bins, after the 'fitful fever' of the evening, slept well." This notorious house was a favourite resort of Londoners in the sixteenth and seventeenth centuries. It was known by the sign of the "Beggars' Bush" previous to the reign of Charles II., when the name became altered to the "Hare and Hounds," in consequence of a hare having been hunted and caught on the premises, where it was afterwards cooked and eaten. The *Beggars' Bush* formed the title of a play brought out in the seventeenth century. In Pepys' "Diary," under date November 20, 1660, is this entry:— "To the new play-house, near Lincoln's Inn Fields (which was formerly Gibbons's Tennis-court), where the play of the *Beggars' Bush* was newly begun; and so we went in and saw it well acted."

In one part of what was the "Rookery"—now Streatham Street, at the rear of Meux's Brewery—stands a block of model lodging-houses, with perfect ventilation and drainage, and rents probably lower than the average paid for the miserable dens that once existed here. These houses were erected by the Society for Improving the Condition of the Working Classes, on ground leased on easy terms from the Duke of Bedford.

Resuming our walk along New Oxford Street, we pass Bloomsbury Street and Duke Street. The first of these streets is formed by a junction of two, named Charlotte Street and Plumtree Street respectively. They were altered into one street and the name changed in 1845. Museum Street, the next thoroughfare eastward, leads from the top of Drury Lane as far as the British Museum. It was originally called Peter Street, but its name was altered soon after the establishment of the Museum. The southern end was called Bow Street, and the northern end Queen Street. At the corner of New Oxford Street and Museum Street is Mudie's Circulating Library. In describing this establishment we cannot do better than quote the words of a writer in *Once a Week*, in 1861 :—" At the present moment the establishment owns no less than 800,000 volumes. If all these were to come home to roost at one time, it would require a library almost as big as the British Museum to hold them. As it is, the house is one mass of books. Up-stairs are contained the main reserves, from which supplies are drafted for the grand saloon down-stairs. This room is itself a sight. It is not a mere store-room, but a hall, decorated with Ionic columns, and such as would be considered a handsome assembly-room in any provincial town. The walls require no ceramic decorations, for they are lined with books, which themselves glow with colour. . . . Light iron galleries give access to the upper shelves, and an iron staircase leads to other books deposited in the well-lit, well-warmed vaults below. We were curious to inquire if volumes ever became exhausted in Mr. Mudie's hard service. Broken backs and torn leaves are treated in an infirmary, and volumes of standard value come out afresh in stouter and more brilliant binding than ever. There is, however, such a thing as a charnel-house in this establishment, where literature is, as it were, reduced to its old bones. Thousands of volumes thus read to death are pitched together in one heap. But would they not do for the butter-man? was our natural query. Too dirty for that. Nor for old trunks? Much too greasy for that. What were they good for, then? For manure! Thus, when worn out as food for the mind, they are put to the service of producing food for our bodies! . . . The great majority of the works circulated by Mr. Mudie consists of books of travel, adventure, biography, history, scientific works, and all the books of *genre*, as they say in painting, which are sought for by the public. . . . Taken altogether, no less than 10,000 volumes are circulating diurnally through this establishment."

The amount of reading which the above figures represent is enormous; and it cannot be denied that, as an educating power, this great Circulating Library holds no mean position among the better classes of society. Its value to authors, moreover,

cannot be lightly estimated, inasmuch as its machinery enables a bountiful supply of their works to be distributed to the remotest parts of the island, thereby increasing the demand for their works, and therefore also their reputation in an ever-widening circle.

Passing through Museum Street, we enter Great Russell Street, which runs from Tottenham Court Road to the north-west corner of Bloomsbury Square. It was built in the year 1670, and was named after the Russells, Earls and Dukes of Bedford. It is now a street of shops, but was formerly, as Strype tells us (circa 1700), "a very handsome, large, and well-built street, graced with the best buildings in all Bloomsbury, and the best inhabited by the nobility and gentry, especially the north side, as having gardens behind the houses, and a prospect of the pleasant fields up to Hampstead and Highgate."

In this street John Le Neve, the antiquary, was born in 1679. Here, at one period, lived Sir Godfrey Kneller; and here the Speaker of the House of Commons, Arthur Onslow, died in 1768. Here, too, lived Admiral Sir Sidney Smith, in 1828; and also the great actor, John Philip Kemble, in a house on the north side, afterwards occupied by Sir Henry Ellis, as principal librarian of the British Museum, but pulled down about the year 1848, to make room for extensions. Here, too, in Queen Anne's reign, stood Montagu House and Thanet House. The first of these mansions occupied the site of the British Museum, which will be best dealt with in a separate chapter.

We learn from Horace Walpole, under date January, 1750, that in this street the Lady Albemarle was "robbed in the evening by nine men." Her loss, however, was made up by the king presenting her with a new gold watch and chain the next day.

In this street died, in 1858, Monsieur Louis Augustin Prevost, a celebrated linguist. The son of a French functionary of the town of Arcy, he was born in 1796, and as a boy was an eye-witness of the famous battle fought near that town. He afterwards went to Paris, and studied at a college at Versailles. In 1823 he entered as a tutor into the family of Mr. Ottley, afterwards Keeper of the Prints in the British Museum, and for some years gave lessons in French and other European languages. In 1843 he was appointed by the Trustees of the Museum to the superintendence of the Catalogue of Chinese Books, which he accomplished after mastering almost incredible difficulties. The remains of Monsieur Prevost were interred at Highgate Cemetery.

CHAPTER XXXVIII.

THE BRITISH MUSEUM.

"Ædes Musis et Apolline dignæ."—Juvenal.

Origin of the Museum—Purchase of Montagu House by the Government—Evelyn's Description of the First Montagu House—Destruction of the Mansion by Fire—Description of the Second Building—Ralph, First Duke of Montagu—The Gardens of Montagu House—The Troops stationed there at the Time of the Gordon Riots—Singular Anecdote of John, Second Duke of Montagu—Sir Hans Sloane and his Public Benefactions—A Skit on the Formation of Sir Hans Sloane's Collection—Appointment of Governors and Trustees of the British Museum—Lord Macaulay's Opinion of the Board of Governors—Original Regulations for the Admission of the Public, and Mr. Hutton's Opinion thereon—More Liberal Arrangements made for Admission—Gradual Extension of the Old Building—The Elgin Marbles—The Royal Library of George III.—The King's Library—The Towneley and Payne-Knight Collections—The Old Museum described—Regulations for Admission—The Old Reading-room.

THIS institution, which occupies the northern side of the eastern portion of Great Russell Street, is far removed from all the other departments under the control of the Government, and is by far the most interesting of all to the people at large, though it can boast of no very great antiquity.

It owes its origin to Sir Hans Sloane, a man of high scientific attainments, who, during a long period of practice as a physician, had accumulated at his house at Chelsea, in addition to a considerable library of books and manuscripts, a vast collection of objects of natural history and works of art. These treasures he directed to be offered to the nation at a certain price after his death, which took place in the year 1753. The offer was accepted, and an Act was passed directing the purchase, not only of Sir Hans Sloane's collection, but also of the Harleian Library of Manuscripts, which we have already mentioned in a previous chapter; and at the same time enacting that the Cottonian Library, which had been presented to the nation by Sir John Cotton, during the reign of William III., and was deposited in Ashburnham House, Dean's Yard, Westminster, should, with those, form one general collection. To these George III. added a large library, collected by the preceding sovereigns since Henry VII. To accommodate the national property thus accumulated, the Government raised, by lottery, the sum of £100,000, of which £20,000 was devoted to the purchase of the above collections; and in 1754 Montagu House, in Great Russell Street, was bought from the two heiresses of the Montagu family, as a repository for the then infant establishment. This mansion, however, was not the first that stood upon the same site. Before proceeding with our description of the Museum it would be well to speak of these two houses.

The first and short-lived Montagu House, erected in 1678 by Robert Hooke, is thus described by John Evelyn, under date November 5, 1679:— "To see Mr. Montagu's new palace, near Bloomsberry, built by our (*i.e.*, the Royal Society's) curator, Mr. Hooke, somewhat after the French

[style]; it is most nobly furnished, and a fine but too much exposed garden." He also records, in his "Diary," a second visit which he paid to the house, October 10, 1683:—"Visited the Duchess of Grafton, not yet brought to bed, and dining with my Lord Chamberlain (her father); went with them to see Montagu House, a palace lately built by Lord Montagu, who had married the most beautiful Countess of Northumberland. It is a stately and ample palace. Signor Verrio's fresco paintings, especially the funeral pile of Dido, on the staircase, the 'Labours of Hercules,' 'Fight with the Centaurs,' his effeminacy with Dejanira, and 'Apotheosis,' or reception among the gods, on the walls and roof of the great room above, I think exceeds anything he has yet done, both for design, colouring, and exuberance of invention, comparable to the greatest of the old masters, or what they so celebrate at Rome. In the rest of the chambers are some excellent paintings of Holbein and other masters. The garden is large, and in good air, but the fronts of the house not answerable to the inside. The court at entry and wings for offices seem too near the street, and that so very narrow and meanly built, that the corridor is not in proportion to the rest, to hide the court from being overlooked by neighbours, all which might have been prevented had they placed the house further into the ground, of which there was enough to spare. But on the whole it is a fine palace, built after the French pavilion way."

But the mansion was not destined to live long. "This night," thus writes Evelyn, in his "Diary," under date January 19, 1686, "was burnt to the ground, my Lord Montagu's Palace, in Bloomsbury, than which for paintings and furniture there was nothing more glorious in England. This happened by the negligence of a servant in airing, as they call it, some of the goods by the fire." It seems the house was at this time occupied by the Earl of Devonshire as a tenant, as we learn from Ellis's "Letters:"—"Whitehall, the 21st January, 1685-6 —"On Wednesday, at one in the morning, a sad fire happened at Montagu House, in Bloomsbury, occasioned by the steward airing some hangings, &c., in expectation of my Lord Montagu's return home, and sending afterwards a woman to see that the fire-pans with charcoal were removed, which she told him she had done, though she never came there. The loss that my Lord Montagu has sustained by this accident is estimated at £40,000, besides £6,000 in plate; and my Lord Devonshire's loss in pictures, hangings, and other furniture is very considerable." The fire is described by Lady Rachel Russell, who was living close by, at Southampton House, in a letter dated the following day to Dr. Fitzwilliam :—" It burnt with so great violence that the whole house was consumed by five o'clock. The wind blew strong this way, so that we lay under fire a great part of the time, the sparks and flames continually covering the house and filling the court." She adds, with a womanly attention to details, that her little boy was almost stifled by the smoke, but would get up to see the fire, and that Lady Devonshire and her youngest child were glad to take refuge for the night with her, the child being carried by his nurse, wrapped up in a blanket.

If the first Montagu House was "somewhat after the French," the second, with its high roofs and dormer windows, was scarcely less foreign in its general design. Nor is that to be wondered at, for it is said to have been designed by a French architect, M. Pougey (or Puget), of Marseilles, eminent as a sculptor, painter, and both civil and naval architect, and that he was sent from Paris expressly to superintend it; but in the "English Encyclopædia" it is stated that the building bore no trace of the peculiar style which induced some to call him the "French Michael Angelo;" and, moreover, in the "Biographie Universelle" no mention is made of his having come to England.

There is a good view of the house in the heyday of its prime in Wilkinson's "Londinia Illustrata," another in Strype's "Survey of London" for 1754, and another curious bird's-eye view may be seen in Stowe's "Survey."

This mansion is described in the "New View of London," in 1708, as "an extraordinary, noble, and beautiful palace, in the occupation of the Duke of Montagu. It (i.e., the shell) was erected in 1677. The building constitutes three sides of a quadrangle, and," the writer quaintly adds, "is composed of fine Brick and Stone Rustick-work, the Roof covered with Slate, and there is an Acroterio (sic) of four Figures in the Front, being the four Cardinal Virtues. From the House the Gardens lie northwards, where is a Fountain, a noble Tarrass (sic), a Gladiator, and several other statues.

The Inside is richly furnished and beautifully finished; the Floors of most Rooms finnier'd (sic); there are great variety of noble paintings, the Staircase and the Cupalo Room particularly curious, being architecture done in Perspective, &c.; and there are many other notable things too numerous to insert here. On the South side of the Court, opposite to the Mansion House is a spacious Piazza, adorned with columns of the Ionic Order, as is the Portal in the middle of a regular and large Frontispiece toward the Street."

"Montagu House," writes the author of the "New Critical Review of the Public Buildings of London," in 1736, "has been long, though ridiculously, esteemed one of the most beautiful buildings about the town. I must own it is grand and expensive, will admit of very noble ranges of apartments within, and fully answers all the dignity of a British nobleman of the first rank; but after I have allowed this, I must add that the entrance into the court-yard is mean and Gothic (!), more like the portal of a monastery than the gate of a palace. . . . I am ready to confess the area (to be) spacious and grand, and the colonnade to the wings graceful and harmonious; but the wings themselves are no way equal to it, and the body of the house has no other recommendation than merely its bulk and the quantity of space that it fills." And then he proceeds to discuss in detail its roofs, "garrets," windows, and the cupola with which it was surmounted, as all open to adverse criticism.

The building was erected on the plan of a first-class French hotel, of red brick, with stone dressings, a lofty domed centre, and pavilion-like wings. In front of the house was a spacious court-yard, enclosed with a high wall, within which was an Ionic colonnade, extending the whole length of the building. The principal entrance, in Great Russell Street, was known as the "Montagu Great Gate;" over it rose an octangular lantern, with clock and cupola; and at each extremity of the wall was a square turret. On each side of the quadrangle were the lodgings of the different officers, by which the colonnade was connected with the main building.

From the pages of the Gentleman's Magazine (May, 1814) we condense the following particulars of the second Montagu House :—" It was erected by Ralph, first Duke of Montagu, who was a great favourite of Charles II., under whom he was twice Ambassador at the Court of Louis XIV. Though constantly in disgrace with James II., he was honoured by William and Anne. It appears that he expended the greater part of his income in erecting this pile after the French taste; on its erection and embellishments a variety of French architects, painters, &c., were engaged to design and embellish it. We are told," adds the writer, "that 'the architecture was conducted by Mons. Pouget, in 1678,' but nothing occurs as to the period when it was brought to a conclusion; yet gardens in the rear. In the former, on the ground-floor, were the hall, grand staircase, and two state-rooms; and in the latter, a grand central saloon, and three state-rooms, right and left. The upper floor was laid out in a similar manner, excepting that the portion over the hall served as a vestibule.

MONTAGU HOUSE, GRAND STAIRCASE. 1830.

from the various combination of features pervading the whole mass, we are induced to fix its main point of execution towards the close of James's reign." The plan of the entire premises was nearly a square, upwards of 200 feet each way. On either side of the principal entrance were porters' lodges, and at each end of the colonnade were entrances to the offices in the wings of the building. The principal or state apartments were divided into two lines, facing both the court-yard and the

The principal doorway in the south front was richly carved with scrolls, &c., and had an elaborate frieze, the centre consisting of a wreath of flowers and fruit, inclosing the initial letter "M," after the quaint fashion of the time, richly ornamented. The roof was lofty, with a high pitch; the centre portion dome-fashion, with rustic quoins and pedimented, dormer windows. On the breaks at the springing of the roof to the centre portion were originally statues, and urns on the apex of the dome.

A full description of the decoration of the interior of the mansion is likewise given in the *Gentleman's Magazine* of the above year; but it will be sufficient for our purpose to state that the principal rooms, one and all, were alike enriched with painted walls and ceilings; the subjects generally were the pagan gods and goddesses, including several of the stories in Ovid's "Metamorphoses," landscapes, fruit and flowers, the execution of which was entrusted to

and shaded by numbers of trees and shrubs. This communicated with a lawn on the north side. On the west side of the lawn was a double avenue of lime-trees; but the garden on this side of the mansion was tasteless and formal. They are stated to have been laid out "after the French manner;" and John Timbs tells us, though we know not on what authority, that the gardens of the houses in its front in Great Russell Street were noted for

FRONT OF MONTAGU HOUSE, GREAT RUSSELL STREET, 1830. (*See page* 491.)

La Fosse, Rousseau, and Jean Baptiste Monnoyer. The stately hall, together with the grand staircase, were the most striking features of the interior architecture, a representation of which is given in Ackermann's "Microcosm of London." There were in all twelve show-rooms on the ground-floor and as many on the first-floor, and these were in general stately and well lighted. On coming into the possession of the nation, prior to the establishment of the Museum, Montagu House underwent some trifling alterations in a few of its details; but, on the whole, it remained much in its original condition down to the time when it was demolished, between the years 1845 and 1849.

On the west side of the house was a flower-garden and a terrace, disposed with much taste,

their fragrance. Strype and Stow add that "the place is esteemed the most healthful in London."

Montagu House and gardens occupied in all about seven acres of ground. In the gardens were encamped, in the year 1780, the troops stationed to quell the Gordon Riots, one of the centres of which was in Bloomsbury. A print of the period, by Paul Sandby, shows the ground in the rear of the mansion laid out with grass, terraces, flower-borders, lawns, and gravel-walks, where the gay world resorted on summer evenings. In the print here referred to, the white tents of the troops are shown, and in front is a grave-looking old gentleman, walking alone with an air of consequence along a path in the direction where now stands Montagu Place, with his wig, and a sword-cane on his shoulders—probably intended for the king. In the foreground is a soldier, conversing with a well-dressed woman, who is seated by his side.

Ralph, Duke of Montagu, mentioned above, married the proud heiress of Henry, Duke of Newcastle, to whom we have before alluded in our account of Clerkenwell.* The duke, who died in the year 1709, was succeeded by his only surviving son by his first marriage, John Montagu, second duke. His grace officiated as Lord High Constable of England at the coronation of George I., and during that reign filled several public situations of the highest importance. At the accession of George II. he was continued in favour, and at his coronation he carried the sceptre with the cross. He died in 1749, when all his honours became extinct. If we may judge from the following anecdote, his grace would seem to have been of a somewhat eccentric turn of mind, for he appears to have made two codicils to his will, one in favour of his servants, and the other of his dogs, cats, &c. Whilst writing the latter one of his cats jumped on his knee. "What!" says he, "have you a mind to be a witness, too? You can't, for you are a party concerned and interested."

A few years after the death of this nobleman—namely, in 1754, as stated above—an Act was passed for vesting Montagu House in trustees, and for enabling them to convey it to the Trustees of the British Museum for a general repository. We have already stated that this national institution originated in the purchase by Government of Sir Hans Sloane's accumulation of objects of natural history, &c. This splendid collection—at which, by the way, Pope sneered at as mere "butterflies"—was fortunately preserved entire after Sloane's death. He generously bequeathed to the public his books, manuscripts, medals, and "butterflies," on certain conditions. The terms were accepted. The valuable manuscripts of Harley, Earl of Oxford—known as the Harleian Library—were added to it; and these two collections, afterwards increased by the Cottonian manuscripts, together formed, as we have said, the nucleus of our great national Museum.

It may not be out of place here to say a few words about Sir Hans Sloane, and of his public benefactions. He was a native of Ireland, but of Scotch extraction, the son of a gentleman who had settled in Ireland in the reign of James I. He was a governor of almost every hospital about London; to each he gave a hundred pounds in his lifetime, and at his death a sum more consider-

able. He formed the plan of a dispensatory, where the poor might be furnished with proper medicines at prime cost; which, with the assistance of the College of Physicians, was afterwards carried into execution. For a quarter of a century he was President of the College of Physicians, as well as physician to the king, and succeeded Sir Isaac Newton as President of the Royal Society. He gave the Company of Apothecaries the entire freehold of their botanical garden at Chelsea; in the centre of which is erected a marble statue of him, admirably executed, by Rysbrack. He helped largely in founding the colony in Georgia, 1732, and also the Foundling Hospital, in 1739, and formed the plan for bringing up the children of the latter. He was the first in England who introduced into general practice the use of bark, not only in fevers, but in a variety of other cases, particularly in nervous disorders, in mortifications, and in violent hæmorrhages. His cabinet of curiosities, which he had taken so much pains to collect, he bequeathed to the public, as above stated, on condition that the sum of £20,000 should be paid to his family; which sum, though large, was not the original cost, and scarce more than the intrinsic value of the gold and silver medals, the ores and precious stones, that were found in it. Besides these, there was his library, consisting of more than 50,000 volumes, many of which were illustrated with cuts, finely engraven, and coloured from nature: 3,500 manuscripts; and an infinite number of rare and curious books. Thus Sir Hans Sloane became the founder of one of the noblest collections in the world. But the wits, who never spare a character, however eminently great and useful, more than once took occasion to ridicule this good man for a taste, the utility of which they did not comprehend, but which was honoured with the unanimous approbation of the British Legislature. Thus Young, in his "Love of Fame:"—

' But what address can be more sublime
Than Sloane—the foremost *toyman* of his time?
His nice ambition lies in curious fancies,
His daughter's portion a rich *shell* enhances,
And Ashmole's baby-house is, in his view,
Britannia's golden mine—a rich Peru!
How his eyes languish! how his thoughts adore
That painted coat which Joseph *never* wore!
He shows, on holidays, a sacred pin,
That touch'd the ruff that touch'd Queen Bess's chin."

Then again, in "Hone's Year Book," there is a skit on the formation of Sir Hans Sloane's collection, which we here quote. It is from a printed tract entitled "An Epistolary Letter from T——H—— to Sir H—— S——, who saved his life

---

* See Vol. II., pp. 331–2.

and desired him to send over all the curiosities he could find in his travels :—

> " Since you, dear doctor, saved my life,
> To bless by turns and plague my wife,
> In conscience I'm obliged to do
> Whatever is enjoined by you.
> According then, to your command,
> That I should search the western land,
> For curious things of every kind,
> And send you all that I could find,
> I've ravaged air, earth, seas, and caverns,
> Men, women, children, towns, and taverns,
> And greater rarities can show
> Than Gresham's children ever knew ;
> Which carrier Dick shall bring you down
> Next time his wagon comes to town.
> I've got three drops of the same shower
> Which Jove in Danaë's lap did pour ;
> From Carthage brought, the sword I'll send
> Which brought Queen Dido to her end ;
> The stone whereby Goliath died,
> Which cures the headache when applied ;
> A whetstone, worn exceeding small,
> Time used to whet his scythe withal ;
> St. Dunstan's tongs, which story shows,
> Did pinch the Devil by the nose ;
> The very shaft, as all may see,
> Which Cupid shot at Anthony ;
> And what above the rest I prize
> A glance from Cleopatra's eyes.
> I've got a ray of Phœbus' shine,
> Found in the bottom of a mine ;
> A lawyer's conscience, large and fair,
> Fit for a judge himself to wear ;
> In a thumb-vial you shall see,
> Close cork'd, some drops of honesty,
> Which, after searching kingdoms round,
> At last were in a cottage found ;
> An antidote, if such there be,
> Against the charms of flattery.
> I ha 'nt collected any Care,
> Of that there's plenty everywhere ;
> But, after wond'rous labour spent,
> I've got one grain of rich content.
> It is my wish, it is my glory,
> To furnish your Nicknackatory ;
> I only wish, whene'er you show 'em,
> You'll tell your friends to whom you owe 'em ;
> Which may your other patients teach
> To do as has done yours,　　　　" T. H."

But to proceed. On the completion of the purchase of the various collections above mentioned, Governors and Trustees, consisting of the most eminent persons in the kingdom, were at once appointed ; among them were the Archbishop of Canterbury, Lord Chancellor, and Secretaries of State, who were declared Trustees for the public. To these were added Lord Cadogan and Mr. Hans Stanley, who had married Sir Hans Sloane's daughters. After their decease, others were to be chosen in their stead, either by themselves, or by the family of Sir Hans Sloane, from time to time, as their perpetual representatives in the trust.

On the purchase of the Cottonian Library it was settled that Mr. Samuel Burrows and Mr. Thomas Hart, the then trustees, and their successors, should be nominated by the Cotton family, as perpetual representatives, in the same manner as those of Sir Hans Sloane. The same arrangement was entered into with respect to the trusteeship of the Harleian collection of manuscripts ; and the Earl of Oxford, the Duke of Portland, and their successors, to be chosen by themselves, or by the Harley family, were made perpetual trustees for the same. These trustees were made a body corporate, by the name of the " Trustees of the British Museum," with power to make statutes, rules, and ordinances ; to choose librarians, officers, and servants, and to appoint their several salaries ; upon this special trust and confidence, " that a free access to the said general repository, and to the collections therein contained, shall be given to all studious and curious persons, at such times and in such manner, and under such regulations, for inspecting and consulting the said collections, as by the said trustees, or the major part of them, in any general meeting assembled, shall be limited for that purpose."

The trustees at the present time are fifty in number. Of these, one is nominated by the Sovereign ; twenty-five are official, among whom the Archbishop of Canterbury, the Lord Chancellor, and the Speaker of the House of Commons are always included ; nine are " family " trustees—the Sloane, Cotton, and Harley families being represented by two each, and the Towneley, Elgin, and Knight families by one each ; whilst the remaining fifteen are chosen by the former thirty-five. Of the Towneley, Elgin, and Knight collections we shall speak in due course.

Lord Macaulay was one of the trustees, and was anxious to improve the administration, but found it apparently a hopeless task. He writes, in his diary, Nov. 25, 1848 :—" After breakfast I went to the Museum. I was in the chair. It was a stupid, useless way of doing business. All boards are bad, and this is the worst of boards. If I live, I will see whether I cannot work a reform here."

The nomination of the subordinate officers rests with the trustees, the candidates being subjected to a test examination before the Civil Service Commissioners. There are two grades, in each of which promotion is supposed to go by seniority ; occasionally, however, an officer is promoted from the lower to the higher grade, but only in a case of singular merit.

After coming into possession of Montagu House, the trustees immediately laid out between twenty and thirty thousand pounds on necessary repairs and alterations.

The Museum was opened to the public for the first time on January 15th, 1759. The establishment then consisted of three departments only, devoted respectively to printed books, manuscripts, and natural history. That the Museum was highly appreciated, even in the earliest stages of its existence, may be easily imagined when we say that Northouck (1772), describing it when first founded, styles it "the wonder of all that beheld it, and confessed, all things considered, to be superior to any other Museum in the world !!"

The regulations for the admission of the public at first bore some resemblance to those which are still observed at the Soane Museum, in Lincoln's Inn Fields*—namely, it was provided that "admission" to such "studious and curious persons" as are desirous to see the Museum should be obtained by means of printed tickets, to be delivered by the porter, upon their application in writing, which writing shall contain their names, condition, and places of abode, also the day and hour at which they desire to be admitted. This list was to be submitted every night to the principal Librarian, or in his absence, to another officer of the Museum, who, if he considered the parties admissible, was to "direct the porter to deliver tickets to them according to their said request, on their applying a second time for the said tickets," observing, however, that not more than ten tickets were delivered for each time of admission." The parties who produced these tickets were to be allowed three hours for their inspection of the Museum, spending one hour in each department, and being taken in charge by a different officer for each. How these regulations operated in some instances may be learned from the account of a visit which was paid to the Museum by Mr. William Hutton, the historian of Birmingham, on the 7th of December, 1784, which he described in his "Journey from Birmingham to London," published in the following year. He says, "The British Museum justly stands in the first class of rarities. I was unwilling to quit London without seeing what I had many years wished to see, but how to accomplish it was the question. I had not one relation in that vast metropolis to direct me, and only one acquaintance; but assistance was not with him. I was given to understand that the door, contrary to other doors, would not open with a silver key;

that interest must be made some time before, and admission granted by a ticket, on a future day. This mode seemed totally to exclude me. As I did not know a right way, I determined to pursue a wrong, which probably might lead me into a right. Assiduity will accomplish weighty matters, or how could Obadiah Roberts count the grains in a bushel of wheat? By good fortune I stumbled upon a person possessed of a ticket for the next day, which he valued at less than two shillings; we struck a bargain in a moment, and were both pleased. And now I feasted upon my future felicity. I was not likely to forget 'Tuesday at eleven, December 7, 1784.' We assembled on the spot, about ten in number, all strangers to me, perhaps to each other. We began to move pretty fast, when I asked with some surprise, whether there were none to inform us what the curiosities were as we went on? A tall, genteel young man in person, who seemed to be our conductor, replied with some warmth, 'What! would you have me tell you everything in the Museum? How is it possible? Besides, are not the names written upon many of them?' I was too much humbled by this reply to utter another word. The company seemed influenced; they made haste, and were silent. No voice was heard but in whispers. The history and the object must go together; if one is wanting, the other is of little value. I considered myself in the midst of a rich entertainment, consisting of ten thousand rarities, but, like Tantalus, I could not taste one. It grieved me to think how much I lost for want of a little information. In about thirty minutes we finished our silent journey through this princely mansion, which would well have taken thirty days. I went out much about as wise as I went in, but with this severe reflection, that for fear of losing my chance, I had that morning abruptly torn myself from three gentlemen, with whom I was engaged in an interesting conversation, had lost my breakfast, got wet to the skin, spent half-a-crown in coach hire, paid two shillings for a ticket, been hackneyed through the rooms with violence, had lost the little share of good humour I brought in, and came away quite disappointed. Hope is the most active of all the human passions. It is also the most delusive. I had laid more stress on the British Museum than on anything I should see in London. It was the only sight that disgusted me."

The system which Hutton has thus described continued for many years longer, probably till 1803, when several alterations in the management were effected. In 1808, when the first "Synopsis," or official guide, was printed, the regulations stated that "on the first four days of the week, 120 persons may be admitted to view the Museum, in eight companies of fifteen each;" but no mention is made of the necessity of their previously obtaining tickets. Two years later a greater advance appears to have been made, for we then find that "the Museum is open for public inspection on the Monday, Wednesday, and Friday in every week (the usual vacations excepted), from ten till four o'clock; and all persons of decent appearance who apply between the hours of ten and two are immediately admitted, and may tarry in the apartments or the Gallery of Antiquities without any limitation of time, except the shutting of the house at four o'clock." From that time the regulations have been constantly growing more liberal, and the corresponding increase in the number of persons admitted, as years have rolled along, has been very striking.

In the year 1850 the numbers were just above a million; and in the following, or "Exhibition year," when multitudes flocked to London from all quarters of the globe, the astonishing total of 2,527,216 visitors was registered—a number at that time surpassing the entire population of the metropolis.

With the commencement of the present century the character of the Museum began to improve, and, gradually, from a stationary, it became an eminently progressive institution. A more liberal system of admission to its treasures, as we have shown, was adopted. The Government annual vote for purchases was increased considerably towards the close of the reign of George IV., and again after the passing of the first Reform Bill.

The acquisition of sundry Egyptian antiquities, for the most part discovered by Belzoni, led to the establishment of a separate Department of Antiquities in the Museum; and in order to provide suitable rooms for their accommodation, a new edifice was erected in the gardens and completed in 1807. This building, which communicated by means of a passage with old Montagu House, was of an entirely different architectural character from it, and comprised a series of thirteen classical saloons. The subsequent addition of the Elgin marbles, for which a grant of £35,000 had been made by Government, and which were for some years exhibited in a wooden shed, rendered necessary a further extension of the building; and lastly, the presentation of the library of George III., in 1821, to the nation, made it imperative to provide a suitable room for its reception, which was one of the conditions of the gift.

Lord Elgin commenced the work of collecting the "marbles" which bear his name during his mission to the Ottoman Porte in the year 1802; but his right to carry them off as spoils, and also his judgment in selecting these particular specimens, was much discussed at the time. When the question of voting a sum of money for them was brought forward in Parliament, the opinions of eminent artists as to his spoils from the Temple of Minerva were sought and collected. It is curious to compare the manner in which each artist expresses his admiration of them. Benjamin West, the then President of the Royal Academy, declared that if he had seen these emanations of genius in his youth, the feeling which he entertained of their perfection would have animated all his labours, and would have led him to infuse more character, expression, and life into his historical compositions. His successor in the President's chair, Sir Thomas Lawrence, expressed his opinion that the statues brought to England by Lord Elgin were superior even to the well-known "Apollo Belvidere," because they united beauty of composition and grandeur of form with a more perfect and correct imitation of nature than is to be found in the "Apollo." He particularly admired in the Elgin Marbles the correct representation of the harmonious variety produced in the human form by the alternate motion and repose of the muscles. Canova declared that Lord Elgin deserved to have altars erected to him as the saviour of the arts, and considered himself fortunate in having visited London, were it only for the opportunity of seeing those masterpieces. In the opinion of Nollekens, the "Theseus" is equalled only by the "Apollo." Flaxman and Chantrey were not quite so decided as to the object of their preference; while Rossi and Westmacott declared that they knew of nothing superior to these "admirable fragments of antiquity."

The gift of the Royal Library to the British Museum by George IV. was certainly a munificent present; but when it is described as a gift "greater than has been bestowed by any sovereign on any nation since the library of the Ptolemies was founded at Alexandria," one cannot help smiling at the loyal exaggeration. The following is the text of the letter by which the gift was accompanied, addressed by the King to Lord Liverpool, then Prime Minister:—

"Pavilion, Brighton, Jan. 15, 1823.

"DEAR LORD LIVERPOOL,—The King, my late revered and excellent father, having formed, during a long series of years, a most valuable and extensive library, consisting of about 120,000 volumes, I have resolved to present this collection to the British nation.

"Whilst I have the satisfaction by this means of advancing the literature of my country, I also feel that I am paying a just tribute to the memory of a parent whose life was adorned with every public and private virtue.

a separate building to be erected to receive the treasure.

In a lecture entitled "Brief Personal Reminiscences of Forty Years in the National Library," delivered in 1875 by Mr. Robert Cowtan, author

SIR HANS SLOANE. *From a Print published in* 1793. (*See page* 490.)

"I desire to add, that I have great pleasure, my lord, in making this communication through you. Believe me, with great regard, your sincere friend,

"G. R.

"To the Earl of Liverpool, K.G., &c."

This letter was communicated to the Houses of Parliament in the following month, and the cheering with which it was received in the House of Commons showed that the people appreciated the king's generosity. The royal library was handed over to the trustees of the Museum, who ordered

of "Memories of the British Museum," &c., the fact of the King's Library being a *gift* to the nation is somewhat negatived. Mr. Cowtan observes that "The books in the 'King's Library,' a kingly room for a kingly collection, were all purchased at the private expense of George III., at the instigation of Dr. Samuel Johnson, who was consulted by Sir Francis Barnard, the king's librarian. These books, which were all large paper copies, included a Bible, which was the first book printed with movable type. There were inscriptions over the door of

THE KING'S LIBRARY.

this room, one in English and one in Latin, stating that the collection was presented to the nation by George IV.; but it was said in the *Quarterly Review* that George IV., not caring much about books (he found books in ladies' faces), was about to sell this collection to a foreign purchaser, when, on the fact becoming known, they were *bought* of him out of some Admiralty funds, and so secured for the nation. So the inscription was like that other 'bully,' which, as Pope said, 'lifted up its head and lied.'"

The design for the King's Library, which was prepared on that occasion by Sir Robert Smirke, the architect of the Museum, formed part of a general plan for rebuilding the whole institution, involving the demolition not only of Montagu House, but of the saloons erected, as we have already mentioned, for the department of antiquities. Sir Robert's proposals were adopted by the trustees, and in the course of twenty-five years were gradually carried into execution.

On the donation, or, at all events, the acquisition of this library, the Government ordered drawings to be prepared for the erection of an entirely new Museum, a portion of one wing of which was to be occupied by the recently-acquired library. This wing, on the eastern side of the Museum garden, was finished in 1828; the northern, southern, and western sides of the quadrangle have since been progressively added.

It may be observed here that in 1827 Charles Lamb, speaking of "poor condemned Montagu House," anticipates the speedy erecting of another and handsomer building in its place; but, as we have just seen, the work of rebuilding had then already commenced. The author of the "Essays of Elia" speaks, however, with great satisfaction of the excellent collection of old plays bequeathed to the Museum by David Garrick.

The Towneley collection of antiquities, comprising a quantity of marble sculptures bought at Rome, Naples, &c., were purchased by the nation at the commencement of the present century. They were collected by Charles Towneley, Esq., who died in 1805, as we have stated in a previous chapter, at his house in Park Street, Westminster. His collection of bronzes, coins, and gems were added to the Museum in 1814. Mr. Richard Payne Knight, the classical scholar, whom we have already mentioned as residing in Soho Square, bequeathed to the Museum his matchless collection of drawings, bronzes, and medals, worth at least £30,000. The collection includes a single volume of drawings by the inimitable Claude, which was purchased by Mr. Knight for £1,600

from a private individual, who a short time before had bought it for £3.

The Museum, as a building, is described in a work published in 1830, as "a large and imposing, rather than a grand or graceful edifice; entered by a simple, if not mean, portal, which opens into a quadrangle, formed on three sides by a long and lofty front and wings, and on the fourth side by a dilapidated Ionic colonnade, never handsome, with the gate in the centre."

The hall, which was approached from the courtyard by a broad flight of steps, was of the Ionic order, and decorated with pilasters, in pairs, with the entablature supporting a horizontal and plain ceiling. Over the great door was a coarse painting of Vesuvius in eruption. From the hall the vestibule was entered through two tall arches, filled with fanciful iron-work and gates. A passage from the vestibule led to the western apartments. The ante-room was comparatively small, with nothing remarkable in its architecture, but the ceiling was richly ornamented with paintings by Rousseau and La Fosse, the subjects by the latter being the "Apotheosis of Iris" and the "Assembly of the Gods."

The staircase was painted with representations of Cæsar and his military retinue; the feasts and sacrifices of Bacchus, and gigantic figures, emblematical of the Nile and the Tiber, with various views of landscapes and pieces of architecture.

The room adjoining the ante-room northward was, till the winter of 1803, the reading-room; but, "having only two windows, which were insufficient to illuminate the most remote parts of the table," another room, both larger and better lighted, was substituted. This apartment had a vaulted ceiling; it was surrounded by shelves of books, and above the cases hung several portraits on the walls. There was a large marble chimney-piece, and the room was lighted by three windows on the north side and one on the west. All the rooms on the north side of the house partook of the same character with the reading-room; they were very spacious, and each was entirely filled with shelves of printed books.

In the Act of Parliament already referred to, it is particularly set forth, that "the collections and libraries are to be reposited, and remain in the Museum, *for the public use;*" and further, "that free access shall be given to this repository *to all studious and curious persons*, at such time, and in such manner, and under such regulations for inspecting and consulting the collections, as the trustees shall think fit." We have already seen in what manner and number the *curious* portion of the public was admitted in obedience to the above law ; and it will doubtless be equally interesting to know what facilities were afforded, at that early period, to the *studious* and the *man of letters.*

In the " Statutes and Rules relating to the inspection and use of the British Museum," published in 1757, it is ordered, " That no one be admitted to make use of the Museum for study, but by leave of the trustees, in a general meeting, or the standing committee ; and that the said leave be not granted for a longer term than half a year, without a fresh application." It is further ordered, " That a particular room be allotted for the persons so admitted, in which they may sit, and read, or write, without interruption, during the time the Museum is kept open ; that a proper officer do constantly attend in the said room, so long as any such person or persons shall be there ; and for the greater ease and convenience of the said persons, as well as security of the collection, it is expected *that notice be given in writing the day before, by each person, to the said officer, what book or manuscript he will be desirous of perusing the following day;* which book or manuscript on such request will be lodged in some convenient place in the said room, and will thence be delivered to him by the officer of the said room," &c.

Since the above period many alterations have been made in the mode of admission, which, at the same time that they have increased the facility of access, have in no wise lessened the precautions so necessary for the safety of the collection.

In Weale's " London and its Vicinity Exhibited " (1851), it is stated that the library contained about 500,000 volumes, and that it was visited by about 70,000 readers during each year, and that every accommodation was afforded in the pursuit of their studies. With regard to the application for admission as a reader being backed " by a proper recommendation," the editor of the above work considers it so very indefinite, as to require, in behalf of the public, some revision on the part of the trustees. " It is left too much to the will of the librarian," he adds, " as to whom he may, in his temper, think a proper person to recommend. My own case may not be singular. In the course of my career as publisher I have contributed to the Museum books not far from a thousand pounds in value ; yet this public servant negatived my recommendation of Mr. Robert Armstrong, an engineer, who, as a scientific man, was desirous of a reading-ticket ; remarking to that gentleman, ' We don't like the recommendations of booksellers.' "

The first apartment specially appropriated for the use of a reading-room was opened towards the close of the year 1757. It was situated in the basement of the old mansion, at the west corner of the building, and here the readers apparently continued to assemble until the year 1810, when they were transferred to a larger and much more commodious apartment, upon the second storey, at that time forming part of the manuscript department. This state of things continued for nearly twenty years, when another transfer took place, two rooms situated at the southern extremity of the east wing of the new building being *temporarily* devoted to the service of the then rapidly increasing body of readers. In 1838 the erection of the north front of the present structure was brought to a completion, when another change in the situation of the " reading-room " was effected. The rooms then brought into use were two in number, at the north-east corner of the building, adjoining to Russell Square. Passing, or slinking in almost surreptitiously, through an iron gate near the lower end of Montagu Place, the " readers " were directed by a porter, seated in a kind of sentry-box, to a narrow door in the lower part of the building. Here a short flight of stone steps, ending in a glass door, led to the rooms placed at their disposal, which were narrow and quite inadequate. The tables, twenty-six in number, were arranged in such a manner as to leave a free passage down the centre and round the sides of the room ; chairs were placed for the accommodation of eight readers at each table, and, as is the case at the present time, book-stands, pens, ink, and blotting-paper were gratuitously furnished.

For a long time the library and reading-room were used by a very few individuals—scholars, historians, antiquaries of the Dryasdust class, and collectors of literary curiosities. The attendants at the reading-room enjoyed quite a sinecure in those " good old days," when perhaps they had not half-a-dozen individuals daily to supply with books. In fact, there was no provision made for a large number of visitors. Indeed, in the rooms of which we are now speaking, accommodation was provided for only 170 persons. The presses round the rooms were filled with books of reference, encyclopædias, dictionaries, lexicons, topographical and geographical works, &c. The rooms themselves, which still form part of the library, have little architectural decoration, beyond what they derive from their ceilings, in each compartment or panel of which there is a rose or flower, which serves as a ventilator, as well as for ornament. The floors are of oak, and have a slip of marble along the centre, and underneath the book-cases ; and the rooms are warmed by hot-water apparatus.

CHAPTER XXXIX.

THE BRITISH MUSEUM (*continued*).

"*Scripta Palatinus quæcunque recepit Apollo.*"—*Horace.*

Commencement of the New Buildings—The Edifice described—The New Reading-room—Rules and Regulations for "Readers"—The Catalogue —Presses and Press-marks—The Chief Books of Reference—A Classic Picture of the Reading-room—Offences for which Readers are expelled—The Printed Book Department—The Grenville Library—Specimens of Early Printed Books—Autographs—Magna Charta, and other Historical Documents—Manuscripts—Newspapers—Acquisition of Books by the Museum under the Copyright Act—The Department of Prints and Drawings—Principal Librarians of the Museum—Mr. J. T. Smith—Celebrated Frequenters of the Reading-room.

THE difference of the appearance of Montagu House from that of the Museum of the present day is very striking, not only with regard to the building in itself, but also as to its situation, relatively to the country and the town. The old house, as we have shown, remained down almost to the close of the last century quite open on the north side, and commanded views of the surrounding fields; whilst the present edifice, although occupying the same site, and indeed covering a much larger space of ground, is almost completely shut in on three sides by streets and squares which are built up close to its walls, so that the only view of the edifice that can be obtained is that of the principal, or southern, front in Great Russell Street.

The new buildings, which were commenced by Sir Robert Smirke, were continued in 1846 by his brother, Mr. Sydney Smirke; the walls of old Montagu House being removed piecemeal as the new edifice progressed; the last portion of it disappeared in 1845. In place of the dull brick wall which separated the old house from Great Russell Street, there was erected a handsome iron railing, partly gilt. Through this the magnificently enriched front of the new building can be surveyed by the passer-by in all its entire length; it presents a recessed portico and two projecting wings; and as the edifice fronts the south, the play of light and shade caused by the forest of Ionic columns with which the whole is faced, is such as no other portico in London possesses. At either extremity of the court-yard is a range of houses for the resident officials of the Museum. In the centre of the iron railing—which is raised upon a granite curb, and is formed of spears painted of a dark copper-colour, with the heads gilt, and an ornamental band—is the principal carriage-gate and foot entrance, strengthened by fluted columns with composite capitals, richly gilt, and surmounted by vases.

The style of architecture adopted throughout the exterior of the new building is the Grecian-Ionic. The southern façade consists of the great entrance portico, eight columns in width, and two intercolumniations in projection. This is approached by a broad flight of steps. On either side is an advancing wing, giving to the entire front an extent

of 370 feet; the whole surrounded by a colonnade of forty-four columns, raised upon a stylobate five feet and a half high. The columns are five feet at their lower diameter, and forty-five feet high; the height from the pavement of the front court-yard to the top of the entablature of the colonnade, upwards of sixty-six feet. Professor Cockerell, in a lecture delivered in 1850, remarked that "since the days of Trajan or Hadrian, no such stones have been used as those recently employed at the British Museum, the front of which is formed by 800 stones, each from five to nine tons weight. Even St. Paul's contains no approach to these magnitudes." In the tympanum of the pediment there is a group of allegorical figures, representing the "Progress of Civilisation," which has been thus described by Sir Richard Westmacott, R.A. :— "Commencing at the western end or angle of the pediment, man is represented as emerging from a rude savage state through the influence of religion. He is next personified as a hunter and tiller of the earth, and labouring for his subsistence. Patriarchal simplicity then becomes invaded, and the worship of the true God defiled. Next, Paganism prevails, and becomes diffused by means of the Arts. The worship of the heavenly bodies, and their supposed influence, led the Egyptians, the Chaldeans, and other nations to study astronomy, typified by the central statue, the key-stone to the composition. Civilisation is now presumed to have made considerable progress. Descending towards the eastern angle of the pediment is the genius of Mathematics, in allusion to science being now pursued on known sound principles. The Drama, Poetry, and Music balance the group of Fine Arts on the western side; the whole composition terminating with Natural History, in which such objects or specimens only are represented as could be made most effective in sculpture."

The building erected by Sir Robert Smirke consists of four ranges of apartments—east, west, north, and south; and these formerly enclosed a hollow square, forming a large open quadrangle. The eastern range, which was completed in 1828, was in use some years previous to the gradual erection of the others. It contains the apartments appropriated to the manuscript collection, and also the Royal Library, of which we have spoken above; a magnificent series of corridors 300 feet in length, and forty wide, with inlaid floors and coffered ceilings. The ground-floor of the northern range of apartments is allotted to the general library, and is less ornate in appearance than the eastern range; but it nevertheless contains one or two rooms of a striking character. The western range was erected partly on the site of the old Gallery of Antiquities, which was opened in 1807, and presents one large apartment, corresponding in length with the Royal Library; this is appropriated to Egyptian and other sculpture. The southern range, the last completed, occupies the exact site of old Montagu House. This range contains the great hall and staircase; on the east of which is a room containing the Grenville library, and on the west a saloon containing sculptured antiquities. The increasing collections of the Museum had rendered it necessary to make various additions to the original design of Sir Robert Smirke, some of them even before that design had been carried out. Of these may be mentioned a gallery or saloon for the Elgin marbles, which was erected on the western side of the western range. The most extensive addition, however, is that erected in the inner quadrangle, under the superintendence of Mr. Sydney Smirke, who had some time previously succeeded his brother, Sir Robert, as architect to the Museum. This new building contains the reading-room and the accommodation prospectively necessary for the annual increase of the collection of printed books. It is one of the principal architectural features of the Museum, and the only one that is visible at a distance, the dome that crowns it forming part of the view of London as seen from Hampstead Heath, and from the Norwood and Sydenham hills near the Crystal Palace. The approach to the room is by a long passage, which is adorned with a bust of Sir Anthony Panizzi, who was some time principal librarian, and at whose suggestion the new reading-room was built. The subject had indeed been under consideration many years previously, and some discussion has arisen as to the real author of the original suggestion. Mr. Hawkins, an architect, who published a pamphlet of " Observations on the Reading-room," in 1858, assigns the earliest notion of building in the above-mentioned quadrangle to Mr. Edward Hawkins, in 1842; but the idea seems to have been ventilated even as early as the years 1836 and 1837, when it was introduced in a series of letters on the Museum, published at that time anonymously in the *Mechanics' Magazine*, but which were subsequently acknowledged by Mr. Watts, one

of the officers of the Printed Book Department. "The space thus unfortunately wasted," says Mr. Watts, speaking of the quadrangle, "would have provided accommodation for the whole library. A reading-room of ample dimensions might have stood in the centre, and have been surrounded on all four sides by galleries for the books, communicating with each other, and lighted from the top."

On crossing the threshold of the reading-room, the visitor finds himself in a large circular apartment crowned with a dome of the most magnificent dimensions, 140 feet in diameter, and 106 feet high. It is the largest dome in the world, with one exception, the Pantheon at Rome. The cylinder or drum which sustains the dome, presents a continuous circular wall of books, which are accessible from the floor, or from low galleries running round the apartment; it comprises in the part open to the " readers " about 20,000 volumes of books of reference and standard works, and in the part round the galleries more than 50,000 volumes of the principal sets of periodical publications, old and new, and in various languages.

" In the decoration of the interior dome "—we use the words of the authorised " Guide to the Museum "—" light colours and the purest gilding have been used. The great room, therefore, has an illuminated and elegant aspect. The decorative work may be shortly described. The inner surface of the dome is divided into twenty compartments by moulded ribs, which are gilded with leaf prepared from unalloyed gold, the soffites being in ornamental patterns, and the edges touching the adjoining margins fringed with a leaf-pattern scalloped edge. Each compartment contains a large circular-headed window, with three panels above, the central one being medallion-shaped, the whole bordered with gilt mouldings and lines, and the field of the panels finished in encaustic azure blue, the surrounding margins being of a warm cream-colour. The details of the windows are treated in like manner—the spandril panels being blue; the enriched column and pilaster caps, the central flowers, the border moulding and lines being all gilded; the margins cream-colour throughout. The moulded rim of the lantern light, which is painted and gilded to correspond, is forty feet diameter. The sash is formed of gilt moulded ribs radiating from a central medallion, in which the royal monogram is alternated with the imperial crown. The cornice, from which the dome springs, is massive and almost wholly gilded, the frieze being formed into panels bounded by lines terminating at the ends with a gilt fret ornament."

The floor of the room is occupied with nineteen

large and sixteen smaller tables, fitted up with ample accommodation for more than 300 readers; two of these are reserved for the exclusive use of ladies, who have been admitted as "readers" since about the year 1854; ladies, however, are always at liberty to take a seat at any other table which they prefer. By the simple expedient of raising the partition down the middle of each of the larger tables so high that a reader cannot see his opposite neigh-

are familiar now," says a writer in the "English Encyclopædia," "to all the readers of Europe and America, and will be familiar, in all probability, centuries hence, from the very labours in which they are aided by the Museum reading-room. . . From the nature of the library around them, not only such men as Carlyle and Thackeray, Kossuth and Montalembert, but the humblest labourer in the literary vineyard, from the most distant corners of

THE READING-ROOM OF THE BRITISH MUSEUM.

bour, privacy is secured to the literary working-bees, and on entering the room when it is quite full, a stranger might at first suppose that it was nearly empty. The tables are all arranged so as to converge towards the centre of the room, near which are two circular ranges of stands for the gigantic Catalogue, the entries of which—mostly printed—fill upwards of 3,000 volumes, and a portion of which is thus, if not at the reader's fingers' ends, yet actually at the end of every table. In the centre is the "quarter-deck" of the chief superintendent, whose position commands a general view of all the tables and their occupants, often between 200 and 300 in number, and comprising among them some of the best known names in the world of literature and learning—"names that

the world, may be certain that on the walls around them there exists some record of his labours, or the copy of some lines traced by his hand."

What a difference exists between the reading-room of to-day and that of a century ago! Not only is its whole aspect changed with regard to the building, the accommodation provided, and the regulations respecting its management and rules for admission, but the increase in the number of its "readers" has kept equal pace with the increase in the thousands who visit the other parts of the Museum. The regulations for its management at the outset, in 1759, were, as we have shown in the previous chapter, of the same cautious and restrictive character with those for the general establishment. Gray, the poet, was one of the first to avail himself of the opening of the room ; and some mention of it will be found in two or three of his letters. Thus, in one, dated August, 1759, he writes, "I often pass four hours in the day in the stillness and solitude of the reading-room;" and in another letter he describes the company, which at that time consisted of only four other readers, two of whom were Prussians, while Dr. Stukeley, the antiquary, and a copyist made up the number.

volumes, one of the best and largest general collections in Europe. Their seats are furnished with every accommodation for writing and reading, and they are met on all sides with attention and civility ; indeed, a nobleman in his private library may often miss facilities to be found in the reading-room of the Museum. The following are the most important directions respecting it, taken from a printed paper which is given to every reader :—

THE BOOK-CASES AT THE BRITISH MUSEUM.

In like manner, Mr. D'Israeli tells us that when his late father, the author of "Curiosities of Literature," &c., first frequented the reading-room, at the end of the last century, his companions never numbered half a dozen. In 1836, after the removal of the readers' quarters to more spacious rooms, the numbers rose to nearly 200 daily ; and on the opening of the present reading-room the number was instantaneously doubled, the daily average in the year 1858 being 424. Those who obtain admission have at their command, arranged on the walls around them, a library of 20,000 volumes, comprising books of reference of all kinds. They may at pleasure, by merely writing for what they want, obtain as many volumes as they please of a printed and manuscript library of about 1,550,000

"The reading-room of the Museum is open every day, except Sundays, Good Friday, Christmas Day, and any Fast or Thanksgiving days appointed by authority ; except also the first four week-days of March and October.

"The Hours throughout the year are from nine in the morning till eight in the evening from September to April ; and till seven during the other months.

"Persons desiring to be admitted to the Reading-room must apply in writing to the Principal Librarian, specifying their profession or business, their place of abode, and, if required, the purpose for which they seek admission.

"Every such application must be made two days at least before admission is required, and must be accompanied by a written recommendation from a householder (whose address can be identified from the ordinary sources of reference), or a person of recognised position, with full signature and address, stated to be given on personal knowledge of the applicant, and certifying that he or she will make proper use of the Reading-room.

"The tickets of admission are renewable at the discretion of the Principal Librarian.

"The tickets of admission given to readers are not transferable, *and each person must, if required, produce his ticket.*

"Persons under twenty-one years of age are not admissible, except under a special order from the trustees.

"Readers, before leaving the room, are to return the books, manuscripts, or maps which they have received to an attendant, and are to obtain the corresponding ticket; *the reader being responsible for such books, manuscripts, or maps so long as the ticket remains uncancelled.*

"It may be sufficient merely to suggest, that *silence* is absolutely requisite in a place dedicated to the purposes of study."

During the winter evenings, the Reading-room is lighted by electricity.

There are various printed catalogues of portions of the collection, such as the King's Library, the Grenville Library, &c., and subsidiary catalogues to the magazines, newspapers, and serial publications, as well as to the Bibles and works illustrative of the Holy Scriptures. But the *magnum opus* is the General Catalogue, to which reference has been already made. The entries were formerly all made in manuscript by an army of scribes, whose daily work was to add to it the names of all the new books which reach the Museum. Since about 1880, however, the additional entries have been printed. These are entered under their author's name, or, where published anonymously, according to the subjects of which they treat. To the title of each book is affixed a "press-mark," which, by certain figures and letters familiar to the practised eyes of the officials, gives a clue to its whereabouts on the shelves of the Collection. Every reader who wants a book must give in writing its full title and "press-mark," in order to enable the attendants to bring it to him when seated at his table. It is to be much wished that there were another *classified* catalogue as well, in order to help the literary explorer when he knows the subject of a book, but is at a loss for the name of the author.

A New General Catalogue, embodying the Old and the Supplemental Catalogues, was compiled between the years 1849 and 1880, and comprised many hundred volumes; and a special catalogue of the printed books from the time of Caxton down to 1640 is now (1883) in course of publication.

The "English Encyclopædia" gives the following curious information concerning the compilation of the Catalogue:—

"The catalogue of the British Museum has been a subject of frequent discussion in the public press, since the committee of the House of Commons in 1835. Before that time, in 1824, the Rev. Thomas Hartwell Horne had been appointed to superintend the preparation of a classed catalogue; but in 1834, his labours, and those of his colleagues, had been suspended, and the Rev. Mr. Baber had been directed to draw up plans for an alphabetical catalogue. A long correspondence on the subject will be found in the Appendices to the Reports of the Commons' Committee, and of the Royal Commission. When, after Mr. Panizzi's appointment to the keepership, the library had been removed from the old to the new building, the question of cataloguing and of printing the catalogue again came up, and a small committee of the Printed Book Department, presided over by Mr. Panizzi, drew up, in 1839, a series of rules for that purpose, which amounted, when they finally received the sanction of the trustees, who re-discussed them, to the number of ninety-one. Objection has been made to their number; but it must be remembered that it was requisite to provide beforehand for all the contingencies to be foreseen in operating on a large library for several hands; and experience shows that the variety in the notions of catalogues is wonderful. In the King's Library Catalogue, for instance, though it is professedly alphabetical, all the novels and tales by anonymous authors, from Amadis de Gaul to Waverley, are entered in a mass, under the singular heading of 'Fabulæ Romanenses.' In such a title as the 'Second Report of the Auxiliary Trinitarian Bible Society, of St. James's, Clerkenwell,' there is hardly a word, except the particles, which has not been selected by some cataloguers as a heading, many taking even the word 'Second'; though it is evident that, on that principle, a set of twenty of these reports would figure in twenty different parts of the same list. It is evident that difficulties of this kind do not diminish when foreign languages are to be treated, which, in the case of the Museum Library, are not few in number. A commencement was made of printing the catalogue compiled on the new principles, and in 1841 the first volume, containing the letter A, appeared under the superintendence of Mr. Panizzi;

but immediately afterwards the printing was suspended, and one of the objects of the Royal
Commission of 1847 was to inquire into the cause
of this suspension. The commission approved of
the step which had been taken, for the reasons
assigned by Mr. Panizzi, that it was evidently
unadvisable to print any portion of an alphabetical
catalogue before the whole was ready for the press.
Since this decision has been arrived at, the revision
of the old catalogues has continued in manuscript,
while all the fresh books added have been dealt
with on the same principles; but, as has already
been stated, the number of volumes in the Museum
before the year 1839 was about 235,000, while the
number since added exceeds 335,000, so that the
bulk of the supplements, had the catalogue been
printed, would in 1859 have already exceeded that
of the principal. The immense labour expended
on this gigantic work would, perhaps, have been
more highly appreciated by the public, had some of
its results been embodied in print. The knowledge and care required in settling the items of an
extensive catalogue might often win a reputation if
exerted in some other direction, but apparently will
never in England win a reputation in this.

"When a new book has been catalogued, the
next step to be taken with it is to place it on one
of the shelves in a press, or book-case, that it may
receive its appropriate 'press-mark,' that is, the
indication of its locality. At the Museum each
press or book-case has a certain number, and the
different shelves are indicated by the letters of the
alphabet. Thus the press-mark '1,340 *a*' indicates
that the book is placed on the '*a*,' or topmost
shelf of press or book-case 1,340. Nothing can
be more simple, yet this simplicity is rare. In
another library in London, for instance, the system
is exactly reversed: the presses are marked with
the letters of the alphabet, and the shelves with
numbers; the consequence is, that as the letters of
the alphabet are soon exhausted, the librarians
have to commence a second series by repeating
them thus, AA, BB, &c.; then a third and a fourth
on some other principle, and long before they have
arrived at as high a number as 1,340, the system
will be found involved in inextricable entanglement.
As the shelves in any book-case never amount
to the number of the letters of the alphabet, no
difficulty of the kind can occur with them. Yet
the system of numbering the presses appears to
have been slow in suggesting itself to librarians in
general. Sir Robert Cotton named his book-cases
after the Twelve Cæsars, and in order to find a
book it was necessary to remember the succession
of Otho, Vitellius, and Vespasian. When his book-

cases outgrew the number of twelve, he abandoned
even this system for a worse, and instead of proceeding in succession with the 'five good Emperors,'
arbitrarily introduced Cleopatra and Faustina. At
the Advocates' Library in Scotland, the presses
were patriotically named after the succession of the
Scottish kings, then the additional presses after
the signs of the zodiac, &c., till necessity drove
them to the adoption of numbers, lest they should
be compelled to make every new attendant go
through a course of the sciences before he could
find a book. The great problem in the arrangement of a library, which is increasing, is so to place
every book as it comes in, that it may receive a
press-mark which will never have to be altered, and
yet to provide that the classes of books shall be
kept together; that a new book of travels in Australia, for instance, shall stand with other books of
travels in Australia, and not with Spanish plays or
Acts of Parliament. A system of this kind would
seem to be peculiarly difficult to establish in a
library which is increasing at the rate of 20,000
volumes a year, and yet at the Museum a plan
of extreme simplicity has been adopted, which is
found to answer its purpose. Let us suppose that
a room has been built which contains 100 book-
cases, each capable of containing 150 volumes, and
therefore that the room will contain 15,000 volumes
in all, but that the possessor has 1,000 volumes only
to place in it at the outset, intending to purchase
for the next fourteen years 1,000 volumes a year.
It is evident that if he numbers his presses from 1
to 100, and proceeds to place his several books,
the very first few volumes that he marks with a
press-mark hamper him in a certain degree as to
the places of all the others. If he assumes that his
purchases of books in English history will finally
occupy a single press, and therefore places an
edition of Hume in press 77, and occupies press 76
on one side of it with ancient history, and press 78
with the history of France; he may find a year
after that his purchases in English history have filled
press 77, and in French history press 78, and that
he requires more room for both, but that the only
space he has left is in press 2, among the Bibles, or
in press 99, which is entirely vacant, but stands
next to the works of Shakespeare. The order
which he has endeavoured to preserve is therefore
spoiled: he must either fill up the vacant spaces
with incongruous books, or shift the position of a
number of them and alter the press-marks. The
problem will be certain to recur over and over again
before the room is filled, and each time the remedy
will be more hard to effect and more wearisome.
One simple change of feature in the arrangements

adopted at the outset will obviate all the difficulty. We have supposed that he has marked his presses with fixed consecutive numbers from 1 to 100; let us suppose that he marks them instead with movable numbers not consecutive, leaving gaps between, and the whole trouble is got over. Assume, for instance, that he places his Hume just in the same position, but marks the press 283, and places the French history still in the next press, but marks that press 315. When, in the course of a year or two, he finds that he wants additional room for English history, and that the last press but one in the room is vacant, he removes the contents of the last press but two into the last press but one, removing the number with it, and by repeating the process obtains a vacant press immediately after his press of English history, which is exactly what is required. Each new press between 283 and 315 he marks with some intermediate number. The process can be repeated as often as requisite, and the gain is obvious; the press-marks remain the same, and, though not consecutive, they stand in sequence, and serve as a ready and easy guide. The books are movable, and yet the press-marks are permanent. The processes we have supposed are precisely those which have actually occurred at the British Museum. When, in 1838, the old library was moved from Montagu House to the new apartments in the northern range, the press-mark of every book, and of every tract in a book (and there are sometimes more than a hundred tracts in a volume), was altered. The task of arranging the library in its new position was entrusted to Mr. Watts, who, in the course of that and the eighteen following years, during which every book that entered the Museum passed through his hands, must have examined and classed upwards of 400,000 volumes. The rapid augmentation of the collection, and the system of marking the presses with consecutive numbers, made it necessary that the accumulations should be arranged in three successive sets or series. The idea of the plan of *in*consecutive numbers occurred to Mr. Watts long before it could be carried into effect, as, in order to carry it out practically, it was required that all, or nearly all, the presses should be of similar height and size, and the presses in the new building often varied considerably. The new scheme, on receiving the sanction of Mr. Panizzi, was finally commenced in the long room by the side of the King's Library. The presses in that room amounted to about 600, but in the numbering a range of numbers was assumed from 3,000 to 12,000. The numbers from the beginning of 3,000 to the end of 4,000 were assigned to Theology; from 5,000 to

6,000, to Jurisprudence; from 7,000 to 8,000, to Philosophy, Science, and Art; from 9,000 to 10,000, to History; from 11,000 to 12,000, to Literature. A particular sub-division was assigned to each century of numbers; it was assumed, for instance, that dramatic literature would occupy a hundred presses, from 11,700 to 11,799, and thus every drama which has been placed on the new system bears in its press-mark 117 for the first three figures of the five. This system, which is known by the name of the elastic system, appears to promise several advantages besides those which have been already derived from it. It is evident, for instance, that if one copy of the title-slips of the books thus placed and marked were arranged in the order of the press-marks instead of that of the author's names, it would *ipso facto* produce a rough classed catalogue; and thus a problem, which has been thought insoluble, would be solved in the simplest manner.

"When the title-slip of a new book has received the press-mark of its locality, it is ready to be entered in the manuscript catalogue, and passes therefore into the hands of the 'Transcribers.' The present catalogues of the Museum are as novel as many other of its arrangements. Formerly, the titles were simply written into an interleaved copy of the printed catalogue, a copy of which was kept in the reading-room. As it could not be calculated beforehand what the insertions were to be, the same difficulty was perpetually recurring with the alphabetical order of the entries as with the classified arrangement of the books, and the only remedy in use was to cancel a sheet whenever required, and re-write the entries over a larger space. The system was not found adequate to the requirements of the Museum, when the augmentations rose to the rate of 20,000 volumes a year. The present system is that of using prepared paper and a kind of stylus, so that four copies of each entry are produced at once. These copies, which are necessarily on thin paper, are mounted on thicker paper by the bookbinder, so as to be equal to considerable wear and tear, and are then fastened on the pages in the volumes of the catalogue, in such a way that, if required, they can be readily taken up again and removed to another page. By this means the exact alphabetical arrangement of the catalogue is continally kept up, to the great advantage of the readers who consult it."

The chief books of reference in the reading-room, as we have already shown, are arranged on shelves round the floor of the building, and are available for readers without the necessity of writing an order for them. They are divided into Theology;

Law; Philosophy; Fine Arts; Biography; Belles Lettres; Poets; Bibliography; Ancient Classics; Geography; Voyages and Travels; Topography; History; Literary Journals and Libraries; Encyclopædias; Dictionaries of Languages; and lastly, Peerages and Genealogical works. To each of these subjects a separate department of the shelves is assigned; and there hangs up on every table in the room a " ground-plan" which will show their order and distribution, so as to save the searcher's time.

Of the scene to be daily witnessed in the reading-room, a classic picture is presented to us by a writer in the " Comprehensive History of England," which we here take the liberty of quoting :—

"So immense an accumulation in every language, of every period, and upon every department of human study, is adequately furnished for the purpose it was designed to serve, and the accommodation of those who use it. An ample reading-room, properly lighted and heated, well served by a numerous staff of attendants, and provided with all the apparatus for reading and writing, leaves the student no cause to regret that by the rules of the institution he can only use the books within the premises, instead of carrying them to his own home. Equally liberal, also, are the terms of admission, so that with a simple recommendation from some literary person or even known respectable householder, an applicant is at once admitted to the full use and range of the collection, let his rank, station, or country be what it may. Here, then, the chief amount of British authorship is daily, weekly, and yearly to be found collected, the veritable living men and women whose names only are known in the provinces, and regarded with veneration and wonderment; and here those works are elaborated which swarm from the press with an abundance and facility at which our ancestors would have been astonished. As intellect also is of no sex, here may be found among the hundreds who regularly assemble within that crystal dome, ladies mingled with gentlemen, but each pursuing his or her separate task apparently unconscious of the presence of another. One is extracting notes from a pile of volumes, or carrying on a hunt of hours or days after a stray fact, date, or name. Another is transcribing from an old smoke-dried or half-burned MS., which none can read but himself. Another is dashing on with pen in full career, and against time, in the lighter departments of literature, where imagination is half the game, and where the work of research is confined to an occasional glance at two or three volumes lying before him. What strange varieties of country, of station, of physiognomy, of intellectual occupation meet daily within these walls; and what results are there produced, from the ponderous folio to the fugitive essay or tale ! No conversation the while—no whispering—nothing is heard but the slight rustle of the pen upon paper, or the occasional roll of the truck-wheels along the oaken floor, conveying volumes too heavy to be carried, while foreigners, astonished at such silence among so great a multitude, cannot comprehend how mind can possibly live in such an atmosphere. But it is a true British characteristic; and, like the awful silence of a British battle-charge, it is the expression of confirmed and concentrated resolve."

It may be as well to add here a list of a few of the offences against the code of rules and regulations for which "readers" have at various times been excluded from the reading-room. Writing (or making marks) in pencil as well as ink, in Museum books, manuscripts, &c., even corrections of the press and the author; damaging book-bindings, &c.; tracing and colouring without permission; leaving the library-books on the tables, instead of returning them, and obtaining the vouchers, or book-tickets; transferring reading-tickets to other persons for their use; taking books out of the reading-room; annoying lady-readers; insulting the officials; disturbing students; carrying lighted cigars into the room; uncleanly habits; conveying away the property of the trustees (for which offence, we need hardly say, a term of imprisonment has followed the exclusion); and also for employing fictitious names and initials in order to gain admission, or for passing under fictitious names and titles after admission gained. For this offence a " reader" of some standing, a foreigner, who had fraudulently assumed a sham title of nobility, in 1874, had his reading-ticket stopped.

Passing from the reading-room to the "printed book department," we will proceed to note down a few of the many interesting works that are here preserved. At the time when the British Museum was first opened, towards the close of the reign of George II., the library of printed books, as we have shown above, had already received a donation which emphatically marked it as the national library of England. This was the royal library, which had been presented to it by the king. The collection, although not large, being estimated only at about 10,500 volumes, was nevertheless rich in interest, from its numerous memorials of the Tudors and the Stuarts. The volumes brought together by Henry VII. comprised a remarkable series of illuminated books on vellum, from the press of the early French printer Anthony

Verard. One of them, a French Boëthius, has a dedication addressed to the King of England, while in another copy in the library, the dedication is to the King of France; but on examination it will be found that, in the King of England's copy, Edward VI., in order that, by standing upon it, he might reach something from a shelf in the room in which they were amusing themselves. At all events, such an anecdote is told; and it is added that the young offender was warmly reproved by

THE TOWNELEY GALLERY. (*See page* 533.)

the word "Engleterre" has been inserted with a pen. A splendid vellum copy of the Bible of 1540 is interesting, as containing in the title-page, said to be from a design by Holbein, a figure of Henry giving the Bible to his subjects. It is something to know that "bluff King Hal" possessed a Bible; but the sacred work does not, it is true, bear marks of having been much used by its royal owner. We will not pretend to say that this is the identical copy of the Bible which was placed upon the floor by a companion of the youthful and pious his royal playmate for his want of reverence for the Scriptures. In the same press is a copy of the New Testament which belonged to Anne Boleyn. There is also King Henry's copy of his "Assertion of the Seven Sacraments," the book which procured for him, from Pope Leo X., the title of "Defender of the Faith," ever since borne by the British sovereigns. Of the three children of Henry who successively came to the throne, there are likewise interesting memorials to be found here—in the Greek Grammar of Edward VI.; in Queen Mary's

COURTYARD OF MONTAGU HOUSE, 1830.

copy of Bandello's novels, which, it is asserted, supplied many of the plots for Shakespeare's plays; and in the volume of the "Lives of the Archbishops of Canterbury," the first book privately printed in England ; the last-named work is handsomely bound in embroidered velvet, and was presented to Queen Elizabeth by its author, Archbishop Parker. Another volume, which must once have belonged to the royal collection, but which came to the Museum through the bequest of a private gentleman, is Queen Elizabeth's copy of the first book printed in Anglo-Saxon, the edition of the Gospels superintended by John Fox, who, as a memorandum in the title-page assures us, personally presented it to the queen. There are numerous memorials of James I., in books offered to him by the universities, the synod of Dort, &c.; and of his unfortunate successor, Charles I., there are the volumes of almanacks in which he scribbled his name when Prince of Wales; then there is Bacon's "Advancement of Learning," printed at Oxford in 1640, which contains twenty-three apophthegms inserted by King Charles with his own hand. Here, too, are some beautifully-bound volumes of the Protestant nuns of Huntingdonshire, the illustrated "Harmony of the Evangelists ;" this work was brought to the king by Nicholas Ferrar, 1635, and a minute account of the delightful reception of it by his Majesty will be found in the "Life of Ferrar." Among the books which belonged to Charles II. is a fine copy of the second edition of the "Pilgrim's Progress." The collection of pamphlets and publications bearing on the state of public affairs during the time of the Civil War, is one of great interest. It was commenced in 1641, at the very outbreak of the rupture between the King and the Parliament, by George Thomason, a bookseller of St. Paul's Churchyard, who, observing the direction which public affairs were taking, and the extraordinary activity of the press, conceived the idea of collecting all the pamphlets and publications on either side, from folios to broadsides, as they made their appearance. "For the twenty years following," says the author of the article in the "Encyclopædia" already quoted, "though we are told it was a heavy burden to himself and his servants, and though at one time it was thought advisable to effect a colourable sale of the collection to the University of Oxford to save it from the Commonwealth, the design appears to have been never relinquished for a day. On one occasion, the king himself sent to borrow a pamphlet, and chancing to drop it in the dirt, sent a courteous apology to Mr. Thomason, who made a memorandum of the circumstance in the volume (one which contains Shawe's 'Broken

Heart') on which the dirt remains to this day to attest the fact. The whole collection at last amounted to about 30,000 pamphlets, bound up in chronological order, in 2,220 volumes. Ill, indeed, was the collector requited. In a statement bound up with his catalogue, and written apparently by his son, we are told that in his lifetime, which lasted till 1666, he refused £4,000 for the collection, supposing that sum not sufficient to reimburse him. His heirs offered it to Charles II. for purchase, and he appears to have directed the royal stationer, Mearne, to buy it on his account, it is not known for what sum, and afterwards to have granted as a favour permission to re-sell it, which the heirs of the Mearne family did not succeed in doing till they disposed of it in 1762 to George III., for £300. The collection, when presented to the Museum, was known there by the name of the 'King's Pamphlets,' the name and merits of the collector who had displayed such sagacity, energy, and perseverance, having sunk into total oblivion."

That portion of the library which passed to the national repository from George III. was originally collected in Buckingham House. There, as we have shown in a previous chapter,[*] Dr. Johnson frequently consulted its books. "It is curious," writes Mr. John Timbs, in his "Autobiography," "that the royal collector (George III.) and his venerable librarian (Mr. Barnard) should have survived almost sixty years after commencing the formation of this, the most complete private library in Europe, steadily appropriating £2,000 per annum towards this object, and adhering with scrupulous attention to the instructions of Dr. Johnson, contained in the admirable letter (see Quarterly Review, June, 1826), printed by order of the House of Commons."

As to the formation of the King's Library, Sir Henry Ellis informs us in his "evidence" on the subject of the Museum collections, that it was commenced in the year 1765, by the purchase of the library of an "eminent character" at Venice, and subsequently enriched by the spoils of the libraries of the Jesuits, consequent on the suppression of that Order on the Continent, when many fine and rare books were to be bought at low prices. It is worthy of remark that the King's Books are kept separate from the rest, and that there is also, as we have already stated, a separate catalogue. In the centre of the King's Library are several upright glazed show-cases, in which are displayed for a time such prints and engravings as may be bequeathed to the Museum, before their final consign-

---

* See ante, p. 64.

ment to the room set apart to the Department of Prints, &c.

Of smaller collections which have found their way, either by bequest or by purchase, on to the shelves of the Museum, may be mentioned a large and choice collection of Bibles belonging to Dr. Charles Combe, bought in 1817 as a nucleus; a large group of books on the topography of Italy, presented by Sir Richard Colt Hoare, in 1825, four batches of tracts on the French Revolution, acquired by purchase, which form a sort of pendant to the Thomason collection spoken of above, and also the Didôt collection, lately purchased in Paris. In 1846 a most valuable addition was made to the library by a bequest of the Right Hon. Thomas Grenville. Mr. Grenville, who had signed the treaty of American Independence in 1783, died in the full possession of his faculties in the last named year, upwards of ninety years of age. In a codicil to his will, dated in October, 1845, he thus expresses himself:—"A great part of my library has been purchased from the profits of a sinecure office given me by the public, and I feel it to be a debt and a duty that I should acknowledge this obligation by giving that library, so acquired, to the British Museum, for the use of the public." It is devoutly to be wished that other holders of sinecures had been equally conscientious. The collection comprised upwards of 20,000 volumes, and is said to have cost more than £54,000. This library is kept in a room entirely set apart for it, on the east side of the entrance-hall. In both the Royal Library and the Grenville Library are a number of tables with show-cases, in which some of the choicest literary treasures are displayed. In the case devoted to the earliest production of the printing-press of Germany, there is a copy of the Latin Bible, known as the "Mazarine Bible," because the copy which first attracted notice in modern times was discovered in the library of Cardinal Mazarine. It is supposed to have been issued from the press of Guttenburg about the year 1455. This book, according to general belief the earliest that was ever printed, is here in company with the Latin Psalter of 1457, printed by Faust and Scheffer; this is said to be the earliest book bearing a date, and it is renowned for the splendour of its initial letter, printed in colours.

Of the specimens of the earliest productions of the printing-press in England, which are here preserved, are, of course, several from the press set up by Caxton in Westminster Abbey, towards the close of the fifteenth century. These include "The Game and Playe of the Chesse"—the first book printed in England—"The Book of the Tales of Cauntyrburye," and the English version of Æsop's Fables. Then there are some real treasures in the various old copies of the Scriptures that have found a safe keeping; and among them are the Elector of Saxony's copy of Martin Luther's translation of the Bible; Myles Coverdale's Bible, bearing the date of 1530, the first printed in England; and Martin Luther's own copy of the German Bible, which is dated 1542. The collection of autographs is very large and valuable, and full of interest, being limited not to those of persons who belong to modern history, but to "all time." Among them are the signatures of W. Shakspere (sic), on a copy of Montaigne's "Essays" translated by Florio, printed in 1603; of Milton, on a copy of Aratus, printed at Paris; of Ben Jonson, on the presentation copy of his "Volpone" to John Florio; of Lord Bacon, on a copy of the works of Fulgentius; of Bentley, and of Martin Luther, 1542, in the copy of the Bible mentioned above. The same copy was afterwards in the possession of Melancthon, who, in 1557, wrote a long note, still preserved, on the fly-leaf of the second volume. Handwritings and letters of Edward IV., V., and VI.; Richard III. (application to the Duke of Gloucester for the loan of a hundred pounds); Richard II. (document concerning the surrender of Brest), Henry VII., Queen Anne Boleyn, Knox, Calvin, Erasmus, Ridley, Cranmer, Latimer, Queen Mary, Bonner, Sir Thomas More, Sir Walter Raleigh, Sir Isaac Newton, Cardinal Wolsey, Galileo, Hampden, Sidney, Burghley, Tasso, Drake, Hawkins, Oliver Cromwell, Queen Elizabeth, Lady Jane Grey, Addison, Leibnitz, Dryden, Franklin, Charles I. and II., James II., Voltaire, George I., II., and III., William III., Queen Anne, Pope, Sully, Marlborough, Gustavus Adolphus, Emperor Charles V., Henry IV. of France, Francis I. of France, Peter the Great, Emperor of Russia, Frederick the Great of Prussia, Napoleon Bonaparte, Catherine de Medici, Mary Queen of Scots (part of her will in her own handwriting in French), Louis XIV. of France, pen-and-ink sketch of Battle of Aboukir by Nelson, Condé, Turenne, Washington, Wellington, Sir Walter Scott, T. B. Macaulay, and Charles Dickens. Some of the autograph stores in the Museum are exhibited under glass cases in the Manuscript Department; many of those which are not so exhibited are published in Sir Henry Ellis's "Original and Royal Letters."

Two documents, which form part and parcel of the history of England, will be found among the historical treasures of the Museum. One of these is superscribed—"Bull of Pope Innocent III., whereby he receives in fee the Kingdom of

England, given to the Roman Church by virtue of a Charter confirmed by the Golden Seal of King John, and takes it into his apostolical protection. Given at St. Peter's, 11 Kalends of May, A.D. 1214, and of the Pontificate of Pope Innocent the 17th year." The rupture between King John and the Pope, as all readers of history know, had lasted for several years. How that in the end the Pope declared that John had forfeited his crown, released his subjects from their allegiance, proclaimed a crusade against England, and commissioned the French king to execute it; and how that John eventually surrendered to the Pontiff, acknowledged his appointment to the primacy of the English Church, consented to do homage to the Pope, and finally drew up the charter cited in the Bull now before us, in which he formally "resigned England and Ireland to God, to St. Peter and St. Paul, and to Pope Innocent and his successors in the apostolical chair, agreeing to hold his dominions as feudatory of the Roman Church, by paying a thousand marks yearly "—all these things are matters of history; and fortunately the actual voucher for the transaction is here to convince the most sceptical.

The other historical deed is a time-worn and highly-valued piece of parchment, bearing the signatures (or copy of the signature) of King John and several of the Barons—the famous Magna Charta. This is enclosed within a glass frame, and has a fragment of the seal, totally defaced, depending from it. After the injury sustained by this unfortunate document, when the library in which it was formerly kept (the Cottonian) was nearly all destroyed by an accidental fire, at Ashburnham House, in 1731, it was carefully extended upon coarse canvas; but through the effects of time and other circumstances, the ink has become very pale, and the writing is now nearly illegible. Many years ago, however, an admirable fac-simile of the deed, in its original state, was made by permission of the trustees; this is surrounded by the arms of the twenty-five barons who witnessed the king's act, and is placed side by side with the original.

Mr. John Timbs, in his "Curiosities of London," says that this copy of Magna Charta is "traditionally stated to have been bought for fourpence, by Sir Robert Cotton, of a tailor, who was about to cut up the parchment into measures! But this anecdote, if true, may refer to another copy of the charter, also preserved at the British Museum in a portfolio of royal and ecclesiastical instruments, marked 'Augustus II., art. 106;' for the original charter is believed to have been presented to Sir Robert Cotton by Sir Edward Dering,

Lieutenant-Governor of Dover Castle; and to be that referred to in a letter dated as far back as May 10, 1630, still extant in the Museum Library, in a volume of correspondence. But it would appear that the original Magna Charta is still a matter of dispute."

Mr. Richard Thomson, the author of "An Historical Essay on the Magna Charta of King John," published in 1829, observes that "The Commissioners on the Public Records regarded the original of Magna Charta, preserved at Lincoln, to be of superior authority to either of those in the British Museum, on account of several words and sentences being inserted in the body of that charta, which in the latter are added at the foot, with reference-marks to the four places where they were to be added. These notes, however, possibly may prove that one of the Museum charters was really the first written, to which those important additions were made immediately previous to the sealing on Runnymede, and therefore the actual original whence the more perfect transcripts were taken."

We have space to notice only two or three other ancient charters in this part of the collection. One of these is the Bull of Pope Leo X., conferring on Henry VIII. the title of "Defender of the Faith." This document was also injured by the fire which partly destroyed the Cottonian Collection. One of the oldest English charters is the title to Battle Abbey, in Sussex, granted by William the Conqueror. This once famous ecclesiastical foundation owed its origin to the battle of Hastings, which decided the Norman conquest, in 1066. The abbey was commenced by the Conqueror the year after.

Another of the treasures of the Cottonian Collection is what antiquaries supposed to be the oldest royal letter in existence—a short note from King Henry V. to the Bishop of Durham, dated 10th of February, 1418.

The history of the Manuscript Department, of which the Harleian, Sloanean, and Cottonian manuscripts formed the nucleus, is in its general outline similar to that of the Printed Book Department, but its development has, of course, not been so immense. It was formed at the outset by the union of four great collections, the three above mentioned, to which shortly afterwards were added the manuscripts of the ancient royal library of England. Old scholastic divinity abounds in this department; but "the great ornament of the collection," says Sir Henry Ellis, "is the 'Codex Alexandrinus,' an ancient Greek copy of the Scriptures, supposed to have been executed by

Thecla, a lady of Alexandria, in the fourth or sixth century, and presented by Cyril Lucar, the Patriarch of Constantinople, to King Charles I. It is generally acknowledged by critics to be one of the two most ancient copies of the Scriptures in existence, and an elaborate edition of the New Testament portion of it was executed by Dr. Woide, and of the Old Testament portion, at the public expense, by the Rev. H. H. Baber, from 1822 to 1837 keeper of the printed books." The department contains also many volumes enriched by the finest illuminators of different countries, in a succession of periods to the sixteenth century; a numerous assemblage of the domestic music-books of Henry VIII.; and the "Basilicon Doron" of King James I., in his own handwriting. This latter work is a treatise on the art of government, addressed by the king to his promising son, Prince Henry, who died young, and "showing how much easier it is to speculate plausibly than to rule well." Among the other literary treasures of the Museum is a copy of the earliest newspaper, so-called the *English Mercurie*, which, by authority, was imprinted at London by her Highness's printer, in 1588; in fact, there are several such papers, printed while the Spanish fleet was hovering about in the English Channel in that year. "These, however," observes D'Israeli, in his "Curiosities of Literature," "were but extraordinary gazettes, and not published regularly. In this obscure origin they were skilfully directed by the policy of that great statesman, Burleigh, who, to inflame the national feeling, gives an extract from a letter from Madrid, which speaks of putting the queen to death, and of the instruments of torture on board of the Spanish fleet." The first newspaper in the collection is printed in Roman type, not in black letter, and contains the usual articles of news like the *London Gazette* of the present day. Under the date of July 26th in that year, for instance, there is a notice of the Scots' Ambassador being introduced to Sir F. Walsingham, and having an audience of her Majesty, to whom he gave a letter from the King, his master, assuring her of his firm adhesion to her interests, and those of the Protestant faith.

The *English Mercurie* came into the possession of the Museum in 1766, through a bequest of Dr. Birch; and from 1796, when George Chalmers first called attention to it, it had been looked on not merely as the first English newspaper, but the first in the world—"an honour," says Sir Henry Ellis, "which it was destined to lose in 1839, when Mr. Thomas Watts, in his letter to Antonio Panizzi, on the reputed earliest newspaper, proved beyond dispute that it was a fabrication, which was subsequently shown to have originated, probably in a frolic, with one of the sons of Lord Hardwicke, the Chancellor, and with Dr. Birch, who was the friend of the family." Many of the genuine early newspapers were acquired by the Museum in the purchase of the library and collections of Dr. Burney; one of the oldest is dated in 1616, and it is mainly occupied with "News out of Holland." Till long after this period occasional pamphlets and tracts served the purpose of the newspaper, which did not assume anything like its present character till after the Revolution of 1688. Macaulay, in his "History of England," describes the earlier efforts of our countrymen at newspaper literature. He mentions that in 1685 nothing like the London daily paper of our time existed, or could exist, for want of capital, skill, and freedom. The political conflicts which preceded the Civil War gave rise to a number of publications, which are thus described: "None exceeded in size a single small leaf. The quantity of matter which one of them contained in a year was not more than is often found in two numbers of the *Times*." With reference to the *London Gazette*, writes Macaulay, "the contents generally were a royal proclamation, two or three Tory addresses, notices of two or three promotions, an account of a skirmish between the Imperial troops and the Janissaries on the Danube, a description of a highwayman, an announcement of a grand cock-fight between two persons of honour, and an advertisement offering a reward for a stray dog. The whole made up two pages of moderate size. Whatever was communicated respecting matters of the highest moment, was communicated in the most meagre and formal style. The most important parliamentary debates, the most important state trials recorded in our history, were passed over in profound silence. In the capital the coffee-houses supplied in some measure the place of a journal. Thither the Londoners flocked, as the Athenians of old flocked to the market-place, to hear whether there was any news. There men might learn how brutally a Whig had been treated the day before in Westminster Hall, or what horrible accounts the letters from Edinburgh gave of the torturing of Covenanters." In 1690 there were nine London newspapers published weekly. In Queen Anne's reign, in 1709, they had increased to eighteen, including one daily paper. In the reign of George I. there were three daily, six weekly, and ten three times a week. The collection of newspapers in the Museum was commenced by Sir Hans Sloane. The Burney Collection was added to these in 1818, at the cost of £1,000.

From 1818 the Stamp Office was directed to supply to the Museum its copies of London newspapers after the lapse of two years, a lapse which had previously converted them into a " perquisite," and consigned them to destruction as waste paper to be sent to the mill. The English country newspapers were not regularly added to the library till about 1820; the Scotch in 1844, and the Irish not until even some years later. Numerous files of

We learn from the " English Encyclopædia " that the donation of the Royal Library to the Museum by George II., in 1757, was accompanied by that of the royal privilege of claiming from the publishers a gratuitous copy of every work printed in the English dominions. This had first been granted to the Crown by an Act of Parliament of the 14th of Charles II., and subsequently renewed after its expiry by the famous Copyright Act of the 8th of

THE NINEVEH GALLERY. (*See page* 531.)

Continental and American newspapers have been added at different times. On the ground floor of the library, surrounding the reading-room, large shelves of newspapers occupy the two sides of a circular passage about 600 feet in length. The newspapers here are not confined to particular languages or dialects, countries, provinces, or cities ; they are in every language, and come from places situated in all parts of the world. But while there are numerous foreign and colonial series of papers complete or nearly so, those of Great Britain generally, and those of London especially, are the most extensive, and probably the most perfect.

For the augmentation of the collection of English books, reliance had been placed, in the earlier stages of the Museum, on its legal rights.

Queen Anne. This does not include privately-printed books, in which department our national collection is not so rich as it should be ; neither does it extend to the printed papers of the House of Commons, one consequence of which is that in our great National Library there is no complete set of Parliamentary Blue-books to be found, and that there never is a specimen less than two or three years old. Dr. Bentley, when keeper of the Royal Library, complained of the constant evasion of the above-mentioned Act by the booksellers ; and the complaints were often renewed by the librarians of the Museum, though from about the year 1818, when Mr. Barber, then keeper of the printed books, gave some curious evidence on the subject before the Copyright Committee, there was certainly a great improvement. The new Copyright Act of 1842 gave a pre-eminence to the Museum among other libraries to which the privilege was conceded, and provided that, in case of non-compliance with the Act, the negligent publisher might be taken before a magistrate and fined. In 1850, the superintendence of this part of the Museum business was transferred to Mr. Panizzi, as keeper of the Printed Book Department, and the strictness with which he

to be found in the British Museum, or apparently anywhere else.

As to whether this library or that of the Louvre in Paris has the most books, is a disputed point; probably we are below the Louvre in manuscripts, and about equal to it in the number of printed books. Owing, however, to the regulation already mentioned referring only to books published in the three kingdoms, it is not every foreign work that

THE MAMMALIA SALOON, 1882. (*See page* 520.)

enforced the Act led to a great augmentation in the number of books received. At present, all is collected that issues from the English press down to the most insignificant work on crochet, a Child's Missionary Magazine, the directory of a country town, or a circulating library novel; and everything that is collected finds its place on the shelves and in the catalogue, in the conviction that it may often be a point of importance to preserve one copy of even a worthless work in a repository where it may instantly be referred to in case of need. A different system prevailed in former days, when it does not seem to have struck a single individual that it might probably be of advantage to preserve a set of the "London Directory" or the "Navy List," and a complete collection of either is, in consequence, not

will be found here. Books published in India and the colonies ought to be sent to the British Museum, but there seems to be some difficulty in the way of enforcing this right. Also with regard to foreign books, a few are sent in order to comply with the regulations for securing the rights of international copyright; but here, too, the rule is not carried out very strictly.

The author of the "Cities and Principal Towns in the World," in 1830, thus speaks of the library: " Regarded as a source of reference, it is deficient in the selection of editions and also in extent, lamentably in arrear of foreign works, and most unmethodically arranged." As we have notified above, the statement here regarding the arrears of foreign works may perhaps hold good even at the present time; but with reference to the general arrangement and selection of books of reference, considerable improvement has been made since the erection of the present reading-room, and the consequent increase in the space devoted to the purposes of the library. At the close of the year 1882 the entire number of volumes in the library amounted to about 1,500,000, besides which there were about 50,000 manuscripts.

Although there is a very large number of prints, drawings, and photographs kept with the collection of printed books and manuscripts, and accessible to students in the reading-room and the apartment attached to the manuscript-room, the most extensive and valuable works of these descriptions are preserved in a separate division of the Museum, called the Department of Prints and Drawings, and are open to the inspection only of persons who hold cards of admission to that department. Members of the Royal Academy are admitted to this room without any recommendation or letter of introduction; they have merely to make a written application, addressed to the principal librarian of the Museum. Other persons are admitted upon applying by letter to the same individual—very much as in the case of readers—and forwarding a written recommendation from some person of standing, either as an artist or otherwise. Drawing and sketching are very freely allowed in this department; and every facility is given for copying; but as the drawings are irreplaceable, and the whole collection intended for "all time," it is scarcely necessary to add that the greatest care of the works entrusted to students is earnestly enjoined. The entrance to this department is in the western range of the building, at the north end of the main gallery of Egyptian antiquities.

For the most part, the Civil Service of the Crown is officered by natives of the United Kingdom; but to this rule the Museum appears to form an exception, as the names of several foreigners figure among its *employés*, and out of its chief librarians, half have been of foreign extraction. None of its earlier heads are men who have left any deep marks behind them, though Mr. Joseph Planta, of Swiss extraction, who held that post in the reign of George III. and George IV., became Secretary of the Treasury, a member of Parliament, and a Privy Councillor. His successor, Sir Henry Ellis, who died in 1869, at the age of upwards of ninety, was, however, a man of deep and varied learning, and is widely known as the editor of the best complete edition of Dugdale's "Monasticon." Sir Antonio Panizzi, to whom, as already stated, is due the erection of the great central reading-room, was a native of Brescello, in Italy. He came to England as a refugee, and, obtaining the patronage of Lord Brougham, was nominated to an assistant-librarianship in the Museum; and, on a vacancy occurring in the keepership of printed books, he received that appointment. Some twenty years later he was promoted to the principal librarianship. On his retirement, in 1866, he was succeeded by Mr. J. Winter Jones, whose knowledge of books and manuscripts was probably unrivalled in England. On his death, which happened in 1878, Mr. Winter Jones was succeeded by Mr. Edward A. Bond, who was at the time keeper of the Manuscript Department.

During the interval between the years 1838 and 1857 the arrangement of the books in the library was under the management of Mr. Thomas Watts, and when the new reading-room was opened in 1857, it was placed under his direction. He presided there until the retirement of Sir A. Panizzi, in 1866, when he became keeper of the Department of Printed Books, an office which he held down to the time of his death, in 1869, when he was succeeded by Mr. Rye, on whose retirement in 1875, Mr. Geo. Bullen was appointed to the office.

One of the former keepers of the Department of Prints and Drawings was Mr. John T. Smith, the author of the "Antiquities of London and Westminster," "Vagabondiana," and other antiquarian works of high merit. He was the son of Mr. Nathaniel Smith, a sculptor, and afterwards a well-known printseller of St. Martin's Lane, and, as we have stated in a previous chapter, was literally born in a hackney-coach in the year 1766, whilst his mother was proceeding to her residence in Great Portland Street. At an early age, young Smith commenced studying drawing at the Royal Academy, and he was for many years a drawing-master, and at one time resided at Edmonton. His name, however, has been handed down to us as the author of some useful and entertaining topographical works on the metropolis, and also of the "Book for a Rainy Day," &c. Mr. Smith died in 1833, having held his post nearly half a century. In the album of a friend, the late Mr. W. Upcott, he wrote a playful account of himself, in which he observed: "I can boast of seven events, some of which *great* men would be proud of. When a boy I received a kiss from the beautiful Mrs. Robinson, was patted on the head by Dr. Johnson, have frequently held Sir Joshua Reynolds's spectacles, partook of a pot of porter with an elephant (at Exeter Change), saved Lady Hamilton from falling when the melancholy news of Lord Nelson's death arrived, three times conversed with George III., and was shut up in a room with Mr. Kean's lion."

It may interest the curious reader to learn the names of some, at least, of the more celebrated literary men of the last two or three generations who have made the library and reading-room the frequent scene of their researches. Among them have been Sir James Mackintosh, Sir Walter Scott, Charles Lamb, Washington Irving, William Godwin, Dean Milman, Leigh Hunt, Hallam, Macaulay, Grote, Tom Campbell, Sir E. Bulwer-Lytton, Edward Jesse, Charles Dickens, Ruskin, Jerrold, Thackeray, Shirley Brooks, Mark Lemon, and Count Stuart d'Albany. Lord Macaulay, it may be added, when at work upon his "History," used to sit day after day, not in the large reading-room, but in the King's Library, where, in virtue of being a trustee, he had the right of taking down with his own hands from the shelves the numerous pamphlets which he desired to consult and search, without the attendance and aid of an assistant. We are told, in his "Life" by Mr. Trevelyan, that

the place where he used to sit was a little desk near the centre of the room, and away from the wall, in order to obtain better light.

Her Majesty the Queen and the Prince Consort on one occasion visited the library. The only object for which Her Majesty asked in the MS. department was the paper signed at the foot by the prince who afterwards became Charles II. This was the piece of paper which, when his father's life was in the balance, he sent to Cromwell with the message, "Fill it up in any way you like, but spare my father."

Among the foreigners of note who have frequented the library and reading-room, either as visitors or as "readers," may be mentioned the names of Guizot, Thiers, Louis Napoleon (who, after his escape from the fortress of Ham, was introduced to the library by Count D'Orsay and the Countess of Blessington, in order to glean materials for his book upon artillery practice), Louis Philippe, when he came to England as an exile, Count Cavour, and Garibaldi.

CHAPTER XL.

THE BRITISH MUSEUM (*continued*).

Rescue of a Discarded Art Treasure—Acquisition of the Natural History Collections—Dr. Gray's Report on the Collection of Mammalia—A Stroll through the Zoological Galleries—Collection of Portraits—Nests of Foreign Birds—Minerals and Fossils—A Gigantic Tortoise—A Fossil Human Skeleton—The Botanical Collection—The Department of Antiquities—Historical Relics—The Portland Vase—Queen Anne's Farthings—The Pulteney Guinea—Greek, Roman, and Etruscan Bronzes—The Slade Collection of Ancient and Modern Glass—Egyptian Mummies—Egyptian Sculptured Antiquities—The Famous Rosetta Stone—Belzoni—Mr. Layard's Assyrian Collections—The Hellenic and Elgin Rooms—Fragments of the Mausoleum at Halicarnassus—The Lycian Gallery—The Temple of Diana at Ephesus—The Græco-Roman Rooms—Mr. Towneley's Choicest Gem—Concluding Remarks.

RETURNING to the entrance-hall, we find ourselves once more at the foot of the principal staircase. Against the wall, near the foot of the stairs, is a statue, executed by Westmacott, of the Hon. Mrs. Damer, holding in her hands a small allegorical figure, sculptured by herself, representing the "Genius of the Thames." On the opposite, or eastern, side of the hall, on each side of the doorway to the Grenville Library, are two marble statues — Shakespeare, by Roubilliac, and Sir Joseph Banks, by Chantrey. In the centre of the hall is a gigantic vase, standing upon a pedestal. It was purchased by the Museum authorities about the year 1859, from a resident of Croydon, in whose garden it had been discovered, broken to fragments. It is of Italian workmanship, and is elaborately ornamented with raised figures of a classical design, illustrative of Bacchanalian subjects. At the top of the staircase commences the suite of rooms appropriated to natural history, mineralogy, zoology, and botany. The depart-

ment of antiquities occupies the whole of the western part of the ground-floor, several rooms connected therewith on the basement, and the western side of the upper floor. We do not pretend in these pages to act the part of *cicerone* in pointing out to our readers all the wonders of the Museum, together with the exact spot in which they are to be found : all that we can do is to ask the reader to accompany us in imagination through the various corridors whilst we endeavour to set before him a few of the most important and interesting objects that are here brought together.

Before, however, commencing our stroll through the galleries, we may simply remark that in the year 1876 extensive alterations were commenced in various parts of the building. Instead of the approach to the reading-room which we have described in the previous chapter, a lobby of half the length is substituted, entered through a new gallery of antiquities. New apartments in the basement are set apart for the display of some of those sculptures which have been for some time stored away and never yet exhibited. A new room above, which is to supersede half of the long approach to the reading-room, will serve for the exhibition of marbles. This alteration will involve the replacing of the ladies'-room in another part of the building. Another alteration will consist of an additional apartment on the upper floor of the building, intended also to be devoted to antiquities. Although the construction of these new rooms will place a large space at the disposal of the trustees, it is believed that this will soon be found insufficient, in consequence of the large additions which are constantly being made.

Sir Hans Sloane's natural history collection, which, however limited it may now appear, was doubtless considered one of the greatest importance at the time it was formed, served as the nucleus of the present extensive departments of zoology, paleontology, mineralogy, and botany. In the infancy of the Museum all miscellaneous artificial curiosities, and even antiquities and anatomical preparations, were consigned to the natural history departments; but all of these have since been separated from it. In 1769 the trustees purchased a fine collection of stuffed birds, which had been brought over from Holland, and many additions to it were afterwards made by purchase and donation. The voyages of discovery by Captain Cook and others, early in the reign of George III., brought numerous acquisitions, and in 1816 the valuable collection of British zoology, which had belonged to Colonel Montague, of Knowle, in Devonshire, and included a very large number of birds, was purchased. General Hardwicke's collection of stuffed birds was bequeathed to the Museum in 1835, since which time still larger acquisitions have been made by presents and purchase, particularly in the case of ornithology, so that the aggregate now forms a collection probably as extensive as any in Europe.

With reference to the collection of mammalia, fishes, reptiles, insects, and crustacea in the British Museum, the late Dr. J. E. Gray, in the year 1849, submitted the following statement to the Commissioners of Inquiry into the constitution and management of the British Museum:—"In 1836 Mr. Gray gave some account of the state of the Museum collections, compared with those on the Continent. Since that period he has had the opportunity of again inspecting those collections, and others in the south and eastern parts of Germany, and the south of France, which he had not then seen, and he considers the statements made at that time to require no corrections; but the comparison is now much more favourable for the British Museum, that collection having been increasing very rapidly—indeed, in a most unexampled manner—while most of the Continental collections have, for the last six or seven years, for some political reason, been nearly stationary; or, at most, increasing a single part of their collections, or receiving specimens from a single locality where they happened to have a collector staying. To enter into a few details, Mr. Gray believes that the Museum collections of mammalia, birds, shells, and lepidopterous insects are much more extensive than any other public collection, and superior to all the public collections together. This is certainly the case with the first and last mentioned groups, and he believes also with the other two. The collections of reptiles, fish, and crustacea are second only to those at Paris, if at all below them, in spite of all the assistance of Baron Cuvier. Our collection in each of these classes contains many species which the Paris collection wants, and our collection of insects, taken as a whole, is much larger and better arranged than that of Paris." Since the above period the collections have continued to increase both in number and importance. In 1880 the authorities decided to transfer the whole of the Natural History collections to a new building erected at South Kensington.

The following account of these collections was written prior to their removal:—Arrived at the top of the grand staircase, we find ourselves in the central saloon, the first of three large rooms devoted to the exhibition of specimens selected from the existing classes of animals. The collection here is extremely varied. Arranged round the walls, in glass cases, are a number of antelopes, sheep, goats, and bats; and above the cases are horns of various kinds of oxen, some of them of gigantic dimensions; whilst in the centre of the room are the towering giraffes, the morse or walrus from the Arctic regions, the rhinoceros, hippopotamus, and the Indian elephant. In two large glass cases are shown stuffed specimens and skeletons of those apes or monkeys which, on the whole, are most like man, and therefore are named "anthropoid apes;" however, it will be perceived that their similarity to man is much greater during their early youth than at an advanced age. To this group of monkeys belong the gorilla and chimpanzee, inhabitants of the forests of Western and Central Africa; and the two kinds of orang-outang from Borneo and Sumatra, brutes possessing an extraordinary strength, which they well know how to use when attacked. Here are numerous specimens of antelopes; they are generally of a sandy colour, and specially fitted to inhabit extensive plains, with tracts of desert. A few of the species live among rocks, where they are as surefooted as the goat. They are most abundant in Africa, especially in the southern districts. A few are found in India. Among the more interesting species may be pointed out the water-buck and sable antelope; the oryx, which, when seen in profile, probably suggested the unicorn mentioned by the ancients; the sassaybe of South Africa; the large-eyed gazelle, so often referred to by Eastern poets; the springbok, so called from its springing bounds, when the white fur of its back opens out like a sheet; the gnu, which at first seems a compound of horse, buffalo, and antelope; the Indian antelope, with its curious cheek-pores; the wood antelopes, with short horns often concealed amongst a brush of hairs; and the chickara of India, with its four little horns. North America and Europe have each a single species, namely, the prong-buck of the United States, and the chamois which frequents the Alps.

Of the varieties of wild sheep from the mountains of Asia, North America, and North Africa, one of the most remarkable is the bearded sheep of Morocco, which has enormous strength in its neck and horns; it sometimes reaches a great size, one specimen exhibited measuring fifty-six inches in a straight line from tip to tip. That these wild sheep are good climbers may be inferred from the fact that one of them was discovered by the Venetian traveller, Marco Polo, in the thirteenth century, on the great Pamir Mountains, at an altitude of 16,000 feet. In three or four cases we find the various kinds of ibex and wild goats of Siberia, India, and Europe, together with some of their domestic varieties; and also the Cashmere and Angora goats, celebrated for the delicate wool growing among their hair, and manufactured into the finest shawls. Several of the larger bats, of which we here see specimens before us, are to be found in Africa, in the islands of the Indian Archipelago, the Pacific, and in Australia; they are called fox-bats, or flying foxes, have blunt, grinding teeth, and eat fruit only. Though bats in general are sombrecoloured, some of these fox-bats have brilliantlycoloured furs. The blood-sucking bats, commonly called vampires, are, we are told, confined to South America, and perhaps it is as well that it should be so, seeing that they delight in attacking animals and "sometimes even men, while sleeping, fanning the victims with their wings." These bats are of small size, have a long tongue, and a deep notch in the lower lip; and the wounds which they inflict, it is stated, often continue to flow after the animals are satiated, and do not readily heal.

In the next room are exhibited the continuation of the collection of hoofed quadrupeds, such as oxen, elands, deer, camels, llamas, horses, as well as the various species of swine. Here also are placed the species of armadillo, manis, and sloth. The four corners of this room are occupied by various specimens of the wild cattle and buffaloes of Europe, Africa, and Asia; by the eland, the largest kind of antelopes acclimatised in England and Ireland; and by the elk, the most bulky species of deer inhabiting North America and some districts of North-eastern Europe. In the centre of this gallery there is a magnificent specimen of the basking shark, captured in March, 1875, near Shanklin, in the Isle of Wight. It is about twenty-eight feet in length, and thirteen feet in its greatest circumference. This shark is an inhabitant of the northern parts of the Atlantic Ocean, and approaches annually the west coast of Ireland, rarely straying to the coasts of England and Scotland. It is of a harmless disposition, its food consisting of small fishes and other marine animals swimming in shoals. On the west coast of Ireland it is chased for the sake of the oil which is extracted from the liver, one fish yielding from a ton to a ton and a half. However, its capture, we are told, is attended with great danger, as one blow from its enormously strong tail is sufficient to stave in the sides of a large boat.

The llamas, of which there are some fine stuffed specimens here, are used as beasts of burden in the Andes of South America, one species furnishing an excellent wool. The wild species are brown, while the domesticated ones are black, white, or brown, and often variegated.

Among the animals in this gallery, classed under the heading of "oxen," may be specified the Lithuanian bison, or aurochs, which in ancient times inhabited the European forests, but is now nearly extinct, a few only having been preserved by the care of the Russian Emperors; the American bison, or "buffalo," which still wanders in gradually diminishing herds over the prairies of North America; the musk-ox, limited to Arctic America, where, with its peculiar head and feet, it manages to find food even during the long winter of those regions; and the yak of Thibet, the tail of which is used as a fly-flap by the Asiatics.

Then we have a continuation of the series of antelopes, such as the bontebok, with its inscribed sides; the fine striped strepsiceros, with spiral horns; the nylghau, often called the horned horse of India; and the anoa of the Celebes. In these cases are also contained some others of the thick-skinned beasts, as Baird's tapir of Central America; the African swine, with warts on the head, and formidable tusks; the babyrussa, with recurved horn-like tusks; the social South American peccaries, with a gland on their back emitting a fœtid odour. All these animals have muscular and callous noses, which fit them well for grubbing in the ground. The curious hyrax, one of the species of which is the "coney" of Scripture: in structure it resembles a diminutive rhinoceros. The "shielded beasts," as the manis, or scaly ant-eaters of India and Africa, with very long claws, which are turned in when they walk; the burrowing armadilloes of South America, which, if danger threatens, can roll themselves into a ball, covered with jointed mail, whence they have derived their name. The ant-eaters of South America, which are covered with hair, and have a very long worm-like tongue which they exert into ant-hills, and, when covered with ants, draw into their mouths.

The next room eastward is called the Saloon of Mammalia. Here there is a very extraordinary collection, which includes the various species of monkeys. One of the most remarkable is the proboscis monkey of Borneo, with its singular long nose. Here also may be noticed the sacred monkey of the Hindoos, which is religiously preserved about their sacred enclosures. Other notable "specimens" in this group are the "colobi," so called from their fore-hands wanting the thumb. Of these the most handsome is the Abyssinian guereza, with long white hairs flowing over its sides, and with the white tail contrasting strongly with the deep black fur. The skin of this monkey is used to ornament the shields of the Abyssinian chiefs. In this saloon are also animals of the feline tribe, such as lions, tigers, leopards, bears, &c. The collection of corals, too, is very perfect. Suspended from the ceiling of this saloon is the skeleton of a whale from New Zealand, a species as important to commerce as the whale of the northern hemisphere. It is stated to be a young

individual, not quite half grown. Near it is the skeleton of the bottle-nosed dolphin, of which a large shoal was taken near Holyhead in 1866. Here is also the skeleton of the narwhal, one of the most singular animals of the whale tribe, distinguished by a long spirally twisted tusk, which projects from the snout in the line of the animal's body. This tusk is developed on one side of the snout only (the left), very rarely on both sides. In the adult male it reaches a length of six or eight feet, but is seldom developed in the female; hence it is probable that its use is the same as that of the antlers in the stag. The ivory of the tusk commands a high price in the market, and was still more valued in former times, when it was believed to be the horn of the unicorn. The narwhal is an inhabitant of the Arctic seas, and rarely strays to more temperate regions.

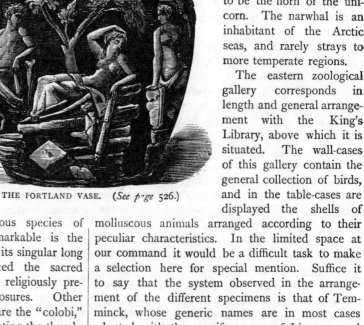

THE PORTLAND VASE. (See page 526.)

The eastern zoological gallery corresponds in length and general arrangement with the King's Library, above which it is situated. The wall-cases of this gallery contain the general collection of birds, and in the table-cases are displayed the shells of molluscous animals arranged according to their peculiar characteristics. In the limited space at our command it would be a difficult task to make a selection here for special mention. Suffice it to say that the system observed in the arrangement of the different specimens is that of Temminck, whose generic names are in most cases adopted, with the specific names of Linnæus, and the English synonyms of Latham. Thus we have, in Cases 1 to 35, the diurnal birds of prey, such as the condor, or great vulture of the Andes, which soars higher than any other bird; the Turkey buzzards, or carrion vultures, which clear away putrifying carcases, and are the most useful scavengers in the warmer parts of America; the eagles, falcons, hawks, and owls. In Cases 36 to 83 we have the perching birds, subdivided into the wide-gaped, as the goatsuckers, the swallows, kingfishers, and the like. Among the tenuirostral birds may be noticed the hoopoes and sun-birds of Africa and

FRONT OF THE BRITISH MUSEUM, 1880.

Asia. The brilliant-plumaged humming-birds come next in order; and then follow the honey-eaters, nuthatches, wrens, wood-warblers, ·thrushes, and chatterers of the American forests, &c. Further on we find cases filled with conirostral birds, including the crows and finches; the scansorial, including the parrots and cuckoos; the gallinaceous birds, as pigeons, turtles, pheasants, and partridges. Lastly, we have the wading and web-footed birds, which comprise the ostriches, trumpeters, storks, cranes, flamingoes, swans, and ducks. An extensive series of cases of eggs of birds, ranged to correspond with the cases of the birds themselves, and placed opposite them, gives completeness to the whole.

In 1874 an important addition was made to the Natural History Department by the acquisition of Mrs. J. E. Craig's collection of shells, comprising some 12,000 specimens, and representing about 4,000 different species. In the same year the collection of beetles formed by Mr. Edward Saunders, and numbering upwards of 7,000 specimens, was purchased for its use.

Above the cases which line the walls of this gallery is a series of portraits, one hundred and thirteen in number, among which are a few of particular interest, notably those of Oliver Cromwell, painted by Walker, and bequeathed to the Museum in the year 1784 by Sir Robert Rich, to whose great-grandfather, Nathaniel Rich, Esq., then serving as a Colonel of Horse in the Parliamentary Army, it was presented by the great "Lord Protector" himself; one of Mary Queen of Scots, by Jansen; and one of Queen Elizabeth, by Zucchero. Here, too, may be seen portraits of Charles II. (by Sir Peter Lely), Sir Isaac Newton, Sir Hans Sloane, and Sir Robert Cotton; Sir William Dugdale, William Camden, and John Speed, the historians; Shakespeare, Algernon Sidney, and Alexander Pope; Philip Dormer, Earl of Chesterfield, and Thomas Britton (the " Musical small-coal man "). But still the British Museum does not even claim, or pretend to contain, a National Portrait Gallery of Eminent Englishmen : we shall find such a gallery, and shall have much to say about it, when we reach South Kensington.

The first room in the northern zoological gallery contains an interesting display of the nests of birds and insects from various countries. " In one group of cases are nests of wasps and bees; some are constructed of clay, or of sand, while others are of paper, made of an admixture of the scrapings of wood and vegetable fibre. Specimens of the various insect fabricators of these structures are, in many instances, attached to the nests. In another case we find the remains of the square lintel of a door of one of the government offices in St. Helena, showing the destruction caused by a species of white ant. Then there are a series of the different stages of development, and of the products, of the Japanese silk-moths, prepared and set up in Japan. Among the more noticeable of the nests of birds are the playing avenues of the Australian bower-birds, the pendulous nests of the American orioles, and the gelatinous nests of the esculent swallow; and that of the San Geronimo swallow, which is a long pendulous tube formed entirely of the seed of a plant, secured together by the saliva of the bird; the hollow for the eggs is at the top, inside the tube; the bird has placed a false entrance on the side to deceive its enemies. Various nests of humming-birds, honey-eaters, tailor-bird, and lyre-tailed menuras are also shown. Another group of cases contains specimens illustrative of the various changes of insects, their nests and structures; the cocoon of the gigantic goliath beetle of Western Africa, the clay nests of various species of white ants, the various vegetable galls, and a series of the nests of spiders; among these the nests of the trap-door spider, and a remarkable flat web, constructed by an Australian species, are shown here. On the walls are suspended some specimens of the large gigantic land-tortoises, which once inhabited in large numbers the Galapagos and the islands of Mauritius, Rodriguez, and Aldabra. They formed a very important article of food to navigators in the seventeenth and eighteenth centuries during the protracted and tedious voyages across the Indian and Pacific Oceans, but are now almost extinct."

The succeeding rooms devoted to zoology, five in number, contain chiefly the various specimens of reptiles, such as serpents, tortoises, crocodiles, and lizards; toads, frogs, and efts; and the various species of marine products, such as star-fishes and sea-wigs. Here, too, are the spiny-rayed and anomalous fishes; insects; crustacea, including such varieties as the crab and lobster; and also sturgeons and pikes, &c.; whilst over the wall-cases, or suspended from the roof, are ranged the larger fish which could not be accommodated within, such as the famous flying sword-fish, sharks, and congers.

On the north side, running parallel with the above-mentioned rooms, is the gallery of minerals and fossils. In no department, probably, is the Museum richer than in its minerals. These occupy the table-cases of four large rooms; the fossil remains of the invertebrate animals being displayed on the floor of the fifth and sixth rooms, and in the wall-cases throughout the entire gallery. In the lobby, at the eastern end of this gallery, is a restored model of the shell of an extinct fossil tortoise, of gigantic size, from the Siwalik Hills, in India. Portions of the shell, and of other parts of the skeleton of several different individuals of this species of tortoise, are deposited in the third room of the gallery, and it is of casts from some of these portions that the restored model is, in a great measure, composed. In this gallery will be found the fossil remains of those gigantic ante-diluvian animals and reptiles, which for so many years have excited the curiosity and stimulated the energies of men learned in geological science —such as the mastodon, the megatherium, the iguanodon, and the megalosaurus; then there are fossil plants, fishes, mammalia, insects, and shells; and perhaps the most extraordinary of all, a fossil human skeleton. This last-named "specimen" was brought from Guadaloupe by Sir Alexander Cochrane, and presented to the Museum by the Lords of the Admiralty. It was found embedded in the solid limestone rock, and much discussion has arisen as to its antiquity; "but," writes Sir Henry Ellis, "the most probable conjecture is that it is not more than a few centuries old." This skeleton (which is described in the "Philosophical Transactions" of the Royal Society) wants the skull, and it is a curious fact, mentioned by Sir Charles Lyell, in his "Travels in North America," that in the Museum at Charleston, South Carolina, he was shown a fossil human skull from Guada-loupe, embedded in solid limestone, "which they say belongs to the same skeleton of a female as that now preserved in the British Museum, where the skull is wanting." Dr. Moultrie, of the Medical College of that State, has described the bones, together with the entire skeleton disen-tombed from the limestone deposit at Guadaloupe, and is of opinion—taking for granted the relation of the skull at Charleston to the headless trunk in London—that the latter is not the skeleton of a Carib, as has been generally supposed, but that of one of the Peruvians, or of a tribe possessing a similar craniological development."

Before proceeding to describe the antiquities, we may say a few words about the botanical collection. This is very extensive, and is exhibited in two rooms, which are entered by a doorway on the eastern side of the central zoological saloon. The collection consists of dried plants, and other botanical specimens, and had its origin in the collection of herbaria formed from time to time by Sir Hans Sloane during his long life, or, at all events, from the year 1687, when he went out to Jamaica as physician to the Duke of Albemarle,

"his chief inducement being the opportunity that it would afford him of studying his favourite science." On his return to England, he brought with him a collection of 800 species of West India plants. These, together with various others pre-sented to or purchased by Sir Hans Sloane, are contained in about 300 volumes. To these have been added the herbarium of Baron von Moll, of Munich; and also that of Sir Joseph Banks. The latter alone formed at one time, it is said, the most valuable assemblage of dried plants in Europe, and is still one of the most important, not only on account of its extent, but as containing the original and authentic specimens of many published species. Besides the above, we learn that additions have since been made from various other sources, which make the entire number of species amount to about 50,000—"sufficient to entitle the Museum collec-tion to rank among the finest in the world."

The department of antiquities is divided into two series: the first, consisting of sculpture, includ-ing inscriptions and architectural remains, occupies the ground-floor of the south-western and western portions of the building, besides some rooms in the basement, not originally designed for exhibition, but now supplying the only space which the exten-sive acquisitions recently made from Assyria and other countries have left available for that purpose. The second series, placed in a suite of rooms on the upper floor, comprises all the smaller remains, of whatever nation or period, such as vases, terra-cottas, bronzes, coins, and medals, and articles of personal or domestic use. To the latter division is attached the collection of ethnographical speci-mens. In the infancy of the Museum, the antiqui-ties being few in number, and of comparatively little value, were considered, with other artificial curiosities, as an appendage to the natural history; the coins, medals, and drawings were at that time appended to the department of manuscripts; and the prints and engravings to the library of printed books. On the purchase of Sir William Hamilton's collection of Greek and Roman antiquities, in 1772, for the sum of £8,400, the augmentations even then were not considered sufficient to require an increase of the establishment; but on the acquisition of the Egyptian monuments at the capitulation of Alexandria, in the year 1801, and the purchase of the Towneley marbles shortly after-wards, additional accommodation was needed, and several new buildings were erected, as we have already shown. It was then that a new department was created, by the name of the Department of Antiquities; and thus, as Sir Henry Ellis writes, "the magnificent collection of ancient sculpture was at length opened for the inspection of strangers and the improvement of artists, an advantage which the students of the Fine Arts had never before enjoyed in this country."

On leaving the rooms containing the botanical specimens, and crossing the central saloon, the visitor enters the Ethnographical room, where will be found a curious and interesting collection of antiquities, and the objects in modern use, belonging to all nations, not of European race. In one table-case are antiquities discovered during excavations in India; in another, a group of Peruvian and Mexican antiquities; whilst others contain dresses and implements in use among the Esquimaux tribes, as well as objects illustrative of the late Arctic expeditions, chiefly collected by Sir John Barrow. With reference to the contents of the wall-cases in this room, we can only remark that they comprise a very miscellaneous assortment of articles, including specimens of wearing apparel, warlike implements, idols, musical instruments, sepulchral vases, pottery, domestic utensils, &c.

The British and Mediæval room contains three collections—namely, the British, consisting of antiquities found in Great Britain and Ireland, extending from the earliest period to the Norman Conquest; the Early Christian; and the Mediæval, comprising all remains of the Middle Ages, both English and foreign. Here we have in abundance such relics of the past as urns and other funeral remains found in tumuli; flint implements of a peculiar pear-shaped form, believed to be the oldest objects of human industry hitherto discovered; stone hammers and axe-heads; implements and weapons made of bronze; also vases and lamps. Among the historical relics in the mediæval collection we may mention the casket made out of Shakespeare's mulberry-tree, at one time in the possession of David Garrick; the punchbowl of Robert Burns; and portions of the frescoes in St. Stephen's Chapel, Westminster, executed in the latter half of the fourteenth century.

Between the two rooms above mentioned is a doorway leading to a small ante-room containing the collection of gold ornaments and gems. Here we find specimens of mediæval and modern jewellery, Greek, Roman, and Etruscan ornaments of an early period. And here also are exhibited the unrivalled collection of cameos and intaglios, formed chiefly by the bequests of the Payne Knight and Cracherode collections, and by the purchase of those of Towneley, Hamilton, Blacas, and Castellani. On one of the cases in this room is placed the celebrated glass vase, placed here in 1810 by its owner, the Duke of Portland, and

thence popularly known as the Portland Vase. It was found in a marble sarcophagus in the Monte del Grano, near Rome, about the middle of the sixteenth century, and was afterwards deposited in the Barberini Palace, where it remained until 1770, when it was purchased by Byres, the antiquary, who sold it to Sir William Hamilton, of whom it was bought, for 1,800 guineas, by the Duchess of Portland, at the sale of whose property it was bought in by the family for £1,029. The ground of the vase is of dark-blue glass, and the design is cut in a layer of opaque white glass, the figures standing out in bold relief. The composition is classical; it is supposed by some to represent the meeting of Peleus and Thetis on Mount Pelion, and Thetis consenting to be the bride of Peleus, in the presence of Poseidon and Eros. On the bottom of the vase, which is detached, is a bust of Atys. This vase is considered one of the principal ornaments of the Museum, and till 1845 it was as perfect as when it was first fashioned. In that year a drunken mechanic, named William Lloyd, found his way into the Museum, and appears to have taken a dislike to the vase, a feeling which he gave vent to by deliberately hurling at it a stone which was lying close at hand; the result was that this peerless vase, as well as the glass case which contained it, was smashed to pieces. The man was at once taken before the magistrate, who sentenced him to pay the cost of damage to the case, but had no power to commit him for breaking the vase, except at the instigation of its ducal owner, who happened at the time to be out of town. In the meantime the money was paid, and the fellow was accordingly discharged. Although the vase was literally smashed into a thousand pieces, the fragments were carefully collected, and a drawing made of them, which is preserved. The fractured pieces were afterwards replaced and cemented together by Mr. Doubleday, a gentleman who had for a long time been engaged at the Museum in repairing pottery and sculpture; and the manner in which he accomplished his task was so far successful that the exquisite form and proportions of the vase have been restored in such a way that scarcely a blemish can be detected. The vase is ten inches high, and its diameter seven inches at the broadest part near the centre, and it has two handles. It diminishes gradually towards the base, and more rapidly upwards into the narrow neck, which again opens towards the lip by a graceful flower-like expansion. Copies of the vase were executed by Wedgwood, and sold at fifty guineas each; the model is said to have cost 500 guineas.

Among the miscellaneous curiosities which are preserved in this room are the gold snuff-box, set with diamonds, and ornamented with a miniature portrait of Napoleon, who, in 1815, presented it to the Hon. Mrs. Damer, the sculptress, by whom it was bequeathed to the Museum; a gold snuff-box, with a cameo lid, presented by Pope Pius VI. to Napoleon, and by him bequeathed to Lady Holland, with a card in Napoleon's handwriting; and also a cast taken from the face of Oliver Cromwell after death.

The medal-room contains a collection of coins and medals superior to almost that of any other country. Sir Hans Sloane's collection, which formed the nucleus, was worth about £7,000 as bullion. To these were added those of Sir Robert Cotton, the Hamilton and Cracherode, valued at several thousand guineas; Roberts's collection of coins from the Conquest to George III.; a series of Papal medals; a collection of Greek coins; a vast collection of foreign coins, presented by Miss Banks; and many others, both by bequest and purchase. Of Queen Anne's farthings here are seven varieties, one only of which was circulated, the others being pattern pieces. Mr. John Timbs, in his "Curiosities," remarks that "the real Queen Anne's farthing, with the figure of Britannia on the reverse, and below it, in the exergue, the date 1714, brings from 7s. to a guinea; but at Baron Bolland's sale, in 1841, a pattern piece fetched £9 9s. The idea that there is but one Queen Anne's farthing in existence, and that only three were struck, is a popular error, several hundreds having been struck. This erroneous belief has caused the British Museum authorities almost as many annoyances as the rarity of a 'tortoiseshell tom-cat.'" In this room are preserved a few coins which have acquired an interest from their former owners or from other circumstances, rather than from their own intrinsic value; and of these we may mention the "Pulteney Guinea," respecting which the following story is told:—"William Pulteney, afterwards Earl of Bath, was remarkable alike for his oratorical talents and his long and consistent opposition to the measures of Sir Robert Walpole, the great Whig minister. On the 11th of February, 1741, a time when party feeling was at its height, Walpole received an intimation in the House of Commons that it was the intention of the Opposition to impeach him. To this menace he replied with his usual composure and self-complacence, merely requesting a fair and candid hearing, and winding up his speech with the quotation—

'Nil conscire sibi, nulli pallescere culpæ.'

With his usual tact Pulteney immediately rose, and observed 'that the right honourable gentleman's logic and Latin were alike inaccurate, and that Horace, whom he had just misquoted, had written 'nullâ pallescere culpâ.' Walpole maintained that his quotation was correct, and a bet was offered. The matter was referred to Nicholas Hardinge, Clerk of the House, an excellent classical scholar, who decided against Sir Robert. The minister accordingly took a guinea from his pocket, and flung it across the house to Pulteney. The latter caught it, and holding it up, exclaimed, 'It's the only money I have received from the Treasury for many years, and it shall be the last.' This guinea having been carefully preserved, finally came into the hands of Sir John Murray, by whom it was presented, in 1828, to the British Museum. The following memorandum, in the handwriting of Pulteney, is attached to it:—'This guinea I desire may be kept as an heirloom. It was won of Sir Robert Walpole in the House of Commons; he asserting the verse in Horace to be "nulli pallescere culpæ," whereas I laid the wager of a guinea that it was "nullâ pallescere culpâ." He sent for the book, and being convinced that he had lost, gave me this guinea. I told him I could take the money without any blush on my side, but believed it was the only money he ever gave in the house where the giver and the receiver ought not equally to blush. This guinea, I hope, will prove to my posterity the use of knowing Latin, and encourage them in their learning.'"

The bronze-room, which we now enter, contains the collection of Greek, Roman, and Etruscan bronzes, with the exception of such as have been found in Great Britain, which are placed in the British and Mediæval room. It was originally composed of the Sloane, Hamilton, Towneley, and Payne Knight collections, to which have been added, in recent years, the bronzes bequeathed by Sir William Temple, and many other interesting objects acquired by purchase or donation, including figures of divinities, furniture, mirrors, lamps and vases, personal ornaments, tripods, candelabra, &c. Several of the objects here exhibited were discovered by Mr. Layard in Assyria; whilst others are from the sepulchres of ancient Etruria, and the excavations at Pompeii and Herculaneum. Here, too, are the exquisite bronzes bequeathed by Mr. R. Payne Knight and Mr. Felix Slade. Among the most recent additions to the contents of this room may be noticed John Milton's watch. This curious timepiece, made by W. Bunting, and worn and used by the poet, was bequeathed to the nation by the late Sir C. Fellows, in 1860; the rest of his collection was added by his widow in 1874.

The two vase-rooms, through which we now pass, contain a large number of Græco-Italian vases painted from the myths or popular poetry of the day; and in the next room (Egyptian room) is dis-

interest, but as furnishing a valuable preparative for the due appreciation of the first series of sculptures (the Egyptian) which we shall find on the ground-floor. The smaller antiquities of Egypt which are

A SLAB FROM THE NINEVEH GALLERY. (*See page* 531.)

played the collections of ancient and more recent glass, including the very valuable bequest made to the Museum in 1868 by Mr. Felix Slade, number-ing about 960 specimens, to which additions have been made since his death out of a fund bequeathed for the purpose, making a total of 1,750 specimens. This room and also the next in order should be carefully inspected, not merely for its own intrinsic

here exhibited comprise divinities, royal person-ages, and sacred animals; sepulchral remains; and miscellaneous objects illustrative of the domestic manners of the Egyptians. They were acquired mainly by purchase from private collections, and by donations from the Prince of Wales, the Duke of Northumberland, the late Sir Gardner Wilkinson, and other travellers in Egypt. Charles Knight, in his "London," remarks that "ancient Egypt here revives before us—Osiris and Isis are no longer mere names; we behold them face to face, as their worshippers beheld them, who are here also represented, and that so numerously, in their mummies and mummy-cases, and who look so life-like from out their portraits upon us that one is half tempted to question them, and many a knotty riddle could no doubt be solved if the humblest of them would

"The preparations for embalming the dead, and ceremonies at funerals," as we learn from Herodotus in the words of the 'Guide to the Museum,' "were looked on as matters of importance by the Egyptians, and large sums were spent upon the sepulchral rites. There were several modes of preparing the mummies, varying not only at different periods, but also with the rank and wealth of the person to be interred. The more costly process was as

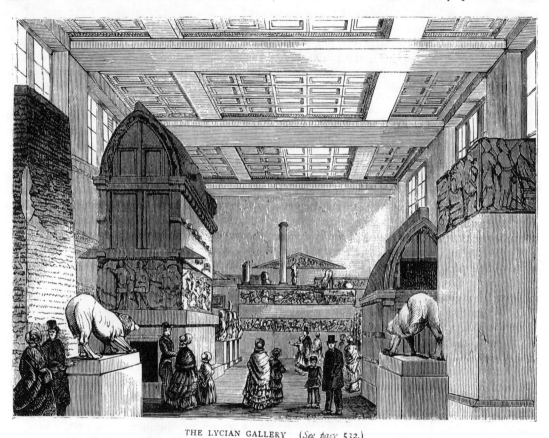

THE LYCIAN GALLERY (See page 532.)

but speak. Yes, here are the very people of Egypt themselves; we see the expression of their faces, the colour of their hair, the outlines of their form; we know their very names, and their professions; this, for instance, is Otaineb, no Egyptian born, but one, no doubt, by naturalisation, as the gods of the country are exhibited on the case, taking especial care of him; Thoth, the Egyptian Mercury, is there seen introducing him to the many deities to whom the different parts of his body are respectively dedicated. This, again, is Hor, or Horus, incense-bearer to the abode of Noum-ra; this, Onkhhapê, a sacred musician; this Khonsaouonkh, a sacerdotal functionary and scribe; this Kotbi, a priestess of the Theban temple of Amoun; that, Har-sont-ioft, a priest of the same building."

follows:—The brain having been extracted, and the viscera removed through an opening cut in the left side with a stone, the body was, in earlier times, prepared with salt and wax—in later times, steeped or boiled in bitumen; then wrapped round with bands of linen, sometimes 700 yards in length; various amulets being placed in different parts, and the whole covered with a linen shroud and sometimes decorated with a network of porcelain bugles. It was then enclosed in a thin case formed of canvas, thickened with a coating of stucco, on which were painted figures of divinities and emblems of various kinds, as well as the name and titles of the deceased, and portions of the ritual of the dead. The whole was then enclosed in a wooden coffin, and sometimes deposited in a stone sarcophagus."

One of the most remarkable objects in the Egyptian collection is part of the mummy-shaped coffin of King Menkara, the Mycerinus of the Greeks, builder of the Third Pyramid. This is not only the oldest coffin in the collection, but one of the earliest inscribed monuments of Egypt. Near it is part of a body, supposed to be that of the king, found in the same pyramid. There is also a small Græco-Egyptian mummy of a child from Thebes; on the external wrapper is painted a representation of the deceased.

In the Egyptian ante-room, at the top of the staircase by which we descend to the ground-floor, the walls are partly covered with casts from sculptured and coloured bas-reliefs in Egypt, painted in imitation of the originals.

Upon the walls of the staircase are placed Egyptian papyri—documents of various character, inscribed on rolls, formed of thin layers or slices of the papyrus plant. The characters presented comprise "chiefly portions or extracts from the 'Ritual of the Dead,' the small pictures in them referring to the subjects of the various chapters; others are solar litanies and magical tracts. Among them is a caricature, and a treatise on arithmetic and geometry, one on medicine, with recipes of the age of Cheops, the romantic tale of a doomed prince, songs, dirges, criminal reports, and several contracts or deeds of sale in the demotic character."

In the vestibule at the foot of the stairs are placed monuments of the first twelve dynasties of Egyptian monarchs. Though small in size, they have considerable interest, being the most ancient sculptures in the Museum. The plaster cast from the head of the colossal statue of Rameses II., at Ibsamboul, placed over the east doorway of the vestibule, seems to keep watch and ward over the assembled treasures.

By a doorway at the foot of the stairs we enter the series of galleries devoted to Egyptian monuments and sculptured antiquities. The collection embraces a wide range of antiquity, commencing as far back as 2,000 years before the Christian era, and closing with the Mohammedan invasion of Egypt, A.D. 640. "The earlier sepulchral monuments," as we learn from the report of Dr. Birch, the keeper of this department, "are chiefly from Memphis, the capital of the most important of the more ancient dynasties, and the ruins of which are on the left bank of the Nile, opposite Cairo. Other early remains are derived from the great burial-place of Abydos. The main portion of the collection, including most of the monuments belonging to the kings of the 18th, 19th, and 20th dynasties, was obtained from the ancient city of Thebes.

which became the capital of Egypt under those monarchs." In the first gallery the larger sculptures belong to the 18th dynasty. It commenced with the expulsion of the "Shepherd Kings" from Lower Egypt, and its monarchs extended their conquests into Æthiopia and Asia, and built great edifices at Thebes. In the centre of the gallery towers aloft the colossal head of King Thothmes III., discovered by Belzoni near the granite sanctuary at Karnak, and near it is the arm of the same figure. Close by is a monument sculptured on four sides, representing in bas-relief the above-named king, supported by the god Muntra and the goddess Athor. In the central recess, on the east side of the gallery, is fixed the tablet of Abydos, said to be an inscription of great value in determining the names and succession of the kings of the various dynasties. It appears originally to have commemorated an offering made by Rameses II. to his predecessors on the throne of Egypt; and it was discovered by Mr. W. Bankes in a chamber of the temple of Abydos, in 1818. Among the curious objects here brought together are several statues of the cat-headed goddess Sekhet (Bubastis), inscribed with the name of the same monarch; the head of a colossal ram, from an avenue of ram-headed sphinxes, which led to a gateway built by King Horus, at Karnak. The king himself is also represented by two statues in black marble, one of which represents him under the protection of the god Amen-ra. The central saloon, through which we now pass, is chiefly occupied by monuments of the age of King Rameses II. Between the columns on the right is a colossal fist, in red granite, from one of the statues which stood before the great temple at Memphis, and close by are three colossal heads; one of these is a cast from a statue of Rameses, at Mitraheny; the next, a head and shoulders from the building called the Memnonium, at Thebes; and the other that of a queen. The principal objects in the southern gallery are the granite sarcophagus of Hapimen, a royal scribe; the elaborately-worked sarcophagus of the Queen of Amasis II., and another of King Nectanebo I., dating some three or four centuries before the Christian era; on the exterior are representations of the sun passing through the heavens in his boat, and on the interior various divinities; then there is a finely-sculptured group, in sandstone, of a male and female figure seated; and also a statue of King Menephtah II., on a throne, with a ram's head on his knees. One of the most interesting and valuable of the objects exhibited in this department is the famous Rosetta Stone. This stone, a black basalt, is inscribed in hieroglyphics, the ancient spoken language of Egypt, and in Greek, with the services of Ptolemy V. Tradition tells us that Professor Porson used to visit the Museum in order to read and decipher this stone, whence he got from the officials the name of "Judge Black-stone."

Several of the most important relics in the Egyptian Galleries were discovered by Belzoni, and came into the possession of the Museum through the bequest of a Mr. Salt, to whom Belzoni had engaged himself. Belzoni was a native of Padua, and came to England early in the present century. He was called "the strong man," a name which he no doubt merited, seeing that he stood nearly seven feet in height, and was well formed and stout in proportion. He exhibited his feats of strength in the minor theatres in the metropolis, and at Edinburgh. It was at Cairo that he became engaged to Mr. Salt, and from that time he was regularly employed in making discoveries, all of which are fully described in Belzoni's "Narrative of the Operations and Recent Discoveries within the Pyramids, Temples, Tombs, and Excavations in Egypt and Nubia ; and of a Journey to the Coast of the Red Sea, in search of the ancient Berenice, and another to the Oasis of Jupiter Ammon ;" this great work was published shortly after his return to England. In 1823, Belzoni, accompanied by his wife, again left England, on another journey of discovery into Africa ; but he died at Benin, on his way thither, from an attack of dysentery, in the same year.

The south end of the Egyptian Galleries opens into the Assyrian transept, which, together with a long and narrow gallery connected with it, running north and south, contain the collection of sculptures excavated, chiefly by Mr. Layard, in the years 1847-50, on the site, or in the vicinity, of ancient Nineveh. To these has been added a further collection, from the same region, excavated in 1853-55 by Mr. Hormuzd Rassam and Mr. W. K. Loftus, under the direction of Sir H. C. Rawlinson, who was at that time Her Majesty's Consul-General at Bagdad. Many of the objects here brought together are covered with pictorial representations of historical events, and inscribed with cuneiform characters. In 1873-4 valuable additions were made to this collection in the shape of a large number of burnt clay tablets, excavated at Kouyunjik, by Mr. George Smith. These tablets have been in part deciphered by Mr. Smith, who has found them to contain Chaldean legends of the creation, fall, deluge, building of the Tower of Babel, &c. The tablets were presented to the Museum by the proprietors of the *Daily Telegraph,* at whose expense Mr. Smith's labours in Assyria were conducted.

Mr. Layard's discoveries, as we learn from his "Nineveh and its Remains," were, for the most part, made in extensive mounds formed by the natural accumulation of the soil over the *débris* of ruined edifices, in the three following localities :— 1. Nimroud, believed to be the ancient Calah of Scripture, on the banks of the Tigris, about twenty miles below the modern Mosul. 2. Khorsabad, a site about ten miles to the north-east of Mosul, which was excavated for the French Government by M. Botta, and from which was procured the greater part of the valuable collection now in the Louvre, though a few specimens of sculpture have also been obtained for the British Museum. 3. Kouyunjik, still indicated by local tradition as the site of Nineveh, nearly opposite Mosul, on the Tigris.

There is monumental evidence that of the various buildings which Mr. Layard excavated, that of the palace of Nimroud was older by several centuries than the edifices of Khorsabad and Kouyunjik. To this palace, the son of a founder added a second ; subsequent additions are recorded in the inscriptions, and the place at last attained the dimensions ascribed to it by Jonah. "If (says Mr. Layard) we take the four great mounds of Nimroud, Kouyunjik, Khorsabad, and Karamles, as the angle of a square, it will be found that its four sides corresponded pretty accurately with the 480 stadia, or sixty miles of the geographer, which makes the three days' journey of the prophet." Within this space there are many mounds, ruins of edifices, vestiges of streets and gardens ; and the face of the country is strewed with fragments of pottery and bricks. As to the number of inhabitants, mentioned in the book of Jonah (chap. iv. 11) to be above 120,000, a number which seems apparently incommensurate with a city of such vast dimensions, Mr. Layard remarks that cities in the East are not like those in Europe ; for such places as London or Paris would not contain above a third of the number of their inhabitants. The women have separate apartments from the men ; there is a separate house for each family ; and gardens and arable land are inclosed by the city walls. Hence it is mentioned in the book of Jonah that there was "much cattle" within the walls of the city, and, of course, there was pasture for them. The existing ruins, Mr. Layard tells us, " show that Nineveh acquired its greatest extent in the time of the kings of the second dynasty, that is, of the kings mentioned in Scripture ; it was then that Jonah visited it, and that reports of its magnificence were carried to the west, and gave rise to the traditions from which the Greek authors mainly derived the information which has been handed down to us."

The monuments obtained by Mr. Layard from Kouyunjik are stated to date from the supposed era of the destruction of Nineveh, and were procured from the remains of a very extensive Assyrian edifice, which appears, from the inscriptions remaining on many of its sculptures, to have been the palace of Sennacherib, who is presumed to have commenced his reign about B.C. 700. For the most part, these remains consist of large slabs of alabaster or limestone, covered with carved figures and inscriptions, which occupied the place of panels in the walls of the palace. One group of slabs, six in number, formed originally part of a series illustrating the architectural works of King Sennacherib, including, probably, the construction of the very edifice from which the slabs were obtained. On two of them is seen the conveyance of a colossal human-headed bull, lying sideways on a sledge, which is propelled, over wooden rollers, partly by ropes in front, partly by a lever behind. On one side is a lofty mound, which labourers are erecting with stones or earth, and which is, perhaps, designed for the platform of the future palace. The workmen are guarded by soldiers, and superintended by Sennacherib himself, in a chariot drawn by two men. A similar mound is represented on the next slab, with an adjoining stone-quarry or clay-pit, where the materials of construction are prepared; whilst on the succeeding one is a portion of a group moving some weighty object. On the next slab is another colossal bull, represented as before; and on the last is depicted the monarch, in his chariot, directing some operation sculptured on a lost portion of the series. The background of the slabs exhibits men carrying axes, saws, ropes, and other implements; and along the top are representations of the natural scenery of the country, water filled with fish, anglers floating on inflated skins, boats, banks lined with trees, and a jungle of reeds, in which are deer, and a wild sow with her young.

By a doorway on the west side of the Nimroud Central Saloon, we pass into the Hellenic Room. Among the marbles here exhibited, the first in importance is a collection discovered by Professor Cockerell, in 1812, among the ruins of the Temple of Apollo, near the ancient Phigalia, in Arcadia. This edifice was erected by Iktinos, the architect of the Parthenon, at Athens, in commemoration of the delivery of the Phigalians from the plague, B.C. 430. The chief part of these treasures consists of twenty-three sculptured slabs, originally belonging to a frieze in the interior of the *cella* of the temple. Eleven of them represent in high relief the con-

test between the Centaurs and Greeks, and the remaining twelve the invasion of Greece by the Amazons.

The Elgin Room, which is next entered, forms the western side of the Museum. Here are arranged the noble sculptures from the Parthenon, a portion of the frieze of the Temple of the Wingless Victory, at Athens, some architectural remains from the Erectheum, together with a number of fragments and casts, all from Athens. The sculptures from the Parthenon, and nearly all the marbles in this room, were obtained by the Earl of Elgin, when Ambassador at Constantinople, in the years 1801–3, by virtue of a firman from the Sublime Porte. We have already spoken of the purchase of the Elgin collection by the Government in a previous chapter.

A doorway at the southern end of the Elgin Room leads into the Mausoleum Room, where are arranged the fragments of the Mausoleum at Halicarnassus, erected by Artemisia, about B.C. 352, over the remains of her husband, Mausolus, Prince of Caria, and discovered by Mr. Newton, in 1857. The structure, we are told, when perfect, " consisted of a lofty basement, on which stood an oblong Ionic edifice, surrounded by columns, and surmounted by a pyramid, on the summit of which was a chariot group in white marble. The edifice which supported the pyramid was encircled by a frieze richly sculptured in high relief, and representing the battle of Greeks and Amazons. The material of the sculptures was Parian marble, and the whole structure was richly ornamented with colour. The tomb of Mausolus was of the class called by the Greeks *heröon*, and so greatly excelled all other sepulchral monuments in size, beauty of design, and richness of decoration, that it was reckoned one of the Seven Wonders of the ancient world, and the name Mausoleum came to be applied to all similar monuments."

Passing through the Greek ante-room, we enter the Lycian Gallery. The antiquities exhibited in this room comprise architectural and sculptural remains obtained from ancient cities in Lycia, one of the south-western provinces of Asia Minor. They were removed from that country in two expeditions, undertaken by Her Majesty's Government in the years 1842–6, under the direction of Sir C. Fellows, by whom the greater part of the marbles in this room were discovered. The building, of which the sculptures and various architectural members here brought together formed a part, has, by some, been considered a trophy in memory of the conquest of Lycia by the Persians, under Harpagos, B.C. 545.

In 1874, an addition was made to the collection in this gallery, in the shape of fragments of columns, bases and capitals, &c., from the Temple of Diana at Ephesus, which had been discovered by Mr. Wood, in explorations made during the two or three previous years. Among the fragments sent hither by Mr. Wood were "the lower drum of a column, nearly entire, with figures sculptured on it in relief, and large fragments of two or more drums, similarly sculptured; also the base of a pilaster, sculptured in relief, on the same scale as the drums." These sculptured drums, it is considered, "are evidently portions of the thirty-six columns of the temple, which Pliny describes as *cælatæ*, or 'sculptured in relief.'" The architectural marbles present many interesting features; some of the smaller fragments, for instance, "retain traces of red colour; while the calcined surface of other marbles, and their charcoal smears, tell the sad story of some ancient conflagration, in which, probably, perished the beautiful timber roof and the staircase, cunningly wrought in vine-wood."

A staircase in the south-west corner of the building leads into the Græco-Roman basement room, to which the basement of the Lycian Room is annexed. In this room are shown figures and reliefs of the Græco-Roman period, miscellaneous objects in marble and other material, and the collection of tessellated pavements and mosaics, which has been formed chiefly from the discoveries at Carthage and Halicarnassus in 1856-8.

The next three rooms, extending along the southern front of the building, are known as the Græco-Roman Rooms, and are appropriated to statues, busts, and bas-reliefs, of quite a mixed class, and mostly of a classic character. Here we find several statues and busts of gods and goddesses, such as Hercules, Venus, Bacchus, Pan, and the like; but we can here notice only a few of them. In an alcove in the centre room is the Towneley Venus, found at Ostia, in 1776; and in the alcove on the opposite side is the celebrated Discobolus, or Quoit-thrower, presumed to be a copy of the famous bronze statue made by the sculptor Myron. In the western room is the beautiful female bust commonly called "Clytie." The bust is represented as emerging from the petals of a flower, and it was esteemed by Mr. Towneley as the gem of his collection. It was bought at Naples, from the Lorrenzano Palace, in 1772. The following curious anecdote connected with this piece of sculpture we quote from Charles Knight's "London:"—"During the Gordon riots, Mr. Towneley, as a Catholic, was marked out by the mob, who intended to attack the house in Park Street, where all his darling treasures were collected. He secured his cabinet of gems, and casting a long and lingering look behind at his marbles, was about to leave them to their fate, when, moved by some irrepressible impulse of affection, he took the bust in question into his arms and hurried off with it to his carriage. Fortunately the attack did not take place, and his 'wife,' as he called the lady represented, returned to her companions."

Passing on through the Roman Gallery, the last of the series of rooms devoted to the department of sculptured antiquities, we arrive once more in the entrance-hall, and so end our perambulation of this great national storehouse. There is, however, one more object which we should mention, and that is the skeleton of, we believe, the largest whale ever captured. This monster of the deep, measuring some hundred feet in length, was for many years an attraction at country fairs throughout the kingdom, a large number of caravans being used for its conveyance and exhibition; and it has at last found a resting-place in the basement of the Museum, under the Grenville Library, where it can be seen on application to the attendants.

It will be evident that the expenses of such an establishment as the British Museum must be very considerable, and that many persons must be occupied in fulfilling the duties attached to it. We have already spoken of the principal librarian as being head and chief, under the trustees, of the whole working body of the establishment. Besides this officer, there are upwards of one hundred persons engaged in the various departments, either as "keepers," or "senior assistants," or "junior assistants;" and in addition, there is a little army of assistants dispersed through the libraries and saloons, perhaps upwards of another hundred strong. Then there are a few "fumatori," or castmakers, and a regular corps of index-makers and bookbinders, constantly employed, as well as a goodly number of household servants. It may, perhaps, be almost needless to remark here that every precaution is taken to ensure the safety of the collection. Like the Bank of England, this building has a detachment of the Guards nightly sent to keep watch and ward against intruders from without; whilst the destruction of the edifice by fire is a thing well nigh impossible, seeing that no light is allowed to be carried about whatever, either by night or by day, and that, through the same fear of fire, all night studies are forbidden.

We conclude this subject with a few general remarks. If we compare it with similar institutions abroad, such as the Bibliothèque Nationale and the Louvre, at Paris, the Royal Libraries of Munich and Berlin, and the Vatican Library at Rome, we may safely claim for our national Museum a very high place. Viewed with reference to its collection of books, both as to quality and in quantity, it stands among the first in the world, combining as it does some 1,500,000 volumes, including nearly all the rarest specimens. Its manuscripts, also, are certainly first-rate in number, being fully equal to those of the Bibliothèque Nationale, though, per-

Towneley, the Payne-Knight, the Crackerode, and the Castellani cabinets, all of which are now incorporated together, and arranged in a mythological series. As a whole the collection ranks with that of Berlin, and though inferior to that of St. Petersburg, especially in respect of gold ornaments, it can hardly acknowledge any other rivals. Then, as to antiquities of a miscellaneous character, thanks, mainly, to Belzoni, who commenced the Egyptian

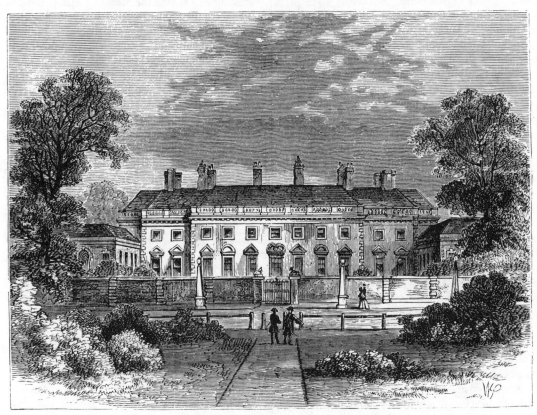

BEDFORD HOUSE, IN 1772 (*See page* 536.)

haps, in intrinsic value, they fall short of the treasures of the Vatican. Our statues from the antique, Greek and Roman, are the finest in the world, and our vases and bronzes are very good, though in modern statuary, just as in pictures, we do not pretend to make a show. Passing on to the other part of our art treasures, a very high rank may be claimed for our prints from the works of the ancient masters, though in topography, both English and foreign, the collection is poor, and our stores of portraits can be hardly said to be more than mediocre. Our coins are acknowledged to be very fine indeed; in Roman gold coins the Museum is superior even to the Bibliothèque Nationale, though inferior to it in Greek coins, and also in medallions. Our collection of gems comprises the Blacas, the

collection, we stand at the head of all; Lord Elgin robbed the Parthenon at Athens to enrich our stores of Greek statuary, as already mentioned; thanks to Mr. Layard, we are extremely rich, far richer than our rivals, in respect of treasures dug up in Assyria and at Nineveh; Sir Charles Fellows has given us a very beautiful collection of Carian and Lycian specimens; Mr. C. T. Newton has brought hither nearly all that was grand from Halicarnassus, including a large part of its celebrated Mausoleum; and more recently, as we have shown, Mr. Wood has contributed some most interesting relics from ancient Ephesus. The Crace Collection of prints of London topography, upon which we have drawn largely in this work, was added in 1881.

BLOOMSBURY SQUARE. (*See page* 536.)

CHAPTER XLI.

BLOOMSBURY SQUARE AND ITS NEIGHBOURHOOD.

——" Around what public works I see !
Lo ! stately streets. Lo ! squares that court the breeze."—*Thomson.*

Southampton (afterwards Bedford) House—The Patriot Lord Russell and his Noble-hearted Wife--An Historic Romance—Lucy, Countess of Bedford—An Episode in the Life of Anne, Wife of the Fifth Earl of Bedford—John; Fourth Duke of Bedford—Invitations to " take Tea and Walk in the Fields"—A Curious Advertisement—Richard Baxter, the Nonconformist Divine—An Anecdote about Dr. Radcliffe—Fashionable Residents—Poor Sir Richard Steele—Pope's Allusion to Bloomsbury Square—Sir Hans Sloane and his " Curiosities"—The Gordon Riots—Attack on Lord Mansfield's House—Charles Knight's Residence in this Square—Isaac D'Israeli, the Author of " Curiosities of Literature"—His Son, Benjamin Disraeli, born here—Edmund Lodge, the Eminent Biographer—Pharmaceutical Society of Great Britain—The Royal Literary Fund—The Famous Mississippi Schemer, Law—The Statue of Charles James Fox—Bloomsbury Market—Southampton Street and Row—National Benevolent Institution—Bloomsbury Place—Thomas Cadell, the Publisher—The Corporation of the Sons of the Clergy—Hart Street—St. George's Church—Archdeacon Nares—The Society of Biblical Archæology.

BLOOMSBURY SQUARE owes its origin to Thomas Wriothesley, Earl of Southampton, the son of Shakespeare's patron and friend, and also the father of Lady Rachel Russell, wife of Lord William Russell, whose tragic death we have recorded as the disgrace of Lincoln's Inn Fields.

Under date of February 9, 1665, Evelyn has the following note in his Diary, touching the building of this square :—" Dined at my Lord Treasurer's, the Earle of Southampton, in Blomesbury, where he was building a noble square or piazza, a little towne ; his owne house stands too low, some noble roomes, a pretty cedar chappell, a naked garden to the north, but good aire." It was at first called Southampton Square ; and Macaulay places it among the head-quarters of the fashion of the metropolis, in the reign of Charles II. " Foreign princes," he tells us, on the authority of the " Travels of the Grand Duke of Cosmo," " were taken to see the square as one of the wonders of England, whilst Soho Square, just built, was a subject of pride, with which the present generation will hardly sympathise."

Southampton House (afterwards called Bedford House), the residence of the above-mentioned earl, stood on the northern side of the square, and a portion of the ground which it occupied is now covered by some of the outbuildings on the east side of the British Museum. The mansion was not only the scene of the childhood and early life, but also, during many of the years of her widowhood, the home of that illustrious and noble woman, Lady Rachel Russell, many of whose " Letters" are dated from within its walls.

Northouck, the topographer, writing of Blooms-bury Square, in 1772, after the house had changed its name, observes :—" The north side is entirely taken up with Bedford House, which is elegant, though low, having but one storey. It was the work of Inigo Jones. Beside the body of the house are two wings, and on each side the proper offices. The square forms a magnificent area

before it, and the grand street in front throws the prospect of it open to Holborn. Behind, it has the advantage of most agreeable gardens, commanding a full view of the rising hills of Hampstead and Highgate ; so that it is hardly possible to conceive a finer situation than that of Bedford House."

One of the wings of the house, we are told, formed a magnificent gallery, in which were copies, by Sir James Thornhill, of the cartoons of Raphael, as large as the originals ; indeed, the mansion was very rich, for that date, in works of art, both sculptures and paintings. When the house was pulled down, about 1802, its contents were sold, and Sir James Thornhill's cartoons were disposed of for a little under £500 ! They would fetch a much higher price in the present day, when high art is better appreciated.

The Wriothesleys, Earls of Southampton, were heads of a family who long enjoyed considerable influence in State affairs, and held many important public offices. As far back as the reign of Edward IV. we find John Wriothsley (as the name was then spelt) occupying the post of " Faucon Herald," and as having letters patent for the office of Garter King-at-Arms in the first year of Richard III. His two sons likewise held offices in the College of Arms, and his grandson, Thomas Wriothesley, who was esteemed "a man of learning, and a good lawyer," was elevated to the peerage as Baron Wriothesley, in 1544, and soon afterwards, on the death of the great Lord Audley, constituted Lord Chancellor of England. Three years later his lordship was advanced to the Earldom of Southampton. His son Henry, second earl, was a friend of Thomas, Duke of Norfolk, and involved himself in trouble by promoting the contemplated marriage of that nobleman with Mary, Queen of Scots, " to whom and her religion (says Dugdale) he stood not a little affected." His successor, Henry, third earl, is not only known to history as the friend of Shakespeare in his early days, when he needed friends, but also as the companion in arms of the Earl of Essex, and a participator in the treason by which that unfortunate nobleman forfeited his life in the reign of Elizabeth. Lord Southampton was also tried, condemned, and attainted ; but his life was spared. Upon the accession of James I. he was released from prison, restored in blood by Act of Parliament, and created by a new patent, in the year 1603, Earl of Southampton, "with the same rights, precedency, and privileges, that he had formerly enjoyed." His son, Thomas, who succeeded as fourth earl, was a staunch supporter of Charles I., and was the Lord Treasurer mentioned by Evelyn in his note quoted above. His lordship died at Southampton House, "near Holburne, in the suburbs of London," in May, 1667, when his honours became extinct. The mansion remained in the possession of his daughter, Lady Rachel Russell, through whose marriage it passed into the possession of the Duke of Bedford, and afterwards, as we have said, came to be called Bedford House.

Lady William Russell, as every reader of English history knows, was a woman distinguished for her ardent and tender affection, "pious, reflecting, firm, and courageous; alike exemplary in prosperity and adversity, when observed by multitudes, or hidden in retirement." Her firm and noble conduct in attending her husband's trial, for the purpose of taking notes and giving him assistance, have been themes of the highest interest and admiration alike to the historian and the artist. The bitterness of their parting is described in the most pathetic language, and a lasting grief is shown in her subsequent correspondence. Lord William Russell, as we have stated in the previous volume,* was executed in Lincoln's Inn Fields, and his widow lived here in retirement till her death, in the reign of George I., at the age of eighty-six.

Lord Russell's father was the first Duke of Bedford. His Grace came of a good old Dorsetshire family, one member of whom is said to have gained a favourable introduction to Court through one of those unexpected incidents which may be attributed solely to good fortune. Sir Bernard Burke, in his "Peerage," relates how that towards the end of the reign of Henry VII., "the Archduke Philip of Austria, only son of the Emperor Maximilian I., and husband of Joanna, daughter of Ferdinand and Isabella, King and Queen of Castile and Aragon, having encountered a violent hurricane in his passage from Flanders to Spain, was driven into Weymouth, where he landed, and was hospitably received by Sir Thomas Trenchard, knight, a gentle-

man of rank in the neighbourhood. Sir Thomas immediately apprised the Court of the circumstance, and in the interim, while waiting for instructions what course to adopt, invited his first cousin, Mr. John Russell, then recently returned from his travels, to wait upon the Prince. The Prince, fascinated by Mr. Russell's companionable qualities, desired that he should accompany him to Windsor, whither the King had invited him on a visit. On the journey the Archduke became still more pleased with his attendant's 'learned discourse and generous deportment,' and recommended him strongly to the King. Mr. Russell was, in consequence, taken immediately into royal favour, and appointed one of the Gentlemen of the Privy Chamber. Becoming subsequently a favourite of Henry VIII., and a companion of that monarch in his French wars, Mr. Russell was appointed to several high and confidential offices." He was finally elevated to the peerage in 1538-9, as Baron Russell of Cheneys, Buckinghamshire; and on the dissolution of the monasteries, in the following year, he obtained a grant of the site of the abbey of Tavistock, and of extensive possessions belonging to it. After the accession of Edward VI., Lord Russell had a grant of the monastery of Woburn, in Bedfordshire, and was created Earl of Bedford. Francis, the second earl, was a person of great eminence during the reign of Elizabeth, and three of his sons likewise greatly distinguished themselves ; he was succeeded in the earldom by his grandson Edward, son of Francis, Lord Russell.

Lucy, Countess of Bedford, to whom Ben Jonson addresses several of his best epigrams, sister and co-heir of the second Lord Warrington, and wife of Edward, the third earl, was distinguished alike by the variety of her attainments, and her liberal patronage of men of genius. Amongst those upon whom this lady specially bestowed her munificence were Ben Jonson, Drayton, Daniel, and Donne ; and they have all paid poetical homage to her merits and her bounty. "Sir Thomas Roe," says Granger, "has addressed a letter to her as one skilled in medals; and she is celebrated by Sir William Temple for projecting the most perfect figure of a garden that he ever saw." She died in 1627. Ben Jonson thus addresses her :—

" Lucy, you brightness of our sphere, who are
    Life of the Muse's day, their morning star !
If works, not th' authors, their own grace should look,
    Whose poems would not wish to be your book?"

William, the fifth earl, to whom we now pass, was, in 1694, created Marquis of Tavistock and Duke of Bedford. He married Anne, daughter and sole heiress of Robert Carr, Earl of Somerset.

---

* See Vol. III., p. 45.

by his too celebrated Countess, Frances Howard, the divorced wife of Essex. "Francis, Earl of Bedford," the father of this nobleman, says Pennant, "was so adverse to the alliance, that he gave his son leave to choose a wife out of any other family but that. Opposition usually stimulates desire; the young couple's affections were only increased. At length the King interposed, and sending the Duke of Lennox to urge the Earl to consent, the match was brought about. Somerset, now reduced to poverty, acted a generous part, selling his house at Chiswick, plate, jewels, and furniture, to raise for his daughter a fortune of £12,000, which the Earl of Bedford demanded, saying, that since her affections were settled, he chose rather to undo himself than make her unhappy." It is said that the lady was ignorant of her mother's dishonour, till informed of it by a pamphlet, which she accidentally found; and it is added, that she was so struck with this detection of her parent's guilt, that she fell down in a fit, and was found senseless with the book open before her. The duke had by this admirable woman seven sons and three daughters, and the eldest surviving son was the celebrated patriot, Lord William Russell, of whom we have already spoken.

John, the fourth Duke of Bedford, to whom we now pass on, was for some time Lord Lieutenant of Ireland, and subsequently our ambassador to the Court of France, in which character he signed, at Fontainebleau, the preliminaries of peace with France and Spain. His Grace is mentioned by Lady Hervey, in her "Letters," as a "rich great person." He nevertheless had the misfortune of being very unpopular in his day, but he hardly deserved all the invectives with which Junius has "damned him to everlasting fame." In 1748 he gave at Bedford House a masqued ball, said to have been one of the most magnificent that ever had been given; the King, the Duke of Cumberland, and many of the nobility, being present in masquerade.

About this time, it is said that the Duchess of Bedford sent out cards to her guests, inviting them to "take tea and walk in the fields;" and sarcastic persons remarked, that it was expected that syllabubs would soon be milked in Berkeley Square, around the statue of his Majesty. In the same style, we are told that Lady Clermont was not more remarkable for her conversational parties than for her *al fresco* gatherings. In May, 1773, when living in St. James's Place, she issued invitations to 300 dear friends "to take tea and walk in the Park."

Having said thus much concerning Bedford House, and the families of its successive owners,

we now proceed to speak of the other parts of Bloomsbury Square. In 1642, we read, among the forts ordered by the Parliament to be raised around London, of "two batteries and a breastwork at Southampton (afterwards Bedford) House," probably in the present square.

Mr. Peter Cunningham, in his "Handbook of London," quotes one of the advertisements from the *London Gazette*, No. 946, which we take the liberty of copying here :—" Lost, from my Lady Baltinglasses (*sic*) house, in the great square of Bloomsbury, the first of this instant December (1674), a great old Indian spaniel or mongrel, as big as a mastiff; he hath curled and black hair all over, except in his fore-feet, which are a little white; he hath also cropt ears, and is bowed and limps a little in one of his fore-feet. If any can bring news thereof, they shall have twenty shillings for their pains."

In this square lived Richard Baxter, the Nonconformist divine, at the time of his persecution by Judge Jefferies; and here his wife died in 1681.

Dr. Mead, in " Richardsoniana," tells an amusing story about Dr. Radcliffe, the celebrated physician, whom we have already had occasion to mention, and who was living in this square when he gave £520 to the poor non-juring clergy. " Dr. Radcliffe," he says, "could never be brought to pay bills without much following and importunity; nor then if there appeared any chance of wearying them out. A paviour, after long and fruitless attempts, caught him just getting out of his chariot at his own door in Bloomsbury Square, and set upon him. 'Why, you rascal !' said the Doctor, 'do you pretend to be paid for such a piece of work? Why, you have spoiled my pavement, and then covered it over with earth, to hide your bad work !' 'Doctor !' said the paviour, 'mine is not the only bad work the earth hides.' 'You dog, you !' said the Doctor, 'are you a wit? You must be poor; come in'—and paid him."

Our readers will have already gathered from Macaulay's remark quoted above, that in Queen Anne's reign this neighbourhood could dispute for the palm of fashion with Lincoln's Inn Fields and Soho Square, and not without good reason; for at this time not only did the Russells live in Bloomsbury Square, but also Lord Paget, Lord Carleton, and the Earl of Northampton. Lord Mansfield's house was at the north-east corner. Lord Ellenborough, when Chief Justice, lived at the corner house of Bloomsbury Square and Orange Street, before he removed to St. James's Square; and Lord Chief Justice Trevor occupied a house on the west side of the square.

At his house here, in 1713, died Philip, second Earl of Chesterfield, the same who figures as a member of the Court of Charles II. and James II., in the "Memoirs" of Count Grammont. In June of the above year, too, Sir Richard Steele was living in this square, as shown by the date of a letter, republished in *fac-simile* in Smith's "Historical and Literary Curiosities." Having already burdened himself—as we have said—with a small house near Jermyn Street, for which he was unable to pay,* Sir Richard, in 1712, could not content himself without taking a much larger, finer, and grander house in Bloomsbury Square ; and here again he got into still greater difficulties than before. It is recorded that, on giving a grand entertainment in his new mansion, he engaged half-a-dozen queer-looking individuals to wait at table on his noble and distinguished guests, to whom he coolly confessed that "his lacqueys were bailiffs in disguise to a man." "I fared like a distressed prince," writes the kindly prodigal, in the *Tatler*, generously complimenting Addison for his assistance — " I fared like a distressed prince who calls in to his aid a powerful neighbour. I was undone by my auxiliary ; when I had once called him in, I could not submit without dependence on him." " Poor needy Prince," writes Thackeray, tenderly ; "think of him with pity in his palace, with his allies from Chancery Lane thus ominously guarding him !" The same incident is said to have occurred a century later to another man of letters, Richard Brinsley Sheridan.†

Pope, who was at this period at the height of his fame, thus alludes to this once fashionable quarter of the town :—

"In Palace-yard, at nine, you'll find me there ;
At ten, for certain, sir, in Bloomsbury-square."

Here, in the early part of the last century, lived Dr. Akenside and Sir Hans Sloane, already mentioned as the founder of the British Museum. The house of the latter was on the south side of the square, and here Dr. Franklin came to see Sloane's " curiosities," " for which," says Franklin, " he paid me handsomely."

In the Gordon Riots of June, 1780, the neighbourhood of Bloomsbury gained a sad notoriety as one of the chief points of attack by the infuriated mob, which, in its zeal for the Protestant faith, very nearly laid London in ruins, being guilty, as Sir N. W. Wraxall remarks, of grosser and more senseless outrages than even the fiends of Paris in the first great Revolution. In the following account he writes with all the vividness of an eye-witness

of these fearful scenes :—" I was personally present at many of the most tremendous effects of the popular fury on the memorable 7th of June, the night on which it attained its highest point. About nine o'clock on that evening, accompanied by three other gentlemen, who, as well as myself, were alarmed at the accounts brought in every moment of the outrages committed, and of the still greater acts of violence meditated, as soon as darkness should favour and ·facilitate their further progress, we set out from Portland Place, in order to view the scene. Having got into a hackney-coach, we drove to Bloomsbury Square, attracted to that spot by a rumour, generally spread, that Lord Mansfield's residence, situate at the north-east, was either already burnt, or destined for destruction. Hart Street and Great Russell Street presented each to the view, as we passed, large fires composed of furniture taken from the houses of magistrates, or other obnoxious individuals. Quitting the coach, we crossed the square, and had scarcely got under the wall of Bedford House, when we heard the door of Lord Mansfield's house burst open with violence. In a few minutes, all the contents of the apartments being precipitated from the windows, were piled up and wrapt in flames. A file of foot-soldiers arriving, drew up near the blazing pile, but without either attempting to quench the fire or to impede the mob, who were, indeed, far too numerous to admit of their being dispersed, or even intimidated, by a small detachment of infantry. The populace remained masters, while we, after surveying the spectacle for a short time, moved on into Holborn, where Mr. Langdale's dwelling-house and warehouses afforded a more appalling picture of devastation. They were altogether enveloped in smoke and flame. In front had assembled an immense multitude of both sexes, many of whom were females, and not a few held infants in their arms. All appeared to be, like ourselves, attracted as spectators solely by curiosity, without taking any part in the acts of violence. The kennel of the street ran down with spirituous liquors, and numbers of the populace were already intoxicated with this beverage. So little disposition, however, did they manifest to riot or pillage, that it would have been difficult to conceive who were the authors and perpetrators of such enormous mischief, if we had not distinctly seen, at the windows of the house, men who, while the floors and rooms were on fire, calmly tore down the furniture and threw it into the street, or tossed it into the flames. They experienced no kind of opposition during a considerable time that we remained at this place ; but a party of the Horse Guards

* See p. 202, *ante*.   † See p. 311. *ante*.

arriving, the terrified crowd instantly began to disperse, and we, anxious to gratify our curiosity, continued our progress on foot, along Holborn, towards Fleet Market."

Lord and Lady Mansfield, we are told, narrowly escaped falling into the hands of the lawless and infuriated mob, and only just succeeded in beating

nevertheless, the author of "Biographiana" states, without reserve or qualification, that "in these disgraceful riots the property and buildings of the metropolis were preserved by the spirited behaviour of the Sovereign." Yet it is difficult to see that the King had any claim to spirited conduct except negatively; at all events, Dr. Johnson wrote at the

ISAAC D'ISRAELI.   (*See page* 542.)

a retreat by a back door. His lordship's valuable library was destroyed; indeed, "even the civilisation of the eighteenth century," writes Mr. D'Israeli, in his "Curiosities of Literature," "could not preserve from the savage and destructive fury of a disorderly mob, in the most polished city of Europe, the valuable papers of the Earl of Mansfield, which were madly consigned to the flames."

Whilst all these riots were proceeding, we are told, George III. was at the Queen's Palace;

time to Mrs. Thrale thus :—"The King said in Council that the magistrates had not done their duty, but that he would do his own; and a proclamation was accordingly published, directing us to keep our servants within doors, as the peace was now to be preserved by force. The soldiers were sent out to different parts, and the town is now quiet." Readers of "Barnaby Rudge" will not have forgotten Charles Dickens' description of the Gordon Riots.

Lord Mansfield was one of Pope's executors, and Lady Lepel Hervey in her "Letters" makes allusions to his " *artful* eloquence "—meaning, elaborate and artificial; for we may be sure that he did not forget the words of Pope to himself—

" Plain truth, dear Murray, needs no flowers of speech."

age than could have been expected, and died in the zenith of his fame; and his memory has been embalmed by the testimonies of some of the wisest and best of his contemporaries. Pope had celebrated him in a well-known distich, and other poets, *haud passibus æquis*, had followed in the

ST. GEORGE'S CHURCH, BLOOMSBURY. (*See page* 544.)

" His lordship's night of life," writes Cradock, " was disturbed by many difficulties; yet he had undoubtedly many blessings to counterbalance them. Though his house was burnt down in Bloomsbury Square, he still possessed an elegant seat and extensive domain in the neighbourhood of London; and his nephew and heir, Lord Stormont, was appointed as the representative of Majesty at the Court of France. He lived to much greater

train. Lord Chesterfield in glowing terms had freely spoken of the rising talents both of Mr. Pitt and Mr. Murray, in a letter to his son: 'No man,' says he, ' can make a figure in this country but by Parliament. Your fate depends on your success as a speaker, and, take my word for it, that success turns much more upon manner than matter. Mr. Pitt, and Mr. Murray, the Solicitor General, are, beyond compare, the best speakers.' "

It has been thought strange that Lord Mansfield's will should be written only by himself on half a sheet of paper, and that the contents there enumerated, in neglect of all the forms of legal practice, should have proved valid for the disposal of half a million of property.

Of other residents of Bloomsbury Square in more recent times, may be mentioned Charles Knight, who, in 1826, lived at No. 29, when helping to lay the foundation of the Society for the Diffusion of Useful Knowledge ; and Isaac D'Israeli, the author of the "Curiosities of Literature," who a little earlier occupied the house No. 6, which, strange to say, appears to have since reverted to Jewish associations, as its late occupant was a Mr. Tabernacle. D'Israeli lived here for many years before he settled down as a country gentleman in Buckinghamshire ; and here his gifted son spent much of his childhood. "In London," says that son, " my father's only amusement was to ramble about among the bookseller's shops ; and if he ever went into a club, it was only to go into the library." With regard to the younger D'Israeli—the future Premier of England—it may be stated that as a child he used to toddle and run about the enclosure of the square with his nursemaid ; and at a fit age was sent to a small school, first at Islington, and afterwards at Walthamstow, at a seminary kept by a clergyman of Unitarian opinions, where he used to keep his schoolfellows awake at night by telling them ghost-stories. In the register of the Portuguese Synagogue for 1805, the name of Benjamin D'Israeli occurs in the January of that year, as having been initiated into the Jewish Church when only eight days old. When about fourteen years of age he exchanged Judaism for Christianity, being baptised at the Church of St. Andrew's, Holborn. He next spent a year or two as a clerk in a solicitor's office in the City, in the neighbourhood of Old Jewry and the present Moorgate Street ; and then, before he was twenty-one, had astonished the world by editing a journal of Radical sentiments, and publishing the novel of "Vivian Grey." Mr. Disraeli, in the course of one of his speeches at Taunton, made an uncomplimentary reference to Daniel O'Connell, then in the zenith of his fame. The agitator, a few days after, returned his invective with interest, and declared, alluding to Disraeli's Hebrew origin, that "he made no doubt that, if his genealogy could be traced, he would be found to be the true heir-at-law of the impenitent thief on the cross." The reply to this outrage was a challenge, not to the speaker, who was known uniformly to decline duelling, but to his son. No duel, however, took

place ; but the correspondence was published in the newspapers. A published letter, written to O'Connell by Disraeli, concluded with the magniloquent boast, " We shall meet at Philippi." This prophecy was fulfilled, in 1837, by the return of Disraeli for Maidstone. Of his subsequent Parliamentary career we have already spoken.*

At his house in this square, in January, 1839, died, at an advanced age, Edmund Lodge, Clarenceux King of Arms, the author of the " Peerage" which bears his name. This eminent biographer became a cornet in the King's Own regiment of Dragoons, in 1772 ; but having a pure taste for antiquities and literature, he left the army, and obtained the situation of Blue Mantle Pursuivant-at-Arms. He was subsequently promoted to the offices of Lancaster Herald, Norroy, and Clarenceux, and was created a Knight of the Hanoverian Guelphic Order. Among his other literary productions may be mentioned, " Illustrations of British History ; " " The Life of Sir Julius Cæsar ; " " Memoirs of Illustrious Personages of Great Britain ; " and many other works of the greatest merit, learning, and research.

The house at the north-west corner of the square forms the head-quarters of the Pharmaceutical Society of Great Britain, which was instituted "for the purposes of uniting the chemists and druggists into one ostensible, recognised, and independent body for protecting their general interests, and for the advancement of pharmacy, by furnishing such a uniform system of education as shall secure to the profession and to the public the safest and most efficient administration of medicine." A royal charter of incorporation was granted in 1843, in which, in addition to the above, the objects of the society were declared to include the providing a fund for the relief of distressed members and associates, and of their widows and orphans. The society has an excellent library and museum, and a laboratory. The museum claims to be very extensive, comprising rare specimens of the animal, vegetable, and mineral kingdoms, and substances and products used in medicine and pharmacy. It contains also groups and series of authenticated specimens, valuable for identifying, comparing, and tracing the origin and natural history of products. The museum includes the valuable collections of Cinchona barks made by eminent foreign naturalists, and formerly belonging to the late Dr. Jonathan Pereira.

In the above house, down to about 1862, was for many years carried on the work of the Royal

Literary Fund. The object of this society, which is now located at No. 7, Adelphi Terrace, is to administer assistance to authors of genius and learning, who may be reduced to distress by unavoidable calamities, or deprived by enfeebled faculties or declining life of the power of literary exertion. This assistance is extended at the death of an author to his widow and children. In the application of this liberality the utmost caution is used, both as to the reality of the distress and the merits of the individual. No writer can come within the views of the society who has not published a work of intelligence and public value, or been an important contributor to periodical literature; and every author, without exception, is excluded whose writings are offensive to morals or religion, and whose personal character is not proved by satisfactory testimony to be beyond suspicion. The business of the society is transacted by a committee; the most anxious consideration is given to the feelings of individuals; all names, and all circumstances which might lead to names, are carefully suppressed, and every precaution taken to avoid distressing publicity. The bounty of this institution is bestowed without regard to national or political distinctions. Here the Council of the Fund showed a small collection of curiosities and treasures, among which were the two daggers employed by Colonel Blood and his accomplice Parrot in their attempts to seize upon the crown and the other regalia in the Tower, in the reign of Charles II.

This square has not been known merely by the names of Southampton and Bloomsbury, but its different sides have been separately named: for instance, at one time the east side was called Seymour Row; the west was known as Allington, or Arlington, Row; and the south side was called Vernon Street. The latter name is still retained in Vernon Place, at the south-east corner of the square. On account of its remoteness from houses, the site now covered by this square, like the fields at the back of old Montagu House, was in former times—particularly in the reign of William III.— often chosen by the "gallants" and "bloods" of the period as a place for the settlement of "affairs of honour" with pistols and swords. Here the financial adventurer named Law, subsequently so famous as the Mississippi schemer, having picked up a quarrel with his antagonist, killed the "magnificent and mysterious Beau Wilson" in a duel.

The centre of the square is laid out in grass plats, planted with plane-trees and shrubs. On the north side of the enclosure, facing Bedford Place, is a fine bronze statue of Charles James Fox, by Sir Richard Westmacott, set up in 1816. This statue, which rests upon a granite pedestal, is considered to be one of Westmacott's best productions. Dignity and repose appear to have been the leading objects of the artist's ideas. "The English sculptors," writes the French author of a "Tour in England" in 1825, "have generally disguised their statues of historical personages by certain anachronisms in costume. Thus we see the Charleses and the Jameses clothed in the Roman toga, the royal periwigs being disregarded, an omission very creditable to the taste of the artist, though in our (French) busts and statues of Louis XIV. a wig usually encircles the brow of *Le Grand Monarque.*" There is nothing offensive, however, in the figure of Charles James Fox, represented as he is in a consular robe, for there was a certain degree of Roman eloquence in the Parliamentary speeches of that great leader. He is represented as seated, with his right arm extended, and supporting Magna Charta. His name forms the only inscription on the pedestal, but that name alone is sufficient to enshrine his memory. The countenance is said to present a striking resemblance to the original. The attitude is dignified, and the statue, as a whole, reflects great credit on the genius of Westmacott.

At the south-west corner of the square was Bloomsbury Market, built by one of the Russell family for the accommodation of that part of the town. Although the market has long been discontinued, it is still kept in remembrance by one of the streets on the site being called Market Street.

Southampton Street, which connects this square with Holborn, witnessed the birth of Colley Cibber, in November, 1671. At the south-west corner of this street, with its principal entrance in Holborn, is the Chief Post and Telegraph Office of the Western Central District. At a short distance eastward is Southampton Row, a broad and well-built thoroughfare extending from High Holborn to Russell Square. It was formerly known as King Street, and is described in the "New View of London," published in 1708, as a "spacious and pleasant street between High Holborne and the fields to the north." At No. 65, on the west side, are the offices of the National Benevolent Institution. This institution was founded by the late Peter Hervé, and established in 1812, with the view of affording relief, by annual pensions, to distressed and aged gentry, merchants, tutors, and governesses, and persons who have been engaged in professional pursuits, or in the higher departments of trade. The unfortunate Dr. Dodd was at one time a resident in this row.

Connecting Southampton Row with the north-east corner of Bloomsbury Square is Bloomsbury Place. At his residence here, in 1802, died Mr. Thomas Cadell, the eminent publisher of the Strand. He was the publisher of the first edition, and of many consecutive editions, of Gibbon's "Decline and Fall of the Roman Empire." At No. 2, in Bloomsbury Place, are the offices of the Corporation of the Sons of the Clergy. This institution was established in 1655, and incorporated by Royal Charter in 1678, for the purpose of "relieving necessitous clergymen, pensioning their widows and aged single daughters, and educating, apprenticing, and providing outfits for their children." The pensions and donations are granted by the Court of Assistants, after investigation of the merits of each case; and it may be interesting to learn that the number benefited by this institution in the course of a year amounts to upwards of one thousand. The Festival of the Sons of the Clergy, which has been already mentioned in our account of St. Paul's Cathedral,* commenced in 1655, and was virtually the basis of the above-mentioned corporation. The proceeds of these festivals are placed at the disposal of the corporation for the apprenticing of the sons and daughters of necessitous clergymen in situations of credit and respectability, and other analogous purposes which the committee may approve. The stewards of the festival contribute a sum of not less than thirty guineas towards the expenses of the festival, and are subsequently elected governors of the corporation.

Hart Street—a fine and broad thoroughfare running from New Oxford Street into the south-west corner of Bloomsbury Square—together with Vernon Place, Theobald's Road, and other streets through the parish of Clerkenwell, now forms a continuous line of route through Northern London to Shoreditch and Hackney. Hart Street was probably so named—like Hart Street, Covent Garden—from an inn bearing the sign of the "White Hart," which may have stood there. On the north side of this street stands the Church of St. George. To use the words of the "Pocket Guide to London," this church "enjoys the privilege of being at once the most pretentious and the ugliest ecclesiastical edifice in the metropolis. All the absurdities of the classic style are here apparent. It was designed by Hawkesmoor, the pupil of Sir C. Wren, and was completed in 1731. The architect chose for his model the description given by Pliny of the tomb of Mausolus, in Caria; but

if the original possessed all the faults of the copy, we can scarcely understand its having been considered one of the seven wonders of the world, unless viewed in the light of a monstrosity. This church has a tower and steeple at the side of the main edifice: upon the former, at the four sides, is a range of Corinthian pillars, placed there apparently for no earthly use. The steeple consists of a series of steps, with the royal arms, guarded by excessively fierce-looking lions and unicorns, and on the summit is a statue of King George I. in a Roman costume." The statue of the king is said to have been the gift of a loyal brewer, Mr. William Hucks, sometime M.P. for Abingdon and Wallingford. On the statue being placed in its exalted situation a wag wrote the following epigram on it:—

"The King of Great Britain was reckoned before
    The 'Head of the Church' by all good Christian people;
But his brewer has added still one title more
    To the rest, and has made him the 'Head of the Steeple!'"

Horace Walpole, who speaks of this steeple as "a master-stroke of absurdity, consisting of an obelisk, crowned with the statue of King George I., and hugged by the royal supporters," treats us with the following version of the same epigram:—

"When Harry the Eighth left the Pope in the lurch,
    The people of England made him 'Head of the Church;'
But George's good subjects, the Bloomsbury people,
    Instead of the Church made him 'Head of the Steeple.'"

The steeple as applied to a building on the Grecian or Roman plan is always absurd, and even Sir C. Wren could not always rescue it from deserved and contemptuous criticism; but Hawkesmoor appears to have been the only architect who ventured to place this part of the structure at the side instead of making it rise out of the building.

The front of the church, facing Hart Street, has a grand portico, elevated on a flight of steps, which support six Corinthian columns. The church is singular from its standing north and south; hence, contrary to the established custom, the altar stands at the north end; so that, in this case at least, the "eastward position" is not rigidly carried out. The fabric is of too recent erection to contain many monuments or objects of interest; there is, however, in it a tablet to the memory of the great Lord Mansfield.

At his residence in Hart Street, in 1829, died Archdeacon Robert Nares, librarian of the MSS. in the British Museum, and the learned editor of part of the "Catalogue of the Harleian Miscellany," and for many years joint editor of the *British Critic.* He was the son of Dr. James Nares,

---

* See Vol. I., p. 262.

many years organist and composer to George II. and George III. He was a busy and voluminous writer, an acute critic, and a Fellow of the Royal and other learned societies.

At No. 11, in this street, are the offices of the Society of Biblical Archæology. This society, which holds its meetings monthly, at No. 9, Conduit Street, Regent Street, was established for the study of such archæological matters as will help to throw additional light on the Holy Scriptures.

CHAPTER XLII.

RED LION SQUARE, AND ITS NEIGHBOURHOOD.

" Where the ' Red Lion' frowns upon the way."—Crabbe.

Red Lion Square in the Last Century—The Old "Red Lyon" Inn—A Quack Doctor's "Puff"—The Fate of the Regicides : Cromwell, Ireton, and Bradshaw—An "Old Lady of Quality"—Lord Raymond, Jonas Hanway, and Sharon Turner, Residents in this Square—An Antiquated Law Court—London Infirmary for Diseases of the Legs—A Batch of Charitable and Provident Institutions—Milton a Resident in this Neighbourhood—Eagle Street—Martin Van Butchell, the Eccentric Quack Doctor—Fisher and Kingsgate Streets—A Royal Misadventure —Messrs. Day and Martin's Blacking Manufactory—The Holborn Amphitheatre—Red Lion Street—Theobald's Road—Lamb's Conduit Street—Lamb's Conduit rebuilt—Its Removal—Lamb's Conduit Fields—Harpur Street—Milman Street—The Chevalier D'Eon—Doughty Street—Charles Dickens a Resident here—John Street Baptist Chapel—St. John's Episcopal Chapel the Head-quarters of Fashionable Evangelicalism—The Gray's Inn Cock-pit—Bedford Row—The Entomological Society—Bedford Street—Featherstone Buildings—Hand Court--Brownlow Street—The Duke's Theatre—Warwick Court.

To the south-east of Bloomsbury Square, surrounded by a nest of narrow alleys between it and Holborn, is Red Lion Square, described by Northouck as a "neat, small square, much longer than it is broad," and having "convenient" streets entering it on three sides, with foot-passages at the corners. It had at that time (1786) not only in the centre a plain obelisk, but a stone watch-house at each corner, all of which have long been swept away. Although respectable, the square has a very dull appearance, which is thus whimsically portrayed by the author of "Critical Observations on the Buildings, &c., of London," published about the middle of the last century :—"I never go into it without thinking of my latter end. The rough sod that 'heaves with many a mouldering heap,' the dreary length of its sides, with the four watch-houses like so many family vaults at the corners, and the naked obelisk that springs from amid the rank grass, like the sad monument of a disconsolate widow for the loss of her first husband, all form together a *memento mori*, more powerful to me than a death's head and cross marrow-bones ; and were but a parson's bull to be seen bellowing at the gate, the idea of a country churchyard, in my mind, would be complete."

Hatton, in 1708, describes it as "a pleasant square of good buildings, between High Holborn south and the fields north ; " and Pennant, writing in 1790, says that in the centre was "a clumsy obelisk, lately vanished."

The "Red Lyon" Inn was in olden times the most important hostelry in Holborn, and accordingly had the honour of giving its name to Red Lion Street and to the adjoining square. If we may draw an inference from the entries in the register of St. Andrew's, Holborn, the inn had behind it a fine row of trees, for we find notices of foundlings being exposed under the "Red Lion Elmes in Holborn." The "Red Lyon" is mentioned in the following "puff" of a quack doctor, at the beginning of the last century :—" Cornelius Tilbury, sworn Chirurgeon in ordinary to K. Charles II., to his late Sovereign K. William, as also to her present Majesty Queen Anne," gives his address as "at the Blue Flower Pot, in Great Lincoln's Inn Fields, at Holbourn Row (where you see at night a light over the door). . . . And for the convenience of those that desire privacy, they may come through the Red Lyon Inn, in Holbourn, between the two Turnstiles, which is directly against my back door, where you will see the sign of the Blue Ball hang over the door. I dispose of my famous Orvietan, either liquid or in powder, what quantity or price you please. . . . This is that Orvietan that expelled that vast quantity of poyson I took before K. Charles II., for which his Majesty presented me with a gold medal and chain."

The story that some of the regicides were buried in Red Lion Square has been extensively believed ; it is told by Mr. Peter Cunningham, with a little variety, as follows :—" The bodies of Oliver Cromwell, Ireton, and Bradshaw were carried from Westminster Abbey to the Red Lion Inn, in Holborn, and the next day dragged on sledges thence to Tyburn." In support of this story he quotes Wood's "Athenæ Oxonienses," and the additional MSS. in the British Museum, where those who are curious in such matters will find the narrative.

On the fate of Cromwell's head we have already quoted at some length in the preceding volume.* It is the opinion of a writer in the *Times*, that if the body of Cromwell was removed from the Abbey and buried in Red Lion Square, it is not probable that another embalmed body could have been procured for the purpose of being sent as its substitute to Tyburn, as has been suggested.

those of Ireton and Bradshaw, whose remains were disinterred at the same time from Westminster Abbey, and exposed on the same gallows. He strengthens this supposition by observing that the contemporary accounts of the last resting-place of these remarkable men simply inform us, that on the anniversary of the death of Charles I. their bodies were borne on sledges to *Tyburn*, and after

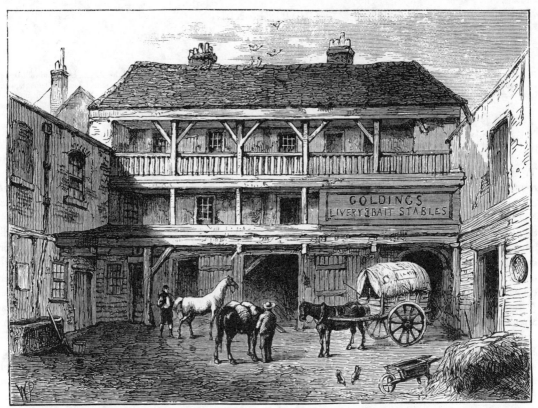

THE OLD "BLACK BULL INN," GRAY'S INN LANE. (*See page* 551.)

Pennant, as we have observed, speaks of the "clumsy obelisk" in Red Lion Square, and mentions that it was inscribed with the following lines:—"Obtusum Obtusioris Ingenii Monumentum. Quid me respicis, viator? Vade." "Could this quaint inscription," asks Mr. Jesse, in his "London," "have any hidden reference to the bones of Cromwell lying beneath it? We think not; but they are meant to mystify; and what, therefore, *do* they mean?" Mr. Jesse is inclined, however, in spite of his scepticism as to the inscription, to agree with those who believe in the tradition that the body of Cromwell was buried beneath this obelisk, and that upon this spot not improbably moulder, not only the bones of the great Protector, but also

hanging till sunset they were cut down and beheaded; that their bodies were then flung into a hole at the foot of the gallows, and their heads fixed upon poles on the roof of Westminster Hall. "From the word *Tyburn* being so distinctly laid down," Mr. Jesse adds, "it has usually been taken for granted that it was intended to designate the well-known place for executing criminals, nearly at the north end of Park Lane, or, as it was anciently styled, Tyburn Lane. However, when we read of a criminal in old times having been executed at *Tyburn*, we are not necessarily to presume that it was at this particular spot, the gallows having unquestionably been shifted at times from place to place, and the word *Tyburn* having been given indiscriminately, for the time being, to each spot. For instance, sixty years before the death of Crom-

* See Vol. III., p. 539.

RED LION SQUARE IN 1780.

well the gallows were frequently erected at the extremity of St. Giles's parish, near the end of the present Tottenham Court Road; while for nearly two centuries the Holborn end of Fetter Lane, within a short distance of Red Lion Square, was no less frequently the place of execution. Indeed, in 1643, only a few years before the exhumation and gibbeting of Cromwell, we find Nathaniel Tomkins executed at this spot for his share in Waller's plot to surprise the City. In addition, however, to these surmises is the curious fact of the bodies of Cromwell and Ireton having been brought in carts, on the night previous to their exposure on the gibbet, to the *Red Lion Inn*, Holborn, from which Red Lion Square derives its name, where they rested during the night. In taking this step, it is surely not unreasonable to presume that the Government had in view the selection of a house in the immediate vicinity of the scaffold, in order that the bodies might be in readiness for the disgusting exhibition of the following morning. Supposing this to have been the case, the place of their exposure and interment could scarcely have been the end of Tyburn Lane, inasmuch as the distance thither from Westminster is actually shorter than the distance from Westminster to Red Lion Square. The object of the Government could hardly have been to create a sensation by parading the bodies along a populous thoroughfare, inasmuch as the ground between St. Giles's Pound and Tyburn, a distance of a mile and a half, was at this period almost entirely open country."

This story of the disposal of Cromwell's body, if true, negatives the well-known lines of Dryden :—

"His ashes in a peaceful urn shall rest."

In Rede's "Anecdotes and Biography," published just before the close of the last century, it is stated that the obelisk was thought to be a memorial erected to Cromwell by an apothecary who was attached to his principles, and had so much influence in the building of the square as to manage the marking out of the ground, thus further contriving to pay this tribute to his favourite. Curiously enough, it has been discovered that an apothecary named Ebenezer Heathcote, who had married the daughter of one of Ireton's sub-commissaries, was living at the King's-gate, Holborn, soon after the Restoration.

Leigh Hunt has left a curious reminiscence of an "old lady of quality," who lived in this square, "a quarter in different esteem once from what it is now." She astounded him one day by letting her false teeth slip out, and clapping them in again.

It was at her house, he adds, that his father one evening met John Wilkes. Not knowing him by sight, and happening to fall into conversation with him, while the latter sat looking down, he said something in Wilkes's disparagement, on which the jovial demagogue looked up in his face, and burst out laughing. In this square lived, in the last century, Lord Raymond, the Chief Justice of the Court of King's Bench. At No. 23, writes Peter Cunningham, lived, and here, in 1786, died the benevolent Mr. Jonas Hanway, the eccentric traveller, remarkable as "the first person who ventured to walk in the streets of London with an umbrella over his head." We have already spoken at some length of this celebrity in dealing with Hanway Street.* The principal rooms in Hanway's house were decorated with paintings and emblematical devices, "in a style," says his biographer, "peculiar to himself. I found," he used to say, when speaking of these ornaments, "that my countrymen and women were not *au fait* in the art of conversation; and that instead of recurring to their cards when the discourse began to flag, the minutes between the time of assembling and the placing of the card-tables are spent in an irksome suspense. To relieve this vacuum in social intercourse, and prevent cards from engrossing the whole of my visitors' minds, I have presented them with objects the most attractive I could imagine; and when that fails there are the cards." At No. 32 in this square, the house at the corner of North Street, lived, for many years in the present century, Sharon Turner, the author of "The Sacred History of the World." He was a solicitor in practice, as well as an historian; he died here in 1847. Besides his "Sacred History," he was the author of the "History of England from the Earliest Period to the Death of Elizabeth," consisting of several works, each published separately and independently—namely, the "History of the Anglo-Saxons," "History of England in the Middle Ages," "History of the Reign of Henry VIII.," and "History of the Reigns of Edward VI., Mary, and Elizabeth." At No. 2 lived Judge Blackstone.

Besides the ordinary Superior Courts, so well known by name to every reader, there is in existence in Red Lion Square, at the house at the north-east corner, an ancient Baronial Court, held under the authority of the Sheriffs of Middlesex. "It is held monthly" (says the *Gentleman's Magazine* in 1829) "before the Sheriff or his deputy. Its power in judgment is as great as that of any of the present Courts of Law. It is more expeditious and less

* See p. 470, *ante*.

expensive; persons seeking to recover debts may do so to any amount at the trifling expense of only six or seven pounds. Nor is it confined to actions of account; it extends to detenue, trover, scandal, &c., and personal service of process is unnecessary. This Court was instituted," adds the writer, "by King Alfred on dividing the kingdom into shires, and subsequently continued and sanctioned by Canute the Dane, by William the Conqueror, and various statutes, including Magna Charta; and is treated upon by several eminent legal authorities, as Judge Hale, Judge Lambert, and many others."

The author of "A Tour through Great Britain" says, "This present year, 1737, an Act was passed for beautifying Red Lyon Square, which had run much to decay." Though the square has at this time a decayed aspect, there is a picturesqueness and a touch of sentiment about it not to be found in squares of a higher grade through which we have passed. The variety of the houses, dilapidated and disfigured as some of them are, is more interesting than the even respectability of continuous brick walls and unbroken roofs. Besides the old Sheriff's Court, mentioned above, several other houses in this square are, or have been, devoted to public and charitable purposes. Here, for instance, at No. 27, are the offices of the Indigent Blind Visiting Society and the British Asylum for Deaf and Dumb Females. The former, which was established in 1834, has for its object the visiting and relieving of the destitute blind at their own homes, and affording elementary education in day classes. It is the only society in London which combines the visitation, relief, and education of the blind. The number of persons benefited annually by this Society is about 700. The British Asylum for Deaf and Dumb Females, which is located at Lower Clapton, was founded in 1851.

The whole of the square, having long since been deserted by the families who used to inhabit it, has become quite a warren, so to speak, of charitable societies, which we have no room to enumerate in detail.

Milton at two different periods of his life was a resident in this immediate neighbourhood, and on both occasions he occupied houses looking upon the green fields. The first time that he resided here was in 1647, when his house "opened backwards into Lincoln's Inn Fields," where it was that he principally employed himself in writing his virulent tirades against monarchy and Charles I. The second occasion of his residing here was after the Restoration, when we are told the front of his humble dwelling looked into Red Lion Fields, the site of the present Red Lion Square.

To the south of Red Lion Square, and parallel to it, half way between the square and Holborn, and separating Dean and Leigh Streets, is Eagle Street. Here was born Martin Van Butchell, the eccentric quack doctor and dentist, of whom we have already spoken in our account of Mount Street, Grosvenor Square.*

At the south-west corner of the square, parallel with the large red-brick church of St. John the Evangelist, is Fisher Street, leading into Kingsgate Street, which opens into Holborn. Hatton, in 1708, says that Kingsgate Street was "so called because the king used to go this way to New Market." This street would seem to have witnessed one royal misadventure at the least; for under date 8th of March, 1668-9, Pepys writes in "Diary:"—"To Whitehall, from whence the King and the Duke of York went by three in the morning, and had the misfortune to be overset with the Duke of York, the Duke of Monmouth, and the Prince [Rupert], at the King's Gate, in Holborne; and the king all dirt, but no hurt. How it came to pass I know not, but only it was dark, and the torches did not, they say, light the coach as they should."

Between Kingsgate and Dean Streets, extending back into Eagle Street, and with their principal entrance facing Holborn, are the extensive premises of Messrs. Day and Martin, the well-known blacking manufacturers. Mr. Charles Day, the founder of this establishment, died in 1836, having made a huge fortune. He had for many years before his death been totally blind, and—apparently touched by that "fellow-feeling" which "makes us wondrous kind"—in his will he directed that £100,000 should be devoted to the establishment of a charity, to be called the "Poor Blind Man's Friend." This institution, as we have already seen, has its offices in Savile Row.

A short distance eastward, between Dean Street and Red Lion Street, is a building which has undergone a variety of uses and vicissitudes. It was erected about the year 1862 as a horse and carriage repository, but the speculation was anything but successful, and in a short time collapsed. The building, which covers a large space of ground, and has an entrance in Holborn, was afterwards converted into a theatre—called first the National, and afterwards the Holborn Amphitheatre—with stage for dramatic representations, and a circus for equestrian performances. It was turned into a skating-rink, and finally re-converted into a theatre, called the Alcazar; but for some reason a licence

* See page 335, *ante*.

has been withheld up to the present time (May, 1883), and it has remained closed.

Red Lion Street, like the Square—as already stated—was so called after the "Red Lion Inn." On the wall of the building at the south-west corner, a public-house called the "Red Lion," is a block of wood let in, with the date "1611." This street—and, indeed, the whole neighbourhood of Red Lion Square, if we may judge by stray allusions in the "London Spy"—would appear to have borne no very high reputation for morality in the reigns of the first and second Georges. Nor does it appear to have been very safe for pedestrians. For instance, in 1760 an apothecary was attacked in Red Lion Street by two ruffians with firearms, who carried him off by force to "Black Mary's Hole."

We gather from King's "Anecdotes of his own Times," that this street was formerly noted for its modellers and dealers in plaster casts, many of whom still linger in the neighbourhood of Gray's Inn Lane and Hatton Garden. Speaking of the Pretender's visit to London, the author says, "He came one evening to my lodgings and drank tea with me; my servant, after he was gone, said to me that he thought my new visitor very like Prince Charles. 'Why,' said I, 'have you ever seen Prince Charles?' 'No, sir,' replied the fellow; 'but this gentleman, whoever he may be, exactly resembles the busts which are sold in Red Lion Street, and are said to be the busts of Prince Charles.' The truth is, these busts were taken in plaster of Paris from his face."

Theobald's Road, which runs parallel with the north side of Red Lion Square, and separates Red Lion Street from Lamb's Conduit Street, was so named, says Mr. Peter Cunningham, "because it led to Theobalds, in Hertfordshire, the favourite hunting-seat of King James I. The king," he adds, "on leaving Whitehall, went through the Strand, up Drury Lane, and so on into Holborn, Kingsgate Street, and Theobald's Road." John Le Neve, author of "Monumenta Anglicana," lived in this road at the time of the publication of that work (1717-19), and here he advertised that his book might be bought.

A conduit, founded by one William Lamb, a gentleman of the Chapel Royal under Henry VIII., gave its name to Lamb's Conduit Street. Lamb, it is stated, here caused several springs to be so connected as to form a head of water, which was conveyed by a leaden pipe, about 2,000 yards in length, to Snow Hill, where he rebuilt a conduit, which had long been in a ruinous state and disused. He is said to have expended a very large sum of money upon these structures, and thus, by his benevolent exertions, conferred an important advantage upon a very populous neighbourhood. "Moreover," as we learn from Stow's "Summary," "he gave to poor women, such as were willing to take pains, 120 pails therewith to carry and serve water." His benefactions for other purposes were also numerous. He was buried in St. Faith's Church, and upon his tomb was inscribed an epitaph in the quaint punning language of the time.

Lamb's Conduit was rebuilt in 1667 from a design by Sir Christopher Wren, and at the expense of Sir Thomas Daws. It was taken down in 1746. Most of the City conduits, it has been remarked, were destroyed by the Great Fire in 1666, and the rest, it is darkly hinted, were swept quietly away in order to force the citizens to have the water of the New River laid on to their houses.

The fields around Lamb's Conduit, a century ago, formed a favourite promenade for the inhabitants of St. Andrew's, Holborn, and St. Giles's. An old English "Herbal," speaking of winter rocket, or cresses, says: "It groweth of its own accord in gardens and fields, by the way-side in divers places, and particularly in *the next pasture to the Conduit Head*, behind Gray's Inn, that brings water to Mr. Lamb's Conduit, in *Holborn*."

A correspondent in *Notes and Queries* (April, 1857) says: "About sixty years since I was travelling from the West of England in one of the old stage-coaches of that day, and my fellow-travellers were an octogenarian clergyman and his daughter. In speaking of the then increasing size of London, the old gentleman said that, when he was a boy, and recovering from an attack of small-pox, he was sent into the country to a row of houses standing on the west side of the upper part of the present Lamb's Conduit Street; that all the space before him was open fields; that a streamlet of water ran under his window; and he saw a man snipe-shooting, who sprang a snipe near to the house, and shot it. . . . I have myself seen a pump reputed to be erected on the Conduit Head, and standing against the corner house of a small turning out of Lamb's Conduit Street, on the right-hand side as you go towards the Foundling, and nearly at the upper end of the street." In this same small turning, now known as Long Yard, may be seen carved on the gable of the first house on the left, the inscription, "Lamb's Conduit, the property of the City of London. This pump is erected for the benefit of the public." The date is obliterated.

On the west side of Lamb's Conduit Street are two or three short streets, which, from the substantial appearance of the houses, would seem to have been formerly the abode of some of the higher classes of society. One of these is Harpur Street, which runs in a line with Theobald's Road, on the north side of Red Lion Square. It was so named after Sir William Harpur, who was Lord Mayor of London in 1562.

Lamb's Conduit Street is crossed by Ormond Street, and terminated at its northern end by Guilford Street. On the east side of the street, and running parallel between it and Gray's Inn Road, are Milman, Doughty, Great James, and John Streets, together with two or three others of little or no importance. In Milman Street, at the house of a friend, on the 21st of May, 1810, died the Chevalier D'Eon, some time equerry to Louis XV., and also Ambassador at the Court of St. James's. During his residence in England, doubts arose respecting his sex, and wagers to a large amount were laid thereon, one of which terminated in a trial before Lord Mansfield. There the witnesses declared that the Chevalier was a woman concealed in man's clothes; and no attempt being made to contradict their evidence, a verdict was given for the plaintiff for the recovery of the wager. After the trial, D'Eon put on female attire, which he continued to wear till his decease, when all doubts regarding his sex were at once set at rest, an examination of the body being made in the presence of several distinguished personages. From the notice of his death in the *Gentleman's Magazine* we learn that in private life the Chevalier was always understood to have been extremely amiable; his natural abilities were great, and his acquirements most numerous. The story which mixed up the name of the Chevalier D'Eon in an intrigue with Queen Charlotte in the early part of her married life, is shown by Mr. W. J. Thoms to be a pure invention of a French scandal-monger, M. Gaillardet.

In Milman Street Bellingham was lodging when, in 1812, he assassinated Mr. Perceval in the lobby of the House of Commons.

In Doughty Street lived Charles Dickens in the earlier days of his first achieved popularity, when as yet he was only "Boz" to the public. Whilst here he wrote, in a letter to a friend, "I always pay my taxes when they 'won't' wait any longer, in order to get a bad name in the parish, and so to escape all 'honours.'" Here was a touch of character; though Mr. Forster tells us that in after life, respectability following in the wake of success, he followed quite a different course, and paid his taxes not only regularly but punctually.

Extending from Doughty Street to Theobald's Road, which forms the northern side of Gray's Inn, is a broad and well-built thoroughfare, called John Street. On the west side of the street is the Baptist chapel where the Hon. and Rev. Baptist Noel preached to crowded congregations, after his secession from the Established Church in 1848. He had previously been for several years the minister of the Episcopal Chapel of St. John, which stood in Chapel Street, Great James Street, at the north end of Bedford Row. The old chapel, which was pulled down soon after Mr. Noel left it, was a plain square brick building, and may be described as having been for half a century the head-quarters of fashionable Evangelicalism, for the string of carriages waiting at its doors about one o'clock on Sundays sometimes extended the entire length of the street. In the early part of the present century the minister of St. John's Chapel was the Rev. Daniel Wilson, afterwards vicar of Islington, and eventually Bishop of Calcutta.

In the rear of Gray's Inn, as we learn from John Timbs, there was formerly a cockpit, which, doubtless, was frequented by the young law-students. The place is still kept in remembrance by Little Cockpit Yard, in the King's Road, close by Great James Street.

The old "Black Bull," in Gray's Inn Lane, of which we give a view on page 546, was a good specimen of the old-fashioned galleried yard.

Bedford Row, which lies between Red Lion Street and Gray's Inn, is a fine specimen of a broad thoroughfare of the early part of the eighteenth century, and must have been a pleasant residence when all to the north was open country as far as Hampstead and Highgate. It does not derive its name, as might be imagined, from the Russell family, but from the town of Bedford, to which— his native place—Sir William Harpur, Lord Mayor of London in 1562, bequeathed the land on which it stands for the foundation of a school and other local charities.

The houses in Bedford Row are now nearly all cut up into chambers and occupied by solicitors. No. 12 was for many years the head-quarters of the Entomological Society. This society was organised in 1833, and the first general meeting of its members was held in the following year, with the Rev. W. Kirby, the "father of British entomology," as its president. Periodical meetings were at first held, at which memoirs were received and read, experiments for the destruction of noxious insects suggested, communications made, and objects exhibited. A collection of insects was also formed, together with a library of books of reference. The valuable collections of Mr. Kirby were presented to the society at its commencement. In 1875, they removed to Chandos Street, Cavendish Square.

At the south end of Bedford Row is Bedford Street, which runs westward into Red Lion Street, former days was not only a favourite public-house sign, but also one of the usual signs of the marriage-mongers in Fleet Street ; and it now figures as the name of one of the London Fire Insurance Offices. Brownlow Street was named after Sir John Brown-

OLD HOUSES IN HOLBORN.

and is connected with High Holborn by three or four narrow streets and courts. One of these, Featherstone Buildings, Mr. Cunningham tells us, was so called from Cuthbert Featherstone, Gentleman Usher and Crier of the King's Bench, who died in 1615. A stone let into the wall is inscribed with the name of the passage, and the date is 1724. The next, Hand Court, is so called from the "Hand-in-Hand" Tavern, which stands at the corner in Holborn. The "Hand-in-Hand" in

low, a parishioner of St. Giles's * in the reign of Charles II. Eastward of this street stood the Duke's Theatre, which occupied a plot of ground abutting on the western boundary of Gray's Inn, formerly used as a yard for mail-carts and post-office omnibuses. It was at first opened about 1866, as the Holborn Theatre, by Mr. Sefton Parry, but subsequently underwent many changes in

* See Vol. III., p. 207.

style and management. Its name later on was altered to "The Mirror," which in turn was changed to the "Duke's." The theatre was eventually burnt down, and the site has been covered by a monster hotel.

Warwick Court, close by the above hotel, was pro-bably so named after the old Earls of Warwick, whose mansion, Warwick House, mentioned in our account of the neighbourhood of Holborn,* stood at a short distance eastward of Gray's Inn Lane. Passing up this court, we find ourselves at the back gate of Gray's Inn, where we stop our journeyings eastward.

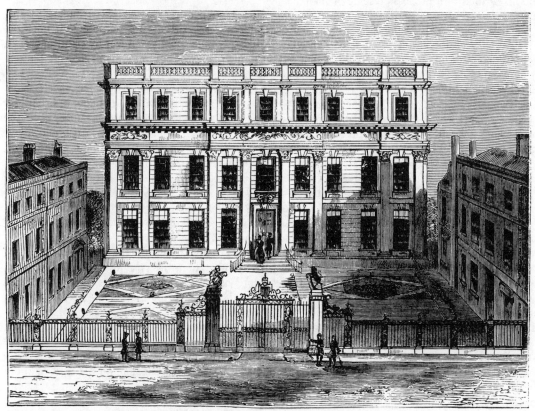

POWIS HOUSE, 1714. (*See page* 556.)

CHAPTER XLIII.

QUEEN SQUARE, GREAT ORMOND STREET, &c.

A "Colony" of French Refugees—Attack on Dr. Challoner's House during the Gordon Riots—Queen Square—The Church of St. George the Martyr—The Parish Burial-ground—Inadequate Accommodation for the Poor—Jonathan Richardson, the Artist—Dr. John Campbell and Dr. Johnson—The Poet Churchill—Dr. Stukeley, the Antiquary—The Alexandra Institution for the Blind—Hospital for Hip Diseases in Childhood—The Ladies' Charity School—National Hospital for the Paralysed and Epileptic—The College for Men and Women—The Aged Poor Society—The Society of St. Vincent de Paul—College of Preceptors—Government District School of Art for Ladies—Great Ormond Street—Noted Residents—Powis House—The Residence of Lord Chancellor Thurlow, and Anecdotes of his Lordship—The Working Men's College—The Hospital of St. John and St. Elizabeth—Provident Surgical Appliance Society—The Residence of Dr. Mead, afterwards the Hospital for Sick Children—The Home for Friendless Girls—The Homœopathic Hospital—The Residence of Zachary Macaulay—The United Kingdom Benefit Society—The Workhouse Visiting Society—Guilford Street—Brunswick and Mecklenburgh Squares.

THE district between Southampton Row and Lamb's Conduit Street was largely inhabited towards the middle and close of the last century by French refugees, who supported themselves by industrial pursuits of a somewhat higher kind than those of Clerkenwell and Soho. Among these were many Roman Catholics, who frequented the only chapel which up to that time existed in

* See Vol. II., p. 549.

Central London, that of the Sardinian Embassy in Lincoln's Inn Fields, which we have already described briefly.* The saintly and learned bishop, Dr. Challoner, was living amongst his people, first in Gloucester Street, Queen Square, and subsequently in Lamb's Conduit Street, at the time of the Gordon Riots. His abode being known, his rooms were invaded by the mob; but the good old man was safe in a retreat a few miles from town, and he escaped with the loss of some of his books and papers.

"Queen Square," writes the fastidious author of a "New Critical Review of the Public Buildings, &c," "is an area of a particular kind, being left open on one side for the sake of the beautiful landscape, which is formed by the hills of Hampstead and Highgate, together with the adjacent fields"— an arrangement which the writer highly approves, on account alike of the inhabitants and of the square as well. "The square," observes the writer of the "Beauties of England and Wales," "forms a parallelogram, and the houses on three of the sides were erected at the commencement of the last century. It was named Queen Square out of compliment to Queen Anne, in whose reign it was built, and whose statue is placed in the midst of the garden at the north side."

At the south-west angle of the square stands the church of St. George the Martyr, erected in 1706 by private subscriptions, as a chapel of ease to the parish of St. Andrew's, Holborn. Northouck tells us that "the persons who built it intended to reimburse themselves by the sale of the pews; but the commissioners for erecting fifty new churches, resolving to make this one of the number, purchased it, assigned to it a district, and had it consecrated in 1723. It was dedicated to St. George in compliment to one of its founders, Sir Streynsham Master, who had been Governor of Fort St. George;" and it is called St. George the Martyr to distinguish it from the other church of the same name in Hart Street.

The parish burial-ground is in the rear of the Foundling Hospital. Speaking of this particular churchyard, Mr. John Timbs, in his "Curiosities," observes—"A strong prejudice formerly existed against new churchyards, and no person was interred here till the ground was broken for Robert Nelson, author of "Fasts and Festivals," whose character for piety reconciled others to the spot: people liked to be buried in company, and in good company." Nancy Dawson, the celebrated hornpipe dancer of Covent Garden and Drury Lane

Theatres, lies here. Here also are buried the good judge, Sir John Richardson, and Zachary Macaulay.

Even in the parish of St. George the Martyr, if a judgment may be formed from Dr. Stallard's work on "London Pauperism," the accommodation in the dwellings of some of the poor is most disgracefully inadequate. It is to be hoped that our children, or, at all events, our grandchildren, will refuse to believe that in the year of grace 1874 a pauper widow, her sister, and six young children were existing—we purposely do not write "living"—in a room seven feet by eight, and eight feet high, a space not more than sufficient for one person.

Queen Square, like the rest of the once fashionable neighbourhood, has had its quota of celebrities among its residents. Here, for instance, lived the worthy Jonathan Richardson, the artist, and friend of Pope, who painted Pope's mother and Lord Bolingbroke. More than one of Pope's letters are addressed to him here. He rests in the burial-ground mentioned above. Sir Godfrey Kneller would often come across from his lodgings in Great Queen Street to spend a quiet evening at Richardson's house.

In Hawkins' "Life of Johnson" we read that Dr. John Campbell's residence for some years before his death was the large new-built house situated at the north-west corner of the square; "whither," adds the author, "particularly on a Sunday evening, great numbers of persons of the first eminence for science and literature were accustomed to resort for the enjoyment of conversation." Boswell has this note on these assemblies:— *Johnson:* I used to go pretty often to Campbell's on a Sunday evening, till I began to consider that the shoals of Scotchmen who flocked about him might probably say, when anything of mine was well done, 'Ay, ay, he has learnt this of *Cawmell.*'" Dr. Campbell was a celebrated biographical and political writer, a friend of Dr. Johnson, and the author of "Hermippus Redivivus," and of other curious works. He was also editor of the "Biographia Britannica." He was, in fact, a voluminous writer, and made a considerable fortune by his pen.

It was in this square that the poet, Charles Churchill, was employed in teaching the *belles lettres* in a lady's school whilst holding the curacy of St. John's, Westminster, and

"Passing rich on forty pounds a year."

In Queen Square, in March, 1765, died the celebrated antiquary, Dr. William Stukeley, whose labours in British archæology obtained for him the name of "the arch-druid." Returning from his house at Kentish Town, he complained that he felt a stroke of palsy, and died a week afterwards. He was buried at East Ham, in Essex. Dr. Stukely was for many years rector of the parish of St. George the Martyr.

Here were shops of sundry booksellers and print-sellers; for at the "Golden Head" in this square, in 1712, the portrait of Cunneshote, one of the Cherokee chiefs then on a visit to this country, was on sale; it was engraved after a painting by Francis Parsons.

Queen Square, as well as Great Ormond Street, into which we shall shortly pass, seems to be a favourite centre of charitable institutions. At the corner of Brunswick Row is the Hospital for Hip Diseases in Childhood, which was founded in 1867. At No. 22 was for many years located the oldest of Ladies' Charity Schools. This institution — for, although called a school, it is in reality one of our oldest charitable institutions—was established in 1702, for "educating, clothing, and maintaining the daughters of respectable parents in reduced and necessitous circumstances." The Ladies' Charity School was removed in 1883 to new quarters at Notting Hill; and the site of the building here is being utilised in an extension of the National Hospital for the Paralysed and Epileptic, which adjoined it. This hospital was instituted in the year 1859. The number of persons annually benefited here amount to about 3,000, of whom a large number of the incurable patients have pensions awarded to them ranging from £10 to £22 each. In 1875-6 a new wing was added to the hospital, founded in memory of the late Johanna Chandler, for the reception of gentlewomen of limited means, governesses, the wives and children of business men, clerks, and other persons of the middle class of society, sufferers from paralysis and other diseases of the nervous system, who are unable to pay the ordinary expenses of medical treatment in their own homes, but are able and willing to pay a portion of their maintenance while in the hospital. In this "memorial wing" hospital life is divested as far as possible of its wearisome monotony by the provision of cheerfully-furnished day-rooms, regulated occupation, and such home comforts as the exigencies of the mode of life permits.

At No. 29 is the "College for Men and Women," with which is incorporated the "Working Women's College," both being offshoots of the "Working Men's College," of which we shall speak presently. It was established in 1874, with the object "of supplying to men and women occupied during the day a higher education than had been hitherto within their reach. The classes are taught, for the most part, gratuitously, and the design is that mutual help and fellowship may be promoted between all members of the college, teachers and students, by the educational work in the classes and the social life in the coffee-room." The classes, which are held every evening (except Saturday), comprise teaching in the following subjects :— Arithmetic, book-keeping, English grammar and language, history, literature, geography, physiology, Latin, French, German, drawing, singing, &c., and the fees range from 2s. to 4s. per class per term. These colleges for the joint education of men and women, though new in England, have long been carried on with much success in America, and the combination of the two sexes in the work of self-culture works well. The house is used by day as a High School for Girls.

No. 31 formed the head-quarters of some Roman Catholic charitable institutions, among which are the Aged Poor Society, and the Society of St. Vincent de Paul, for visiting and relieving distress among the labouring classes. This society is widely spread over all the large cities of the Continent both in Catholic and in Protestant countries.

A large double house on the south side of the square is the College of Preceptors, founded in 1846, and enjoying a royal charter. Its object is to afford to commercial and other public and private schools those tests of results which were afforded to other schools by the university local examinations. In 1870 and 1881 the number of persons examined by the college were respectively 2,412 and 16,000, showing an increase of several thousands, and at the same time affording conclusive evidence of the practical use of the examinations, many of the persons who submit to these tests of fitness being teachers themselves. In the adjoining house is another educational institution— the Government District School of Art for Ladies, under the patronage of Her Majesty. Another establishment is the School of Ecclesiastical Embroidery at No. 32. At the commencement of the present reign the square was inhabited almost entirely by private families of the upper classes; but gradually these mansions have been turned into hospitals and other institutions, for which the quiet of the place fits it admirably. The building now occupied as the College of Preceptors was originally part of Queen Anne's nursery; and Gloucester Street, close by, was named after her little short-lived son. It may be mentioned here that Sir John Karslake, the late Attorney-General, was born and brought up in this square, of which his father was an old and respected inhabitant.

Great Ormond Street, which we now enter, and which runs from Queen Square eastward into Lamb's Conduit Street, dates its erection from the commencement of the last century. Hatton, in 1708, speaks of it as "a street of fine new buildings;" and it is described by the author of a "New Critical Review of the Public Buildings, &c.," in the reign of George II., as a "place of pleasure;" he adds that "the side of it next the fields is, beyond question, one of the finest situations about town." Many of the large red-brick-built houses have in their time been the residences of some of the great men of the age. Dr. Hickes, the author of the "Thesaurus," at one time lived here; as also did Robert Nelson, the author of "Fasts and Festivals."

Dr. Stukeley, the antiquary, whom we have already mentioned, lived at one time "next door to the Duke of Powis;" his "Itinerarium Curiosum" (1724) is dated from thence. In 1773 Dr. Hawkesworth was living in this street. The celebrated writer, politician, poet, and convert from infidelity, Soame Jenyns, many years M.P. for Cambridge, was a native of this street.

In this street, as Cradock tells us, in his "Miscellaneous Memoirs," lived Mr. Bankes, the great conveyancer, of Lincoln's Inn, and friend of Lord Mansfield. He was Chancellor of York, and a Commissioner of Customs, and had a country house at Mortlake, where he kept a pack of hounds. He "gave up the law for hunting, and was more convivial than studious." He laid the foundations of the fortune of the Bankeses of Dorsetshire, which was cemented by an alliance, in the next generation, with Lord Eldon.

Powis House stood near the north-west end of the street, on the site now occupied by Powis Place. Mr. Peter Cunningham tells us that it was built in the latter part of the reign of William III., by William Herbert, Marquis of Powis, son of the first marquis, who was outlawed for his adherence to James II. It was mysteriously burnt down in January, 1714, while the Duc d'Aumont, its then tenant, was entertaining the ambassador of Venice and the envoys of Sweden and Tuscany at dinner, about three o'clock in the afternoon. The alarm of fire was raised in one of the upper rooms, and in less than two hours the whole place was burnt to the ground, the plate and a few of the most valuable pictures alone being saved. "How the fire began," writes Northouck, "was then and still is a mystery. Many reports were circulated on the occasion, one of which was that the house was designedly burnt, to afford a pretence for removing the ambassador to Somerset House (where he was afterwards accommodated), which lying on the banks of the Thames, any person might have more private access to him by water. Others said that the Pretender came over with the ambassador, and had private interviews with the queen and some of her ministers; but that his residence here being suspected, the house was fired to favour his escape in the confusion."

The house was insured; but the French king's dignity would not permit him, it is said, to suffer a fire-office to pay for the neglect of the domestics of his representatives,[*] and it was accordingly afterwards rebuilt magnificently, at his majesty's cost. Northouck describes it, in 1773, as having long been tenanted first by Lord Chancellor Hardwicke, and then occupied by the Spanish ambassador. He adds: "It stands back from the street, is fronted with stone in a majestic style; eight lofty Corinthian pilasters reach to the entablature over the first storey, which supports the attic storey, which has been censured as out of proportion; and the house stands greatly in need of wings, to render it complete." The same is the opinion of the author of the "New Critical Review of the Public Buildings," already quoted. The following additional details of Powis House we glean from Mr. P. Cunningham's "Handbook:"—"The front was surmounted on the coping by urns and statues. Over the street door was a phœnix, still standing (but without the head) in the tympanum of the pediment of the house, No. 51. The ornament above the capitals of the pilasters was the Gallic cock. The staircase was painted by Giacomo Amiconi, a Venetian painter of some reputation in this country. He chose the story of Holofernes, and painted the personages of his story in Roman dresses. On the top was a great reservoir, used as a fishpond and a resource against fire. The house was taken down in 1777." There is a large engraving of the mansion by Thomas Bowles, dated 1714, the year after the destruction of the first building by fire.

A large house on the north side, No. 45, now the Working Men's College, was during the last century the residence of Lord Chancellor Thurlow. The house is chiefly noticeable for its deep bay-windows, and its old-fashioned iron railings on each side of the steps leading to the doorway. Within, most of the rooms are large and lofty, and the principal staircase is broad and spacious.

---

* *European Magazine* for June, 1804, p. 429.

Under an arched recess upon the staircase there stood formerly a bust of Lord Thurlow. It was from this house, on the night of the 24th of March, 1784, the day before the dissolution of Parliament, that the Great Seal of England, one of the emblems of the supreme authority of the occupant of the woolsack, was stolen. The story of the theft is thus told by Mr. Cunningham :—"The thieves got in by scaling the garden-wall and forcing two iron bars out of the kitchen window. They then made their way up to the chancellor's study, broke open the drawers of his lordship's writing-table, ransacked the room, and carried away the Great Seal, rejecting the pouch as of little value, and the mace as too unwieldy. The thieves were discovered, but the seal, being of silver, had got into circulation through the melting-pot, and patents and other important public documents were delayed until a new one was made." In another version of the tale it was stated that the thieves effected their escape without having been heard by any of the family ; and though a reward was offered for their discovery they could never be traced, nor was the Great Seal ever recovered. A Cabinet Council was immediately called, and a new seal was ordered to be made, and such expedition was used, that by noon the next day the new Great Seal was finished in a rough fashion, and was used as a makeshift until another was prepared, which it took the artist a whole year to complete. An accident similar to the above befell Lord Nottingham, Lord Chancellor in the year 1577, when the official mace was stolen. The story of its recovery, quite a romance of its kind, is told by Hone, in his "Year Book."

Many good stories are told about the haughty and eccentric Lord Thurlow, a few of which we offer to our readers.

When, by the death of his publisher, Mr. Payne, of Pall Mall, George Crabbe found himself poor and unknown in London, reduced to the necessity of asking assistance, he applied, among other great men, to Lord Thurlow, to whom he wrote more than once. "To the first letter, which enclosed a copy of verses," writes the poet's son, " Lord Thurlow returned for answer a cold and polite note, regretting that his avocations did not leave him leisure to read verses. The great talents and discriminating judgment of Lord Thurlow made Crabbe feel this repulse with double bitterness ; and he addressed to his lordship some strong but not disrespectful lines, intimating that in former times the encouragement of literature had been considered as a duty appertaining to the illustrious station which he held. Of this effusion the lord

chancellor," adds the filial biographer, " took no notice whatever." It is satisfactory to learn from the same source that a year later—not, however, till he had found a friend in Edmund Burke— Crabbe received from Lord Thurlow an invitation to breakfast at his house in Great Ormond Street, when the latter apologised to the poet for his neglect, and placed in his hands on leaving a sealed letter containing a bank-note for £100, with a promise of further aid of another kind as soon as he should enter holy orders.

Lord Thurlow's personal appearance was often the subject of amusing and laughable remarks. It is asserted that he was singularly ugly ; so ugly that when his portrait was shown to Lavater, the physiognomist, he observed—" Whether that man is on earth or in another place that should be nameless, I know not ; but wherever he is, he is a born tyrant, and will rule if he can." The Duke of Norfolk had, at Arundel Castle, a fine breed of owls, one of whom, from its excessive ugliness, he named Lord Thurlow ; and it is said that great fun was caused by a messenger coming to the duke in a lobby of the House of Peers with the news that "Lord Thurlow had just laid an egg."

For the following anecdote, relative to Lord Chancellor Thurlow, whilst living in Great Ormond Street, we are indebted to Mr. Cradock's amusing " Memoirs : "—

"Soon after Mr. Thurlow was made Lord Chancellor, he addressed his brother, the Bishop of Durham, in the following words :—' Tom, there is to be a drawing-room on Thursday, where I am obliged to attend ; and as I have purchased Lord Bathurst's coach, but have no leisure to give orders about the necessary alterations, do you see and get all ready for me.' The bishop, always anxious to obey the *sic volo, sic jubeo*, of his brother, immediately bestirred himself, and everything was considered as completed in due time ; but when the carriage came to the door, the bishop found that Lord Bathurst's arms had never been altered. Knowing his brother's hasty temper, he happily hit immediately on the only expedient to prevent a storm : the door was held open till the Lord Chancellor arrived, and as soon as he was seated and had fully examined the interior, he stretched out his hand, and most kindly exclaimed, ' Brother, the whole is finished entirely to my satisfaction, and I thank you.' The same expedient, as to the door, was resorted to again at his return from St. James's, and of course no time was lost to remedy all defects." Doubtless, the very next day the arms and crest of the Bathursts were superseded by those which Garter King of Arms had assigned to

Lord Thurlow ; for, being the first gentleman of his race, he probably inherited none.

Lord Thurlow, it is well known, was rough and plain-spoken to a degree, not to say occasionally wanting in common courtesy ; and yet sometimes, when the fit took him, he could unbend, much like Dr. Johnson, who, by the way, was himself an

carriage, and saw them safely to their lodgings in what was then the fashionable street of Church Row. The circumstance being related to Lord Thurlow, the Lord Chancellor took an early opportunity of calling on the young man, to thank him in person, and finding him at breakfast, sat down and joined him at his morning meal, where he

LORD THURLOW.

occasional guest here with his lordship. Mr. Cradock, in his "Memoirs," for instance, records a slight incident which shows him in an amiable light. Though there never was a Lady Thurlow, yet he had two daughters, of whom he was fond and proud. One evening, as they were coming away from the Assembly Rooms at Hampstead, there was a slight riot in Well Walk among the servants in waiting. The young ladies being alarmed, a young officer stepped forward and offered his assistance and protection, which they were glad to accept. He handed them to their

made himself particularly agreeable. It was not till after his lordship was gone that the young man found out that he had been entertaining a lord chancellor unawares.

Notwithstanding his eccentricity, Lord Thurlow will ever be looked upon as a great lawyer and magistrate. When he last offered in the House of Lords to deliver a judgment in a divorce case, the whole house rose in honour to his years and learning. Dr. Johnson said he was a splendid fellow ; and Sheridan declared that "no man was half so wise as Thurlow looked."

QUEEN SQUARE, 1810.

The Working Men's College, of which we now proceed to speak, had its origin in a very humble manner. In 1848, a barrister of Lincoln's Inn, Mr. John Malcolm Ludlow, proposed to the then newly-appointed chaplain of Lincoln's Inn, the Rev. F. D. Maurice, that some district near should be taken in hand by the lawyers whom Mr. Ludlow could get together, for the purpose of holding educational classes, Bible readings, &c., among the working classes. This was in a building in Little Ormond Yard, not far from the present college. In course of time this party of gentlemen, with some others, formed "The Society for Promoting Working Men's Associations," and built the Hall of Association, under the workshops of the Tailors' Association, in Castle Street. Here were begun classes and lectures, to both of which women were admitted. In 1854 Mr. Maurice drew up a lengthy plan for the formation of a College for Working Men, in which it was agreed "that the education should be regular and organic, not taking the form of mere miscellaneous lectures, or even of classes not related to each other." It was also agreed that the teachers, and, by degrees, the pupils, should form an organic body, so that the name of "college" should be at least as applicable to the institution as to University College or King's College. And it was also determined that the college should, in some sense or other, immediately or ultimately be self-governed and self-supported. Mr. Maurice's plan having been duly discussed, a circular was distributed, setting forth the nature and objects of the college. In the meantime a house —No. 31, Red Lion Square—had been taken; and the infant establishment consisted of a principal, a council of teachers, and students. The first "term" opened on October 31, 1854, the candidates for admission as members numbering upwards of 100, Mr. Maurice filling the presidential chair. Many other names of men of note have since been added to the lists. In 1856 the college became "affiliated" to the London University. In the following year —the lease of the house in Red Lion Square having expired—the College took up its quarters in Great Ormond Street. In course of time, owing to the increase in the number of students, and for other reasons, the adjoining house, No. 44, was purchased, and added to the College property; and in 1870, partly out of funds contributed by friends, and partly by money advanced on loan, some large additional buildings were erected at the end of the grounds in the rear of the house, to serve as class-rooms, lecture-hall, museum, &c. There is also an excellent library, and a room set apart for general sociable conversation among the members.

In 1874 the college was incorporated, under the name of the "Working Men's College Corporation," under the provisions of an Act of Parliament, and thus permanently settled its status; and the debt which arose from taking the present house, and also by the erection of the additional buildings, was nearly extinguished by the "Maurice Memorial Fund" having been placed at the disposal of the council as a Domus-fund. Professor Maurice, the founder, continued to be the Principal of the College till his death, in 1872, when he was succeeded by Mr. Thomas Hughes, and he by Sir John Lubbock in 1883. Besides the College proper, here are also the Working Men's College Adult Evening School and the International Collegiate School.

One or two doors westward is the Hospital of St. John and St. Elizabeth. This is a Roman Catholic charity for the relief of the sick poor of the metropolis. The church connected with the institution is a large and handsome building, and was erected by Sir George Bowyer, as a knight of the Order of St. John. The hospital was founded in 1856, and was for some time under the direction of the late Cardinal Wiseman. Considerable alteration was subsequently made in the building, and it was re-opened in 1868.

The house lately standing at the corner of Powis Place, and incorporated into the Hospital for Sick Children, was the last home of Dr. Richard Mead, the celebrated physician and "archiator" of King George II., who died there in 1754. Born at Stepney in 1673, Dr. Mead lived to become the friend of Drs. Radcliffe, Garth, and Arbuthnot, and he had sufficiently established his reputation as a physician as to be called in consultation to the sick room of Queen Anne, two days before her death. On the accession of George II. Dr. Mead was appointed Physician in Ordinary. He had in the meantime held several important positions, including the post of Physician to St. Thomas's Hospital. The doctor's last, and perhaps the most useful, of all his works is his "Medical Precepts and Cautions."

Dr. Mead, no less celebrated as a patron of artistic and literary genius than in his own walk of life, was one of the first collectors of a private gallery, which he threw open freely to art-students and to private amateurs. His house, indeed, may be said to have been the first academy of painting in London. At the bottom of the garden at the back of his house the doctor had constructed a museum, in which was brought together a large collection of pictures and antiquities, besides which he had an extensive and valuable library. His doors were always open to the poor and indigent for advice; men of intellect were sure of finding from Dr. Mead all help and aid. He kept continually in his pay a number of scholars and artists of all kinds, who were continually at work for him, or, rather, for the public. No foreigner of taste and learning came to London without being introduced to him, and being asked to dine at his table. His library was open to every one who wished to consult it, and he allowed his books to be borrowed by the studious. Dr. Mead's library, medals, and pictures were sold by auction and dispersed after his death, in 1754.

The Hospital for Sick Children was established in the year 1852 in the above-mentioned old-fashioned mansion, with its spacious garden behind. The retrospect, in looking back over the time during which the hospital has existed, shows a marvellous progress. At its first opening only one child—a little girl—came to be admitted as a patient, and at the end of a month only eight in-patients and twenty-four out-patients had applied. For some years there was a struggle, not only for funds, but for existence, on the part of the new institution. Happily, some influential people took up the children's cause. The Bishop of London, Lord Carlisle, and Lord Shaftesbury said many a good word for it. Charles Dickens, as brilliant as he was large-hearted, advocated it by tongue and pen. Who, having read "Our Mutual Friend," will have forgotten "Little Johnny's" removal to "a place where there are none but children; a place set up on purpose for children; where the good doctors and nurses pass their lives with children, talk to none but children, touch none but children, comfort and cure none but children?" Notwithstanding all that was said and written in its favour, little money at first seemed to be forthcoming, but much sympathy and kind encouragement also, the best impetus that can be given to a really good cause, aware of its own value —publicity. In course of time the first annual report appeared, announcing as patroness of the Children's Hospital the most exalted mother in the realm—the Queen, and then definitely stating the objects. These were—" 1. The medical and surgical treatment of poor children. 2. The attainment and diffusion of knowledge regarding the diseases of children. 3. The training of nurses for children." It had above thirty beds, and in the first five years of its existence had given out-door and in-door relief to above 50,000 children, when want of funds threatened to arrest its merciful work. A public dinner was arranged at the Freemasons' Hall; Charles Dickens undertook to preside. From his speech on the occasion we get a picture of the hospital, drawn in his own masterly manner. After some preliminary remarks, he proceeded: "Within a quarter of a mile of this place where I speak stands a courtly old house where once, no doubt, blooming children were born, and grew up to be men and women, and married, and brought their own blooming children back to patter up the old oak staircase which stood but the other day, and to wonder at the old oak carvings on the chimney-pieces. In the airy wards into which the old state drawing-rooms and family bed-chambers of that house are now converted are such little patients, that the attendant nurses look like reclaimed giantesses, and the kind medical practitioner like an amiable Christian ogre. Grouped about the little low tables in the centre of the rooms are such tiny convalescents, that they seem to be playing at having been ill. On the dolls' beds are such diminutive creatures, that each poor sufferer is supplied with its tray of toys; and, looking round, you may see how the little, tired, flushed cheek has toppled over half the brute creation on its way to the ark, or how one little dimpled arm has mowed down (as I saw myself) the whole tin soldiery of Europe. On the walls of these rooms are graceful, pleasant, bright childish pictures. At the beds' heads are pictures of the figure which is the universal embodiment of all mercy and compassion, the figure of Him who was once a child Himself, and a poor one. Besides these little creatures on the beds, you may learn in that place that the number of small out-patients brought to that house for relief is no fewer than 10,000 in the compass of one single year. In the room in which these are received you may see against the wall a box on which it is written that it has been calculated that if every grateful mother who brings a child there will drop a penny into it, the hospital funds may possibly be increased in a year by so large a sum as forty pounds." That night added £3,000 to the resources of the hospital, and Dickens afterwards read publicly for the same charitable purpose his " Christmas Carol." Year by year the number of out-patients increase enormously, whilst the in-patients are still limited by the want of sufficient funds. Nevertheless, as the list of subscribers swells, and one or two legacies fall in, the number of tiny beds is added to by twos and threes. In an article in Dickens' *All the Year Round* (1863), we read :—" Steadily as it has advanced, generously and wisely as it has been supported, it is yet but the small beginning of a work of duty. In the first five of its ten years of existence, it received into its beds more than 1,100 children seriously and dangerously ill, and gave the best help of medicine to 30,000 who were nursed at home. In the second half of its life, nearly 2,000 sick children have been sedulously tended in the little beds of the hospital, and almost 50,000 have received, as out-patients, gratuitous advice and medicine. The help is gratuitous; need of help is the sole recommendation necessary."

Since the above period the work of the hospital has become increasingly well known, and its borders have expanded along with its sphere of usefulness. First came the purchase of the house and garden adjoining that in which the hospital had been established; then came the addition of a room for convalescents; then the admission of women to be trained as nurses, and the institution of lectures on the diseases of children. The children who were recovering were sent to Brighton or to Mitcham for the fresh air they needed; and Cromwell House, at Highgate, has been occupied as a convalescent home for the children leaving the hospital.

In 1875, a further extension of the hospital was completed by the erection of a magnificent block of buildings in the rear of the old house, from the designs of Mr. E. M. Barry, R.A. It is an imposing brick-built structure, decorated with terracotta, and flanked by octagonal towers, which are made to play an important part in the fulfilment of the sanitary requirements of the place. Immediately facing the entrance—which is in Powis Place—is a beautifully decorated chapel, with walls of polished alabaster, and a roof supported by columns of alabaster and marble. This chapel was the gift of an anonymous donor, and it has been set apart, without actual consecration, for the religious services of the house, the services being conducted by the ladies who undertake the administration of the hospital, and the congregation consisting of the nurses and such of the little patients as are able to attend. On either side of the entrance, on the ground floor and on the first floor, is a spacious ward, each one being named, by special permission, after some member of the royal family. On the upper floor there are a number of smaller wards, to afford quiet to single patients after operations, or to admit of the separation of infectious disease (if it should accidentally break out) from the main body of the hospital. This new building affords space for 112 beds, and upon its construction the best architectural and sanitary knowledge has been brought to bear. It may be well to record here that the nurses are under the supervision of trained ladies, who are called "sisters," who reside in the hospital and are provided with board, but whose services are otherwise gratuitous. There is a "sister"

to each ward, and one to the out-patient department, and under the sisters there are paid nurses, in the proportion of at least one to every ten patients. These nurses, however skilful in their calling, are engaged upon probation, and are not retained unless they are found to possess tact and aptitude in the management of children—a circumstance, it has been remarked, which renders it curious and interesting to observe that they are all little women.

In 1882 Dr. Mead's house was pulled down, in order to complete the rebuilding of the Hospital according to the original plan and design of Mr. Barry. This charity, being unendowed, is dependent entirely on voluntary contributions for its support and maintenance.

On the west side of Powis Place is a large and handsome stone building, called the Homœopathic Hospital. In what is now the east wing of the edifice (then No. 50) the family of the Macaulays were living in the early part of the present century. It was then occupied by Zachary Macaulay, and in it his celebrated son, the future essayist, orator, and historian, Lord Macaulay, spent some portion of his early manhood.

Mr. G. O. Trevelyan, in his "Life of Lord Macaulay," draws a most pleasant picture of the interior of this house, when the younger brothers and sisters of the future essayist were still in the school-room, the fun and mirth of the week days, however, being softened down by the regular visit on Sundays to St. John's Chapel, Bedford Row, to sit under the ministry of Daniel Wilson. "It was round the house in Great Ormond Street that the dearest associations of the family were gathered," writes Mr. Trevelyan, who tells us how his mother, Lord Macaulay's sister, drove thither when dying to look once more on its well-known walls. Here the family lived very quietly, Mr. Z. Macaulay having met with reverses in business; and here he was living when the "Essay on Milton," contributed by his son, the future Lord Macaulay, to the *Edinburgh Review,* made him at once the "talk of the town." "The family table in Bloomsbury," writes Mr. Trevelyan, "was at once covered with cards of invitation from every quarter of London."

At No. 27, on the south side of the street, are the offices of the United Kingdom Benefit Society, one of the oldest and best conducted societies of the kind in the metropolis. It was instituted in 1839, and was originally located in Castle Street, Long Acre, but removed to Great Ormond Street about 1865. The society, which was formed for the purpose of affording relief to its members in case of sickness, and of an allowance to the family in case of death, is enrolled agreeably to Act of Parliament, and has upon its books a very large number of members.

Addison, in the *Spectator* (No. 9), lets us into the character of this street in his time. He writes in a tone half serious and half jesting :—" There are, at present, in several parts of this city, what are called street clubs, in which the chief inhabitants of the street converse together every night. I remember, upon my inquiring after lodgings in Great Ormond Street, the landlord, to recommend that quarter of the town, told me there was at that time a very good club in it. He also told me upon further discourse with him, that two or three noisy country squires, who were settled there the year before, had considerably sunk the price of house-rent, and that the club (to prevent the like inconvenience for the future) had thoughts of taking every house that became vacant into their own hands, till they had found for it a tenant of a sociable nature and good conversation."

In New Ormond Street is an institution called the Workhouse Visiting Society. It was established to promote the moral and spiritual improvement of workhouse inmates (of whom there are upwards of 117,000 in England and Wales), and to provide a centre of communication and information for all persons interested in that object. The society is in connection with the National Association for the Promotion of Social Science. It was founded in 1858, and has already enlisted a large number of persons in its interests, who labour among the various classes which are to be met with in our workhouses. The objects of this society are being carried out in all parts of England, and the work has been extended to Ireland. Besides the work of visiting carried on by the members, a scheme has also been started by them for the formation of workhouse libraries. The society has also a Home for Incurable and Infirm Women, which was opened in 1861. The occupation of those in the home consists of housework, cooking, and laundry-work, for a month in turn, with needlework, and two hours of instruction in the evening : they also assist the nurse in attendance on the aged patients in the infirm ward. Two girls also, for a month at a time, are attached to the infant nursery of the Children's Hospital in Great Ormond Street. There is a considerable degree of liberty allowed to the girls in the Home, as it is desired to treat them and trust them as they will have to be trusted in situations.

Guilford Street, into which we now pass, runs parallel with Great and New Ormond Streets, and extends from Russell Square to Gray's Inn Road.

"Its site," says Malcolm, "was formerly a path, which led from Gray's Inn Lane by the Foundling Hospital, the gardens of Great Ormond Street, and the back of Queen Square, to Baltimore House (afterwards inhabited by the Duke of Bolton and the Earl of Roslyn), and it was generally bounded by stagnant water at least twelve feet lower than the square." In the first half of the present century, however, the street had become the residence of a large number of the most successful barristers, and even of several members of the judicial bench. In it lived, long after he had attained the dignity of Lord Chief Baron of the Exchequer, the late Right Hon. Sir Frederick Pollock. Here, too, lived Sir Edward Sugden (afterwards Lord St. Leonard's, and Lord High Chancellor of England) whilst in the full tide of his professional success. At No. 71, two doors off, resided Mr. Serjeant Wilde, another Chancellor in embryo, the future Lord Truro.

A great part of the north side of Guilford Street—in fact, the whole space between Brunswick and Mecklenburgh Squares—is occupied by the grounds surrounding the Foundling Hospital, of which institution we shall speak in a future volume. We may, however, mention here that a small inn, named the "Boat," in the then open fields to the rear of the hospital, was the rendezvous of Lord George Gordon and the other ringleaders of the mob of "No Popery" zealots who, in the year 1780, set half London on fire, and caused a panic of a week's duration.

Both Brunswick and Mecklenburgh Squares are of comparatively modern growth, and are highly respectable, but not in any way fashionable. Macaulay more than once contrasts with Holland House and West-end society "the quiet folks who live in Mecklenburgh and Brunswick Squares." In Brunswick Square, as one of them tells us, the great historian would pace up and down with his sisters Margaret and Hannah for a couple of hours at a time, talking incessantly on politics and literature, or "deep in the mazes of the most subtle metaphysics." John Leech, the well-known artist, and contributor to *Punch*, was at one time living in this square ; and Mecklenburgh Square has numbered among its residents Lord Kingsdown and Mr. G. A. Sala. The house-fronts of Brunswick Square have been described as "brick walls with holes in them," as is the case with the majority of the squares in this neighbourhood ; it is blocked up on the east side by the grounds of the Foundling Hospital, which form, on the other hand, the west boundary of Mecklenburgh Square. The east side of the latter is architecturally embellished, and the enclosure contains some very fine trees.

HOSPITAL FOR SICK CHILDREN, GREAT ORMOND STREET. (*See page* 562.)

CHAPTER XLIV.

RUSSELL AND BEDFORD SQUARES, &c.

"Fountains and trees our wearied pride do please,
Even in the midst of gilded palaces;
And in our towns the prospect gives delight,
Which opens round the country to our sight."—*Spratt.*

The Site of Russell Square at the Beginning of the Present Century—Statue of Francis, Fifth Duke of Bedford—General Appearance of the Square—Bolton House—A Pair of Eccentric Peers—Lord Chancellor Loughborough—Other Distinguished Residents—Bedford Place—Montagu Place—Keppel Street—Bedford Square—Lord Eldon and the Prince Regent—The "Princess Olivia of Cumberland"—Gower Street—The Toxophilite Society—Jack Bannister, the Actor—The Eccentric Henry Cavendish—University College—Flaxman's Models—The Graphic Club—University College Hospital—Dr. Williams' Library.

ON the demolition of Bedford House, the adjoining lands were laid out for building purposes, and Russell and Bedford Squares were erected about the year 1804, and were named after the Russells, Earls and Dukes of Bedford. For some time previously—as we have already shown in our account of Bloomsbury Square, Great Ormond Street, and other places in the locality—many of the houses in the immediate neighbourhood were very extensively inhabited by judges and successful lawyers; and on the building of the above squares the houses were so largely taken up by members of the legal profession, on account of their nearness to Lincoln's Inn, that in course of time the epithet of "Judge-land" came to be applied to this particular part of Bloomsbury, in much the same manner as in late years Pall Mall and its neighbourhood came to be called "Club-land."

Russell Square, which we enter at the western end of Guilford Street, occupies part of what in 1720 was called Southampton Fields, but what in later times became known as Long Fields. At the beginning of the present century, Long Fields lay waste and useless. There were nursery grounds northward; towards the north-west were the grounds of the Toxophilite Society; Bedford House, with its lawn and magnificent gardens planted with lime-trees, occupied the south side; whilst Baltimore House, which later on came to be called Bolton House, stood on the east side, at the corner of Guilford Street.   This square is one of the largest in the metropolis; in fact, it is the next largest to Lincoln's Inn Fields.   The houses are of brick, with the lower part in some cases cemented. Something of an architectural character is given to a block on the west side, between Montagu Place

resting on a plough, while in the other he holds some ears of corn.   There are four emblematical figures at the corners of the pedestal, which is adorned in bas-relief with various rural attributes. The statue—a very fine specimen of Sir Richard Westmacott's best style—was erected in 1809.

SIR THOMAS LAWRENCE'S HOUSE, RUSSELL SQUARE.   (*See page* 566.)

and Keppel Street, but the majority of the houses are better inside than out.   On the south side of the central enclosure, looking down Bedford Place, and facing the monument to Fox in Bloomsbury Square, is a statue which recalls to mind one of those illustrious statesmen of ancient Rome, whose time was divided between the labours of the Senate and those of their Sabine farms.   The statue represents that eminent and patriotic agriculturist, Francis, the fifth Duke of Bedford, with one hand

A writer in the *St. James's Magazine* thus speaks of this locality : "Russell Square is, under ordinary circumstances, a very nice place to walk in.   If those troublesome railway vans and goods wagons would not come lumbering and clattering, by way of Southampton Row, through the square, and up Guilford Street, on their way to King's Cross, 'La Place Roussell' would be as cosy and tranquil as 'La Place Royale' in Paris.   It has the vastness of Lincoln's Inn Fields without its dinginess."

The handsome mansion on the south-east side of the square, at the corner of Guilford Street, was built, in 1759, for the eccentric and profligate Lord Baltimore; and, as we have already stated, it was at first called Baltimore House. Hither his lordship decoyed a young milliner, Sarah Woodcock, and was prosecuted for having caused her ruin, but acquitted. He died in 1771 at Naples, whence his remains were brought to London, and lay in state, as we have mentioned, at Exeter Change. The house was subsequently occupied by the equally eccentric Duke of Bolton, whose name was then given to it. Northouck remarks, wittily and truly, that "it was either built without a plan, or else has had very whimsical owners; for the door has been shifted to different parts of the house, until at last it is lost to all outward appearance, being now (1776) carried into the stable-yard!"

The Duke of Bolton, who was, of course, known as Lord Henry Powlett during his elder brother's life, served in early life in the navy, in which, however, if we may believe Sir N. W. Wraxall, "he had gained no laurels." He was supposed generally to be the Captain Whiffle so humorously described by Smollett in his "Roderick Random." His mother was Miss Lavinia Fenton, an actress in her day (well known for her impersonation of "Polly Peachum").

Bolton House was afterwards occupied by Lord Loughborough when Lord Chancellor, as also by Sir John Nicholl and Sir Vicary Gibbs.

On the 21st of June, 1799, George III., with the Queen and several members of the Royal Family, assembled at Bolton House, when occupied by Lord Loughborough, and after partaking of a cold collation, proceeded to view the Foundling Hospital. Lord Loughborough, though an Erskine by birth, was a "paltry and servile politician," according to Lord Holland. He died soon after his elevation to the Earldom of Rosslyn, and George III. pronounced his funeral oration by declaring that "he had not left a greater rogue behind him."

When the square was laid out for building, Bolton House was the only mansion standing, and this was incorporated into the rest of the square, though somewhat incongruously; and though it is now divided into two large residences, it still retains its name of Bolton House.

Passing to the other mansions in the square, we may state that Sir Samuel Romilly lived and died (by his own hand) at No. 21; Chief-Justice Abbot (Lord Tenterden) at No. 28; Mr. Justice Holroyd at No. 46; Mr. T. (afterwards Lord) Denman at

No. 50; and at No. 12, Mr. W. Tooke, F.R.S., the writer on currency and political economy, M.P. for Truro in 1835-7.

At No. 67 lived for some time the lawyer, poet, philanthropist, and man of letters, Sir Thomas N. Talfourd, a judge of the Court of Common Pleas, who died suddenly, in 1854, in the court-house at Stafford, while addressing the grand jury.

A person no less distinguished, though in quite another way, Sir Thomas Lawrence, the courtly painter, and President of the Royal Academy, resided at No. 65 for a quarter of a century. He died there in 1830, after a very short illness. Concerning the residence of Sir Thomas Lawrence, there is a note in the *Gentleman's Magazine* for January, 1818, by the Rev. John Mitford, which says:—"We shall never forget the Cossacks, mounted on their small white horses, with their long spears grounded, standing as sentinels at the door of this great painter, whilst he was taking the portrait of their general, Platoff."

Bedford Place, connecting Russell Square with Bloomsbury Square, was built between 1801 and 1805 on the site of Bedford House. Here, at the house of Mr. Henry Fry, died, in 1811, Richard Cumberland, the author of *The West Indian*. In Upper Bedford Place, on the opposite side of Russell Square, in 1826, and for some years later, lived Mr. Richard Bethell, afterwards Lord Chancellor and Lord Westbury.

At No. 4, Montagu Place, between Russell and Bedford Squares, in 1841, lived the late Sir John T. Coleridge, father of Lord Coleridge; he had previously resided in Torrington Square, and afterwards in Park Crescent, Regent's Park. To the north-west of Russell Square are Woburn and Torrington Squares, in the latter of which was the residence of Sir Harris Nicolas, editor of Nelson's Despatches and Letters, and a distinguished antiquary and genealogist. He died at Boulogne in 1848.

Running parallel with Montagu Place, and with Store Street, forming a communication with Tottenham Court Road, is Keppel Street. This is chiefly noticeable as containing a chapel for Anabaptists.

Bedford Square, on the west side of the British Museum, stands on a part of the Bedford estate, and covers some considerable portion of the old "rookery" of St. Giles's; it is about six acres in extent, or exactly half the size of Lincoln's Inn Fields. In the reign of George IV. and William IV. it was extensively occupied by lawyers who had climbed to the top of their profession, and also by very many of the judges, among whom were Chief Justice Sir Nicholas Tindall, Sir John Richardson,

Mr. Justice Burrough, Mr. Justice Bayley, Mr. Justice Littledale, Baron Graham, Baron J. A. Park, and Mr. Justice Patteson. No. 7 was for many years occupied by Sir Robert Harry Inglis, the venerable M.P. for Oxford University.

At No. 6 lived Lord Chancellor Eldon from 1804 down to 1816; and here occurred the memorable interview between his lordship and the Prince Regent, afterwards George IV., which has been so often told, though it will bear telling here again in the words of Mr. Peter Cunningham :—"The Prince came alone to the Chancellor's house, and upon the servant opening the door, observed that as his lordship had the gout, he knew he must be at home, and therefore desired that he might be shown up to the room where the Chancellor was sitting or lying. The servant said he was too ill to be seen, and that he had also positive orders to show in *no one*. The Prince then asked to be shown the staircase, which he immediately ascended, and pointed first to one door and then to another, asking, ' Is that your master's room ? ' The servant answered ' No,' until he came to the right one, upon which he opened the door, seated himself by the Chancellor's bedside, and asked him to appoint his friend Jekyll, the great wit, to the vacant office of Master in Chancery. The Chancellor refused—there could be no more unfit appointment. The Prince, perceiving the humour of the Chancellor, and that he was firm to his determination not to appoint him, threw himself back in the chair and exclaimed, ' How I do pity Lady Eldon !' ' Good God !' said the Chancellor, ' what is the matter ?' ' Oh, nothing !' answered the Prince, ' except that she will never see you again, for here I remain until you promise to make Jekyll a Master in Chancery.' Jekyll, of course, obtained the appointment."

In March, 1816, during the riots at the West-end on account of the rejection of the Corn-Law Alteration Bill, some portion of the mob proceeded to Bedford Square, and broke the windows of the house of the unpopular Tory Lord Chancellor.

In Alfred Place, Bedford Square, was living in 1820 Olivia Serres, *née* Wilmott, when she came forward before the world to claim royal rank and precedence as "the Princess Olivia of Cumberland," declaring that she was the legitimate daughter of Henry Frederick, Duke of Cumberland, youngest brother of George III., who had created her, by a somewhat informal document in his own hand-writing, Duchess of Lancaster. Her claim to this title was discussed more than once in the House of Commons, and was revived after her death by her children ; but it was finally negatived by a decree

of the Court for Divorce and Matrimonial Causes, in June, 1866. The "Princess" died in 1834, and was buried in the churchyard of St. James's, Piccadilly.

Gower Street, which runs from the north-east corner of Bedford Square into the Euston Road, is a broad thoroughfare, nearly a third of a mile in length, but dull and monotonous in appearance. Mr. James Grant, in his "Travels in Town," is not far from the mark when he describes this as "a street which scarcely exhibits any signs of being an inhabited place. . . . . Here and there," he writes, "you see a solitary pedestrian, or perchance a one-horse chaise. The stranger in passing along this street feels an emotion of melancholy come over him, caused by its dulness and unbroken monotony, and wonders how people can betray so entire a disregard of the truth as to represent the metropolis as a place of business and bustle, of noise and din."

"This street," observes a writer in *Once a Week*, in 1867, "was still so perfectly free from smoke forty years ago that grapes were ripened by the sun in the open air in the garden of one at least of the houses. Lord Eldon used often to speak of the fine fruit which he raised in his garden here, and also mentioned in Court the sad effect of the smoke upon it. A still more extraordinary fact is that even so late as the year 1800, Mr. William Bentham, of Upper Gower Street, had nearly twenty-five dozen of the finest and most delicious nectarines, all fit for the table, gathered off three trees in his garden, and that the same plot of ground continued, even long after, to produce the richest-flavoured celery in great abundance."

In 1791 the Toxophilite Society began to hold its meetings in grounds on the eastern side of Gower Street, under lease from the Duke of Bedford ; and they continued here till 1805, when they were driven away westwards, the land being "required for building purposes." We shall meet with them again when we come to the Regent's Park.

Gower Street in its time has numbered among its residents a few remarkable men. At No. 65, Jack Bannister, the actor, lived and died. "In the drama," as we learn from a memoir in the *Mirror*, "he was affecting, because he was natural and simple ; in society, he was distinguished by the same characteristics. His unaffected hilarity in conversation, the flexibility of his mind in adapting itself to every subject which arose, and the almost puerile good humour with which he recalled and recited the incidents of his earliest life and observation, formed altogether a picture equally singular and interesting. In these moments he showed himself to the greatest advantage; his animated countenance displayed at once the intelligence of a man, the sweetness of a woman, and the innocent sportiveness of a child. His social virtues will never be forgotten; they assured to him the respect and the esteem of all; he enjoyed upon earth full reward of his talents and good qualities, while his hopes of an hereafter were cherished with a warmth and confidence resulting from a true and lively faith."

A house at the corner of Montagu Place and Gower Street was for some years the town residence of the eccentric philosopher, the Hon. Henry Cavendish, who was well known for his chemical researches. Few visitors were admitted there, but some found their way across the threshold, and have reported that books and apparatus formed its chief furniture. For the former, however, Cavendish set apart a separate mansion in Dean Street, Soho. Here he had collected a large and carefully-chosen library of works on science, which he threw open to all engaged in research; and to this house he went for his own books, as one would go to a circulating library, signing a formal receipt for such of the volumes as he took with him. Cavendish, it is asserted, lived comfortably, but made no display; and his few guests were treated on all occasions to the same fare, and it was not very sumptuous. A Fellow of the Royal Society reports that "if any one dined with Cavendish he invariably gave them a leg of mutton and nothing else." Another Fellow says that Cavendish "seldom had company at his house, but on one occasion three or four scientific men were to dine with him, and when his housekeeper came to ask what was to be got for dinner, he said, 'A leg of mutton!' 'Sir, that will not be enough for five.' 'Well, then, get two,' was the reply."

Dr. Thomas Thomson writes of Cavendish:— " He was shy and bashful to a degree bordering on disease. He could not bear to have any person introduced to him, or to be pointed out in any way as a remarkable man. One Sunday evening he was standing at Sir Joseph Banks's, in a crowded room, conversing with Mr. Hatchett, when Dr. Ingenhousz, who had a good deal of pomposity of manner, came up with an Austrian gentleman in his hand, and introduced him formally to Mr. Cavendish. He mentioned the titles and qualifications of his friend at great length, and said that he had been particularly anxious to be introduced to a philosopher so profound and so universally known and celebrated as Mr. Cavendish. As soon as Dr. Ingenhousz had finished, the Austrian gentleman began to speak,

assuring Mr. Cavendish that his principal reason for coming to London was to see and converse with one of the greatest ornaments of the age, and one of the most illustrious philosophers that ever existed. To all these high-flown speeches Mr. Cavendish answered not a word, but stood with his eyes cast down, quite abashed and confounded. At last, spying an opening in the crowd, he darted through it with all the speed of which he was master, nor did he stop till he reached his carriage, which drove him directly home."

Sir Humphry Davy, in addition to the eloquent eulogium passed on Mr. Cavendish soon after his death, left this less studied but more graphic sketch of the philosopher amongst his papers :— " Cavendish was a great man, with extraordinary singularities. His voice was squeaking, his manner nervous, he was afraid of strangers, and seemed, when embarrassed, even to articulate with difficulty. He wore the costume of our grandfathers; was enormously rich, but made no use of his wealth. He gave me once some bits of platinum for my experiments, and came to see my results on the decomposition of the alkalis, and seemed to take an interest in them; but he encouraged no intimacy with any one. . . . He lived latterly the life of a solitary, came to the club dinner, and to the Royal Society, but received nobody at his own house. He was acute, sagacious, and profound, and, I think, the most accomplished British philosopher of his time." He died in 1810.

On the east side of Gower Street is University College, which was founded in the year 1826, for the purpose of affording "literary and scientific education at a moderate expense;" divinity being excluded. The credit of the idea of a university for London, in which the ancient languages should be taught, free from those artificial restrictions which bound Oxford and Cambridge so tightly, has generally been given to Lord Brougham and the other Whig politicians of his time. Cyrus Redding, however, in his " Recollections," claims the praise for Tom Campbell, the poet, who certainly took an active part in its foundation, and even journeyed—indolent as he was by nature— to Berlin in order to observe with his own eyes the professional system of Prussia, and to mature a plan for the government of the university. Testimony to the same effect was eventually borne by Lord Brougham himself.

The foundation-stone of the college was laid on Monday, the 30th of April, 1827, by H.R.H. the Duke of Sussex, who had long been associated with the leaders of the Whig party. The architect was Mr. William Wilkins, R.A., the designer of the National Gallery. The Duke of Sussex, on laying the stone, said, "May God bless this undertaking which we have so happily commenced, and make it prosper for honour, happiness, and glory, not only of the metropolis, but of the whole country." He also expressed a hope that the undertaking would excite the old universities to fresh exertions, and force them to reform abuses. An "oration," or prayer, was then offered up by the Rev. Dr. Maltby, afterwards Bishop of Durham. The ceremony was followed by a dinner at Freemasons' Hall, nearly all the chief Whigs of the day being among the guests.

The building was opened on the 1st of October in the following year, under the title of the University of London. Its constitution then was that of a joint-stock company, and the original deed of settlement provided for a dividend not exceeding four per cent. on the share capital—a dividend which, as a matter of fact, was never paid, inasmuch as from the first the expenditure of the college absorbed all that portion of the receipts in which it was supposed the dividend would be found. Thomas Campbell, then in the height of his celebrity, was appointed Lecturer on Poetry on the first opening of the institution. As the title of "University" was nothing more than a title, conveying with it none of the privileges we are accustomed to associate with the name, not even the power of granting degrees, the House of Commons in 1836 prayed for a charter of incorporation conferring such privileges and power. In answer, the Government of the day founded what is now known as the University of London, and proposed to the old institution to take the name of University College. To this proposal the proprietors, on the recommendation of the council, agreed, only stipulating that their college—as they had hoped would be done for their university—should be incorporated by royal charter. The idea seems to have been that by this means would be extinguished all the pecuniary rights of the proprietors. As this, however, was not effected, the charter, indeed, not referring to the subject at all, and as it was thought that from these rights there might at some future time arise inconvenience to the college, a private Act of Parliament was applied for with a view to settle the matter once and for all. This was obtained in 1869, and had not only the result desired, but also the effect of considerably enlarging the powers of the institution in several directions—among others, in the education of women, and instruction in the Fine Arts.

The governing body of the college consists of a council, elected by its members, who in their turn comprise the Governors, the Fellows, and the Life Governors, the first of whom, as representing the registered proprietors of the original shares, although, as we have said, all their pecuniary rights have been abolished, retain the privilege of nominating their successors. The Council itself consists of a President, Vice-President, and Treasurer, and not more than twenty-one or less than sixteen other members, six of whom, eligible to re-election, retire every year. The powers of this body are very wide—comprising, indeed, the sole and entire management of the college, both in the financial and educational departments, and also the government of the hospital to the same degree. There is, however, a subordinate body known as the Senate, and consisting of the professorial staff, which, having no voice in the government of the College, and no existence, indeed, under the Act of Parliament, is yet empowered to advise with the council on various subjects of management, especially of the libraries and museum, and has, moreover, a good deal to say to any contemplated addition or alteration in its own numbers. In connection with the larger establishment is a school, which stands to it in the light of a feeder, a considerable number of well-instructed pupils yearly passing up into the ranks of its students. The head master stands in all respects on the same footing as the professors of the college, and, like them, is subject to the regulations and control of the council. There are three faculties in the college—of arts and laws, of science, and of medicine—besides a department of civil and mechanical engineering. In the first two faculties are numbered thirty-one professorships, and of the eleven scientific chairs therein included, but one is endowed, the chair of physiology, although the professor of geology receives a yearly sum of £31 from the Goldsmid Fund.

The college comprises a central façade and two wings, and has a total length of about 400 feet. In the centre, which looks to the west, is an immense Corinthian portico, formed by twelve columns supporting the pediment, and elevated on a lofty plinth, approached by numerous steps effectively arranged. Behind the pediment is a cupola, with a lantern light, and in the great hall beneath it are placed on view the original models of the principal works of John Flaxman, which were presented to the institution some ten years after the death of the sculptor by his sister-in-law, Miss Denman, to whom, with the late Miss Flaxman, belonged the remaining works of the great

English sculptor—in the shape of drawings, models in plaster and wax, and other interesting relics—which were disposed of by public auction in April, 1876, and realised a sum of more than £2,000. In the vestibule of the college is Flaxman's restoration of the Farnese Hercules; beneath the dome is his grand life-size group of " Michael and Satan;" and around the walls are his various monumental and other bas-reliefs. In an adjoining room was placed Flaxman's " Shield of Achilles " and other works.

In the ground-floor are lecture-rooms, cloisters for the exercise of the pupils, two semi-circular theatres, the chemical laboratory, and museum of *materia medica*. In the upper floor, besides the great hall above mentioned, are museums of natural history and anatomy, two theatres, two libraries, and other rooms set apart for the purposes of the college. The principal library is richly decorated in the Italian style; it is large and valuable, containing upwards of 68,000 volumes and 16,000 pamphlets, to which has lately been added a fine collection of works on mathematics, physics, and astronomy, the gift of the late Mr. J. T. Graves. The laboratory, completed from the plan of Professor Donaldson in 1845, is stated to combine all the recent improvements of our own schools with that of Professor Liebig, at Giessen.

At University College the Graphic Club, composed of artists, painters, and engravers, used to hold their monthly meetings for the purpose of interchange of thought on matters connected with the fine arts. The club was originally established by the late Mr. John Burnet and his friends; and it numbered among its members J. M. W. Turner, Prout, Landseer, Clarkson Stanfield, and other departed worthies.

On the opposite side of Gower Street, facing the college gates, is the North London, or University College Hospital. It was founded soon after the college itself, under the presidency of Lord Brougham, for the relief of poor sick and maimed persons, and the delivery of poor married women; and also for furthering the objects of the college, by affording improved means of practical instruction in medicine and surgery to the medical students of the college under the superintendence of its professors. The building, which was erected from the designs of Mr. Alfred Ainger, affords accommodation for 160 beds, fourteen of which, in two separate wards, are devoted exclusively to the use of children under twelve years of age. The total number of persons relieved yearly is about 20,000, at the cost of £15,000; whilst the income from subscriptions and other sources amounts to not

quite half that sum, thus leaving a yearly deficit of nearly £8,000 to be provided for.

In Grafton Street East, and nearly opposite the hospital, is the Dissenters' Library, which was originally founded in Cripplegate,* in the year 1711, by Dr. Daniel Williams, a Presbyterian minister, for the use of the Presbyterian, Independent, and Baptist persuasions, with a salary for a librarian and housekeeper. In pursuance of his will, a building was erected in Redcross Street, with space for 40,000 volumes (though the original collection did not comprise more than 16,000 volumes), and an apartment for the curator. In the library was also a register in which Dissenters might record the births of their children. When the premises in Redcross Street were required for the extension of the Metropolitan Railway, in 1865, the library was temporarily transferred to a hired house in Queen Square, Bloomsbury, where it remained for eight years, until a home was found for it here. The site of the new library cost £4,000, and the new building in which it is lodged £7,000 more. It is a plain and substantial Gothic building. The basement includes, besides offices, strong rooms for the custody of manuscripts. On the ground floor are the entrance-hall, committee-rooms, waiting-rooms, &c. The library occupies the whole first floor, which is lofty and well lighted. The upper portion of the building is occupied by the librarian. The architect was Mr. T. Chatfield Clarke, and the structure is as nearly fireproof as possible.

The library, a very rich collection of theological works, and especially of Nonconformist literature, was first actually opened in 1729, and the new library was completed and opened in September, 1873. It now comprises about 30,000 volumes, among which are various editions of the Bible, also the first folio edition of Shakespeare; but there are no Caxtons or Wynkyn de Wordes. The library is open to respectable persons of every class daily throughout the year, excepting during the month of August and in Christmas week; on Good Friday and Whit Monday it is also closed. Books are allowed to be taken out under proper restrictions. Upon the walls of the library are portraits of Richard Baxter, by Riley; of Matthew Henry, of Wm. Tyndale, of Joseph Priestley, by Fuseli; of John Milton, and of Isaac Watts. The trustees, twenty-three in number, must all be Presbyterians; and it may be added that each trustee makes a present of books to the library.

Of Dr. Williams's ministerial career we have already spoken in our account of Redcross Street;

* See Vol. II., p. 239.

UNIVERSITY COLLEGE, GOWER STREET. (*See page* 568.)

but it may be added that he was one of the friends and fellow-workers of Baxter, and an advocate of what was known as "occasional conformity." He lived very frugally, but having married two rich wives, was able to lay by money towards his favourite scheme. He bequeathed money to the University of Glasgow for the support of eight students for the ministry, besides other sums in aid of the maintenance of poor ministers and their widows. He took care that his library should be open to persons of all denominations. Dr. Williams was among those who urged the Nonconformist body to refuse the concessions offered to them in conjunction with the Roman Catholics, and became one of the firmest supporters of the House of Brunswick.

A portion of Dr. Williams's estates, bequeathed for 2,000 years, was appropriated to the following objects :—The formation of a library; exhibitions at Glasgow University, and divinity scholarships; also to the establishment of schools for poor children in various parts of England and Wales; to the payment of poor Dissenting ministers; Christian teachers in Ireland, the West Indies, and New England; and to the distribution of the Doctor's own works among suitable persons.

CHAPTER XLV.

GORDON AND TAVISTOCK SQUARES, &c.

"Lucus in urbe fuit mediâ, gratissimus umbrâ."—*Virgil, Æn.,* i.

Gordon Square—The "Catholic and Apostolic Church"—A Scene in the Chapel of the "Irvingites"—Memoir of the Rev. Edward Irving—University Hall—Tavistock Square—Dickens' Amateur Theatricals at Tavistock House—Tavistock Place—The "Building in which the Earth was Weighed—St. Andrew's Chapel—Great Coram Street—The Russell Literary and Scientific Institution—Thackeray and Dickens—Burton Street and Crescent—John Britton, the Topographer—Robert Owen, the Socialist—Major Cartwright, the Champion of Parliamentary Reform—Mr. Burton, the Builder—Judd Street—Sir Andrew Judde—Regent Square—Argyle Square—The New Jerusalem Church—Liverpool Street—The Cabinet Theatre.

GORDON SQUARE was so called after Alexander, fourth Duke of Gordon, whose daughter, the Lady Georgiana Gordon, married, as his second wife, John, sixth Duke of Bedford, whose first wife was a daughter of the noble house of Torrington.

The south-west corner of Gordon Square is occupied by a very large and noble Gothic building, the Metropolitan Church or Cathedral of the "Catholic and Apostolic Church," as the followers of Edward Irving style themselves. It was built about the year 1850, from the designs of Mr. R. Brandon and Mr. Ritchie. The exterior is of Early-English design, and the Decorated interior has a triforium in the aisle-roof, after the manner of our early churches and cathedrals. The ceilings are highly enriched, and some of the windows are filled with stained glass; the northern doorway and porch and the southern wheel-window are very fine. A beautiful side chapel has been added on the south, styled a "Lady Chapel;" but the name is inappropriate, as devotion to the Virgin Mary forms no part of the Irvingite creed. Grouped around the church are some Gothic houses, with projections and gables, pointed-headed windows, and traceried balconies.

Previous to the building of the Catholic and Apostolic Church, the "Irvingites" had their headquarters for some years in a chapel in Newman Street, which, as we have already stated, had previously served as Benjamin West's studio.

"The scene in this chapel," writes Mr. James Grant, in his "Travels in Town," "was one which might well have made angels weep. I myself have repeatedly, in the course of one morning's service, witnessed no fewer than from four to seven exhibitions, in the way of speaking with tongues [he means, of course, 'unknown tongues']. There was one young lady who . . . spoke three different times in this way in less than an hour; and sounds more wild or more unearthly than those she uttered it has never been my lot to hear." The writer, however, whilst regretting Mr. Irving's novel and strange views, defends him zealously from the charge so frequently brought against him in his life-time, of aiding in an imposture, certifying to his single-heartedness and honesty. He adds that the late Mr. Henry Drummond, of Albury, M.P. for Surrey, and a son of the Prime Minister Spencer Perceval, were among those who frequented this chapel, and that Mr. Irving himself, as the "minister" of it, was styled its "angel."

Irving first propounded or exhibited the strange doctrine which became associated with his name in the parish of Row, and the town of Port Glasgow, in Scotland; but afterwards settled in London, preaching first in a chapel in Hatton Garden, and afterwards in the Scotch Church in Regent Square, which was built expressly for him. Here, we are informed, "the religious services were interrupted by the harangues of the inspired; women started up and in strange tones poured forth a jargon of words which none could understand, but which were assumed to be inspired by the same power that had imparted the gift of tongues on the day of Pentecost; even the lame were commanded to walk, and the dead to rise to life by those confident thaumaturgists, who were astonished at the non-compliance of their patients, and in whom, want of faith alone, they declared, had been the cause of the failure. And of all the deluded none exceeded Mr. Irving himself, whose morbid intellect it inspired with fresh activity, and to whose eloquence it furnished a new and exciting theme. The latter days, he declared, had come; the miraculous powers of the Church were restored; the millennium itself was at hand. But the Church of Scotland could no longer tolerate the unsoundness of his preaching and the extravagant displays of his congregation; and in 1830 he was deposed from his local cure, as minister of the Scots Church in Regent Square, by the presbytery of London, and finally, in the year 1833, from his standing as an ordained minister, by the presbytery of his native Annan. For these exclusions, however, Mr. Irving cared little, surrounded as he was by prophets and prophetesses, who were of higher account with him than presbyteries and general assemblies; and on his expulsion from Regent Square he betook himself to a building in Newman Street, which his people had fitted up as a place of worship, and where he organised his congregation into a separate and distinct Church. They were now placed under a fourfold ministry of apostles, prophets, evangelists, and pastors, Mr. Irving himself being ordained as the 'angel' of the Church in Newman Street. In 1834 he died, at the age of forty-two, worn out by a life of intellectual excitement and by the feverish labours of his latter years in supporting and propagating the doctrines of his new system."[*]

Irving's oratorical powers, and the novelty of the doctrines promulgated by him, "drew" immense congregations, and he became the "observed of all observers." We are told that his figure, air, costume, and uncapped head attracted the gaze, if not the admiration, of the young and old. He was a tall, gaunt figure, with dress of unusual cut, with his hat generally in his hand; a head of black hair, starting in all directions like the projecting quills of the "fretful porcupine;" lank cheeks, and eyes apparently directed to the two sides of the street rather than to his pathway, which was usually in the middle of the road.

* "Comprehensive History of England," vol. iv., p. 769.

Mr. Grant, in his "Travels in Town," tells us that the Irvingite body, in spite of having diminished in numbers since the death of its founder, has seven churches in the metropolis besides its central place of worship, in allusion, doubtless, to the "Seven Churches" of the Book of Revelation.

On the west side of Gordon Square, and in the rear of University College, is University Hall. It was designed by Professor Donaldson in 1849, and was built for the purpose of instructing such young men as chose to reside there in theology and moral philosophy, subjects which are excluded from the college curriculum. The architecture is Elizabethan or Tudor, in red brick and stone, and the grouping of the windows is effectively managed.

Tavistock Square, which lies on the east side of Gordon Square, is named from the Duke of Bedford's second title, Marquis of Tavistock. Tavistock House, long the residence of James Perry, editor of the *Morning Chronicle* during its palmiest days, became in later times the abode of Charles Dickens, who took possession of it in October, 1851, having removed hither from Devonshire Terrace, Marylebone. Here he almost immediately set to work upon the first number of "Bleak House," which he had long been meditating. Here his children's private theatricals were commenced on Twelfth Night in 1854, being renewed annually till the actors ceased to be children any longer. They were often aided by Mr. Mark Lemon, Douglas Jerrold, and Mr. Planché, and among the audience were Sir Edwin Landseer, Clarkson Stanfield, and the other friends of "Boz" in his early days. But it was not only at Christmas that Dickens delighted in his private theatricals. In the summer of 1855, for instance, he threw open his little theatre to several gatherings of a larger and outer circle of friends, amongst whom were Lord Campbell, Peter Cunningham, Lord Lytton, William M. Thackeray, and Thomas Carlyle. He described himself on his play-bills as "Lessee and Manager, Mr. Crummles;" his poet was Wilkie Collins, "in an entirely new and original domestic melodrama;" and his scene-painter was Clarkson Stanfield. The performances included "The Lighthouse," by Mr. W. Collins; and it may be recorded here that the scene of the Eddystone Lighthouse in this little play, afterwards carefully framed, and hung up in the hall at Gad's Hill, near Rochester, Dickens' last home, fetched a thousand guineas at the sale of the great novelist's effects. It was at supper, after one of these performances, that Lord Campbell told the company that he would rather have written "Pickwick" than be Lord Chief Justice and a Peer of Parliament.

"The best of the performances," writes Mr. John

ster, "were 'Tom Thumb' and 'Fortunio,' in 1854 and 1855, Dickens himself now first joining in the revel, and Mark Lemon bringing into it his own clever children, and a very mountain of child-pleasing fun in himself. Dickens had become very intimate with him, and his merry, genial ways had given him unbounded popularity with the young ones, who had no such a favourite as 'Uncle' Mark. In Fielding's burlesque he was the giantess Glumdalca, and Dickens was the Ghost of Gaffer Thumb, the names by which they appeared respectively being the 'Infant Phenomenon' and the 'Modern Garrick.' But the youngest actors carried off the palm. There was a Lord Grizzle, at whose ballad of Miss Villikins, introduced by desire, Thackeray rolled off his chair in a burst of laughter that became absurdly contagious. Yet even this, with hardly less fun from the Noodles, Doodles, and King Arthurs, was not so good as the pretty, fantastic, comic grace of Dollalolla, Huncamunca, and Tom. The girls wore steadily the airs which are irresistible when put on by little children ; and an actor, not out of his fourth year, who went through the comic songs and the tragic exploits without a wrong note or a victim unslain, represented the small helmeted hero." There is, it may be added, a most amusing paper in *Macmillan's Magazine* on these "Amateur Theatricals at Tavistock House," written by one who had been a member of the juvenile company. In the getting-up of these amusements Dickens was happy to secure the help of Mr. J. R. Planché in costume, and the "priceless help" of Clarkson Stanfield in his scenery.

Southward of the square is Tavistock Place, which has had among its residents some men of note in their day. At No. 9 lived John Pinkerton, the historian. " Here," says Mr. Peter Cunningham, " his depraved mode of life was the cause of continual quarrels with abandoned women." No. 34 was for some time the residence of Francis Douce, the antiquary, the author of a " Dissertation on the Dance of Death," and "Illustrations of Shakespeare and of Ancient Manners." John Galt afterwards resided in the same house. Here he wrote his autobiography and many other literary works, including a " Life of Byron." No. 37, more recently the residence of Sir Matthew Digby Wyatt, is worthy of a note, as having been the residence of Francis Baily, President of the Royal Astronomical Society, and also the spot where, in 1851, the weight of the world was ascertained by him. With reference to this building, Sir John Herschel writes : " The house stands isolated in a garden, so as to be free from any material tremor from passing carriages. A small observatory was constructed in the upper part. The building in which the earth was weighed, and its bulk and figure calculated, the standard measure of the British nation perpetuated, and the pendulum experiments rescued from their chief source of inaccuracy, can never cease to be an object of interest."

Close by is St. Andrew's Chapel, which was for some time famous for the antics of the musical " Archdeacon" Dunbar. At the time of its erection, early in the present century, this chapel was considered a prodigy of Gothic art and beauty.

Parallel with Tavistock Place, on the south side, and extending from Woburn Place to Brunswick Square, is Great Coram Street, so named after Captain Coram, the founder of the Foundling Hospital. In this street is a building of some architectural pretensions, the centre having a handsome portico with four pillars. It is called the Russell Literary and Scientific Institution, and is somewhat similar in plan to the London Institution, though on a smaller and less ambitious scale. The house was erected on speculation for the purpose of holding assemblies and balls, and was purchased in the year 1808 from Mr. James Burton, the builder, by the managers of the institution. There is here an extensive and valuable library, consisting of the most useful works in ancient and modern literature ; and the reading-room is well managed and attended.

In 1837, Thackeray, then newly married, took up his residence in this street, where he lived for two years, occupying himself with his literary contributions to *Fraser*, and an occasional illustration. It was while residing here that he one day called on Dickens, with an offer to illustrate " Pickwick "— an offer which was " declined with thanks," and possibly turned the course of his life into a different channel. Had his offer been accepted, he probably would have become an artist, and possibly an R.A. ; but " Vanity Fair " would never have been written.

On the north side of Tavistock Place are Burton Street and Burton Crescent. In the former, at No. 15, lived Mrs. Davidson, who, as Miss Duncan, attained high repute on the stage by her performances in *The Honeymoon* and other dramas, but who lived to see her fame decline. Often would she walk to and from the theatre twice a day, to rehearsal and performance, in wet and cold weather, whilst her husband was either in bed or at a gaming-table.

In this street, as Mr. Grant tells us in his " Travels in Town," there was formerly one of the chapels of the sect founded by Emmanuel Swedenborg, called the New Jerusalem Church.

At Burton Cottage, Burton Street, lived John Britton, F.S.A., the topographer, antiquary, and man of letters, who has already been briefly mentioned in our account of Red Lion Street, Clerkenwell.* John Britton was a native of Kington St. Michael, Wiltshire, where his father was a small farmer and kept a village shop. At an early age he came to London, and, as we have said, was apprenticed to a wine-merchant. At that time, and even on reaching manhood, his education was very imperfect; he, nevertheless, formed the acquaintance of various persons connected with the humbler walks of literature, and was induced to embark in a small way on authorship himself, by compiling some common street song-books, &c. Becoming acquainted with Mr. Wheble, the publisher of the *Sporting Magazine*, for which he had prepared some short notices, he obtained his introduction into the career which he so long and honourably pursued. Wheble, whilst residing at Salisbury, had issued the prospectus of a work to be called the "Beauties of Wiltshire," but was not able to carry it on ; but now, finding that Britton was a native of that county, Wheble proposed to him to compile the work he had announced. Among Britton's acquaintances was a young man named Brayley, of about his own age, but somewhat better taught; they had assisted each other in their studies, and they now entered upon a sort of literary partnership. In due time the "Beauties of Wiltshire" was completed, and at the invitation of the publishers the joint authors immediately afterwards set to work on the "Beauties of Bedfordshire." Eventually the "Beauties" of all the other counties of England were published, in twenty-six volumes, but only the first nine were written by the original authors. In 1805, Mr. Britton produced the first part of a more elaborate work, the "Architectural Antiquities of England," which in the end formed five splendid volumes. From this time Mr. Britton's course was one of laborious and persevering authorship in the path which he made for many years in a special manner his own—that of architectural and topographical description. Of the many works of this character which he produced, the most important is the "Cathedral Antiquities of England." Mr. Britton died in 1857, at an advanced age.

No. 4, Crescent Place, which intersects Burton Street, was for some years the home of Robert Owen, the Socialist. Like Mr. Britton, Owen was of humble origin. He was for some time a successful cotton-spinner at Lanark, in Scotland,

during which period he attended with benevolent care to the welfare of the persons employed and to the education of their children. He here introduced many improvements, since adopted in other schools, so as to make instruction at once attractive and useful; and founded, if not the first, one of the earliest of the infant schools. About this time he published his "New View of Society, or Essays on the Formation of Human Character," and subsequently a "Book of the New Moral World," in which he developed a theory of modified Communism. In 1823, this eccentric philanthropist went to North America, where he attempted, but unsuccessfully, to found a settlement. The latter years of his life, which were spent in England, were devoted to various objects, all more or less visionary, "the foretelling of the millennium on earth; the establishing of a system of morality, independent of religion; and a vindication of his claims to be able to hold conversations with the spirits of the dead, particularly with the late Duke of Kent." He died in 1858, at his birthplace in North Wales.

Burton Crescent is only noticed in the "Handbook of London" as containing "a statue of Major Cartwright, by Clarke, of Birmingham, which is a disgrace to art." This Major Cartwright was one of the earliest advocates and champions of Parliamentary reform. In "A Book for a Rainy Day" it is stated that he was born at Marnham, Nottinghamshire, in 1740. "In the year 1758 he entered the naval service, under the command of Lord Howe; was promoted to a lieutenancy in September, 1762, and continued on active service until the spring of 1771. Then retiring to recruit his health, he remained at Marnham till invited by his old Commander-in-chief, in the year 1775 or 1776 ; but not approving of the war with America, he declined accepting the proffered commission. About the same time he became major of the regiment of Nottinghamshire Militia, then for the first time raised in that county, in which he served seventeen years. When George III. arrived at the year of the Jubilee, a naval promotion of twenty lieutenants to the rank of commanders took place, and the name of J. C. standing the twentieth on the list, he was commissioned as a commander accordingly. In the year 1802 he published 'The Trident,' a work in quarto, having for its object to promote that elevation of character which can alone preserve the vital spirit of a navy, as well as to furnish an inexhaustible patronage of the arts." The major, who often distinguished himself at the Covent Garden hustings, lived to a ripe old age, and was much esteemed by all who knew him.

---

* See Vol. II., p 323.

He died at his residence in Burton Crescent in the year 1824.

Burton Street and Burton Crescent preserve the name of the builder, who may be regarded as the creator of all this district, James Burton, of whom Mr. Britton thus writes in his "Autobiography:" —"The career of Mr. Burton was like that of many other ardent and speculating persons. In his first undertaking of building Russell Square, Bedford Place, Upper Bedford Place, &c., he was eminently successful, and might have retired from the working world with a handsome fortune; but he was tempted to embark in further speculations by engaging to cover a large tract of ground belonging to the Skinners' Company: this proved a failure, and he sustained serious losses. During this time he became connected with John Nash, the sycophant architect and companion of the Prince Regent and after King. That architect, like Mr. Burton, was an active, speculating man; and among other plans for the improvement of London, his designs for Regent Street, the Regent's Park, St. James's Park, and Buckingham Palace, were accepted and acted upon. Mr. Burton was intimately connected with Nash in carrying into effect much of the New Road, and also the Regent's Park, in the latter of which he built a handsome villa for himself, where he resided some years. At a previous time he had embarked in gunpowder works in Kent, and built a country seat near Tunbridge. Soon afterwards he ventured on the perilous task of building and forming the new town of St. Leonard's; to convey occupants to which he established coaches to run between that place and the metropolis. These were hazardous and losing schemes, and the very worthy but daring builder was, consequently, involved in ruin. Amongst a large family, his son, Decimus Burton, was eminently successful as an architect, and designed many handsome buildings in London.

To the east of Burton Crescent, and connecting Brunswick Square with the Euston Road, is Judd Street. Sir Andrew Judd, or Judde, after whom the street was named, was a native of Tunbridge in Kent, and was Lord Mayor of London in 1551. He bequeathed a large part of his wealth towards founding and endowing a public school in his native town. Among the lands so bequeathed were certain "sand-hills on the back side of Holborn," then let for grazing purposes at a few pounds a year, but now covered with houses, and bringing in an income of several thousands a year. Sir Andrew Judde lies buried in St. Helen's, Bishopsgate, and his school now flourishes among the best grammar schools in the kingdom.

On the east side of Hunter Street, behind the Foundling Hospital, is Regent Square, which is chiefly noticeable for containing the Scotch Presbyterian Church, where, as we have already stated, the Rev. Edward Irving and his peculiar doctrines and "tongues" attracted large and fashionable congregations in the early part of this century. The church, which stands at the corner of Compton Street, is Gothic in style, and was built in 1824-25, by Mr. (afterwards Sir William) Tite, the architect, who adopted as his model the principal front of York Minster; the twin towers are 120 feet in height. On the east side of the square is St. Peter's, commonly called Regent Square Church. Here, too, is a charitable institution, wholly dependent upon voluntary contributions; it is called the Home of Hope, and has been established "for the reception of such young women, before they become mothers, as are unfitted, from their previous good character and position, for the general wards of a workhouse."

Passing in the direction of King's Cross, by a few streets of little or no importance, we arrive in Argyle Square, which, with its trees and greensward, has quite a refreshing appearance after escaping from some of the narrow streets which surround it. Here is the New Jerusalem Church, which was opened in 1844 for the followers of Swedenborg, whom we have mentioned above. The church is in the Anglo-Norman style of architecture, and was built from the designs of Mr. Hopkins; it has two towers and spires, each terminating with a bronze cross; the intervening gable has a stone cross, and a wheel-window over a deeply-recessed doorway. The interior of the church has a vaulted roof; the altar arrangements are somewhat peculiar, and there is an organ and choir.

Liverpool Street, Sidmouth Street, and a few others in the neighbourhood, were named after the Ministers in office at the date of their erection. In Liverpool Street, a little to the eastward of Argyle Square, is a small building which has been occasionally used for amateur theatrical performances. It was originally an auction-room, but has since been turned into the King's Cross, or, as it is sometimes called, "Cabinet Theatre."

Having now arrived at King's Cross, which has been already fully described in these pages,* we shall in the succeeding chapters travel over the outlying portions of London, on the south-west and west frontier of the great metropolis, commencing our journey anew at Hyde Park Corner.

---

* See Vol. III., p. 539.